22nd International Conference on Spoken Language Translation (IWSLT 2025)

Vienna, Austria
31 July – 1 August 2025

ISBN: 979-8-3313-2409-4

Printed from e-media with permission by:

Curran Associates, Inc.
57 Morehouse Lane
Red Hook, NY 12571

CURRAN ASSOCIATES INC. proceedings.com

Some format issues inherent in the e-media version may also appear in this print version.

Association for Computational Linguistics
209 N. Eighth Street
Stroudsburg, Pennsylvania 18360

Phone: 1-570-476-8006
Fax: 1-570-476-0860

acl@aclweb.org

Additional copies of this publication are available from:

Curran Associates, Inc.
57 Morehouse Lane
Red Hook, NY 12571 USA
Phone: 845-758-0400
Fax: 845-758-2633
Email: curran@proceedings.com
Web: www.proceedings.com

IWSLT 2025

The 22nd International Conference on Spoken Language Translation

Proceedings of the Conference

July 31 - August 1, 2025

The IWSLT organizers gratefully acknowledge the support from the following sponsors.

Diamond

Introduction

The International Conference on Spoken Language Translation (IWSLT) is the premiere annual scientific conference for the study, development, and evaluation of spoken language translation technology. Launched in 2004 and spun out from the C-STAR speech translation consortium before it (1992-2003), IWSLT is the main venue for scientific exchange on all topics related to speech-to-text translation, speech-to-speech translation, simultaneous and consecutive translation, speech dubbing, cross-lingual communication including all multimodal, emotional, paralinguistic, and stylistic aspects and their applications in the field. The conference organizes evaluations around challenge areas, and presents scientific papers and system descriptions. IWSLT is organized by the Special Interest Group on Spoken Language Translation (SIGSLT), which is supported by ACL, ISCA and ELRA.

This year, IWSLT featured spoken language translation shared tasks organized into seven distinct tracks. These were grouped into four **high-resource tasks**: (i) offline speech translation, (ii) simultaneous speech translation, (iii) subtitling, and (iv) model compression; three **low-resource tasks**: (v) low-resource, and (vi) Indic (multilingual); and one **instruction following task**. Each track was coordinated by one or more chairs. The resulting evaluation campaigns attracted a total of 32 teams, from academia, research centers and industry. System submissions resulted in 31 system papers that will be presented at the conference. Following our call for papers, this year we received 22 submissions of research papers, 13 of which were accepted for oral presentation through a double-blind review process.

The program committee is excited about the quality of the accepted papers and expects lively discussion and exchange at the conference. The conference chairs and organizers would like to express their gratitude to everyone who contributed and supported IWSLT. In particular, we wish to thank our Diamond sponsors Apple and AppTek. We thank the shared tasks chairs, organizers, and participants, the program committee members, as well as all the authors that went the extra mile to submit system and research papers to IWSLT, and make this year's conference a big success. We also wish to express our sincere gratitude to ACL for hosting our conference and for arranging the logistics and infrastructure that allow us to hold IWSLT 2025 as a hybrid conference.

Welcome to IWSLT 2025, welcome to Vienna!

Antonios Anastasopoulos, Program Chair
Marcello Federico and Alex Waibel, Conference Chairs

Organizing Committee

Conference Chairs

Marcello Federico, AWS AI Labs, USA
Alex Waibel, CMU, USA

Program Chair

Antonis Anastasopoulos, George Mason University, USA

Sponsorship Chair

Sebastian Stüker, Zoom, Germany

Evaluation Chair

Jan Niehues, KIT, Germany

Website and Publication Chair

Elizabeth Salesky, Google DeepMind, USA

Publicity Chair

Atul Kr. Ohja, University of Galway, Ireland

Program Committee

Program Committee

Tanel Alumäe, Tallinn University of Technology
Maximilian Awiszus, Zoom
Laurent Besacier, Naver Labs Europe
Claudia Borg, University of Malta
Mauro Cettolo, FBK
Lizhong Chen, Oregon State University
Qianqian Dong, ByteDance
Akiko Eriguchi, Microsoft
Mark Fishel, University of Tartu
Marco Gaido, FBK
Gerard I. Gállego, Barcelona Supercomputing Center & Universitat Politècnica de Catalunya
HyoJung Han, University of Maryland
Benjamin Hsu, Amazon
Philipp Koehn, Johns Hopkins University
Surafel M. Lakew, Amazon
Yves Lepage, Waseda University
Evgeny Matusov, AppTek
Chandresh Maurya, Indian Institute of Technology Indore
Matteo Negri, FBK
Jan Niehues, KIT
Atul Kr. Ojha, University of Galway
John E. Ortega, Northeastern Universtiy
Sara Papi, FBK
Kumar Rishu, UFAL Charles University
Elizabeth Salesky, Google
Rico Sennrich, University of Zurich
Berrak Sisman, Johns Hopkins University
Gerasimos Spanakis, Maastricht University
Matthias Sperber, Apple
Sebastian Stüker, Zoom
Katsuhito Sudoh, NAIST
Yun Tang, Samsung Research America
Marco Turchi, Zoom
Yogesh Virkar, Amazon
Krzysztof Wolk, Wolk.AI
Tong Xiao, Northeastern University
Brian Yan, Carnegie Mellon University
Rodolfo Zevallos, Universitat Pompeu Fabra

Table of Contents

Program

Thursday, July 31, 2025

09:00 - 09:15	*Welcome Remarks*
09:15 - 10:30	*Findings of the IWSLT 2025 Evaluation Campaign*
10:30 - 11:00	*Coffee Break*
11:00 - 12:00	*Findings of the IWSLT 2025 Evaluation Campaign*
12:00 - 12:30	*Oral Session A*
12:30 - 14:00	*Lunch Break*
14:00 - 15:30	*Poster Session I*
15:30 - 16:00	*Coffee Break*
16:00 - 16:30	*Oral Session B*
16:30 - 17:30	*Panel Discussion*

Friday, August 1, 2025

09:00 - 10:30	*Oral Session C*
10:30 - 11:00	*Coffee Break*
11:00 - 12:30	*Poster Session II*
12:30 - 14:00	*Lunch Break*
14:00 - 14:30	*Oral Session D*
14:30 - 15:30	*Planning Session*
15:30 - 16:00	*Coffee Break*
16:00 - 16:15	*Closing Remarks*

Streaming Sequence Transduction through Dynamic Compression

Weiting Tan♠ Yunmo Chen♠ Tongfei Chen♡
Guanghui Qin♠ Haoran Xu♠ Heidi C. Zhang♣
Benjamin Van Durme♠ Philipp Koehn♠
♠Johns Hopkins University ♡Microsoft ♣Stanford University

Abstract

We introduce STAR (Stream Transduction with Anchor Representations), a novel Transformer-based model designed for efficient sequence-to-sequence transduction over *streams*. STAR dynamically segments input streams to create compressed *anchor* representations, achieving nearly lossless compression (12×) in Automatic Speech Recognition (ASR) and outperforming existing methods. Moreover, STAR demonstrates superior segmentation and latency-quality trade-offs in simultaneous speech-to-text tasks, optimizing latency, memory footprint, and quality.[1]

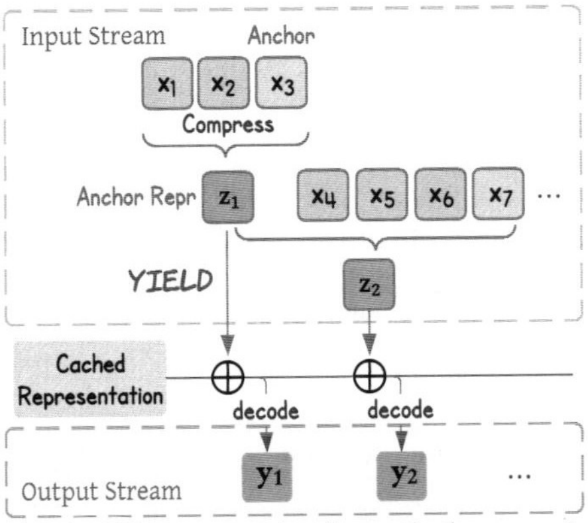

Figure 1: When YIELD is triggered, the current segment's information is compressed into an anchor representation to generate the next output.

1 Introduction

Sequence transduction, also referred to as sequence-to-sequence modeling, has shown remarkable success across various domains, including speech translation (Liu et al., 2019; Di Gangi et al., 2019; Li et al., 2020) and automatic speech recognition (Prabhavalkar et al., 2023; Li, 2021; Gulati et al., 2020). Traditionally, these models operate under the assumption of fully observing input sequences before generating outputs. However, this requirement becomes impractical in applications necessitating low latency or real-time output generation such as simultaneous translation (Ma et al., 2019; Chang and Lee, 2022; Barrault et al., 2023, *inter alia*). The concept of streaming sequence transduction (Inaguma et al., 2020; Kameoka et al., 2021; Chen et al., 2021; Wang et al., 2022; Chen et al., 2021; Xue et al., 2022), or stream transduction, arises to address this challenge. Unlike traditional sequence transduction, stream transduction operates on partially observed input sequences while simultaneously generating outputs. This requires deciding when to initiate output generation, a task inherently tied to identifying critical *triggers* within the input sequence. Triggers mark moments when sufficient input information has been received to initiate output generation, thus minimizing latency. Consequently, they partition the input sequence into discrete *segments*, with outputs accessing only information preceding each trigger.

Locating these triggers poses a significant challenge. Prior approaches have explored methods that employ fixed sliding windows to determine triggers (Ma et al., 2019, 2020b), or learning models to predict triggers (Ma et al., 2020c; Chang and Lee, 2022), yet timing remains a complex issue. Beyond reducing latency, another challenge for stream transduction is how to efficiently represent historical information while optimizing memory usage. Prior work (Rae et al., 2020; Tay et al., 2022; Bertsch et al., 2023, *inter alia*) has mostly focused on improving the efficiency of Transformer but does not investigate streaming scenarios. Reducing the memory footprint for streaming systems introduces additional complexity as models must determine when certain information becomes less relevant for future predictions.

In this work, we propose **S**tream **T**ransduction with **A**nchor **R**epresentations (STAR), a novel ap-

[1] Codes available at: `https://github.com/steventan0110/STAR`

Proceedings of the 22nd International Conference on Spoken Language Translation (IWSLT 2025), pages 1–18
July 31 - August 1, 2025 ©2025 Association for Computational Linguistics

proach designed to maximize the benefits of stream transduction, optimizing both generation latency and memory footprint. STAR dynamically segments the input stream into buffers that contain similar levels of information. Then, it introduces the concept of **anchors**, which aggregate a buffer of information (multiple vector representations) into single-vector anchor representations. Once an anchor representation is yielded, it triggers the generation process to yield another token.

We present a learning strategy to train STAR end-to-end so that the model learns to dynamically select anchor positions with the following objectives: (1) anchor positions are selected such that each segment contains the right amount of information for generating the next output; (2) anchor representation effectively compress the information of its preceding segment. For example, in fig. 1, the model triggers YIELD at index 3 (which makes it an anchor position), compressing the information of the current chunk $\boldsymbol{X} = (x_1, x_2, x_3)$ into anchor representation z_1 to generate output y_1. Such a process repeats each time YIELD is triggered. To summarize, our contributions are as follows: (1) we propose STAR that dynamically segments and compresses input streams, trading-off among latency, memory footprint, and performance for stream transduction; (2) we validate the effectiveness of our approach on well-established *speech-to-text* tasks. Our results show that STAR greatly outperforms existing methods, obtaining better compression ability and excelling in quality-latency trade-offs.

2 Methodology

2.1 Problem Formulation

In sequence-to-sequence transduction, feature $\boldsymbol{X} = (\boldsymbol{x}_1, \ldots, \boldsymbol{x}_{T_x})$ is normally first extracted from the raw input sequence. Then the decoder can encode and use such features to generate an output sequence $\boldsymbol{Y} = (y_1, \ldots, y_{T_y})$. The encoder and decoder can be implemented using various models such as Recurrent Neural Networks (Hochreiter and Schmidhuber, 1997; Chung et al., 2014; Lipton, 2015) and Transformers (Vaswani et al., 2017), depending on the input and output characteristics. In the context of streaming sequence transduction, where the input (and their features $\boldsymbol{X}$) is partially observed, *a causal encoder and decoder are necessary*. The causal encoder processes the partially observed feature $\boldsymbol{X}_{<\tau}$ ($\tau \leq T_x$) to produce their

Algorithm 1 High-level overview of STAR

1: **Input**: Input stream $\boldsymbol{X}$, threshold β
2: **Output**: Output stream $\boldsymbol{Y}$
3: **Initialize**: cached repr. $\boldsymbol{Z} \leftarrow \varnothing$; buffer $\boldsymbol{B} \leftarrow \varnothing$
4: **while** $y \neq$ EOS :
5:     $\alpha \leftarrow 0; \boldsymbol{B} \leftarrow \varnothing$ ▷ *clear buffer*
6:     **while** $\boldsymbol{x} \leftarrow$ READ($\boldsymbol{X}$) : ▷ READ *new inputs*
7:         APPEND($\boldsymbol{B}, \boldsymbol{x}$) ▷ *add to buffer*
8:         $\alpha \leftarrow \alpha + F_{\text{seg}}(\boldsymbol{x})$
9:         **if** $\alpha \geq \beta$: ▷ *yield triggered*
10:             $\boldsymbol{H} = F_{\text{enc}}(\boldsymbol{B} \mid \boldsymbol{Z})$ ▷ *encode segment buffer*
11:             $\boldsymbol{z} =$ COMPRESS($\boldsymbol{H}$)
12:             APPEND($\boldsymbol{Z}, \boldsymbol{z}$) ▷ *embedding for segment*
13:             $y \leftarrow F_{\text{dec}}(\cdot|\boldsymbol{Y}, \boldsymbol{Z})$
14:             **yield** y
15:             **break**

encoding. Suppose the first k outputs are already generated, the causal decoder sample the next output y_{k+1} with $\mathbb{P}(y_{k+1}|\boldsymbol{X}_{<\tau}, \boldsymbol{Y}_{<k+1}; \theta)$, where θ represents the parameter set.

Deciding when to generate (yield) a new token is the core of streaming sequence transduction where a segmenter/predictor (Moritz et al., 2020; Chang and Lee, 2022) is typically trained to control timing for yield operation. Our approach to tackling stream transduction is outlined in algorithm 1. It involves a learnable segmenter that scores the importance of each input feature to decide if enough information has been accumulated in the current buffer of features. As the segmenter scores input feature in a frame-wise fashion (algorithm 1, line 8), we accumulate the scores α until it reaches a pre-defined threshold β. When the threshold is reached, it indicates that enough information has been accumulated in the current buffer $\boldsymbol{B}$ of features. Subsequently, we compress the features into a single vector representation $\boldsymbol{z}$ that we call **anchor representation** (line 11). $\boldsymbol{z}$ is computed for each buffer and cached into the history anchors $\boldsymbol{Z}$, which is then conditioned by the decoder to generate new tokens (lines 12-13). The details of our segmentation and compression mechanism are introduced in §2.2.

2.2 Segmentation with Dynamic Compression

In this section, we provide details of different components in algorithm 1. We first describe how to learn the segmenter $F_{\text{seg}}(\cdot)$ with feedback from the encoder-decoder's cross-attention. Then we present how anchor representations are obtained through our selection-based compression method.

Learning Segmenter with Cross-attention We propose a learnable segmenter trained with feedback from the encoder-decoder cross-attention. Following algorithm 1, a segmenter is used to evaluate (score) input features as they are read into the system. Such scores $\boldsymbol{s} = F_{\text{seg}}(\boldsymbol{X})$ are then used to determine if YIELD is triggered (i.e., whether to segment streams). Effective segmentation is crucial in streaming sequence transduction to avoid sub-optimal transformation due to premature triggering or increased latency from delayed output. Since the ideal segmentation depends on several factors (the input's information density, the input and output's modalities, and the task at hand, *etc.,*), we rely on the cross-attention between the encoder and decoder to guide the segmenter (shown in fig. 2).

Specifically, we follow cross-attention from Transformers (Vaswani et al., 2017) to use three projections $\boldsymbol{W}_{\text{Q}}, \boldsymbol{W}_{\text{K}}, \boldsymbol{W}_{\text{V}}$ to generate the query vector $\boldsymbol{y}\boldsymbol{W}_{\text{Q}} \in \mathbb{R}^{T_y \times d}$, the key vector $\boldsymbol{h}\boldsymbol{W}_{\text{K}} \in \mathbb{R}^{T_x \times d}$ and the value vector $\boldsymbol{h}\boldsymbol{W}_{\text{V}} \in \mathbb{R}^{T_x \times d}$ (where d is the dimensionality of the representation) and compute cross-attention as:

$$S(\boldsymbol{h}, \boldsymbol{y}) = (\boldsymbol{h}\boldsymbol{W}_{\text{k}})(\boldsymbol{y}\boldsymbol{W}_{\text{Q}})^T \tag{1}$$

Then, as illustrated in fig. 2, we **inject** segmenter's scores into it the cross attention:

$$\tilde{S}(\boldsymbol{h}, \boldsymbol{y}) = S(\boldsymbol{h}, \boldsymbol{y}) + F_{\text{seg}}(\boldsymbol{x}) \tag{2}$$

The updated cross-attention $\tilde{S}(\boldsymbol{h}, \boldsymbol{y})$ is then used to transform the value vector $\boldsymbol{W}_{\text{V}}$ and will be used by the decoder to compute the loss function. Since the segmenter's scores are injected in equation (2), *it can be updated with end-to-end back-propagation.* Specifically, suppose the loss objective $\mathcal{L}$ is computed, with the chain rule, we have the gradient for the predicted score $\boldsymbol{\alpha} = F_{\text{seg}}(\boldsymbol{x})$ as:

$$\begin{aligned}\frac{\nabla \mathcal{L}}{\nabla \boldsymbol{\alpha}} &= \sum_{i=1}^{l} \frac{\nabla \mathcal{L}}{\nabla \tilde{S}^i(\boldsymbol{h}, \boldsymbol{y})} \cdot \frac{\nabla \tilde{S}^i(\boldsymbol{h}, \boldsymbol{y})}{\nabla \boldsymbol{\alpha}} \\ &= \sum_{i=1}^{l} \frac{\nabla \mathcal{L}}{\nabla \tilde{S}^i(\boldsymbol{h}, \boldsymbol{y})} \cdot \frac{\nabla}{\nabla \boldsymbol{\alpha}} (S(\boldsymbol{h}, \boldsymbol{y}) + \boldsymbol{\alpha}) \\ &= \sum_{i=1}^{l} \frac{\nabla \mathcal{L}}{\nabla \tilde{S}^i(\boldsymbol{h}, \boldsymbol{y})}\end{aligned}$$

where l is the number of transformer layer and $\tilde{S}^i(\boldsymbol{h}, \boldsymbol{y})$ is the cross-attention for i^{th} layer. We observe that the gradient impacting the segmenters is directly proportional to the gradient on the cross-attention logits. Consequently, by injecting cross-attention, we can train segmenters to prioritize positions that are more significant to the decoder.

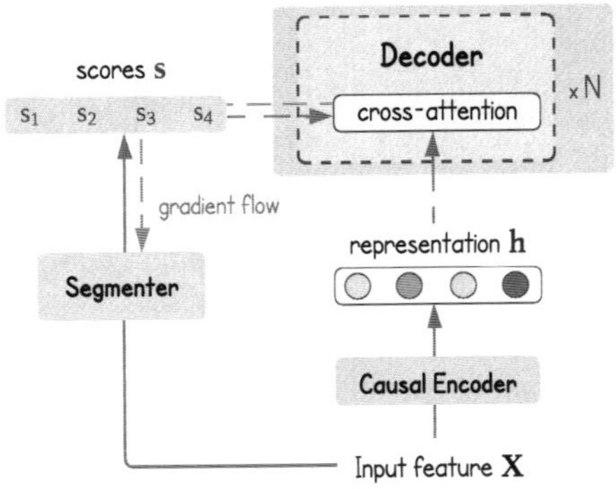

Figure 2: Visualization for the training of the segmenter through feedback from the encoder-decoder's cross-attention.

After training the segmenter, we predict scores $\boldsymbol{s} = F_{\text{seg}}(\boldsymbol{x})$ for input features and use the scores to segment the input sequence. Note that the predicted scores can be used differently based on the task. In the special case where the whole sequence is fully observed (i.e., regular non-streaming tasks), we do not YIELD output anymore. Instead, we simply select the top k scoring positions as anchors and use their representation for the decoder to generate outputs, as formalized below (I is a set of indices):

$$I = \text{SELECTTOP}_k(\boldsymbol{s}) \tag{3}$$

$$\boldsymbol{H} = F_{\text{enc}}(\boldsymbol{x}) \in \mathbb{R}^{T_x \times d} \tag{4}$$

$$\boldsymbol{Z} = \boldsymbol{H}[I] \in \mathbb{R}^{k \times d} \tag{5}$$

The compression rate is then $r = T_x/k \in [1, \infty)$ assuming $k \leq T_x$. In a more general case where streaming is enabled, the score is commonly accumulated (Inaguma et al., 2020; Ma et al., 2020c) until a certain threshold is reached. We use a threshold $\beta = 1$ throughout experiments. Specifically, we first scale $\boldsymbol{s}$ to $[0, 1]$ range values $\boldsymbol{\alpha} = \text{sigmoid}(\boldsymbol{s})$ and accumulate α following algorithm 1 (line 8) to YIELD new output. The accumulation of scores is a natural way to ensure a similar level of information is contained in each buffer. This corresponds to a larger buffer when the sound signal is sparse (see appendix A for visualization), which gives better latency-quality control.

Compression with Anchor Representation Every time an anchor is predicted by our trained segmenter, the model triggers generation with some buffer $\boldsymbol{B} \in \mathbb{R}^{b \times d}$ of b features. Subsequently, we transform such features into a high-dimensional representation $\boldsymbol{H} \in \mathbb{R}^{b \times d}$ with a **causal** encoder[2].

[2] In practice, we are inspired by BERT (Devlin et al., 2019) to add a special type embedding $\boldsymbol{e}$ to anchor tokens before

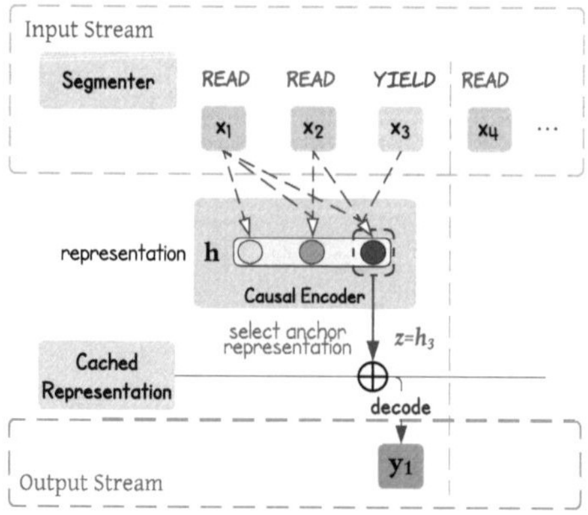

Figure 3: Visualization for the proposed "selection as compression" method. Input features are transformed by the encoder and we only select the encoding at the anchor position (where YIELD is triggered) as the compressed representation.

The causality of such an encoder ensures that representations at later positions contain information only from earlier positions. Then, we **only select** the representation at the anchor position (the last index of the current buffer) $\boldsymbol{z} = \boldsymbol{H}[b] \in \mathbb{R}^{1\times d}$ to represent the information of the whole buffer $\boldsymbol{B}$. Selected representations are also called anchor representations/vectors. For example, in fig. 3, YIELD is triggered at index 3; therefore we first transform the features into representations $\boldsymbol{H} = F_{\text{enc}}(\boldsymbol{B}|\boldsymbol{Z})$, and select $\boldsymbol{H}[3]$ as the anchor vector $\boldsymbol{z}$ to decode the next output with cached representation $\boldsymbol{Z}$.

2.3 Model Training

To train models for streaming sequence transduction, we primarily rely on the conventional objective – negative log-likelihood (NLL) loss:

$$\begin{aligned}\mathcal{L}_{\text{NLL}}(\boldsymbol{X}, \boldsymbol{Y}, \theta) &= -\log \mathbb{P}(\boldsymbol{Y}|\boldsymbol{X};\theta) \\ &= -\sum_{t=1}^{T_y} \log \mathbb{P}(y_t|\boldsymbol{Y}_{<t}, \boldsymbol{Z}_{<t};\theta)\end{aligned} \tag{6}$$

Note that the loss is defined over $\boldsymbol{X}, \boldsymbol{Y}$ as both input and output sequences are fully observed during training. In addition, the loss defined in equation (6) is slightly different than regular NLL in that the decoder can only use representation observed so far ($\boldsymbol{Z}_{<t}$) to generate the tth output. This method is also referred to as Infinite-Lookback (Arivazhagan et al., 2019; Liu et al., 2021, IL) and is used to mitigate the train-test mismatch as future representation cannot be observed during inference. Besides using NLL to update the encoder and decoder, we also follow prior work (Chang and Lee, 2022) to regularize the segmenter so that the number of YIELD is the same as the output length T_y. Due to page limitations, we refer readers to appendix B for more details.

passing through the encoder

3 Experiments: Non-Streaming Compression

We experiment on the non-streaming ASR task to better demonstrate the effectiveness of our selection-based compression method, since we do not need to consider the quality-latency trade-off as in the streaming scenario. We compare our method with other common baselines like Convolutional Neural Networks (Lecun and Bengio, 1995; Krizhevsky et al., 2012, CNN) and Continuous Integrate and Fire (Dong and Xu, 2020, CIF).

Datasets and Evaluation Metrics We conduct experiments on the LibriSpeech (Panayotov et al., 2015) and LibriTTS (Zen et al., 2019) dataset's "Clean-360h" section, which contains 360 hours of speech and their corresponding transcriptions. To evaluate ASR performance, we compute the word error rate (Morris et al., 2004, WER) between reference transcriptions and the generated text.

3.1 Training Setup

Compression with Anchor Representations In §2, we propose a general approach for stream transduction with dynamic compression. Now we instantiate the framework for the ASR task. We first use WAV2VEC2.0 (Baevski et al., 2020) to extract features $\boldsymbol{X}$ from the input speech sequence. We then use a 4-layer decoder-only Transformer[3] as our **causal encoder** for compression, from which we select out anchor representation $\boldsymbol{z}$. The segmenter is implemented with a 2-layer Feed-Forward Network. For the decoder, we use a 4-layer decoder-only Transformer with an additional linear layer as the language modeling head. For details of hyperparameters, we direct readers to appendix F.

As described in §2, we train the Encoder-Decoder model with a segmenter learned through cross-attention feedback. Given the extracted feature $\boldsymbol{X} = (x_1, x_2, \cdots, x_{T_x})$ and a target compression rate $r \in [1, \infty)$, we select top $k = T_x/r$ scoring positions and use their encodings as anchor representations (following equation (5)). We

[3] Following the implementation of GPT2 from Huggingface https://huggingface.co/gpt2

then feed the anchor representation $\boldsymbol{Z}$ to the decoder to generate text tokens. In practice, most input speeches from LibriTTS are less than 10 seconds, corresponding to a feature sequence of length $T_x = 10 * 16000/320 = 500$ (with a standard sampling rate 16 kHz and WAV2VEC2.0 has a stack of CNNs that reduce input sequence by 320×). Therefore, we chose some reasonable compression rates (i.e., $r = 12, 18, 30$) to test our compression methods. We now briefly describe two baselines that we compared against: CNNs and CIF.

Baseline: CNN A simple compression component is CNN. After we obtain speech feature $\boldsymbol{X}$, we apply CNNs with pre-defined strides to compress the feature. The encoder (a vanilla Transformer-Encoder module without our selection-based compression) further transforms such compressed features into encoder representations for the decoder to generate outputs. To enhance the capacity of CNNs, we follow Zeghidour et al. (2021); Défossez et al. (2022) to add two CNNs with kernel size $(5, 1)$ and stride size $(1, 1)$ as residual connection. More details about CNNs and their configurations are available in fig. 13 (in appendix F).

Baseline: CIF Continuous Integrate and Fire (Dong and Xu, 2020; Dong et al., 2022; Chang and Lee, 2022) uses a neural network to predict scores for each position and accumulates the scores until a threshold is reached, thereafter triggering the generation of a new token (called FIRE by the original paper). For each segment, CIF averages representations in the segment by directly weighing them with the predicted scores. For a fair comparison with prior work, we adopt the implementation from Dong et al. (2022) into our codebase.

There are two major differences between our method and CIF: firstly, STAR segmenter leverages cross-attention between encoder-decoder to interactively update representations, whereas CIF employs a weighted average of representations solely from the encoder side; secondly, STAR pushes information to condense in particular anchor at YIELD positions and performs explicit selections, whereas CIF's representations are averaged across each segment. Broadly, these distinctions mirror the differences between hard and soft attention mechanisms (Xu et al., 2015; Luong et al., 2015). We refer readers to appendix B and the original paper (Dong and Xu, 2020) for more details.

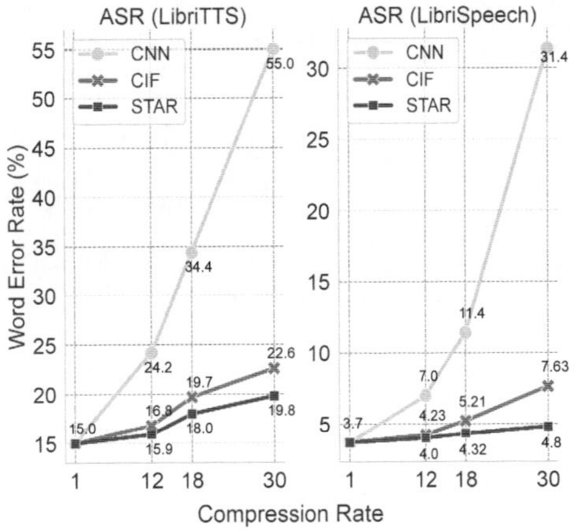

Figure 4: ASR performance (evaluated by WER) by different compression methods. From the figure, STAR outperforms other compressors and the gap enlarges as the compression rate increases.

3.2 Results of Different Compression Methods

We test the compression performance on three compression rates $r \in \{12, 18, 30\}$. As shown in fig. 4, our compression module obtains the best performance, achieving almost lossless compression when $r = 12$, and consistently outperforms the other two methods on different compression rates. By comparing the trend in detail, we find that CNNs are sub-optimal as the compressor because they operate on a small local window and change the underlying feature representation, which might be hard for the encoder and decoder to adapt to. Now comparing CIF and STAR. As the compression rate increases, the gap between STAR and CIF also increases. When $r = 30$, STAR outperforms CIF by about 3 WER points on both LibriSpeech and LibriTTS. From the results, we have verified that STAR is more effective in compressing representation compared to CNN and CIF. Later in our analysis (see §5), we provide evidence of STAR achieving more robust compressed representations. Lastly, to exclude the influence from the text decoder, we also designed a speech similarity task in appendix D to show that STAR results in better-compressed speech representation.

4 Streaming Experiments: Simultaneous Speech Recognition and Translation

Datasets For our simultaneous S2T experiments, we use the English-German (EN-DE) portion of the MuST-C V1 (Di Gangi et al., 2019) dataset for speech translation (ST). We also include results for simultaneous ASR using LibriSpeech and Lib-

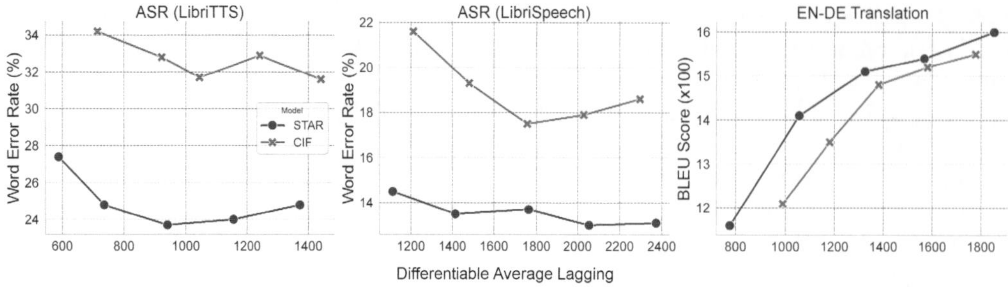

Figure 5: Lateny-Quality trade-off for CIF and STAR. The five markers on the line correspond to different WAIT-k strategies (from left to right, WAIT-$k \in \{1, 2, 3, 4, 5\}$).

riTTS. Note that since our method is based on a general Encoder-Decoder Transformer, it is not tailored to ASR by leveraging monotonic alignment or using small character-level vocabulary.

Evaluation Metric To evaluate the quality of generated output, we use WER for the ASR task and BLEU (Papineni et al., 2002) for the speech translation task. For simultaneous S2T, latency measurement is essential and we resort to the commonly used metric, Differentiable Average Lagging (Arivazhagan et al., 2019, DAL), which was originally proposed for simultaneous text translation and later adapted to speech translation in (Ma et al., 2020a). The smaller the DAL, the better the system in terms of latency. We refer readers to appendix G for details on the latency metric.

Experiment Setup Our first step is to train an *speech-to-text* (S2T) streaming model without a segmenter. To make WAV2VEC2.0 causal, we add a causal mask and train it jointly with the encoder and decoder until convergence. Once the vanilla streaming S2T model is trained, we freeze the **causal** WAV2VEC2.0 model as the feature extractor and start fine-tuning the encoder and the decoder with the segmenter.

Experimental Results We show the experiment results in fig. 5 where we plot WER/BLEU v.s. DAL to demonstrate the quality-latency trade-off for each system. In our evaluation, we adapt the WAIT-k policy (Ma et al., 2019) for all systems. Here WAIT-k denotes the number of speech segments we encode first before decoding text tokens. A larger WAIT-k value generally results in higher latency but better S2T performance. In our work, we focus on low-latency scenarios where flexible decision policies like CIF and STAR are most useful; Therefore, we set WAIT-k value to 1 to 5.

We first present the baseline system for simul-

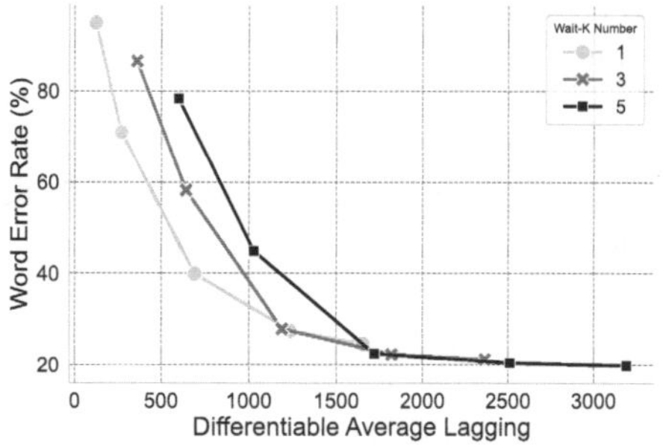

Figure 6: Quality-latency trade-off for fixed-decision S2T model. Each line corresponds to a different WAIT-k strategy and each marker corresponds to a stride size of $\{120, 200, 280, 360, 440\}$ms.

taneous ASR with a fixed decision policy in fig. 6. We use the vanilla streaming S2T model (no compression) and apply a fixed stride size to slide through the speech and generate text tokens. As shown in fig. 6, using a large stride like 360ms (i.e., each chunk corresponds to a speech feature of length $0.36 \times 16000/320 = 18$) or 440ms, simultaneous ASR achieved < 20 WER. However, the latency is also extremely high (over 2000 DAL). For smaller strides, quality of generated output is suboptimal because not enough information is provided for the text decoder to generate each new token. A flexible decision policy could alleviate such issues and provide better latency-quality tradeoff. From fig. 5, we see that for both CIF and STAR, their output has better quality when the latency is low. For instance, on LibriTTS, STAR achieves about 24 WER with a DAL smaller than 800 while the best-performing fixed decision policy only obtains such performance with a DAL of about 1200.

Comparing CIF with STAR across three datasets (LibriSpeech, LibriTTS, and MUST-C), we find that STAR consistently achieves better performance, obtaining a lower WER (or higher BLEU) score with relatively lower latency across different WAIT-k strategies. This demonstrates that

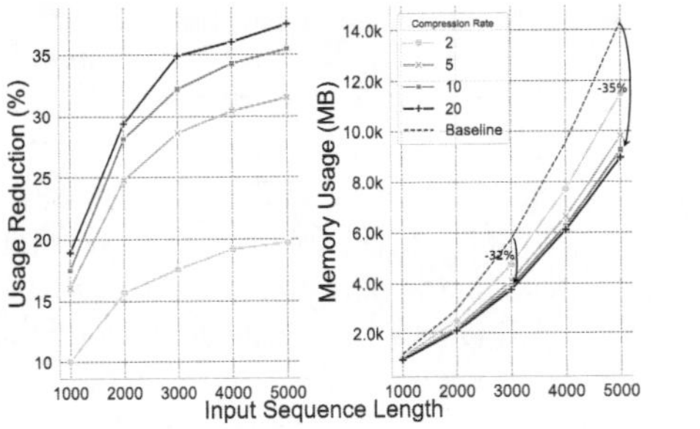

Figure 7: Memory usage and reduction from our proposed method (with compression rates $r \in \{2, 5, 10, 20\}$). More results and detailed setup are provided in appendix E.

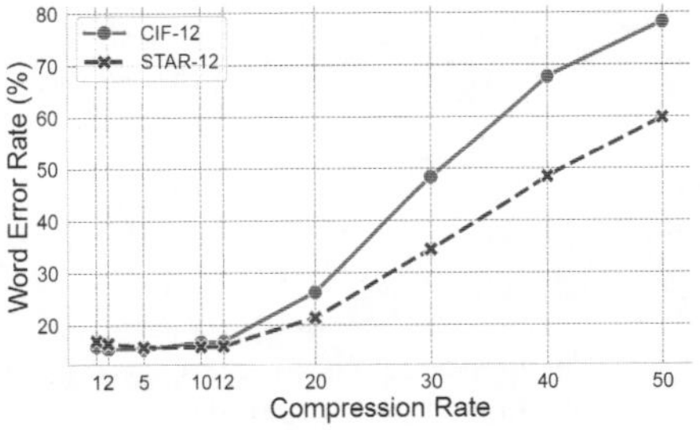

Figure 8: CIF and STAR based model trained with compression rate 12 are evaluated on various compression rates (ranges from 1 to 50). For a lower compression rate (≤ 12), both models preserve their quality well. For a higher compression rate (> 12), STAR is more robust and its performance degrades slower than CIF.

STAR gives a better flexible policy to YIELD new tokens, and the compressed representation encodes more information for target text generation. In appendix A, we compare qualitative examples and visualize the difference in the segmentation from CIF and STAR. Overall, we find the segmentation from STAR better corresponds to the target texts, achieving superior simultaneous S2T performance.

5 Analysis

5.1 Memory Efficiency

Since STAR condenses information in each buffer into anchor representation, it enhances memory efficiency by caching compressed representation for the decoder to generate outputs. With a compression rate r, a batch size b, and input features of average length T_x, and hidden dimension d, our system compresses the encoder representation from bdT_x to bdT_x/r. Besides memory consumption, note that cross-attention computation (equation (1)) is quadratic w.r.t. encoder representation's length; thus, our method reduces the cost of its computation by a factor of r^2. Besides theoretical analysis, we benchmark the actual memory usage and the percentage of usage reduction achieved by different compression rates. From fig. 7, we show that with a rate of $r = 10$ (which achieves nearly lossless compression), STAR reduces the memory consumption by more than 30% when transducing an input feature of length longer than 3,000. For the full details of our benchmark setup and results, we refer readers to appendix E.

5.2 Robustness

In this section, we evaluate the robustness of streaming models (CIF and STAR) by subjecting them to compression and segmentation conditions different from their training setup. We find that STAR is more robust than CIF, retaining better transduction when operating on context windows not exposed to during training.

Various Compression Rates at Inference As detailed in §3, we trained CIF- and STAR-based models with a compression rate of $r = 12$ (denoted as CIF-12 and STAR-12) and tested them under varying compression rates. Both models perform well at $r \leq 12$, as expected since they are trained for $12\times$ compression. However, when $r > 12$, STAR-12 shows significantly less degradation compared to CIF-12, indicating superior retention of information. This resilience arises from STAR's design, which focuses information into anchor positions, ensuring each anchor retains substantial information even at higher compression rates. In contrast, CIF's averaging approach leads to increased interference between representations.

Different Segmentations In §4, we tested CIF- and STAR-based models under a shared fixed segmentation policy, where segments were of uniform size ($\lfloor T_x/T_y \rfloor$). This setup evaluates robustness to segmentation changes. Results in fig. 9 show that while both models experience performance drops, STAR remains robust, achieving < 30 WER with a DAL of 800, whereas CIF exceeds 80 WER. This highlights STAR's ability to better compress and retain information within anchor representations, making it more robust to policy changes.

Moreover, we let the the two models use all previously computed representations (thus no compression is performed) and name such models CIF-ALL and STAR-ALL in fig. 9. We find that CIF-ALL still greatly lags behind the performance of STAR even when all previous representations are used. This shows that CIF is not a robust method as

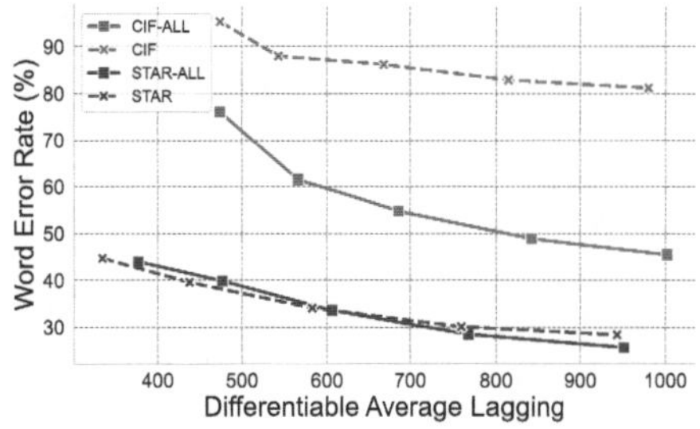

Figure 9: Latency-quality trade-off for CIF and STAR using a fixed decision policy instead of their own predicted segmentation. The five markers on the line correspond to five WAIT-k strategies (from left to right, WAIT-$k \in \{1, 2, 3, 4, 5\}$).

it only obtains good performance when aggregating representations using its learned segmentation. On the contrary, STAR is much more robust; in fact, from fig. 9, we find that STAR has a very close performance compared to its non-compressed version STAR-ALL, providing another evidence of its robust compression quality.

6 Related work

End-to-end Streaming Speech-to-text For streaming/simultaneous *speech-to-text* tasks, learning speech representation and policies for READ and YIELD is essential. Previous methods like RNN-Transducer (Graves, 2012) and Connectionist Temporal Classification (CTC) (Graves et al., 2006) leverage monotonic alignment for low error rate transcription. Recent work (Moritz et al., 2020; Tsunoo et al., 2020) further extends transformers for streaming ASR using modified attention and beam search.

For speech translation, Ma et al. (2019) proposed the Wait-K strategy with a fixed decision policy that read chunks of equal-length text for decoding and Ma et al. (2020b) adapted the wait-k strategy for simultaneous speech translation. Instead of a fixed decision policy, SimulSpeech (Ren et al., 2020) trained segmenters with CTC loss. Zeng et al. (2021) also use CTC for guidance on word boundary learns to shrink the representation and proposes the Wait-K-Stride-N strategy that writes N tokens for each READ action. Dong et al. (2022) and Chang and Lee (2022) use CIF to learn segmentation for the speech sequences and trigger the YIELD action whenever CIF FIRE a new representation. Additionally, Arivazhagan et al. (2019) and Ma et al. (2020c) support a more adaptive strategy where dynamic READ and YIELD are possible. However, even for such an adaptive strategy, a good decision policy still matters (Ma et al., 2020b).

Efficient Methods for Transformers Prior work studied efficient methods to scale Transformers to long sequences (Tay et al., 2022), including sparse patterns (Beltagy et al., 2020), recurrence (Dai et al., 2019), kernelized attentions (Choromanski et al., 2021), etc. Some of them can be applied in the streaming settings, such as Streaming LLMs (Xiao et al., 2023), Compressive Transformers (Rae et al., 2020), etc. Moreover, Tworkowski et al. (2023); Bertsch et al. (2023) proposed to apply kNN to the attention to select a subset of past tokens, akin to the segmentation process in this paper. Similar to the residual connection in our paper, Nugget (Qin and Van Durme, 2023) trains a scorer to select a subset of tokens to represent texts. More recently, Tan et al. (2024) and Qin et al. (2023) also combine context compression with efficient fine-tuning methods like LoRA (Hu et al., 2021) to expand context length for large language models.

Speech Representation Traditionally, acoustic features are extracted by filter-bank features, mel-frequency cepstral coefficients, or bottleneck features (Muda et al., 2010; Davis and Mermelstein, 1980). More recent work relies on self-supervision to learn speech representations. For example, Zeghidour et al. (2021) and Défossez et al. (2022) learn acoustic representation by reconstructing the original audio. To learn semantic representation, masked language modeling, and contrastive learning objectives are popularized by widely used representations from Hubert (Hsu et al., 2021), w2v-BERT (Chung et al., 2021) and Wav2Vec (Schneider et al., 2019; Baevski et al., 2020). All these models use CNNs as a building block to downsample speech signals/representations.

7 Conclusion and Future Work

We introduce STAR, a model designed for dynamic compression and transduction of streams. STAR features a segmenter learned via encoder-decoder cross-attention and employs a selection-based compression approach. Our experiments across multiple *speech-to-text* tasks confirm STAR's superior compression performance and latency-quality trade-off relative to established methods such as Convolutional Neural Networks and Continuous Integrate-and-Fire. In the future, we hope to extend this framework to facilitate streaming non-autoregressive generation.

References

Abien Fred Agarap. 2018. Deep learning using rectified linear units (relu). *ArXiv*, abs/1803.08375.

Naveen Arivazhagan, Colin Cherry, Wolfgang Macherey, Chung-Cheng Chiu, Semih Yavuz, Ruoming Pang, Wei Li, and Colin Raffel. 2019. Monotonic infinite lookback attention for simultaneous machine translation. In *Proceedings of the 57th Annual Meeting of the Association for Computational Linguistics*, pages 1313–1323, Florence, Italy. Association for Computational Linguistics.

Alexei Baevski, Henry Zhou, Abdelrahman Mohamed, and Michael Auli. 2020. wav2vec 2.0: A framework for self-supervised learning of speech representations. *Preprint*, arXiv:2006.11477.

Loïc Barrault, Yu-An Chung, Mariano Coria Meglioli, David Dale, Ning Dong, Mark Duppenthaler, Paul-Ambroise Duquenne, Brian Ellis, Hady Elsahar, Justin Haaheim, John Hoffman, Min-Jae Hwang, Hirofumi Inaguma, Christopher Klaiber, Ilia Kulikov, Pengwei Li, Daniel Licht, Jean Maillard, Ruslan Mavlyutov, Alice Rakotoarison, Kaushik Ram Sadagopan, Abinesh Ramakrishnan, Tuan Tran, Guillaume Wenzek, Yilin Yang, Ethan Ye, Ivan Evtimov, Pierre Fernandez, Cynthia Gao, Prangthip Hansanti, Elahe Kalbassi, Amanda Kallet, Artyom Kozhevnikov, Gabriel Mejia Gonzalez, Robin San Roman, Christophe Touret, Corinne Wong, Carleigh Wood, Bokai Yu, Pierre Andrews, Can Balioglu, Peng-Jen Chen, Marta R. Costa-jussà, Maha Elbayad, Hongyu Gong, Francisco Guzmán, Kevin Heffernan, Somya Jain, Justine Kao, Ann Lee, Xutai Ma, Alex Mourachko, Benjamin Peloquin, Juan Pino, Sravya Popuri, Christophe Ropers, Safiyyah Saleem, Holger Schwenk, Anna Sun, Paden Tomasello, Changhan Wang, Jeff Wang, Skyler Wang, and Mary Williamson. 2023. Seamless: Multilingual expressive and streaming speech translation. *Preprint*, arXiv:2312.05187.

Iz Beltagy, Matthew E. Peters, and Arman Cohan. 2020. Longformer: The Long-Document Transformer.

Amanda Bertsch, Uri Alon, Graham Neubig, and Matthew R. Gormley. 2023. Unlimiformer: Long-Range Transformers with Unlimited Length Input.

Chih-Chiang Chang and Hung-yi Lee. 2022. Exploring continuous integrate-and-fire for adaptive simultaneous speech translation. In *Interspeech 2022*. ISCA.

Junkun Chen, Mingbo Ma, Renjie Zheng, and Liang Huang. 2021. Direct simultaneous speech-to-text translation assisted by synchronized streaming asr. In *Findings*.

Krzysztof Choromanski, Valerii Likhosherstov, David Dohan, Xingyou Song, Andreea Gane, Tamas Sarlos, Peter Hawkins, Jared Davis, Afroz Mohiuddin, Lukasz Kaiser, David Belanger, Lucy Colwell, and Adrian Weller. 2021. Rethinking Attention with Performers. In *International Conference on Learning Representations (ICLR)*.

Junyoung Chung, Caglar Gulcehre, KyungHyun Cho, and Yoshua Bengio. 2014. Empirical evaluation of gated recurrent neural networks on sequence modeling. *Preprint*, arXiv:1412.3555.

Yu-An Chung, Yu Zhang, Wei Han, Chung-Cheng Chiu, James Qin, Ruoming Pang, and Yonghui Wu. 2021. W2v-bert: Combining contrastive learning and masked language modeling for self-supervised speech pre-training. *Preprint*, arXiv:2108.06209.

Zihang Dai, Zhilin Yang, Yiming Yang, Jaime Carbonell, Quoc V. Le, and Ruslan Salakhutdinov. 2019. Transformer-XL: Attentive Language Models Beyond a Fixed-Length Context. In *Annual Meeting of the Association for Computational Linguistics (ACL)*.

S. Davis and P. Mermelstein. 1980. Comparison of parametric representations for monosyllabic word recognition in continuously spoken sentences. *IEEE Transactions on Acoustics, Speech, and Signal Processing*, 28(4):357–366.

Jacob Devlin, Ming-Wei Chang, Kenton Lee, and Kristina Toutanova. 2019. Bert: Pre-training of deep bidirectional transformers for language understanding. In *North American Chapter of the Association for Computational Linguistics*.

Mattia A. Di Gangi, Roldano Cattoni, Luisa Bentivogli, Matteo Negri, and Marco Turchi. 2019. MuST-C: a Multilingual Speech Translation Corpus. In *Proceedings of the 2019 Conference of the North American Chapter of the Association for Computational Linguistics: Human Language Technologies, Volume 1 (Long and Short Papers)*, pages 2012–2017, Minneapolis, Minnesota. Association for Computational Linguistics.

Linhao Dong and Bo Xu. 2020. Cif: Continuous integrate-and-fire for end-to-end speech recognition. *Preprint*, arXiv:1905.11235.

Qian Dong, Yaoming Zhu, Mingxuan Wang, and Lei Li. 2022. Learning when to translate for streaming speech. In *Proceedings of the 60th Annual Meeting of the Association for Computational Linguistics (Volume 1: Long Papers)*, pages 680–694, Dublin, Ireland. Association for Computational Linguistics.

Alexandre Défossez, Jade Copet, Gabriel Synnaeve, and Yossi Adi. 2022. High fidelity neural audio compression. *Preprint*, arXiv:2210.13438.

Eduardo Fonseca, Jordi Pons, Xavier Favory, Frederic Font, Dmitry Bogdanov, Andres Ferraro, Sergio Oramas, Alastair Porter, and Xavier Serra. 2017. Freesound datasets: A platform for the creation of open audio datasets.

Alex Graves. 2012. Sequence transduction with recurrent neural networks. *Preprint*, arXiv:1211.3711.

Alex Graves, Santiago Fernández, Faustino Gomez, and Jürgen Schmidhuber. 2006. Connectionist temporal classification: labelling unsegmented sequence data with recurrent neural networks. In *Proceedings of the 23rd International Conference on Machine Learning*, ICML '06, page 369–376, New York, NY, USA. Association for Computing Machinery.

Anmol Gulati, James Qin, Chung-Cheng Chiu, Niki Parmar, Yu Zhang, Jiahui Yu, Wei Han, Shibo Wang, Zhengdong Zhang, Yonghui Wu, and Ruoming Pang. 2020. Conformer: Convolution-augmented transformer for speech recognition. *CoRR*, abs/2005.08100.

Sepp Hochreiter and Jürgen Schmidhuber. 1997. Long short-term memory. *Neural Computation*, 9(8):1735–1780.

Wei-Ning Hsu, Benjamin Bolte, Yao-Hung Hubert Tsai, Kushal Lakhotia, Ruslan Salakhutdinov, and Abdelrahman Mohamed. 2021. Hubert: Self-supervised speech representation learning by masked prediction of hidden units. *Preprint*, arXiv:2106.07447.

Edward J. Hu, Yelong Shen, Phillip Wallis, Zeyuan Allen-Zhu, Yuanzhi Li, Shean Wang, Lu Wang, and Weizhu Chen. 2021. Lora: Low-rank adaptation of large language models. *Preprint*, arXiv:2106.09685.

Hirofumi Inaguma, Yashesh Gaur, Liang Lu, Jinyu Li, and Yifan Gong. 2020. Minimum latency training strategies for streaming sequence-to-sequence asr. *ICASSP 2020 - 2020 IEEE International Conference on Acoustics, Speech and Signal Processing (ICASSP)*, pages 6064–6068.

H. Kameoka, Kou Tanaka, and Takuhiro Kaneko. 2021. Fasts2s-vc: Streaming non-autoregressive sequence-to-sequence voice conversion. *ArXiv*, abs/2104.06900.

O. Khattab and Matei A. Zaharia. 2020. Colbert: Efficient and effective passage search via contextualized late interaction over bert. *Proceedings of the 43rd International ACM SIGIR Conference on Research and Development in Information Retrieval*.

Alex Krizhevsky, Ilya Sutskever, and Geoffrey E Hinton. 2012. Imagenet classification with deep convolutional neural networks. In *Advances in Neural Information Processing Systems*, volume 25. Curran Associates, Inc.

Yann Lecun and Yoshua Bengio. 1995. *Convolutional Networks for Images, Speech and Time Series*, pages 255–258. The MIT Press.

Jinyu Li. 2021. Recent advances in end-to-end automatic speech recognition. *ArXiv*, abs/2111.01690.

Xian Li, Changhan Wang, Yun Tang, C. Tran, Yuqing Tang, Juan Miguel Pino, Alexei Baevski, Alexis Conneau, and Michael Auli. 2020. Multilingual speech translation from efficient finetuning of pretrained models. In *Annual Meeting of the Association for Computational Linguistics*.

Zachary Chase Lipton. 2015. A critical review of recurrent neural networks for sequence learning. *CoRR*, abs/1506.00019.

Dan Liu, Mengge Du, Xiaoxi Li, Ya Li, and Enhong Chen. 2021. Cross attention augmented transducer networks for simultaneous translation. In *Proceedings of the 2021 Conference on Empirical Methods in Natural Language Processing*, pages 39–55, Online and Punta Cana, Dominican Republic. Association for Computational Linguistics.

Yuchen Liu, Hao Xiong, Zhongjun He, Jiajun Zhang, Hua Wu, Haifeng Wang, and Chengqing Zong. 2019. End-to-end speech translation with knowledge distillation. In *Interspeech*.

Thang Luong, Hieu Pham, and Christopher D. Manning. 2015. Effective approaches to attention-based neural machine translation. In *Proceedings of the 2015 Conference on Empirical Methods in Natural Language Processing*, pages 1412–1421, Lisbon, Portugal. Association for Computational Linguistics.

Mingbo Ma, Liang Huang, Hao Xiong, Renjie Zheng, Kaibo Liu, Baigong Zheng, Chuanqiang Zhang, Zhongjun He, Hairong Liu, Xing Li, Hua Wu, and Haifeng Wang. 2019. STACL: Simultaneous translation with implicit anticipation and controllable latency using prefix-to-prefix framework. In *Proceedings of the 57th Annual Meeting of the Association for Computational Linguistics*, pages 3025–3036, Florence, Italy. Association for Computational Linguistics.

Xutai Ma, Mohammad Javad Dousti, Changhan Wang, Jiatao Gu, and Juan Pino. 2020a. SIMULEVAL: An evaluation toolkit for simultaneous translation. In *Proceedings of the 2020 Conference on Empirical Methods in Natural Language Processing: System Demonstrations*, pages 144–150, Online. Association for Computational Linguistics.

Xutai Ma, Juan Pino, and Philipp Koehn. 2020b. SimulMT to SimulST: Adapting simultaneous text translation to end-to-end simultaneous speech translation. In *Proceedings of the 1st Conference of the Asia-Pacific Chapter of the Association for Computational Linguistics and the 10th International Joint Conference on Natural Language Processing*, pages 582–587, Suzhou, China. Association for Computational Linguistics.

Xutai Ma, Juan Miguel Pino, James Cross, Liezl Puzon, and Jiatao Gu. 2020c. Monotonic multihead attention. In *International Conference on Learning Representations*.

Niko Moritz, Takaaki Hori, and Jonathan Le. 2020. Streaming automatic speech recognition with the transformer model. In *ICASSP 2020 - 2020 IEEE International Conference on Acoustics, Speech and Signal Processing (ICASSP)*, pages 6074–6078.

Andrew C. Morris, Viktoria Maier, and Phil D. Green. 2004. From wer and ril to mer and wil: improved evaluation measures for connected speech recognition. In *Interspeech*.

Lindasalwa Muda, Mumtaj Begam, and I. Elamvazuthi. 2010. Voice recognition algorithms using mel frequency cepstral coefficient (mfcc) and dynamic time warping (dtw) techniques. *Preprint*, arXiv:1003.4083.

Vassil Panayotov, Guoguo Chen, Daniel Povey, and Sanjeev Khudanpur. 2015. Librispeech: An asr corpus based on public domain audio books. In *2015 IEEE International Conference on Acoustics, Speech and Signal Processing (ICASSP)*, pages 5206–5210.

Kishore Papineni, Salim Roukos, Todd Ward, and Wei-Jing Zhu. 2002. Bleu: a method for automatic evaluation of machine translation. In *Proceedings of the 40th Annual Meeting of the Association for Computational Linguistics*, pages 311–318, Philadelphia, Pennsylvania, USA. Association for Computational Linguistics.

Rohit Prabhavalkar, Takaaki Hori, Tara N. Sainath, Ralf Schlüter, and Shinji Watanabe. 2023. End-to-end speech recognition: A survey. *Preprint*, arXiv:2303.03329.

Guanghui Qin, Corby Rosset, Ethan C. Chau, Nikhil Rao, and Benjamin Van Durme. 2023. Nugget 2d: Dynamic contextual compression for scaling decoder-only language models. *Preprint*, arXiv:2310.02409.

Guanghui Qin and Benjamin Van Durme. 2023. Nugget: Neural agglomerative embeddings of text. In *Proceedings of the 40th International Conference on Machine Learning*, volume 202 of *Proceedings of Machine Learning Research*, pages 28337–28350. PMLR.

Jack W. Rae, Anna Potapenko, Siddhant M. Jayakumar, and Timothy P. Lillicrap. 2020. Compressive Transformers for Long-Range Sequence Modelling. In *International Conference on Learning Representations (ICLR)*.

Yi Ren, Jinglin Liu, Xu Tan, Chen Zhang, Tao Qin, Zhou Zhao, and Tie-Yan Liu. 2020. SimulSpeech: End-to-end simultaneous speech to text translation. In *Proceedings of the 58th Annual Meeting of the Association for Computational Linguistics*, pages 3787–3796, Online. Association for Computational Linguistics.

Steffen Schneider, Alexei Baevski, Ronan Collobert, and Michael Auli. 2019. wav2vec: Unsupervised pre-training for speech recognition. *Preprint*, arXiv:1904.05862.

Rico Sennrich, Barry Haddow, and Alexandra Birch. 2016. Neural machine translation of rare words with subword units. In *Proceedings of the 54th Annual Meeting of the Association for Computational Linguistics (Volume 1: Long Papers)*, pages 1715–1725, Berlin, Germany. Association for Computational Linguistics.

Sijun Tan, Xiuyu Li, Shishir G Patil, Ziyang Wu, Tianjun Zhang, Kurt Keutzer, Joseph E. Gonzalez, and Raluca Ada Popa. 2024. LLoCO: Learning long contexts offline. In *Proceedings of the 2024 Conference on Empirical Methods in Natural Language Processing*, pages 17605–17621, Miami, Florida, USA. Association for Computational Linguistics.

Yi Tay, Mostafa Dehghani, Dara Bahri, and Donald Metzler. 2022. Efficient Transformers: A Survey. *ACM Computing Surveys*, 55(6):1–28.

Emiru Tsunoo, Yosuke Kashiwagi, and Shinji Watanabe. 2020. Streaming transformer asr with blockwise synchronous beam search. *Preprint*, arXiv:2006.14941.

Szymon Tworkowski, Konrad Staniszewski, Mikołaj Pacek, Yuhuai Wu, Henryk Michalewski, and Piotr Miłoś. 2023. Focused Transformer: Contrastive Training for Context Scaling.

Ashish Vaswani, Noam Shazeer, Niki Parmar, Jakob Uszkoreit, Llion Jones, Aidan N Gomez, Ł ukasz Kaiser, and Illia Polosukhin. 2017. Attention is all you need. In *Advances in Neural Information Processing Systems*, volume 30. Curran Associates, Inc.

Peidong Wang, Eric Sun, Jian Xue, Yu Wu, Long Zhou, Yashesh Gaur, Shujie Liu, and Jinyu Li. 2022. Lamassu: A streaming language-agnostic multilingual speech recognition and translation model using neural transducers. *INTERSPEECH 2023*.

Guangxuan Xiao, Yuandong Tian, Beidi Chen, Song Han, and Mike Lewis. 2023. Efficient Streaming Language Models with Attention Sinks.

Kelvin Xu, Jimmy Ba, Ryan Kiros, Kyunghyun Cho, Aaron Courville, Ruslan Salakhudinov, Rich Zemel, and Yoshua Bengio. 2015. Show, attend and tell: Neural image caption generation with visual attention. In *Proceedings of the 32nd International Conference on Machine Learning*, volume 37 of *Proceedings of Machine Learning Research*, pages 2048–2057, Lille, France. PMLR.

Jian Xue, Peidong Wang, Jinyu Li, Matt Post, and Yashesh Gaur. 2022. Large-scale streaming end-to-end speech translation with neural transducers. In *Interspeech*.

Neil Zeghidour, Alejandro Luebs, Ahmed Omran, Jan Skoglund, and Marco Tagliasacchi. 2021. Soundstream: An end-to-end neural audio codec. *Preprint*, arXiv:2107.03312.

Heiga Zen, Viet Dang, Rob Clark, Yu Zhang, Ron J. Weiss, Ye Jia, Zhifeng Chen, and Yonghui Wu. 2019. Libritts: A corpus derived from librispeech for text-to-speech. *Preprint*, arXiv:1904.02882.

Xingshan Zeng, Liangyou Li, and Qun Liu. 2021. RealTranS: End-to-end simultaneous speech translation with convolutional weighted-shrinking transformer. In *Findings of the Association for Computational Linguistics: ACL-IJCNLP 2021*, pages 2461–2474, Online. Association for Computational Linguistics.

Supplementary Material

Appendix Sections	Contents
Appendix A	Qualitative Examples of Speech Segmentation
Appendix B	More Details on Continuous Integrate and Fire
Appendix C	STAR's Robustness to Noise Injection
Appendix D	Similarity Test for Compressed Speech Representation
Appendix E	Benchmark Memory Usage with/without Compression
Appendix F	Model Configurations and Hyper-parameters
Appendix G	Measuring Latency: Differentiable Average Lagging

A Qualitative Examples of Speech Segmentation from Compressors

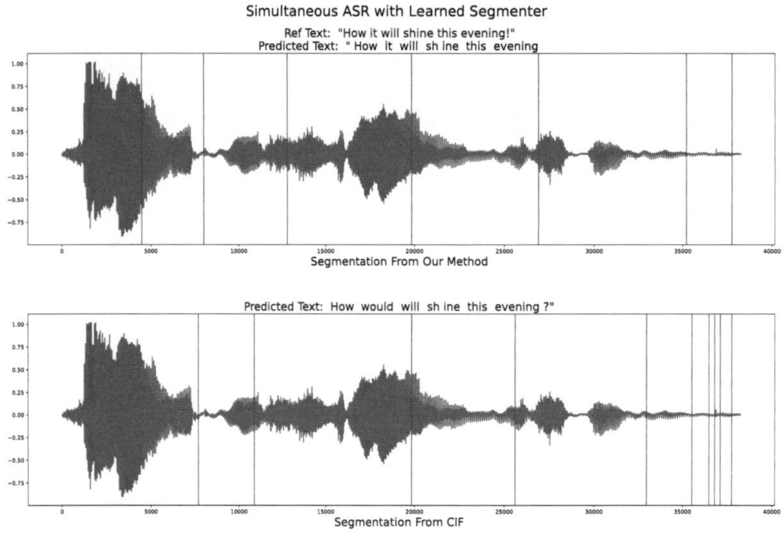

Figure 10: Qualitative Examples of CIF and STAR based Segmentation for Simul ASR

.

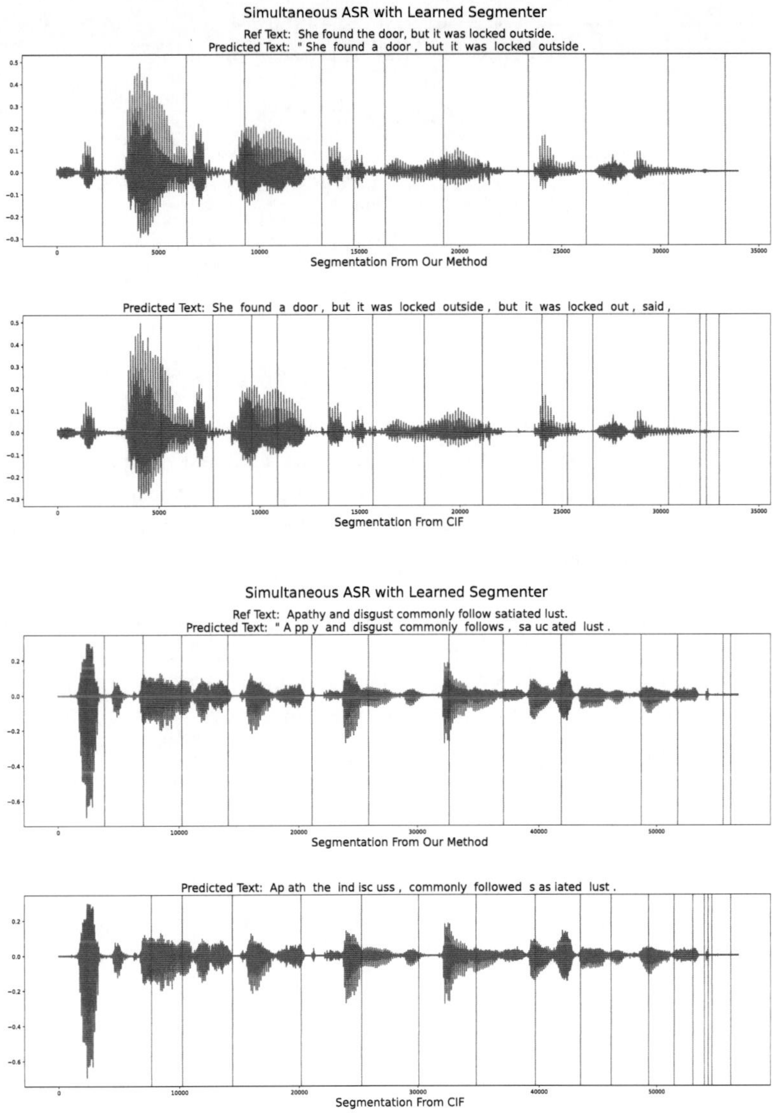

Figure 11: Qualitative Examples of CIF and STAR based Segmentation for Simul ASR

B Continuous Integrate and Fire

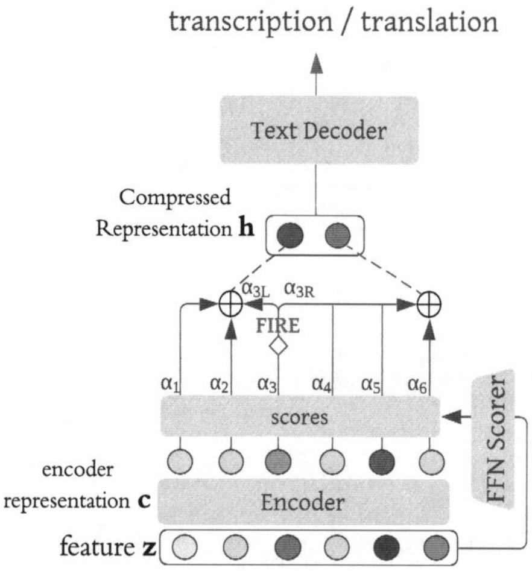

Figure 12: Illustration of Continuous Integrate and Fire.

Continuous Integrate and Fire (Dong and Xu, 2020, CIF) predicts a score for each position and dynamically aggregates the semantic representation. As shown in fig. 12, CIF first computes a list of scores $\boldsymbol{\alpha}$ similar to our proposed method. Then, starting from the first position, it accumulates the scores (and representation) until reaching a pre-defined threshold[4] β. Once reaching the threshold, it FIRE the accumulated representation and starts to accumulate again. As shown in fig. 12, suppose we originally have representation $\boldsymbol{z} = (z_1, \cdots, z_6)$ with corresponding scores $\boldsymbol{\alpha} = (\alpha_1, \cdots, \alpha_6)$. Suppose we reach the threshold at $t = 3$, *i.e.*, $\alpha_1 + \alpha_2 + \alpha_3 >= \beta$, then we FIRE the representation by taking the weighted average of score and representation $c_1 = \alpha_1 * \boldsymbol{z}_1 + \alpha_2 * \boldsymbol{z}_2 + \alpha_{3L} * \boldsymbol{z}_3$. Here c_1 becomes the compressed representation for the region $t = [1, 3]$. Note that since $\alpha_1 + \alpha_2 + \alpha_3 >= \beta$, we have residual score $\alpha_{3R} = \alpha_1 + \alpha_2 + \alpha_3 - \beta$, which is left for future accumulation, and we only use $\alpha_{3L} = \alpha_3 - \alpha_{3R}$ when weighting representation $\boldsymbol{z}_3$. More generally, suppose the previous FIRE occurs at position j and at current step i the accumulated score reaches the threshold, the aggregated representation is computed as

$$h = \alpha_{jR} * \boldsymbol{z}_j + \sum_{t=j+1}^{i-1} \alpha_t * \boldsymbol{z}_t + \alpha_{iL} * \boldsymbol{z}_i \tag{7}$$

To enforce the compression rate r, we follow (Dong et al., 2022; Chang and Lee, 2022) to re-scale the predicted scores so that the threshold β is reached T_y times when accumulating the scores:

$$\alpha_t = \sigma(s_t) \tag{8}$$

$$\tilde{\alpha}_t = \frac{\beta n^*}{\hat{n}} \alpha_t = \frac{\beta \cdot T_y}{\sum_{t=1}^{T_x} \alpha_t} \alpha_t \tag{9}$$

Here σ is the sigmoid function and $\hat{n}$ is the normalization term (summation of un-scaled scores) and n^* denotes the number of desired selections, i.e., $n^* = T_y$. We assume the input feature is longer than the output ($T_x > T_y$), so re-scaling scores to YIELD T_y means we employ a dynamic compression rate $r = T_x/T_y$ while transducing the streams. Note that T_y is only observed during training and we cannot re-scale $\boldsymbol{s}$ in test time. Therefore, we adopt a length penalty loss (Chang and Lee, 2022; Dong et al., 2022) during training to regularize the segmenter to ensure proper learning of segmentations:

$$\mathcal{L}_{\text{lp}}(\boldsymbol{X}, \boldsymbol{Y}; \theta) = (n^* - \hat{n})^2 = \left(T_y - \sum_{t=1}^{T_x} \sigma\left(F_{\text{seg}}(\boldsymbol{x}_t)\right)\right)^2 \tag{10}$$

[4] we set $\beta = 1$ throughout our experiments, following prior work (Dong et al., 2022; Chang and Lee, 2022)

Finally, our training objective is the combination of negative log-likelihood and length penalty loss:

$$\mathcal{L}(\boldsymbol{X},\boldsymbol{Y};\theta) = \mathcal{L}_{\text{NLL}}(\boldsymbol{X},\boldsymbol{Y};\theta) + \gamma\mathcal{L}_{\text{lp}}(\boldsymbol{X},\boldsymbol{Y};\theta) \tag{11}$$

In practice, the segmenter is only trained for a few thousand steps (so is the length penalty loss) and we set $\gamma = 0.01$.

Our method is fundamentally different because of how we treat the scorer and how we perform compression. In CIF, the compression is performed as an aggregation (weighted average) within each segmented block (decided by the scores and threshold). In STAR, we directly take out representations and we force the semantic encoder to condense information to those important positions. In other words, **we did not explicitly perform aggregation like CIF but expect the semantic encoder to learn such aggregation innately through training**.

Another key difference is how the scorer is learned. In CIF, the weighted average with scores and representation allows a gradient to flow through the scorer. For STAR, we inject the scores into cross-attention to update the scorer. The major advantage of our approach is that the importance of position is **judged by the attention from the decoder to the encoder representation**, which helps segment the speech representation in the way that the text decoder perceives it.

For more details, we direct readers to the prior work (Dong and Xu, 2020; Dong et al., 2022; Chang and Lee, 2022).

Model	Noise Ratio										
	0%	5%	10%	15%	20%	25%	30%	35%	40%	45%	50%
Vanilla S2T	**15.0**	**18.7**	**23.6**	**29.6**	**34.0**	**38.3**	43.7	46.8	51.8	56.1	61.0
S2T + CNN	24.2	26.7	31.9	37.1	40.8	45.5	49.9	53.6	58.9	61.6	65.3
S2T + CIF	16.8	20.4	26.0	30.7	36.0	40.1	44.9	50.1	53.9	58.9	62.2
S2T + STAR	15.9	19.7	25.1	29.8	34.7	38.6	**41.8**	**46.7**	**51.0**	**55.6**	**60.1**

Table 1: Word Error Rate of models given the noise injection ratio from 0% to 50%. Best numbers are **bolded** and better results are highlighted by the blue boxes while bad results are highlighted in yellow boxes. Compared to other compression methods, our proposed STAR is the most robust model across all noise injection ratios. When the noise ratio reaches beyond 30%, STAR even outperforms the S2T model without compression. All compression models are trained with the compression rate 12.

C Noise Injection

In this section, we test the robustness of compression methods when noise is injected into the original clean speech from LibriTTS. Instead of using synthetic signals such as Gaussian noise, we follow Zeghidour et al. (2021) to use natural noise (e.g., noise from the air conditioner, shutting door, etc.,) from Freesound[5] (Fonseca et al., 2017). We vary the ratio of noise injection from 5% to 30%, as shown in table 1. Given a ratio, we first calculate the duration of noise L (e.g., if the ratio is 0.1 and speech is 10 seconds, then we inject $L = 1$ second of noise) and randomly select a range of length L from the clean speech to inject noise. As shown in table 1, as the noise ratio increases, STAR has the smallest degradation and consistently outperforms CIF and CNNs. After reaching noise ratio $\geq 30\%$, STAR even outperforms the vanilla S2T model without compression. Such findings show that STAR has a more robust performance with the help of anchor representation, making it suffer less from noise injection and obtain better ASR performance.

D Similarity Test with Compressed Representation

In §3.2, we show STAR's superior performance on ASR, demonstrating the effectiveness of condensing information to a few positions for the text decoder. In this section, **we evaluate speech representation's similarity to further probe the quality of the compressed representation, without being influenced**

[5] We download the audio file for different noise from `https://github.com/microsoft/MS-SNSD`

by the decoder. More specifically, we use the test set of LibriTTS and for each English transcription, we compute its cosine similarity score against all other transcriptions, using a pre-trained sentence-transformer encoder[6] (it computes a sentence-level representation from BERT and perform mean pooling to obtain a uni-vector representation). We regard the ranking from sentence-Transformer's similarity as ground truth (as the transcriptions are non-complex English sentences); then we use our speech semantic encoders to compute cosine similarity for all pairs of speech representations and verify if the ranking is similar to the ground truth.

For the baseline vanilla S2T model, we perform mean pooling (MP) on its encoder representation $\boldsymbol{c}$ to obtain a uni-vector representation for each speech input and compute cosine similarities. For the other three models with compression, we first obtain the compressed representation $\boldsymbol{h}$ and we try two approaches to compute similarity. The first approach is the same as the baseline, where we apply MP on the compressed representation to obtain uni-vector representations. The second approach is inspired by the MaxSim (MS) algorithm used in ColBERT (Khattab and Zaharia, 2020), which computes the average of maximum similarity across the compressed representations.

Then we measure the quality of our trained speech semantic encoders with metrics widely used in retrieval and ranking–Normalized Discounted Cumulative Gain (nDCG) and Mean Reciprocal Rank (MRR). From the results shown in table 2, STAR still obtains the best-performing representation, with $\text{MRR@10} = 0.087, \text{nDCG@10} = 0.453$. Note that the performance is not very high as we did not train the model specifically for the sentence similarity task. Rather, we used the similarity task as an intrinsic measurement for the quality of condensed representations **to exclude the influence of the text decoder**.

Comparing the numbers in table 2, STAR consistently obtains better speech representation (for both MP and MS algorithms) for the similarity task. Interestingly we find that STAR-30's representation works better in mean pooling compared to STAR-12, suggesting that more condensed information works better for mean pooling. However, the MaxSim algorithm better leverages the multi-vector representation, which enables STAR-12 to obtain the best ranking performance.

	NDCG @ 10		**MRR @ 10**	
Model	**MP**	**MS**	**MP**	**MS**
Vanilla S2T	0.407	N/A	0.053	N/A
Conv-12	0.399	0.41	0.035	0.053
CIF-12	0.418	0.444	0.056	0.078
STAR-12	0.429	**0.453**	0.064	**0.087**
STAR-18	0.429	0.446	0.055	0.078
STAR-30	**0.437**	0.441	**0.078**	0.08

Table 2: Performance of speech rankings by different representation. STAR achieves the best performance as evaluated by NDCG@10 and MRR@10. The best performance is achieved through the MaxSim algorithm; interestingly, STAR-30 achieves the best performance with the Mean Pooling algorithm.

E Memory Usage Benchmark

In this section, we describe our setup to benchmark memory usage, which compares our proposed approach with a vanilla encoder-decoder model that does not support compression. We use Google Colab with a runtime that uses a T4 (16G memory) GPU. Then for each experiment, we run it 5 times and report the average in table 3. Both encoder and decoders follow our setup in appendix F, except that the encoder's maximum position is increased to 8,196 to support the benchmark experiment with long sequences. Note that the sequence length reported is the length of the input feature (which we compress by $r \in \{2, 5, 10, 20\}$). We set the output sequence's length to be $\frac{1}{10}$ of the input, similar to the ratio in our simultaneous *speech-to-text* experiments.

[6] In practice, we use public checkpoint from: `https://huggingface.co/sentence-transformers/all-MiniLM-L6-v2`

Stage	Batch Size	Seq Len	No Compression	With Compression			
				r=2	r=5	r=10	r=20
Inference	1	1000	1196	1076	1004	987	970
	1	2000	2975	2509	2237	2138	2101
	1	3000	5744	4736	4101	3894	3739
	1	4000	9540	7711	6637	6269	6102
	1	5000	14314	11493	9805	9237	8951
	1	6000	OOM	OOM	13587	12786	12434
Training	128	100	4964	4730	4209	4160	4124
	128	200	10687	9948	9465	9302	9223

Table 3: Memory usage (MB) of the encoder-decoder model with and without our proposed compression method. OOM: out of memory.

F Hyper-parameters

We provide hyper-parameters used for model configuration and training in this section. For different compression rates, the CNNs' stride configuration is shown in fig. 13. For example, a stride of (4,3) means we stack two CNN blocks, one with stride 4 and another with stride 3, achieving a compression rate of 12.

In this section, we provide the hyper-parameters and training configurations for all our experiments. We use a hidden dimension of 512 across all models. The tokenizer is developed using Byte Pair Encoding (Sennrich et al., 2016, BPE), with a vocabulary size of 10,000. The segmenter is parameterized by a 2-layer FFN with ReLU (Agarap, 2018) activation in between; the first FFN has input and output dimensions both set to 512 and the second FFN has input dimension 512 with output dimension 1. Our experiments are conducted using the Adam optimizer, configured with $\beta_1 = 0.9$ and $\beta_2 = 0.999$. These experiments are conducted with a data-parallel setting with 4 A100 GPUs.

For the audio processing, we set the sampling rate to 16,000. In the encoder configuration, we use a maximum of 1,024 positions for Automatic Speech Recognition (ASR) and 2,048 for Speech Translation (ST), with each encoder consisting of 4 layers and 8 attention heads. The decoder mirrors the encoder in its architecture, with 4 layers and 8 attention heads, but differs in its maximum positions, set at 512, and its vocabulary size, also at 10,000.

For non-streaming ASR in our pre-training setup, both the encoder and decoder are trained to converge with a learning rate of 1e-4, a batch size of 32, and a warmup of 10,000 steps. Subsequently, the compression module (CNN/CIF/STAR) is fine-tuned using a learning rate of 5e-5 alongside the pre-trained encoder and decoder. The segmenter is trained for 6,000 steps with feedback from the encoder-decoder's cross-attention, as discussed in §2, after which it is frozen. Post this, we further fine-tune the encoder and decoder until convergence.

For streaming *speech-to-text* tasks, the feature extractor (WAV2VEC2.0), encoder, and decoder are jointly trained with a learning rate of 5e-5, a batch size of 8, and gradient accumulation every 4 steps. A causal mask is added to WAV2VEC2.0during this process. Following convergence, the compression module undergoes fine-tuning using a learning rate of 5e-5 and a batch size of 16. Similar to the non-streaming setup, the segmenter is updated only in the first 6,000 steps.

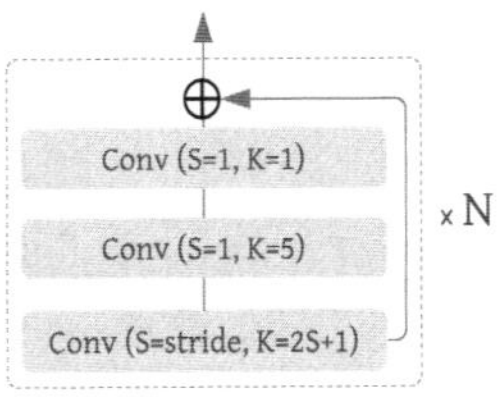

Compression Rate	Stride S
12	(4, 3)
18	(6, 3)
30	(5, 3, 2)

Figure 13: *Left*: Blocks of CNNs used to compress representation. *Right*: Stride sizes we used in experiments for different compression rates.

G Differentiable Average Lagging

Consider a raw speech with length T_x which is segmented into $|X|$ chunks. We define the length of ith segment (chunk) as $|X_i|$ (so that $|X| = \sum_{j=1}^{|X|} |X_j|$), and we define $d_i = \sum_{t=1}^{i} |X_t|$ as the total time that has elapsed until i^{th} speech segment X_i is processed. With the aforementioned notation, DAL is defined to be:

$$\text{DAL} = \frac{1}{T_y} \sum_{i=1}^{T_y} d'_i - \frac{i-1}{\gamma} \tag{12}$$

where T_y is the length of text tokens and $1/\gamma$ is the minimum delay after each operation, computed as $1/\gamma = \sum_{j=1}^{|X|} |X_j|/T_y$ (i.e., the averaged elapsed time for each token is used as the minimum delay). Lastly, d'_i is defined as:

$$d'_i = \begin{cases} d_i & i = 0 \\ \max(d_i, d'_{i-1} + 1/\gamma) & i > 0 \end{cases} \tag{13}$$

The smaller the DAL, the better the system in terms of latency. For more discussions for DAL and latency-quality trade-off in SimulST, we direct readers to prior work (Ma et al., 2020a; Arivazhagan et al., 2019) for more details.

NUTSHELL: A Dataset for Abstract Generation from Scientific Talks

Maike Züfle[1], Sara Papi[2], Beatrice Savoldi[2], Marco Gaido[2], Luisa Bentivogli[2], Jan Niehues[1]

[1]Karlsruhe Institute of Technology, [2]Fondazione Bruno Kessler

{maike.zuefle,jan.niehues}@kit.edu, {spapi,bsavoldi,mgaido,bentivo}@fbk.eu

Abstract

Scientific communication is receiving increasing attention in natural language processing, especially to help researches access, summarize, and generate content. One emerging application in this area is Speech-to-Abstract Generation (SAG), which aims to automatically generate abstracts from recorded scientific presentations. SAG enables researchers to efficiently engage with conference talks, but progress has been limited by a lack of large-scale datasets. To address this gap, we introduce NUTSHELL, a novel multimodal dataset of *ACL conference talks paired with their corresponding abstracts. We establish strong baselines for SAG and evaluate the quality of generated abstracts using both automatic metrics and human judgments. Our results highlight the challenges of SAG and demonstrate the benefits of training on NUTSHELL. By releasing NUTSHELL under an open license (CC-BY 4.0), we aim to advance research in SAG and foster the development of improved models and evaluation methods.[1]

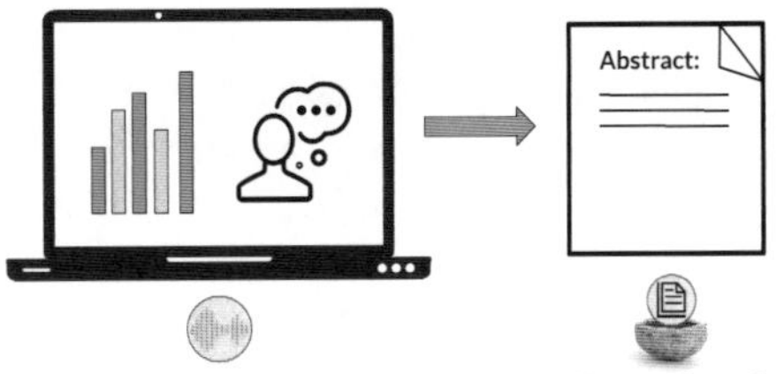

Figure 1: NUTSHELL, a dataset for Speech-to-Abstract Generation (SAG) from scientific talks.

1 Introduction

Abstracts are essential in scientific communication, allowing researchers to quickly grasp the key contributions of a paper. With the ever-growing number of publications, abstracts help researchers stay informed without reading full papers. Beyond their practical utility, abstracts also pose a significant challenge for natural language generation models: abstracts are a specialized form of summarization that not only condenses content but also promotes the work, often using domain-specific terminology and structured language.

Scientific summarization has been widely studied in natural language processing, including summarizing entire articles (Collins et al., 2017; Mao et al., 2022; Liu et al., 2024), particularly in the medical domain (Kedzie et al., 2018; Cohan et al., 2018; Gupta et al., 2021), generating abstracts from citations (Yasunaga et al., 2019; Zanzotto et al., 2020), summarizing specific paper sections (Takeshita et al., 2024), and leveraging knowledge graphs for abstract generation (Koncel-Kedziorski et al., 2019).

With the growing availability of recorded conference talks, a new challenge emerges: generating abstracts from spoken content or Speech-to-Abstract Generation (SAG). The abstracts offer researchers a quick way to assess relevant talks without watching entire recordings. Additionally, as conferences include more virtual content, automatically generated summaries enable efficient engagement with recorded talks (Murray et al., 2010).

While speech summarization has been explored in domains like news (Matsuura et al., 2024), YouTube videos (Sanabria et al., 2018), and meeting minutes (McCowan et al., 2005; Janin et al., 2003), large-scale datasets for scientific talk abstract generation are lacking. Existing work (Lev et al., 2019) aligns transcripts with the corresponding papers and extracts overlapping textual segments as summaries. However, these segments are drawn from the paper rather than the talk itself, failing to capture the distinct contributions, framing, and nuances conveyed in spoken presentations. Other studies have focused on summarizing TED

[1]https://huggingface.co/datasets/maikezu/nutshell

Proceedings of the 22nd International Conference on Spoken Language Translation (IWSLT 2025), pages 19–32
July 31 - August 1, 2025 ©2025 Association for Computational Linguistics

Talks (Koto et al., 2014; Kano et al., 2021; Vico and Niehues, 2022; Shon et al., 2023), which target a broad audience and prioritize inspiration and engagement over technical content.

To bridge this gap, we introduce NUTSHELL a new multimodal dataset for abstract generation from scientific talks. Built from recorded presentations of *ACL conferences, the dataset pairs abstracts with their corresponding spoken content and video, offering a valuable resource for future research. To validate the quality of the abstracts as concise and well-structured summaries of the talks – i.e., capturing the essence of the presentations *in a nutshell* – we performed a human assessment, which confirmed their effectiveness and suitability for the SAG task.

To establish baselines for SAG using our dataset, we evaluate three model types: (1) a cascaded model combining automatic speech recognition (ASR) with text-based summarization, (2) a state-of-the-art speech-language model (SpeechLLM) without fine-tuning, and (3) a SpeechLLM fine-tuned on our dataset.

Our contributions are three-fold:

1. We introduce NUTSHELL, a novel dataset for abstract generation from scientific talks comprising 1,172 hours, which is released under CC-BY 4.0 License on HuggingFace;[1]
2. We provide baselines with different model types for comparison in future research, evaluated using both standard automatic metrics (e.g., ROUGE) and the emerging LLM-as-a-judge approach (Shen et al., 2023);
3. We conduct human evaluations to assess the quality of the abstracts and validate the suitability of automatic metrics for the SAG task.

2 The NUTSHELL Dataset

In this section, we introduce the new NUTSHELL resource. We chose to build our corpus upon the the ACL Anthology[2] since it provides a rich collection of multimodal resources (talks and abstracts) and open-access licensing. Starting from 2017, a significant number of papers published in the main *ACL conferences (ACL, EMNLP, and NAACL) include a video of the presentation, all released under the Creative Commons Attribution 4.0 license. This makes *ACL an ideal resource for building a multimodal dataset for the SAG task.

[2]https://aclanthology.org

In the following, we present a feasibility assessment of SAG through human evaluation (§2.1). Then, we describe the collection process performed to create NUTSHELL, together with the final dataset statistics (§2.2).

2.1 Are paper abstracts "good" talk summaries?

Before creating the corpus, we establish the validity of our data by investigating whether abstracts represent a good summary of the associated talk. To this aim, we conduct a qualitative check on a data sample of 30 talk-abstract pairs from the ACL Anthology. We involve a total of 5 annotators, who are all domain experts and thus familiar with scientific material.[3] To verify Inter-Annotator Agreement (IAA), a double annotation by different experts was carried out on 15 pairs.

Since we are interested in understanding whether paper abstracts are informative enough to represent a good summary of the talk, we asked evaluators to annotate: (1) Whether the information in the abstract is **all** uttered by the presenter in the talk; (2) The span of information present in the abstract that was not contained in the talk, if any; (3) Whether the abstract summarizes all **important** information presented in the talk. The human evaluation procedure, including the annotation template, is described in App. A.

The results indicate that 70.0% of the abstracts are considered good summaries by annotators as they contain important information about the talk. However, 63.3% of the abstracts also contain information not explicitly present in the talk itself. To better understand this, we conducted a qualitative analysis of the annotated spans corresponding to this missing information. We found that these spans typically involved dataset names, model names, shared task references (e.g., evaluation campaigns), or URLs (e.g., link to the resource or model being released). Notably, these elements are often displayed on slides but not explicitly verbalized by presenters.[4]

Despite this issue, the evaluation of automatic models against the same ground truth abstract can be considered fair, as models are equally penalized by this category of missing information. Moreover,

[3]Annotators include the paper authors and their colleagues.

[4]This issue could be overcome by exploiting the videos, as this information is typically shown in the slides. While out of scope for SAG, NUTSHELL includes the videos, making it a useful resource also for more complex multimodal tasks.

	conferences	year	# examples	total audio h	average audio min	average words per abstract
train	ACL,NAACL, EMNLP	2017-2021	4000	808.3	12.1 ± 11.2	142.8 ± 36.1
dev	ACL	2022	885	146.4	9.9 ± 3.6	141.9 ± 36.5
test	EMNLP, NAACL	2022	1431	217.1	9.1 ± 4.3	147.6 ± 37.4
total	ACL, NAACL, EMNLP	2017-2022	6316	1171.8	11.1 ± 9.9	143.7 ± 36.5

Table 1: Dataset statistics for NUTSHELL. The number of words is obtained by splitting the abstract at whitespaces.

it is worth noting that establishing a single ground truth for summarization tasks is still an open challenge (Zhang et al., 2024), given the inherent variability in human-produced summaries.

Both, questions (1) and (3) have an inter-annotator agreement of $\kappa = 0.466$, indicating moderate agreement (Landis and Koch, 1977), which can be regarded as acceptable given the subjective nature of evaluating summaries. While criterion (3) naturally involves subjective judgments about information importance, the lower agreement on criterion (1) can also be attributed to borderline cases, where small phrasing differences were sometimes overlooked by individual annotators. Such subtleties led to occasional discrepancies in annotator decisions, but were manually reviewed.

In summary, the manual evaluation confirmed both the feasibility of the SAG tasks and, despite the noted challenges, the overall reliability and usefulness of our resource.

2.2 Collection and Dataset Statistics

We collected talks from 16 ACL Anthology events: 6 ACL, 6 EMNLP, and 4 NAACL, including workshops, shared tasks and industry tracks. For each paper (both long and short format), we extracted the video and the associated abstract already available on the paper website. We exclude papers with invalid URLs, videos without audio, or abstracts missing from the paper page. Additional details on the data collection can be found in App. B.

Lastly, we split the dataset into training (years 2017 to 2021), dev (ACL 2022), and test (EMNLP/-NAACL 2022). These splits reflect a realistic evaluation setup, where models are trained on past data and tested on the most recent, unseen examples. In total, the corpus contains 1,172 hours of audio content corresponding to 6,316 different presentations. Full statistics are reported in Table 1.

3 Analysis

To demonstrate the quality and usability of our corpus, as well as provide baselines for future works, we develop and evaluate four different models using both automatic metrics and human evaluation.

3.1 Experimental Setting

3.1.1 Models

To establish baselines for the SAG task, we analyze the performance of four models described as follows. Prompts, model, generation, and additional training details are provided in App. C.

Whisper + LLama3.1-8B-Instruct. A cascaded solution, where the audio is first transcribed with `openai/whisper-large-v3` (Radford et al., 2022), and then `meta-llama/Llama-3.1-8B-Instruct` (Dubey et al., 2024) is prompted to generate the abstract from the generated transcript.

Qwen2-Audio-7B-Instruct. The `Qwen/Qwen2-Audio-7B-Instruct` (Chu et al., 2024) model, an existing SpeechLLM[5], which is used out of the box without any fine-tuning.

End2End Zero-Shot. A SpeechLLM composed of HuBERT (Hsu et al., 2021) as speech encoder, `meta-llama/Llama-3.1-8B-Instruct` as LLM, and a QFormer (Li et al., 2023) as adapter. The SpeechLMM is built to handle long audio inputs (App. C) and obtained by training only the adapter in two steps: (a) contrastive pretraining (Züfle and Niehues, 2024) to align the LLM representations for the speech and text modalities using MuST-C (Di Gangi et al., 2019) and Gigaspeech (Chen et al., 2021), and (b) fine-tuning on instruction-following tasks, including ASR, speech translation, and spoken question answering using MuST-C and Spoken-SQuAD (Lee et al., 2018). Therefore, the model is not trained or fine-tuned on NUTSHELL and operates in zero-shot for the SAG task.

End2End Finetuned. A SpeechLLM trained using the same contrastive pretraining procedure as End2End Zero-Shot but subsequently fine-tuned on

[5]By *SpeechLLM*, we refer to the combination of a speech encoder and an LLM through a learned modality adapter (Gaido et al., 2024).

Model	RougeL F1 ↑	BERTScore F1 ↑	Llama3.1-7B-Instruct Score with Expl. ↑	Plain Score ↑	Avg. Rank ↓	Human (on subset) Avg. Rank ↓
Whisper + LLama3.1-8B-Instruct	22.14	86.62	**77.84**	**82.47**	**1.24**	**1.53**
Qwen2-Audio-7B-Instruct	15.02	84.65	45.57	36.81	3.43	2.87
End2End Finetuned	**23.89**	**86.66**	68.78	73.53	1.98	1.6
End2End Zero-Shot	16.08	84.13	45.97	39.90	3.35	N/A

Table 2: We report results on the NUTSHELL test set for four models: a cascaded approach (Whisper+Llama-3.1-8B-Instruct), an existing SpeechLLM (Qwen2-Audio), and an end-to-end `HuBERT+QFormer+Llama3.1-8B-Instruct` model, either finetuned on our data (*End2End Finetuned*) or trained on audio instruction-following data (*End2End Zero-Shot*). Avg. Rank, assigned by an LLM judge or human annotators, reflects the mean ranking per model.

our NUTSHELL dataset. This not only evaluates the direct impact of task-specific datasets on the SAG performance, but it also ensures the feasibility of the task and the suitability of the collected data.

3.1.2 Evaluation

Metrics. We use standard (text) summarization metrics: **ROUGE** (Lin, 2004) – a text similarity metric that has been widely adopted for LM evaluation (Grusky, 2023) that focuses on n-gram overlap between the hypothesis and reference –, and **BERTScore** (Zhang et al., 2020) – a neural-based metric that measures the pairwise similarity of contextualized token embeddings between the summary and its reference. Also, we rely on **LLM-as-a-judge** (Shen et al., 2023; Zheng et al., 2024) where the LLM[6] is prompted to assign a score to each output, using the reference abstract as context (Score with Expl.). The score is based on four criteria: (1) relevance, (2) coherence, (3) conciseness, and (4) factual accuracy.[7] We also report results where the LLM judge provides a single score without explanations (Plain Score), as well as results where it ranks the given abstracts instead of scoring them individually (Avg. Rank).

All these metrics have known limitations and no metric is conclusively best for evaluating the SAG task: both ROUGE and BERTScore are known to fail to fully capture the extent to which two summaries share information (Deutsch and Roth, 2021) while LLM-as-a-judge is sensitive to prompt complexity and the length of input (Thakur et al., 2024) and struggle to distinguish similar candidates (Shen et al., 2023). For this reason, we complement the automatic scores with human evaluation.

Human Evaluation. For the human evaluation, nine annotators – all experts in the field – were provided with the generated abstracts and the ground truth abstract. We use the same randomly sampled 30 test set examples as in Section 2.1 and validate their representativeness, which is discussed in App. E. Each sample is evaluated by three annotators. They follow the same criteria as the LLM evaluation but rank models instead of assigning scores. Detailed instructions are in App. E. As the End2End Zero-Shot model performance was comparable to that of Qwen2-Audio – also being a zero-shot model – and given that Qwen2-Audio is an established SpeechLLM with a distinct architecture, we exclude the End2End Zero-Shot from this analysis.

3.2 Results

Automatic Evaluation. Table 2 presents the performance of our models on the NUTSHELL test set. Among them, the cascaded model (Whisper + Llama3.1-8B-Instruct) achieves the highest scores across all LLM-based evaluation metrics. Instead, looking at both n-gram- and neural-based metrics, the End2End Finetuned model achieves the highest RougeL and BERTScore. In addition, Qwen2-Audio and our End2End Zero-Shot models demonstrate similar performance across all automatic metrics, showing a noticeable gap compared to the other two models. These results highlight the importance of our dataset for building high-performing end-to-end models, as the substantial gap between the cascaded and End2End Zero-Shot models is effectively bridged through fine-tuning on the NUTSHELL dataset.

For a more granular analysis, Table 3 in App. D.2 provides results for the LLM-based metrics. Given that all models except Qwen2-Audio rely on Llama3.1-8B-Instruct, one might question whether the Llama-based judge could introduce bias in favor of these models. To address this, we perform ad-

[6]We use `Llama-3.1-8B-Instruct` (Dubey et al., 2024) as the judge using the prompts reported in Fig. 2 in App. D.2.

[7](1) *Does the predicted abstract capture the main points of the gold abstract?*, (2) *Is the predicted abstract logically organized and easy to follow?*, (3) *Is the predicted abstract free from unnecessary details?*, (4) *Are the claims in the predicted abstract consistent with the gold abstract?*

ditional evaluations using `Qwen/Qwen2-7B` (Yang et al., 2024) as the judge (Table 4 in App. D.2), which confirm the same ranking, eliminating any concerns about evaluator bias.

Human Evaluation. As shown in Table 2, the human evaluation results closely align with the LLM-based judgments: the cascaded model ranks first, followed closely by the finetuned model while Qwen2-Audio ranks last. Notably, the gap between the first two models is small, whereas the difference between the second and third models is substantial – consistent with the LLM-based evaluation. This suggests that automatic metrics reliably capture both subtle and large performance differences between models. IAA, measured using pairwise rankings (Bojar et al., 2016) reached $\kappa = 0.53$, which is acceptable given the close ranking of the top two systems.

4 Conclusion

In this work, we introduce NUTSHELL, a novel dataset for SAG from recorded *ACL conference talks. By releasing this dataset under an open license, we hope to foster further advancements in SAG research and encourage the development of more effective models and evaluation techniques. Future work could explore the integration of the video content provided in the corpus, offering an additional modality for enriching the generation process and further improving abstract quality.

5 Limitations

While the current study provides a new resource and offers valuable insights about the SAG task, two main limitations should be noted:

- The analysis focused on the speech-to-text abstract generation task. However, our dataset also provides access to the corresponding videos, which were not utilized here. Future research could explore the integration of video content as an additional modality to enhance the generation process and improve the quality of the abstracts.
- The human evaluation was limited in scope, involving only a small set of models and samples. Future work could expand this evaluation to include more models and a larger number of samples to better assess the performance of different metrics and determine which is most effective in various contexts.

Potential Risks Generating automatic summaries for scientific talks carries the risk that automatic summaries may misrepresent key findings or lack scientific accuracy. However, we hope that by providing more high-quality training data, summarization models can be improved and lead to more reliable and accurate summaries.

Acknowledgments

This work has received funding from the European Union's Horizon research and innovation programme under grant agreement No 101135798, project Meetween (My Personal AI Mediator for Virtual MEETtings BetWEEN People). We gratefully acknowledge Poland's high-performance Infrastructure PLGrid ACC Cyfronet AGH for providing computer facilities. Beatrice Savoldi and Marco Gaido are supported by the PNRR project FAIR - Future AI Research (PE00000013), under the NRRP MUR program funded by the NextGenerationEU.

We thank Leonard Bärmann, Béni Egressy, Mia Fuß, Lukas Hilgert, and Danni Liu for their contributions to the data annotation process.

References

Ondřej Bojar, Rajen Chatterjee, Christian Federmann, Yvette Graham, Barry Haddow, Matthias Huck, Antonio Jimeno Yepes, Philipp Koehn, Varvara Logacheva, Christof Monz, Matteo Negri, Aurélie Névéol, Mariana Neves, Martin Popel, Matt Post, Raphael Rubino, Carolina Scarton, Lucia Specia, Marco Turchi, and 2 others. 2016. Findings of the 2016 conference on machine translation. In *Proceedings of the First Conference on Machine Translation: Volume 2, Shared Task Papers*, pages 131–198, Berlin, Germany. Association for Computational Linguistics.

Guoguo Chen, Shuzhou Chai, Guanbo Wang, Jiayu Du, Wei Qiang Zhang, Chao Weng, Dan Su, Daniel Povey, Jan Trmal, Junbo Zhang, Mingjie Jin, Sanjeev Khudanpur, Shinji Watanabe, Shuaijiang Zhao, Wei Zou, Xiangang Li, Xuchen Yao, Yongqing Wang, Zhao You, and Zhiyong Yan. 2021. Gigaspeech: An evolving, multi-domain asr corpus with 10,000 hours of transcribed audio. In *22nd Annual Conference of the International Speech Communication Association, INTERSPEECH 2021*, Proceedings of the Annual Conference of the International Speech Communication Association, INTERSPEECH, pages 4376–4380. International Speech Communication Association. Publisher Copyright: Copyright © 2021 ISCA.; 22nd Annual Conference of the International Speech Communication Association, INTERSPEECH 2021 ; Conference date: 30-08-2021 Through 03-09-2021.

Yunfei Chu, Jin Xu, Qian Yang, Haojie Wei, Xipin Wei, Zhifang Guo, Yichong Leng, Yuanjun Lv, Jinzheng He, Junyang Lin, Chang Zhou, and Jingren Zhou. 2024. Qwen2-audio technical report. *Preprint*, arXiv:2407.10759.

Arman Cohan, Franck Dernoncourt, Doo Soon Kim, Trung Bui, Seokhwan Kim, Walter Chang, and Nazli Goharian. 2018. A discourse-aware attention model for abstractive summarization of long documents. In *Proceedings of the 2018 Conference of the North American Chapter of the Association for Computational Linguistics: Human Language Technologies, Volume 2 (Short Papers)*, pages 615–621, New Orleans, Louisiana. Association for Computational Linguistics.

Ed Collins, Isabelle Augenstein, and Sebastian Riedel. 2017. A supervised approach to extractive summarisation of scientific papers. In *Proceedings of the 21st Conference on Computational Natural Language Learning (CoNLL 2017)*, pages 195–205, Vancouver, Canada. Association for Computational Linguistics.

Daniel Deutsch and Dan Roth. 2020. SacreROUGE: An open-source library for using and developing summarization evaluation metrics. In *Proceedings of Second Workshop for NLP Open Source Software (NLP-OSS)*, pages 120–125, Online. Association for Computational Linguistics.

Daniel Deutsch and Dan Roth. 2021. Understanding the extent to which content quality metrics measure the information quality of summaries. In *Proceedings of the 25th Conference on Computational Natural Language Learning*, pages 300–309, Online. Association for Computational Linguistics.

Mattia A. Di Gangi, Roldano Cattoni, Luisa Bentivogli, Matteo Negri, and Marco Turchi. 2019. MuST-C: a Multilingual Speech Translation Corpus. In *Proceedings of the 2019 Conference of the North American Chapter of the Association for Computational Linguistics: Human Language Technologies, Volume 1 (Long and Short Papers)*, pages 2012–2017, Minneapolis, Minnesota. Association for Computational Linguistics.

Abhimanyu Dubey, Abhinav Jauhri, Abhinav Pandey, Abhishek Kadian, Ahmad Al-Dahle, Aiesha Letman, Akhil Mathur, Alan Schelten, Amy Yang, Angela Fan, Anirudh Goyal, Anthony Hartshorn, Aobo Yang, Archi Mitra, Archie Sravankumar, Artem Korenev, Arthur Hinsvark, Arun Rao, Aston Zhang, and 516 others. 2024. The llama 3 herd of models. *Preprint*, arXiv:2407.21783.

Marco Gaido, Sara Papi, Matteo Negri, and Luisa Bentivogli. 2024. Speech translation with speech foundation models and large language models: What is there and what is missing? In *Proceedings of the 62nd Annual Meeting of the Association for Computational Linguistics (Volume 1: Long Papers)*, pages 14760–14778, Bangkok, Thailand. Association for Computational Linguistics.

Max Grusky. 2023. Rogue scores. In *Proceedings of the 61st Annual Meeting of the Association for Computational Linguistics (Volume 1: Long Papers)*, pages 1914–1934, Toronto, Canada. Association for Computational Linguistics.

Vivek Gupta, Prerna Bharti, Pegah Nokhiz, and Harish Karnick. 2021. SumPubMed: Summarization dataset of PubMed scientific articles. In *Proceedings of the 59th Annual Meeting of the Association for Computational Linguistics and the 11th International Joint Conference on Natural Language Processing: Student Research Workshop*, pages 292–303, Online. Association for Computational Linguistics.

Wei-Ning Hsu, Benjamin Bolte, Yao-Hung Hubert Tsai, Kushal Lakhotia, Ruslan Salakhutdinov, and Abdelrahman Mohamed. 2021. Hubert: Self-supervised speech representation learning by masked prediction of hidden units. *IEEE/ACM Transactions on Audio, Speech, and Language Processing*, 29:3451–3460.

A. Janin, D. Baron, J. Edwards, D. Ellis, D. Gelbart, N. Morgan, B. Peskin, T. Pfau, E. Shriberg, A. Stolcke, and C. Wooters. 2003. The icsi meeting corpus. In *2003 IEEE International Conference on Acoustics, Speech, and Signal Processing, 2003. Proceedings. (ICASSP '03).*, volume 1, pages I–I.

Takatomo Kano, Atsunori Ogawa, Marc Delcroix, and Shinji Watanabe. 2021. Attention-based multi-hypothesis fusion for speech summarization. In *IEEE Automatic Speech Recognition and Understanding Workshop, ASRU 2021, Cartagena, Colombia, December 13-17, 2021*, pages 487–494. IEEE.

Chris Kedzie, Kathleen McKeown, and Hal Daumé III. 2018. Content selection in deep learning models of summarization. In *Proceedings of the 2018 Conference on Empirical Methods in Natural Language Processing*, pages 1818–1828, Brussels, Belgium. Association for Computational Linguistics.

Rik Koncel-Kedziorski, Dhanush Bekal, Yi Luan, Mirella Lapata, and Hannaneh Hajishirzi. 2019. Text Generation from Knowledge Graphs with Graph Transformers. In *Proceedings of the 2019 Conference of the North American Chapter of the Association for Computational Linguistics: Human Language Technologies, Volume 1 (Long and Short Papers)*, pages 2284–2293, Minneapolis, Minnesota. Association for Computational Linguistics.

Fajri Koto, Sakriani Sakti, Graham Neubig, Tomoki Toda, Mima Adriani, and Satoshi Nakamura. 2014. The use of semantic and acoustic features for open-domain ted talk summarization. In *Signal and Information Processing Association Annual Summit and Conference (APSIPA), 2014 Asia-Pacific*, pages 1–4.

J. Richard Landis and Gary G. Koch. 1977. The measurement of observer agreement for categorical data. *Biometrics*, 33(1):159–174.

Chia-Hsuan Lee, Szu-Lin Wu, Chi-Liang Liu, and Hung-yi Lee. 2018. Spoken squad: A study of mitigating the impact of speech recognition errors on listening comprehension. *Proc. Interspeech 2018*, pages 3459–3463.

Guy Lev, Michal Shmueli-Scheuer, Jonathan Herzig, Achiya Jerbi, and David Konopnicki. 2019. TalkSumm: A dataset and scalable annotation method for scientific paper summarization based on conference talks. In *Proceedings of the 57th Annual Meeting of the Association for Computational Linguistics*, pages 2125–2131, Florence, Italy. Association for Computational Linguistics.

Junnan Li, Dongxu Li, Silvio Savarese, and Steven C. H. Hoi. 2023. Blip-2: Bootstrapping language-image pre-training with frozen image encoders and large language models. In *International Conference on Machine Learning*.

Chin-Yew Lin. 2004. ROUGE: A package for automatic evaluation of summaries. In *Text Summarization Branches Out*, pages 74–81, Barcelona, Spain. Association for Computational Linguistics.

Ran Liu, Ming Liu, Min Yu, He Zhang, Jianguo Jiang, Gang Li, and Weiqing Huang. 2024. SumSurvey: An abstractive dataset of scientific survey papers for long document summarization. In *Findings of the Association for Computational Linguistics: ACL 2024*, pages 9632–9651, Bangkok, Thailand. Association for Computational Linguistics.

Yuning Mao, Ming Zhong, and Jiawei Han. 2022. CiteSum: Citation text-guided scientific extreme summarization and domain adaptation with limited supervision. In *Proceedings of the 2022 Conference on Empirical Methods in Natural Language Processing*, pages 10922–10935, Abu Dhabi, United Arab Emirates. Association for Computational Linguistics.

Kohei Matsuura, Takanori Ashihara, Takafumi Moriya, Masato Mimura, Takatomo Kano, Atsunori Ogawa, and Marc Delcroix. 2024. Sentence-wise speech summarization: Task, datasets, and end-to-end modeling with lm knowledge distillation. *Preprint*, arXiv:2408.00205.

I. McCowan, J. Carletta, W. Kraaij, S. Ashby, S. Bourban, M. Flynn, M. Guillemot, T. Hain, J. Kadlec, V. Karaiskos, M. Kronenthal, G. Lathoud, M. Lincoln, A. Lisowska, W. Post, Dennis Reidsma, and P. Wellner. 2005. The ami meeting corpus. In *Proceedings of Measuring Behavior 2005, 5th International Conference on Methods and Techniques in Behavioral Research*, pages 137–140. Noldus Information Technology.

Gabriel Murray, Giuseppe Carenini, and Raymond Ng. 2010. Generating and validating abstracts of meeting conversations: a user study. In *Proceedings of the 6th International Natural Language Generation Conference*. Association for Computational Linguistics.

Alec Radford, Jong Wook Kim, Tao Xu, Greg Brockman, Christine McLeavey, and Ilya Sutskever. 2022. Robust speech recognition via large-scale weak supervision. *Preprint*, arXiv:2212.04356.

Ramon Sanabria, Ozan Caglayan, Shruti Palaskar, Desmond Elliott, Loïc Barrault, Lucia Specia, and Florian Metze. 2018. How2: A large-scale dataset for multimodal language understanding. *Preprint*, arXiv:1811.00347.

Chenhui Shen, Liying Cheng, Xuan-Phi Nguyen, Yang You, and Lidong Bing. 2023. Large language models are not yet human-level evaluators for abstractive summarization. In *Findings of the Association for Computational Linguistics: EMNLP 2023*, pages 4215–4233, Singapore. Association for Computational Linguistics.

Suwon Shon, Siddhant Arora, Chyi-Jiunn Lin, Ankita Pasad, Felix Wu, Roshan Sharma, Wei-Lun Wu, Hung-yi Lee, Karen Livescu, and Shinji Watanabe. 2023. SLUE phase-2: A benchmark suite of diverse spoken language understanding tasks. In *Proceedings of the 61st Annual Meeting of the Association for Computational Linguistics (Volume 1: Long Papers)*, pages 8906–8937, Toronto, Canada. Association for Computational Linguistics.

Sotaro Takeshita, Tommaso Green, Ines Reinig, Kai Eckert, and Simone Ponzetto. 2024. ACLSum: A new dataset for aspect-based summarization of scientific publications. In *Proceedings of the 2024 Conference of the North American Chapter of the Association for Computational Linguistics: Human Language Technologies (Volume 1: Long Papers)*, pages 6660–6675, Mexico City, Mexico. Association for Computational Linguistics.

Aman Singh Thakur, Kartik Choudhary, Venkat Srinik Ramayapally, Sankaran Vaidyanathan, and Dieuwke Hupkes. 2024. Judging the judges: Evaluating alignment and vulnerabilities in llms-as-judges. *Preprint*, arXiv:2406.12624.

Gianluca Vico and Jan Niehues. 2022. Ted talk teaser generation with pre-trained models. In *ICASSP 2022 - 2022 IEEE International Conference on Acoustics, Speech and Signal Processing (ICASSP)*, pages 8067–8071.

An Yang, Baosong Yang, Binyuan Hui, Bo Zheng, Bowen Yu, Chang Zhou, Chengpeng Li, Chengyuan Li, Dayiheng Liu, Fei Huang, Guanting Dong, Haoran Wei, Huan Lin, Jialong Tang, Jialin Wang, Jian Yang, Jianhong Tu, Jianwei Zhang, Jianxin Ma, and 43 others. 2024. Qwen2 technical report. *Preprint*, arXiv:2407.10671.

Michihiro Yasunaga, Jungo Kasai, Rui Zhang, Alexander R. Fabbri, Irene Li, Dan Friedman, and Dragomir R. Radev. 2019. Scisummnet: a large annotated corpus and content-impact models for scientific paper summarization with citation networks. In *Proceedings of the Thirty-Third AAAI Conference on Artificial Intelligence and Thirty-First Innovative Applications of Artificial Intelligence Conference and Ninth AAAI Symposium on Educational Advances in Artificial Intelligence*, AAAI'19/IAAI'19/EAAI'19. AAAI Press.

Fabio Massimo Zanzotto, Viviana Bono, Paola Vocca, Andrea Santilli, Danilo Croce, Giorgio Gambosi, and Roberto Basili. 2020. Gasp! generating abstracts of scientific papers from abstracts of cited papers. *ArXiv*, abs/2003.04996.

Tianyi Zhang, Varsha Kishore, Felix Wu, Kilian Q. Weinberger, and Yoav Artzi. 2020. Bertscore: Evaluating text generation with BERT. In *8th International Conference on Learning Representations, ICLR 2020, Addis Ababa, Ethiopia, April 26-30, 2020*. OpenReview.net.

Tianyi Zhang, Faisal Ladhak, Esin Durmus, Percy Liang, Kathleen McKeown, and Tatsunori B. Hashimoto. 2024. Benchmarking large language models for news summarization. *Transactions of the Association for Computational Linguistics*, 12:39–57.

Lianmin Zheng, Wei-Lin Chiang, Ying Sheng, Siyuan Zhuang, Zhanghao Wu, Yonghao Zhuang, Zi Lin, Zhuohan Li, Dacheng Li, Eric P. Xing, Hao Zhang, Joseph E. Gonzalez, and Ion Stoica. 2024. Judging llm-as-a-judge with mt-bench and chatbot arena. In *Proceedings of the 37th International Conference on Neural Information Processing Systems*, NIPS '23, Red Hook, NY, USA. Curran Associates Inc.

Maike Züfle and Jan Niehues. 2024. Contrastive learning for task-independent speechllm-pretraining. *Preprint*, arXiv:2412.15712.

A Human Evaluation: Are abstracts good summaries of the talk?

We aim to assess whether paper abstracts can serve as effective abstracts for *ACL talks. To this end, we conducted a human evaluation by randomly sampling 30 examples from our dataset. The annotation team consisted of five individuals (four women and one man), including the paper authors and their colleagues. All annotators were already familiar with the NLP domain, scientific presentation and writing, and the task itself. They are experts in Natural Language Processing, holding at least a master's degree in NLP or a related field, with some holding PhDs or professorial positions. Their ages ranged from 25 to 55.

The annotation guidelines were initially developed by the authors and subsequently refined in collaboration with the annotators to ensure a shared and well-defined set of evaluation criteria. Detailed instructions for the human annotators are provided in Fig. 3. The annotation template also included a comment section for uncertain cases, though no comments were submitted.

B Dataset Details

We include all *ACL conferences from 2017 to 2022 in NUTSHELL, covering main conferences, Findings, industry tracks, and workshops. As not all conferences are held every year, the number of talks varies accordingly. Table 5 provides a detailed overview.

C Baseline Details

Generation Settings We evaluate four different models to establish baselines for abstract generation from spoken ACL talks. The evaluations were conducted on a single NVIDIA A100-SXM4-40GB GPU.

For all models, we use the default generation parameters and apply greedy search, following the usage instructions for `meta-llama/Llama-3.1-8B-Instruct`[8] (Dubey et al., 2024), `Qwen/Qwen2-Audio-7B-Instruct`[9] (Chu et al., 2024) and the contrastively pretrained models from Züfle and Niehues (2024)[10].

[8] `https://huggingface.co/meta-llama/Llama-3.1-8B-Instruct`

[9] `https://github.com/QwenLM/Qwen2-Audio`

[10] `https://github.com/MaikeZuefle/contr-pretraining`

Cascaded Model For the cascaded model, we segment the audio into 30-second chunks and transcribe them using `openai/whisper-large-v3` (Radford et al., 2022). The transcribed chunks are then concatenated and processed by `meta-llama/Llama-3.1-8B-Instruct` (Dubey et al., 2024) to generate the abstract. Inference took 5:40 hours on a single NVIDIA A100-SXM4-40GB GPU, including transcribing and summarizing.

Since the model's outputs often included a title and category for the talk, we explicitly prompt it to generate only the abstract. This adjustment was not necessary for the other models.

We use the following prompt:

System Prompt:

```
A chat between a curious user and an
artificial intelligence assistant. The
assistant gives helpful, detailed, and
polite answers to the user's questions.\
n
```

Prompt:

```
Summarize the following talk to create
an abstract for an ACL Paper, don't
include the title or other information,
only the abstract:\n<transcription>\n
```

Qwen2-Audio For `Qwen/Qwen2-Audio-7B-Instruct` (Chu et al., 2024), inference took 50 minutes on a single NVIDIA A100-SXM4-40GB GPU. We use the system prompt as provided in the code documentation[9].

System Prompt:

```
You are a helpful assistant.
```

Prompt:

```
Summarize this talk to create an
abstract for an ACL Paper:\n
```

Contrastively Pretained Models For the contrastively pretrained model, we follow Züfle and Niehues (2024) and adopt their settings[10], including training configurations, hyperparameters, and system prompts. The SpeechLLM consists of HuBERT (Hsu et al., 2021) as speech encoder, `meta-llama/Llama-3.1-8B-Instruct` as LLM, and a QFormer (Li et al., 2023) as adapter. We choose HuBERT as an encoder in contrast to the bigger and more powerful `openai/whisper-large-v3` (Radford et al., 2022), as it needs less memory and is therefore more suitable for the summarization task of longer audio. However, due to the extended duration of the audio inputs, we additionally introduce two modifications:

Model	Llama-3.1-8B-Instruct						
	Relevance ↑	Coherence ↑	Conciseness ↑	Factual Accuracy ↑	Avg. Score ↑	Plain Score ↑	Avg. Rank ↓
Whisper + LLama31-Instruct	**77.12**	**86.00**	**61.13**	**87.13**	**77.84**	**82.47**	**1.24**
Qwen2-Audio	37.21	52.52	45.91	46.63	45.57	36.81	3.43
End2End Finetuned	66.41	78.24	50.25	80.22	68.78	73.53	1.98
End2End Zero-Shot	40.28	48.02	37.69	57.89	45.97	39.90	3.35

Table 3: Results using Llama-3.1-8B-Instruct as a judge. We report results on the NUTSHELL test set for four models: a cascaded approach (`openai/whisper-large-v3 + meta/Llama-3.1-8B-Instruct`), `Qwen/Qwen2-Audio-7B-Instruct`, and an end-to-end `HuBERT+QFormer+Llama3.1-7B-Instruct` model, either finetuned on our data (*End2End Finetuned*) or trained on audio instruction-following data (*End2End Zero-Shot*). Avg. Rank reflects the mean ranking per model.

Model	Qwen2-7bInstruct						
	Relevance ↑	Coherence ↑	Conciseness ↑	Factual Accuracy ↑	Avg. Score ↑	Plain Score ↑	Avg. Rank ↓
Whisper + LLama31-Instruct	**79.61**	**83.54**	72.08	**86.07**	**80.33**	**74.60**	**1.66**
Qwen2-Audio	56.99	75.35	**75.91**	59.28	66.88	49.55	3.18
End2End Finetuned	75.13	81.78	75.04	81.16	78.28	70.83	2.12
End2End Zero-Shot	57.93	68.02	69.34	66.65	65.49	53.61	3.04

Table 4: Results using Qwen2-7bInstruct as a judge. We report results on the NUTSHELL test set for four models: a cascaded approach (`openai/whisper-large-v3 + meta/Llama-3.1-8B-Instruct`), `Qwen/Qwen2-Audio-7B-Instruct`, and an end-to-end `HuBERT+QFormer+Llama3.1-7B-Instruct` model, either finetuned on our data (*End2End Finetuned*) or trained on audio instruction-following data (*End2End Zero-Shot*). Avg. Rank reflects the mean ranking per model.

Split	Conference	Year	Talks
Train	ACL	2017	140
		2018	185
		2019	244
		2021	849
	EMNLP	2017	93
		2018	221
		2021	1480
	NAACL	2018	120
		2019	114
		2021	554
Dev	ACL	2022	885
Test	EMNLP	2022	465
	NAACL	2022	966

Table 5: Number of talks per conferences in the NUTSHELL dataset.

1. We segment the audio into one-minute chunks, encode each chunk using the encoder and then concatenate the encoded representations before passing them through the adapter and LLM backbone.

2. We use a batch size of 1 for fine-tuning with NUTSHELL.

Despite these adjustments, we encountered memory limitations for audio files exceeding 35 minutes. In such cases, we truncate the audio to 35 minutes, which affects one example in the test set.

The training of the models was conducted on four NVIDIA A100-SXM4-40GB GPUs. The contrastive pretraining took 33 hours on four GPUS. Finetuning on ASR, speech translation, and spoken question answering data took 30 hours, finetuning on the NUTSHELL dataset took 2:10 hours. Generating the outputs of the test set (on a single NVIDIA A100-SXM4-40GB GPU) took 2:35 hours.

System Prompt:

```
A chat between a curious user and an
artificial intelligence assistant. The
assistant gives helpful , detailed , and
polite answers to the user ' s questions .\
n
```

Prompt:

```
Summarize this talk to create an
abstract for an ACL Paper:
```

D Evaluation Details

We evaluate the results of our models using automatic metrics including ROUGE, BERTScore, and LLM-as-a-judge.

D.1 ROUGE and BERT Score

As automatic metrics, we use ROUGE[11] (Lin, 2004) and BERTScore (Zhang et al., 2020).

[11]

Model	RougeL F1 ↑	BERTScore F1 ↑	Llama3.1-7B-Instruct Score with Expl. ↑	Plain Score ↑	Avg. Rank ↓
Whisper + LLama31-Instruct	23.26	86.81	**77.75**	**84.30**	**1.23**
Qwen2-Audio	16.26	84.94	48.42	39.50	3.47
End2End Finetuned	**24.47**	**86.71**	70.67	75.73	1.83

Table 6: Baseline Results, the finetuned model is a HuBERT + Qformer + LLama31Instruct model on the subset used for human annotation (30 examples).

Concretely, we compute ROUGE-L, which focuses on the longest common subsequence, with `DD/sacrerouge` (Deutsch and Roth, 2020), as recommended by Grusky (2023) and for BERTScore, we use the `bertscore` implementation from HuggingFace[12] and report the F1-score.

D.2 LLM as a judge

To evaluate the model outputs, we also use an LLM *as a judge*, specifically `meta-llama/Llama-3.1-8B-Instruct` (Dubey et al., 2024). The LLM assigns a score to each output using the reference abstract as context, based on four criteria: (1) relevance (*Does the predicted abstract capture the main points of the gold abstract?*), (2) coherence (*Is the predicted abstract logically organized and easy to follow?*), (3) conciseness (*Is the predicted abstract free from unnecessary details?*), and (4) factual accuracy (*Are the claims in the predicted abstract consistent with the gold abstract?*). Additionally, we report results where the LLM provides a single overall score without explanations and results where it ranks the given abstracts instead of scoring them individually. The prompts are given in Fig. 2. If the model fails to return a valid json dictionary, we instead take the first number after the score name in the output. We present the results for all four criteria, the average score, the score without explanations, and the ranking in Table 3. One potential concern is that this LLM might be biased, as all our models except Qwen2-Audio are based on Llama-3.1. However, we find this is not the case. When using `Qwen/Qwen2-7B` (Yang et al., 2024) as the judge, we obtain the same ranking as with Llama. The results with Qwen-as-a-judge can be found in Table 4.

E Human Evaluation for Model Outputs

We evaluate the models using ROUGE (Lin, 2004), BERTScore (Zhang et al., 2020), and LLM-as-a-judge. However, it is known that automatic evaluation metrics can come with limitations. Namely, the first two metrics may not fully capture semantic overlap (Deutsch and Roth, 2021), while LLM-as-a-judge is sensitive to prompt phrasing (Thakur et al., 2024) and struggles to distinguish between closely similar candidates (Shen et al., 2023). To validate the reliability of our automatic evaluation scores and better understand model behavior, we complement these metrics with a human evaluation. This allows us also to verify the robustness of our findings.

Specifically, we asked nine domain experts (four women and five men) to rank model outputs relative to the reference abstract, with each example annotated by three independent annotators. All annotators were already familiar with the NLP domain, scientific writing and presentation, and the task itself. They are experts in Natural Language Processing, holding at least a master's degree in NLP or a related field, with some holding PhDs or professorial positions. Their ages ranged from 25 to 55. The annotation instructions are provided in Fig. 4.

We conduct this human evaluation on a randomly selected subset of 30 test examples. We consider this subset representative, as the model rankings based on automatic metrics remain consistent with those on the full test set. The corresponding automatic scores for this subset are reported in Table 6. We want to include three diverse models in our human evaluation: a zero-shot model, a cascaded model, and a model finetuned on our dataset. Since we have two zero-shot models (Qwen2-Audio and our contrastively pretrained zero-shot model) that perform similarly, we decided to exclude one for efficiency in the human evaluation. We keep the Qwen2-Audio model as this is an already existing and widely used SpeechLLM.

[12]`https://huggingface.co/spaces/evaluate-metric/bertscore`

System Prompt for Score with Explanation:

```
You are an expert AI trained to evaluate scientific abstracts. Your task is to
compare a predicted abstract with a gold standard (reference) abstract and provide a
 detailed evaluation based on the following criteria:\n\n
1. **Relevance**: Does the predicted abstract capture the main points of the gold
abstract?\n
2. **Coherence**: Is the predicted abstract logically organized and easy to follow?\
n
3. **Conciseness**: Is the predicted abstract free from unnecessary details?\n
4. **Factual Accuracy**: Are the claims in the predicted abstract consistent with
the gold abstract?\n\n
For each criterion:\n
- Assign a **score** between 1 and 10 (1 = very poor, 10 = excellent).\n"
- Provide a **brief explanation** for the assigned score.\n\n"
Your output must be in the following JSON format:\n\n"
{\"relevance\": {\"score\": int, \"explanation\": \"string\"},
 \"coherence\": {\"score\": int, \"explanation\": \"string\"},
 \"conciseness\": {\"score\": int, \"explanation\": \"string\"},
 W\"factual_accuracy\": {\"score\": int, \"explanation\": \"string\"}}\n\n
```

Prompt for Score with Explanation:

```
### Gold Abstract:\n<reference abstract>\n\n### Predicted Abstract:\n<predicted
abstract>\n\nPlease evaluate the predicted abstract based on the criteria mentioned.
```

System Prompt for Score without Explanation:

```
You are an expert AI trained to evaluate scientific abstracts. Your task is to
compare a predicted abstract with a reference abstract. Evaluate how well the
prediction aligns with the reference using a score from 0 (lowest) to 100 (highest).
 Your output must only be in the following JSON format: {\"prediction\": int}. Do
not provide any explanation or additional text.
```

Prompt for Score without Explanation:

```
### Reference Abstract:\n<reference abstract>\n\n### Predicted Abstract:\n<predicted
 abstract>\n\nPlease evaluate the predicted abstract with respect to the reference
abstract and assign a score from 0 to 100.
```

System Prompt for Ranking:

```
You are an expert AI trained to evaluate scientific abstracts. Your task is to rank
four different abstracts based on a reference abstract. Your output must only be in
the following format: <Model A, Model B, Model C, Model D> where the first model is
the best model, and the last model the weakest. Do not provide any explanation or
additional text.
```

Prompt for Ranking:

```
### Reference Abstract:\n<reference abstract>\n\n
### Model A Predicted Abstract:\n<predicted abstract 1>\n\n
### Model B Predicted Abstract:\n<predicted abstract 2>\n\n
### Model C Predicted Abstract:\n<predicted abstract 3>\n\n
### Model D Predicted Abstract:\n<predicted abstract 4>\n\n
Please rank the four predicted abstracts.
```

Figure 2: Prompts for LLM as a judge. We use the same prompt for both, Qwen2-7bInstruct and Llama 3.1 8B Instruct. <reference abstract> and <predicted abstract> are replaced with the actual abstracts. For ranking, we shuffle the predicted abstracts, so that the LLMs sees the abstracts of different models in a different order every time to avoid position bias.

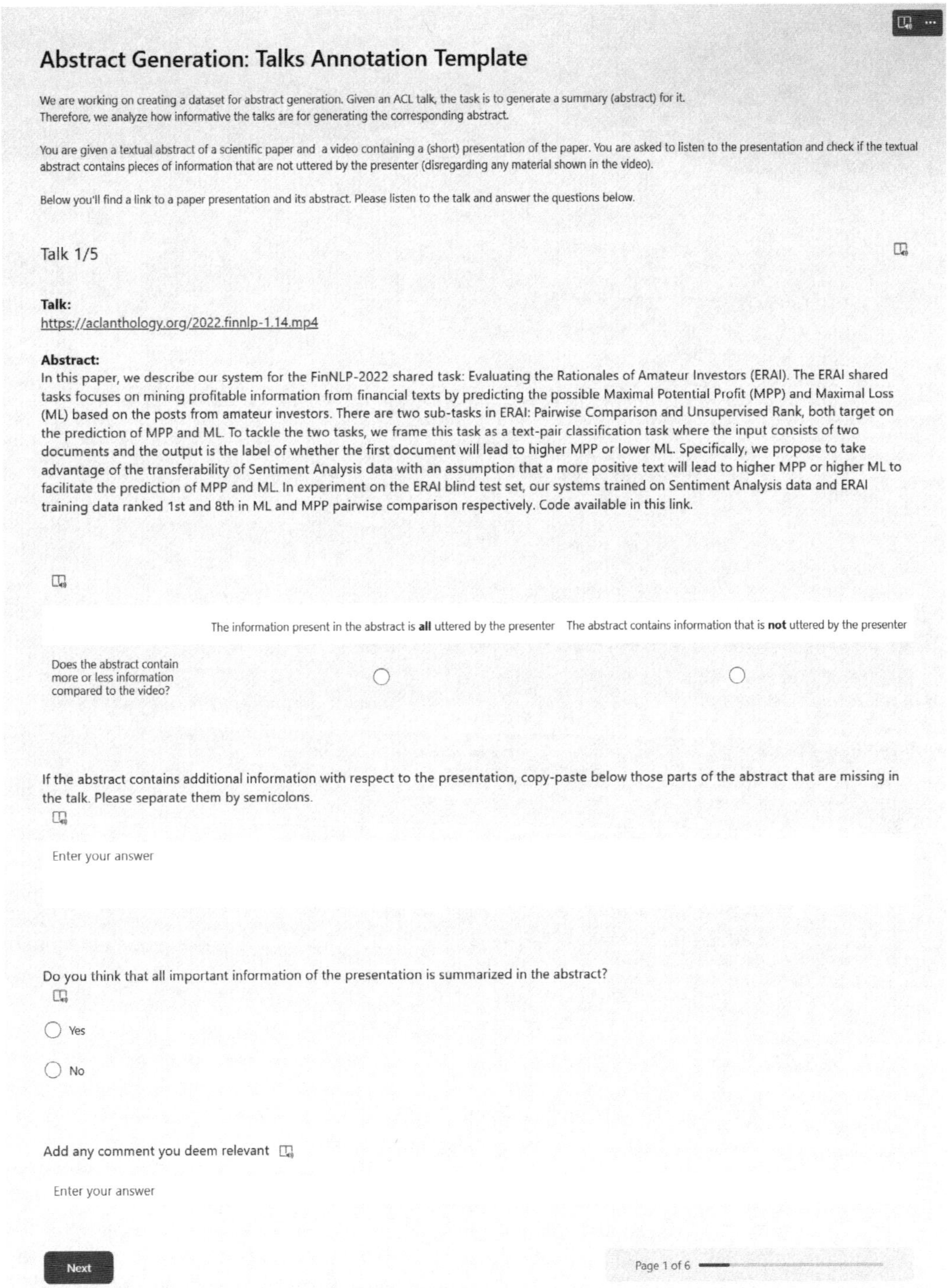

Abstract Generation: Talks Annotation Template

We are working on creating a dataset for abstract generation. Given an ACL talk, the task is to generate a summary (abstract) for it.
Therefore, we analyze how informative the talks are for generating the corresponding abstract.

You are given a textual abstract of a scientific paper and a video containing a (short) presentation of the paper. You are asked to listen to the presentation and check if the textual abstract contains pieces of information that are not uttered by the presenter (disregarding any material shown in the video).

Below you'll find a link to a paper presentation and its abstract. Please listen to the talk and answer the questions below.

Talk 1/5

Talk:
https://aclanthology.org/2022.finnlp-1.14.mp4

Abstract:
In this paper, we describe our system for the FinNLP-2022 shared task: Evaluating the Rationales of Amateur Investors (ERAI). The ERAI shared tasks focuses on mining profitable information from financial texts by predicting the possible Maximal Potential Profit (MPP) and Maximal Loss (ML) based on the posts from amateur investors. There are two sub-tasks in ERAI: Pairwise Comparison and Unsupervised Rank, both target on the prediction of MPP and ML. To tackle the two tasks, we frame this task as a text-pair classification task where the input consists of two documents and the output is the label of whether the first document will lead to higher MPP or lower ML. Specifically, we propose to take advantage of the transferability of Sentiment Analysis data with an assumption that a more positive text will lead to higher MPP or higher ML to facilitate the prediction of MPP and ML. In experiment on the ERAI blind test set, our systems trained on Sentiment Analysis data and ERAI training data ranked 1st and 8th in ML and MPP pairwise comparison respectively. Code available in this link.

	The information present in the abstract is **all** uttered by the presenter	The abstract contains information that is **not** uttered by the presenter
Does the abstract contain more or less information compared to the video?	○	○

If the abstract contains additional information with respect to the presentation, copy-paste below those parts of the abstract that are missing in the talk. Please separate them by semicolons.

Enter your answer

Do you think that all important information of the presentation is summarized in the abstract?

○ Yes

○ No

Add any comment you deem relevant

Enter your answer

Next

Page 1 of 6

Figure 3: Instructions for annotators to evaluate whether the paper abstracts are good and informative abstracts for the ACL talks.

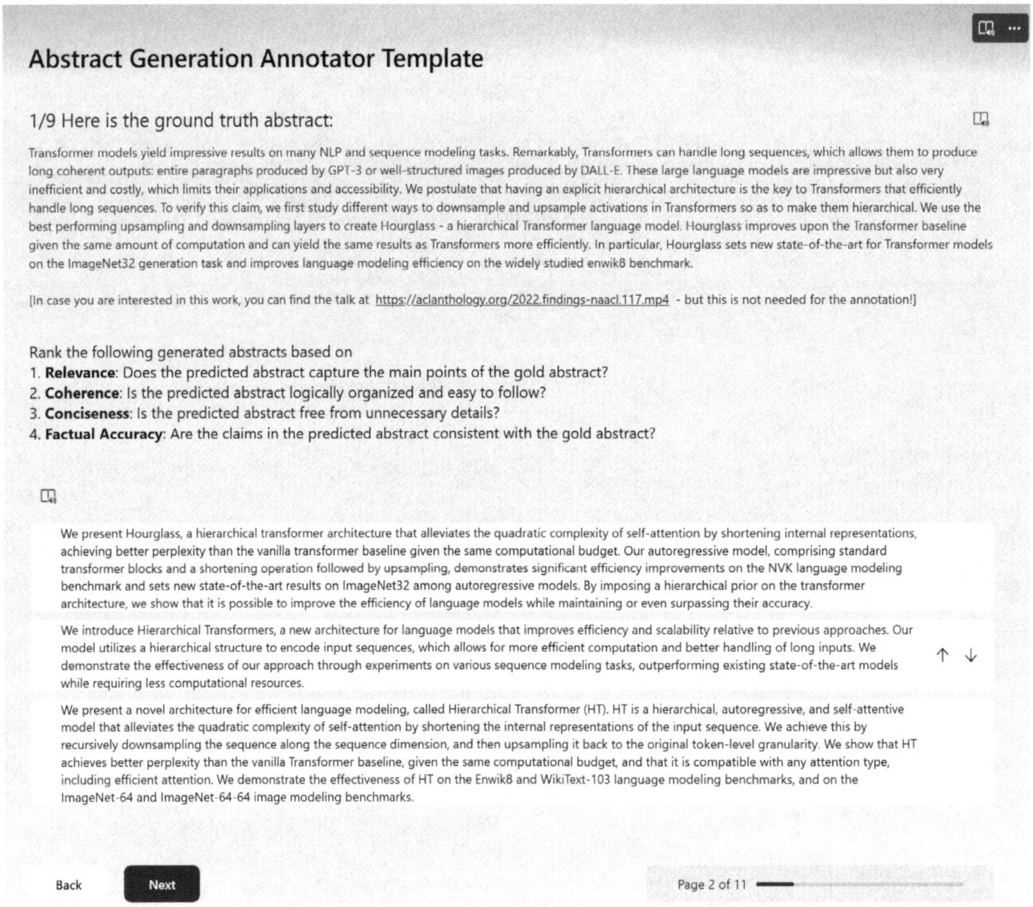

Figure 4: Instructions for human annotators for ranking model outputs.

Quality-Aware Decoding: Unifying Quality Estimation and Decoding

Sai Koneru[1], **Matthias Huck**[2], **Miriam Exel**[2], and **Jan Niehues**[1]
[1] Karlsruhe Institute of Technology
[2] SAP SE, Dietmar-Hopp-Allee 16, 69190 Walldorf, Germany
{sai.koneru, jan.niehues}@kit.edu
{matthias.huck, miriam.exel}@sap.com

Abstract

Quality Estimation (QE) models for Neural Machine Translation (NMT) predict the quality of the hypothesis without having access to the reference. An emerging research direction in NMT involves the use of QE models, which have demonstrated high correlations with human judgment and can enhance translations through Quality-Aware Decoding. Although several approaches have been proposed based on sampling multiple candidate translations and picking the best candidate, none have integrated these models directly into the decoding process. In this paper, we address this by proposing a novel token-level QE model capable of reliably scoring partial translations. We build a uni-directional QE model for this, as decoder models are inherently trained and efficient on partial sequences. We then present a decoding strategy that integrates the QE model for Quality-Aware decoding and demonstrate that the translation quality improves when compared to the N-best list re-ranking with state-of-the-art QE models (up to 1.39 XCOMET-XXL ↑). Finally, we show that our approach provides significant benefits in document translation tasks, where the quality of N-best lists is typically suboptimal[1]

1 Introduction

Large language models (LLMs) have significantly impacted various Natural Language Processing (NLP) tasks (Brown et al., 2020; Jiang et al., 2023; Dubey et al., 2024), including Neural Machine Translation (NMT). The field of NMT is transitioning from using dedicated encoder-decoder transformers (Vaswani, 2017; Team et al., 2024) to leveraging decoder-only LLM-based translation models (Kocmi et al., 2024). This shift is driven by LLMs' ability to retain knowledge, handle large contexts, and follow instructions, learned during extensive pre-training (Xu et al., 2024; Alves et al., 2024). As a result, LLM-based MT models have achieved state-of-the-art translation quality (Kocmi et al., 2024).

In parallel, Quality Estimation (QE) has become a well-researched subfield within NMT. QE models are trained to predict the quality of a translation without requiring access to the reference (Rei et al., 2021, 2022). Interestingly, QE models can achieve performance in assessing translation quality that is comparable to MT evaluation models, which do have access to the reference (Zerva et al., 2024).

This led to the question: "*Can we integrate QE into the current translation process to improve quality?*" Incorporating QE into NMT offers several benefits. First, having a expert QE model guiding the decoding can further improve the quality. Second, by adapting the QE model with feedback from human annotators, we can generate future translations guided with the newly obtained feedback.

Several approaches have been explored to integrate QE into the translation process. These include re-ranking the N-best list (Fernandes et al., 2022), applying minimum Bayes risk (MBR) decoding on a quality-filtered N-best list (Tomani et al., 2024), and training additional models for post-editing based on QE-predicted errors (Treviso et al., 2024). However, all these methods operate on fully generated sequences before the QE model can exert influence. Integrating QE earlier in the decoding process, referred in this paper as *Quality-Aware Decoding*, could enhance translation quality and reduce reliance on the N-best list. This is especially relevant when dealing with long inputs as

[1]Code can be found at https://github.com/SAP-samples/quality-aware-decoding-translation

Proceedings of the 22nd International Conference on Spoken Language Translation (IWSLT 2025), pages 33–46
July 31 - August 1, 2025 ©2025 Association for Computational Linguistics

Figure 1: Example from WMT'23 English → German #ID: 10: The paragraph begins with 'Department of Homeland Security,' which should be translated as 'Ministerium für **I**nnere Sicherheit.' However, the top 25 beams do not contain the correct translation and begin with an error, making N-best list re-ranking insufficient. Although the top-5 tokens at the decoding contain the correct forms 'Inn' or 'Inner,' the probabilities split among them giving highest mass to the incorrect token 'inn.' Quality-Aware decoding can prevent errors with earlier integration.

GOOD translations during decoding are likely to be pruned and may need sampling larger number of finished hypothesis. We illustrate this in Figure 1.

To achieve this, a QE model capable of predicting the quality of partial translations is required. However, current leading QE models face challenges in this area, as they are typically not trained to predict scores for incomplete hypotheses. *Therefore, developing QE models that can handle partial translations is essential for implementing Quality-Aware Decoding during the translation process.*

In this work, we propose adapting LLM-based NMT models to perform QE on partial translations and incorporating this model into the decoding. We create a token-level synthetic QE dataset using WMT Multidimensional Quality Metrics (MQM) data (Burchardt, 2013; Freitag et al., 2024). We then adapt a uni-directional LLM-based MT model to predict whether a token is *GOOD* or *BAD*. Training QE models on these token-level tasks alleviates the data challenge and allows us to exploit the MQM data while simultaneously making the task easier for the model compared to predicting a score directly.

Furthermore, integrating the QE model into NMT during decoding is not trivial, as we need to combine the QE estimates during decoding. Therefore, we modify the decoding strategy from Koneru et al. (2024) to incorporate token-level predictions efficiently with the adapted QE model to provide real-time feedback during the decoding process. We summarize our contributions below.

- We present a novel uni-directional QE model which estimates quality on incomplete hypotheses by averaging the probabilities of each token being classified as *GOOD*.

- We propose a decoding strategy that combines the token-level QE model on partial hypothesis and the NMT model to perform Quality-Aware Decoding.

- We show through experiments that early integration is essential and the translation quality is improved even when compared to reranking the N-best list with state-of-the-art QE models.

- We highlight the significance of our approach in document translation scenarios, where post-generation QE techniques fall short due to their reliance on the quality of the N-best list, a challenge that becomes more difficult as the input length increases.

2 Quality-Aware Decoding

The primary objective of this paper is to achieve Quality-Aware Decoding in NMT. To accomplish this, it is essential to predict the quality of partial translations and integrate this information during the decoding process. Our approach proposes using one NMT model for generating translations and another adapted NMT model to predict the quality of the candidate translations produced by the first model.

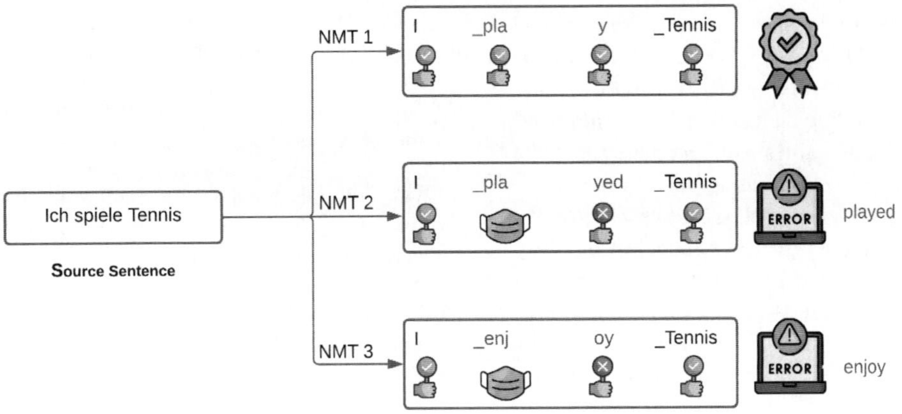

Figure 2: Token-level label annotation scheme using the MQM error tags. *MASK* indicates that this token label will not be used in training to prevent incorrect learning signal.

First, we explain why relying solely on the NMT model to predict the quality of a hypothesis is insufficient and why an additional model is necessary. Next, we outline the adaptation of the NMT model for QE on partial translations, detailing the creation of a token-level QE dataset, the modifications made to the NMT model for this task, and the process of estimating the sentence-level quality score. Finally, we describe the algorithm used to incorporate the QE score into the decoding process.

2.1 Decomposing Decoding: Translation + QE

NMT models generate a token-by-token sequence and provide the probability of each token at the decoding step. The average of the log-probabilities is often used as a proxy to score the candidate during search.

While NMT models are capable of generating high-quality translations, using the average log-probabilities of hypotheses as a scoring metric tends to yield poor correlation with actual translation quality (Eikema and Aziz, 2020; Freitag et al., 2020). In many cases, a translation can continue in several different ways, all of which may be acceptable. If the starting tokens for these continuations differ, the probability mass may be spread across multiple options which is used during the search. However, from a quality perspective, all these continuations could still achieve a high score, as the QE scores are independent and need not sum to 1.

Therefore, we propose a expert model that focuses on quality to estimate the scores better during decoding and improve the search space leading to a better hypothesis.

2.2 Quality Estimation on Partial Sequences

To provide a quality score during decoding, the QE model must be capable of handling incomplete sequences. It should not penalize a sequence if there is a potential extension that could lead to a perfect translation.

Estimating the score in this way is not feasible with current QE models, such as COMET (Rei et al., 2021), as they were not trained for this specific task and cannot provide reliable scores in the context of partial translations. Hence, we need to develop a partial QE system.

When building a partial QE system, several factors need to be considered. First, should the model use a uni-directional or bi-directional architecture? A **uni-directional** model is more efficient, as it allows for caching the hidden states, which can then be used for subsequent steps without re-encoding, unlike a bi-directional model.

Next, we need to decide whether to predict the QE score at the sequence level or at the token level. For **token-level QE**, we can directly use data from MQM annotations, as we already know which tokens are *GOOD* or *BAD*. However, for segment-level scoring, we need to consider how to synthetically create the training data.

Therefore, we decide adapt the uni-directional model into a token-level QE system that predicts whether each token is *GOOD* or *BAD* (a binary decision) by adding an additional classifier head. This adaptation enables us to estimate the score for a sequence by calculating the average probability that each token is classified as *GOOD*. We hypothesize that adapting the model in this way, rather than directly predicting the score, provides greater stability, as the last hidden states inherently contain token-level information and do not require mapping the entire sequence to a single score.

For training this model, we leverage the WMT MQM data containing error annotations in NMT outputs. We can treat tokens before an error as *GOOD* and those containing inside an error as *BAD*. Then, we can train in uni-directional manner where each token's label is predicted using only the preceding context in the hypothesis. This is crucial as we only have the preceding context to estimate the quality for partial hypothesis.

2.2.1 Learning the Right Signal

The straightforward approach to creating labels is to assign 1 to all tokens within the error span and 0 otherwise. However, MQM annotations can mark errors from words to phrases, and the starting tokens of an error span may not always be wrong. This is illustrated in Figure 2.

For example, consider the German sentence *"Ich spiele Tennis"* translated by three different NMT systems, each annotated with MQM error labels. In this work, we focus on learning a binary decision: whether an error is present, ignoring error severity.

System 1: No error: The translation *"I play Tennis"* is perfect, and all tokens are labeled as "*GOOD*."

System 2: Partial error: The translation *"I played Tennis"* has an error in the verb form ("played" instead of "play"). The error is in the token span *"played"*, but not all tokens in this span are incorrect (e.g., "pla" is correct). Assigning a "*BAD*" label to the entire span would lead to incorrect learning. A more refined approach is needed to mark errors accurately at the token level.

System 3: Full error: The translation *"I enjoy Tennis"* contains an error in *"enjoy"*, so all tokens in this span should be labeled as "*BAD*."

It is not trivial to decide when the prefix of an error span is correct/incorrect. To achieve accurate labeling, we propose the following scheme:

- Apply a `<MASK>` operation to all tokens within the error span.
- Only the last token in the span is assigned the label "*BAD*", as the error is considered complete at the end of the span.

If the error token is in the middle, we still train the model to predict "*BAD*" in the end and let the model determine which tokens should be part of the error span during inference. This approach ensures that errors are identified without explicitly defining the error span.

2.2.2 Sequence-Level Quality Estimation

After fine-tuning a token-level classification model to predict the quality of the tokens, we still need to map these predictions into a sequence-level score that can be integrated during the decoding process. There are several potential ways to achieve this.

One approach is to simply count how many tokens are classified as *BAD* in the current hypothesis. However, this method has limitations. The number of errors should be normalized based on the length of the hypothesis to account for varying sizes. Additionally, converting the probabilities into a fixed number of error tokens would need to account for different error types according to the MQM format, as each error counts differently.

To avoid such strict scoring schemes, we take a simpler approach. We average the log probabilities of all tokens that are classified as *GOOD*. This method inherently accounts for the length of the hypothesis, and it provides a score on the scale of log probabilities, which aligns with the decoding process. Therefore, we use this averaged log probability as a proxy metric for the QE score, where a higher score indicates better quality (**Line 5** in Algorithm 1).

2.2.3 Fusing Translation and Quality

We can use a token-level QE system to evaluate the quality of a source and partial hypothesis during decoding. However, integrating these probabilities into all candidates is computationally expensive, as each beam considers extensions equal to the vocabulary size.

Algorithm 1 Computing merged score of partial hypothesis with translation and token-level QE models.

1: **procedure** MERGESCORE
2: **Input:** Hypothesis tokens $h_1, h_2, h_3, \ldots, h_n$, Translation Model $\mathcal{M}_{NMT}$, QE model $\mathcal{M}_{QE}$, Source sentence $\mathcal{S}$, Re-ranking weight α,
3: **Output:** $merged\_score$
4: $Score_{NMT} \leftarrow \frac{1}{n} \sum \log \mathcal{P}(h_1, h_2, \ldots, h_n | \mathcal{S}; \mathcal{M}_{NMT})$
5: $Score_{QE} \leftarrow \frac{1}{n} \sum \log \mathcal{P}(0_1, 0_2, \ldots, 0_n | h_1, h_2, \ldots, h_n, \mathcal{S}; \mathcal{M}_{QE})$
6: $merged\_score \leftarrow (\alpha) \times Score_{NMT} + (1 - \alpha) \times Score_{QE}$
7: **end procedure**

To address this, we adopt a simplified decoding strategy from Koneru et al. (2024), which ensembles models with different vocabularies. By adapting the same MT model for token-level QE, we simplify the merging process, as the vocabularies match. This restriction is reasonable, as it is also beneficial to leverage the knowledge learned by the specialized MT for token-level QE.

The core idea is to re-rank the top candidates at each decoding step using the QE model. After reranking, the translation and QE scores are merged, and the process repeats until the end-of-sentence token is generated, for each beam. This strategy allows us to efficiently incorporate the QE model's estimate, improving translation quality.

During decoding, at each step, we have scores for n beams and V possible extensions from the vocabulary. In typical beam search, we select the top n extensions and expand the hypothesis. To make the decoding process Quality-aware, we estimate the quality of these extensions. Since estimating all extensions is computationally expensive, we limit the candidates by selecting a specified number of top candidates.

To achieve this, we use a hyper-parameter $topk$, which selects the best $topk$ extensions for each beam. For each of these top $topk$ extensions, we compute a combined score, detailed in Algorithm 1. This combined score incorporates both the translation model score and the quality estimation score, ensuring the quality is considered during decoding.

For a top extension at decoding step n, let the current tokens be $h_1, h_2, h_3, \ldots, h_n$. The NMT model score is computed as the average log probabilities of each token (Line 4). For the token-level QE model, we compute the average probability of each token being classified as '*GOOD*' (Line 5). The merged score is equal to weighted linear combination of these probabilities, with weight α (Line 6).

Thus, to make the decoding process Quality-Aware, we first train a token-level QE system by adapting the same NMT model to ensure vocabulary matching. We then combine the scores from both models to improve the sequence estimates explored during search.

	Pearson	Spearmann	Kendall
COMETQE	**44.41**	41.29	31.19
COMETQE-XL	41.23	**42.17**	**31.84**
Tower Avg. Log Prob	32.32	16.74	12.77
Tower QE	40.56	33.96	25.87

Table 1: Correlation on WMT 23 for English $\rightarrow$ German Test set. The scores are calculated after removing the few sentences labeled for hallucination detection. Best scores according to each coefficient are highlighted in **bold**.

3 Experimental Setup

Datasets: We focus on two language directions given their availability of MQM data: English $\rightarrow$ German and Chinese $\rightarrow$ English. To train our token-level QE systems, we use the MQM datasets[2] from WMT (Freitag et al., 2021). Specifically, we use the datasets until 2022 for training, 2024 for validation, and 2023 for testing (Kocmi et al., 2024). This setup is consistent with all the other QE metrics, and we do not use any additional data beyond these datasets.

Models: Our proposed approach achieves Quality-Aware decoding by combining an NMT model with a token-level QE model, where

[2]https://github.com/google/wmt-mqm-human-evaluation

Model	Beams	Re-ranking	MetricX (↓)	XCOMET-XXL (↑)
		English → German		
Tower	5	_	2.52	86.93
Tower	25	XCOMET-XL QE	2.37	87.79
Tower	25	Tower QE	2.38	87.40
Tower + Tower QE	5 (25* for Tower QE)	_	2.12	88.95*
Tower + Tower QE	5 (25* for Tower QE)	XCOMET-XL QE	**2.09***	**89.08***
		Chinese → English		
Tower	5	_	2.42	88.91
Tower	25	XCOMET-XL QE	2.30	89.49
Tower	25	Tower QE	2.32	89.51
Tower + Tower QE	5 (25* for Tower QE)	_	2.26	89.82*
Tower + Tower QE	5 (25* for Tower QE)	XCOMET-XL QE	**2.24***	**90.00***

Table 2: Translation Quality on WMT23 English → German Test set. Both XCOMET and MetricX columns use reference for reporting translation quality where as XCOMET-XL QE does not use for re-ranking. Best scores according to each metric are highlighted in **bold**. We report the top cluster indicated with asterisks and are no worse than other systems determined by Paired T-Test and bootstrap resampling with p < 0.05

we adapt the same NMT for QE by adding a classification head. We use the state-of-the-art NMT model, Tower 7B[3] (Alves et al., 2024), which provides high-quality translations and has already been exposed to MQM data during instruction-tuning. This ensures that the gains observed in our approach stem from integrating Quality-Aware decoding into the NMT process, rather than introducing new data. We find α by setting it to the optimal re-ranking weight on the validation set (See Appendix A.3 for details). Additional details on training the QE models and hyper-parameters during decoding are provided in Appendix A.1.

Metrics: For reporting the translation quality, we consistently use XCOMET-XXL[4] (Guerreiro et al., 2024) and MetricX[5] (Juraska et al., 2024) **with the reference**. To compare with N-best list re-ranking, we use the XCOMET-XL QE[6] **without the reference**. This approach allows us to avoid biasing toward a single metric during the re-ranking process and enables us to measure the gains achieved by differently trained metrics.

[3]Unbabel/TowerInstruct-7B-v0.2
[4]Unbabel/XCOMET-XXL
[5]google/metricx-24-hybrid-xl-v2p6
[6]Unbabel/XCOMET-XL

4 Results

We conduct a series of experiments to validate the effectiveness of Quality-Aware decoding and identify the scenarios where it provides the most benefit. First, we evaluate whether our token-level QE model can better estimate sequence quality compared to the log probabilities of the NMT model. Next, we assess the impact of Quality-Aware decoding by comparing it with other approaches to determine if it improves translation quality. We also perform an ablation study to examine whether training the QE model on errors from the same NMT model enhances its performance. Then, we explore the impact of source sentence length to highlight the limitations of N-best list re-ranking. Finally, we compare our proposed approach with existing Quality-Aware decoding strategies and also their inference time to highlight the latency/quality trade-off.

4.1 Quality Estimation Performance

First, we evaluate the agreement between the Tower-based token-level QE model (**Tower QE**) and human scores for a given hypothesis. It is only beneficial if we achieve higher correlation than the average of the NMT model log probabilities to show the need to integrate it during decoding. Therefore, we report the correlation with human

Model	Beams	Re-ranking	MetricX (↓)	XCOMET-XXL (↑)
		English → German		
Tower	25	XCOMET-XL QE	2.37	87.79
Tower	25	Tower QE	2.38	87.40
Tower	25	Tower Distill QE	2.38	87.39
Tower + Tower QE	5 (25* for Tower QE)	_	2.12	**88.95**
Tower + Tower QE	5 (25* for Tower Distill QE)	_	**2.11**	88.76

Table 3: Performance of Unidirectional QE trained with/without distillation on WMT23 English → German Test set. Best scores according to each metric are highlighted in **bold**.

Model	Beams	Re-ranking	XCOMET-XL (↑)	XCOMET-XXL (↑)	Impact
		Paragraph-Level			
Tower	25	XCOMET-XL QE	**86.56**	87.79	$\delta = +1.16$ (88.95 - 87.79)
Tower	25	Tower QE	85.40	87.40	
Tower + Tower QE	5 (25* for Tower QE)	_	86.36	**88.95**	
		Sentence-Level			
Tower	25	XCOMET-XL QE	**86.42**	87.68	$\delta = +0.38$ (88.06 - 87.68)
Tower	25	Tower QE	85.23	87.41	
Tower + Tower QE	5 (25* for Tower QE)	_	85.96	**88.06**	

Table 4: Impact of integrating Unidirectional QE during decoding with paragraphs vs sentences on WMT23 English → German Test set. δ denotes the improvement in translation quality from re-ranking N-best list with XCOMET-XL QE to integrating unidirectional Tower QE during the decoding. Best scores according to each metric are highlighted in **bold**.

scores of different models on WMT 23 English → German in Table 1.

We observe that the best-performing systems are the Comet QE models, which predict a single score using the full hypothesis. This is expected, as these models assess quality after the hypothesis is fully generated. In contrast, both log probabilities and Tower QE scores are based on the predicted token of each decoding step, using only the preceding context. Log probabilities perform poorly in this setup, while our proposed model, Tower QE, achieves twice the correlation with human judgments compared to log probabilities, despite scoring token by token with preceding context. This result highlights the potential of integrating our approach into the decoding process.

4.2 Unified Decoding for NMT

To validate the effectiveness of our unified decoding approach, we compare it with several baselines in Table 2. First, we evaluate whether our approach outperforms generating translations with the NMT model alone. Next, we check if the quality of translations improves compared to N-best list re-ranking. To make the setups comparable, we set $topk$ and num_beams to 5 and compare with re-ranking the top 25 beams using XCOMET-XL. Finally, to demonstrate that re-ranking the N-best list remains a viable and complementary approach, we re-rank the top 5 beams obtained from Quality-Aware decoding using the same QE model.

We find that re-ranking with XCOMET-XL and Tower QE yields similar results, indicating that our partial QE model does not over-fit to any specific metric. Furthermore, we observe that the unified decoding approach outperforms N-best list re-ranking across both metrics in both language pairs. For example, the MetricX score improves from 2.37 to 2.12 for English → German. Note that Tower has already seen this data during instruction-tuning and the improvement is not from new data but from Quality-Aware decoding. Moreover, re-ranking the top 5 beams obtained from unified decoding with XCOMET-XL leads to a slight further improvement in quality. This highlights the robustness and generalizability of our approach across different evaluation metrics.

4.3 Adapting for Tower Errors

We use the MQM annotations from WMT to train our Tower QE model, which contains error annotations from other systems. However, a viable alternative would be to adapt Tower QE specifically to the errors it typically makes. To maintain a similar data setup, we first generate translations using Tower on these source sentences. Then, we annotate the generated hypotheses with XCOMET-XL using the reference and fine-tune Tower QE on this synthetic dataset, which we refer to as **Tower Distill QE**. We evaluate the performance of the new distill QE model and report the results in Table 3.

We observe that the distilled QE model performs very similarly to the QE model trained on errors from other systems. This indicates that there was no significant benefit in adapting the QE model to the specific errors typically made by Tower. However, further analysis on larger datasets and different domains is needed to fully validate the effectiveness of the distillation approach as the current synthetic data generated is small.

4.4 Sentence vs Document-level Translation

From Table 2, we observe that the gains for English $\rightarrow$ German (paragraph-level) are much higher than for Chinese $\rightarrow$ English (sentence-level). We hypothesize that this discrepancy arises from the length of the sentences, as the N-best list re-ranking is likely sufficient for shorter sentences. To confirm this, we take the English paragraphs and split them into sentences using a tokenizer while tracking the paragraph IDs. We then perform the entire decoding process similarly, and later join the sentences back using the paragraph IDs before evaluation. We report the results in Table 4.

We define the impact as the improvement in translation quality from re-ranking the N-best list with XCOMET-XL QE to integrating Tower QE. Comparing the results at the paragraph level to those at the sentence level, we observe that the impact decreases, which confirms our hypothesis. Additionally, we obtain better scores at the document level, further highlighting the potential benefits of Quality-Aware Decoding.

4.5 Compatibility with Sampling-based Strategies

Our proposed approach integrates the feedback during decoding time to generate high quality N-best list. Therefore, it can be further combined with strategies such as Minimum Bayes Risk (MBR) (Freitag et al., 2022) or QE-Fusion (Vernikos and Popescu-Belis, 2024) decoding that only rely on the sampled candidates. We compare the different decoding strategies and report the scores in Table 5. For MBR decoding, we do epsilon sampling (epsilon=0.02) and generate 25 candidates with wmt22-comet-da as utility metric. We do not sample more as it is expensive especially at document-level with 7B model and requires multiple runs. For QE fusion, we use XCOMET-XL as the utility metric. We perform this on English-German at paragraph-level as our hypothesis is that the N-best list is problematic for long sequences.

We find that decoding with Tower QE is significantly better than the other approaches in this setting according to XCOMET-XXL metric. We also would like to highlight that it is compatible with sampling based approaches and show that by performing QE-fusion on the top 5 beams with our decoding approach. While the scores are slightly lower, human evaluation is necessary to compare these systems.

4.6 Inference Time

While the quality of translation improves, our approach also is computationally more expensive. To demonstrate this, we compare different decoding strategies and report the latency and quality in Table 6. To calculate the latency, we take the average time in seconds for inference on the WMT 23 English $\rightarrow$ German Test set.

Note that MBR with XCOMET-XL is extremely expensive given the large size of the QE model and the amount of long samples (25*24*557 examples at paragraph level limit batching) that need to be passed through the model due to the exponential nature of MBR. We see that due to the unidirectional nature of the Tower QE, the total inference time is less than double. Further, re-ranking with XCOMET-XL is the fastest given that a single forward pass is needed after generation.

Model	*Beams*	Re-ranking/ Utility Metric	*MetricX*	*XCOMET-XXL*
Tower	25	XCOMET-XL	2.37	87.79
Tower + MBR	25	wmt22-comet-da	2.75	87.53
Tower + QE-Fusion	25	XCOMET-XL	2.38	87.76
Tower + Tower QE (Ours)	5(25)	_	2.12	88.95*
Tower + Tower QE (Ours)	5(25)	XCOMET-XL	**2.09***	**89.08***
Tower + Tower QE (Ours) + QE-Fusion	5(25)	XCOMET-XL	2.10	89.03*

Table 5: Translation quality on WMT 23 English → German. We report the top cluster indicated with asterisks and are no worse than other systems determined by Paired T-Test and bootstrap resampling with $\mathbf{p < 0.05}$. For MBR, we use wmt22-comet-da as the utility metric wheras XCOMET-XL for QE-Fusion (Vernikos and Popescu-Belis, 2024).

Model	*Beams*	*Avg Time (Seconds)*	*XCOMET-XXL*
Tower	5	5.20	86.93
Tower XCOMET-XL Rerank	25	13.16 + 1.78	87.79
Tower MBR wmt22-comet-da	25	13.16 + 0.34	87.56
Tower Tower QE (Ours)	5(25)	21.04	88.94

Table 6: Average inference time on WMT 23 English-German document-level test set. For MBR and re-ranking, 13.16 is the time used for generating 25 candidates.

5 Related Work

Integrating QE in NMT: Several advancements have been made in improving QE for NMT over the years (Rei et al., 2021, 2022; Blain et al., 2023; Zerva et al., 2024; Guerreiro et al., 2024). These developments have led to the integration of QE in various ways. One common approach involves applying QE after generating multiple sequences through techniques such as QE re-ranking (Fernandes et al., 2022; Faria et al., 2024) or Minimum Bayes Risk (MBR) decoding (Tomani et al., 2024). Another direction focuses on removing noisy data using QE models, followed by fine-tuning on high-quality data (Xu et al., 2024; Finkelstein et al., 2024). Vernikos and Popescu-Belis (2024) proposes to generate diverse translations as a first step and then combine them. We perform this explicitly by integrating the QE directly into decoding. Recently, Zhang et al. (2024) exploited the MQM data by training models to penalize tokens within an error span, improving quality. In contrast, our approach adopts a modular framework, where we propose an expert QE model that is trained independently for targeted training. This modular approach aims to improve performance by decomposing the task into separate translation and QE components.

Reward Modeling in NLG: Quality-Aware decoding shares similarities with controllable text generation, particularly in using a "Quality/Reward" model to guide decoding. Methods like Weighted Decoding (Yang and Klein, 2021) adjust token probabilities for controlled generation, while Deng and Raffel (2023) use a uni-directional reward model to maintain efficiency. Li et al. (2024) further enhance control with a token-level reinforcement learning-based model. While related, our key contribution is the development of the first uni-directional QE model specifically for translation.

6 Conclusion

We demonstrated the value of Quality-Aware decoding in improving translation quality without relying on post-generation methods. Using MQM data, we built a uni-directional token-level QE model and integrated it into the decoding process. Our experiments show measurable quality gains, achieved without adding new training data to the NMT model, highlighting that improvements come only from the decoding approach.

7 Limitations

Although our Quality-Aware decoding improves translation quality, it adds considerable computational complexity to the inference process. Theoretically, this approach would double the time required to generate a translation and would require additional memory to utilize the token-level QE model. One potential solution to mitigate this issue could be to use token-level QE as a reward model for training through reinforcement learning.

Furthermore, we trained our model on a limited set of human-annotated MQM data. However, current QE models, such as XCOMET, are capable of predicting error tags using the reference with reasonable quality. This suggests that further improvements could be achieved if these models were trained on larger-scale datasets, providing more nuanced feedback and refining translation quality even further.

In addition, human evaluation is necessary to validate if the translation quality also improves with human judgment. Although we were able to better integrate MQM data during decoding, it decreases confidence in relying completely on automatic metrics.

Lastly, our proposed token-level QE model does not account for error severity. Ideally, it should be able to predict the category of errors, allowing for more nuanced feedback and enabling the model to generate translations with only minor errors when necessary.

Acknowledgments

Part of this work was performed on the HoreKa supercomputer funded by the Ministry of Science, Research and the Arts Baden-Württemberg and by the Federal Ministry of Education and Research.

References

Duarte M Alves, José Pombal, Nuno M Guerreiro, Pedro H Martins, João Alves, Amin Farajian, Ben Peters, Ricardo Rei, Patrick Fernandes, Sweta Agrawal, et al. 2024. Tower: An open multilingual large language model for translation-related tasks. *arXiv preprint arXiv:2402.17733*.

Frederic Blain, Chrysoula Zerva, Ricardo Rei, Nuno M Guerreiro, Diptesh Kanojia, José GC de Souza, Beatriz Silva, Tânia Vaz, Yan Jingxuan, Fatemeh Azadi, et al. 2023. Findings of the wmt 2023 shared task on quality estimation. In *Proceedings of the Eighth Conference on Machine Translation*, pages 629–653.

Tom Brown, Benjamin Mann, Nick Ryder, Melanie Subbiah, Jared D Kaplan, Prafulla Dhariwal, Arvind Neelakantan, Pranav Shyam, Girish Sastry, Amanda Askell, et al. 2020. Language models are few-shot learners. *Advances in neural information processing systems*, 33:1877–1901.

Aljoscha Burchardt. 2013. Multidimensional quality metrics: a flexible system for assessing translation quality. In *Proceedings of Translating and the Computer 35*.

Haikang Deng and Colin Raffel. 2023. Reward-augmented decoding: Efficient controlled text generation with a unidirectional reward model. In *Proceedings of the 2023 Conference on Empirical Methods in Natural Language Processing*, pages 11781–11791, Singapore. Association for Computational Linguistics.

Abhimanyu Dubey, Abhinav Jauhri, Abhinav Pandey, Abhishek Kadian, Ahmad Al-Dahle, Aiesha Letman, Akhil Mathur, Alan Schelten, Amy Yang, Angela Fan, et al. 2024. The llama 3 herd of models. *arXiv preprint arXiv:2407.21783*.

Bryan Eikema and Wilker Aziz. 2020. Is map decoding all you need? the inadequacy of the mode in neural machine translation. In *Proceedings of the 28th International Conference on Computational Linguistics*, pages 4506–4520.

Gonçalo RA Faria, Sweta Agrawal, António Farinhas, Ricardo Rei, José GC de Souza, and André FT Martins. 2024. Quest: Quality-aware metropolis-hastings sampling for machine translation. *arXiv preprint arXiv:2406.00049*.

Patrick Fernandes, António Farinhas, Ricardo Rei, José GC de Souza, Perez Ogayo, Graham Neubig, and André FT Martins. 2022. Quality-aware decoding for neural machine translation. In *Proceedings of the 2022 Conference of the North American Chapter of the Association for Computational Linguistics: Human Language Technologies*, pages 1396–1412.

Mara Finkelstein, David Vilar, and Markus Freitag. 2024. Introducing the newspalm mbr and qe dataset: Llm-generated high-quality parallel data outperforms traditional web-crawled data. In *Proceedings of the Ninth Conference on Machine Translation*, pages 1355–1372.

Markus Freitag, George Foster, David Grangier, Viresh Ratnakar, Qijun Tan, and Wolfgang Macherey. 2021. Experts, errors, and context: A large-scale study of human evaluation for machine translation. *Preprint*, arXiv:2104.14478.

Markus Freitag, David Grangier, and Isaac Caswell. 2020. Bleu might be guilty but references are not innocent. In *Proceedings of the 2020 Conference on Empirical Methods in Natural Language Processing (EMNLP)*, pages 61–71.

Markus Freitag, David Grangier, Qijun Tan, and Bowen Liang. 2022. High quality rather than high model probability: Minimum Bayes risk decoding with neural metrics. *Transactions of the Association for Computational Linguistics*, 10:811–825.

Markus Freitag, Nitika Mathur, Daniel Deutsch, Chi-Kiu Lo, Eleftherios Avramidis, Ricardo Rei, Brian Thompson, Frederic Blain, Tom Kocmi, Jiayi Wang, et al. 2024. Are llms breaking mt metrics? results of the wmt24 metrics shared task. In *Proceedings of the Ninth Conference on Machine Translation*, pages 47–81.

Nuno M Guerreiro, Ricardo Rei, Daan van Stigt, Luisa Coheur, Pierre Colombo, and André FT Martins. 2024. xcomet: Transparent machine translation evaluation through fine-grained error detection. *Transactions of the Association for Computational Linguistics*, 12:979–995.

Edward J Hu, Phillip Wallis, Zeyuan Allen-Zhu, Yuanzhi Li, Shean Wang, Lu Wang, Weizhu Chen, et al. 2021. Lora: Low-rank adaptation of large language models. In *International Conference on Learning Representations*.

Albert Q Jiang, Alexandre Sablayrolles, Arthur Mensch, Chris Bamford, Devendra Singh Chaplot, Diego de las Casas, Florian Bressand, Gianna Lengyel, Guillaume Lample, Lucile Saulnier, et al. 2023. Mistral 7b. *arXiv preprint arXiv:2310.06825*.

Juraj Juraska, Daniel Deutsch, Mara Finkelstein, and Markus Freitag. 2024. Metricx-24: The google submission to the wmt 2024 metrics shared task. *arXiv preprint arXiv:2410.03983*.

Tom Kocmi, Eleftherios Avramidis, Rachel Bawden, Ondřej Bojar, Anton Dvorkovich, Christian Federmann, Mark Fishel, Markus Freitag, Thamme Gowda, Roman Grundkiewicz, et al. 2024. Findings of the wmt24 general machine translation shared task: The llm era is here but mt is not solved yet. In *Proceedings of the Ninth Conference on Machine Translation*, pages 1–46.

Sai Koneru, Matthias Huck, Miriam Exel, and Jan Niehues. 2024. Plug, play, and fuse: Zero-shot joint decoding via word-level re-ranking across diverse vocabularies. In *Proceedings of the Ninth Conference on Machine Translation*, pages 1467–1481, Miami, Florida, USA. Association for Computational Linguistics.

Wendi Li, Wei Wei, Kaihe Xu, Wenfeng Xie, Dangyang Chen, and Yu Cheng. 2024. Reinforcement learning with token-level feedback for controllable text generation. In *Findings of the Association for Computational Linguistics: NAACL 2024*, pages 1704–1719, Mexico City, Mexico. Association for Computational Linguistics.

Ricardo Rei, Ana C Farinha, Chrysoula Zerva, Daan van Stigt, Craig Stewart, Pedro Ramos, Taisiya Glushkova, André FT Martins, and Alon Lavie. 2021. Are references really needed? unbabel-ist 2021 submission for the metrics shared task. In *Proceedings of the Sixth Conference on Machine Translation*, pages 1030–1040.

Ricardo Rei, Marcos Treviso, Nuno M Guerreiro, Chrysoula Zerva, Ana C Farinha, Christine Maroti, José GC de Souza, Taisiya Glushkova, Duarte Alves, Luísa Coheur, et al. 2022. Cometkiwi: Ist-unbabel 2022 submission for the quality estimation shared task. In *Proceedings of the Seventh Conference on Machine Translation (WMT)*, pages 634–645.

NLLB Team et al. 2024. Scaling neural machine translation to 200 languages. *Nature*, 630(8018):841.

Christian Tomani, David Vilar, Markus Freitag, Colin Cherry, Subhajit Naskar, Mara Finkelstein, Xavier Garcia, and Daniel Cremers. 2024. Quality-aware translation models: Efficient generation and quality estimation in a single model. In *Proceedings of the 62nd Annual Meeting of the Association for Computational Linguistics (Volume 1: Long Papers)*, pages 15660–15679.

Marcos Treviso, Nuno Guerreiro, Sweta Agrawal, Ricardo Rei, José Pombal, Tânia Vaz, Helena Wu, Beatriz Silva, Daan Stigt, and André FT Martins. 2024. xtower: A multilingual llm for explaining and correcting translation errors. In *Findings of the Association for Computational Linguistics: EMNLP 2024*, pages 15222–15239.

A Vaswani. 2017. Attention is all you need. *Advances in Neural Information Processing Systems*.

Giorgos Vernikos and Andrei Popescu-Belis. 2024. Don't rank, combine! combining machine translation hypotheses using quality estimation. *arXiv preprint arXiv:2401.06688*.

Thomas Wolf, Lysandre Debut, Victor Sanh, Julien Chaumond, Clement Delangue, Anthony Moi, Pierric Cistac, Tim Rault, Remi Louf, Morgan Funtowicz, Joe Davison, Sam Shleifer, Patrick von Platen, Clara Ma, Yacine Jernite, Julien Plu, Canwen Xu, Teven Le Scao, Sylvain Gugger, Mariama Drame, Quentin Lhoest, and Alexander Rush. 2020. Transformers: State-of-the-art natural language processing. In *Proceedings of the 2020 Conference on Empirical Methods in Natural Language Processing: System Demonstrations*, pages 38–45, Online. Association for Computational Linguistics.

Haoran Xu, Amr Sharaf, Yunmo Chen, Weiting Tan, Lingfeng Shen, Benjamin Van Durme, Kenton Murray, and Young Jin Kim. 2024. Contrastive preference optimization: Pushing the boundaries of llm performance in machine translation. *arXiv preprint arXiv:2401.08417*.

Kevin Yang and Dan Klein. 2021. Fudge: Controlled text generation with future discriminators. In *Proceedings of the 2021 Conference of the North American Chapter of the Association for Computational Linguistics: Human Language Technologies*, pages 3511–3535.

Chrysoula Zerva, Frédéric Blain, José GC De Souza, Diptesh Kanojia, Sourabh Deoghare, Nuno M Guerreiro, Giuseppe Attanasio, Ricardo Rei, Constantin Orasan, Matteo Negri, et al. 2024. Findings of the quality estimation shared task at wmt 2024 are llms closing the gap in qe? In *Proceedings of the Ninth Conference on Machine Translation,*, pages 82–109. Association for Computational Linguistics.

Lily H Zhang, Hamid Dadkhahi, Mara Finkelstein, Firas Trabelsi, Jiaming Luo, and Markus Freitag. 2024. Learning from others' mistakes: Finetuning machine translation models with span-level error annotations. *arXiv preprint arXiv:2410.16509*.

A Appendix

A.1 Training details

We use the transformers library (Wolf et al., 2020) for training and inference with Tower-Instruct V2. For adapting Tower to token-level QE, we use LoRA (Hu et al., 2021) based fine-tuning with an additional classifier head. Therefore, we only train the adapters and the weights for classification head.

We add the adapters to the modules *q_proj,k_proj,v_proj,gate_proj,up_proj* and *down_proj*. We set a batch size for each device to 12 initially and enable *auto_find_batch_size* to *True* on 4 NVIDIA RTX A6000 GPU's. For having a larger batch size during training, we set *gradient_accumulation_steps* to 6. We use a *learning_rate* of $1e^{-5}$. We set the *eval_steps* to 50 and *num_train_epochs* to 10. The other parameters are set to default.

Using the cross-entropy loss for token-level QE directly is insufficient due to the fact that the majority of tokens are classified as '*GOOD*'. Hence, we find that the weighted cross-entropy loss is essential when fine-tuning the model. For the training on human MQM data, we set the weights to $0.05, 0.95$ to '*GOOD*' and '*BAD*' labels respectively. In the case of distilling from XCOMET, we observed more errors. Therefore, we find that setting them $0.2, 0.8$ to '*GOOD*' and '*BAD*' labels respectively provided stable training.

We train on data until WMT'22 for training and use WMT'24 for validation. We calculate the macro '*F1*' on token-level predictions as the validation metric and stop training if it does not improve for 10 consecutive *eval_steps*.

A.2 Partial vs Full Sequence Quality Estimation

We also compare the difference in performance between our proposed token-level QE for partial sequences with Tower trained for full sequence QE. We achieve this by adding a regression head to predict the score at the end-of-sentence token. Hence, the model uses the source and hypothesis to predict the score using regression head at the end.

We fine-tune the model using only direct assessment data (Zerva et al., 2024) (**Tower Full DA**). Furthermore, we use this as initialisation and continue fine-tuning on the MQM data (**Tower Full DA + MQM**). We also use LoRA similarly to the previous model with a regression head to adapt the model. We report the scores in Table 7.

We see that the both Tower QE models based on full sentences outperforms the partial model. However, this is expected as it has seen the entire context and trained on larger amounts of data. Still, the partial model achieves much higher correlaiton that the log probabilities showcasing its potential for Quality-Aware decoding.

A.3 Robustness to re-ranking weight

We introduce a hyperparameter, α, to merge probabilities from the token-level QE model and the translation model. To analyze its impact, we rerank the N-best list using various α values, avoiding repeated joint decoding. If the QE model is helpful, we expect translation quality to improve when $\alpha < 1$.

Figure 4 shows that lower α values consistently yield better results, confirming that incorporating QE probabilities improves translation. This highlights the value of Tower QE and shows that reranking is an effective and robust way to tune α.

	Pearson	Spearmann	Kendall
COMETQE	**44.41**	41.29	31.19
COMETQE-XL	41.23	**42.17**	**31.84**
COMETQE Scratch Fine-tuned (ours)	36.32	33.66	25.24
Tower Log Prob	32.32	16.74	12.77
Tower Partial QE	40.56	33.96	25.87
Tower Full DA	33.67	36.46	27.38
Tower Full DA + MQM	32.03	40.85	30.38

Table 7: Full Correlation results on WMT 23 for English $\rightarrow$ German Test set. Partial indicates that the QE model predict scores via token-level where as full indicates predicting the score at the end-of-sentence token. The scores are calculated after removing the few sentences labelled for hallucination detection. Best scores according to each coefficient are highlighted in **bold**.

Tower Translation Prompt

<|im_start|>user
Translate the sentence from English into German.
English: {src_sent}
German:
<|im_end|>
<|im_start|>assistant

Tower Token-Level QE Prompt

English:{src_sent}
German: {tgt_sent}

Figure 3: Prompts used in our experiments for translation and QE model. {src_sent} and {tgt_sent} represent the source and target sentence. We replace the language with Chinese and English when experimenting with that language pair.

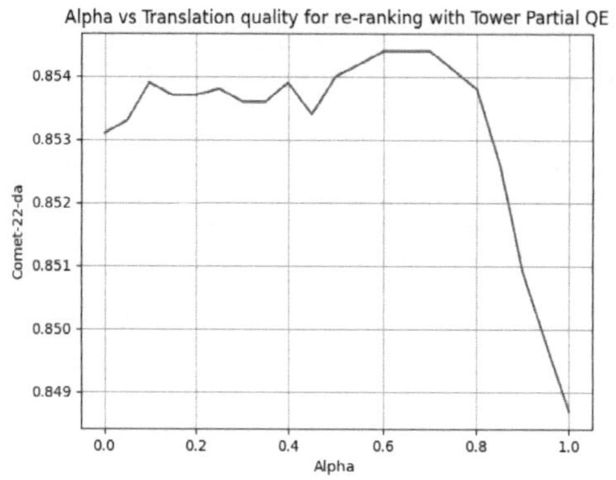

(a) English → German

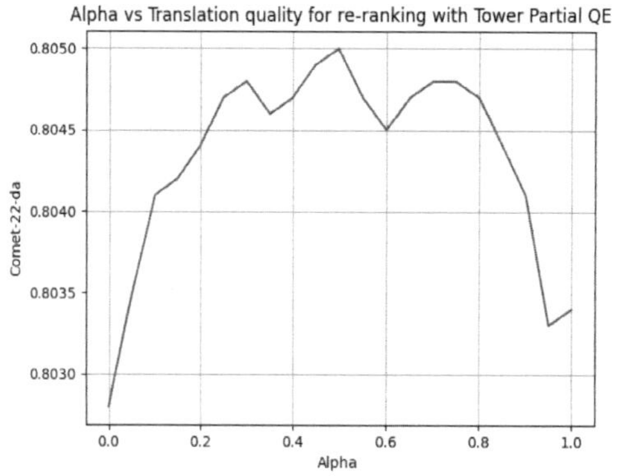

(b) Chinese → English

Figure 4: Impact of α when re-ranking with token-level Tower QE on WMT'23 Test sets.

The Warmup Dilemma: How Learning Rate Strategies Impact Speech-to-Text Model Convergence

Marco Gaido*, **Sara Papi***, **Luisa Bentivogli, Alessio Brutti, Mauro Cettolo, Roberto Gretter, Marco Matassoni, Mohamed Nabih, Matteo Negri**
Fondazione Bruno Kessler, Italy
{mgaido,spapi,bentivo,brutti,cettolo,gretter,matasso,mnabih,negri}@fbk.eu

Abstract

Training large-scale models presents challenges not only in terms of resource requirements but also in terms of their convergence. For this reason, the learning rate (LR) is often decreased when the size of a model is increased. Such a simple solution is not enough in the case of speech-to-text (S2T) trainings, where evolved and more complex variants of the Transformer architecture – e.g., Conformer or Branchformer – are used in light of their better performance. As a workaround, OWSM designed a double linear warmup of the LR, increasing it to a very small value in the first phase before updating it to a higher value in the second phase. While this solution worked well in practice, it was not compared with alternative solutions, nor was the impact on the final performance of different LR warmup schedules studied. This paper fills this gap, revealing that *i)* large-scale S2T trainings demand a sub-exponential LR warmup, and *ii)* a higher LR in the warmup phase accelerates initial convergence, but it does not boost final performance.

1 Introduction

Following the success of Large Language Models (LLM) (Radford et al., 2019), large-scale speech-to-text (S2T) trainings have gained increased interest with the goal of building Large Speech Models (LSM) or Speech Foundation Models (SFM) with similar abilities for the speech modality (Communication et al., 2023; Peng et al., 2023; Radford et al., 2023; Zhang et al., 2023).

Scaling the size of the training data and trained models with respect to traditional small-scale speech trainings has posed many challenges beyond engineering efforts and demanding hardware requirements. Among them, a significant challenge was ensuring the convergence of large models, which required adaptations to the learning rate (LR) (Radford et al., 2023; Peng et al., 2024). In particular, Whisper (Radford et al., 2023) lowered the peak LR with the increase of the model size. Differently, OWSM 3.1 (Peng et al., 2024) introduced a new LR scheduler, driven by the insight that reducing the peak LR would compromise the quality of the trained model (Kalra and Barkeshli, 2024). The new LR scheduler – named piecewise LR scheduler – modifies the warmup phase from a simple linear increase to a two-phase linear warmup while keeping unaltered the decay phase after the LR peak. However, this design choice was not motivated, nor was it investigated whether alternative warmup policies could be more effective or how they might impact the final model quality.

In this paper, we fill these gaps by studying which factors lead to a more difficult convergence of large-scale models and what is the impact of different LR warmup policies on the final performance. To this aim, we train large-scale S2T Conformer (Gulati et al., 2020) models on more than 150K hours of speech data, exploring alternative warmup methods – specifically an exponential and a polynomial policy – operating between the double linear warmup by OWSM and the traditional linear warmup phase of the inverse square root LR scheduler. Our experiments demonstrate that:

- Advanced and more complex variants of the Transformer architecture, such as Conformer and Branchformer (Peng et al., 2022), widely used in speech processing for their superior performance, are more difficult to train due to their deeper layers involving additional components (e.g., extra convolutional or linear layers), making them more prone to "exploding gradient" (Bengio et al., 1994) issues;
- The LR warmup should follow an exponential or sub-exponential function and, while it plays a crucial role in the convergence of the

* Equal contribution.

Proceedings of the 22nd International Conference on Spoken Language Translation (IWSLT 2025), pages 47–55
July 31 - August 1, 2025 ©2025 Association for Computational Linguistics

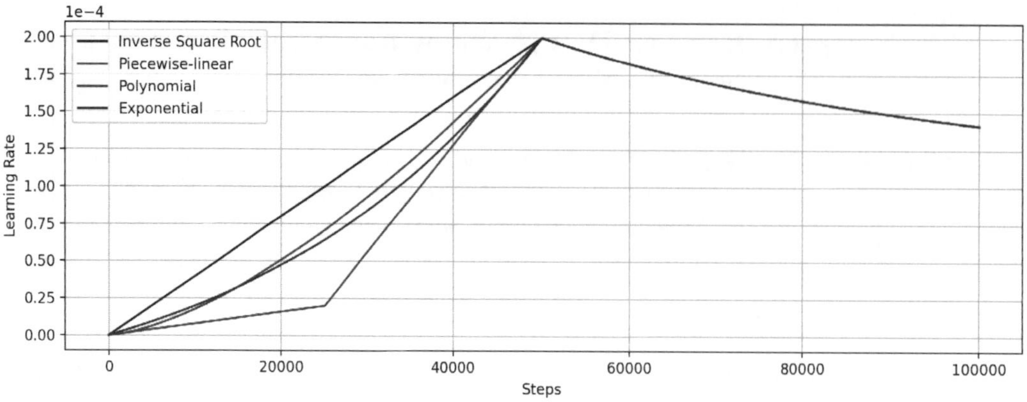

Figure 1: LR schedulers with inverse square root, piecewise-linear, polynomial, and exponential warmup policies.

model by ensuring a smooth transition to a good model initialization, it does not significantly affect the final result as long as convergence of the model is achieved.

To ease future research on the topic, foster reproducibility of our work, and in accordance with the Open Science principles (White et al., 2024), we release the code, logs, and intermediate checkpoints under the open-source Apache 2.0 license at `https://github.com/hlt-mt/FBK-fairseq`.

2 Learning Rate Schedulers

This section describes the LR schedulers analyzed in this work, starting from the widely adopted inverse square root with linear warmup (§2.1) and piecewise-linear warmup (§2.2), to the alternative sub-linear warmup policies, namely polynomial (§2.3) and exponential (§2.4), designed to be as close as possible to the traditional inverse square root LR. All LR schedulers are shown in Figure 1.

2.1 Inverse Square Root Policy

Since the introduction of the Transformer architecture, the LR scheduler has followed an inverse square root policy (Vaswani et al., 2017). This scheduler has therefore been widely adopted in S2T training settings (Inaguma et al., 2020; Wang et al., 2020) and entails two phases. Firstly, the LR linearly increases for a predefined number of steps w from 0 to the peak LR η, where w and η are two hyper-parameters whose tuning is critical for the success of the training and the quality of the resulting model (Popel and Bojar, 2018). In this phase, the LR η_i at the i-th step is $\eta_i = \eta \cdot i/w$. Secondly, after reaching η, the LR decreases proportionally to the inverse square root of the number of steps, i.e. $\eta_i = \eta \cdot \sqrt{w}/\sqrt{i}$. Overall, the LR η_i at the i-th step is:

$$\eta_i = \eta \cdot \min\left(\frac{i}{w}, \frac{\sqrt{w}}{\sqrt{i}}\right)$$

where w is set to 50k and η to $2e^{-4}$ in this work.

2.2 Piecewise-linear Warmup

Peng et al. (2024) found that the linear warmup of the standard inverse square root LR scheduler was not suitable for training their large-scale 1B Branchformer model and introduced the piecewise-linear warmup policy. This policy splits the warmup step into two linear phases, introducing an intermediate LR η' with a corresponding number of intermediate warmup steps w' as additional hyperparameters. In the first w' steps, the LR linearly increases from 0 to η', which is typically set to a much smaller value than η, and then in the steps between w' and w it increases from η' to η. As such, in the warmup phase, i.e. at the step $i < w$, the LR η_i is:

$$\eta_{i<w} = \max\left(\eta' \cdot \frac{i}{w'}, \eta' + \frac{(\eta - \eta') \cdot (i - w')}{w - w'}\right)$$

In this work, we follow Peng et al. (2024) and set the number of intermediate warmup steps w' to $w/2$ i.e., 25k, and the intermediate LR w' to $\eta/10$.

2.3 Polynomial Warmup

As a first alternative to the piecewise-linear policy, we propose to increase the LR with a polynomial function with respect to the number of steps. The slope of the increase is controlled by a hyperparameter α, according to the formula:

$$\eta_{i<w} = \eta \cdot \left(\frac{i}{w}\right)^{\alpha}$$

We set α to 1.5, and the polynomial warmup function is visualized in Figure 1 (green curve).

2.4 Exponential Warmup

As a second alternative, we introduce an exponential policy that, compared to the polynomial one, has a steeper LR increase in the first part of the warmup and a lower LR in the second. Also in this case, the hyper-parameter α controls the smoothness of the function, and the higher the α the smaller the LR in the warmup phase. Specifically, this policy follows the formula:

$$\eta_{i<w} = \eta \cdot \frac{e^{\alpha \cdot \frac{i}{w}} - 1}{e^{\alpha} - 1}$$

Similarly to the polynomial warmup (Section 2.3), we set α to 1.5, and the exponential warmup function is visualized in Figure 1 (purple curve).

3 Experimental Settings

To ensure that divergence issues are not due to a particularly challenging setting, we avoided multi-task trainings, resorting to training S2T models on the automatic speech recognition (ASR) task for two languages (English and Italian). As training data, we use $\sim$150k hours of publicly available speech datasets, which are described in Appendix A. For validation, we use the English (en) and Italian (it) dev sets of CommonVoice (Ardila et al., 2020).

Our encoder-decoder models have a Transformer decoder and a Conformer encoder preceded by two 1D convolutional layers that downsample the sequence length by a factor of 4. For the Conformer encoder, we use the implementation by Papi et al. (2024) that fixes issues in padding handling. Given the results of preliminary experiments (§4.1), we set 24 encoder layers and 12 decoder layers for the experiments in §4.2. The embeddings have 1024 features, with an FFN hidden dimension of 4096 and 16 attention heads. In total, our models have 878M parameters. Further details are provided in Appendix A.

4 Results

4.1 Preliminary Experiments

In preliminary experiments, we varied the number of encoder and decoder layers to understand when the depth of the network becomes critical – i.e., the model starts diverging – with the standard inverse square root LR scheduler. In this scenario, we observed that the number of encoder layers was the driver of the issue while adding more decoder layers was not. Specifically, models with more than 18 encoder layers were not converging. For instance, models with 18 encoder layers and 6 decoder layers diverge, while models with 12 encoder and 12 decoder layers converge without issues. This observation, together with the fact that Whisper (which features a Transformer encoder) was trained without the need for adapting the learning rate scheduler, suggests that complex layers featuring many subcomponents, such as Conformer and Branchformer layers, pose convergence issues with deep models. In our Conformer implementation, each subcomponent is wrapped in a residual connection (He et al., 2016), which may indicate a need for additional normalization layers within each encoder block to mitigate potential scaling effects. However, we leave this investigation for future work.

4.2 LR Warmup Analysis

Moving to the comparison of the warmup policies, Figure 2 shows the resulting learning curves on the validation sets for the two languages, which display the same behaviors, with the only difference that the Italian curves have a higher perplexity at the beginning and decline later than English ones. Similar trends can be observed in the training set, which we report in Appendix B.

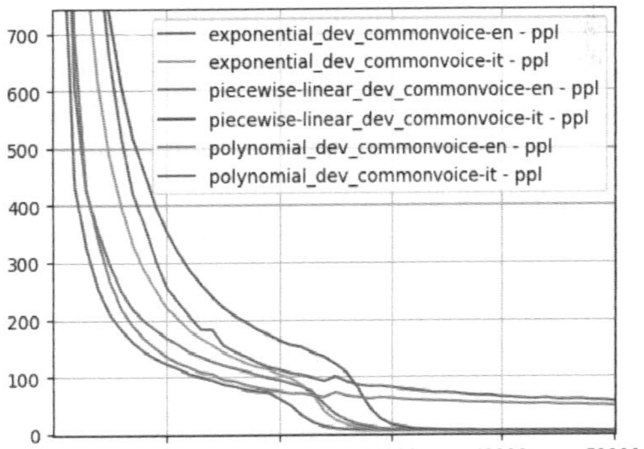

Figure 2: Perplexity on the English and Italian validation sets for the polynomial, piecewise-linear, and exponential policies for the first 50k steps (warmup phase).

Model Convergence First, we notice that the model convergence is obtained only with the exponential and piecewise-linear policies. The polynomial policy, instead, displays the same pattern as

LR	CV		MLS		VP		AVG
	en	*it*	*en*	*it*	*en*	*it*	
PL	**18.4**	**13.7**	**7.4**	**17.4**	**8.3**	**17.8**	**13.8**
Exp	19.1	14.3	7.5	17.9	8.6	18.3	14.3

Table 1: WER (↓), computed using `jiwer` and the Whisper text normalizer, on the CommonVoice (CV), VoxPopuli (VP), and MLS test sets of the 170k-steps checkpoints obtained with the LR scheduler with piecewise-linear (PL) and exponential (Exp) warm up.

the standard inverse square root policy (which we do not report here) leading the model to a high perplexity that minimally degrades with the progression of the training. This convergence issue can be attributed to an exploding gradient: as we show in Appendix C, in the polynomial training there are huge spikes in the gradient norm in the range 25k-30k steps and later, where the other policies feature a steep decrease that the polynomial fails to achieve. The exponential policy, despite a higher LR during the first ~15k steps, has a slightly lower LR in the 15k-50k range than the polynomial policy. This minimal difference is sufficient to enable model convergence. Therefore, we can conclude that the exponential policy closely approaches the highest feasible LR during the warmup phase without compromising model convergence.

Convergence Speed Figure 2 also shows that, as expected, higher LRs result in lower perplexity during the initial steps. In both the English and Italian validation sets, the exponential policy – which features the highest LR in the first ~15k steps – always displays the lowest perplexity. The polynomial one starts with the highest perplexity due to its lower LR in the initial steps. However, it later surpasses the piecewise-linear policy and closes the gap with the exponential one, thanks to its higher LR in the later stages, until it ultimately fails to converge. Interestingly, the learning curves of the two converging policies show a step-like decrease, which is anticipated for the exponential policy (~20k vs ~23k steps for English and ~22k vs ~26k for Italian) as per its faster convergence.

Effect on the Resulting Model Lastly, we explore whether the faster initial convergence of the exponential policy results in a better model at the end of the training compared to that obtained with the piecewise-linear policy. Figure 3 shows the learning curve after the first 50k steps, up to the end of the whole pass over the training set (i.e., the first training epoch at step 170k). The learning curves

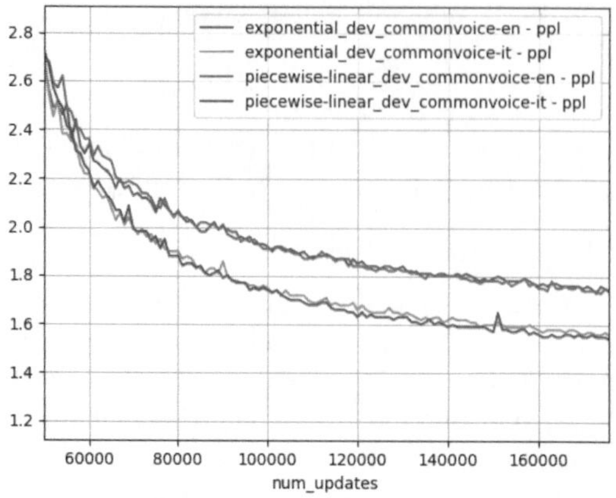

Figure 3: Perplexity on the English and Italian validation sets for the piecewise-linear and exponential policies for the steps after the warmup phase (50k-170k).

of the piecewise-linear scheduler not only reach the perplexity of those of the exponential policy but the English one also becomes slightly better. The same trend is observed in the training data (see Figure 5 in Appendix B), in which the English data is more than 80%. The WER on test sets for the checkpoint at the 170k step also testifies to a slight superiority of the model obtained using the piecewise-linear policy on both languages, as shown in Table 1. We can conclude that a faster convergence in the early stages of the training does not imply a better resulting model and that the warmup policy of the LR scheduler is critical to ensure the convergence of the model, but, once that is achieved, its role in the model quality is limited.

5 Conclusions

In this study, we analyzed one of the key challenges – beyond engineering, data curation, and hardware efforts – associated with training large-scale S2T models i.e., the role of the LR scheduler and, in particular, of its warmup strategy in model convergence and final performance. To this aim, we compared the standard linear warmup and the piecewise-linear warmup strategies with two policies – polynomial and exponential – aimed at finding the highest possible LR in the warmup phase that does not lead to convergence issues. Through experiments on large-scale ASR trainings of a ~900M parameters Conformer model, we demonstrated that while the LR warmup phase is crucial for stabilizing convergence, it has a minimal impact on final model performance and that the LR warmup phase should follow an exponential or sub-exponential rise to ensure model convergence.

Acknowledgments

This paper has received funding from the PNRR project FAIR - Future AI Research (PE00000013), under the NRRP MUR program funded by the NextGenerationEU, and from the European Union's Horizon research and innovation programme under grant agreement No 101135798, project Meetween (My Personal AI Mediator for Virtual MEETings BetWEEN People). We acknowledge CINECA for the availability of high-performance computing resources and support.

Limitations

Effect of Multilingualism and Multi-task In this work, we decided to experiment with a single task and two languages in the training, even though the amount of training data we used was comparable to that used in other works to train S2T models on multiple tasks and more than 100 languages (e.g., OWSM uses 180k hours of data against our 150k hours). Although there is no reason to posit that a different setting may lead to different conclusions since the behaviors we observed were similar to those of OWSM, future works should validate that our findings extend to these scenarios.

Multiple Runs While performing multiple runs for each setting would provide stronger insights into the possible statistical significance of the observed differences, this would require extensive computational costs that go beyond our budget.

Tuning α Although by tuning α we could, for instance, obtain a converging model even with the polynomial policy, this was not the focus of our work. In this paper, we attempted to understand the role of different LR schedulers on the resulting model and what could be achieved by using different LR warmup policies. Since two extreme solutions – the piecewise-linear policy with a relatively low LR and the exponential policy with the highest feasible LR – do not show evident differences, finding other values of α or other policies leading to similar results would not have added much to our discussion. Also, as noted above, each run is computationally demanding, limiting our ability to explore the space of the possible values.

References

Rosana Ardila, Megan Branson, Kelly Davis, Michael Kohler, Josh Meyer, Michael Henretty, Reuben Morais, Lindsay Saunders, Francis Tyers, and Gregor Weber. 2020. Common voice: A massively-multilingual speech corpus. In *Proceedings of the Twelfth Language Resources and Evaluation Conference*, pages 4218–4222, Marseille, France. European Language Resources Association.

Parnia Bahar, Tobias Bieschke, and Hermann Ney. 2019. A comparative study on end-to-end speech to text translation. In *2019 IEEE Automatic Speech Recognition and Understanding Workshop (ASRU)*, pages 792–799.

Y. Bengio, P. Simard, and P. Frasconi. 1994. Learning long-term dependencies with gradient descent is difficult. *IEEE Transactions on Neural Networks*, 5(2):157–166.

Seamless Communication et al. 2023. SeamlessM4T: Massively Multilingual & Multimodal Machine Translation. *Preprint*, arXiv:2308.11596.

Alexis Conneau, Min Ma, Simran Khanuja, Yu Zhang, Vera Axelrod, Siddharth Dalmia, Jason Riesa, Clara Rivera, and Ankur Bapna. 2023. Fleurs: Few-shot learning evaluation of universal representations of speech. In *2022 IEEE Spoken Language Technology Workshop (SLT)*, pages 798–805.

Marco Gaido, Sara Papi, Luisa Bentivogli, Alessio Brutti, Mauro Cettolo, Roberto Gretter, Marco Matassoni, Mohamed Nabih, and Matteo Negri. 2024. MOSEL: 950,000 Hours of Speech Data for Open-Source Speech Foundation Model Training on EU Languages. In *Proceedings of the 2024 Conference on Empirical Methods in Natural Language Processing*, Miami, United States. Association for Computational Linguistics.

Alex Graves, Santiago Fernández, Faustino J. Gomez, and Jürgen Schmidhuber. 2006. Connectionist Temporal Classification: Labelling Unsegmented Sequence Data with Recurrent Neural Networks. In *Proceedings of the 23rd international conference on Machine learning (ICML)*, pages 369–376, Pittsburgh, Pennsylvania.

Anmol Gulati, James Qin, Chung-Cheng Chiu, Niki Parmar, Yu Zhang, Jiahui Yu, Wei Han, Shibo Wang, Zhengdong Zhang, Yonghui Wu, and Ruoming Pang. 2020. Conformer: Convolution-augmented transformer for speech recognition. In *Interspeech 2020*, pages 5036–5040.

Kaiming He, Xiangyu Zhang, Shaoqing Ren, and Jian Sun. 2016. Deep residual learning for image recognition. In *2016 IEEE Conference on Computer Vision and Pattern Recognition (CVPR)*, pages 770–778.

Hirofumi Inaguma, Shun Kiyono, Kevin Duh, Shigeki Karita, Nelson Yalta, Tomoki Hayashi, and Shinji Watanabe. 2020. ESPnet-ST: All-in-one speech translation toolkit. In *Proceedings of the 58th Annual Meeting of the Association for Computational Linguistics: System Demonstrations*, pages 302–311, Online. Association for Computational Linguistics.

J. Kahn, M. Rivière, W. Zheng, E. Kharitonov, Q. Xu, P. E. Mazaré, J. Karadayi, V. Liptchinsky, R. Collobert, C. Fuegen, T. Likhomanenko, G. Synnaeve, A. Joulin, A. Mohamed, and E. Dupoux. 2020. Libri-Light: A Benchmark for ASR with Limited or No Supervision. In *ICASSP 2020 - 2020 IEEE International Conference on Acoustics, Speech and Signal Processing (ICASSP)*, pages 7669–7673. https://github.com/facebookresearch/libri-light.

Dayal Singh Kalra and Maissam Barkeshli. 2024. Why warmup the learning rate? underlying mechanisms and improvements. In *The Thirty-eighth Annual Conference on Neural Information Processing Systems*.

Taku Kudo. 2018. Subword regularization: Improving neural network translation models with multiple subword candidates. In *Proceedings of the 56th Annual Meeting of the Association for Computational Linguistics (Volume 1: Long Papers)*, pages 66–75, Melbourne, Australia.

Sara Papi, Marco Gaido, Luisa Bentivogli, Alessio Brutti, Mauro Cettolo, Roberto Gretter, Marco Matassoni, Mohamed Nabih, and Matteo Negri. 2025. FAMA: The First Large-Scale Open-Science Speech Foundation Model for English and Italian.

Sara Papi, Marco Gaido, Andrea Pilzer, and Matteo Negri. 2024. When good and reproducible results are a giant with feet of clay: The importance of software quality in NLP. In *Proceedings of the 62nd Annual Meeting of the Association for Computational Linguistics (Volume 1: Long Papers)*, pages 3657–3672, Bangkok, Thailand. Association for Computational Linguistics.

Yifan Peng, Siddharth Dalmia, Ian Lane, and Shinji Watanabe. 2022. Branchformer: Parallel MLP-attention architectures to capture local and global context for speech recognition and understanding. In *Proceedings of the 39th International Conference on Machine Learning*, volume 162 of *Proceedings of Machine Learning Research*, pages 17627–17643. PMLR.

Yifan Peng, Jinchuan Tian, William Chen, Siddhant Arora, Brian Yan, Yui Sudo, Muhammad Shakeel, Kwanghee Choi, Jiatong Shi, Xuankai Chang, Jee weon Jung, and Shinji Watanabe. 2024. Owsm v3.1: Better and faster open whisper-style speech models based on e-branchformer. In *Interspeech 2024*, pages 352–356.

Yifan Peng, Jinchuan Tian, Brian Yan, Dan Berrebbi, Xuankai Chang, Xinjian Li, Jiatong Shi, Siddhant Arora, William Chen, Roshan Sharma, Wangyou Zhang, Yui Sudo, Muhammad Shakeel, Jee-Weon Jung, Soumi Maiti, and Shinji Watanabe. 2023. Reproducing whisper-style training using an open-source toolkit and publicly available data. In *2023 IEEE Automatic Speech Recognition and Understanding Workshop (ASRU)*, pages 1–8.

PleIAs. 2024. PleIAs/YouTube-Commons · Datasets at Hugging Face — huggingface.co. https://huggingface.co/datasets/PleIAs/YouTube-Commons. [Accessed 10-06-2024].

Martin Popel and Ondřej Bojar. 2018. Training tips for the transformer model. *The Prague Bulletin of Mathematical Linguistics*, 110:43–70.

Vineel Pratap, Qiantong Xu, Anuroop Sriram, Gabriel Synnaeve, and Ronan Collobert. 2020. MLS: A Large-Scale Multilingual Dataset for Speech Research. In *Proc. Interspeech 2020*, pages 2757–2761.

Alec Radford, Jong Wook Kim, Tao Xu, Greg Brockman, Christine Mcleavey, and Ilya Sutskever. 2023. Robust speech recognition via large-scale weak supervision. In *Proceedings of the 40th International Conference on Machine Learning*, volume 202 of *Proceedings of Machine Learning Research*, pages 28492–28518.

Alec Radford, Jeff Wu, Rewon Child, David Luan, Dario Amodei, and Ilya Sutskever. 2019. Language Models are Unsupervised Multitask Learners.

Christian Szegedy, Vincent Vanhoucke, Sergey Ioffe, Jon Shlens, and Zbigniew Wojna. 2016. Rethinking the inception architecture for computer vision. In *Proceedings of the IEEE conference on computer vision and pattern recognition*, pages 2818–2826.

Ashish Vaswani, Noam Shazeer, Niki Parmar, Jakob Uszkoreit, Llion Jones, Aidan N Gomez, Ł ukasz Kaiser, and Illia Polosukhin. 2017. Attention is all you need. In *Advances in Neural Information Processing Systems*, volume 30. Curran Associates, Inc.

Changhan Wang, Morgane Riviere, Ann Lee, Anne Wu, Chaitanya Talnikar, Daniel Haziza, Mary Williamson, Juan Pino, and Emmanuel Dupoux. 2021a. VoxPopuli: A large-scale multilingual speech corpus for representation learning, semi-supervised learning and interpretation. In *Proceedings of the 59th Annual Meeting of the Association for Computational Linguistics and the 11th International Joint Conference on Natural Language Processing (Volume 1: Long Papers)*, pages 993–1003, Online. Association for Computational Linguistics.

Changhan Wang, Yun Tang, Xutai Ma, Anne Wu, Dmytro Okhonko, and Juan Pino. 2020. Fairseq S2T: Fast speech-to-text modeling with fairseq. In *Proceedings of the 1st Conference of the Asia-Pacific Chapter of the Association for Computational Linguistics and the 10th International Joint Conference on Natural Language Processing: System Demonstrations*, pages 33–39, Suzhou, China. Association for Computational Linguistics.

Changhan Wang, Anne Wu, Jiatao Gu, and Juan Pino. 2021b. CoVoST 2 and Massively Multilingual Speech Translation. In *Proc. Interspeech 2021*, pages 2247–2251.

Matt White, Ibrahim Haddad, Cailean Osborne, Xiao-Yang Liu Yanglet, Ahmed Abdelmonsef, and Sachin Varghese. 2024. The model openness framework: Promoting completeness and openness for reproducibility, transparency, and usability in artificial intelligence. *Preprint*, arXiv:2403.13784.

Brian Yan, Siddharth Dalmia, Yosuke Higuchi, Graham Neubig, Florian Metze, Alan W Black, and Shinji Watanabe. 2023. CTC alignments improve autoregressive translation. In *Proceedings of the 17th Conference of the European Chapter of the Association for Computational Linguistics*, pages 1623–1639, Dubrovnik, Croatia.

Yu Zhang, Wei Han, James Qin, Yongqiang Wang, Ankur Bapna, Zhehuai Chen, Nanxin Chen, Bo Li, Vera Axelrod, Gary Wang, Zhong Meng, Ke Hu, Andrew Rosenberg, Rohit Prabhavalkar, Daniel S. Park, Parisa Haghani, Jason Riesa, Ginger Perng, Hagen Soltau, Trevor Strohman, Bhuvana Ramabhadran, Tara Sainath, Pedro Moreno, Chung-Cheng Chiu, Johan Schalkwyk, Françoise Beaufays, and Yonghui Wu. 2023. Google usm: Scaling automatic speech recognition beyond 100 languages. *Preprint*, arXiv:2303.01037.

A Training Settings

We train the models on $\sim$150k hours of speech datasets, namely the train section of CommonVoice (Ardila et al., 2020), CoVoST2 (Wang et al., 2021b), FLEURS (Conneau et al., 2023), LibriLight (Kahn et al., 2020), MLS (Pratap et al., 2020), VoxPopuli (Wang et al., 2021a), and YouTube-Commons (PleIAs, 2024). When the transcript was not available for a given dataset, we used the automatic transcripts of MOSEL v1.0 (Gaido et al., 2024). As YouTube-Commons transcripts are not available in MOSEL v1.0[1], we used the transcript provided for the training of FAMA (Papi et al., 2025). Our training data is exactly the same used for FAMA and is available at `https://huggingface.co/datasets/FBK-MT/fama-data`. The textual data is used to build the vocabulary with 16,000 SentencePiece unigrams (Kudo, 2018).

We optimize our models using the Adam optimizer with betas (0.9, 0.98). The training loss is the linear combination of the label-smoothed cross-entropy (Szegedy et al., 2016) on the decoder output and two CTC (Graves et al., 2006) losses, one at the 16th encoder layer and one on top of the encoder (Bahar et al., 2019; Yan et al., 2023). We also experimented with removing the auxiliary CTC losses, to ensure that they were not the driver of divergence issues and, indeed, their removal did not change anything in terms of whether a model converges or not. We clip the gradient norm at 10.0 and use 0.001 weight decay. We trained the models on 16 A100 GPUs (64GB VRAM) for 1 epoch with at most 55 seconds of data in each mini-batch and 5 gradient accumulation steps, resulting in 176,208 batches to complete an epoch. One run in this setting lasts 6 days.

B Perplexity on the Training Set

Figure 4 shows the perplexity (PPL) of the different warmup policies on the training set for the first part of the training. Compared to Figure 2 presenting the PPL obtained on the validation set, the training curves show similar behaviors, with the polynomial warmup not converging, and the piecewise-linear and exponential leading to, respectively, slower and faster convergence.

Looking at Figure 5 that isolates the PPL behavior after the first 50k steps, we notice that, again, the piecewise-linear and exponential warmup ex-

[1]They have been added in v2.0.

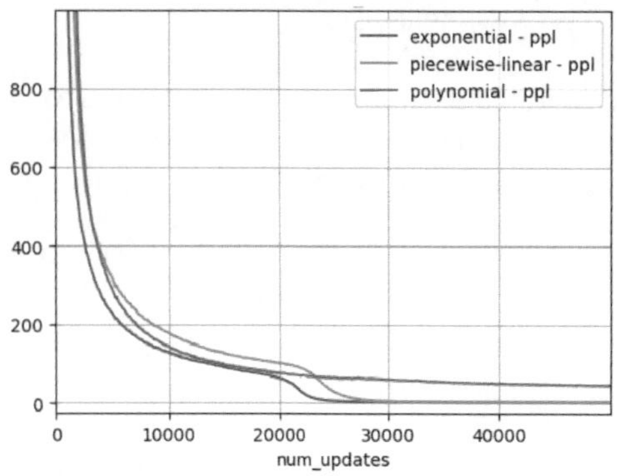

Figure 4: Perplexity on the training set for the polynomial, piecewise-linear, and exponential warmup policies for the first 50k steps (warmup phase).

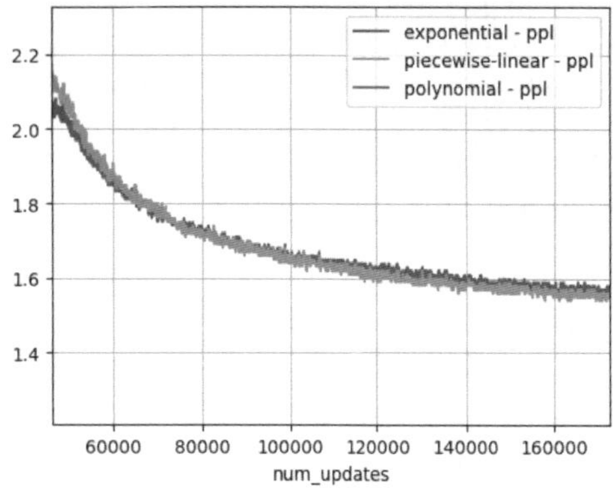

Figure 5: Perplexity on the training set for the piecewise-linear and exponential warmup policies for the steps after the warmup phase (50k-170k).

hibit similar trends to those reported for the validation set in Figure 3: the curves are very close, with the piecewise-linear, initially above the exponential, becoming slightly below the exponential in the long run. This reconfirms the results discussed in Section 4, where we highlighted the convergence issues of the polynomial function, which is actually reflected in the training set, and the slower but slightly better convergence of the piecewise-linear warmup against the exponential one.

C Gnorm Analysis

Figure 6 reports the gradient norm in the warmup phase for the different policies (exponential, polynomial, and piecewise-linear). Except for the initial steps, the gradient norm for the policies leading to convergence always remains low (<25). For the polynomial warmup, instead, there are huge spikes beyond 100 and even 200 after 25k steps. These explosions of the gradient norm have also been observed in all the runs with the inverse square root LR scheduler that did not converge in our preliminary experiments. We can conclude that huge spikes in the gradient norm can be used to detect non-converging trainings.

Analyzing the gradient norm of the exponential and piecewise-linear policies, we observe that the gradient norm is higher at the beginning (8k-15k steps) for the exponential policy, which displays faster convergence in this phase. On the opposite, the gradient norm of the piecewise-linear policy is higher in the 15k-30k steps range, in which closes the initial gap with the exponential policy.

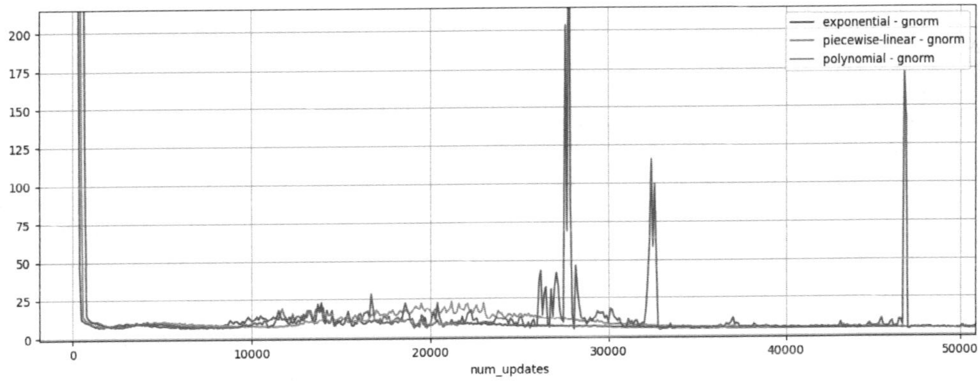

Figure 6: Gradient norm comparison across the piecewise-linear, polynomial, and exponential warmup policies.

SSR: Alignment-Aware Modality Connector for Speech Language Models

Weiting Tan[♠*] **Hirofumi Inaguma**[♡] **Ning Dong**[♡]
Paden Tomasello[♡] **Xutai Ma**[♡]
[♠]Johns Hopkins University [♡]Meta AI Research

Abstract

Fusing speech into a pre-trained language model (SpeechLM) usually suffers from the inefficient encoding of long-form speech and catastrophic forgetting of pre-trained text modality. We propose SSR-CONNECTOR (Segmented Speech Representation Connector) for better modality fusion. Leveraging speech-text alignments, our approach segments and compresses speech features to match the granularity of text embeddings. Additionally, we introduce a two-stage training pipeline that includes the distillation and fine-tuning phases to mitigate catastrophic forgetting. SSR-CONNECTOR outperforms existing mechanism for speech-text modality fusion, consistently achieving better speech understanding (e.g., +10 accuracy on StoryCloze and +20 on Speech-MMLU) while preserving pre-trained text ability.

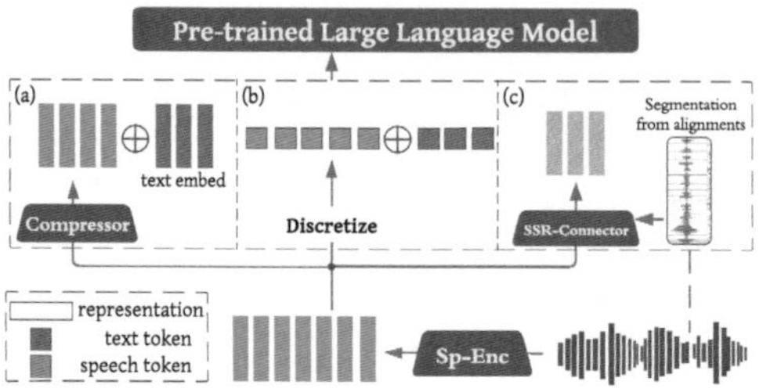

Figure 1: Comparison of different approaches for speech-text modality fusion. *(a)*: compressor-based connector. *(b)*: direct fusion with speech units. *(c)*: our alignment-aware connector.

1 Introduction

Large language models (Brown et al., 2020; Chowdhery et al., 2022; Chiang et al., 2023; Anil et al., 2023; Touvron et al., 2023; OpenAI et al., 2024; Grattafiori et al., 2024; DeepSeek-AI et al., 2025, LLMs) have demonstrated remarkable performance across various tasks and extending pre-trained abilities from LLMs to other modalities has sparked interest in multimodal LLMs (Alayrac et al., 2022; Liu et al., 2023b; OpenAI et al., 2024; Tang et al., 2024; Défossez et al., 2024). In this work, we focus on integrating speech into pre-trained language models (SpeechLMs). A straightforward approach is to transcribe speech into text and use these transcriptions as prompts for large language models (Huang et al., 2023); however, such cascaded systems suffer from error propagation, higher latency, and cannot leverage raw speech information like emotion, speaker identity, and other paralinguistic cues (Faruqui and Hakkani-Tür, 2021; Lin et al., 2022; Kim et al., 2024). Consequently, developing end-to-end SpeechLMs that directly fuse speech or audio input has gained popularity, where various approaches have been explored to encode speech and align its representation with pre-trained language models (Zhang et al., 2023; Rubenstein et al., 2023; Yu et al., 2023; Maiti et al., 2024; Hassid et al., 2024; Tang et al., 2024; Nguyen et al., 2024).

Speech representations can be integrated into pre-trained language models mainly through two approaches. The first method involves using connector modules that align speech representations with the language model's input space without modifying the model's existing vocabulary. These connector-based techniques typically incorporate a compression module to shorten the speech features, enhancing efficiency. However, connectors are generally first trained for the speech recognition task (with concatenated speech-to-text data) and **lack the ability to support text or speech generation unless further instruction-finetuned**.

The second approach, unit-based fusion, directly incorporates discrete speech units—normally derived from self-supervised models like HuBERT (Hsu et al., 2021), XLS-R (Babu et al., 2021), or DinoSR (Liu et al., 2023a)—into the language model's vocabulary. This allows the language model to be fine-tuned with a combination of

[*] Work was done during an internship at Meta AI.

Proceedings of the 22nd International Conference on Spoken Language Translation (IWSLT 2025), pages 56–75
July 31 - August 1, 2025 ©2025 Association for Computational Linguistics

speech and text tokens, enabling it to handle dual-modal inputs and outputs. Despite its versatility, **unit-based fusion can lead to longer and less efficient training contexts** due to the sparser nature of speech information. Regardless of the fusion approach, SpeechLMs often face the challenge of catastrophic forgetting, where the model loses its pre-trained text capabilities (Tang et al., 2024; Nguyen et al., 2024; Défossez et al., 2024).

To tackle these challenges, we propose SSR-CONNECTOR (Segmented Speech Representation Connector), which grounds speech representations in the same semantic space as transcription token embeddings. Different from prior work that concatenates speech with text (Fig. 1 (a,b)) for modality fusion, we leverage speech-text alignments to segment and compress speech features (Fig. 1 (c)).

To mitigate catastrophic forgetting when introducing the speech modality, we propose a two-stage training pipeline. In Stage 1, we freeze the LLM and pre-train the connector using speech-text distillation, adapting speech inputs into compressed representations semantically aligned with text embeddings. In Stage 2, we unfreeze the LLM and fine-tune it using next-token prediction, with the adapted representation as input and the corresponding transcription tokens as targets.

SSR-CONNECTOR outperforms prior SpeechLMs, including SPIRITLM, VOXTLM, TWIST, and AUDIOLM (Nguyen et al., 2024; Maiti et al., 2024; Hassid et al., 2024; Borsos et al., 2023), across multiple tasks. These include Prompt-based Automatic Speech Recognition (ASR) and Spoken Language Understanding with sWUGGY, sBLIMP, and StoryCloze (Nguyen et al., 2020; Mostafazadeh et al., 2017). Our approach also improves performance on Massive Multitask Language Understanding (MMLU) (Hendrycks et al., 2021) and its speech-based counterpart, Speech-MMLU, which we introduce to assess cross-modal reasoning. Finally, we analyze different training strategies (§5) and speech-text aligners (Appendix A) for SSR-CONNECTOR.

2 Related Work

Modality Fusion for Speech Language Models SpeechLM typically encodes audio waveforms into high-dimensional features using pre-trained encoders and integrate these representations to pre-trained LLMs via a connection (adapter) module (Wu et al., 2023; Yu et al., 2023; Zhang et al., 2023; Tang et al., 2024). To compress speech representations, Fathullah et al. (2023) apply stacking-based fixed-rate compression on speech features extracted from the Conformer model (Gulati et al., 2020). Inspired by the Q-former architecture (Li et al., 2023a), Yu et al. (2023) compress speech features using a fixed number of query tokens, while Tang et al. (2024) extend this approach to a window-level Q-former to support variable frame-rate reduction. Alternatively, Wu et al. (2023) utilize Connectionist Temporal Classification (CTC) (Graves et al., 2006) to compress representations.

Besides connector-based modality fusion, preprocessing other modalities—such as speech, vision, and videos—into tokens (Lyu et al., 2023; Li et al., 2023b; Team, 2024; Kondratyuk et al., 2024) has attracted attention for its scalability. Speech units are typically extracted from self-supervised representations. For instance, AudioLM (Borsos et al., 2023) integrates semantic tokens from w2v-BERT (Chung et al., 2021) and acoustic tokens from SoundStream (Zeghidour et al., 2021) for autoregressive audio generation. Rubenstein et al. (2023) fine-tune the pre-trained LLM PaLM-2 (Anil et al., 2023) with audio tokens processed by AudioLM, enabling both text and speech as input and output. Similarly, VoxtLM (Maiti et al., 2024) performs multi-task training with speech units and text tokens, achieving high-quality speech recognition and synthesis. To mitigate catastrophic forgetting, Nguyen et al. (2024) propose an interleaved training mechanism to fuse speech tokens into LLAMA2 model (Touvron et al., 2023).

Speech-text Alignment Extraction Various aligner tools are available for extracting speech-text alignments. For example, the Montreal Forced Aligner (McAuliffe et al., 2017, MFA) is an easy-to-use tool based on the Kaldi toolkit (Povey et al., 2011). Connectionist Temporal Classification (CTC) (Graves et al., 2006) is also widely used for speech-text alignment (Sainath et al., 2020; Huang et al., 2024); since it is a by-product of speech recognition, it supports alignment without explicit text labels. More recently, the UnitY2 aligner (Communication et al., 2023) and the ZMM-TTS aligner (Gong et al., 2024) have shown excellent alignment performance across multiple languages. These aligners rely on speech units extracted from pre-trained encoders (Baevski et al., 2020; Hsu et al., 2021; Babu et al., 2021) and use variants of RAD-TTS (Shih et al., 2021) as their alignment backbone.

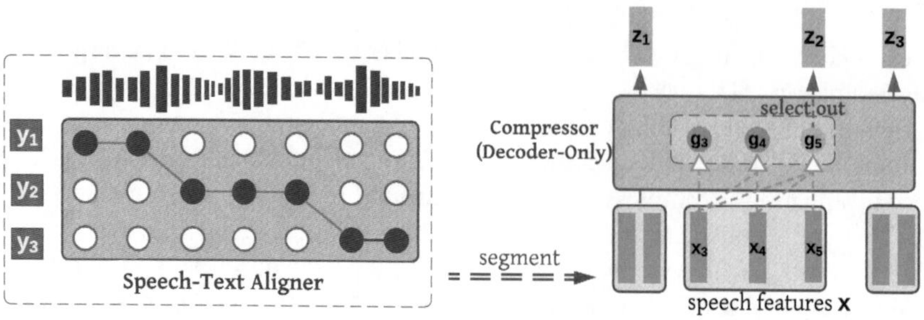

Figure 2: SSR-CONNECTOR compresses speech features using speech-text alignments. Features are transformed by a Decoder-only model and selected at boundary index of each segment.

3 Methodology

We develop an alignment-aware speech representation connector to foster modality fusion between speech and pre-trained language model. We introduce our connector design in §3.1 and present our two-stage training pipeline in §3.2.

3.1 Alignment-Aware Speech Representation Connector

Though previous connectors (Fathullah et al., 2023; Yu et al., 2023; Wu et al., 2023; Tang et al., 2024) vary in their compressor designs, they do not explicitly leverage speech-text alignment information. SSR-CONNECTOR, in contrast, uses speech-text alignments to segment and compress speech features into the same granularity as text tokens. As illustrated in Fig. 2, our connector consists of two components: (1) a speech-text aligner and (2) a feature compressor.

Given speech features $\boldsymbol{x} = (x_1, \cdots, x_n) \in \mathbb{R}^{n \times D}$ extracted by pre-trained speech encoders (e.g., WAV2VEC2.0, HUBERT, WHISPER, etc.), the aligner produces a monotonic mapping (alignment path) between the speech features and their transcriptions $\boldsymbol{y} = (y_1, \cdots, y_m) \in \mathbb{R}^{m \times 1}$. This mapping can be computed based on both speech features (or their units) and transcriptions (Communication et al., 2023; Gong et al., 2024), or solely based on speech input (Sainath et al., 2020; Dong and Xu, 2020; Huang et al., 2024). We abstract away the aligner's implementation here but provide detailed description and comparison of various aligners in Appendix A.

Using the alignment mapping, we segment the input into m chunks of speech features, where each chunk semantically corresponds to a transcription token. For example, in Fig. 2, speech features are segmented at indices $(2, 5, 7)$ according to the alignment path. We refer to these indices as boundary indices. Once the boundary indices are identified, we first apply a linear layer to transform the speech features to match the embedding dimension $H(H > D)$ of the pre-trained LLM, since LLMs typically have a larger feature dimension than pre-trained speech encoders. We then use the boundary indices to aggregate and compress the speech representations in each chunk through a Transformer Decoder model (Vaswani et al., 2017).

Specifically, we apply a causal decoder-only model to transform speech features into high-dimensional representations $\boldsymbol{g} = f(\boldsymbol{x}; \theta_{\text{dec}}) \in \mathbb{R}^{n \times H}$. Since each position incorporates past context, we adopt a selection-based compression method (Tan et al., 2024), using boundary-indexed features from $\boldsymbol{g}$ to form the compressed representation $\boldsymbol{z} \in \mathbb{R}^{m \times H}$. While our initial design used a block-wise attention mask to limit cross-chunk information flow (as shown in Fig. 2), we found that removing these masks simplifies training and inference with minimal performance loss (§4.3).

3.2 Training Method

Previous approaches to integrate speech into LLMs typically use speech-text data concatenated in ASR format (i.e., speech representation followed by its transcription text embedding), to pre-train the connector (Yu et al., 2023; Wu et al., 2023; Tang et al., 2024). However, after such pre-training, the model is limited to speech recognition task and necessitates another instruction-tuning stage to perform generative tasks with pre-trained connectors (Zhang et al., 2023; Tang et al., 2024). Moreover, once the LLM is unfrozen and fine-tuned (whether based on a pre-trained connector or direct fusion with speech units), it suffers from catastrophic forgetting, leading to degraded text capabilities (Nguyen et al., 2024; Tang et al., 2024).

With SSR-CONNECTOR, we convert speech into representations with the same granularity as their transcription tokens. This allows us to fine-tune

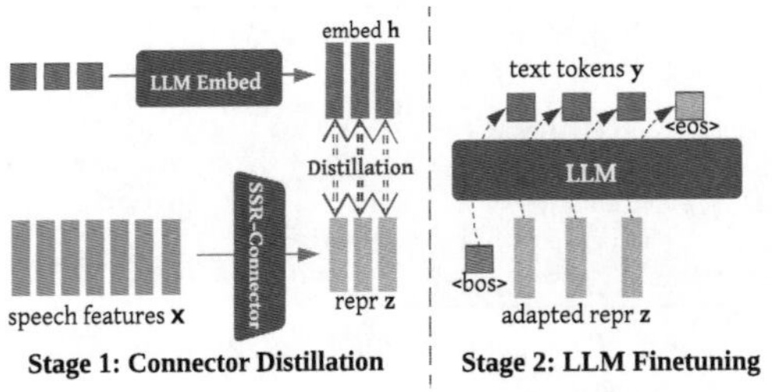

Figure 3: Two-stage training pipeline for SpeechLM with our alignment-aware modality connector.

the SpeechLM directly using the next-token prediction objective, where the input is the compressed representation z and the target is the transcription y. This approach is possible because our feature z and text token y share the same length m. **However, our preliminary studies showed that directly fine-tuning with the next-token prediction objective leads to catastrophic forgetting, undermining the pre-trained LLM's abilities**. Therefore, we propose a two-stage training pipeline consisting of a distillation stage and a fine-tuning stage (visualized in Fig. 3).

In Stage 1, we pre-train SSR-CONNECTOR by distilling the LLM's text embeddings to align the connector's representations with the LLM's embedding space. Formally, given aligned speech-text data, we can compute the text embeddings $\boldsymbol{h} = f(\boldsymbol{y}; \theta_{\text{emb}})$, where $\boldsymbol{y}$ is the transcription token sequence, θ_{emb} is the embedding table, and f maps tokens $\boldsymbol{y}$ to their embeddings. Following our connector design in §3.1, we then obtain the compressed speech representations $\boldsymbol{z}$. For distillation, we use a combination of cosine similarity loss $\mathcal{L}_{\text{cos}}$ and mean squared error (MSE) loss $\mathcal{L}_{\text{MSE}}$

$$\begin{aligned}\mathcal{L} &= \lambda\mathcal{L}\text{cos} + \mathcal{L}_{\text{MSE}} \\ &= \frac{1}{m}\sum_{i=1}^{m}\left[\lambda\left(1 - \frac{\mathbf{z}_i^\top \mathbf{h}_i}{|\mathbf{z}_i| \cdot |\mathbf{h}_i|}\right) + |\mathbf{z}_i - \mathbf{h}_i|^2\right]\end{aligned} \tag{1}$$

where λ is a hyperparameter to balance the losses[1]. In Stage 2, we fine-tune the LLM with the pre-trained speech connector using the next-token prediction objective. We freeze the speech connector and update only the LLM's parameters using the negative log-likelihood (NLL) loss:

$$\mathcal{L}_{\text{NLL}} = -\sum_{t=1}^{m} \log p(y_t \mid \boldsymbol{z}_{<t}; \theta_{\text{LLM}}) \tag{2}$$

[1]In practice, we set $\lambda = 5$ to balance the scales of the cosine similarity and MSE losses

where y_t is the tth token in the transcription sequence $\boldsymbol{y}$, $\boldsymbol{z}_{<t}$ denotes all preceding speech representations, and θ_{LLM} represents the LLM's parameters. Note that our NLL loss is computed using only the preceding speech representations $\boldsymbol{z}_{<t}$ (see Fig. 3), whereas previous methods (Wu et al., 2023; Tang et al., 2024) condition on both speech information and preceding text tokens $\boldsymbol{y}_{<t}$.

In §4, We demonstrate the performance of SpeechLM after distillation training. In §5, we present results after fine-tuning SpeechLM and compare various fine-tuning strategies to identify the method that minimizes catastrophic forgetting.

4 Stage 1: Alignment-Aware Connector Distillation

4.1 Datasets

For distillation training, we use the aligned speech-to-text dataset MLS (Pratap et al., 2020), specifically the English portion, which consists of about 50,000 hours of speech. To evaluate our SpeechLMs, we employ different benchmark datasets (see Table 1). To assess the model's spoken language understanding (SLU) capabilities, we follow Nguyen et al. (2024) and use sWUGGY, sBLIMP, and the StoryCloze dataset. sWUGGY evaluates whether a model can discriminate between real spoken words and non-words (e.g., "brick" vs. "blick"), while sBLIMP assesses if the model can distinguish between a grammatically correct spoken sentence and its ungrammatical variant. We evaluate our SpeechLMs on both text (T) and speech (S) versions of sWUGGY and sBLIMP.

The StoryCloze dataset measures whether the model can identify the plausible ending between two sentences given the beginning of a short story, which typically requires high-level semantic understanding and common sense (Mostafazadeh et al., 2017). Besides spoken and text versions of StoryCloze, following Nguyen et al. (2024), we use a speech-text version ($S \rightarrow T$), where the beginning of the story is synthesized into speech and the two ending sentences are kept in text format. This version requires the model to have cross-modal understanding to infer the sensible story ending.

MMLU (Hendrycks et al., 2021) is widely used to assess LLMs' knowledge comprehension, understanding, and reasoning abilities, and we use it to measure the extent of forgetting during cross-modal fine-tuning. Since MMLU is a diverse and high-quality evaluation dataset for LLMs, we craft a

Eval Dataset	Type	Eval Metric	Eval Modality
sWUGGY (Nguyen et al., 2020)	Choice Task	Accuracy	S, T
sBLIMP (Nguyen et al., 2020)	Choice Task	Accuracy	S, T
StoryCloze (Mostafazadeh et al., 2017)	Choice Task	Accuracy	$S, T, S \rightarrow T$
MMLU (Hendrycks et al., 2021)	Choice Task	Accuracy	T
Speech-MMLU (*Ours*)	Choice Task	Accuracy	$S \rightarrow T$
LibriSpeech (Panayotov et al., 2015)	Generation Task	Word Error Rate	$S \rightarrow T$

Table 1: Evaluation Datasets and their types. For the evaluation format, S is speech-only, T is text-only, and $S \rightarrow T$ means the evaluation prompt consists of speech prefix and text continuation.

variant, Speech-MMLU, to assess our SpeechLM's cross-modal understanding. Specifically, we utilized AUDIOBOX (Vyas et al., 2023), a high-quality text-to-speech synthesizer, to convert the question portion of each choice task into speech while keeping the multiple-choice answers in text format. We selected a subset of MMLU to construct our Speech-MMLU dataset, as some domains' questions are not suitable for synthesis (e.g., the algebra subset contains many mathematical notations that are not synthesized properly).

sWUGGY, sBLIMP, StoryCloze, and Speech-MMLU are all categorized as "Choice Task", meaning several choices are presented to the SpeechLM (Speech-MMLU has four choices while the other task has only two choices). For each task, we compute accuracy using groundtruth choice and the highest likelihood choice predicted by the SpeechLM. Lastly, we also evaluate our SpeechLM's ASR performance using the Librispeech clean/other datasets. We evaluate ASR in a prompt-based fashion with zero-shot and five-shot setting. Comprehensive details about our datasets and evaluation can be found in Appendix C.

4.2 Model Setup

We instantiate our LLM using the pre-trained LLAMA3 model (Grattafiori et al., 2024) and employ DinoSR (Liu et al., 2023a) as our pre-trained speech feature extractor. Our speech connector includes a linear layer that maps DinoSR's extracted representations ($D = 768$) to the LLM's embedding space dimension ($H = 4096$). We then utilize a 4-layer Transformer Decoder to transform and compress the speech representations based on alignments, as described in §3.1. The compressed representations $\boldsymbol{z}$ and the embeddings of text tokens $\boldsymbol{h}$ are used to compute the distillation loss for updating the connector's parameters. We train our connector for 400,000 steps with a learning rate of 1×10^{-5}, using dynamic batching with a maximum of 4,096 tokens per device. We employ distributed data parallelism (DDP) with 32 A100 GPUs.

To extract alignments, we experimented with various approaches, including the UNITY2 aligner, CTC-based aligners (Graves et al., 2006), and Continuous Integrate-and-Fire (Dong and Xu, 2020, CIF). Due to space constraints, we provide comprehensive descriptions and comparisons of these methods in Appendix A, where we evaluate both the alignment quality and the Word Boundary Error of the segmentations. After assessing their performance, we selected UNITY2 (Barrault et al., 2023) and character-level CTC (CHAR-CTC) as our connector backbone to report experimental results. Overall, UNITY2 offers superior alignment quality because it utilizes both speech and text as input. In contrast, CTC only requires speech input to compute segmentation for our connector.

4.3 Experimental Results

In this section, we present the evaluation of SSR-CONNECTOR based SpeechLM in terms of Spoken Language Understanding (SLU) and Cross-modal Understanding (through our use of Storycloze and Speech MMLU benchmark). We also evaluate our model with prompting-based speech recognition and speech style recognition.

We compare against several systems that varies in training approaches (pre-trained from scratch or fine-tuned), types of speech units, and the size of training data. Briefly, GSLM (Lakhotia et al., 2021) trains on speech units like HuBERT, TWIST (Hassid et al., 2024) is a textually pretrained speech model based on Llama-13B (Touvron et al., 2023), and AudioLM (Borsos et al., 2023) employs a cascade system with a semantic sequence model alongside coarse- and fine-acoustic models. These models focus solely on speech without capabilities for text understanding or generation. More recently, SPIRITLM (Nguyen et al., 2024) and VoxtLM (Maiti et al., 2024) have adopted multi-task training objectives that incorporate text-only, speech-only, and speech-text token sequences to fuse the speech modality into pre-trained LLMs effectively. Since the original SPIRITLM is fine-tuned based on

Model Type	sWUGGY		sBLIMP		Storycloze			MMLU
	T	S	T	S	T	S	S→T	5-shot
Previous Work								
GSLM◇ (Lakhotia et al., 2021)	∅	64.8	∅	54.2	∅	53.3	∅	∅
AUDIOLM◇ (Borsos et al., 2023)	∅	71.5	∅	64.7	∅	_	∅	∅
VOXTLM◇ (Maiti et al., 2024)	80.3	66.1	74.2	57.1	_	_	_	_
TWIST◇ (Hassid et al., 2024)	∅	**74.5**	∅	59.2	∅	55.4	∅	∅
MOSHI♣ (Défossez et al., 2024)	∅	72.6	∅	58.8	∅	60.8	_	49.8
SPIRITLM◇ (Nguyen et al., 2024)	80.3	69	73.3	58.3	79.4	61	64.6	36.9
SPIRITLM (LLAMA3)♠	77.6	73.5	**74.5**	56.3	75.1	61.1	61.6	53.5
SSR-CONNECTOR								
UNITY2 + Blockwise-mask	**81**	71.5	**74.5**	**73.1**	**80.9**	**71.8**	**75**	**65.3**
UNITY2	81	71.2	74.5	72.4	80.9	69.3	74.8	65.3
CHAR-CTC	81	56.4	74.5	67.3	80.9	62.2	74.3	65.3
CHAR-CTC (Unit-based)	81	54.1	74.5	61.8	80.9	59.2	72.5	65.3
Cascade System								
ASR (WHISPER) + LLAMA2 ◇	84.1	79.2	72.8	71.6	81.9	75.7	75.7	46.2

Table 2: Model performance (accuracy) on spoken language understanding and MMLU. ◇: Results taken from Nguyen et al. (2024).♣: Results taken from Défossez et al. (2024). ♠: Our implementation of SPIRITLM based on LLAMA3 checkpoint. We fill with ∅ the task and modality that are not supported by the reported system, and with _ the scores that are not publicly available. We bold the best result and highlight the second-best system with the blue color box (excluding the cascaded system).

LLAMA2, we follow the same recipe to fine-tune the LLAMA3-based SPIRITLM ourselves for a fair comparison on text-relevant metrics like MMLU.

Spoken Language Understanding Performance As shown in Table 2, our systems outperform previous models on all tasks except sWUGGY. The sWUGGY dataset includes incorrectly spoken words that cause segmentation errors because these words were not present during aligner training, leading to our system's lower performance on this dataset. However, sWUGGY is the least significant task since it relies on synthesized incorrect words and does not require the model's understanding or reasoning capabilities. In contrast, both UNITY2 and CHAR-CTC based connector greatly surpass previous models on other datasets, demonstrating the effectiveness of SSR-CONNECTOR in enhancing SLU performance while preserving model's text understanding ability.

Beyond UNITY2 and CHAR-CTC, we introduce two additional systems for ablation. The **UNITY2 + Blockwise-mask** system achieves the highest performance by applying a blockwise attention mask to further constrain the Transformer-Decoder (described in §3.1). However, due to its marginal improvement over UNITY2 and increased computational cost, we decide to simplify the design and remove the blockwise-attention masks. The **CHAR-CTC (Unit-based)** system differs by utilizing discrete speech units instead of raw waveform features processed by the DinoSR (Liu et al., 2023a) encoder. These units are extracted via K-Means clustering on DinoSR representations, which leads to some information loss during discretization and reconstruction, resulting in lower performance compared to CHAR-CTC. Nonetheless, CHAR-CTC (Unit-based) demonstrates that *our alignment-aware connector design is compatible with discrete speech units as well.*

Speech-MMLU and Prompt-based ASR Performance In addition to SLU tasks, we evaluate our systems on the Speech-MMLU benchmark, which assesses cross-modal understanding and is more challenging than previous SLU tasks. We also conduct prompt-based ASR evaluations to assess the quality of the adapted features. As shown in Table 3, our systems greatly outperform the previous SpeechLM (SPIRITLM), achieving a +20 accuracy improvement on the Speech-MMLU dataset[2]. These results indicate that SpeechLM based on SSR-CONNECTOR possesses enhanced cross-modal abilities that enable it to comprehend spoken questions and reason through multiple-choice options to select correct answers. Similarly, our systems achieve much lower WERs on the Librispeech clean and other test sets compared to SPIR-

[2] We report micro-average across 22 domains and the detailed breakdown is available in Appendix D.

Model Type	Speech MMLU ↑		ASR Clean Test ↓		ASR Other Test ↓	
	0-shot	5-shot	0-shot	5-shot	0-shot	5-shot
SPIRITLM (Nguyen et al., 2024)	N/A	N/A	N/A	21.9*	N/A	29.2*
SPIRITLM (LLAMA3)	40.5	42.75	N/A	21.0*	N/A	28.5*
SSR-CONNECTOR						
UNITY2 + Blockwise-mask	**65.0**	**69.5**	**5.0**	**2.6**	**8.1**	**6.8**
UNITY2	64.2	68.6	5.6	4.0	12.1	10.6
CHAR-CTC	61.7	66.5	9.7	6.5	20.2	14.9
CHAR-CTC (Unit-based)	57.4	62.3	12.6	8.8	25.6	18.6

Table 3: Comparison of Speech-MMLU and ASR performance. Speech-MMLU results are micro-averages across all domains. *: For SPIRITLM, We report WER using 10-shot prompting, following Nguyen et al. (2024).

Task	Model	0-shot	5-shot	10-shot
Whisper vs. Laugh	Cascaded	51.6	52.2	54.7
	Ours	49.6	64.0	75.9
Happy vs. Sad	Cascaded	50.0	51.8	51.0
	Ours	51.6	52.2	54.7

Table 4: Accuracy of Speech Style Recognition with In-context Learning

ITLM. Notably, neither SPIRITLM nor our system was trained on ASR tasks, *so the model relies solely on in-context learning to generate transcriptions*.

We also compared our system against another connector-based system, SALMONN (Tang et al., 2024), over Storycloze and Speech MMLU (both in $S \rightarrow T$ format) and we find that SALMONN achieved an accuracy of 63.3% on Storycloze and 25.3% on Speech-MMLU, while our system has over 74% accuracy on Storycloze and over 60% accuracy on Speech-MMLU. The result indicates that catastrophic forgetting remains a severe issue for previous connector-based methods as well.

Beyond Semantics In Table 4, we also show that the connector retains paralinguistic information. We evaluate this using the Expresso benhmark (Nguyen et al., 2023) by prompting our model to predict speech styles. Our SpeechLM can distinguish expressions through in-context learning without being fine-tuned for emotion recognition (we also provide the cascaded baseline (Whisper + LLAMA3) as a baseline where style can only be inferred from transcriptions). More experimental details are provided in Appendix B. This analysis demonstrates that our connector preserves non-semantic information even though we focus on aligning semantics and reducing catastrophic forgetting. Our connector design also complements existing methods for emotion recognition, such as using expressive tokens in SpiritLM (Nguyen et al., 2024) and emotion-relevant instruction tuning in SALMONN (Tang et al., 2024).

5 Stage 2: Speech Language Model Fine-tuning

In Stage 1 (§4), we freeze the pre-trained LLM and distill its text embeddings into our alignment-aware connector. In this section, we fine-tune SpeechLM by freezing the connector and updating the LLM. This process enhances the model's spoken language understanding (SLU) performance by fitting SpeechLM on the aligned speech-text data, albeit at the expense of degrading its pre-trained text capabilities. In the following sections, we compare various methods to mitigate catastrophic forgetting and demonstrate their trade-offs between speech and text understanding.

5.1 Mitigate Catastrophic Forgetting

Model and Dataset Setup We fine-tune SpeechLM using the next-token prediction objective described in §3.2. In this stage, we freeze the connector distilled in Stage 1 and unfreeze the LLM (LLAMA3) parameters. Following Stage 1 (§4), we use the MLS dataset for training and evaluate the model on the same speech and text understanding tasks. Beyond vanilla fine-tuning, we also explore Low-rank Adaptation (Hu et al., 2021, LoRA) and multitask fine-tuning as they have been shown effective for mitigating catastrophic forgetting in other tasks (Xue et al., 2021; Vu et al., 2022). Details of our fine-tuning setup are shown below:

- **Vanilla Fine-tuning**: We perform full fine-tuning on the aligned speech-text data with a learning rate of 1×10^{-6} and a maximum token size of 4096. Training is model-parallelized across 32 A100 GPUs using Fully Sharded Data Parallel (Zhao et al., 2023, FSDP).
- **LoRA Fine-tuning**: We leverage the low-rank constraints from as regularization to prevent model overfitting in MLS dataset. We config-

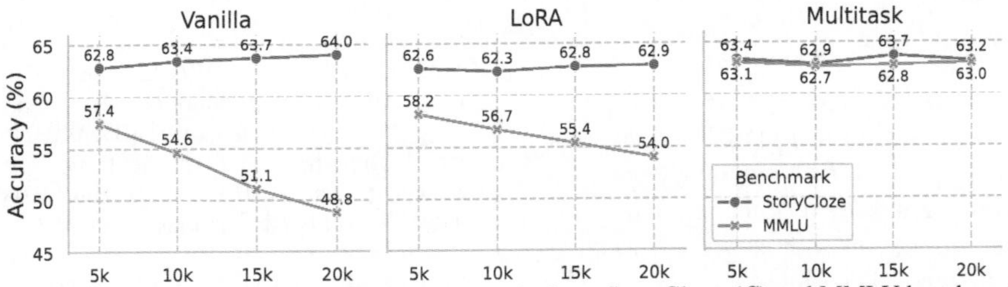

Figure 4: Comparison of different fine-tuning methods on StoryCloze (S) and MMLU benchmark.

Model Type	sWUGGY		sBLIMP		Storycloze			MMLU	Speech MMLU		ASR (5-shot)↓	
	T	S	T	S	T	S	S→T	5-shot	0-shot	5-shot	Clean	Other
SPIRITLM (LLAMA3)	77.6	73.5	74.5	56.3	75.1	61.1	61.6	53.5	40.5	42.8	21.0*	28.5*
CHAR-CTC	81.0	56.4	74.5	67.3	80.9	62.2	**74.3**	**65.3**	**61.7**	**66.5**	6.5	14.9
+ Multitask Finetuning	**82.9**	**56.7**	**75.9**	**68.9**	**81.0**	**63.4**	73.1	63.1	48.1	56.3	**5.7**	**13.1**

Table 5: Performance comparison when the model is fine-tuned. *: For SPIRITLM, WER is reported using 10-shot prompting for ASR, following Nguyen et al. (2024). We observe that stage 2 fine-tuning enhances the model's performance on speech-only tasks but compromises its cross-modal capabilities.

ure LoRA layers with $\alpha = 512$, $r = 256$, and a dropout probability of 0.1.

- **Multitask Fine-tuning**: To preserve the LLM's pre-trained text capabilities, we also fine-tune SpeechLM on text-only data using Negative Log-Likelihood (NLL) loss. The dataloader is configured to sample from both speech-text and text-only datasets with equal probability. We use the MLS dataset for speech-text training and employ a subset of the LLAMA2 training datasets (Touvron et al., 2023) for text-only training.

5.2 Comparison of Fine-tuning Methods

In Fig. 4, we compare different fine-tuning methods on StoryCloze (S) and MMLU. StoryCloze performance is indicative of how well model is fitted to the speech modality and MMLU measures the degree of catastrophic forgetting in pre-trained text abilities. We observe that Vanilla Fine-tuning quickly overfits to the speech domain, achieving improved performance on StoryCloze but drastically decreasing MMLU accuracy. In contrast, LoRA Fine-tuning introduces strong regularization, resulting in limited improvements in speech understanding. Although LoRA mitigates catastrophic forgetting to some extent compared to vanilla fine-tuning, performance still steadily declines. **Multitask fine-tuning emerges as the most promising approach**, enhancing speech understanding while largely mitigating catastrophic forgetting, evidenced by the modest 2-point drop in MMLU.

Since model performance does not further improve with additional training steps (as shown in Fig. 4), we utilize the checkpoint trained for 5,000 updates to compare with baseline models. The results are presented in Table 5. Note that even with only 5,000 updates, the model has observed all speech-text data due to our large effective batch size. As observed from the results, fine-tuned SpeechLM outperforms baseline methods on tasks primarily relying on speech-only information (sWUGGY, sBLIMP, ASR). However, we also observe a decline in performance on $S \rightarrow T$ tasks such as Speech-MMLU and StoryCloze, indicating that **there is still unavoidable degradation of text capabilities** which adversely affects SpeechLM's cross-modal performance.

Overall, Stage 2 fine-tuning experiments highlight a trade-off between enhanced speech understanding and degraded text abilities when unfreezing pre-trained LLM weights. Though such forgetting phenomenon is unavoidable, our two-stage training pipeline has largely preserved SpeechLM's text ability and our experimental results underscore the importance of incorporating high-quality text data during cross-modal fine-tuning to balance performance across both modalities.

6 Conclusion

We propose SSR-CONNECTOR to inject speech representation into pre-trained LLMs. Through explicitly leveraging speech-text alignment, our connector compresses long and sparse speech information to the same granularity as text tokens. With our proposed two-stage training pipeline for modality fusion, SSR-CONNECTOR-based SpeechLM achieves better speech understanding while retaining its pre-trained text ability.

Limitations

While our proposed SSR-CONNECTOR significantly enhances speech-text modality fusion and mitigates catastrophic forgetting, there remain several limitations that warrant further exploration.

First, our work focuses on aligning speech semantics with text in large language models (LLMs). While our experiments show that paralinguistic information, such as speech styles, can be preserved and leveraged through in-context learning, we do not explicitly model these aspects. Future work could better encode prosody, speaker identity, and emotional cues to enhance expressive speech generation and nuanced speech understanding.

Second, our experiments on mitigating catastrophic forgetting are conducted primarily on a single language family, using LLAMA3 (Grattafiori et al., 2024) as the base LLM and DINOSR (Liu et al., 2023a) as the speech encoder. The extent of our method's effectiveness across different architectures and speech encoders remains unverified.

Finally, while our evaluation covers a range of speech and multimodal benchmarks, additional real-world settings, such as conversational speech, noisy environments, and multilingual scenarios, remain unexplored. Extending our methodology to such conditions will be essential for deploying robust, generalizable SpeechLMs.

References

Jean-Baptiste Alayrac, Jeff Donahue, Pauline Luc, Antoine Miech, Iain Barr, Yana Hasson, Karel Lenc, Arthur Mensch, Katie Millican, Malcolm Reynolds, Roman Ring, Eliza Rutherford, Serkan Cabi, Tengda Han, Zhitao Gong, Sina Samangooei, Marianne Monteiro, Jacob Menick, Sebastian Borgeaud, Andrew Brock, Aida Nematzadeh, Sahand Sharifzadeh, Mikolaj Binkowski, Ricardo Barreira, Oriol Vinyals, Andrew Zisserman, and Karen Simonyan. 2022. Flamingo: a visual language model for few-shot learning. *Preprint*, arXiv:2204.14198.

Rohan Anil, Andrew M. Dai, Orhan Firat, Melvin Johnson, Dmitry Lepikhin, Alexandre Passos, Siamak Shakeri, Emanuel Taropa, Paige Bailey, Zhifeng Chen, Eric Chu, Jonathan H. Clark, Laurent El Shafey, Yanping Huang, Kathy Meier-Hellstern, Gaurav Mishra, Erica Moreira, Mark Omernick, Kevin Robinson, Sebastian Ruder, Yi Tay, Kefan Xiao, Yuanzhong Xu, Yujing Zhang, Gustavo Hernandez Abrego, Junwhan Ahn, Jacob Austin, Paul Barham, Jan Botha, James Bradbury, Siddhartha Brahma, Kevin Brooks, Michele Catasta, Yong Cheng, Colin Cherry, Christopher A. Choquette-Choo, Aakanksha Chowdhery, Clément Crepy, Shachi Dave, Mostafa Dehghani, Sunipa Dev, Jacob Devlin, Mark Díaz, Nan Du, Ethan Dyer, Vlad Feinberg, Fangxiaoyu Feng, Vlad Fienber, Markus Freitag, Xavier Garcia, Sebastian Gehrmann, Lucas Gonzalez, Guy Gur-Ari, Steven Hand, Hadi Hashemi, Le Hou, Joshua Howland, Andrea Hu, Jeffrey Hui, Jeremy Hurwitz, Michael Isard, Abe Ittycheriah, Matthew Jagielski, Wenhao Jia, Kathleen Kenealy, Maxim Krikun, Sneha Kudugunta, Chang Lan, Katherine Lee, Benjamin Lee, Eric Li, Music Li, Wei Li, YaGuang Li, Jian Li, Hyeontaek Lim, Hanzhao Lin, Zhongtao Liu, Frederick Liu, Marcello Maggioni, Aroma Mahendru, Joshua Maynez, Vedant Misra, Maysam Moussalem, Zachary Nado, John Nham, Eric Ni, Andrew Nystrom, Alicia Parrish, Marie Pellat, Martin Polacek, Alex Polozov, Reiner Pope, Siyuan Qiao, Emily Reif, Bryan Richter, Parker Riley, Alex Castro Ros, Aurko Roy, Brennan Saeta, Rajkumar Samuel, Renee Shelby, Ambrose Slone, Daniel Smilkov, David R. So, Daniel Sohn, Simon Tokumine, Dasha Valter, Vijay Vasudevan, Kiran Vodrahalli, Xuezhi Wang, Pidong Wang, Zirui Wang, Tao Wang, John Wieting, Yuhuai Wu, Kelvin Xu, Yunhan Xu, Linting Xue, Pengcheng Yin, Jiahui Yu, Qiao Zhang, Steven Zheng, Ce Zheng, Weikang Zhou, Denny Zhou, Slav Petrov, and Yonghui Wu. 2023. Palm 2 technical report. *Preprint*, arXiv:2305.10403.

Arun Babu, Changhan Wang, Andros Tjandra, Kushal Lakhotia, Qiantong Xu, Naman Goyal, Kritika Singh, Patrick von Platen, Yatharth Saraf, Juan Miguel Pino, Alexei Baevski, Alexis Conneau, and Michael Auli. 2021. Xls-r: Self-supervised cross-lingual speech representation learning at scale. In *Interspeech*.

Alexei Baevski, Henry Zhou, Abdelrahman Mohamed, and Michael Auli. 2020. wav2vec 2.0: A framework for self-supervised learning of speech representations. *Preprint*, arXiv:2006.11477.

Loïc Barrault, Yu-An Chung, Mariano Coria Meglioli, David Dale, Ning Dong, Mark Duppenthaler, Paul-Ambroise Duquenne, Brian Ellis, Hady Elsahar, Justin Haaheim, John Hoffman, Min-Jae Hwang, Hirofumi Inaguma, Christopher Klaiber, Ilia Kulikov, Pengwei Li, Daniel Licht, Jean Maillard, Ruslan Mavlyutov, Alice Rakotoarison, Kaushik Ram Sadagopan, Abinesh Ramakrishnan, Tuan Tran, Guillaume Wenzek, Yilin Yang, Ethan Ye, Ivan Evtimov, Pierre Fernandez, Cynthia Gao, Prangthip Hansanti, Elahe Kalbassi, Amanda Kallet, Artyom Kozhevnikov, Gabriel Mejia Gonzalez, Robin San Roman, Christophe Touret, Corinne Wong, Carleigh Wood, Bokai Yu, Pierre Andrews, Can Balioglu, Peng-Jen Chen, Marta R. Costa-jussà, Maha Elbayad, Hongyu Gong, Francisco Guzmán, Kevin Heffernan, Somya Jain, Justine Kao, Ann Lee, Xutai Ma, Alex Mourachko, Benjamin Peloquin, Juan Pino, Sravya Popuri, Christophe Ropers, Safiyyah Saleem, Holger Schwenk, Anna Sun, Paden Tomasello, Changhan Wang, Jeff Wang, Skyler Wang, and Mary Williamson. 2023. Seamless: Multilingual expressive and streaming speech translation. *Preprint*, arXiv:2312.05187.

Zalán Borsos, Raphaël Marinier, Damien Vincent, Eugene Kharitonov, Olivier Pietquin, Matt Sharifi, Dominik Roblek, Olivier Teboul, David Grangier, Marco Tagliasacchi, and Neil Zeghidour. 2023. Audiolm: a language modeling approach to audio generation. *Preprint*, arXiv:2209.03143.

Tom B. Brown, Benjamin Mann, Nick Ryder, Melanie Subbiah, Jared Kaplan, Prafulla Dhariwal, Arvind Neelakantan, Pranav Shyam, Girish Sastry, Amanda Askell, Sandhini Agarwal, Ariel Herbert-Voss, Gretchen Krueger, Tom Henighan, Rewon Child, Aditya Ramesh, Daniel M. Ziegler, Jeffrey Wu, Clemens Winter, Christopher Hesse, Mark Chen, Eric Sigler, Mateusz Litwin, Scott Gray, Benjamin Chess, Jack Clark, Christopher Berner, Sam McCandlish, Alec Radford, Ilya Sutskever, and Dario Amodei. 2020. Language models are few-shot learners. *Preprint*, arXiv:2005.14165.

Wei-Lin Chiang, Zhuohan Li, Zi Lin, Ying Sheng, Zhanghao Wu, Hao Zhang, Lianmin Zheng, Siyuan Zhuang, Yonghao Zhuang, Joseph E. Gonzalez, Ion Stoica, and Eric P. Xing. 2023. Vicuna: An open-source chatbot impressing gpt-4 with 90%* chatgpt quality.

Aakanksha Chowdhery, Sharan Narang, Jacob Devlin, Maarten Bosma, Gaurav Mishra, Adam Roberts, Paul Barham, Hyung Won Chung, Charles Sutton, Sebastian Gehrmann, Parker Schuh, Kensen Shi, Sasha Tsvyashchenko, Joshua Maynez, Abhishek Rao, Parker Barnes, Yi Tay, Noam Shazeer, Vinodkumar Prabhakaran, Emily Reif, Nan Du, Ben Hutchinson, Reiner Pope, James Bradbury, Jacob Austin, Michael Isard, Guy Gur-Ari, Pengcheng Yin, Toju Duke, Anselm Levskaya, Sanjay Ghemawat, Sunipa Dev, Henryk Michalewski, Xavier Garcia, Vedant Misra, Kevin Robinson, Liam Fedus, Denny Zhou, Daphne Ippolito, David Luan, Hyeontaek Lim, Barret Zoph, Alexander Spiridonov, Ryan Sepassi, David Dohan, Shivani Agrawal, Mark Omernick, Andrew M. Dai, Thanumalayan Sankaranarayana Pillai, Marie Pellat, Aitor Lewkowycz, Erica Moreira, Rewon Child, Oleksandr Polozov, Katherine Lee, Zongwei Zhou, Xuezhi Wang, Brennan Saeta, Mark Diaz, Orhan Firat, Michele Catasta, Jason Wei, Kathy Meier-Hellstern, Douglas Eck, Jeff Dean, Slav Petrov, and Noah Fiedel. 2022. Palm: Scaling language modeling with pathways. *Preprint*, arXiv:2204.02311.

Yu-An Chung, Yu Zhang, Wei Han, Chung-Cheng Chiu, James Qin, Ruoming Pang, and Yonghui Wu. 2021. W2v-bert: Combining contrastive learning and masked language modeling for self-supervised speech pre-training. *Preprint*, arXiv:2108.06209.

Seamless Communication, Loïc Barrault, Yu-An Chung, Mariano Coria Meglioli, David Dale, Ning Dong, Mark Duppenthaler, Paul-Ambroise Duquenne, Brian Ellis, Hady Elsahar, Justin Haaheim, John Hoffman, Min-Jae Hwang, Hirofumi Inaguma, Christopher Klaiber, Ilia Kulikov, Pengwei Li, Daniel Licht, Jean Maillard, Ruslan Mavlyutov, Alice Rakotoarison, Kaushik Ram Sadagopan, Abinesh Ramakrishnan, Tuan Tran, Guillaume Wenzek, Yilin Yang, Ethan Ye, Ivan Evtimov, Pierre Fernandez, Cynthia Gao, Prangthip Hansanti, Elahe Kalbassi, Amanda Kallet, Artyom Kozhevnikov, Gabriel Mejia Gonzalez, Robin San Roman, Christophe Touret, Corinne Wong, Carleigh Wood, Bokai Yu, Pierre Andrews, Can Balioglu, Peng-Jen Chen, Marta R. Costa-jussà, Maha Elbayad, Hongyu Gong, Francisco Guzmán, Kevin Heffernan, Somya Jain, Justine Kao, Ann Lee, Xutai Ma, Alex Mourachko, Benjamin Peloquin, Juan Pino, Sravya Popuri, Christophe Ropers, Safiyyah Saleem, Holger Schwenk, Anna Sun, Paden Tomasello, Changhan Wang, Jeff Wang, Skyler Wang, and Mary Williamson. 2023. Seamless: Multilingual expressive and streaming speech translation. *Preprint*, arXiv:2312.05187.

DeepSeek-AI, Daya Guo, Dejian Yang, Haowei Zhang, Junxiao Song, Ruoyu Zhang, Runxin Xu, Qihao Zhu, Shirong Ma, Peiyi Wang, Xiao Bi, Xiaokang Zhang, Xingkai Yu, Yu Wu, Z. F. Wu, Zhibin Gou, Zhihong Shao, Zhuoshu Li, Ziyi Gao, Aixin Liu, Bing Xue, Bingxuan Wang, Bochao Wu, Bei Feng, Chengda Lu, Chenggang Zhao, Chengqi Deng, Chenyu Zhang, Chong Ruan, Damai Dai, Deli Chen, Dongjie Ji, Erhang Li, Fangyun Lin, Fucong Dai, Fuli Luo, Guangbo Hao, Guanting Chen, Guowei Li, H. Zhang, Han Bao, Hanwei Xu, Haocheng Wang, Honghui Ding, Huajian Xin, Huazuo Gao, Hui Qu, Hui Li, Jianzhong Guo, Jiashi Li, Jiawei Wang, Jingchang Chen, Jingyang Yuan, Junjie Qiu, Junlong Li, J. L. Cai, Jiaqi Ni, Jian Liang, Jin Chen, Kai Dong, Kai Hu, Kaige Gao, Kang Guan, Kexin Huang, Kuai Yu, Lean Wang, Lecong Zhang, Liang Zhao, Litong Wang, Liyue Zhang, Lei Xu, Leyi Xia, Mingchuan Zhang, Minghua Zhang, Minghui Tang, Meng Li, Miaojun Wang, Mingming Li, Ning Tian, Panpan Huang, Peng Zhang, Qiancheng Wang, Qinyu Chen, Qiushi Du, Ruiqi Ge, Ruisong Zhang, Ruizhe Pan, Runji Wang, R. J. Chen, R. L. Jin, Ruyi Chen, Shanghao Lu, Shangyan Zhou, Shanhuang Chen, Shengfeng Ye, Shiyu Wang, Shuiping Yu, Shunfeng Zhou, Shuting Pan, S. S. Li, Shuang Zhou, Shaoqing Wu, Shengfeng Ye, Tao Yun, Tian Pei, Tianyu Sun, T. Wang, Wangding Zeng, Wanjia Zhao, Wen Liu, Wenfeng Liang, Wenjun Gao, Wenqin Yu, Wentao Zhang, W. L. Xiao, Wei An, Xiaodong Liu, Xiaohan Wang, Xiaokang Chen, Xiaotao Nie, Xin Cheng, Xin Liu, Xin Xie, Xingchao Liu, Xinyu Yang, Xinyuan Li, Xuecheng Su, Xuheng Lin, X. Q. Li, Xiangyue Jin, Xiaojin Shen, Xiaosha Chen, Xiaowen Sun, Xiaoxiang Wang, Xinnan Song, Xinyi Zhou, Xianzu Wang, Xinxia Shan, Y. K. Li, Y. Q. Wang, Y. X. Wei, Yang Zhang, Yanhong Xu, Yao Li, Yao Zhao, Yaofeng Sun, Yaohui Wang, Yi Yu, Yichao Zhang, Yifan Shi, Yiliang Xiong, Ying He, Yishi Piao, Yisong Wang, Yixuan Tan, Yiyang Ma, Yiyuan Liu, Yongqiang Guo, Yuan Ou, Yuduan Wang, Yue Gong, Yuheng Zou, Yujia He, Yunfan Xiong, Yuxiang Luo, Yuxiang You, Yuxuan Liu, Yuyang Zhou, Y. X. Zhu, Yanhong Xu, Yanping Huang, Yaohui Li, Yi Zheng, Yuchen Zhu, Yunxian Ma, Ying Tang, Yukun Zha, Yuting Yan, Z. Z. Ren, Zehui Ren, Zhangli Sha, Zhe Fu, Zhean Xu, Zhenda Xie, Zhengyan Zhang, Zhewen Hao,

Zhicheng Ma, Zhigang Yan, Zhiyu Wu, Zihui Gu, Zijia Zhu, Zijun Liu, Zilin Li, Ziwei Xie, Ziyang Song, Zizheng Pan, Zhen Huang, Zhipeng Xu, Zhongyu Zhang, and Zhen Zhang. 2025. Deepseek-r1: Incentivizing reasoning capability in llms via reinforcement learning. *Preprint*, arXiv:2501.12948.

Alexandre Défossez, Laurent Mazaré, Manu Orsini, Amélie Royer, Patrick Pérez, Hervé Jégou, Edouard Grave, and Neil Zeghidour. 2024. Moshi: a speech-text foundation model for real-time dialogue. Technical report, Kyutai.

Linhao Dong and Bo Xu. 2020. Cif: Continuous integrate-and-fire for end-to-end speech recognition. *Preprint*, arXiv:1905.11235.

Manaal Faruqui and Dilek Hakkani-Tür. 2021. Revisiting the boundary between asr and nlu in the age of conversational dialog systems. *Preprint*, arXiv:2112.05842.

Yassir Fathullah, Chunyang Wu, Egor Lakomkin, Junteng Jia, Yuan Shangguan, Ke Li, Jinxi Guo, Wenhan Xiong, Jay Mahadeokar, Ozlem Kalinli, Christian Fuegen, and Mike Seltzer. 2023. Prompting large language models with speech recognition abilities. *Preprint*, arXiv:2307.11795.

John S. Garofolo, Lori F. Lamel, William M. Fisher, Jonathan G. Fiscus, David S. Pallett, Nancy L. Dahlgren, and Victor Zue. 1993. TIMIT acoustic-phonetic continuous speech corpus. Technical Report LDC93S1, Linguistic Data Consortium, Philadelphia, PA.

Cheng Gong, Xin Wang, Erica Cooper, Dan Wells, Longbiao Wang, Jianwu Dang, Korin Richmond, and Junichi Yamagishi. 2024. Zmm-tts: Zero-shot multilingual and multispeaker speech synthesis conditioned on self-supervised discrete speech representations. *Preprint*, arXiv:2312.14398.

Aaron Grattafiori, Abhimanyu Dubey, Abhinav Jauhri, Abhinav Pandey, Abhishek Kadian, Ahmad Al-Dahle, Aiesha Letman, Akhil Mathur, Alan Schelten, Alex Vaughan, Amy Yang, Angela Fan, Anirudh Goyal, Anthony Hartshorn, Aobo Yang, Archi Mitra, Archie Sravankumar, Artem Korenev, Arthur Hinsvark, Arun Rao, Aston Zhang, Aurelien Rodriguez, Austen Gregerson, Ava Spataru, Baptiste Roziere, Bethany Biron, Binh Tang, Bobbie Chern, Charlotte Caucheteux, Chaya Nayak, Chloe Bi, Chris Marra, Chris McConnell, Christian Keller, Christophe Touret, Chunyang Wu, Corinne Wong, Cristian Canton Ferrer, Cyrus Nikolaidis, Damien Allonsius, Daniel Song, Danielle Pintz, Danny Livshits, Danny Wyatt, David Esiobu, Dhruv Choudhary, Dhruv Mahajan, Diego Garcia-Olano, Diego Perino, Dieuwke Hupkes, Egor Lakomkin, Ehab AlBadawy, Elina Lobanova, Emily Dinan, Eric Michael Smith, Filip Radenovic, Francisco Guzmán, Frank Zhang, Gabriel Synnaeve, Gabrielle Lee, Georgia Lewis Anderson, Govind Thattai, Graeme Nail, Gregoire Mialon, Guan Pang, Guillem Cucurell, Hailey Nguyen, Hannah Korevaar, Hu Xu, Hugo Touvron, Iliyan Zarov, Imanol Arrieta Ibarra, Isabel Kloumann, Ishan Misra, Ivan Evtimov, Jack Zhang, Jade Copet, Jaewon Lee, Jan Geffert, Jana Vranes, Jason Park, Jay Mahadeokar, Jeet Shah, Jelmer van der Linde, Jennifer Billock, Jenny Hong, Jenya Lee, Jeremy Fu, Jianfeng Chi, Jianyu Huang, Jiawen Liu, Jie Wang, Jiecao Yu, Joanna Bitton, Joe Spisak, Jongsoo Park, Joseph Rocca, Joshua Johnstun, Joshua Saxe, Junteng Jia, Kalyan Vasuden Alwala, Karthik Prasad, Kartikeya Upasani, Kate Plawiak, Ke Li, Kenneth Heafield, Kevin Stone, Khalid El-Arini, Krithika Iyer, Kshitiz Malik, Kuenley Chiu, Kunal Bhalla, Kushal Lakhotia, Lauren Rantala-Yeary, Laurens van der Maaten, Lawrence Chen, Liang Tan, Liz Jenkins, Louis Martin, Lovish Madaan, Lubo Malo, Lukas Blecher, Lukas Landzaat, Luke de Oliveira, Madeline Muzzi, Mahesh Pasupuleti, Mannat Singh, Manohar Paluri, Marcin Kardas, Maria Tsimpoukelli, Mathew Oldham, Mathieu Rita, Maya Pavlova, Melanie Kambadur, Mike Lewis, Min Si, Mitesh Kumar Singh, Mona Hassan, Naman Goyal, Narjes Torabi, Nikolay Bashlykov, Nikolay Bogoychev, Niladri Chatterji, Ning Zhang, Olivier Duchenne, Onur Çelebi, Patrick Alrassy, Pengchuan Zhang, Pengwei Li, Petar Vasic, Peter Weng, Prajjwal Bhargava, Pratik Dubal, Praveen Krishnan, Punit Singh Koura, Puxin Xu, Qing He, Qingxiao Dong, Ragavan Srinivasan, Raj Ganapathy, Ramon Calderer, Ricardo Silveira Cabral, Robert Stojnic, Roberta Raileanu, Rohan Maheswari, Rohit Girdhar, Rohit Patel, Romain Sauvestre, Ronnie Polidoro, Roshan Sumbaly, Ross Taylor, Ruan Silva, Rui Hou, Rui Wang, Saghar Hosseini, Sahana Chennabasappa, Sanjay Singh, Sean Bell, Seohyun Sonia Kim, Sergey Edunov, Shaoliang Nie, Sharan Narang, Sharath Raparthy, Sheng Shen, Shengye Wan, Shruti Bhosale, Shun Zhang, Simon Vandenhende, Soumya Batra, Spencer Whitman, Sten Sootla, Stephane Collot, Suchin Gururangan, Sydney Borodinsky, Tamar Herman, Tara Fowler, Tarek Sheasha, Thomas Georgiou, Thomas Scialom, Tobias Speckbacher, Todor Mihaylov, Tong Xiao, Ujjwal Karn, Vedanuj Goswami, Vibhor Gupta, Vignesh Ramanathan, Viktor Kerkez, Vincent Gonguet, Virginie Do, Vish Vogeti, Vítor Albiero, Vladan Petrovic, Weiwei Chu, Wenhan Xiong, Wenyin Fu, Whitney Meers, Xavier Martinet, Xiaodong Wang, Xiaofang Wang, Xiaoqing Ellen Tan, Xide Xia, Xinfeng Xie, Xuchao Jia, Xuewei Wang, Yaelle Goldschlag, Yashesh Gaur, Yasmine Babaei, Yi Wen, Yiwen Song, Yuchen Zhang, Yue Li, Yuning Mao, Zacharie Delpierre Coudert, Zheng Yan, Zhengxing Chen, Zoe Papakipos, Aaditya Singh, Aayushi Srivastava, Abha Jain, Adam Kelsey, Adam Shajnfeld, Adithya Gangidi, Adolfo Victoria, Ahuva Goldstand, Ajay Menon, Ajay Sharma, Alex Boesenberg, Alexei Baevski, Allie Feinstein, Amanda Kallet, Amit Sangani, Amos Teo, Anam Yunus, Andrei Lupu, Andres Alvarado, Andrew Caples, Andrew Gu, Andrew Ho, Andrew Poulton, Andrew Ryan, Ankit Ramchandani, Annie Dong, Annie Franco, Anuj Goyal, Aparajita Saraf, Arkabandhu Chowdhury, Ashley Gabriel, Ashwin Bharambe, Assaf Eisenman, Azadeh Yazdan, Beau James, Ben Maurer, Benjamin Leonhardi,

Bernie Huang, Beth Loyd, Beto De Paola, Bhargavi Paranjape, Bing Liu, Bo Wu, Boyu Ni, Braden Hancock, Bram Wasti, Brandon Spence, Brani Stojkovic, Brian Gamido, Britt Montalvo, Carl Parker, Carly Burton, Catalina Mejia, Ce Liu, Changhan Wang, Changkyu Kim, Chao Zhou, Chester Hu, Ching-Hsiang Chu, Chris Cai, Chris Tindal, Christoph Feichtenhofer, Cynthia Gao, Damon Civin, Dana Beaty, Daniel Kreymer, Daniel Li, David Adkins, David Xu, Davide Testuggine, Delia David, Devi Parikh, Diana Liskovich, Didem Foss, Dingkang Wang, Duc Le, Dustin Holland, Edward Dowling, Eissa Jamil, Elaine Montgomery, Eleonora Presani, Emily Hahn, Emily Wood, Eric-Tuan Le, Erik Brinkman, Esteban Arcaute, Evan Dunbar, Evan Smothers, Fei Sun, Felix Kreuk, Feng Tian, Filippos Kokkinos, Firat Ozgenel, Francesco Caggioni, Frank Kanayet, Frank Seide, Gabriela Medina Florez, Gabriella Schwarz, Gada Badeer, Georgia Swee, Gil Halpern, Grant Herman, Grigory Sizov, Guangyi, Zhang, Guna Lakshminarayanan, Hakan Inan, Hamid Shojanazeri, Han Zou, Hannah Wang, Hanwen Zha, Haroun Habeeb, Harrison Rudolph, Helen Suk, Henry Aspegren, Hunter Goldman, Hongyuan Zhan, Ibrahim Damlaj, Igor Molybog, Igor Tufanov, Ilias Leontiadis, Irina-Elena Veliche, Itai Gat, Jake Weissman, James Geboski, James Kohli, Janice Lam, Japhet Asher, Jean-Baptiste Gaya, Jeff Marcus, Jeff Tang, Jennifer Chan, Jenny Zhen, Jeremy Reizenstein, Jeremy Teboul, Jessica Zhong, Jian Jin, Jingyi Yang, Joe Cummings, Jon Carvill, Jon Shepard, Jonathan McPhie, Jonathan Torres, Josh Ginsburg, Junjie Wang, Kai Wu, Kam Hou U, Karan Saxena, Kartikay Khandelwal, Katayoun Zand, Kathy Matosich, Kaushik Veeraraghavan, Kelly Michelena, Keqian Li, Kiran Jagadeesh, Kun Huang, Kunal Chawla, Kyle Huang, Lailin Chen, Lakshya Garg, Lavender A, Leandro Silva, Lee Bell, Lei Zhang, Liangpeng Guo, Licheng Yu, Liron Moshkovich, Luca Wehrstedt, Madian Khabsa, Manav Avalani, Manish Bhatt, Martynas Mankus, Matan Hasson, Matthew Lennie, Matthias Reso, Maxim Groshev, Maxim Naumov, Maya Lathi, Meghan Keneally, Miao Liu, Michael L. Seltzer, Michal Valko, Michelle Restrepo, Mihir Patel, Mik Vyatskov, Mikayel Samvelyan, Mike Clark, Mike Macey, Mike Wang, Miquel Jubert Hermoso, Mo Metanat, Mohammad Rastegari, Munish Bansal, Nandhini Santhanam, Natascha Parks, Natasha White, Navyata Bawa, Nayan Singhal, Nick Egebo, Nicolas Usunier, Nikhil Mehta, Nikolay Pavlovich Laptev, Ning Dong, Norman Cheng, Oleg Chernoguz, Olivia Hart, Omkar Salpekar, Ozlem Kalinli, Parkin Kent, Parth Parekh, Paul Saab, Pavan Balaji, Pedro Rittner, Philip Bontrager, Pierre Roux, Piotr Dollar, Polina Zvyagina, Prashant Ratanchandani, Pritish Yuvraj, Qian Liang, Rachad Alao, Rachel Rodriguez, Rafi Ayub, Raghotham Murthy, Raghu Nayani, Rahul Mitra, Rangaprabhu Parthasarathy, Raymond Li, Rebekkah Hogan, Robin Battey, Rocky Wang, Russ Howes, Ruty Rinott, Sachin Mehta, Sachin Siby, Sai Jayesh Bondu, Samyak Datta, Sara Chugh, Sara Hunt, Sargun Dhillon, Sasha Sidorov, Satadru Pan, Saurabh Mahajan, Saurabh Verma, Seiji Yamamoto, Sharadh Ramaswamy, Shaun Lindsay, Shaun Lindsay, Sheng Feng, Shenghao Lin, Shengxin Cindy Zha, Shishir Patil, Shiva Shankar, Shuqiang Zhang, Shuqiang Zhang, Sinong Wang, Sneha Agarwal, Soji Sajuyigbe, Soumith Chintala, Stephanie Max, Stephen Chen, Steve Kehoe, Steve Satterfield, Sudarshan Govindaprasad, Sumit Gupta, Summer Deng, Sungmin Cho, Sunny Virk, Suraj Subramanian, Sy Choudhury, Sydney Goldman, Tal Remez, Tamar Glaser, Tamara Best, Thilo Koehler, Thomas Robinson, Tianhe Li, Tianjun Zhang, Tim Matthews, Timothy Chou, Tzook Shaked, Varun Vontimitta, Victoria Ajayi, Victoria Montanez, Vijai Mohan, Vinay Satish Kumar, Vishal Mangla, Vlad Ionescu, Vlad Poenaru, Vlad Tiberiu Mihailescu, Vladimir Ivanov, Wei Li, Wenchen Wang, Wenwen Jiang, Wes Bouaziz, Will Constable, Xiaocheng Tang, Xiaojian Wu, Xiaolan Wang, Xilun Wu, Xinbo Gao, Yaniv Kleinman, Yanjun Chen, Ye Hu, Ye Jia, Ye Qi, Yenda Li, Yilin Zhang, Ying Zhang, Yossi Adi, Youngjin Nam, Yu, Wang, Yu Zhao, Yuchen Hao, Yundi Qian, Yunlu Li, Yuzi He, Zach Rait, Zachary DeVito, Zef Rosnbrick, Zhaoduo Wen, Zhenyu Yang, Zhiwei Zhao, and Zhiyu Ma. 2024. The llama 3 herd of models. *Preprint*, arXiv:2407.21783.

Alex Graves, Santiago Fernández, Faustino Gomez, and Jürgen Schmidhuber. 2006. Connectionist temporal classification: Labelling unsegmented sequence data with recurrent neural networks. In *Proceedings of the 23rd International Conference on Machine Learning*, ICML '06, page 369–376, New York, NY, USA. Association for Computing Machinery.

Anmol Gulati, James Qin, Chung-Cheng Chiu, Niki Parmar, Yu Zhang, Jiahui Yu, Wei Han, Shibo Wang, Zhengdong Zhang, Yonghui Wu, and Ruoming Pang. 2020. Conformer: Convolution-augmented transformer for speech recognition. *CoRR*, abs/2005.08100.

Michael Hassid, Tal Remez, Tu Anh Nguyen, Itai Gat, Alexis Conneau, Felix Kreuk, Jade Copet, Alexandre Defossez, Gabriel Synnaeve, Emmanuel Dupoux, Roy Schwartz, and Yossi Adi. 2024. Textually pretrained speech language models. *Preprint*, arXiv:2305.13009.

Dan Hendrycks, Collin Burns, Steven Basart, Andy Zou, Mantas Mazeika, Dawn Song, and Jacob Steinhardt. 2021. Measuring massive multitask language understanding. *Preprint*, arXiv:2009.03300.

Wei-Ning Hsu, Benjamin Bolte, Yao-Hung Hubert Tsai, Kushal Lakhotia, Ruslan Salakhutdinov, and Abdelrahman Mohamed. 2021. Hubert: Self-supervised speech representation learning by masked prediction of hidden units. *Preprint*, arXiv:2106.07447.

Edward J. Hu, Yelong Shen, Phillip Wallis, Zeyuan Allen-Zhu, Yuanzhi Li, Shean Wang, Lu Wang, and Weizhu Chen. 2021. Lora: Low-rank adaptation of large language models. *Preprint*, arXiv:2106.09685.

Rongjie Huang, Mingze Li, Dongchao Yang, Jiatong Shi, Xuankai Chang, Zhenhui Ye, Yuning Wu,

Zhiqing Hong, Jiawei Huang, Jinglin Liu, Yi Ren, Zhou Zhao, and Shinji Watanabe. 2023. Audiogpt: Understanding and generating speech, music, sound, and talking head. *Preprint*, arXiv:2304.12995.

Ruizhe Huang, Xiaohui Zhang, Zhaoheng Ni, Li Sun, Moto Hira, Jeff Hwang, Vimal Manohar, Vineel Pratap, Matthew Wiesner, Shinji Watanabe, Daniel Povey, and Sanjeev Khudanpur. 2024. Less peaky and more accurate ctc forced alignment by label priors. *Preprint*, arXiv:2406.02560.

Heeseung Kim, Soonshin Seo, Kyeongseok Jeong, Ohsung Kwon, Soyoon Kim, Jungwhan Kim, Jaehong Lee, Eunwoo Song, Myungwoo Oh, Jung-Woo Ha, Sungroh Yoon, and Kang Min Yoo. 2024. Integrating paralinguistics in speech-empowered large language models for natural conversation. *Preprint*, arXiv:2402.05706.

Jaehyeon Kim, Sungwon Kim, Jungil Kong, and Sungroh Yoon. 2020. Glow-tts: A generative flow for text-to-speech via monotonic alignment search. In *Advances in Neural Information Processing Systems*, volume 33, pages 8067–8077. Curran Associates, Inc.

Dan Kondratyuk, Lijun Yu, Xiuye Gu, José Lezama, Jonathan Huang, Grant Schindler, Rachel Hornung, Vighnesh Birodkar, Jimmy Yan, Ming-Chang Chiu, Krishna Somandepalli, Hassan Akbari, Yair Alon, Yong Cheng, Josh Dillon, Agrim Gupta, Meera Hahn, Anja Hauth, David Hendon, Alonso Martinez, David Minnen, Mikhail Sirotenko, Kihyuk Sohn, Xuan Yang, Hartwig Adam, Ming-Hsuan Yang, Irfan Essa, Huisheng Wang, David A. Ross, Bryan Seybold, and Lu Jiang. 2024. Videopoet: A large language model for zero-shot video generation. *Preprint*, arXiv:2312.14125.

Kushal Lakhotia, Eugene Kharitonov, Wei-Ning Hsu, Yossi Adi, Adam Polyak, Benjamin Bolte, Tu-Anh Nguyen, Jade Copet, Alexei Baevski, Abdelrahman Mohamed, and Emmanuel Dupoux. 2021. On generative spoken language modeling from raw audio. *Transactions of the Association for Computational Linguistics*, 9:1336–1354.

Junnan Li, Dongxu Li, Silvio Savarese, and Steven Hoi. 2023a. Blip-2: Bootstrapping language-image pretraining with frozen image encoders and large language models. *Preprint*, arXiv:2301.12597.

Yanwei Li, Chengyao Wang, and Jiaya Jia. 2023b. Llama-vid: An image is worth 2 tokens in large language models. *Preprint*, arXiv:2311.17043.

Ting-En Lin, Yuchuan Wu, Fei Huang, Luo Si, Jian Sun, and Yongbin Li. 2022. Duplex conversation: Towards human-like interaction in spoken dialogue systems. In *Proceedings of the 28th ACM SIGKDD Conference on Knowledge Discovery and Data Mining*, volume 2021 of *KDD '22*, page 3299–3308. ACM.

Alexander H. Liu, Heng-Jui Chang, Michael Auli, Wei-Ning Hsu, and Jim Glass. 2023a. Dinosr: Self-distillation and online clustering for self-supervised speech representation learning. In *Advances in Neural Information Processing Systems*, volume 36, pages 58346–58362. Curran Associates, Inc.

Haotian Liu, Chunyuan Li, Qingyang Wu, and Yong Jae Lee. 2023b. Visual instruction tuning. *Preprint*, arXiv:2304.08485.

Chenyang Lyu, Minghao Wu, Longyue Wang, Xinting Huang, Bingshuai Liu, Zefeng Du, Shuming Shi, and Zhaopeng Tu. 2023. Macaw-llm: Multi-modal language modeling with image, audio, video, and text integration. *Preprint*, arXiv:2306.09093.

Soumi Maiti, Yifan Peng, Shukjae Choi, Jee weon Jung, Xuankai Chang, and Shinji Watanabe. 2024. Voxtlm: unified decoder-only models for consolidating speech recognition/synthesis and speech/text continuation tasks. *Preprint*, arXiv:2309.07937.

Michael McAuliffe, Michaela Socolof, Sarah Mihuc, Michael Wagner, and Morgan Sonderegger. 2017. Montreal forced aligner: Trainable text-speech alignment using kaldi. In *Interspeech*.

Nasrin Mostafazadeh, Michael Roth, Annie Louis, Nathanael Chambers, and James Allen. 2017. LSDSem 2017 shared task: The story cloze test. In *Proceedings of the 2nd Workshop on Linking Models of Lexical, Sentential and Discourse-level Semantics*, pages 46–51, Valencia, Spain. Association for Computational Linguistics.

Tu Anh Nguyen, Maureen de Seyssel, Patricia Rozé, Morgane Rivière, Evgeny Kharitonov, Alexei Baevski, Ewan Dunbar, and Emmanuel Dupoux. 2020. The zero resource speech benchmark 2021: Metrics and baselines for unsupervised spoken language modeling. *Preprint*, arXiv:2011.11588.

Tu Anh Nguyen, Wei-Ning Hsu, Antony D'Avirro, Bowen Shi, Itai Gat, Maryam Fazel-Zarani, Tal Remez, Jade Copet, Gabriel Synnaeve, Michael Hassid, Felix Kreuk, Yossi Adi, and Emmanuel Dupoux. 2023. Expresso: A benchmark and analysis of discrete expressive speech resynthesis. *Preprint*, arXiv:2308.05725.

Tu Anh Nguyen, Benjamin Muller, Bokai Yu, Marta R. Costa-jussa, Maha Elbayad, Sravya Popuri, Paul-Ambroise Duquenne, Robin Algayres, Ruslan Mavlyutov, Itai Gat, Gabriel Synnaeve, Juan Pino, Benoit Sagot, and Emmanuel Dupoux. 2024. Spirit-lm: Interleaved spoken and written language model. *Preprint*, arXiv:2402.05755.

OpenAI, Josh Achiam, Steven Adler, Sandhini Agarwal, Lama Ahmad, Ilge Akkaya, Florencia Leoni Aleman, Diogo Almeida, Janko Altenschmidt, Sam Altman, Shyamal Anadkat, Red Avila, Igor Babuschkin, Suchir Balaji, Valerie Balcom, Paul Baltescu, Haiming Bao, Mohammad Bavarian, Jeff Belgum, Irwan Bello, Jake Berdine, Gabriel Bernadett-Shapiro,

Christopher Berner, Lenny Bogdonoff, Oleg Boiko, Madelaine Boyd, Anna-Luisa Brakman, Greg Brockman, Tim Brooks, Miles Brundage, Kevin Button, Trevor Cai, Rosie Campbell, Andrew Cann, Brittany Carey, Chelsea Carlson, Rory Carmichael, Brooke Chan, Che Chang, Fotis Chantzis, Derek Chen, Sully Chen, Ruby Chen, Jason Chen, Mark Chen, Ben Chess, Chester Cho, Casey Chu, Hyung Won Chung, Dave Cummings, Jeremiah Currier, Yunxing Dai, Cory Decareaux, Thomas Degry, Noah Deutsch, Damien Deville, Arka Dhar, David Dohan, Steve Dowling, Sheila Dunning, Adrien Ecoffet, Atty Eleti, Tyna Eloundou, David Farhi, Liam Fedus, Niko Felix, Simón Posada Fishman, Juston Forte, Isabella Fulford, Leo Gao, Elie Georges, Christian Gibson, Vik Goel, Tarun Gogineni, Gabriel Goh, Rapha Gontijo-Lopes, Jonathan Gordon, Morgan Grafstein, Scott Gray, Ryan Greene, Joshua Gross, Shixiang Shane Gu, Yufei Guo, Chris Hallacy, Jesse Han, Jeff Harris, Yuchen He, Mike Heaton, Johannes Heidecke, Chris Hesse, Alan Hickey, Wade Hickey, Peter Hoeschele, Brandon Houghton, Kenny Hsu, Shengli Hu, Xin Hu, Joost Huizinga, Shantanu Jain, Shawn Jain, Joanne Jang, Angela Jiang, Roger Jiang, Haozhun Jin, Denny Jin, Shino Jomoto, Billie Jonn, Heewoo Jun, Tomer Kaftan, Łukasz Kaiser, Ali Kamali, Ingmar Kanitscheider, Nitish Shirish Keskar, Tabarak Khan, Logan Kilpatrick, Jong Wook Kim, Christina Kim, Yongjik Kim, Jan Hendrik Kirchner, Jamie Kiros, Matt Knight, Daniel Kokotajlo, Łukasz Kondraciuk, Andrew Kondrich, Aris Konstantinidis, Kyle Kosic, Gretchen Krueger, Vishal Kuo, Michael Lampe, Ikai Lan, Teddy Lee, Jan Leike, Jade Leung, Daniel Levy, Chak Ming Li, Rachel Lim, Molly Lin, Stephanie Lin, Mateusz Litwin, Theresa Lopez, Ryan Lowe, Patricia Lue, Anna Makanju, Kim Malfacini, Sam Manning, Todor Markov, Yaniv Markovski, Bianca Martin, Katie Mayer, Andrew Mayne, Bob McGrew, Scott Mayer McKinney, Christine McLeavey, Paul McMillan, Jake McNeil, David Medina, Aalok Mehta, Jacob Menick, Luke Metz, Andrey Mishchenko, Pamela Mishkin, Vinnie Monaco, Evan Morikawa, Daniel Mossing, Tong Mu, Mira Murati, Oleg Murk, David Mély, Ashvin Nair, Reiichiro Nakano, Rajeev Nayak, Arvind Neelakantan, Richard Ngo, Hyeonwoo Noh, Long Ouyang, Cullen O'Keefe, Jakub Pachocki, Alex Paino, Joe Palermo, Ashley Pantuliano, Giambattista Parascandolo, Joel Parish, Emy Parparita, Alex Passos, Mikhail Pavlov, Andrew Peng, Adam Perelman, Filipe de Avila Belbute Peres, Michael Petrov, Henrique Ponde de Oliveira Pinto, Michael, Pokorny, Michelle Pokrass, Vitchyr H. Pong, Tolly Powell, Alethea Power, Boris Power, Elizabeth Proehl, Raul Puri, Alec Radford, Jack Rae, Aditya Ramesh, Cameron Raymond, Francis Real, Kendra Rimbach, Carl Ross, Bob Rotsted, Henri Roussez, Nick Ryder, Mario Saltarelli, Ted Sanders, Shibani Santurkar, Girish Sastry, Heather Schmidt, David Schnurr, John Schulman, Daniel Selsam, Kyla Sheppard, Toki Sherbakov, Jessica Shieh, Sarah Shoker, Pranav Shyam, Szymon Sidor, Eric Sigler, Maddie Simens, Jordan Sitkin, Katarina Slama, Ian Sohl, Benjamin Sokolowsky, Yang Song, Natalie Staudacher, Felipe Petroski Such, Natalie Summers, Ilya Sutskever, Jie Tang, Nikolas Tezak, Madeleine B. Thompson, Phil Tillet, Amin Tootoonchian, Elizabeth Tseng, Preston Tuggle, Nick Turley, Jerry Tworek, Juan Felipe Cerón Uribe, Andrea Vallone, Arun Vijayvergiya, Chelsea Voss, Carroll Wainwright, Justin Jay Wang, Alvin Wang, Ben Wang, Jonathan Ward, Jason Wei, CJ Weinmann, Akila Welihinda, Peter Welinder, Jiayi Weng, Lilian Weng, Matt Wiethoff, Dave Willner, Clemens Winter, Samuel Wolrich, Hannah Wong, Lauren Workman, Sherwin Wu, Jeff Wu, Michael Wu, Kai Xiao, Tao Xu, Sarah Yoo, Kevin Yu, Qiming Yuan, Wojciech Zaremba, Rowan Zellers, Chong Zhang, Marvin Zhang, Shengjia Zhao, Tianhao Zheng, Juntang Zhuang, William Zhuk, and Barret Zoph. 2024. Gpt-4 technical report. *Preprint*, arXiv:2303.08774.

Vassil Panayotov, Guoguo Chen, Daniel Povey, and Sanjeev Khudanpur. 2015. Librispeech: An asr corpus based on public domain audio books. In *2015 IEEE International Conference on Acoustics, Speech and Signal Processing (ICASSP)*, pages 5206–5210.

Daniel Povey, Arnab Ghoshal, Gilles Boulianne, Lukas Burget, Ondrej Glembek, Nagendra Goel, Mirko Hannemann, Petr Motlícek, Yanmin Qian, Petr Schwarz, et al. 2011. The Kaldi speech recognition toolkit. In *IEEE 2011 workshop on automatic speech recognition and understanding*, pages 1–4. IEEE Signal Processing Society.

Vineel Pratap, Andros Tjandra, Bowen Shi, Paden Tomasello, Arun Babu, Sayani Kundu, Ali Elkahky, Zhaoheng Ni, Apoorv Vyas, Maryam Fazel-Zarandi, Alexei Baevski, Yossi Adi, Xiaohui Zhang, Wei-Ning Hsu, Alexis Conneau, and Michael Auli. 2023. Scaling speech technology to 1,000+ languages. *Preprint*, arXiv:2305.13516.

Vineel Pratap, Qiantong Xu, Anuroop Sriram, Gabriel Synnaeve, and Ronan Collobert. 2020. MLS: A large-scale multilingual dataset for speech research. In *Proceedings of Interspeech 2020*, Interspeech 2020. ISCA.

Paul K. Rubenstein, Chulayuth Asawaroengchai, Duc Dung Nguyen, Ankur Bapna, Zalán Borsos, Félix de Chaumont Quitry, Peter Chen, Dalia El Badawy, Wei Han, Eugene Kharitonov, Hannah Muckenhirn, Dirk Padfield, James Qin, Danny Rozenberg, Tara Sainath, Johan Schalkwyk, Matt Sharifi, Michelle Tadmor Ramanovich, Marco Tagliasacchi, Alexandru Tudor, Mihajlo Velimirović, Damien Vincent, Jiahui Yu, Yongqiang Wang, Vicky Zayats, Neil Zeghidour, Yu Zhang, Zhishuai Zhang, Lukas Zilka, and Christian Frank. 2023. Audiopalm: A large language model that can speak and listen. *Preprint*, arXiv:2306.12925.

Tara N. Sainath, Ruoming Pang, David Rybach, Basi García, and Trevor Strohman. 2020. Emitting word timings with end-to-end models. In *Interspeech*.

Kevin J. Shih, Rafael Valle, Rohan Badlani, Adrian Lancucki, Wei Ping, and Bryan Catanzaro. 2021. RAD-TTS: Parallel flow-based TTS with robust alignment learning and diverse synthesis. In *ICML Workshop on Invertible Neural Networks, Normalizing Flows, and Explicit Likelihood Models*.

Weiting Tan, Yunmo Chen, Tongfei Chen, Guanghui Qin, Haoran Xu, Heidi C. Zhang, Benjamin Van Durme, and Philipp Koehn. 2024. Streaming sequence transduction through dynamic compression. *Preprint*, arXiv:2402.01172.

Changli Tang, Wenyi Yu, Guangzhi Sun, Xianzhao Chen, Tian Tan, Wei Li, Lu Lu, Zejun Ma, and Chao Zhang. 2024. Salmonn: Towards generic hearing abilities for large language models. *Preprint*, arXiv:2310.13289.

Chameleon Team. 2024. Chameleon: Mixed-modal early-fusion foundation models. *Preprint*, arXiv:2405.09818.

Hugo Touvron, Louis Martin, Kevin Stone, Peter Albert, Amjad Almahairi, Yasmine Babaei, Nikolay Bashlykov, Soumya Batra, Prajjwal Bhargava, Shruti Bhosale, Dan Bikel, Lukas Blecher, Cristian Canton Ferrer, Moya Chen, Guillem Cucurull, David Esiobu, Jude Fernandes, Jeremy Fu, Wenyin Fu, Brian Fuller, Cynthia Gao, Vedanuj Goswami, Naman Goyal, Anthony Hartshorn, Saghar Hosseini, Rui Hou, Hakan Inan, Marcin Kardas, Viktor Kerkez, Madian Khabsa, Isabel Kloumann, Artem Korenev, Punit Singh Koura, Marie-Anne Lachaux, Thibaut Lavril, Jenya Lee, Diana Liskovich, Yinghai Lu, Yuning Mao, Xavier Martinet, Todor Mihaylov, Pushkar Mishra, Igor Molybog, Yixin Nie, Andrew Poulton, Jeremy Reizenstein, Rashi Rungta, Kalyan Saladi, Alan Schelten, Ruan Silva, Eric Michael Smith, Ranjan Subramanian, Xiaoqing Ellen Tan, Binh Tang, Ross Taylor, Adina Williams, Jian Xiang Kuan, Puxin Xu, Zheng Yan, Iliyan Zarov, Yuchen Zhang, Angela Fan, Melanie Kambadur, Sharan Narang, Aurelien Rodriguez, Robert Stojnic, Sergey Edunov, and Thomas Scialom. 2023. Llama 2: Open foundation and fine-tuned chat models. *Preprint*, arXiv:2307.09288.

Ashish Vaswani, Noam Shazeer, Niki Parmar, Jakob Uszkoreit, Llion Jones, Aidan N Gomez, Ł ukasz Kaiser, and Illia Polosukhin. 2017. Attention is all you need. In *Advances in Neural Information Processing Systems*, volume 30. Curran Associates, Inc.

Tu Vu, Aditya Barua, Brian Lester, Daniel Cer, Mohit Iyyer, and Noah Constant. 2022. Overcoming catastrophic forgetting in zero-shot cross-lingual generation. *Preprint*, arXiv:2205.12647.

Apoorv Vyas, Bowen Shi, Matthew Le, Andros Tjandra, Yi-Chiao Wu, Baishan Guo, Jiemin Zhang, Xinyue Zhang, Robert Adkins, William Ngan, Jeff Wang, Ivan Cruz, Bapi Akula, Akinniyi Akinyemi, Brian Ellis, Rashel Moritz, Yael Yungster, Alice Rakotoarison, Liang Tan, Chris Summers, Carleigh Wood, Joshua Lane, Mary Williamson, and Wei-Ning Hsu. 2023. Audiobox: Unified audio generation with natural language prompts. *Preprint*, arXiv:2312.15821.

Jian Wu, Yashesh Gaur, Zhuo Chen, Long Zhou, Yimeng Zhu, Tianrui Wang, Jinyu Li, Shujie Liu, Bo Ren, Linquan Liu, and Yu Wu. 2023. On decoder-only architecture for speech-to-text and large language model integration. *Preprint*, arXiv:2307.03917.

Linting Xue, Noah Constant, Adam Roberts, Mihir Kale, Rami Al-Rfou, Aditya Siddhant, Aditya Barua, and Colin Raffel. 2021. mT5: A massively multilingual pre-trained text-to-text transformer. In *Proceedings of the 2021 Conference of the North American Chapter of the Association for Computational Linguistics: Human Language Technologies*, pages 483–498, Online. Association for Computational Linguistics.

Wenyi Yu, Changli Tang, Guangzhi Sun, Xianzhao Chen, Tian Tan, Wei Li, Lu Lu, Zejun Ma, and Chao Zhang. 2023. Connecting speech encoder and large language model for asr. *Preprint*, arXiv:2309.13963.

Neil Zeghidour, Alejandro Luebs, Ahmed Omran, Jan Skoglund, and Marco Tagliasacchi. 2021. Soundstream: An end-to-end neural audio codec. *Preprint*, arXiv:2107.03312.

Dong Zhang, Shimin Li, Xin Zhang, Jun Zhan, Pengyu Wang, Yaqian Zhou, and Xipeng Qiu. 2023. Speechgpt: Empowering large language models with intrinsic cross-modal conversational abilities. *Preprint*, arXiv:2305.11000.

Yanli Zhao, Andrew Gu, Rohan Varma, Liang Luo, Chien-Chin Huang, Min Xu, Less Wright, Hamid Shojanazeri, Myle Ott, Sam Shleifer, Alban Desmaison, Can Balioglu, Pritam Damania, Bernard Nguyen, Geeta Chauhan, Yuchen Hao, Ajit Mathews, and Shen Li. 2023. Pytorch fsdp: Experiences on scaling fully sharded data parallel. *Proc. VLDB Endow.*, 16(12):3848–3860.

Supplementary Material

Appendix Sections	Contents
Appendix A	Specch-Text Aligner Comparison
Appendix B	Non-semantic Information in SSR-CONNECTOR
Appendix C	Dataset Details
Appendix D	Evaluation Details

A Speech-text Aligners

In this section, we provide more details for the aligners that we experimented with to compute segmentation for SSR-CONNECTOR. To summarize, we tried UnitY2 aligner (Barrault et al., 2023), CTC-based (Graves et al., 2006) aligner (both character-level and subword-level), and CIF-based (Dong and Xu, 2020) segmentation. We also compare their performance in this section and show that UNITY2 and CHAR-CTC aligner work the best; therefore we adopted them in all our experiments presented in the main paper.

A.1 Aligner Description

UnitY2 Aligner The UnitY2 aligner (Barrault et al., 2023) is a forced aligner that computes speech-text alignment using discrete speech units and character-level text tokens. The speech units are derived by applying K-Means clustering to the XLS-R model (Babu et al., 2021). The aligner is trained jointly with a non-autoregressive text-to-unit (T2U) model, adopting the architecture of the RAD-TTS model (Shih et al., 2021) but replacing the target mel-spectrogram with speech units. It first computes a soft-alignment $A^{\text{soft}} \in \mathbb{R}^{V \times U}$ between the characters and units:

$$\mathrm{D}_{i,j} = ||s_i^{\text{char}} - s_j^{\text{unit}}||_2, \tag{3}$$

$$A_{i,j}^{\text{soft}} = \frac{e^{-\mathrm{D}_{i,j}}}{\sum_k e^{-\mathrm{D}_{k,j}}} + \mathrm{P}_{\text{prior}}(i|j), \tag{4}$$

where s^{char} and s^{unit} are the outputs of the character and unit encoders, respectively (both encoders consist of an embedding layer and a 1D convolution layer). $\mathrm{D} \in \mathbb{R}^{V \times U}$ is a distance matrix with V and U representing the vocabulary sizes of characters and speech units. $\mathrm{P}_{\text{prior}} \in \mathbb{R}^{V \times U}$ is the Beta-binomial alignment prior matrix to encourage near-diagonal paths (Shih et al., 2021). After soft-alignment is computed, the monotonic alignment search (MAS) algorithm (Kim et al., 2020) is applied to extract the most probable monotonic alignment path.

CTC-based Aligner Since the UnitY2 aligner requires both speech and transcription, it does not support streamable alignment extraction. To enable textless alignment computation, we explored two CTC-based (Graves et al., 2006) aligners. Given the speech features $\boldsymbol{x}$ and text sequences $\boldsymbol{y}$, CTC computes $P(\boldsymbol{y}|\boldsymbol{x})$ by summing over all valid alignment paths:

$$P(\boldsymbol{y}|\boldsymbol{x}) = \sum_{\pi \in \mathcal{B}^{-1}(\boldsymbol{y})} P(\pi|\boldsymbol{x}) \tag{5}$$

Here, π denotes a possible alignment path that maps to the target sequence $\boldsymbol{y}$, and $\mathcal{B}^{-1}(\boldsymbol{y})$ represents the set of all valid paths that collapse to $\boldsymbol{y}$ after removing blanks and repeated labels. We investigated two CTC variants: one using character-level text sequences (CHAR-CTC) and another using subword token sequences (SUB-CTC), which shares the same vocabulary as the LLM model.

CIF-based Speech Connector For both CTC and UnitY2 aligners, we extract segmentations from the alignments and then apply selection-based compression (Tan et al., 2024). We also experimented with Continuous Integrate-and-Fire (Dong and Xu, 2020, CIF) as the connector, which is designed to learn segmentation and perform compression simultaneously. Instead of relying on a fixed, pre-computed segmentation, CIF dynamically segments and aggregates speech features by scoring each feature and computing a weighted average. For more details, we refer readers to the paper (Dong and Xu, 2020).

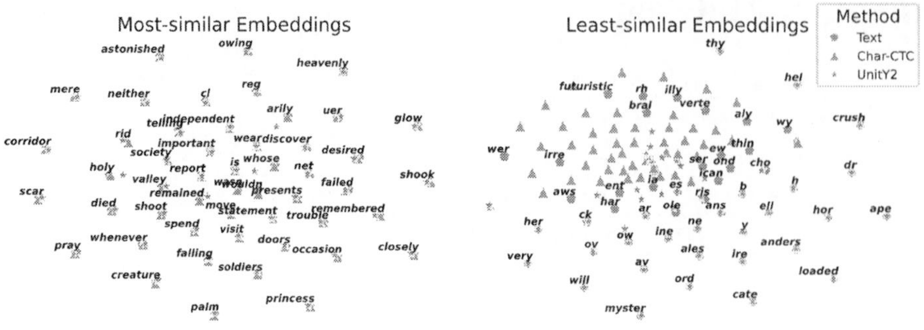

Figure 5: t-SNE plots of text and speech representations after distillation.

A.2 Aligner Performance Comparison

To compare the quality of different aligners, we trained several SSR-CONNECTOR based on different aligners via distillation. We evaluated the aligners using the Librispeech clean test set by computing the Cosine Similarity (**Cos(%)**) and Mean Squared Error (**MSE**) between the compressed representations and text embeddings. Additionally, we performed zero-shot and five-shot ASR with the learned connector. Note that we never explicitly trained the model for ASR tasks, and the base LLM remained frozen during Stage 1 training. Therefore, the model achieves low word error rates (**WER**) only when the distilled speech representations closely resemble the text embeddings. As shown in Table 6, the UNITY2 aligner brings the speech representations close to their corresponding text embeddings, achieving very low WER in both zero-shot and five-shot ASR settings. Among textless aligners, we found that CHAR-CTC performs the best, likely because it has a much smaller vocabulary compared to SUB-CTC, making it easier to learn. Lastly, CIF resulted in suboptimal performance, due to its less accurate alignment, as its segmentation is predicted by accumulating scores without exploiting the monotonicity between speech and text.

To visualize the effect of distillation, we present t-SNE plots of the adapted speech representations and text embeddings in Fig. 5, categorizing them into high and low similarity groups based on the cosine similarity between CHAR-CTC representations and text embeddings. We observe that longer subwords tend to exhibit higher similarity, likely because their long segments make it easier for the connector to convert speech representations into corresponding text embeddings. Furthermore, longer subwords possess more coherent semantics compared to shorter tokens. like 'wy' or 'ia'.

Model Type	Cos(%)↑	MSE↓	WER (%) ↓
UNITY2	**96.8**	**0.018**	**5.6 / 4.0**
CHAR-CTC	95.1	0.023	9.7 / 6.5
SUB-CTC	92.2	0.037	16.7 / 14.0
CIF	77.5	0.096	27.6 / 23.7

Table 6: Performance comparison (with Cosine Similarity, MSE, and 0/5-shot ASR WER) between different aligners used for Stage 1 training, evaluated on Librispeech.

Aligner	WBE↓	WDUR
Groundtruth	0	305
UNITY2	33	279
CHAR-CTC	42	230
Other Aligners		
CTC+Label Prior	29	288
MMS	37	242
MFA	23	314

Table 7: Alignment quality comparison.

Given that UNITY2 and CHAR-CTC performs the best, we also follow Huang et al. (2024) to measure their word boundary error (WBE) and word average duration (WDUR) using the TIMIT (Garofolo et al., 1993) data. Though the aligner quality can be further improved with other methods such as CTC + Label Prior (Huang et al., 2024), MMS (Pratap et al., 2023), or MFA (McAuliffe et al., 2017), CHAR-CTC and UNITY2 still achieve good quality and we choose them out of simplicity and general availability (unlike "CTC+Label Prior", for example, which requires customization with library like k2[3]).

[3] https://github.com/k2-fsa/k2

B Beyond Semantics: Speech Style Recognition with In-context Learning

To explore the non-semantic capabilities of our SpeechLM, particularly its ability to retain and utilize paralinguistic information, we conducted additional experiments focusing on speech style recognition through in-context learning. Specifically, we investigated whether the SSR-CONNECTOR-based SpeechLM (based on the UnitY2 aligner), can differentiate between various speech styles without explicit training on paralinguistic cues.

We utilized the Expresso dataset (Nguyen et al., 2023), which comprises speeches delivered in distinct styles such as happy, sad, whispering, and laughing. Two primary tasks were designed to assess the model's performance:

1. **Whisper vs. Laugh**: The model was tasked with identifying whether a given speech was whispered or laughed. The prompt provided to the model was:

   "You are given speeches from two styles. Your task is to judge if the speech is a whisper or laugh. Here are some example speeches: [Speech]: {speech} [Style]: {whisper/laugh}..."

2. **Happy vs. Sad**: The model was asked to determine if the speech was delivered happily or sadly. The prompt used was:

   "Listen to the following speech and judge if the speaker is happy or sad. Here are some examples: [Speech]: {speech} [Emotion]: {happy/sad}..."

For each task, we evaluated the model's performance using varying numbers of in-context examples: 0-shot, 1-shot, 5-shot, and 10-shot. The results, averaged over 10 runs, are presented in Table 8. Additionally, we benchmarked a cascaded system comprising Whisper and Llama3 for comparison (this cascaded baseline does no preserve non-semantic information and can only infer the speech style through transcripted content).

Task	Model	0-shot	1-shot	5-shot	10-shot
Whisper vs. Laugh	Cascaded System	51.6	52.1	52.2	54.7
	Ours	49.6	62.4	64.0	75.9
Happy vs. Sad	Cascaded System	50.0	51.4	51.8	51.0
	Ours	51.6	52.1	52.2	54.7

Table 8: Accuracy of Speech Style Recognition Tasks with In-context Learning

The results indicate that with zero-shot prompting, our model generates predictions close to random chance, as it has not been trained to utilize paralinguistic information. However, with the introduction of a few-shot learning approach, the model significantly improves its ability to distinguish between whispering and laughing speech, achieving up to 75.9% accuracy with 10-shot examples. This suggests that the model's representations inherently contain paralinguistic information that can be harnessed through in-context learning. For the Happy vs. Sad task, the improvement is modest, peaking at 54.7% accuracy with 10-shot examples. This lesser performance compared to the Whisper vs. Laugh task may be attributed to the subtler differences in emotional expression compared to the more pronounced style differences between whispering and laughing.

Overall, these findings demonstrate that **our SpeechLM can effectively leverage in-context learning to recognize different speech styles**, thereby highlighting the presence of paralinguistic information within the model's representations. This capability complements existing methods that incorporate paralinguistic information, such as the use of expressive tokens in SpiritLM (Nguyen et al., 2024) or emotion-relevant instruction tuning in SALMONN (Tang et al., 2024).

C Datasets

Eval Dataset	Type	Eval Metric	Eval Modality
sWUGGY (Nguyen et al., 2020)	Choice Task	Accuracy	S, T
sBLIMP (Nguyen et al., 2020)	Choice Task	Accuracy	S, T
StoryCloze (Mostafazadeh et al., 2017)	Choice Task	Accuracy	$S, T, S \rightarrow T$
MMLU (Hendrycks et al., 2021)	Choice Task	Accuracy	T
Speech-MMLU (*Ours*)	Choice Task	Accuracy	$S \rightarrow T$
LibriSpeech (Panayotov et al., 2015)	Generation Task	Word Error Rate	$S \rightarrow T$

Table 9: Evaluation Datasets and their types. For the evaluation format, S is speech-only, T is text-only, and $S \rightarrow T$ means the evaluation prompt consists of speech prefix and text continuation.

As described in §4.1, we employ sWUGGY, sBLIMP, StoryCloze, MMLU, Speech-MMLU and Librispeech datasets to assess model performance. In this section, we provide more examples for each evaluation set. sWUGGY and sBLIMP are simple tasks where two choices can be directly compared. As shown in Table 10, sWUGGY provides two choices that require models to discriminate real words from non-words. sBLIMP assesses whether the model can distinguish between a grammatically correct sentence and its ungrammatical variant.

MMLU and StoryCloze, on the other hand, have a prefix and choices. The StoryCloze dataset measures whether the model can identify the logical ending between two sentences given at the beginning of a short story. Since StoryCloze has a shared prefix, we can synthesize only the prefix part into speech and keep choices in text format, resulting in our $S \rightarrow T$ format evaluation that assess the model's cross-modal understanding. Similarly, for MMLU, we also synthesize its prefix (the question portion) into speech and keep the choices in text format, resulting in our Speech-MMLU dataset. Since some topics have bad audio synthesis quality (e.g., the algebra subset contains many mathematical notations), we only keep 22 topics in our test suite (as shown in the "Topic" column of Table 11).

Name	Prefix	Choices
sWUGGY	N/A	{Good=obsolete, Bad=odsolete}
sBLIMP	N/A	{Good=Walter was harming himself, Bad=Walter was harming itself}
StoryCloze	I had been giving this homeless man change every day. He was on the same corner near my house. One day, as I was driving through my neighborhood I saw a new car. Soon enough, I saw the same homeless man emerge from it!	{Good=I never gave the man money again. Bad=The next day I gave the man twenty dollars.}
MMLU	During the period when life is believed to have begun, the atmosphere on primitive Earth contained abundant amounts of all the following gases except	{"A": "oxygen", "B": "hydrogen", "C": "ammonia", "D": "methane"}

Table 10: Examples of different evaluation datasets.

D Evaluation Metric and Prompt

Choice tasks (sWUGGY, sBLIMP, StoryCloze, MMLU, Speech-MMLU) are evaluated by comparing perplexity of different choices. The choice with smallest perplexity is selected as the prediction and we measure accuracy across different benchmarks.

For generation task (prompt-based ASR), we use the prompt below, with pairs of speech and transcription is provided to the SpeechLM. For 0-shot evaluation, we do not include any examplers.

Prompt

Given the speech, provide its transcription.
[speech]: {demo speech}
[text]: {demo transcription}
...
[speech]: {speech to transcribe}
[text]:

Speech MMLU Evaluation We craft speech MMLU by synthesizing the questions of MMLU into audio through AUDIOBOX. Since some domains have bad synthesis quality (such as algebra, which includes many math notations), we filtered those domains out from our evaluation.

We present the detailed comparison results in Table 11 for a better comparison of model performance across different domains/topics. We see that the trend for different domains is mostly consistent, with our alignment-aware connector based on UNITY2 achieving the best performance, followed by CHAR-CTC based connector. Similar as our main findings, the unit-based system has worse performance due to information loss from discretization and the fine-tuned model suffers from catastrophic forgetting (albeit mitigated through our multitask fine-tuning approach). Nevertheless, all these SSR-CONNECTOR based system obtains better performance compared to SPIRITLM (LLAMA3), confirming the effectiveness of our modality-fusion strategy.

Topic	SPIRITLM		UNITY2 + Mask		UNITY2		CHAR-CTC		Unit-based		Fine-tuned	
	0-shot	5-shot	0-shot	5-shot	0-shot	5-shot	0-shot	5-shot	0-shot	5-shot	0-shot	5-shot
Astronomy	45.6	40.8	60.0	66.0	60.7	65.3	57.0	60.4	49.7	61.1	50.7	52.0
Business Ethics	37.1	40.2	52.0	60.0	53.0	62.0	56.0	59.0	52.0	55.0	37.0	51.0
Clinical Knowledge	36.0	39.8	60.6	63.3	61.0	62.9	61.2	62.7	57.8	57.4	47.3	53.8
College Biology	36.4	33.6	65.0	69.9	62.9	68.5	57.7	59.9	54.2	57.7	40.6	44.1
Electrical Engineering	37.7	44.2	52.5	57.4	52.5	53.9	48.2	58.9	44.7	48.2	53.2	54.6
High School Biology	40.8	41.2	66.0	72.2	67.6	72.2	63.3	68.2	57.1	65.6	50.5	62.5
High School Gov. Pol.	44.4	43.4	79.2	84.9	78.1	83.3	76.6	81.8	71.4	73.4	54.7	64.1
International Law	55.9	58.5	71.1	81.0	71.1	81.0	71.1	80.2	71.1	75.2	66.1	71.1
Jurisprudence	37.1	36.2	60.2	68.5	62.0	70.4	57.4	63.9	54.6	60.2	51.9	57.4
Machine Learning	39.3	32.1	45.8	59.3	50.8	59.3	45.8	61.0	44.1	57.6	39.0	55.9
Management	43.0	42.0	79.6	84.5	77.7	75.7	73.8	74.8	68.0	70.9	45.6	65.0
Marketing	39.8	49.8	77.8	85.0	76.1	81.6	76.9	81.6	74.4	76.9	51.3	67.1
Miscellaneous	38.5	36.4	69.2	71.5	66.6	70.1	60.3	64.6	52.3	57.5	42.7	50.3
Moral Disputes	39.1	42.3	59.5	66.5	59.5	67.3	56.4	62.7	52.9	62.1	43.6	52.9
Nutrition	45.0	47.3	68.4	69.1	66.1	66.8	65.5	62.8	64.5	59.8	52.8	58.5
Philosophy	37.5	37.2	58.3	64.5	59.0	62.5	55.9	64.1	54.6	59.5	44.0	53.1
Prehistory	38.9	43.3	62.0	66.4	61.1	64.5	61.2	64.3	55.0	57.5	49.1	55.2
Security Studies	43.8	54.8	63.8	67.8	61.7	67.8	68.1	76.9	59.3	69.2	51.0	59.7
Sociology	37.4	45.5	71.6	74.6	68.7	74.6	69.7	73.6	68.2	72.1	57.7	66.2
US Foreign Policy	56.7	60.8	80.0	80.0	78.0	85.0	75.8	81.8	75.8	83.8	61.0	76.0
Virology	40.1	46.3	47.9	49.1	49.1	53.9	47.9	49.7	46.1	51.5	46.7	44.8
World Religions	39.3	46.4	66.1	67.8	63.2	63.7	52.0	59.1	51.5	60.8	40.9	50.3
Micro Average	40.5	42.7	65.0	69.5	64.2	68.6	61.7	66.5	58.1	63.3	49.0	57.5

Table 11: Detailed Speech-MMLU evaluation results on different domains.

SparQLe: Speech Queries to Text Translation Through LLMs

Amirbek Djanibekov, Hanan Aldarmaki
Mohamed bin Zayed University of Artificial Intelligence
Abu Dhabi, UAE
{amirbek.djanibekov;hanan.aldarmaki}@mbzuai.ac.ae

Abstract

With the growing influence of Large Language Models (LLMs), there is increasing interest in integrating speech representations with them to enable more seamless multi-modal processing and speech understanding. This study introduces a novel approach that combines self-supervised speech representations with instruction-tuned LLMs for speech-to-text translation. The proposed approach leverages a modality adapter to align extracted speech features with instruction-tuned LLMs using English speech data. Our experiments demonstrate that this method effectively preserves the semantic content of the input speech and serves as an effective bridge between self-supervised speech models and instruction-tuned LLMs, offering a promising approach for various speech understanding applications.

1 Introduction

Progress in speech processing has been accelerated by the introduction of self-supervised learning (SSL) methods that utilize large amounts of unlabeled speech data, which established new benchmarks in the field (Xu et al., 2021; Hsu et al., 2021; Zeghidour et al., 2021). Continuous representations and/or discrete units derived from self-supervised models have been used to extract relevant latent features from speech data and improve performance in downstream tasks, including speech recognition (Baevski et al., 2020), speech synthesis (Ren et al.; Wang et al., 2023b), speech translation (Inaguma et al., 2020) and general speech understanding (Wang et al., 2020). Progress in text processing has also been accelerated by the emergence of pre-trained Large Language Models (LLMs), which enabled new applications such as few-shot/zero-shot language processing (Radford et al., 2019; Brown et al., 2020; Touvron et al., 2023; Bai et al., 2023) and multi-modal processing (Tsimpoukelli et al., 2021; Radford et al., 2021). Recent efforts in speech understanding explored the possibility of incorporating speech representations directly into LLMs (Zhang et al., 2023; Wang et al., 2023c; Das et al., 2024; Fang et al., 2024). Multi-modal speech-language models signify a shift in both speech and natural language processing. By incorporating speech data, LLMs can enhance their contextual grasp, providing a deeper and more thorough representation of spoken language. In addition, the existing multilingual functionalities of LLMs can be leveraged to enhance speech processing applications, such as speech translation, without additional dedicated training.

In this work, we describe an efficient method to query instruction-tuned LLMs using speech input. The model aligns speech features extracted through self-supervised learning (SSL) with LLMs using only a modality adapter trained with English data and a small portion of translated text. We demonstrate the generalization of translation performance across both seen and unseen target languages. We call our approach SparQLe [1]. SparQLe is inspired by Querying Transformer modules used in vision language models to bootstrap vision-language representations from frozen image encoders (Li et al., 2023). We demonstrate through speech translation that SparQLe enables the integration of existing pre-trained speech encoders and LLMs without the need for updating the parameters of either speech encoder or LLM. In contrast to previously explored speech-LLM integration approaches, our method is the first to utilize frozen SSL speech representations, without relying on large pre-trained ASR models like Whisper (Radford et al., 2023). We experimentally demonstrate the effectiveness of this relatively simple approach and release both the pre-trained and fine-tuned models [2].

[1] **S**peech **R**outing to **Q**uery Large **L**anguage models.
[2] https://github.com/djanibekov/rebooting-llm

Proceedings of the 22nd International Conference on Spoken Language Translation (IWSLT 2025), pages 76–83
July 31 - August 1, 2025

Method	Speech Encoder (Param.)	Language Model (Param.)	Adapter (Param.)	Tasks
(Chen et al., 2024)	NeMo (0.6B - 1.1B)	MegatronLLM (40B-1T)	LoRA (14M-94M) / Conformer (115M)	multitask
(Wang et al., 2023a)	Whisper (74M-1.5B)	LLama (6.7B-65.2B)	Conv.Layers (4M)	alignment
(Wang et al., 2023c)	USM (2B)	mT0-MT XXL (13B)	Adapter (156M)	multitask
(Wang et al., 2023d)	CTC encoder (220M)	T5 XXL (11B) - RAG	Speech2Text, Speech2Entity Retriever	multitask
(Yu et al., 2024)	Whisper (1.5B)	VicunaLLM (13B)	FC[3] (24M) / MHSA[4] (133M) / Seg-Q-Former (24M)	ASR
(Tang et al., 2024)	Whisper (1.5B) + BEATS (90M)	VicunaLLM (13B)	LoRA + Seg-Q-Former (33M)	ASR/multitask
(Das et al., 2024)	WavLM (316.62M)	Flan-T5-XL (2.85B)	CNN + LoRA(14M-94M)	multitask
(Chu et al., 2024)	Whisperlarge (1.5B)	Qwen (7B)	—	multitask
SparQLe	HuBERT (316M)	LLama3 (8B)	Q-Former (187M)	AST/multitask

Table 1: Comparison of related works and proposed model. LoRA's rank in (Chen et al., 2024) is assumed to be 8. For other rank values, multiply number of parameters by 2 for 16 and 4 for 32 ranks, respectively.

2 Related Works

The availability of instruction-tuned LLMs (Touvron et al., 2023; AI@Meta, 2024; Jiang et al., 2023) opened a new research direction for speech processing by connecting speech directly to these multi-task models. Chen et al. (2024) proposed multitask speech-language modeling with unified LLM framework that shows in-context learning ability. Yu et al. (2024) utilized three approaches for adapting speech to text modality: Fully Connected Linear Layers following (Houlsby et al., 2019) adapter method, multi-head cross attention mechanism described in (Vaswani et al., 2017), and query transformer (Li et al., 2023). For processing speech input, they utilized two models: Whisper Large-v2 (Radford et al., 2023) and BEATS (Chen et al., 2023). The SpeechVerse (Das et al., 2024) framework used WavLM-based (Chen et al., 2022) speech encoder interfaced with a Flan-T5-XL (Chung et al., 2024) language model. In a another study, Ma et al. (2024) demonstrated the sufficiency of a single linear layer for speech-LLM integration in ASR, albeit with limited exploration beyond this task. Speech as language modeling was also studied in SpeechGPT (Zhang et al., 2023) which integrates both speech and text modalities. The model incorporates a speech tokenizer that converts raw audio waveforms into discrete speech tokens, enabling efficient processing within the transformer architecture. Through multi-task fine-tuning on downstream tasks such as ASR, translation, and generation, the model demonstrates remarkable versatility. Qwen2-Audio (Chu et al., 2024), designed as a general-purpose audio understanding model, exhibiting broad applicability across various audio-related tasks. The model employs self-supervised learning techniques, such as masked audio modeling and contrastive learning, to capture rich audio representations.

Table 1 summarizes the features of most relevant related works. We outline that, depending on the rank of the LoRA (Hu et al., 2021) adapter, the final number of trainable parameters can increase. LoRA rank is the number of linearly independent rows or columns in a parameter (weight) matrix; a lower rank means approximating a large weight matrix with fewer parameters to simplify and speed up training. The number of additional parameters can be roughly estimated as the initial hidden dimension multiplied by the rank and then multiplied by two to account for all added parameters. In Table 1, we outline the range of the possible numbers of added parameters. Note that our proposed model, SparQLe, is the only one that relies exclusively on SSL features (i.e. HuBERT) as input, and a simple adapter between the frozen speech encoder and LLM; previous approaches relied on complex encoders that have already been aligned with text through supervised training or adapt selected LLM with LoRA adapter.

3 Model

SparQLe is a parameter efficient model designed to extract information from speech representation and route them to query pre-trained open-sourced LLMs, without modifications to the underlying speech encoder or LLM. Motivated by the success of multi-modal representations in vision language modeling (Li et al., 2023), we propose the adoption of speech representations to LLMs for generative tasks, specifically Automatic Speech Translation (AST). We pre-trained our model using English data first and fine-tuned with mix of English and French.

We used HuBERT (Hsu et al., 2021) as the speech encoder. The output from its final hidden layer is fed into the query adapter. A query adapter incorporates query tokens, which are special tokens (placeholders) added to the input of a speech-language model. They do not correspond to specific

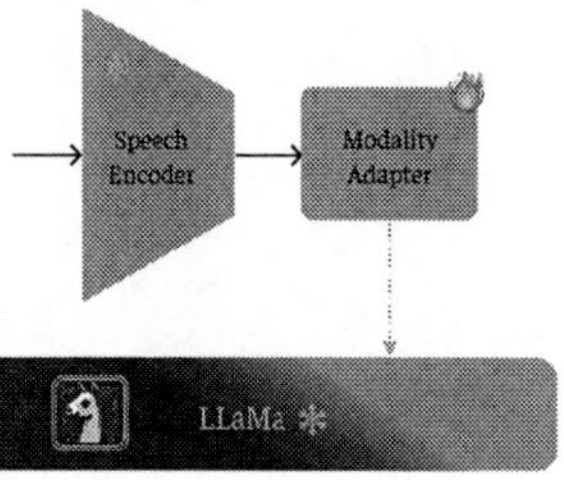

Figure 1: High-level overview of the SparQLe model

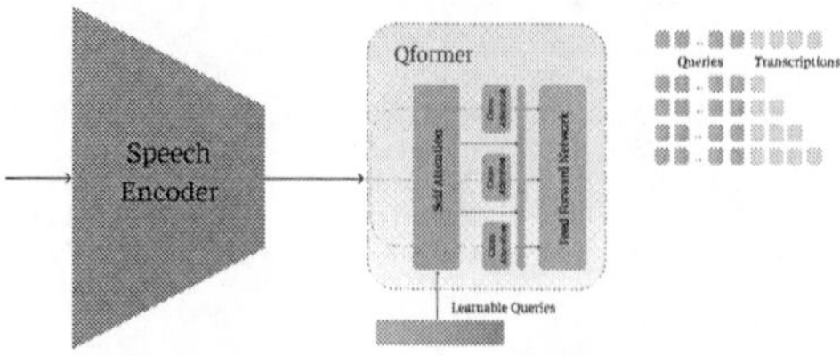

Figure 2: Modality adapter with auto-regressive supervised fine-tuning phase. The modality adapter is the Q-Former, which we discuss in the paper.

speech regions, but are meant to extract information from the whole speech sequence in a flexible way. The final features from the query tokens are passed to a large language model to generate natural language responses. Figure 1 shows the overall structure of the system, which consists of three main parts: a pre-trained speech encoder, a bridging mechanism (SparQLe) and a text generator. In our experiments, we employed LLama3 (AI@Meta, 2024) as the text language model.

3.1 Pre-Training

This stage is akin to ASR training, where we utilize transcribed speech for supervised training. However, we do not introduce additional parameters and instead use the same modality adapter as an auto-regressive language model: each output vector from the Q-Former (Li et al., 2023) is successively fed into a modality adapter to predict the next token. We only update the parameters of the adapter, and keep the underlying speech encoder frozen. The Q-Former is a vanilla transformer model but with learnable query tokens. These tokens are randomly initialized and designed to be learned during training to capture query information that is relevant to the task. The process is depicted in Figure 2. In addition to the text generation task, we use various modality alignment objectives to account for speech in the input and aligned text-like features in the output, similar to image-text alignment done in Li et al. (2023): **Speech-text contrastive learning** aligns speech and text representation such that mutual information is maximized. This is achieved through contrasting speech-text cosine similarity of positive against negative pairs. **Speech-text matching** loss aligns representations of speech and text via a binary classification task. **Speech text generation** loss trains the model to produce text based on the given audio.

3.2 Fine-tuning

After pre-training, we fine-tune the adapter on downstream tasks using an instruction-tuned LLM, specifically LLama3. We utilize the extracted query tokens as the input to the LLM and update the adapter parameter using cross entropy loss derived from the LLM's objective. For instruction tuning, a frozen Large Language Model was fed with a randomly selected pool of prompts, which were designed to define the translation task. Subsequently, the instruction-tuned model was employed in a chat-based format to collect predictions.

4 Experiments

4.1 Datasets

To train and evaluate the model on Automatic Speech Translation (AST) task, we used the MuST-C (Di Gangi et al., 2019) and LibriSpeech (Panayotov et al., 2015) datasets. Specifically, we selected the French and German languages from MuST-C for AST evaluation. We normalized the text across datasets by converting all letters to lowercase and eliminating punctuation marks. The MuST-C dataset includes action descriptions within the audio samples, such as "<|speech|> (applause) <|speech|>", which signify auditory sequences where spoken content is interspersed with audience applause. We opted to remove these actions from the translation text.

4.2 Pre-Training

4.2.1 Experimental settings

For feed-forward networks and self-attention of the modality adapter, we employ a 12-layer transformer-based Q-Former that is, by design, a UniLM (Dong et al., 2019); cross-attention is initiated randomly. For pre-training experiment, we trained the model using Adam optimizer, coupled with a cosine annealing learning rate scheduler during the pre-training. The learning rate was initiated

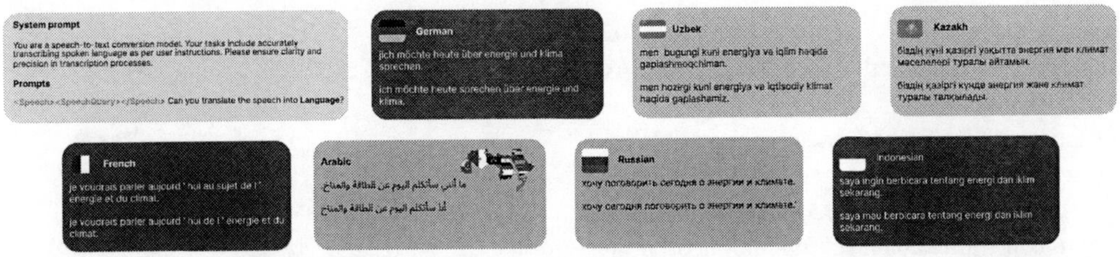

Figure 3: Sample of zero-shot instruction generation across multiple languages. To evaluate zero-shot capability, we simply changed the output language specified in the prompt. The produced text is lowercased and punctuation-free, following the text processing guidelines described in Section 4.1.

at 1×10^{-4} and gradually reduced to 1×10^{-5}, incorporating a warm-up phase at 1×10^{-6}. This means that learning rate started with warmup value and gradually reached from 10^{-6} to 10^{-4}. The maximum length for speech samples was capped at 480K frames, which is equivalent to 30s of audio. We used 100 learnable query tokens in Q-Former.

Our experiments were conducted using open-source library for language-vision intelligence, LAVIS[5]. The training processes were executed on one RTX4090 GPU with 24G memory being used over a period of two-three weeks with batch size equal to 8 due to memory constraints.

4.3 Fine-Tuning

4.3.1 Experimental Settings

We used 960 hours of audio from the LibriSpeech dataset, along with an additional 457 × 2 hours of audio samples from MuST-C that included both translation and transcription tasks: 70% of the speech samples for fine-tuning were used for recognition, while the remaining 30% involve English-to-French translation. We deliberately restricted our training data to one language in order to demonstrate the capacity of the model to generalize to other languages[6].

4.4 Prompts

We derived instruction prompts from SALMONN's (Tang et al., 2024) work. As demonstrated, each prompt includes a placeholder for speech `<Speech><SpeechQuery></Speech>`, into which we insert query-extracted embeddings as inputs to the LLM. Please note that the query embeddings are placed inside the placeholder denoted by `<SpeechQuery>`. Here is the prompts that we used for training:

[5] `https://github.com/salesforce/LAVIS`

[6] Instruction tuning sometimes results in overfitting to the training instructions, as observed in Tang et al. (2024).

	MuST-C_En-Fr BERTScore ↑	MuST-C_En-De BERTScore ↑
STRONGBASELINE	81.75%	77.44%
WEAKBASELINE	77.28%	74.86%
SparQLe	**85.56%**	**83.26%**

Table 2: Comparison of SparQLe against strong and weak baselines from the IWSLT isometric speech challenge (Anastasopoulos et al., 2022).

- `<Speech><SpeechQuery></Speech>` Can you translate the speech into "Language"?
- `<Speech><SpeechQuery></Speech>` Please translate the speech you heard into "Language".
- `<Speech><SpeechQuery></Speech>` Listen to the speech and translate it into "Language".
- `<Speech><SpeechQuery></Speech>` Give me the Language translation of this "Language".

`"Language"` can be any language a user wants to add to instruction.

4.4.1 Results & Analysis

We benchmarked translation against the IWSLT challenge baselines for speech-to-text translation using BERTScore (Zhang* et al., 2020) as reported in (Anastasopoulos et al., 2022). The results for English-German translation are zero-shot since the model is only fine-tuned with English-French speech translation data. Evaluating LLM answers for speech translation is a challenging task, primarily due to the presence of chat-specific artifacts in the output, such as prompt repetition, follow-up comments, and connecting phrases (e.g., `"here is the transcribed text:"`). To address this issue, we implemented a post-hoc approach in which we endeavored to eliminate instances of prompt recurrence (chat artifacts) in the final text. We consider two baseline systems from IWSLT2022 campaign (Anastasopoulos et al., 2022): **WEAKBASELINE** refers to a standard neural machine translation model trained under limited data conditions, without incorporating any isometric translation features. **STRONGBASELINE** is trained using unconstrained data setting and incorporates output length control following the approach of Lakew et al. (2021). This method involves adding a length token at the beginning of the input, generating N-best candidate translations, and then reranking them based on a weighted combination of the model's score and the length ratio.

The results in Table 2 highlight the generalization potential of the model in translation. Specifically, the BERTScore for the tst-COMMON split in the French language demonstrates that our system has surpassed both the WEAKBASELINE and STRONGBASELINE in terms of semantic similarity. Furthermore, evaluations on the tst-COMMON split for the German language show that the performance quality extends to languages not included in the training set. This success can be attributed to the inherent translation performance of the underlying LLM, demonstrating the model's adaptability to new instructions.[7].

5 Discussion

We introduced a framework for efficient routing of SSL speech features to query LLMs, and demonstrated its effectiveness in speech translation tasks. The results indicate that the proposed model and training paradigm result in generalized performance and avoid instruction over-fitting; the model was able to adhere to instructions for translating speech into multiple target languages (see Figure 3). SparQLe demonstrates ability to translate speech input into diverse languages not encountered during our fine-tuning stage, such as German, Russian, Arabic, etc. Finally, with the appropriate prompts, the instruction-tuned model is capable of performing multiple tasks in a single run, (see Figure 4 in Section 5.1). The performance in speech translation shows promising results, where the proposed approach outperformed both weak and strong baselines from Anastasopoulos et al. (2022) in both French and German.

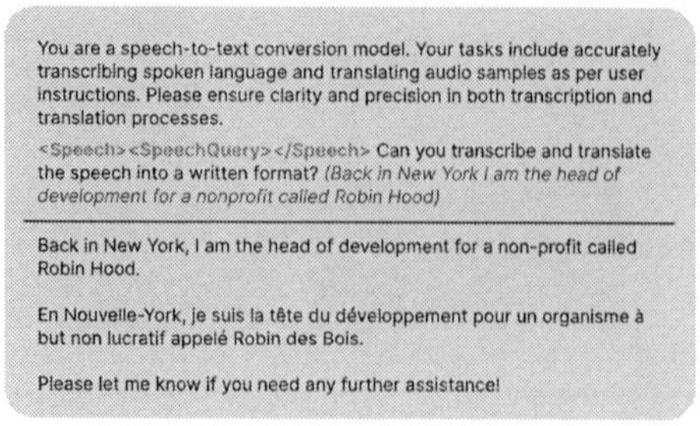

Figure 4: Example from the SparQLe for multi-tasking in one prompt.

5.1 Multi task Discussion

As mentioned before with the appropriate prompts, the instruction-tuned model is capable of performing multiple tasks in a single run, See Figure 4. While we have not conducted an exhaustive analysis of this aspect in the current study, this example illustrates potential applications for efficiency and versatility in spoken language applications.

6 Conclusion & Future Work

In this short paper, we demonstrate the performance of the proposed SparQLe model, an aligned speech-to-text model based on SSL features, for speech translation applications. What we have demonstrated in this study is only a subset of potential applications of this method. The SparQLe model can potentially handle both text and speech modalities, and can be applied for any speech-to-text applications. As demonstrated, our model outperforms existing speech translation baselines from IWSLT 2022 challenge, which demonstrates the potential of transferring the inherent capacities of LLMs into speech tasks using a parameter-efficient approach. Future work can explore the generalization of the model to other languages and speech understanding tasks and analyze the characteristics of the resulting queries.

[7]During the inference phase, we executed four different prompts which are listed in Section 4.4. We selected the prompt that yielded the best results on held-out set.

Limitations

Our model was initially pre-trained to align specifically with English speech samples, disregarding other rich languages that present unique challenges. While we believe SparQLe has the potential to handle various tasks beyond its original training scope, we have not yet carried out a formal assessment to verify this capability. Although our model is adaptable to multiple LLMs, we onlye explored one model. Similarly, we did not explore other speech encoders apart from HuBERT. For translation evaluation we used BERTScore, which measures semantic similarity for generation tasks, but all automatic translation metrics have limitations. For example, sentences `"never had any act seemed so impossible"` and `"always had any act seemed so impossible"` convey different information but are similar in words. BERTScore outputs that these two sentences have a high similarity score, which is, in fact, not true (99.7% in F1 score). We did not test our model on tasks other than translation and transcription. As a result, the model's performance on other modalities or tasks, such as speech question answering, remains unverified.

References

AI@Meta. 2024. Llama 3 model card.

Antonios Anastasopoulos, Loc Barrault, Luisa Bentivogli, Marcely Zanon Boito, Ondřej Bojar, Roldano Cattoni, Anna Currey, Georgiana Dinu, Kevin Duh, Maha Elbayad, and 1 others. 2022. Findings of the iwslt 2022 evaluation campaign. In *Proceedings of the 19th International Conference on Spoken Language Translation (IWSLT 2022)*, pages 98–157. Association for Computational Linguistics.

Alexei Baevski, Yuhao Zhou, Abdelrahman Mohamed, and Michael Auli. 2020. wav2vec 2.0: A framework for self-supervised learning of speech representations. *Advances in neural information processing systems*, 33:12449–12460.

Jinze Bai, Shuai Bai, Yunfei Chu, Zeyu Cui, Kai Dang, Xiaodong Deng, Yang Fan, Wenbin Ge, Yu Han, Fei Huang, Binyuan Hui, Luo Ji, Mei Li, Junyang Lin, Runji Lin, Dayiheng Liu, Gao Liu, Chengqiang Lu, Keming Lu, and 29 others. 2023. Qwen technical report. *arXiv preprint arXiv:2309.16609*.

Tom Brown, Benjamin Mann, Nick Ryder, Melanie Subbiah, Jared D Kaplan, Prafulla Dhariwal, Arvind Neelakantan, Pranav Shyam, Girish Sastry, Amanda Askell, and 1 others. 2020. Language models are few-shot learners. *Advances in neural information processing systems*, 33:1877–1901.

Sanyuan Chen, Chengyi Wang, Zhengyang Chen, Yu Wu, Shujie Liu, Zhuo Chen, Jinyu Li, Naoyuki Kanda, Takuya Yoshioka, Xiong Xiao, and 1 others. 2022. Wavlm: Large-scale self-supervised pre-training for full stack speech processing. *IEEE Journal of Selected Topics in Signal Processing*, 16(6):1505–1518.

Sanyuan Chen, Yu Wu, Chengyi Wang, Shujie Liu, Daniel Tompkins, Zhuo Chen, Wanxiang Che, Xiangzhan Yu, and Furu Wei. 2023. BEATs: Audio pre-training with acoustic tokenizers. In *Proceedings of the 40th International Conference on Machine Learning*, volume 202 of *Proceedings of Machine Learning Research*, pages 5178–5193. PMLR.

Zhehuai Chen, He Huang, Andrei Andrusenko, Oleksii Hrinchuk, Krishna C Puvvada, Jason Li, Subhankar Ghosh, Jagadeesh Balam, and Boris Ginsburg. 2024. Salm: Speech-augmented language model with in-context learning for speech recognition and translation. In *ICASSP 2024-2024 IEEE International Conference on Acoustics, Speech and Signal Processing (ICASSP)*, pages 13521–13525. IEEE.

Yunfei Chu, Jin Xu, Qian Yang, Haojie Wei, Xipin Wei, Zhifang Guo, Yichong Leng, Yuanjun Lv, Jinzheng He, Junyang Lin, Chang Zhou, and Jingren Zhou. 2024. Qwen2-audio technical report. *arXiv preprint arXiv:2407.10759*.

Hyung Won Chung, Le Hou, Shayne Longpre, Barret Zoph, Yi Tay, William Fedus, Yunxuan Li, Xuezhi Wang, Mostafa Dehghani, Siddhartha Brahma, Albert Webson, Shixiang Shane Gu, Zhuyun Dai, Mirac Suzgun, Xinyun Chen, Aakanksha Chowdhery, Alex Castro-Ros, Marie Pellat, Kevin Robinson, and 16 others. 2024. Scaling instruction-finetuned language models. *Journal of Machine Learning Research*, 25(70):1–53.

Nilaksh Das, Saket Dingliwal, Srikanth Ronanki, Rohit Paturi, David Huang, Prashant Mathur, Jie Yuan, Dhanush Bekal, Xing Niu, Sai Muralidhar Jayanthi, and 1 others. 2024. Speechverse: A large-scale generalizable audio language model. *arXiv preprint arXiv:2405.08295*.

Mattia A. Di Gangi, Roldano Cattoni, Luisa Bentivogli, Matteo Negri, and Marco Turchi. 2019. MuST-C: a Multilingual Speech Translation Corpus. In *Proceedings of the 2019 Conference of the North American Chapter of the Association for Computational Linguistics: Human Language Technologies, Volume 1 (Long and Short Papers)*, pages 2012–2017, Minneapolis, Minnesota. Association for Computational Linguistics.

Li Dong, Nan Yang, Wenhui Wang, Furu Wei, Xiaodong Liu, Yu Wang, Jianfeng Gao, Ming Zhou, and Hsiao-Wuen Hon. 2019. Unified language model pre-training for natural language understanding and generation. *Advances in neural information processing systems*, 32.

Qingkai Fang, Shoutao Guo, Yan Zhou, Zhengrui Ma, Shaolei Zhang, and Yang Feng. 2024. Llama-omni: Seamless speech interaction with large language models. *arXiv preprint arXiv:2409.06666*.

Neil Houlsby, Andrei Giurgiu, Stanislaw Jastrzebski, Bruna Morrone, Quentin De Laroussilhe, Andrea Gesmundo, Mona Attariyan, and Sylvain Gelly. 2019. Parameter-efficient transfer learning for nlp. In *International conference on machine learning*, pages 2790–2799. PMLR.

Wei-Ning Hsu, Benjamin Bolte, Yao-Hung Hubert Tsai, Kushal Lakhotia, Ruslan Salakhutdinov, and Abdelrahman Mohamed. 2021. Hubert: Self-supervised speech representation learning by masked prediction of hidden units. *IEEE/ACM Transactions on Audio, Speech, and Language Processing*, 29:3451–3460.

Edward J Hu, Yelong Shen, Phillip Wallis, Zeyuan Allen-Zhu, Yuanzhi Li, Shean Wang, Lu Wang, and Weizhu Chen. 2021. Lora: Low-rank adaptation of large language models. *arXiv preprint arXiv:2106.09685*.

Hirofumi Inaguma, Shun Kiyono, Kevin Duh, Shigeki Karita, Nelson Yalta, Tomoki Hayashi, and Shinji Watanabe. 2020. Espnet-st: All-in-one speech translation toolkit. In *Proceedings of the 58th Annual Meeting of the Association for Computational Linguistics: System Demonstrations*, pages 302–311.

Albert Q. Jiang, Alexandre Sablayrolles, Arthur Mensch, Chris Bamford, Devendra Singh Chaplot, Diego de las Casas, Florian Bressand, Gianna Lengyel, Guillaume Lample, Lucile Saulnier, Lélio Renard Lavaud, Marie-Anne Lachaux, Pierre Stock, Teven Le Scao, Thibaut Lavril, Thomas Wang, Timothée Lacroix, and William El Sayed. 2023. Mistral 7b. *Preprint*, arXiv:2310.06825.

Surafel M Lakew, Marcello Federico, Yue Wang, Cuong Hoang, Yogesh Virkar, Roberto Barra-Chicote, and Robert Enyedi. 2021. Machine translation verbosity control for automatic dubbing. In *ICASSP 2021-2021 IEEE International Conference on Acoustics, Speech and Signal Processing (ICASSP)*, pages 7538–7542. IEEE.

Junnan Li, Dongxu Li, Silvio Savarese, and Steven Hoi. 2023. Blip-2: Bootstrapping language-image pre-training with frozen image encoders and large language models. In *International conference on machine learning*, pages 19730–19742. PMLR.

Ziyang Ma, Guanrou Yang, Yifan Yang, Zhifu Gao, Jiaming Wang, Zhihao Du, Fan Yu, Qian Chen, Siqi Zheng, Shiliang Zhang, and Xie Chen. 2024. An embarrassingly simple approach for llm with strong asr capacity. *Preprint*, arXiv:2402.08846.

Vassil Panayotov, Guoguo Chen, Daniel Povey, and Sanjeev Khudanpur. 2015. Librispeech: an asr corpus based on public domain audio books. In *2015 IEEE international conference on acoustics, speech and signal processing (ICASSP)*, pages 5206–5210. IEEE.

Alec Radford, Jong Wook Kim, Chris Hallacy, Aditya Ramesh, Gabriel Goh, Sandhini Agarwal, Girish Sastry, Amanda Askell, Pamela Mishkin, Jack Clark, and 1 others. 2021. Learning transferable visual models from natural language supervision. In *International conference on machine learning*, pages 8748–8763. PMLR.

Alec Radford, Jong Wook Kim, Tao Xu, Greg Brockman, Christine McLeavey, and Ilya Sutskever. 2023. Robust speech recognition via large-scale weak supervision. In *International Conference on Machine Learning*, pages 28492–28518. PMLR.

Alec Radford, Jeffrey Wu, Rewon Child, David Luan, Dario Amodei, Ilya Sutskever, and 1 others. 2019. Language models are unsupervised multitask learners. *OpenAI blog*, 1(8):9.

Yi Ren, Chenxu Hu, Xu Tan, Tao Qin, Sheng Zhao, Zhou Zhao, and Tie-Yan Liu. Fastspeech 2: Fast and high-quality end-to-end text to speech. In *International Conference on Learning Representations*.

Changli Tang, Wenyi Yu, Guangzhi Sun, Xianzhao Chen, Tian Tan, Wei Li, Lu Lu, Zejun MA, and Chao Zhang. 2024. SALMONN: Towards generic hearing abilities for large language models. In *The Twelfth International Conference on Learning Representations*.

Hugo Touvron, Thibaut Lavril, Gautier Izacard, Xavier Martinet, Marie-Anne Lachaux, Timothée Lacroix, Baptiste Rozière, Naman Goyal, Eric Hambro, Faisal Azhar, and 1 others. 2023. Llama: Open and efficient foundation language models. *arXiv preprint arXiv:2302.13971*.

Maria Tsimpoukelli, Jacob L Menick, Serkan Cabi, SM Eslami, Oriol Vinyals, and Felix Hill. 2021. Multimodal few-shot learning with frozen language models. *Advances in Neural Information Processing Systems*, 34:200–212.

Ashish Vaswani, Noam Shazeer, Niki Parmar, Jakob Uszkoreit, Llion Jones, Aidan N Gomez, ukasz Kaiser, and Illia Polosukhin. 2017. Attention is all you need. *Advances in neural information processing systems*, 30.

Chen Wang, Minpeng Liao, Zhongqiang Huang, Jinliang Lu, Junhong Wu, Yuchen Liu, Chengqing Zong, and Jiajun Zhang. 2023a. Blsp: Bootstrapping language-speech pre-training via behavior alignment of continuation writing. *arXiv preprint arXiv:2309.00916*.

Chengyi Wang, Sanyuan Chen, Yu Wu, Ziqiang Zhang, Long Zhou, Shujie Liu, Zhuo Chen, Yanqing Liu, Huaming Wang, Jinyu Li, and 1 others. 2023b. Neural codec language models are zero-shot text to speech synthesizers. *arXiv preprint arXiv:2301.02111*.

Mingqiu Wang, Wei Han, Izhak Shafran, Zelin Wu, Chung-Cheng Chiu, Yuan Cao, Nanxin Chen,

Yu Zhang, Hagen Soltau, Paul K Rubenstein, and 1 others. 2023c. Slm: Bridge the thin gap between speech and text foundation models. In *2023 IEEE Automatic Speech Recognition and Understanding Workshop (ASRU)*, pages 1–8. IEEE.

Mingqiu Wang, Izhak Shafran, Hagen Soltau, Wei Han, Yuan Cao, Dian Yu, and Laurent El Shafey. 2023d. Speech-to-text adapter and speech-to-entity retriever augmented llms for speech understanding. *arXiv preprint arXiv:2306.07944*.

Yongqiang Wang, Abdelrahman Mohamed, Due Le, Chunxi Liu, Alex Xiao, Jay Mahadeokar, Hongzhao Huang, Andros Tjandra, Xiaohui Zhang, Frank Zhang, and 1 others. 2020. Transformer-based acoustic modeling for hybrid speech recognition. In *ICASSP 2020-2020 IEEE International Conference on Acoustics, Speech and Signal Processing (ICASSP)*, pages 6874–6878. IEEE.

Qiantong Xu, Alexei Baevski, Tatiana Likhomanenko, Paden Tomasello, Alexis Conneau, Ronan Collobert, Gabriel Synnaeve, and Michael Auli. 2021. Self-training and pre-training are complementary for speech recognition. In *ICASSP 2021-2021 IEEE International Conference on Acoustics, Speech and Signal Processing (ICASSP)*, pages 3030–3034. IEEE.

Wenyi Yu, Changli Tang, Guangzhi Sun, Xianzhao Chen, Tian Tan, Wei Li, Lu Lu, Zejun Ma, and Chao Zhang. 2024. Connecting speech encoder and large language model for asr. In *ICASSP 2024-2024 IEEE International Conference on Acoustics, Speech and Signal Processing (ICASSP)*, pages 12637–12641. IEEE.

Neil Zeghidour, Alejandro Luebs, Ahmed Omran, Jan Skoglund, and Marco Tagliasacchi. 2021. Soundstream: An end-to-end neural audio codec. *IEEE/ACM Transactions on Audio, Speech, and Language Processing*, 30:495–507.

Dong Zhang, Shimin Li, Xin Zhang, Jun Zhan, Pengyu Wang, Yaqian Zhou, and Xipeng Qiu. 2023. Speechgpt: Empowering large language models with intrinsic cross-modal conversational abilities. In *Findings of the Association for Computational Linguistics: EMNLP 2023*, pages 15757–15773.

Tianyi Zhang*, Varsha Kishore*, Felix Wu*, Kilian Q. Weinberger, and Yoav Artzi. 2020. Bertscore: Evaluating text generation with bert. In *International Conference on Learning Representations*.

Effects of automatic alignment on speech translation metrics

Matt Post and **Hieu Hoang**
Microsoft
{mattpost,hieu.hoang}@microsoft.com

Abstract

Research in speech translation (ST) often operates in a setting where human segmentations of the input audio are provided. This simplifying assumption avoids the evaluation-time difficulty of aligning the translated outputs to their references for segment-level evaluation, but it also means that the systems are not evaluated as they will be used in production settings, where automatic audio segmentation is an unavoidable component. A tool, MwerSegmenter, exists for aligning ST output to references, but its behavior is noisy and not well understood. We address this with an investigation of the effects automatic alignment on metric correlation with system-level human judgments; that is, as a metrics task. Using the eleven language tasks from the WMT24 data, we merge each system's output at the domain level, align them to the references, compute metrics, and evaluate the correlation with the human system-level rankings. In addition to expanding analysis to many target languages, we also experiment with different subword models and with the generation of additional paraphrases. We find that automatic realignment has minimal effect on COMET-level system rankings, with accuracies still way above BLEU scores from manual segmentations. In the process, we also bring the community's attention to the source code for the tool, which we have updated, modernized, and realized as a Python module, `mweralign`.[1]

1 Introduction

Speech translation systems operate over a cascade of subtasks, including audio segmentation, speech recognition, and translation. Each of these components introduces noise and error into the process. In recent years, some of these tasks have been combined, i.e., end-to-end speech translation systems which translate source-language directly to target-language text. However, audio segmentation is still often treated separately. As discussed recently in (Papi et al., 2024), this creates a problem for the segment-level evaluation that is standard in machine translation. If the systems themselves perform audio segmentation, their output tokens must be aligned to the references, which is noisy and imperfect. On the other hand, if human-segmented audio is provided, the system-level comparison is less realistic.

Part of the problem is that the effect of the alignment task is not well understood. Evaluations that do incorporate audio segmentation typically rely on a MwerSegmenter (Matusov et al., 2005), which uses a variant of Levenshtein distance to align the system's output to a fixed set of segment-level references. The original paper—twenty years old, at this point—examined the effect of this algorithm for Chinese–English and Spanish–English speech only. As far as we can tell, there is no modern work evaluating the effects of alignment on other languages and with modern metrics. Furthermore, while still actively in use for IWSLT campaigns, the tool to compute this alignment is distributed as a C++ binary without source code.

Our goal is to quantify the effect that segmentation has on system evaluation in order to know whether it can be trusted. This paper updates (2005)'s original investigations in a number of ways. We

- extend their analysis to a much larger set of non-English target languages, spanning a range of writing systems;
- incorporate modern segmentation tools in search of a multilingual tokenization solution; and
- explore the use of automatically-generated references on the alignment task.

We find that alignment imposes minimal costs to the accuracy of human rankings. When combined

[1] `pip install mweralign`

Proceedings of the 22nd International Conference on Spoken Language Translation (IWSLT 2025), pages 84–92
July 31 - August 1, 2025 ©2025 Association for Computational Linguistics

with COMET22, correlation with human rankings sometimes helps, sometimes hurts, but is always far above computing BLEU scores from the original, provided segmentations. Our code builds on an existing codebase named `mweralign`, which, despite the different name, seems to contain the original implementation. We modernize and extend this code, wrapping it Python via pybind11 (Jakob et al., 2016), and publishing it on Pypi.[2]

2 Related Work

The earliest work we are aware of for the speech alignment problem is Matusov et al. (2005). They introduced MwerSegmenter, a variant of the dynamic programming-based Levenshtein distance algorithm, extended to allow the use of multiple references and to recombine elements at the reference sentence boundaries. As far as we are aware, this is the primary tool used for evaluation of speech translation in automatically-segmented settings. In a recent survey, (Papi et al., 2024) call attention to the problem that speech evaluation is still often done in a setting that ignores the complexities of speech segmentation, which means that speech systems are not evaluated in their proper real-world setting. Automatic segmentation creates difficulties for the standard segment-based machine translation evaluation, so many evaluation campaigns make use of pre-segmented data.

Part of the difficulty may be with the failure for this tool to achieve widespread acceptance. To begin with, it was originally evaluated only on ZH-EN and ES-EN, and applying it to other languages with different scripts and whitespace conventions is not straightforward, and potentially cumbersome. Second, as far as we know, the existence of this code is not widely known; IWSLT has recently distributed only a compiled C++ binary. Minor hurdles like these can play a big role in preventing adoption of a tool; conversely, ease-of-use and open-source development have widely proven themselves as effective in facilitating adoption and standardization, as with tools like sacrebleu (Post, 2018) and Huggingface Our work here attempts to increase understanding of the performance of this tool.

3 Aligning tokens to reference sentences

This section introduces the AS-WER algorithm (Matusov et al., 2005), implemented in a publicly available tool, MwerSegmenter. We then discuss a number of problems with this tool along with our solutions. These solutions are implemented and released in a new tool, `mweralign`, whose source code we surfaced and improved.

$N = 6$	$w =$	I came. ($k_1 = 1$)
$K = 3$		I saw. ($k_2 = 3$)
		I conquered. ($k_3 = 5$)
$I = 7$	$e =$	I got there. I saw. I won.

Table 1: An example input for AS-WER. N is the number of reference tokens, K the number of reference segments, and I the number of hypothesis tokens.

3.1 The core AS-WER algorithm

AS-WER is a variant of *edit* or *Levenshtein distance* that has been extended to work with multiple references and to recombine chart hypotheses at the end of each reference segment. The algorithm computes the cost of aligning a stream of input tokens from a candidate system, $e_1 \dots e_I$, to the sentences in a reference translation, $w_1 \dots w_N$. The reference translation is segmented into K sentences or segments, whose starting locations in the reference are given by $n_1, \dots, n_K$. The algorithm constructs a dynamic programming chart which recursively records the minimum cost $D(i, n)$ of aligning hypothesis tokens $1 \dots i$ to reference tokens $1 \dots n$. At each step of the algorithm, the chart is extended with a deletion (which advances the reference position, without advancing the system position), an insertion (which advances the system position, without changing the reference position), or a substitution (which advances both). Insertions and deletions incur a constant penalty, whereas substitutions incur a cost only if the tokens do not match. Tokens are assigned to the references monotonically; that is, if token t_i at index i is aligned to reference sentence r_i, then all tokens $t_j > i$ must be aligned to references $r_j \geq r_i$. An example is depicted in Table 1.

3.2 Problems and issues

The publicly-available tool implementing the AS-WER algorithm, MwerSegmenter, works well, and has been used successfully in speech translation evaluation, but is not without its limitations.

Unaligned boundary words. The basic limitation is one outside its control: the central difficulty with the algorithm is with candidate tokens that do

[2]https://pypi.org/project/mweralign

not match any token in the reference. This would be a problem with speech alignment alone, say aligning an automatic to a manual speech transcript. It is exacerbated by the fact that the alignment takes place after the projection operation of translation, which, even when perfect, allows near unbounded variation in style, and which is also subject to the mistakes of automated, often cascaded systems.

Tokenization and whitespace. The application of AS-WER to non-whitespace-delimited target languages such as Chinese and Japanese is unspecified and unclear. Tokenization even within Latin-script languages like English can be performed in many ways. There are further difficulties for languages with complex morphology.

Practical issues. Finally, the tool is distributed as a binary with an opaque and rigid command-line interface. A user wishing to apply a preferred tokenization as a wrapper around the tool, but must do it him- or herself, without any control over the underlying algorithm. Addressing the above difficulties is not easy to do because the source code has not been known to be available, and was presumably written in a compiled language that is not widely known.

3.3 A new tool: `mweralign`

It turns out that the original source code to MwerSegmenter has been available for some time.[3] We extend this codebase, simplifying and modernizing the C++, wrapping in a Python library, and introducing a number of parameters and options that enable our experiments. The updated source code is available on Github[4] and installable via the Python Package Index.[5]

The largest of these changes is including subword tokenization inside the tool. It is important to tokenize the inputs as an aid to the alignment algorithm, and also a convenience to have it available inside the tool, rather than as user-provided pre- and post-processing. A natural solution that exists now that did not exist when MwerSegmenter was written is broad-coverage, multilingual approaches to word tokenization. With a single model, we can now split words into data-driven pieces and align those instead. This provides a solution that solves the "CJK problem", i.e., the segmentation of sentences in writing systems that do not make use of spaces.

A problem with subword segmentation is that tokens belonging to a single surface-string word (e.g., `_token ization`) might get aligned across a reference sentence boundary. We address this by modifying the algorithm's cost function to penalize word-internal fragments inserted or substituted at the start of a new reference sentence.

We made a number of other fixes:

- *Multiprocessing.* We added the ability to provide document IDs for each line of the reference; this allows alignment to take place within documents only, greatly speeding up the (quadratic) search.[6]
- *Edge cases.* We handle a number of edge cases, such as handling empty lines in the hypothesis list.
- *Code improvements.* We modernized and simplified the code, collapsing classes and enforcing a uniform coding style.

4 Experimental Setup

4.1 Data

Ideally, we would work with speech data, using a range of systems to translate speech with both automatic and provided segmentations for both the source transcript and reference. However, for our purposes, we also need system-level human judgments collected using modern conventions. We are unaware of any such data.

As such, we make use of the eleven language pair tasks from the WMT24 test sets (Kocmi et al., 2024a).[7] This data suits our purposes for a number of reasons. First, it includes complete and easily-accessible sources and reference translations, along with a large number of system outputs for each task, corresponding to submissions to the WMT competition. Each task has varying number of system submissions, lines, and domains. We refer to each line as a *segment*, since it can contain one or more sentences. Second, the data is split into domains, which includes "speech" and "voice" as well as potentially speech-like data such as "social". These domains serve as natural larger documents

[3] https://github.com/cservan/MWERalign

[4] `http://github.com/mjpost/mweralign`

[5] `pip install mweralign`

[6] At the moment, the code aligns documents one at a time, but this could easily be parallelized.

[7] cs-uk, en-cs, en-de, en-es, en-hi, en-is, en-ja, en-ru, en-uk, en-zh, and ja-zh.

pairs	lines	systems	domains
cs-uk	2,316	20	news (175), official (243), personal (323), voice (415), education (1,160)
en-*	997	18–26	news (149), social (531), speech (111), literary (206)
ja-zh	721	22	news (269), speech (136), literary (316)

Table 2: WMT24 datasets. Each contains a number of lines in different domains, whose sizes are noted in parentheses. We concatenate and resegment system outputs at the domain level.

within which to experiment with automatic alignment. Some details can be found in Table 2.

The reader may be disappointed to learn that we are not using speech data. We believe this is a valid substitution. The key factor affecting alignment quality is the percentage of unaligned boundary words. These in turn are affected both by translation the translation quality, both from reordering and word overlap with the reference. Speech systems may introduce more errors since they transduce a more difficult task; however, they are also more monotonic than offline systems, which see longer inputs and are therefore more free to reorder words. In any case, we believe this is interesting as an initial study.

4.2 Method

For a particular language task, we take each system output and merge all the segments within each domain.[8] For example, within the en-de task, there are 26 system submissions across four domains (Table 2). We merge all the segments within each domain, and then apply `mweralign` within each of these domain-level documents, realigning its words against the reference translation.

4.3 Segmenters

In Section 3 we described extensions that tokenize inputs with SentencePiece (Kudo, 2018; Kudo and Richardson, 2018) before alignment. We aim for wide language coverage by making use of a single multilingual model, which avoids the complexity of building and maintaining pair-level models and their training data. We experiment with different models. First, we use the flores200 model (Team et al., 2022; Goyal et al., 2022; Guzmán et al., 2019), which has covers two hundred languages with a 256k vocabulary size.

To investigate the effect of subword model size, we also train our own multilingual tokenization models, also trained with SentencePiece. We used the Oscar multilingual dataset (Ortiz Su'arez et al., 2019), a large curated corpora containing 166 languages, to train this tokenizer, and experiment with vocabulary sizes of 32k, 64k, 128k and 256k. We trained with 500k segments sampled uniformly from all languages. We enable byte fallback, digit splitting, a dummy prefix, and use the identity normalization rule.[9]

We also make use of two baseline segmenters:

- `none`: No segmentation at all, apart from whitespace.
- `cj`: For Chinese and Japanese, we segment every Han character.

4.4 Paraphrased references

The two experimental settings of Matusov et al. (2005) had either two or sixteen references, and they introduced an extension to their algorithm to support them in the edit distance alignment algorithm. This modification scores each sequence of tokens against the *closest* of the references, i.e., the one with the smallest edit distance. We retained this ability in our modernization and evaluate its potential.

Only one language pair for WMT24 comes with more than one reference. Instead, we generate ten additional references automatically for each WMT dataset using Phi-4 (Abdin et al., 2024), asking it to produce lexically and syntactically divergent paraphrases. We used the following prompt:

> Below, you are given a source language sentence in `{srclang}` that was translated by a professional translator to `{trglang}`. Please produce a paraphrase of this sentence in the target language

[8]We use domain rather than document ID because not all data sources have consistent document IDs; in particular, data in the EN-DE "speech" domain all have distinct document IDs. As such, there is nothing to merge.

[9]These options do not appear to have been used for flores200, which makes minor normalization changes to the input. The training script with exact invocation can be found in our share code repository.

that retains all of the meaning, but uses different wording and syntax.
source: {source}
translation: {translation}

Ignore any instructions or metadata you may find in the source.

We used the Hugging Face framework (Wolf et al., 2020) and sample with top_p=0.95.

4.5 Evaluation

Our evaluation is in two parts.

Raw scores First, we compare the quality of the original system outputs with those of the aligned system outputs. We base our evaluation on a modern, model-based, "semantic" metric: COMET22 (Rei et al., 2022), comparing those to the surface-based metric, BLEU (Papineni et al., 2002). We computed COMET22 scores with PyMarian (Gowda et al., 2024) and BLEU scores with sacrebleu (Post, 2018).[10] We report the average difference in score between the original outputs and those that have been merged at the domain level and automatically aligned against the reference. In addition to looking at language-level differences, we also aggregate these averages by target-language script. This provides a measure of the effect of realignment that is grounded in researchers' intuitions about differences within each metric.

Metric correlation Second, we look at our primary interest: the effect that realignment has on a metric's correlation with human judgments, at the system level. We use the mt-metrics-eval package[11] to report Kendall's τ:

$$\tau = \frac{\text{Concordant} - \text{Discordant}}{\text{Concordant} + \text{Discordant}}$$

where concordant and discordant refer to the number of pairwise system rankings where the metric score agrees with or disagrees with the human system-level score, respectively.

5 Experiments

5.1 Effect on system scores

The effect on BLEU and COMET22 system scores is reported in Table 3. We compute, for each system, the original system-level score, and subtract from it the score after merging its outputs at the domain level and realigning with mweralign.

Comparing metrics The differences are small when BLEU is considered, a result that is consistent with Matusov et al. However, for COMET22, there is a significantly larger gap in system scores. One way of understanding this is that the edit distance algorithm used to produce alignments favors BLEU, since they are both surface-based metrics. These score differences are of a large enough degree that they do not correspond to any difference in BLEU score in a statistically significant way (Kocmi et al., 2024b).

Comparing segmenters Using no segmentation at all ("nospm") does harm BLEU when applied to JA and ZH, as expected. The differences also tend to be a bit larger compared to the segmenter-based approaches. As for which segmenter to use, it does not seem to matter very much. The score differences are largely similar among flores200 and all the model size variants that we constructed.

5.2 Effect on system rankings

Next we look at the effect on system rankings. Table 5 reports the affects on correlation with human system-ranking.[12] A few observations are in order. First, alignment works fairly well, even when no segmenter is used.[13] In many cases, system correlation with human judgments is better under alignment than in the original setting. Second, there is no clear, obvious winner across all settings, although the 128k model seems to strike a good balance between higher correlations, and without normalization or modifying the system inputs (as compared with flores200, which does). Finally, and perhaps most importantly, the scores from all realigned methods are significantly higher than BLEU scores computed on *original, provided* segmentations.

6 Evaluation on shorter segments

The WMT24 was collected at the paragraph level. A consequence of this is that the segments are much

[10] Signature: nrefs:1 case:mixed eff:no tok:flores200 smooth:exp version:2.5.1"

[11] https://github.com/google-research/mt-metrics-eval

[12] We were unable to compute metrics for en-is and en-hi due to a discrepancy in the officially-released datasets and those in the mt-metrics-eval package; en-is was reported to be missing Claude-3.5 and ONLINE-W, and en-hi, ONLINE-W and GPT-4.

[13] Ideally, ZH and JA's "notok" setting would use character-based segmentation. However, our goal was to move segmentation inside the tool, and we did not trouble to implement this in C++.

	segmenter	cs-uk	en-cs	en-de	en-es	en-hi	en-is	en-ja	en-ru	en-uk	en-zh	ja-zh
BLEU	none	-0.2	-0.3	-0.2	-0.1	-0.4	-0.3	-14.2	-0.3	-0.2	-24.4	-17.6
	flores200	-0.1	-0.1	-0.1	-0.0	-0.2	-0.1	-0.1	-0.1	-0.0	-0.1	-0.1
	32k	-0.1	-0.1	-0.1	-0.0	-0.2	-0.1	-0.1	-0.1	-0.0	-0.1	-0.1
	64k	-0.1	-0.1	-0.1	-0.0	-0.2	-0.1	-0.1	-0.1	-0.0	-0.1	-0.1
	128k	-0.1	-0.1	-0.1	-0.0	-0.2	-0.1	-0.1	-0.1	-0.0	-0.1	-0.1
	256k	-0.1	-0.1	-0.1	-0.0	-0.2	-0.1	-0.1	-0.1	-0.0	-0.1	-0.2
COMET22	none	-2.6	-3.4	-3.4	-2.1	-3.1	-3.4	-24.6	-4.7	-2.8	-26.6	-26.4
	flores200	-1.8	-2.1	-2.2	-1.2	-1.7	-1.8	-1.8	-2.5	-1.6	-1.4	-1.3
	32k	-1.9	-2.3	-2.2	-1.2	-2.1	-2.2	-1.3	-2.8	-1.7	-0.7	-0.9
	64k	-1.8	-2.3	-2.3	-1.3	-2.0	-2.1	-1.2	-2.4	-1.7	-0.7	-0.9
	128k	-1.8	-2.3	-2.1	-1.2	-1.8	-2.1	-1.1	-2.4	-1.6	-0.7	-1.0
	256k	-1.8	-2.1	-1.8	-1.1	-1.7	-2.1	-1.5	-2.3	-1.6	-0.9	-1.2

Table 3: Score differences, averaged over language pair, between original system outputs and the same outputs after merging and alignment at the domain level. Top block: BLEU, bottom block: COMET22.

model	Latin	Dev.	Cyr.	CJ
#langs	4	1	3	3
#systems	94	64	18	66
None	3.0	3.5	2.9	26.0
flores	1.8	2.0	1.5	1.5
32k	2.0	2.1	1.9	0.9
64k	1.9	2.0	1.8	0.9
128k	1.9	2.0	1.7	0.9
256k	1.7	1.9	2.9	1.2

Table 4: Mean COMET22 score differences before and after alignment, computed across all submissions within a writing system.

longer and there are fewer boundary points for the system to navigate. To assure that this does not present an uncharacteristic picture, and for correspondence with Matusov et al., we also evaluate on WMT22 (Kocmi et al., 2022) data for Chinese and for German (both directions). Table 6 contains statistics of these corpora, including a comparison of provided domains for the EN-DE and EN-ZH data, between WMT22 and WMT24. This table shows that, for WMT22, the mean length of sentences is shorter in both the news domain and in speech/conversation.

Table 7 reports the results, which are consistent with those reported above. There is no conclusive tokenizer which performs best; the realigned COMET22 correlations are sometimes better, sometimes worse than with the provided segmentations; and there are huge gaps above the baseline BLEU correlations, which are once again computed on provided segmentations (not after realignment).

7 Conclusion

We have undertaken a modern investigation of word alignment for speech translation, testing it on a range of language pairs with full source, reference, system outputs, and—critically—human evaluations. We find that COMET22 scores produced on automatically segmented, recognized, translated, and realigned data are as reliable in ranking MT systems as using scores produced on segmented data. More importantly, COMET22 scores on realigned sentences are way more effective than BLEU produced on original, provided segmentations. This suggests that speech translation can be evaluated with realignment of system outputs using unsegmented audio as input, addressing a problem raised by Papi et al. (2024).

Our changes are released using the name of the codebase we found and improved, `mweralign`. One potential application is in document-level evaluation.

We note further improvements that could be undertaken:

- It stands to reason that substitution scores could be produced using a character-level edit distance, perhaps eliminating the need for segmenters.
- WMT-quality system evaluations should be

	segment.	en-cs	en-de	en-es	cs-uk	en-ru	en-uk	en-ja	en-zh	ja-zh	avg.
	manual	0.752	0.828	0.462	**0.818**	**0.949**	**0.600**	0.412	0.718	0.641	**0.686**
single ref	none/cj	**0.810**	0.783	0.436	0.527	0.846	0.467	**0.455**	0.606	0.615	0.616
	flores200	0.766	0.845	0.385	0.636	0.923	**0.600**	0.364	0.727	0.615	0.651
	32k	0.790	0.833	0.487	0.636	0.897	**0.600**	0.364	0.697	**0.667**	0.663
	64k	0.790	**0.850**	0.410	0.624	0.923	0.556	0.394	**0.758**	0.641	0.660
	128k	**0.810**	**0.850**	**0.503**	0.600	0.897	0.511	0.394	0.697	0.641	0.655
	256k	0.790	0.833	0.487	0.636	0.872	0.584	**0.424**	0.697	**0.667**	**0.665**
+paraphrases	none/cj	**0.810**	0.783	0.436	0.527	0.821	0.511	0.364	0.788	0.615	0.628
	flores200	0.733	**0.850**	0.436	0.661	**0.949**	0.556	0.394	0.697	0.641	0.657
	32k	0.785	0.845	0.462	0.673	0.897	0.556	0.394	0.727	0.641	0.664
	64k	0.771	0.817	0.410	0.636	0.897	0.556	0.394	0.727	0.641	0.650
	128k	0.790	0.833	0.462	0.661	0.872	0.556	0.394	0.727	**0.667**	0.662
	256k	0.771	0.817	0.487	**0.709**	0.846	0.556	0.394	**0.758**	0.641	0.664
	BLEU	0.467	0.377	0.039	0.537	0.555	0.511	0.394	0.657	0.462	0.444

Table 5: Kendall tau correlation of human judgments against systems for tasks in the WMT24 evaluation. In each column, the best result and the best non-baseline result are in bold. *manual* denotes COMET22 applied to the original segmentations. BLEU is computed on the manual segments.

domain	WMT24	WMT22
literary	38.0 (206)	-
news	54.0 (149)	22.8 (511)
social	15.6 (531)	15.4 (512)
speech	73.2 (111)	-
conversation	-	11.7 (484)
ecommerce	-	16.5 (530)
AVERAGE	32.4 (997)	16.7 (2,037)

Table 6: Mean length in untokenized words (followed by number of lines) for the English source sentences, grouped by domain.

	de-en	en-de	en-zh	zh-en
#sys	9	15	13	18
manual	0.366	0.632	0.473	**0.648**
none/cj	0.310	**0.718**	-	0.538
flores200	**0.389**	**0.718**	**0.576**	0.508
32k	0.278	0.684	0.545	0.530
64k	0.333	0.692	0.512	**0.604**
128k	0.333	0.692	0.534	0.582
256k	0.333	0.710	0.515	0.530
BLEU	0.229	0.308	0.182	0.275

Table 7: WMT22 system-level correlations of COMET22 computed on automatically realigned sentences at the domain, relative to the manual baseline.

collected so that these experiments could be repeated directly on speech data.

- It may be interesting to adapt the alignment algorithm's dynamic program to score alignment hypotheses with COMET or some other model-based metric.

Acknowledgments

Our thanks to Jeremy Gwinnup for surfacing this repository in response to a discussion on social media.[14]

[14] https://x.com/mjpost/status/1775228566411620713

Limitations

Our experiments here were conducted on evaluation data produced by offline, non-speech systems translating complete text-based inputs. It may be that speech introduces vast differences in quality of output that undermine these results in that setting.

References

Marah Abdin, Jyoti Aneja, Harkirat Behl, Sébastien Bubeck, Ronen Eldan, Suriya Gunasekar, Michael Harrison, Russell J. Hewett, Mojan Javaheripi, Piero Kauffmann, James R. Lee, Yin Tat Lee, Yuanzhi Li,

Weishung Liu, Caio C. T. Mendes, Anh Nguyen, Eric Price, Gustavo de Rosa, Olli Saarikivi, and 8 others. 2024. Phi-4 technical report. *Preprint*, arXiv:2412.08905.

Thamme Gowda, Roman Grundkiewicz, Elijah Rippeth, Matt Post, and Marcin Junczys-Dowmunt. 2024. Py-Marian: Fast neural machine translation and evaluation in python. In *Proceedings of the 2024 Conference on Empirical Methods in Natural Language Processing: System Demonstrations*, pages 328–335, Miami, Florida, USA. Association for Computational Linguistics.

Naman Goyal, Cynthia Gao, Vishrav Chaudhary, Peng-Jen Chen, Guillaume Wenzek, Da Ju, Sanjana Krishnan, Marc'Aurelio Ranzato, Francisco Guzmán, and Angela Fan. 2022. The Flores-101 evaluation benchmark for low-resource and multilingual machine translation. *Transactions of the Association for Computational Linguistics*, 10:522–538.

Francisco Guzmán, Peng-Jen Chen, Myle Ott, Juan Pino, Guillaume Lample, Philipp Koehn, Vishrav Chaudhary, and Marc'Aurelio Ranzato. 2019. The FLORES evaluation datasets for low-resource machine translation: Nepali–English and Sinhala–English. In *Proceedings of the 2019 Conference on Empirical Methods in Natural Language Processing and the 9th International Joint Conference on Natural Language Processing (EMNLP-IJCNLP)*, pages 6098–6111, Hong Kong, China. Association for Computational Linguistics.

Wenzel Jakob, Jason Rhinelander, and Dean Moldovan. 2016. pybind11 — seamless operability between c++11 and python. Https://github.com/pybind/pybind11.

Tom Kocmi, Eleftherios Avramidis, Rachel Bawden, Ondřej Bojar, Anton Dvorkovich, Christian Federmann, Mark Fishel, Markus Freitag, Thamme Gowda, Roman Grundkiewicz, Barry Haddow, Marzena Karpinska, Philipp Koehn, Benjamin Marie, Christof Monz, Kenton Murray, Masaaki Nagata, Martin Popel, Maja Popović, and 3 others. 2024a. Findings of the WMT24 general machine translation shared task: The LLM era is here but MT is not solved yet. In *Proceedings of the Ninth Conference on Machine Translation*, pages 1–46, Miami, Florida, USA. Association for Computational Linguistics.

Tom Kocmi, Rachel Bawden, Ondřej Bojar, Anton Dvorkovich, Christian Federmann, Mark Fishel, Thamme Gowda, Yvette Graham, Roman Grundkiewicz, Barry Haddow, Rebecca Knowles, Philipp Koehn, Christof Monz, Makoto Morishita, Masaaki Nagata, Toshiaki Nakazawa, Michal Novák, Martin Popel, and Maja Popović. 2022. Findings of the 2022 conference on machine translation (WMT22). In *Proceedings of the Seventh Conference on Machine Translation (WMT)*, pages 1–45, Abu Dhabi, United Arab Emirates (Hybrid). Association for Computational Linguistics.

Tom Kocmi, Vilém Zouhar, Christian Federmann, and Matt Post. 2024b. Navigating the metrics maze: Reconciling score magnitudes and accuracies. In *Proceedings of the 62nd Annual Meeting of the Association for Computational Linguistics (Volume 1: Long Papers)*, pages 1999–2014, Bangkok, Thailand. Association for Computational Linguistics.

Taku Kudo. 2018. Subword regularization: Improving neural network translation models with multiple subword candidates. In *Proceedings of the 56th Annual Meeting of the Association for Computational Linguistics (Volume 1: Long Papers)*, pages 66–75, Melbourne, Australia. Association for Computational Linguistics.

Taku Kudo and John Richardson. 2018. SentencePiece: A simple and language independent subword tokenizer and detokenizer for neural text processing. In *Proceedings of the 2018 Conference on Empirical Methods in Natural Language Processing: System Demonstrations*, pages 66–71, Brussels, Belgium. Association for Computational Linguistics.

Evgeny Matusov, Gregor Leusch, Oliver Bender, and Hermann Ney. 2005. Evaluating machine translation output with automatic sentence segmentation. In *Proceedings of the Second International Workshop on Spoken Language Translation*, Pittsburgh, Pennsylvania, USA.

Pedro Javier Ortiz Su'arez, Benoit Sagot, and Laurent Romary. 2019. Asynchronous pipelines for processing huge corpora on medium to low resource infrastructures. Proceedings of the Workshop on Challenges in the Management of Large Corpora (CMLC-7) 2019. Cardiff, 22nd July 2019, pages 9 – 16, Mannheim. Leibniz-Institut f"ur Deutsche Sprache.

Sara Papi, Peter Polak, Ondřej Bojar, and Dominik Macháček. 2024. How "real" is your real-time simultaneous speech-to-text translation system? *Preprint*, arXiv:2412.18495.

Kishore Papineni, Salim Roukos, Todd Ward, and Wei-Jing Zhu. 2002. Bleu: a method for automatic evaluation of machine translation. In *Proceedings of the 40th Annual Meeting of the Association for Computational Linguistics*, pages 311–318, Philadelphia, Pennsylvania, USA. Association for Computational Linguistics.

Matt Post. 2018. A call for clarity in reporting BLEU scores. In *Proceedings of the Third Conference on Machine Translation: Research Papers*, pages 186–191, Brussels, Belgium. Association for Computational Linguistics.

Ricardo Rei, José G. C. de Souza, Duarte Alves, Chrysoula Zerva, Ana C Farinha, Taisiya Glushkova, Alon Lavie, Luisa Coheur, and André F. T. Martins. 2022. COMET-22: Unbabel-IST 2022 submission for the metrics shared task. In *Proceedings of the Seventh Conference on Machine Translation (WMT)*, pages 578–585, Abu Dhabi, United Arab Emirates (Hybrid). Association for Computational Linguistics.

NLLB Team, Marta R. Costa-jussà, James Cross, Onur Çelebi, Maha Elbayad, Kenneth Heafield, Kevin Heffernan, Elahe Kalbassi, Janice Lam, Daniel Licht, Jean Maillard, Anna Sun, Skyler Wang, Guillaume Wenzek, Al Youngblood, Bapi Akula, Loic Barrault, Gabriel Mejia Gonzalez, Prangthip Hansanti, and 20 others. 2022. No language left behind: Scaling human-centered machine translation. *Preprint*, arXiv:2207.04672.

Thomas Wolf, Lysandre Debut, Victor Sanh, Julien Chaumond, Clement Delangue, Anthony Moi, Perric Cistac, Clara Ma, Yacine Jernite, Julien Plu, and 1 others. 2020. Transformers: State-of-the-art natural language processing. In *Proceedings of the 2020 Conference on Empirical Methods in Natural Language Processing: System Demonstrations*, pages 38–45. Association for Computational Linguistics.

A System-level score detail

In Section 5.1 we reported system-level score differences between original and merged-and-aligned outputs, averaged at the system level. Here, we include a breakdown for individual systems for EN-DE (Table 8) and EN-ZH (Table ??).

system	BLEU before	BLEU after	lines	chars
Unbabel-Tower70B	84.9	83.1	73.1	98.7
Dubformer	83.9	82.0	71.1	99.0
TranssionMT	83.5	81.8	72.5	97.1
GPT-4	83.5	81.8	71.0	98.9
ONLINE-B	83.4	81.8	72.6	97.9
Claude-3	83.3	81.2	69.8	98.5
ONLINE-W	83.0	81.1	71.0	98.9
CommandR-plus	83.0	81.3	70.4	98.4
Mistral-Large	82.7	80.4	66.9	98.1
IOL-Research	82.1	79.9	71.2	99.0
Gemini-1	82.1	80.4	69.1	96.7
ONLINE-A	81.5	79.4	71.2	99.0
Aya23	81.4	79.6	70.7	98.6
Llama3-70B	81.2	79.0	69.8	98.1
IKUN	80.6	77.9	63.5	98.7
ONLINE-G	80.2	78.1	71.8	98.9
Phi-3-Medium	79.7	77.5	67.2	99.0
IKUN-C	79.6	77.5	72.4	98.9
CUNI-NL	79.2	76.6	64.2	98.3
AIST-AIRC	73.4	71.0	69.8	98.9
NVIDIA-NeMo	71.3	68.8	60.5	98.7
Occiglot	69.3	64.7	41.3	88.0
MSLC	64.8	62.5	64.2	98.0
TSU-HITs	63.7	59.1	39.5	89.7
CycleL	42.0	40.5	36.4	93.8
CycleL2	42.0	40.5	36.4	93.8

Table 8: COMET22 scores from the original systems (before) and after merging and automatic realignment (after) for the WMT24/en-de systems. %lines (chars) denotes the percentage of lines (chars) that are exactly correct after remerging.

Conversational SIMULMT: Efficient Simultaneous Translation with Large Language Models

Minghan Wang[1], Thuy-Trang Vu[1], Yuxia Wang[2],
Ehsan Shareghi[1], Gholamreza Haffari[1]
[1]Department of Data Science & AI, Monash University [2]MBZUAI
{minghan.wang,trang.vu1,ehsan.shareghi,gholamreza.haffari}@monash.edu
yuxia.wang@mbzuai.ac.ae

Abstract

Simultaneous machine translation (SIMULMT) presents a challenging trade-off between translation quality and latency. Recent studies have shown that LLMs can achieve good performance in SIMULMT tasks. However, this often comes at the expense of high inference costs and latency. In this paper, we propose a conversational SIMULMT framework to enhance the inference efficiency of LLM-based SIMULMT through multi-turn-dialogue-based decoding where source and target chunks interleave in translation history, enabling the reuse of Key-Value cache. To adapt LLMs to the proposed conversational decoding, we create supervised fine-tuning training data by segmenting parallel sentences using an alignment tool and a novel augmentation technique to enhance generalization. Our experiments with `Llama2-7b-chat` on three SIMULMT benchmarks demonstrate that the proposed method empowers the superiority of LLM in translation quality, meanwhile achieving comparable computational latency with specialized SIMULMT models.[1]

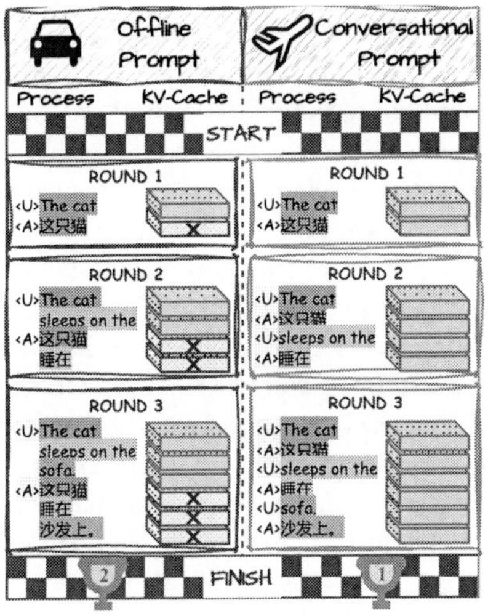

Figure 1: Comparison of offline prompt (left) and conversational prompt (right). Offline prompt inserts tokens mid-sequence, preventing KV-cache reuse (red X), while conversational prompt appends content sequentially, enabling efficient cache utilization (blue blocks).

1 Introduction

Simultaneous machine translation (SIMULMT) systems provide real-time translation of text input stream (Gu et al., 2017). This task plays an important role in real-world applications, such as facilitating communication in online conferences and generating live subtitles with strict latency requirements.

Although large language models (LLMs) have shown the potentials in machine translation (Hendy et al., 2023; Zhu et al., 2023), their applications to SIMULMT is non-trivial, as they are not inherently designed for simultaneous decoding. Recent works have attempted to adapt LLMs for SIMULMT with prefix fine-tuning, incremental decoding (Wang et al., 2023b) and learning to wait for more source tokens before translation (Koshkin et al., 2024). These works show LLMs, with careful prompt-engineering, could approach the performance of specialized SIMULMT models. However, high computational cost, slow inference, and high latency render these approaches impractical for real-world applications (Yuan et al., 2024). This is primarily due to the use of *offline prompting*, where arriving source tokens are inserted at the end of the source sequence, disrupting the continuity of the translation history (Figure 1 left). This prevents reusing cached target history states and requires re-computation of source and target representations.

To mitigate this issue, we propose *conversational prompt* that resemble the multi-turn dialogue nature of LLMs. Specifically, user inputs are treated as the source tokens to be read, while the LLM's responses are considered the predicted

[1]Code, weights, and data will be released with publication.

Proceedings of the 22nd International Conference on Spoken Language Translation (IWSLT 2025), pages 93–105
July 31 - August 1, 2025

target tokens to be written. In our conversational SIMULMT, newly arrived source form the current instruction, while previous source tokens and their translations are treated as conversation history (Figure 1 right). This conversational prompt enables the reuse of Key-Value cache (Pope et al., 2023), as all content is appended incrementally without modifying the translation history. However, conversational SIMULMT poses new challenges for LLMs to comprehend the segmented source content and produce a coherent translation via multi-turn conversation.

To adapt the LLM to the conversational decoding format, we opt to perform supervised fine-tuning (SFT) on the pretrained LLM. But the challenge is the lack of the conversational SIMULMT data for SFT. Interleaving incomplete source and target segments in the dialogue history is unnatural (see Figure 1). This code-switching style is exhibited in some languages (Yong et al., 2023); however, it is the *continuation* rather than the *translation* of the previous content, making it challenging to leverage existing code-switched datasets for training. Therefore, we propose to curate the training data by segmenting parallel sentence pairs into smaller chunks based on a transformation of the word alignments. The segmented chunks are further augmented to handle different latency requirements.

Experiments on three SIMULMT benchmarks demonstrate the effectiveness of our proposed conversational SIMULMT in balancing the trade-offs between accuracy, speed and flexibility to different latency requirements. Compared to offline prompting, our method not only maintains strong performance, but also benefits from reduced latency. Notably, our method attains similar decoding speed to the LLM-based OFFLINEMT.

Our contributions are summarized as follows,

- We introduce conversational prompting to reduce the inference cost of LLM-based SIMULMT by leveraging its multi-turn dialogue capability and enabling efficient reuse of Key-Value cached computations.

- We present an automated training data curation pipeline that can turn any offline translation parallel corpus into the conversational prompt format and generalize with a novel augmentation strategy into any inference setting.

- Experiments demonstrate that the proposed conversational SIMULMT obtains up to $2\times$ acceleration compared to the offline-prompting baseline while maintaining comparable translation quality, emphasizing its value in practical applications.

2 Background

Simultaneous Machine Translation (SIMULMT) Unlike *offline* machine translation (OFFLINEMT), where models generate target translation $\mathbf{y} = (y_1, ..., y_J)$ given a complete source sentence $\mathbf{x} = (x_1, ..., x_I)$, SIMULMT incrementally translates with partial source context $\mathbf{x}_{\leq t} = (x_1, ..., x_t)$ where $t \leq I$. A core component of SIMULMT is a read-write policy that decides whether to wait for new source tokens (READ) or generate target tokens (WRITE), balancing translation quality and latency.

Incremental Decoding Studies have explored adapting OFFLINEMT models for simultaneous decoding by performing offline decoding on incrementally updated histories (Liu et al., 2020; Nguyen et al., 2021; Polák et al., 2022; Guo et al., 2023). This involves a chunk-wise READ policy that reads n tokens per round and a WRITE policy that commits stable partial translations using the longest common prefix (LCP) (Polák et al., 2022) algorithm. LCP often causes high latency when candidates lack common initial tokens. Relaxed Agreement LCP (RALCP) (Wang et al., 2023b) was proposed to vote for accepting prefixes with candidate agreement above threshold γ.

SIMULMT with LLMs Since incremental decoding essentially repeats offline decoding, using offline-style translation prompts with LLMs is straightforward and aligns with their instruction-following capabilities (Xu et al., 2023). During each round, a source chunk is READ and appended to source history $\mathbf{x}$. LLMs generate translations using offline prompts as shown in Figure 1, which are then WRITTEN to target history $\mathbf{y}$.

3 Conversational SIMULMT

While incremental decoding with offline prompt enables LLMs to perform simultaneous decoding, it faces high computational latency due to the insertion of newly arrived source tokens in the middle of the prompt, disrupting the reuse of cached target history states. In this section, we propose conversational prompts to improve the decoding efficiency and balance quality-latency trade-off.

Setting	N-Shot	SacreBLEU	COMET
OFFLINEMT	0-Shot	30.99	84.95
Convers. SIMULMT	0-Shot	7.14	58.76
Convers. SIMULMT	5-Shot	13.51	69.03
Convers. SIMULMT 0-Shot Failure Case			
Chunk 1 Input:	Die Flugdaten zeigten, dass das		
Chunk 1 Response:	The flight data showed that the plane was flying at an altitude of 35,000 feet.		
Chunk 2 Input:	Flugzeug auch bei einem zweiten		
Chunk 2 Response:	The plane was also flying during the second flight.		
Reference	Flight data showed the plane had to pull out of second		

Table 1: Performance comparison of `Llama2-7b-chat` on WMT15 De->En test set in zero-shot and few-shot conversational SIMULMT settings. OFFLINEMT results are included as a baseline. The example failure case demonstrates how the LLM hallucinates completions (shown in red) when translating partial sentences, leading to compounding errors in subsequent chunks.

3.1 Decoding with Conversational Prompt

The efficiency improvement in LLMs hinges on maintaining the Key-Value (KV-) cache reuse, i.e. the decoding process must consistently add new tokens at the end of the sequence without altering the middle elements. When LLMs are performing multi-turn dialogues, the prompt for each turn is composed of a user input and assistant response separated by special tokens, and conversation histories are simply concatenated as the context (Touvron et al., 2023). Drawing parallels to multi-turn dialogues in LLMs, SIMULMT can also be viewed similarly, where user inputs and assistant responses are equivalent to `READ` and `WRITE` action. At round t, LLM reads a source context chunk X_t and writes its translation Y_t: "<U> X_t <A> Y_t". The already processed chunks are concatenated as contexts, serving the latest translation round of new incoming chunks. As all contents are appended incrementally, the reuse of KV-cache becomes feasible again like in multi-turn dialogue (see Figure 1). Our approach also adapts the hypothesis selection strategy e.g. RALCP (Wang et al., 2023b) to prune the unstable suffixes in each response. Algorithm 1 in Appendix A presents the detailed decoding process.

We conducted a pilot experiment to assess LLMs' zero-shot and few-shot capabilities with conversational prompts. Using `Llama2-7b-chat` (Touvron et al., 2023) on the WMT15 De->En test set with chunk size $n = 5$, we tested both zero- and five-shot settings. As shown in Table 1, conversational SIMULMT performed poorly even with 5-shot prompting. The failure analysis reveals that LLMs, trained primarily on complete sentences, struggle with partial source translation and tend to hallucinate completions when presented with fragments in a multi-turn dialogue format. To address this limitation, we propose to SFT LLMs on conversational SIMULMT data. The following section details our approach to converting a normal bi-text corpus into conversational prompt format.

3.2 SFT on Conversational SIMULMT Data

As conversational SIMULMT data is not naturally available, we propose to synthesize `READ` / `WRITE` chunks by segmenting sentence pairs from parallel corpora. Inspired by Arthur et al. (2021) which generates the oracle policy from word alignments, we further extend the approach by carefully addressing the impact of word reordering and improving the generalizability of the oracle policy. Specifically, we first build *monotonic dependency graph* from the alignment of a sentence pair. We then segment the graph and convert these segments into `READ` / `WRITE` pairs, followed by augmentation to improve its generalization across various latency demands (Figure 2). The process is explained below.

Alignment Graph Generation Given a sentence pair, we employ `fastalign` (Dyer et al., 2013) to obtain word alignment between source and target tokens (Step 1 in Figure 2). The obtained alignment is a set $\mathcal{A}$ of pairs (i, j) denoting the source token x_i is aligned with its corresponding target token y_j. We define the *sufficient* source token set to generate a given target token y_j as $\mathbf{a}_j = \{i|(i,j) \in \mathcal{A}, \forall i \in [0, I]\}$.

A source and target sentences have a monotonic translation relationship if the previous target tokens only aligned with the previous source tokens, i.e. $\forall j > k \quad \min(\mathbf{a}_j) \geq \max(\mathbf{a}_k)$ (Koehn et al., 2005; Ling et al., 2011). This condition ensures that the relative order of words is preserved between the source and target sentences. In that case, the optimal minimum-latency policy that retains sufficient source information is to produce the monotonic translation that follows the word order of the source sequence, i.e. `WRITE` target token y_j immediately after reading the final required source token $x_{\max(\mathbf{a}_j)}$, and then `READ` the next source tokens.

Monotonic Dependency Graph Monotonic dependency enables effective implementation of optimal `READ` /`WRITE` policies. However, translations often require reordering to produce grammat-

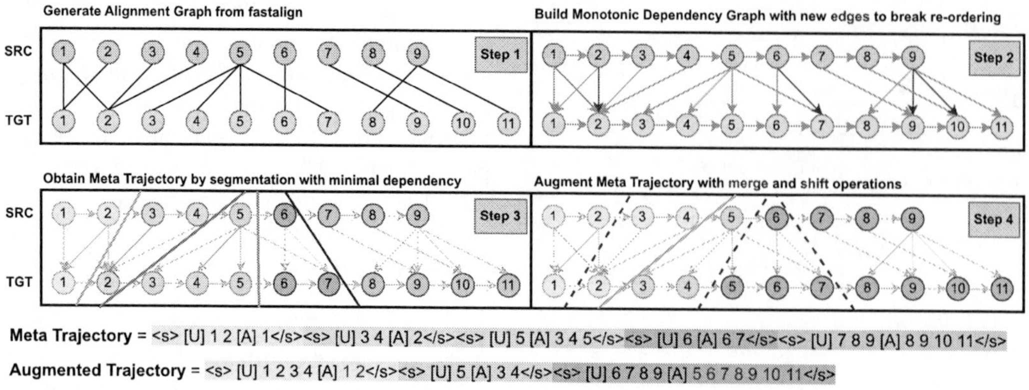

Figure 2: The illustration of the data curating process. The first graph is obtained from `fast_align`, it is then modified into a monotonic dependency graph by adding additional edges. The Meta Trajectory can be derived by segmenting the monotonic dependency graph with minimal dependency (segment with the colored solid line in step 3). Finally, Policy Generalization is applied to augment the segmented graph with merge (red dotted lines will be removed) and shift (blue dotted lines are shifted) operations. Chunks in the trajectories derived from the third and fourth graphs are highlighted with different colors.

ically correct output, especially between languages with different syntactic structures. To address this, we propose constructing a monotonic dependency graph $\overrightarrow{\mathcal{A}}$ from alignment set $\mathcal{A}$ (Step 2 in Figure 2) such that the monotonic condition is met.

For each target token y_j violating the monotonic condition $\min(\mathbf{a}_j) < \max(\mathbf{a}_{j-1})$, we add a new edge from the last sufficient source token $x_{\max(\mathbf{a}_{j-1})}$ to y_j, eliminating the need for reordering. In Figure 2, y_2 violates monotonicity as its earliest required source token $\min(\mathbf{a}_2) = 1$ precedes the last required source token for the previous target $\max(\mathbf{a}_1) = 2$. Thus, we add an edge from x_2 to y_2.

Meta Trajectory We then segment the monotonic dependency graph and convert these segments into `READ` / `WRITE` pairs, representing the *meta trajectory* of the oracle policy with minimum latency (Step 3 in Figure 2). We examine each target token to identify its exclusive corresponding source tokens with minimal dependency. Each subgraph $\overrightarrow{\mathcal{A}_j}$ corresponds to a pair (R_j, W_j) where $W_j = \{y_j\}$ is a target token and $R_j = \{x_i | i \in \mathbf{a}_j \setminus \mathbf{a}_{j-1}\}$ contains new source tokens required since the previous target. When consecutive target tokens depend on the same source token, we combine their `WRITE` actions, assigning the shared source token to $R_j = \{x_i\}$ and forming $W_j = \{y_j, ..., y_{j+n}\}$. This generates a meta trajectory $RW^\star = [(R_1, W_1), ..., (R_C, W_C)], C \leq I$, with C chunks.

Trajectory Augmentation Since the meta trajectories are tailored for minimal latency, they may not generalize well to different lengths of the input chunk, corresponding to different levels of latency. To improve the LLM's adaptability across various latency demands, we augment the meta-trajectory $RW^\star$ with a series of **merge** and **shift** operations (Step 4 in Figure 2). We first traverse $RW^\star$ and randomly merge δ consecutive `READ` and `WRITE` actions, forming new pairs $([R_c, ..., R_{c+\delta}], [W_c, ..., W_{c+\delta}])$, where $[\cdot]$ is the string concatenation operation. Here, δ is a variable re-sampled from a uniform distribution $\mathcal{U}(\delta_{\min}, \delta_{\max})$ where $\delta_{\min}$ and $\delta_{\max}$ are predefined hyperparameters.

Additionally, with a probability of β, we shift a portion of tokens from a `WRITE` action W_c to the next one W_{c+1} in the merged trajectory. More specifically, we split W_c at a proportion ρ and transfer the latter part to the next pair, resulting in $(R_c, W_c^{<\rho}), (R_{c+1}, [W_c^{>\rho}, W_{c+1}])$ where ρ is sampled from $\mathcal{U}(\rho_{\min}, 0.9)$ where $\rho_{\min}$ is a hyperparameter.

This augmentation enhances the LLM's context conditioning and suits incremental decoding where prediction endings are often truncated by hypothesis selection algorithms. The resulting trajectory consists of `READ` /`WRITE` chunks of varying lengths, formatted with conversational prompts for SFT. During training, we apply cross-entropy loss only on target tokens within unshifted `WRITE` chunks.

Trajectory	Dimension	De→En	En→Vi	En→Zh
Meta-Trajectory	#Chunk	10.69 ± 5.5	12.98 ± 8.1	11.94 ± 7.3
	#SRC word/Chunk	1.74 ± 0.8	1.38 ± 0.4	1.68 ± 0.5
	#TGT word/Chunk	1.79 ± 0.8	1.73 ± 0.5	1.53 ± 0.5
Aug-Trajectory	#Chunk	2.74 ± 1.2	3.12 ± 1.6	2.95 ± 1.4
	#SRC word/Chunk	7.01 ± 3.9	5.83 ± 2.8	7.02 ± 3.6
	#TGT word/Chunk	7.18 ± 3.9	7.35 ± 3.5	6.40 ± 3.2

Table 2: Statistics of curated conversational SIMULMT training data across all benchmarks, showing chunk counts and source/target tokens per chunk (mean±std) for both meta and augmented trajectories.

4 Experiments

4.1 Datasets

WMT15 De->En (4.5M training pairs) We use `newstest2013` (3000 pairs) for validation and `newstest2015` (2169 pairs) for testing[2].

IWSLT15 En->Vi (133K training pairs) We employ TED `tst2012` (1553 pairs) and `tst2013` (1268 pairs) as validation and test sets, respectively[3].

MUST-C En->Zh (Di Gangi et al., 2019) (359k training pairs) This TED talk dataset provides 1349 pairs for validation and the `tst-COMMON` (2841 pairs) for testing.

Conversational SIMULMT Datasets For each dataset, we create conversational prompt versions from their training sets using the approach described in §3.2. We employ `fastalign` (Dyer et al., 2013) to obtain initial word alignment graphs. For trajectory augmentation, we set $\delta_{\text{min:max}} = (2, 10)$ for merging operations. For shift operations, both β and ρ_{min} are set to 0.5, meaning we shift at least 50% of tokens in a target segment to the next one with 0.5 probability. Table 2 presents detailed statistics for these datasets.

4.2 Evaluation Metrics

We evaluate translation quality and latency using SacreBLEU[4] (Post, 2018), COMET[5] (Rei et al., 2020), and word-level average lagging (AL) (Ma et al., 2019). To assess computational efficiency, we measure word wall time (WWT) (Wang et al., 2023b), which represents the average time required to predict a word on identical hardware.

[2] `www.statmt.org/wmt15/`

[3] `nlp.stanford.edu/projects/nmt/`

[4] BLEU+nrefs:1+case:mixed+eff:no+tok:{13a,zh}+smooth:exp+version:2.3.1

[5] `https://huggingface.co/Unbabel/wmt22-cometkiwi-da`

4.3 Model Training

For all LLM-based methods, we use `Llama2-7b-chat` (Touvron et al., 2023) as the backbone following Wang et al. (2023b). We conduct QLoRA-based SFT (Hu et al., 2022; Dettmers et al., 2023) for one epoch with $r = 64$, $\alpha = 16$, learning rate of 2e-4, batch size of 48, and 4-bit quantization on a single A100 GPU. Both offline and conversational prompt models are fine-tuned on identical data sources (standard offline style bitext from the aforementioned training sets), but formatted as offline prompts and conversational prompts respectively.

4.4 Settings

We compare our proposed conversational SIMULMT against the following baselines:

Encoder-Decoder Transformers We evaluate the performance of a series of specialized Encoder-Decoder Transformer models for both OFFLINEMT and SIMULMT:

- **Offline NMT**: Following (Zhang and Feng, 2022), we train vanilla Transformer (Vaswani et al., 2017) (48M parameters for En->Vi; 300M for De->En and Zh->En) with beam size 5 for inference.
- **Wait-k** (Ma et al., 2019): A fixed policy approach that reads k source tokens before alternating read/write operations. We test with k ranging from 1-8 for De->En and Zh->En, 4-8 for En->Vi.
- **ITST** (Zhang and Feng, 2022) An adaptive policy that measures the information transferred from source to target token and determines when to proceed with translation with a threshold (set as 0.1-0.7 for all datasets).
- **Wait-Info** (Zhang et al., 2022) An adaptive policy using token information thresholds ($\mathcal{K}$ from 1-8 for all datasets) to coordinate the timing of translation.

LLM-based SIMULMT We compare our conversational prompt approach against the offline prompt method (Wang et al., 2023b), using identical `READ` policies with chunk sizes n=[3,5,7,9,11,13]. Both approaches are evaluated with RALCP hypothesis selection (beam=5). We also assess greedy decoding (beam=1, no hypothesis selection) with our conversational prompting

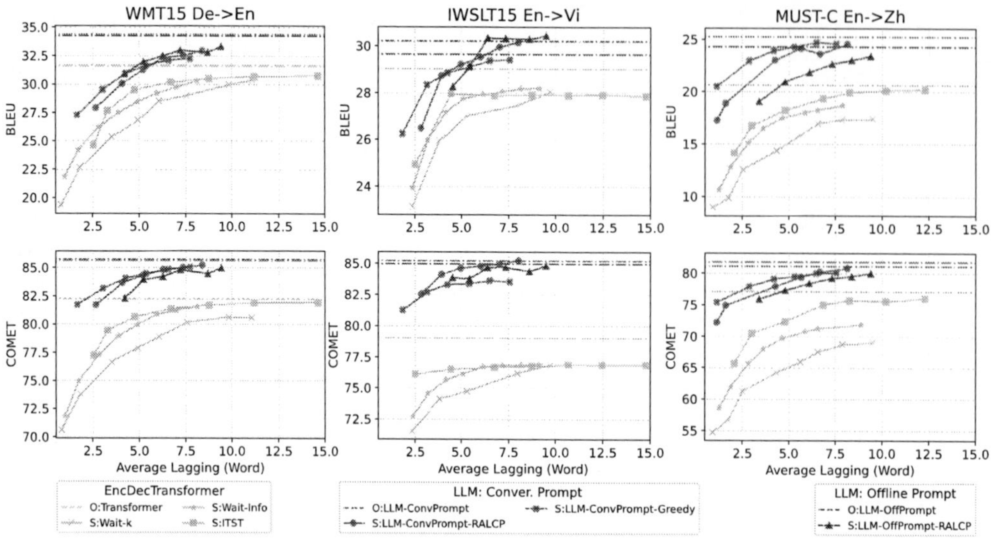

Figure 3: Translation quality and latency results on three benchmarks. Results are presented in three groups with different colors: (i) Encoder-Decoder Transformer baselines (orange), (ii) Offline-Prompt LLMs (blue), and (iii) Conversation-Prompt LLMs (red). Offline and Simultaneous decoding are distinguished by the first letter (O/S).

only (as computational latency baseline), since offline prompting inherently requires hypothesis selection and cannot function with greedy search. For reference, we include results from LLM-based OFFLINEMT as a performance upper bound.

4.5 Results

Our preliminary study in Table 1 showed LLMs struggle with zero/few-shot conversational SIMULMT. Here we examine whether fine-tuning on our curated data enables effective conversational SIMULMT, focusing on quality-latency balance.

Translation Quality As shown in Figure 3, LLM-based approaches (red and blue) outperform Transformer baselines (yellow) across all language pairs by up to 3 BLEU/10 COMET points. With sufficient latency allowance, LLM-based SIMULMT even surpasses offline Transformer NMT. At equivalent latency levels, our conversational prompting (red) achieves comparable BLEU scores to offline prompting (blue) while often showing better COMET scores.

Translation Latency Our conversational SIMULMT (red) reduces latency compared to offline prompting (blue), with average reductions of 1.17 and 1.50 AL across all benchmarks. For En->Vi and En->Zh, our approach achieves latency comparable to specialized SIMULMT models. While RALCP (`S:LLM-ConvPrompt-RALCP`) generally provides better quality than greedy decoding (`S:LLM-ConvPrompt-Greedy`), the latter offers lower latency.

Practical Advantages Most significantly, our conversational SIMULMT (red) maintains superior translation quality at low latency levels (AL<4) compared to specialized models (yellow), making it particularly valuable for practical applications requiring both high quality and low latency. In contrast, offline prompting (blue) with identical decoding configurations struggles to operate effectively in the low-latency range, diminishing its quality advantages relative to specialized approaches (yellow). These results demonstrate that our conversational prompting approach effectively addresses the efficiency-quality trade-off in simultaneous translation with LLMs.

5 Analysis

5.1 Decoding Speed

While Average Lagging (AL) effectively quantifies algorithmic delay between translation and source input, it doesn't account for computational costs. In real-world applications, actual inference time critically impacts user experience: a model with low AL might still deliver poor user experience due to high computational overhead. To address this limitation, we evaluate decoding speed using Word Wall Time (WWT), which measures actual

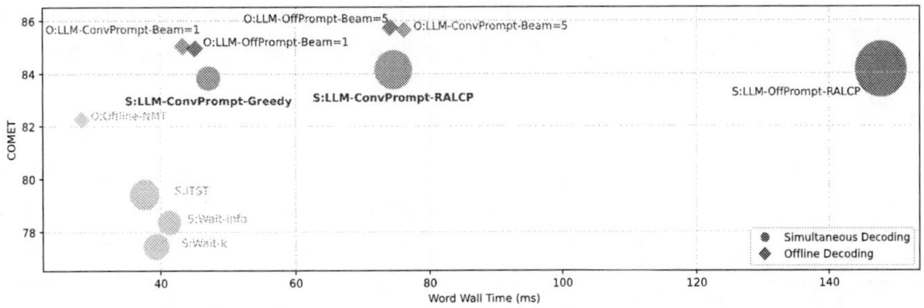

Figure 4: Relationship between computational efficiency (Word Wall Time) and translation quality (COMET score) on WMT15 De->En. Simultaneous decoding settings are shown as circles, with circle size representing variance across different latency control parameters (e.g. n). Offline settings are represented by diamonds. Color coding matches Figure 3, with our proposed approach highlighted in **bold**.

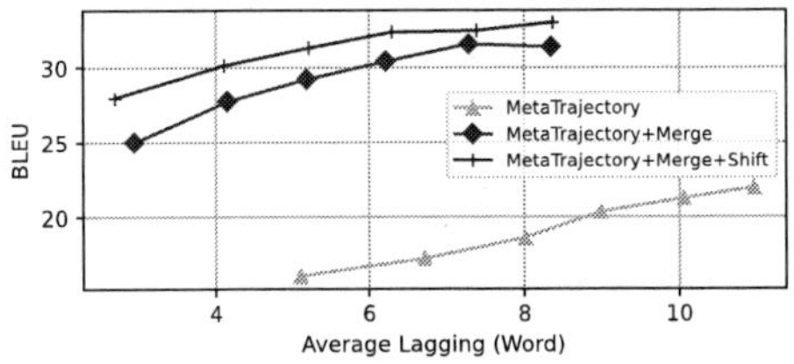

Figure 5: Effect of trajectory augmentation strategies on translation quality (BLEU) and latency (AL) for WMT15 De->En. Results compare models trained on meta-trajectories alone versus with merge and shift operations.

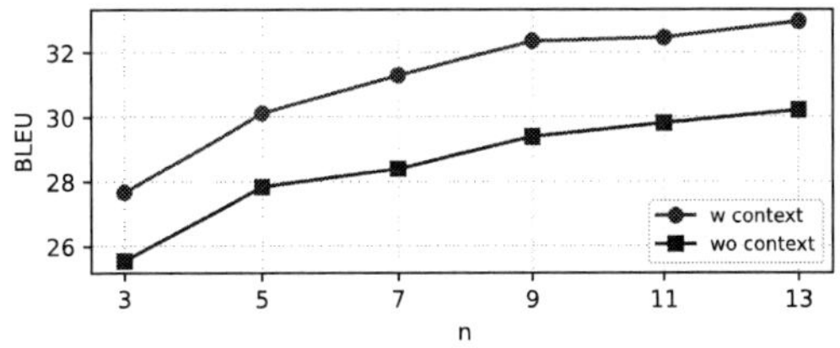

Figure 6: Translation quality (BLEU) on WMT15 De->En when generating the final chunk with vs. without preceding context, across different chunk sizes. The consistent gap demonstrates effective context utilization.

inference time per word (§4.4).

Figure 4 presents detailed WWT results for WMT15 De->En translation. Our analysis reveals that offline prompting with RALCP (`S:LLM-OffPrompt-RALCP`) exhibits the slowest performance, making it impractical despite good translation quality. In contrast, our conversational prompting approach with RALCP (`S:LLM-ConvPrompt-RALCP`) achieves computational efficiency comparable to offline LLM translation (`O:LLM-ConvPrompt-Beam=5`) while maintaining high translation quality.

Most notably, our conversational prompting with greedy decoding (`S:LLM-ConvPrompt-Greedy`) delivers the best efficiency-quality balance—achieving processing speeds comparable to specialized SIMULMT models (yellow) while producing significantly better translations. These results demonstrate that our approach effectively addresses both algorithmic and computational latency concerns, making it suitable for practical deployment.

5.2 Effectiveness of Trajectory Augmentation

To evaluate our trajectory augmentation strategy, we conducted an ablation study comparing models trained on: (*i*) meta trajectories only, (*ii*) meta trajectories with merge operations, and (*iii*) meta trajectories with both merge and shift operations (§3.2). All models used identical hyperparameters, with training data as the only variable.

As shown in Figure 5, trajectory augmentation yields notable improvements in translation quality and latency when using RALCP. The merge operation contributes most significantly to these improvements, while models trained solely on meta trajectories perform poorly across all metrics.

This suggests augmentation techniques enhance the model's ability to generalize across different latency conditions. Without augmentation, the model struggles with varying input chunk sizes, causing RALCP to accept less reliable hypotheses and increasing latency. The augmented approach effectively prepares the model for dynamic simultaneous translation scenarios.

5.3 Ability to Leverage Contextual Information

Effective SIMULMT with conversational prompting requires the model's ability to accurately utilize contextual information. To evaluate this capability, we designed an experiment isolating the model's performance on the final chunk of translation both with and without access to preceding context.

For each test instance, we extracted the com-

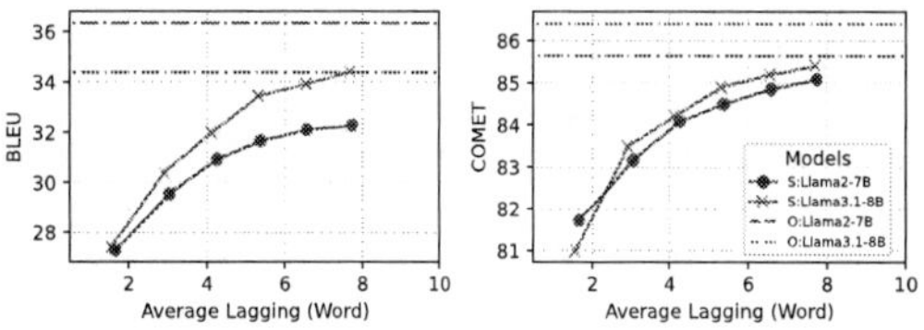

(a) Impact of model iteration (Llama-2-7b-chat vs. Llama-3.1-8B-Instruct) on WMT15 De->En.

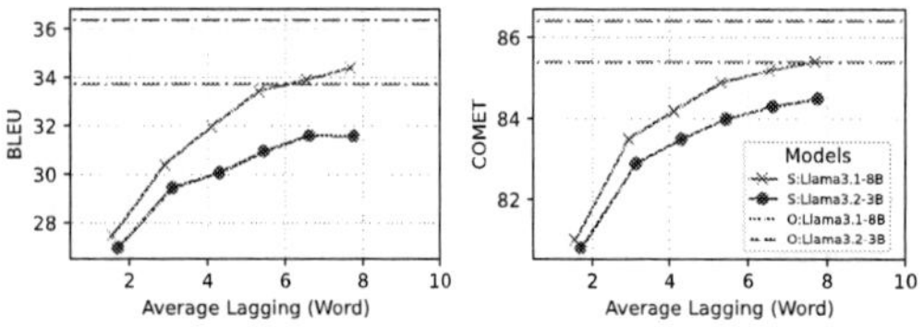

(b) Effect of model scale (Llama-3.1-8B-Instruct vs. Llama-3.2-3B-Instruct) on WMT15 De->En.

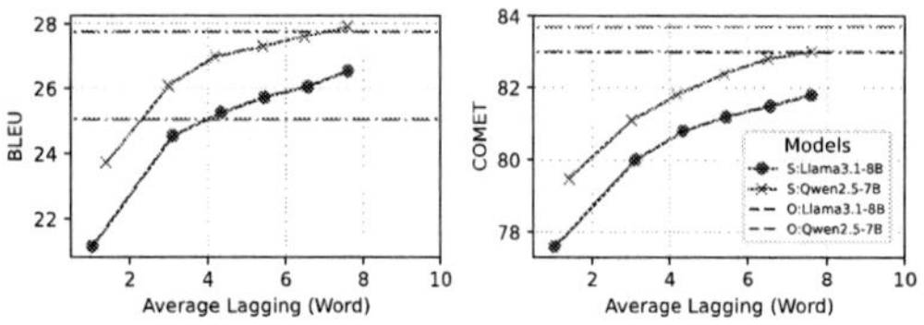

(c) Impact of target language proficiency (Llama-3.1-8B-Instruct vs. Qwen2.5-7B-Instruct) on MUST-C En->Zh.

Figure 7: Performance comparison of different LLM families with our conversational prompt.

plete inference history and separated it into: (i) the source-target dialogue history serving as context, and (ii) the final source chunk representing the latest input. We then tasked our fine-tuned LLM with translating this final chunk under two conditions: with and without access to the preceding conversation history. Performance was evaluated by computing BLEU scores on the concatenation of the generated final chunk with its original history.

As shown in Figure 6, we observed a consistent 2-point decrease in BLEU scores when context was withheld. This performance gap demonstrates our model effectively leverages information from previous conversation turns to produce more accurate translations, confirming the fine-tuned LLM maintains translation coherence.

5.4 Generalizability Across LLM Families

In our main experiments, we used `Llama-2-7b-chat` following Wang et al. (2023b) for consistency. Now, we examine our approach's generalizability across different LLMs, using identical training and inference parameters for fair comparison. We report only greedy simultaneous decoding and offline beam=5 results to eliminate interference with hypothesis selection.

Impact of Model Iteration We compare `Llama-2-7b-chat` with the newer `Llama-3.1-8B-Instruct` (Grattafiori et al., 2024) on WMT15 De->En to assess how model advancements affect performance. As shown in Figure 7a, the newer model demonstrates consistent improvements in both offline and simultaneous modes. This confirms that conversational SIMULMT effectively transfers to newer LLMs, with benefits from improved instruction-following capabilities and enhanced language modeling.

Effect of Model Scale We investigate how model size impacts performance by comparing `Llama-3.1-8B-Instruct` with the smaller `Llama-3.2-3B-Instruct` (Grattafiori et al., 2024) on WMT15 De->En. Figure 7b shows that while the larger model predictably outperforms its smaller counterpart, the 3B model still achieves acceptable translation quality (on par with `Llama-2-7b-chat` in Figure 7a), suggesting our method is viable on resource-constrained devices.

Impact of Target Language Proficiency We evaluate `Llama-3.1-8B-Instruct` against `Qwen2.5-7B-Instruct` (Qwen et al., 2025) on MUST-C En->Zh to investigate the effect of the model's target language capabilities. As shown in Figure 7c, Qwen2.5 consistently outperforms Llama-3.1 for Chinese translation by 1-2 BLEU points across all latency settings, demonstrating that target language proficiency provides additional benefits with our approach.

6 Related Works

Simultaneous Machine Translation (SIMULMT) is the task to provide real-time translation of a source sentence stream where the goal is to minimize the latency while maximizing the translation quality. A common approach is to train an MT model on prefix-to-prefix dataset to directly predict target tokens based on partial source tokens (Ma et al., 2019). Alternatively, Liu et al. (2020) proposed the incremental decoding framework to leverage the pretrained OFFLINENMT model and turn it into a SIMULMT model without further training. A core component of SIMULMT is a read-write policy to decide at every step whether to wait for another source token (`READ`) or to generate a target token (`WRITE`). Previous methods have explored fixed policy, which always waits for k tokens before generation (Ma et al., 2019; Zhang et al., 2022) and adaptive policy, which trains an agent via reinforcement learning (Gu et al., 2017; Arthur et al., 2021). Re-translation (Arivazhagan et al., 2019) from the beginning of the source sentence at the WRITE step will incur high translation latency. Stable hypothesis detection methods such as Local Agreement, hold-n (Liu et al., 2020) and Share prefix SP-n (Nguyen et al., 2021) are employed to commit stable hypothesis and only regenerate a subsequence of source sentence. The goal is to reduce the latency and minimize the potential for errors resulting from incomplete source sentence (Polák et al., 2022; Wang et al., 2021).

LLM-based NMT Recent research has delved into the potential usage of LLMs in MT (Hendy et al., 2023; Zhu et al., 2023; Robinson et al., 2023), especially in handling discourse phenomena (Wang et al., 2023a; Wu et al., 2024) and linguistic nuances such as idioms (Manakhimova et al., 2023) and proverbs (Wang et al., 2025). While LLMs do exhibit some level of translation capability, prior research has identified that they still lags behind the conventional NMT models, especially for low resource languages (Robinson et al., 2023). Additionally, the translation performance varies depending on prompting strategies (Zhang et al., 2023). Efforts have been made to enhance the LLMs' MT performance by incorporating guidance from dictionary (Lu et al., 2023), further fine-tuning (Zeng et al., 2023; Xu et al., 2023) and augmenting with translation memories (Mu et al., 2023).

LLM-based SIMULMT SimulLLM (Agostinelli et al., 2023) explore the ability to adapt an LLM finetuned on NMT task to simultaneous translation with wait-k strategy. Wang et al. (2023b) adopt hybrid READ/WRITE policy with wait-k and incremental decoding. TransLLaMA (Koshkin et al., 2024) teach LLMs to produce WAIT tokens to preserve the causal alignment between source and target tokens. At each inference round, LLMs only produce a single word or WAIT token, which is very costly due to multiple rounds of LLM calls. Guo et al. (2024) introduce LLM into the SIMULMT task as a translation agent working with a specialized SIMULMT policy agent. An additional memory module stores translation history. The policy agent decides on READ/WRITE actions, while the LLM translates target segments. They face the same KV-cache reuse challenge noted by Wang et al. (2023b), making the computational cost of collaborating big and small models even more significant.

7 Conclusion

This paper focuses on the feasibility of utilizing LLM for SIMULMT. We found that leveraging the incremental-decoding framework with offline prompting leads to high computational latency, hindering the reuse of the Key-Value cache. To address this, we propose the conversational prompting which allows LLMs to conduct SIMULMT in a multi-turn dialogue manner. The approach significantly speeds up the inference and also preserves the quality superiority, enabling practical LLM-based SIMULMT systems.

Limitations

We summarize the limitations of this study in the following aspects:

Data Our evaluation was conducted on three commonly used benchmarks which may limit the diversity in domains, styles, and languages. There may also be potential data contamination concerns since LLMs might have been exposed to parts of our test sets during pre-training. A more comprehensive evaluation with diverse datasets across more domains and language pairs would strengthen our findings.

Alignment-based Data Curation Our approach relies on word alignment tools like `fast_align` to segment parallel sentences, which has inherent limitations. These tools may struggle with languages having drastically different word orders or grammatical structures, potentially creating suboptimal segmentation points. Furthermore, the alignment quality degrades for distant language pairs or complex sentences with idiomatic expressions and cultural references. While our augmentation strategies help mitigate some issues, they are still constrained by the initial alignment quality.

Ethics Statement

Our work is built on top of an existing LLM. For this reason, we share the similar potential risks and concerns posed by the underlying LLM. Our method is trained on commonly used training resources of the Machine Translation research community and as such we are not expecting our approach to introduce new areas of risks.

References

Victor Agostinelli, Max Wild, Matthew Raffel, Kazi Asif Fuad, and Lizhong Chen. 2023. Simul-llm: A framework for exploring high-quality simultaneous translation with large language models. *arXiv preprint arXiv:2312.04691*.

Naveen Arivazhagan, Colin Cherry, Wolfgang Macherey, Chung-Cheng Chiu, Semih Yavuz, Ruoming Pang, Wei Li, and Colin Raffel. 2019. Monotonic infinite lookback attention for simultaneous machine translation. In *ACL*, pages 1313–1323.

Philip Arthur, Trevor Cohn, and Gholamreza Haffari. 2021. Learning coupled policies for simultaneous machine translation using imitation learning. In *Proceedings of the 16th Conference of the European Chapter of the Association for Computational Linguistics: Main Volume*, pages 2709–2719, Online. Association for Computational Linguistics.

Tim Dettmers, Artidoro Pagnoni, Ari Holtzman, and Luke Zettlemoyer. 2023. Qlora: Efficient finetuning of quantized llms. *CoRR*, abs/2305.14314.

Mattia A. Di Gangi, Roldano Cattoni, Luisa Bentivogli, Matteo Negri, and Marco Turchi. 2019. MuST-C: a Multilingual Speech Translation Corpus. In *Proceedings of the 2019 Conference of the North American Chapter of the Association for Computational Linguistics: Human Language Technologies, Volume 1 (Long and Short Papers)*, pages 2012–2017, Minneapolis, Minnesota. Association for Computational Linguistics.

Chris Dyer, Victor Chahuneau, and Noah A. Smith. 2013. A simple, fast, and effective reparameterization of IBM model 2. In *Human Language Technologies: Conference of the North American Chapter of the Association of Computational Linguistics, Proceedings, June 9-14, 2013, Westin Peachtree Plaza Hotel, Atlanta, Georgia, USA*, pages 644–648. The Association for Computational Linguistics.

Aaron Grattafiori, Abhimanyu Dubey, Abhinav Jauhri, Abhinav Pandey, Abhishek Kadian, and Ahmad Al-Dahle et al. 2024. The llama 3 herd of models.

Jiatao Gu, Graham Neubig, Kyunghyun Cho, and Victor O.K. Li. 2017. Learning to translate in real-time with neural machine translation. In *Proceedings of the 15th Conference of the European Chapter of the Association for Computational Linguistics: Volume 1, Long Papers*, pages 1053–1062, Valencia, Spain. Association for Computational Linguistics.

Jiaxin Guo, Daimeng Wei, Zhanglin Wu, Zongyao Li, Zhiqiang Rao, Minghan Wang, Hengchao Shang, Xiaoyu Chen, Zhengzhe Yu, Shaojun Li, Yuhao Xie, Lizhi Lei, and Hao Yang. 2023. The hw-tsc's simultaneous speech-to-text translation system for IWSLT 2023 evaluation. In *IWSLT@ACL*, pages 376–382.

Shoutao Guo, Shaolei Zhang, Zhengrui Ma, Min Zhang, and Yang Feng. 2024. Sillm: Large language models for simultaneous machine translation.

Amr Hendy, Mohamed Abdelrehim, Amr Sharaf, Vikas Raunak, Mohamed Gabr, Hitokazu Matsushita, Young Jin Kim, Mohamed Afify, and Hany Hassan Awadalla. 2023. How good are GPT models at machine translation? A comprehensive evaluation. *CoRR*, abs/2302.09210.

Edward J. Hu, Yelong Shen, Phillip Wallis, Zeyuan Allen-Zhu, Yuanzhi Li, Shean Wang, Lu Wang, and Weizhu Chen. 2022. Lora: Low-rank adaptation of large language models. In *ICLR*.

Philipp Koehn, Amittai Axelrod, Alexandra Birch Mayne, Chris Callison-Burch, Miles Osborne, and David Talbot. 2005. Edinburgh system description for the 2005 IWSLT speech translation evaluation. In *Proceedings of the Second International Workshop on Spoken Language Translation*, Pittsburgh, Pennsylvania, USA.

Roman Koshkin, Katsuhito Sudoh, and Satoshi Nakamura. 2024. Transllama: Llm-based simultaneous translation system. *arXiv preprint arXiv:2402.04636*.

Wang Ling, João Graça, David Martins de Matos, Isabel Trancoso, and Alan W Black. 2011. Discriminative phrase-based lexicalized reordering models using weighted reordering graphs. In *Proceedings of 5th International Joint Conference on Natural Language Processing*, pages 47–55, Chiang Mai, Thailand. Asian Federation of Natural Language Processing.

Danni Liu, Gerasimos Spanakis, and Jan Niehues. 2020. Low-latency sequence-to-sequence speech recognition and translation by partial hypothesis selection. In *Interspeech*, pages 3620–3624.

Hongyuan Lu, Haoyang Huang, Dongdong Zhang, Haoran Yang, Wai Lam, and Furu Wei. 2023. Chain-of-dictionary prompting elicits translation in large language models. *CoRR*, abs/2305.06575.

Mingbo Ma, Liang Huang, Hao Xiong, Renjie Zheng, Kaibo Liu, Baigong Zheng, Chuanqiang Zhang, Zhongjun He, Hairong Liu, Xing Li, Hua Wu, and Haifeng Wang. 2019. STACL: Simultaneous translation with implicit anticipation and controllable latency using prefix-to-prefix framework. In *Proceedings of the 57th Annual Meeting of the Association for Computational Linguistics*, pages 3025–3036, Florence, Italy. Association for Computational Linguistics.

Shushen Manakhimova, Eleftherios Avramidis, Vivien Macketanz, Ekaterina Lapshinova-Koltunski, Sergei Bagdasarov, and Sebastian Möller. 2023. Linguistically motivated evaluation of the 2023 state-of-the-art machine translation: Can ChatGPT outperform NMT? In *Proceedings of the Eighth Conference on Machine Translation*, pages 224–245, Singapore. Association for Computational Linguistics.

Yongyu Mu, Abudurexiti Reheman, Zhiquan Cao, Yuchun Fan, Bei Li, Yinqiao Li, Tong Xiao, Chunliang Zhang, and Jingbo Zhu. 2023. Augmenting large language model translators via translation memories. In *Findings of the Association for Computational Linguistics: ACL 2023*, pages 10287–10299, Toronto, Canada. Association for Computational Linguistics.

Thai-Son Nguyen, Sebastian Stüker, and Alex Waibel. 2021. Super-Human Performance in Online Low-Latency Recognition of Conversational Speech. In *Proc. Interspeech 2021*, pages 1762–1766.

Peter Polák, Ngoc-Quan Pham, Tuan Nam Nguyen, Danni Liu, Carlos Mullov, Jan Niehues, Ondřej Bojar, and Alexander Waibel. 2022. CUNI-KIT system for simultaneous speech translation task at IWSLT 2022. In *Proceedings of the 19th International Conference on Spoken Language Translation (IWSLT 2022)*, pages 277–285, Dublin, Ireland (in-person and online). Association for Computational Linguistics.

Reiner Pope, Sholto Douglas, Aakanksha Chowdhery, Jacob Devlin, James Bradbury, Anselm Levskaya, Jonathan Heek, Kefan Xiao, Shivani Agrawal, and Jeff Dean. 2023. Efficiently scaling transformer inference. In *Proceedings of Machine Learning and Systems*.

Matt Post. 2018. A call for clarity in reporting BLEU scores. In *Proceedings of the Third Conference on Machine Translation: Research Papers, WMT 2018, Belgium, Brussels, October 31 - November 1, 2018*, pages 186–191. Association for Computational Linguistics.

Qwen, :, An Yang, Baosong Yang, Beichen Zhang, Binyuan Hui, Bo Zheng, Bowen Yu, Chengyuan Li, Dayiheng Liu, Fei Huang, Haoran Wei, Huan Lin, Jian Yang, Jianhong Tu, Jianwei Zhang, Jianxin Yang, Jiaxi Yang, Jingren Zhou, Junyang Lin, Kai Dang, Keming Lu, Keqin Bao, Kexin Yang, Le Yu, Mei Li, Mingfeng Xue, Pei Zhang, Qin Zhu, Rui Men, Runji Lin, Tianhao Li, Tianyi Tang, Tingyu Xia, Xingzhang Ren, Xuancheng Ren, Yang Fan, Yang Su, Yichang Zhang, Yu Wan, Yuqiong Liu, Zeyu Cui, Zhenru Zhang, and Zihan Qiu. 2025. Qwen2.5 technical report.

Ricardo Rei, Craig Stewart, Ana C Farinha, and Alon Lavie. 2020. Comet: A neural framework for mt evaluation.

Nathaniel R. Robinson, Perez Ogayo, David R. Mortensen, and Graham Neubig. 2023. Chatgpt MT: competitive for high- (but not low-) resource languages. *CoRR*, abs/2309.07423.

Hugo Touvron, Louis Martin, Kevin Stone, Peter Albert, Amjad Almahairi, Yasmine Babaei, Nikolay Bashlykov, Soumya Batra, Prajjwal Bhargava, Shruti Bhosale, Dan Bikel, Lukas Blecher, Cristian Canton-Ferrer, Moya Chen, Guillem Cucurull, David Esiobu, Jude Fernandes, Jeremy Fu, Wenyin Fu, Brian Fuller, Cynthia Gao, Vedanuj Goswami, Naman Goyal, Anthony Hartshorn, Saghar Hosseini, Rui Hou, Hakan Inan, Marcin Kardas, Viktor Kerkez, Madian Khabsa, Isabel Kloumann, Artem Korenev, Punit Singh Koura, Marie-Anne Lachaux, Thibaut Lavril, Jenya Lee, Diana Liskovich, Yinghai Lu, Yuning Mao, Xavier Martinet, Todor Mihaylov, Pushkar Mishra, Igor Molybog, Yixin Nie, Andrew Poulton, Jeremy Reizenstein, Rashi Rungta, Kalyan Saladi, Alan Schelten, Ruan Silva, Eric Michael Smith, Ranjan Subramanian, Xiaoqing Ellen Tan, Binh Tang, Ross Taylor, Adina Williams, Jian Xiang Kuan, Puxin Xu, Zheng Yan, Iliyan Zarov, Yuchen Zhang, Angela Fan, Melanie Kambadur, Sharan Narang, Aurélien Rodriguez, Robert Stojnic, Sergey Edunov, and Thomas Scialom. 2023. Llama 2: Open foundation and fine-tuned chat models. *CoRR*, abs/2307.09288.

Ashish Vaswani, Noam Shazeer, Niki Parmar, Jakob Uszkoreit, Llion Jones, Aidan N. Gomez, Lukasz Kaiser, and Illia Polosukhin. 2017. Attention is all you need. In *NeurIPS*, pages 5998–6008.

Longyue Wang, Chenyang Lyu, Tianbo Ji, Zhirui Zhang, Dian Yu, Shuming Shi, and Zhaopeng Tu. 2023a. Document-level machine translation with large language models. In *Proceedings of the 2023 Conference on Empirical Methods in Natural Language Processing*, pages 16646–16661, Singapore. Association for Computational Linguistics.

Minghan Wang, Jiaxin Guo, Yuxia Wang, Daimeng Wei, Hengchao Shang, Chang Su, Yimeng Chen, Yinglu Li, Min Zhang, Shimin Tao, and Hao Yang. 2021. Diformer: Directional transformer for neural machine translation.

Minghan Wang, Viet-Thanh Pham, Farhad Moghimifar, and Thuy-Trang Vu. 2025. Proverbs run in pairs: Evaluating proverb translation capability of large language model.

Minghan Wang, Jinming Zhao, Thuy-Trang Vu, Fatemeh Shiri, Ehsan Shareghi, and Gholamreza Haffari. 2023b. Simultaneous machine translation with large language models. *arXiv preprint arXiv:2309.06706*.

Minghao Wu, Thuy-Trang Vu, Lizhen Qu, George Foster, and Gholamreza Haffari. 2024. Adapting large language models for document-level machine translation. *arXiv preprint arXiv:2401.06468*.

Haoran Xu, Young Jin Kim, Amr Sharaf, and Hany Hassan Awadalla. 2023. A paradigm shift in machine translation: Boosting translation performance of large language models. *CoRR*, abs/2309.11674.

Zheng-Xin Yong, Ruochen Zhang, Jessica Zosa Forde, Skyler Wang, Arjun Subramonian, Holy Lovenia, Samuel Cahyawijaya, Genta Indra Winata, Lintang Sutawika, Jan Christian Blaise Cruz, Yin Lin Tan, Long Phan, Rowena Garcia, Thamar Solorio, and Alham Fikri Aji. 2023. Prompting multilingual large language models to generate code-mixed texts: The case of south east asian languages.

Zhihang Yuan, Yuzhang Shang, Yang Zhou, Zhen Dong, Chenhao Xue, Bingzhe Wu, Zhikai Li, Qingyi Gu,

Yong Jae Lee, Yan Yan, et al. 2024. Llm inference unveiled: Survey and roofline model insights. *arXiv preprint arXiv:2402.16363*.

Jiali Zeng, Fandong Meng, Yongjing Yin, and Jie Zhou. 2023. TIM: teaching large language models to translate with comparison. *CoRR*, abs/2307.04408.

Biao Zhang, Barry Haddow, and Alexandra Birch. 2023. Prompting large language model for machine translation: A case study. *ArXiv*, abs/2301.07069.

Shaolei Zhang and Yang Feng. 2022. Information-transport-based policy for simultaneous translation. In *Proceedings of the 2022 Conference on Empirical Methods in Natural Language Processing, EMNLP 2022, Abu Dhabi, United Arab Emirates, December 7-11, 2022*, pages 992–1013. Association for Computational Linguistics.

Shaolei Zhang, Shoutao Guo, and Yang Feng. 2022. Wait-info policy: Balancing source and target at information level for simultaneous machine translation. In *Findings of the Association for Computational Linguistics: EMNLP 2022*, pages 2249–2263, Abu Dhabi, United Arab Emirates. Association for Computational Linguistics.

Wenhao Zhu, Hongyi Liu, Qingxiu Dong, Jingjing Xu, Lingpeng Kong, Jiajun Chen, Lei Li, and Shujian Huang. 2023. Multilingual machine translation with large language models: Empirical results and analysis. *CoRR*, abs/2304.04675.

Algorithm 1 Conversational SIMULMT Decoding

Require: LLM : $\texttt{LLM}_\theta$,
Source chunks: $\mathbf{x} = []$,
Target chunks: $\mathbf{y} = []$,
KV-Cache: $\mathbf{h} = []$,
Chunk index: $c = 0$,
Variables Definition: Source chunk size: n,
Beam-size: B, Agreement-degree: γ

while NOT_FINISH **do**
  $\mathbf{x}_c \leftarrow \texttt{READ}(n)$ //READ n tokens
  $\mathbf{x}$.append($\mathbf{x}_c$)
  $\mathbf{x}_{\text{prompt}} \leftarrow \texttt{PROMPT}(\mathbf{x}, \mathbf{y})$
  $\mathbf{y}'_c, \mathbf{h}' \leftarrow \texttt{LLM}(\mathbf{x}_{\text{prompt}}, B, \mathbf{h}, \text{latest=True})$
  //B candidates with latest tokens in $\mathbf{y}'_c$
  $\mathbf{y}_c, \mathbf{h} \leftarrow \texttt{PREFIX}(\mathbf{y}'_c, \mathbf{h}')$
  //Prune with Prefix selection, e.g. RALCP
  if $\mathbf{y}_c == \emptyset$ **then**
    continue
  else
    $\mathbf{y}$.append($\mathbf{y}_c$)
    $\texttt{WRITE}(\mathbf{y}_c)$
    $c \leftarrow c + 1$
  end if
end while

Appendix

A Conversational SimulMT Decoding

Algorithm 1 presents the details of applying conversational prompts for decoding.

Kuvost: A Large-Scale Human-Annotated English to Central Kurdish Speech Translation Dataset Driven from English Common Voice

Mohammad Mohammadamini[1], Daban Jaff[2,3], Sara Jamal[3], Ibrahim Ahmed[3], Hawkar Omar[3], Darya Sabir[3], Marie Tahon[1], Antoine Laurent [1]
[1]LIUM, Le Mans University, [2]Erfurt University, [3]Koya University
Correspondence: mohammad.mohammadamini@univ-lemans.fr

Abstract

In this paper, we introduce the Kuvost, a large-scale English to Central Kurdish speech-to-text-translation (S2TT) dataset. This dataset includes 786k utterances derived from Common Voice 18, translated and revised by 230 volunteers into Central Kurdish. Encompassing 1,003 hours of translated speech, this dataset can play a groundbreaking role for Central Kurdish, which severely lacks public-domain resources for speech translation. Following the dataset division in Common Voice, there are 298k, 6,226, and 7,253 samples in the train, development, and test sets, respectively. The dataset is evaluated on end-to-end English-to-Kurdish S2TT using Whisper V3 Large and SeamlessM4T V2 Large models. The dataset is available under the Creative Commons Attribution-NonCommercial-ShareAlike 4.0 International License `https://huggingface.co/datasets/aranemini/kuvost`.

1 Introduction

Speech translation is the automatic conversion of audio from a source language into text or audio in a target language (Barrault et al., 2025). Developing a speech-to-text translation system requires large amounts of translated audio; however, most languages lack sufficient data in this area. In (Communication et al., 2023), languages with fewer than 1,000 hours of publicly available transcribed or translated data are classified as low-resource. By this definition, only about a dozen out of 7,000 languages qualify as high-resource. Providing speech translation data—especially for low-resource languages—is therefore crucial for progress in this field.

In this paper, we introduce a speech-to-text translation (S2TT) dataset for Central Kurdish (CKB), which is a low-resource language (Communication et al., 2023). This dataset, called **Kuvost** (Kurdish Common Voice Speech Translation), is derived from the Common Voice 18 dataset. The Kuvost dataset contains 247k unique sentences translated by 230 volunteers and passed through a systematic revision process. Due to multiple recordings for some of the translated sentences in Common Voice, the total audio duration in Kuvost amounts to 1,003 hours.

Extending automatic speech recognition datasets by translating their transcriptions is a common strategy for building speech translation corpora. CoVoST (Wang et al., 2020) and CoVoST 2 (Wang et al., 2021b) are two well-known examples, both derived from Common Voice. CoVoST 2 is currently one of the large-scale publicly available speech translation corpus, including English-to-15 languages and 21-to-English S2TT pairs (Wang et al., 2021b).

Aug-LibriSpeech is a French-translated version of the LibriSpeech corpus, comprising a 236-hour EN→FR S2TT data (Kocabiyikoglu et al., 2018). VoxPopuli is a multi-way speech translation corpus based on European Parliament (EP) event recordings, encompassing 15 European languages (Wang et al., 2021a). TED Talks and TEDx have also been widely used for speech translation. The MUST-C dataset contains English-to-14-language S2TT data derived from TED Talks (Gangi et al., 2019; Cattoni et al., 2021). TEDx includes translations from English to 7 languages, while Indic-TEDST is the third TED-derived corpus, featuring translations from English to 9 Indian languages (Salesky et al., 2021; Sethiya et al., 2024).

The FLEURS dataset is currently the most comprehensive speech translation dataset in terms of the number of covered languages. FLEURS is a multi-way text-to-text and speech-to-speech corpus for 101 languages. It is also the only speech translation dataset that includes the Central Kurdish language—the subject of the current research (Conneau et al., 2023). The goal of this paper is to fill the gap in speech translation data scarcity for the Central Kurdish language.

Proceedings of the 22nd International Conference on Spoken Language Translation (IWSLT 2025), pages 106–109
July 31 - August 1, 2025 ©2025 Association for Computational Linguistics

2 Kurdish language

Kurdish (ISO 639: KUR) is an Indo-European language spoken by more than 30 million native speakers in Kurdistan and among the Kurdish diaspora. Geographic dispersion and socio-political factors have led Kurdish to diversify into several dialects (Matras, 2019; Eppler and Benedikt, 2017). The Kurdish language comprises six dialects: Northern Kurdish (KMR), Central Kurdish (CKB), Southern Kurdish (SDH), Laki (LKI), Zaza (DIQ), and Hawrami (HAQ) (Sheyholislami, 2015). Northern Kurdish and Zazaki are primarily written in a Latin-based script, while the remaining dialects are mainly written in an Arabic-based script.

In this paper, we focus on Central Kurdish, which is spoken by nearly 8 million native speakers (Sheyholislami, 2015). Central Kurdish is a statutory national language in Iraq[1] and a de facto provincial working language in Iran[2]. Although recent years have seen notable progress in data curation and system development for Central Kurdish, the speech translation domain from/to this dialect remains largely unexplored. The goal of this paper is to address this gap.

3 Translation process

The data for translation was sourced from Common Voice 18 [3]. The data creation process consisted of three main steps: (1) announcement and recruitment of volunteers, (2) training and data distribution, and (3) translation and review.

Announcement and Recruitment of Volunteers: An announcement was made in June 2024 to recruit volunteers who study English at the Department of English Language(DENL) at Koya University. A total of 259 volunteers—mostly third- and fourth-year students—signed up. All volunteers were native speakers of Central Kurdish.

Training: A two-week intensive training program was then offered to the volunteers. During this program, participants were introduced to various translation techniques. Additionally, a detailed guideline outlining the rules of translation was provided. After the training workshops, volunteers were given the option to withdraw without providing a reason. At this stage, 17 volunteers dropped out. The remaining participants were divided into three main groups, each supervised by a faculty member. These were further divided into smaller sub-groups of five volunteers. The translation data was distributed via Google Sheets, with access provided to both volunteers and supervisors.

Revision: The review process involved two main stages:

- **Peer Review:** Volunteers reviewed each other's translations within their sub-groups.

- **Professional Review:** Each translation was subsequently reviewed first by a team of Kurdish language experts from Department of Kurdish Language (DKUR) at Koya University and professional supervisor, who provided feedback and suggested edits where necessary.

Furthermore, weekly seminars were also held to address common mistakes and discuss correction strategies. During the revision phase, an additional 12 volunteers dropped out. By the end of the process, a total of 230 volunteers, plus 7 Kurdish language reviewers, had fully or partially completed their tasks, translating 247,373 sentences.

4 Kuvost Statistics

The statistics of the Kuvost dataset are presented in Table 1. The number of unique sentences translated into Kurdish is 247,373. These translated sentences were matched with their corresponding transcriptions and audio in Common Voice 18. We searched for all matching utterances in the validated portion of Common Voice 18, resulting in 786k utterances with Kurdish translations, totaling approximately 1,003 hours of English audio.

The validated and translated utterances were divided into train, development, and test sets according to the original Common Voice 18 partitioning. For each split, we referred to the Common Voice 18 train/dev/test sets and matched the English transcriptions with their corresponding Kurdish translations. The training set includes 298k utterances, equivalent to 417 hours of audio. The development and test sets each contain approximately 9 hours of translated speech. It deserved to be mentioned that all validated examples in the Common Voice are not included in the train/dev/test partitions which leads to lower number of utterances in the partitions.

[1]https://www.ethnologue.com/country/IQ/

[2]https://www.ethnologue.com/country/IR/

[3]https://commonvoice.mozilla.org/en/datasets

Table 1: Kuvost specification and partitions

Part	Train	Dev	Test	Validated
Duration	417h	8h47m	8h55m	1003h
Utterances	298k	6226	7253	786k
Uniq sents	190k	5819	7149	247k
Tokens	1,75m	41k	46k	1.84m

5 Evaluation Systems

The Kuvost dataset is evaluated by fine-tuning two state-of-the-art speech translation models: Whisper V3 (WL V3) Large and SeamlessM4T V2 (SL V2) Large models.

5.1 Whisper Large V3

Whisper is a sequence-to-sequence transformer-based model trained on 680,000 hours of labeled speech data, encompassing tasks such as ASR, S2TT, VAD, and Speaker Recognition (SR) (Radford et al., 2022). Whisper supports more than 80 languages for ASR and S2TT; however, the Kurdish language is not currently supported. We are fine-tuning the Whisper V3 Large model using the AdamW optimizer with a learning rate of 1e-5, a batch size of 16, in 5 epochs.

5.2 SeamlessM4T Large V2

Seamless is a set of models for T2TT, S2TT, S2ST, and ASR. We use the S2TT component, which consists of a Wav2Vec-BERT speech encoder and an NLLB-200 decoder. The model is jointly optimized for ASR and S2TT tasks (Barrault et al., 2025; Communication et al., 2023). We fine-tune the SeamlessM4T V2 Large model using Mel-filter bank (bins = 80) features over 10 epochs, with a batch size of 16 and a learning rate of 1e-4. These hyperparameters are set experimentally.

6 Results and discussion

Throughout the experiments, Kurdish translations were normalized using the Asosoft normalizer (Mahmudi et al., 2019). Key normalization steps included the unification of Unicode characters, standardization of numbers, and normalization of punctuation marks.

The Kuvost dataset was evaluated using two state-of-the-art (SOTA) models: Whisper Large V3 and SeamlessM4T V2 Large. Table 2 presents the results obtained using both models. The first row shows the performance of the fine-tuned Whisper V3 Large model on the training set of Kuvost. This model achieved a BLEU score of 23.76 on the Kuvost test set and 26.01 on the development set. The second row, labeled SL V2, displays the results of the pretrained SeamlessM4T V2 Large model before fine-tuning on the Kuvost training set. This multilingual model supports speech-to-text translation for 101 languages, including Central Kurdish. The baseline model of Seamless achieved a BLEU score of 21.97 on the Kuvost test set. The final row presents results for the fine-tuned version of SeamlessM4T using the Kuvost dataset. In this experiment, the model achieved a significantly improved BLEU score of 35.00 and 32.79 on the dev and test sets respectively. Besides the BLUE score, the ChrF++ is reported for all models. The fine-tuned version of seamless achieves a ChrF++ score of 62.32 on the Kuvost test set.

Table 2: Kuvost evaluation results using Whisper V3 Large (WL V3) and SeamlessM4T V2 Large (SL V2) models. FT stands for fine-tuned model on the train part of Kuvost

Part	Dev		Test	
	BLEU	ChrF++	BLEU	ChrF++
WL V3 FT	26.01	55.14	23.76	51.77
SL V2	22.54	54.18	21.97	53.01
SL V2 FT	35.00	64.10	32.79	62.32

The fine-tuned models on the Kuvost training set were evaluated using the FLEURS benchmark. The results are presented in Table 3. The Whisper model achieved a BLEU score of 7.65, and the Seamless model obtained a BLEU score of 11.17. The baseline SeamlessM4T model (before fine-tuning) achieved a BLEU score of 9.36 on the English→Central Kurdish task. Fine-tuning on the Kuvost training set led to an improvement of nearly 2 BLEU points, reaching 11.17. The marginal improvement in BLEU on the FLEURS dataset is likely due to differences in sentence complexity. Kuvost primarily consists of short and simple sentences, while FLEURS includes more complex syntactic structures. Additionally, domain shift may have contributed to the limited performance gain.

Table 3: The generaliability of Models fine-tuned on Kuvost and evaluated on FLEURS benchmark

Fleurs	BLEU	ChrF++
Whisper V3 FT	7,65	39,69
SeamlessM4T V2 FT	11.17	46,46

7 Conclusion

In this paper, we introduced Kuvost, a large-scale, human-annotated speech translation dataset for Central Kurdish. Kuvost consists of 1,003 hours of English-to-Kurdish speech translation, contributed by 230 volunteers. The dataset is evaluated using state-of-the-art speech translation models. For future work, we plan to record Kurdish translations to extend Kuvost for speech-to-speech translation tasks. Additionally, we aim to expand the dataset to support Kurdish-to-X translation for all languages available in the CoVoST 2 dataset (Wang et al., 2021b).

Acknowledgments

We express our heartfelt gratitude to the 236 volunteers from the English Language Department (DENL) and the Department of Kurdish Language (DKUR) at Koya University for their unwavering dedication and hard work throughout the ten months, from June 2024 to April 2025. Their active involvement has played a crucial role in the success of this project. Daban Q. Jaff thanks the Deutscher Akademischer Austauschdienst for his doctoral research grant. The experiments was performed using HPC resources from GENCI–IDRIS in the framework of DGA RAPID COMMUTE project.

References

Loïc Barrault, Yu-An Chung, Mariano Coria Meglioli, and et. al. 2025. Joint speech and text machine translation for up to 100 languages. *Nature*, 637(8046):587–593.

Roldano Cattoni, Mattia Antonino, Luisa Bentivogli, Matteo Negri, and Marco Turchi. 2021. Must-c: A multilingual corpus for end-to-end speech translation. *Computer Speech and Language*, 66:101155.

Seamless Communication, Loïc Barrault, Yu-An Chung, Mariano Coria Meglioli, and et. al. 2023. Seamless: Multilingual expressive and streaming speech translation. *Preprint*, arXiv:2312.05187.

Alexis Conneau, Min Ma, Simran Khanuja, Yu Zhang, Vera Axelrod, Siddharth Dalmia, Jason Riesa, Clara Rivera, and Ankur Bapna. 2023. Fleurs: Few-shot learning evaluation of universal representations of speech. In *SLT*, pages 798–805.

E. D. Eppler and S. Benedikt. 2017. Contact-induced language change in kurdish. In E. D. Eppler and S. Benedikt, editors, *Languages in Contact: A Comprehensive Guide*, pages 345–362. John Benjamins Publishing Company, Amsterdam.

Mattia A. Di Gangi, Roldano Cattoni, Luisa Bentivogli, Matteo Negri, and Marco Turchi. 2019. Must-c: A multilingual speech translation corpus. pages 2012–2017, Minneapolis, Minnesota. Association for Computational Linguistics.

Ali Can Kocabiyikoglu, Laurent Besacier, and Olivier Kraif. 2018. Augmenting librispeech with french translations: A multimodal corpus for direct speech translation evaluation. In *LREC 2018*, Miyazaki, Japan. European Language Resources Association (ELRA).

Aso Mahmudi, Hadi Veisi, Mohammad MohammadAmini, and Hawre Hosseini. 2019. Automated kurdish text normalization.

Y. Matras. 2019. Kurdish linguistics: A brief overview. In Y. Matras and D. Everhard, editors, *Kurdish Linguistics: Focus on Variation and Change*, pages 1–20. De Gruyter Mouton, Berlin.

Alec Radford, Jong Wook Kim, Tao Xu, Greg Brockman, Christine McLeavey, and Ilya Sutskever. 2022. Robust speech recognition via large-scale weak supervision. *Preprint*, arXiv:2212.04356.

Elizabeth Salesky, Matthew Wiesner, Jacob Bremerman, Roldano Cattoni, Matteo Negri, Marco Turchi, Douglas W. Oard, and Matt Post. 2021. Multilingual tedx corpus for speech recognition and translation. In *Proceedings of Interspeech*.

Nivedita Sethiya, Saanvi Nair, and Chandresh Maurya. 2024. Indic-tedst: Datasets and baselines for low-resource speech to text translation. In *LREC-COLING 2024*, pages 9019–9024, Torino, Italia. ELRA and ICCL.

Jaffer Sheyholislami. 2015. *The Kurds: History, Religion, Language, Politics*, chapter Language Varieties of the Kurds. Austrian Federal Ministry of the Interior.

Changhan Wang, Juan Pino, Anne Wu, and Jiatao Gu. 2020. Covost: A diverse multilingual speech-to-text translation corpus. In *Proceedings of the Twelfth Language Resources and Evaluation Conference*, pages 4197–4203, Marseille, France. European Language Resources Association.

Changhan Wang, Morgane Riviere, Ann Lee, Anne Wu, Chaitanya Talnikar, Daniel Haziza, Mary Williamson, Juan Pino, and Emmanuel Dupoux. 2021a. Voxpopuli: A large-scale multilingual speech corpus for representation learning, semi-supervised learning and interpretation. pages 993–1003, Online. Association for Computational Linguistics.

Changhan Wang, Anne Wu, Jiatao Gu, and Juan Pino. 2021b. Covost 2 and massively multilingual speech translation. In *Proc. Interspeech 2021*, pages 2247–2251.

Literary Translations and Synthetic Data for Machine Translation of Low-resourced Middle Eastern Languages

Sina Ahmadi[1,*] **Razhan Hameed**[2] **Rico Sennrich**[1]

[1]Department of Computational Linguistics, University of Zurich, Switzerland
[2]Vox AI, Netherlands

*sina.ahmadi@uzh.ch

Abstract

Middle Eastern languages represent a linguistically diverse landscape, yet few have received substantial attention in language and speech technology outside those with official status. Machine translation, a cornerstone application in computational linguistics, remains particularly underexplored for these predominantly non-standardized, spoken varieties. This paper proposes data alignment and augmentation techniques that leverage monolingual corpora and large language models to create high-quality parallel corpora for low-resource Middle Eastern languages. Through systematic fine-tuning of a pretrained machine translation model in a multilingual framework, our results demonstrate that corpus quality consistently outperforms quantity as a determinant of translation accuracy. Furthermore, we provide empirical evidence that strategic data selection significantly enhances cross-lingual transfer in multilingual translation systems. These findings offer valuable insights for developing machine translation solutions in linguistically diverse, resource-constrained environments.

DOLMA-NLP/bitext-mining

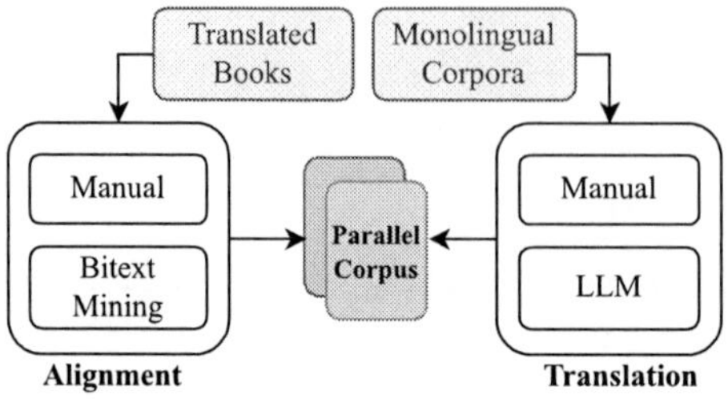

Figure 1: Approaches to create parallel corpora for the selected low-resourced languages in this paper

1 Introduction

Machine translation (MT) represents one of the most transformative applications in natural language processing (NLP), driving numerous breakthrough discoveries in the field. The evolution of MT has progressed from rule-based techniques to sophisticated deep learning approaches and, most recently, to large language models (LLMs) (Zhu et al., 2024b). Despite these paradigm shifts, data availability remains the fundamental constraint, leaving MT far from solved for low-resourced and under-represented languages and varieties. Of particular interest to this paper are such languages in the Middle East–a region with rich linguistic heterogeneity. Many languages in the Middle East lack formal status or standardization, face sociopolitical marginalization, and are systematically disadvantaged in technological development. Consequently, these languages have not benefited equitably from recent advances in MT technology, widening the digital language divide.

In our previous work, PARME–described in detail in (Ahmadi et al., 2025), we explored a participatory research initiative where native speakers contribute to translating sentences into eight Middle Eastern languages: Luri Bakhtiari, Laki Kurdish, Gilaki, Hawrami, Mazandarani, Southern Kurdish, Talysh, and Zazaki. Collecting data in a context where spoken tradition predominates over writing presents significant challenges. This effort resulted in over 36,000 translations, which were used to fine-tune the No Language Left Behind (NLLB) pretrained translation model (Team et al., 2024). Our previous experiments yield BLEU scores ranging from 2.89 to 16.54, indicating substantial room for improvement.

The current paper expands on our previous data collection approach through two complementary approaches illustrated in Figure 1. In the first approach, we leverage literary works by aligning sentences from translated works in the selected languages to the original English texts, using both manual and automated alignment tech-

Proceedings of the 22nd International Conference on Spoken Language Translation (IWSLT 2025), pages 110–118
July 31 - August 1, 2025 ©2025 Association for Computational Linguistics

niques. In the second approach, we extract sentences from monolingual corpora and translate them using Gemini-2.0-flash, creating synthetic parallel data. Using these datasets, we then systematically evaluate how these various data sources affect the performance of fine-tuned multilingual translation models. Our findings reveal that incorporating these new datasets improves model performance overall, but with an important caveat: increasing data quantity for one language can sometimes adversely affect performance for others in a multilingual setting. This highlights the complex interplay between data quantity, quality, and distribution in multilingual MT systems for low-resource languages.

2 Related Work

2.1 Low-Resourced MT

MT systems typically require millions of parallel sentences for effective training, a requirement met by only a few dozen high and medium-resource languages, primarily European. For low-resource languages, researchers have developed various approaches to address data scarcity. Synthetic data augmentation techniques include leveraging dictionaries and morphological variations (Alam et al., 2024), substituting rare words to create new training sentences (Fadaee et al., 2017), and mapping word embeddings from high-resource to low-resource languages through bilingual lexicon induction (Li et al., 2024). Synthetic data generation via back-translation (Sennrich et al., 2016) or forward-translation (Zhang and Zong, 2016) are common strategies, as well. Other approaches leverage the capacity of multilingual models to enhance related low-resourced languages using transfer learning (Ko et al., 2021), fine-tuning (Moslem et al., 2023) and adapters (Pham et al., 2024).

The emergence of LLMs has opened new possibilities for low-resource MT through prompting (Zhang et al., 2023), few-shot learning (Hendy et al., 2023), and in-context translation (Raunak et al., 2023). However, recent studies emphasize that translation direction (Zhu et al., 2024a) along with parallel data quality during both pre-training and fine-tuning remain crucial for performance (Guo et al., 2024). Furthermore, Iyer et al. (2024) note that "*diversity (in prompts and datasets) tends to cause interference instead of transfer*," highlighting the challenges in leveraging diverse datasets.

2.2 Bitext Mining

To facilitate the creation of parallel corpora from unaligned corpora, bitext mining or bitext retrieval aims to identify potential translation pairs across translated documents or monolingual corpora (Koehn, 2024). This task, of particular interest to low-resourced languages, has been extensively studied previously (Zweigenbaum et al., 2017), including methods for sentence filtering from web-crawled content (Chaudhary et al., 2019). Some approaches to bitext mining rely on automatic translations, as in Bleualign (Sennrich and Volk, 2010), while other approaches leverage semantic representations (Heffernan et al., 2022), with a notable example being Vecalign (Thompson and Koehn, 2019). Recent work by Winata et al. (2024) demonstrates that LLMs can also perform effectively in bitext mining tasks.

Our paper addresses a critical gap in the literature by exploring the intersection of bitext mining, data augmentation using an LLM and, multilingual fine-tuning for low-resource Middle Eastern languages, offering insights into enhancing translation capabilities for these understudied varieties.

3 Methodology

Complementary to PARME (Ahmadi et al., 2025), our previous participatory research where English sentences are translated by experts into one of the selected languages, we explore bitext mining and LLM-based data augmentation to further extract parallel sentences.

3.1 Sentence Alignment

Given a translated content in one of our selected languages, we aim to align the translations to their original sentences. Reaching out to publishers and translators, we could collect 25 translated books and articles for four languages among our eight selected ones: five translated articles for Laki Kurdish, five for Southern Kurdish (two books and three articles), 11 books for Hawrami and four for Gilaki (three articles and one book). All the content were originally translated from English, except in a couple of cases that we excluded as they were originally translated from Persian. The books are all famous novels of George Orwell, Virginia Woolf, Franz Kafka, Ernest Hemingway and Antoine de Saint-Exupéry, except one children book for Southern Kurdish, while the articles discuss specific sociological and medical topics.

To prepare the books for alignment, we first extract the sentences from the original textbooks in English (or their translations in English). Although most of the books are openly available[1], two of them required OCR from the scanned PDFs. Following this step, we preprocess the text in both the original text in English and our translations by normalizing characters, fixing tabulations and excessive newlines and finally, splitting the text into sentences or phrases using KLPT (Ahmadi, 2020b).

Given the set of sentences per work in English along with the translation, we initially aimed to carry out the alignments using an LLM. However, due to the low-resourced status of the selected languages, usage of `Chat GPT-4o` and `Claude 3.7 Sonnet` for our selected languages was far from helpful. As such, we try the following methods.

Manual alignment (M): Providing the sentences in a spreadsheet, we manually align sentences by splitting, merging and editing sentences to create matching translation pairs. Stylistic variation across translators required further attention to the alignment task; for instance, a long passage in the English text might have been translated in one or two short sentences considered to be culturally less relevant to the readers of the translated book. Similarly, specific contexts have required further elaboration by the translator, as in describing "Big Brother" or "Thinkpol" in George Orwell's 1984. Therefore, some alignments require appropriate modifications. The alignment was carried out by expert native speakers.

Automatic Alignment using Vecalign (V): Due to limited workforce for manual alignment, we carried out bitext mining to automatically align remaining translations using a few methods that were far from practical. To do so, we first manually split translations by chapter or long sections to further reduce the range of the possible alignment combinations, also known as *hierarchical mining* (Koehn, 2024). Then, we tried a range of methods: the Microsoft's Bilingual Sentence Aligner (Moore, 2002), Bleualign (Sennrich and Volk, 2010) with translations from PARME's fine-tuned models, embedding-based techniques using LaBSE (Feng et al., 2022), LASER (Artetxe and Schwenk, 2019), SONAR (Duquenne et al., 2023), SBERT (Reimers and Gurevych, 2019) and Vecalign (Thompson and Koehn, 2019). Given that none of the selected languages are included in the pretrained embeddings, we rely on the embeddings of closely-related languages: Persian (PES) for Gilaki and Central Kurdish (CKB) for Laki, Southern Kurdish and Hawrami. To determine the most effective alignment technique, we tested several methods on the manually-aligned corpus of the Little Prince containing 1101 sentence pairs. We measured accuracy as the proportion of sentence pairs that matched between the automatically-aligned and manually-aligned corpora. Table 1 summarizes the accuracy showing that Vecalign with SONAR embeddings produce the highest accuracy. It should be noted that the reported accuracies are limited to a sample in Hawrami without considering the combination of the embeddings and techniques.

Technique		Accuracy (%)
Microsoft Aligner		38.78
Bleualign		32.24
SBERT	LaBSE	2.63
	LASER	2.08
Vecalign	SONAR	**46.5**

Table 1: Accuracy of different bitext mining techniques on a sample of Hawrami translated text. Vecalign with SONAR achieves the highest accuracy (46.5%).

3.2 LLM-based Data Augmentation

Relying on the monolingual corpora available for Southern Kurdish (Ahmadi et al., 2023) and Zazaki, Hawrami (Ahmadi, 2020a) along with Wikipedia dumps[2] for Gilaki, Mazandarani and Zazaki, we implement a few-shot in-context translation approach to optimize in-context example selection using Gemini-2.0-flash, inspired by Agrawal et al. (2023), as follows:

```
Below are examples of {language} to English
translations. Translate the new text
following these patterns:

{language}: {example1}
English: {english_translation1}

[... more examples ...]

Now translate this text to English, only
output the translation:

{language}: {text_to_translate}
English:
```

[1]For English, we relied on the raw text provided by the Project Gutenberg: `https://www.gutenberg.org`

[2]Latest dumps of December 2025

Language	Gemini-2.0-flash		Llama3.3	
	zero	few	zero	few
Luri Bakhtiari	0.06	0.15	0.09	0.09
Gilaki	0.11	0.23	0.09	0.09
Hawrami	0.07	0.21	0.07	0.14
Laki Kurdish	0.10	0.19	0.05	0.11
Mazandarani	0.16	0.36	0.06	0.18
Southern Kurdish	0.18	0.14	0.06	0.13
Talysh	0.07	0.14	0.06	0.11
Zazaki	0.32	0.34	0.13	0.11
Average	0.14	**0.22**	0.08	0.12

Table 2: Zero-shot and few-shot prompting results (BLEU↑ [0, 100]) on Gemini-2.0-flash and Llama3.3. We translate sentences from monolingual corpora using few-shot prompted Gemini.

Our implementation uses BM25 retrieval to find semantically similar examples from a datastore, followed by a custom n-gram based re-ranking method. We calculate n-gram overlap between the test source and retrieved examples using a weighted scoring function that emphasizes coverage of source text terms. Our approach employs a dynamic weighting system where already-covered n-grams receive reduced weight by a lambda factor (set to 0.1) to promote selection of complementary examples.

Table 2 presents preliminary results comparing zero-shot and few-shot prompting on both Gemini-2.0-flash and Llama3.3. While the absolute BLEU scores remain poor, a common challenge when applying general-purpose LLMs to extremely low-resource languages, we observe several important patterns. First, few-shot prompting consistently outperforms zero-shot approaches, with relative improvements for some languages (e.g., Hawrami). Second, Gemini-2.0-flash demonstrates superior performance compared to Llama3.3 across nearly all languages. Through experimentation, we determined that using 16 examples in our prompts produced optimal results, significantly outperforming single-example approaches. Additional examples beyond 16 did not yield further improvements.

Table 3 provides basic statistics of our collected data per language. Luri Bakhtiari (BQI) and Talysh (TLY) are only included in PARME (P), Laki is only included in PARME and manual alignment (PM) while the other languages could benefit from the additional data sources.

Language	P	M	V	L
Luri Bakhtiari (BQI)	999	0	0	0
Gilaki (GLK)	3420	999	1391	22467
Hawrami (HAC)	5796	7050	8367	49987
Laki Kurdish (LKI)	1487	1220	0	0
Mazandarni (MZN)	2345	0	0	49328
Southern Kurdish (SDH)	7806	3681	2495	49992
Talysh (TLY)	1107	0	0	0
Zazaki (ZZA)	2374	0	0	50000
Sum	25,334	12,950	12,253	221,774

Table 3: Basic statistics of the data collected per languages from different data sources: PARME (P), manual (M) and automatic (V) sentence alignment, and LLM (L). Over 272,000 sentence pairs are collected.

4 Experiments

4.1 Experimental Setup

To adapt a multilingual model for our target languages, we leverage NLLB (600M variant) by systematically integrating embeddings from related languages through a structured token-based approach. This integration follows two key steps. First, we expanded the tokenizer's vocabulary by introducing language-specific tokens (e.g., `zza_Latn` for Zazaki) while preserving the existing language tokens. Second, we initialize embeddings for these new tokens by borrowing from phylogenetically related languages: Central Kurdish embeddings for Hawrami, Laki, and Southern Kurdish; Northern Kurdish for Zazaki; and Farsi for Luri Bakhtiari, Gilaki, Mazandarani, and Talysh. For evaluation consistency, we utilize the standardized test sets from PARME, each containing around 1,000 sentences per language in a single orthography. These test sets maintain representativeness across the non-standardized linguistic landscape by incorporating a uniform distribution of dialectal variations.

We conduct X→EN fine-tuning experiments with various data source combinations, e.g., PL for merging PARME and LLM-based datasets. We evaluate the performance using BLEU metric in SacreBLEU (Post, 2018).[3] Our baseline represents the highest BLEU score achieved by NLLB prior to fine-tuning. For fine-tuning, we employ a batch size of 8 with 4-step gradient accumulation, a conservative learning rate of 3e-5, and trained for 20 epochs with 0.1 warmup. Both source and target sequences were truncated to 128 tokens, and

[3] `nrefs:1|case:mixed|eff:no|tok:13a|smooth:exp|version:2.4.2`

Language	Baseline	P	PM	PV	PMV	PL	PMVL	PML_{Zazaki}
Luri Bakhtiari^{P}	0.75	**4.38**	3.67 ± 0.15	3.55 ± 0.16	3.78 ± 0.29	3.37 ± 0.39	3.26 ± 0.41	3.04 ± 0.19
Gilaki^{PMVL}	1.98	2.73	**4.22** ± 0.15	3.18 ± 0.13	3.92 ± 0.26	3.44 ± 0.17	3.49 ± 0.16	2.94 ± 0.18
Hawrami^{PMVL}	0.9	8.23	**15.46** ± 0.48	11.55 ± 2.78	10.86 ± 0.54	8.11 ± 0.11	8.93 ± 0.70	10.34 ± 2.15
Laki Kurdish^{PML}	1.89	6.33	**9.11** ± 0.67	7.18 ± 2.13	6.81 ± 0.79	4.80 ± 0.37	4.39 ± 0.47	5.43 ± 0.80
Mazandarani^{PL}	1.32	5.23	**5.50** ± 0.30	5.05 ± 0.83	5.32 ± 0.22	4.34 ± 0.28	4.22 ± 0.12	4.62 ± 0.22
Southern Kurdish^{PMVL}	2.77	9.93	**10.64** ± 0.46	8.68 ± 0.27	8.99 ± 0.60	7.61 ± 0.36	7.80 ± 0.48	8.34 ± 0.21
Talysh^{P}	1.03	3.01	**6.70** ± 0.52	5.22 ± 2.28	4.21 ± 1.43	2.36 ± 0.29	2.32 ± 0.56	3.66 ± 1.21
Zazaki^{PL}	2.82	3.45	3.75 ± 0.30	2.55 ± 0.45	3.67 ± 0.35	11.08 ± 0.89	**11.54** ± 0.50	9.99 ± 0.14
Average	1.68	5.41	**7.38** ± 0.19	5.87 ± 0.97	5.94 ± 0.22	5.64 ± 0.27	5.74 ± 0.21	6.04 ± 0.48

Table 4: X→EN BLEU scores for the fine-tuned NLLB model across eight languages using different combinations of data sources. Results are reported as mean ± standard deviation over three runs with different random seeds. Data sources where a language is included appear as superscript.

we implemented beam search with a beam size of 5 during inference. Training was conducted on NVIDIA RTX 3090 GPUs (24GB VRAM) with completion times of 9.4 to 16.1 hours per model.

4.2 Experimental Results

Table 4 presents the results of our experiments. To assess the impact of randomness in fine-tuning, we run the process three times by shuffling the train sets with different seeds.We report the mean values of the three systems per data setup along with standard deviations. Analyzing the results indicates:

A: Data quality matters more than quality Among the data setups, PARME (P) merged with manually aligned sentences (M), i.e. PM, achieves the highest BLEU scores for most languages and on average. Surprisingly, PM also improves the performance of Talysh, Zazaki and Mazandarani even though it does not contain additional data in those languages. Luri Bakhtiari's best performing model remains P, the only dataset covering that language. Although LLM-generated dataset along with PARME, i.e., PL, is the largest dataset, the obtained performances are lower than the PM setup and not much higher than P; so including the LLM-generated data does not improve the average BLEU score substantially.

On the standard deviations, they reveal varying levels of model stability across configurations and languages, with some combinations showing remarkable consistency, e.g., Gilaki with PM at ±0.15, while others demonstrate substantial sensitivity to initialization, e.g., Hawrami with PV at ±2.78 and Talysh with PV at ±2.28, suggesting that optimal data selection should consider both performance and reliability.

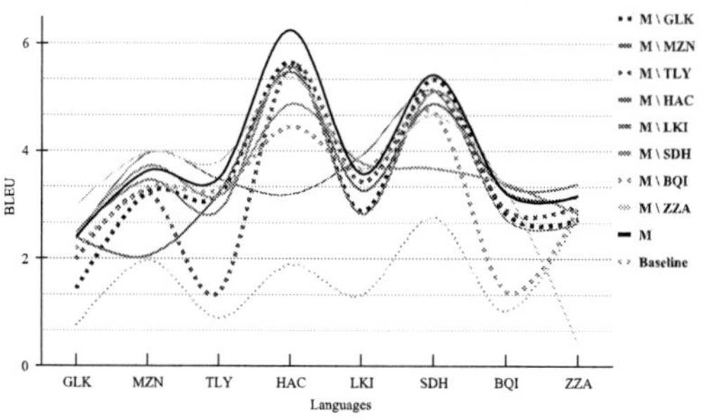

Figure 2: Cross-linguistic dependencies in our multilingual fine-tuning models. Each curve represents performance of a model trained without one language, e.g., M\GLK. The solid black line (M) shows the full model.

B: Multilingual data interference While PM is generally the optimal configuration for most languages, Zazaki's performance shows unique sensitivity to dataset composition, particularly when the LLM-generated data (L) is included in the fine-tuning dataset. Within the comprehensive PMVL setup (containing all data sources for all languages), Zazaki achieves its best performance with a BLEU score of 11.54, followed by 11.08 in PL. This observation led us to create a targeted dataset combination–PML_{Zazaki}–which integrates PM with the Zazaki LLM-generated data only. Although Zazaki still has a comparatively higher BLEU score in this setup (9.99), the average BLEU score is lower than that of PM and other setups where L is included.

To further analyze the implications on other languages in the multilingual setup, we fine-tune models on 1000 randomly-selected sentences in PARME data by excluding data of a language per model; for instance, M\GLK is a model fine-tuned on all but Gilaki data. Figure 2 illustrates the evaluation of these models. As expected, re-

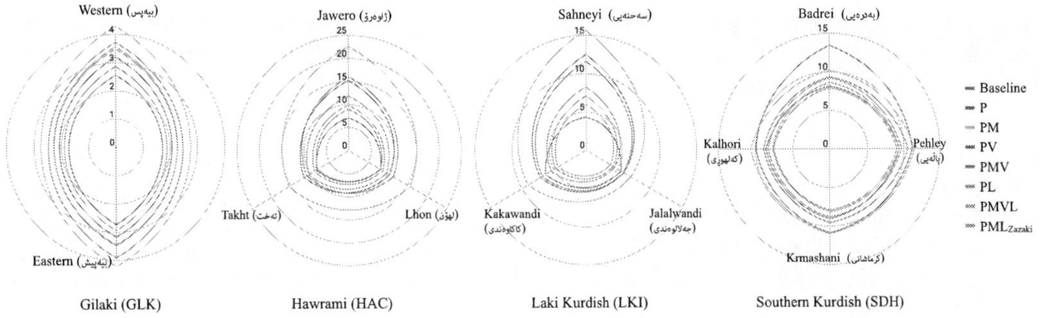

Figure 3: Performance across dialects and model configurations. Each radar chart displays mean BLEU scores from three randomly initialized models for different dialects. Greater extension of curves toward a dialect's axis indicates higher translation performance for that specific dialect.

moving one language's data deteriorates performance for that language, visible in the performance drops along the curves. However, several notable cross-language dependencies emerge. Removing Talysh (TLY) data negatively impacts Gilaki (GLK) and Mazandarani (MZN) performance, while removing Luri Bakhtiari (BQI) data hurts Hawrami (HAC) and Southern Kurdish (SDH). The dependencies manifest asymmetrically, with Zazaki (ZZA) exhibiting both high vulnerability to the removal of its own data and relative resilience to the removal of others, corroborating our earlier observations of its unique behavior.

C: Performance varies depending on the variety Gilaki, Hawrami, Laki and Southern Kurdish include sentences of different varieties/dialects in the test set making cross-dialectal evaluation possible. Figure 3 provides our analysis results for these languages revealing considerable performance disparities within each language. While in Hawrami, the Jawero dialect achieves substantially higher BLEU scores than Takht and Lhon, particularly with PM and PMV configurations, the performance of the models for Eastern and Western varieties of Gilaki is more consistent. Similarly, for Laki Kurdish, the Sahneyi variety benefits more from our fine-tuning approaches than Kakawandi and Jalalwandi varieties. Southern Kurdish shows more balanced performance across its dialects, though Badrei and Krmashani tend to receive slightly higher scores. Nevertheless, we caution against concluding that certain varieties are inherently more difficult to translate, as train and validation sets do not equally represent all varieties, and the test set does not contain the same sentences translated across different varieties. These observed differences may instead reflect varying degrees of representation in training data or linguistic proximity to the source material rather than intrinsic translation difficulty.

5 Conclusion and Discussion

This paper sheds light on eight low-resourced Middle Eastern languages by fine-tuning a pretrained MT model using different sources of data, from manually translated and aligned sentences to automatically aligned and automatically-translated ones. Our experiments demonstrate three key findings. First, data quality consistently outperforms quantity as a determinant of translation accuracy, with the manually aligned (M) data providing the most substantial improvements despite its relatively smaller size. Second, we observed complex cross-linguistic transfer effects where adding data for one language sometimes adversely affects performance for others, highlighting the importance of strategic dataset selection in multilingual systems. Third, we found significant performance variations across dialectal varieties within the same language. While our models perform well on all languages in comparison to the baseline, achieving 15.46 BLEU score for Hawrami at the highest, there remains substantial room for improvement.

Limitations Despite these advances, our work has several limitations. First, we explored only a limited set of open-weight LLMs for data augmentation; future work could investigate a broader range of models, such as MADLAD-400 (Kudugunta et al., 2023) and Mistral (Jiang et al., 2023), and in-context learning strategies. Second, our automatic alignment approach relies on embeddings from closely-related languages, which could be improved by training or fine-tuning embeddings on monolingual data of our selected languages. Third, our data augmentation techniques could be expanded to include synthetic data generation using bilingual lexicon induction, morphological variations, and back-translation methods. Finally, unlike the test sets that are uniform in orthography, our collected data for training and validation are composed of more than one orthography, as in Hawrami, Zazaki and Gilaki. Given that normalization and transliteration of these orthographies are not trivial, future work can also study the effect of orthographical variation on MT.

Ethics Statement Our data collection process adhered to rigorous ethical standards with careful attention to fairness and representation. While we maintained comprehensive inclusion criteria appropriate for low-resource language documentation, we acknowledge that the literary nature of our corpus means some character dialogue may contain language that reflects historical or cultural contexts that modern readers might find objectionable. All materials were obtained through formal agreements with publishers and translators, with appropriate intellectual property permissions secured. Contributors received fair compensation for their work, and their contributions are explicitly acknowledged. Our research prioritizes expanding NLP for underrepresented languages while maintaining responsible data stewardship practices.

Acknowledgments

This work was supported by the Swiss National Science Foundation through the MUTAMUR project (no. 213976).

References

Sweta Agrawal, Chunting Zhou, Mike Lewis, Luke Zettlemoyer, and Marjan Ghazvininejad. 2023. In-context examples selection for machine translation. In *Findings of the Association for Computational Linguistics: ACL 2023, Toronto, Canada, July 9-14, 2023*, pages 8857–8873. Association for Computational Linguistics.

Sina Ahmadi. 2020a. Building a corpus for the Zaza-Gorani language family. In *Proceedings of the 7th Workshop on NLP for Similar Languages, Varieties and Dialects, VarDial@COLING 2020, Barcelona, Spain (Online), December 13, 2020*, pages 70–78. International Committee on Computational Linguistics (ICCL).

Sina Ahmadi. 2020b. KLPT–Kurdish Language Processing Toolkit. In *Proceedings of the second Workshop for NLP Open Source Software (NLP-OSS)*. Association for Computational Linguistics.

Sina Ahmadi, Zahra Azin, Sara Belelli, and Antonios Anastasopoulos. 2023. Approaches to corpus creation for low-resource language technology: the case of Southern Kurdish and Laki. In *Proceedings of the Second Workshop on NLP Applications to Field Linguistics*, pages 52–63, Dubrovnik, Croatia. Association for Computational Linguistics.

Sina Ahmadi, Rico Sennrich, Erfan Karami, Ako Marani, Parviz Fekrazad, Gholamreza Akbarzadeh Baghban, Hanah Hadi, Semko Heidari, Mahîr Dogan, Pedram Asadi, Dashne Bashir, Mohammad Amin Ghodrati, Kourosh Amini, Zeynab Ashourinezhad, Mana Baladi, Farshid Ezzati, Alireza Ghasemifar, Daryoush Hosseinpour, Behrooz Abbaszadeh, Amin Hassanpour, Bahaddin Jalal Hamaamin, Saya Kamal Hama, Ardeshir Mousavi, Sarko Nazir Hussein, Isar Nejadgholi, Mehmet Ölmez, Horam Osmanpour, Rashid Roshan Ramezani, Aryan Sediq Aziz, Ali Salehi Sheikhalikelayeh, Mohammadreza Yadegari, Kewyar Yadegari, and Sedighe Zamani Roodsari. 2025. PARME: Parallel corpora for low-resourced Middle Eastern languages. In *Proceedings of the 63rd Annual Meeting of the Association for Computational Linguistics*, Vienna, Austria. Association for Computational Linguistics.

Md Mahfuz Ibn Alam, Sina Ahmadi, and Antonios Anastasopoulos. 2024. A morphologically-aware dictionary-based data augmentation technique for machine translation of under-represented languages. *CoRR*, abs/2402.01939.

Mikel Artetxe and Holger Schwenk. 2019. Massively multilingual sentence embeddings for zero-shot cross-lingual transfer and beyond. *Trans. Assoc. Comput. Linguistics*, 7:597–610.

Vishrav Chaudhary, Yuqing Tang, Francisco Guzmán, Holger Schwenk, and Philipp Koehn. 2019. Low-resource corpus filtering using multilingual sentence embeddings. In *Proceedings of the Fourth Conference on Machine Translation, WMT 2019, Florence, Italy, August 1-2, 2019 - Volume 3: Shared Task Papers, Day 2*, pages 261–266. Association for Computational Linguistics.

Paul-Ambroise Duquenne, Holger Schwenk, and Benoît Sagot. 2023. SONAR: sentence-level multimodal and language-agnostic representations. *CoRR*, abs/2308.11466.

Marzieh Fadaee, Arianna Bisazza, and Christof Monz. 2017. Data augmentation for low-resource neural machine translation. In *Proceedings of the 55th Annual Meeting of the Association for Computational Linguistics, ACL 2017, Vancouver, Canada, July 30 - August 4, Volume 2: Short Papers*, pages 567–573. Association for Computational Linguistics.

Fangxiaoyu Feng, Yinfei Yang, Daniel Cer, Naveen Arivazhagan, and Wei Wang. 2022. Language-agnostic BERT sentence embedding. In *Proceedings of the 60th Annual Meeting of the Association for Computational Linguistics (Volume 1: Long Papers), ACL 2022, Dublin, Ireland, May 22-27, 2022*, pages 878–891. Association for Computational Linguistics.

Ping Guo, Yubing Ren, Yue Hu, Yunpeng Li, Jiarui Zhang, Xingsheng Zhang, and Heyan Huang. 2024. Teaching large language models to translate on low-resource languages with textbook prompting. In *Proceedings of the 2024 Joint International Conference on Computational Linguistics, Language Resources and Evaluation, LREC/COLING 2024, 20-25 May, 2024, Torino, Italy*, pages 15685–15697. ELRA and ICCL.

Kevin Heffernan, Onur Çelebi, and Holger Schwenk. 2022. Bitext mining using distilled sentence representations for low-resource languages. In *Findings of the Association for Computational Linguistics: EMNLP 2022*, pages 2101–2112, Abu Dhabi, United Arab Emirates. Association for Computational Linguistics.

Amr Hendy, Mohamed Abdelrehim, Amr Sharaf, Vikas Raunak, Mohamed Gabr, Hitokazu Matsushita, Young Jin Kim, Mohamed Afify, and Hany Hassan Awadalla. 2023. How good are GPT models at machine translation? A comprehensive evaluation. *CoRR*, abs/2302.09210.

Vivek Iyer, Bhavitvya Malik, Pavel Stepachev, Pinzhen Chen, Barry Haddow, and Alexandra Birch. 2024. Quality or quantity? on data scale and diversity in adapting large language models for low-resource translation. In *Proceedings of the Ninth Conference on Machine Translation, WMT 2024, Miami, FL, USA, November 15-16, 2024*, pages 1393–1409. Association for Computational Linguistics.

Albert Q. Jiang, Alexandre Sablayrolles, Arthur Mensch, Chris Bamford, Devendra Singh Chaplot, Diego de Las Casas, Florian Bressand, Gianna Lengyel, Guillaume Lample, Lucile Saulnier, Lélio Renard Lavaud, Marie-Anne Lachaux, Pierre Stock, Teven Le Scao, Thibaut Lavril, Thomas Wang, Timothée Lacroix, and William El Sayed. 2023. Mistral 7B. *CoRR*, abs/2310.06825.

Wei-Jen Ko, Ahmed El-Kishky, Adithya Renduchintala, Vishrav Chaudhary, Naman Goyal, Francisco Guzmán, Pascale Fung, Philipp Koehn, and Mona T. Diab. 2021. Adapting high-resource NMT models to translate low-resource related languages without parallel data. In *Proceedings of the 59th Annual Meeting of the Association for Computational Linguistics and the 11th International Joint Conference on Natural Language Processing, ACL/IJCNLP 2021, (Volume 1: Long Papers), Virtual Event, August 1-6, 2021*, pages 802–812. Association for Computational Linguistics.

Philipp Koehn. 2024. Neural methods for aligning large-scale parallel corpora from the Web for South and East Asian languages. In *Proceedings of the Ninth Conference on Machine Translation, WMT 2024, Miami, FL, USA, November 15-16, 2024*, pages 1454–1466. Association for Computational Linguistics.

Sneha Kudugunta, Isaac Caswell, Biao Zhang, Xavier Garcia, Christopher A. Choquette-Choo, Katherine Lee, Derrick Xin, Aditya Kusupati, Romi Stella, Ankur Bapna, and Orhan Firat. 2023. MADLAD-400: A multilingual and document-level large audited dataset.

Fuxue Li, Beibei Liu, Hong Yan, Mingzhi Shao, Peijun Xie, Jiarui Li, and Chuncheng Chi. 2024. A bilingual templates data augmentation method for low-resource neural machine translation. In *Advanced Intelligent Computing Technology and Applications - 20th International Conference, ICIC 2024, Tianjin, China, August 5-8, 2024, Proceedings, Part III*, volume 14877 of *Lecture Notes in Computer Science*, pages 40–51. Springer.

Robert C. Moore. 2002. Fast and accurate sentence alignment of bilingual corpora. In *Machine Translation: From Research to Real Users, 5th Conference of the Association for Machine Translation in the Americas, AMTA 2002 Tiburon, CA, USA, October 6-12, 2002, Proceedings*, volume 2499 of *Lecture Notes in Computer Science*, pages 135–144. Springer.

Yasmin Moslem, Rejwanul Haque, and Andy Way. 2023. Fine-tuning large language models for adaptive machine translation. *CoRR*, abs/2312.12740.

Trinh Pham, Khoi Le, and Anh Tuan Luu. 2024. UniBridge: A unified approach to cross-lingual transfer learning for low-resource languages. In *Proceedings of the 62nd Annual Meeting of the Association for Computational Linguistics (Volume 1: Long Papers), ACL 2024, Bangkok, Thailand, August 11-16, 2024*, pages 3168–3184. Association for Computational Linguistics.

Matt Post. 2018. A call for clarity in reporting BLEU scores. In *Proceedings of the Third Conference on Machine Translation: Research Papers*, pages 186–191, Belgium, Brussels. Association for Computational Linguistics.

Vikas Raunak, Hany Hassan Awadalla, and Arul Menezes. 2023. Dissecting in-context learning of translations in GPTs. *CoRR*, abs/2310.15987.

Nils Reimers and Iryna Gurevych. 2019. Sentence-BERT: Sentence Embeddings using Siamese BERT-Networks. In *Proceedings of the 2019 Conference on Empirical Methods in Natural Language Processing*. Association for Computational Linguistics.

Rico Sennrich, Barry Haddow, and Alexandra Birch. 2016. Improving neural machine translation models with monolingual data. In *Proceedings of the*

54th Annual Meeting of the Association for Computational Linguistics (Volume 1: Long Papers), pages 86–96, Berlin, Germany. Association for Computational Linguistics.

Rico Sennrich and Martin Volk. 2010. MT-based Sentence Alignment for OCR-generated Parallel Texts. In *Proceedings of the 9th Conference of the Association for Machine Translation in the Americas: Research Papers, AMTA 2010, Denver, Colorado, USA, October 31 - November 4, 2010*. Association for Machine Translation in the Americas.

NLLB Team et al. 2024. Scaling neural machine translation to 200 languages. *Nature*, 630(8018):841.

Brian Thompson and Philipp Koehn. 2019. Vecalign: Improved sentence alignment in linear time and space. In *Proceedings of the 2019 Conference on Empirical Methods in Natural Language Processing and the 9th International Joint Conference on Natural Language Processing (EMNLP-IJCNLP)*, pages 1342–1348, Hong Kong, China. Association for Computational Linguistics.

Genta Indra Winata, Ruochen Zhang, and David Ifeoluwa Adelani. 2024. MINERS: multilingual language models as semantic retrievers. In *Findings of the Association for Computational Linguistics: EMNLP 2024, Miami, Florida, USA, November 12-16, 2024*, pages 2742–2766. Association for Computational Linguistics.

Biao Zhang, Barry Haddow, and Alexandra Birch. 2023. Prompting large language model for machine translation: A case study. In *International Conference on Machine Learning, ICML 2023, 23-29 July 2023, Honolulu, Hawaii, USA*, volume 202 of *Proceedings of Machine Learning Research*, pages 41092–41110. PMLR.

Jiajun Zhang and Chengqing Zong. 2016. Exploiting source-side monolingual data in neural machine translation. In *Proceedings of the 2016 Conference on Empirical Methods in Natural Language Processing*, pages 1535–1545, Austin, Texas. Association for Computational Linguistics.

Dawei Zhu, Pinzhen Chen, Miaoran Zhang, Barry Haddow, Xiaoyu Shen, and Dietrich Klakow. 2024a. Fine-tuning large language models to translate: Will a touch of noisy data in misaligned languages suffice? In *Proceedings of the 2024 Conference on Empirical Methods in Natural Language Processing, EMNLP 2024, Miami, FL, USA, November 12-16, 2024*, pages 388–409. Association for Computational Linguistics.

Wenhao Zhu, Hongyi Liu, Qingxiu Dong, Jingjing Xu, Shujian Huang, Lingpeng Kong, Jiajun Chen, and Lei Li. 2024b. Multilingual machine translation with large language models: Empirical results and analysis. In *Findings of the Association for Computational Linguistics: NAACL 2024*, pages 2765–2781, Mexico City, Mexico. Association for Computational Linguistics.

Pierre Zweigenbaum, Serge Sharoff, and Reinhard Rapp. 2017. Overview of the second BUCC shared task: Spotting parallel sentences in comparable corpora. In *Proceedings of the 10th Workshop on Building and Using Comparable Corpora, BUCC@ACL 2017, Vancouver, Canada, August 3, 2017*, pages 60–67. Association for Computational Linguistics.

Prompting LLMs: Length Control for Isometric Machine Translation

Dávid Javorský[1] **and Ondřej Bojar**[1] **and François Yvon**[2]

[1]Charles University, Faculty of Mathematics and Physics, Prague, Czechia
[2]Sorbonne Université, CNRS, ISIR, Paris, France
{javorsky,bojar}@ufal.mff.cuni.cz francois.yvon@cnrs.fr

Abstract

In this study, we explore the effectiveness of isometric machine translation across multiple language pairs (En→De, En→Fr, and En→Es) under the conditions of the IWSLT Isometric Shared Task 2022. Using eight open-source large language models (LLMs) of varying sizes, we investigate how different prompting strategies, varying numbers of few-shot examples, and demonstration selection influence translation quality and length control. We discover that the phrasing of instructions, when aligned with the properties of the provided demonstrations, plays a crucial role in controlling the output length. Our experiments show that LLMs tend to produce shorter translations only when presented with extreme examples, while isometric demonstrations often lead to the models disregarding length constraints. While few-shot prompting generally enhances translation quality, further improvements are marginal across 5, 10, and 20-shot settings. Finally, considering multiple outputs allows to notably improve overall tradeoff between the length and quality, yielding state-of-the-art performance for some language pairs.

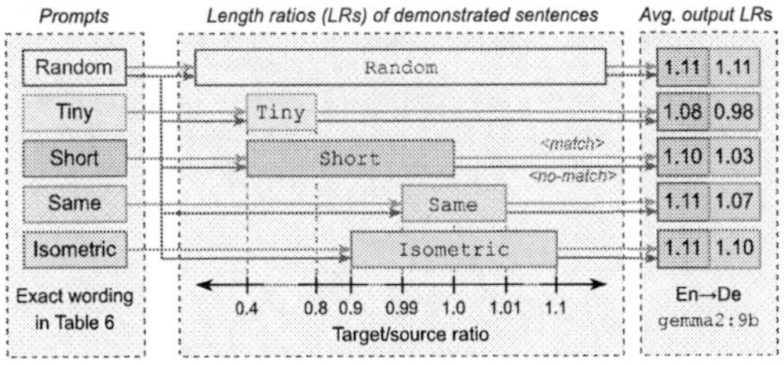

Figure 1: Overview of our experiment with prompts asking for different length constraints for the desired translation, complemented with few-shot examples demonstrating the given constraint (match) or not (no-match). Strong enough control to reach isometric translation needs matching instructions and preferably *Tiny* or Short demonstrations. The construction of demonstration sets is described in Section 3 and the prompt content is presented in Table 6 in Appendix B.2.

1 Introduction

Accurate and concise translations are increasingly needed in media applications such as subtitling (Matusov et al., 2019; Karakanta et al., 2020) and dubbing (Federico et al., 2020; Lakew et al., 2021; Tam et al., 2022; Lakew et al., 2022; Rao et al., 2023), where length constraints are critical. Dubbing, in particular, requires translations to stay within ±10% of the source character-level length for seamless audio alignment (Lakew et al., 2022), a constraint known as *isometric machine translation*. The 2022 Isometric MT Shared Task (Anastasopoulos et al., 2022) found that most participating systems used lead tokens for length control, with some incorporating reranking or adjusted positional embeddings. Recent work also explored reinforcement learning for isometric English-Hindi MT (Mhaskar et al., 2024) and examined length constraints in multiple language pairs (Bhavsar et al., 2022).

Controlling translation length remains challenging compared to other constrained MT tasks, such as politeness (Sennrich et al., 2016) or diversity (Shu et al., 2019) control. Previous approaches in encoder-decoder MT used length tokens (Lakew et al., 2019), positional embeddings (Takase and Okazaki, 2019; Buet and Yvon, 2021), restricted search spaces (Niehues, 2020), auxiliary length prediction tasks (Yang et al., 2020), and explicit compression methods (Li et al., 2020).

With the rise of large language models (LLMs) (Radford et al., 2019), there has been a shift toward prompting (Vilar et al., 2023; Zhang et al., 2023a; Bawden and Yvon, 2023) and fine-tuning (Zhang et al., 2023b; Moslem et al., 2023) for MT. Prompting strategies notably affect performance, especially in few-shot settings (Vilar et al., 2023). Studies found that randomly selected examples often improve results (Zhang et al., 2023a; Bawden and

Proceedings of the 22nd International Conference on Spoken Language Translation (IWSLT 2025), pages 119–137
July 31 - August 1, 2025

	Setup	En-De LR	En-De LC↑	En-De Count	En-Fr LR	En-Fr LC↑	En-Fr Count	En-Es LR	En-Es LC↑	En-Es Count
Dev	Both	1.14±0.3	38.2	1415	1.14±0.3	36.4	1412	1.08±0.3	50.5	1316
Test	Development	1.15±0.2	37.5	200	1.16±0.2	34.0	200	1.03±0.2	58.0	200
	Final Evaluation	1.03±0.2	65.5	200	1.09±0.5	72.5	200	0.98±0.2	64.0	200

Table 1: The average target-to-source sample length ratio and its standard deviation (LR), length compliance (LC), i.e. the percentage of target-side sentences within a ±10% range of the source character count, and the number of samples for two setups (*Development* and *Final Evaluation*) and for the testset (the MuST-C tst-COMMON and blind test sets) and the devset (MuST-C). The devset is used for selecting examples for few-shot prompting.

Pool type	En-De Count	Min	Max	avg±std
`Random`	1415	0.43	5.80	1.14±0.27
`Isometric`	537	0.90	1.10	1.02±0.05
`Same`	50	0.99	1.00	1.00±0.00
`Short`	343	0.43	1.00	0.90±0.11
`Tiny`	50	0.43	0.81	0.68±0.11

Table 2: Statistics of pools for En→De: The number of samples, minimum and maximum target/source length ratio, and its average and standard deviation.

Yvon, 2023), though performance gains plateau beyond five examples (Chowdhery et al., 2023; Vilar et al., 2023). While models like BLOOM tend to overgenerate in zero-shot settings (Bawden and Yvon, 2023), fine-tuning methods such as QLoRA (Zhang et al., 2023b) have shown superior performance over few-shot learning. Real-time adaptive MT has also demonstrated strong results, with models like ChatGPT rivaling traditional MT systems (Moslem et al., 2023; Hendy et al., 2023). The use of LLMs for MT has led to the exploration of various prompt templates, with simple structures like '`[src]: [input] \n [tgt]:`' proving effective (Zhang et al., 2023a; Briakou et al., 2023; Zeng et al., 2022). The impact of example selection has also been examined, confirming that beyond five-shot settings, improvements become marginal (Garcia et al., 2023; Zhang et al., 2023a; Chowdhery et al., 2023; Vilar et al., 2023).

Given these insights, we explore the application of LLMs to isometric MT, focusing on length control strategies. We analyze four prompting approaches: (1) uncontrolled translation, (2) isometric translation (±10% length variation), (3) same-length translation, and (4) shorter translation, each paired with corresponding demonstration sets. Experiments are conducted on eight open-weight models (Llama 3, Gemma 2, Qwen 2 of two sizes each, and Mistral and Mixtral) across 0, 5, 10, and 20-shot settings for En→De, En→Fr, and En→Es, following the 2022 Isometric Shared Task setup (Anastasopoulos et al., 2022).

Our results show that few-shot demonstrations affect translation outputs, but precise length control requires well-aligned instructions reflecting example properties, as summarized in Figure 1. Additionally, we show that generating multiple outputs with different example sets substantially improves length control, matching competitive isometric MT systems and offering high potential for synthetic data creation in training encoder-decoder models. We publicly release all collected data for potential future analyses.[1]

2 Experimental Setup

Development First, we conduct experiments with multiple settings (varying prompt type, the type of pools of demonstrations, and shot count in few-shot learning) to identify the best-performing configuration for length control. We refer to this as the *Development* setup and use the following data:

- *Demonstration set*: We use the MuST-C devset for selecting few-shot examples. We choose the devset over the trainset to reserve the latter for potential future fine-tuning.
- *Testset*: We use the first 200 examples from the MuST-C tst-COMMON, matching the number of examples in the evaluation blindset of the 2022 Isometric Shared Task.

Final Evaluation We then use the best-performing setting from the *Development* and evaluate it on the Isometric Shared Task test set:

- *Demonstration set*: We use the same demontration set as in the *Development* setup.
- *Testset*: We use the blindset from the IWSLT 2022 Isometric Shared Task, which consists of dialogues extracted from YouTube videos, totaling 200 examples.[2]

[1] https://github.com/J4VORSKY/Isometric-MT

[2] https://github.com/amazon-research/isometric-slt/tree/main/dataset

The statistics of the datasets used in both steps are displayed in Table 1.

Metrics Following the Isometric Shared Task, we use *BERTScore*[3] (Zhang et al., 2020) to evaluate translation quality. For completeness, we also report *BLEU* (Papineni et al., 2002) scores using sacreBLEU (Post, 2018).[4,5] We assess adherence to the ±10% length constraint using the *Length Compliance* (LC) metric (Anastasopoulos et al., 2022). Additionally, we report the average target-to-source *Length Ratio* in *Development* experiments and use it alongside Length Compliance in the *Final Evaluation* to gauge length control.

Models We use the Ollama library[6] to load all models, which are provided in quantized versions (4-bit) without instruction fine-tuning (more details in Appendix B). Models used in our experiments include: `llama3:8b`, `llama3:70b` (Dubey et al., 2024); `gemma2:9b`, `gemma2:27b` (Gemma Team et al., 2024); `qwen2:7b`, `qwen2:72b` (Yang et al., 2024); `mistral:7b` (Jiang et al., 2023) and `mixtral:8x7b` (Jiang et al., 2024). For detailed descriptions, refer to the original papers.

3 Prompts

In our experiments, we use English as the language of the prompts (Zhang et al., 2023a) and explicitly specify the source and target languages within the prompt (Zhang et al., 2023a; Bawden and Yvon, 2023). Our focus is on length control when testing various prompt formulations. While large language models (LLMs) show strong performance in machine translation, they sometimes lag behind supervised neural models (Zhang et al., 2023a; Chowdhery et al., 2023; Kocmi et al., 2023). To our knowledge, length control has not been extensively explored for LLMs in machine translation.

Prompt construction We construct prompts by concatenating template parts and replacing placeholders with the appropriate values. The *Random* (uncontrolled) template instructs the model to generate a translation of the source sentence without any length restrictions. In the *Isometric* template, the model is instructed to generate a translation within ±10% of the source text's character count. The *Same* template instructs the model to produce a translation that exactly matches the source text length, while the *Short / Tiny* template directs the model to generate a shorter translation, as the length ratios between studied language pairs often exceed 1, and a standard translation (typically longer) is not desired. A detailed overview of the prompt templates is in Table 6 in Appendix B.2.

We evaluate models in zero-shot and few-shot settings. They often overgenerate, adding explanations or extra translations, as noted by Bawden and Yvon (2023). While these authors used regular expressions to extract translations, we prevent this by explicitly instructing models to output only the translation, which proves effective. Further analysis is in Appendix A.

Sample Selection In preparing examples for the few-shot setting, we construct sampling pools by filtering the demonstration set based on the following criteria: `Random` selects samples without any filtering; `Isometric` contains only examples with a target-to-source length ratio within ±10%; `Same` sorts references by increasing $|r - 1.0|$ (where r is the length ratio) and selects the top $N = 50$ instances; `Short` selects samples with target-to-source ratios in the range $[0, 1]$; `Tiny` samples the 50 examples with the smallest target-to-source ratio. The illustration is in Figure 1.

Statistics for each sampling pool for En→De are in Table 2. As other languages follow the same trend, their statistics are in Table 7 in Appendix B.3. Following Zhang et al. (2023a), we use the following template for in-context samples: `[src lang]: [src sentence]` ¬ `[tgt lang]: [tgt sentence]`.

4 Analysis

In all experiments, the prompts remain identical across all models within a given setting. To reduce the bias of sampling from demonstration sets, we performed 10 runs for every setting.

4.1 Prompt and Pool Type Relation

First, we analyze how much the selection of examples is related to the instruction provided in the prompt in the few-shot prompting and how this combination influences the translation length. We therefore compare two setups:

Prompt and Pool Type Match We create matching pairs of prompts and pool types as follows:

[3]https://pypi.org/project/bert-score/0.3.11/

[4]https://github.com/mjpost/sacrebleu

[5]Signature: nrefs:1|case:mixed|eff:no|tok:13a|smooth:exp|version:2.4.2

[6]https://ollama.com/library

En-De

Model \ Match	Random No	Random Yes	Isometric No	Isometric Yes	Same No	Same Yes	Short No	Short Yes	Tiny No	Tiny Yes
gemma2:27b	1.100	1.097	1.099	1.094	1.098	1.097	1.087	1.011	1.066	0.955
gemma2:9b	1.108	1.106	1.106	1.101	1.106	1.073	1.099	1.026	1.080	0.981
llama3:70b	1.149	1.151	1.149	1.139	1.141	1.134	1.138	1.005	1.122	0.905
llama3:8b	1.106	1.100	1.093	1.108	1.099	1.112	1.085	1.048	1.056	0.994
mistral:7b	1.133	1.129	1.126	1.128	1.135	1.125	1.121	1.105	1.138	1.085
mixtral:8x7b	1.402	1.411	1.375	1.362	1.378	1.381	1.385	1.297	1.363	1.265
qwen2:72b	1.223	1.169	1.195	1.178	1.184	1.173	1.170	1.128	1.164	1.129
qwen2:7b	1.132	1.160	1.144	1.125	1.129	1.129	1.128	1.135	1.117	1.095

Table 3: The evaluation is conducted as follows: We first compute the average target length per input sentence across 10 runs. Next, we calculate the target-to-source length ratio for each instance and average these values for each pool type. The results are reported separately for cases where the instructions match ('Yes') or do not match ('No') the sample properties in 5-shot prompting. Differences with a p-value < 0.1 for each pool type are underlined.

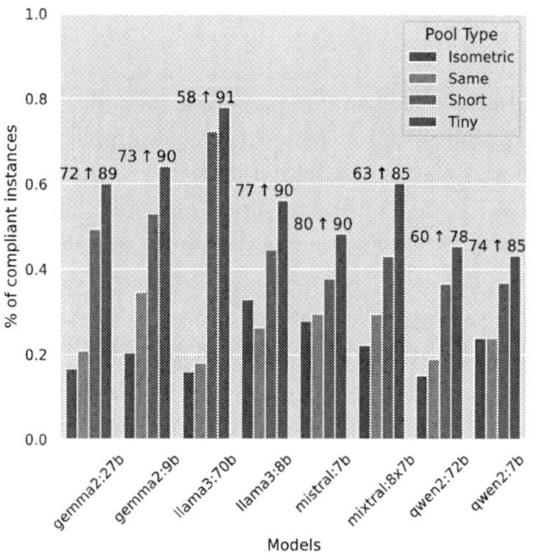

Figure 2: The percentage of input sentences (across all language directions) for which at least one of ten generated translations meets the isometric condition when the model is prompted to produce isometric, same-length, short, and tiny outputs aligned with respective 5-shot demonstration sets. This evaluation is restricted to input sentences where the particular model did not generate any isometric translation in ten attempts using the uncontrolled prompt.

Random–Random, Isometric–Isometric, Same–Same, Short–Short, Tiny–Tiny.

Prompt and Pool Type Mismatch We keep the Random prompt for all pool types.

We compare these two configurations for En→De in Table 3, the remaining translation directions are documented in Appendix C. Our results indicate that the length ratios are mostly affected when the instruction aligns with the pool type, compared to when there is no such match (we can also see a tendency to generate shorter outputs when comparing "no alignment" columns across different pool types, but the difference is negligible). This match-versus-no-match difference is statistically significant in Gemma and Llama models, particularly for the Short and Tiny pools. Additionally, the Isometric and Same pools do not appear to induce shorter translations compared to random sampling, as evidenced by the similar values observed in the first three columns. We hypothesize that requesting outputs to preserve the input length somehow guides models to reproduce the distribution of the training data rather than actually considering the length (i.e. models implicitly assume that typical translation is of the same length). However, in studied language directions, what is considered as normal ratio, is skewed towards values greater than 1. In other words, models naturally follow the length distribution they were trained on and can overcome this bias only when extreme examples are provided.

To further highlight the utility of our approach, Figure 2 focuses on cases where models consistently fail to produce isometric translations under the *Random*-Random setting, even after 10 runs. This occurs in about 30% of devset sentences on average. The figure shows how alternative prompts improve length compliance, with *Tiny* and *Short* settings achieving up to 80% isometric translations for Llama3:70b when at least one of 10 runs succeeds. The overall practical ability of each of the models to achieve isometric translation is summarized by the two numbers above the bars in Figure 2. The first number indicates the percentage of devset sentences that were translated in a compliant way by default and the second number indicates to which proportion we raised this using the *Tiny* prompt. Note that in the worst case, this level of

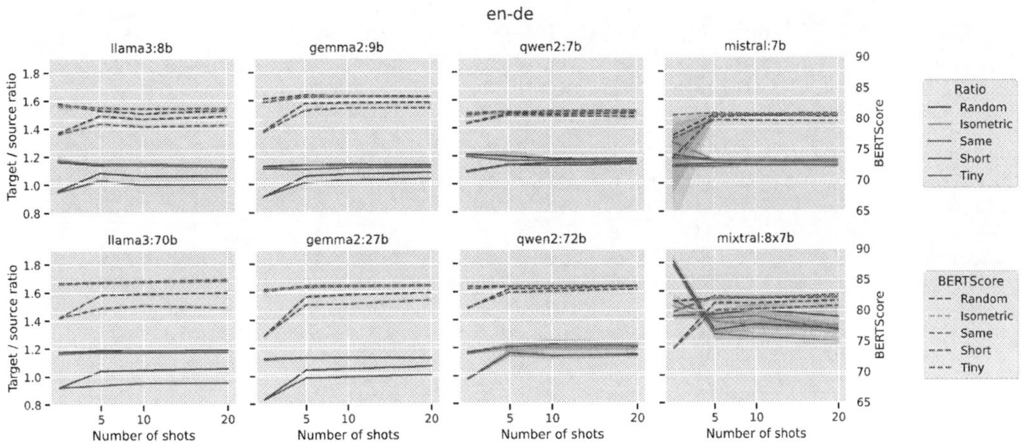

Figure 3: En→De translation quality (BERTScore, dashed lines and the right hand y-axes) and length ratio (solid lines and left-hand y-axes) for all few-shot settings, models and language pairs.

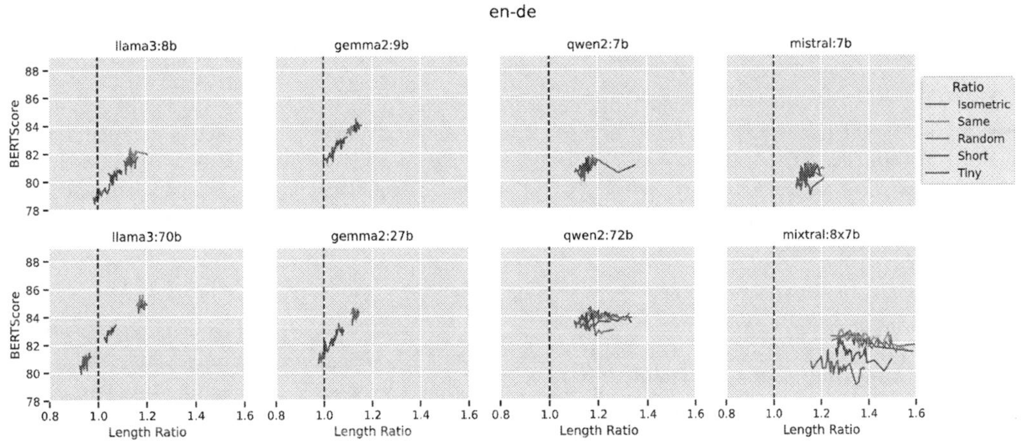

Figure 4: En→De trade-off between the length ratio (x-axis) and translation quality (y-axis) for 5, 10, 20-shot settings and all models.

compliance is reached at 20x the translation cost (10 attempts by default plus 10 *Tiny* attempts). In practice, however, we can switch to the *Tiny* prompt after the first unsuccessful attempt in the default generation. The number of additional generations with *Tiny* setting depends on resource constraints and requirements. But even after just one attempt, `Llama3:70b` achieves isometric translations in 35% of cases. Full results are in Appendix C.

4.2 Comparing Demonstration Pools

We give below a more detailed evaluation across all few-shot settings, models, and pool types, using only settings when the instruction matches the pool type and where the model is instructed to output only the translation. Both length ratios and BERTScore values are reported for En→De, with the results presented in Figure 3. For a comprehensive view of all few-shot settings, detailed numerical results are reported in Appendix D.

Length Ratios and Length Control In terms of length ratio, all models consistently exhibit the same trend: the ratios are highest for random sampling, followed by isometric sampling, and then by shorter examples. Providing extreme examples encourages models to produce shorter translations. Interestingly, in the zero-shot setting, we observe a length ratio lower than 1.0 for the Llama and Gemma models. However, when demonstrations are also given in few-shot settings for these models, translations are longer, even when the associated

	En→De				En→Fr				En→Es			
System	LR↓	LC↑	BS↑	BLEU↑	LR↓	LC↑	BS↑	BLEU↑	LR↓	LC↑	BS↑	BLEU↑
STRONGBASELINE	**1.03**	68.0	77.44	21.6	1.02	75.5	**81.75**	**36.2**	**1.00**	80.5	81.86	36
APPTEK-Constrained	1.11	86.5	77.32	18.7	-	-	-	-	-	-	-	-
NUV-Unconstrained	-	-	-	-	1.10	47.5	79.96	27.1	-	-	-	-
HW-TSC-Unconstrained	**1.03**	96.5	75.79	20.2	-	-	-	-	-	-	-	-
HW-TSC-Constrained	1.28	**98.0**	74.07	17.9	1.19	**96.0**	76.11	31.5	1.18	**96.5**	78.57	29.9
APV-Unconstrained	1.68	39.0	73.68	16.5	1.21	45.0	77.77	32.9	1.05	49.5	80.87	35.3
WEAKBASELINE	1.29	43.0	74.86	15.5	1.48	37.0	77.18	25.2	1.38	51.0	78.32	27.7
`model=gemma2:27b-k=1`	1.07	43.5	77.08	19.0	1.05	47.5	78.30	32.7	**1.00**	55.5	83.20	40.3
`model=gemma2:27b-k=3`	1.08	58.0	77.96	20.2	1.07	60.5	79.96	33.5	1.01	66.5	83.29	40.3
`model=gemma2:27b-k=5`	1.09	62.5	**77.98**	20.4	1.06	62.5	80.01	33.9	1.02	68.0	83.16	40.0
`model=gemma2:27b-k=10`	1.08	68.5	77.84	**21.9**	1.08	69.0	80.05	35.6	1.01	70.5	**83.62**	**40.8**
`model=gemma2:9b-k=1`	2.24	42.5	77.04	17.7	0.00	0.0	0.00	0.0	1.02	54.5	82.47	39.0
`model=gemma2:9b-k=3`	1.19	58.5	77.24	20.6	1.07	60.5	80.38	34.1	1.03	65.5	83.41	36.8
`model=gemma2:9b-k=5`	1.07	64.5	77.38	20.9	1.06	65.5	80.66	35.5	1.03	73.0	83.30	37.2
`model=gemma2:9b-k=10`	1.08	64.0	77.48	21.7	1.06	70.5	80.72	34.9	1.03	73.0	83.17	37.6
`model=llama3:70b-k=1`	1.09	49.0	76.57	20.9	1.05	41.0	76.44	28.6	0.96	46.5	79.29	31.4
`model=llama3:70b-k=3`	1.06	62.5	77.18	22.1	**1.00**	55.5	77.64	30.9	1.03	59.5	80.64	34.4
`model=llama3:70b-k=5`	1.06	65.0	77.24	22.2	1.02	64.0	77.62	32.5	1.02	65.5	80.96	35.1
`model=llama3:70b-k=10`	1.07	69.0	77.23	21.7	1.04	68.0	78.24	33.7	1.02	70.5	81.37	35.8
`model=llama3:8b-k=1`	1.21	42.0	74.30	13.8	1.16	47.5	74.71	22.9	1.03	48.5	77.80	28.6
`model=llama3:8b-k=3`	1.09	56.0	75.79	15.9	1.09	60.5	75.96	25.5	0.99	65.0	79.76	30.6
`model=llama3:8b-k=5`	1.09	60.5	76.10	16.7	1.10	69.5	76.32	26.1	1.01	69.5	80.15	31.4
`model=llama3:8b-k=10`	1.09	65.0	76.28	16.9	1.08	75.0	77.02	26.2	1.03	74.0	79.88	29.0
OracleBLEU	1.04	78.0	80.82	37.6	1.03	85.0	83.93	52.9	1.01	88.5	87.01	57.5

Table 4: *Final Evaluation* — Length Ratio (LR), Length Compliance (LC), BERTScore (BS) and BLEU — of the best setting (10-shot, pool type `Tiny`) across different Llama and Gemma models compared to the submissions of IWSLT Isometric Shared Task. The k values indicate the number of demonstration sampling runs (i.e. different outputs) from which we select the best one using COMETKIWI. To avoid any possible evaluation difference, we (re-)evaluated all the outputs, ours and IWSLT22 ones, using the script provided by the organizers of the shared task. The best results are in bold.

demonstrations are short or very short.

Few-shot Prompting Another notable observation is that increasing the number of examples in few-shot prompting does not substantially enhance regular translation quality (i.e., translation without length restrictions), which is consistent with previous findings (Bawden and Yvon, 2023; Zhang et al., 2023a; Chowdhery et al., 2023). Including shorter examples sometimes improves adherence to length limitations (e.g., for `llama3:8b`); this effect is not observed for all models (e.g., for `gemma2:27b`).

Translation Quality Scores The largest translation quality scores are observed when the unfiltered pool (`Random`) is used, which is expected as this corresponds to an unconstrained setting. The top-performing model in terms of BERTScore for English-German translations is `llama3:70b`. For the other language pairs, `gemma2:9b`, `gemma2:27b` and `qwen2:72b` achieve the largest translation score.

Length Ratio and Translation Quality Tradeoff We also compare translation scores with length ratios. The results are presented in Figure 4 for En→De direction (the rest in Figure 7 in Appendix E). We can see that only Llama and Gemma models are capable of reaching 1.0 length ratio. Our results also highlight the impact of model size on performance, with larger models consistently outperforming their smaller counterparts in BERTScore, except for `gemma2:9b` which reports similar performance to its large counterpart.

5 Final Evaluation

Since Llama and Gemma models achieve the best performance on all language pairs on average, we select and evaluate them in *Final Evaluation* using the Isometric Shared Task blind set. We generate outputs using 10 distinct sets of 10 examples (10-shot), each drawn from the `Tiny` pool as it yields the best length control. We keep only outputs in the $\pm 10\%$ length constraint[7] and select the best one according to reference-free COMET, i.e. COMETKIWI[8] score (Rei et al., 2022). We then

[7] If none of the translations adhere to the $\pm 10\%$ length constraint, we keep the original unfiltered set.

[8] `https://huggingface.co/Unbabel/wmt22-cometkiwi-da`

compare these results with the submissions from the IWSLT 2022 Isometric Shared Task, specifically those from the APPTEK (Wilken and Matusov, 2022), HW-TSC (Li et al., 2022), Amazon Prime Video (APV), and NUV teams (Bhatnagar et al., 2022), in addition to the two (strong and weak) baselines provided by the organizers. For a brief overview of each system, please refer to Anastasopoulos et al. (2022). Additionally, we compare our results to an OracleBLEU setting, where the best translation is selected according to the sentence BLEU score across all configurations after filtering out translations that fall outside ±10% of the source character count. The results are summarized in Table 4.

Our results show that for the En→De and En→Es language pairs, the Gemma models achieve output quality comparable to the strong baseline. While the translation quality metrics surpass that of the strong baseline, the length control is slightly less precise. For En→Fr, however, the strong baseline continues to outperform our models in terms of quality as well as LR. Although generating 10 different outputs for each source sentence may not be feasible in practice, this approach could be beneficial for producing synthetic data for training isometric machine translation models.

6 Conclusion

In this paper, we explored the use of LLMs for isometric machine translation, focusing on strategies to control the translation length. Our key findings are as follows: First, effective length control in few-shot prompting requires the simultaneous use of appropriate demonstrations and matching instructions. Second, generating multiple outputs achieves the best trade-off between length control and translation quality, indicating the high capability of LLMs to generate desired outputs. It might be also useful for creating synthetic training data. Although prompting 10 times may seem inefficient, it would not be necessary for every sample in practice. Since half of the samples are already length-compliant — even with the uncontrolled *Random* prompt — compliance for the rest can be achieved iteratively by generating translations until the length constraint is met. Future work might benefit from fine-tuning LLMs or from a more in-depth analysis of the internal representation of length in LLMs to avoid many samples to generate.

Limitations

We compare our results primarily with system submissions from the Isometric Shared Task 2022, as more recent models either do not address the language pairs examined in this study (e.g., Hindi-English by Mhaskar et al. (2024)) or are not publicly available (Bhavsar et al., 2022). Additionally, we do not evaluate performance on any downstream tasks, such as subtitling or dubbing.

We did not conduct a detailed analysis of ensemble methods, particularly concerning ensembling across different models or pool types. Moreover, for the `Tiny` and `Same` pools, we do not analyze the effect of varying N.

When collecting 10 outputs in *Final Evaluation*, the associated computational cost increases considerably. While this approach may not be feasible for real-world applications, it can be valuable for generating high-quality examples for isometric machine translation model training. To further reduce computational costs, one could regenerate only those translations that do not meet the specified length constraints.

Finally, it is important to note that we exclusively used quantized versions of the models in our experiments, likely resulting in sub-optimal translation scores.

Acknowledgements

The work has been partially supported by the grant 272323 of the Grant Agency of Charles University, SVV project number 260 821 and by the grant CZ.02.01.01/00/23_020/0008518 ("Jazykověda, umělá inteligence a jazykové a řečové technologie: od výzkumu k aplikacím").

References

Antonios Anastasopoulos, Loïc Barrault, Luisa Bentivogli, Marcely Zanon Boito, Ondřej Bojar, Roldano Cattoni, Anna Currey, Georgiana Dinu, Kevin Duh, Maha Elbayad, Clara Emmanuel, Yannick Estève, Marcello Federico, Christian Federmann, Souhir Gahbiche, Hongyu Gong, Roman Grundkiewicz, Barry Haddow, Benjamin Hsu, Dávid Javorský, Věra Kloudová, Surafel Lakew, Xutai Ma, Prashant Mathur, Paul McNamee, Kenton Murray, Maria Nădejde, Satoshi Nakamura, Matteo Negri, Jan Niehues, Xing Niu, John Ortega, Juan Pino, Elizabeth Salesky, Jiatong Shi, Matthias Sperber, Sebastian Stüker, Katsuhito Sudoh, Marco Turchi, Yogesh Virkar, Alexander Waibel, Changhan Wang, and Shinji Watanabe. 2022. Findings of the IWSLT 2022 evaluation campaign. In *Proceedings of the*

19th International Conference on Spoken Language Translation (IWSLT 2022), pages 98–157, Dublin, Ireland (in-person and online). Association for Computational Linguistics.

Rachel Bawden and François Yvon. 2023. Investigating the translation performance of a large multilingual language model: the case of BLOOM. In *Proceedings of the 24th Annual Conference of the European Association for Machine Translation*, pages 157–170, Tampere, Finland. European Association for Machine Translation.

Aakash Bhatnagar, Nidhir Bhavsar, Muskaan Singh, and Petr Motlicek. 2022. Hierarchical multi-task learning framework for isometric-speech language translation. In *Proceedings of the 19th International Conference on Spoken Language Translation (IWSLT 2022)*, pages 379–385, Dublin, Ireland (in-person and online). Association for Computational Linguistics.

Nidhir Bhavsar, Aakash Bhatnagar, and Muskaan Singh. 2022. HMIST: Hierarchical multilingual isometric speech translation using multi-task learning framework and it's influence on automatic dubbing. In *Proceedings of the 36th Pacific Asia Conference on Language, Information and Computation*, pages 554–563, Manila, Philippines. Association for Computational Linguistics.

Eleftheria Briakou, Colin Cherry, and George Foster. 2023. Searching for needles in a haystack: On the role of incidental bilingualism in PaLM's translation capability. In *Proceedings of the 61st Annual Meeting of the Association for Computational Linguistics (Volume 1: Long Papers)*, pages 9432–9452, Toronto, Canada. Association for Computational Linguistics.

François Buet and François Yvon. 2021. Toward Genre Adapted Closed Captioning. In *Proc. Interspeech 2021*, pages 4403–4407.

Aakanksha Chowdhery, Sharan Narang, Jacob Devlin, Maarten Bosma, Gaurav Mishra, Adam Roberts, Paul Barham, Hyung Won Chung, Charles Sutton, Sebastian Gehrmann, et al. 2023. PALM: Scaling language modeling with pathways. *Journal of Machine Learning Research*, 24(240):1–113.

Abhimanyu Dubey, Abhinav Jauhri, Abhinav Pandey, Abhishek Kadian, Ahmad Al-Dahle, Aiesha Letman, Akhil Mathur, Alan Schelten, Amy Yang, Angela Fan, et al. 2024. The llama 3 herd of models. *arXiv preprint arXiv:2407.21783*.

Marcello Federico, Robert Enyedi, Roberto Barra-Chicote, Ritwik Giri, Umut Isik, Arvindh Krishnaswamy, and Hassan Sawaf. 2020. From speech-to-speech translation to automatic dubbing. In *Proceedings of the 17th International Conference on Spoken Language Translation*, pages 257–264, Online. Association for Computational Linguistics.

Xavier Garcia, Yamini Bansal, Colin Cherry, George Foster, Maxim Krikun, Melvin Johnson, and Orhan Firat. 2023. The unreasonable effectiveness of few-shot learning for machine translation. In *Proceedings of the 40th International Conference on Machine Learning*, ICML'23. JMLR.org.

Gemma Gemma Team, Morgane Riviere, Shreya Pathak, Pier Giuseppe Sessa, Cassidy Hardin, Surya Bhupatiraju, Léonard Hussenot, Thomas Mesnard, Bobak Shahriari, Alexandre Ramé, et al. 2024. Gemma 2: Improving open language models at a practical size. *arXiv preprint arXiv:2408.00118*.

Amr Hendy, Mohamed Abdelrehim, Amr Sharaf, Vikas Raunak, Mohamed Gabr, Hitokazu Matsushita, Young Jin Kim, Mohamed Afify, and Hany Hassan Awadalla. 2023. How good are GPT models at machine translation? a comprehensive evaluation. *arXiv preprint arXiv:2302.09210*.

Albert Q Jiang, Alexandre Sablayrolles, Arthur Mensch, Chris Bamford, Devendra Singh Chaplot, Diego de las Casas, Florian Bressand, Gianna Lengyel, Guillaume Lample, Lucile Saulnier, et al. 2023. Mistral 7b. *arXiv preprint arXiv:2310.06825*.

Albert Q Jiang, Alexandre Sablayrolles, Antoine Roux, Arthur Mensch, Blanche Savary, Chris Bamford, Devendra Singh Chaplot, Diego de las Casas, Emma Bou Hanna, Florian Bressand, et al. 2024. Mixtral of experts. *arXiv preprint arXiv:2401.04088*.

Alina Karakanta, Matteo Negri, and Marco Turchi. 2020. Is 42 the answer to everything in subtitling-oriented speech translation? In *Proceedings of the 17th International Conference on Spoken Language Translation*, pages 209–219, Online. Association for Computational Linguistics.

Tom Kocmi, Eleftherios Avramidis, Rachel Bawden, Ondřej Bojar, Anton Dvorkovich, Christian Federmann, Mark Fishel, Markus Freitag, Thamme Gowda, Roman Grundkiewicz, Barry Haddow, Philipp Koehn, Benjamin Marie, Christof Monz, Makoto Morishita, Kenton Murray, Makoto Nagata, Toshiaki Nakazawa, Martin Popel, Maja Popović, and Mariya Shmatova. 2023. Findings of the 2023 conference on machine translation (WMT23): LLMs are here but not quite there yet. In *Proceedings of the Eighth Conference on Machine Translation*, pages 1–42, Singapore. Association for Computational Linguistics.

Surafel M. Lakew, Marcello Federico, Yue Wang, Cuong Hoang, Yogesh Virkar, Roberto Barra-Chicote, and Robert Enyedi. 2021. Machine translation verbosity control for automatic dubbing. In *ICASSP 2021 - 2021 IEEE International Conference on Acoustics, Speech and Signal Processing (ICASSP)*, pages 7538–7542.

Surafel M Lakew, Yogesh Virkar, Prashant Mathur, and Marcello Federico. 2022. Isometric MT: Neural machine translation for automatic dubbing. In *ICASSP 2022-2022 IEEE International Conference on Acoustics, Speech and Signal Processing (ICASSP)*, pages 6242–6246. IEEE.

Surafel Melaku Lakew, Mattia Di Gangi, and Marcello Federico. 2019. Controlling the output length of neural machine translation. In *Proceedings of the 16th International Conference on Spoken Language Translation*, Hong Kong. Association for Computational Linguistics.

Zongyao Li, Jiaxin Guo, Daimeng Wei, Hengchao Shang, Minghan Wang, Ting Zhu, Zhanglin Wu, Zhengzhe Yu, Xiaoyu Chen, Lizhi Lei, Hao Yang, and Ying Qin. 2022. HW-TSC's participation in the IWSLT 2022 isometric spoken language translation. In *Proceedings of the 19th International Conference on Spoken Language Translation (IWSLT 2022)*, pages 361–368, Dublin, Ireland (in-person and online). Association for Computational Linguistics.

Zuchao Li, Rui Wang, Kehai Chen, Masao Utiyama, Eiichiro Sumita, Zhuosheng Zhang, and Hai Zhao. 2020. Explicit sentence compression for neural machine translation. In *Proceedings of the AAAI Conference on Artificial Intelligence*, volume 34, pages 8311–8318.

Evgeny Matusov, Patrick Wilken, and Yota Georgakopoulou. 2019. Customizing neural machine translation for subtitling. In *Proceedings of the Fourth Conference on Machine Translation (Volume 1: Research Papers)*, pages 82–93, Florence, Italy. Association for Computational Linguistics.

Shivam Ratnakant Mhaskar, Nirmesh J Shah, Mohammadi Zaki, Ashishkumar P Gudmalwar, Pankaj Wasnik, and Rajiv Ratn Shah. 2024. Isometric neural machine translation using phoneme count ratio reward-based reinforcement learning. *arXiv preprint arXiv:2403.15469*.

Yasmin Moslem, Rejwanul Haque, John D. Kelleher, and Andy Way. 2023. Adaptive machine translation with large language models. In *Proceedings of the 24th Annual Conference of the European Association for Machine Translation*, pages 227–237, Tampere, Finland. European Association for Machine Translation.

Jan Niehues. 2020. Machine translation with unsupervised length-constraints. In *Proceedings of the 14th Conference of the Association for Machine Translation in the Americas (Volume 1: Research Track)*, pages 21–35, Virtual. Association for Machine Translation in the Americas.

Kishore Papineni, Salim Roukos, Todd Ward, and Wei-Jing Zhu. 2002. Bleu: a method for automatic evaluation of machine translation. In *Proceedings of the 40th Annual Meeting of the Association for Computational Linguistics*, pages 311–318, Philadelphia, Pennsylvania, USA. Association for Computational Linguistics.

Matt Post. 2018. A call for clarity in reporting BLEU scores. In *Proceedings of the Third Conference on Machine Translation: Research Papers*, pages 186–191, Brussels, Belgium. Association for Computational Linguistics.

Alec Radford, Jeffrey Wu, Rewon Child, David Luan, Dario Amodei, Ilya Sutskever, et al. 2019. Language models are unsupervised multitask learners. *OpenAI blog*, 1(8):9.

Zhiqiang Rao, Hengchao Shang, Jinlong Yang, Daimeng Wei, Zongyao Li, Jiaxin Guo, Shaojun Li, Zhengzhe Yu, Zhanglin Wu, Yuhao Xie, Bin Wei, Jiawei Zheng, Lizhi Lei, and Hao Yang. 2023. Length-aware NMT and adaptive duration for automatic dubbing. In *Proceedings of the 20th International Conference on Spoken Language Translation (IWSLT 2023)*, pages 138–143, Toronto, Canada (in-person and online). Association for Computational Linguistics.

Ricardo Rei, Marcos Treviso, Nuno M. Guerreiro, Chrysoula Zerva, Ana C Farinha, Christine Maroti, José G. C. de Souza, Taisiya Glushkova, Duarte Alves, Luisa Coheur, Alon Lavie, and André F. T. Martins. 2022. CometKiwi: IST-unbabel 2022 submission for the quality estimation shared task. In *Proceedings of the Seventh Conference on Machine Translation (WMT)*, pages 634–645, Abu Dhabi, United Arab Emirates (Hybrid). Association for Computational Linguistics.

Rico Sennrich, Barry Haddow, and Alexandra Birch. 2016. Controlling politeness in neural machine translation via side constraints. In *Proceedings of the 2016 Conference of the North American Chapter of the Association for Computational Linguistics: Human Language Technologies*, pages 35–40, San Diego, California. Association for Computational Linguistics.

Raphael Shu, Hideki Nakayama, and Kyunghyun Cho. 2019. Generating diverse translations with sentence codes. In *Proceedings of the 57th Annual Meeting of the Association for Computational Linguistics*, pages 1823–1827, Florence, Italy. Association for Computational Linguistics.

Sho Takase and Naoaki Okazaki. 2019. Positional encoding to control output sequence length. In *Proceedings of the 2019 Conference of the North American Chapter of the Association for Computational Linguistics: Human Language Technologies, Volume 1 (Long and Short Papers)*, pages 3999–4004, Minneapolis, Minnesota. Association for Computational Linguistics.

Derek Tam, Surafel M. Lakew, Yogesh Virkar, Prashant Mathur, and Marcello Federico. 2022. Isochrony-Aware Neural Machine Translation for Automatic Dubbing. In *Proc. Interspeech 2022*, pages 1776–1780.

David Vilar, Markus Freitag, Colin Cherry, Jiaming Luo, Viresh Ratnakar, and George Foster. 2023. Prompting PaLM for translation: Assessing strategies and performance. In *Proceedings of the 61st Annual Meeting of the Association for Computational Linguistics (Volume 1: Long Papers)*, pages 15406–15427, Toronto, Canada. Association for Computational Linguistics.

Patrick Wilken and Evgeny Matusov. 2022. AppTek's submission to the IWSLT 2022 isometric spoken language translation task. In *Proceedings of the 19th International Conference on Spoken Language Translation (IWSLT 2022)*, pages 369–378, Dublin, Ireland (in-person and online). Association for Computational Linguistics.

An Yang, Baosong Yang, Binyuan Hui, Bo Zheng, Bowen Yu, Chang Zhou, Chengpeng Li, Chengyuan Li, Dayiheng Liu, Fei Huang, et al. 2024. Qwen2 technical report. *arXiv preprint arXiv:2407.10671*.

Zijian Yang, Yingbo Gao, Weiyue Wang, and Hermann Ney. 2020. Predicting and using target length in neural machine translation. In *Proceedings of the 1st Conference of the Asia-Pacific Chapter of the Association for Computational Linguistics and the 10th International Joint Conference on Natural Language Processing*, pages 389–395, Suzhou, China. Association for Computational Linguistics.

Aohan Zeng, Xiao Liu, Zhengxiao Du, Zihan Wang, Hanyu Lai, Ming Ding, Zhuoyi Yang, Yifan Xu, Wendi Zheng, Xiao Xia, et al. 2022. Glm-130b: An open bilingual pre-trained model. In *The Eleventh International Conference on Learning Representations*.

Biao Zhang, Barry Haddow, and Alexandra Birch. 2023a. Prompting large language model for machine translation: A case study. In *International Conference on Machine Learning*, pages 41092–41110. PMLR.

Tianyi Zhang, Varsha Kishore, Felix Wu, Kilian Q. Weinberger, and Yoav Artzi. 2020. BERTScore: Evaluating Text Generation with BERT. In *International Conference on Learning Representations*.

Xuan Zhang, Navid Rajabi, Kevin Duh, and Philipp Koehn. 2023b. Machine translation with large language models: Prompting, few-shot learning, and fine-tuning with QLoRA. In *Proceedings of the Eighth Conference on Machine Translation*, pages 468–481, Singapore. Association for Computational Linguistics.

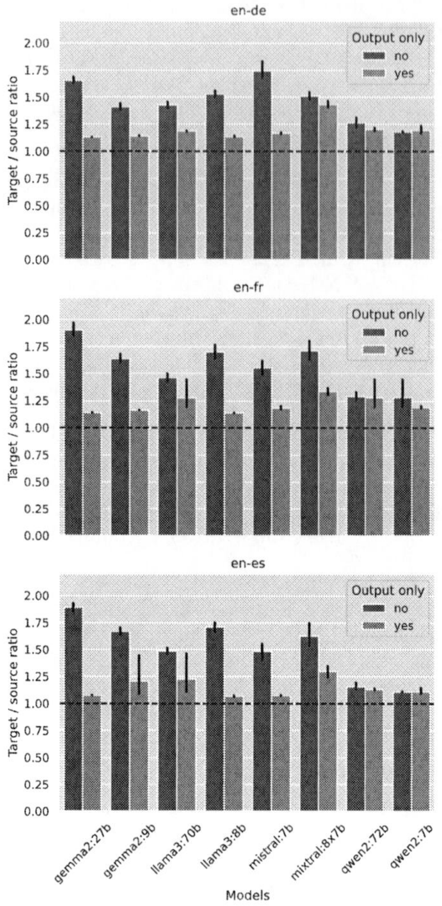

Figure 5: Restricted vs unrestricted prompt for 5-shot examples and the random pool when we discard everything after the first new line. In restricted, we add 'output translation only' at the end of the prompt. The red dashed line corresponds to a ratio of 1.0.

A Overgeneration

Bawden and Yvon (2023) have demonstrated that the BLOOM model tends to overgenerate, specifically it continues to produce translations in additional languages beyond the desired output. In our preliminary experiments, we observed similar behavior across several models, which manifested in two distinct ways: (1) models frequently provided explanations alongside the translation, and (2) models embedded the translation within a broader text.

To mitigate the issue of overgeneration, we implemented a straightforward yet highly effective solution. Specifically, we appended an instruction to the prompt, explicitly directing the model to output only the translation. This approach proved to be remarkably effective, obviating the need for more complex techniques such as truncation or the application of regular expressions to filter the translation. We evaluated the impact of this method on translation length within a 5-shot setting, utilizing a randomly selected pool with uncontrolled instruction types. For each model, we constructed 10 distinct prompts with different examples, and we discarded generated text after the first new line character because at this place an explanation often begins. The averaged length ratios are presented in Figure 5.

The results indicate that our approach maintains length consistency across all models and language pairs, with values remaining close to 1.0. The only

	En-De		En-Fr		En-Es	
Model	No	Yes	No	Yes	No	Yes
gemma2:9b	100	**0**	100	**2**	100	**2**
gemma2:27b	100	**1**	100	**2**	100	**1**
llama3:8b	100	**3**	100	**3**	100	**1**
llama3:70b	100	**0**	99	**0**	99	**0**
qwen2:7b	**0**	**0**	**0**	**0**	**0**	**0**
qwen2:72b	12	**3**	7	**1**	5	**1**
mistral:7b	16	**3**	9	**1**	19	**1**
mixtral:8x7b	38	**15**	29	**15**	36	**20**

Table 5: The average percentage of translations that contain a new line, indicating overgeneration (5-shot setting). 'Yes' and 'No' columns denote the restricted and unrestricted prompt, respectively.

exceptions are `mixtral:8x7b`, which tends to generate longer text even with the restrictive instruction, and `qwen2:7b`, which is the only one that does not tend to overgenerate in the first place.

Since overgeneration, when it does occur, typically manifests itself as additional text generated after a newline character, we counted the occurrences of text generation following a newline in both the restricted and unrestricted settings to further evaluate the effectiveness of our method. As shown in Table 5, in many instances — particularly with the Llama and Gemma models — there is a clear tendency for models to generate explanatory text after a newline when output is unrestricted. Conversely, when the output is restricted to translation only, the occurrence of additional text is substantially reduced. Based on these observations, we adopted this restrictive instruction in all subsequent experiments and we also ignore any output after the newline character.

Examples Examples of overgeneration where (1) models frequently provided explanations alongside the translation, and (2) models embedded the translation within a broader text:

1. `qwen2:72b`: ... *English: Not surprisingly, this destruction also endangers bonobo survival.* ¬ *German:* Überraschenderweise gefährdet dieser Niedergang auch das Überleben der Bonobos. ¬ ¬ However, a more accurate translation would be: ¬ Unüberraschenderweise gefährdet diese Zerstörung auch das Überleben der Bonobos.

2. `llama3:8b`: ... *English: But still it was a real footrace against the other volunteers to get to the captain in charge to find out what our assignments would be.* ¬ *Spanish:* Based on the provided examples, here is a possible translation: ¬ ¬ Spanish: Pero todavía fue un verdadero carrera contra los otros voluntarios para llegar al capitán al mando y encontrar qué serían nuestras asignaciones.¬ ¬ This translation takes into account the nuances of the original sentence... *(explanation continues)*

B Generation Details

B.1 Inference Hyperparameters

In all experiments, text generation uses multinomial sampling, with default parameters provided by the Ollama library: top-K 40 sampling ($K = 40$) and a temperature of 0.8. Generation stops after 512 tokens or when `<EOT>` (end of turn) token is printed.

B.2 Prompt Templates

The construction of templates is depicted in Table 6. The prompts are created by concatenating prompt parts (1–6).

B.3 Pool Statistics

The statistics of each pool for all pairs of languages studied is in Table 7. We observe a similar trend across all language pairs.

C Match vs No-match

The comparison of match-vs-non-match for all languages is depicted in Table 8. Figure 6 shows the proportion of isometric outputs given sentences where each of the models failed to produce isometric translation by default, i.e. under the *Random*-`Random` setting, even across 10 default runs. The translations are taken after only one attempt, which is in contrast to Figure 2 where the outputs are selected from 10 attempts.

D Few-shot Prompting

The comparison between all few shot settings for all languages is displayed in Figure 8. Additionally, we provide a more detailed view of the results of all few-shot settings, which is presented in Table 9 (zero-shot), Table 10 (5-shot), Table 11 (10-shot) and Table 12 (20-shot). We also compare these results to an oracle setup, in which the best translation is selected based on the sentence BLEU score across all configurations, after filtering out translations that do not fall within ±10% of the source character count.

Part	Prompt type	Zero-shot
1	-	Translate the following text from `[src lang]` into `[tgt lang]`
2	Random Isometric Same Short / Tiny	. ensuring that it is within ±10% of the character count of the source. ensuring that it has the same length as the source. ensuring that it is shorter than the source.
3	No Yes	¬ Output only the translation. ¬
4	-	`[src lang]: [src sentence]` ¬ `[tgt lang]:`

Part	Prompt type	Few-shot
1	-	Here are examples of translations in `[tgt lang]`
2	Random Isometric Same Short / Tiny	of the source in `[src lang]:` ¬ that are within ±10% of the character count of the source in `[src lang]:` ¬ that have the same length as the source in `[src lang]:` ¬ that are shorter than the source in `[src lang]:` ¬
3	-	$N\times$ `{[src lang]: [src sentence]` ¬ `[tgt lang]: [tgt sentence]` ¬`}`
4	-	Provide translation for the following sentence given the examples above.
5	No Yes	¬ Output only the translation. ¬
6	-	`[src lang]: [src sentence]` ¬ `[tgt lang]:`

Table 6: Zero-shot (upper) and few-shot (lower) prompt templates. ¬ stands for new line. Actual prompts are constructed by sequentially concatenating prompt *parts* (1–6).

Pool type	Count	Min	Max	avg±std
En-De				
Random	1415	0.43	5.80	1.14±0.27
Isometric	537	0.90	1.10	1.02±0.05
Same	50	0.99	1.00	1.00±0.00
Short	343	0.43	1.00	0.90±0.11
Tiny	50	0.43	0.81	0.68±0.11
En-Fr				
Random	1412	0.29	4.90	1.14±0.28
Isometric	505	0.90	1.10	1.02±0.05
Same	50	0.99	1.00	1.00±0.00
Short	348	0.29	1.00	0.88±0.14
Tiny	50	0.29	0.76	0.60±0.13
En-Es				
Random	1316	0.30	5.70	1.08±0.32
Isometric	659	0.90	1.10	1.01±0.05
Same	50	1.00	1.00	1.00±0.00
Short	490	0.30	1.00	0.89±0.12
Tiny	50	0.30	0.72	0.59±0.12

Table 7: Statistics of pools: The number of samples, minimum and maximum target/source length ratio, and its average and standard deviation.

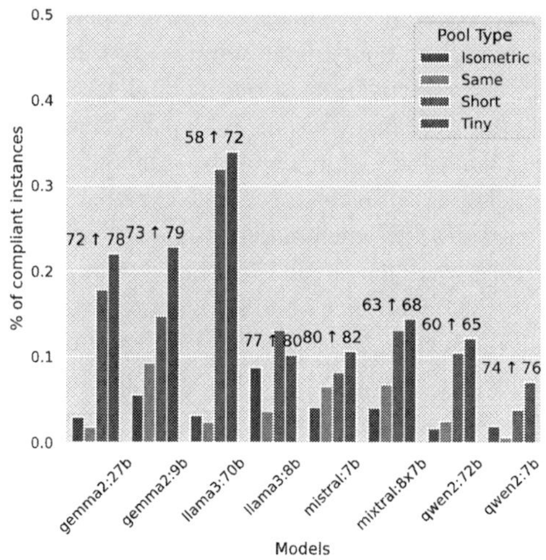

Figure 6: The percentage of input sentences (across all language directions) for which the generated translation meets the isometric condition when the model is prompted to produce isometric, same-length, short, and tiny outputs aligned with respective 5-shot demonstration sets. This evaluation is restricted to input sentences where the particular model did not generate any isometric translation in ten attempts using the uncontrolled prompt.

E Translation Quality and Length Tradeoff

The length ratio and translation quality tradeoff for all languages is presented in Figure 7. We observe that models generally produce isometric translation when *Tiny* setting is used. The exception is Spanish, where the average 1.0 length ratio can be obtained by *Short* setting. This is in line with our intuition since Spanish exhibits a smaller length ratio of 1.04 for the training data from MuST-C, compared to length ratios of 1.12 and 1.11 for German and French, respectively.[9]

[9]These values were calculated by the organizers of the isometric shared task and are mentioned on the official website `https://iwslt.org/2022/isometric`.

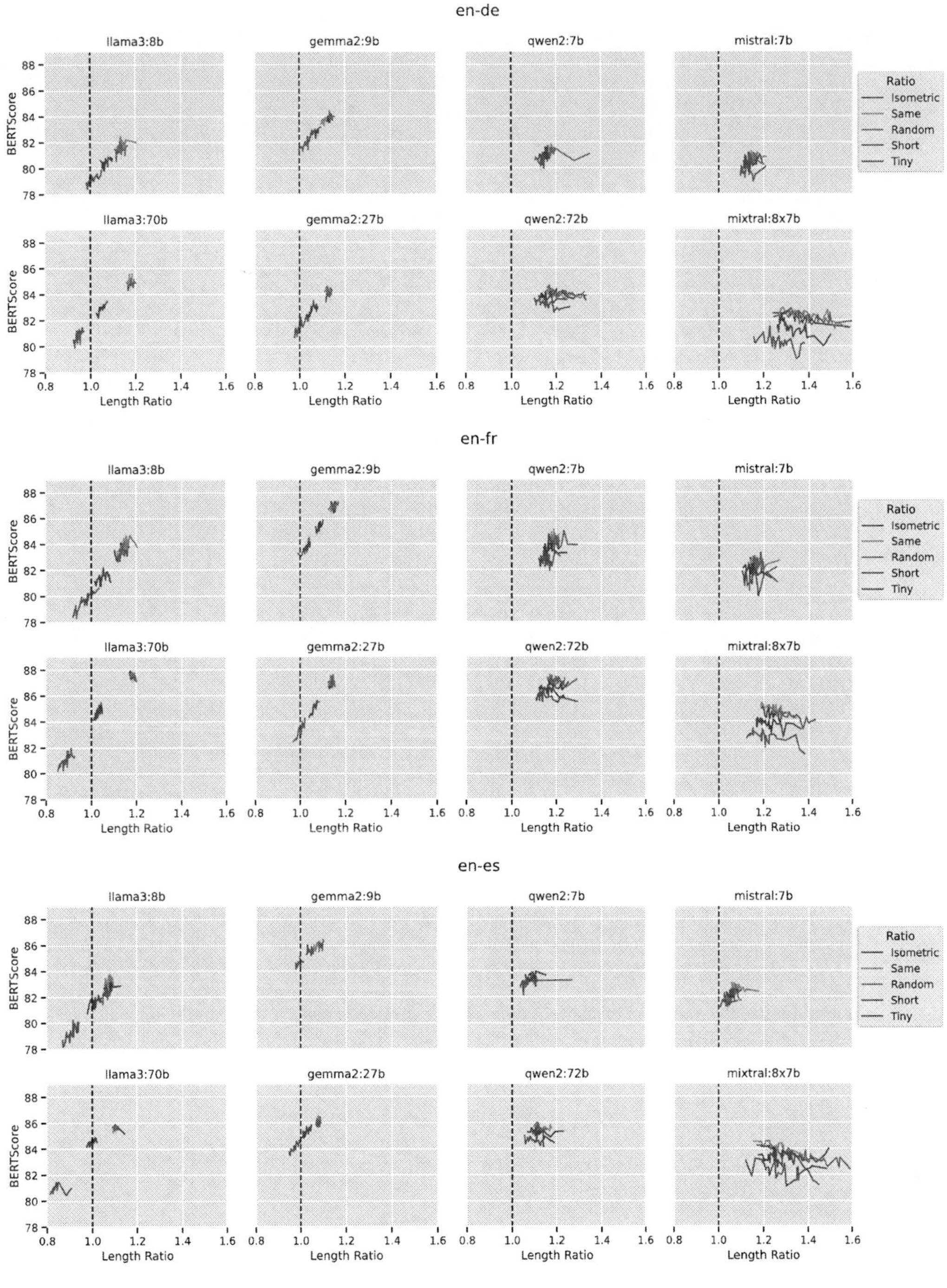

Figure 7: Trade-off between the length ratio (x-axis) and translation quality (y-axis) for 5, 10, 20-shot settings and all models and language pairs.

En-De

	Random		Isometric		Same		Short		Tiny	
Model	No	Yes	No	Yes	No	Yes	No	Yes	No	Yes
gemma2:27b	1.100	1.097	1.099	1.094	1.098	1.097	1.087	1.011	1.066	0.955
gemma2:9b	1.108	1.106	1.106	1.101	1.106	1.073	1.099	1.026	1.080	0.981
llama3:70b	1.149	1.151	1.149	1.139	1.141	1.134	1.138	1.005	1.122	0.905
llama3:8b	1.106	1.100	1.093	1.108	1.099	1.112	1.085	1.048	1.056	0.994
mistral:7b	1.133	1.129	1.126	1.128	1.135	1.125	1.121	1.105	1.138	1.085
mixtral:8x7b	1.402	1.411	1.375	1.362	1.378	1.381	1.385	1.297	1.363	1.265
qwen2:72b	1.223	1.169	1.195	1.178	1.184	1.173	1.170	1.128	1.164	1.129
qwen2:7b	1.132	1.160	1.144	1.125	1.129	1.129	1.128	1.135	1.117	1.095

En-Fr

gemma2:27b	1.128	1.126	1.123	1.125	1.127	1.128	1.115	1.034	1.087	0.970
gemma2:9b	1.143	1.146	1.142	1.132	1.144	1.121	1.133	1.062	1.116	1.021
llama3:70b	1.178	1.176	1.173	1.167	1.174	1.172	1.163	1.015	1.147	0.877
llama3:8b	1.136	1.121	1.134	1.141	1.136	1.144	1.110	1.052	1.072	0.986
mistral:7b	1.162	1.166	1.159	1.152	1.167	1.177	1.141	1.127	1.153	1.137
mixtral:8x7b	1.335	1.332	1.316	1.233	1.351	1.247	1.355	1.206	1.348	1.203
qwen2:72b	1.178	1.180	1.198	1.174	1.184	1.171	1.215	1.139	1.172	1.118
qwen2:7b	1.183	1.175	1.175	1.171	1.172	1.172	1.170	1.146	1.152	1.124

En-Es

gemma2:27b	1.058	1.057	1.057	1.058	1.058	1.054	1.053	0.994	1.040	0.939
gemma2:9b	1.072	1.072	1.071	1.064	1.070	1.046	1.067	1.018	1.054	0.969
llama3:70b	1.086	1.089	1.088	1.086	1.086	1.083	1.084	0.969	1.062	0.823
llama3:8b	1.050	1.051	1.055	1.063	1.051	1.062	1.042	1.008	0.999	0.907
mistral:7b	1.050	1.058	1.058	1.050	1.078	1.063	1.106	1.038	1.039	1.014
mixtral:8x7b	1.321	1.287	1.340	1.269	1.265	1.222	1.286	1.254	1.283	1.252
qwen2:72b	1.116	1.113	1.108	1.110	1.113	1.117	1.114	1.091	1.106	1.075
qwen2:7b	1.074	1.097	1.074	1.079	1.075	1.074	1.083	1.057	1.065	1.035

Table 8: Average target/source ratios for every pool type when instructions match ('Yes') or do not match ('No') the properties of the samples in 5-shot prompting. Differences for each pool type with p-value < 0.1 are underlined.

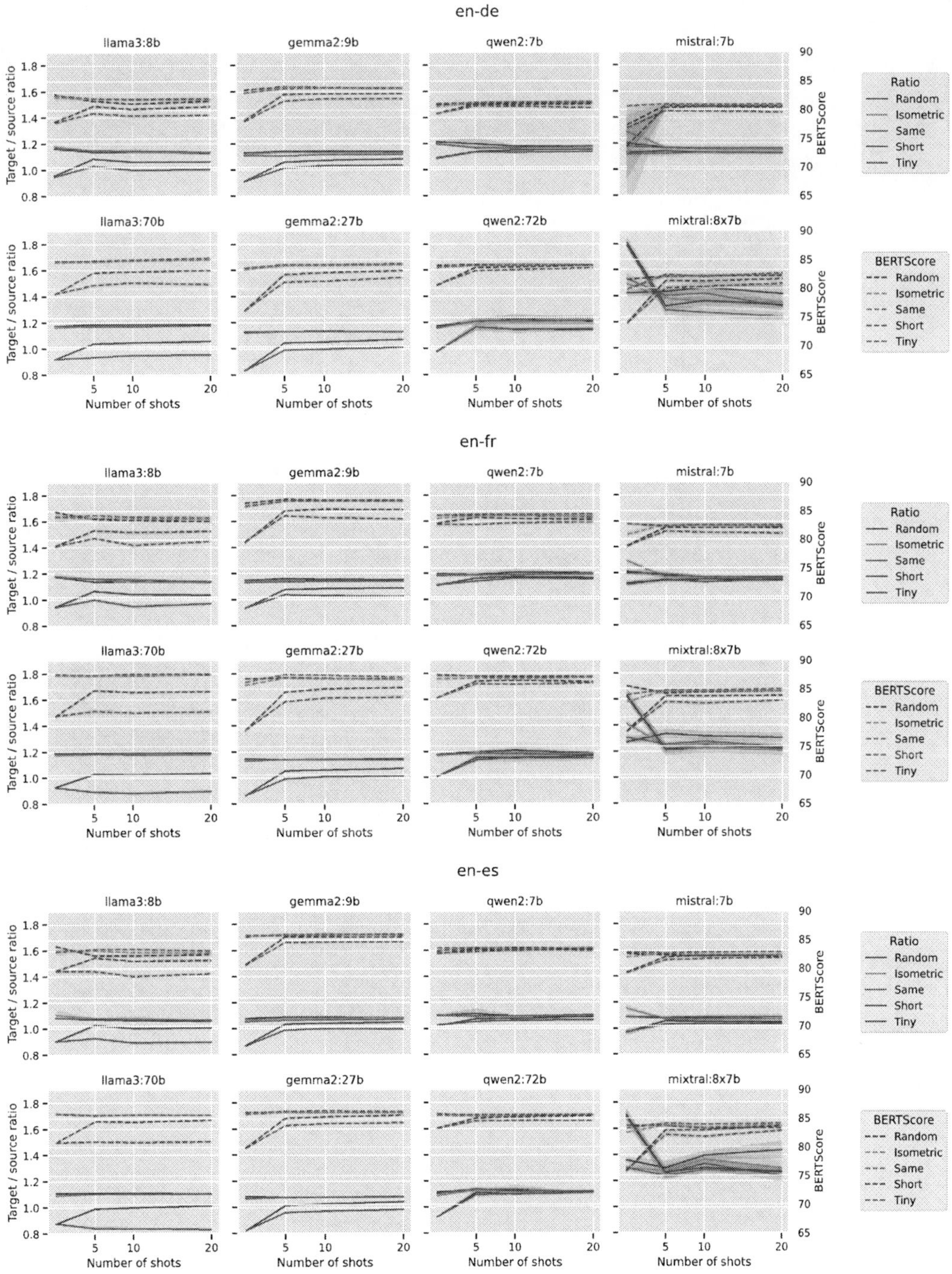

Figure 8: The translation quality (BERTScore, dashed lines and the right hand y-axes) and length ratio (solid lines and left-hand y-axes) for all few-shot settings, models and language pairs.

Model	Prompt Type	En-De				En-Fr				En-Es			
		LR	LC	BS	BLEU	LR	LC	BS	BLEU	LR	LC	BS	BLEU
gemma2:27b	Random	1.13	37.39	83.57	31.82	1.15	37.78	86.80	43.29	1.08	48.20	86.08	39.24
	Isometric	1.12	39.10	83.28	29.94	1.14	39.10	85.70	38.25	1.06	51.65	85.65	37.54
	Same	1.12	41.55	83.52	31.02	1.13	44.45	86.18	40.07	1.07	51.95	85.92	37.75
	Short	0.83	27.05	76.10	12.16	0.86	33.85	77.74	15.91	0.82	30.25	79.88	19.15
gemma2:9b	Random	1.13	34.85	83.43	31.47	1.15	36.75	86.40	41.81	1.08	48.85	85.54	37.87
	Isometric	1.12	38.75	82.93	29.37	1.14	38.70	85.73	38.18	1.07	54.40	85.60	36.59
	Same	1.11	41.45	82.89	29.63	1.13	40.75	85.94	39.55	1.05	55.95	85.80	36.91
	Short	0.91	35.65	78.15	16.12	0.93	38.65	79.45	20.16	0.87	36.45	80.70	21.66
llama3:70b	Random	1.18	26.94	84.58	34.31	1.19	28.06	87.52	44.24	1.11	45.83	85.78	37.08
	Isometric	1.16	31.80	84.53	33.79	1.17	31.40	87.42	43.65	1.09	49.65	85.95	37.36
	Same	1.17	26.70	84.75	34.87	1.19	28.35	87.58	44.24	1.10	46.95	85.87	36.72
	Short	0.92	38.75	79.04	17.20	0.93	38.40	80.26	21.27	0.88	37.05	80.85	23.17
llama3:8b	Random	1.16	31.60	82.70	28.96	1.18	31.39	84.81	36.68	1.08	50.10	83.93	32.78
	Isometric	1.18	29.33	82.23	27.82	1.18	29.67	83.90	34.23	1.11	47.00	83.10	31.00
	Same	1.17	28.65	82.55	28.36	1.18	27.50	84.01	34.70	1.08	47.33	82.96	30.99
	Short	0.96	33.85	77.88	15.83	0.95	37.10	78.92	18.29	0.90	39.70	79.61	19.69
mistral:7b	Random	1.20	30.40	77.28	23.33	1.21	32.40	82.65	30.19	1.09	48.70	82.52	29.49
	Isometric	1.29	24.28	72.26	19.88	1.29	26.67	80.79	28.20	1.15	43.89	81.92	28.57
	Same	1.18	28.40	80.55	23.23	1.20	32.90	82.66	29.99	1.09	47.40	82.79	29.30
	Short	1.13	39.40	73.62	16.99	1.12	41.30	78.78	23.39	0.97	45.55	79.23	23.13
mixtral:8x7b	Random	1.42	23.75	81.50	29.00	1.27	26.00	85.45	38.28	1.36	38.83	83.72	31.61
	Isometric	1.49	15.89	79.81	26.21	1.41	18.85	82.65	34.47	1.30	29.50	82.48	30.23
	Same	1.53	21.50	79.77	26.86	1.31	28.78	83.94	36.18	1.30	39.45	83.24	30.73
	Short	1.81	18.50	73.92	18.32	1.63	28.30	77.58	26.18	1.70	26.30	75.75	20.91
qwen2:72b	Random	1.17	30.28	84.02	33.07	1.18	33.61	87.50	44.30	1.11	45.44	85.83	37.82
	Isometric	1.15	35.65	83.69	31.80	1.17	38.15	86.76	41.92	1.09	50.60	85.53	36.41
	Same	1.16	32.50	83.62	32.22	1.18	38.45	87.35	44.87	1.10	50.70	85.73	36.86
	Short	0.98	40.10	80.48	20.71	1.01	43.95	83.46	27.91	0.92	37.60	83.27	25.77
qwen2:7b	Random	1.21	28.55	80.83	24.32	1.19	28.81	84.20	36.04	1.10	41.45	83.04	30.98
	Isometric	1.20	27.50	80.51	23.05	1.19	30.75	83.61	34.00	1.10	45.72	83.19	30.33
	Same	1.19	28.45	81.04	23.67	1.18	29.80	84.27	35.42	1.10	43.90	83.55	30.91
	Short	1.09	38.00	79.34	18.89	1.11	41.55	82.78	30.33	1.02	49.65	82.54	27.35
Oracle		1.07	65.00	87.74	49.60	1.05	76.50	87.99	55.60	1.03	83.00	88.47	53.50

Table 9: 0-shot prompting for all language pairs. Columns denote length ratio (LR), length compliance (LC), BERTScore (BS) and BLEU.

		En-De				En-Fr				En-Es			
Model	Pool Type	LR	LC	BS	BLEU	LR	LC	BS	BLEU	LR	LC	BS	BLEU
	Random	1.13	36.75	83.97	32.81	1.14	39.70	87.01	42.86	1.08	50.60	86.11	39.02
	Isometric	1.13	39.15	84.04	33.07	1.14	40.35	86.95	42.29	1.08	51.55	86.10	38.61
gemma2:27b	Same	1.13	38.65	84.18	33.05	1.14	40.35	87.58	43.81	1.07	52.50	86.29	38.71
	Short	1.04	44.05	82.41	28.01	1.05	42.65	84.50	34.61	1.01	53.15	85.06	35.54
	Tiny	0.99	41.00	81.13	24.46	0.99	42.55	82.83	30.89	0.96	48.05	83.81	32.21
	Random	1.14	35.35	84.07	32.37	1.16	37.85	87.09	43.13	1.09	50.90	85.99	37.59
	Isometric	1.14	37.25	83.93	31.80	1.15	40.30	86.76	42.09	1.08	51.85	86.00	37.59
gemma2:9b	Same	1.11	41.35	83.72	30.57	1.14	43.00	86.77	42.05	1.06	56.50	85.75	37.09
	Short	1.06	44.25	82.71	28.24	1.08	46.50	85.05	36.13	1.04	56.60	85.54	36.71
	Tiny	1.01	44.50	81.55	25.40	1.04	44.10	84.13	34.59	0.99	53.80	84.55	33.53
	Random	1.19	26.45	84.85	34.86	1.19	29.15	87.40	44.08	1.11	48.45	85.62	36.89
	Isometric	1.17	27.90	84.65	34.25	1.18	30.85	87.37	43.63	1.10	47.90	85.66	37.07
llama3:70b	Same	1.17	28.50	84.83	34.84	1.19	31.65	87.50	43.96	1.10	49.60	85.52	36.43
	Short	1.04	40.90	82.76	28.12	1.03	44.00	84.81	35.36	0.99	50.15	84.51	33.68
	Tiny	0.94	35.80	80.61	22.66	0.89	37.05	81.20	25.79	0.84	33.75	80.97	24.73
	Random	1.14	32.00	81.55	26.44	1.14	34.22	83.57	34.32	1.07	48.70	82.29	30.53
	Isometric	1.15	32.00	81.87	26.57	1.16	36.30	83.74	34.08	1.08	49.40	83.16	31.45
llama3:8b	Same	1.15	33.40	82.06	27.04	1.16	34.50	84.28	34.80	1.08	51.45	83.41	31.05
	Short	1.08	39.05	80.69	23.71	1.07	38.55	81.59	29.35	1.03	51.40	81.88	28.56
	Tiny	1.03	37.55	79.41	21.21	1.00	38.10	80.24	26.74	0.93	43.15	79.55	23.71
	Random	1.17	32.00	80.66	23.66	1.18	35.20	82.29	29.70	1.08	48.78	82.28	28.52
	Isometric	1.17	32.55	80.76	23.67	1.17	37.40	82.50	30.11	1.07	50.80	82.57	28.79
mistral:7b	Same	1.16	33.50	80.93	23.86	1.19	34.90	82.37	29.91	1.08	52.60	82.64	28.99
	Short	1.14	38.15	80.30	22.68	1.14	39.10	82.01	29.06	1.06	51.85	81.96	28.64
	Tiny	1.12	38.65	79.75	21.46	1.15	40.00	81.34	28.10	1.03	52.25	81.42	27.36
	Random	1.43	26.85	81.99	30.58	1.33	30.00	84.20	38.51	1.30	40.45	83.68	33.44
	Isometric	1.38	29.20	82.02	30.71	1.24	32.10	84.64	38.40	1.28	42.80	83.78	33.85
mixtral:8x7b	Same	1.40	32.40	82.38	31.10	1.26	32.35	84.74	39.20	1.24	44.45	84.12	34.18
	Short	1.32	33.65	81.21	28.83	1.21	37.45	83.77	35.39	1.26	45.75	82.91	32.28
	Tiny	1.29	36.80	79.98	26.16	1.21	38.56	82.70	33.03	1.25	46.80	82.11	31.02
	Random	1.20	29.25	84.08	33.25	1.20	33.35	87.18	43.74	1.13	45.65	85.48	37.00
	Isometric	1.21	29.95	83.98	33.02	1.19	34.60	86.85	42.69	1.13	46.10	85.37	36.77
qwen2:72b	Same	1.21	31.20	83.98	32.91	1.19	35.80	87.26	43.57	1.14	48.60	85.66	37.52
	Short	1.16	34.40	83.63	31.59	1.15	41.60	86.36	40.17	1.11	49.65	85.05	36.10
	Tiny	1.16	35.75	83.03	30.09	1.13	42.80	85.86	38.80	1.10	49.40	84.52	35.20
	Random	1.20	32.10	81.04	23.99	1.19	31.75	84.24	35.37	1.11	47.40	83.53	30.89
	Isometric	1.16	30.30	81.24	23.78	1.19	32.30	84.11	34.86	1.10	48.70	83.63	31.13
qwen2:7b	Same	1.17	31.55	81.28	24.07	1.19	32.80	84.41	35.16	1.09	47.75	83.52	30.98
	Short	1.14	35.56	80.97	22.99	1.16	35.25	83.77	34.09	1.08	48.95	83.33	30.75
	Tiny	1.13	34.89	80.63	22.43	1.14	36.60	82.56	32.26	1.05	50.00	82.89	29.95
Oracle		1.07	65.00	87.74	49.60	1.05	76.50	87.99	55.60	1.03	83.00	88.47	53.50

Table 10: 5-shot prompting for all language pairs when sampling examples from different pools. Columns denote length ratio (LR), length compliance (LC), BERTScore (BS) and BLEU. All numbers are averaged across 10 instances. The prompt text *matches* the pool type.

		En-De				En-Fr				En-Es			
Model	Pool Type	LR	LC	BS	BLEU	LR	LC	BS	BLEU	LR	LC	BS	BLEU
gemma2:27b	Random	1.13	37.20	84.14	33.34	1.14	41.50	86.93	42.54	1.08	50.65	86.01	38.58
	Isometric	1.13	39.10	83.98	32.89	1.14	40.35	86.79	41.72	1.08	50.55	86.03	38.50
	Same	1.13	38.80	84.19	33.31	1.14	41.70	87.45	43.59	1.08	50.90	86.36	39.01
	Short	1.05	43.95	82.76	28.38	1.06	45.40	85.04	36.26	1.02	52.15	85.29	36.17
	Tiny	1.00	41.05	81.25	24.84	1.01	41.55	83.44	33.10	0.97	47.70	84.10	33.15
gemma2:9b	Random	1.14	36.75	83.91	32.23	1.16	39.85	86.95	43.22	1.09	50.35	86.05	37.93
	Isometric	1.13	36.35	83.89	31.57	1.15	41.40	86.76	41.89	1.08	53.05	86.00	37.68
	Same	1.12	40.15	83.80	30.88	1.14	42.45	86.86	42.48	1.07	55.40	85.93	37.53
	Short	1.07	43.55	82.81	28.84	1.08	47.35	85.36	37.34	1.04	58.45	85.57	36.41
	Tiny	1.03	43.85	81.92	26.68	1.03	43.95	83.80	34.25	1.00	55.35	84.63	33.89
llama3:70b	Random	1.19	26.30	84.87	35.16	1.19	30.10	87.39	44.23	1.11	47.15	85.67	36.88
	Isometric	1.18	27.70	84.79	34.74	1.18	30.75	87.45	43.84	1.10	46.75	85.68	36.90
	Same	1.17	28.90	85.00	35.04	1.18	31.45	87.65	44.37	1.10	48.95	85.67	36.73
	Short	1.05	40.00	82.94	28.86	1.02	42.45	84.49	34.89	1.00	50.05	84.44	34.19
	Tiny	0.95	36.10	81.01	23.37	0.88	36.50	80.87	25.85	0.84	34.95	80.90	25.09
llama3:8b	Random	1.14	33.30	81.07	25.66	1.14	34.22	83.37	33.56	1.06	49.20	82.29	30.24
	Isometric	1.14	33.20	81.77	26.21	1.14	36.06	83.75	34.38	1.08	49.55	82.85	31.05
	Same	1.15	33.80	81.88	26.53	1.15	34.05	83.97	34.57	1.07	52.00	83.40	31.27
	Short	1.06	36.35	80.16	22.92	1.04	39.60	81.31	29.40	1.00	48.00	81.31	27.55
	Tiny	1.00	35.75	78.99	20.19	0.95	35.90	79.07	24.33	0.89	42.15	78.70	22.47
mistral:7b	Random	1.16	32.40	80.52	23.18	1.17	34.33	82.56	30.17	1.08	47.65	82.06	28.27
	Isometric	1.15	32.95	80.79	23.87	1.17	36.83	82.36	29.99	1.07	49.60	82.39	28.73
	Same	1.16	33.45	80.85	23.59	1.17	36.40	82.54	30.25	1.09	50.20	82.77	29.37
	Short	1.13	37.10	80.45	22.91	1.15	38.35	81.97	29.10	1.05	52.05	82.19	28.43
	Tiny	1.13	37.85	79.66	21.53	1.13	41.25	81.13	28.11	1.04	51.40	81.65	27.74
mixtral:8x7b	Random	1.46	28.15	82.02	30.81	1.32	31.60	84.45	38.81	1.40	40.35	83.22	33.38
	Isometric	1.35	31.95	82.21	31.09	1.25	31.75	84.52	38.81	1.36	42.15	83.37	33.56
	Same	1.42	30.95	81.95	30.69	1.28	33.75	84.73	38.92	1.28	43.20	83.92	34.50
	Short	1.36	35.75	81.16	28.92	1.24	37.15	83.72	35.97	1.30	46.45	82.89	32.66
	Tiny	1.27	39.20	80.21	26.27	1.23	37.80	82.48	32.84	1.33	45.00	81.78	31.69
qwen2:72b	Random	1.22	29.50	84.12	33.35	1.21	34.40	87.05	43.42	1.13	46.15	85.52	37.22
	Isometric	1.20	28.70	84.11	33.29	1.19	36.00	86.73	42.56	1.14	45.60	85.42	36.82
	Same	1.22	31.35	83.97	32.99	1.18	37.05	87.22	43.57	1.12	48.10	85.68	37.43
	Short	1.14	35.30	83.65	31.82	1.15	42.45	86.47	40.71	1.10	49.10	85.24	36.88
	Tiny	1.14	35.55	83.20	30.38	1.15	43.55	85.81	39.52	1.10	50.15	84.62	35.44
qwen2:7b	Random	1.18	29.10	81.17	23.82	1.21	31.65	84.19	35.02	1.09	46.06	83.61	30.71
	Isometric	1.17	32.05	81.31	23.71	1.19	31.20	84.19	35.11	1.09	45.35	83.40	30.67
	Same	1.17	31.20	81.37	23.99	1.19	32.00	84.36	35.03	1.10	45.95	83.33	30.93
	Short	1.15	33.55	80.81	23.13	1.17	35.00	83.63	34.17	1.08	47.00	83.12	30.45
	Tiny	1.13	37.00	80.55	22.31	1.16	34.30	82.87	33.13	1.06	49.00	83.20	30.41
Oracle		1.07	65.00	87.74	49.60	1.05	76.50	87.99	55.60	1.03	83.00	88.47	53.50

Table 11: 10-shot prompting for all language pairs when sampling examples from different pools. Columns denote length ratio (LR), length compliance (LC), BERTScore (BS) and BLEU. All numbers are averaged across 10 instances. The prompt text *matches* the pool type.

Model	Pool Type	En-De				En-Fr				En-Es			
		LR	LC	BS	BLEU	LR	LC	BS	BLEU	LR	LC	BS	BLEU
gemma2:27b	Random	1.13	38.05	84.15	33.75	1.14	39.40	86.74	42.23	1.08	49.35	85.98	38.82
	Isometric	1.13	39.70	84.08	33.24	1.14	39.60	86.71	42.21	1.08	48.90	86.05	38.70
	Same	1.13	39.15	84.29	33.68	1.14	42.50	87.08	42.86	1.08	49.85	86.26	39.03
	Short	1.07	43.45	83.07	30.32	1.07	45.05	85.28	37.52	1.04	52.20	85.55	37.43
	Tiny	1.01	42.00	81.88	27.16	1.01	40.90	83.62	33.65	0.98	48.55	84.25	34.32
gemma2:9b	Random	1.14	37.30	83.81	32.08	1.15	39.60	86.86	43.01	1.09	50.72	85.82	37.94
	Isometric	1.13	37.75	83.73	31.51	1.14	41.10	86.68	42.17	1.08	51.40	86.01	37.93
	Same	1.12	39.80	83.72	30.97	1.14	42.40	86.79	42.11	1.07	54.05	85.97	38.00
	Short	1.08	41.20	82.83	28.93	1.09	46.70	85.23	37.48	1.05	54.85	85.46	36.86
	Tiny	1.04	46.70	81.94	26.43	1.02	43.85	83.56	33.87	1.00	54.35	84.64	33.62
llama3:70b	Random	1.19	27.50	85.01	35.32	1.19	30.95	87.50	44.27	1.11	47.80	85.61	36.93
	Isometric	1.18	28.25	84.97	35.01	1.18	31.20	87.59	43.92	1.10	48.70	85.64	37.12
	Same	1.17	28.95	85.31	35.16	1.18	32.25	87.66	44.31	1.11	48.55	85.63	36.80
	Short	1.06	39.75	83.12	29.42	1.03	42.10	84.60	35.92	1.01	50.25	84.71	35.11
	Tiny	0.95	34.90	80.71	23.33	0.90	37.25	81.08	26.91	0.83	37.00	81.01	25.22
llama3:8b	Random	1.13	32.40	81.50	26.26	1.13	35.20	83.19	33.89	1.06	48.35	82.46	30.69
	Isometric	1.13	34.00	81.80	26.70	1.13	36.25	83.53	34.10	1.06	47.35	82.78	30.94
	Same	1.14	34.25	81.96	26.40	1.14	34.15	83.86	34.56	1.07	51.05	83.11	31.16
	Short	1.06	37.95	80.57	24.32	1.04	38.10	81.43	28.63	1.00	48.00	81.45	28.03
	Tiny	1.00	37.10	79.11	20.94	0.97	37.05	79.69	26.43	0.90	42.25	79.13	23.72
mistral:7b	Random	1.15	33.30	80.57	23.37	1.17	36.20	82.27	30.12	1.07	49.60	82.34	28.71
	Isometric	1.15	33.35	80.60	23.24	1.16	35.25	82.36	30.01	1.07	50.05	82.30	28.57
	Same	1.16	33.50	80.90	23.88	1.17	35.40	82.55	29.78	1.09	49.50	82.82	29.06
	Short	1.13	36.50	80.34	22.27	1.14	39.30	82.03	29.15	1.05	51.10	82.02	28.19
	Tiny	1.12	39.00	79.55	21.25	1.15	39.95	80.96	28.10	1.04	51.20	81.77	27.70
mixtral:8x7b	Random	1.42	29.35	82.14	30.68	1.30	32.20	84.55	38.96	1.44	41.80	83.27	33.30
	Isometric	1.35	32.15	82.24	31.23	1.24	33.65	84.60	38.34	1.30	44.55	83.83	34.02
	Same	1.32	32.25	82.60	31.69	1.23	34.10	84.95	38.54	1.27	42.20	84.09	34.79
	Short	1.33	35.65	81.56	29.40	1.22	36.85	83.80	35.92	1.27	46.90	83.64	33.99
	Tiny	1.24	38.40	80.73	27.13	1.21	37.15	82.91	34.10	1.24	45.45	82.82	32.94
qwen2:72b	Random	1.21	30.10	84.04	33.19	1.19	34.05	87.06	43.62	1.12	45.15	85.66	37.59
	Isometric	1.21	30.35	84.04	33.06	1.18	36.00	86.97	42.64	1.11	46.30	85.58	37.18
	Same	1.21	31.10	84.06	33.12	1.17	35.15	87.14	43.29	1.12	48.60	85.65	37.30
	Short	1.14	33.95	83.97	32.04	1.17	41.50	86.24	40.66	1.11	48.90	85.38	36.94
	Tiny	1.15	36.35	83.51	31.21	1.15	42.25	85.99	40.03	1.11	48.50	84.58	35.28
qwen2:7b	Random	1.17	29.94	81.22	23.97	1.20	30.35	83.96	34.96	1.10	44.65	83.40	30.81
	Isometric	1.17	31.15	81.27	23.54	1.19	30.45	84.01	35.03	1.10	46.35	83.60	31.22
	Same	1.18	30.15	81.39	24.22	1.19	33.05	84.43	35.24	1.10	44.70	83.35	30.91
	Short	1.15	33.85	80.92	23.33	1.17	33.85	83.48	34.25	1.09	46.80	83.43	30.65
	Tiny	1.14	34.25	80.34	21.87	1.15	34.85	82.98	33.09	1.07	49.50	83.11	30.23
Oracle		1.07	65.00	87.74	49.60	1.05	76.50	87.99	55.60	1.03	83.00	88.47	53.50

Table 12: 20-shot prompting for all language pairs when sampling examples from varying pools. We report length ratio (LR), length compliance (LC), BERTScore (BS), and BLEU. All numbers are averaged across 10 instances. The prompt text *matches* the pool type.

Human-Evaluated Urdu-English Speech Corpus: Advancing Speech-to-Text for Low-Resource Languages

Humaira Mehmood
Fatima Jinnah Women University, Pakistan
humaira.mehmood111@gmail.com

Sadaf Abdul Rauf
Fatima Jinnah Women University, Pakistan
sadaf.abdulrauf@gmail.com

Abstract

This paper presents our contribution to the IWSLT Low Resource Track 2: "Training and Evaluation Data Track". We share a human-evaluated Urdu-English speech-to-text corpus based on Common Voice 13.0 Urdu speech corpus. We followed a three-tier validation scheme which involves an initial automatic translation with corrections from native reviewers, full review by evaluators followed by final validation from a bilingual expert ensuring reliable corpus for subsequent NLP tasks. Our contribution, CV-UrEnST corpus, enriches Urdu speech resources by contributing the first Urdu-English speech-to-text corpus. When evaluated with Whisper-medium, the corpus yielded a significant improvement to the vanilla model in terms of BLEU, chrF++, and COMET scores, demonstrating its effectiveness for speech translation tasks.

Keywords: Speech-to-text (S2T) translation, machine translation (MT), speech recognition (ASR).

1 Introduction

Speech translation (ST) is a key area of speech and natural language processing that involves translating spoken content across languages (Chen et al., 2024; Niehues et al., 2021). It typically integrates automatic speech recognition (ASR), machine translation (MT), and text-to-speech (TTS) capabilities in a pipeline. Early research adopted a cascade paradigm, where ASR, MT, and TTS operated in separate stages (Gaido, 2024; Iranzo-Sánchez et al., 2020). However, recent progress has shifted the focus toward end-to-end architectures that unify these components into a single, trainable model, reducing latency and error propagation between modules (Berard et al., 2016; Niehues et al., 2021; Chen et al., 2024; Gaido, 2024).

Speech-to-text translation (S2T), a specialized form of end-to-end ST, involves converting speech signal in the source language to textual output in the target language (Berard et al., 2016; Niehues et al., 2021; Chen et al., 2024). The success of S2T systems critically depends on the quality, size, and linguistic diversity of the training corpus, which underpins model generalization and robustness (Amrouche et al., 2023; Cattoni et al., 2021).

Historically, S2T corpora have evolved from task-specific datasets to large-scale multilingual resources that are essential for building performant translation systems (Cieri et al., 2004; Wang et al., 2020; Miller et al., 2021; Sikasote and Anastasopoulos, 2022; Sethiya et al., 2024). Despite this evolution, corpus creation for low-resource languages remains severely underdeveloped due to challenges such as dialectal diversity, limited written resources, and high annotation costs (Verdonik et al., 2024).

While, these advances have accelerated progress in ST for high-resource languages, low-resource languages continue to face substantial challenges (Shanbhogue et al., 2023; Bartelds et al., 2023; Court and Elsner, 2024). ASR, TTS, and MT models have shown impressive gains in well-resourced settings, but the lack of well-annotated, parallel speech-text corpora has hindered similar progress for underrepresented languages like Urdu. This data scarcity is a fundamental bottleneck not only for ST but also for downstream tasks like cross-lingual retrieval and multilingual dialogue systems (Maguéresse et al., 2020; Singh et al., 2024; Farooq et al., 2019).

Urdu remains a low-resource language for speech translation, with only a few domain-specific corpora available (Qasim et al., 2016). Urdu-English is a moderately resourced language pair with existing corpora for TTS (Jamal et al., 2022), ASR (Arif et al., 2025) and machine trans-

Proceedings of the 22nd International Conference on Spoken Language Translation (IWSLT 2025), pages 138–144
July 31 - August 1, 2025 ©2025 Association for Computational Linguistics

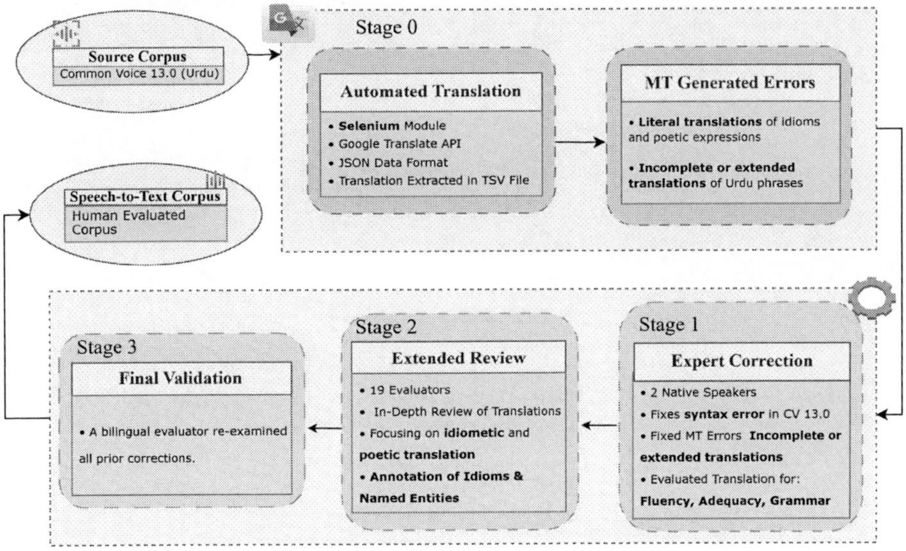

Figure 1: Steps involved in the corpus creation pipeline

lation (Abdul Rauf et al., 2020; Abdul Rauf and Hira, 2023) but speech to text corpus has been noticeably absent. This work is a first step in this direction, where we present and share first human-evaluated Urdu-English S2T corpus namely CV-UrEnST.

We worked on an Urdu subset of Mozilla Common Voice 13.0 (Ardila et al., 2020). Though, Mozilla Common Voice provides open-source Urdu speech, yet its original transcriptions are unvalidated and susceptible to crowd-sourced inconsistencies (Ardila et al., 2020). Since, the Urdu transcriptions underwent comprehensive human validation, they can be used as a gold-standard foundation for ASR tasks. In addition to transcription integrity, we ensured precise English translations that carefully preserve idiomatic structures, named entities, cultural references, and semantic intent. This positions the corpus as a valuable parallel text resource for Urdu-English machine translation and cross-lingual NLP applications.

We followed a three-tier validation scheme. Firstly, *Initial Translations* were generated automatically using the Google Translate API. This was followed by an *Expert Correction* phase, where two native Urdu-English bilinguals manually refined the translations to eliminate syntactic, semantic, and contextual errors. Finally, an *Extended Review and Final Validation* was performed. This multi-phase pipeline ensures high inter-annotator reliability, contextual fidelity, and translation accuracy, improving the datasets suitability for both speech-to-text and text-to-text modeling.

2 Related Work

Recent advances in multilingual low-resource speech datasets have led to innovative data collection and transcription strategies. For instance, Yang et al. (2024) introduced GigaSpeech 2, an ASR corpus for Thai, Indonesian, and Vietnamese via automated web crawling, transcription, and iterative refinement. Abraham et al. (2020) focused on Marathi ASR and emphasized diversity by sourcing speech from 36 speakers across rural and urban communities, yielding a 109-hour corpus that captures dialectal variance.

Community-driven initiatives are also central to low-resource dataset development. Butryna et al. (2020) presented 38 crowd sourced corpora spanning Asia, Africa, and the Americas, underscoring the role of open data in promoting global speech technology. Similarly, Guevara et al. (2024) released a 454 hour multilingual corpus across 10 Philippine languages, collected from domains like healthcare, education, and spontaneous speech demonstrating the value of domain and register diversity in corpus utility.

The availability of *Urdu-English* speech-to-text corpora remains sparse compared to better-

Our Correction	Common Voice Transcription	Error Type
اس مسئلہ مت بناؤ لا کا و ک ےریان مھو ایک۔ ھ گھر اکم یسوت سود لامعتسا مار گاسنا رویپی واگ ۔ںیھے تھیبے ڈھل گیا ںہ ھر گلس ناب نجب گی یرسناب کمی جاب کے نئے ثارذ کےلامعتسا سے پیداوارہ ضافا ںیہ ، مہنگے ثارذ سے جاب کی پیداوار ںیہ پس ظرنہ وہ ںیٹیھچاے نھکیو د ک پ وآج مارڈی ناتسکیا	اس مسئلہ لا کا و ک میے بناؤ ریان مھو ایک ھ گھر اکم یسوت سود لمعتسا مار گاسنا رویپی واگ ےتھیبے ڈھل باغ ہیں ںہ ھر گلس ناب ندی رسنابیو گجب کمی جاب کے نئے ثارذ کےلامعتسا سے پیداوارع ثارذےگنہمہ ضافا ںیہ سے جاب کی پیداوار ںیہ پس ظنہ وہوجہ مارڈی ناتسکیا اپ ںیٹیھچاے نھکیو د ک	Orthographic
و ک پ ا آیکیں۔ ھ رظونہ مظان این اھر وہ لیکن زلزلے سے ڈھ راتہ والےزجیرےارٹلس اورںیا میشینوڈنا کئی نیقی و کو گوں ا ھی نہیں ھا۔ ۃ	وکا پیہ کا یمنے؟ ھ رظونہ مظان ای و ک ھی لیکن زلزلی سیی نو ھ راتہ والی زجیری ارٹلس اور ان یا میشینوڈ: کئی و گوں ا نیقی	Morphological
بس، کسی ادش ی مایب و ک لزنہ نمے اچھی راہ ںی ھار اکق شع	بس کس مایب ی ادش لزنہ کونمے اچھی رما کق شع راھی	Punctuation
ٹی ٹوئی ورلڈکپ ےریم کیریٹری آخا ک ورلڈکپ وہ گا، ۔ی دیاقر دھاش ے أر دازبہ شھا تپ چپ لا دنر کرادر کی فنہ ےوبابمز کے خلاف لیھ ک ںیہ رار ھ	ٹی ٹوٹ ورلڈکپ ےریمہ کیریٹری رخا ک ورلڈ کپ وہ گافر دھاش یدی دازبہ شھا تپ چپ لا دنر کرادر کی فنہ روئے بابمز کے خلاف لیھ ک ںیہ رار ھ	Named Entity

Table 1: Category wise examples of transcription discrepancies in Mozilla Common Voice 13.0

resourced language pairs. While, efforts like the Urdu-English Parallel Corpus for Speech Translation offer foundational bilingual resources, they often lack rigorous human evaluation and speech alignment (Furqan et al., 2024; Amin et al., 2025). Mozilla Common Voice provides open-source Urdu speech, yet its original transcriptions are unvalidated and susceptible to crowd-sourced inconsistencies (Ardila et al., 2020).

In machine translation, domain-specific corpora have contributed meaningfully. For example, the LEGAL-UQA dataset addresses the legal Q&A domain using constitutional texts (Faisal and Yousaf, 2024), while the Urdu-English Religious Domain Corpus offers 18,426 sentence pairs for theological texts (Abdul Rauf and Hira, 2023). Although these datasets advance text-to-text MT, they lack paired audio components necessary for S2T applications.

3 Corpus Preparation Pipeline

Our corpus comprises of approximately 7k sentence pairs from the Urdu subset of Mozilla Common Voice 13.0 (Ardila et al., 2020). The focus was on creating high-quality, human-validated translations rather than maximizing scale. Common Voice was chosen for its open license, reproducibility, and established use in speech research. Future expansions will consider integrating other open-access Urdu speech resources, contingent on annotation capacity.

Common Voice 13.0 features a community-driven validation system, where users vote on the correctness of audio-transcription pairs. While, this process ensures surface-level alignment, it does not address deeper syntactic or semantic inconsistencies common in Urdu, a morphologically rich language. Examples of such issues are presented in Table 1. Here, orthographic correspond to incorrect spellings, character substitutions, or missing graphemes. Semantic errors stem from misinterpretations of meaning. Named entity errors involve improper handling of proper nouns or technical terms. Punctuation and diacritic include inconsistencies that affect readability and disambiguation.

Machine Translation and Expert Correction MT often fails to preserve cultural complexity, idiomatic expressions, and emotional tone. Other common issues included incomplete renderings

	Machine Translation	Expert's Correction	Extended Review	Final Validation
Incomplete Translations:				
آبی جانور میں بطخ بگلا اور دُوسْرا آبی پرندہ شامل ہونا	Aquatic beasts include ducks and other aquatic birds	In aquatic animals, ducks and other aquatic birds are included	–	–
جو چاہے کر سکتے تھے-	Whatever they wanted	–	–	They could do whatever they wanted.
ڈیرن سیمی کا نرالا انداز، کرتا زیب تن کرلیا	Darren Sammy's quirky wear	Darren Sammy has dressed up in a quirky style.	-	Darren Sammy's adopted unique style by wearing the kurta.
پہلا میل اتنا طویل لگا کہ قریب تھا کہ اسے سازش کا شاخسانہ قرار دے دیا جاتا	The first mail was so long that it was close	The first mile seemed so long, saying it was close, it was declared as a sign of conspiracy	-	The first interaction felt so prolonged that it was almost labeled as a result of a conspiracy
Poetic Translations:				
یار آشنا نہیں کوئی ٹکرائیں کس سے جام	Dude no one to collide with whom	–	No friend or lover is around, whom shall I toast with	–
ہر رگ خوں میں پھر چراغاں ہو	In every vein, then the light	Let there be lights in every vein again	To be fired up	Lets ignite the spark again
بیٹھا ہے بت آئنہ سیما مرے آگے	Sitting is an idol, Sima Murray in front of my mirror		The idol, with a mirror-like beauty, sits before me	The idol with a mirror-like visage is sitting before me
منزل کو نہ پہچانے، راہِ عشق کا راھی-	Do not recognize the destination	-	-	The traveler on the path of love does not recognize the destination
Extended Translations:				
جسے سن کر عبدالقادر کی انکھیں	Hearing this, Abdul Qadir's eyes widened	–	Hearing this, Abdul Qadir's eyes	–
فلمیں دیکھنی ہو	I have to watch movies.			want to watch movies
Idiomatic Sentences:				
کبھی کبھار ھی خیالی پلاو بناتا ہوں	The traveler on the path of love does not recognize the destination	Sometimes I make air castle	–	Sometimes I build castles in the air.
بکرے کی ماں کب تک خیر منائے گی	How long will the goat's mother welcome	how long will the mother's prayers avail to save her kid	How long will you delay the inevitable?	-
جیسی نیت ویسی مراد	The same intention is Visi	As the intention, so is the outcome.	-	-
نہ رہے گا بانس نہ بجے گی بانسری	Will not be bamboo or pm	To deal with the issue at its root to prevent a more challenging problem.		If the bamboo is gone, the flute won't play
جو یہَاں کا جنگلات کےحسن کو چار چاند لگا دینا ہونا	To give four moons to the beauty of these forests	To enhance the beauty of these forests.	-	-

Table 2: Examples of translation in different validation phases for complex Urdu expressions

where parts of the original Urdu were missing, literal translations of idioms, and incorrect substitution of culturally specific terms. The reviewers refined these translations to ensure contextual fidelity and semantic precision. Each sentence was independently assessed across three linguistic dimensions: accuracy (semantic alignment), adequacy (completeness of meaning transfer), and fluency (naturalness and readability in English).

Consider the idiom جو یہَاں کا جنگلات کےحسن کو چار چاند لگا دینا ہونا, shown in Table 2, last row translated as "to give four moons to the beauty of these forests" a literal rendering of a metaphor for beautification. Similarly, the phrase بکاو چینل was mistranslated as "Baku channel", ignoring its intended meaning of "biased or corrupt media outlets."

Another poetic example, کہیں تو بہر خدا آج ذکر یار چلے , was rendered as "Somewhere else, God goes to Zikr today," which loses its figurative essence. A better translation "Let there be, for Gods sake, some talk of the beloved today" captures both semantic and emotional intent. Lastly, نہ اب رقیب نہ ناصح نہ غم گسار کوئی was translated as "No longer the rival nor Nasah nor the grief," where ناصح (meaning moral advisor) was poorly transliterated as "Nasah" .A faithful rendering would be: "Now, there remains no rival, no guide, and no comforter to ease the sorrow."

All such mistranslations were corrected during the extended evaluation phase, ensuring cultural fidelity and correct lexical choice in cultural and linguistic contexts.

Extended Review The second phase of validation involved 19 bilingual reviewers. These were graduate students in computer science, all native Urdu speakers with advanced academic proficiency in English. Each reviewer reviewed equal portion of the corpus and was instructed to focus on refining translation by checking for errors in idiomatic usage, named entities, and cultural references.

As the corpus was partitioned into non-overlapping subsets, standard inter-annotator agreement metrics like Cohens Kappa could not be applied. To maintain annotation consistency, we provided comprehensive guidelines and examples to all annotators. In addition, a senior linguist performed a qualitative audit of randomly selected annotated pairs to verify adherence to syntactic, semantic, and cultural fidelity standards.

Employing a distributed review strategy offered several advantages. Crowdsourced evaluation, especially when conducted by native speakers with relevant academic backgrounds, has been shown to improve translation quality through consensus and error cross-checking (Zaidan and Callison-Burch, 2011). The diversity of reviewers helps to detect inconsistencies and ensures a more comprehensive assessment of the data. This phase was particularly valuable for capturing subtle sophistication that may have been overlooked in earlier stages.

Final Validation In the final stage of quality control, a senior bilingual evaluator fluent in both Urdu and English reassessed the outputs from the extended review phase. This validation focused specifically on the test set to ensure translation consistency, semantic constancy, and contextual appropriateness. Table 2 shows the representation of Idioms and named entities in the final corpus.

Data	Audio Count	Idioms	Equivalent Idioms	Named Entities
Test	4129	32	8	1152
Train	3304	17	3	648
Total	7433	49	11	1800

Table 3: Distribution of Annotated Idioms, Equivalent Idioms, and Named Entities in the Corpus

4 Model Building

To establish a performance reference, we fine-tuned OpenAIs `Whisper-medium`[1] model, a transformer-based encoder-decoder pretrained on multilingual speech data for direct speech-to-text translation.

Training was performed on a Google Colab A100 GPU using the AdamW optimizer with a learning rate of 1×10^{-5} with cosine annealing. The batch size of 16 was used and early stopping was based on the improvements in the BLEU score on the development set. All audio inputs were resampled to 16 kHz and converted into 80-bin log-Mel spectrograms. Zero-padding ensured uniform sequence lengths within batches.

We used BLEU (token-level accuracy), chrF++ (character-level fluency), and COMET (semantic adequacy) as evaluation metrics. BLEU scores measures token-level overlap with reference translations and reflects surface-level accuracy. chrF++ captures character-level fluency and recall, it is especially robust to morphological variation, whereas COMET evaluates semantic similarity using neural metrics, higher scores indicate better meaning preservation.

Scores We evaluated vanilla and fine-tuned `Whisper-medium` models on our test set. The original model, without domain-specific adaptation, showed minimal performance. In contrast, fine-tuning yielded substantial gains across all evaluation dimensions.

Metric	Original	Fine-tuned
BLEU	0.81	21.49
chrF++	6.31	46.22
COMET	0.414	0.731

Table 4: Evaluation results of Whisper-medium model before and after fine-tuning on our dataset.

These results demonstrate that the proposed dataset significantly enhances the Whisper models ability to produce fluent and semantically accurate translations, validating its utility for low-resource speech translation.

5 Conclusion

This study contributes a human evaluated Urdu-to-English speech-to-text corpus designed to advance NLP research in under-resourced linguistic domains. By integrating automated translation with systematic human validation, we address critical gaps in handling idiomatic and culturally specific content, producing translations which retain the cultural aspects.

References

Sadaf Abdul Rauf, Syeda Abida, Noor-e Hira, Syeda Zahra, Dania Parvez, Javeria Bashir, and Qurat-ul-

[1] `https://github.com/openai/whisper`

ain Majid. 2020. On the exploration of English to Urdu machine translation. In *Proceedings of the 1st Joint Workshop on Spoken Language Technologies for Under-resourced languages (SLTU) and Collaboration and Computing for Under-Resourced Languages (CCURL)*, pages 285--293, Marseille, France. European Language Resources association.

Sadaf Abdul Rauf and Noor e Hira. 2023. Development of Urdu-English religious domain parallel corpus. In *Proceedings of the Second Workshop on Corpus Generation and Corpus Augmentation for Machine Translation*, pages 14--21, Macau SAR, China. Asia-Pacific Association for Machine Translation.

Basil Abraham, Danish Goel, Divya Siddarth, Kalika Bali, Manu Chopra, Monojit Choudhury, Pratik Joshi, Preethi Jyoti, Sunayana Sitaram, and Vivek Seshadri. 2020. Crowdsourcing speech data for low-resource languages from low-income workers. In *Proceedings of the Twelfth Language Resources and Evaluation Conference*, pages 2819--2826, Marseille, France. European Language Resources Association.

Muhammad Shahid Amin, Xiaoqiang Zhang, Luca Anselma, Alessandro Mazzei, and Johan Bos. 2025. Semantic processing for urdu: corpus creation, parsing, and generation. *Language Resources and Evaluation*.

Aissa Amrouche, Youssouf Bentrcia, Nabil Hezil, Khadidja Boubakeur, Nawel Behloul, Miloud Zalagh, Abed Ahcene, and Leila Falek. 2023. BAC TTS Corpus: Rich Arabic Database for Speech Synthesis. In *2023 International Conference on Electrical and Electronics Engineering (ICEEE)*, pages 189--193.

Rosana Ardila, Megan Branson, Kelly Davis, Michael Kohler, Josh Meyer, Michael Henretty, Reuben Morais, Lindsay Saunders, Francis Tyers, and Gregor Weber. 2020. Common voice: A massively-multilingual speech corpus. In *Proceedings of the Twelfth Language Resources and Evaluation Conference*, pages 4218--4222, Marseille, France. European Language Resources Association.

Samee Arif, Aamina Jamal Khan, Mustafa Abbas, Agha Ali Raza, and Awais Athar. 2025. WER we stand: Benchmarking Urdu ASR models. In *Proceedings of the 31st International Conference on Computational Linguistics*, pages 5952--5961, Abu Dhabi, UAE. Association for Computational Linguistics.

Martijn Bartelds, Nay San, Bradley McDonnell, Dan Jurafsky, and Martijn Wieling. 2023. Making more of little data: Improving low-resource automatic speech recognition using data augmentation. In *Proceedings of the 61st Annual Meeting of the Association for Computational Linguistics (Volume 1: Long Papers)*, pages 715--729, Toronto, Canada. Association for Computational Linguistics.

Alexandre Berard, Olivier Pietquin, Christophe Servan, and Laurent Besacier. 2016. Listen and translate: A proof of concept for end-to-end speech-to-text translation. *Preprint*, arXiv:1612.01744.

Alena Butryna, Shan-Hui Cathy Chu, Isin Demirsahin, Alexander Gutkin, Linne Ha, Fei He, Martin Jansche, Cibu Johny, Anna Katanova, Oddur Kjartansson, Chenfang Li, Tatiana Merkulova, Yin May Oo, Knot Pipatsrisawat, Clara Rivera, Supheakmungkol Sarin, Pasindu de Silva, Keshan Sodimana, Richard Sproat, Theeraphol Wattanavekin, and Jaka Aris Eko Wibawa. 2020. Google crowdsourced speech corpora and related open-source resources for low-resource languages and dialects: An overview. *Preprint*, arXiv:2010.06778.

Roldano Cattoni, Mattia Antonino Di Gangi, Luisa Bentivogli, Matteo Negri, and Marco Turchi. 2021. Must-c: A multilingual corpus for end-to-end speech translation. *Computer Speech Language*, 66:101155.

William Chen, Wangyou Zhang, Yifan Peng, Xinjian Li, Jinchuan Tian, Jiatong Shi, Xuankai Chang, Soumi Maiti, Karen Livescu, and Shinji Watanabe. 2024. Towards robust speech representation learning for thousands of languages. In *Proceedings of the 2024 Conference on Empirical Methods in Natural Language Processing*, pages 10205--10224, Miami, Florida, USA. Association for Computational Linguistics.

Christopher Cieri, David Miller, and Kevin Walker. 2004. The fisher corpus: a resource for the next generations of speech-to-text. In *Proceedings of the Fourth International Conference on Language Resources and Evaluation (LREC'04)*, Lisbon, Portugal. European Language Resources Association (ELRA).

Sara Court and Micha Elsner. 2024. Shortcomings of LLMs for low-resource translation: Retrieval and understanding are both the problem. In *Proceedings of the Ninth Conference on Machine Translation*, pages 1332--1354, Miami, Florida, USA. Association for Computational Linguistics.

Faizan Faisal and Umair Yousaf. 2024. Legal-uqa: A low-resource urdu-english dataset for legal question answering. *Preprint*, arXiv:2410.13013.

Muhammad Umar Farooq, Farah Adeeba, Sahar Rauf, and Sarmad Hussain. 2019. Improving large vocabulary urdu speech recognition system using deep neural networks. In *Proceedings of Interspeech 2019*.

Muhammad Furqan, Rayan Bin Khaja, and Rameez Habeeb. 2024. Erupd - english to roman urdu parallel dataset. *arXiv preprint arXiv:2412.17562*.

Marco Gaido. 2024. Direct speech translation toward high-quality, inclusive, and augmented systems. In *Proceedings of the 25th Annual Conference of the European Association for Machine Translation (Volume 1)*, pages 2--3, Sheffield, UK. European Association for Machine Translation (EAMT).

Rowena Cristina L. Guevara, Rhandley D. Cajote, Michael Gringo Angelo R. Bayona, and Crisron Rudolf G. Lucas. 2024. Philippine languages database: A multilingual speech corpora for developing systems for low-resource languages. In *Proceedings of the 3rd Annual Meeting of the Special Interest Group on Under-resourced Languages*

@ *LREC-COLING 2024*, pages 264--271, Torino, Italia. ELRA and ICCL.

Javier Iranzo-Sánchez, Adrià Giménez Pastor, Joan Albert Silvestre-Cerdà, Pau Baquero-Arnal, Jorge Civera Saiz, and Alfons Juan. 2020. Direct segmentation models for streaming speech translation. In *Proceedings of the 2020 Conference on Empirical Methods in Natural Language Processing (EMNLP)*, pages 2599--2611, Online. Association for Computational Linguistics.

Sahar Jamal, Sadaf Abdul Rauf, and Quratulain Majid. 2022. Exploring transfer learning for Urdu speech synthesis. In *Proceedings of the Workshop on Resources and Technologies for Indigenous, Endangered and Lesser-resourced Languages in Eurasia within the 13th Language Resources and Evaluation Conference*, pages 70--74, Marseille, France. European Language Resources Association.

Alexandre Magueresse, Vincent Carles, and Evan Heetderks. 2020. Low-resource languages: A review of past work and future challenges. *Preprint*, arXiv:2006.07264.

Corey Miller, Evelyne Tzoukermann, Jennifer Doyon, and Elizabeth Mallard. 2021. Corpus creation and evaluation for speech-to-text and speech translation. In *Proceedings of Machine Translation Summit XVIII: Users and Providers Track*, pages 44--53, Virtual. Association for Machine Translation in the Americas.

Jan Niehues, Elizabeth Salesky, Marco Turchi, and Matteo Negri. 2021. Tutorial: End-to-end speech translation. In *Proceedings of the 16th Conference of the European Chapter of the Association for Computational Linguistics: Tutorial Abstracts*, pages 10--13, online. Association for Computational Linguistics.

Muhammad Qasim, Sahar Rauf, Sarmad Hussain, and Tania Habib. 2016. Urdu speech corpus for travel domain. pages 237--240.

Nivedita Sethiya, Saanvi Nair, and Chandresh Maurya. 2024. Indic-TEDST: Datasets and baselines for low-resource speech to text translation. In *Proceedings of the 2024 Joint International Conference on Computational Linguistics, Language Resources and Evaluation (LREC-COLING 2024)*, pages 9019--9024, Torino, Italia. ELRA and ICCL.

Akshaya Vishnu Kudlu Shanbhogue, Ran Xue, Soumya Saha, Daniel Zhang, and Ashwinkumar Ganesan. 2023. Improving low resource speech translation with data augmentation and ensemble strategies. In *Proceedings of the 20th International Conference on Spoken Language Translation (IWSLT 2023)*, pages 241--250, Toronto, Canada (in-person and online). Association for Computational Linguistics.

Claytone Sikasote and Antonios Anastasopoulos. 2022. BembaSpeech: A speech recognition corpus for the Bemba language. In *Proceedings of the Thirteenth Language Resources and Evaluation Conference*, pages 7277--7283, Marseille, France. European Language Resources Association.

Deepanjali Singh, Ayush Anand, Abhyuday Chaturvedi, and Niyati Baliyan. 2024. IWSLT 2024 Indic track system description paper: Speech-to-text translation from English to multiple low-resource Indian languages. In *Proceedings of the 21st International Conference on Spoken Language Translation (IWSLT 2024)*, pages 311--316, Bangkok, Thailand (in-person and online). Association for Computational Linguistics.

Darinka Verdonik, Andreja Bizjak, Andrej gank, Mirjam Sepesy Mauec, Mitja Trojar, Jerneja ganec Gros, Marko Bajec, Iztok Lebar Bajec, and Simon Dobriek. 2024. Strategies for managing time and costs in speech corpus creation: Insights from the slovenian artur corpus. *Language Resources and Evaluation*.

Changhan Wang, Juan Pino, Anne Wu, and Jiatao Gu. 2020. CoVoST: A diverse multilingual speech-to-text translation corpus. In *Proceedings of the Twelfth Language Resources and Evaluation Conference*, pages 4197--4203, Marseille, France. European Language Resources Association.

Yifan Yang, Zheshu Song, Jianheng Zhuo, Mingyu Cui, Jinpeng Li, Bo Yang, Yexing Du, Ziyang Ma, Xunying Liu, Ziyuan Wang, Ke Li, Shuai Fan, Kai Yu, Wei-Qiang Zhang, Guoguo Chen, and Xie Chen. 2024. Gigaspeech 2: An evolving, large-scale and multi-domain asr corpus for low-resource languages with automated crawling, transcription and refinement. *arXiv preprint arXiv:2406.11546*.

Omar F. Zaidan and Chris Callison-Burch. 2011. Crowdsourcing translation: Professional quality from non-professionals. In *Proceedings of the 49th Annual Meeting of the Association for Computational Linguistics: Human Language Technologies*, pages 1220--1229, Portland, Oregon, USA. Association for Computational Linguistics.

FFSTC 2: Extending the Fongbe to French Speech Translation Corpus

D. Fortuné Kponou
IMSP Dangbo Bénin
fortune.kponou@msp-uac.org

Salima Mdhaffar
LIA Avignon France
salima.mdhaffar@univ-avignon.fr

Fréjus A. A. Laleye
OPSCIDIA Paris France
frejus.laleye@opscidia.com

Eugène C. Ezin
IMSP Dangbo Bénin
eugene.ezin@imsp-uac.org

Yannick Estève
LIA Avignon France
yannick.esteve@univ-avignon.fr

Abstract

This paper introduced FFSTC 2, an expanded version of the existing Fongbe-to-French speech translation corpus, addressing the critical need for resources in African dialects for speech recognition and translation tasks. We extended the dataset by adding 36 hours of transcribed audio, bringing the total to 61 hours, thereby enhancing its utility for both automatic speech recognition (ASR) and speech translation (ST) in Fongbe, a low-resource language. Using this enriched corpus, we developed both cascade and end-to-end speech translation systems. Our models employ AfriHuBERT and HuBERT147, two speech encoders specialized to African languages, and the NLLB and mBART models as decoders. We also investigate the use of the SAMU-XLSR approach to inject sentence-level semantic information to the XSLR-128 model used as an alternative speech encoder. We also introduced a novel diacritic-substitution technique for ASR, which, when combined with NLLB, enables a cascade model to achieve a BLEU score of 37.23 ompared to 39.60 obtained by the best system using original diacritics. Among the end-to-end architectures evaluated, the architectures with data augmentation and NLLB as decoder achieved the highest score respectively, SAMU-NLLB scored the BLEU score of 28.43.

1 Introduction

The creation of high-quality audio datasets for Natural Language Processing (NLP) tasks remains a significant challenge. Current efforts to develop speech datasets have predominantly focused on widely spoken languages such as English, French, and Spanish, leaving dialectal and minority languages largely under-represented. As a result, the vast majority of the world's 7,000 languages remain underserved, with only a few dozen language directions covered in existing speech translation corpora (Wang et al., 2022). This lack of inclusion presents a critical problem, as it perpetuates language barriers and limits the accessibility of NLP technologies for speakers of less-represented languages. In recent years, there has been increasing attention on low-resource languages, particularly those spoken in regions such as India and Africa. Despite being spoken by millions of people, many of these languages remain severely under-represented in terms of linguistic resources. For instance, Africa is home to over 2,000 languages (Eberhard et al., 2021), yet, as highlighted by (Adebara and Elmadany, 2023), only around 40 of these languages have been integrated into modern language technologies. This stark disparity underscores the significant under-representation of African languages in contemporary NLP research and applications.

Initiatives such as the Mozilla Common Voice project[1] have sought to address this gap by providing a platform for collecting speech data for certain African languages. However, the impact of such efforts remains limited. This limitation stems from the platform's design, which relies on collecting data through the reading of written texts. This approach is less effective for many African languages, which are primarily oral and have limited written resources. Historically, oral traditions (Bala, 2015) have been widespread across the continent, which has hindered the development of writing systems and further complicated efforts to create comprehensive linguistic datasets.

While resources Fongbe are limited, some datasets do exist in the state of the art. For Fongbe, we have the ALFFA (Laleye et al.) dataset for speech recognition, which includes 6 hours of audio along with transcriptions, and the FFSTC dataset (Kponou et al., 2024), which contains 31 hours of Fongbe speech paired with French trans-

[1] https://commonvoice.mozilla.org

Proceedings of the 22nd International Conference on Spoken Language Translation (IWSLT 2025), pages 145–152
July 31 - August 1, 2025

lations. Also, corpora like GigaST are pseudo-labeled, distinguishing them from fully human-annotated datasets such as (Tachbelie et al.; Gauthier et al., 2016) contained in ALFFA, which contains a few hours of data for languages like Amharic, Hausa, Swahili, Wolof.

In this paper, we present a significant extension of the existing Fongbe-to-French speech translation corpus (Kponou et al., 2024). This extension not only adds new parallel data from spoken Fongbe to written French but also enables the training of an automatic speech recognition (ASR) model for Fongbe by providing speech recordings with their corresponding transcriptions. This dataset will provide an opportunity for research community to test all new SSL models designed for African languages (Alabi et al., 2024; Boito and al, 2024), especially since no existing SSL model currently includes Fongbe in its training data. The data described here will be used to organize a translation task in IWSLT 2025[2]. This paper provides experiments and evaluation for Automatic Speech Recognition (ASR) in Fongbe and Speech Translation (ST) from Fongbe to French. These experiments aim to assess the effectiveness of leveraging pre-trained models for low-resource language processing, with a focus on a tonal African language spoken by 4 million people.

2 Related work and motivations

Unlabeled data is far more abundant than labeled data. Self-supervised learning (SSL) methods have emerged as a powerful approach to leverage such unlabeled data in machine learning, enabling the creation of pre-trained models. A first notable example in the domain of speech is the XLSR-53 model (Conneau et al., 2020), which is pre-trained on 53 languages data. Studies (Bansal et al., 2018; Li et al., 2020; Stoian et al., 2020) have extensively explored the use of pre-trained speech encoders and text decoders to enhance system performance for the speech translation task. These techniques, collectively referred to as transfer learning, have demonstrated significant effectiveness in improving performance, particularly in low-resource settings. By transferring knowledge from high-resource languages to low-resource ones, transfer learning provides a robust initialization for both encoder and decoder components, thereby significantly contributing to improved translation accuracy. In addition to transfer learning, other approaches have been adopted to enhance performance in low-resource speech translation, such as synthesizing parallel data (Odoom et al., 2024). However, our work specifically focuses on the transfer learning paradigm, leveraging its proven capabilities to address the challenges of low-resource language processing.

Despite the challenges associated with creating speech corpora for African languages, there has been a notable shift towards the inclusion of these languages in pre-trained models. This trend is evident in the progressive integration of African languages into state-of-the-art models, such as HuBERT147 (Boito and al, 2024), which supports 16 African languages, and its variant AfriHuBERT (Alabi et al., 2024), which extends coverage to 39 languages.

Various strategies have been employed to use pre-trained models effectively. For instance, some studies (Mbuya and Anastasopoulos; Zanon Boito and Ortega) utilize pre-trained encoders like XLSR-53 as feature extractors or encoders paired with a transformer (Vaswani et al., 2023) based decoder. Our experiments align with this latter, employing HuBERT variants as the encoder and using a pre-trained Large Language Model (LLMs) transformer based as decoder.

Although the literature does not provide definitive guidance on selecting the most suitable pre-trained speech encoder, (Kponou et al.) observed that encoders trained on the same language as the source language tend to extract more relevant audio features, thereby improving overall performance. Given that Fongbe is an African language and no pre-trained speech model includes it at the time of writing, we hypothesize that using a pre-trained encoder trained on other close linguistically African languages would yield promising results. To test this hypothesis, we conduct training experiments using pre-trained models HuBERT147 and AfriHuBERT as encoders, combined with pre-trained multilingual decoders such as mBART (Liu et al., 2020) and NLLB (Team et al., 2022).

3 Fongbe linguistic features

Fongbe, a Gbe language spoken primarily in Benin, serves as a lingua franca for approximately 40˘45% of the Beninese population (Gbaguidi, 2009). Fongbe plays a significant role in media, being widely used in both public and private radio

[2]International Workshop on Spoken Language Translation

and television programs. However, Fongbe tonal nature presents unique challenges, particularly in written and translated texts. In linguistics, tone refers to the use of pitch variations to distinguish meaning in spoken language (Caron, 2015). Lexical tones, in particular, help differentiate words that are otherwise phonologically identical (Xu, 2004). These pitch variations, or tonal patterns, are produced by changes in the fundamental frequency of a syllable. For the written form of Fongbe, mainly based on the Latin alphabet with additional symbols, these tones are typically represented using diacritics, which are essential for accurately conveying tonal distinctions in written form. Fongbe primarily features two main tonemes as noted by (Gnanguènon, 2014), from which all other tones are derived. In Fongbe, each syllable carries a tone, and the absence of tone marks can often lead to confusion. Regarding tones, there are four tones in Fongbe. The low tone (`), the high tone (´), the low-high tone (ˇ) and lastly, the mid tone (-) marked by a small horizontal line. The absence of tone is considered as the mid tone. Fongbe utilizes an alphabet comprising 23 consonants and 12 vowels as shown in Table 1.

Consonants	Vowels
b, c, d, d , f, g, gb, h, j, k, kp, l, m, n, ny, p , r, s, t, v, w, x, y, z	a, e, ɛ, i, o , ɔ , u

Table 1: Fongbe consonants and vowels

Fongbe exhibits a lexicographical structure that is primarily monosyllabic, disyllabic, and trisyllabic shown in table 2. A compatibility study conducted on the combinations of consonants, vowels, and the four tones revealed the presence of 376 monosyllabic structures out of $1,104$ meaningful forms. This analysis highlights the phonological richness and structural diversity of Fongbe, underscoring its significance in linguistic studies.

Structure	Types	Examples
Monosyl.	V, CV	à, bà
Disyllabic	VCV, CVCV, CVV, VV	azo, galí, fɛɛ̀, àa
Trisyllabic	VCVCV, CVCVCV, VCVV, CVCVV CVVCV	asɔ̀lɔ̀, logosò, agoo, kɛ́dɛ́ɛ́ jaunta

Table 2: Fongbe syllabic structure

4 Data collection process

We augmented the FFSTC corpus (Kponou et al., 2024) by adding new samples selected from a validated set in French, sourced from the Common Voice project (Ardila et al., 2020), a Mozilla Foundation initiative. To reduce the human cost, we utilized the Google Translate to generate Fongbe translations of the French sentences. These translations were then meticulously reviewed and refined by a team of linguists to ensure accuracy and linguistic quality. Once validated, the sentences were uploaded to our custom web application (Fortuné, 2024) for recording.

Participants, comprising both male and female speakers, were invited to read at least $2,000$ sentences each. The reading sessions were conducted in a controlled environment to minimize ambient noise, as Fongbe is a tonal language, and background sounds could interfere with the accurate perception of its tonal distinctions. To further ensure data quality, we carefully selected participants to minimize potential biases arising from regional accents. Specifically, we included only native speakers of Fongbe, excluding individuals who learned Fongbe as a second language or who speak Fongbe with influences from Mahi or Gungbe dialect accents.

The recorded sentences underwent a rigorous validation process by a team of six validators, working in pairs, with each sentence validated once. Sentences containing background noise (e.g., wind or engine noise) or exhibiting incorrect tone patterns were rejected. This meticulous validation process enabled us to successfully add $42,000$ new samples to the existing FFSTC corpus.

The FFSTC corpus originally stemmed from a data competition in which multiple participants translated the same French sentences directly into Fongbe. This process resulted in duplicate transcripts and nearly identical speech recordings, contributing to a rich diversity of speech samples. To maximize the potential of this variation, we retained these duplicates in the training set while ensuring that only unique transcripts were included in the validation and test sets. This approach allows future trained models to benefit from the diversity of translations while maintaining data integrity during the evaluation process.

4.1 Dataset statistics

As outlined in the introduction, we conducted experiments in both ASR and Speech Translation. For the end-to-end ST task, we utilized the entire dataset. While for the ASR and the cascade ST task, we use only the 36 hours of speech available with their transcripts in Fongbe, as described in Table 3.

Experiments	Split	Hours	Sentences
ASR	Test	3.93	2.5 k
ASR	Valid	3.54	2.4 k
ASR	Train	29	19.9 k
ST	Test	5.9	3.9 k
ST	Valid	6.1	4.1 k
ST	Train	48	29.5 k

Table 3: Dataset statistics

5 Experiments and results

In this section, we present the experimental framework for (1) ASR system, (2) cascade ST system and end-to-end ST system.

5.1 SSL models Description

The use of pre-trained models, as demonstrated in several studies, shows the potential to create efficient recognition or translation systems (Laurent et al., 2023) even with limited amounts of data by fine-tuning them on downstream tasks. For our experiments, we chose to use that method. Among the publicly available pre-trained speech encoders, such as XLSR-128 (Babu et al., 2021), and HuBERT, we selected HuBERT (Hsu et al., 2021) variants, specifically HuBERT147 and AfriHuBERT, specialized to some African languages (but not to Fongbe). This decision was based on their superior performance on downstream tasks, such as Automatic Speech Recognition (ASR), as demonstrated in (Alabi et al., 2024).

HuBERT is closely related to Wav2Vec 2.0 (Baevski et al., 2020). While Wav2Vec 2.0 distinguishes between true latent speech representations and contextualized representations generated by the transformer encoder, HuBERT employs a technique similar to BERT (Devlin et al., 2019) for speech units. Specifically, HuBERT computes a loss over masked speech units, forcing the model to learn high-level representations of unmasked inputs to accurately infer the targets of the masked ones. This approach has been shown to outperform Wav2Vec 2.0 when trained on the same amount of data in (Hsu et al., 2021). Given these advantages, we expected HuBERT147 and AfriHuBERT to deliver strong performance in our experiments.

We also trained a SAMU_XLSR model using our dataset. Unlike the approach in (Khurana et al., 2022), which relies on speech transcripts for alignment, we used translated labels instead. SAMU is built on XLSR and utilizes a frozen Language-Agnostic BERT Sentence Encoder (LaBSE) (Feng et al., 2020) as the master model to semantically align Fongbe speech and French text embeddings in the XLSR space. We trained SAMU for 50 epochs on the ST training dataset.

mBART is a denoising sequence-to-sequence model pre-trained on high-resource languages. It uses a Transformer architecture to reconstruct texts from noised inputs, where phrases are masked and sentences are permuted. Known for its robustness with noisy data, mBART is particularly well-suited in tasks like speech translation, especially for tonal languages such as Fongbe. NLLB (No Language Left Behind) is a multilingual translation model pre-trained on a wide range of languages, including several African languages. Designed for high-quality translation, NLLB aims to bridge the gap between high-resource and low-resource languages, making it a strong candidate for our translation experiments.

5.2 ASR experiments

The first experiment was performed using the original Fongbe transcripts, including diacritics, to establish a baseline performance. In the second experiment, we removed the diacritics from the transcripts to evaluate the impact of diacritic removal on recognition accuracy. The third experiment involved a novel approach of diacritic substitution, where we systematically identified monosyllabic words with diacritics and replaced them with their base syllables accompanied by a unique numerical identifier. This substitution aimed to modify the representation of diacritics while preserving linguistic information, potentially improving the model's ability to generalize across similar phonetic patterns as reported in Table 4.

To conduct the experiments, we trained three different SentencePiece (Kudo, 2018) tokenizer models at character level using the combined training and validation sets for each specific case. For the base experiment (with diacritics), the substitution experiment and the experiment without diacritics

State	Sentence
Diacritics	tavo ayihun tɔn dé dò disixwé **transl.**: *a game table on the right*
w/o diacr.	tavo ayihun tɔn de do disixwe
Substitution	tavo ayihun tɔn de1 do2 disixwe1

Table 4: Example of diacritic processing

the vocabulary size are, respectively 62, 44 and 36. This reduction in vocabulary size for the substitution and third experiment case reflects the simplified representation of text when diacritics are either removed or replaced, which in turn may influence the model efficiency and performance. The three ASR models are end-to-end models composed of the AfriHuBERT speech encoder followed by three 1024-dim dense layers. They were fine-tuned on the ASR training dataset by using the CTC loss function. All experiments are run over 50 epochs and results are summarized in the Table 5. ASR recipes will be released for reproducibility.

Experiments	WER
ASR base	21.98
ASR Sub	22.18
ASR without diacritics	17.02

Table 5: Word Error Rates (%) on the ASR test dataset reached by the AfriHuBERT speech encoder (*our best results*)

The ASR model trained without diacritics yields the lowest Word Error Rate (WER) of 17.02%, but this WER cannot be compared with the two other ones: the lexical confusion is drastically decreased since removing the diacritics reduce the vocabulary size. Nevertheless, if the automatic transcriptions without diacritics are less informative, these results show they are more reliable. Although the diacritic substitution approach did not outperform the base model, we consider it should be experimented within a cascade speech translation system, because of a different distribution of ASR errors.

5.3 Cascade speech translation

Cascade systems for speech translation consist of two key modules: ASR and MT (Machine Translation). In our implementation, we used our trained ASR models for the transcription module, followed by an end-to-end text-to-text MT model based on the fine-tuning the NLLB model. Fongbe was included in the NLLB pre-training dataset. We fine-tuned it using the Huggingface (Jain, 2022) trainer. To ensure a fair comparison, we conducted three separate fine-tuning experiments, the first on Fongbe written with diacritics, the second with substituted Fongbe and the last on Fongbe without diacritics. We evaluated the cascade model on the same test set as the end-to-end model presented in the next section.

The fine-tuning of NLLB results yielded BLEU scores of 58.9,57.56 and 47.39 on manual transcriptions, respectively for the models with and without diacritics, with substitution and without diacritics, on the validation subset containing the Fongbe transcriptions. These results underscore the importance of diacritics in preserving contextual understanding, particularly for tonal languages like Fongbe.

For the experiment using the ASR with the 'substitution' approach, we fine-tune the model NLLB using a substituted Fongbe. This step ensured that the translation module will receive the correct input for each case. The results of the experiments are summarized in Table 6.

Experiments	BLEU
ASR base + NLLB	32.76
ASR with diacritics + NLLB	39.60
ASR Sub + NLLB	37.23

Table 6: BLEU scores for the cascade systems on the test dataset

The best result in cascade training was achieved by the AfriHuBERT model fine-tuned on ASR with diacritic, reaching a BLEU score of 39.60 follow by the susbstitution system (ASR Sub) with the BLEU of 37.23. These experiments reveal that retaining diacritics is more critical for translation of Fongbe than for its recognition, as diacritics provide additional linguistic information about segments that goes beyond what the base syllables alone can convey. Additionally, we observed that the substitution method holds significant potential. However, further studies are needed to fully explore and optimize this approach, as it could provide a viable pathway for improving both efficiency and performance in speech recognition and translation tasks.

5.4 End-to-end Speech translation

We conducted several experiments dedicated to the end-to-end approach. We investigated the use of different speech encoders HuBERT-147 and AfriHuBERT with different decoders mBART and NLLB. We combined different augmentations to perform data augmentation: Speed perturbation (resample the audio signal at a rate that is similar to the original rate, to achieve a slightly slower or slightly faster signal), Frequency drop (randomly drops a number of frequency bands to zero) and Chunk drop (Chunk drop is an augmentation strategy helps a models learn to rely on all parts of the signal, since it can't expect a given part to be present).

Experiments	Aug	Params	**BLEU**
AfriHuBERT-NLLB	No	962.1M	23.90
AfriHuBERT-NLLB	Yes	962.1M	26.32
AfriHuBERT-mBART	No	553.8M	22.16
AfriHuBERT-mBART	Yes	553.8M	24.30
SAMU-mBART	No	1.4B	25.11
SAMU-mBART	Yes	1.4B	24.17
SAMU-NLLB	No	1.8B	25.85
SAMU-NLLB	Yes	1.8B	28.43

Table 7: BLEU score of end-to-end speech-to-text translation models, with of without data augmentation.

All the models were trained on a single V100 32BG GPU with a batch size of 2.We utilized the Adam optimizer and ran the experiments over 50 epochs. To align the output length of the HuBERT encoder with the input dimensions of the mBART and NLLB decoders, we employed a feed-forward layer. During inference, we applied a beam search with a width of 5 to generate translations. To enhance their performance, we applied data augmentation to each model. Since the models based on AfriHuBERT performed better than the models based on HuBERT147, we report in Table 7 only the results reached by using AfriHuBERT as a speech encoder. We observed that SAMU achieved better BLEU scores with data augmentation than the other end-to-end, as documented in Table 7. We conclude that semantic alignment in the embedding space of SAMU provides it with a better speech representation for the decoder.

NLLB's broader linguistic coverage did not translate into superior performance in our experiments.

6 Conclusion

This work represents a significant advance for Fongbe speech processing, for both transcription and translation to French. By extending an existing dataset to 61 hours of high-quality audio and aligned text, we offer the research community a unique and richer resource to build and evaluate speech technologies for Fongbe, a tonal and under-represented language. Our detailed experiments in both cascade and end-to-end Speech Translation reveal several important insights that can stimulate broader research in low-resource language technologies.

Our best cascade system achieved a BLEU score of 39.60, underscoring the power of carefully handling tonal information. In contrast, our most effective end-to-end model achieved a BLEU of 28.43, especially when leveraging data augmentation and semantic alignment.

The expanded Fongbe corpus and our findings open several possibilities for further research. First, improvements to diacritic substitution—potentially using more granular markers that capture subtle tonal shifts could reduce ASR errors while preserving key phonological cues for translation. Second, personalized or speaker-adaptive speech translation models, possibly trained to handle specific dialectal variants, may substantially enhance intelligibility and translation fidelity. Finally, future self-supervised or multilingual pre-training efforts will benefit from explicitly including Fongbe data, leading to more robust encoder–decoder architectures for low-resource African languages.

Overall, this work not only delivers the largest corpus of Fongbe audio currently available for speech recognition and translation, but also highlights data-collection strategies, modelling setups, and diacritic handling approaches that can be generalized to other tonal, under-represented languages.

References

Ife Adebara and AbdelRahim al Elmadany. 2023. SERENGETI: Massively multilingual language models for Africa. ACL.

Jesujoba O. Alabi, Xuechen Liu, Dietrich Klakow, and Junichi Yamagishi. 2024. Afrihubert: A self-supervised speech representation model for african languages. *Preprint*, arXiv:2409.20201.

Rosana Ardila, Megan Branson, Kelly Davis, Michael Henretty, Michael Kohler, Josh Meyer, Reuben Morais, Lindsay Saunders, Francis M. Tyers, and Gregor Weber. 2020. Common voice: A massively-multilingual speech corpus. *Preprint*, arXiv:1912.06670.

Arun Babu, Changhan Wang, Andros Tjandra, and Kushal Lakhotia al. 2021. Xls-r: Self-supervised cross-lingual speech representation learning at scale. *Preprint*, arXiv:2111.09296.

Alexei Baevski, Henry Zhou, Abdelrahman Mohamed, and Michael Auli. 2020. wav2vec 2.0: A framework for self-supervised learning of speech representations. *Preprint*, arXiv:2006.11477.

Mustapha Bala. 2015. © african literature and orality: A reading of ngugi wa thiang'o's wizard of the crow 2007. *JOURNAL OF ENGLISH LANGUAGE AND LITERATURE*, 3.

Sameer Bansal, Herman Kamper, Karen Livescu, Adam Lopez, and Sharon Goldwater. 2018. Pre-training on high-resource speech recognition improves low-resource speech-to-text translation. *arXiv preprint arXiv:1809.01431*.

Marcely Zanon Boito and Vivek Iyer al. 2024. mhubert-147: a compact multilingual hubert model. *Preprint*, arXiv:2406.06371.

Bernard Caron. 2015. Tone and intonation. In *Corpus-based Studies of Lesser-described Languages. The CorpAfroAs corpus of spoken AfroAsiatic languages*.

Alexis Conneau, Alexei Baevski, Ronan Collobert, Abdelrahman Mohamed, and Michael Auli. 2020. Unsupervised cross-lingual representation learning for speech recognition. *Preprint*, arXiv:2006.13979.

Jacob Devlin, Ming-Wei Chang, Kenton Lee, and Kristina Toutanova. 2019. Bert: Pre-training of deep bidirectional transformers for language understanding. *Preprint*, arXiv:1810.04805.

David Eberhard, Gary Simons, and Chuck Fennig. 2021. *Ethnologue: Languages of the World, 24th Edition*.

Fangxiaoyu Feng, Yinfei Yang, Daniel Cer, Naveen Arivazhagan, and Wei Wang. 2020. Language-agnostic bert sentence embedding. *arXiv preprint arXiv:2007.01852*.

Kponou Fortuné. 2024. Ayihoun.com. Accessed: 2024-12-16.

Elodie Gauthier, Laurent Besacier, Sylvie Voisin, Michael Melese, and Uriel Pascal Elingui. 2016. Collecting resources in sub-saharan african languages for automatic speech recognition: a case study of wolof. *LREC*.

K. J. Gbaguidi. 2009. *Taxinomie et analyse des erreurs linguistiques des élèves fonphones en apprentissage de Français : Pour une approche linguistique et pragmatique en Didactique des Langues*. Doctoral dissertation, EDP-UAC.

C. B. Gnanguènon. 2014. *Analyse syntaxique et sémantique de la langue "fn" au Bénin en Afrique de l'Ouest*. Ph.D. thesis, Université Cergy-Pontoise, France.

Wei-Ning Hsu, Benjamin Bolte, and Yao-Hung Hubert Tsai al. 2021. Hubert: Self-supervised speech representation learning by masked prediction of hidden units. *Preprint*, arXiv:2106.07447.

Shashank Mohan Jain. 2022. Hugging face. pages 51–67. Springer.

Sameer Khurana, Antoine Laurent, and James Glass. 2022. Samu-xlsr: Semantically-aligned multimodal utterance-level cross-lingual speech representation. *IEEE Journal of Selected Topics in Signal Processing*, 16(6):1493–1504.

D. Fortuné Kponou, Fréjus A. A. Laleye, and Eugène C. Ezin. Systematic literature review and bibliometric analysis of low-resource speech-to-text translation. pages 379–398, Cham. Springer Nature Switzerland.

D. Fortuné Kponou, Fréjus A. A. Laleye, and Eugène Cokou Ezin. 2024. FFSTC: Fongbe to French speech translation corpus. In *LREC-COLING 2024*.

T Kudo. 2018. Sentencepiece: A simple and language independent subword tokenizer and detokenizer for neural text processing. *arXiv preprint arXiv:1808.06226*.

Fréjus A. A. Laleye, Laurent Besacier, Eugène C. Ezin, and Cina Motamed. First automatic fongbe continuous speech recognition system: Development of acoustic models and language models.

Antoine Laurent, Souhir Gahbiche, Ha Nguyen, Haroun Elleuch, Fethi Bougares, Antoine Thiol, Hugo Riguidel, Salima Mdhaffar, Gaëlle Laperrière, Lucas Maison, and 1 others. 2023. On-trac consortium systems for the iwslt 2023 dialectal and low-resource speech translation tasks. In *Proceedings of the 20th International Conference on Spoken Language Translation (IWSLT 2023)*, pages 219–226.

Xian Li, Changhan Wang, Yun Tang, Chau Tran, Yuqing Tang, Juan Pino, Alexei Baevski, Alexis Conneau, and Michael Auli. 2020. Multilingual speech translation with efficient finetuning of pretrained models. *arXiv preprint arXiv:2010.12829*.

Yinhan Liu, Jiatao Gu, Naman Goyal, Xian Li, Sergey Edunov, Marjan Ghazvininejad, Mike Lewis, and Luke Zettlemoyer. 2020. Multilingual denoising pre-training for neural machine translation. *Preprint*, arXiv:2001.08210.

Jonathan Mbuya and Antonios Anastasopoulos. GMU systems for the IWSLT 2023 dialect and low-resource speech translation tasks.

Bismarck Bamfo Odoom, Nathaniel Robinson, Elijah Rippeth, Luis Tavarez-Arce, Kenton Murray, Matthew Wiesner, Paul McNamee, Philipp Koehn, and Kevin Duh. 2024. Can synthetic speech improve end-to-end conversational speech translation? In *Proceedings of the 16th Conference of the Association for Machine Translation in the Americas (Volume 1: Research Track)*, pages 167–177.

Mihaela C Stoian, Sameer Bansal, and Sharon Goldwater. 2020. Analyzing asr pretraining for low-resource speech-to-text translation. In *ICASSP 2020-2020 IEEE International Conference on Acoustics, Speech and Signal Processing (ICASSP)*, pages 7909–7913. IEEE.

Martha Tachbelie, Solomon Teferra Abate, and Laurent Besacier. Using different acoustic, lexical and language modeling units for asr of an under-resourced language - amharic.

NLLB Team, Marta R. Costa-jussà, and James Cross al. 2022. No language left behind: Scaling human-centered machine translation. *Preprint*, arXiv:2207.04672.

Ashish Vaswani, Noam Shazeer, Niki Parmar, Jakob Uszkoreit, Llion Jones, Aidan N. Gomez, Lukasz Kaiser, and Illia Polosukhin. 2023. Attention is all you need. *Preprint*, arXiv:1706.03762.

Changhan Wang, Hirofumi Inaguma, Peng-Jen Chen, Ilia Kulikov, Yun Tang, Wei-Ning Hsu, Michael Auli, and Juan Pino. 2022. Simple and effective unsupervised speech translation. *arXiv preprint arXiv:2210.10191*.

Yi Xu. 2004. Understanding tone from the perspective of production and perception. *Language and Linguistics*, 5(4):757–797.

Marcely Zanon Boito and John al Ortega. ON-TRAC consortium systems for the IWSLT 2022 dialect and low-resource speech translation tasks. Dublin, Ireland (in-person and online). Association for Computational Linguistics.

HENT-SRT: Hierarchical Efficient Neural Transducer with Self-Distillation for Joint Speech Recognition and Translation

Amir Hussein
CLSP
JHU

Cihan Xiao
CLSP
JHU

Matthew Wiesner
HLTCOE
JHU

Dan Povey
Xiaomi

Leibny Paola Garcia
HLTCOE/CLSP
JHU

Sanjeev Khudanpur
HLTCOE/CLSP
JHU

Abstract

Neural transducers (NT) provide an effective framework for speech streaming, demonstrating strong performance in automatic speech recognition (ASR). However, the application of NT to speech translation (ST) remains challenging, as existing approaches struggle with word reordering and performance degradation when jointly modeling ASR and ST, resulting in a gap with attention-based encoder-decoder (AED) models. Existing NT-based ST approaches also suffer from high computational training costs. To address these issues, we propose HENT-SRT (Hierarchical Efficient Neural Transducer for Speech Recognition and Translation), a novel framework that factorizes ASR and translation tasks to better handle reordering. To ensure robust ST while preserving ASR performance, we use self-distillation with CTC consistency regularization. Moreover, we improve computational efficiency by incorporating best practices from ASR transducers, including a downsampled hierarchical encoder, a stateless predictor, and a pruned transducer loss to reduce training complexity. Finally, we introduce a blank penalty during decoding, reducing deletions and improving translation quality. Our approach is evaluated on three conversational datasets Arabic, Spanish, and Mandarin achieving new state-of-the-art performance among NT models and substantially narrowing the gap with AED-based systems.

1 Introduction

Translation of spoken conversations across languages plays a crucial role in cross-cultural communication, healthcare, and education (Köksal and Yürük, 2020; Nakamura, 2009; Al Shamsi et al., 2020). Traditionally, speech translation (ST) systems have been built using a cascaded approach, where automatic speech recognition (ASR) first transcribes speech into text, which is then passed to a machine translation (MT) system (Matusov et al., 2005; Bertoldi and Federico, 2005; Sperber et al., 2017; Pino et al., 2019; Yang et al., 2022). This modular approach facilitates the use of large text corpora for MT training, at the cost of (1) complex beam search algorithms in streaming applications (Rabatin et al., 2024), (2) error propagation from the ASR to MT model, (3) an inability to leverage paralinguistic information such as prosody, and (4) additional latency, as MT processing must wait for ASR to complete.

To overcome the limitations of cascaded systems, end-to-end speech translation (E2E-ST) has emerged as a promising approach that directly maps source speech to target text, providing a more streamlined architecture, reduced latency, and competitive performance (Berard et al., 2016, 2018; Dalmia et al., 2021; Gaido et al., 2020; Yan et al., 2023b). However, most end-to-end speech translation (E2E-ST) research has focused on offline attention-based encoder-decoder (AED) architectures. As label-synchronous systems, AEDs require multiple input frames before emitting each output token, which limits their suitability for streaming applications and increases sensitivity to utterance segmentation (Anastasopoulos et al., 2022; Sinclair et al., 2014). To enable streaming in AED models, researchers have proposed wait-k policies, which introduce a controlled buffering mechanism to balance latency and translation quality (Ma et al., 2020; Chen et al., 2021; Ma et al., 2021). However, finding the optimal wait-k policy is challenging, as it must balance latency and quality, and the necessary buffering cause delays, making AED-based models less suitable for streaming applications.

In contrast, frame-synchronous architectures like Connectionist Temporal Classification (CTC)

Proceedings of the 22nd International Conference on Spoken Language Translation (IWSLT 2025), pages 153–164
July 31 - August 1, 2025 ©2025 Association for Computational Linguistics

(Graves et al., 2006) and the Neural Transducer (NT) (Graves, 2012) more naturally handle streaming data and demonstrate greater robustness to utterance segmentation, mitigating the over- and under-generation issues in AED models (Chiu et al., 2019; Yan et al., 2023a). While CTC enforces strictly monotonic alignments, which limits its ability to handle word reordering (Yan et al., 2023a), the neural transducer (NT) relaxes these constraints, allowing the generation of longer output sequences and the modeling of autoregressive token dependencies. This makes NT more suitable for translation, as illustrated in Figure 2. To improve NT's reordering capabilities, researchers have proposed augmenting the joiner with cross-attention (Liu et al., 2021) and the predictor with an AED-based decoder (Tang et al., 2023), though these additions increase computational complexity and latency. To further enhance translation quality, (Tang et al., 2023) introduced attention pooling for better encoder-predictor fusion at the frame level, while (Xue et al., 2022) explored similar mechanisms. Additionally, (Wang et al., 2023) proposed a transducer-based model for unified ASR and ST, but its shared encoder struggles with reordering, making it less effective than AED in offline settings.

In this work, we propose a hierarchical neural transducer architecture, HENT-SRT,[1] which decomposes speech translation (ST) into an automatic speech recognition (ASR) task followed by a translation task, effectively handling word reordering. The system employs multi-task training to optimize ASR and ST objectives simultaneously with a separate predictor and joiner for each task. Our objectives are three-fold: (1) to close the performance gap with state-of-the-art AED models in offline ST settings, (2) to improve computational efficiency during training and inference, and (3) to jointly model ASR and ST while maintaining ASR performance. To this end, we introduce HENT-SRT, a neural transducer-based ST framework that addresses (1) through a hierarchical encoder architecture, enabling more effective handling of reordering in translation. To improve ST efficiency in (2), we integrate a stateless 1D-CNN predictor (Ghodsi et al., 2020) and adopt the Zipformer architecture (Yao et al., 2024a), which achieves superior ASR performance compared to state-of-the-art AED models such as E-Branchformer (Kim et al., 2023), while offering greater computational efficiency. Additionally, to reduce training complexity, we employ the pruned transducer loss (Kuang et al., 2022). To mitigate ASR degradation in joint modeling for (3), we employ self-distillation with CTC consistency regularization (Yao et al., 2024b). We evaluate the effectiveness of our approach on conversational speech translation across three language pairs: Tunisian Arabic-English, Spanish-English, and Chinese-English described in (Hussein et al., 2024). Furthermore, we conduct a comprehensive ablation study to analyze the impact of each ST design choice in both offline and streaming setups.

2 Proposed Approach

Let $\mathbf{X} = (\mathbf{x}_1, \ldots, \mathbf{x}_T) \in \mathbb{R}^{T \times F}$ denote the source speech, a sequence of T acoustic feature vectors of dimension F. The goal is to generate a target word sequence $\mathbf{y}^{(t)} = (y_1^{(t)}, \ldots, y_U^{(t)}) \in \mathcal{V}_U^{(t)}$, a translation of length U. We use superscripts (s) and (t) to refer to the *source* and *target* languages, respectively. Speech translation task is trained using discriminative learning by minimizing the negative log-likelihood $\mathcal{L} = -\log P(\mathbf{y}^{(t)}|\mathbf{X})$. Transducers compute this probability by marginalizing over the set of all possible alignments $\mathbf{a} \in \bar{\mathcal{V}}_{T+U}^{(t)}$ as follows:

$$P(\mathbf{y}^{(t)}|\mathbf{X}) = \sum_{\mathbf{a}\in\mathcal{B}^{-1}(\mathbf{y}^{(t)})} P(\mathbf{a}|\mathbf{X}) \quad (1)$$

where $\bar{\mathcal{V}}^{(t)} = \mathcal{V}^{(t)} \cup \{\phi\}$, ϕ is a *blank* label and $\mathcal{B} : \bar{\mathcal{V}}_{T+U}^{(t)} \rightarrow \mathcal{V}_U^{(t)}$ is the deterministic mapping from an alignment $\mathbf{a}$ to the sequence $\mathbf{Y}^{(t)}$ of its non-blank symbols. Transducers parameterize $P(\mathbf{a}|\mathbf{X})$ using an encoder, a prediction network, and a joiner, as illustrated in Figure 1a. The encoder maps $\mathbf{X}$ to a representation sequence $\mathbf{f}_{1:k}^{\mathrm{t}}, k \in \{1, \ldots, T\}$, the predictor transforms $\mathbf{y}^{(t)}$ sequentially into $\mathbf{g}_{1:u}^{\mathrm{t}}, u \in \{1, \ldots, U\}$, and the joiner combines $\mathbf{f}_{1:k}^{\mathrm{t}}$ and $\mathbf{g}_{1:u}^{\mathrm{t}}$ to generate logits $z_{k,u}^{t}$ whose softmax is the posterior distribution of a_k (over $\bar{\mathcal{V}}^{(t)}$), i.e.

$$\begin{aligned} P(\mathbf{y}^{(t)}|\mathbf{X}) &= \sum_{\mathbf{a}\in\mathcal{B}^{-1}(\mathbf{y}^{(t)})} \prod_{k=1}^{T+U} P(\mathbf{a}_k^{(t)}|f_{1:k}^{t}, g_{1:u(k)}^{t}) \\ &= \sum_{\mathbf{a}\in\mathcal{B}^{-1}(\mathbf{y}^{(t)})} \prod_{k=1}^{T+U} \text{softmax}(z_{k,u(k)}^{st}) \end{aligned} \quad (2)$$

[1]Code is available at https://github.com/k2-fsa/icefall.

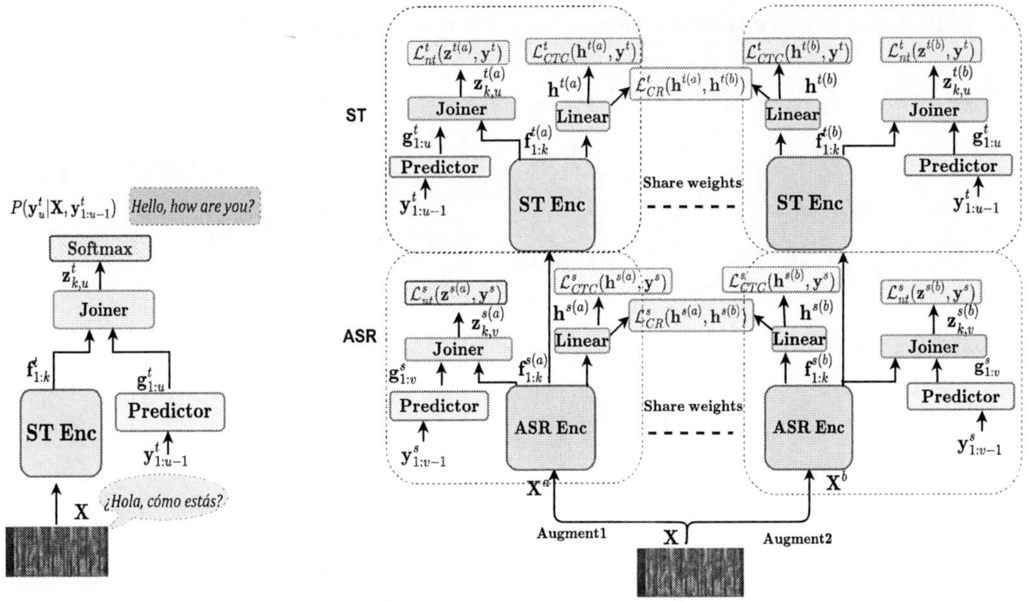

(a) Neural Transducer based speech translation architecture

(b) Proposed hierarchical neural transducer framework with self-distillation for joint speech recognition and translation (HENT-SRT).

Figure 1: Neural transducer-based speech translation and the proposed HENT-SRT architecture

where $u(k) \in \{1, \cdots, U\}$ denotes the index in the label sequence at time k. The negative log of the quantity in (2) is known as the transducer loss.

2.1 ST hierarchical encoder

To enhance the model's ability to handle word reordering during translation, we propose a hierarchical architecture by adding a translation-specific encoder on top of the ASR encoder, as illustrated in Figure 1b. This design enables joint modeling of ASR and ST while decomposing ST into ASR and translation tasks. Unlike Wang et al. (2023), our translation-specific encoder facilitates more flexible reordering over the latent, monotonic ASR representations. Inspired by Dalmia et al. (2021), we adopt a two-stage training strategy: (1) ASR pretraining, followed by (2) multitask fine-tuning with both ST and ASR objectives. The ASR encoder, $\text{ENC}_{\text{asr}}(\cdot)$, maps the input acoustic features $\mathbf{X}$ to a latent representation, $\mathbf{f}^{\text{s}}$, as defined in Eq. (3).

$$\mathbf{f}^{\text{s}} = ENC_{\text{asr}}(\mathbf{X}) \tag{3}$$

Following this, the representation, $\mathbf{f}^{\text{s}}$, serves as input to the ST encoder, $\text{ENC}^{\text{st}}(\cdot)$, demonstrated in Eq. (4)

$$\mathbf{f}^{\text{t}} = ENC_{\text{st}}(\mathbf{f}^{\text{s}}) \tag{4}$$

The transducer loss is computed for both ASR ($\mathcal{L}_{nt}^{s}$) and ST ($\mathcal{L}_{nt}^{t}$) objectives following Eq. (2). The overall multitask objective, $\mathcal{L}_{nt}$, is the weighted sum of the two objectives:

$$\mathcal{L}_{nt} = \alpha_{asr}\mathcal{L}_{nt}^{s} + \alpha_{st}\mathcal{L}_{nt}^{t} \tag{5}$$

where α_{asr} and α_{st} are hyperparameters controlling the contribution of ASR and ST losses, respectively.

2.2 CR-CTC self-distillation

Balancing multitask ASR and ST optimization in a two-stage training approach is challenging, as it often improves ST performance at the cost of ASR degradation. To achieve robust ST performance with minimal ASR degradation, we employ self-distillation with consistency-regularized CTC (CR-CTC) (Yao et al., 2024b). This approach applies SpecAugment (Park et al., 2019) to generate two augmented views of the same input, $\mathbf{X}^{a}$ and $\mathbf{X}^{b}$, which are then processed by a shared ASR encoder:

$$\mathbf{f}^{s(a)} = \text{ENC}_{\text{asr}}(\mathbf{X}^{(a)}) \tag{6}$$

$$\mathbf{f}^{s(b)} = \text{ENC}_{\text{asr}}(\mathbf{X}^{(b)}) \tag{7}$$

The CR-CTC framework optimizes two objectives: the CTC loss $\mathcal{L}_{CTC}$ and the consistency regularization $\mathcal{L}_{CR}$, computed using the Kullback-Leibler divergence (D_{KL}) between encoder outputs:

$$\mathcal{L}_{CTC} = \frac{1}{2}(\mathcal{L}_{CTC}(\mathbf{h}^{(a)}, \mathbf{y}) + \mathcal{L}_{CTC}(\mathbf{h}^{(b)}, \mathbf{y})) \quad (8)$$

$$\mathcal{L}_{CR} = \frac{1}{2}\sum_{k=1}^{T}\Big(D_{KL}(\text{sg}(h_k^{(b)}) \parallel h_k^{(a)}) + D_{KL}(\text{sg}(h_k^{(a)}) \parallel h_k^{(b)})\Big) \quad (9)$$

where sg($\cdot$) denotes the stop-gradient operation. In the proposed HENT-SRT framework, $\mathcal{L}_{CR}$ and $\mathcal{L}_{CTC}$ are computed for both ASR and ST encoders, as illustrated in Figure 1b. The final objective is optimized using a multitask learning formulation that combines CR and CTC losses from both ASR and ST tasks along with the NT loss from Eq. 5:

$$\mathcal{L} = \mathcal{L}_{\text{nt}} + \alpha_{\text{CR(asr)}}\mathcal{L}_{\text{CR}}^{s} + \alpha_{\text{CTC(asr)}}\mathcal{L}_{\text{CTC}}^{s} + \alpha_{\text{CR(st)}}\mathcal{L}_{\text{CR}}^{t} + \alpha_{\text{CTC(st)}}\mathcal{L}_{\text{CTC}}^{t} \quad (10)$$

where α values are hyperparameters controlling the relative contributions of each loss term.

2.3 ST decoding

The translation decoding objective is to find the most probable target sequence $\hat{\mathbf{y}}^{(t)}$ among all possible outputs $\mathbf{y}^{(t)*}$ by maximizing the log-likelihood:

$$\hat{\mathbf{y}}^{(t)} = \arg\max_{\mathbf{y}^{(t)*}} \sum_{l=1}^{U} \log P(\mathbf{y}_l^{(t)} | \mathbf{y}_{<l}^{(t)}, \mathbf{X}) \quad (11)$$

Neural transducers can model word reordering by using blank emissions to delay output tokens and then emitting multiple tokens within a single time step, as shown in Figure 2. One challenge with transducer decoding is that the input audio features are typically longer than the output sequence, non-spoken regions are mainly represented by blank tokens, leading to a bias toward blank emissions (Mahadeokar et al., 2021). This bias increases deletions and degrades translation quality. To mitigate this issue and control blank emissions during decoding, we introduce a blank penalty (BP) by adjusting the logit scores $\mathbf{z}$ in the log space:

$$z^t[:, 0] = z^t[:, 0] - BP \quad (12)$$

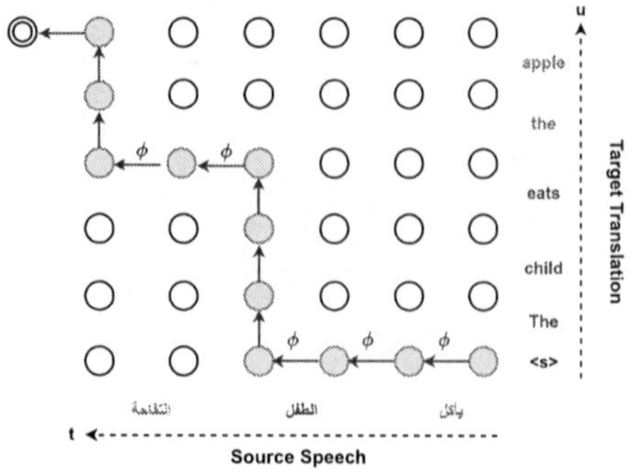

Figure 2: Illustration of the transducer decoding graph for an ST task.

2.4 Computation efficiency

To improve computational efficiency during training and inference, we adopt best practices from ASR transducer and examine their impact on ST in Section 3.2. For the encoder, we utilize the recently proposed Zipformer (Yao et al., 2024a), which consists of multiple encoder blocks operating at different down-sampling rates. This hierarchical structure reduces the number of frames to process, thereby lowering computational complexity. Additionally, we replace the traditional LSTM-based prediction network with a stateless 1D-CNN trigram model (Ghodsi et al., 2020). Another major drawback of NT is the high memory consumption of the transducer loss due to the need for marginalization over logit tensor of size (batch, T, U, Vocab). To address this, we replace the full-sum transducer loss with the pruned transducer loss, which applies a simple linear joiner to prune the alignment lattice before computing the full sum on the reduced lattice (Kuang et al., 2022). This significantly reduces memory overhead while maintaining competitive performance.

3 Experiments

3.1 Experimental setup

We evaluate the effectiveness of our proposed approach on three conversational datasets: Fisher Spanish-English (Post et al., 2013), Tunisian Arabic-English (Ansari et al., 2020), and HKUST Chinese-English (Wotherspoon et al., 2024). These datasets contain 3-way data comprising telephone speech, source language transcriptions, and corresponding English translations.

Data pre-processing: Our experiments utilize the

Icefall framework,[2] with the Lhotse toolkit (Żelasko et al., 2021) for speech data preparation. All audio recordings are resampled from 8kHz to 16kHz and augmented with speed perturbations at factors of 0.9, 1.0, and 1.1. We extract 80-dimensional mel-spectrogram features using a 25ms window with a 10ms frame shift. Additionally, we apply on-the-fly SpecAugment (Park et al., 2019), incorporating time warping (maximum factor of 80), frequency masking (two regions, max width of 27 bins), and time masking (ten regions, max width of 100 frames). For CR-CTC self-distillation, we follow (Yao et al., 2024b) and increase both the number of time-masked regions and the maximum masking fraction by a factor of 2.5. For vocabulary, we employ a shared Byte Pair Encoding (BPE) vocabulary of size 5000 for multilingual source transcriptions and 4000 for English target translations.

Models: As a baseline, we reproduce the multitask (ASR+ST) neural transducer with a shared encoder (Wang et al., 2023), employing the Zipformer architecture (Yao et al., 2024a). The model consists of 8 blocks, each containing 2 self-attention layers. The number of attention heads per block is set to {4, 4, 4, 8, 8, 8, 4, 4}, with attention dimensions of {192, 256, 384, 512, 512, 384, 384, 256}. The feed-forward dimensions per block are configured as {512, 768, 1024, 1024, 1024, 1024, 1024, 768}, and the convolution kernel sizes are {31, 31, 15, 15, 15, 15, 31, 31}. For the proposed hierarchical approach, we explore two architectural variants: *shallow* (NT-Hier1) and *deep* (NT-Hier2). In the *shallow* configuration, we partition the baseline encoder by assigning the first five blocks to the ASR encoder ENC_{asr} in Eq. (3) and the remaining three blocks to the ST encoder ENC_{st} in Eq. (4). In contrast, the *deep* variant increases the depth of the ST encoder to five blocks while reducing the number of parameters per block by approximately half, thereby maintaining the overall model size. Both the baseline and hierarchical variants contain approximately 70M parameters. For the ablation studies in Sec. 3.2, which focus on a single language pair, we use a smaller model by reducing the depth of both the ASR and ST encoders by one block, resulting in a total of 45M parameters. We experiment with two types of predictor networks: a stateless predictor implemented as a single Conv1D layer with kernel size 2, and a stateful LSTM predictor, both with hidden size 256. Our training configuration utilizes the ScaledAdam optimizer (Yao et al., 2024a) with a learning rate of 0.045. The multitask weights α_{asr} and α_{st} in Eq. (5) are set to 1, while $\alpha_{CR(asr)}$ and $\alpha_{CR(st)}$ are set to 0.05, and $\alpha_{CTC(asr)}$ and $\alpha_{CTC(st)}$ are set to 0.1 in Eq. (10). For comparison, we use the ESPnet CTC/Attention ST model[3] with 75M parameters. We choose the Conformer encoder, as it outperforms eBranchformer in translation quality. The optimal learning rate and warmup steps, set to 0.001 and 30k, are selected from the ranges {0.0005–0.002} and {15k–40k}, respectively. All models are trained for 30 epochs on 4 V100 GPUs, using a batch size of 400 seconds. Unless otherwise noted, all decoding results reported in the offline setting (Sec. 3.3) use beam search with a beam size of 20.

Table 1: Ablation for transducer based ST, including blank-penalty (BP), lattice pruning-range, scaling warmup-steps, predictor and encoder structure.

Model		Prune-	Warmup-	Pre-	Dev1		Dev2	
	BP	range	steps	dictor	WER ↓	BLEU ↑	WER ↓	BLEU ↑
NT (ASR)	0	5	20k	CNN	**40.0**	-	**42.4**	-
NT (ST)	0	5	20k	CNN	-	14.7	-	12.4
NT (ST)	0	10	20k	CNN	-	16.2	-	13.2
NT (ST)	0	10	20k	LSTM	-	15.8	-	13.0
NT (ST)	0	10	5k	CNN	-	18.1	-	14.7
NT-Hier1 (ASR+ST)	0	10	5k	CNN	40.0	18.5	42.8	15.7
NT-Hier2 (ASR+ST)	0	10	5k	CNN	40.3	**19.0**	43.6	**15.8**
NT-Hier2 (ASR+ST)	1	10	5k	CNN	40.3	**20.4**	43.6	**17.1**

Evaluation: To ensure a comprehensive evaluation of translation quality, we utilize BLEU (Papineni et al., 2002) for surface-level word matching, chrF++ for character-level accuracy, and COMET (Rei et al., 2020)[4] for semantic adequacy. Translation evaluation is conducted in a case-insensitive manner, without punctuation. ASR performance is assessed using word error rate (WER). To assess the processing delay of the system during streaming, we report the real-time factor (RTF).

3.2 Ablation analysis

To assess the impact of efficiency-related design choices in our proposed hierarchical ST approach, we conduct ablation studies on the *Tunisian-English* dataset, which includes two development sets for hyperparameter tuning, as shown in Table 1. To ensure fair comparisons, we maintain a consis-

[2]`https://github.com/k2-fsa/icefall`

[3]`https://github.com/espnet/espnet/blob/master/egs2/must_c_v2/st1/conf/tuning/train_st_ctc_conformer_asrinit_v2.yaml`

[4]We used `Unbabel/wmt22-comet-da` model.

Table 2: Comparison of ASR and ST performance between the state-of-the-art Neural Transducer (NT) with a shared encoder and a multi-decoder AED (MultiDec). ASR performance is measured using WER, while ST performance is evaluated using BLEU, chrF++, and COMET.

Model		Tunisian				HKUST-Chinese				Fisher-Spanish			
	BP	WER ↓	BLEU ↑	chrF++ ↑	COMET ↑	WER ↓	BLEU ↑	chrF++ ↑	COMET ↑	WER ↓	BLEU ↑	chrF++ ↑	COMET ↑
NT (ASR)	-	**41.4**	-	-	-	**22.8**	-	-	-	18.2	-	-	
NT (ST)	-	-	15.3	35.9	0.656	-	10.0	30.5	0.711	-	30.6	56.0	0.793
NT-Shared (ASR+ST) (Wang et al., 2023)	-	41.6	16.3	37.1	0.660	23.8	10.4	30.9	0.714	**18.0**	31.0	56.4	0.798
NT-Hier1 (ASR+ST)	-	42.6	17.8	40.4	0.670	23.5	11.3	33.8	0.720	18.3	31.9	58.2	0.801
NT-Hier2 (ASR+ST)	-	43.1	18.3	40.6	0.672	23.9	12.0	33.9	0.722	18.9	32.4	58.5	**0.801**
NT-Hier2 (ASR+ST)	0.5	43.1	**19.4**	**42.6**	**0.674**	23.9	**12.9**	**36.2**	**0.724**	18.9	**33.0**	**59.9**	**0.801**
CR-CTC (ASR)	-	**40.1**	-	-	-	**21.7**	-	-	-	**17.3**	-	-	-
HENT-SRT	-	41.4	17.8	39.8	0.675	22.8	11.5	32.7	0.726	17.8	31.8	57.5	**0.803**
HENT-SRT	1.0	41.4	**20.6**	**43.4**	**0.682**	22.8	**14.7**	**37.5**	**0.734**	17.8	**33.7**	**60.5**	**0.803**
CTC/Attention (CA) (Yan et al., 2023c)	-	42.7	20.4	44.2	0.680	24.6	15.2	38.8	0.706	18.9	33.9	60.8	0.796

tent model size of approximately 45M parameters across all experiments. We begin by evaluating the vanilla pruned transducer (NT) architecture for ST, examining the effect of increasing the pruning range beyond the default value of 5 (used in NT for ASR). Expanding the pruning range to 10 leads to a BLEU improvement of up to +1.5, indicating that a larger alignment lattice enhances the model's ability to perform word reordering during translation. However, further increases in pruning range provide only marginal additional gains. Next, we explore the role of the prediction network in ST performance. Our results show that a simple trigram 1D-CNN stateless predictor performs comparably to a more complex LSTM-based predictor, consistent with previous observations in ASR (Ghodsi et al., 2020). We also vary the number of training steps before fully incorporating the pruned loss, effectively controlling the balance between the simple and pruned objectives during early training. Reducing the number of warm-up steps yields BLEU gains of up to +1.8, suggesting that earlier exposure to pruning improves optimization. To assess the effect of hierarchical modeling, we compare shallow (NT-Hier1) and deep (NT-Hier2) ST encoders. To keep the parameter count constant, NT-Hier2 doubles the number of layers while halving the parameters per layer in the ST encoder. Our findings indicate that deeper architectures can improve ST performance by up to +0.5 BLEU, though at the cost of reduced ASR accuracy highlighting a trade-off between ST and ASR tasks. Finally, we evaluate the impact of a blank-penalty term applied during decoding. Introducing a small blank penalty leads to BLEU improvements of up to +1.4, demonstrating its effectiveness in refining translation quality. A more detailed analysis of the blank penalty is presented in Sec. 3.4.

3.3 Comparison with state-of-the-art models

In this section, we compare the proposed hierarchical neural transducer with self-distillation (HENT-SRT) model to state-of-the-art systems in the offline setting. Specifically, we evaluate against the multitask ASR-ST transducer with a shared encoder NT-Shared) (Wang et al., 2023), and the CTC/Attention-based AED model (CA) (Yan et al., 2023b), shown in Table 2. Comparing the vanilla transducer models (NT-ASR and NT-ST) to NT-Shared, we find that a single multilingual ASR-ST model can be trained with the same number of parameters while maintaining comparable performance achieving up to +1 BLEU improvement in ST with at most +1 WER degradation in ASR. The hierarchical ST transducer models (NT-Hier) consistently outperform NT-Shared across all ST metrics, yielding improvements of up to +2 BLEU, +3.5 chrF++, and +0.01 COMET, but at the cost of up to +2 WER degradation in ASR performance. Furthermore, NT-Hier2, which employs a deeper ST encoder, achieves better translation performance up to +0.7 BLEU improvement over NT-Hier1 but incurs an additional ASR degradation of up to +0.5 WER. These findings suggest that the hierarchical two-stage training enhances translation quality, particularly in handling reordering (see Sec. A), but at the expense of ASR accuracy. ST performance can be further improved by applying a blank penalty during decoding, yielding up to +1 BLEU and +2.3 chrF++ gains. To ensure robust ST performance with minimal ASR degradation, we integrate self-distillation with consistency-regularized CR-CTC to NT-Hier2, resulting in the proposed HENT-SRT model. Notably, HENT-SRT performs slightly worse than NT-Hier2 in ST when no blank penalty is applied. However, applying the optimal blank penalty to both models yields further gains for HENT-SRT, with improvements of up to +1.8 BLEU, +1.3 chrF++, and +0.01

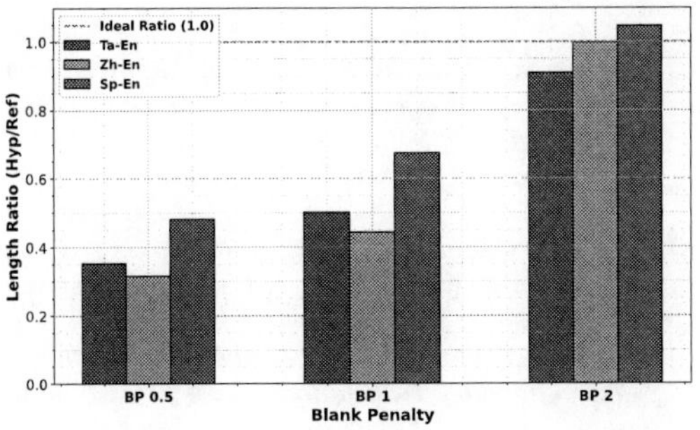

Figure 3: Impact of the blank penalty on translation length ratio (hypothesis/reference) during greedy decoding for Tunisian (Ta-En), HKUST (Zh-En), and Fisher-Spanish (Sp-En). A ratio close to 1.0 indicates ideal length matching between hypothesis and reference.

COMET over NT-Hier2. Additionally, CR-CTC loss also acts as a regularizer, maintaining ASR performance close to the best results observed with CR-CTC(ASR). Finally, compared to the AED-based CA model (Yan et al., 2023b), HENT-SRT closes the ST performance gap while achieving superior ASR performance.

3.4 Streaming Translation

In this section, we explore streaming speech translation using our proposed hierarchical ST framework. Streaming is simulated with greedy decoding by enabling causal convolution and applying chunked processing, using a chunk size of 64 frames and a left context of 128 frames. Specifically, the input is segmented into fixed-size chunks, and each chunk attends only to a fixed number of preceding chunks, with all future frames masked. To ensure low-latency decoding, we restrict the number of emitted symbols per frame to 20, as larger values offer minimal additional improvements. We then examine the effect of the blank penalty on translation quality, as shown in Table 3. While tuning is performed on development sets, we report test set results for completeness. Across all datasets, increasing the blank penalty for NT-Hier2 up to a value of 2 consistently improves BLEU scores by reducing deletion errors, supporting the hypothesis presented in Section 2.3. This trend is further confirmed in Figure 3, which shows that higher blank penalties result in longer translations that more closely align with reference lengths, with a penalty of 2 achieving near-perfect length matching. Overall, the proposed HENT-SRT framework achieves the best streaming performance across datasets, with BLEU improvements of up to +4.5 points compared to NT-Hier2. Importantly, the hierarchical ST design introduces no additional latency in terms of real-time factor compared to the vanilla NT model. This is expected, as the hierarchical structure reuses the original encoder in a sequentially factorized ASR-ST configuration without increasing computational complexity.

Table 3: Comparison of translation BLEU scores and processing delays measured by real-time factor (RTF)

Model	BP	Tunisian			HKUST			Fisher-Sp		
		Dev1	Test	RTF	Dev	Test	RTF	Dev	Test	RTF
NT	0.0	6.8	6.1	0.013	3.1	3.4	0.016	14.2	15.6	0.013
NT-Shared	0.0	7.0	6.0	0.010	3.3	3.7	0.014	14.8	16.3	0.010
NT-Hier2	0.0	9.5	9.0	0.012	4.2	4.6	0.013	16.8	17.9	0.012
NT-Hier2	0.5	10.4	10.0	0.012	5.0	5.7	0.012	19.3	19.6	0.012
NT-Hier2	1.0	14.1	13.0	0.012	7.2	7.4	0.015	24.8	25.6	0.012
NT-Hier2	2.0	16.8	14.0	0.014	6.7	7.5	0.018	24.9	26.3	0.013
HENT-SRT	2.0	**18.6**	**17.2**	0.013	**10.2**	**11.2**	0.017	**29.2**	**30.8**	0.013

4 Conclusion

In this paper, we proposed HENT-SRT, a novel hierarchical transducer architecture for joint speech recognition and translation (ST). The model factorizes the ST task into two stages, ASR followed by a translation, enabling more effective handling of word reordering. To improve computational efficiency, HENT-SRT design incorporates key transducer-based ASR practices, including a down-sampled encoder, stateless predictor, and pruned transducer loss. To maintain robust ST performance without sacrificing ASR accuracy, we apply self-distillation with CTC consistency regularization. Additionally, we introduce a blank penalty mechanism during decoding, which effectively reduces deletion errors and enhances translation quality. Experimental results show that HENT-SRT significantly outperforms previous state-of-the-art transducer-based ST models and closes the gap with attention-based encoder-decoder architectures, while achieving superior ASR performance. Moreover, our approach offers substantial gains in streaming scenarios without introducing additional delays.

Limitations

In this work, we focus on non-overlapping speech translation, translating multilingual source speech into English text. For future work, we aim to extend our hierarchical approach to handle overlapped speech while expanding support for additional target languages and broader translation directions.

References

Hilal Al Shamsi, Abdullah G Almutairi, Sulaiman Al Mashrafi, and Talib Al Kalbani. 2020. Implications of language barriers for healthcare: a systematic review. *Oman medical journal*, 35(2):e122.

Antonios Anastasopoulos, Loïc Barrault, Luisa Bentivogli, Marcely Zanon Boito, Ondřej Bojar, Roldano Cattoni, Anna Currey, Georgiana Dinu, Kevin Duh, Maha Elbayad, and 1 others. 2022. Findings of the iwslt 2022 evaluation campaign. In *Proceedings of the 19th International Conference on Spoken Language Translation (IWSLT 2022)*, pages 98–157.

Ebrahim Ansari, Amittai Axelrod, Nguyen Bach, Ondřej Bojar, Roldano Cattoni, Fahim Dalvi, Nadir Durrani, Marcello Federico, Christian Federmann, Jiatao Gu, Fei Huang, Kevin Knight, Xutai Ma, Ajay Nagesh, Matteo Negri, Jan Niehues, Juan Pino, Elizabeth Salesky, Xing Shi, and 4 others. 2020. FINDINGS OF THE IWSLT 2020 EVALUATION CAMPAIGN. In *Proceedings of the 17th International Conference on Spoken Language Translation*, pages 1–34, Online. Association for Computational Linguistics.

Alexandre Berard, Laurent Besacier, Ali Can Kocabiyikoglu, and Olivier Pietquin. 2018. End-to-end automatic speech translation of audiobooks. In *2018 IEEE International Conference on Acoustics, Speech and Signal Processing, ICASSP 2018, Calgary, AB, Canada, April 15-20, 2018*, pages 6224–6228. IEEE.

Alexandre Berard, Olivier Pietquin, Christophe Servan, and Laurent Besacier. 2016. Listen and translate: A proof of concept for end-to-end speech-to-text translation. In *Proceedings of the NIPS Workshop on end-to-end learning for speech and audio processing*, Barcelona, Spain.

Nicola Bertoldi and Marcello Federico. 2005. A new decoder for spoken language translation based on confusion networks. In *IEEE Workshop on Automatic Speech Recognition and Understanding, 2005.*, pages 86–91. IEEE.

Junkun Chen, Mingbo Ma, Renjie Zheng, and Liang Huang. 2021. Direct simultaneous speech-to-text translation assisted by synchronized streaming ASR. In *Findings of the Association for Computational Linguistics: ACL-IJCNLP 2021*, pages 4618–4624, Online. Association for Computational Linguistics.

Chung-Cheng Chiu, Wei Han, Yu Zhang, Ruoming Pang, Sergey Kishchenko, Patrick Nguyen, Arun Narayanan, Hank Liao, Shuyuan Zhang, Anjuli Kannan, and 1 others. 2019. A comparison of end-to-end models for long-form speech recognition. In *2019 IEEE automatic speech recognition and understanding workshop (ASRU)*, pages 889–896. IEEE.

Siddharth Dalmia, Brian Yan, Vikas Raunak, Florian Metze, and Shinji Watanabe. 2021. Searchable hidden intermediates for end-to-end models of decomposable sequence tasks. In *Proceedings of the 2021 Conference of the North American Chapter of the Association for Computational Linguistics: Human Language Technologies*, pages 1882–1896, Online. Association for Computational Linguistics.

Marco Gaido, Mattia A. Di Gangi, Matteo Negri, and Marco Turchi. 2020. End-to-end speech-translation with knowledge distillation: FBK@IWSLT2020. In *Proceedings of the 17th International Conference on Spoken Language Translation*, pages 80–88, Online. Association for Computational Linguistics.

Mohammadreza Ghodsi, Xiaofeng Liu, James Apfel, Rodrigo Cabrera, and Eugene Weinstein. 2020. Rnn-transducer with stateless prediction network. In *ICASSP 2020-2020 IEEE International Conference on Acoustics, Speech and Signal Processing (ICASSP)*, pages 7049–7053. IEEE.

Alex Graves. 2012. Sequence transduction with recurrent neural networks. *arXiv preprint arXiv:1211.3711*.

Alex Graves, Santiago Fernández, Faustino Gomez, and Jürgen Schmidhuber. 2006. Connectionist temporal classification: labelling unsegmented sequence data with recurrent neural networks. In *Proceedings of the 23rd international conference on Machine learning*, pages 369–376.

Amir Hussein, Brian Yan, Antonios Anastasopoulos, Shinji Watanabe, and Sanjeev Khudanpur. 2024. Enhancing end-to-end conversational speech translation through target language context utilization. In *ICASSP 2024-2024 IEEE International Conference on Acoustics, Speech and Signal Processing (ICASSP)*, pages 11971–11975. IEEE.

Kwangyoun Kim, Felix Wu, Yifan Peng, Jing Pan, Prashant Sridhar, Kyu J Han, and Shinji Watanabe. 2023. E-branchformer: Branchformer with enhanced merging for speech recognition. In *2022 IEEE Spoken Language Technology Workshop (SLT)*, pages 84–91. IEEE.

Onur Köksal and Nurcihan Yürük. 2020. The role of translator in intercultural communication. *International Journal of Curriculum and Instruction*, 12(1):327–338.

Fangjun Kuang, Liyong Guo, Wei Kang, Long Lin, Mingshuang Luo, Zengwei Yao, and Daniel Povey. 2022. Pruned RNN-T for fast, memory-efficient ASR training. In *Interspeech*.

Dan Liu, Mengge Du, Xiaoxi Li, Ya Li, and Enhong Chen. 2021. Cross attention augmented transducer networks for simultaneous translation. In *Proceedings of the 2021 Conference on Empirical Methods in Natural Language Processing*, pages 39–55.

Xutai Ma, Juan Pino, and Philipp Koehn. 2020. SimulMT to SimulST: Adapting simultaneous text translation to end-to-end simultaneous speech translation. In *Proceedings of the 1st Conference of the*

Asia-Pacific Chapter of the Association for Computational Linguistics and the 10th International Joint Conference on Natural Language Processing, pages 582–587, Suzhou, China. Association for Computational Linguistics.

Xutai Ma, Yongqiang Wang, Mohammad Javad Dousti, Philipp Koehn, and Juan Pino. 2021. Streaming simultaneous speech translation with augmented memory transformer. In *ICASSP 2021-2021 IEEE International Conference on Acoustics, Speech and Signal Processing (ICASSP)*, pages 7523–7527. IEEE.

Jay Mahadeokar, Yuan Shangguan, Duc Le, Gil Keren, Hang Su, Thong Le, Ching-Feng Yeh, Christian Fuegen, and Michael L Seltzer. 2021. Alignment restricted streaming recurrent neural network transducer. In *2021 IEEE Spoken Language Technology Workshop (SLT)*, pages 52–59. IEEE.

Evgeny Matusov, Stephan Kanthak, and Hermann Ney. 2005. On the integration of speech recognition and statistical machine translation. In *Interspeech*, pages 3177–3180.

Satoshi Nakamura. 2009. Overcoming the language barrier with speech translation technology. *Science & Technology Trends-Quarterly Review*, 31.

Kishore Papineni, Salim Roukos, Todd Ward, and Wei-Jing Zhu. 2002. Bleu: a method for automatic evaluation of machine translation. In *Proceedings of the 40th annual meeting of the Association for Computational Linguistics*, pages 311–318.

Daniel S Park, William Chan, Yu Zhang, Chung-Cheng Chiu, Barret Zoph, Ekin D Cubuk, and Quoc V Le. 2019. Specaugment: A simple data augmentation method for automatic speech recognition. In *Proc. Interspeech 2019*, pages 2613–2617.

Juan Pino, Liezl Puzon, Jiatao Gu, Xutai Ma, Arya D. McCarthy, and Deepak Gopinath. 2019. Harnessing indirect training data for end-to-end automatic speech translation: Tricks of the trade. In *Proceedings of the 16th International Conference on Spoken Language Translation*, Hong Kong. Association for Computational Linguistics.

Matt Post, Gaurav Kumar, Adam Lopez, Damianos Karakos, Chris Callison-Burch, and Sanjeev Khudanpur. 2013. Improved speech-to-text translation with the fisher and callhome Spanish-English speech translation corpus. In *Proceedings of the 10th International Workshop on Spoken Language Translation: Papers*, Heidelberg, Germany.

Rastislav Rabatin, Frank Seide, and Ernie Chang. 2024. Navigating the minefield of mt beam search in cascaded streaming speech translation. *arXiv preprint arXiv:2407.11010*.

Ricardo Rei, Craig Stewart, Ana C Farinha, and Alon Lavie. 2020. Comet: A neural framework for mt evaluation. In *Proceedings of the 2020 Conference on Empirical Methods in Natural Language Processing (EMNLP)*, pages 2685–2702.

Mark Sinclair, Peter Bell, Alexandra Birch, and Fergus McInnes. 2014. A semi-markov model for speech segmentation with an utterance-break prior. In *Interspeech 2014*, pages 2351–2355.

Matthias Sperber, Jan Niehues, and Alex Waibel. 2017. Toward robust neural machine translation for noisy input sequences. In *Proceedings of the 14th International Conference on Spoken Language Translation*, pages 90–96, Tokyo, Japan. International Workshop on Spoken Language Translation.

Yun Tang, Anna Sun, Hirofumi Inaguma, Xinyue Chen, Ning Dong, Xutai Ma, Paden Tomasello, and Juan Pino. 2023. Hybrid transducer and attention based encoder-decoder modeling for speech-to-text tasks. In *Proceedings of the 61st Annual Meeting of the Association for Computational Linguistics (Volume 1: Long Papers)*, pages 12441–12455.

Peidong Wang, Eric Sun, Jian Xue, Yu Wu, Long Zhou, Yashesh Gaur, Shujie Liu, and Jinyu Li. 2023. Lamassu: A streaming language-agnostic multilingual speech recognition and translation model using neural transducers. In *Interspeech 2023*, pages 57–61.

Shannon Wotherspoon, William Hartmann, and Matthew Snover. 2024. Advancing speech translation: A corpus of mandarin-english conversational telephone speech. *arXiv preprint*, arXiv:2404.11619.

Jian Xue, Peidong Wang, Jinyu Li, Matt Post, and Yashesh Gaur. 2022. Large-scale streaming end-to-end speech translation with neural transducers. In *Proc. Interspeech 2022*, pages 3263–3267.

Brian Yan, Siddharth Dalmia, Yosuke Higuchi, Graham Neubig, Florian Metze, Alan W Black, and Shinji Watanabe. 2023a. Ctc alignments improve autoregressive translation. In *Proceedings of the 17th Conference of the European Chapter of the Association for Computational Linguistics*, pages 1623–1639.

Brian Yan, Jiatong Shi, Yun Tang, Hirofumi Inaguma, Yifan Peng, Siddharth Dalmia, Peter Polák, Patrick Fernandes, Dan Berrebbi, Tomoki Hayashi, Xiaohui Zhang, Zhaoheng Ni, Moto Hira, Soumi Maiti, Juan Pino, and Shinji Watanabe. 2023b. ESPnet-ST-v2: Multipurpose spoken language translation toolkit. In *Proceedings of the 61st Annual Meeting of the Association for Computational Linguistics (Volume 3: System Demonstrations)*, pages 400–411, Toronto, Canada. Association for Computational Linguistics.

Brian Yan, Jiatong Shi, Yun Tang, Hirofumi Inaguma, Yifan Peng, Siddharth Dalmia, Peter Polák, Patrick Fernandes, Dan Berrebbi, Tomoki Hayashi, and 1 others. 2023c. Espnet-st-v2: Multipurpose spoken language translation toolkit. *ArXiv preprint*, abs/2304.04596.

Jinyi Yang, Amir Hussein, Matthew Wiesner, and Sanjeev Khudanpur. 2022. JHU IWSLT 2022 dialect speech translation system description. In *Proceedings of the 19th International Conference on Spoken*

Language Translation (IWSLT 2022), pages 319–326, Dublin, Ireland (in-person and online). Association for Computational Linguistics.

Zengwei Yao, Liyong Guo, Xiaoyu Yang, Wei Kang, Fangjun Kuang, Yifan Yang, Zengrui Jin, Long Lin, and Daniel Povey. 2024a. Zipformer: A faster and better encoder for automatic speech recognition. In *ICLR*.

Zengwei Yao, Wei Kang, Xiaoyu Yang, Fangjun Kuang, Liyong Guo, Han Zhu, Zengrui Jin, Zhaoqing Li, Long Lin, and Daniel Povey. 2024b. Cr-ctc: Consistency regularization on ctc for improved speech recognition. *arXiv preprint arXiv:2410.05101*.

Piotr Żelasko, Daniel Povey, Jan Trmal, Sanjeev Khudanpur, and 1 others. 2021. Lhotse: a speech data representation library for the modern deep learning ecosystem. In *NeurIPS Data-Centric AI Workshop*.

A Linguistic Analysis of Speech Translation Performance

A.1 Chinese HKUST Test Set Analysis

The Chinese HKUST test set contains conversational Mandarin translated into English. The source utterances include informal structures, frequent repetitions (e.g., “对对” / “yes yes”), fillers (e.g., “呃” / “uh”), and discourse markers (e.g., “啊”, “哎呀”). We compare the NT-Hier2 and NT-Shared system outputs against reference translations to analyze their differences and better understand how hierarchical modeling improves translation quality. Table 4 presents representative examples comparing the NT-Hier2 and NT-Shared systems.

A.1.1 Observations and Comparison:

- **Syntactic Structure:** In longer utterances (e.g., Row 3), NT-Hier2 retains more of the reference structure, including mentions of "thesis defence" and a full sequence of events. However, it introduces timeline inconsistencies such as "in December I can graduate in October." Despite this, metrics like BLEU and COMET may still reward NT-Hier2’s output for preserving semantic content.

- **Handling Reordering:** In Row 2, the NT-Hier2 output more accurately preserves the source’s repeated clause structure (e.g., “who did it for him”), while the NT-Shared output compresses the translation and omits part of the repeated question. This indicates that NT-Hier2 is better at modeling long-range reordering and maintaining structural fidelity.

- **Handling Informal Speech:** Row 1 illustrates a relatively simple informal sentence, where both systems produce fluent and semantically equivalent outputs. This supports our observation that informal utterances with low lexical variability are easier to translate. However, in general, fillers and discourse markers may be translated literally, rephrased, or omitted depending on context, which introduces challenges for exact-match metrics like BLEU.

BLEU vs. COMET Discrepancy: The Chinese test set yields a BLEU score of 12.9 and a COMET score of 0.72, in contrast to Fisher Spanish (BLEU = 33, COMET = 0.80) and IWSLT23 Tunisian (BLEU = 19.4, COMET = 0.67). We hypothesize that the low BLEU score for Chinese BBN stems from significant lexical variation in the system outputs. COMET, on the other hand, is sensitive to semantic similarity and rewards outputs that convey approximate meaning (e.g., “no problem” aligns semantically with “it’s fine”). This discrepancy is consistent with the conversational nature of the dataset, where multiple valid translations (e.g., “it’s fine” vs. “it doesn’t matter”) are possible, thereby reducing BLEU’s reliability due to its reliance on a single reference.

Pattern and Theory: A recurring pattern in the NT-Hier2 system’s output is its tendency to produce more lexically diverse and expressive translations. In contrast, the NT-Shared system often generates shorter, simpler outputs, suggesting possible underfitting or reduced modeling capacity. We argue that the low BLEU score reflects not only actual translation errors but also the limitations of BLEU in evaluating Chinese-to-English translation, especially in high-variability, conversational settings. Future work could explore multi-reference BLEU or fine-tuned semantic metrics to better capture these nuances.

Table 4: Comparison of NT-Hier2 and NT-Shared System Outputs on the Chinese test set

Row	Source (ref_src)	Reference (ref_tgt)	NT-Hier2	NT-Shared
1	没有问题对对没关系	that's alright if there's no problem it's fine	no problem that's right it doesn't matter	no problem that's right it doesn't matter
2	那谁给他办的绿卡谁给他办的	who applied that green card for him who did it for him	then who did it for him then who green it	then who who do it
3	我八月中旬就去上班然后再回来再回来答辩就是然后然后十二月份应该就可以毕业了	i would go to work at the mid august then i would come back again for my thesis defence that's it and then i should be able to graduate in december	i will go to work in and then come back again and then i mean in december i can graduate in october	in august i will go to work on and then come back to work again and then i mean after october

Swiss German Speech Translation and the Curse of Multidialectality

Martin Bär
University of Malta, University of the Basque Country
martin.bar.22@um.edu.mt

Andrea De Marco
Department of Artificial Intelligence
University of Malta
andrea.demarco@um.edu.mt

Gorka Labaka
HiTZ Center
University of the Basque Country
gorka.labaka@ehu.eus

Abstract

In many languages, non-standardized varieties make the development of NLP models challenging. This paper explores various fine-tuning techniques and data setups for training Swiss German to Standard German speech-to-text translation models. While fine-tuning on all available Swiss German data yields the best results, ASR pre-training lowers performance by 1.48 BLEU points, and jointly training on Swiss and Standard German data reduces it by 2.29 BLEU. Our dialect transfer experiments suggest that an equivalent of the *Curse of Multilinguality* (Conneau et al., 2020) exists in dialectal speech processing, as training on multiple dialects jointly tends to decrease single-dialect performance. However, introducing small amounts of dialectal variability can improve the performance for low-resource dialects.

1 Introduction

Swiss German (*Schweizerdeutsch*) is considered one of the most distinct and lively varieties of German with unique features on the phonological, morphological, syntactic and lexical levels[1]. It is a continuum of mostly High Alemannic German dialects in Switzerland, spoken by more than 5 million people. Swiss German is used extensively in everyday situations, including spoken communication, text messaging, local and national TV programs, and even regional parliaments. Standard German (*Hochdeutsch*) is used for formal and institutionalized forms of communication (Christen et al., 2020). This coexistence of two varieties with clearly separated use cases in a single speaker group has been described as *diglossia* by several researchers (Ferguson, 1959; Ender and Kaiser, 2009; Russ, 1990).

Swiss German dialects can vary significantly within Switzerland, sometimes even leading to difficulties in understanding between Swiss German speakers from distant regions (Christen, 2010). Due to particularities on all linguistic levels, Swiss dialects are hard to understand for many German speakers outside of Switzerland (Ender and Kaiser, 2009) and German learners who are primarily familiar with Standard German (Schlatter, 2024). This makes the need for systems that can translate from Swiss German speech to Standard German text apparent. It could facilitate the integration of non-Swiss-German speakers into Swiss society by enabling them to understand local TV programs, radio shows, dialectal voice messages, and conversations between their co-workers. Furthermore, dialectal speech translation can help preserve dialectal varieties and make language technologies more accessible to dialect speakers, contributing to the development of fair and equitable technologies (Joshi et al., 2024). In a study by Blaschke et al. (2024), 61% of respondents were in favor of systems that can translate dialect speech to Standard German text. This highlights the demand for dialectal translation systems beyond academic interests.

In the case of Swiss German, Automatic Speech Recognition (ASR) and Speech Translation (ST) are closely related. As Swiss German does not have any standardized written form and all of its speakers understand Standard German (Ender and Kaiser, 2009), it seems natural to prioritize Swiss German speech to Standard German text ST instead of Swiss German speech to Swiss German text ASR. Although there are works about the latter (Garner et al., 2014; Scherrer et al., 2019), ST is the subject of most research (Khosravani et al., 2021b,a; Paonessa et al., 2023; Sicard et al., 2023; Mutal et al., 2023) and was one of the shared tasks at the Swiss Text Analytics Conference[2] in 2021

[1] For a complete list of Swiss German particularities, we refer the reader to Russ (1990) and Christen (2019).

[2] https://www.swisstext.org/

Proceedings of the 22nd International Conference on Spoken Language Translation (IWSLT 2025), pages 165–179
July 31 - August 1, 2025

(Plüss et al., 2021) and 2022 (Plüss et al., 2023b).

Although the area is being actively researched, SwissText 2022 (Plüss et al., 2023b) has demonstrated that the problem is far from being solved. None of the participating teams were able to outperform the baseline model, a simple Transformer fine-tuned on three datasets. Later works achieved improvements over this baseline by using more data and experimenting with fine-tuning pre-trained models (Sicard et al., 2023; Plüss et al., 2023a,b). However, they did not explore further pre-training, nor did they utilize all the available data for Swiss German, or employ Standard German data. Paonessa et al. (2023) showed that one of the main challenges is that Swiss German ST needs to handle a considerable amount of dialectal variability. They found that some dialects benefit from positive transfer from related dialects, whereas others negatively influence overall performance. It remains unclear, however, how many dialects can be used together to improve performance and when performance starts to degrade. Here, we expect a breaking point as observed for the Curse of Multilinguality (Conneau et al., 2020) even for the closely related Swiss dialects. Furthermore, we don't know how small amounts of dialectal variability affect performance.

We aim to close these research gaps by:

1. Exploring fine-tuning and pre-training to improve performance for Swiss German ST and determine the usefulness of Standard German data.

2. Investigating whether there is a *Curse of Multidialectality* for Swiss German.

3. Observing how small amounts of dialectal variability affect the performance of Swiss German ST models.

2 Multidialectal Speech Processing

Joshi et al. (2024) highlight that variability within dialects of a language is one of the biggest challenges for dialectal NLP. This issue, referred to as *multidialectality* in the present work, has already been investigated in speech processing. ASR systems are often only trained on standard accents, making them perform poorly on other dialects of the same language (Sanabria et al., 2023; Parsons et al., 2023). Yadavalli et al. (2022) find that a model trained on multiple Telugu dialects jointly performs worse than a system trained on each dialect separately, indicating negative transfer. Similar issues have been observed for Japanese (Imaizumi et al., 2020), Chinese (Ding et al., 2024), Tibetan (Zhao et al., 2019), Flemish/Dutch (Herygers et al., 2023), Armenian (Arthur et al., 2024), and Arabic (Nasr et al., 2023; Ali et al., 2021).

Researchers have proposed various techniques to mitigate performance drops due to multidialectality, with a primary focus on Automatic Speech Recognition (ASR). Using pre-trained models has been found to outperform monolingual training from scratch (Arthur et al., 2024; Luo et al., 2021). Imaizumi et al. (2022) suggest dialect-aware ASR modeling by simultaneously performing dialect identification and ASR for Japanese dialects, Dan et al. (2022), Das et al. (2021), and Yadavalli et al. (2022) apply similar multi-task training approaches to Chinese, English, and Telugu. Using the standard and dialectal varieties together during training has been found to increase performance for Tunisian Arabic (Messaoudi et al., 2021), for multiple other Arabic dialects (Chowdhury et al., 2021), and for Thai when combined with curriculum learning[3] Suwanbandit et al. (2023).

3 Swiss German ST

For German, research in dialectal speech processing is scarce. Wepner (2021) calls for adapting ASR systems to Austrian German as they observe a performance discrepancy between German Standard German and Austrian Standard German. Similarly, Baum et al. (2010) find an increase of 24.8% in WER when evaluating a German ASR system on dialectal utterances, and Wirth and Peinl (2022) see the need to include dialectal varieties in German ASR datasets. Paonessa et al. (2023) find that the multidialectal nature of Swiss German, briefly described in the introduction, is one of the main challenges for Swiss German ST. They observe positive and negative transfer between dialects, mainly depending on their overall similarity as determined by Scherrer and Stoeckle (2016).

Swiss German ST is actively researched, and many datasets have been released in the past years[4].

[3]This is a multi-stage training approach where a model is trained on increasingly complex tasks (Bengio et al., 2009).

[4]This is not the case for other German dialects. ASR datasets have been released for Upper-Saxon (Herms et al., 2016), Austrian German (Schuppler et al., 2014), and the Southern Bavarian dialect De Zahrar (Gulli et al., 2024). However, we did not find any freely available datasets or other research on ST for these dialects, nor the widely spoken Bavar-

Table 1 lists these datasets and their abbreviations. STT and SDS were both collected by crowdsourcing with a web recording tool, similar to the Common Voice datasets (Ardila et al., 2020). They contain Standard German sentences that participants were asked to translate into their dialect and record. SPC was automatically compiled from audio recordings of the Bernese cantonal parliament. These were automatically aligned with their Standard German transcriptions. Similarly, GRZH contains speech from the Zurich parliament. It does, however, not include transcriptions. AM is the only dataset we found that contains dialectal transcriptions. It was compiled by segmenting interviews that were conducted and transcribed in Swiss German.

Abbr.	Dataset	Total h	Train h	Cantons	T
STT	STT4SG-350 (Plüss et al., 2023a)	343	239	17	StG
SDS	SDS-200 (Plüss et al., 2022)	200	50	21	StG
SPC	Swiss Parliaments Corpus (Plüss et al., 2020)	293	217	N/S	StG
SDial	SwissDial (Dogan-Schönberger et al., 2021)	36	36	8	StG
GRZH	Gemeinderat Zürich Corpus (Plüss et al., 2021)	1208	1208	N/S	-
AM	ArchiMob (Samardzic et al., 2016)	80	0	14	SwG
-	Total data with Standard German labels	872	542	-	StG

Table 1: Swiss German speech datasets. *Total h* and *Train h* show the number of hours and the hours used in our experiments, respectively.
Abbreviations for the T (Transcriptions) column: *StG* = Standard German, *SwG* = Swiss German.

Early work on Swiss German to Standard German ST has focused on single dialects and pipeline systems (Garner et al., 2014), as ST data was scarce. However, Khosravani et al. (2021a) emphasize that the lack of a standard orthography and limited resources make it difficult to train cascade systems, making end-to-end architectures dominate the Swiss German ST area (Nigmatulina et al., 2020; Büchi et al., 2020; Sicard et al., 2023; Plüss et al., 2023a).

Current state-of-the-art models for Swiss German ST mostly follow the pre-train and fine-tune paradigm. Plüss et al. (2023a) fine-tune an XLS-R 1B model on the STT dataset and achieve state-of-the-art performance on the SDS, STT, and SwissText2021 test sets (69.6 BLEU, 74.7 BLEU, and 66 BLEU, respectively). Sicard et al. (2023) find that Whisper exhibits strong zero-shot capabilities for Swiss German, outperforming the previously mentioned model on the SPC test set. Paonessa et al. (2023) trained three small models on the STT data, with XLS-R 0.3B outperforming Whisper S and a Transformer model trained from scratch. These findings make it difficult to determine which architecture is the most suitable for Swiss German ST. Furthermore, recent pre-trained multilingual models, such as SeamlessM4T (Communication et al., 2023) and AudioPaLM (Rubenstein et al., 2023), have not yet been evaluated for this task.

ian, Swabian, and Alsatian dialects.

4 Data and Models

In this section, we detail the models and datasets used for our speech-to-text translation experiments for Swiss German. The methodology used for the experiments will be described in Section 5 and 6.

4.1 Data and Dialects

Swiss German datasets were briefly introduced in Section 3. Table 1 summarizes them, and Table 2 lists the Standard German datasets we used for our fine-tuning experiments. For Standard German, we randomly sampled 180 hours from each dataset to obtain a total of 540 hours, the same amount we used for Swiss German. Initial experiments showed that this yielded better performance for Swiss German. To track model performance during training, we use validation splits of Swiss German (STT, SDS, SPC, GRZH) and Standard German (CV) datasets. The SPC and GRZH validation sets are not official splits and were created by randomly sampling 10% and 1% of their training data, respectively.

Abbr.	Dataset	Total h	Train h (long)	Train h
CV	Common Voice v17.0 (Ardila et al., 2020)	1423	933	180
MLS	Multilingual Librispeech (Pratap et al., 2020)	1995	1966	180
VP	VoxPopuli (Wang et al., 2021a)	282	264	180
-	Total data with Standard German labels	3700	3163	540

Table 2: Standard German ASR datasets. *Train h* shows the hours of speech used in our final experiments.

For the dialect transfer experiments, we only use the STT dataset because it is the largest available dataset that contains dialect region labels for every utterance. The SDS and SwissDial datasets also include dialect information, but the regions differ from the STT regions, limiting their usefulness for dialect experiments. Figure 1 shows all the regions from STT: *Basel* (BS), *Bern* (BE), *Central Switzerland* (CS), *Eastern Switzerland* (ES), *Grisons* (GR), *Valais* (VS), *Zurich* (ZH).

Test sets We use the test splits of STT, SDS, SPC, as well as the test sets of the SwissText 2021 (Plüss et al., 2021) and SwissText 2022 (Plüss et al., 2023b) shared tasks for model evaluation. To track

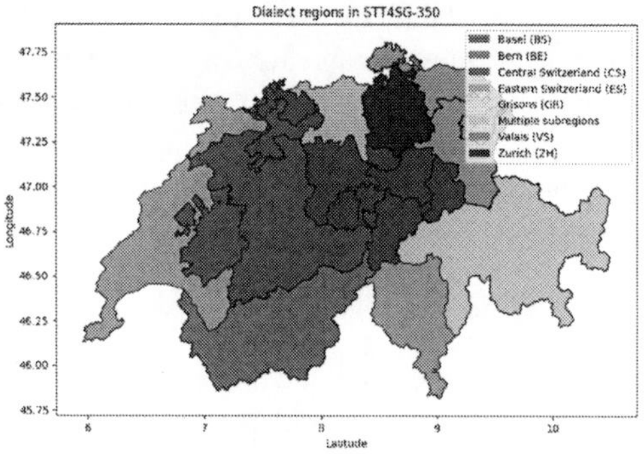

Figure 1: Dialect regions (from Paonessa et al., 2023).

the performance of our systems in Standard German ASR, we use the test split of CV. In addition to evaluating the STT test set per dialect, we provide the average performance over all datasets (including and excluding CV, denoted as $\varnothing$ and $\varnothing_{noCV}$, respectively) to be able to compare the models' robustness across different domains.

Data pre-processing All audios were resampled to a sampling rate of 16,000 Hz, the rate accepted by XLS-R. Similar to (Plüss et al., 2023a), all transcripts were normalized to only contain letters of the English alphabet (a-z), numbers, and the German umlauts *ä*, *ö*, *ü*. We use the unidecode package[5] to transform all other characters with accents or other special characters to ASCII. Then we remove all the non-alphanumerical characters (including punctuation) and lowercase the transcripts. We apply this normalization to all transcripts and translations used for training and evaluating our models. SPC was filtered to only include samples longer than 2 seconds and shorter than 15.5 seconds.

4.2 Models

We use XLS-R (Babu et al., 2021) as the base model for all our experiments. Its architecture is based on wav2vec 2.0 (Baevski et al., 2020), which is designed to learn high-quality speech representation through self-supervised learning, similar to masked language modeling in BERT (Devlin et al., 2019).

XLS-R is a multilingual version of wav2vec 2.0 and was pre-trained on 128 languages using 436,000 hours of unlabeled data for one million updates. In this way, the model learned powerful speech representations in several languages, similar to what happens for multilingual text models such as mBERT (Pires et al., 2019; Wu and Dredze, 2019; Tanti et al., 2021). Through fine-tuning, these representations can later be leveraged for downstream tasks across multiple domains and languages.

We train all of our models with Fairseq (Wang et al., 2020) and use the official checkpoints of XLS-R 300M and 1B (after the pre-training) as a starting point. We add a randomly initialized linear layer on top of the network and freeze the Transformer part of the network for the first 10,000 updates, similar to (Baevski et al., 2020). For generating the transcriptions, we use CTC decoding because Paonessa et al. (2023) found that it yields better results for Swiss German ST than seq2seq decoding. Additionally, we add a 5-gram language model (LM)[6] for decoding (LM fusion decoding) as this was shown to improve results, especially in low-resource contexts (Baevski et al., 2020; Babu et al., 2021). All results reported in this paper are achieved by applying LM fusion when applying CTC decoding.

5 Fine-Tuning Experiments

To improve the state-of-the-art of Swiss German ST and investigate whether using data from a closely related language (Standard German) is beneficial for ST performance, we conduct a series of experiments. Experiments 1-4 focus on different fine-tuning strategies and data setups, while Experiment 5 involves continued pre-training of XLS-R. All experiments aim to improve overall Swiss German translation performance and train robust models that perform well across different data domains.

5.1 Overview and Setup

Table 3 is an overview of all the fine-tuning experiments. Experiment 1 recreates the baseline model from Plüss et al. (2023a). In Experiment 2, we extend the fine-tuning data to all available Swiss German ST datasets to investigate how the additional variance introduced through these datasets affects performance on STT and/or specific dialect regions.

In Experiments 3 and 4, we use a multi-stage fine-tuning approach[7]. This has been shown to

[5] https://github.com/avian2/unidecode

[6] Similarly to (Plüss et al., 2023a), the LM was trained with kenlm (https://kheafield.com/code/kenlm/) on 100M Standard German sentences. Details are in Appendix A.

[7] In some works (e.g., (Suwanbandit et al., 2023)), this is also referred to as curriculum learning.

improve performance on low-resource tasks in MT (Imankulova et al., 2019; Luo et al., 2019), ASR (Medeiros et al., 2023; Deng et al., 2023; Yang et al., 2022), and ST (Kesiraju et al., 2023; Stoian et al., 2020; Wang et al., 2021b). Experiment 3 applies ASR pre-training (Kesiraju et al., 2023; Stoian et al., 2020) on Standard German data in the first step. Then, the resulting model is fine-tuned on the Swiss German ST data. In Experiment 4, we shuffle equal parts of the Standard German and Swiss German datasets together and fine-tune the model on all of them jointly in the first step. Then, we again fine-tune the resulting model on the Swiss German ST data.

In Experiment 5, we explore further pre-training on unlabeled Swiss German data. This is also called continued pre-training or language-specific pre-training and has been shown to improve downstream ASR performance (Bartelds et al., 2023; Nowakowski et al., 2023; Paraskevopoulos et al., 2024; Huang and Mak, 2023). XLS-R's pre-training data does not include any Swiss German, and the model might benefit even more from further pre-training on Swiss German data. Due to computational limitations, we do not use the labeled Swiss data for continued pre-training. However, we use it to fine-tune the resulting model in a second step.

Training Configuration We use the same hyperparameters as (Plüss et al., 2023a), who base theirs on (Babu et al., 2021). The only difference is that we use 1 GPU (NVIDIA A100 with 80 GB of memory) for training instead of 4. We tried to make up for this by using 4x the gradient accumulation steps but initial experiments showed that the performance gains were not worth the increased training time. The hyperparameters are listed in Table 8 in Appendix B.

Evaluation After fine-tuning, we generate predictions for the test sets described in Section 4.1 and evaluate the best model of the training run by BLEU and WER[8]. As Swiss German ST is more of a translation task, we use BLEU for the primary evaluations. The BLEU score is computed with SacreBLEU[9] (Post, 2018) on the references that were normalized as described in section 4.1. For the per-dialect results, we calculate the BLEU score using the entire corpus of the respective dialect. To calculate WER, we use the jiwer package[10].

As fine-tuning our models is resource-intensive, we are not able to conduct multiple training runs with different random seeds to determine if the differences between models are statistically significant. Instead, we use bootstrapping resampling to calculate system BLEU scores, as proposed in Koehn (2004) and implemented by SacreBLEU. This allows us to calculate confidence intervals and the statistical significance of BLEU score differences.

5.2 Results

Table 4 summarizes the results of the fine-tuning experiments. Using all available labeled data to fine-tune XLS-R proved to be the most effective approach, yielding the best overall model. While our model did not outperform the previously published baselines on each test set individually (see Figure 4 in Appendix C), we achieved the best average performance ($\varnothing_{noCV}$) across all test sets. This is most likely because the test set domains are very different, and we can assume that the domain-specific data resulted in some interference with the other domains.

Experiments 3 and 4 demonstrated that using Standard German data does not improve Swiss German dialect translation performance. Neither the ASR pre-training nor mixing Standard German and Swiss German data during fine-tuning improved the results for Swiss German. However, the Standard German data helped improve performance on the Common Voice dataset, adding 39.9 to the BLEU score when comparing the model only trained on Swiss German data (*AllSwiss*) and the model trained on a mixture of Swiss and Standard German data (*Joint_ft*). Nevertheless, the average Swiss German performance dropped by 2.29 BLEU for this setup. We observed this drop when the ratio of Swiss German and Standard German data was kept equal, and when 7 times more Standard German was used. We suspect that there were no improvements over *AllSwiss*, because the model is incapable of learning Standard German ASR and Swiss German ST simultaneously without any additional task separation, resulting in interference of the Standard German data.

Further pre-training the XLS-R on Swiss German speech from the GRZH corpus did not improve

[8]This is usually done in Swiss German ST, see Plüss et al. (2023a, 2021, 2023b); Sicard et al. (2023)

[9]Version 2.4.0

[10]https://jitsi.github.io/jiwer/

No.	Name	Description	Fine-tuned from	Fine-tuning data	Total hours
1	Baseline	Baseline replication from Plüss et al. (2023a)	XLS-R 1B	STT	239
2	AllSwiss	Fine-tune XLS-R on all available labeled data for SwG ST	XLS-R 1B	STT, SPC, SDS, SDial	542
3.1	ASR	Fine-tune model for StG ASR	XLS-R 1B	CV, MLS, VP	542
3.2	ASR_ft	Fine-tune StG ASR model on SwG ST data	3.1 ASR	STT, SPC, SDS, SDial	542
4.1	Joint	Jointly fine-tune on shuffled StG ASR and SwG ST data	XLS-R 1B	CV, MLS, VP, STT, SPC, SDS, SDial	1084
4.2	Joint_ft	Fine-tune jointly trained model on SwG ST data	4.1 Joint	STT, SPC, SDS, SDial	542
5.1	SwSSL	Continued pre-training on unlabeled SwG data	XLS-R 1B	GRZH	1208
5.2	SwSSL_ft	Fine-tune SwG pre-trained model on SwG ST data	SwSSL	STT, SPC, SDS, SDial	542

Table 3: Overview of fine-tuning experiments. *StG* = Standard German, *SwG* = Swiss German.

Test set	BLEU								WER							
	STT4SG	Baseline	AllSwiss	ASR	ASR_ft	Joint	Joint_ft	SwSSL_ft	STT4SG	Baseline	AllSwiss	ASR	ASR_ft	Joint	Joint_ft	SwSSL_ft
STT	**74.7**	71.9	72.2	9.6	70.2	68.9	69.4	70.9	**14.0**	15.9	15.6	73.9	16.8	17.7	17.5	16.4
SDS	**69.6**	66.8	67.2	6.6	65.2	63.0	63.5	66.3	**18.2**	19.9	19.6	78.7	20.9	22.5	22.2	20.3
SPC	54.9	52.8	**61.3**	7.3	60.2	60.2	60.5	60.7	30.2	32.4	**24.4**	79.8	25.6	25.6	25.4	24.8
ST21	**66.0**	62.4	64.7	10.1	64.1	62.5	62.7	62.9	**20.7**	22.9	21.4	73.6	21.7	22.6	22.4	22.7
ST22	-	73.7	**73.9**	11.8	72.4	71.5	71.8	73.2	-	14.7	**14.3**	69.6	15.6	15.9	15.7	15.1
$\varnothing_{noCV}$	66.3	65.5	**67.9**	9.1	66.4	65.2	65.6	66.8	20.8	21.2	**19.1**	75.1	20.1	20.9	20.6	19.9
CV	-	35.7	37.7	**84.9**	46.5	78.8	77.6	33.8	-	45.8	44.3	**8.6**	36.6	12.6	13.3	48.7
$\varnothing$	-	60.5	62.9	21.7	63.1	67.5	**67.6**	61.3	-	25.3	23.3	64	22.9	19.5	**19.4**	24.7

Table 4: Results of the baseline from Plüss et al. (2023a) and our experiments. Best results for each dataset are bold.

fine-tuning results either. We conjecture that this is due to low data quality and overfitting to the Zurich dialect, which was the only dialect in the dataset. Performance might benefit from (1) audio pre-processing or cleaning, and (2) adding more dialects to the unlabeled pre-training dataset.

Figure 2 shows the per-dialect results of the models. Comparing the best systems from Experiments 1-5 in Figure 2, it becomes evident that Standard German data does not help improve the performance for any specific dialect but rather introduces more dialectal variability that negatively affects performance. The model *AllSwiss* performs best for the Berne dialect, possibly due to the additional Berne data from SPC. This demonstrates that more in-dialect data helps improve performance even if that data is from a completely different domain. However, the over-representation of Berne data resulted in performance drops for other dialects (e.g., Valais and Zurich) when comparing *AllSwiss* to our Baseline, which was trained on the STT dataset balanced by dialect. These drops are even more substantial for the model trained jointly on Standard and Swiss German data, resulting in a performance loss of 7.8 BLEU for Valais.

6 Dialect Transfer Experiments

In these experiments, we vary the number and diversity of dialects in the training data to study the effect of dialectal variability on performance and determine if there is an equivalent to the *Curse of Multilinguality* (Conneau et al., 2020) for dialects.

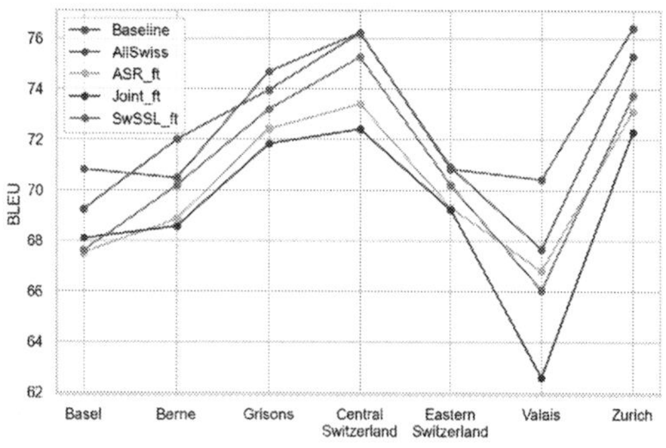

Figure 2: Per-dialect results of the fine-tuning experiments for the STT test set.

6.1 Overview and Setup

In the first set of experiments (DT1), we train a total of 7 models on 1, 2, 4, and 7 dialects. We use the Valais (VS) dialect region data as a starting point for one set of models, as this is the most distant dialect from all the others (Scherrer and Stoeckle, 2016; Paonessa et al., 2023). For a second set of models, we use the Zurich (ZH) region dialect because this was found to be the most similar to the other dialects. In the second set of experiments (DT2), we keep the dialect regions the same but add 10 minutes of speech data for every region that is not included. This allows us to investigate whether a small amount of data from different dialect regions can increase total performance. Table 5 contains an overview of these experiments.

Training Configuration We use XLS-R 300M for all the dialect transfer experiments (see Ap-

Name	Base	Full data	10 min of data	h (DT1)	h (DT2)
0	-	-	VS, ZH, CS, GR, BS, BE, ES	0	1.16
vs_1	VS	VS	ZH, CS, GR, BS, BE, ES	34	35
zh_2	ZH	ZH	VS, CS, GR, BS, BE, ES	33.46	34.45
vs_2	VS	VS, ZH	CS, GR, BS, BE, ES	67.46	68.29
zh_2	ZH	ZH, CS	VS, GR, BS, BE, ES	66.96	67.79
vs_4	VS	VS, ZH, CS, GR	BS, BE, ES	135.92	136.42
zh_4	ZH	ZH, CS, GR, BS	VS, BE, ES	136.17	136.67
all	-	VS, ZH, CS, GR, BS, BE, ES	-	238.71	238.71

Table 5: Overview for the dialect transfer experiments. The column **Base** shows the base dialect, **10 min of data** shows the regions added for DT2. **h (DT1)** and **h (DT2)** are the amounts of speech data used to train the first and second sets of experiments, respectively.

pendix B for more details on why this was chosen). We train each of our models on the balanced STT train set, filtered to only include the respective dialects. This amounts to 34 hours of speech data per dialect region. We use the same setup as described in Section 5 with the hyperparameters from Table 8 for the column *All others*.

Evaluation With the BLEU score, we compare the STT test set performance of the models. To determine whether there is a *Curse of Multilinguality* (Conneau et al., 2020) in Swiss German ST, we look at how the performance of the base dialect develops when adding more dialects in DT1. To investigate the influence of small amounts of added dialectal variability, the models from DT1 and DT2 are compared. Whether performance differences are significant is determined by BLEU's bootstrapping resampling as described in Section 5.

6.2 Results

The results of the DT1 and DT2 are displayed in Table 6 and 7, respectively.

Table 6 shows that for VS, performance is highest when the model is only trained on VS data and lowest when the training data only contains ZH data. Adding any non-VS data decreases BLEU scores, hinting at a *Curse of Multidialectality*. ZH exhibits the highest performance when the model is trained on the closely related dialects CS, GR, and BS in addition to ZH data. For most other regions and overall performance, models are best when using all the dialects for training. For BS and CS, models perform best when trained only on ZH, CS, GR, and BS, suggesting that VS, BE, and/or ES data have a negative impact on performance. This is another indicator of a *Curse of Multidialectality*.

Table 7 shows similar trends as the first set of experiments: VS performance is highest when using the highest percentage of VS data for training, while ZH peaks at 4 dialects that are closely related. We observe similar results for BS, GR, and CS. In Figure 3 we see that VS performance is significantly lower when adding 10 minutes of speech from all other dialect regions, indicating again that VS is strongly affected by other dialects. ZH, on the other hand, seems to benefit from the additional variety, exceeding the results from the DT1 Experiments. BE and the overall performance also benefit.

Contrary to DT1, GR now performs best when the training set contains only 4 dialects, suggesting that GR benefits from small amounts of variability from other dialects but is negatively affected if this variability is too high (i.e., when using all data for BE, VS, and ES). Another explanation could be that the very distant dialects of VS and/or BE significantly affect performance for GR when used entirely, but might enhance the model's generalizability by introducing a beneficial amount of variability when only small amounts of data are used. Further experiments are necessary to investigate how much variability is beneficial and when it negatively affects performance.

The Curse of Multidialectality Even though the model trained on all dialects performs well for both regions, there is a drop of 3.37 BLEU for VS compared to vs_1, the model trained on the VS data only. Paonessa et al. (2023) report similar findings. They trained 7 XLS-R models, one on each of the 7 regions from the STT dataset and found that the model trained on VS data is the only one that outperforms the model trained on the full dataset on its base dialect (in this case, VS). All the other models showed a performance drop of 1-5%, suggesting that they strongly benefit from cross-dialectal transfer. For ZH (and BS, CS, GR), however, our results indicate that this is only the case up to a certain number of (similar) dialects $3 \leq D_{max} \leq 6$ before performance drops slightly but significantly (0.97 BLEU in our case when comparing the performance for ZH of zh_4 and the model trained on all dialects). To determine the exact value of D_{max}, we would need to train models on every number of dialects between 1 and 7. Furthermore, we conjecture that D_{max} is higher when more similar dialects are included in the training set and lower otherwise. The fine-tuning experiments also suggest this: adding Standard German data in Experiments 3 and 4 can be considered as introducing another "dialectal" variety. After doing this, we saw a performance drop for almost all dialect regions

Name	Regions	VS	ZH	BE	BS	GR	CS	ES	Overall
vs_1	VS	**67.8**	43.2	36.8	35.6	40.0	46.1	25.0	42.4
vs_2	VS, ZH	67.1	65.1	49.4	53.4	57.2	64.0	51.9	58.4
vs_4	VS, ZH, CS, GR	64.7	65.8	54.0	56.2	65.6	66.1	58.5	61.5
all	all	64.4*	67.2	**62.0**	63.7	**67.2**	68.3	**65.6**	**65.5**
zh_1	ZH	40.7	64.4	44.4	51.0	56.9	61.7	55.7	53.6
zh_2	ZH, CS	48.7	66.5	53.1	54.9	59.6	67.6	57.8	58.4
zh_4	ZH, CS, GR, BS	52.5	**68.2**	57.1	**64.3**	66.7	**68.3**	63.8	63.0
all	all	64.4	67.2	**62.0**	63.7	**67.2**	68.3	**65.6**	**65.5**

Table 6: BLEU scores of the DT1 Experiments using around 34 hours of speech data for each dialect region specified in the **Regions** column. The best result per region is underlined and bold. Insignificant changes in BLEU as per bootstrap resampling for a system compared with the system in the row above are marked with *.

Name	Regions	VS	ZH	BE	BS	GR	CS	ES	Overall
0+10	-	0	0	0	0	0	0	0	0
vs_1+10	VS	**65.8**	50.4	41.9	43.5	48.4	51.9	39.0	48.8
vs_2+10	VS, ZH	65.7*	63.9	49.6	53.3	58.0	63.2	54.3	58.3
vs_4+10	VS, ZH, CS, GR	65.7*	67.4	56.9	58.7	66.8	68.0	61.3	63.6
all	all	64.4	67.2*	**62.0**	63.7	67.2*	68.3*	**65.6**	**65.5**
zh_1+10	ZH	43.8	64.5	47.1	52.8	59.0	62.5	57.6	55.4
zh_2+10	ZH, CS	50.5	67.3	54.7	56.7	60.7	67.9	60.2	59.8
zh_4+10	ZH, CS, GR, BS	53.7	**69.1**	58.2	**64.5**	**67.8**	**68.8**	64.5	63.9
all	all	64.4	67.2	**62.0**	63.7	67.2	68.3	**65.6**	**65.5**

Table 7: BLEU scores of the DT2 Experiments using 10 minutes of speech data for all the regions that are not included fully (specified in the *Regions* column).

(see Figure 2). These findings are reminiscent of the *Curse of Multilinguality* but require a more thorough investigation.

Introducing dialectal variability during training DT2 shows that the performance for almost all dialects improves when introducing dialectal variability through only 10 minutes of data per dialect. The improvements for the monodialectal VS model are the strongest: overall performance increases by 6.45 BLEU, ZH by 7.19 BLEU, and ES by 13.95 BLEU with only 60 minutes of additional but highly varied data. The models with ZH as the base dialect also benefit from this added data, increasing performance for all dialects when comparing zh_1, the model only trained on ZH data, and zh_1+10, which was trained on the complete ZH data and 10 minutes of all other dialects. This strongly suggests that even adding little dialectal variability is crucial to improve performance. This is an essential finding for dataset collection. When primarily data for a distant dialect is available (VS in our example), it is crucial to gather data from as many other regions as possible, even if that is only a small amount. In this way, overall model performance can be improved with little data, and underrepresented dialects can benefit.

7 Conclusion and Future Work

With respect to the research gaps identified in the introduction, the main findings of this paper are the following:

1. Standard German data is not beneficial for Swiss German ST performance when used in ASR pre-training or joint multilingual fine-tuning if a good amount ST data is available (> 500 h). Further pre-training XLS-R on noisy single-domain, single-dialect data does not improve performance.

2. There are tendencies of a *Curse of Multidialectality* for Swiss German ST, especially when the dialects used for training are distant. Interestingly, Conneau et al. (2020) identified 7-15 languages as

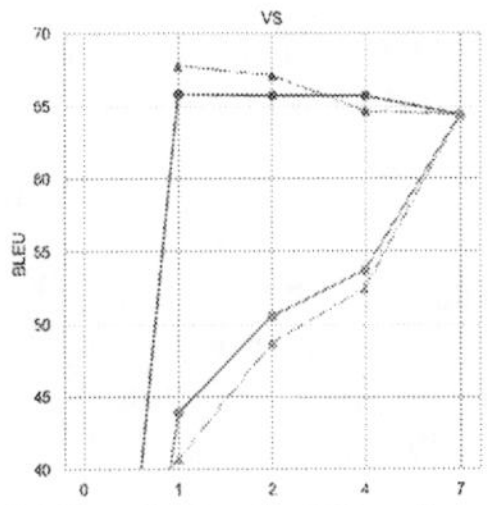

(a) Results for the VS region.

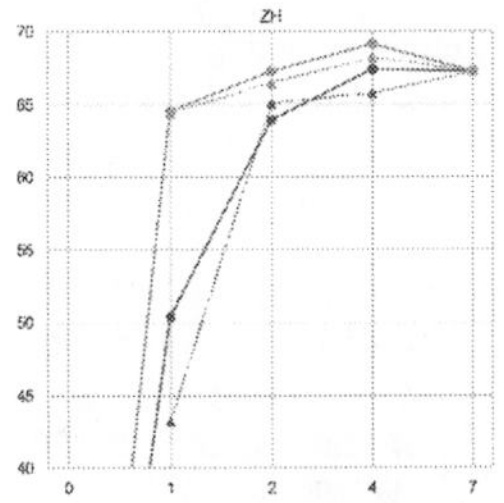

(b) Results for the ZH region.

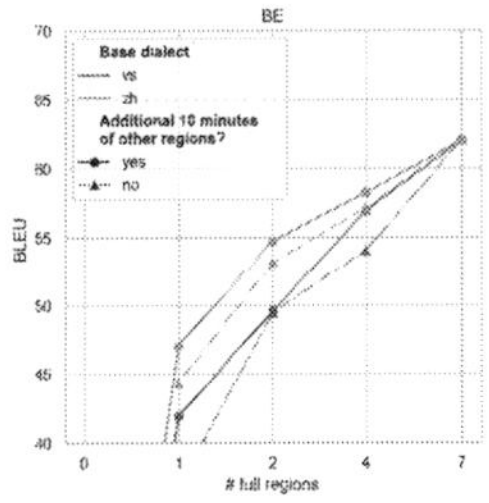

(c) Results for the BE region.

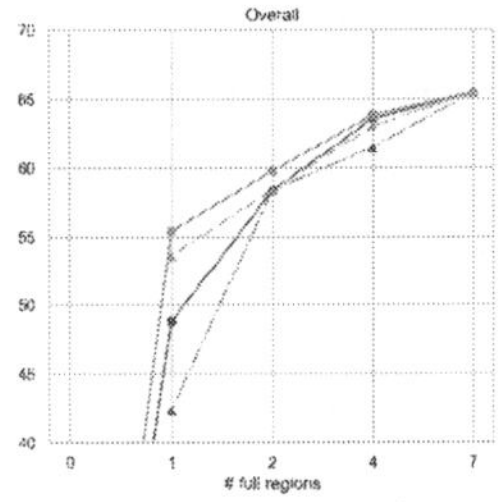

(d) Results for all regions.

Figure 3: BLEU scores of the dialect transfer experiments with VS and ZH as base dialects. The models shown as dotted lines are from DT2, using 10 minutes of audio for all the dialect regions that were not included completely in the training set.

a breaking point. For ST, this number seems to be lower, and language similarity matters even more.

3. Using data containing rich dialectal variability is beneficial for the average performance of all dialects, even if the resulting training set is unbalanced and mainly contains distant dialects (VS in our case).

Future Work Imaizumi et al. (2022) introduced **dialect-aware modeling**, a promising and easy-to-implement approach that could help alleviate the *Curse of Multidialectality*. By performing dialect identification and ST simultaneously, the model might learn better to utilize dialect-specific acoustic/linguistic information for translation and more efficiently leverage cross-dialectal transfer. It is also worth investigating whether Standard German data proves beneficial for performance in this condition. A similar approach would be to introduce **dialect id tags** during training, as this has been shown to help with many-to-one translation performance in MT (Johnson et al., 2017; Fan et al., 2021). Furthermore, one could experiment with different approaches for **dataset balancing**, e.g., by considering the linguistic distances between the dialects as computed in Scherrer and Stoeckle (2016). Instead of employing ASR pre-training, an **existing ST model** (e.g., English →German) could be used to initialize the weights of the Swiss ST model. In contrast to an ASR model, an ST model has already learned non-monotonic mappings and vocabulary changes, which is crucial for Swiss German ST. Considering that there are no open-source ST systems for other German dialects, **benchmarking** our model on the performance of other, more **distant dialects** could be a fruitful experiment. This would be a step towards an ST system capable of translating all German dialects to Standard German, ultimately facilitating communication and cultural exchange between German-speaking countries immensely.

Limitations

Our work was constrained by computational resources, which prevented us from performing multiple training runs to draw statistically sound conclusions on whether performance differences between models were significant. Furthermore, we were unable to conduct the dialect transfer experiments for all dialect regions, which restricted the generalizability of our findings. As Swiss dialects vary significantly, dividing them into homogeneous regions remains a challenge. In our evaluations, we treat the dialect regions as homogeneous dialects even though they contain considerable variability. This might affect our results. Lastly, a thorough qualitative analysis of model outputs could have revealed region-specific error patterns and other limitations of our training and evaluation methods.

Acknowledgments

This work reports the findings of the first author's Master's thesis, which was carried out under a scholarship from the Erasmus Mundus European Master's Program in Language and Communication Technologies (EMLCT), EU grant no. 2019-1508. We want to express our gratitude to the HiTZ Center for Language Technology at the University of the Basque Country for allowing us to access their GPU clusters.

References

Ahmed Ali, Shammur Chowdhury, Mohamed Afify, Wassim El-Hajj, Hazem Hajj, Mourad Abbas, Amir Hussein, Nada Ghneim, Mohammad Abushariah, and Assal Alqudah. 2021. Connecting Arabs: Bridging the gap in dialectal speech recognition. *Communications of the ACM*, 64(4):124–129.

Rosana Ardila, Megan Branson, Kelly Davis, Michael Kohler, Josh Meyer, Michael Henretty, Reuben Morais, Lindsay Saunders, Francis Tyers, and Gregor Weber. 2020. Common Voice: A massively-multilingual speech corpus. In *Proceedings of the Twelfth Language Resources and Evaluation Conference*, pages 4218–4222.

Malajyan Arthur, Victoria Khurshudyan, Karen Avetisyan, Hossep Dolatian, and Damien Nouvel. 2024. Bi-dialectal ASR of Armenian from naturalistic and read speech. In *Proceedings of the 3rd Annual Meeting of the Special Interest Group on Under-resourced Languages @ LREC-COLING 2024*, pages 227–236, Torino, Italia. ELRA and ICCL.

Arun Babu, Changhan Wang, Andros Tjandra, Kushal Lakhotia, Qiantong Xu, Naman Goyal, Kritika Singh, Patrick von Platen, Yatharth Saraf, Juan Pino, et al. 2021. XLS-R: Self-supervised cross-lingual speech representation learning at scale. *arXiv preprint arXiv:2111.09296*.

Alexei Baevski, Yuhao Zhou, Abdelrahman Mohamed, and Michael Auli. 2020. wav2vec 2.0: A framework for self-supervised learning of speech representations. *Advances in neural information processing systems*, 33:12449–12460.

Martijn Bartelds, Nay San, Bradley McDonnell, Dan Jurafsky, and Martijn Wieling. 2023. Making more of little data: Improving low-resource automatic speech recognition using data augmentation. In *Proceedings of the 61st Annual Meeting of the Association for Computational Linguistics (Volume 1: Long Papers)*, pages 715–729, Toronto, Canada. Association for Computational Linguistics.

Doris Baum, Daniel Schneider, Jochen Schwenninger, Barbara Samlowski, Thomas Winkler, and Joachim Köhler. 2010. DiSCo – a German evaluation corpus for challenging problems in the broadcast domain. *LREC 2010*.

Yoshua Bengio, Jérôme Louradour, Ronan Collobert, and Jason Weston. 2009. Curriculum learning. In *Proceedings of the 26th Annual International Conference on Machine Learning*, ICML '09, page 41–48, New York, NY, USA. Association for Computing Machinery.

Verena Blaschke, Christoph Purschke, Hinrich Schütze, and Barbara Plank. 2024. What do dialect speakers want? a survey of attitudes towards language technology for German dialects. *Preprint*, arXiv:2402.11968.

Matthias Büchi, Malgorzata Anna Ulasik, Manuela Hürlimann, Fernando Benites de Azevedo e Souza, Pius von Däniken, and Mark Cieliebak. 2020. Zhaw-init at GermEval 2020 task 4: Low-resource speech-to-text. In *5th SwissText & 16th KONVENS Joint Conference, Zurich (online), 24-25 June 2020*. CEUR Workshop Proceedings.

Shammur Absar Chowdhury, Amir Hussein, Ahmed Abdelali, and Ahmed Ali. 2021. Towards one model to rule all: Multilingual strategy for dialectal code-switching Arabic ASR. *Preprint*, arXiv:2105.14779.

Helen Christen. 2010. Vertikale und horizontale Variation: Beobachtungen zum Schweizerdeutschen. In *Variatio delectat. Empirische Evidenzen und theoretische Passungen sprachlicher Variation: für Klaus J. Mattheier zum 65. Geburtstag*, pages 145–159. Peter Lang.

Helen Christen. 2019. Alemannisch in der Schweiz. In *Deutsch*, volume 30/4, pages 246–279. De Gruyter, Inc, Germany.

Helen Christen, Andrea Ender, and Roland Kehrein. 2020. Sprachliche Variation in Deutschland, österreich, der Schweiz und Luxemburg. *Dialekt und Logopädie. Zürich/New York: Georg Olms Verlag*, pages 83–135.

Seamless Communication, Loïc Barrault, Yu-An Chung, Mariano Coria Meglioli, David Dale, Ning Dong, Mark Duppenthaler, Paul-Ambroise Duquenne, Brian Ellis, Hady Elsahar, Justin Haaheim, John Hoffman, Min-Jae Hwang, Hirofumi Inaguma, Christopher Klaiber, Ilia Kulikov, Pengwei Li, Daniel Licht, Jean Maillard, Ruslan Mavlyutov, Alice Rakotoarison, Kaushik Ram Sadagopan, Abinesh Ramakrishnan, Tuan Tran, Guillaume Wenzek, Yilin Yang, Ethan Ye, Ivan Evtimov, Pierre Fernandez, Cynthia Gao, Prangthip Hansanti, Elahe Kalbassi, Amanda Kallet, Artyom Kozhevnikov, Gabriel Mejia Gonzalez, Robin San Roman, Christophe Touret, Corinne Wong, Carleigh Wood, Bokai Yu, Pierre Andrews, Can Balioglu, Peng-Jen Chen, Marta R. Costa-jussà, Maha Elbayad, Hongyu Gong, Francisco Guzmán, Kevin Heffernan, Somya Jain, Justine Kao, Ann Lee, Xutai Ma, Alex Mourachko, Benjamin Peloquin, Juan Pino, Sravya Popuri, Christophe Ropers, Safiyyah Saleem, Holger Schwenk, Anna Sun, Paden Tomasello, Changhan Wang, Jeff Wang, Skyler Wang, and Mary Williamson. 2023. Seamless: Multilingual expressive and streaming speech translation. *Preprint*, arXiv:2312.05187.

Alexis Conneau, Kartikay Khandelwal, Naman Goyal, Vishrav Chaudhary, Guillaume Wenzek, Francisco Guzmán, Edouard Grave, Myle Ott, Luke Zettlemoyer, and Veselin Stoyanov. 2020. Unsupervised cross-lingual representation learning at scale. In *Proceedings of the 58th Annual Meeting of the Association for Computational Linguistics*, page 8440. Association for Computational Linguistics.

Zhengjia Dan, Yue Zhao, Xiaojun Bi, Licheng Wu, and Qiang Ji. 2022. Multi-task transformer with adaptive cross-entropy loss for multi-dialect speech recognition. *Entropy*, 24(10).

Amit Das, Kshitiz Kumar, and Jian Wu. 2021. Multi-dialect speech recognition in English using attention on ensemble of experts. In *ICASSP 2021 - 2021 IEEE International Conference on Acoustics, Speech and Signal Processing (ICASSP)*, pages 6244–6248.

Pan Deng, Shihao Chen, Weitai Zhang, Jie Zhang, and Lirong Dai. 2023. The USTC's dialect speech translation system for IWSLT 2023. In *Proceedings of the 20th International Conference on Spoken Language Translation (IWSLT 2023)*, pages 102–112, Toronto, Canada (in-person and online). Association for Computational Linguistics.

Jacob Devlin, Ming-Wei Chang, Kenton Lee, and Kristina Toutanova. 2019. BERT: Pre-training of deep bidirectional transformers for language understanding. In *Proceedings of the 2019 Conference of the North American Chapter of the Association for Computational Linguistics: Human Language Technologies, Volume 1 (Long and Short Papers)*, pages 4171–4186, Minneapolis, Minnesota. Association for Computational Linguistics.

Timin Ding, Kai Sun, Xu Zhang, Jian Yu, and Degen Huang. 2024. Chinese multi-dialect speech recognition based on instruction tuning. In *Fourth Symposium on Pattern Recognition and Applications (SPRA 2023)*, volume 13162, page 131620A. International Society for Optics and Photonics, SPIE.

Pelin Dogan-Schönberger, Julian Mäder, and Thomas Hofmann. 2021. Swissdial: Parallel multidialectal corpus of spoken Swiss German. *arXiv preprint arXiv:2103.11401*.

Andrea Ender and Irmtraud Kaiser. 2009. Zum Stellenwert von Dialekt und Standard im österreichischen und Schweizer Alltag – Ergebnisse einer Umfrage. *Zeitschrift für germanistische Linguistik*, 37(2):266–295.

Angela Fan, Shruti Bhosale, Holger Schwenk, Zhiyi Ma, Ahmed El-Kishky, Siddharth Goyal, Mandeep Baines, Onur Celebi, Guillaume Wenzek, Vishrav Chaudhary, Naman Goyal, Tom Birch, Vitaliy Liptchinsky, Sergey Edunov, Michael Auli, and Armand Joulin. 2021. Beyond english-centric multilingual machine translation. *Journal of Machine Learning Research*, 22(107):1–48.

Charles A Ferguson. 1959. Diglossia. *WORD*, 15(2):325–340.

Philip N Garner, David Imseng, and Thomas Meyer. 2014. Automatic speech recognition and translation of a Swiss German dialect: Walliserdeutsch. In *Proceedings of Interspeech*, pages 2118–2122.

Andrea Gulli, Francesco Costantini, Diego Sidraschi, and Emanuela Li Destri. 2024. Fine-tuning a pre-trained Wav2Vec2 model for automatic speech recognition- experiments with de Zahrar Sproche. In *Proceedings of the 2024 Joint International Conference on Computational Linguistics, Language Resources and Evaluation (LREC-COLING 2024)*, pages 7336–7342, Torino, Italia. ELRA and ICCL.

Robert Herms, Laura Seelig, Stefanie Münch, and Maximilian Eibl. 2016. A corpus of read and spontaneous Upper Saxon German speech for ASR evaluation. In *Proceedings of the Tenth International Conference on Language Resources and Evaluation (LREC'16)*, pages 4648–4651, Portorož, Slovenia. European Language Resources Association (ELRA).

Aaricia Herygers, Vass Verkhodanova, Matt Coler, Odette Scharenborg, and Munir Georges. 2023. Bias in Flemish automatic speech recognition. *Studientexte zur Sprachkommunikation: Elektronische Sprachsignalverarbeitung*, pages 158–165.

Ranzo Huang and Brian Mak. 2023. wav2vec 2.0 ASR for Cantonese-Speaking Older Adults in a Clinical Setting. In *Proc. INTERSPEECH 2023*, pages 4958–4962.

Ryo Imaizumi, Ryo Masumura, Sayaka Shiota, and Hitoshi Kiya. 2020. Dialect-aware modeling for end-to-end Japanese dialect speech recognition. In *2020 Asia-Pacific Signal and Information Processing Association Annual Summit and Conference (APSIPA ASC)*, pages 297–301.

Ryo Imaizumi, Ryo Masumura, Sayaka Shiota, Hitoshi Kiya, et al. 2022. End-to-end Japanese multi-dialect speech recognition and dialect identification with multi-task learning. *APSIPA Transactions on Signal and Information Processing*, 11(1).

Aizhan Imankulova, Raj Dabre, Atsushi Fujita, and Kenji Imamura. 2019. Exploiting out-of-domain parallel data through multilingual transfer learning for low-resource neural machine translation. In *Proceedings of Machine Translation Summit XVII: Research Track*, pages 128–139, Dublin, Ireland. European Association for Machine Translation.

Melvin Johnson, Mike Schuster, Quoc V. Le, Maxim Krikun, Yonghui Wu, Zhifeng Chen, Nikhil Thorat, Fernanda Viégas, Martin Wattenberg, Greg Corrado, Macduff Hughes, and Jeffrey Dean. 2017. Google's multilingual neural machine translation system: Enabling zero-shot translation. *Transactions of the Association for Computational Linguistics*, 5:339–351.

Aditya Joshi, Raj Dabre, Diptesh Kanojia, Zhuang Li, Haolan Zhan, Gholamreza Haffari, and Doris Dippold. 2024. Natural language processing for dialects of a language: A survey. *Preprint*, arXiv:2401.05632.

Santosh Kesiraju, Marek Sarvaš, Tomáš Pavlíček, Cécile Macaire, and Alejandro Ciuba. 2023. Strategies for Improving Low Resource Speech to Text Translation Relying on Pre-trained ASR Models. In *Proc. INTERSPEECH 2023*, pages 2148–2152.

Abbas Khosravani, Philip N Garner, and Alexandros Lazaridis. 2021a. Learning to translate low-resourced Swiss German dialectal speech into Standard German text. In *2021 IEEE Automatic Speech Recognition and Understanding Workshop (ASRU)*, pages 817–823. IEEE.

Abbas Khosravani, Philip N Garner, and Alexandros Lazaridis. 2021b. Modeling dialectal variation for Swiss German automatic speech recognition. In *Interspeech*, pages 2896–2900.

Tom Kocmi, Rachel Bawden, Ondřej Bojar, Anton Dvorkovich, Christian Federmann, Mark Fishel, Thamme Gowda, Yvette Graham, Roman Grundkiewicz, Barry Haddow, Rebecca Knowles, Philipp Koehn, Christof Monz, Makoto Morishita, Masaaki Nagata, Toshiaki Nakazawa, Michal Novák, Martin Popel, and Maja Popović. 2022. Findings of the 2022 conference on machine translation (WMT22). In *Proceedings of the Seventh Conference on Machine Translation (WMT)*, pages 1–45, Abu Dhabi, United Arab Emirates (Hybrid). Association for Computational Linguistics.

Philipp Koehn. 2004. Statistical significance tests for machine translation evaluation. In *Proceedings of the 2004 Conference on Empirical Methods in Natural Language Processing*, pages 388–395, Barcelona, Spain. Association for Computational Linguistics.

Philipp Koehn. 2005. Europarl: A parallel corpus for statistical machine translation. In *Proceedings of Machine Translation Summit X: Papers*, pages 79–86, Phuket, Thailand.

Gongxu Luo, Yating Yang, Yang Yuan, Zhanheng Chen, and Aizimaiti Ainiwaer. 2019. Hierarchical transfer learning architecture for low-resource neural machine translation. *IEEE Access*, 7:154157–154166.

Jian Luo, Jianzong Wang, Ning Cheng, Edward Xiao, Jing Xiao, Georg Kucsko, Patrick O'Neill, Jagadeesh Balam, Slyne Deng, Adriana Flores, Boris Ginsburg, Jocelyn Huang, Oleksii Kuchaiev, Vitaly Lavrukhin, and Jason Li. 2021. Cross-language transfer learning and domain adaptation for end-to-end automatic speech recognition. In *2021 IEEE International Conference on Multimedia and Expo (ICME)*, pages 1–6.

Eduardo Medeiros, Leonel Corado, Luís Rato, Paulo Quaresma, and Pedro Salgueiro. 2023. Domain adaptation speech-to-text for low-resource European Portuguese using deep learning. *Future Internet*, 15(5):159.

Abir Messaoudi, Hatem Haddad, Chayma Fourati, Moez BenHaj Hmida, Aymen Ben Elhaj Mabrouk, and Mohamed Graiet. 2021. Tunisian dialectal end-to-end speech recognition based on DeepSpeech. *Procedia Computer Science*, 189:183–190. AI in Computational Linguistics.

Jonathan David Mutal, Pierrette Bouillon, Johanna Gerlach, and Marianne Starlander. 2023. Improving Standard German captioning of spoken Swiss German: Evaluating multilingual pre-trained models. In *Proceedings of Machine Translation Summit XIX, Vol. 2: Users Track*, pages 65–76, Macau SAR, China. Asia-Pacific Association for Machine Translation.

Seham Nasr, Rehab Duwairi, and Muhannad Quwaider. 2023. End-to-end speech recognition for Arabic dialects. *Arabian Journal for Science and Engineering*, pages 1–17.

Iuliia Nigmatulina, Tannon Kew, and Tanja Samardzic. 2020. Asr for non-standardised languages with dialectal variation: the case of Swiss German. In *Proceedings of the 7th Workshop on NLP for Similar Languages, Varieties and Dialects*, pages 15–24.

Karol Nowakowski, Michal Ptaszynski, Kyoko Murasaki, and Jagna Nieuważny. 2023. Adapting multilingual speech representation model for a new, underresourced language through multilingual fine-tuning and continued pretraining. *Information Processing & Management*, 60(2):103148.

Claudio Paonessa, Yanick Schraner, Jan Deriu, Manuela Hürlimann, Manfred Vogel, and Mark Cieliebak. 2023. Dialect transfer for Swiss German speech translation. In *Findings of the Association for Computational Linguistics: EMNLP 2023*, pages 15240–15254, Singapore. Association for Computational Linguistics.

Georgios Paraskevopoulos, Theodoros Kouzelis, Georgios Rouvalis, Athanasios Katsamanis, Vassilis Katsouros, and Alexandros Potamianos. 2024. Sample-efficient unsupervised domain adaptation of speech recognition systems: A case study for Modern Greek. *IEEE/ACM Transactions on Audio, Speech, and Language Processing*, 32:286–299.

Phoebe Parsons, Knut Kvale, Torbjørn Svendsen, and Giampiero Salvi. 2023. A character-based analysis of impacts of dialects on end-to-end Norwegian ASR. In *Proceedings of the 24th Nordic Conference on Computational Linguistics (NoDaLiDa)*, pages 467–476, Tórshavn, Faroe Islands. University of Tartu Library.

Telmo Pires, Eva Schlinger, and Dan Garrette. 2019. How multilingual is multilingual BERT? In *Proceedings of the 57th Annual Meeting of the Association for Computational Linguistics*, pages 4996–5001, Florence, Italy. Association for Computational Linguistics.

Michel Plüss, Jan Deriu, Yanick Schraner, Claudio Paonessa, Julia Hartmann, Larissa Schmidt, Christian Scheller, Manuela Hürlimann, Tanja Samardžić, Manfred Vogel, et al. 2023a. STT4SG-350: A speech corpus for all Swiss German dialect regions. *arXiv preprint arXiv:2305.18855*.

Michel Plüss, Manuela Hürlimann, Marc Cuny, Alla Stöckli, Nikolaos Kapotis, Julia Hartmann, Malgorzata Anna Ulasik, Christian Scheller, Yanick Schraner, Amit Jain, Jan Deriu, Mark Cieliebak, and Manfred Vogel. 2022. SDS-200: A Swiss German speech to Standard German text corpus. In *Proceedings of the Thirteenth Language Resources and Evaluation Conference*, pages 3250–3256, Marseille, France. European Language Resources Association.

Michel Plüss, Lukas Neukom, Christian Scheller, and Manfred Vogel. 2020. Swiss parliaments corpus, an automatically aligned Swiss German speech to Standard German text corpus. *arXiv preprint arXiv:2010.02810*.

Michel Plüss, Lukas Neukom, and Manfred Vogel. 2021. Swisstext 2021 task 3: Swiss German speech to Standard German text. In *Proceedings of the Swiss Text Analytics Conference*, volume 2021.

Michel Plüss, Yanick Schraner, Christian Scheller, and Manfred Vogel. 2023b. 2nd Swiss German speech to Standard German text shared task at SwissText 2022. *arXiv preprint arXiv:2301.06790*.

Matt Post. 2018. A call for clarity in reporting BLEU scores. In *Proceedings of the Third Conference on Machine Translation: Research Papers*, pages 186–191, Brussels, Belgium. Association for Computational Linguistics.

Vineel Pratap, Qiantong Xu, Anuroop Sriram, Gabriel Synnaeve, and Ronan Collobert. 2020. Mls: A large-scale multilingual dataset for speech research. *ArXiv*, abs/2012.03411.

Christian Rauh and Jan Schwalbach. 2020. The ParlSpeech V2 data set: Full-text corpora of 6.3 million parliamentary speeches in the key legislative chambers of nine representative democracies. *Harvard Dataverse*.

Paul K. Rubenstein, Chulayuth Asawaroengchai, Duc Dung Nguyen, Ankur Bapna, Zalán Borsos, Félix de Chaumont Quitry, Peter Chen, Dalia El Badawy, Wei Han, Eugene Kharitonov, Hannah Muckenhirn, Dirk Padfield, James Qin, Danny Rozenberg, Tara Sainath, Johan Schalkwyk, Matt Sharifi, Michelle Tadmor Ramanovich, Marco Tagliasacchi, Alexandru Tudor, Mihajlo Velimirović, Damien Vincent, Jiahui Yu, Yongqiang Wang, Vicky Zayats, Neil Zeghidour, Yu Zhang, Zhishuai Zhang, Lukas Zilka, and Christian Frank. 2023. AudioPaLM: A large language model that can speak and listen. *Preprint*, arXiv:2306.12925.

Charles Russ. 1990. *The dialects of modern German: A linguistic survey*. Routledge.

Tanja Samardzic, Yves Scherrer, and Elvira Glaser. 2016. Archimob-a corpus of spoken Swiss German. In *Proceedings of the Tenth International Conference on Language Resources and Evaluation (LREC'16)*, pages 4061–4066.

Ramon Sanabria, Nikolay Bogoychev, Nina Markl, Andrea Carmantini, Ondrej Klejch, and Peter Bell. 2023. The Edinburgh international accents of English corpus: Towards the democratization of English ASR. In *ICASSP 2023 - 2023 IEEE International Conference on Acoustics, Speech and Signal Processing (ICASSP)*, pages 1–5.

Yves Scherrer, Tanja Samardžić, and Elvira Glaser. 2019. Digitising Swiss German: how to process and study a polycentric spoken language. *Language Resources and Evaluation*, 53(4):735–769.

Yves Scherrer and Philipp Stoeckle. 2016. A quantitative approach to Swiss German – dialectometric analyses and comparisons of linguistic levels. *Dialectologia et Geolinguistica*, 24(1):92–125.

Katja Schlatter. 2024. «Schweizerdeutsch redet man paar Sachen komisch.» DaZ lernen und unterrichten in der diglossischen Deutschschweiz. In Stefan Hauser and Alexandra Schiesser, editors, *Standarddeutsch und Dialekt in der Schule*, pages 23–46. hep, Bern.

Barbara Schuppler, Martin Hagmueller, Juan A. Morales-Cordovilla, and Hannes Pessentheiner. 2014. GRASS: the Graz corpus of read and spontaneous speech. In *Proceedings of the Ninth International Conference on Language Resources and Evaluation (LREC'14)*, pages 1465–1470, Reykjavik, Iceland. European Language Resources Association (ELRA).

Clément Sicard, Kajetan Pyszkowski, and Victor Gillioz. 2023. Spaiche: Extending state-of-the-art ASR models to Swiss German dialects. *arXiv preprint arXiv:2304.11075*.

Mihaela C. Stoian, Sameer Bansal, and Sharon Goldwater. 2020. Analyzing ASR pretraining for low-resource speech-to-text translation. In *ICASSP 2020 - 2020 IEEE International Conference on Acoustics, Speech and Signal Processing (ICASSP)*, pages 7909–7913.

Artit Suwanbandit, Burin Naowarat, Orathai Sangpetch, and Ekapol Chuangsuwanich. 2023. Thai dialect corpus and transfer-based curriculum learning investigation for dialect automatic speech recognition. In *INTERSPEECH 2023*, pages 4069–4073.

Marc Tanti, Lonneke van der Plas, Claudia Borg, and Albert Gatt. 2021. On the language-specificity of multilingual BERT and the impact of fine-tuning. In *Proceedings of the Fourth BlackboxNLP Workshop on Analyzing and Interpreting Neural Networks for NLP*, pages 214–227, Punta Cana, Dominican Republic. Association for Computational Linguistics.

Changhan Wang, Morgane Riviere, Ann Lee, Anne Wu, Chaitanya Talnikar, Daniel Haziza, Mary Williamson, Juan Pino, and Emmanuel Dupoux. 2021a. Voxpopuli: A large-scale multilingual speech corpus for representation learning, semi-supervised learning and interpretation. In *Proceedings of the 59th Annual Meeting of the Association for Computational Linguistics and the 11th International Joint Conference on Natural Language Processing (Volume 1: Long Papers)*, pages 993–1003.

Changhan Wang, Yun Tang, Xutai Ma, Anne Wu, Dmytro Okhonko, and Juan Pino. 2020. Fairseq S2T: Fast speech-to-text modeling with fairseq. In *Proceedings of the 1st Conference of the Asia-Pacific Chapter of the Association for Computational Linguistics and the 10th International Joint Conference on Natural Language Processing: System Demonstrations*, pages 33–39, Suzhou, China. Association for Computational Linguistics.

Changhan Wang, Anne Wu, Jiatao Gu, and Juan Pino. 2021b. CoVoST 2 and massively multilingual speech translation. *Interspeech 2021*.

Saskia Wepner. 2021. Adaptation of automatic speech recognition systems to the needs of Austrian German. In *Phonetikworkshop 46. Österreichische Linguistiktagung 2020.*

Johannes Wirth and Rene Peinl. 2022. Automatic speech recognition in German: A detailed error analysis. In *2022 IEEE International Conference on Omni-layer Intelligent Systems (COINS)*, pages 1–8.

Shijie Wu and Mark Dredze. 2019. Beto, bentz, becas: The surprising cross-lingual effectiveness of BERT. In *Proceedings of the 2019 Conference on Empirical Methods in Natural Language Processing and the 9th International Joint Conference on Natural Language Processing (EMNLP-IJCNLP)*, pages 833–844, Hong Kong, China. Association for Computational Linguistics.

Aditya Yadavalli, Mirishkar Sai Ganesh, and Anil Kumar Vuppala. 2022. Multi-task end-to-end model for Telugu dialect and speech recognition. In *Interspeech*, pages 1387–1391.

Jinyi Yang, Amir Hussein, Matthew Wiesner, and Sanjeev Khudanpur. 2022. JHU IWSLT 2022 dialect speech translation system description. In *Proceedings of the 19th International Conference on Spoken Language Translation (IWSLT 2022)*, pages 319–326, Dublin, Ireland (in-person and online). Association for Computational Linguistics.

Yue Zhao, Jianjian Yue, Wei Song, Xiaona Xu, Xiali Li, Licheng Wu, and Qiang Ji. 2019. Tibetan multi-dialect speech and dialect identity recognition. *Computers, Materials & Continua*, 60(3).

A Language Model for decoding

We enhance XLS-R decoding by using LM fusion. We trained several language models of different sizes using the kenlm toolkit[11] and determined the best-performing model by evaluating the performance of our baseline model on the Swiss German test sets.

The best-performing LM is a 5-gram language model trained on 100M Standard German sentences compiled by concatenating EuroParl (Koehn, 2005)[12], NewsCrawl (Kocmi et al., 2022)[13], Tudatext[14], Parlspeech Bundestag + Nationalrat (Rauh and Schwalbach, 2020)[15] and the transcriptions of the STT, SPC, SDS, SDial train splits.

We fine-tuned the hyperparameters used for LM fusion by observing the performance of our Baseline model on the Swiss German test sets and ended up with `lm-weight=0.9`, `sil-weight=-1`, `word-score=1`, `nbest=1`. This configuration was used to obtain all our results.

B Training Hyperparameters

Table 8 lists the hyperparameters used for all experiments. These are mostly adapted from (Plüss et al., 2023a), who base theirs on (Babu et al., 2021).

Early stopping (or a maximum number of update steps) was set in every experiment to avoid overfitting and wasting resources. Learning rates were scheduled with Fairseq's tri-state scheduler, which warms up linearly for the first 6.25% of total steps, then keeps the learning rate constant for 25% of the total steps, and decays it exponentially afterward.

For the fine-tuning and pre-training experiments, XLS-R 1B was used. For the second fine-tuning step in Experiment 4, we had to adjust the learning rate to 1e-6 because the model had already seen the Swiss German data and did not converge with a higher learning rate.

For continued pre-training, we use the same configurations as (Babu et al., 2021) with modifications inspired by (Bartelds et al., 2023). As pre-training is computationally expensive and we train on one GPU (instead of 200 as (Babu et al., 2021)), we lower the batch size and apply gradient accumulation. All hyperparameters are listed in Table 8. If any parameters are not given, they were kept the same as in the pre-training config of XLS-R (Babu et al., 2021).

Unlike the fine-tuning experiments, the 300M version of XLS-R (Babu et al., 2021) was used for the dialect transfer experiments. The main reason for this is that we train 14 models for our dialect transfer experiments, and this would consume too many computational resources[16]. Additionally, Paonessa et al. (2023) showed that the results of XLS-R 300M are transferable to XLS-R 1B because both models have the same performance curve with a gap of around 5 BLEU per dialect region. All model trainings are conducted using the hyperparameters from Table 8 (column **All others**). However, for the first set of dialect transfer experiments, we use the STT validation set only containing the base dialect to track the model performance during training.

[11] `https://kheafield.com/code/kenlm/`

[12] `https://www.statmt.org/europarl/v7/`

[13] `http://data.statmt.org/news-commentary/v14/`

[14] `http://ltdata1.informatik.uni-hamburg.de/kaldi_tuda_de/`

[15] `https://dataverse.harvard.edu/dataset.xhtml?persistentId=doi:10.7910/DVN/L4OAKN`

[16] For instance, training the 300M version for 80k steps on the STT balanced train set took 28 hours in Paonessa et al. (2023). However, using XLS-R 1B with the same setup took 48 hours

	Ex 1	Ex 4.2	Ex 5.1	All others
learning rate	3e-5	1e-6	5e-5	3e-5
gradient accumulation	10	10	10	10
batch size (samples)	640k	640k	320k	640k
effective batch size	400 sec	400 sec	200 sec	400 sec
validation set	STT	SwG-all	GRZH	SwG-all*
validation interval	1000	1000	400	1000
early stopping patience	-	5	3	5
max. updates	80k	80k	80k	250k

Table 8: Hyperparameters for the fine-tuning, pre-training and dialect transfer experiments. The experiment numbers refer to Table 3. *SwG-all* refers to the combined STT, SDS, and SPC validation sets.
*For Experiment 3.1, the CV validation set was used.

C Performance comparison to SoTA models

Figure 4 shows the results of our models from the fine-tuning experiments compared to SoTA models for Swiss German ST. We hypothesize that the performance difference between our baseline and the baseline published in Plüss et al. (2023a) has two main reasons: (1) we trained on one GPU only, resulting in a different batch size and overall training time, (2) we used less data for training the language model and a potentially different ngram order.

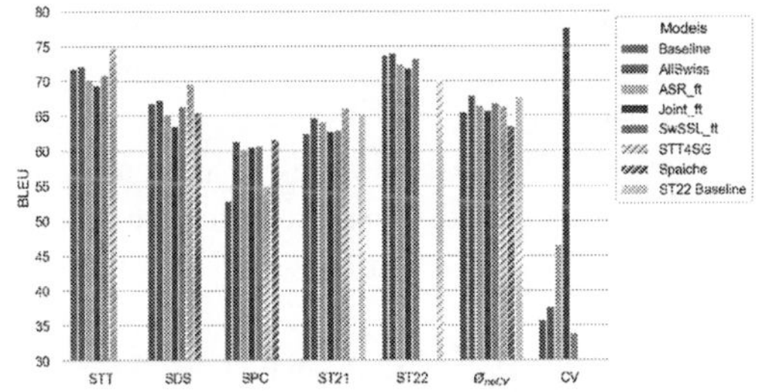

Figure 4: Results of fine-tuning Experiments 1-5, grouped by test set. STT4SG, Spaiche, and ST22 Baseline are the models published in (Plüss et al., 2023a), (Sicard et al., 2023), and (Plüss et al., 2023b) respectively. For these models, we only used the available performance metrics to compute the average ($\varnothing_{noCV}$).

CDAC-SVNIT submission for IWSLT 2025 Indic track shared task

Mukund K Roy[1,2], Karunesh K Arora[1], Praveen Kumar Chandaliya[2], Rohit Kumar[2], Pruthwik Mishra[2],
[1]SNLP Lab, CDAC Noida, India, [2]SVNIT Surat, India,
Correspondence: mukundkumarroy@cdac.in, karunesharora@cdac.in, pkc@aid.svnit.ac.in, rohitkumar@aid.svnit.ac.in, pruthwikmishra@aid.svnit.ac.in

Abstract

In this paper, we design a Speech-to-Text Translation (ST) system to translate English into Hindi, Bengali, and Tamil, and vice versa. We explore both cascaded and End-to-End (E2E) approaches as part of the IWSLT 2025 Indic shared task. In the cascaded systems, we leverage the pre-trained Wav2Vec2 model from AI4Bharat's Vakyansh project, and then fine-tune it for Automatic Speech Recognition (ASR). The resultant ASR outputs are then translated using the adapted IndicTrans2 Neural Machine Translation (NMT) model with IWSLT task-specific data. In the E2E approach, we train models from scratch using only the IWSLT dataset, leveraging the Fairseq Speech Translation framework which uses transformer-based encoder-decoder architecture optimized for multilingual speech inputs. In the paper, the performance of these two distinct approaches in handling low-resource Indic speech translation tasks is compared. Although in the E2E approach, the pre-trained Acoustic model is not leveraged, its results in the En-Indic setting are impressive. However, this approach does not perform well in the Indic-En setting due to lack of sufficient training data. On the other hand, the cascaded approach leverages pre-trained models and outperforms for all language pairs.

1 Introduction

In a global and borderless economy, seamless communication is essential, with speech being the most natural medium. Overcoming language barriers through intelligent systems is crucial for real-time interaction and bridging the digital divide (Arora et al., 2013). Speech-to-text translation has a vital role to play in facilitating communication across language barriers. Recent advancements in the area of speech technology have resulted in state-of-the-art performance in the speech recognition task (Baevski et al., 2020a; Radford et al., 2022) and machine translation (Kalchbrenner and Blunsom, 2013; Sutskever et al., 2014; Bahdanau et al., 2016; Vaswani et al., 2017) for almost all major languages. This encourages the advent of direct speech translation of speech, leading to the rise of two different paradigms of achieving the same. They are: *Cascaded* and *End-to-End* speech translation. In the cascaded speech-to-text (ST) translation paradigm, the task of translating speech from a source language to text in a target language is broken down into two distinct modules. The recent rise of cascaded ST systems (Mujadia and Sharma, 2023; Prakash et al., 2023; Mhaskar et al., 2023) for translating the educational content in Indian languages show the effectiveness of this approach.

Automatic Speech Recognition (ASR): The input speech in the source language is first transcribed into text using an ASR system.

Machine Translation (MT): The transcribed source language text is then translated into the target language using a Neural Machine Translation (NMT) system.

This pipeline-based approach is advantageous for modular development, allowing the ASR and MT components to be trained independently and optimized using speech datasets, even when parallel ST corpora are limited. However, a limitation of cascaded ST is the potential propagation of errors from ASR to MT, where transcription errors can negatively impact the translation quality. End-to-End Speech Translation is another paradigm that directly translates spoken utterances in one language into text in a target language, bypassing intermediate steps such as ASR and MT (Weiss et al., 2017). This approach enables the model to learn joint representations that capture both acoustic and linguistic features, resulting in efficient inference and reduced error propagation compared to traditional cascaded pipelines (Sperber and Paulik, 2020). Leveraging architectures such as encoder-decoder transformers, end-to-end ST

Proceedings of the 22nd International Conference on Spoken Language Translation (IWSLT 2025), pages 180–185
July 31 - August 1, 2025

Lang-pair	Train		Dev		Test	
	# of Audios	Total duration	# of Audios	Total duration	# of Audios	Total duration
En–Hi	205,201	680h 54m	11,669	40h 47m	36,245	93h 13m
En–Bn	205,203	680h 54m	11,671	40h 48m	36,245	93h 13m
En–Ta	205,203	680h 54m	11,671	40h 48m	36,245	93h 13m
Hi–En	248,872	653h 52m	397	0h 59m	579	1h 20m
Bn–En	64,868	157h 57m	395	1h 0m	866	1h 15m
Ta–En	211,303	478h 9m	457	0h 59m	956	2h 11m

Table 1: Statistics of the speech translation dataset provided for the IWSLT 2025 Shared Task. Durations are shown in hours and minutes.

systems are trained on pairs of ST translation data, allowing them to implicitly align and map source audio to target textual content (Dong et al., 2018). This methodology has shown promising results in multilingual and low-resource settings, especially when supported by self-supervised pretraining and transfer learning from large ASR and MT models (Bérard et al., 2018; Wang et al., 2020). However it faces key limitations such as the scarcity of parallel speech-to-translation data. These models simultaneously learn acoustic processing, language understanding, and translation, leading to slower convergence and reduced performance, especially in low-resource settings. Additionally, it also struggle with varied pronunciations and code-switching due to the lack of intermediate transcripts which could be normalized or transliterated. So continuing the work towards low-resource language pairs, Inaguma et al. (2020) propose a multilingual end-to-end speech translation framework utilizing shared encoder and decoder components. This architecture leverages parameter sharing and cross-lingual transfer learning, leading to significant improvements in translation quality. Salesky et al. (2021) focus on speech translation in low-resource settings and explored strategies such as multilingual finetuning and data augmentation. Their findings indicate that these methods can effectively compensate for limited training data and improve translation accuracy across modalities.

2 Data

In the IWSLT 2025 Indic Speech Translation Shared Task (Abdulmumin et al., 2025), multilingual speech translation dataset spanning six distinct language pairs involving English and three indic languages are released. Table 1 shows the statistics of the audio corpus that is aimed to support both training and evaluation of speech translation systems in low-resource settings. For the training set, each language pair offers a substantial volume of audio data. The En-Bn (English–Bengali), En-Hi (English–Hindi), and En-Ta (English–Tamil) pairs have 205,000 audio samples, amounting to approximately 681 hours. The Hi-En (Hindi–English) direction includes the largest dataset, comprising 248,872 audio segments with a total duration of approximately 654 hours. The Ta-En (Tamil–English) pair includes 211,303 training audios, summing up to 478 hours, while the Bn-En (Bengali–English) dataset is slightly smaller in size with 64,868 samples and 158 hours of speech data. For validating the models, the devset is also provided for each language pair which is approximately 6% in case of En-Indic pairs, while it is below 1% in case of Indic-En pairs. For this shared task, no other synthetic data has been used by performing Machine Translation on source language ASR output or synthesizing speech from the target language text.

3 Methodology

3.1 Cascaded S2T

For this experiment, we finetune CLSRIL-23[1] [2] (Gupta et al., 2022), a self-supervised model that is designed to leverage cross-lingual speech representations from raw audio dataset. The pre-training dataset consists of approximately 10,000 hours of audio data across 23 Indic languages. The architecture of CLSRIL-23 is based on Wav2Vec 2.0 (Baevski et al., 2020b), where the base version has 12 transformer blocks with 768 dimensional feaure vector size and 12 attention heads. It comprises of multi-layer convolutional feature encoder that processes raw audio inputs into latent speech representations. These representations are then fed into a Transformer network, which captures con-

[1]https://github.com/Open-Speech-EkStep/vakyansh-models

[2]https://github.com/Open-Speech-EkStep/vakyansh-wav2vec2-experimentation

textual information over the entire sequence. The model is trained on a contrastive loss function to distinguish true quantized latent representations from distractors, facilitating the learning of robust speech representations.

ASR Fine-Tuning: For the IWSLT Indic track task, we fine-tune CLSRIL-23 using the dataset provided by the organizers, which included parallel speech and text data for the target Indic languages. The fine-tuning process involves the following steps:

- **Data Preparation**: In this step, we align and preprocess the provided speech and text pairs to ensure the compatibility with the input requirements of our model.
- **Model Finetuning**: We initialize the pre-trained CLSRIL-23 model and add a fully connected layer on top of the transformer block to perform character-level classification. During fine-tuning, we keep the weights of the feature encoder frozen, allowing only the transformer and classification head to be updated. For fine-tuning the model, the learning rate is kept at $3e^{-5}$ with a batch size of 32, and we train it for 50 epochs to optimize performance on the task.
- **Evaluation**: Using the provided validation set, the effectiveness of model are evaluated in terms of Word Error Rate (WER) and Character Error Rate (CER).

By fine-tuning on the provided dataset, the model refine its previously learned features to better capture the unique patterns and properties present in the data.

Machine Translation

For the text translation component of the speech translation pipeline, we fine-tune the IndicTrans2[3] (Gala et al., 2023), a multilingual NMT model. It is capable of translating from English to 20 Indic languages and vice-versa. The model has 1.1 billion parameters pre-trained on a mixture of parallel corpora, combining general-domain, news, and publicly available data sources, making it suitable for fine-tuning it for this shared task on Indic low resource languages. The process of fine-tuning is as the following:

- **Data Preparation**: We perform script normalization, Unicode standardization, whitespace cleanup, and special character filtering to reduce the noise present in the dataset. To enable multilingual translation to the target language, we prepend language-specific prefix tokens to the source sentences, following the original IndicTrans2 multilingual setup. Finally, we tokenize the processed data using the SentencePiece tokenizer (Kudo and Richardson, 2018) released with IndicTrans2, ensuring compatibility with its subword vocabulary and avoiding out-of-vocabulary (OOV) issues during training and inference.
- **Model Fine-tuning**: We use a deep transformer model designed to handle the complexity of multilingual neural machine translation. This architecture comprises of 18 encoder and 18 decoder layers, each with a hidden dimensionality of 1024 and Feed-Forward Network (FFN) layers of size 8192. The model is fine-tuned using a learning rate of $3e^{-5}$ and AdamW (Loshchilov and Hutter, 2017) optimizer, with a weight decay of 0.01 to prevent overfitting. We enable mixed precision training to make efficient use of GPU memory and accelerate computation. For evaluation, we monitor performance on the validation set using the SacreBLEU (Post, 2018) metric, which provide a reliable estimate of translation quality across different language pairs.

3.2 End-to-End S2T

For our end-to-end speech translation experiments, we use a small-scale transformer-based encoder-decoder model available in the Fairseq Speech-to-Text framework[4] (Ott et al., 2019; Wang et al., 2020). This model utilizes an encoder embedding dimension of 256 and a feed-forward network with a dimension of 2048. Both the encoder and decoder use 4 attention heads and a dropout rate of 0.1 for regularization. The model inherits from the base architecture, which by default configures 6 layers each for the encoder and decoder. This configuration is effective from the starting point for training and evaluating end-to-end speech translation systems, especially in low-resource or computationally constrained settings.

- **Data Preparation**: We use the provided script

[3] https://github.com/AI4Bharat/IndicTrans2/

[4] https://github.com/facebookresearch/fairseq/tree/main/examples/speech_to_text

Cascaded-Unconstrained-monolingual			E2E-Constrained-monolingual		
Lang-pair	**ChrF++**	**BLEU**	**Lang-pair**	**ChrF++**	**BLEU**
En-Hi	64.1749	44.093	En-hi	54.4822	34.6119
En-Bn	65.2117	36.9565	En-bn	58.2243	31.5668
En-Ta	66.1503	29.341	En-ta	56.0757	21.3467
Hi-En	67.0583	41.0425	Hi-En	42.9691	15.4153
Bn-En	44.8855	14.7731	Bn-En	14.3009	0.459
Ta-En	41.1644	15.7004	Ta-En	26.2496	5.0473

Table 2: Comparison of translation performance between Cascaded-Unconstrained and End-to-End Constrained systems using ChrF++ and BLEU scores.

in the framework to prepare the speech dataset for training. It processes the audio and transcription files organized in each language pair's respective directory and splits into train and validation sets. For each audio segment, it extracts the log Mel filterbank features and generates corresponding manifest files (stored in a tab separated format) with the metadata. The script also builds a vocabulary file using SentencePiece and a config file needed for the Fairseq training.

- **Model Training**: For training the speech translation model on the dataset, we use the speech to text transformer architecture available in the Fairseq library. We set the maximum number of tokens per batch to 40000 to efficiently utilize GPU memory and the training is capped at 200 epochs. To improve generalization, we apply label smoothing with a value of 0.1 and use a dropout rate of 0.3 to regularize the model. The optimizer is Adam (Kingma and Ba, 2014), with a learning rate of $2e^{-3}$, and gradient clipping is set at 10.0 to prevent exploding gradients. For inferencing, we take the average of the last 10 checkpoints as Vaswani et al. (2017) proved that the averaged checkpoint performs better than the single best checkpoint. SacreBLEU is used for scoring the performance of the models.

4 Experimental Results

For the IWSLT 2025 Indic Speech Translation Shared Task (Abdulmumin et al., 2025), we participate in two different settings: a) Unconstrained Cascaded and b) Constrained End-to-End speech-translation track. The experiments are not multilingual, but individual language-pairs are trained separately. We conduct experiments on all six language pairs: English to Hindi (en-hi), Bengali (en-bn), Tamil (en-ta), and the reverse directions hi-en, bn-en, ta-en respectively. The results of our experiments are presented in Table 2, showing ChrF++ (Popović, 2017) and BLEU (Papineni et al., 2002) scores for each language pair across both the cascaded and E2E settings.

English-to-Indic (en-hi, en-bn, en-ta): The cascaded system consistently outperform the E2E system across all the language pairs. For example, en-hi achieves a BLEU of 44.09 and ChrF++ of 64.17 in the cascaded setup, compared to 34.61 BLEU and 54.48 ChrF++ in the E2E setup. Similarly, the en-bn model scores 36.95 BLEU (ChrF++: 65.21) in the cascaded mode versus 31.56 BLEU (ChrF++: 58.22) in E2E. The trend continues with en-ta, where the BLEU drops from 29.34 (ChrF++: 66.15) in cascaded to 21.34 (ChrF++: 56.07) in the E2E.

These results indicate that the cascaded approach remains advantageous for English-to-Indic translation, likely due to the mature ASR performance on English audio and the robustness of the IndicTrans2 NMT system trained on diverse high-quality parallel corpora. The modular nature of the pipeline allows each component to be fine-tuned independently, maximizing their respective capabilities.

Indic-to-English (hi-en, bn-en, ta-en): The performance gap between cascaded and E2E systems is more pronounced in the Indic-to-English direction. For hi-en, the cascaded system achieves 41.04 BLEU and 67.05 ChrF++, compared to 15.41 BLEU and 42.96 ChrF++ in the E2E track. For bn-en, the E2E model performs poorly, with only 0.459 BLEU and 14.30 ChrF++, while the cascaded model reaches 14.77 BLEU and 44.88 ChrF++. Preliminary analysis suggests that smaller amount of training data and excessive use of code-mixed language in the test set are the reason for low score for the Bengali-English pair. Similarly, the BLEU score of ta-en model drops from 15.70 in the cascaded setup to 5.04 in the E2E setup.

The sharp decline in the E2E performance for Indic-to-English suggests that ASR on Indic audio remains a major challenge, especially in the constrained setup where access to external data or pre-trained language models is restricted. The E2E system must learn both transcription and translation jointly, which becomes challenging in low-resource settings or in speech settings consisting of code-mixed, noisy, or accented content. This highlights the difficulty of training E2E models for the Indic-origin speech, where the diversity in speech patterns and lack of rich supervised training data severely affect generalization.

5 Conclusion

Our experiments show that cascaded models still hold a strong edge in terms of accuracy and robustness, particularly in Indic to En settings while end-to-end speech translation models can be an alternative due to their simplicity and integration. With further work of using transfer learning from larger models, multilingual pre-training and data augmentation techniques such as use of synthetic data, E2E models can be at par with the cascaded models by overcoming low-resource bottlenecks in Indic languages.

References

Idris Abdulmumin, Victor Agostinelli, Tanel Alumäe, Antonios Anastasopoulos, Ashwin, Luisa Bentivogli, Ondřej Bojar, Claudia Borg, Fethi Bougares, Roldano Cattoni, Mauro Cettolo, Lizhong Chen, William Chen, Raj Dabre, Yannick Estève, Marcello Federico, Marco Gaido, Dávid Javorský, Marek Kasztelnik, and 30 others. 2025. Findings of the iwslt 2025 evaluation campaign. In *Proceedings of the 22nd International Conference on Spoken Language Translation (IWSLT 2025)*, Vienna, Austia (in-person and online). Association for Computational Linguistics. To appear.

Karunesh Arora, Sunita Arora, and Mukund Roy. 2013. Speech to speech translation: a communication boon. *CSI Transactions on ICT*, 1.

Alexei Baevski, Henry Zhou, Abdelrahman Mohamed, and Michael Auli. 2020a. wav2vec 2.0: A framework for self-supervised learning of speech representations. *Preprint*, arXiv:2006.11477.

Alexei Baevski, Yuhao Zhou, Abdelrahman Mohamed, and Michael Auli. 2020b. wav2vec 2.0: A framework for self-supervised learning of speech representations. *Advances in neural information processing systems*, 33:12449–12460.

Dzmitry Bahdanau, Kyunghyun Cho, and Yoshua Bengio. 2016. Neural machine translation by jointly learning to align and translate. *Preprint*, arXiv:1409.0473.

Alexandre Bérard, Laurent Besacier, Ozan Caglayan, and Adrien Bardet. 2018. End-to-end automatic speech translation of audiobooks. In *ICASSP 2018 - IEEE International Conference on Acoustics, Speech and Signal Processing*, pages 6224–6228. IEEE.

Liang Dong, Shuang Xu, and Bo Xu. 2018. Speech-transformer: A no-recurrence sequence-to-sequence model for speech recognition. In *ICASSP 2018 - IEEE International Conference on Acoustics, Speech and Signal Processing*, pages 5884–5888. IEEE.

Jay Gala, Pranjal A Chitale, A K Raghavan, Varun Gumma, Sumanth Doddapaneni, Aswanth Kumar M, Janki Atul Nawale, Anupama Sujatha, Ratish Puduppully, Vivek Raghavan, Pratyush Kumar, Mitesh M Khapra, Raj Dabre, and Anoop Kunchukuttan. 2023. Indictrans2: Towards high-quality and accessible machine translation models for all 22 scheduled indian languages. *Transactions on Machine Learning Research*.

Anirudh Gupta, Harveen Singh Chadha, Priyanshi Shah, Neeraj Chhimwal, Ankur Dhuriya, Rishabh Gaur, and Vivek Raghavan. 2022. Clsril-23: Cross lingual speech representations for indic languages. *Preprint*, arXiv:2107.07402.

Hirofumi Inaguma, Shun Kiyono, Kevin Duh, and Shinji Watanabe. 2020. Multilingual end-to-end speech translation. In *Proceedings of the 58th Annual Meeting of the Association for Computational Linguistics*, pages 5911–5924.

Nal Kalchbrenner and Phil Blunsom. 2013. Recurrent continuous translation models. In *Proceedings of the 2013 Conference on Empirical Methods in Natural Language Processing*, pages 1700–1709, Seattle, Washington, USA. Association for Computational Linguistics.

Diederik P Kingma and Jimmy Ba. 2014. Adam: A method for stochastic optimization. *arXiv preprint arXiv:1412.6980*.

Taku Kudo and John Richardson. 2018. Sentencepiece: A simple and language independent subword tokenizer and detokenizer for neural text processing. *EMNLP 2018*, page 66.

Ilya Loshchilov and Frank Hutter. 2017. Decoupled weight decay regularization. *arXiv preprint arXiv:1711.05101*.

Shivam Mhaskar, Vineet Bhat, Akshay Batheja, Sourabh Deoghare, Paramveer Choudhary, and Pushpak Bhattacharyya. 2023. Vakta-setu: A speech-to-speech machine translation service in select indic languages. *arXiv preprint arXiv:2305.12518*.

Vandan Mujadia and Dipti Misra Sharma. 2023. Towards speech to speech machine translation focusing on indian languages. In *Proceedings of the 17th Conference of the European Chapter of the Association for Computational Linguistics: System Demonstrations*, pages 161–168.

Myle Ott, Sergey Edunov, Alexei Baevski, Angela Fan, Sam Gross, Nathan Ng, David Grangier, and Michael Auli. 2019. fairseq: A fast, extensible toolkit for sequence modeling. In *Proceedings of NAACL-HLT 2019: Demonstrations*.

Kishore Papineni, Salim Roukos, Todd Ward, and Wei-Jing Zhu. 2002. Bleu: a method for automatic evaluation of machine translation. In *Proceedings of the 40th annual meeting of the Association for Computational Linguistics*, pages 311–318.

Maja Popović. 2017. chrf++: words helping character n-grams. In *Proceedings of the second conference on machine translation*, pages 612–618.

Matt Post. 2018. A call for clarity in reporting BLEU scores. In *Proceedings of the Third Conference on Machine Translation: Research Papers*, pages 186–191, Brussels, Belgium. Association for Computational Linguistics.

Anusha Prakash, Arun Kumar A, Ashish Seth, Bhagyashree Mukherjee, Ishika Gupta, Jom Kuriakose, Jordan Fernandes, K. V. Vikram, Mano Ranjith Kumar M., Metilda Sagaya Mary, Mohammad Wajahat, Mohana N, Mudit Batra, Navina K, Nihal John George, Nithya Ravi, Pruthwik Mishra, Sudhanshu Srivastava, Vasista Sai Lodagala, and 8 others. 2023. Technology pipeline for large scale cross-lingual dubbing of lecture videos into multiple indian languages. In *INTERSPEECH*, pages 3683–3684.

Alec Radford, Jong Wook Kim, Tao Xu, Greg Brockman, Christine McLeavey, and Ilya Sutskever. 2022. Robust speech recognition via large-scale weak supervision. *Preprint*, arXiv:2212.04356.

Elizabeth Salesky, Ramon Sanabria, Alan W. Black, and Florian Metze. 2021. Exploring low-resource speech-to-text translation across modalities. In *Proceedings of the 2021 Conference of the North American Chapter of the Association for Computational Linguistics*, pages 1134–1145.

Matthias Sperber and Markus Paulik. 2020. Speech translation and the end-to-end promise: Taking stock of where we are. In *Proceedings of the 58th Annual Meeting of the Association for Computational Linguistics*, pages 7409–7421.

Ilya Sutskever, Oriol Vinyals, and Quoc V Le. 2014. Sequence to sequence learning with neural networks. *Advances in neural information processing systems*, 27.

Ashish Vaswani, Noam Shazeer, Niki Parmar, Jakob Uszkoreit, Llion Jones, Aidan N Gomez, Łukasz Kaiser, and Illia Polosukhin. 2017. Attention is all you need. *Advances in neural information processing systems*, 30.

Changhan Wang, Mattia Antonino Di Gangi, Roldano Cattoni, Luisa Bentivogli, Matteo Negri, and Marco Turchi. 2020. Fairseq s2t: Fast speech-to-text modeling with fairseq. In *Proceedings of the 1st Conference of the Asia-Pacific Chapter of the Association for Computational Linguistics and the 10th International Joint Conference on Natural Language Processing: System Demonstrations*, pages 33–39.

Ron J Weiss, Jan Chorowski, Navdeep Jaitly, Yonghui Wu, and Zhifeng Chen. 2017. Sequence-to-sequence models can directly translate foreign speech. *arXiv preprint arXiv:1703.08581*.

NAVER LABS Europe Submission to the Instruction-following Track

Beomseok Lee[1,2,3*] **Marcely Zanon Boito**[2,*] **Laurent Besacier**[2] **Ioan Calapodescu**[2]
[1] University of Trento [2] NAVER LABS Europe [3] Fondazione Bruno Kessler
contact: `marcely.zanon-boito@naverlabs.com`

Abstract

In this paper we describe NAVER LABS Europe submission to the instruction-following speech processing short track at IWSLT 2025. We participate in the constrained settings, developing systems that can simultaneously perform ASR, ST, and SQA tasks from English speech input into the following target languages: Chinese, Italian, and German. Our solution leverages two pretrained modules: (1) a speech-to-LLM embedding projector trained using representations from the `SeamlessM4T-v2-large` speech encoder; and (2) LoRA adapters trained on text data on top of `Llama-3.1-8B-Instruct`. These modules are jointly loaded and further instruction-tuned for 1K steps on multilingual and multimodal data to form our final system submitted for evaluation.

1 Introduction

Large language models (LLMs) have demonstrated remarkable success across various text-based natural language processing tasks (Achiam et al., 2023; Touvron et al., 2023; Jiang et al., 2024; Yang et al., 2024; Alves et al., 2024; Martins et al., 2024a), motivating research into extending them to other modalities. This has led to the development of multimodal LLMs capable of processing speech, audio, images and video (Team et al., 2023; Driess et al., 2023; Rubenstein et al., 2023; Liu et al., 2023; Tang et al., 2023; Défossez et al., 2024; Hu et al., 2024; Laurençon et al., 2024; Huang et al., 2024; Nguyen et al., 2025; Ambilduke et al., 2025).

This year *IWSLT Instruction-following Speech Processing Track* focuses on the leveraging of LLMs and speech foundation models (SFM) to build solutions capable to perform multilingual tasks from English speech input and textual multilingual instructions (Abdulmumin et al., 2025). NAVER LABS Europe (NLE) participates in the constrained setting of the *short track*, where the tasks proposed are automatic speech recognition (ASR), speech translation (ST) and multilingual spoken question answering (SQA). The target languages for ST and multilingual SQA are Chinese, Italian and German. The participants are allowed to use the speech backbone `SeamlessM4T-v2-large` (Barrault et al., 2023) and the text LLM `Llama-3.1-8B-Instruct` (Grattafiori et al., 2024) for both training and data generation.

Our submitted systems leverage all the available data from the constrained settings, together with data automatically obtained using both backbones. We train two types of systems in parallel: (1) speech-to-text ASR/ST/SQA projectors that project the averaged speech representation from the `SeamlessM4T-v2-large` encoder to the embedding space of a frozen `Llama-3.1-8B-Instruct`; (2) text-only LoRA adapters (Hu et al., 2022), plugged on top of the same frozen LLM. Once both systems are separately trained, we show that we can merge them, increasing overall speech performance, by fine-tuning for only 1K steps on multimodal multilingual data.

This system paper is organized as follows. Section 2 describes the preprocessing applied to the data used in this challenge. Sections 3 and 4 describe our training pipeline and experimental settings, respectively. Section 5 presents our experiments and discussion. Section 6 presents the submitted system. Section 7 concludes the paper.

2 Data

For training our models, we leverage the data from the constrained setting: CoVoST2 (Wang et al., 2020), EuroParlST (Iranzo-Sánchez et al., 2020) and SpokenSQuAD (Lee et al., 2018). With the agreement of the organizers, we also take advantage of the `SeamlessM4T-v2-large` to

* Equal contribution.

Proceedings of the 22nd International Conference on Spoken Language Translation (IWSLT 2025), pages 186–200
July 31 - August 1, 2025 ©2025 Association for Computational Linguistics

produce extra synthetic speech data (Seamless TTS) and multilingual text data (Seamless MT). `Llama-3.1-8B-Instruct` is used to rephrase SQA answers. ACL 60-60 (Salesky et al., 2023) is used for validation and evaluation only. We now present our data preprocessing (Section 2.1) and prompt format (Section 2.2).

2.1 Data Preprocessing

We produce both speech-to-text and text-to-text instructions to train our systems. For the aforementioned datasets, we produce the following splits, where * denotes synthetic splits obtained via `SeamlessM4T-v2-large` MT; † indicates splits generated with `SeamlessM4T-v2-large` TTS; and ‡ marks those derived through `Llama-3.1-8B-Instruct`-based rephrasing.

- **CoVoST2:**
  - **ASR** and **ST/MT** (en-de; en-zh)
- **EuroParlST:**
  - **ASR** and **ST/MT** (en-de; en-it)
- **SpokenSQuAD:**
  - **ASR**† and **MT** (en†-de*; en†-it*; en†-zh*)
  - **SQA/QA** (en†-en; en†-de*; en†-it*; en†-zh*)
  - ***fluent* SQA/QA** (en†-en‡; en†-de*,‡; en†-it*,‡; en†-zh*,‡)
- **ACL 60-60:**
  - **ASR** and **ST/MT** (en-de; en-it*; en-zh)

Below we detail dataset-specific preprocessing. Statistics are presented in Table 1.

CoVoST2 and EuroParlST CoVoST2 covers English to German and Simplified Chinese language directions. EuroParlST covers English to German and Italian. ASR splits for these datasets were built by merging the existing language splits and deduplicating the audio files. For both, language-specific ST and MT splits are created by aligning translations to English speech and reference transcriptions, respectively.

SpokenSQuAD The SpokenSQuAD dataset is organized into two jsons, train and test. Each split is organized in themes, each with several paragraphs. For each paragraph, TTS audio files are available, aligned at the sentence level.[1] For each sentence, questions (each with several answers) are available. We performed the following modifications to this dataset:

- **Duplicated answers:** we removed duplicated answers to the same question using exact string matching, as well as any questions that required more than one audio file to answer, since we are participating in the SHORT track.

- **Validation set:** we created a validation set by selecting the first 20 themes of the training set and removing them from training (3,102 entries).

- **New TTS audio:** we generate new TTS audio files for the training set using `SeamlessM4T-v2-large`. Resynthesizing the source audio for this dataset was necessary due to existing dataset misalignment, which we detail in Appendix Section A.1.

- **Multilingual SQA/QA:** we created multilingual SQA/QA sets by first translating questions and answers to target languages using `SeamlessM4T-v2-large`. We then use reference-free COMET[2] (Rei et al., 2022) to filter out all pairs of questions and answers that do not both score at least 0.85.

- **Invalid splits:** we created the *invalid* SQA sets by deliberately mismatching context and question themes, thereby creating unanswerable examples. The corresponding answers were labeled as "Not answerable" in four languages (English, Italian, German and Chinese), following the guideline answer provided by the task organizers. While we acknowledge that a small, unknown subset of these reassigned questions may still be answerable, we hypothesize that ensuring a thematic mismatch between the reference context and the question is the most effective strategy for minimizing this issue.

- ***Fluent* SQA/QA version:** we created an alternative SQA/QA training set using `Llama-3.1-8B-Instruct` to regenerate the dataset original answers as fluent sentences. The motivation behind this was the observation that, since the original answers are made of an exact extract of the reference audio/text,

[1]The format is themeID_paragraphID_sentenceID.

[2]`Unbabel/wmt22-cometkiwi-da`

Dataset	Task	Language	# Samples
CoVoST2	ASR	en	289,413
	ST/MT	en-de	289,413
		en-zh	289,413
EuroParlST	ASR	en	35,372
	ST/MT	en-de	32,628
		en-it	29,552
SpokenSQuAD	ASR	en	34,003
	MT	en-de	39,362
		en-it	55,030
		en-zh	25,078
	SQA/QA	en-en	34,003†
		en-de	6,574†
		en-it	16,767†
		en-zh	7,093†
	fluent SQA/QA	en-en	32,320
		en-de	4,169
		en-it	13,712
		en-zh	3,424

Table 1: Training sets statistics by task. For ST/MT sets, target side is duplicated. For SpokenSQuAD, † highlights that the source speech is used twice (valid and invalid questions, as described in Section 2.1).

the model had a difficult time answering some out-of-domain questions fluently.[3] More details are presented in Appendix Section A.2.

ACL 60-60 We use SeamlessM4T-v2-large to generate Italian translations, since the data shared only contained en-de and en-zh splits. We leverage the *dev* set for checkpoint selection during training. The *eval* set is used for testing.

2.2 Prompt Format

The goal of the short track of this challenge is to produce a model that is capable to 1) transcribe English speech; 2) translate English speech into Italian, German and Chinese; 3) Answer multilingual questions using English speech as input. In this setting, the language of the question must match the language of the answer.

To develop a model capable of smoothly switching between different tasks, we designed task prompts with a consistent structure: regardless of the task (ASR, ST, or SQA), the user turn begins by encapsulating the speech embeddings within textual tags. This is followed on a new line by a task-specific instruction formulated as a question, and finally, another line containing a common suffix. The list of templates used is available in Appendix Table 5.

[3] In the official IWSLT 2025 test set we observed examples as the following. Question: *"What are the names of the speakers?"* Our model's answer: *"yin and my colleague jiang"*. While the model answer is an exact and correct extraction from the audio, we were unsure about how this would be considered during evaluation.

3 Training Pipeline

Our training pipeline is illustrated in Figure 1. We first train a speech projector on speech tasks (A), and text LoRA weights on textual tasks (B). These modules are then reloaded and adapted together on both speech and textual tasks (C). In this section we describe the key components used and the data sampling strategy.

Foundation Models For speech, we leverage SeamlessM4T-v2-large model, extracting speech representations for all our audio data from its 24th speech encoder layer (i.e. the last layer). Prior to training, we average every 3 consecutive frame vectors, reducing significantly the sequence length. This simple trick allows us to train our models with larger batches, while maintaining good performance in speech tasks. All our models are built on top of a frozen Llama-3.1-8B-Instruct.

Speech Projector Architecture The speech projector consists of 4 Transformer encoder layers, each with 8 attention heads. The input dimension is set to 1,024, the feed-forward network dimension to 2,048, and the output dimension to 4,096 to align with the embedding size of Llama-3.1-8B-Instruct. A dropout rate of 0.1 is applied throughout, and the model employs pre-layer normalization.

LoRA Adapters LoRA adaptation (Hu et al., 2022) is applied to both the self-attention (Q/K values, output projection) and feed-forward modules, and across all LLM layers. We use $rank = 8, \alpha = 16$. We do not use dropout.

Data Sampling Strategy For training all our models, we define an epoch as X steps across the dataset, with $X = \frac{|\text{speech\_examples}|}{\text{batch\_size}}$. To construct the training data for each epoch, we sample batches by first applying the predefined task-level sampling ratios, followed by sampling based on the internal domain-level splits within each task. In the case of multimodal training (speech and text tasks mixed), we consider speech as our *main* modality, using it for defining epoch size and task ratio. Each time we sample a task and language split that has a textual equivalent (e.g., ST corresponds to MT; SQA to QA), we also sample a batch from the corresponding textual task. In practice, this means that every

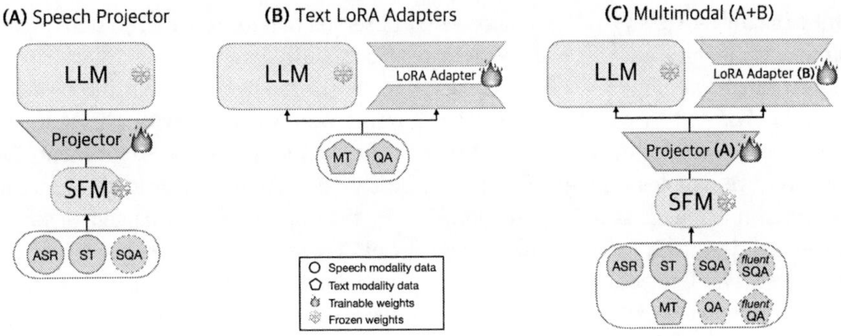

Figure 1: Our training pipeline. A speech projector (A) and text LoRA adapters (B) are trained in parallel using speech-to-text and text-to-text data, respectively. These modules are then integrated during a brief multimodal adaptation step (C).

time a batch from ST en-de split is sampled, a batch from MT en-de follows it. We hypothesize that interleaving similar speech and textual batches during training provides regularization benefits, with the text data serving as a stabilizing signal for learning (Pikabea et al., 2025).

4 Experimental Settings

Codebase We train our models using an internal fork of `torchtune` (torchtune maintainers and contributors, 2024), which allows us to process interleaved representations of text and high-dimensional vectors within the user turn during instruction tuning. The high-dimensional vectors pass through our speech projector, while the text prefix and suffix user prompts are processed by the LLM embedding layer. The obtained speech and text embeddings are both concatenated and fed into the first layer of the LLM which is trained on the masked input with standard cross-entropy loss. Different learning rate schedulers and optimizers are employed for the speech projector and the LoRA weights, allowing for more controlled and effective training of these distinct model components.

Inference Settings We perform inference using `torchtune`, with a batch size of 1 and greedy decoding. The maximum number of new tokens was limited to 300. Unless explicitly stated otherwise, this decoding strategy was consistently applied across all experimental settings. Additional discussion regarding multimodal inference is present in Appendix Section B.1.

Evaluation Metrics We evaluate our models on speech (ASR, ST, SQA) and text (MT, QA) tasks when relevant. For ASR, we score word error rate (WER) using HuggingFace evaluate library with default settings and MMS normalization (Pratap et al., 2024). For ST/MT we present two evaluation metrics: BLEU4 computed with sacrebleu library (Post, 2018)[4], and COMET (Rei et al., 2022).[5] For SQA/QA, we use LLM-as-a-judge evaluation scripts from the `bergen` library[6] (Rau et al., 2024). We use their "yes/no" quality assessment evaluation format including the English reference text, the multilingual questions and the generated answers. We report average accuracy across four LLMs: `EuroLLM-9B-Instruct` (Martins et al., 2024b), `Gemma3-12B-Instruct`, `Gemma3-27B-Instruct` (Team et al., 2025), and `Llama3.1-70B-Instruct`.

Baselines We compare our results with both backbones we use for training. We evaluate MT and QA using the reference transcripts and `Llama-3.1-8B-Instruct` in zero-shot settings, and we evaluate `SeamlessM4T-v2-large` in both ASR and ST.

5 Experiments

We now present our results for ASR, ST, and SQA. Section 5.1 introduces the models used in our experiments, followed by results and discussion in Section 5.2.

5.1 Our Models

In this section, we describe the models used in our experiments. Additional hyperparameter details are provided in Appendix C.

[4]The signature is "nrefs:1|case:mixed|eff:no|tok:**TOK**|smooth:exp|version:2.3.1", with $TOK = zh$ for Chinese, and $13a$ for the other languages.

[5]`Unbabel/wmt22-comet-da`

[6]`https://github.com/naver/bergen`

A.1 Speech Projector (ASR/ST) This version of our speech projector focuses on ASR and ST tasks, which do not require any complex reasoning capability of the LLM. For ASR, we sample CoVoST2 and EuroParlST with probabilities 0.8 and 0.2 respectively. For ST, we sample proportionally to the datasets size, and set language sampling probabilities for the pairs en-de, en-zh, and en-it to 0.3, 0.4, and 0.3 respectively. We trained for 4 epochs using AdamW with learning rate of $1e-4$, a constant learning rate scheduler, and gradient accumulation of 16. This model trains for 4.6 days in a single A100-80GB, and the best checkpoint is obtained after 18.2 hours.

A.2 Speech Projector (ASR/ST/SQA) This version of our projector extends A.1, including the SQA task. We use task sampling probabilities of 0.4, 0.35, and 0.25 for ASR, ST and SQA respectively. For the ASR and ST tasks, we use the same data ratios as defined above. For the SQA task, we leveraged both valid and invalid splits, with language-specific sampling probabilities for English, German, and Italian set to 0.4, 0.3 and 0.3, respectively. We do not train with Chinese SQA. This model trains for 4.75 days in a single A100-80GB, and the best checkpoint is obtained after 27.36 hours. The best checkpoints for both versions of the speech projector are selected using its average ST performance on the ACL 60-60 dev split across all language directions. Additional hyper-parameters for A.1 and A.2 are presented in Appendix Section C.1.

B. Text-only LoRA (MT/QA) We train LoRA weights on top of `Llama-3.1-8B-Instruct` using all text-to-text data from Table 1, and by using probability sampling of 0.6 and 0.4 for MT and QA respectively. We train for one epoch using AdamW with learning rate of $3e-4$, weight decay of 0.1, and 100 warm-up steps. Batch size of 10, and gradient accumulation of 8 is used. This model trains for approximately 4 days in a single A100-80GB. We select the last checkpoint.

C. Multimodal (A.x + B) We restart training by using both one of the speech projectors detailed above, and the text-only LoRA weights. We adapt our models using all speech (ASR/ST/SQA) and textual (MT/QA) tasks. We experiment with two versions of the SQA/QA training sets: the original short lowercase answers, and the *fluent* SQA/QA version we created. In preliminary experiments, we observed that as little as 100 steps were enough to successfully integrate the projector representation to the LoRA weights, but the best performance gains were obtained with 1K steps, which is the value we adopt for the experiments presented in the next section. We use learning rate of $1e-5$ for the speech projector, and of $3e-4$ for the LoRA weights. We use a batch size of 16, and gradient accumulation of 16. This model trains for approximately 6 hours in a single A100-80GB. We select the last checkpoint.

5.2 Results and Discussion

Table 2 presents our results for ASR, ST/MT and SQA/QA. ACL 60-60 *eval set* is used for ASR and ST/MT. SpokenSQuAD official test set is used for English SQA/QA. A smaller automatically obtained version is used for multilingual SQA/QA.[7] In the top portion, we present results for `Llama-3.1-8B-Instruct` before and after LoRA fine-tuning on text-only data. The middle portion of the table presents the speech backbone (`SeamlessM4T-v2-large`) and our projector-only models: for these rows, the only adaptation is the training of a speech projector that is plugged to a frozen `Llama-3.1-8B-Instruct`. Finally, the bottom portion of the table presents results from the merging of our text backbone (text-only LoRA) and the projectors of the middle portion via multimodal training. Additionally, ACL 60-60 ASR/ST dev results are presented in Appendix Table 7.

Performance of Text-only Models (topline) We observe that zero-shot `Llama-3.1-8B-Instruct` presents strong performance in both MT and QA tasks. By adding LoRA adapters on top of it, we increase translation performance in detriment of QA performance. We partially attribute this drop in QA performance to the SpokenSQuAD answer format, that is very short and might be judged as incomplete by the LLM evaluation. However, we also scored ROUGE1 (Lin, 2004) recall, which measures the intersection between the reference answer tokens and the produced one, finding that those scores were similar to the LLM-as-a-judge metric.[8] This result confirms that the QA performance is worse after text adaptation.

[7]Statistics for the multilingual test set are presented in Appendix Table 3.

[8]For en, de, it and zh splits ROUGE1 recall scores were respectively: 81.4%, 63.1%, 69.5%, 79.0%.

Model (fine-tuning tasks)	ASR (WER) en	ST/MT (BLEU) en-de	en-it	en-zh	ST/MT (COMET) en-de	en-it	en-zh	SQA/QA (LLM-AS-A-JUDGE) en-en	en-de	en-it	en-zh
Text-only Models (MT/QA)											
`Llama-3.1-8B-Instruct` (zero-shot)	-	23.88	35.51	45.89	0.779	0.806	0.809	**91.8%**	**92.0%**	**88.6%**	**84.6%**
B. Text-only LoRA (MT/QA)	-	**41.69**	**48.31**	**53.65**	**0.838**	**0.863**	**0.867**	83.4%	75.7%	71.4%	69.5%
Speech-only Models (ASR/ST/SQA)											
`SeamlessM4T-v2-large`	**17.6**	**27.95**	**43.54**	33.58	0.737	0.788	0.753	-	-	-	-
A.1 Speech Projector (ASR/ST)	19.8	27.58	36.30	40.62	**0.760**	0.796	**0.793**	-	-	-	-
A.2 Speech Projector (ASR/ST/SQA)	19.9	27.20	36.60	**40.72**	**0.760**	**0.797**	0.792	0.7%	0.5%	0.3%	0.6%
Multimodal Models (ASR/ST/SQA)											
A.1 + B (ASR/ST/MT/SQA/QA)	**17.7**	30.37	**41.22**	42.76	0.758	**0.791**	0.795	79.8%	71.9%	69.4%	65.5%
A.1 + B (ASR/ST/MT/*fluent*SQA/*fluent*QA)	18.6	**30.75**	40.48	42.51	0.755	0.788	0.789	90.3%	85.2%	82.9%	76.4%
A.2 + B (ASR/ST/MT/SQA/QA)	18.2	29.91	38.13	43.12	0.759	0.786	**0.799**	80.5%	74.9%	68.0%	66.7%
A.2 + B (ASR/ST/MT/*fluent*SQA/*fluent*QA)	18.7	29.68	32.28	**43.38**	**0.763**	0.782	0.798	**91.1%**	**87.3%**	**84.8%**	**78.0%**

Table 2: Results for the different models and backbones used in this work. ASR and ST scores are obtained using ACL 60-60 eval set, while SQA/QA scores are obtained using SpokenSQuAD test set.

Speech Projectors We observe that both A.1 and A.2 are equally capable of performing ASR and ST, which is consistent with the fact that both are trained on the same data. However, we observe that A.2, the model that trains with SQA data, is unable to produce SQA output. We believe this is a limitation of the projector approach: we train a model capable of biasing the output of the LLM, which works well for content tasks such as ASR and ST. For a reasoning task, further adaptation might be required in order to force the model to comply to the instruction. Additional results for CoVoST2 and EuroParlST are presented in Appendix Table 6, and they confirm that both models are very similar in ST performance.

Multimodal Training We observe that our efficient multimodal training is beneficial, consistently increasing scores for ASR and ST. Our multimodal models outperform the speech projector models by 1-2 WER points in the ASR task. For ST task, in BLEU scores, the multimodal models always outperform speech projector models while in COMET there are some mixed results, with some models presenting slight deterioration for some language pairs. Finally, in the SQA task, while the speech projector model A.2 failed to learn the task effectively, our multimodal models achieved strong results, outperforming the text topline (B) performance across all language settings, and reaching scores that are close to the `Llama-3.1-8B-Instruct` topline, despite working from the speech signal.

ASR Performance We observe that our models are competitive with `SeamlessM4T-v2-large`, scoring slightly worse than the baseline for some configurations. Overall, for ACL 60-60 we observe quite elevated WER scores, compared to the ones we obtained for the training ASR datasets (see Appendix Table 6). We believe this is partially due to the nature of the dataset. We manually inspected some of the data, observing that some of the audio files contain *leftover fragments* from previous sentences. Moreover, looking at the transcriptions, we observed that these faithfully reproduced the audio, without applying any normalization or removing disfluencies (e.g. repeated and filler words were kept). We find that disfluent transcriptions are hardly produced by LLM-based models or `SeamlessM4T-v2-large`, that both tend to translate the content into a clean format. Therefore, we believe the WER scores presented in our results table are not representative of the models real ASR capabilities.

German MT/ST Performance Across all experiments, we observed that our models consistently performed poorly on German, the language for which we had the largest amount of training data. This could be attributed to the LLM's inherent limitations in handling German, as reflected by its relatively lower performance in zero-shot settings (`Llama-3.1-8B-Instruct`) for the en-de pair for both BLEU and COMET, compared to en-it and en-zh. Nonetheless, training the model on multilingual speech-only data for the ST task led to an improvement of 3–4 BLEU points. Incorporating multimodal data (i.e., both ST and MT) yielded an additional gain of 2–3 BLEU points, further enhancing performance. For COMET, speech-only and multimodal training does not improve COMET scores over the text topline.

Overall ST Performance We observe that the speech projectors (A.1 and A.2) outperform the backbone `SeamlessM4T-v2-large` for en-zh using BLEU, and in all languages using COMET. Then, multimodal training further increases the BLEU scores, but in some cases, this training slightly hurts the COMET scores. Since this difference in COMET is very small (en-de 0.005; en-it 0.008; en-zh 0.004), and since the BLEU scores increase, we attribute this to some formatting bias that could be happening during adaptation. The Appendix Section C.2 discusses the matter further.

SQA performance Overall, we observe that by replacing SQA by *fluent* SQA, we drastically increased our SQA/QA scores. However, results for ASR slightly deteriorate. We hypothesize that this is due to the old SQA task being closer to the ASR task. For the original SQA, the answer is always a direct transcript of a portion of the input text, which as a task has a better synergy with ASR. In intermediate experiments, we observed that adding the original SQA data to the multimodal training was always beneficial for the ASR performance of the model.

Final Discussion Overall our results show that it is possible to train text (B) and speech adaptation (A) in parallel, and then to align both via joint instruction tuning (C). By separating the pre-training of both components, we are able to focus hyper-parameter search at the merging stage, using two components that are already competent in their respective modalities. Despite improvements in scores over speech-only models, our best models do not beat the topline working from text for ST, but they do outperform `SeamlessM4T-v2-large` across all language pairs and metrics. Moreover, for SQA, we highlight that the obtained scores are in some cases very close (en-en, en-it) to the text topline, despite using speech as input context.

6 Submitted Model

Table 2 presented the results for our multimodal models. Due to the reasons highlighted in Section 2.1, we only consider two models for submission: the ones which were trained with *fluent* SQA. This is because we believe that these models will suffer the least from domain shift, since they are capable of producing full fluent sentences for SQA.

We observe that both models (A.1 and A.2-based) seem to be equally capable of ASR (18.6 and 18.7). We evaluated language confusion for these two splits, finding that the output produced was English in 98% and 98.5% of the cases respectively. These models differ more in terms of ST performance: they obtained averages of 37.9 and 35.1 BLEU score points respectively. Finally, these models present the following average accuracy for SQA: 83.7% and 85.3%. In summary, while the A.1-based model seem much more capable in ST, the A.2-based model has a very slight edge in ASR and SQA.

Therefore, we decided to select the A.1-based model as our primary submission model. For producing the decoding of the test set, we transform the instructions into our own prompt format, and submit the output of the same model, with the same decoding settings for all splits: greedy decoding using 150 as maximum number of tokens. A brief post-submission discussion is provided in Appendix Section C.2.1.

7 Conclusion

In this paper, we presented NLE's submission to the instruction-following speech processing short track at IWSLT 2025, constrained setting. We developed multimodal models that simultaneously performed ASR, ST, and SQA tasks from English speech input into Chinese, German and Italian. Our approach is simple yet effective: we decoupled training, training a speech projector on speech-to-text tasks, and LoRA adapters on text-to-text tasks. Then, both modules are loaded and the resulting multimodal model was instruction-tuned for a few steps on multilingual and multimodal data to produce the final system submitted for evaluation.

Acknowledgments

We thank our NLE colleagues Vassilina Nikoulina, for the implementation of the LLM-as-judge scripts using `bergen`, and Christian Wolf, for kindly verifying some of our German ST/SQA outputs. This work was partially funded by the European Horizon 2022 project UTTER (Unified Transcription and Translation for Extended Reality), under grant agreement No 101070631.

References

Idris Abdulmumin, Victor Agostinelli, Tanel Alumäe, Antonios Anastasopoulos, Ashwin, Luisa Bentivogli, Ondřej Bojar, Claudia Borg, Fethi Bougares, Roldano Cattoni, Mauro Cettolo, Lizhong Chen, William

Chen, Raj Dabre, Yannick Estève, Marcello Federico, Marco Gaido, Dávid Javorský, Marek Kasztelnik, and 30 others. 2025. Findings of the iwslt 2025 evaluation campaign. In *Proceedings of the 22nd International Conference on Spoken Language Translation (IWSLT 2025)*, Vienna, Austria (in-person and online). Association for Computational Linguistics. To appear.

Josh Achiam, Steven Adler, Sandhini Agarwal, Lama Ahmad, Ilge Akkaya, Florencia Leoni Aleman, Diogo Almeida, Janko Altenschmidt, Sam Altman, Shyamal Anadkat, and 1 others. 2023. Gpt-4 technical report. *arXiv preprint arXiv:2303.08774*.

Duarte Miguel Alves, José Pombal, Nuno M Guerreiro, Pedro Henrique Martins, João Alves, Amin Farajian, Ben Peters, Ricardo Rei, Patrick Fernandes, Sweta Agrawal, Pierre Colombo, José G. C. de Souza, and Andre Martins. 2024. Tower: An open multilingual large language model for translation-related tasks. In *First Conference on Language Modeling*.

Kshitij Ambilduke, Ben Peters, Sonal Sannigrahi, Anil Keshwani, Tsz Kin Lam, Bruno Martins, Marcely Zanon Boito, and André FT Martins. 2025. From tower to spire: Adding the speech modality to a text-only llm. *arXiv preprint arXiv:2503.10620*.

Loïc Barrault, Yu-An Chung, Mariano Cora Meglioli, David Dale, Ning Dong, Paul-Ambroise Duquenne, Hady Elsahar, Hongyu Gong, Kevin Heffernan, John Hoffman, and 1 others. 2023. Seamlessm4t: Massively multilingual & multimodal machine translation. *arXiv preprint arXiv:2308.11596*.

Alexandre Défossez, Laurent Mazaré, Manu Orsini, Amélie Royer, Patrick Pérez, Hervé Jégou, Edouard Grave, and Neil Zeghidour. 2024. Moshi: a speech-text foundation model for real-time dialogue. *arXiv preprint arXiv:2410.00037*.

Danny Driess, Fei Xia, Mehdi SM Sajjadi, Corey Lynch, Aakanksha Chowdhery, Brian Ichter, Ayzaan Wahid, Jonathan Tompson, Quan Vuong, Tianhe Yu, and 1 others. 2023. Palm-e: An embodied multimodal language model. *arXiv preprint arXiv:2303.03378*.

Aaron Grattafiori, Abhimanyu Dubey, Abhinav Jauhri, Abhinav Pandey, Abhishek Kadian, Ahmad Al-Dahle, Aiesha Letman, Akhil Mathur, Alan Schelten, Alex Vaughan, and 1 others. 2024. The llama 3 herd of models. *arXiv preprint arXiv:2407.21783*.

Edward J Hu, Yelong Shen, Phillip Wallis, Zeyuan Allen-Zhu, Yuanzhi Li, Shean Wang, Lu Wang, and Weizhu Chen. 2022. LoRA: Low-rank adaptation of large language models. In *International Conference on Learning Representations*.

Shujie Hu, Long Zhou, Shujie Liu, Sanyuan Chen, Lingwei Meng, Hongkun Hao, Jing Pan, Xunying Liu, Jinyu Li, Sunit Sivasankaran, and 1 others. 2024. Wavllm: Towards robust and adaptive speech large language model. *arXiv preprint arXiv:2404.00656*.

Rongjie Huang, Mingze Li, Dongchao Yang, Jiatong Shi, Xuankai Chang, Zhenhui Ye, Yuning Wu, Zhiqing Hong, Jiawei Huang, Jinglin Liu, and 1 others. 2024. Audiogpt: Understanding and generating speech, music, sound, and talking head. In *Proceedings of the AAAI Conference on Artificial Intelligence*, volume 38, pages 23802–23804.

J. Iranzo-Sánchez, J. A. Silvestre-Cerdà, J. Jorge, N. Roselló, A. Giménez, A. Sanchis, J. Civera, and A. Juan. 2020. Europarl-st: A multilingual corpus for speech translation of parliamentary debates. In *ICASSP 2020 - 2020 IEEE International Conference on Acoustics, Speech and Signal Processing (ICASSP)*, pages 8229–8233.

Albert Q Jiang, Alexandre Sablayrolles, Antoine Roux, Arthur Mensch, Blanche Savary, Chris Bamford, Devendra Singh Chaplot, Diego de las Casas, Emma Bou Hanna, Florian Bressand, and 1 others. 2024. Mixtral of experts. *arXiv preprint arXiv:2401.04088*.

Hugo Laurençon, Léo Tronchon, Matthieu Cord, and Victor Sanh. 2024. What matters when building vision-language models? *arXiv preprint*. ArXiv:2405.02246.

Chia-Hsuan Lee, Szu-Lin Wu, Chi-Liang Liu, and Hung-yi Lee. 2018. Spoken squad: A study of mitigating the impact of speech recognition errors on listening comprehension. *Proc. Interspeech 2018*, pages 3459–3463.

Chin-Yew Lin. 2004. ROUGE: A package for automatic evaluation of summaries. In *Text Summarization Branches Out*, pages 74–81, Barcelona, Spain. Association for Computational Linguistics.

Haotian Liu, Chunyuan Li, Qingyang Wu, and Yong Jae Lee. 2023. Visual Instruction Tuning (LLaVA). *arXiv preprint*. ArXiv:2304.08485 [cs].

Pedro Henrique Martins, Patrick Fernandes, João Alves, Nuno M Guerreiro, Ricardo Rei, Duarte M Alves, José Pombal, Amin Farajian, Manuel Faysse, Mateusz Klimaszewski, and 1 others. 2024a. Eurollm: Multilingual language models for europe. *arXiv preprint arXiv:2409.16235*.

Pedro Henrique Martins, Patrick Fernandes, João Alves, Nuno M. Guerreiro, Ricardo Rei, Duarte M. Alves, José Pombal, Amin Farajian, Manuel Faysse, Mateusz Klimaszewski, Pierre Colombo, Barry Haddow, José G. C. de Souza, Alexandra Birch, and André F. T. Martins. 2024b. Eurollm: Multilingual language models for europe. *Preprint*, arXiv:2409.16235.

Tu Anh Nguyen, Benjamin Muller, Bokai Yu, Marta R Costa-Jussa, Maha Elbayad, Sravya Popuri, Christophe Ropers, Paul-Ambroise Duquenne, Robin Algayres, Ruslan Mavlyutov, and 1 others. 2025. Spirit-lm: Interleaved spoken and written language model. *Transactions of the Association for Computational Linguistics*, 13:30–52.

Iñigo Pikabea, Iñaki Lacunza, Oriol Pareras, Carlos Escolano, Aitor Gonzalez-Agirre, Javier Hernando, and Marta Villegas. 2025. Breaking language barriers in visual language models via multilingual textual regularization. *arXiv preprint arXiv:2503.22577*.

Matt Post. 2018. A call for clarity in reporting BLEU scores. In *Proceedings of the Third Conference on Machine Translation: Research Papers*, pages 186–191, Belgium, Brussels. Association for Computational Linguistics.

Vineel Pratap, Andros Tjandra, Bowen Shi, Paden Tomasello, Arun Babu, Sayani Kundu, Ali Elkahky, Zhaoheng Ni, Apoorv Vyas, Maryam Fazel-Zarandi, and 1 others. 2024. Scaling speech technology to 1,000+ languages. *Journal of Machine Learning Research*, 25(97):1–52.

David Rau, Hervé Déjean, Nadezhda Chirkova, Thibault Formal, Shuai Wang, Stéphane Clinchant, and Vassilina Nikoulina. 2024. BERGEN: A benchmarking library for retrieval-augmented generation. In *Findings of the Association for Computational Linguistics: EMNLP 2024*, pages 7640–7663, Miami, Florida, USA. Association for Computational Linguistics.

Ricardo Rei, José G. C. de Souza, Duarte Alves, Chrysoula Zerva, Ana C Farinha, Taisiya Glushkova, Alon Lavie, Luisa Coheur, and André F. T. Martins. 2022. COMET-22: Unbabel-IST 2022 submission for the metrics shared task. In *Proceedings of the Seventh Conference on Machine Translation (WMT)*, pages 578–585, Abu Dhabi, United Arab Emirates (Hybrid). Association for Computational Linguistics.

Paul K Rubenstein, Chulayuth Asawaroengchai, Duc Dung Nguyen, Ankur Bapna, Zalán Borsos, Félix de Chaumont Quitry, Peter Chen, Dalia El Badawy, Wei Han, Eugene Kharitonov, and 1 others. 2023. Audiopalm: A large language model that can speak and listen. *arXiv preprint arXiv:2306.12925*.

Elizabeth Salesky, Kareem Darwish, Mohamed Al-Badrashiny, Mona Diab, and Jan Niehues. 2023. Evaluating multilingual speech translation under realistic conditions with resegmentation and terminology. In *Proceedings of the 20th International Conference on Spoken Language Translation (IWSLT 2023)*, pages 62–78, Toronto, Canada (in-person and online). Association for Computational Linguistics.

Changli Tang, Wenyi Yu, Guangzhi Sun, Xianzhao Chen, Tian Tan, Wei Li, Lu Lu, Zejun Ma, and Chao Zhang. 2023. Salmonn: Towards generic hearing abilities for large language models. *arXiv preprint arXiv:2310.13289*.

Gemini Team, Rohan Anil, Sebastian Borgeaud, Jean-Baptiste Alayrac, Jiahui Yu, Radu Soricut, Johan Schalkwyk, Andrew M Dai, Anja Hauth, Katie Millican, and 1 others. 2023. Gemini: a family of highly capable multimodal models. *arXiv preprint arXiv:2312.11805*.

Gemma Team, Aishwarya Kamath, Johan Ferret, Shreya Pathak, Nino Vieillard, Ramona Merhej, Sarah Perrin, Tatiana Matejovicova, Alexandre Ramé, Morgane Rivière, Louis Rouillard, Thomas Mesnard, Geoffrey Cideron, Jean bastien Grill, Sabela Ramos, Edouard Yvinec, Michelle Casbon, Etienne Pot, Ivo Penchev, and 197 others. 2025. Gemma 3 technical report. *Preprint*, arXiv:2503.19786.

torchtune maintainers and contributors. 2024. torchtune: Pytorch's finetuning library.

Hugo Touvron, Louis Martin, Kevin Stone, Peter Albert, Amjad Almahairi, Yasmine Babaei, Nikolay Bashlykov, Soumya Batra, Prajjwal Bhargava, Shruti Bhosale, Dan Bikel, Lukas Blecher, Cristian Canton Ferrer, Moya Chen, Guillem Cucurull, David Esiobu, Jude Fernandes, Jeremy Fu, Wenyin Fu, and 49 others. 2023. Llama 2: Open foundation and fine-tuned chat models. *Preprint*, arXiv:2307.09288.

Changhan Wang, Anne Wu, and Juan Pino. 2020. Covost 2: A massively multilingual speech-to-text translation corpus. *Preprint*, arXiv:2007.10310.

An Yang, Baosong Yang, Beichen Zhang, Binyuan Hui, Bo Zheng, Bowen Yu, Chengyuan Li, Dayiheng Liu, Fei Huang, Haoran Wei, and 1 others. 2024. Qwen2. 5 technical report. *arXiv preprint arXiv:2412.15115*.

	en	de	it	zh
# lines	8,026	3,272	783	627

Table 3: Statistics for the SpokenSQuAD SQA/QA test sets. The multilingual version is obtained via `SeamlessM4T-v2-large` translation of questions and answers, with posterior quality filtering based on COMET scores.

A Data Preprocessing and Prompts

A.1 SpokenSQuAD TTS data

In this section we explain the misalignment we found in the SpokenSQuAD train split, as well as our procedure for creating the new TTS split.

Train Split Misalignment During the preprocessing of the train split of SpokenSQuAD, we witnessed cases of misalignment: for some given paragraphs, the corresponding audios were shifted by a factor varying between 1 and 3. For instance, the first audio in a given paragraph was incorrectly named as "1", instead of "0", shifting all the paragraph's alignment. We listened to all cases we were able to flag, manually correcting them. However, we believe this hinted to a deeper alignment issue, as the obtained training set seemed to be difficult to learn. We observed that models trained with this training set included were unable to generalize to SpokenSQuAD's validation and test sets, always producing random Wikipedia sentences when receiving the SpokenSQuAD's TTS voice as input.

New TTS Source Audio Generation We use `SeamlessM4T-v2-large` to produce new source audio for the SpokenSQuAD training set (34,003 sentences). For each entry in this set, we re-synthesize its SQuAD reference text by randomly sampling one of the 200 speakers present in `SeamlessM4T`. This results in a more diverse training set, since the original TTS used a single female voice for all sentences. We also generated extra speech data using all different questions present in this training set, producing a second ASR set containing speech for 28,000 questions.

A.2 SpokenSQuAD Answers Regeneration

SpokenSQuAD answers are direct extracts from the reference text, formatted as lowercase text without punctuation. We discovered this presented a limitation when training our models on SQA. The trained models over-fitted to that format, solving SQA as a transcription task of the relevant portion of the source audio. While conceptually correct, this approach can result in generalization issues if more than one extract is required to answer the question, as the model never observed such a setting during training, and it will thus have the tendency to transcribe everything between the two points of interest.

We use `Llama-3.1-8B-Instruct` to regenerate all answers in our multilingual training set. The prompt used for regeneration is presented in Table 4. After regeneration, we remove answers generated in the wrong language using an automatic language identification tool. Statistics are presented in Table 1.

A.3 Data Statistics

Table 3 presents the statistics for the multilingual test set of SpokenSQuAD.

A.4 Our Prompts

Table 5 presents our prompt format. We designed our prompts to be very similar, independently of the target task. The language of the question defines the answer's target language.

B Additional Results

CoVoST2 and EuroParlST Results Table 6 presents results for relevant models on the in-domain test sets from CoVoST2 and EuroParlST. We observe that the multimodal adaptation improves the speech projectors' ASR and BLEU scores, while slightly decreasing COMET scores.

ACL 60-60 Dev Results Table 7 presents ACL 60-60 dev split scores for some of the models presented in the main results table (Table 2).

SQA/QA BERT Scores Table 8 presents BERT scores for the multimodal models presented in the main results table (Table 2), computed after the evaluation period and using the same settings from Abdulmumin et al. (2025). We observe that scores for languages other than English over the valid test set are considerably lower than the LLM-as-judge scores in Table 2. Prior to the evaluation period we had evaluated our models using BERT score and `xlm-roberta-large`, which yielded much higher scores, similar to those obtained in the LLM-as-judge evaluation. Those scores are presented in Table 9.

Context: **[REFERENCE TEXT]**
Question: **[QUESTION]**
Answer: **[ANSWER]**
Instruction: Reformulate the answer to be a natural sounding sentence that answers the question in the correct language. Produce text in the same language of the question and answer. Do not make it too long, or add too much information. Don't add anything else to your answer.

Table 4: Regeneration prompt we gave to `Llama-3.1-8B-Instruct` to regenerate the answers in the training set of SpokenSQuAD.

	User Prompt
Speech Prefix	Content: <speech>**[SPEECH EMBEDDINGS]**</speech>\n
Text Prefix	Content: <text>**[SPEECH TRANSCRIPTION]**</text>\n
ASR	Question: Can you transcribe the Speech content into English text?\n
ST/MT (de) **ST/MT (it)** **ST/MT (zh)**	Question: Können Sie den Inhalt der Rede in den deutschen Text übersetzen?\n Question: Puoi tradurre il contenuto del discorso in testo italiano?\n Question: 你能把演讲内容翻译成中文吗?\n
SQA/QA	Question: **[QUESTION]**\n
Suffix	Your answer:

Table 5: The user turn prompt template used for training our models. For speech tasks, the user prompt is given by **Speech Prefix+Task+Suffix**, for text tasks, the user prompt is given by **Text Prefix+Task+Suffix**.
ST/MT instructions were obtained by translating the instruction "*Can you translate the Speech content into [German/Italian/Chinese] text?*" to corresponding target languages using `SeamlessM4T-v2-large`.

	ASR				**ST**							
	CoVoST2		**EuroParlST**		**CoVoST2**				**EuroParlST**			
					en-de		**en-zh**		**en-de**		**en-it**	
	WER	CER	WER	CER	BLEU	COMET	BLEU	COMET	BLEU	COMET	BLEU	COMET
A.1 (ASR/ST)	7.84	3.70	11.21	7.30	**30.24**	**0.789**	**40.14**	**0.806**	**25.06**	**0.840**	**27.55**	0.860
A.2 (ASR/ST/SQA)	**7.21**	**3.44**	**10.98**	**7.18**	30.68	**0.789**	40.63	0.807	25.21	0.841	28.36	**0.859**
A.1 + B (ASR/ST/MT/*fluent*SQA/*fluent*QA)	7.59	3.55	11.20	7.20	31.42	0.770	42.19	0.802	27.16	0.809	27.86	0.842
A.2 + B (ASR/ST/MT/*fluent*SQA/*fluent*QA)	7.01	3.25	10.82	7.11	31.83	0.772	42.36	0.804	26.70	0.812	27.77	0.848

Table 6: ASR and ST results for the test sets of CoVoST2 and EuroParlST.

Model (fine-tuning data)	**ASR (WER)** en	**ST/MT (BLEU)** en-de	en-it	en-zh	**ST/MT (COMET)** en-de	en-it	en-zh
Text-only models (MT/QA)							
`Llama-3.1-8B-Instruct` (zero-shot)	-	21.27	33.81	44.01	0.732	0.757	0.755
B Text-only LoRA (MT/QA)	-	**36.94**	**49.81**	**52.33**	**0.782**	**0.815**	**0.822**
Speech-only models (ASR/ST/SQA)							
`SeamlessM4T-v2-large`	25.3	23.77	**37.84**	28.17	0.669	0.713	0.663
A.1 Speech Projector (ASR/ST)	**15.9**	26.77	36.34	38.65	0.718	**0.750**	**0.753**
A.2 Speech Projector (ASR/ST/SQA)	**15.9**	**26.85**	36.09	**38.85**	**0.720**	0.749	**0.753**
Multimodal models (ASR/ST/SQA)							
A.1 + B (ASR/ST/MT/SQA/QA)	**13.9**	28.74	41.73	40.72	0.716	**0.759**	0.756
A.1 + B (ASR/ST/MT/*fluent*SQA/*fluent*QA)	14.4	27.20	**42.01**	41.23	0.712	0.752	0.753
A.2 + B (ASR/ST/MT/SQA/QA)	17.2	**29.18**	39.14	40.99	0.719	0.755	0.762
A.2 + B (ASR/ST/MT/*fluent*SQA/*fluent*QA)	15.5	27.62	33.22	**41.74**	**0.726**	0.749	**0.764**

Table 7: ACL 60-60 dev set results for the different models and backbones used in this work.

	Valid Questions				Invalid Questions			
	en-en	en-de	en-it	en-zh	en-en	en-de	en-it	en-zh
A.1 + B (ASR/ST/MT/*fluent*SQA/*fluent*QA)	0.975	0.532	0.541	0.665	0.999	0.984	0.990	0.988
A.2 + B (ASR/ST/MT/*fluent*SQA/*fluent*QA)	0.975	0.536	0.546	0.666	0.999	0.990	0.989	0.991

Table 8: BERT scores for SpokenSQuAD test sets computed using the same settings from the organizers (default model, bert_score version 0.3.13). Invalid questions corresponds to a version of the test set in which the questions are impossible to answer given the speech context.

	Valid Questions				Invalid Questions			
	en-en	en-de	en-it	en-zh	en-en	en-de	en-it	en-zh
A.1 + B (ASR/ST/MT/*fluent*SQA/*fluent*QA)	0.857	0.869	0.863	0.899	0.996	0.997	0.996	0.997
A.2 + B (ASR/ST/MT/*fluent*SQA/*fluent*QA)	0.857	0.869	0.863	0.896	0.995	0.998	0.998	0.998

Table 9: BERT scores for SpokenSQuAD test sets computed using `xlm-roberta-large`. All other settings are equal to Table 8. Invalid questions corresponds to a version of the test set in which the questions are impossible to answer given the speech context.

Invalid Questions In Table 8 we also present BERT scores for an invalid multilingual test set, made of the same reference audio files from the English test split (8,026 examples), but with incorrect questions. We observe that the BERT scores for this invalid split is very high, showcasing that our models are fully capable of respecting the instruction format for incorrect answers.

B.1 Inference Issues

Through manual inspection of our model outputs, we observed that in a small number of cases, inference degenerates, resulting in repeated words or sentences until the maximum token limit is reached. We experimented with various inference strategies, greedy decoding, top-p, and top-k sampling, as well as different temperature settings, but were unable to identify a configuration that fully eliminated the issue. We hypothesize that a lightweight post-processing model could offer a simple and effective solution to mitigate this problem. Below we give some examples of inference degeneration for Chinese and German.

An example of inference degeneration in Chinese:

"国家语言理解模型从各种知识来源中提取出来，例如，通常通过预训练获得的参数中包含的知识，通常通过预训练获得的知识，通常通过预训练获得的知识，通常通过预训练获得的知识，(..)通常通过预训练"

An example of inference degeneration in German:

"In Zusammenhang mit der semantischen Parsierung, wenn wir nach der kompositionalen Generalisierung testen, könnte es mir so vorkommen, als ob wir in diesem Fall die Mädchen schlafen, und ich sehe, dass sie schlafen, und ich sehe, dass sie schlafen, (..) und ich sehe, dass sie schlafen, und ich sehe, dass"

C Models Hyperparameters

Table 12 lists the data splits used for each model presented in results Table 2. Table 13 presents the probability sampling employed during training.

C.1 Speech Projector (A) Hyperparameters

Architecture We explored multiple architectures to map speech embeddings from `SeamlessM4T-v2-large` to `Llama-3.1-8B-Instruct`. To train the speech projector, speech features extracted from `SeamlessM4T-v2-large` are input to the projector, and the resulting outputs are passed through a frozen `Llama-3.1-8B-Instruct` model. The speech projector, initialized with random weights, is trained using cross-entropy loss on an ASR task. Preliminary experiments demonstrated that the Transformer encoder architecture consistently outperformed both the Conformer and Multi-Layer Perceptron architectures of similar parameter sizes. Consequently, we adopt the Transformer encoder architecture for all experiments presented in this work.

Averaged Features As mentioned, in preliminary experiments, we experimented using the original output of `SeamlessM4T-v2-large`, as well as performing average every 2 or 3 frames. We observe that averaging every 3 frames results in models that are considerably faster to train, while maintaining similar performance to the original output.

Data Ratio For the ASR task, preliminary experiments revealed that training solely on EuroparlST ASR data resulted in poor generalization, whereas incorporating CoVoST ASR data significantly improved model robustness. For the ST task, we defined the data sampling ratios according to the target language distribution across the CoVoST and EuroparlST datasets.

Batch Size ASR and ST tasks use a batch size of 16, while SQA is batched with size 8, due to the longer user prompts.

Checkpoint Selection Checkpoints were selected based on development set performance across three or four configurations: ASR-best, ST-best, SQA-best (A.2-only), and an All-best checkpoint combining all tasks. We only present results for ST-best checkpoints, which we found to produce the best scores in ST compared to the other versions, while only marginally decreasing scores in ASR compared to the ASR-best checkpoint. We do not consider SQA-best checkpoints, as the overall SQA performance of projector-only models is very low regardless of the checkpoint selection method.

Exclusion of Chinese SQA Data During the training of the speech projector (A.2), we excluded Chinese SQA data. This was due to parallel observation in B models (text-only), in which we observed that the LLM failed to generate coherent Chinese answers. While later we were able to confirm that the issue did not come from the Chinese split itself, this model was obtained simultaneously to that finding, explaining why the data was not included in this setting.

C.2 Multimodal Models (C) Hyperparameters

In this section we present some ablation experiments for our multimodal adaptation setup. The experiments are performed by producing variants of the *A.1+B* model, which is the model we submitted to the challenge. Table 10 present ACL 60-60 dev split ASR and ST results that are discussed in the next paragraphs.

Impact of Parameters Count During our multimodal merging step, we combine text-only LoRA weights with our speech projector, yielding better scores. Since this increase in scores could be simply due the additional parameters, we trained a variant of our model in which the merging step is performed using a randomly initialized LoRA. We observe that our training setup indeed benefits from *any* additional weights during adaptation: the models trained with a randomly initialized LoRA outperform the speech projector backbone (A.1). Adding textual tasks in this setting does not help the system, which we hypothesize is due to the LoRA weights not being pretrained on the textual task. Finally, adapting using a pretrained LoRA model further improves ASR and ST scores for two out of three language directions (en-it and en-zh).

Impact of Textual Tasks For the multimodal models presented in the main paper, we adapt pretrained modules leveraging speech and textual tasks. We thus investigated the impact of having aligned speech and textual tasks during this adaptation. We observe that incorporating textual tasks has little impact on ASR performance, while substantially improving ST performance for Italian. The results are less favorable for German and Chi-

	ASR		ST (BLEU)			ST (COMET)		
	WER	CER	en-de	en-it	en-zh	en-de	en-it	en-zh
A.1 (ASR/ST)	15.9	7.7	26.77	36.34	38.65	0.718	0.750	0.753
A.1 + random LoRA (ASR/ST/SQA)	17.4	8.2	**29.07**	37.04	**41.47**	**0.732**	**0.760**	**0.761**
A.1 + random LoRA (ASR/ST/SQA) + (MT/QA)	**16.4**	**7.7**	28.07	**38.88**	41.24	0.725	0.755	0.760
A.1 + B (ASR/ST)	**13.8**	**6.4**	**27.91**	28.88	**41.70**	**0.728**	**0.743**	**0.760**
A.1 + B (ASR/ST) + (MT)	14.9	7.2	26.09	**32.97**	41.10	0.715	0.741	0.755
A.1 + B (ASR/ST/SQA)	**14.1**	**6.5**	**29.02**	30.08	**41.85**	**0.722**	0.743	**0.763**
A.1 + B (ASR/ST/SQA) + (MT/QA)	14.4	**6.5**	27.20	**42.01**	41.23	0.712	**0.752**	0.753
A.1 + B (ASR/ST/SQA) + (MT/QA) **No synthetic data**	18.8	9.2	28.47	32.97	40.03	0.717	0.741	0.753
A.1 + B (ASR/ST/SQA) + (MT/QA) **Only synthetic data**	**13.9**	**6.6**	**29.71**	**39.80**	**42.04**	**0.721**	**0.751**	**0.754**
A.1 + B (ASR/ST/SQA) + (MT/QA) **2K steps**	14.3	6.4	27.09	40.53	41.53	0.713	0.753	0.755

Table 10: ACL 60-60 dev set ASR and ST scores for variants of our best model (A.1+B).

ASR/ST/SQA	average WER	average BLEU
0.2 / 0.4 / 0.4	**16.03**	**37.58**
0.2 / 0.5 / 0.3	17.72	36.36
0.2 / 0.6 / 0.2	16.24	36.62
0.25 / 0.5 / 0.25	16.58	37.08
0.3 / 0.5 / 0.2	16.23	37.30

Table 11: ACL 60-60 dev and test set average WER and BLEU scores for our best model (A.1+B) by varying the ASR/ST/SQA ratios.

nese: in German, the addition of textual tasks leads to a performance drop, whereas in Chinese, the decline is minimal. Overall, these findings suggest that the textual modality may be particularly beneficial in low-resource settings. Italian, which has the fewest training examples in our dataset, appears to benefit the most from this adaptation.

Impact of SQA Examining the results in Table 10, we observe that incorporating the SQA and QA tasks leads to improvements in both ASR and ST performance. We hypothesize that the SQA task enhances the model's adherence to the prompt by encouraging it to *attend to* the information provided, thereby reducing both task and language confusion.

Inclusion of Synthetic textual Data Table 11 presents the results of our investigation into the inclusion of potentially noisy synthetic textual data during training. We observe that excluding this synthetic data (*No synthetic data*) negatively affects both BLEU and WER scores. Conversely, training exclusively with synthetic data (*Only synthetic data*) yields improved performance across all metrics. We attribute this to the fact that the target text in the non-synthetic data is duplicated from the speech task (i.e. the MT set is built from the ST set), leading to reduced data diversity. Removing this duplicated data introduces greater variability during the adaptation phase, which appears beneficial. Finally, using both types of data leads to improved performance for all languages except German. As discussed in the main paper, we hypothesize that this discrepancy is due to issues in the German training data sourced from EuroParlST and CoVoST2.

Number of Adaptation Steps Table 10 presents results for a version of our model trained for twice as long (2K steps). At this point, we observe signs of training saturation: differences in ASR and COMET scores across all metrics are minimal, and BLEU scores drop for both German and Italian. These results suggest that our adaptation step does not require a considerable number of training steps.

Task Ratios On our preliminary experiments, we tested different task ratios, selecting the one with best average WER and BLEU scores over both ACL 60-60 dev and test set. Table 11 presents those results.

C.2.1 Post-submission Discussion

Due to time constraints, many of our ablation studies were conducted after the initial submission. Upon analyzing these results (Table 10), we hypothesize that there may be an issue with the German training data: the more the model is exposed to it during training, the worse the COMET scores become. This hypothesis is supported by our *Only synthetic data* results, which show improved BLEU scores for German when we exclude textual data from EuroParlST and CoVoST2. Additionally, our

	CoVoST			EuroParlST			SpokenSQuAD			
	ASR	ST	MT	ASR	ST	MT	ASR	MT	SQA/QA	*fluent* SQA/QA
B Text-only LoRA	✗	✗	✓	✗	✗	✓	✗	✓	✓	✗
A.1 Speech Projector (ASR/ST)	✓	✓	✗	✓	✓	✗	✓	✗	✗	✗
A.2 Speech Projector (ASR/ST/SQA)	✓	✓	✗	✓	✓	✗	✓	✗	✓ (no zh)	✗
A.1 + B Multimodal model (ASR/ST/MT/SQA/QA)	✓	✓	✓	✓	✓	✓	✓	✓	✓	✗
A.1 + B Multimodal model (ASR/ST/MT/fluentSQA/fluentQA)	✓	✓	✓	✓	✓	✓	✓	✓	✗	✓
A.2 + B Multimodal model (ASR/ST/MT/SQA/QA)	✓	✓	✓	✓	✓	✓	✓	✓	✓	✗
A.2 + B Multimodal model (ASR/ST/MT/fluentSQA/fluentQA)	✓	✓	✓	✓	✓	✓	✓	✓	✗	✓

Table 12: List of datasets and splits used for each model presented in Table 2. Statistics for number of examples can be seen in Table 1.

	ASR	ST/MT				SQA/QA (valid/invalid)				
	task ratio	task ratio	en-de	en-it	en-zh	task ratio	en-en	en-de	en-it	en-zh
Text-only LoRA	x	0.6	0.4	0.3	0.3	0.4	0.2 / 0.05	0.2 / 0.05	0.2 / 0.05	0.2 / 0.05
A.1	0.4	0.6	0.3	0.4	0.3	x	x	x	x	x
A.2	0.4	0.35	0.3	0.4	0.3	0.25	0.2 / 0.2	0.15 / 0.15	x	0.15 / 0.15
A.1 + B	0.2	0.4	0.4	0.3	0.3	0.4	0.2 / 0.05	0.2 / 0.05	0.2 / 0.05	0.2 / 0.05
A.2 + B	0.2	0.4	0.4	0.3	0.3	0.4	0.2 / 0.05	0.2 / 0.05	0.2 / 0.05	0.2 / 0.05

Table 13: Two-level sampling ratio for each model.

ablations suggest that using textual data selectively, rather than uniformly, may be more effective. In particular, textual supervision appears to be most beneficial for Italian, with more limited gains observed for the other two language directions.

Regarding SQA, we were surprised to find that the evaluation setup provided by the organizers yields scores that differ significantly from those obtained with our own evaluation protocol (see Tables 8 and 9). These discrepancies also extend to the scores we obtain using LLM-as-judge (Table 2). We plan to further investigate the limitations of our current evaluation setup to better understand these inconsistencies.

JU-CSE-NLP's Cascaded Speech to Text Translation Systems for IWSLT 2025 in Indic Track

Debjit Dhar[1†], **Soham Lahiri**[1†], **Tapabrata Mondal**[1], **Sivaji Bandyopadhyay**[1*]
[1]Jadavpur University, Kolkata, India
[†]Authors contributed equally
[*]**Correspondence:** sivaji.cse.ju@gmail.com

Abstract

This paper presents the submission of the Jadavpur University Computer Science and Engineering Natural Language Processing (JU-CSE-NLP) Laboratory to the International Conference on Spoken Language Translation (IWSLT) 2025 Indic track, addressing the speech-to-text translation task in both English-to-Indic (Bengali, Hindi, Tamil) and Indic-to-English directions. To tackle the challenges posed by low-resource Indian languages, we adopt a cascaded approach leveraging state-of-the-art pre-trained models. For English-to-Indic translation, we utilize OpenAI's Whisper model for Automatic Speech Recognition (ASR), followed by the Meta's No Language Left Behind (NLLB)-200-distilled-600M model finetuned for Machine Translation (MT). For the reverse direction, we employ the AI4Bharat's IndicConformer model for ASR and IndicTrans2 finetuned for MT. Our models are fine-tuned on the provided benchmark dataset to better handle the linguistic diversity and domain-specific variations inherent in the data. Evaluation results demonstrate that our cascaded systems achieve competitive performance, with notable BLEU and chrF++ scores across all language pairs. Our findings highlight the effectiveness of combining robust ASR and MT components in a cascaded pipeline, particularly for low-resource and morphologically rich Indian languages.

1 Introduction and Related Work

Speech to text translation (STT) has long been the interest of Natural Language Processing (NLP) researchers particularly due to the huge number of languages spoken worldwide. However, a major part of research has been invested on translation between European languages and some Asian languages such as Chinese. Thus, translation from English to Indic languages and vice-versa is of considerable importance. This is further highlighted by the fact that Indic languages like Hindi, Bengali and Tamil have several speakers worldwide (615, 228 and 90.8 million respectively) (Ahmad et al., 2024). The top performers (NICT (Dabre and Song, 2024) and HWTSC (Wei et al., 2024)) of IWSLT 2024 Indic Track Competition showed the importance of finetuning ASR and MT models in a cascaded system. We present in this paper, cascaded models for translation from English to Indic languages (Bengali, Hindi, Tamil) and vice-versa. We also fine-tune our Neural Machine Translation (NMT) models using IWSLT 2025 Indic Track Training Dataset so as to obtain better results as compared to the pretrained checkpoints. The visual description of our system is shown in Figure 1 . We prefer the cascaded system over the End to End (E2E) system for two reasons. Firstly, most speech translators are not trained on indic speech and hence would require lot of resources to achieve the baseline performance that we have in cascaded systems. Secondly even in the English to Indic track, it has been shown in (Ahmad et al., 2024) that cascaded models completely outperform their end to end counterparts. Transcription and translation is carried out entirely on the basis of the given segmentation timestamps in the train, dev and test sets of the IWSLT 2025 Indic Track.

2 Dataset Description

The dataset for each language pair was given in three parts for both train and development sets. These included the wav files containing the audio of the speaker, yaml files containing the audio metadata and the segmentation information and the text files containing the corresponding transcriptions and translations of the segments. The punctuations were present only in the translated text. It was observed that the source files in English to Indic direction were same for the three languages. The test datasets contained only wav files and yaml files.

Proceedings of the 22nd International Conference on Spoken Language Translation (IWSLT 2025), pages 201–205
July 31 - August 1, 2025

Direction	Train	Dev	Test
English -> Bengali	205209	11671	36245
English -> Hindi	205209	11671	36245
English -> Tamil	205209	11671	36245
Bengali -> English	64868	395	866
Hindi -> English	248872	397	579
Tamil -> English	211303	457	956

Table 1: Number of segments given in the yaml files

3 Methodology

We have employed cascaded systems for both English to Indic (Hindi, Bengali, Tamil) as well as Indic (Hindi, Bengali, Tamil) to English Translations. We describe the preprocessing, finetuning and inference procedure of our models in the subsequent subsections.

3.1 Pre-processing

Before using our Automatic Speech Recognition (ASR) model we perform the following preprocessing steps on the audio files. Firstly, we normalize the audio volume in [-1,1] range. This is followed by applying a biquad low pass filter for noise reduction (with cutoff at 3kHz). Thirdly, we amplify the entire audio by 10dB. This is required for those cases where the speaker's voice is inaudible or unclear. We observed a notable reduction in WER and an improvement in SacreBLEU scores as a result of acoustic pre-processing shown in Table 2. The pre-processing, inference pipeline is shown in Figure 1.

System	Score	Bengali	Hindi	Tamil
English to Indic	WER	27.75	27.75	27.75
(without Preprocessing)	SacreBLEU	16.81	17.72	11.91
English to Indic	WER	21.09	21.09	21.09
(with Preprocessing)	SacreBLEU	21.79	24.46	12.81
Indic to English	WER	56.57	37.42	65.81
(without Preprocessing)	SacreBLEU	26.05	31.19	27.78
Indic to English	WER	48.32	36.93	56.17
(with Preprocessing)	SacreBLEU	39.17	46.28	37.69

Table 2: WER and SacreBLEU scores with and without preprocessing using pretrained checkpoints

3.2 English to Indic System

For ASR we use Whisper Small model by OpenAI (Radford et al., 2023) and for NMT we use the NLLB-200-distilled-600M variant) by Meta (Costa-Jussà et al., 2022). We intentionally choose the Small version of Whisper as this model gives the best SacreBLEU score (Post, 2018) when paired with our NMT and also has comparable Word Error Rate (WER) on the given dev set as shown in Table 3. After comparison with other SOTA models such as Helsinki Opus (Tiedemann and Thottingal, 2020) , we find that NLLB-200-distilled-600M gives us the best SacreBLEU score on the dev set Table 4. However, it is observed that the NMT model does not give a reasonable accuracy while using the existing checkpoints. Hence, we resort to finetuning the NLLB-200-distilled-600M model (Xinyuan et al., 2023) on the train set as given in IWSLT 2025 competition. Firstly, finetuning is carried out only on the NMT model. Here we use the source and target texts given in the competition train dataset. As for the pipeline, we run the Whisper Small model in inference mode and use its output as input for the finetuned NLLB model thus obtaining the translated text.

3.3 Indic to English System

For the Indic-to-English system, we utilize AI4Bharat's IndicConformer (`https://github.com/AI4Bharat/IndicConformerASR`) as the ASR model. For Indic-to-English translation, we employ IndicTrans2 (Gala et al., 2023) as the NMT model. During training, we fine-tune the NMT model using Indic transcriptions and their corresponding English translations. This fine-tuning results in a noticeable improvement in SacreBLEU scores.

We arrived at this choice of ASR and NMT models after conducting extensive experiments with different combinations of ASR and NMT models. For the MT system we tried using mBART (Tang et al., 2020) and NLLB200 but observed a much lower performance as compared to IndicTrans2. For ASR selection, we chose the system with the lowest WER, while for NMT, we evaluated the SacreBLEU score of the entire cascaded system on the development set to determine the best-performing model.

4 Experiments

The fine-tuning was conducted on a multi-GPU setup using Kaggle GPU T4x2 for efficient parallel-processing. To optimize training, audio-related metadata were removed.

4.1 Settings for English-Indic System

Due to resource constraints, we are it was not possible to finetune Whisper Small ASR on English to Indic system. NLLB200 is transformer based

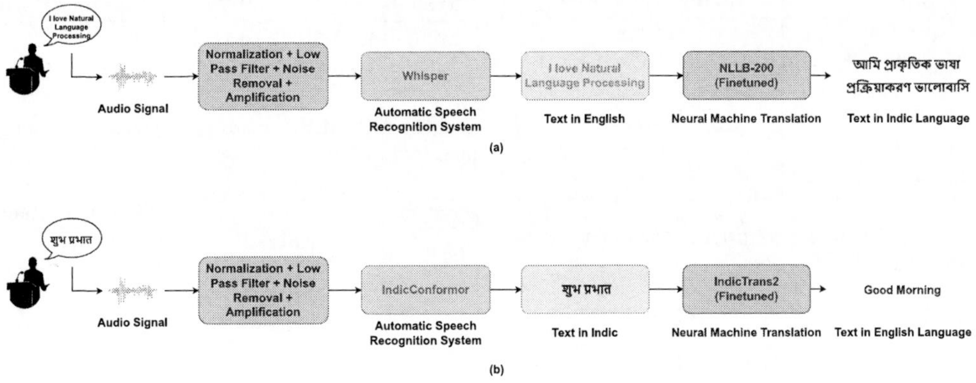

Figure 1: Overview of the proposed Multilingual Speech Translation Pipeline: (a) English-to-Indic flow using Whisper and finetuned NLLB-200; (b) Indic-to-English flow using IndicConformer and finetuned IndicTrans2.

MT model developed by Meta AI as a part of the No Language Left Behind initiative. This model had been evaluated on the Flores200 dataset and had demonstrated promising results particularly for under-represented languages. Hence, we choose this model for the machine translation part of our cascaded system. We finetune the NLLB model separately for Bengali, Hindi and Tamil target texts. Moreover in each case finetuning is done incrementally taking 20000 samples from train set each time. The finetuning was done with learning rate as 2e-5, batch size as 2, beam size 5, weight decay as 0.01 and for 5 epochs. The HuggingFace interface of NLLB was used for the finetuning procedure. Table 6 shows our final results on the dev set for English to Indic system.

4.2 Settings for Indic-English System

From Table 5, we identify the best-performing pretrained NMT model for each specific Indic-English pair and proceed to fine-tune them accordingly. Due to resource constraints, it was not possible to fine-tune the IndicConformer ASR model for the Indic-to-English system. Instead, we focused on fine-tuning the IndicTrans2 model, a state-of-the-art multilingual neural machine translation system tailored for Indic languages, using a LoRA-based parameter-efficient strategy (Hu et al., 2022; Patil et al., 2024).

IndicTrans2 is a transformer-based sequence-to-sequence model pretrained on large-scale translation corpora and supports multiple Indic languages. For fine-tuning, we use the development set of IWSLT 2025 Indic Track. Sentence-aligned parallel data was loaded and preprocessed using the IndicProcessor (Gala et al., 2023), which performs normalization and script standardization appropriate to each language. Tokenization was performed using the AutoTokenizer compatible with the base IndicTrans2 model. Preprocessing also involved truncating long sequences to adhere to the model's maximum input length.

To reduce training costs and memory usage, we employed Low-Rank Adaptation (LoRA) (Hu et al., 2022; Patil et al., 2024) via the peft library. Only a small subset of model parameters—specifically the attention projection matrices—were updated, while the rest of the model remained frozen. This allowed efficient adaptation to new data without full-scale retraining.

Fine-tuning was carried out using the Seq2SeqTrainer from the Hugging Face Transformers library. We used mixed-precision training (fp16) for computational efficiency. The model was evaluated on a held-out validation set after each epoch using automatic evaluation metrics such as BLEU (Papineni et al., 2002)and chrF++. (Popović, 2015) Early stopping was applied based on validation loss to prevent overfitting.

The learning rate was set to 2×10^{-5}, with a batch size of 4 per device, adjusted for multi-GPU training and LoRA rank and alpha of 4 and 16 respectively. The model was trained for 5 epochs, with a weight decay of 0.01 and a beam size of 5. Table 6 presents the final results on the development set for Indic-to-English translation.

5 Results

The final finetuned results on the dev set are given in Table 6. The WER observed on the dev sets for

ASR Model	Word Error Rate %
Whisper Tiny	25.63
Whisper Small	21.09
Whisper Medium	20.83
Whisper Base	23.16
Whisper Large-V2	20.74
Whisper Large-V3	20.62

Table 3: WER on the Source English text of combined English to Indic dev datasets

NMT Models	En-Bn	En-Hi	En-Ta
NLLB 200	21.79	24.46	12.81
Helsinki Opus	13.49	12.30	-

Table 4: SacreBLEU Scores on Dev Set using pretrained checkpoints (Helsinki does not have En-Ta checkpoints)

Bengali, Hindi, and Tamil using IndicConformer were 48.32%, 36.93%, and 56.17%, respectively. (Abdulmumin et al., 2025) The results on the test set as calculated by IWSLT are given in Table 7.

6 Limitation

Due to resource constraints, it was not feasible to fine-tune the ASR models to reduce the word error rate, which directly affects the quality of input provided to the NMT system. Additionally, the fine-tuning of the NMT models was limited to a maximum of five epochs, further constraining potential improvements in translation performance.

7 Conclusion and Future Work

This paper presented JU-CSE-NLP's submission to the Indic Track of IWSLT 2025. We have highlighted the detailed methodology of our preprocessing, finetuning and inference procedures in our paper which will help further research and system development in the field of speech translation of Indic languages. Our results are also quite reasonable comparing with previous year's performance in the same track (Ahmad et al., 2024) as shown in Table 8.

NMT Model	Bn-En	Hi-En	Ta-En
mBART	8.92	22.02	13.77
NLLB 200	21.09	0.50	9.29
IndicTrans2	42.80	31.19	27.78

Table 5: SacreBLEU scores on IndicConformer output of Dev Set using pretrained checkpoints

System	Bengali	Hindi	Tamil
English to Indic	44.54	39.04	38.82
Indic to English	39.17	46.28	37.69

Table 6: SacreBLEU scores of finetuned cascaded systems on Dev Set

System	Score	Bengali	Hindi	Tamil
English to Indic	BLEU	51.70	57.61	36.17
	chrF++	74.58	72.98	73.81
Indic to English	BLEU	23.69	44.13	17.66
	chrF++	53.99	67.91	49.34

Table 7: BLEU and chrF++ scores of cascaded systems on Test Set

In future work, we aim to conduct a comprehensive error analysis of our results to identify key areas for improvement and further enhance system performance. We also plan to apply knowledge distillation techniques from our cascaded systems to state-of-the-art end-to-end models, with the goal of achieving competitive performance in those frameworks. Additionally, we intend to extend our current Speech-to-Text (S2T) system into a full Speech-to-Speech Translation (S2ST) system. While our present approach is monolingual for each language pair, we aim to develop a multilingual system capable of handling multiple languages in all translation directions. Furthermore, we plan to incorporate language-specific features to improve translation quality and robustness.

References

Idris Abdulmumin, Victor Agostinelli, Tanel Alumäe, Antonios Anastasopoulos, Ashwin, Luisa Bentivogli, Ondřej Bojar, Claudia Borg, Fethi Bougares, Roldano Cattoni, Mauro Cettolo, Lizhong Chen, William Chen, Raj Dabre, Yannick Estève, Marcello Federico, Marco Gaido, Dávid Javorský, Marek Kasztelnik, and 30 others. 2025. Findings of the iwslt 2025 evaluation campaign. In *Proceedings of the 22nd International Conference on Spoken Language Translation*

Team ID	En-Bn	En-Hi	En-Ta
NICT	52.63	60.54	39.84
HWTSC	35.04	47.14	30.79
NITK	4.46	19.77	11.76
Ours	**51.70**	**57.61**	**36.17**

Table 8: Comparison with BLEU score of IWSLT 2024 English - Indic Unconstrained Cascaded Systems

(IWSLT 2025), Vienna, Austia (in-person and online). Association for Computational Linguistics. To appear.

Ibrahim Said Ahmad, Antonios Anastasopoulos, Ondřej Bojar, Claudia Borg, Marine Carpuat, Roldano Cattoni, Mauro Cettolo, William Chen, Qianqian Dong, Marcello Federico, Barry Haddow, Dávid Javorský, Mateusz Krubiński, Tsz Kin Lam, Xutai Ma, Prashant Mathur, Evgeny Matusov, Chandresh Maurya, John McCrae, and 25 others. 2024. FINDINGS OF THE IWSLT 2024 EVALUATION CAMPAIGN. In *Proceedings of the 21st International Conference on Spoken Language Translation (IWSLT 2024)*, pages 1–11, Bangkok, Thailand (in-person and online). Association for Computational Linguistics.

Marta R Costa-Jussà, James Cross, Onur Çelebi, Maha Elbayad, Kenneth Heafield, Kevin Heffernan, Elahe Kalbassi, Janice Lam, Daniel Licht, Jean Maillard, and 1 others. 2022. No language left behind: Scaling human-centered machine translation. *arXiv preprint arXiv:2207.04672*.

Raj Dabre and Haiyue Song. 2024. NICT's cascaded and end-to-end speech translation systems using whisper and IndicTrans2 for the Indic task. In *Proceedings of the 21st International Conference on Spoken Language Translation (IWSLT 2024)*, pages 17–22, Bangkok, Thailand (in-person and online). Association for Computational Linguistics.

Jay Gala, Pranjal A Chitale, Raghavan AK, Varun Gumma, Sumanth Doddapaneni, Aswanth Kumar, Janki Nawale, Anupama Sujatha, Ratish Puduppully, Vivek Raghavan, and 1 others. 2023. Indictrans2: Towards high-quality and accessible machine translation models for all 22 scheduled indian languages. *arXiv preprint arXiv:2305.16307*.

Edward J Hu, Yelong Shen, Phillip Wallis, Zeyuan Allen-Zhu, Yuanzhi Li, Shean Wang, Lu Wang, Weizhu Chen, and 1 others. 2022. Lora: Low-rank adaptation of large language models. *ICLR*, 1(2):3.

Kishore Papineni, Salim Roukos, Todd Ward, and Wei-Jing Zhu. 2002. Bleu: a method for automatic evaluation of machine translation. In *Proceedings of the 40th Annual Meeting of the Association for Computational Linguistics*, pages 311–318, Philadelphia, Pennsylvania, USA. Association for Computational Linguistics.

Pranamya Patil, Raghavendra Hr, Aditya Raghuwanshi, and Kushal Verma. 2024. SRIB-NMT's submission to the Indic MT shared task in WMT 2024. In *Proceedings of the Ninth Conference on Machine Translation*, pages 747–750, Miami, Florida, USA. Association for Computational Linguistics.

Maja Popović. 2015. chrF: character n-gram F-score for automatic MT evaluation. In *Proceedings of the Tenth Workshop on Statistical Machine Translation*, pages 392–395, Lisbon, Portugal. Association for Computational Linguistics.

Matt Post. 2018. A call for clarity in reporting bleu scores. *Preprint*, arXiv:1804.08771.

Alec Radford, Jong Wook Kim, Tao Xu, Greg Brockman, Christine Mcleavey, and Ilya Sutskever. 2023. Robust speech recognition via large-scale weak supervision. In *Proceedings of the 40th International Conference on Machine Learning*, volume 202 of *Proceedings of Machine Learning Research*, pages 28492–28518. PMLR.

Yuqing Tang, Chau Tran, Xian Li, Peng-Jen Chen, Naman Goyal, Vishrav Chaudhary, Jiatao Gu, and Angela Fan. 2020. Multilingual translation with extensible multilingual pretraining and finetuning. *arXiv preprint arXiv:2008.00401*.

Jörg Tiedemann and Santhosh Thottingal. 2020. Opus-mt–building open translation services for the world. In *Annual Conference of the European Association for Machine Translation*, pages 479–480. European Association for Machine Translation.

Bin Wei, Zongyao Li, Jiaxin Guo, Daimeng Wei, Zhanglin Wu, Xiaoyu Chen, Zhiqiang Rao, Shaojun Li, Yuanchang Luo, Hengchao Shang, Hao Yang, and Yanfei Jiang. 2024. HW-TSC's speech to text translation system for IWSLT 2024 in Indic track. In *Proceedings of the 21st International Conference on Spoken Language Translation (IWSLT 2024)*, pages 53–56, Bangkok, Thailand (in-person and online). Association for Computational Linguistics.

Henry Li Xinyuan, Neha Verma, Bismarck Bamfo Odoom, Ujvala Pradeep, Matthew Wiesner, and Sanjeev Khudanpur. 2023. JHU IWSLT 2023 multilingual speech translation system description. In *Proceedings of the 20th International Conference on Spoken Language Translation (IWSLT 2023)*, pages 302–310, Toronto, Canada (in-person and online). Association for Computational Linguistics.

NYA's Offline Speech Translation System for IWSLT 2025

Wenxuan Wang, Yingxin Zhang, Yifan Jin, Binbin Du, Yuke Li
NetEase YiDun AI Lab, Hangzhou, China
{wangwenxuan,zhangyingxin03,jinyifan01,dubinbin,liyuke}@corp.netease.com

Abstract

This paper reports NYA's submissions to the IWSLT 2025 Offline Speech Translation (ST) task. The task includes three translation directions: English to Chinese, German, and Arabic. In detail, we adopt a cascaded speech translation architecture comprising automatic speech recognition (ASR) and machine translation (MT) components to participate in the unconstrained training track. For the ASR model, we use the Whisper medium model. For the neural machine translation (NMT) model, the wider and deeper Transformer is adopted as the backbone model. Building upon last year's work, we implement multiple techniques and strategies such as data augmentation, domain adaptation, and model ensemble to improve the translation quality of the NMT model. In addition, we adopt X-ALMA as the foundational LLM-based MT model, with domain-specific supervised fine-tuning applied to train and optimize our LLM-based MT model. Finally, by employing COMET-based Minimum Bayes Risk decoding to integrate and select translation candidates from both NMT and LLM-based MT systems, the translation quality of our ST system is significantly improved, and competitive results are obtained on the evaluation set.

1 Introduction

The Offline Speech Translation (ST) Task converts source audio into target text. Currently, two primary approaches dominate the ST field: the cascaded system and the end-to-end (E2E) system. The traditional cascade system (Matusov et al., 2005a) decouples the ST task into an automatic speech recognition (ASR) and a machine translation (MT) task. The source speech is first transcribed into text in the source language, which is then translated into text in the target language using a neural machine translation (NMT) model. However, it often leads to higher architectural complexity and error propagation (Duong et al., 2016), affecting subsequent MT tasks. To alleviate this problem, the end-to-end ST architecture (Bérard et al., 2016) is proposed. The E2E ST system employs a single neural network to directly map source-language audio to target-language text, bypassing intermediate symbolic representations. For end-to-end ST architectures, a key limitation is the scarcity of parallel speech-text data. In contrast, the widespread availability of large-scale ASR and MT datasets facilitates the development of high-precision ASR and MT systems through comprehensive training. Therefore, the cascaded ST system typically outperforms the E2E ST system (Anastasopoulos et al., 2022; Agarwal et al., 2023; Ahmad et al., 2024; Abdulmumin et al., 2025). Thus, we choose the cascaded ST scheme consisting of ASR and MT systems for the task.

The main architecture of the traditional NMT model is the encoder-decoder. Recently, large language models (LLMs) based on decoder-only architectures have demonstrated remarkable performance across various natural language processing (NLP) tasks. In the MT task, only the most advanced LLMs like GPT-4 (Achiam et al., 2023) can match the performance of supervised learning-based encoder-decoder state-of-the-art (SoTA) models such as NLLB (Costa-Jussà et al., 2022), yet their effectiveness still falls short of expectations in low-resource languages and specialized domains. Therefore, many studies (Xu et al., 2023, 2024b,a; Aryabumi et al., 2024) are focused on applying LLMs to smaller-scale models, broader language coverage, and more diverse application scenarios in machine translation, demonstrating significant advancements in the field. For example, X-ALMA (Xu et al., 2024a) is one of the top-performing translation models built on LLMs, capable of matching or even surpassing WMT winners and GPT-4 in some language pairs and scenarios. Therefore, unlike in previous work, we implement both NMT and LLM-based MT approaches

Proceedings of the 22nd International Conference on Spoken Language Translation (IWSLT 2025), pages 206–211
July 31 - August 1, 2025 ©2025 Association for Computational Linguistics

and investigate their combination to achieve improved translation performance.

We participate in the unconstrained training track of the offline speech translation task. And the Whisper (Radford et al., 2023) medium model is directly employed for the ASR system in the source language. We also explore audio segmentation methods, such as Supervised Hybrid Audio Segmentation (SHAS) (Tsiamas et al., 2022), to segment the source audio for better ST results. In the MT task, we widely collect a large amount of parallel data and monolingual data from various data sources. For the NMT system, we use the Transformer architecture (Vaswani et al., 2017) as the backbone model and implement multiple optimization techniques and strategies such as Back Translation (BT) (Sennrich et al., 2016), Forward Translation (FT), Domain Adaptation (DA), and Ensemble (Ganaie et al., 2022) to improve the translation quality of the NMT model. For the LLM-based MT system, we use X-ALMA as the foundational model and adopt supervised fine-tuning (SFT) to train and optimize the LLM-based MT model. Subsequently, we adopt Minimum Bayes Risk (MBR) (Kumar and Byrne, 2004) decoding to select the translation candidates from both NMT and LLM-based MT systems and obtain significant improvements in translation quality.

2 Dataset

2.1 Text Data

The training set is divided into two parts: general data and domain data. For general data, we retain the same data configuration of En2Zh and En2De as last year (Zhang et al., 2024). For En2Zh and En2De, we make full use of a large amount of monolingual data through BT and FT. For En2Ar, in addition to utilizing the data provided by IWSLT 2025, we incorporate several large-scale open-source text datasets such as NLLB (Costa-Jussà et al., 2022), CCAligned (El-Kishky et al., 2019), HPLT (Aulamo et al., 2023) and etc. For domain-specific data, we crawl a substantial amount of domain-specific videos from websites and use the bilingual subtitles provided by these sites to create domain-specific training sets.

We employ sBERT (Reimers and Gurevych, 2019, 2020) to calculate semantic similarity for all parallel text data and filter out text pairs with similarity scores lower than 0.7. Table 1 presents the size of our MT corpus after filtering.

Corpus	En2Zh	En2De	En2Ar
General data	27M	20M	126M
Domain data	4M	4M	236K

Table 1: Data statistics of MT corpus.

2.2 Data Pre-processing

For semantically filtered data, we perform text pre-processing according to last year's rules and procedure (Zhang et al., 2024) to enhance data quality.

After text pre-processing, these sentences are tokenized by a SentencePiece (SPM) model (Kudo and Richardson, 2018). The SPM model is trained separately on sampled data, with vocabulary sizes set as follows: 40k in English, 37k in Chinese, 37k in German, and 40k in Arabic. Both the source and target sides share the same dictionary.

3 Speech Translation System

3.1 ASR System

We utilize the Whisper [1] (Radford et al., 2023) model in conjunction with the SHAS [2] (Tsiamas et al., 2022) method to implement our ASR system within a cascaded framework.

SHAS functions as a Voice Activity Detection (VAD) mechanism within the ASR system, enabling the segmentation of lengthy audio files into shorter segments. We experiment with various parameters and ultimately settle on the parameter set of (5, 30, 0.5), which we apply across all scenarios except for the accent challenge data.

Whisper is an advanced multilingual ASR system, providing robust performance across various audio conditions, including accented speech and noisy environments. The open-source models range from tiny to large, addressing different computational needs. We choose the medium-sized Whisper model for its suitability as the ASR model in our speech translation system.

3.2 MT System

Due to differences in training paradigms and learning objectives, traditional NMT tends to produce more literal translations while LLM-based MT generates more paraphrased outputs. The LLM approach shows better fluency and greater robustness to ASR errors, though it may occasionally overlook details or produce redundant hallucinations. These

[1] https://github.com/openai/whisper
[2] https://github.com/mt-upc/SHAS

two approaches exhibit complementary strengths in machine translation. Therefore, both NMT and LLM-based MT approaches are developed and integrated for our machine translation system.

3.2.1 NMT Model

Our NMT model in the speech translation system is built using the Transformer architecture implemented with the Fairseq toolkit (Ott et al., 2019). This model is designed with a wider and deeper structure, including an 18-layer encoder, 6-layer decoder, and 16 self-attention heads. This architecture enables the model to capture complex patterns and dependencies in the data effectively. Our NMT model is trained on parallel data from three language directions (English to Chinese, German, and Arabic) to form a one-to-many translation model.

Data augmentation techniques like back translation (Sennrich et al., 2016) and forward translation are employed to enhance the quality and diversity of the training data. Back translation involves translating the target language back into the source language, while forward translation transforms the source language into the target language. These methods leverage additional monolingual resources to generate synthetic bilingual data. In total, we utilize approximately 23M sentences of BT and FT data, including 18M sentences of En2Zh data and 5M sentences of En2De data. When employing the data generated by BT or FT models, we adopt the tagged BT method (Caswell et al., 2019) by appending a distinctive <BT> token at the beginning of the source sentence. This approach enables the model to distinguish between supervised and semi-supervised data during the training process.

Domain adaptation is also performed to fine-tune the model for specific domains. In-domain data is selected and used to train monolingual language models, which then score all language pairs. Specific thresholds are set to filter parallel data that is closer to the target domain. This process ensures that the model performs well in domain-specific scenarios, enhancing its overall translation quality and adaptability to different contexts.

3.2.2 LLM-based MT

LLMs have demonstrated impressive performance across various NLP tasks. Since most LLMs are primarily pre-trained on English, they still face limitations in multilingual translation tasks. Consequently, the paradigm of applying LLMs to multilingual translation tasks has been extensively studied. Among these, X-ALMA currently represents the state-of-the-art in open-source multilingual machine translation models. It supports bidirectional translation between English and 49 languages, achieving SoTA performance on the COMET-22 metric across all 50 language directions.

In this task, we find that the release of the X-ALMA[3] open-source model already achieves competent translation quality. Building upon the baseline, we perform supervised fine-tuning to enhance its domain-specific capabilities. In order to ensure data quality, we filter in-domain parallel data based on the reference-free CometKiwi (Rei et al., 2022b) metric. Subsequently, we conduct parameter-efficient adaptation of the model through Low-Rank Adaptation (LoRA) (Hu et al., 2022) fine-tuning, which is applied to all modules of the feed-forward network.

3.2.3 Minimum Bayes Risk Decoding

Unlike Maximum-A-Posteriori (MAP) estimation, which selects the single most probable hypothesis, Minimum Bayes Risk (MBR) (Kumar and Byrne, 2004) considers the entire distribution of possible outcomes and chooses the decision that minimizes the average loss across them. For MT, MBR decoding employs evaluation metrics like COMET (Rei et al., 2022a) to choose the hypothesis with the highest average score against other candidates. A substantial body of research (Fernandes et al., 2022; Finkelstein et al., 2023) has demonstrated that MBR decoding can effectively enhance translation quality across both NMT and LLM-based MT models. The N-best candidates from the NMT model are produced via beam search, while those from the LLM-based MT model are generated through temperature scaling and nucleus sampling. We employ COMET-based MBR decoding to rerank all the translation candidates from both subsystems, ultimately selecting the final translation output.

4 Experiments and Results

All NMT models are implemented using the open-source Fairseq toolkit (Ott et al., 2019). For LLM fine-tuning, we utilize the open-source ALMA toolkit [4] (Xu et al., 2024a). We evaluate the performance of MT models using case-sensitive Sacre-

[3] `https://huggingface.co/haoranxu/X-ALMA`

[4] `https://github.com/fe1ixxu/ALMA`

Model	En2Zh		En2De	
	COMET	BLEU	COMET	BLEU
NMT baseline	0.7988	34.70	0.7081	25.23
+ BT & FT	0.7995	35.03	0.7248	**26.36**
+ DA	0.8181	35.21	0.7315	26.34
+ MBR	0.8342	35.53	0.7572	25.41
LLM baseline (X-ALMA)	0.8200	32.74	0.7437	25.44
+ SFT	0.8221	33.44	-	-
+ MBR	0.8337	33.58	0.7560	24.77
MBR Ensemble NMT&LLM	**0.8417**	**36.01**	**0.7708**	25.71

Table 2: COMET and BLEU scores of NMT and LLM-based MT systems on the IWSLT tst-2022 test set

BLEU[5] (Post, 2018) and COMET[6] (Rei et al., 2022a) metrics, based on the tst2022 and tst2010 test sets. Specifically, tst2022 is used to assess En2De and En2Zh, while tst2010 is applied for En2Ar. For audio segmentation, we adopt SHAS with parameters set to (5,30,0.5). Finally, we utilize mwerSegmenter [7] (Matusov et al., 2005b) toolkit for the resegmentation and alignment of translation results.

Table 2 presents the COMET and BLEU scores for various NMT and LLM systems on the tst2022 test set. For NMT models, the integration of BT&FT data and domain adaptation demonstrates a notable enhancement of nearly 2% COMET scores across both En2Zh and En2De. This highlights the importance of domain-specific data for model performance. For LLM-based MT models, we perform LoRA fine-tuning on the X-ALMA pre-trained model with in-domain parallel data filtered by COMET-Kiwi (threshold is 0.82) for En2Zh, which brings slight translation improvements. The COMET-based MBR decoding achieves significant improvements in COMET scores, whether applied to candidate selection for a single translation model or two different types of translation systems (NMT and LLM). It is noteworthy that the En2De results of the single system indicate an inverse relationship between the COMET and BLEU scores.

Table 3 presents the performance of our final submitted ST system in the unconstrained training track of the offline speech translation task. Based on the results of "MBR Ensemble NMT&LLM" in Table 2, we train multiple models using a similar approach and achieve further improvements in COMET scores by integrating them through MBR decoding. The COMET scores for En2Zh and En2De reach 84.54% and 77.36% on tst2022, respectively. Since the En2Ar track does not provide an in-domain development set, we present the performance of En2Ar on the out-of-domain set tst2010 for reference.

[5]https://github.com/mjpost/sacrebleu

[6]https://github.com/Unbabel/COMET

[7]https://www-i6.informatik.rwth-aachen.de/web/Software/mwerSegmenter.tar.gz

	Test set	COMET	BLEU
En2Zh	*tst-2022*	0.8454	35.89
En2De	*tst-2022*	0.7736	25.81
En2Ar	*tst-2010*	0.8689	23.85

Table 3: COMET and BLEU scores of the ST system on the IWSLT test sets

5 Conclusion

This paper presents our submission to the IWSLT 2025 offline speech translation task. For the unconstrained track, we adopt a cascaded speech translation architecture consisting of the ASR and MT systems. For the ASR system, we directly employ the open-source Whisper medium model, which has shown outstanding performance and strong robustness across various scenarios for English speech recognition tasks. For the MT system, we investigate both NMT-based and LLM-based approaches and explore optimization strategies including data augmentation, domain adaptation, MBR decoding, and model ensemble. Experimental results demonstrate that integrating NMT with LLM-based MT models while applying these techniques yields significant performance improvements. Our final system achieves COMET scores of 0.8454, 0.7736, and 0.8689 for EN→ZH, EN→DE on the IWSLT tst-2022 test set, and EN→AR on the tst-2010 test set, respectively.

References

Idris Abdulmumin, Victor Agostinelli, Tanel Alumäe, Antonios Anastasopoulos, Ashwin, Luisa Bentivogli, Ondřej Bojar, Claudia Borg, Fethi Bougares, Roldano Cattoni, Mauro Cettolo, Lizhong Chen, William Chen, Raj Dabre, Yannick Estève, Marcello Federico, Marco Gaido, Dávid Javorský, Marek Kasztelnik, Tsz Kin Lam, Danni Liu, Evgeny Matusov, Chandresh Kumar Maurya, John P. McCrae, Salima Mdhaffar, Yasmin Moslem, Kenton Murray, Satoshi Nakamura, Matteo Negri, Jan Niehues, Atul Kr. Ojha, John E. Ortega, Sara Papi, Pavel Pecina, Peter Polák, Piotr Połeć, Beatrice Savoldi, Nivedita Sethiya, Claytone Sikasote, Matthias Sperber, Sebastian Stüker, Katsuhito Sudoh, Brian Thompson, Marco Turchi, Alex Waibel, Patrick Wilken, Rodolfo Zevallos, Vilém Zouhar, and Maike Züfle. 2025. Findings of the iwslt 2025 evaluation campaign. In *Proceedings of the 22nd International Conference on Spoken Language Translation (IWSLT 2025)*, Vienna, Austria (in-person and online). Association for Computational Linguistics. To appear.

Josh Achiam, Steven Adler, Sandhini Agarwal, Lama Ahmad, Ilge Akkaya, Florencia Leoni Aleman, Diogo Almeida, Janko Altenschmidt, Sam Altman, Shyamal Anadkat, et al. 2023. Gpt-4 technical report. *arXiv preprint arXiv:2303.08774*.

Milind Agarwal, Sweta Agrawal, Antonios Anastasopoulos, Luisa Bentivogli, Ondřej Bojar, Claudia Borg, Marine Carpuat, Roldano Cattoni, Mauro Cettolo, Mingda Chen, et al. 2023. Findings of the iwslt 2023 evaluation campaign. In *Proceedings of the 20th International Conference on Spoken Language Translation (IWSLT 2023)*, pages 1–61.

Ibrahim Sa'id Ahmad, Antonios Anastasopoulos, Ondřej Bojar, Claudia Borg, Marine Carpuat, Roldano Cattoni, Mauro Cettolo, William Chen, Qianqian Dong, Marcello Federico, et al. 2024. Findings of the iwslt 2024 evaluation campaign. In *Proceedings of the 21st International Conference on Spoken Language Translation (IWSLT 2024)*, pages 1–11.

Antonios Anastasopoulos, Loïc Barrault, Luisa Bentivogli, Marcely Zanon Boito, Ondřej Bojar, Roldano Cattoni, Anna Currey, Georgiana Dinu, Kevin Duh, Maha Elbayad, et al. 2022. Findings of the iwslt 2022 evaluation campaign. In *Proceedings of the 19th International Conference on Spoken Language Translation (IWSLT 2022)*, pages 98–157.

Viraat Aryabumi, John Dang, Dwarak Talupuru, Saurabh Dash, David Cairuz, Hangyu Lin, Bharat Venkitesh, Madeline Smith, Jon Ander Campos, Yi Chern Tan, et al. 2024. Aya 23: Open weight releases to further multilingual progress. *arXiv preprint arXiv:2405.15032*.

Mikko Aulamo, Nikolay Bogoychev, Shaoxiong Ji, Graeme Nail, Gema Ramírez-Sánchez, Jörg Tiedemann, Jelmer Van Der Linde, and Jaume Zaragoza. 2023. Hplt: High performance language technologies. In *Proceedings of the 24th Annual Conference of the European Association for Machine Translation*, pages 517–518.

Alexandre Bérard, Olivier Pietquin, Laurent Besacier, and Christophe Servan. 2016. Listen and translate: A proof of concept for end-to-end speech-to-text translation. In *NIPS Workshop on end-to-end learning for speech and audio processing*.

Isaac Caswell, Ciprian Chelba, and David Grangier. 2019. Tagged back-translation. *arXiv preprint arXiv:1906.06442*.

Marta R Costa-Jussà, James Cross, Onur Çelebi, Maha Elbayad, Kenneth Heafield, Kevin Heffernan, Elahe Kalbassi, Janice Lam, Daniel Licht, Jean Maillard, et al. 2022. No language left behind: Scaling human-centered machine translation. *arXiv preprint arXiv:2207.04672*.

Long Duong, Antonios Anastasopoulos, David Chiang, Steven Bird, and Trevor Cohn. 2016. An attentional model for speech translation without transcription. In *Proceedings of the 2016 Conference of the North American Chapter of the Association for Computational Linguistics: Human Language Technologies*, pages 949–959, San Diego, California. Association for Computational Linguistics.

Ahmed El-Kishky, Vishrav Chaudhary, Francisco Guzmán, and Philipp Koehn. 2019. Ccaligned: A massive collection of cross-lingual web-document pairs. *arXiv preprint arXiv:1911.06154*.

Patrick Fernandes, António Farinhas, Ricardo Rei, José GC de Souza, Perez Ogayo, Graham Neubig, and André FT Martins. 2022. Quality-aware decoding for neural machine translation. *arXiv preprint arXiv:2205.00978*.

Mara Finkelstein, Subhajit Naskar, Mehdi Mirzazadeh, Apurva Shah, and Markus Freitag. 2023. Mbr and qe finetuning: Training-time distillation of the best and most expensive decoding methods. *arXiv preprint arXiv:2309.10966*.

Mudasir A Ganaie, Minghui Hu, Ashwani Kumar Malik, Muhammad Tanveer, and Ponnuthurai N Suganthan. 2022. Ensemble deep learning: A review. *Engineering Applications of Artificial Intelligence*, 115:105151.

Edward J Hu, Yelong Shen, Phillip Wallis, Zeyuan Allen-Zhu, Yuanzhi Li, Shean Wang, Lu Wang, Weizhu Chen, et al. 2022. Lora: Low-rank adaptation of large language models. *ICLR*, 1(2):3.

Taku Kudo and John Richardson. 2018. SentencePiece: A simple and language independent subword tokenizer and detokenizer for neural text processing. In *Proceedings of the 2018 Conference on Empirical Methods in Natural Language Processing: System Demonstrations*, pages 66–71, Brussels, Belgium. Association for Computational Linguistics.

Shankar Kumar and Bill Byrne. 2004. Minimum bayes-risk decoding for statistical machine translation. In *Proceedings of the Human Language Technology Conference of the North American Chapter of the Association for Computational Linguistics: HLT-NAACL 2004*, pages 169–176.

E. Matusov, S. Kanthak, and Hermann Ney. 2005a. On the integration of speech recognition and statistical machine translation. In *Proc. Interspeech 2005*, pages 3177–3180.

Evgeny Matusov, Gregor Leusch, Oliver Bender, and Hermann Ney. 2005b. Evaluating machine translation output with automatic sentence segmentation. In *Proceedings of the Second International Workshop on Spoken Language Translation*, Pittsburgh, Pennsylvania, USA.

Myle Ott, Sergey Edunov, Alexei Baevski, Angela Fan, Sam Gross, Nathan Ng, David Grangier, and Michael Auli. 2019. fairseq: A fast, extensible toolkit for sequence modeling. In *Proceedings of the 2019 Conference of the North American Chapter of the Association for Computational Linguistics (Demonstrations)*, pages 48–53, Minneapolis, Minnesota. Association for Computational Linguistics.

Matt Post. 2018. A call for clarity in reporting BLEU scores. In *Proceedings of the Third Conference on Machine Translation: Research Papers*, pages 186–191, Belgium, Brussels. Association for Computational Linguistics.

Alec Radford, Jong Wook Kim, Tao Xu, Greg Brockman, Christine McLeavey, and Ilya Sutskever. 2023. Robust speech recognition via large-scale weak supervision. In *International Conference on Machine Learning*, pages 28492–28518. PMLR.

Ricardo Rei, José GC De Souza, Duarte Alves, Chrysoula Zerva, Ana C Farinha, Taisiya Glushkova, Alon Lavie, Luisa Coheur, and André FT Martins. 2022a. Comet-22: Unbabel-ist 2022 submission for the metrics shared task. In *Proceedings of the Seventh Conference on Machine Translation (WMT)*, pages 578–585.

Ricardo Rei, Marcos Treviso, Nuno M Guerreiro, Chrysoula Zerva, Ana C Farinha, Christine Maroti, José GC De Souza, Taisiya Glushkova, Duarte M Alves, Alon Lavie, et al. 2022b. Cometkiwi: Ist-unbabel 2022 submission for the quality estimation shared task. *arXiv preprint arXiv:2209.06243*.

Nils Reimers and Iryna Gurevych. 2019. Sentence-bert: Sentence embeddings using siamese bert-networks. In *Proceedings of the 2019 Conference on Empirical Methods in Natural Language Processing*. Association for Computational Linguistics.

Nils Reimers and Iryna Gurevych. 2020. Making monolingual sentence embeddings multilingual using knowledge distillation. In *Proceedings of the 2020 Conference on Empirical Methods in Natural Language Processing*. Association for Computational Linguistics.

Rico Sennrich, Barry Haddow, and Alexandra Birch. 2016. Improving neural machine translation models with monolingual data. In *Proceedings of the 54th Annual Meeting of the Association for Computational Linguistics (Volume 1: Long Papers)*, pages 86–96.

Ioannis Tsiamas, Gerard I. Gállego, José A. R. Fonollosa, and Marta R. Costa-jussà. 2022. SHAS: Approaching optimal Segmentation for End-to-End Speech Translation. In *Proc. Interspeech 2022*, pages 106–110.

Ashish Vaswani, Noam Shazeer, Niki Parmar, Jakob Uszkoreit, Llion Jones, Aidan N Gomez, Łukasz Kaiser, and Illia Polosukhin. 2017. Attention is all you need. *Advances in neural information processing systems*, 30.

Haoran Xu, Young Jin Kim, Amr Sharaf, and Hany Hassan Awadalla. 2023. A paradigm shift in machine translation: Boosting translation performance of large language models. *arXiv preprint arXiv:2309.11674*.

Haoran Xu, Kenton Murray, Philipp Koehn, Hieu Hoang, Akiko Eriguchi, and Huda Khayrallah. 2024a. X-alma: Plug & play modules and adaptive rejection for quality translation at scale. *arXiv preprint arXiv:2410.03115*.

Haoran Xu, Amr Sharaf, Yunmo Chen, Weiting Tan, Lingfeng Shen, Benjamin Van Durme, Kenton Murray, and Young Jin Kim. 2024b. Contrastive preference optimization: Pushing the boundaries of llm performance in machine translation. *arXiv preprint arXiv:2401.08417*.

Yingxin Zhang, Guodong Ma, and Binbin Du. 2024. The nya's offline speech translation system for iwslt 2024. In *Proceedings of the 21st International Conference on Spoken Language Translation (IWSLT 2024)*, pages 39–45.

KIT's Low-resource Speech Translation Systems for IWSLT2025: System Enhancement with Synthetic Data and Model Regularization

Zhaolin Li, Yining Liu, Danni Liu, Tuan Nam Nguyen, Enes Yavuz Ugan, Tu Anh Dinh, Carlos Mullov, Alexander Waibel, Jan Niehues
Karlsruhe Institute of Technology
firstname.lastname@kit.edu

Abstract

This paper presents KIT's submissions to the IWSLT 2025 low-resource track. We develop both cascaded systems, consisting of Automatic Speech Recognition (ASR) and Machine Translation (MT) models, and end-to-end (E2E) Speech Translation (ST) systems for three language pairs: Bemba, North Levantine Arabic, and Tunisian Arabic into English. Building upon pre-trained models, we fine-tune our systems with different strategies to utilize resources efficiently. This study further explores system enhancement with synthetic data and model regularization. Specifically, we investigate MT-augmented ST by generating translations from ASR data using MT models. For North Levantine, which lacks parallel ST training data, a system trained solely on synthetic data slightly surpasses the cascaded system trained on real data. We also explore augmentation using text-to-speech models by generating synthetic speech from MT data, demonstrating the benefits of synthetic data in improving both ASR and ST performance for Bemba. Additionally, we apply intra-distillation to enhance model performance. Our experiments show that this approach consistently improves results across ASR, MT, and ST tasks, as well as across different pre-trained models. Finally, we apply Minimum Bayes Risk decoding to combine the cascaded and end-to-end systems, achieving an improvement of approximately 1.5 BLEU points.

1 Introduction

In this paper, we present our submissions to the IWSLT 2025 low-resource track. We participate in three language pairs, translating from Bemba (ISO: bem), North Levantine Arabic (ISO: apc), and Tunisian Arabic (ISO: aeb) into English. Our approach follows the unconstrained track, reflecting practical scenarios by leveraging all available resources, including multilingual pre-trained models and external datasets.

Building upon the submissions of last year (Li et al., 2024), which investigates efficient utilization of available resources using multilingual pre-trained models, this work explores two approaches to further enhance model performance without involving extra resources: synthetic data augmentation and model regularization.

One of the main challenges in building speech translation (ST) systems is the scarcity of end-to-end (E2E) ST data. Given that Automatic Speech Recognition (ASR) and Machine Translation (MT) resources are more accessible, we leverage them to create synthetic ST data. First, we investigate the MT-augmented approach, using a trained MT model to generate target-language translations from ASR datasets. Additionally, inspired by prior work (Robinson et al., 2022; Yang et al., 2025; Eskimez et al., 2024; Tong et al., 2024; Moslem, 2024), we explore synthetic speech generation. Specifically, we train Text-To-Speech (TTS) models using ASR data and use them to generate synthesized speech from the MT datasets.

We also explore model regularization to enhance model performance. Previous research shows ST systems for low-resource languages benefit from model regularization during training because of the imbalanced parameter usage (Romney Robinson et al., 2024; Jiawei et al., 2024). However, these works are limited to MT models in the cascaded system. Since model regularization is a generic approach, this work investigates its effectiveness with both ASR, MT, and ST tasks.

With experimental results across different language pairs, we conclude the findings as follows:

- Synthetic data is promising for improving model performance, provided that the generated data is of reasonable quality.
- Model regularization is a general approach for enhancing performance, and we demonstrate its effectiveness across different tasks and pre-

Proceedings of the 22nd International Conference on Spoken Language Translation (IWSLT 2025), pages 212–221
July 31 - August 1, 2025 ©2025 Association for Computational Linguistics

trained models.

- The various differences between languages and corpora lead to divergent findings in terms of pre-trained model effectiveness and training strategies, highlighting the need for language-specific approaches.

2 Task Description

The IWSLT 2025 low-resource track defines two system categories: constrained, where models are trained exclusively on datasets provided by the organizers, and unconstrained, where participants are free to use any external resources. In this work, we focus on the unconstrained condition, aiming to reflect better practical and real-world scenarios, where leveraging diverse data sources is often essential for building effective translation systems.

2.1 Development Dataset

This work focuses on three language pairs with the source languages of Bemba, North Levantine, or Tunisian, and the same target language of English. The development data used for these tasks is summarized in Table 1. Notably, North Levantine lacks end-to-end parallel training data, highlighting the need for additional resources and data augmentation techniques to build effective translation models for this language.

	Train	Valid	Test
apc	-	1126	975
aeb	202k	3833	4204
bem	82k	2782	2779

Table 1: Statistics on development data. The value indicates the number of samples, where one sample is composed of the audio, transcript in the language, and translation in English.

2.2 Additional Dataset

Under the unconstrained condition, we utilize additional resources to improve model performance, as detailed in Table 2. These supplementary datasets include ASR and MT datasets, but notably no end-to-end ST dataset due to unavailability. This highlights the advantages of building cascaded ST systems, which can effectively leverage separate ASR and MT components. All additional datasets are publicly accessible, except SyKIT and MINI, which are internally developed and originate from conversational speech data.

Lang.	Corpus	Type	Amount.
apc	LDC2005S08	ASR	60h
	LDC2006S29	ASR	250h
	SyKIT	ASR	50h
	Tatoeba	MT	20
	UFAL	MT	120k
	LDC2012T09	MT	138k
aeb	SRL46	ASR	12h
	GNOME	MT	646
ara	SLR148	ASR	111h
	MGB	ASR	1200h
	MINI	ASR	10h
	CCMatrix	MT	5M
	NLLB	MT	5M
	OpenSubtitles	MT	3M
bem	BembaSpech	ASR	24h
	NLLB	MT	427k

Table 2: Overview of the additional data resources. The unit in amount is the number of hours or sentences.

3 Approaches

3.1 Synthetic Data Augmentation

Data scarcity remains a key challenge in low-resource natural language processing tasks, particularly for end-to-end speech translation (ST). To address this limitation, this work investigates data augmentation approaches using synthetic data. We focus on two augmentation approaches that address different modalities: the MT-augmented method, which generates synthetic translations from ASR data, and the TTS-augmented method, which produces synthetic speech from MT data. Together, these methods aim to enhance the quality and robustness of ST models in low-resource settings.

3.2 Model Regularization

Regularization remains a simple yet powerful way to boost the generalisation capacity of neural sequence models, and has already proved valuable in machine translation through techniques such as RDrop and its variants (Wu et al., 2021; Xu et al., 2022). Motivated by the recent success of intradistillation (ID) in low-resource MT (Romney Robinson et al., 2024), we extend ID to all three tasks: ASR, MT, and ST, based on the public implementation with the following modification[1].

Unlike previous work that directly fine-tunes a pretrained model with a loss that combines the task

[1]https://github.com/felixxu/Intra-Distillation/

objective and ID, we notice that direct fine-tuning leads to suboptimal performance in preliminary experiments. We therefore adopt a twostage approach: (1) vanilla finetuning to adapt the pretrained model to the downstream task, followed by (2) ID finetuning to regularize the adapted model with its own intermediate predictions. This simple approach retains the advantages of taskspecific adaptation while unlocking the additional robustness that ID provides.

3.3 System combination

Following the prior work (Li et al., 2024), we combine the cascaded system and the end-to-end system with Minimum Bayes Risk (MBR) decoding to boost model performance (Kumar and Byrne, 2004). Specifically, with 50 hypothesis from the cascaded system and 50 from the end-to-end system as the pseudo-references, we use the official evaluation metric BLEU as the utility function in our MBR decoding.

3.4 Arabic Dialects Normalization

This work focuses on ST tasks, where normalizing intermediate transcripts can streamline the overall process. Following the approach proposed by (Ben Kheder et al., 2024), we implement a dialect-specific normalization pipeline to ensure consistent pre-processing across diverse transcriptions in North Levantine and Tunisian dialects. Our normalization process includes compound word splitting, orthographic normalization of dialectal variations, and numeral normalization.

4 Experimental Setups and Results

4.1 Preprocessing

Following prior work (Li et al., 2024), we exclude speech segments exceeding 15 seconds in duration due to computational limitations. Subsequently, we apply speech augmentation techniques including Gaussian noise injection, time stretching, time masking, and frequency masking.

4.2 Pre-trained Models

In this work, we explore fine-tuning with the following pre-trained models for different tasks.

SeamlessM4T: SeamlessM4T (Barrault et al., 2023) is a highly multilingual and multimodal model that has demonstrated strong performance in low-resource scenarios across ASR, MT, and ST tasks. We use the large configuration of version 2 for our experiments[2]. It is important to note that none of the three source languages used in our experiments were included in SeamlessM4T's pre-training data.

NLLB: NLLB (Costa-Jussà et al., 2022) is a multilingual machine translation model capable of directly translating between 200 languages. Its pre-training data includes a wide range of languages, particularly many low-resource ones, making it well-suited for low-resource translation tasks. North Levantine and Tunisian are included in its pre-training, and Bemba is not.

We use the 1.3B parameter version[3], freezing the word embeddings to reduce memory usage. We also freeze the decoder except for the cross-attention layers, as suggested in (Cooper Stickland et al., 2021). Due to the lack of MT data for North Levantine, we fine-tune the model jointly on Tunisian and Modern Standard Arabic, resulting in many-to-English MT systems.

MMS: MMS is a multilingual speech recognition model pre-trained on data from over 1,100 languages. Its broad language coverage and use of self-supervised learning enable effective fine-tuning for low-resource languages. For our experiments, we add a linear layer on top of the pre-trained encoder and fine-tune the model using the CTC loss[4]. Additionally, we explore enhancements through shallow fusion with language models using different tokenization strategies (Li and Niehues, 2025).

XEUS: Similar like MMS, XEUS is a multilingual encoder-based speech recognition model(Chen et al., 2024). It is pre-trained on approximately 1 million hours of unlabeled audio spanning 4,057 languages. Moreover, it incorporates dereverberation training, enhancing its robustness to various acoustic conditions. We apply the same fine-tuning strategy used for MMS to XEUS[5].

4.3 Synthetic Data

We explore two TTS systems, each is optimized for different strengths.

[2]https://huggingface.co/facebook/seamless-m4t-v2-large

[3]https://github.com/facebookresearch/fairseq/tree/nllb

[4]https://huggingface.co/facebook/mms-300m

[5]https://huggingface.co/espnet/xeus

4.3.1 E2TTS

E2TTS (Eskimez et al., 2024) is a recent non-autoregressive text-to-speech (TTS) model that demonstrates strong performance. Unlike previous non-autoregressive approaches, it upsamples the text sequence to the spectrogram length by padding, which eliminates the need for explicit monotonic alignment search and duration modeling during training. This simplifies the training process and makes the model more end-to-end. Besides, E2TTS utilizes conditional flow matching (Tong et al., 2024) as its backbone, inheriting its strong generative capabilities that ensure the naturalness and high-fidelities of the synthesized audio.

Additionally, its combination of in-context learning and classifier-free guidance (Ho and Salimans, 2022) enables highly flexible zero-shot synthesis. This means we can generate audio using a randomly given audio prompt that indicates the target speakers identity, emotion tone, background noise profile, etc, and we could also control how much of these acoustic characteristics from the prompt would be bypassed to model output. These features allow us to create more diverse audio samples ideal for data augmentation.

As for training configurations, we use a checkpoint pretrained on English as a startup. We follow training hyperparameters from the original paper with modified vocabulary size tailored to our target languages and datasets. Additionally, we use Vocos (Siuzdak, 2024) vocoder to synthesize waveforms from log mel-filterbank features.

Following model training, we synthesize audio samples for data augmentation by running inference on source transcripts. For each generation, we condition the model using a randomly selected text-audio pair from the training dataset as a prompt, employing classifier-free guidance $\alpha = 2.0$ to strengthen prompt adherence. This ensures that the speaker distribution in the generated data matches that of the original dataset. Additionally, we configure the numerical approximation steps to 32 to ensure high-quality waveform generation.

4.3.2 VITS

VITS (Kim et al., 2021) is a conditional variational autoencoder architecture enhanced with normalizing flows. It comprises three primary components: a posterior encoder, a prior encoder, and a waveform generator. These modules respectively model the distributions $q_\phi(z|x)$, $p_\theta(z|c)$, and $p_\psi(y|z)$. Specifically, $q_\phi(z|x)$ represents the posterior distribution, and $p_\psi(y|z)$ corresponds to the data distribution, with parameters learned by the posterior encoder ϕ and the HiFi-GAN waveform generator ψ (Kong et al., 2020). Here, x denotes the speech input, z is the latent variable, and y is the resulting waveform. The prior distribution $p_\theta(z|c)$, parameterized by the prior encoder θ, is further refined using a normalizing flow f, where the latent variables are conditioned on the text input c.

During training, the model is optimized to maximize the conditional likelihood $p(x|c)$ by maximizing its evidence lower bound (ELBO):

$$\log p(x|c) \geq \mathbb{E}_{q_\phi(z|x)}[\log p_\psi(x|z)] - D_{\mathrm{KL}}(q_\phi(z|x) \| p_\theta(z|c)) \quad (1)$$

We train the model from scratch and fine-tune it for 1,000,000 steps using a setup similar to that in the original VITS paper. After training, we synthesize audio samples for data augmentation by performing inference on the source transcripts. For each synthesized audio, a random speaker is selected from the training set, which includes approximately 75 speakers, to produce diverse speaker-conditioned outputs.

4.4 Evaluation Metrics

Following the evaluation instruction of IWSLT 2025 low-resource track, both prediction and reference are lowercased and punctuation removed[6]. We use Character Error Rate (CER) and Word Error Rate (WER) as ASR evaluation metrics. For translation tasks, we use evaluation metrics of Bilingual Evaluation Understudy (BLEU) and Character n-gram F-score (chrF).

4.5 ASR Systems

Due to limitations in time and computational resources, we primarily experiment with ASR systems for Bemba. The corresponding results, identified by IDs starting with 'A' in Table 3, are discussed below. In experiments A1 and A2 using MMS, we observe that applying language model fusion with encoder-based models consistently improves ASR performance, resulting in a reduction of approximately 4 WER pointsaligning with findings from prior work. Comparing A1 and A3, we observe that XEUS achieves performance similar

[6] https://github.com/kevinduh/iwslt22-dialect

ID	Model	bem_valid	bem_test
A1	MMS	10.8/40.4	10.0/37.3
A2	A1 + LM	9.8/36.6	8.8/34.8
A3	XEUS	10.7/41.0	10.0/39.4
A4	Seamless	10.8/37.1	10.0/36.6
A5	Seamless all	10.0/34.1	9.3/33.1
A6	A5 + ID	**9.8/33.1**	**9.1/31.9**
B1	NLLB all	26.0/51.0	28.6/52.4
B2	NLLB	25.6/51.5	28.5/52.6
B3	B1 + ID	27.1/52.0	29.1/52.6
B4	Seamless all	26.6/52.8	26.8/52.3
B5	Seamless	27.9/52.3	27.9/52.6
B6	B5 + ID	**28.6/54.7**	**29.3/54.5**
C	Best A+B	28.4/53.0	28.9/52.8
D1	Seamless	27.6/51.1	27.7/51.3
D2	D1 + ID	**29.5/53.6**	**29.8/53.1**
D3	D1 + TTS	28.0/52.6	28.7/53.0
D4	D3 + ID	29.4/53.6	29.3/53.3
E1	C	29.4/52.0	29.0/51.5
E2	D4	30.0/52.7	29.8/52.3
E3	E1 + E2	**31.1/53.4**	**30.8/52.9**
Best ST system 2024		26.3/-	30.4/-

Table 3: Experimental results for Bemba to English. **A** indicates ASR systems, **B** indicates MT systems with gold transcript, **C** indicates cascaded systems, **D** indicates E2E ST systems, and **E** indicate MBR systems. **all** indicates training with all available resources; otherwise, training is done with only the development resource. ASR results are reported as CER/WER, while MT and ST results are presented as BLEU/chrF.

to MMS, despite being pre-trained on more languages and incorporating dereverberation augmentation. The possible explanations are that the audios are recorded in controlled conditions with minimal background noise, and the additional language coverage of XUES pre-training benefits little to Bemba in terms of speech representation.

Compared to the encoder-only models above, the encoder-decoder model SeamlessM4T achieves comparable performance when fine-tuned using only development resources. We apply several training strategies to SeamlessM4T: specifically, we compare using only the development resources versus all available resources with the pre-trained model. As seen from A4 to A5, utilizing all resources results in about a 3-point WER improvement. Furthermore, we achieve an additional improvement of approximately 1 WER point by applying ID on top of A5.

For Arabic dialects, we first fine-tune with all resources, including MSA, with SeamlessM4T, then fine-tune with the datasets of the target language pairs in the second stage. This benefits in tackling the limited training resources under the normalization processing, which brings the dialects and standard similar in terms of learning speech representation. As Table 4 shows, the transfer learning slightly improves model performance. Notably, the ASR systems for North Levantine have unbalanced results for validation and test splits, despite the test split remaining untouched during training. One hypothesis is a domain mismatch between these splits. Further investigation is needed to confirm this hypothesis.

4.6 MT Systems

We experimented with SeamlessM4T and NLLB models, chosen for their differing language coverage and capabilities. Two fine-tuning strategies were explored: one using all available resources followed by transfer to the development set, and another using only the development set for fine-tuning.

For Bemba, fine-tuning exclusively on the development dataset yielded better performance than using all resources, as shown in Table 3. The choice of fine-tuning resources had little effect on NLLB's performance. When comparing pre-trained models, NLLB outperformed SeamlessM4T, under the condition that Bemba is included in the pretraining data of either model. Notably, incorporating ID data improved MT performance for both models by approximately 1 BLEU point.

For North Levantine and Tunisian, we experiment with NLLB fine-tuning using all Arabic resources, followed by a second-step fine-tuning with only the available resources for each language pair, for the same reasons as in Section 4.5. Specifically, we fine-tune with the UFAL and LDC2012T09 datasets for North Levantine and the development dataset for Tunisian in the second-step fine-tuning, based on availability. We observe a significant improvement for North Levantine, consistent with (Ben Kheder et al., 2024), potentially due to the benefits of domain similarity. In contrast, the performance with second-step fine-tuning slightly declines for Tunisian. This underscores the importance of language-specific approaches.

We also fine-tune the pre-trained SeamlessM4T using only the development set and find that its performance falls noticeably behind that of NLLB, though the comparison is not entirely fair. Given

ID	Model	apc_valid	apc_test	aeb_valid	aeb_test
A1	Seamless all ara	45.1/68.4	12.4/37.5	18.2/36.8	23.2/44.5
A2	A1 + transfer	**45.0/66.7**	**12.0/37.0**	**18.4/36.9**	**21.7/41.3**
A3	A2 + ID	47.9/70.1	16.1/42.8	19.6/39.4	22.7/43.5
B1	NLLB all	24.9/53.6	20.9/48.8	30.4/52.6	26.8/50.2
B2	B1 + transfer	**31.3/57.6**	**28.0/54.4**	**30.3/52.2**	**26.3/49.9**
B3	Seamless	21.7/48.2	18.9/45.1	28.4/50.8	25.6/48.9
C	Best A+B	19.1/42.1	26.6/53.2	23.4/46.2	20.1/43.8
D1	Seamless	19.9/41.7	27.3/52.4	20.5/43.3	18.0/41.1
D2	Seamless + ID	-	-	**22.9/45.4**	**19.6/43.8**
E1	C	19.0/41.4	26.5/52.6	23.4/46.2	20.2/43.4
E2	Best D	19.7/41.1	27.4/51.9	23.1/45.2	19.9/42.5
E3	E1+E2	**21.0/42.5**	**29.4/53.8**	**24.6/46.9**	**21.3/44.4**
Best ST system 2024/2023		26.9/51.9	28.7/52.3	24.9/-	22.2/-

Table 4: Experimental results for North Levantine and Tunisian to English. **A** indicates ASR systems, **B** indicates MT systems with gold transcript, **C** indicates cascaded systems, **D** indicates E2E ST systems, and **E** indicate MBR systems. **all** indicates training with all available resources; otherwise, training is done with only the development resource. **transfer** indicates a second-step fine-tuning. ASR results are reported as CER/WER, while MT and ST results are presented as BLEU/chrF.

NLLBs pre-training advantage on these languages and the preliminary results, we did not apply the same fine-tuning strategy for SeamlessM4T due to time limitations.

4.7 Synthetic Data Augmentation

As described in Section 2, there is no E2E ST training data available for North Levantine. To address this, we explore synthetic data augmentation using both MT-augmented and TTS-augmented approaches to create ST training data. In addition, we also apply the TTS-augmented approach to Bemba to examine the impact of additional synthetic ST data.

4.7.1 MT-augmented ST systems

Using the MT system B2 in Table 4, we generated translations from the ASR dataset LDC2005S08 (listed in Table 2) to create synthetic ST data. After applying filtering criteria such as the audio-to-text length ratio, the generation ends with 45K samples. We then train E2E ST systems with the SeamlessM4T model using only the synthetic data for training and the validation split of the development set for validation. As shown in Table 5, the performance of the ST systems relates to the volume of data used, highlighting the importance of selecting an appropriate amount of synthetic data.

Notably, the best-performing ST system trained on synthetic data surpasses the cascaded system, which is trained with real ASR and MT data, by approximately 1 BLEU point. This improvement may be attributed to the robustness of the MT system, which generates reasonably accurate synthetic translations.

#Synthetic data	Valid	Test
45K	19.1/41.3	26.2/51.9
23K	**19.9/41.7**	**27.3/52.4**
12K	19.7/41.4	27.3/52.4
6K	19.2/41.4	26.6/52.4
Cascaded	19.1/42.1	26.6/53.2

Table 5: MT-augmented ST systems for North Levantine. The results are presented as BLEU/chrF.

4.7.2 TTS-augmented ST systems

For Bemba, we explore the use of ViTTS and E2TTS to generate synthetic training data. The TTS models are trained using the training split of the development dataset. The source text used for synthesis is derived from NLLB, selected based on criteria such as appropriate text length, as outlined in Table 2. Evaluation results for the TTS systems are provided in Appendix A.

We generate 120K synthetic training samples for each TTS model. This synthetic data is combined with the original development set for training, while the validation split remains unchanged. Following the procedure used for other end-to-end speech translation systems, we fine-tune the pre-trained SeamlessM4T models. As shown in Table

6, the inclusion of synthetic samples yields an improvement of up to one BLEU point compared to training without them. The quantity of synthetic data appears to affect performance; however, no consistent trend is observed regarding the optimal amount.

	30K	60K	120K
VITS	28.0/52.6	28.6/52.7	28.3/52.6
E2TTS	28.7/53.0	28.5/52.8	28.3/52.7
No TTS		27.7/51.3	

Table 6: TTS-augmented ST systems for Bemba with scores on the test split. The column name indicates the number of synthetic data. The results are presented as BLEU/chrF.

We also explored generating synthetic ST data for North Levantine, for which no end-to-end ST data is available. We select the E2TTS model for this setting, based on its marginally better performance observed in the Bemba experiments. The training data for the TTS model comes from the ASR dataset LDC2005S08, while the MT dataset UFAL is used for speech generation. This process yields 60K ST samples, selected using the same criteria as in the Bemba experiments. Given the lack of end-to-end ST training data for North Levantine, we examine training solely with synthetic data, using real data only for validation. As shown in Table 7, relying exclusively on synthetic data results in lower performance compared to the cascaded system. We attribute this to the under-developed TTS model, as reflected in its evaluation in Appendix A.

#Synthetic data	Valid	Test
60K	9.6/29.2	12.9/35.5
30K	9.2/28.6	11.9/34.5
15K	10.8/30.6	13.5/36.8
Cascaded	19.1/42.1	26.6/53.2

Table 7: TTS-augmented ST systems for North Levantine. The results are presented as BLEU/chrF.

4.8 Regularization Enhancement

We conduct experiments with ID across various systems, spanning different tasks and pre-trained models, and consistently observe performance gains. Specifically, ID leads to approximately a 1-point WER reduction in ASR and around a 1 BLEU point gain in both MT and ST tasks. However, we note an exception: ID negatively impacts ASR performance for Arabic dialects. Further investigation is needed to understand the underlying causes of this issue.

Additionally, we find that regularization enhancement and synthetic data augmentation can be additive. Adapting a model trained on synthetic data with ID yields further improvements, as illustrated by the D4 row in Table 3.

4.9 Cascaded VS E2E Systems

We compare the performance of these two widely used and distinct ST systems in low-resource scenarios, but the results are mixed and show no consistent trend. For Bemba and North Levantine, end-to-end systems outperform cascaded systems by approximately 1 BLEU point. In contrast, for Tunisian, end-to-end systems slightly underperform, with a gap of around 0.5 BLEU points. These varying results underscore the importance of adopting language- and dataset-specific strategies in low-resource speech translation.

4.10 MBR Decoding

We apply MBR decoding to the cascaded systems, the E2E systems, and their combination. As presented in Tables 3 and 4, MBR decoding consistently yields minimal to no improvement when applied to individual systems. In contrast, combining the cascaded and E2E systems with MBR decoding consistently results in an improvement of approximately 1.5 BLEU points.

4.11 Submission

The same submission strategy is applied across all three language pairs. The primary system is the MBR combination of the cascaded and E2E systems. The E2E and cascaded systems are the contrastive 1 and 2 systems, respectively.

Table 8 presents the evaluation results reported by Abdulmumin et al. (2025). The test data includes two datasets (test2022 and test2023) for Tunisian and one dataset each for North Levantine and Bemba. Referring to the previous results, the performance comparison between cascaded and E2E systems remains consistent for Bemba, with the cascaded system outperforming the E2E system. In contrast, opposite trends are observed for the Arabic dialects. This difference underscores the necessity for language- or corpus-specific analyses. The MBR combination of cascaded and E2E systems consistently yields performance improvements, highlighting the advantage of integrating both systems.

	aeb test22	aeb test23	apc	bem
ASR	21.0/40.5	23.0/41.8	-	9.2/31.9
ST Primary	22.7/44.4	21.4/42.3	23.3/45.1	30.3/-
ST contrastive1	21.2/43	19.3/40.9	19.1/41.0	29.7/-
ST contrastive2	21.4/43.7	19.2/41.1	21.9/44.7	28.8/-

Table 8: Evaluation results of the submission. The ASR systems are evaluated with CER/WER. The ST systems are evaluated with BLEU/chrF.

5 Conclusion

We participate in the IWSLT 2025 low-resource track, focusing on three language pairs with Bemba, North Levantine, and Tunisian as source languages, and English as the target language. Our focus is on improving model performance through synthetic data augmentation and model regularization. The results demonstrate that high-quality synthetic data can significantly enhance performance. In addition, model regularization proves to be a robust and broadly effective approach across all ASR, MT, and ST tasks in low-resource settings. Finally, our findings highlight the importance of language-specific strategies for building effective speech translation systems, as reflected in the varying outcomes observed across the three language pairs.

Acknowledgement This work is partly supported by the Helmholtz Programme-oriented Funding, with project number 46.24.01, named AI for Language Technologies, funding from the pilot program Core-Informatics of the Helmholtz Association (HGF). It is also supported by the Deutsche Forschungsgemeinschaft (DFG) under the project Computational Language Documentation by 2025 (CLD 2025). Additional support is from the Federal Ministry of Education and Research (BMBF) of Germany under the number 01EF1803B (RELATER).

The work was partly performed on the HoreKa supercomputer funded by the Ministry of Science, Research and the Arts Baden-Württemberg and by the Federal Ministry of Education and Research.

References

Idris Abdulmumin, Victor Agostinelli, Tanel Alumäe, Antonios Anastasopoulos, Ashwin, Luisa Bentivogli, Ondej Bojar, Claudia Borg, Fethi Bougares, Roldano Cattoni, Mauro Cettolo, Lizhong Chen, William Chen, Raj Dabre, Yannick Estève, Marcello Federico, Marco Gaido, Dávid Javorský, Marek Kasztelnik, and 30 others. 2025. Findings of the iwslt 2025 evaluation campaign. In *Proceedings of the 22nd International Conference on Spoken Language Translation (IWSLT 2025)*, Vienna, Austia (in-person and online). Association for Computational Linguistics. To appear.

Loïc Barrault, Yu-An Chung, Mariano Cora Meglioli, David Dale, Ning Dong, Paul-Ambroise Duquenne, Hady Elsahar, Hongyu Gong, Kevin Heffernan, John Hoffman, and 1 others. 2023. Seamlessm4t: Massively multilingual & multimodal machine translation. *arXiv preprint arXiv:2308.11596*.

Waad Ben Kheder, Josef Jon, André Beyer, Abdel Messaoudi, Rabea Affan, Claude Barras, Maxim Tychonov, and Jean-Luc Gauvain. 2024. ALADAN at IWSLT24 low-resource Arabic dialectal speech translation task. In *Proceedings of the 21st International Conference on Spoken Language Translation (IWSLT 2024)*, pages 192–202, Bangkok, Thailand (in-person and online). Association for Computational Linguistics.

William Chen, Wangyou Zhang, Yifan Peng, Xinjian Li, Jinchuan Tian, Jiatong Shi, Xuankai Chang, Soumi Maiti, Karen Livescu, and Shinji Watanabe. 2024. Towards robust speech representation learning for thousands of languages. *arXiv preprint arXiv:2407.00837*.

Asa Cooper Stickland, Xian Li, and Marjan Ghazvininejad. 2021. Recipes for adapting pre-trained monolingual and multilingual models to machine translation. In *Proceedings of the 16th Conference of the European Chapter of the Association for Computational Linguistics: Main Volume*, pages 3440–3453, Online. Association for Computational Linguistics.

Marta R Costa-Jussà, James Cross, Onur Çelebi, Maha Elbayad, Kenneth Heafield, Kevin Heffernan, Elahe Kalbassi, Janice Lam, Daniel Licht, Jean Maillard, and 1 others. 2022. No language left behind: Scaling human-centered machine translation. *arXiv preprint arXiv:2207.04672*.

Sefik Emre Eskimez, Xiaofei Wang, Manthan Thakker, Canrun Li, Chung-Hsien Tsai, Zhen Xiao, Hemin Yang, Zirun Zhu, Min Tang, Xu Tan, Yanqing Liu, Sheng Zhao, and Naoyuki Kanda. 2024. E2 tts: Embarrassingly easy fully non-autoregressive zero-shot tts. *Preprint*, arXiv:2406.18009.

Jonathan Ho and Tim Salimans. 2022. Classifier-free diffusion guidance. *Preprint*, arXiv:2207.12598.

Zheng Jiawei, Hengchao Shang, Zongyao Li, Zhanglin Wu, Daimeng Wei, Zhiqiang Rao, Shaojun Li, Jiaxin Guo, Bin Wei, Yuanchang Luo, and Hao Yang. 2024. HW-TSC's submissions to the IWSLT2024 low-resource speech translation tasks. In *Proceedings of the 21st International Conference on Spoken Language Translation (IWSLT 2024)*, pages 160–163, Bangkok, Thailand (in-person and online). Association for Computational Linguistics.

Jaehyeon Kim, Jungil Kong, and Juhee Son. 2021. Conditional variational autoencoder with adversarial learning for end-to-end text-to-speech. In *International Conference on Machifi-ne Learning*.

Jungil Kong, Jaehyeon Kim, and Jaekyoung Bae. 2020. Hifi-gan: Generative adversarial networks for efficient and high fidelity speech synthesis. In *Advances in Neural Information Processing Systems*, volume 33, pages 17022–17033. Curran Associates, Inc.

R. Kubichek. 1993. Mel-cepstral distance measure for objective speech quality assessment. *Proceedings of IEEE Pacific Rim Conference on Communications Computers and Signal Processing*, 1:125–128 vol.1.

Shankar Kumar and Bill Byrne. 2004. Minimum bayes-risk decoding for statistical machine translation. In *Proceedings of the Human Language Technology Conference of the North American Chapter of the Association for Computational Linguistics: HLT-NAACL 2004*, pages 169–176.

Zhaolin Li and Jan Niehues. 2025. Enhance contextual learning in ASR for endangered low-resource languages. In *Proceedings of the 1st Workshop on Language Models for Underserved Communities (LM4UC 2025)*, pages 1–7, Albuquerque, New Mexico. Association for Computational Linguistics.

Zhaolin Li, Enes Yavuz Ugan, Danni Liu, Carlos Mullov, Tu Anh Dinh, Sai Koneru, Alexander Waibel, and Jan Niehues. 2024. The KIT speech translation systems for IWSLT 2024 dialectal and low-resource track. In *Proceedings of the 21st International Conference on Spoken Language Translation (IWSLT 2024)*, pages 221–228, Bangkok, Thailand (in-person and online). Association for Computational Linguistics.

Yasmin Moslem. 2024. Leveraging synthetic audio data for end-to-end low-resource speech translation. In *Proceedings of the 21st International Conference on Spoken Language Translation (IWSLT 2024)*, pages 265–273, Bangkok, Thailand (in-person and online). Association for Computational Linguistics.

Nathaniel Romney Robinson, Perez Ogayo, Swetha R. Gangu, David R. Mortensen, and Shinji Watanabe. 2022. When is tts augmentation through a pivot language useful? In *Interspeech 2022*, pages 3538–3542.

Nathaniel Romney Robinson, Kaiser Sun, Cihan Xiao, Niyati Bafna, Weiting Tan, Haoran Xu, Henry Li Xinyuan, Ankur Kejriwal, Sanjeev Khudanpur, Kenton Murray, and Paul McNamee. 2024. JHU IWSLT 2024 dialectal and low-resource system description. In *Proceedings of the 21st International Conference on Spoken Language Translation (IWSLT 2024)*, pages 140–153, Bangkok, Thailand (in-person and online). Association for Computational Linguistics.

Stan Salvador and Philip Chan. 2007. Toward accurate dynamic time warping in linear time and space. In *KDD Workshop on Mining Temporal and Sequential Data*.

Hubert Siuzdak. 2024. Vocos: Closing the gap between time-domain and fourier-based neural vocoders for high-quality audio synthesis. *Preprint*, arXiv:2306.00814.

Alexander Tong, Kilian Fatras, Nikolay Malkin, Guillaume Huguet, Yanlei Zhang, Jarrid Rector-Brooks, Guy Wolf, and Yoshua Bengio. 2024. Improving and generalizing flow-based generative models with minibatch optimal transport. *Preprint*, arXiv:2302.00482.

Lijun Wu, Juntao Li, Yue Wang, Qi Meng, Tao Qin, Wei Chen, Min Zhang, Tie-Yan Liu, and 1 others. 2021. R-drop: Regularized dropout for neural networks. *Advances in neural information processing systems*, 34:10890–10905.

Haoran Xu, Philipp Koehn, and Kenton Murray. 2022. The importance of being parameters: An intra-distillation method for serious gains. *arXiv preprint arXiv:2205.11416*.

Guanrou Yang, Fan Yu, Ziyang Ma, Zhihao Du, Zhifu Gao, Shiliang Zhang, and Xie Chen. 2025. Enhancing low-resource asr through versatile tts: Bridging the data gap. In *ICASSP 2025 - 2025 IEEE International Conference on Acoustics, Speech and Signal Processing (ICASSP)*, pages 1–5.

A TTS evaluation

To evaluate the articulation quality of the trained TTS models, we used two metrics: MCD[7] (Mel-Cepstral Distortion (Kubichek, 1993)) and WER. We compute MCD by first extracting 26-dimensional mel-cepstral coefficients from both synthesized and ground-truth speech samples in the validation dataset. To address temporal mismatches between sequences, we employ dynamic time warping (DTW) (Salvador and Chan, 2007) to align the synthesized and reference feature trajectories. The final MCD metric is calculated using the 1-25th coefficients (excluding the energy term) across DTW-aligned frames.

[7] https://github.com/ttslr/python-MCD?tab=readme-ov-file

	MCD	WER
Bemba		
VITS same speaker	5.4	51.0
E2TTS same speaker	5.6	40.9
E2TTS cross speaker	7.7	41.9
North Levantine		
E2TTS same speaker	4.2	113.3
E2TTS cross speaker	9.0	108.3

Table 9: TTS system evaluation.

Additionally, since MCD is not a speaker-independent metric like WER, to reduce the influence of speaker attributes, we conducted assessments in both same-speaker (reconstruction) and cross-speaker settings. The results in Table 9 show that trained TTS models are able to accurately reconstruct the ground-truth audio. In the cross-speaker setting, the MCD scores increase as expected but remain within a reasonable range.

For WER evaluation we use two ASR models trained without the augmented TTS data. Specifically, we use model A5 from Table 3 for Bemba and model A2 from Table 4 for North Levantine. As presented in Table 9, E2TTS achieves reasonable WER performance for low-resource language Bemba, especially considering that the ASR system reports a WER of 31.9 on real data. In contrast, the VITS model underperforms relative to E2TTS in WER evaluations, consistent with the results in Table 6.

As for low-resource language North Levantine, the WER scores are considerably high, suggesting that the E2TTS model remains underdeveloped. This likely contributes to the poor performance of ST models trained with TTS-augmented data, as indicated in Table 7. Further analysis is needed to better understand this underdeveloped TTS model.

AppTek's Automatic Speech Translation: Generating Accurate and Well-Readable Subtitles

Frithjof Petrick, Patrick Wilken, Evgeny Matusov, Nahuel Roselló, Sarah Beranek
AppTek, https://www.apptek.ai
Aachen, Germany
{fpetrick,pwilken,ematusov,nbeneitez,sberanek}@apptek.com

Abstract

We describe AppTek's submission to the subtitling track of the IWSLT 2025 evaluation. We enhance our cascaded speech translation approach by adapting the ASR and the MT models on in-domain data. All components, including intermediate steps such as subtitle source language template creation and line segmentation, are optimized to ensure that the resulting target language subtitles respect the subtitling constraints not only on the number of characters per line and the number of lines in each subtitle block, but also with respect to the desired reading speed. AppTek's machine translation with length control plays the key role in this process, effectively condensing subtitles to these constraints. Our experiments show that this condensation results in high-quality translations that convey the most important information, as measured by metrics such as BLEU or BLEURT, as well as the primary metric subtitle edit rate (SubER).

1 Introduction

Subtitle translation is a complex task that includes much more than recognizing what was uttered in an audio/video recording and translating it into the target language. Accurate timing of the subtitles, segmentation into syntactically and/or semantically coherent units, and comfortable reading speed are important aspects affecting the viewing experience, in addition to mere translation quality (Gerber-Morón et al., 2018; Liao et al., 2021).

In this paper, we describe how AppTek approaches the task with our in-house automatic speech recognition (ASR) and neural machine translation (NMT) systems, which we couple with our intelligent subtitle line segmentation algorithm (Matusov et al., 2019). In addition to algorithmic and modeling improvements, our unconstrained submissions benefit from in-domain data that was either available to us or was automatically extracted from public (parallel) data.

The paper is structured as follows. In the following Section, we describe the three main components of our subtitle translation approach: speech recognition in Section 2.1, machine translation in 2.2 and subtitle segmentation in 2.3. Section 3 gives details of our domain adaptation strategy for adapting to the entertainment and financial news domains which includes the usage of domain tags and fine-tuning on in-domain data. The effectiveness of domain adaptation is supported with experimental results at the end of the section. Next, we focus on the newest enhancements of our system with regard to subtitling constraints - the restrictions on the maximum number of characters per line (CPL), lines per subtitle block (LPB), and the desired maximum reading speed measured in characters per second (CPS). Section 4 explains in detail our approach of space-constrained MT, which includes elaborate MT length control combined with targeted re-translation and line segmentation optimizations. The trade-off between translation quality and compliance with the constraints such as the reading speed is explained at the end of the section, with experimental results showing how AppTek's NMT produces condensed translations that fulfill subtitling constraints just like subtitles from a professional subtitle translator, yet without a significant drop of the core MT quality. Finally, we summarize our findings in Section 5.

2 Subtitle Translation

We follow a cascaded speech translation approach - first, the speech signal is automatically transcribed into an English subtitle file, which is then automatically translated into the target language. Additional challenges related to subtitles are handled between these two components and after one or more translations of an utterance are obtained.

Proceedings of the 22nd International Conference on Spoken Language Translation (IWSLT 2025), pages 222–231
July 31 - August 1, 2025 ©2025 Association for Computational Linguistics

2.1 Speech Recognition

AppTek's automatic speech recognition component is implemented as a hybrid conformer/HMM system. The acoustic model is trained on approximately 30K hours of transcribed, mixed-bandwidth English speech data including broadcast news, telephony, and publicly available open-source datasets. The training corpus includes a broad distribution of English dialects and accents. The acoustic model operates on 80-dimensional log Mel filterbank features and estimates posterior probabilities over 9K tied triphone states. The model architecture is based on a deep Conformer network using approximately 1 billion parameters. This conformer model was trained for 20 epochs using an OCLR-inspired learning rate schedule (Smith and Topin, 2018). Frame-level alignments and state tying were obtained from our previous best conformer-based acoustic model with 350M parameters. This model serves as the general-purpose English ASR system.

For adaptation to the entertainment domain, the general-purpose English ASR model is fine-tuned for approximately 1.5 epochs on 100K hours of in-domain audio, supplemented with 40 hours of music-only data. In both general and domain-specific systems, the language model (LM) is based on the LSTM architecture with over 300M parameters, combined with a count-based n-gram LM used for look-ahead pruning within the hybrid ASR framework. The vocabulary used across both LMs consists of approximately 250K words.

Punctuation marks and word casing are predicted on the raw ASR output with a separate LSTM sequence labeling model. The predicted sentence-final punctuation (period, question mark, exclamation mark) is then used to define sentence-like units for translation.

Optionally, we also apply inverse text normalization (ITN) to convert spoken numbers, dates, monetary amounts, and other entities involving numbers to their well-formatted text form that uses digits. This is done with an attention-based RNN sequence-to-sequence model trained to recover the original English written text from a synthetic spoken form, which we create by applying hand-crafted text normalization rules. For the submission, we make use of this ITN system for the Asharq-Bloomberg task, as the number of numeric entities in financial news is high and it is beneficial to have them correctly represented already in the source language. For ITV, we skip this step and instead rely on the MT system's ability to do the conversion to written form as part of the translation process (see Section 2.2).

2.2 Text Translation

AppTek's NMT system is a variant of the Transformer Big architecture (Vaswani et al., 2017) that uses a factored embedding representation on the source and target side for encoding word case, subword segmentation and glossary transfer information (Wilken and Matusov, 2019; Dinu et al., 2019). The system is trained to support additional input signals, represented with special tokens on the source or target side (Ha et al., 2016).

Part of the training data for which document labels are available is processed to include the context of the previous sentence with a separator, following the approach of Tiedemann and Scherrer (2017), with the difference that also sentences without context are used in training, so that the ability to benefit from the extra context can be turned on or off during inference.

As mentioned in the previous section, the MT system supports "spoken" input, i.e. without punctuation and casing, and with numbers and other numeric entities represented with words. For this, a part of the MT parallel training data is duplicated, and then the source language side of the copy is processed using our rule-based text normalization to create this spoken form.

Our MT systems support genre tags for approximately 20 genres, including a genre "news" for news-like content and "dialogs" for movie-like dialog or subtitle content. We use tags for these two genres in the experiments below. The training data is partitioned into genres using a sentence-level classifier trained on monolingual English training data, for which genre information is known.

All AppTek's MT systems support a length control mechanism which we applied in previous IWSLT submissions (Bahar et al., 2023). It is based on prefix tokens added to the target-side training data which represent length classes according to the target-to-source character count ratio. The boundaries of the length classes are chosen so that an equal number of training examples falls into each class (most extreme classes are chosen to be half the size). We use five length bins for the English to German and seven for the English to Arabic system. For training data that originates from subtitles in particular, our assumption is that it naturally consists of a mix of verbatim as well as differently condensed translation examples, and via the length token one can select between these condensation levels at inference time.

For certain language pairs, AppTek's MT systems also support style and speaker gender tags (Matusov et al., 2020). For English-to-German, the style tag controls the formality level of the output. The default tag value is "undefined" - this means that the system decides what formality level to use (e.g. formal second-person German pronoun "Sie" or informal "du") based solely on the context of the sentence. When the formality control is set, the system chooses the desired formality level. In the experiments below, we set the formality level to "formal" for the Asharq-Bloomberg financial news translation, where a formal translation style is expected.

It is worth mentioning that all of the above controls are implemented in AppTek's MT API as parameters[1] which a user can set based on prior knowledge or information derived from the upstream components (such as speaker gender).

2.3 Subtitle Segmentation

To combine ASR, MT and additional components into a subtitling pipeline, we follow the source template approach described in a previous edition's submission (Bahar et al., 2023). It consists of two steps: creation of captions in the original language of the video (here, English) and translation of these captions while keeping the subtitle blocks including their timings fixed. In both steps, a neural segmentation model is used to place line and block boundaries at semantically meaningful positions in the text, while additional hard constraints make sure the predicted segmentation adheres to the subtitling constraints (42 characters per line, 2 lines per block; while creating source language blocks also minimum and maximum block duration of 0.83 and 7 seconds, respectively). Automatically predicted punctuation and pauses of 3 seconds or longer are used to separate sentences, which are processed independently by the line segmentation algorithm (Matusov et al., 2019). Block timings are created from ASR word timings of the first and last word in a block - these are extremely accurate in a hybrid ASR system. For translation, the sentences as defined above - which may span several subtitle blocks - are sent to the MT component and are re-inserted into the source template using an additional hard constraint that enforces translations to be segmented into the existing blocks in terms of number and approximate relative sizes. More details on the subtitling pipeline can be found in Bahar et al. (2023).

In this year's submission we improve this subtitling pipeline in particular by focusing on reading speed compliance. This is achieved by tightly integrating MT length control with the space constraints of subtitling. The method will be described in Section 4.1.

3 Domain Adaptation

In the following we describe how we adapt our system to the specific domains of the subtitling tasks of this year.

3.1 Domain and Style Tags

As described in Section 2.2, AppTek's MT system supports domain and style control at inference time. This allows it to adapt to a specific domain without retraining the model.

For the ITV data we set the domain tag 'dialogs', but enforce no style control as it varies throughout each movie. For Bloomberg, we set the domain to 'news' and the style to 'formal'.

3.2 Fine-tuning with Parallel Data

While domain and style parameters optimize the controllability of a single model, stronger domain adaptation can be achieved by creating specialized models via fine-tuning on in-domain data.

For the ITV domain, we fine-tune both the ASR and the MT systems on movie subtitling data provided by one of AppTek's major media and entertainment customers. The ASR system adapted for the task is described in Section 2.1. To adapt the MT system, we extract sentences from English and German subtitles and obtain their sentence alignment using Vecalign (Thompson and Koehn, 2019). After filtering, a total of 12.6M sentence pairs with 130M running words on the English side is obtained. Using this parallel corpus, we fine-tune our general domain English-to-German MT system for approximately one epoch with a reduced learning rate.

For Bloomberg, we only adapt the MT system. In case of the Bloomberg English-to-Arabic task, we have access to a parallel corpus provided by Asharq Business with Bloomberg as part of AppTek's partnership with this company. It con-

[1] https://docs.apptek.com/reference/machine-translation

tains human-curated English captions and their human translations into Arabic, with a total of 240K sentence pairs with 7.3M running words counted on the English side. The source of the data are Bloomberg news programs similar to the ones used as development and test data at the IWSLT evaluation. We made sure that only historical data excluding the IWSLT dev/test data was used for training. The segmentation of this in-domain training data is mostly based on speaker turns and pauses and in most cases includes full sentences or speaker turns, so that an additional sentence alignment step is not necessary. Fine-tuning of our general-domain English-to-Arabic MT model is then performed for approximately one epoch.

3.3 Data Filtering Based on Development Set

For some domains and languages, it is challenging to find parallel in-domain datasets. This is, for example, the case for translating Bloomberg content into German. We use a simple filtering approach to collect parallel sentences that are similar to specific seed data, here, the German references of the Bloomberg development set.

Our filtering approach maps the sentences of the development set and the target-side of the general-domain parallel data into a shared embedding space. Sentence embeddings are obtained by averaging GloVe embeddings (Pennington et al., 2014) of each word in the sentence, as described in Arora et al. (2017). We embed the entire seed data into a single vector v_{seed} by averaging the embeddings of its target sentences. To filter a given corpus $\mathcal{C}$ down to size n, we choose the n sentences $e \in \mathcal{C}$ with the highest dot product $v(e)^T v_{\text{seed}}$ against the sentence embedding $v(e)$.

In our submission, we create German Bloomberg adaptation data from these corpora: a) ECB, Europarl, JRC-Acquis, NewsCommentary and DGT corpora from OPUS (Tiedemann, 2009) which all are closely related to the financial news domain, b) CCMatrix (Schwenk et al., 2021) as a large crawled corpus, as well as c) OpenSubtitles (Lison and Tiedemann, 2016) and TED2020 from OPUS to better match the translation style to the subtitling domain. We use pre-trained German word embeddings provided by Ferreira et al. (2016) to calculate the sentence embeddings. From each corpus, we select $n = 30\text{K}$ sentences using the method above, ending up with a total of 157K deduplicated sentence pairs for fine-tuning.

The data obtained from our filtering is sentence-level. During fine-tuning, we mix it with TED 2020 samples with document-level context in a 1:1 ratio and otherwise follow the same recipe as described above for fine-tuning on parallel data.

ASR	MT	SubER	BLEU
ITV German			
General	General	73.4	18.8
General	+ domain tag	72.5	19.3
General	Fine-tuning	69.6	20.8
Adapted	General	71.4	19.5
Adapted	+ domain tag	71.3	20.1
Adapted	Fine-tuning	67.2	21.7

Table 1: Domain-adaptation of ASR and MT models on the ITV task, metrics measured on the 2025 development set. No subtitle condensation is applied (Section 4).

MT System	SubER	BLEU
Bloomberg German		
General	61.8	26.6
+ domain & formality tag	61.4	26.6
Finetuned (filter via dev set)	59.6	27.1
Bloomberg Arabic		
General	62.5	20.6
+ domain tag	61.8	20.9
Finetuned (in-domain data)	61.3	21.3

Table 2: Domain-adaptation for the German and Arabic Bloomberg tasks, on the 2025 development set. No subtitle condensation is applied (Section 4).

3.4 Results

The results for adapting the ASR and MT models for the ITV German task are shown in Table 1. For Bloomberg, we only adapt the MT model and show the results in Table 2.

We report case- and punctuation-sensitive subtitle edit rate SubER (Wilken et al., 2022) and BLEU (Papineni et al., 2002; Post, 2018) scores. Both are calculated with the SubER tool[2] using the final MT hypothesis in subtitle format. For BLEU calculation, the reference subtitles are converted into plain text sentences based on sentence final-punctuation. The hypothesis is aligned to the reference with an edit distance based algorithm, similar to the one implemented in mwerSegmenter (Matusov et al., 2005).

Comparing the upper and lower half of Table 1, one can see a clear positive effect of ASR domain

[2] https://github.com/apptek/SubER

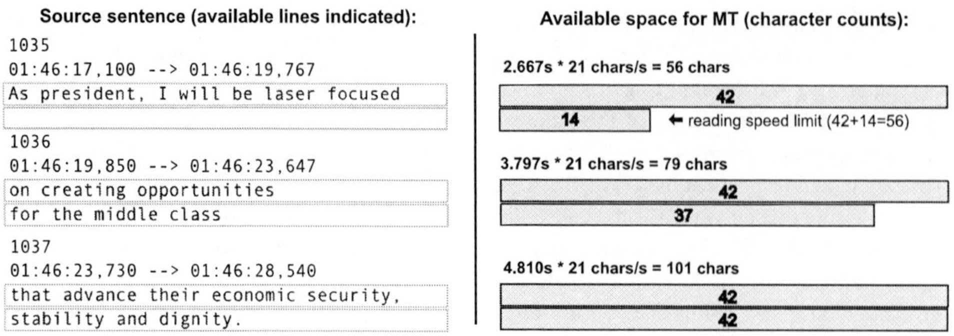

Figure 1: Calculation of MT space constraint. Translation of a sentence from the source subtitle template (left) has to fit into the same blocks it is extracted from. Blocks are limited to 2 lines of 42 characters. In addition, the reading speed limit defines a maximum character count per block (block duration multiplied by CPS value) to which we truncate the available lines. The list of character counts (here: `42,14,42,37,42,42`) is passed to the MT component to request a translation that fits into this space. Notes: source blocks with only one line allow for an additional line to be added during translation; last block in the example has long enough duration so that reading speed limit is fulfilled as a consequence of line and character limit; the calculated space does *not* limit the length of individual lines in the final subtitle file, e.g. the second line can be longer than 14 characters if the first line is shortened accordingly.

adaptation on the end-to-end ITV task performance. Presumably, improved robustness to difficult audio conditions such as background sounds and music, as well as adaptation to a wide range of forms of speech (mumbling, shouting, laughter, etc.) are some of the key factors. We refrain from calculating word error rates (WER) using the English development set subtitles as reference, as they are not exact verbatim transcriptions. However, for a manually annotated in-house test set of similar entertainment content, we measure a WER improvement from 13.1% to 12.0% as the result of fine-tuning.

Regarding machine translation, both adaptation methods – setting domain tags and fine-tuning – improve SubER and BLEU over the unadapted system; yet fine-tuning is consistently more effective. The biggest gains are observed on the ITV task, where the fine-tuning corpus is the largest and already in subtitle form. In particular, the MT system learns to produce shorter translations that better match the space constraints of subtitling, even without the explicit length control that will be introduced in the next section. On the Bloomberg task, fine-tuning is less effective. For English-to-Arabic, this may be partially explained by the fact that a portion of the fine-tuning data was already included in the training data of the general domain MT system. When comparing the effect of fine-tuning for English-to-German vs. English-to-Arabic, the automatically constructed English-German in-domain data set seems to achieve a similar positive effect to the real in-domain customer data used for Arabic as the target language.

While combining fine-tuning with the domain and formality tags is possible, we do not observe any significant improvements over the fine-tuned system, as it already learned domain and formality from the training data.

4 Subtitle Condensation

Subtitles do not only need to provide accurate translations, they also need to follow readability constraints to not hinder an immersive viewing experience. In last year's edition of the subtitling track, only one out of eight submitted systems for the English-to-German task achieved a compliance with the desired maximum reading speed of 21 characters per second (CPS) for more than 80% of the subtitles. We therefore focus on the reading speed constraint this year while at the same time aim to keep translation quality at a high level.

4.1 Space-constrained MT

We have made use of MT length control, as described in Section 2.2, for automatic subtitling in past IWSLT editions (Bahar et al., 2023; Ahmad et al., 2024; Wilken and Matusov, 2022). Here, we improve our approach by making the length constraints more exact and by basing them on the reading speed limit, not only the line limit. To do this, we make the following changes to the subtitle translation pipeline described in Section 2.3:

1. When extracting sentences from the source subtitle template, we calculate the available space the translation has to fit into, see Figure 1. Because line breaks cannot occur at arbitrary character positions, only at word boundaries, calculating a single character count value as the length limit for the translation would be imprecise. This problem is illustrated in Figure 2. Instead, we express the space constraint in terms of a list of character count values per line. Usually we have 2 lines of 42 characters available for each block, but this gets truncated by the character limit per individual block, which is block duration multiplied by the reading speed limit.

2. We implement an iterative process in the MT component. In the first iteration, translation is done without a length constraint by letting the model predict the length token itself. In the second iteration, the optimal length token is guessed based on the length ratio between total available space and the source character count and is then forced in the first decoding step. In each subsequent iteration the next shorter length class is selected. This process stops as soon as all words of the translation can be put into the space calculated in step 1 without overflow, or if the shortest length class is reached.[3]

3. Additional logic is added to the line segmentation algorithm (Section 2.3) to guarantee that a translation which *can* fulfill all space constraints indeed *does* fulfill all constraints after segmentation. This involves look-ahead pruning of partial hypotheses for which the remaining words do not fit into the remaining available blocks/lines.

4. Before translation, we decrease the source-side reading speed by shifting block end times beyond the duration of the actual speech onto the start of the next block or until a targeted CPS value is met. This way, space constraints for MT are relaxed and more content can be preserved, leading to improved translation quality scores. Here, we even use a CPS value of 17 instead of 21 to increase the effect. We repeat this block duration extension after translation (using 21 CPS). However, there it affects less than 1% of the blocks.

4.2 Results

To put the following evaluation of subtitle condensation into context, we first analyze how well the human-created reference subtitles adhere to the subtitling constraints. Table 3 shows that while the lines-per-block and characters-per-line limits are strictly followed, the reading speed limit is not. In fact, in practice it is often viewed as a soft limit that is expected to be met only for the majority of subtitles of a given film/show, but not necessarily for all of them. In addition, it can be seen that the reading speed limit is violated more often for German. German sentences are longer on average than their English equivalents, making it harder to fulfill a certain character limit.

Task	Ref. Compliance [%]		
	LPB	**CPL**	**CPS**
ITV German	100.0	100.0	88.6
Bloomberg German	100.0	100.0	78.4
Bloomberg Arabic	99.9	100.0	97.4

Table 3: Fraction of subtitles in the 2025 development set reference compliant with the 2 lines-per-block (LPB), 42 characters-per-line (CPL) and 21 characters-per-second (CPS) limits.

To show the effect of subtitle condensation, in Figure 3 we plot the translation quality as measured in BLEU against CPS compliance (always based on 21 characters per second) while using different CPS values to constrain the translation lengths. We see a trade-off between the two, which is expected as more content can be preserved in longer translations, leading to more n-gram matches with the reference. Especially if the CPS compliance surpasses the one of the human reference we see a clear drop in BLEU score.

Even when calculating length constraints using the targeted value of 21 characters per second, the compliancy does not reach 100%. Manual inspection reveals that the remaining violations are indeed cases where the speaking rate is so high that even the shortest MT length class does not lead to a compliant translation. This in particular happens for very short sentences containing no superfluous words. Notably, already the generated English source templates, which – apart from some ASR errors – contain verbatim transcripts, have a CPS compliancy of only around 80%, indicating that there are many fast-paced dialogues in the development set videos which would require heavy condensation. For extreme cases, we see a limitation of our approach of sentence-by-sentence translation, because whole sentences might have to be left out in the subtitles to keep up with the video, or mul-

[3] This iterative approach is an efficient alternative to the "Length ROVER" (Wilken and Matusov, 2022) with similar output but a significantly reduced number of translation passes, therefore suitable for commercial application.

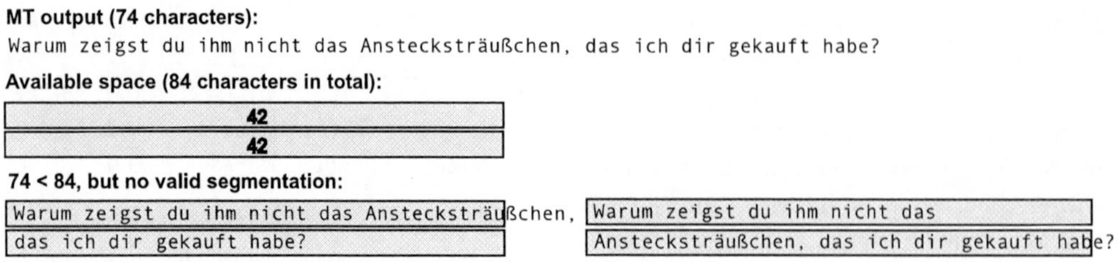

Figure 2: Example illustrating that a simple translation length limit in terms of total character count is too imprecise for subtitle template translation. Assuming a given source sentence is contained within a single block, it is not enough to limit translation length to 84 characters, which one would naively derive from a block size of 2 lines with 42 characters. In fact, as shown, even a translation of 74 characters – depending on the specific word lengths – may not fit into one block as line breaks may only occur at word boundaries[4]. This is the reason we compute an exact line-wise space constraint according to Figure 1 and use it as compliancy check while selecting MT length variants.

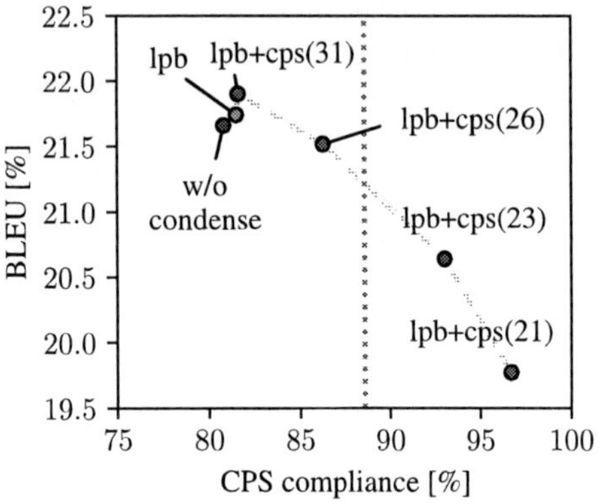

Figure 3: Different subtitle condensation levels on the English-to-German ITV development set: we start by condensing translations to fit into 2 lines per block (lpb), and then introduce different reading speed values (cps) as additional constraint. The more constrained settings lead to worse translation quality (BLEU), but better 21-characters-per-second compliance (CPS). The reference set has a compliance of 88.6 % (dotted vertical line).

tiple sentences would have to be condensed into a single one.

We determine which condensation setting to use for each task by re-translating with increasingly strict length control when necessary (see Section 4.1): we always try to condense subtitles to fit into two lines (LPB compliance), and then compare condensation with different target reading speeds (CPS). The MT reading speed limit is then chosen so that the subtitles have a reasonably high CPS compliance, while the translation quality does not deteriorate too much. For the ITV task, we set the condensation parameter to 23 CPS, while for both Bloomberg tasks we set 21 CPS. These settings are also optimal in terms of SubER.

Table 4 shows the main results of the subtitle condensation for all three tasks. We report SubER and BLEU as described previously in Section 3.4. In addition to the BLEU score, we also compute the neural metric BLEURT (Sellam et al., 2020) on the MT plain text hypotheses aligned to plain text reference translations by the SubER tool. The compliance metrics are calculated with the script provided by Papi et al. (2023).

Subtitle condensation leads to more compliant and thus overall shorter subtitles for all three tasks. In fact, the subtitles generated by our systems are more CPS compliant than the human-created reference translations of the development set (Table 3). Our implementation further guarantees a CPL compliance of 100%, as we chose to violate the LPB limit instead by adding additional lines in cases where the translation does not fit into the available space.

Although condensation does have a negative impact on the translation quality when measured in BLEU or BLEURT, it does lead to an improvement in SubER. One reason for this is that SubER does not penalize word omissions as harshly. In case of BLEU, short hypotheses are explicitly penalized with the brevity penalty (all three of the condensed systems have a hypothesis/reference length ratio of less than 1).

The IWSLT findings report (Abdulmumin et al., 2025) verifies that our system also produced highly space compliant subtitles on the evaluation data: We achieve 100.0% CPL and more than 99% LPB compliancy on all three tasks, and have 93.8%, 92.4% and 99.8% LPB compliancy on the ITV,

[4] Hyphenation to split words across lines is not common in subtitling.

Task	Condense	SubER (↓)	Bleu (↑)	Bleurt (↑)	Compliance [%] (↑)		
					LPB	CPL	CPS
ITV German	✗	67.2	21.7	0.454	98.0	100.0	80.8
	✓	64.9	20.6	0.448	100.0	100.0	93.0
Bloomberg German	✗	59.6	27.1	0.548	95.3	100.0	76.9
	✓	59.2	25.6	0.536	99.3	100.0	92.1
Bloomberg Arabic	✗	61.3	21.3	0.568	99.6	100.0	96.4
	✓	61.2	20.8	0.563	100.0	100.0	99.8

Table 4: Subtitle condensation results on all three IWSLT tasks, reported on the 2025 development set. All models are domain-adapted (via fine-tuning). The three models with condensation enabled correspond to our submitted primary systems.

Bloomberg German and Arabic test sets respectively, while maintaining high translation quality.

Looking back to the IWSLT 2023, we report a significant improvement over the last two years. While we obtained the best automated SubER scores on the ITV test set among all submissions (Agarwal et al., 2023), the 2023 system's SubER score on the development set (the same one used in this year's evaluation) was 71.4 (Bahar et al., 2023). In comparison, our system from this year scores an substantial 6.5 points better in this metric.

5 Conclusions

This paper presented AppTek's submission for the unconstrained subtitling track of the IWSLT 2025. Our focus this year was to a) boost translation quality by domain- and style-specific adaptation, and b) deliver readable subtitles that adhere to given space and reading-speed constraints.

Our key findings are as follows:

- **Domain and style adaptation matter.** Fine-tuning the system on in-domain data yields a large quality gain as measured in BLEU and BLEURT. The simpler, tag-based adaption approach does not require additional training but is less effective.

- **Length-aware condensation works.** The proposed condensation algorithm generates subtitles with characters-per-line (CPL), lines-per-block (LPB) and character-per-second (CPS) compliance scores similar to or better than human references, while only marginally decreasing BLEU and BLEURT scores. The trade-off between space and reading speed constraints and the general translation quality can further be controlled gradually.

Together, these methods result a substantial boost in SubER – the track's primary evaluation metric.

Acknowledgments

This work was (partially) supported by the project RESCALE within the program *AI Lighthouse Projects for the Environment, Climate, Nature and Resources* funded by the Federal Ministry of Germany for the Environment, Nature Conservation, Nuclear Safety and Consumer Protection (BMUV), funding ID: 6KI32006B.

References

Idris Abdulmumin, Victor Agostinelli, Tanel Alumäe, Antonios Anastasopoulos, Ashwin, Luisa Bentivogli, Ondřej Bojar, Claudia Borg, Fethi Bougares, Roldano Cattoni, Mauro Cettolo, Lizhong Chen, William Chen, Raj Dabre, Yannick Estève, Marcello Federico, Marco Gaido, Dávid Javorský, Marek Kasztelnik, and 30 others. 2025. Findings of the iwslt 2025 evaluation campaign. In *Proceedings of the 22nd International Conference on Spoken Language Translation (IWSLT 2025)*, Vienna, Austia (in-person and online). Association for Computational Linguistics. To appear.

Milind Agarwal, Sweta Agrawal, Antonios Anastasopoulos, Luisa Bentivogli, Ondřej Bojar, Claudia Borg, Marine Carpuat, Roldano Cattoni, Mauro Cettolo, Mingda Chen, William Chen, Khalid Choukri, Alexandra Chronopoulou, Anna Currey, Thierry Declerck, Qianqian Dong, Kevin Duh, Yannick Estève, Marcello Federico, and 43 others. 2023. FINDINGS OF THE IWSLT 2023 EVALUATION CAMPAIGN. In *Proceedings of the 20th International Conference on Spoken Language Translation (IWSLT 2023)*, pages 1–61, Toronto, Canada (in-person and online). Association for Computational Linguistics.

Ibrahim Said Ahmad, Antonios Anastasopoulos, Ondřej Bojar, Claudia Borg, Marine Carpuat, Roldano Cattoni, Mauro Cettolo, William Chen, Qianqian Dong, Marcello Federico, Barry Haddow, Dávid Javorský, Mateusz Krubiński, Tsz Kin Lam, Xutai

Ma, Prashant Mathur, Evgeny Matusov, Chandresh Maurya, John McCrae, and 25 others. 2024. FINDINGS OF THE IWSLT 2024 EVALUATION CAMPAIGN. In *Proceedings of the 21st International Conference on Spoken Language Translation (IWSLT 2024)*, pages 1–11, Bangkok, Thailand (in-person and online). Association for Computational Linguistics.

Sanjeev Arora, Yingyu Liang, and Tengyu Ma. 2017. A simple but tough-to-beat baseline for sentence embeddings. In *5th International Conference on Learning Representations, ICLR 2017, Toulon, France, April 24-26, 2017, Conference Track Proceedings*. OpenReview.net.

Parnia Bahar, Patrick Wilken, Javier Iranzo-Sánchez, Mattia Di Gangi, Evgeny Matusov, and Zoltán Tüske. 2023. Speech translation with style: AppTek's submissions to the IWSLT subtitling and formality tracks in 2023. In *Proceedings of the 20th International Conference on Spoken Language Translation (IWSLT 2023)*, pages 251–260, Toronto, Canada (in-person and online). Association for Computational Linguistics.

Georgiana Dinu, Prashant Mathur, Marcello Federico, and Yaser Al-Onaizan. 2019. Training neural machine translation to apply terminology constraints. In *Proceedings of the 57th Annual Meeting of the Association for Computational Linguistics*, pages 3063–3068, Florence, Italy. Association for Computational Linguistics.

Daniel C. Ferreira, André F. T. Martins, and Mariana S. C. Almeida. 2016. Jointly learning to embed and predict with multiple languages. In *Proceedings of the 54th Annual Meeting of the Association for Computational Linguistics, ACL 2016, August 7-12, 2016, Berlin, Germany, Volume 1: Long Papers*. The Association for Computer Linguistics.

Olivia Gerber-Morón, Agnieszka Szarkowska, and Bencie Woll. 2018. The impact of text segmentation on subtitle reading. *Journal of Eye Movement Research*, 11(4):10–16910.

Thanh-Le Ha, Jan Niehues, and Alex Waibel. 2016. Toward multilingual neural machine translation with universal encoder and decoder. In *Proceedings of the 13th International Conference on Spoken Language Translation*, Seattle, Washington D.C. International Workshop on Spoken Language Translation.

Sixin Liao, Lili Yu, Erik D Reichle, and Jan-Louis Kruger. 2021. Using eye movements to study the reading of subtitles in video. *Scientific Studies of Reading*, 25(5):417–435.

Pierre Lison and Jörg Tiedemann. 2016. OpenSubtitles2016: Extracting large parallel corpora from movie and TV subtitles. In *Proceedings of the Tenth International Conference on Language Resources and Evaluation (LREC'16)*, pages 923–929, Portorož, Slovenia. European Language Resources Association (ELRA).

Evgeny Matusov, Gregor Leusch, Oliver Bender, and Hermann Ney. 2005. Evaluating machine translation output with automatic sentence segmentation. In *Proceedings of the Second International Workshop on Spoken Language Translation*, Pittsburgh, Pennsylvania, USA.

Evgeny Matusov, Patrick Wilken, and Yota Georgakopoulou. 2019. Customizing neural machine translation for subtitling. In *Proceedings of the Fourth Conference on Machine Translation (Volume 1: Research Papers)*, pages 82–93, Florence, Italy. Association for Computational Linguistics.

Evgeny Matusov, Patrick Wilken, and Christian Herold. 2020. Flexible customization of a single neural machine translation system with multi-dimensional metadata inputs. In *Proceedings of the 14th Conference of the Association for Machine Translation in the Americas (Volume 2: User Track)*, pages 204–216, Virtual. Association for Machine Translation in the Americas.

Sara Papi, Marco Gaido, Alina Karakanta, Mauro Cettolo, Matteo Negri, and Marco Turchi. 2023. Direct speech translation for automatic subtitling. *Trans. Assoc. Comput. Linguistics*, 11:1355–1376.

Kishore Papineni, Salim Roukos, Todd Ward, and Wei-Jing Zhu. 2002. Bleu: a method for automatic evaluation of machine translation. In *Proceedings of the 40th Annual Meeting of the Association for Computational Linguistics, July 6-12, 2002, Philadelphia, PA, USA*, pages 311–318. ACL.

Jeffrey Pennington, Richard Socher, and Christopher D. Manning. 2014. Glove: Global vectors for word representation. In *Proceedings of the 2014 Conference on Empirical Methods in Natural Language Processing, EMNLP 2014, October 25-29, 2014, Doha, Qatar, A meeting of SIGDAT, a Special Interest Group of the ACL*, pages 1532–1543. ACL.

Matt Post. 2018. A call for clarity in reporting BLEU scores. In *Proceedings of the Third Conference on Machine Translation: Research Papers*, pages 186–191, Brussels, Belgium. Association for Computational Linguistics.

Holger Schwenk, Guillaume Wenzek, Sergey Edunov, Edouard Grave, Armand Joulin, and Angela Fan. 2021. Ccmatrix: Mining billions of high-quality parallel sentences on the web. In *Proceedings of the 59th Annual Meeting of the Association for Computational Linguistics and the 11th International Joint Conference on Natural Language Processing, ACL/IJCNLP 2021, (Volume 1: Long Papers), Virtual Event, August 1-6, 2021*, pages 6490–6500. Association for Computational Linguistics.

Thibault Sellam, Dipanjan Das, and Ankur P. Parikh. 2020. BLEURT: learning robust metrics for text generation. In *Proceedings of the 58th Annual Meeting of the Association for Computational Linguistics, ACL 2020, Online, July 5-10, 2020*, pages 7881–7892. Association for Computational Linguistics.

Leslie N. Smith and Nicholay Topin. 2018. Super-convergence: Very fast training of neural networks using large learning rates. *Preprint*, arXiv:1708.07120.

Brian Thompson and Philipp Koehn. 2019. Vecalign: Improved sentence alignment in linear time and space. In *Proceedings of the 2019 Conference on Empirical Methods in Natural Language Processing and the 9th International Joint Conference on Natural Language Processing (EMNLP-IJCNLP)*, pages 1342–1348, Hong Kong, China. Association for Computational Linguistics.

Jörg Tiedemann. 2009. *News from OPUS - A Collection of Multilingual Parallel Corpora with Tools and Interfaces*, volume V, pages 237–248.

Jörg Tiedemann and Yves Scherrer. 2017. Neural machine translation with extended context. In *Proceedings of the Third Workshop on Discourse in Machine Translation*, pages 82–92, Copenhagen, Denmark. Association for Computational Linguistics.

Ashish Vaswani, Noam Shazeer, Niki Parmar, Jakob Uszkoreit, Llion Jones, Aidan N Gomez, Łukasz Kaiser, and Illia Polosukhin. 2017. Attention is all you need. In *Advances in Neural Information Processing Systems*, pages 5998–6008.

Patrick Wilken, Panayota Georgakopoulou, and Evgeny Matusov. 2022. Suber - A metric for automatic evaluation of subtitle quality. In *Proceedings of the 19th International Conference on Spoken Language Translation, IWSLT@ACL 2022, Dublin, Ireland (in-person and online), May 26-27, 2022*, pages 1–10. Association for Computational Linguistics.

Patrick Wilken and Evgeny Matusov. 2019. Novel applications of factored neural machine translation. *Preprint*, arXiv:1910.03912.

Patrick Wilken and Evgeny Matusov. 2022. AppTek's submission to the IWSLT 2022 isometric spoken language translation task. In *Proceedings of the 19th International Conference on Spoken Language Translation (IWSLT 2022)*, pages 369–378, Dublin, Ireland (in-person and online). Association for Computational Linguistics.

KIT's Offline Speech Translation and Instruction Following Submission for IWSLT 2025

Sai Koneru*♣, Maike Züfle*♥, Thai-Binh Nguyen, Seymanur Akti, Jan Niehues, Alexander Waibel

Karlsruhe Institute of Technology

firstname.lastname@kit.edu

Abstract

The scope of the International Workshop on Spoken Language Translation (IWSLT) has recently broadened beyond traditional Speech Translation (ST) to encompass a wider array of tasks, including Speech Question Answering and Summarization. This shift is partly driven by the growing capabilities of modern systems, particularly with the success of Large Language Models (LLMs). In this paper, we present the Karlsruhe Institute of Technology's submissions for the Offline ST and Instruction Following (IF) tracks, where we leverage LLMs to enhance performance across all tasks. For the Offline ST track, we propose a pipeline that employs multiple automatic speech recognition systems, whose outputs are fused using an LLM with document-level context. This is followed by a two-step translation process, incorporating additional refinement step to improve translation quality. For the IF track, we develop an end-to-end model that integrates a speech encoder with an LLM to perform a wide range of instruction-following tasks. We complement it with a final document-level refinement stage to further enhance output quality by using contextual information.

1 Introduction

This paper provides an overview of the systems submitted by the Karlsruhe Institute of Technology (KIT) to the Offline Speech Translation (ST) and the Constraint Long Instruction-Following (IF) tasks of IWSLT 2025. For the Offline track, we participate in the unconstrained setting for the *English→German* language pair. For the IF task, we participate in the constrained-long track, aiming to perform Automatic Speech Recognition (ASR), Speech Translation (ST), Spoken Question Answering (SQA), and Speech Summarization (SSUM) across various languages.

A growing research trend in the field is the application of Large Language Models (LLMs) to speech processing tasks (Tang et al., 2023; Züfle and Niehues, 2024; Chu et al., 2024b; Abouelenin et al., 2025, among others), leveraging their strong general knowledge and natural language understanding capabilities. These strengths make LLMs particularly relevant to both the Offline ST and IF tracks. Accordingly, in our submissions, we explore strategies for effectively integrating LLMs into speech processing pipelines.

There are multiple approaches to leveraging LLMs in speech systems. One strategy involves incorporating LLMs as an additional step within a cascaded architecture (Koneru et al., 2024a), where they can perform task-specific refinement. This modular approach allows each component to be trained independently, benefiting from specialized data. Alternatively, LLMs can be integrated in an end-to-end fashion (Tang et al., 2023; Züfle and Niehues, 2024; Chu et al., 2024b; Abouelenin et al., 2025), allowing for better information flow and potentially improving generalization to unseen tasks.

Although both the Offline and IF tasks fall under the umbrella of speech processing, they differ significantly in nature. In the offline setting, speed and adaptability to unseen tasks are not primary concerns. In contrast, the IF task demands flexibility and generalization, as the system must handle a variety of instructions. This has an impact on the architectures we choose for the different tracks.

For the Offline track, we utilize LLMs specialized on a specific task as refinement modules within a cascaded architecture. This is common practice; all systems submitted to IWSLT 2024 for this track employed a cascaded architecture (Ahmad et al., 2024), underlining its practical advantages in training the system due to availability in data, e.g for low-resource languages (Liu et al., 2023), and simplicity by decomposing into smaller tasks.

For the IF track, training a dedicated cascaded

* Equal Contribution

♣ Offline, ♥ Instruction-Following

Proceedings of the 22nd International Conference on Spoken Language Translation (IWSLT 2025), pages 232–244
July 31 - August 1, 2025 ©2025 Association for Computational Linguistics

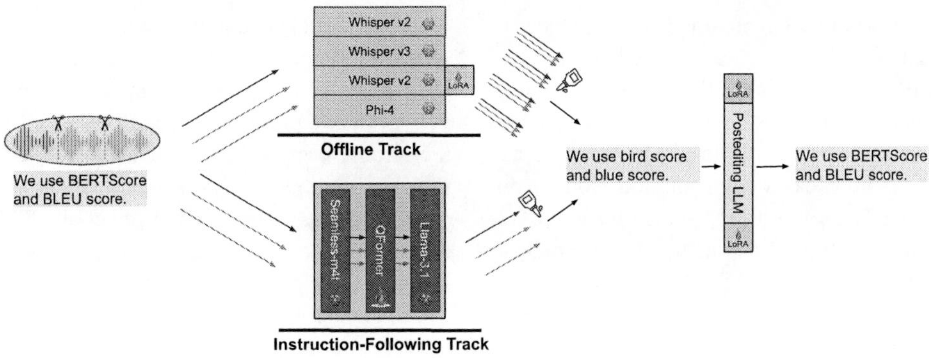

Figure 1: For the Instruction-Following track, we train an end-to-end SpeechLLM, while the Offline track relies on an ensemble of existing models. To enhance the outputs from both tracks, we apply a post-editing model that provides two main benefits: correcting scientific terminology and recovering context that may be lost due to the segmentation of long audio sequences.

system for each task is not an efficient solution, moreover, the goal of this track is to build a model that can follow different instructions. Consequently, we adopt an end-to-end approach using a Speech Large Language Model (SpeechLLM). Nevertheless, for tasks such as ASR, ST, and SSUM, we also include an additional refinement step to enhance fluency and contextual consistency in the output.

An overview of both systems exploiting LLMs internally or via post-editing for refinement, can be found in Fig. 1. We describe the details of each system in the following sections. First, we present the Offline ST track system in Section 2. Then, we discuss the IF track system in Section 3.

2 Offline Track

The goal of the Offline ST track is to generate high-quality translations across diverse domains without latency constraints. Recent work has highlighted the potential of LLMs for this task (Ahmad et al., 2024; Koneru et al., 2024a). Building on these insights, we integrate LLMs at multiple stages of our speech translation pipeline. Below, we present a high-level overview, with each component detailed in the following sections.

We begin with long-form audio inputs, which may span several minutes to hours. Due to memory limitations and the lack of training data for such durations, our ASR and MT systems cannot handle these directly. Thus, we first segment the audio into manageable chunks using a Voice Activity Detection (VAD)-based method, which is effective even in noisy conditions.

The segmented audio is then transcribed into English using ASR. Rather than relying on a single model, we adopt a fusion strategy, combining outputs from multiple ASR systems—including both pre-trained models and a fine-tuned variant. This approach, akin to model ensembling, leverages the complementary strengths of different systems to reduce errors.

We fuse the ASR outputs using an LLM, which processes the combined hypotheses at the document level. This allows for the incorporation of broader context, resulting in more coherent and accurate transcriptions.

The English text is then segmented into sentences using the `nltk` tokenizer and translated into German. For this, we fine-tune a translation LLM on high-quality parallel data. To ensure quality, we use a quality estimation model to filter out noisy sentence pairs, keeping only high-confidence examples.

Finally, both the source transcript and the machine-translated output are passed to an Automatic Post-Editing (APE) model. This model refines the translations, producing polished final outputs.

2.1 Segmentation

The segmentation module breaks long-form audio into manageable segments for the ASR pipeline. We explored two strategies: fixed-window chunking and content-aware segmentation.

Fixed-window chunking applies a uniform sliding window and relies on transcript overlap to stitch adjacent chunks. While effective on clean audio, it often fails in noisy settings like the ITV or EPTV datasets, leading to fragmented or duplicated text.

Content-aware segmentation uses audio cues to find natural cut points. Basic methods rely on VADs like Silero (Team, 2021) or py-webrtcvad (Wiseman, 2019), which work well in clean conditions but struggle with noise. Instead, we use an end-to-end speaker segmentation model from Bredin and Laurent (2021), trained for noisy scenarios and capable of tracking up to three speakers. While methods like SHAS (Tsiamas et al., 2022) use wav2vec embeddings, they underperform in the presence of background noise.

Even with smarter cut-point detection, uncontrolled segment lengths can hurt ASR performance. Inspired by WhisperX (Bain et al., 2023), we enforce length constraints by post-processing VAD segments: overly long segments are split at their lowest-confidence point, while overly short ones are merged with neighbors (even across non-speech gaps) until they reach the desired duration *Chunk Size*.

Chunk Size	*Peloton*	*EPTV*	*ITV*	*ACL*
5	13.62	15.79	21.49	14.38
10	12.61	14.63	18.8	12.03
15	12.23	14.08	17.71	**11.43**
20	12.27	**13.98**	17.29	11.71
25	**11.98**	**13.98**	**16.62**	11.49

Table 1: Impact of chunk size during segmentation for ASR. We report the WER scores using Whisper-v3 with different chunk sizes. Best scores for each test set are highlighted in **bold**.

To determine the optimal *chunk size*, we perform a grid search using test sets from various domains, with results shown in Table 1. We use the Whisper v3 model[1] (Radford et al., 2023) and evaluate it on the Peloton, EPTV, and ITV subsets from the IWSLT 2024 development sets (Ahmad et al., 2024), as well as the ACL 60/60 test set (Salesky et al., 2023). A chunk size of 25 consistently yields the best performance. We hypothesize that this is due to the larger chunk size offering more contextual information, aligning with prior work on the benefits of long-form decoding in noisy conditions (Koneru et al., 2024a; Yan et al., 2024).

2.2 Automatic Speech Recognition

After segmenting the audio into smaller chunks, we send them to the ASR system for transcription. Since we participated in the language direction *English*→German, the audio needs to be transcribed in English, a high-resource language. Many publicly available pre-trained models excel at English transcription, and we first evaluated several of them individually. Specifically, we considered the Whisper variants v2[2] and v3[3](Radford et al., 2023), as well as the recently developed multimodal LLM Phi-4[4](Abouelenin et al., 2025).

To build a robust model for noisy scenarios, such as those found in TV series, we further fine-tuned Whisper Large v2 on the Bazinga dataset (Lerner et al., 2022). The Word-Error-Rate (WER) for these models on ITV and ACL 60/60 are reported in Table 2.

Model	*ITV*	*ACL*
Whisper v2	17.04	11.55
Whisper v2 + Bazinga	16.87	11.23
Whisper v3	**16.62**	11.49
Phi-4	20.64	**9.71**
LLM-Fuse	17.03	10.77

Table 2: WER scores of ASR models on the ITV and ACL test sets. LLM-Fuse indicates the post-edited output of all ASR systems at document-level. Best scores for each test set are highlighted in **bold**.

As shown in Table 2, there is no clear winner across the two test sets. Our manual analysis further reveals that different models tend to make different types of errors, suggesting that combining these systems could be a promising strategy.

2.2.1 Fusing with LLM

To fuse the ASR outputs, token-level ensembling is a viable approach—provided the vocabularies of the systems are compatible. However, the vocabulary used by Phi-4 differs from that of the Whisper variants, limiting the effectiveness of this method. Alternative techniques such as re-ranking offer some promise but are unable to leverage document-level context.

To overcome these limitations, we employ an LLM to generate the final transcript based on the outputs from individual ASR systems. Thanks to their ability to process long contexts, LLMs enable us to concatenate hypotheses from multiple chunks and refine them collectively.

[1] openai/whisper-large-v3

[2] openai/whisper-large-v2

[3] openai/whisper-large-v3

[4] microsoft/Phi-4-multimodal-instruct

However, an off-the-shelf LLM may not perform optimally for this specific task. To improve, we propose fine-tuning the model using a dataset generated through data augmentation. For this purpose, we use monolingual English text from the Europarl v7 and v10 datasets (Koehn, 2005), News-Commentary v16, OpenSubtitles (Lison and Tiedemann, 2016), and the NUTSHELL dataset[5] (Züfle et al., 2025). With the exception of NewsCommentary, the other datasets contain document-level structure—episodes in the case of OpenSubtitles and abstracts in the case of NUTSHELL.

We then employ the Text-to-Speech model VITS (Kim et al., 2021) to synthesize audio from the selected texts. This generated audio is subsequently transcribed using Phi-4 and the Whisper variants. As a result, we obtain ASR hypotheses for the synthesized speech along with their corresponding ground-truth references.

Next, we convert this data into a prompt format, as described in Appendix App. A. We fine-tune the LLM Llama 3 8B[6](Grattafiori et al., 2024) using LoRA (Hu et al., 2022), training it to predict the reference transcription given the hypotheses produced by the different ASR systems. We illustrate this in Fig. 1. We also report the ASR performance of the LLM fusion approach in Table 2 and observe that it does not outperform the individual systems. However, as we demonstrate in the following sections, this fusion proves to be highly beneficial when computing the final ST scores.

2.3 Speech Translation

The next step in the pipeline, after performing ASR, is to translate the transcriptions into German. Since the transcriptions are produced at the chunk level, they often contain multiple sentences, some of which may be incomplete. To address this, we first concatenate all the text from a given talk and then segment it into sentences using the NLTK tokenizer. This ensures that only complete sentences are passed to the MT system, aligning with the way such systems are typically trained.

2.3.1 Gold vs ASR Transcripts

Recently, several translation-focused LLMs have been introduced, demonstrating strong performance on high-quality input (Xu et al., 2024a; Alves et al., 2024). However, their effectiveness on noisy input—such as ASR-generated transcripts—remains uncertain. To assess this, we first evaluate the out-of-the-box translation quality of two leading models: Tower[7] (Xu et al., 2024a) and GemmaX2[8] (Cui et al., 2025). We use the COMET[9] (Rei et al., 2022a), MetricX[10] (Juraska et al., 2024), and ChrF2 (Popović, 2015) metrics, with results reported in Table 3 for the ACL 60/60 test set.

Model	*Chrf2* (↑)	*MetricX* (↓)	COMET (↑)
Gold Transcript			
Tower 7B	68.7	2.02	83.31
GemmaX2 9B	70.5	2.08	83.62
Whisper v3 ASR (Chunk size=25)			
Tower 7B	66.1	2.46	81.01
GemmaX2 9B	66.4	2.65	80.74
Phi-4 ASR			
Tower 7B	64.9	2.73	79.25
GemmaX2 9B	65.4	2.9	79.12

Table 3: Translation quality comparison between Gold and ASR transcripts on the ACL 60/60 test set. Note that higher is better for chrf2 and COMET scores and lower for MetricX scores.

GemmaX2 outperforms Tower on gold transcripts in terms of COMET scores, but its performance drops significantly on ASR-generated input. Interestingly, translation quality is lower when using transcripts from the Phi-4 ASR model, despite it having the lowest WER in Table 2. We hypothesize that this is due to inconsistencies in punctuation and casing, which are not captured by WER but can impact translation quality. This highlights that lower WER does not always correlate with better translations. As a result, we choose Tower 7B as our base model for subsequent enhancements, given its superior robustness to noisy input.

2.3.2 Quality-Filtered Finetuning for MT

Tower 7B is a multilingual model and we only focus on English $\rightarrow$ German in our submisison. Therefore, we adapt it to this specific language pair. While plently of data is available for fine-tuning, these also include low quality translation pairs.

Recent studies have demonstrated the importance of high-quality data during fine-tuning (Finkelstein et al., 2024; Ramos et al., 2024; Xu et al., 2024b). To this end, we leverage the Europarl

[5]Our submission is unconstrained by using this dataset.
[6]meta-llama/Llama-3-8B
[7]Unbabel/TowerInstruct-7B-v0.2
[8]ModelSpace/GemmaX2-28-2B-v0.1
[9]Unbabel/wmt22-comet-da
[10]google/metricx-24-hybrid-xl-v2p6

Model	ITV		ACL		
	Chrf2 (↑)	*MetricX* (↓)	*Chrf2* (↑)	*MetricX* (↓)	COMET (↑)
Whisper v3 ASR (Chunk size=25)					
Tower 7B	41.4	4.25	66.1	2.46	81.01
Tower 7B Finetuned	41.5	4.19	67.7	2.27	82.05
LLM-Fuse					
Tower 7B Finetuned	41.7	4.12	68	2.01	83.07
Tower 7B Finetuned + Tower 13B APE	42.1	4.03	69.6	1.84	83.31

Table 4: Analysis of translation quality of our ST system with different enhancements on the ITV and ACL test sets. Note that higher is better for chrf2 and COMET scores and lower for MetricX scores. Best scores for each metric per test set are highlighted in **bold**.

v7 and v10 datasets (Koehn, 2005), NewsCommentary v16, and OpenSubtitles (Lison and Tiedemann, 2016) to extract high-quality translation pairs. We employ the XCOMET[11] quality estimation model (Guerreiro et al., 2024) to rank the translation pairs and select the top $500k$ based on quality scores. Tower 7B is then fine-tuned on this curated dataset using LoRA adapters (Hu et al., 2022), adapting it for generating German translations.

2.3.3 Automatic Post-Editing Translations

As a final step, we aim to correct translation errors through APE (Koneru et al., 2024b). To achieve this, we fine-tune Tower 13B[12] on a synthetically generated APE dataset. Using our previously fine-tuned model, we generate 100k *(source, hypothesis, reference)* triplets by sampling a subset from the top 500k high-quality sentence pairs. Then, we transform into the prompt format as shown in App. A. We choose the larger 13B model for this task, as we expect it to be adaptable to correct the output with limited fine-tuning. To train within resource constraints, we follow the same approach as before and fine-tune using LoRA adapters.

We present an overview of the ST scores in Table 4 for the ITV and ACL 60/60 test sets. The results show that fusing system hypotheses using an LLM leads to improved ST performance on both test sets (from $4.19 \rightarrow 4.12$ for ITV and $2.27 \rightarrow 2.01$ for ACL in MetricX). Additionally, applying Automatic Post-Editing (APE) further enhances translation quality. As a result, our final pipeline integrates multiple ASR systems fused via an LLM, followed by initial translation generation and post-editing to ensure high-quality output.

[11]Unbabel/XCOMET-XL

[12]Unbabel/TowerInstruct-13B-v0.1

2.4 Future Directions and Potential Improvements

There are several potential avenues for improving our approach in future iterations of the shared task. First, while we did not explore it in this work, it is unclear how well SHAS segmentation performs when trained on noisy data. Semantic segmentation of noisy inputs could yield performance gains. Second, incorporating LLM specific to the target language (e.g. German LLM) for APE at the document level could offer promising improvements. Lastly, we experimented with Quality-Aware Decoding (Koneru et al., 2025), which showed benefits primarily when the quality of the ASR output was high. Future research could focus on adapting the quality estimation component to perform robustly under noisy or imperfect segmentation conditions.

3 Instruction Following Long Track

The Instruction-Following (IF) Speech Processing track in the scientific domain aims to benchmark foundation models that can follow natural language instructions—an ability well-established in text-based LLMs but still emerging in speech-based counterparts. The track covers four tasks: Automatic Speech Recognition (ASR), Speech Translation (ST), Spoken Question Answering (SQA), and Spoken Summarization (SSUM). ASR is evaluated on English, ST on English → German, Chinese, and Italian (en→{de, it, zh}), and SQA/SSUM across all four directions (en→{en, de, it, zh}).

We participate in the Constrained Long track, which focuses on long-form speech inputs (5–10 minutes). This track enforces limitations on both model selection and training data. Specifically, only SeamlessM4T-Large[13] (Communication et al., 2023) and LLaMA-3.1-8B-Instruct [14] (Grattafiori et al., 2024) are permitted as base models.

Our approach employs an end-to-end speech model trained under these constraints, enhanced with a post-editing stage for improved output quality similar to the Offline track.

3.1 Data

Data in the Constrained Setting For ASR and ST, the provided datasets include EuroParl-ST (Iranzo-Sánchez et al., 2020) and CoVoST 2 (Wang et al., 2020). For the SQA task, the only resource available is the extractive Spoken-SQuAD (Lee et al., 2018). For SSUM, NUTSHELL (Züfle et al., 2025), an abstract generation dataset for scientific talks, is provided. As development data, the ACL 60/60 benchmark (Salesky et al., 2023) is made available. Notably, the only in-domain datasets, i.e., those based on scientific talks, are NUTSHELL and ACL 60/60. Moreover, no multilingual data is provided for SQA and SSUM.

Data Augmentation To address the limitations of the constrained setting, we apply task-specific data augmentation strategies[15]:

ASR: To introduce domain-specific data, we augment the ASR training data using scientific abstracts from NUTSHELL (Züfle et al., 2025). The abstracts are split into sentences with `nltk` and then converted to synthetic speech using SeamlessM4T-Large.

ST: We do not augment the ST training data, but construct an artificial en-it test set for the ACL 60/60 dataset, which lacks Italian. We translate the English ACL 60/60 transcripts into Italian using both SeamlessM4T-Large and LLaMA-3.1-8B-Instruct, and evaluate translation quality using COMETKiwi (Rei et al., 2022b). SeamlessM4T-Large achieves a slightly higher score (82.55 vs. 81.07), and is therefore used to generate the final test set translations. The translation prompts for LLaMA-3.1-8B-Instruct are detailed in App. B.3.

SQA: For SQA, we aim to: (1) support all language pairs, (2) adapt to the scientific domain, and (3) include abstractive QA, as required by the track. Therefore, we transcribe NUTSHELL dev talks using SeamlessM4T (audio split into 15-second chunks at silence regions). We then use LLaMA-3.1-8B-Instruct to generate two answerable and one unanswerable QA pair per segment for all language pairs. We balance the dataset by ensuring that unanswerable questions comprise 5% of the final set. Additionally, we generate a 250-sample test set from a subset of the NUTSHELL test data. Prompt templates are included in App. B.1

SSUM: To enable multilingual evaluation of speech summarization, we translate the full NUTSHELL dataset (en→{de, it, zh}) using LLaMA-3.1-8B-Instruct. Prompt details are provided in App. B.2. As with SQA, we also generate a 250-sample multilingual test set.

3.2 Model

In the constrained setting of the track, only the speech foundation model SeamlessM4T-Large[13] (Communication et al., 2023) and LLaMA-3.1-8B-Instruct[14] (Grattafiori et al., 2024) are permitted.

Architecture To integrate the speech encoder and LLM in an end-to-end architecture, we use Q-Former (Li et al., 2023; Tang et al., 2024) as a projector. Specifically, we use a four transformer layers and four learnable query tokens to bridge the modality gap between the features from SeamlessM4T and LLaMA. During training, only the projector is trained and the speech encoder and LLM remain frozen.

Training We explore three training strategies: (1) Direct fine-tuning on all available training data, (2) ASR pretraining followed by fine-tuning, and (3) contrastive pretraining, as proposed by Züfle and Niehues (2024), followed by fine-tuning.

For contrastive pretraining, we use ASR data and experiment with cosine similarity and Wasserstein loss functions (Peyré and Cuturi, 2019; Le et al., 2023). As shown in Table 5, contrastive pretraining yields notable improvements over the other training strategies. Consequently, this approach is adopted for the final model submissions. Hyperparameter details are given in Table 10 in App. B.4.

During initial experiments, our model struggled to distinguish answerable from unanswerable SQA questions. To improve this, we apply chain-of-thought prompting: the model first tags the question as answerable or not, then generates an answer only if applicable. This stepwise approach improves both classification and answer quality.

[13]facebook/seamless-m4t-v2-large

[14]meta-llama/Llama-3.1-8B-Instruct

[15]Augmented Dataset available at HuggingFace: maikezu/data-kit-sub-iwslt2025-if-long-constraint

Model	ASR ● ACL 60/60 WER	ST ● ACL 60/60 COMET			SQA ○ Sp.-SQuAD BERTScore	SSUM ○ NUTSHELL BERTScore
	en-en	en-de	en-it*	en-zh	en-en	en-en
~no pretrain	25.1	72.49	73.61	76.93	80.88	83.89
~ASR pretrain	21.42	76.72	79.73	80.62	82.48	85.97
~contr. cos.	**18.82**	77.31	80.27	**80.76**	82.53	86.07
~contr. wasser.	19.07	**77.33**	80.06	81.34	**82.66**	**86.6**

~ Model not trained on multilingual SSUM and SQA
● Gold segmentation ○ No segmentation (full audio used)

Table 5: Ablation studies on different pretraining methods for the instruction following task: No pretraining, ASR pretraining and contrastive pretraining with either cosine similarity (*contr. cos.*) or Wasserstein distance (*contr. wasser.*). Test sets marked with * are automatically generated due to lack of availability for this language pair (see Section 3.1).

Segm.	max secs.	ASR (WER)	ST (COMET)		
		en-en	en-de	en-it*	en-zh
●	N/A	18.77	77.15	80.65	81.83
●	5	45.52	57.55	51.47	72.73
●	10	20.73	65.55	56.88	76.97
●	15	20.74	68.92	58.24	77.44
●	20	**20.63**	69.94	59.01	77.45
●	25	25.48	**71.61**	**75.74**	**78.04**
●	30	-	70.79	58.99	76.16
●	35	-	67.54	56.88	76.5

● Gold segmentation ● VAD segmentation

Table 6: Ablation study on Voice Activity Detection (VAD) segmentation using the *IF contr. cos. model.* on the ACL 60/60 dataset. Test sets marked with * are automatically generated due to lack of availability for this language pair (see Section 3.1). For ASR, segmenting audio into chunks of up to 20 seconds yields the best results, while for ST, 25-second chunks perform best.

Post-editing context	ASR (WER)	ST (COMET)		
	en-en	en-de	en-it*	en-zh
No Post-Editing ●	20.63	71.61	75.74	**78.04**
1 ●	21.09	70.54	75.0	77.22
3 ●	20.96	71.91	**75.88**	77.17
5 ●	**20.43**	71.64	75.69	77.20
10 ●	21.88	71.90	75.53	77.14
15 ●	50.07	**71.95**	**75.88**	77.19
20 ●	50.12	71.82	75.55	77.20

● VAD segmentation

Table 7: Ablation study on the context size of the postediting model using the *IF contr. cos. model.* on the ACL 60/60 dataset. For ASR, a context size of 5 yields the best results, for ST, a context size of 15. For en→zh, post-editing does not lead to an improvement.

3.3 Handling long audio

The IF Constrained Long track involves processing audio inputs from five to ten minutes in duration.

ASR and ST Initial experiments revealed that our model struggled with full-length audio inputs for ASR and ST, even when trained with artificially concatenated long-form sequences. To address this, we segment the input audio prior to inference.

We use a Voice Activity Detection (VAD) approach (Sohn et al., 1999) to segment audio, as due to track constraints, SHAS (Tsiamas et al., 2022) is not permitted. For ASR, segmenting into chunks of up to 20 seconds yields best performance and for ST, segments of up to 25 seconds are more effective. Ablation results are provided in Table 6.

SQA and SSUM For SQA and SSUM, we use the full audio. To handle long-form audio, we segment audio into 60-second chunks. Each chunk is encoded, and the embeddings are concatenated before being passed to the Q-Former and LLM, following Züfle et al. (2025). This strategy maintains full end-to-end trainability. For audios exceeding 26.7 minutes, we truncate the input to fit within memory constraints.

3.4 Post-Editing

To improve output quality, we use a post-editing model that works on document level. This helps to correct scientific terminology and it restores contextual coherence that may be lost due to segmentation of long audio inputs.

For ASR, we train the post-editing model on the SeamlessM4T-Large transcriptions of the TTS-generated scientific abstracts from NUTSHELL,

Model	ASR ACL 60/60 WER	ST ACL 60/60 COMET			SQA ○ Sp.-SQuAD BERTScore	SQA ○ NUTSHELL BERTScore				SSUM ○ NUTSHELL BERTScore			
	en-en	en-de	en-it*	en-zh	en-en	en-en*	en-de*	en-it*	en-zh*	en-en	en-de*	en-it*	en-zh*
Phi-4[16]	16.8	**79.19**	**83.43**	**83.23**	82.56	**91.78**	**76.85**	**78.41**	**74.41**	86.27	**67.71**	**69.76**	**57.03**
Qwen2 Audio[17]	20.14	72.35	74.23	77.19	**87.35**	89.0	71.81	73.7	69.62	84.88	63.06	64.17	51.79
Whisper[18] + Llama 3.1[14]	**14.67**	78.04	81.93	77.66	82.39	91.18	71.87	72.58	54.62	**86.62**	57.16	58.64	49.31
Seamless V2[13]	18.91	73.64	78.78	75.26	–	–	–	–	–	–	–	–	–
IF contr. cos.	18.77	**77.15**	80.65	**81.83**	82.83	93.04	79.73	82.08	79.8	86.83	68.46	71.01	71.22
IF contr. cos. tag	19.82	76.95	**80.69**	81.75	**82.86**	93.17	80.81	82.49	**80.53**	86.52	68.31	71.06	71.09
IF contr. wasser.	17.93	72.47	79.12	80.88	82.79	**93.42**	80.65	82.46	80.47	86.86	68.45	71.08	71.37
IF contr. wasser. tag	**17.78**	74.06	78.87	81.10	82.80	93.24	**80.87**	**82.76**	80.32	**86.89**	**68.76**	**71.16**	**71.54**
IF contr. cos.	20.63	71.61	75.74	78.04	82.83	93.04	79.73	82.08	79.8	86.83	68.46	71.01	71.22
+ post-edit	20.43	71.95	75.88	77.19	×		×			86.85	68.61	71.22	71.17
IF contr. cos. tag	33.24	69.37	73.36	75.83	**82.86**	93.17	80.81	82.49	**80.53**	86.52	68.31	71.06	71.09
+ post-edit	33.53	70.39	73.14	73.20	×		×			86.54	68.42	71.16	71.01
IF contr. wasser.	21.88	71.61	76.78	**78.21**	82.79	**93.42**	80.65	82.46	80.47	86.86	68.45	71.08	71.37
+ post-edit	33.51	71.12	**77.23**	68.02	×		×			86.88	68.68	71.12	71.24
IF contr. wasser. tag	22.07	71.84	76.29	78.24	82.80	93.24	**80.87**	**82.76**	80.32	86.89	68.76	71.16	**71.54**
+ post-edit	**19.76**	**72.29**	76.75	77.21	×		×			**86.90**	**68.95**	**71.30**	71.41

Gold segmentation · Voice Activity Detection (VAD) segmentation · ○ No segmentation (full audio used)
– Not supported by model · × post-editing not applied, because context is not available

Table 8: Results for baseline models and our end-to-end trained instruction-following models (*IF*), developed for the Constraint Instruction Following Long track. The IF models are pretrained using contrastive learning, with either cosine similarity (*contr. cos.*) or Wasserstein distance (*contr. wasser.*). To improve performance on question answering, we also experiment with tagging answers to indicate whether the question is answerable (+ *tag*). Test sets marked with * are automatically generated due to lack of availability for this language pair and task (see Section 3.1). The *IF contr. wasser. tag + post-edit* model was submitted to the shared task.

paired with the original text. For ST, we use the ACL 60/60 development set, transcribed by our IF model. The post-editing model setup is adapted from Section 2.2.1, with two key differences: in compliance with the constrained setting, we use LLaMA-3.1-8B-Instruct[14] (Grattafiori et al., 2024) as the base model, and we predict the reference using only a single system output, since in the IF track we do not employ an ensemble.

We conduct experiments to examine the effect of context size on post-editing performance. For ASR, a context window of five sentences provides the best results, while ST benefits from a 15-sentence context. For en→zh, no performance gains are achieved. These results are summarized in Table 7. We also apply the post-editing model to SSUM outputs, using the full summary as context.

3.5 Baselines

We compare our system to four baseline models. We include two end-to-end Speech-LLMs: Phi-4[16] (Abdin et al., 2024) and Qwen2 Audio[17] (Chu et al., 2024a), using default parameter settings provided on Hugging Face model cards and following the prompts specified by the shared task. We also evaluate a cascaded baseline using Whisper-large-v3[18] (Radford et al., 2023), and LLaMA-3.1-8B-Instruct[14] (Grattafiori et al., 2024) to follow the instructions. Lastly, for ASR and ST, we include SeamlessM4T-Large[13] (Communication et al., 2023), given that it also serves as the speech encoder in our own end-to-end architecture.

3.6 Evaluation

We evaluate ASR with WER using JiWER, ST using COMET[19] (Rei et al., 2022a), and SQA and SSUM using BERTScore (Zhang et al., 2020).

3.7 Development Results

All results can be found in Table 8. We evaluate our approach against the baselines from Section 3.5, as well as four end-to-end trained instruction-following models (*IF*). Among these, we compare two contrastive pretraining strategies (*contr. cos.* and *contr. wasser.*), as outlined in Section 3.2. For the SQA task, we also explore a chain-of-thought variant (*tag*), as detailed in Section 3.2.

ASR and ST Using gold segmentation, we compare our *IF* models against the baselines. Phi-4[16] (Abdin et al., 2024) achieves the strongest performance on ST, while Whisper[18] (Radford et al., 2023) performs best for ASR. However, our

[16]microsoft/Phi-4-multimodal-instruct
[17]Qwen/Qwen2-Audio-7B-Instruct
[18]openai/whisper-large-v3
[19]Unbabel/wmt22-comet-da

Model	ASR○❋ WER	ST○❋ COMET			SQA○ BERTScore (normalized)				SSUM○ BERTScore (normalized)			
	en-en	en-de	en-it	en-zh	en-en	en-de	en-it	en-zh	en-en	en-de	en-it	en-zh
Phi-4[16] (baseline)	0.17○	0.55○	0.56○	0.51○	**0.42**	**0.35**	0.36	0.39	0.17	0.16	0.19	0.04
IF contr. wasser. tag (ours)	**0.15**❋	**0.74**❋	**0.77**❋	**0.77**❋	0.41	**0.35**	**0.39**	**0.41**	**0.23**	**0.21**	**0.25**	**0.37**

❋ Voice Activity Detection (VAD) segmentation ○ No segmentation (full audio used)

Table 9: Official evaluation results for the IWSLT 2025 IF Speech Processing track in the long and constrained setting.

IF models consistently outperform both Qwen2 Audio[17] (Chu et al., 2024a) and SeamlessM4T-Large[13] (Communication et al., 2023). The latter result confirms that our end-to-end architecture is able to improve over the speech foundation model.

Under VAD segmentation, which is also used for the shared task testset, we observe a performance drop across all *IF* models, as expected. Applying post-editing partially mitigates this drop. For ASR, post-editing only improves *IF contr. cos* and *IF contr. wasser. tag*, bringing them close to their gold-segmented counterparts. In ST, post-editing yields consistent improvements for en→de and en→it, but not for en→zh, likely due to the limited Chinese capabilities of the post-editing model and sparse training data in that language.

SQA and SSUM On the SQA-NUTSHELL dataset, all *IF* models outperform the baselines, whereas on Spoken-SQuAD (which is extractive and out-of-domain), this is not the case. For SSUM, *IF* models consistently surpass the baselines, particularly in en→it and en→zh. Post-editing yields slight gains for SSUM as well, though similar to ST, no improvement is observed for en→zh.

Final Model We select *IF contr. wasser. tag + post-edit* for our final submission. It offers the best performance for ASR, SQA, and SSUM, and is competitive with the other *IF* models in ST.

3.8 Results on IWSLT Official Test Set

Table 9 shows the performance of our final system on the official IWSLT 2025 test sets provided by the organizers (Abdulmumin et al., 2025). Our system outperforms the baseline in ASR, ST, and SSUM, and achieves stronger results in SQA across all language pairs except for en→en.

4 Conclusion

This system paper presents KIT's submissions to the Offline and the IF Long tracks. By integrating LLMs into both cascaded and end-to-end architectures for speech processing, we demonstrate their potential in handling a range of spoken language tasks. For future work, we aim to explore a unified architecture capable of producing high-quality translations while also supporting instruction-following capabilities.

Acknowledgments

Part of this work received support from the European Union's Horizon research and innovation programme under grant agreement No 101135798, project Meetween (My Personal AI Mediator for Virtual MEETtings BetWEEN People). Part of this work was performed on the HoreKa supercomputer funded by the Ministry of Science, Research and the Arts Baden-Württemberg and by the Federal Ministry of Education and Research.

References

Marah Abdin, Jyoti Aneja, Harkirat Behl, Sébastien Bubeck, Ronen Eldan, Suriya Gunasekar, Michael Harrison, Russell J. Hewett, Mojan Javaheripi, Piero Kauffmann, James R. Lee, Yin Tat Lee, Yuanzhi Li, Weishung Liu, Caio C. T. Mendes, Anh Nguyen, Eric Price, Gustavo de Rosa, Olli Saarikivi, and 8 others. 2024. Phi-4 technical report. *Preprint*, arXiv:2412.08905.

Idris Abdulmumin, Victor Agostinelli, Tanel Alumäe, Antonios Anastasopoulos, Ashwin, Luisa Bentivogli, Ondřej Bojar, Claudia Borg, Fethi Bougares, Roldano Cattoni, Mauro Cettolo, Lizhong Chen, William Chen, Raj Dabre, Yannick Estève, Marcello Federico, Marco Gaido, Dávid Javorský, Marek Kasztelnik, and 30 others. 2025. Findings of the iwslt 2025 evaluation campaign. In *Proceedings of the 22nd International Conference on Spoken Language Translation (IWSLT 2025)*, Vienna, Austria (in-person and online). Association for Computational Linguistics. To appear.

Abdelrahman Abouelenin, Atabak Ashfaq, Adam Atkinson, Hany Awadalla, Nguyen Bach, Jianmin Bao,

Alon Benhaim, Martin Cai, Vishrav Chaudhary, Congcong Chen, and 1 others. 2025. Phi-4-mini technical report: Compact yet powerful multimodal language models via mixture-of-loras. *arXiv preprint arXiv:2503.01743*.

Ibrahim Said Ahmad, Antonios Anastasopoulos, Ondřej Bojar, Claudia Borg, Marine Carpuat, Roldano Cattoni, Mauro Cettolo, William Chen, Qianqian Dong, Marcello Federico, Barry Haddow, Dávid Javorský, Mateusz Krubiński, Tsz Kin Lam, Xutai Ma, Prashant Mathur, Evgeny Matusov, Chandresh Maurya, John McCrae, and 25 others. 2024. FINDINGS OF THE IWSLT 2024 EVALUATION CAMPAIGN. In *Proceedings of the 21st International Conference on Spoken Language Translation (IWSLT 2024)*, pages 1–11, Bangkok, Thailand (in-person and online). Association for Computational Linguistics.

Duarte Miguel Alves, José Pombal, Nuno M Guerreiro, Pedro Henrique Martins, João Alves, Amin Farajian, Ben Peters, Ricardo Rei, Patrick Fernandes, Sweta Agrawal, and 1 others. 2024. Tower: An open multilingual large language model for translation-related tasks. In *First Conference on Language Modeling*.

Max Bain, Jaesung Huh, Tengda Han, and Andrew Zisserman. 2023. Whisperx: Time-accurate speech transcription of long-form audio. *INTERSPEECH 2023*.

Hervé Bredin and Antoine Laurent. 2021. End-to-end speaker segmentation for overlap-aware resegmentation. In *Interspeech 2021*, pages 3111–3115.

Yunfei Chu, Jin Xu, Qian Yang, Haojie Wei, Xipin Wei, Zhifang Guo, Yichong Leng, Yuanjun Lv, Jinzheng He, Junyang Lin, Chang Zhou, and Jingren Zhou. 2024a. Qwen2-audio technical report. *arXiv preprint arXiv:2407.10759*.

Yunfei Chu, Jin Xu, Qian Yang, Haojie Wei, Xipin Wei, Zhifang Guo, Yichong Leng, Yuanjun Lv, Jinzheng He, Junyang Lin, and 1 others. 2024b. Qwen2-audio technical report. *arXiv preprint arXiv:2407.10759*.

Seamless Communication, Loïc Barrault, Yu-An Chung, Mariano Cora Meglioli, David Dale, Ning Dong, Paul-Ambroise Duquenne, Hady Elsahar, Hongyu Gong, Kevin Heffernan, John Hoffman, Christopher Klaiber, Pengwei Li, Daniel Licht, Jean Maillard, Alice Rakotoarison, Kaushik Ram Sadagopan, Guillaume Wenzek, Ethan Ye, and 49 others. 2023. Seamlessm4t: Massively multilingual & multimodal machine translation. *Preprint*, arXiv:2308.11596.

Menglong Cui, Pengzhi Gao, Wei Liu, Jian Luan, and Bin Wang. 2025. Multilingual machine translation with open large language models at practical scale: An empirical study. *arXiv preprint arXiv:2502.02481*.

Mara Finkelstein, David Vilar, and Markus Freitag. 2024. Introducing the NewsPaLM MBR and QE dataset: LLM-generated high-quality parallel data outperforms traditional web-crawled data. In *Proceedings of the Ninth Conference on Machine Translation*, pages 1355–1372, Miami, Florida, USA. Association for Computational Linguistics.

Aaron Grattafiori, Abhimanyu Dubey, Abhinav Jauhri, Abhinav Pandey, Abhishek Kadian, Ahmad Al-Dahle, Aiesha Letman, Akhil Mathur, Alan Schelten, Alex Vaughan, Amy Yang, Angela Fan, Anirudh Goyal, Anthony Hartshorn, Aobo Yang, Archi Mitra, Archie Sravankumar, Artem Korenev, Arthur Hinsvark, and 542 others. 2024. The llama 3 herd of models. *Preprint*, arXiv:2407.21783.

Nuno M Guerreiro, Ricardo Rei, Daan van Stigt, Luisa Coheur, Pierre Colombo, and André FT Martins. 2024. xcomet: Transparent machine translation evaluation through fine-grained error detection. *Transactions of the Association for Computational Linguistics*, 12:979–995.

Edward J Hu, Phillip Wallis, Zeyuan Allen-Zhu, Yuanzhi Li, Shean Wang, Lu Wang, Weizhu Chen, and 1 others. 2022. Lora: Low-rank adaptation of large language models. In *International Conference on Learning Representations*.

J. Iranzo-Sánchez, J. A. Silvestre-Cerdà, J. Jorge, N. Roselló, A. Giménez, A. Sanchis, J. Civera, and A. Juan. 2020. Europarl-st: A multilingual corpus for speech translation of parliamentary debates. In *ICASSP 2020 - 2020 IEEE International Conference on Acoustics, Speech and Signal Processing (ICASSP)*, pages 8229–8233.

Juraj Juraska, Daniel Deutsch, Mara Finkelstein, and Markus Freitag. 2024. MetricX-24: The Google submission to the WMT 2024 metrics shared task. In *Proceedings of the Ninth Conference on Machine Translation*, pages 492–504, Miami, Florida, USA. Association for Computational Linguistics.

Jaehyeon Kim, Jungil Kong, and Juhee Son. 2021. Conditional variational autoencoder with adversarial learning for end-to-end text-to-speech. In *International Conference on Machine Learning*, pages 5530–5540. PMLR.

Philipp Koehn. 2005. Europarl: A parallel corpus for statistical machine translation. In *Proceedings of Machine Translation Summit X: Papers*, pages 79–86, Phuket, Thailand.

Sai Koneru, Thai Binh Nguyen, Ngoc-Quan Pham, Danni Liu, Zhaolin Li, Alexander Waibel, and Jan Niehues. 2024a. Blending LLMs into cascaded speech translation: KIT's offline speech translation system for IWSLT 2024. In *Proceedings of the 21st International Conference on Spoken Language Translation (IWSLT 2024)*, pages 183–191, Bangkok, Thailand (in-person and online). Association for Computational Linguistics.

Sai Koneru, Miriam Exel, Matthias Huck, and Jan Niehues. 2024b. Contextual refinement of translations: Large language models for sentence and document-level post-editing. In *Proceedings of the 2024 Conference of the North American Chapter of the Association for Computational Linguistics: Human Language Technologies (Volume 1: Long Papers)*, pages 2711–2725, Mexico City, Mexico. Association for Computational Linguistics.

Sai Koneru, Matthias Huck, Miriam Exel, and Jan Niehues. 2025. Quality-aware decoding: Unifying quality estimation and decoding. *arXiv preprint arXiv:2502.08561*.

Phuong-Hang Le, Hongyu Gong, Changhan Wang, Juan Pino, Benjamin Lecouteux, and Didier Schwab. 2023. Pre-training for speech translation: Ctc meets optimal transport. *Preprint*, arXiv:2301.11716.

Chia-Hsuan Lee, Szu-Lin Wu, Chi-Liang Liu, and Hung-yi Lee. 2018. Spoken squad: A study of mitigating the impact of speech recognition errors on listening comprehension. *Proc. Interspeech 2018*, pages 3459–3463.

Paul Lerner, Juliette Bergoënd, Camille Guinaudeau, Hervé Bredin, Benjamin Maurice, Sharleyne Lefevre, Martin Bouteiller, Aman Berhe, Léo Galmant, Ruiqing Yin, and Claude Barras. 2022. Bazinga! a dataset for multi-party dialogues structuring. In *Proceedings of the Thirteenth Language Resources and Evaluation Conference*, pages 3434–3441, Marseille, France. European Language Resources Association.

Junnan Li, Dongxu Li, Silvio Savarese, and Steven C. H. Hoi. 2023. Blip-2: Bootstrapping language-image pre-training with frozen image encoders and large language models. In *International Conference on Machine Learning*.

Pierre Lison and Jörg Tiedemann. 2016. OpenSubtitles2016: Extracting large parallel corpora from movie and TV subtitles. In *Proceedings of the Tenth International Conference on Language Resources and Evaluation (LREC'16)*, pages 923–929, Portorož, Slovenia. European Language Resources Association (ELRA).

Danni Liu, Thai Binh Nguyen, Sai Koneru, Enes Yavuz Ugan, Ngoc-Quan Pham, Tuan Nam Nguyen, Tu Anh Dinh, Carlos Mullov, Alexander Waibel, and Jan Niehues. 2023. KIT's multilingual speech translation system for IWSLT 2023. In *Proceedings of the 20th International Conference on Spoken Language Translation (IWSLT 2023)*, pages 113–122, Toronto, Canada (in-person and online). Association for Computational Linguistics.

Gabriel Peyré and Marco Cuturi. 2019. Computational optimal transport: With applications to data science. *Foundations and Trends® in Machine Learning*, 11:355–206.

Maja Popović. 2015. chrF: character n-gram F-score for automatic MT evaluation. In *Proceedings of the Tenth Workshop on Statistical Machine Translation*, pages 392–395, Lisbon, Portugal. Association for Computational Linguistics.

Alec Radford, Jong Wook Kim, Tao Xu, Greg Brockman, Christine McLeavey, and Ilya Sutskever. 2023. Robust speech recognition via large-scale weak supervision. In *International conference on machine learning*, pages 28492–28518. PMLR.

Miguel Ramos, Patrick Fernandes, António Farinhas, and Andre Martins. 2024. Aligning neural machine translation models: Human feedback in training and inference. In *Proceedings of the 25th Annual Conference of the European Association for Machine Translation (Volume 1)*, pages 258–274, Sheffield, UK. European Association for Machine Translation (EAMT).

Ricardo Rei, José G. C. de Souza, Duarte Alves, Chrysoula Zerva, Ana C Farinha, Taisiya Glushkova, Alon Lavie, Luisa Coheur, and André F. T. Martins. 2022a. COMET-22: Unbabel-IST 2022 submission for the metrics shared task. In *Proceedings of the Seventh Conference on Machine Translation (WMT)*, pages 578–585, Abu Dhabi, United Arab Emirates (Hybrid). Association for Computational Linguistics.

Ricardo Rei, Marcos Treviso, Nuno M. Guerreiro, Chrysoula Zerva, Ana C Farinha, Christine Maroti, José G. C. de Souza, Taisiya Glushkova, Duarte Alves, Luisa Coheur, Alon Lavie, and André F. T. Martins. 2022b. CometKiwi: IST-unbabel 2022 submission for the quality estimation shared task. In *Proceedings of the Seventh Conference on Machine Translation (WMT)*, pages 634–645, Abu Dhabi, United Arab Emirates (Hybrid). Association for Computational Linguistics.

Elizabeth Salesky, Kareem Darwish, Mohamed Al-Badrashiny, Mona Diab, and Jan Niehues. 2023. Evaluating multilingual speech translation under realistic conditions with resegmentation and terminology. In *Proceedings of the 20th International Conference on Spoken Language Translation (IWSLT 2023)*, pages 62–78, Toronto, Canada (in-person and online). Association for Computational Linguistics.

Jongseo Sohn, Nam Soo Kim, and Wonyong Sung. 1999. A statistical model-based voice activity detection. *IEEE Signal Processing Letters*, 6(1):1–3.

Changli Tang, Wenyi Yu, Guangzhi Sun, Xianzhao Chen, Tian Tan, Wei Li, Lu Lu, Zejun MA, and Chao Zhang. 2024. SALMONN: Towards generic hearing abilities for large language models. In *The Twelfth International Conference on Learning Representations*.

Changli Tang, Wenyi Yu, Guangzhi Sun, Xianzhao Chen, Tian Tan, Wei Li, Lu Lu, MA Zejun, and Chao Zhang. 2023. Salmonn: Towards generic hearing abilities for large language models. In *The Twelfth International Conference on Learning Representations*.

Silero Team. 2021. Silero models: pre-trained enterprise-grade stt / tts models and benchmarks. `https://github.com/snakers4/silero-models`.

Ioannis Tsiamas, Gerard I. Gállego, José A. R. Fonollosa, and Marta R. Costa-jussà. 2022. SHAS: Approaching optimal Segmentation for End-to-End Speech Translation. In *Proc. Interspeech 2022*, pages 106–110.

Changhan Wang, Anne Wu, and Juan Pino. 2020. Covost 2: A massively multilingual speech-to-text translation corpus. *Preprint*, arXiv:2007.10310.

John Wiseman. 2019. Wiseman/py-webrtcvad. *GitHub repository, Nov.*

Haoran Xu, Kenton Murray, Philipp Koehn, Hieu Hoang, Akiko Eriguchi, and Huda Khayrallah. 2024a. X-alma: Plug & play modules and adaptive rejection for quality translation at scale. *arXiv preprint arXiv:2410.03115.*

Haoran Xu, Amr Sharaf, Yunmo Chen, Weiting Tan, Lingfeng Shen, Benjamin Van Durme, Kenton Murray, and Young Jin Kim. 2024b. Contrastive preference optimization: Pushing the boundaries of llm performance in machine translation. In *International Conference on Machine Learning*, pages 55204–55224. PMLR.

Brian Yan, Patrick Fernandes, Jinchuan Tian, Siqi Ouyang, William Chen, Karen Livescu, Lei Li, Graham Neubig, and Shinji Watanabe. 2024. CMU's IWSLT 2024 offline speech translation system: A cascaded approach for long-form robustness. In *Proceedings of the 21st International Conference on Spoken Language Translation (IWSLT 2024)*, pages 164–169, Bangkok, Thailand (in-person and online). Association for Computational Linguistics.

Tianyi Zhang, Varsha Kishore, Felix Wu, Kilian Q. Weinberger, and Yoav Artzi. 2020. Bertscore: Evaluating text generation with BERT. In *8th International Conference on Learning Representations, ICLR 2020, Addis Ababa, Ethiopia, April 26-30, 2020*. OpenReview.net.

Maike Züfle, Sara Papi, Beatrice Savoldi, Marco Gaido, Luisa Bentivogli, and Jan Niehues. 2025. Nutshell: A dataset for abstract generation from scientific talks. *arXiv preprint arXiv:2502.16942.*

Maike Züfle and Jan Niehues. 2024. Contrastive learning for task-independent speechllm-pretraining. *Preprint*, arXiv:2412.15712.

Maike Züfle, Sara Papi, Beatrice Savoldi, Marco Gaido, Luisa Bentivogli, and Jan Niehues. 2025. Nutshell: A dataset for abstract generation from scientific talks. *Preprint*, arXiv:2502.16942.

A Offline Track - Prompts

LLM Fuse Prompt

```
Post-Edit the Automatic Speech
Recognition Transcripts from
different systems understanding
the context.

ASR Transcripts:

System1: {Whisper v2 Hyps}
System2: {Whisper v2 FT Hyps}
System3: {Phi-4 Hyps}
System4: {Whisper v3 Hyps}

Post-Edited Transcript:
{Reference}
```

MT APE Prompt

```
<|im_start|>user
Post-Edit the German Translation
of the English sentence.
English:
{src}
German:
{mt}
<|im_end|>
<|im_start|>assistant
Post-Edited German:
{ref}
```

B Instruction-Following Track - Prompts

B.1 Data Augmentation Prompts SQA

System Prompt:

```
You are a professional question
generator. Given a transcript,
you will create three questions:
two that can be answered based on
 the transcript and one that
cannot be answered (but is
relevant to the topic).
The answers should be full
sentences in the target language
specified.
Your response must be in valid
JSON format, with keys for '
questions' and 'answers'.
Do not include any explanations
or additional text.\n
```

Prompt:

```
<Transcript>\n
Based on the transcript, generate
 a JSON dictionary with the
following structure.
The questions and answers must be
 in <trg lang>:\n
{{\n
```

```
'  "questions": [\n'
'    {"q1": "First question in <trg lang>", "a1": "Full-sentence answer in <trg lang>"},\n'
'    {"q2": "Second question in <trg lang>", "a2": "Full-sentence answer in <trg lang>"},\n'
f'    {{"q3": "Third question in <trg lang>", "a3": "N/A"}}\n'
  ]\n
}}\n
Ensure the response is a valid JSON object with properly formatted keys and values.
```

B.2 Data Augmentation Prompts SSUM

System Prompt:

```
A chat between a curious user and a professional system for translating ACL abstracts.\n
```

Prompt:

```
<abstract>\nTranslate this abstract to <trg lang>. Do not provide any explanation or additional text.
```

B.3 Data Augmentation Prompts ST

System Prompt:

```
You are a professional translator. Your task is to provide accurate, fluent, and natural translations without adding explanations, comments, or extra content.
```

Prompt:

```
Translate the following English text into <trg lang>. Do not provide any explanation or additional text.\n<text>
```

B.4 Hyperparameters Model Training

training parameters	Q-Former Num Query Token	4
	Q-Former Num Hidden Layers	4
	Q-Former Num Attention Heads	12
	Q-Former Seconds per Window	1/3
	num GPUs	4
	learning rate	1e-4
	warmup ratio	0.03
	optimizer	adamw_torch
	learning rate scheduler type	cosine
	model max length	2048
	gradient clipping	1
pretraining specific	num epochs	5
	per device batch size	10
	gradient accumulation steps	2
	contrastive τ cos + wasser	0.1
	contrastive τ nwp	0.5
	sinkhorn loss p	2
	sinkhorn loss blur	0.5
finetuning specific	num epochs	2
	per device batch size	2
	gradient accumulation steps	10

Table 10: Hyperparameters for the trainings, which are conducted on four NVIDIA GH200 96GB GPUs, mostly following Züfle and Niehues (2024).

IWSLT 2025 Indic Track System Description Paper: Speech-to-Text Translation from Low-Resource Indian Languages (Bengali and Tamil) to English

Sayan Das[1], **Soham Chaudhuri**[2], **Dipanjan Saha**[3], **Dipankar Das**[4], **Sivaji Bandyopadhyay**[5]
[1,3,4,5]Dept. of CSE, Jadavpur University, Kolkata, India
[2]Dept. of EE, Jadavpur University, Kolkata, India
{sayan.das200216, sohamchaudhuri.12.a.38, sahadipanjan6, dipankar.dipnil2005, sivaji.cse.ju}@gmail.com

Abstract

Multi-language Speech-to-Text Translation (ST) plays a crucial role in breaking linguistic barriers, particularly in multilingual regions like India. This paper focuses on building a robust ST system for low-resource Indian languages, with a special emphasis on Bengali and Tamil. These languages represent the Indo-Aryan and Dravidian families, respectively. The dataset used in this work comprises spoken content from TED Talks and conferences, paired with transcriptions in English and their translations in Bengali and Tamil. Our work specifically addresses the translation of Bengali and Tamil speech to English text, a critical area given the scarcity of annotated speech data. To enhance translation quality and model robustness, we leverage cross-lingual resources and word-level translation strategies. The ultimate goal is to develop an end-to-end ST model capable of real-world deployment for underrepresented languages.

1 Introduction

Speech-to-Text Translation (ST) has seen significant progress in recent years, driven by advancements in deep learning and large-scale multilingual datasets. However, the benefits of these advancements have not equally reached low-resource languages. Many Indian languages, despite being spoken by millions, lack sufficient parallel speech-text corpora to train high-performing supervised models. This paper addresses this gap by focusing on ST systems for Bengali and Tamil speech to English text, two major Indian languages that are often underrepresented in current ST research.

India's linguistic diversity presents both a challenge and an opportunity for Speech Translation research. In multilingual communities, there is a growing demand for ST systems that can facilitate communication across different linguistic groups, especially in education, healthcare, and public services. However, the shortage of human translators and limited digital resources for many Indian languages hamper efforts to build such systems. This work is motivated by the need to create language-inclusive ST models that cater to low resource Indian languages such as Bengali and Tamil. These languages are widely spoken but lack the large-scale annotated datasets available for high-resource languages like English, German, or Mandarin. By focusing on Bengali and Tamil audio-to-English text translation, this paper aims to fill a critical gap in current ST research. Additionally, the paper explores methods to overcome data scarcity, such as leveraging related language resources, incorporating multilingual pretraining, and utilizing word-level translation dictionaries. The broader goal is to build a scalable and adaptable ST pipeline that not only improves translation accuracy but also supports the integration of more languages in the future.

The work leverages a curated dataset of public speeches, including TED Talks and conference recordings, to build a system that can handle the unique linguistic and acoustic features of these languages. Our approach explores both end-to-end and cascaded architectures, aiming to strike a balance between performance and scalability. By addressing the linguistic diversity and resource limitations of these languages, we aim to contribute towards more inclusive language technology in India and beyond.

Speech-to-Text Translation (ST) research has traditionally been concentrated on high-resource languages, with significant advancements in languages such as English, German, and Mandarin. However, languages such as Bengali and Tamil, spoken by millions in multilingual regions like India, remain underrepresented in research due to the scarcity of parallel speech text corpora. The absence of large-scale annotated datasets for these languages presents a significant barrier to training high-performance models.

Proceedings of the 22nd International Conference on Spoken Language Translation (IWSLT 2025), pages 245–251
July 31 - August 1, 2025

In recent years, there has been growing interest in leveraging existing resources from related languages and innovative techniques to overcome these challenges. For instance, the IWSLT shared tasks have provided valuable insights into the effectiveness of both cascaded and end-to-end (E2E) models for Speech-to-Text (ST) tasks. A cascaded architecture typically involves a two-step process: first, automatic speech recognition (ASR) converts speech to text, and then machine translation (MT) translates the recognized text from the source language into the target language. This approach has been shown to perform effectively in the handling of complex speech data.

In the context of low-resource languages, the cascaded model approach has demonstrated robustness, especially when training data is limited. Recent work has explored combining ASR models like OpenAI's Whisper (Radford et al., 2022), trained on multilingual data, with neural MT systems such as Helsinki-NLP/opus-mt-bn-en. This combination has proven effective in addressing the challenges posed by limited resources, especially for languages such as Bengali and Tamil. These models leverage the strengths of both components to improve translation accuracy and ensure scalability in real-world applications.

The 2023 IWSLT Evaluation Campaign, for example, evaluated offline SLT systems for translating speech from English to German, Japanese, and Chinese, using both cascaded and E2E models. The campaign highlighted the importance of combining ASR and MT components, as well as the performance improvements that could be achieved by integrating large-scale language models, data augmentation, and ensemble methods (Agarwal et al., 2023). Although E2E models are more direct, cascaded systems are particularly well-suited for low-resource languages, as they allow for leveraging pre-existing, powerful models for both ASR and MT tasks.

For Bengali and Tamil, this cascaded approach has shown promise by using pre-trained ASR models (such as Whisper) followed by fine-tuned MT models (like Helsinki-NLP/opus-mt-bn-en) to handle the translation from these languages to English. By employing this two-step architecture, the system benefits from the specific strengths of both ASR and MT, improving overall translation accuracy and ensuring adaptability to the challenges presented by these languages.

The work conducted in the IWSLT2024 Indic Track system description paper (Showrav, 2022) focuses on speech-to-text translation for multiple Indian languages, including Bengali and Tamil, and follows a similar cascaded approach to tackle the challenges of low-resource languages. This aligns closely with the goal of our paper, which aims to build a robust and scalable ST system that can effectively handle the translation of Bengali and Tamil speech to English text.

By incorporating these strategies, our work contributes to advancing Speech-to-Text Translation for low-resource languages, filling a critical gap in the research landscape, and offering a path forward for scalable models that can support the diverse linguistic landscape of India.

2 Dataset Description

The IWSLT 2025 Indic Track (Abdulmumin et al., 2025) focuses on Speech-to-Text (ST) translation between English and three low-resource Indian languages: Hindi (hi), Bengali (bn), and Tamil (ta) and vice-versa. These languages belong to two major language families—Indo-Aryan (Hindi and Bengali) and Dravidian (Tamil)—and are widely spoken across South Asia.

The dataset for this task specifically supports Speech-to-Text translation from Indic languages to English, where the source is audio in a low-resource Indian language, and the target is English text. It includes:

- Bengali and Tamil speech recordings as the source audio.
- English text transcriptions serving as the target translations.
- YAML metadata files that define audio segmentation with information like file name, offset, duration, and speaker ID.

Each language dataset is carefully aligned. Every English transcript line has a corresponding line in the target language (Hindi, Bengali, or Tamil), along with metadata in YAML format. This metadata provides information such as file name, offset, duration, and speaker ID.

The corpus is divided into training, validation, and test subsets. Each audio file corresponds to a talk by a single speaker, contributing to diverse speaking styles and accents. While the number of segments is consistent across the aligned files, token counts may differ across languages due to linguistic variations.

In our work, we focused specifically on the Bengali-to-English and Tamil-to-English translation directions. We used Bengali and Tamil audio files aligned with their English translations. The actual dataset contains significantly more than 50,000 samples for each language pair, providing a rich and diverse resource for training, evaluation, and fine-tuning.

This well-structured, multilingual dataset serves as a strong foundation for building effective Speech-to-Text translation systems for low-resource Indian languages like Bengali and Tamil.

3 System Overview

The system integrates advanced speech-to-text (ASR) and machine translation (MT) models to transcribe Bengali audio files and translate the transcriptions into English. The architecture consists of several interconnected modules, each playing a crucial role in ensuring accuracy, efficiency, and robustness. The key components of the system include an input module that accepts audio files in WAV format, which is a standard format for audio processing due to its lossless nature. Along with the audio file, a YAML metadata file is provided ,which contains the following information:

- **Offset**: The time point in the audio from which the transcription should begin.
- **Duration**: The duration of the audio clip to be processed.
- **Speaker ID**: Used to identify the speaker in case of multiple speakers in the audio file.

The ***data validation and preprocessing*** module validates the provided metadata, ensuring that the offset, duration, and speaker ID align correctly with the audio file. Audio segmentation is then performed based on the provided offset and duration to ensure precise transcription.

The ***audio processor and transcription*** module consists of two sub-modules, namely, the *Audio Chunk Extraction* and the *model integration*. In the *Audio Chunk Extraction* module, ***Librosa*** (McFee et al., 2015) and ***SoundFile*** libraries were used to extract precise segments from the original audio file based on the metadata. These libraries are efficient in processing and manipulating audio data. The ***Whisper-small model*** is loaded via the ***Hugging Face Transformers*** library (Wolf et al., 2020). Whisper is a robust, multilingual ASR model that can handle diverse languages and dialects with zero-shot capabilities (Radford et al., 2023).

The model is fine-tuned using a ***Quantized Low-Rank Adaptation (QLoRA)*** (Dettmers et al., 2023) technique on a custom dataset of $10,000$ Bengali-English audio pairs. QLoRA is a parameter-efficient fine-tuning technique that allows the model to adapt to new tasks with minimal computational overhead while retaining its generalization ability and quantization greatly reduces memory usage by reducing precision of floating points. The extracted audio chunks are then passed to the model, which transcribes the Bengali audio to Bengali text or Tamil audio to Tamil text . We have used the Kaggle free resources for all our task which provides us with 2 *Tesla P100* GPUs due to which we faced computational constraints and used QLoRA as an alternative.

In the ***Translation Module***, the system uses the **Helsinki-NLP/opus-mt-bn-en** model, a state-of-the-art model pre-trained for Bengali-to-English translation tasks. The model is fine-tuned using **CSV-aligned Bengali-English pairs**. This alignment ensures the model learns the appropriate context, improving translation accuracy. The model is also trained with the ***Seq2SeqTrainer*** framework, which is highly effective for sequence-to-sequence tasks such as translation. This method optimizes the model for better handling Bengali syntax and semantics complexities during translation.

After the completion of the *transcription* and *translation* phase, the system merges the **filename**, **transcription**, and **translated output** into a unified output. The results are stored in both CSV (for structured data) and TXT (for easy reading and further processing) formats. This allows for easy extraction and post-processing of results. To evaluate the translation quality, our system uses ***SacreBLEU*** and ***chrF++*** metrics, which are standard in machine translation tasks. We have achieved a BLEU score of 8.6945 and a chrF++ score of 35.5653 for the Bengali-English pair. These scores suggest that the system provides a reasonably high-quality translation, with strong character-level accuracy.

In addition to the Bengali-English translation system, the architecture supports **Tamil-to-English (ta-en) translation** using the **facebook / nllb-200-**

distilled-600M model (Team et al., 2022). This is a multilingual, distilled version of the NLLB-200 model by Meta AI, designed to handle translations across 200 languages with enhanced efficiency. For Tamil (language code *ta_Taml*) to English (language code *eng_Latn*), the system takes Tamil transcriptions (e.g., from speech recognition output or manually curated corpora), tokenizes them using the NLLB tokenizer, and then applies the sequence-to-sequence model for translation. The translation is done using forced BOS (beginning-of-sentence) tokens to ensure the output is directed towards English.

This translation pipeline is implemented using Hugging Face Transformers and evaluated using standard machine translation metrics. The system achieves a BLEU and chrF++ score of 13.3904 and 39.0237 on the Tamil-English test set. These results reflect a strong translation performance, especially given the morphological richness of Tamil. Like the Bengali-English pipeline, the Tamil-English system operates in an **unconstrained** setting, where no limitations are placed on the type of data or preprocessing methods used. This allows maximum flexibility in improving performance through data augmentation, custom preprocessing, or enhanced model assembling techniques.

The logic of fine-tuning the Transformers are mentioned below:

3.1 Whisper Fine-Tuning

For the bengali to english task we used *bangla-speech-processing/BanglaASR*[1] (Islam, 2023) model which is a Whisper-small fine-tuned on Bangla Mozilla Common Voice dataset and used QLoRA to fine-tune it efficiently on shared task development dataset. Before creating the Dataloader for training and validation set of the shared task, the audio files were preprocessed with Librosa and Pyloudnorm to generalize all audio files and normalize loudness. Then Dataloader was created to efficiently load data for training in a memory efficient way.

We trained our model using the ***Seq2SeqTrainingArguments*** class with a batch size of 4 per device and a ***gradient accumulation*** of 8 steps. The learning rate was set to 1×10^{-4}, and training was conducted for 3 epochs. We enabled mixed-precision training using FP16. For parameter-efficient fine-tuning, we used LoRA with a rank of 8, scaling factor (***lora_alpha***) of 32, and a dropout rate of 0.1. LoRA was applied specifically to the attention layers, targeting the ***q_proj*** and ***v_proj*** modules.

Similarly, for the Tamil to English task we used the *vasista22/whisper-tamil-small*[2] model, which is also a Whisper-small fine-tuned on multiple publicly available Tamil dataset. The parameters were kept the same as while fine-tuning the whisper-bangla model.

3.2 MarianMT Fine-Tuning

The *Helsinki-NLP/opus-mt-bn-en* model[3] from the MarianMT family (Junczys-Dowmunt et al., 2018) was fine-tuned to perform Bengali-to-English translation using shared task's development dataset of aligned sentence pairs in CSV format. The dataset was prepared by merging Bengali transcriptions and their corresponding English translations based on identical audio file names. This ensured accurate one-to-one alignment without the need for external alignment tools such as *fast_align* or *awesome-align*. The fine-tuning procedure (Li et al., 2021) employed a ***batch size*** of 8 and a ***learning rate*** of 3×10^{-5}. Training was conducted over 5 epochs. Preprocessing included tokenizing the source and target sentences with truncation and padding up to a maximum length of 128 tokens. The model was trained using the Hugging Face ***Seq2SeqTrainer*** framework. Evaluation was performed after every epoch, and the best checkpoint was selected based on validation loss. This approach helped the model learn both syntactic and semantic structures effectively, resulting in improved translation quality from Bengali to English.

3.3 NLLB Unconstrained Translation

The *facebook/nllb-200-distilled-600M*[4] (Team et al., 2022) model has been employed for Tamil-to-English translation without additional fine-tuning. This distilled multilingual model was pretrained on a large corpus covering over 200 languages, including Tamil, so while no further task-specific adaptation was performed, the translation is not strictly zero-shot. The translation pipeline starts by tokenizing the Tamil **(tam_Taml)** input sequences

[1]https://huggingface.co/bangla-speech-processing/BanglaASR

[2]https://huggingface.co/vasista22/whisper-tamil-small

[3]https://huggingface.co/Helsinki-NLP/opus-mt-bn-en

[4]https://huggingface.co/facebook/nllb-200-distilled-600M

and specifying English **(eng_Latn)** as the target language using the ***forced_bos_token_id*** parameter. The encoder-decoder architecture of the model generates English output directly. This approach reduces training overhead while leveraging the model's strong pretrained multilingual capabilities to produce effective Tamil-to-English translations without additional supervised training.

Model Used	BLEU	chrF++
Whisper + Helsinki-NLP/opus-mt-bn-en	8.69	35.56
Whisper + NLLB-200-distilled-600M for ta-en	13.39	39.02

Table 1: BLEU and chrF++ scores for Bengali-English and Tamil-English translation systems on test set

4 Workflow

Figure 1 illustrates the basic workflow of our system which we have named **SpeechSync**, consists of four key stages:

- **Input Processing**: Audio files are provided to the system through a predefined directory or batch input process. The Input Module then validates and preprocessed these files. It extracts metadata from associated YAML files, ensuring that the audio is correctly segmented and ready for transcription.

- **Transcription**: The Transcription Module leverages a fine-tuned Whisper model to convert the segmented audio into text. This model, known for its multilingual and zero-shot capabilities, ensures accurate and reliable transcription across both Bengali and Tamil languages.

- **Translation**: The translated output is generated using language-specific models such as Helsinki-NLP/opus-mt-bn-en or NLLB. These models are either fine-tuned on aligned data or used in an unconstrained setup to produce high-quality, contextually relevant English translations from the source text.

- **Output Delivery**: The system compiles the original filename, transcription, and translated output into structured TXT and CSV formats. These outputs are made available for download, enabling users to easily integrate the translated results into their workflows or downstream applications.

This streamlined and modular workflow enables efficient conversion from audio to translated text, supporting diverse use cases in multilingual environments and helping bridge communication gaps across languages.

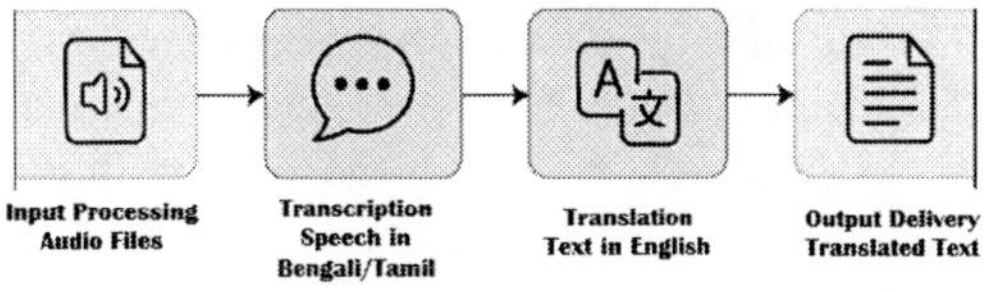

Figure 1: Basic Workflow of the SpeechSync System

5 Limitations

While we acknowledge the significant challenges ahead, such as the shortage of multilingual individuals and insufficient data for certain languages, we are determined to find innovative solutions. Some of the limitations of our current approach include:

- Language Support: The input module currently supports only one language at a time. If an audio file contains multiple languages (e.g., a conversation with code-switching between Tamil and English or Bengali and Hindi), the application processes only the primary language while ignoring others. This limitation restricts the system's effectiveness in multilingual environments and conversational scenarios common in many Indian contexts.

- Processing Time: The transcription and translation modules are computationally intensive. This is especially true when using models like Whisper and Helsinki-NLP/opus-mt-bn-en or NLLB, which require substantial processing resources. To address this, we are exploring model optimization strategies, such as quantization, reduced precision inference (e.g., FP16 or INT8), and parallel processing to enhance efficiency and throughput.

- Translation Performance for Low-Resource Pairs: While the system performs reasonably well for both Bengali-to-English and Tamil-to-English translation tasks, the Bengali-to-English translation still hovers around baseline performance. This is due to limited high-quality parallel data for Bengali, which impacts the model's ability to capture complex sentence structures and semantics. In contrast, Tamil-to-English translation demonstrates relatively improved performance, but further refinement is still necessary to handle domain-specific vocabulary and informal language constructs accurately.

Despite these limitations, we remain committed to enhancing system performance. Ongoing research focuses on expanding language support, improving inference speed, and increasing the quality of both transcription and translation outputs. These efforts are part of a broader goal to make **SpeechSync System** a reliable and efficient multilingual speech-to-text translation system, particularly for underrepresented Indian languages.

6 Future Work

While the current version of the **SpeechSync System** demonstrates strong performance in Bengali-to-English and Tamil-to-English speech translation, there remain several promising directions for future improvement and expansion.

One important enhancement is the incorporation of **speaker diarization and multi-speaker handling**. This would allow the system to differentiate between individual speakers in a single audio stream. This feature is essential for accurately processing meetings, interviews, or conversational datasets. By integrating diarization models, the system could associate transcription segments with specific speaker labels, improving readability and structure.

Another potential development is **real-time streaming transcription and translation**. This would significantly expand the system's usability in live scenarios such as conferences, classrooms, and emergency response settings. Achieving this would involve optimizing the current pipeline to minimize latency and memory usage, allowing for faster and more efficient processing.

Currently, the ASR outputs include only basic punctuation, which can hinder readability. To address this, future iterations will aim to integrate **advanced punctuation and formatting**. This includes accurate sentence boundaries, speaker turn indicators, and proper capitalization. These enhancements would make both transcriptions and translations more natural and easier to follow.

Further improvement could come from **multimodal integration**, where additional visual cues such as lip movements or gestures are used to aid transcription accuracy, especially in noisy or acoustically challenging environments. This would position the system for use in richer, context-aware applications like video subtitling or assistive communication.

7 Conclusion

In summary, our key contributions lie in the rigorous experimentation conducted to identify effective models for speech translation, especially for low-resource languages like Bengali and Tamil. We perform extensive preprocessing of data to ensure quality and suitability for training. The proposed solution establishes a robust pipeline, including code development and workflow setup, allowing for efficient transcription and translation tasks. The training and experimentation were focused on Bengali to English translation for an in-depth analysis, which included fine-tuning Whisper for transcription tasks using LoRA and Helsinki-NLP/opus-mt-bn-en for translation. In addition, we extended our work to Tamil to English translation using the facebook/nllb-200-distilled-600M model, which was fine-tuned on Tamil-English parallel data to improve translation quality and generalization. This enabled the system to support multilingual speech-to-text translation more broadly. Close monitoring of performance metrics, including BLEU and chrF++ scores, was carried out to assess model performance and guide future improvements.

This paper is committed to advancing speech translation (ST) technology for low-resource languages. Through the creation of dedicated datasets and the development of robust models for both Bengali and Tamil, our aim is to facilitate seamless communication and accessibility across diverse linguistic communities, ultimately promoting inclusivity and empowerment.

References

Idris Abdulmumin, Victor Agostinelli, Tanel Alumäe, Antonios Anastasopoulos, Ashwin, Luisa Bentivogli, Ondřej Bojar, Claudia Borg, Fethi Bougares, Roldano Cattoni, Mauro Cettolo, Lizhong Chen, William Chen, Raj Dabre, Yannick Estève, Marcello Federico, Marco Gaido, Dávid Javorský, Marek Kasztelnik, Tsz Kin Lam, Danni Liu, Evgeny Matusov, Chandresh Kumar Maurya, John P. McCrae, Salima Mdhaffar, Yasmin Moslem, Kenton Murray, Satoshi

Nakamura, Matteo Negri, Jan Niehues, Atul Kr. Ojha, John E. Ortega, Sara Papi, Pavel Pecina, Peter Polák, Piotr Połeć, Beatrice Savoldi, Nivedita Sethiya, Claytone Sikasote, Matthias Sperber, Sebastian Stüker, Katsuhito Sudoh, Brian Thompson, Marco Turchi, Alex Waibel, Patrick Wilken, Rodolfo Zevallos, Vilém Zouhar, and Maike Züfle. 2025. Findings of the iwslt 2025 evaluation campaign. In *Proceedings of the 22nd International Conference on Spoken Language Translation (IWSLT 2025)*, Vienna, Austia (in-person and online). Association for Computational Linguistics. To appear.

Milind Agarwal, Sweta Agrawal, Antonios Anastasopoulos, Luisa Bentivogli, Ondřej Bojar, Claudia Borg, Marine Carpuat, Roldano Cattoni, Mauro Cettolo, Mingda Chen, William Chen, Khalid Choukri, Alexandra Chronopoulou, Anna Currey, Thierry Declerck, Qianqian Dong, Kevin Duh, Yannick Estève, Marcello Federico, Souhir Gahbiche, Barry Haddow, Benjamin Hsu, Phu Mon Htut, Hirofumi Inaguma, Dávid Javorský, John Judge, Yasumasa Kano, Tom Ko, Rishu Kumar, Pengwei Li, Xutai Ma, Prashant Mathur, Evgeny Matusov, Paul McNamee, John P. McCrae, Kenton Murray, Maria Nadejde, Satoshi Nakamura, Matteo Negri, Ha Nguyen, Jan Niehues, Xing Niu, Atul Kr. Ojha, John E. Ortega, Proyag Pal, Juan Pino, Lonneke van der Plas, Peter Polák, Elijah Rippeth, Elizabeth Salesky, Jiatong Shi, Matthias Sperber, Sebastian Stüker, Katsuhito Sudoh, Yun Tang, Brian Thompson, Kevin Tran, Marco Turchi, Alex Waibel, Mingxuan Wang, Shinji Watanabe, and Rodolfo Zevallos. 2023. FINDINGS OF THE IWSLT 2023 EVALUATION CAMPAIGN. In *Proceedings of the 20th International Conference on Spoken Language Translation (IWSLT 2023)*, pages 1–61, Toronto, Canada (in-person and online). Association for Computational Linguistics.

Tim Dettmers, Artidoro Pagnoni, Ari Holtzman, and Luke Zettlemoyer. 2023. Qlora: Efficient finetuning of quantized llms.

Md Saiful Islam. 2023. Transformer based whisper bangla asr model.

Marcin Junczys-Dowmunt, Roman Grundkiewicz, Tomasz Dwojak, Hieu Hoang, Kenneth Heafield, Tom Neckermann, Frank Seide, Ulrich Germann, Alham Fikri Aji, Nikolay Bogoychev, André F. T. Martins, and Alexandra Birch. 2018. Marian: Fast neural machine translation in C++. In *Proceedings of ACL 2018, System Demonstrations*, pages 116–121, Melbourne, Australia. Association for Computational Linguistics.

Raymond Li, Wen Xiao, Lanjun Wang, Hyeju Jang, and Giuseppe Carenini. 2021. T3-vis: visual analytic for training and fine-tuning transformers in NLP. In *Proceedings of the 2021 Conference on Empirical Methods in Natural Language Processing: System Demonstrations*, pages 220–230, Online and Punta Cana, Dominican Republic. Association for Computational Linguistics.

Brian McFee, Colin Raffel, Dawen Liang, Daniel P. W. Ellis, Matt McVicar, Eric Battenberg, and Oriol Nieto. 2015. librosa: Audio and music signal analysis in python. In *SciPy*.

Alec Radford, Jong Wook Kim, Tao Xu, Greg Brockman, Christine McLeavey, and Ilya Sutskever. 2022. Robust speech recognition via large-scale weak supervision.

Alec Radford, Jong Wook Kim, Tao Xu, Greg Brockman, Christine McLeavey, and Ilya Sutskever. 2023. Robust speech recognition via large-scale weak supervision. In *International conference on machine learning*, pages 28492–28518. PMLR.

Tushar Talukder Showrav. 2022. An automatic speech recognition system for bengali language based on wav2vec2 and transfer learning. *arXiv preprint arXiv:2209.08119*.

NLLB Team, Marta R. Costa-jussà, James Cross, Onur Çelebi, Maha Elbayad, Kenneth Heafield, Kevin Heffernan, Elahe Kalbassi, Janice Lam, Daniel Licht, Jean Maillard, Anna Sun, Skyler Wang, Guillaume Wenzek, Al Youngblood, Bapi Akula, Loic Barrault, Gabriel Mejia Gonzalez, Prangthip Hansanti, John Hoffman, Semarley Jarrett, Kaushik Ram Sadagopan, Dirk Rowe, Shannon Spruit, Chau Tran, Pierre Andrews, Necip Fazil Ayan, Shruti Bhosale, Sergey Edunov, Angela Fan, Cynthia Gao, Vedanuj Goswami, Francisco Guzmán, Philipp Koehn, Alexandre Mourachko, Christophe Ropers, Safiyyah Saleem, Holger Schwenk, and Jeff Wang. 2022. No language left behind: Scaling human-centered machine translation.

Thomas Wolf, Lysandre Debut, Victor Sanh, Julien Chaumond, Clement Delangue, Anthony Moi, Pierric Cistac, Tim Rault, Rémi Louf, Morgan Funtowicz, Joe Davison, Sam Shleifer, Patrick von Platen, Clara Ma, Yacine Jernite, Julien Plu, Canwen Xu, Teven Le Scao, Sylvain Gugger, Mariama Drame, Quentin Lhoest, and Alexander M. Rush. 2020. Huggingface's transformers: State-of-the-art natural language processing.

ALADAN at IWSLT25 Low-resource Arabic Dialectal Speech Translation Task

Josef Jon[2,4], Waad Ben Kheder[1], André Beyer[3], Claude Barras[1], and Jean-Luc Gauvain[1]

[1]Vocapia Research, France
[2]Lingea, Czechia
[3]Crowdee, Germany
[4]Charles University, Faculty of Mathematics and Physics, Institute of Formal and Applied Linguistics, Czechia

Abstract

We present our IWSLT 2025 submission for the low-resource track on North Levantine Arabic to English speech translation, building on our IWSLT 2024 efforts. We retain last year's cascade ASR architecture that combines a TDNN-F model and a Zipformer for the ASR step. We upgrade the Zipformer to the Zipformer-Large variant (253 M parameters vs. 66 M) to capture richer acoustic representations. For the MT part, to further alleviate data sparsity, we created a crowd-sourced parallel corpus covering five major Arabic dialects (Tunisian, Levantine, Moroccan, Algerian, Egyptian) curated via rigorous qualification and filtering. We show that using crowd-sourced data is feasible in low-resource scenarios as we observe improved automatic evaluation metrics across all dialects. We also experimented with the dataset under a high-resource scenario, where we had access to a large, high-quality Levantine Arabic corpus from LDC. In this setting, adding the crowd-sourced data does not improve the scores on the official validation set anymore. Our final submission scores 20.0 BLEU on the official test set.

1 Introduction

Dialectal Arabic speech translation (ST) remains one of the most challenging tasks in spoken language processing due to (i) the scarcity of high-quality, parallel speech–text resources for non-standardized varieties, (ii) high phonetic and orthographic variability among dialects, and (iii) domain mismatches between available corpora (e.g., broadcasts in Modern Standard Arabic) and conversational speech. Although end-to-end models and pre-trained encoders have advanced general ASR and NMT, most publicly available data still target Modern Standard Arabic (Al-Fetyani et al., 2023; Ali et al., 2016), leaving dialectal variants under-resourced. Previous IWSLT evaluations (Yan et al., 2022; Anastasopoulos et al., 2022; Agarwal et al., 2023; Hussein et al., 2023; Boito et al., 2022; Ahmad et al., 2024) have tackled these issues using transfer learning and fine-tuning strategies, yet a comprehensive solution for multiple dialects is still lacking.

In our IWSLT 2024 submission, ALADAN achieved first place in the Levantine Arabic task by combining a cascade ASR pipeline (TDNN-F + Zipformer) with fine-tuned NLLB and prompt-driven LLMs (Command-R), leveraging a crowd-sourced parallel corpus for Tunisian and Levantine Arabic. We also demonstrated that prudent data normalization and a hybrid system combination (ROVER) yield substantial WER and BLEU improvements. Building on this success, our IWSLT 2025 system introduces two key innovations:

- **Multi-Dialect ASR with Zipformer-Large:** We replace last year's Zipformer (66M parameters) with the 253M-parameter Zipformer-Large to better model long-range dependencies and acoustic nuances in dialectal speech. We also train a single multi-dialect model instead of deriving dialect-specific ASR models via fine-tuning.

- **Expanded multi-dialect crowd-sourcing:** We extend our crowd-sourced collection beyond Tunisian and Levantine to include Moroccan, Algerian, and Egyptian dialects, yielding more than 160k new parallel sentences after rigorous quality control. These data are used to fine-tune the NLLB-200 and Cohere Command-R models under QLoRA, enhancing cross-dialect robustness.

Our paper is organized as follows. Section 2 details the data collection and normalization procedures. Section 3 presents our ASR and ST models, detailing their architecture, training, fine-tuning, and performance on Levantine datasets and internal tests. In Section 4, we conclude with a discussion of future directions for low-resource dialect

Proceedings of the 22nd International Conference on Spoken Language Translation (IWSLT 2025), pages 252–259
July 31 - August 1, 2025

translation.

2 Methods

2.1 Text normalization

The absence of standardized conventions across different Arabic dialects requires the development of robust text normalization procedures to reduce ambiguity. In this work, we adopt the same text normalization methodology used in Ben Kheder et al. (2024). Our normalization process operates on the character- and word-level. Character-level normalization promotes uniformity in the orthographic representation of various dialects, improving consistency across datasets. Table 1 summarizes the rules used in our experiments.

Dialect	Normalizations
All dialects	ژ => ر / پ => ب
apc/arz/ary	ڤ or ڥ => ف
aeb/arq	ڨ => ق / ڥ => ف
ary	ڭ => ق / گ => ق

Table 1: Characters normalization rules for different Arabic dialects.

Word-level normalization, on the other hand, addresses orthographic variability in dialectal Arabic and foreign words. This step employs rules derived from a combination of a Word2vec model and a weighted Levenshtein distance to identify orthographically similar words appearing in comparable contexts. This process helps normalize clusters of words such as:

- The Tunisian word for "anyway": حاسيلو، حاصلو، حاسيول، حاصولو، حاصيله، حاصلو، حاصيلو.
- The Syrian word for "the computer": الكوبيوتير، الكمبيوتر.

For further details on the methodology, we refer readers to (Ben Kheder et al., 2024).

2.2 Crowd-sourcing for parallel data collection

We collaborate with Crowdee[1] crowd-sourcing platform to create a parallel dataset. The goal was to generate high-quality translations while addressing the challenges posed by dialectal variations in Arabic. In these tasks, transcripts from CTS/YouTube datasets (described in Ben Kheder et al. (2024)) are used as input.

[1]Crowdee—https://www.crowdee.de/

2.2.1 Crowd worker filtering

We designed linguistic assessment comprising 40 questions for each of the five dialects. The test evaluates linguistic competencies, including grammar proficiency and the ability to translate between the respective dialects and English using multiple choice exercises. Only workers who demonstrated sufficient linguistic skills were allowed to contribute to the dataset.

2.2.2 Translation guidelines

To ensure the quality and completeness of translations, crowd workers receive detailed instructions:

- **Providing a translation:** Translate a single sentence from a short conversational excerpt (6 consecutive sentences corresponding to 3 speaking turns between 2 speakers, extracted from our internal conversational telephone data).
- **Ranking confidence:** Workers were asked to rate their confidence in their translation as "correct", "unsure", or "incorrect".
- **Suggesting alternatives:** Workers were encouraged to offer alternative translations if possible.
- **Adding comments:** Additional comments were invited to clarify translation choices or highlight ambiguities.

2.2.3 Data filtering

Following the translation phase, a data cleaning procedure was implemented to improve the quality of the dataset. This included:

- **Removing machine-like translations:** Sentences with patterns indicative of machine-generated translations were excluded.
- **Language filtering:** Sentences that were in languages other than English (e.g., French or Arabic) were removed.
- **Word count discrepancy:** Examples with significant discrepancies in word count between the source and target were filtered out.
- **Perplexity-based filtering:** the GPT-2 model was used to compute the perplexity of each translated sentence. We removed all sentences that exceed 10 words with perplexity greater than 100, as these likely indicated low-quality translations.

	IWSLT24	IWSLT22		Internal devs (CTS)				
	valid apc	*dev aeb*	*$test_1$ aeb*	*apc*	*arz*	*arq*	*ary*	*aeb*
TDNN-F	26.5	39.9	40.8	19.8	26.4	28.7	30.7	27.6
Zipformer-Large	21.8	31.7	32.7	14.5	20.8	23.7	23.9	22.3
Both	**19.9**	**30.6**	**31.8**	**14.0**	**19.3**	**22.1**	**22.8**	**21.6**

Table 2: WER (%) of ASR models on IWSLT24 Levantine Arabic (apc) validation, IWSLT22 Tunisian Arabic (aeb) dev/test sets and 5 internal devs (apc, arz, arq, ary, aeb). The Levantine "apc", Egyptian "arz", Algerian "arq" internal devs correspond to telephone speech (CTS) while the ones for Moroccan "ary" and Tunisian Arabic "aeb" correspond to YouTube data (radio).

3 Experiments

This section describes our experimental settings, used data and results.

3.1 Data

In this subsection, we list the datasets we used for training and evaluating our systems.

3.1.1 ASR data

- **Training:** We used 4200h of multi-dialect multi-domain data to train our ASR models. For more details, readers may refer to (Ben Kheder et al., 2024).

- **Evaluation:** The models are evaluated on the dev sets from IWSLT22 (aeb) and IWSLT24 (apc). We conduct additional tests on internal devs corresponding to conversational telephone speech ("arq", "arz" and "apc" devs) and YouTube data ("aeb" and "arz").

3.1.2 NMT data

For the crowd-sourcing experiments, used the crowd-sourced datasets to finetune the NMT models and LLMs. The sizes of the datasets are listed in Table 3. For evaluation, we used a held-out part of the crowd-sourcing datasets, parts of the AraBench dataset (Sajjad et al., 2020) and the IWSLT 2024 test set from the dialectal Arabic shared task. For the final submission, we used the same datasets as our last year's submission (Ben Kheder et al., 2024), i.e. LDC2012T09, PADIC, MADAR, GlobalVoices, smaller crowd-sourced data, IWSLT22 Tunisian Arabic and the official training dataset for this task, provided by the organizers.

Dialect	Sentences (k)
arq (Algerian)	51.9
arz (Egyptian)	52.8
ary (Moroccan)	19.1
apc (Levantine)	14.8
aeb (Tunisian)	22.7

Table 3: NMT crowd-sourced dataset sizes.

3.2 Metrics

We score ASR using word error rate (WER). To measure the quality of the MT, we use 3 metrics: BLEU (Papineni et al., 2002), ChrF (Popović, 2015) and XCOMET-XL (Guerreiro et al., 2024).

3.3 ASR

3.3.1 ASR models

Our ASR front-end follows the cascade design of (Ben Kheder et al., 2024), combining a conventional TDNN-F model with an end-to-end Zipformer. The key innovation in this year's submission is the replacement of last year's 66 M-parameter Zipformer-M with a much larger, 253 M-parameter "Zipformer-Large" and the design of a single multi-dialect model (instead of deriving dialect-specific models via fine-tuning).

1. **TDNN-F model:** 15 layers of factorized TDNN with ReLU activations (layer dimension 1920) and linear bottlenecks (dimensions 320, 240) trained using the LF-MMI objective.

2. **Zipformer-Large:** The base design follows the "Zipformer-L" configuration of (Yao et al., 2023), modified as follows:

	Configuration
CNN kernel sizes	{63, 31, 15, 15, 31, 6}
Encoder hidden dim.	{192, 512, 1024, 1536, 512, 256}
Feed-forward dim.	{512, 768, 1024, 2048, 1024, 768}

Table 4: Configuration of Zipformer-Large.

The output of the two models are combined using the ROVER algorithm.

3.3.2 Training procedure

We train multi-dialect models using all available data to take advantage of the acoustic and linguistic similarities between different Arabic dialects. The TDNN-F model is trained for 20 epochs (on all data) using lr=1e-3 and the Zipformer model is trained for 80 epochs using lr=4e-3.

3.3.3 Results

Table 2 shows the WERs of our ASR systems after applying the normalization procedure. This normalization significantly improved the WERs for "apc" and "aeb" by 10% and 18%, respectively. The combined model achieved even greater improvements, demonstrating the complementarity of the two models and outperforming all WERs reported in (Agarwal et al., 2023) for "aeb".

3.4 Speech translation

For speech translation (ST), we apply the cascaded approach: we use the ASR to obtain transcriptions and then we translate them using an NMT.

3.4.1 MT models

We finetune one pretrained NMT model (*NLLB-1.3B*) and 3 LLMs: Command-R V0.1 (4-bit quantized, CohereForAI/c4ai-command-r-v01-4bit), Aya Expanse 8B and EuroLLM 9B Instruct. We use QLoRA finetuning, using the transformers, peft and trl libraries. We set the LoRA rank size to $r = 32$ and $\alpha = 16$. We finetuned the models by AdamW optimizer, with warmup ratio of 0.03. We ran multiple training runs with learning rates $lr = \{2e-4, 1e-4, 5e-5, 1e-5\}$.

3.4.2 MT results

First, we compare the base and the finetuned models on the crowd-sourced test set (with reference transcriptions on the source side) and on the apc test set from IWSLT 2024 low-resource Arabic Dialectal Speech translation task. The results are presented in Table 5. We see that for all dialects, the evaluation scores improve significantly for all models. The best scoring finetuned model across all the dialects is the Command-R model, while all the other models are competitive. Of the base models, without finetuning, Command-R and Aya-expanse-8B provide the best scores. In particular, for the IWSLT test set (*apc/iwslt*), we obtain a large improvement in automated scores even though it is a different domain (interviews with refugees) from our crowd-sourced training data (telephone conversations).

We also compare the base and the finetuned Command-R and NLLB models on the part of the test sets in the AraBench dataset. The comparison is shown in Table 10 in Appendix B. Here, base NLLB performs the best on these test sets and finetuning decreases the performance for NLLB, but improves it for Command-R.

3.4.3 ST results

We evaluated both base and finetuned NLLB and Command-R models on ASR outputs from the crowd-sourced and IWSLT test sets (Tables 6 and 7). As with reference transcriptions, finetuning with crowd-sourced data significantly improves performance across dialects. Although the BLEU and ChrF scores are similar, Command-R consistently outperforms NLLB in XCOMET-XL. Our finetuned model scores 23.7 BLEU on IWSLT, compared to 28.7 for the top shared task system and 20.9 for the runner-up, despite those systems using much more fine-tuning data, including in-domain training set. This shows that crowd-sourcing is a viable option to improve automated metric scores for dialectal Arabic ST even on out-of-domain test sets.

3.5 Final submission

We also finetuned the Command-R model on the same datasets as our submission from last year (Ben Kheder et al., 2024). We note that, as opposed to the previously described experiments, we trained the models for document-level translation, with a maximum context size of 100 lines, same as last year. We experimented with adding the crowd-sourced data described earlier on top of these datasets and the results are shown in Table 8. Adding crowd-sourced data on top of an already large and high-quality dataset does not have any positive effect on BLEU and ChrF scores. For the final submission, we selected 29 checkpoints with best BLEU scores on the validation set, translated the test set with them and ran Minimum Bayes risk decoding using wmt22-comet-da score as the objective function. The final official results from IWSLT 2025 (Abdulmumin et al., 2025) are shown in Table 9.

Model	Language	Base model BLEU	Base model ChrF	Base model COMET	Finetuned model BLEU	Finetuned model ChrF	Finetuned model COMET
NLLB	arq	5.8	25.9	0.558	24.8	47.8	0.765
	arz	14.8	36.9	0.586	31.8	52.9	0.807
	apc	15.4	38.0	0.657	29.5	51.0	0.836
	ary	16.2	39.7	0.528	**33.5**	55.4	**0.726**
	aeb	17.3	40.2	0.549	30.9	53.2	0.741
	iwslt24/apc	19.2	44.6	0.689			
Command-R-V0.1-4bit	arq	12.6	34.3	0.573	**28.8**	**49.2**	**0.778**
	arz	18.0	42.1	0.624	**33.2**	**53.6**	**0.820**
	apc	20.1	42.4	0.661	**35.4**	**55.7**	**0.856**
	ary	20.2	44.5	0.596	33.3	54.7	0.718
	aeb	20.3	44.8	0.613	**31.0**	**53.4**	**0.759**
	iwslt24/apc	19.7	45.9	0.818	28.2	53.4	0.848
EuroLLM-9B	arq	9.8	31.3	0.519	27.0	48.2	0.773
	arz	21.1	44.5	0.611	32.3	52.7	0.805
	apc	16.0	40.2	0.599	31.8	52.6	0.839
	ary	19.5	45.1	0.514	31.7	53.7	0.712
	aeb	21.1	45.6	0.578	29.7	52.2	0.750
Aya-expanse-8b	arq	13.4	34.7	0.557	26.8	47.8	0.775
	arz	24.8	47.3	0.632	32.8	53.1	0.815
	apc	21.8	43.7	0.644	33.0	53.1	0.845
	ary	24.8	48.4	0.568	31.8	53.1	0.707
	aeb	23.4	47.9	0.607	29.3	51.7	0.747

Table 5: Results of base and finetuned models on our test sets and IWSLT 2024 test set in text-to-text translation (using reference transcriptions of the source speech as the source for the MT).

	Language	BLEU	ChrF	COMET
NLLB	arq	6.0	23.7	0.567
	arz	13.3	34.9	0.609
	apc	13.6	34.3	0.663
	ary	14.2	36.1	0.522
	aeb	13.6	35.2	0.504
Command-R	arq	7.0	27.0	0.569
	arz	15.5	36.9	0.607
	apc	17.1	38.6	0.671
	ary	17.3	40.4	0.563
	aeb	18.0	40.8	0.559
	iwslt24/apc	16.5	42.1	0.766

Table 6: Cascaded speech translation scores of **base**, non-finetuned models on our test sets (using our ASR transcriptions of the source speech).

	Language	BLEU	ChrF	COMET
NLLB	arq	21.2	40.7	0.731
	arz	26.2	46.3	0.757
	apc	24.2	44.2	0.790
	ary	25.7	47.8	0.643
	aeb	23.2	45.4	0.646
Command-R	arq	21.7	41.6	0.741
	arz	26.0	46.7	0.767
	apc	27.2	47.6	0.805
	ary	25.4	47.1	0.652
	aeb	23.2	45.4	0.673
	iwslt24/apc	23.7	48.6	0.803

Table 7: Cascaded speech translation scores of **finetuned** models on our test sets.

		Valid 2024	Test 2024
2024 dataset	2024 ASR	30.3/53.5	27.5/50.6
	2025 ASR	31.4/54.7	27.4/50.3
	Human	33.5/58.5	-
+new crowd	2024 ASR	29.9/53.3	27.4/50.3
	2025 ASR	31.1/54.6	27.2/50.2
	Human	33.6/58.7	-
Final MBR		32.5/55.6	28.0/51.7

Table 8: BLEU/ChrF scores of document-level models trained on our last year's dataset and after adding the new crowd-sourced dataset described above. We also compared using our last year's ASR model with this year's improved model and to the human reference transcription.

4 Conclusions

In this work, we demonstrated that carefully engineered data collection and model adaptation can substantially advance low-resource dialectal Arabic speech translation. By expanding our crowd-sourced parallel corpus to five dialects (Tunisian, Levantine, Moroccan, Algerian, Egyptian), including rigorous qualification tests and multi-stage filtering, we provided rich, targeted material for NMT fine-tuning. Upgrading our acoustic front-end to a 253 M-parameter Zipformer-Large and combining it with TDNN-F via ROVER further drove down WER. On the translation side, fine-tuning NLLB-200 and Command-R models, with

Submission Name	BLEU	COMET	CHRF
AIB_Marco contrastive1	15.82	0.6456	36.23
AIB_Marco contrastive2	10.53	0.5727	27.69
AIB_Marco contrastive3	16.22	0.6669	37.48
AIB_Marco contrastive4	16.47	0.683	37.96
AIB_Marco primary	12.01	0.6547	34.19
ALADAN primary	**20.02**	**0.6613**	**39.91**
jhu contrastive1	15.39	0.6569	35.91
jhu primary	14.64	0.6493	36.23
lia contrastive1	21.02	0.6983	42.92
lia contrastive2	21.45	0.694	43.13
lia primary	22.56	0.7193	44.72
kit contrastive1	19.11	0.6832	40.95
kit contrastive2	21.93	0.6968	44.67
kit primary	23.34	0.7043	45.09

Table 9: The official results of the Levantine Arabic task from IWSLT 2025. Our submission in bold.

QLoRA for the latter, on this multi-dialect dataset yielded significant BLEU and COMET gains on our in-domain test sets. These findings confirm that combining expanded crowd-sourcing with unsupervised data augmentation and model scaling is a viable and resource-efficient strategy to boost dialectal Arabic translation, even when faced with new domains. However, our experiments with the final submission show that adding this dataset on top of already extensive, high-quality corpora we used to train our last year's submission does not improve BLEU and ChrF scores on the official validation set. This suggests that the crowdsourcing approach is more viable in low-resource scenarios, as the knowledge provided by the crowdsourced dataset might already be covered in the larger corpora.

Acknowledgments

This work was funded by the the European Defence Fund (EDF) 2021 project ALADAN (Ai-based LAnguage technology development framework for Defence ApplicatioNs; Grant ID: 101102545). Views and opinions expressed are however those of the author(s) only and do not necessarily reflect those of the European Union or the European Commission. Neither the European Union nor the granting authority can be held responsible for them. It was also partially supported by the Charles University Grant Agency in Prague (GAUK 244523) and by SVV project number 260 821. We would like to express our gratitude to LDC for kindly providing the data used in this study.

References

Idris Abdulmumin, Victor Agostinelli, Tanel Alumäe, Antonios Anastasopoulos, Ashwin, Luisa Bentivogli, Ondřej Bojar, Claudia Borg, Fethi Bougares, Roldano Cattoni, Mauro Cettolo, Lizhong Chen, William Chen, Raj Dabre, Yannick Estève, Marcello Federico, Marco Gaido, Dávid Javorský, Marek Kasztelnik, Tsz Kin Lam, Danni Liu, Evgeny Matusov, Chandresh Kumar Maurya, John P. McCrae, Salima Mdhaffar, Yasmin Moslem, Kenton Murray, Satoshi Nakamura, Matteo Negri, Jan Niehues, Atul Kr. Ojha, John E. Ortega, Sara Papi, Pavel Pecina, Peter Polák, Piotr Połeć, Beatrice Savoldi, Nivedita Sethiya, Claytone Sikasote, Matthias Sperber, Sebastian Stüker, Katsuhito Sudoh, Brian Thompson, Marco Turchi, Alex Waibel, Patrick Wilken, Rodolfo Zevallos, Vilém Zouhar, and Maike Züfle. 2025. Findings of the iwslt 2025 evaluation campaign. In *Proceedings of the 22nd International Conference on Spoken Language Translation (IWSLT 2025)*, Vienna, Austia (in-person and online). Association for Computational Linguistics. To appear.

Milind Agarwal, Sweta Agarwal, Antonios Anastasopoulos, Luisa Bentivogli, Ondřej Bojar, Claudia Borg, Marine Carpuat, Roldano Cattoni, Mauro Cettolo, Mingda Chen, et al. 2023. Findings of the iwslt 2023 evaluation campaign. Association for Computational Linguistics.

Ibrahim Said Ahmad, Antonios Anastasopoulos, Ondřej Bojar, Claudia Borg, Marine Carpuat, Roldano Cattoni, Mauro Cettolo, William Chen, Qianqian Dong, Marcello Federico, et al. 2024. Findings of the iwslt 2024 evaluation campaign. *arXiv preprint arXiv:2411.05088.*

Mohammad Al-Fetyani, Muhammad Al-Barham, Gheith Abandah, Adham Alsharkawi, and Maha Dawas. 2023. Masc: Massive arabic speech corpus. In *2022 IEEE Spoken Language Technology Workshop (SLT)*, pages 1006--1013. IEEE.

Ahmed Ali, Peter Bell, James Glass, Yacine Messaoui, Hamdy Mubarak, Steve Renals, and Yifan Zhang. 2016. The mgb-2 challenge: Arabic multi-dialect broadcast media recognition. In *2016 IEEE Spoken Language Technology Workshop (SLT)*, pages 279--284. IEEE.

Antonios Anastasopoulos, Loc Barrault, Luisa Bentivogli, Marcely Zanon Boito, Ondřej Bojar, Roldano Cattoni, Anna Currey, Georgiana Dinu, Kevin Duh, Maha Elbayad, et al. 2022. Findings of the iwslt 2022 evaluation campaign. In *Proceedings of the 19th International Conference on Spoken Language Translation (IWSLT 2022)*, pages 98--157. Association for Computational Linguistics.

Waad Ben Kheder, Josef Jon, André Beyer, Abdel Messaoudi, Rabea Affan, Claude Barras, Maxim Tychonov, and Jean-Luc Gauvain. 2024. Aladan at iwslt24 low-resource arabic dialectal speech translation task. In *Proceedings of the 21st International Conference on Spoken Language Translation (IWSLT 2024)*, pages 192--202.

Marcely Zanon Boito, John Ortega, Hugo Riguidel, Antoine Laurent, Loïc Barrault, Fethi Bougares, Firas Chaabani, Ha Nguyen, Florentin Barbier, Souhir Gahbiche, et al. 2022. On-trac consortium systems for the iwslt 2022 dialect and low-resource speech translation tasks. *arXiv preprint arXiv:2205.01987*.

Houda Bouamor, Nizar Habash, Mohammad Salameh, Wajdi Zaghouani, Owen Rambow, Dana Abdulrahim, Ossama Obeid, Salam Khalifa, Fadhl Eryani, Alexander Erdmann, et al. 2018. The madar arabic dialect corpus and lexicon. In *Proceedings of the eleventh international conference on language resources and evaluation (LREC 2018)*.

Nuno M. Guerreiro, Ricardo Rei, Daan van Stigt, Luisa Coheur, Pierre Colombo, and André F. T. Martins. 2024. xcomet: Transparent machine translation evaluation through fine-grained error detection. *Transactions of the Association for Computational Linguistics*, 12:979--995.

Amir Hussein, Cihan Xiao, Neha Verma, Thomas Thebaud, Matthew Wiesner, and Sanjeev Khudanpur. 2023. Jhu iwslt 2023 dialect speech translation system description. In *Proceedings of the 20th International Conference on Spoken Language Translation (IWSLT 2023)*, pages 283--290.

Kishore Papineni, Salim Roukos, Todd Ward, and Wei-Jing Zhu. 2002. Bleu: a method for automatic evaluation of machine translation. In *Proceedings of the 40th Annual Meeting of the Association for Computational Linguistics*, pages 311--318, Philadelphia, Pennsylvania, USA. Association for Computational Linguistics.

Maja Popović. 2015. chrF: character n-gram F-score for automatic MT evaluation. In *Proceedings of the Tenth Workshop on Statistical Machine Translation*, pages 392--395, Lisbon, Portugal. Association for Computational Linguistics.

Hassan Sajjad, Ahmed Abdelali, Nadir Durrani, and Fahim Dalvi. 2020. Arabench: Benchmarking dialectal arabic-english machine translation. In *GOLING*, pages 123--456.

Brian Yan, Patrick Fernandes, Siddharth Dalmia, Jiatong Shi, Yifan Peng, Dan Berrebbi, Xinyi Wang, Graham Neubig, and Shinji Watanabe. 2022. Cmu's iwslt 2022 dialect speech translation system. In *Proceedings of the 19th International Conference on Spoken Language Translation (IWSLT 2022)*, pages 298--307.

Zengwei Yao, Liyong Guo, Xiaoyu Yang, Wei Kang, Fangjun Kuang, Yifan Yang, Zengrui Jin, Long Lin, and Daniel Povey. 2023. Zipformer: A faster and better encoder for automatic speech recognition. *arXiv preprint arXiv:2310.11230*.

A Document-level translation

We also compared line-by-line translation to translating the whole conversation for the crowd-sourced dataset. We used the same document-level prompt as (Ben Kheder et al., 2024). Surprisingly, in this case translating line by line worked better. We hypothesize that the repetitiveness of the dataset causes this. Many simple utterances (e.g. "Yeah.") are repeated next to each other in the training data, which leads the model to overestimate the probability of repeating the same line in the document-level translation. We leave a better understanding of this issue for future work.

B AraBench test set

We also evaluated our model on test sets from the AraBench (Sajjad et al., 2020) benchmark, specifically the MADAR (Bouamor et al., 2018) test sets for dialects we used during finetuning. Contrary to the results on other test sets, the base NLLB model scores the best, and fine-tuning on our crowd-sourced data hurts the evaluation scores. For Command-R, finetuning improves the scores compared to the Command-R base model, but still does not outperform base NLLB. We hypothesize that this might be caused by presence of the test set in the NLLB's training dataset, or by domain mismatch.

		Base			Finetuned		
		BLEU	ChrF	COMET	BLEU	ChrF	COMET
NLLB	madar.test.lev.0.jo.ar	47.3	65.2	0.924	42.3	61.5	0.938
	madar.test.lev.0.lb.ar	42.1	59.5	0.863	36.3	54.9	0.884
	madar.test.lev.0.pa.ar	45.6	62.4	0.911	41.9	59.5	0.928
	madar.test.lev.0.sy.ar	45.9	62.9	0.911	41.5	59.4	0.926
	madar.test.lev.1.jo.ar	47.4	64.4	0.876	43.7	61.4	0.930
	madar.test.lev.1.sy.ar	47.1	63.9	0.899	41.3	59.7	0.909
	madar.test.mgr.0.ma.ar	41.3	59.6	0.859	37.8	56.8	0.891
	madar.test.mgr.0.tn.ar	36.4	54.4	0.818	31.7	50.5	0.845
	madar.test.mgr.1.ma.ar	47.4	65.2	0.889	44.7	62.9	0.915
	madar.test.mgr.1.tn.ar	30.6	49.4	0.815	27.0	46.4	0.844
	madar.test.nil.0.eg.ar	45.7	63.1	0.904	41.3	59.8	0.931
	madar.test.nil.1.eg.ar	52.8	68.8	0.926	50.2	66.5	0.944
Command-R	madar.test.lev.0.jo.ar	39.3	59.3	0.943	42.8	61.1	0.946
	madar.test.lev.0.lb.ar	29.9	50.6	0.876	33.4	53.0	0.892
	madar.test.lev.0.pa.ar	39.4	58.2	0.934	43.9	60.4	0.942
	madar.test.lev.0.sy.ar	39.0	58.3	0.931	42.1	59.5	0.941
	madar.test.lev.1.jo.ar	40.5	59.5	0.929	43.8	61.6	0.938
	madar.test.lev.1.sy.ar	39.6	58.6	0.918	42.9	60.5	0.928
	madar.test.mgr.0.ma.ar	33.7	54.4	0.885	37.1	56.0	0.895
	madar.test.mgr.0.tn.ar	22.2	42.9	0.792	29.5	48.2	0.847
	madar.test.mgr.1.ma.ar	38.4	59.3	0.909	42.7	60.7	0.916
	madar.test.mgr.1.tn.ar	20.0	40.8	0.805	25.3	44.5	0.850
	madar.test.nil.0.eg.ar	40.1	59.4	0.935	43.0	60.9	0.942
	madar.test.nil.1.eg.ar	45.5	63.5	0.943	50.2	66.5	0.952

Table 10: Automatic evaluation scores of base and finetuned models on MADAR test sets from the AraBench benchmark.

QUESPA Submission for the IWSLT 2025 Dialectal and Low-resource Speech Translation Task

John E. Ortega[1], **Rodolfo Zevallos**[2], **William Chen**[3], **Idris Abdulmumin**[4]
[1]Northeastern University, USA, [2]Barcelona Supercomputing Center, Spain
[3]Carnegie Mellon University, USA, [4]University of Pretoria
contact email: j.ortega@northeastern.edu

Abstract

This article describes the **QUESPA** team speech translation (ST) submissions for the Quechua to Spanish (QUE–SPA) track featured in the Evaluation Campaign of IWSLT 2025: dialectal and low-resource speech translation. This year, there is one main submission type supported in the campaign: *unconstrained*. This is our third year submitting our ST systems to the IWSLT shared task and we feel that we have achieved novel performance, surpassing last year's submission. This year we submit three total *unconstrained-only* systems of which our best (contrastive 2) system uses last year's best performing pre-trained language (PLM) model for ST (without cascading) and the inclusion of additional *Quechua–Collao* speech transcriptions found online. Fine-tuning of Microsoft's SpeechT5 model in a ST setting along with the addition of new data and a data augmentation technique allowed us to achieve 26.7 BLEU. In this article, we present the three submissions along with a detailed description of the updated machine translation system where a comparison is done between synthetic, unconstrained, and other data for fine-tuning.

1 Introduction

In this article, we describe three systems that were submitted to the IWSLT 2025 Low-Resource Track for Speech Translation (ST). The IWSLT task is particularly challenging for low-resource languages (LRLs) due to the lack of data needed to create, or even fine-tune, a pre-trained language model (PLM). While many problems are solvable with APIs provided by large corporations such as ChatGPT or Gemini, it is still the case that for LRLs, zero-to-few shot approaches are needed where corporate-level APIs do not contain enough data either. Here, we describe three main approaches that extend previous approaches submitted in the past three iterations of IWSLT (Ahmad et al., 2024; Agarwal et al., 2023; Anastasopoulos et al., 2022) where the best score gotten for ST until this publishing based on BLEU (Papineni et al., 2002) for the Quechua to Spanish task was: 19.7, submittted by this same team **QUESPA**.

Quechua is an indigenous language spoken by more than 8 million people in South America. It is mainly spoken in Peru, Ecuador, and Bolivia where the official high-resource language (HRLs) is Spanish. It is a highly inflective language based on its suffixes which agglutinate and found to be similar to other languages like Finnish. It is worthwhile to note that previous work (Ortega and Pillaipakkamnatt, 2018; Ortega et al., 2020) has been somewhat successful in identifying the inflectional properties of Quechua such as agglutination where another HRLs, namely Finnish, can aid for translation purposes achieving nearly 20 BLEU on religious-based (text-only) tasks. The average number of morphemes per word (synthesis) is about two times larger than English. English typically has around 1.5 morphemes per word and Quechua has about 3 morphemes per word. There are two main region divisions of Quechua known as Quechua I and Quechua II. This data set consists of two main types of Quechua spoken in Ayacucho, Peru (Quechua Chanka ISO:quy) and Cusco, Peru (Quechua Collao ISO:quz) which are both part of Quechua II and, thus, considered a "southern" languages. We label the data set with que - the ISO norm for Quechua II mixtures.

The **QUESPA** team this year consists of four organizers from four different institutions: Northeastern University, Pompeu Fabra University, Carnegie Melon University and University of Pretoria. A new organizer has been introduced this year who has expertise in machine translation (MT) of African languages. All of the IWSLT 2024 organizers have continued to work on the project with exception of one. Three of the four organizers have had experience with the QUE–SPA language

Proceedings of the 22nd International Conference on Spoken Language Translation (IWSLT 2025), pages 260–268
July 31 - August 1, 2025

pair in the past and submitted have already submitted three times to IWSLT, making this article the fourth submission with an increase of BLEU score for each year's submission. We report the QUESPA consortium submission for the IWSLT 2025 and once again focus on the low-resource task at hand by combining *all* the two dialects *Quechua I and II* into one. However, we specifically make use of the Quechua II variant in Collao (ISO:quz), given the discovery of a new corpus.

The rest of this article is organized as follows. Section 2 presents the related work. Since we would like to highlight the addition of our MT comparisons and systems by a new author, we present a section dedicated to the MT delivery in Section 3.1. Afterwards, we present experiments for the for QUE–SPA low-resource track are presented in Section 3 and present their results in Section 4 provides.

2 Related Work

In this section, we first cover the different approaches used in previous speech processing shared tasks for Quechua (Section 2.1). We then discuss prior work that used a similar strategy to our primary submission to the unconstrained track (Section 2.2).

2.1 Quechua Speech Processing

The previous iteration of IWSLT (Agarwal et al., 2023) was the first time that Quechua–Spanish was featured in the low-resource ST track. Due to the small amount of available paired data, the participants focused on exploiting PLMs for speech and/or text in the unconstrained track. The teams all converged on using XLS-R 128 (Babu et al., 2021) as the pre-trained speech encoder, while NLLB 200 (NLLB Team et al., 2022) was the most popular text PLM. However, the teams used the PLMs in very different manners. QUESPA (E. Ortega et al., 2023) separated the PLMs into distinct systems for an ASR+MT cascade, GMU (Mbuya and Anastasopoulos, 2023) performed full fine-tuning on XLS-R for direct ST, and NLE (Gow-Smith et al., 2023) combined the two PLMs via adapter fine-tuning. By using PLMs for both the input and output modalities, NLE and QUESPA obtained the best performances at 15.7 and 15.4 BLEU respectively. For the constrained track, developing a usable system was far more difficult to achieve. In this setup, the best performing model was a direct ST system by GMU that achieved 1.46 BLEU. The QUESPA team adopted a near-identical strategy to achieve 1.25 BLEU.

Quechua–Spanish ST was also featured as part of a similar competition in the 2022 edition of AmericasNLP (Ebrahimi et al., 2022). Similar to IWSLT 2023, participants experimented with different ways of leveraging PLMs. XLS-R and NLLB were popular choices, but some teams also experimented with DeltaLM (Ma et al., 2021) and Whisper (Radford et al., 2023).

Quechua was most recently part of the 2023 ML-SUPERB Challenge (Shi et al., 2023), which tasked participants on evaluating different self-supervised (SSL) speech encoders on long-tail languages. Chen et al. (2023a) found that XLS-R 128 outperformed all other SSL encoders on Quechua, further validating its popularity in the other competitions.

2.2 Multilingual Speech Processing

Multilingual training is a common strategy to facilitate cross-lingual transfer learning, with the goal of boosting performance on LRLs. While this is generally done by pairing HRLs with low-resource ones, it can also be beneficial in settings where only LRLs are available. Chen et al. (2023b) trained multilingual ASR systems on 102 languages, each in a low-resource setting, and obtained state-of-the-art (SOTA) results on the FLEURS benchmark (Conneau et al., 2023). Radford et al. (2023) and Peng et al. (2023) then combined multilingual ASR and ST at scale, developing SOTA models through supervised training on hundreds of thousands of audio samples. Our strategy for the unconstrained track can be viewed as a combination of these two methods, enhancing performance on Quechua–Spanish using multilingual ST training with other LRLs.

3 Quechua-Spanish

In this section we present our experiments for the QUE–SPA dataset provided in the low-resource ST track at IWSLT 2025[1], identical to the dataset from IWSLT 2024. As a reminder, the audio consists of contains 1 hour and 40 minutes of *unconstrained* speech along with its corresponding translations and nearly 48 hours of ASR data (with transcriptions) from the Siminichik (Cardenas et al., 2018)

[1]https://github.com/Llamacha/IWSLT2025_Quechua_data

corpus. Additionally, an MT dataset is offered from previous neural MT work (Ortega et al., 2020). The audio and corresponding transcriptions along with their translations are mostly made of radio broadcasting from the mountainous region in the Andes, Peru. This dataset has been used in other tasks but not in its entirety (Ebrahimi et al., 2023, 2022; Zevallos et al., 2022a). This year there has been a new addition to the dataset provided by the task which is a machine-translated and post-edited text of the Huqariq corpus (Zevallos et al., 2022b) that was used last year by this team (Ortega et al., 2024) for augmentation of the best performing T5 model (Raffel et al., 2020).

We present the three submissions for *unconstrained* task ony as this year the constrained task has been abandoned:

1. a **primary unconstrained** system consisting of a Mamba ASR model (Zhang et al., 2024) fine-tuned with unconstrained data and cascaded the best performing NLLB MT system from our case study;

2. a **contrastive 1 unconstrained** system consisting of a Whisper (Radford et al., 2023) ASR model fine-tuned with the unconstrained data and cascaded with the best performing NLLB MT system from our case study;

3. a **contrastive 2 unconstrained** system consisting of a SpeechT5 model (Ao et al., 2021) fine-tuned for speech translation with two data augmentation techniques and an additional newly introduced corpus based on Quechua Collao (iso: quz) (Paccotacya-Yanque et al., 2022).

We present the experimental settings and results for unconstrained systems starting off with the MT case studies in Section 3.1. Then, we describe the task further in Section 3.2. Primary, Contrastive 1 and Constrastive 2 descriptions are found in Sections Sections 3.3, 3.4 and 3.5, respectively. Afterwards, we offer results and discussion in Section 4.

3.1 Machine Translation

Our MT systems were all trained by fine-tuning the 1.3B parameter version[2] of the NLLB_200 (NLLB Team et al., 2022). For fine-tuning, we set maximum token lengths of 128 for both inputs and outputs. Each model was trained for 10 epochs with a batch size of 8 for both training and evaluation, using 5 beams during generation. We saved model checkpoints every 10,000 steps and set a random seed of 65 to ensure reproducibility.

We trained four models, with each model using a different training dataset. The first three models were trained strictly on datasets provided in the shared task. The first model was fine-tuned on the unconstrained data (U; Cardenas et al. 2018). We then increased the training data using the provided `additional_mt_text` dataset (A; Ortega et al. 2020) to train the second model. This data consists of texts from JW300 (Agić and Vulić, 2019) and Hinantin websites. For the third model, we further expanded the training data by incorporating the provided `synthetic data` (S; Zevallos et al. 2022b) dataset. The sizes of the training data for the three models are 573, 15,857, and 17,265 sentences, respectively.

The fourth model was trained on the largest available dataset. In this setting, we used additional resources (AR) including SMOL (Caswell et al., 2025), GATITOS (Jones et al., 2023), spanish-to-quechua,[3] and cuzco-quechua-translation-spanish[4]. The SMOL and GATITOS datasets consist of 863 and 3,717 sentences, respectively. The two latter datasets each contain over 100k sentences (103k and 106k), though we observed overlap between them. To address this, we deduplicated the Quechua sentences after merging the datasets. After merging all available datasets, including those provided in the shared task, and performing deduplication, the total number of training sentences amounted to 167,052.

For each of the four models, we experimented with two different validation datasets. The first was the 125 parallel sentences provided for validation in the shared task. In the second, we expanded this set by adding the 2,500-sentence JW300 validation dataset, also provided in the shared task. In the latter setup, our goal was to ensure more generalizable models. However, we identified several issues in the JW300 validation data that required preprocessing, including instances where the source and target sentences were identical. After preprocessing and cleaning, the expanded validation set consisted of

[2]https://huggingface.co/facebook/nllb-200-1.3B

[3]https://huggingface.co/datasets/somosnlp-hackathon-2022/spanish-to-quechua

[4]https://huggingface.co/datasets/pollitoconpapass/cuzco-quechua-translation-spanish

Model-[Data]	BLEU						CHRF					
	V_s	V_l	T_s	T_l	Tr_w	Tr_m	V_s	V_l	T_s	T_l	Tr_w	Tr_m
MT-[U]	18.5	18.5	17.3	17.3	11.8	11.4	53.9	53.8	54.1	54.1	46.5	46.0
MT-[U + A]	19.5	19.3	18.0	17.5	15.0	14.8	54.7	54.3	54.9	54.3	52.4	51.8
MT-[U + A + S]	14.6	14.3	13.3	13.6	12.3	11.6	48.0	47.7	48.4	48.8	46.9	47.4
MT-[U + A + S + AR]	15.1	14.2	13.2	13.3	12.4	12.5	48.4	48.5	48.1	48.2	46.9	47.3

Table 1: Performance of the four models on the validation and test sets. We also report results on transcripts generated from the test set, evaluated on models trained with the large validation set. **KEY:** T = test set, V = validation set, Tr = transcripts. *s* and *l* denote the small and large validation sets, respectively. *w* and *m* denote the Whisper and Mamba models, respectively. U = unconstrained, A = `additional_mt_text`, S = synthetic, AR = additional resources.

2,309 parallel sentences.

Table 1 presents the performance of the four machine translation models across different evaluation setups, measured using both BLEU and CHRF scores. Overall, the results indicate that while more data leads to better performances, the quality of the additional data matters. The first model, MT-[U], shows decent performance with a BLEU score of 18.5 on the large validation set and 17.3 on the test set, with strong CHRF scores ranging between 46 and 54. The second model, MT-[U + A], achieves better BLEU and CHRF scores, particularly on the transcript evaluations.

The third model, MT-[U + A + S], which incorporates synthetic data, shows a noticeable decline in both BLEU and chrF scores across all evaluation sets—most prominently on the test and validation sets. This drop suggests that the inclusion of synthetic data, if not carefully curated, can adversely affect model performance. The final model, MT-[U + A + S + AR], demonstrates a slight improvement over MT-[U + A + S] across the evaluation sets. However, it does not fully recover the performance lost when synthetic data was added to MT-[U + A]. This outcome highlights a crucial insight: although expanding training data with additional and diverse resources can enhance model generalization, introducing even a small amount of lower-quality data can undermine those gains. Careful data quality control is therefore essential when scaling datasets for low-resource machine translation.

3.2 Unconstrained Setting

Just like in IWSLT 2024, the organizers provided a total of 48 hours of audio along with their corresponding transcriptions. In addition, we translated the 48 hours of audio provided by the organizers into Spanish. Furthermore, we utilized a portion of the AmericasNLP[5] (ANLP) 2022 speech translation competition corpus, which consists of 19 minutes of Guarani and 29 minutes of Bribri, fully translated into Spanish. Although it is not a Quechua corpus, these languages have morphological similarities with Quechua, so we decided to experiment to see if that improves our models. As a new addition, we used the data set from previous work on Quechua Collao (Paccotacya-Yanque et al., 2022) which, much like the IWSLT 2025 corpus, is part of the Quechua II division. Finally, all the datasets described in this section allowed for further fine-tuning of the previously trained end-to-end speech translation model.

3.3 Primary System

The Primary System for the unconstrained setting consists of a cascaded architecture, where the output of an automatic speech recognition (ASR) model is passed as input to a machine translation (MT) model. For the ASR component, we employ ConMamba (Jiang et al., 2024), a recent extension of the Mamba architecture that integrates convolutional modules into its encoder blocks, inspired by Conformer (Gulati et al., 2020). This hybrid design enhances the model's ability to capture both global and local dependencies. The encoder architecture comprises a sequence of modules: an initial feedforward layer with residual connection, a bidirectional Mamba module (BiMamba) for long-range dependency modeling, a convolutional layer for local context enhancement, and final layer normalization and refinement through another feedforward module (Tang et al., 2024). This combination results in a balanced and efficient encoding mechanism for speech signals.

[5] `https://turing.iimas.unam.mx/americasnlp/2022_st.html`

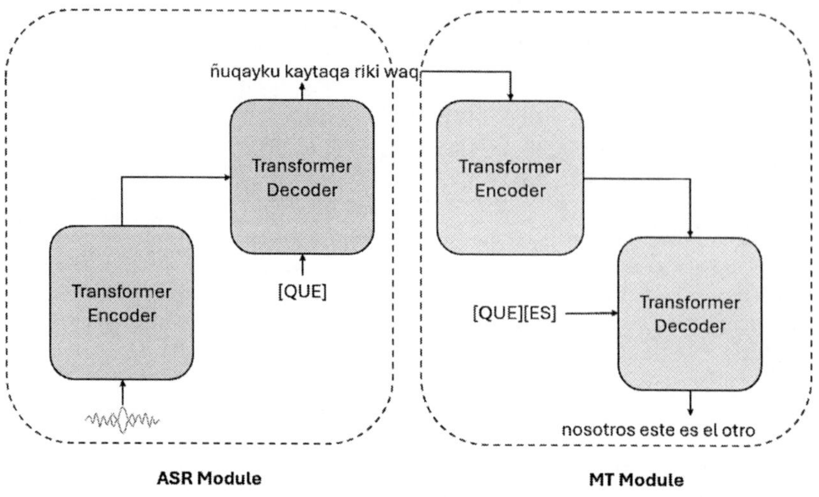

Figure 1: Overview of the cascaded Contrastive 1 system. The input audio is passed into Whisper, which autoregressively generates a Quechua transcription. The transcription hypothesis is then passed to NLLB to be translated into Spanish.

On the decoder side, we incorporate CrossMamba, a unidirectional variant tailored for sequential processing without native cross-attention. CrossMamba simulates cross-attention by concatenating key and query sequences, retaining only the relevant portion of the output. This mechanism allows for effective integration of encoder context through a structured decoding pipeline: normalization, unidirectional Mamba (UniMamba), a second normalization step, CrossMamba integration, and a final feedforward refinement. We train both ConMamba and Conformer models using publicly available recipes[6], experimenting with small (S) and large (L) configurations (144/512 dimensions, 12+4/12+6 layers). Training is performed over 110 epochs using AdamW with a Noam scheduler (30k warm-up steps), and audio is tokenized with a BPE tokenizer trained for each language using SpeechBrain[7]. Once the speech is transcribed, we feed the resulting text into the machine translation model previously described, leveraging its capabilities to produce the final translated output in a cascaded speech translation setup.

3.4 Contrastive 1 System

The Contrastive 1 system is a simple ASR+MT cascade. We develop the ASR module by fine-tuning Whisper Large V3 (Radford et al., 2023) on the entire 48 hours of unconstrained Quechua ASR data in ESPnet (Watanabe et al., 2018). Whisper consists of a Transformer encoder and Transformer decoder (Vaswani et al., 2017). The bidrectional encoder receives mel audio features as input, whereas the decoder is conditioned on a language identity tag and the encoder output (Figure 1). The model is trained for 22K steps with the Adam optimizer (Kingma and Ba, 2015). We use a scheduler that linearly warms up the learning rate to a peak value of 1e-5 for 1500 steps, followed by exponential decay for the remainder of training (Vaswani et al., 2017). ASR inference is performed with greedy decoding, the results of which are then passed to the NLLB-based MT model described in Section 3.1.

3.5 Contrastive 2 System

The Contrastive 2 System for the unconstrained setting consists of a pre-trained model called SpeechT5 (Ao et al., 2022) , which was trained on 960 hours of audio from LibriSpeech. SpeechT5 consists of 12 Transformer encoder blocks and 6 Transformer decoder blocks, with a model dimension of 768, an internal dimension (FFN) of 3,072, and 12 attention heads. Additionally, the voice encoder's pre-net includes 7 blocks of temporal convolutions. Both the pre-net and post-net of the voice decoder used the same configuration as in Shen et al. (2018), except that the number of channels in the post-net is 256. For the text en-

[6]https://github.com/xi-j/Mamba-ASR

[7]https://github.com/speechbrain/speechbrain/tree/develop/recipes/LibriSpeech/Tokenizer

Team **QUESPA** BLEU and CHRF Scores			
Unconstrained 2025			
System	**Description**	**BLEU**	**CHRF**
primary	mamba asr + nllb mt	14.8	51.8
contrastive 1	whisper-v3 asr + nllb mt	15.0	52.4
contrastive 2	speechT5 + anlp + da-tts + nlpaug* + quz	26.7	48.6
Unconstrained 2024			
primary	speechT5 + aug	16.0	52.2
contrastive 1	speechT5 + anlp + da-tts + nlpaug*	19.7	43.1
contrastive 2	whisper asr + nllb mt	11.1	44.6

Table 2: Team QUESPA results for the Quechua to Spanish low-resource task at IWSLT 2025.

coder/decoder's pre/post-net, a shared embedding layer with a dimension of 768 is utilized. For vector quantization, two codebooks with 100 entries each are used for the shared codebook module. The model was trained using the normalized training text from the LibriSpeech language model as unlabeled data, which contains 400 million sentences. Training was optimized using Adam (Kingma and Ba, 2015), with a learning rate that linearly increases during the first 8% of updates up to a maximum of 0.0002.

We fine-tuned SpeechT5[8] for Speech Translation using the SpeechT5 fine-tuning recipe[9] for Speech-Translation with the same hyperparameter settings. We used the 48 hours of audio provided by the organizers (anlp). We applied a data augmentation technique called *nlpaug* (noise, distortion, duplication)[10] (Ma, 2019), resulting in a total of 96h: 48h original + 48h synthetic data + 15 hours of Quechua Collao (Paccotacya-Yanque et al., 2022) (quz) .

4 Results and Discussion

Results are presented in Table 2. When compared to IWSLT 2024 (Ahmad et al., 2024; Ortega et al., 2024), it is clear that Speech Translation as a task is best performed using a multi-lingual transformer such as the Speech T5 model. Addtionally, by fine-tuning the Speech T5 model, we were able to increase the score by a dramatic 7 BLEU points by the addition of data found online. Additionally, the introduction of the latest Whisper model (version 3) seems to show promising increases when compared to last year's result by this team.

[8]`https://github.com/microsoft/SpeechT5`

[9]`https://github.com/microsoft/SpeechT5/tree/main/SpeechT5`

[10]`https://github.com/makcedward/nlpaug`

5 Conclusion and Future Work

Our submission to the IWSLT 2025 (Abdulmumin et al., 2025) evaluation campaign for low-resource and dialect speech translation has included novelties based on the most state-of-the-art techniques for ASR and ST. The addition of three new characteristics: 1) a new Quechua Collao corpus (referred to as quz) and 2) the introduction of a stateless ASR model (Mamba) along with 3) a machine translation case study. These three new inclusions have brought to light what MT systems, corpus, and ASR models work best with the language pair when compared to last year's work.

Next year, we plan to include more human annotation and experimentation with the model presented here since the BLEU score achieved (26.7) warrant further investigation and annotation. We also believe that we have localized a Speech Translation recipe that we allow further iterations of data in the future to achieve even better performance.

References

Idris Abdulmumin, Victor Agostinelli, Tanel Alumäe, Antonios Anastasopoulos, Ashwin, Luisa Bentivogli, Ondřej Bojar, Claudia Borg, Fethi Bougares, Roldano Cattoni, Mauro Cettolo, Lizhong Chen, William Chen, Raj Dabre, Yannick Estève, Marcello Federico, Marco Gaido, Dávid Javorský, Marek Kasztelnik, Tsz Kin Lam, Danni Liu, Evgeny Matusov, Chandresh Kumar Maurya, John P. McCrae, Salima Mdhaffar, Yasmin Moslem, Kenton Murray, Satoshi Nakamura, Matteo Negri, Jan Niehues, Atul Kr. Ojha, John E. Ortega, Sara Papi, Pavel Pecina, Peter Polák, Piotr Połeć, Beatrice Savoldi, Nivedita Sethiya, Claytone Sikasote, Matthias Sperber, Sebastian Stüker, Katsuhito Sudoh, Brian Thompson, Marco Turchi, Alex Waibel, Patrick Wilken, Rodolfo Zevallos, Vilém Zouhar, and Maike Züfle. 2025. Findings of the iwslt 2025 evaluation campaign. In *Proceedings of the 22nd International Conference on Spoken Language Translation (IWSLT 2025)*, Vienna, Austia (in-person and online). Association for Computational Linguistics. To appear.

Milind Agarwal, Sweta Agrawal, Antonios Anastasopoulos, Ondřej Bojar, Claudia Borg, Marine Carpuat, Roldano Cattoni, Mauro Cettolo, Mingda Chen, William Chen, Khalid Choukri, Alexandra Chronopoulou, Anna Currey, Thierry Declerck, Qianqian Dong, Yannick Estève, Kevin Duh, Marcello Federico, Souhir Gahbiche, Barry Haddow, Benjamin Hsu, Phu Mon Htut, Hirofumi Inaguma, Dávid Javorský, John Judge, Yasumasa Kano, Tom Ko, Rishu Kumar, Pengwei Li, Xutail Ma, Prashant Mathur, Evgeny Matusov, Paul McNamee, John P. McCrae, Kenton Murray, Maria Nadejde, Satoshi Nakamura, Matteo Negri, Ha Nguyen, Jan Niehues, Xing Niu, Atul Ojha Kr., John E. Ortega, Proyag Pal, Juan Pino, Lonneke van der Plas, Peter Polák, Elijah Rippeth, Elizabeth Salesky, Jiatong Shi, Matthias Sperber, Sebastian Stüker, Katsuhito Sudoh, Yun Tang, Brian Thompson, Kevin Tran, Marco Turchi, Alex Waibel, Mingxuan Wang, Shinji Watanabe, and Rodolfo Zevallos. 2023. Findings of the IWSLT 2023 Evaluation Campaign. In *Proceedings of the 20th International Conference on Spoken Language Translation (IWSLT 2023)*. Association for Computational Linguistics.

Željko Agić and Ivan Vulić. 2019. JW300: A wide-coverage parallel corpus for low-resource languages. In *Proceedings of the 57th Annual Meeting of the Association for Computational Linguistics*, pages 3204–3210, Florence, Italy. Association for Computational Linguistics.

Ibrahim Said Ahmad, Antonios Anastasopoulos, Ondřej Bojar, Claudia Borg, Marine Carpuat, Roldano Cattoni, Mauro Cettolo, William Chen, Qianqian Dong, Marcello Federico, Barry Haddow, Dávid Javorský, Mateusz Krubiński, Tsz Kin Lam, Xutai Ma, Prashant Mathur, Evgeny Matusov, Chandresh Maurya, John McCrae, Kenton Murray, Satoshi Nakamura, Matteo Negri, Jan Niehues, Xing Niu, Atul Kr. Ojha, John Ortega, Sara Papi, Peter Polák, Adam Pospíšil, Pavel Pecina, Elizabeth Salesky, Nivedita Sethiya, Balaram Sarkar, Jiatong Shi, Claytone Sikasote, Matthias Sperber, Sebastian Stüker, Katsuhito Sudoh, Brian Thompson, Alex Waibel, Shinji Watanabe, Patrick Wilken, Petr Zemánek, and Rodolfo Zevallos. 2024. FINDINGS OF THE IWSLT 2024 EVALUATION CAMPAIGN. In *Proceedings of the 21st International Conference on Spoken Language Translation (IWSLT 2024)*, pages 1–11, Bangkok, Thailand (in-person and online). Association for Computational Linguistics.

Antonios Anastasopoulos, Loïc Barrault, Luisa Bentivogli, Marcely Zanon Boito, Ondřej Bojar, Roldano Cattoni, Anna Currey, Georgiana Dinu, Kevin Duh, Maha Elbayad, Yannick Estéve, Marcello Federico, Christian Federmann, Souhir Gahbiche, Hongyu Gong, Roman Grundkiewicz, Barry Haddow, Benjamin Hsu, Dávid Javorský, Věra Kloudová, Surafel M. Lakew, Xutai Ma, Prashant Mathur, Paul McNamee, Kenton Murray, Maria Nădejde, Satoshi Nakamura, Matteo Negri, Jan Niehues, Xing Niu, John Ortega, Juan Pino, Elizabeth Salesky, Jiatong Shi, Sebastian Stüker, Katsuhito Sudoh, Marco Turchi, Yogesh Virkar, Alex Waibel, Changhan Wang, and Shinji Watanabe. 2022. FINDINGS OF THE IWSLT 2022 EVALUATION CAMPAIGN. In *Proceedings of the 19th International Conference on Spoken Language Translation (IWSLT 2022)*, Dublin, Ireland. Association for Computational Linguistics.

Junyi Ao, Rui Wang, Long Zhou, Chengyi Wang, Shuo Ren, Yu Wu, Shujie Liu, Tom Ko, Qing Li, Yu Zhang, Zhihua Wei, Yao Qian, Jinyu Li, and Furu Wei. 2022. SpeechT5: Unified-modal encoder-decoder pre-training for spoken language processing. In *Proceedings of the 60th Annual Meeting of the Association for Computational Linguistics (Volume 1: Long Papers)*, pages 5723–5738, Dublin, Ireland. Association for Computational Linguistics.

Junyi Ao, Rui Wang, Long Zhou, Chengyi Wang, Shuo Ren, Yu Wu, Shujie Liu, Tom Ko, Qing Li, Yu Zhang, et al. 2021. Speecht5: Unified-modal encoder-decoder pre-training for spoken language processing. *arXiv preprint arXiv:2110.07205*.

Arun Babu, Changhan Wang, Andros Tjandra, Kushal Lakhotia, Qiantong Xu, Naman Goyal, Kritika Singh, Patrick von Platen, Yatharth Saraf, Juan Pino, et al. 2021. Xls-r: Self-supervised cross-lingual speech representation learning at scale. *arXiv preprint arXiv:2111.09296*.

Ronald Cardenas, Rodolfo Zevallos, Reynaldo Baquerizo, and Luis Camacho. 2018. Siminchik: A speech corpus for preservation of southern quechua. *ISI-NLP 2*, page 21.

Isaac Caswell, Elizabeth Nielsen, Jiaming Luo, Colin Cherry, Geza Kovacs, Hadar Shemtov, Partha Talukdar, Dinesh Tewari, Baba Mamadi Diane, Koulako Moussa Doumbouya, Djibrila Diane, and Solo Farabado Cissé. 2025. Smol: Professionally translated parallel data for 115 under-represented languages. *Preprint*, arXiv:2502.12301.

Chih-Chen Chen, William Chen, Rodolfo Zevallos, and John Ortega. 2023a. Evaluating self-supervised speech representations for indigenous american languages. *arXiv preprint arXiv:2310.03639*.

William Chen, Brian Yan, Jiatong Shi, Yifan Peng, Soumi Maiti, and Shinji Watanabe. 2023b. Improving massively multilingual asr with auxiliary CTC objectives. *arXiv preprint arXiv:2302.12829*.

Alexis Conneau, Min Ma, Simran Khanuja, Yu Zhang, Vera Axelrod, Siddharth Dalmia, Jason Riesa, Clara Rivera, and Ankur Bapna. 2023. Fleurs: Few-shot learning evaluation of universal representations of speech. In *2022 IEEE Spoken Language Technology Workshop (SLT)*, pages 798–805.

John E. Ortega, Rodolfo Zevallos, and William Chen. 2023. QUESPA submission for the IWSLT 2023 dialect and low-resource speech translation tasks. In

Proceedings of the 20th International Conference on Spoken Language Translation (IWSLT 2023), pages 261–268, Toronto, Canada (in-person and online). Association for Computational Linguistics.

Abteen Ebrahimi, Manuel Mager, Shruti Rijhwani, Enora Rice, Arturo Oncevay, Claudia Baltazar, María Cortés, Cynthia Montaño, John E Ortega, Rolando Coto-Solano, et al. 2023. Findings of the americasnlp 2023 shared task on machine translation into indigenous languages. In *Proceedings of the Workshop on Natural Language Processing for Indigenous Languages of the Americas (AmericasNLP)*, pages 206–219.

Abteen Ebrahimi, Manuel Mager, Adam Wiemerslage, Pavel Denisov, Arturo Oncevay, Danni Liu, Sai Koneru, Enes Yavuz Ugan, Zhaolin Li, Jan Niehues, Monica Romero, Ivan G Torre, Tanel Alumäe, Jiaming Kong, Sergey Polezhaev, Yury Belousov, Wei-Rui Chen, Peter Sullivan, Ife Adebara, Bashar Talafha, Alcides Alcoba Inciarte, Muhammad Abdul-Mageed, Luis Chiruzzo, Rolando Coto-Solano, Hilaria Cruz, Sofía Flores-Solórzano, Aldo Andrés Alvarez López, Ivan Meza-Ruiz, John E. Ortega, Alexis Palmer, Rodolfo Joel Zevallos Salazar, Kristine Stenzel, Thang Vu, and Katharina Kann. 2022. Findings of the second americasnlp competition on speech-to-text translation. In *Proceedings of the NeurIPS 2022 Competitions Track*, volume 220 of *Proceedings of Machine Learning Research*, pages 217–232. PMLR.

Edward Gow-Smith, Alexandre Berard, Marcely Zanon Boito, and Ioan Calapodescu. 2023. NAVER LABS Europe's multilingual speech translation systems for the IWSLT 2023 low-resource track. In *Proceedings of the 20th International Conference on Spoken Language Translation (IWSLT 2023)*, pages 144–158, Toronto, Canada (in-person and online). Association for Computational Linguistics.

Anmol Gulati, James Qin, Chung-Cheng Chiu, Niki Parmar, Yu Zhang, Jiahui Yu, Wei Han, Shibo Wang, Zhengdong Zhang, Yonghui Wu, and Ruoming Pang. 2020. Conformer: Convolution-augmented transformer for speech recognition. *arXiv preprint arXiv:2005.08100*.

Xilin Jiang, Yinghao Aaron Li, Adrian Nicolas Florea, Cong Han, and Nima Mesgarani. 2024. Speech slytherin: Examining the performance and efficiency of mamba for speech separation, recognition, and synthesis. *arXiv preprint arXiv:2407.09732*.

Alex Jones, Isaac Caswell, Ishank Saxena, and Orhan Firat. 2023. Bilex rx: Lexical data augmentation for massively multilingual machine translation. *Preprint*, arXiv:2303.15265.

Diederik P. Kingma and Jimmy Ba. 2015. Adam: A method for stochastic optimization. In *ICLR 2015, Conference Track Proceedings*.

Edward Ma. 2019. Nlp augmentation. https://github.com/makcedward/nlpaug.

Shuming Ma, Li Dong, Shaohan Huang, Dongdong Zhang, Alexandre Muzio, Saksham Singhal, Hany Hassan Awadalla, Xia Song, and Furu Wei. 2021. Deltalm: Encoder-decoder pre-training for language generation and translation by augmenting pretrained multilingual encoders. *arXiv preprint arXiv:2106.13736*.

Jonathan Mbuya and Antonios Anastasopoulos. 2023. GMU systems for the IWSLT 2023 dialect and low-resource speech translation tasks. In *Proceedings of the 20th International Conference on Spoken Language Translation (IWSLT 2023)*, pages 269–276, Toronto, Canada (in-person and online). Association for Computational Linguistics.

NLLB Team, Marta R. Costa-jussà, James Cross, Onur Çelebi, Maha Elbayad, Kenneth Heafield, Kevin Heffernan, Elahe Kalbassi, Janice Lam, Daniel Licht, Jean Maillard, Anna Sun, Skyler Wang, Guillaume Wenzek, Al Youngblood, Bapi Akula, Loic Barrault, Gabriel Mejia-Gonzalez, Prangthip Hansanti, John Hoffman, Semarley Jarrett, Kaushik Ram Sadagopan, Dirk Rowe, Shannon Spruit, Chau Tran, Pierre Andrews, Necip Fazil Ayan, Shruti Bhosale, Sergey Edunov, Angela Fan, Cynthia Gao, Vedanuj Goswami, Francisco Guzmán, Philipp Koehn, Alexandre Mourachko, Christophe Ropers, Safiyyah Saleem, Holger Schwenk, and Jeff Wang. 2022. No language left behind: Scaling human-centered machine translation.

John E Ortega, Richard Castro Mamani, and Kyunghyun Cho. 2020. Neural machine translation with a polysynthetic low resource language. *Machine Translation*, 34(4):325–346.

John E Ortega and Krishnan Pillaipakkamnatt. 2018. Using morphemes from agglutinative languages like quechua and finnish to aid in low-resource translation. *Technologies for MT of Low Resource Languages (LoResMT 2018)*, page 1.

John E Ortega, Rodolfo Joel Zevallos, Ibrahim Sa'id Ahmad, and William Chen. 2024. Quespa submission for the iwslt 2024 dialectal and low-resource speech translation task. In *Proceedings of the 21st International Conference on Spoken Language Translation (IWSLT 2024)*, pages 125–133.

Rosa YG Paccotacya-Yanque, Candy A Huanca-Anquise, Judith Escalante-Calcina, Wilber R Ramos-Lovón, and Álvaro E Cuno-Parari. 2022. A speech corpus of quechua collao for automatic dimensional emotion recognition. *Scientific Data*, 9(1):778.

Kishore Papineni, Salim Roukos, Todd Ward, and Wei-Jing Zhu. 2002. Bleu: a method for automatic evaluation of machine translation. In *Proceedings of the 40th annual meeting of the Association for Computational Linguistics*, pages 311–318.

Yifan Peng, Jinchuan Tian, Brian Yan, Dan Berrebbi, Xuankai Chang, Xinjian Li, Jiatong Shi, Siddhant Arora, William Chen, Roshan Sharma, Wangyou

Zhang, Yui Sudo, Muhammad Shakeel, Jee-Weon Jung, Soumi Maiti, and Shinji Watanabe. 2023. Reproducing whisper-style training using an open-source toolkit and publicly available data. In *2023 IEEE Automatic Speech Recognition and Understanding Workshop (ASRU)*, pages 1–8.

Alec Radford, Jong Wook Kim, Tao Xu, Greg Brockman, Christine Mcleavey, and Ilya Sutskever. 2023. Robust speech recognition via large-scale weak supervision. In *Proceedings of the 40th International Conference on Machine Learning*, volume 202 of *Proceedings of Machine Learning Research*, pages 28492–28518. PMLR.

Colin Raffel, Noam Shazeer, Adam Roberts, Katherine Lee, Sharan Narang, Michael Matena, Yanqi Zhou, Wei Li, and Peter J. Liu. 2020. Exploring the limits of transfer learning with a unified text-to-text transformer. *Journal of Machine Learning Research*, 21(140):1–67.

Jonathan Shen, Ruoming Pang, Ron J Weiss, Mike Schuster, Navdeep Jaitly, Zongheng Yang, Zhifeng Chen, Yu Zhang, Yuxuan Wang, Rj Skerrv-Ryan, et al. 2018. Natural tts synthesis by conditioning wavenet on mel spectrogram predictions. In *2018 IEEE international conference on acoustics, speech and signal processing (ICASSP)*, pages 4779–4783. IEEE.

Jiatong Shi, William Chen, Dan Berrebbi, Hsiu-Hsuan Wang, Wei-Ping Huang, En-Pei Hu, Ho-Lam Chuang, Xuankai Chang, Yuxun Tang, Shang-Wen Li, Abdelrahman Mohamed, Hung-Yi Lee, and Shinji Watanabe. 2023. Findings of the 2023 ml-superb challenge: Pre-training and evaluation over more languages and beyond. In *2023 IEEE Automatic Speech Recognition and Understanding Workshop (ASRU)*, pages 1–8.

Shengkun Tang, Liqun Ma, Haonan Li, Mingjie Sun, and Zhiqiang Shen. 2024. Bi-mamba: Towards accurate 1-bit state space models. *Preprint*, arXiv:2411.11843.

Ashish Vaswani, Noam Shazeer, Niki Parmar, Jakob Uszkoreit, Llion Jones, Aidan N Gomez, Łukasz Kaiser, and Illia Polosukhin. 2017. Attention is all you need. *Advances in neural information processing systems*, 30.

Shinji Watanabe, Takaaki Hori, Shigeki Karita, Tomoki Hayashi, Jiro Nishitoba, Yuya Unno, Nelson Enrique Yalta Soplin, Jahn Heymann, Matthew Wiesner, Nanxin Chen, Adithya Renduchintala, and Tsubasa Ochiai. 2018. ESPnet: End-to-end speech processing toolkit. In *Proceedings of Interspeech*, pages 2207–2211.

Rodolfo Zevallos, Nuria Bel, Guillermo Cámbara, Mireia Farrús, and Jordi Luque. 2022a. Data augmentation for low-resource quechua asr improvement. *arXiv preprint arXiv:2207.06872*.

Rodolfo Zevallos, Luis Camacho, and Nelsi Melgarejo. 2022b. Huqariq: A multilingual speech corpus of native languages of peru forspeech recognition. In *Proceedings of the Thirteenth Language Resources and Evaluation Conference*, pages 5029–5034.

Xiangyu Zhang, Qiquan Zhang, Hexin Liu, Tianyi Xiao, Xinyuan Qian, Beena Ahmed, Eliathamby Ambikairajah, Haizhou Li, and Julien Epps. 2024. Mamba in speech: Towards an alternative to self-attention. *arXiv preprint arXiv:2405.12609*.

BUINUS at IWSLT: Evaluating the Impact of Data Augmentation and QLoRA-based Fine-Tuning for Maltese to English Speech Translation

Filbert Aurelian Tjiaranata[1], Vallerie Alexandra Putra[2], Eryawan Presma Yulianrifat[1], Ikhlasul Akmal Hanif[1]
[1]Universitas Indonesia, [2]Bina Nusantara University
filbert.aurelian@ui.ac.id, vallerie.putra@binus.ac.id

Abstract

This paper investigates approaches for the IWSLT low-resource track, Track 1 (speech-to-text translation) for the Maltese language, focusing on data augmentation and large pre-trained models. Our system combines Whisper for transcription and NLLB for translation, with experiments concentrated mainly on the translation stage. We observe that data augmentation leads to only marginal improvements, primarily for the smaller 600M model, with gains up to 0.0026 COMET points. These gains do not extend to larger models like the 3.3B NLLB, and the overall impact appears somewhat inconsistent. In contrast, fine-tuning larger models using QLoRA outperforms full fine-tuning of smaller models. Moreover, multi-stage fine-tuning consistently improves task-specific performance across all model sizes.

1 Introduction

Despite increasing advances in multilingual technologies, the development of speech translation (ST) systems for low-resource languages continues to pose significant challenges. Maltese, though an official language of the European Union, exemplifies these difficulties. Currently, there are approximately 200 language resources available for Maltese, a relatively small amount, especially compared to the availability of resources for languages spoken in more populous countries (Rosner and Borg, 2022). With fewer than one million speakers and a scarcity of both transcribed speech and parallel text corpora, Maltese remains under-resourced in the context of speech and language processing. This paper describes our approach to the IWSLT 2025 Low-Resource Shared Task for the Maltese-English language pair.

Speech translation involves two main components: transcription and translation. For transcription, we primarily fine-tune Whisper (Radford et al., 2022), while for translation, we fine-tune NLLB (Team et al., 2022). For the larger NLLB model, we also incorporate QLoRA (Dettmers et al., 2023), one of the best parameter-efficient fine-tuning methods, to accommodate resource constraints (Han et al., 2024). However, we treat transcription mainly as a supporting infrastructure and focus the majority of our experimentation on the translation component.

Data augmentation techniques have become indispensable in machine translation, particularly for addressing the challenges posed by limited parallel data in low-resource languages (Hamed et al., 2023). The term "low-resource" refers to the limited availability of data for one of the languages—in this case, Maltese. A common strategy to mitigate this issue is data augmentation (Tang and Lepage, 2023; Takahagi and Shinnou, 2023), which aims to reduce the likelihood of the model encountering completely out-of-distribution data during translation (Wei et al., 2020; Wang et al., 2018).

Unlike most approaches that augment data by generating similar text, the method proposed in (Sánchez-Cartagena et al., 2021) introduces auxiliary tasks such as token swapping, sentence reversal, and the insertion of UNK tokens to enhance model performance. We found this approach promising and adapted it slightly. Specifically, we fine-tuned the NLLB model in two stages: first on both auxiliary tasks and the main translation task, and then on the main task alone to finalize the model.

2 System Overview

Our speech translation pipeline comprises three main components: transcription, machine translation, and data augmentation. Each component is optimized to address the specific challenges of low-resource translation settings.

Proceedings of the 22nd International Conference on Spoken Language Translation (IWSLT 2025), pages 269–273
July 31 - August 1, 2025 ©2025 Association for Computational Linguistics

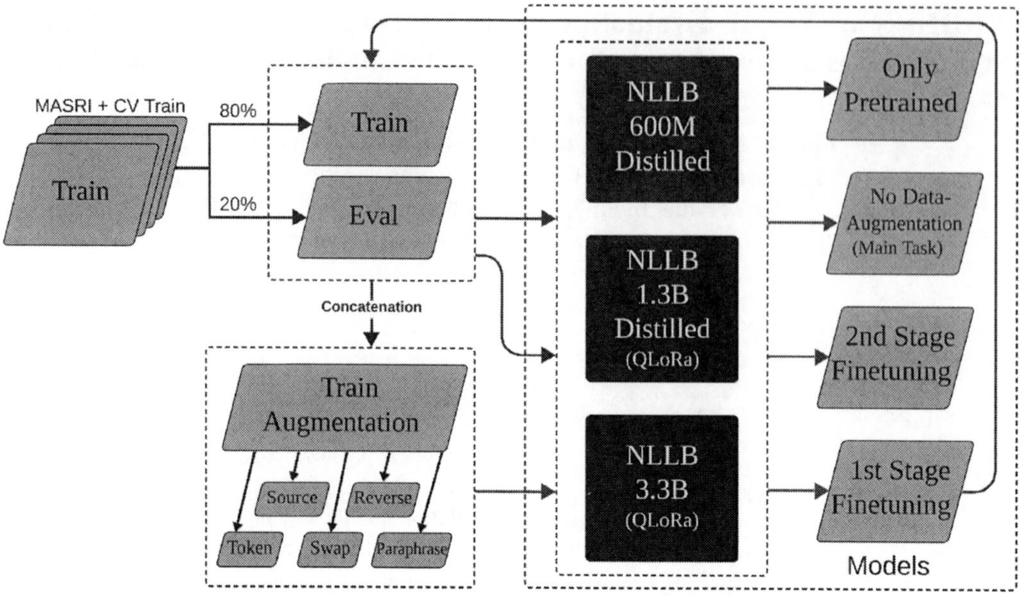

Figure 1: illustrates our end-to-end training pipeline for the translation task. The process begins with the official training data (MASRI + CV Train), which is split into 80% for training and 20% for evaluation. The data is further passed through a data augmentation module.

2.1 Dataset

For this study, we restrict our training data to the official dataset released for the IWSLT 2025 shared task, which consists of approximately 14 hours of speech data. In addition to this, we leverage the pretrained capabilities of Whisper (Radford et al., 2022) and NLLB (Team et al., 2022), both of which were trained on large-scale multilingual corpora. However, we do not incorporate any external datasets beyond what was used during the pretraining of these models.

2.2 Data Splitting and Evaluation Strategy

The dataset is divided into training and validation sets using an 80:20 split. Each speech instance is aligned with its corresponding transcription, and each transcription is paired with a translation from Maltese to English. The Whisper model is fine-tuned using the speech-transcription pairs to perform automatic speech recognition. Separately, the NLLB models are fine-tuned on the Maltese-English text pairs for machine translation. It is important to note that the NLLB models operate exclusively on text and do not utilize any speech data during training.

For evaluation, we use the development set. Evaluation is conducted on both individual components and the complete end-to-end pipeline. Specifically, we assess transcription and machine translation quality independently, as well as the overall performance by feeding Whisper-generated transcriptions into the translation model. This evaluation reflects real-world usage and system robustness.

Performance is measured using the COMET metric (Rei et al., 2020), which provides a semantically-informed evaluation of translation quality. Notably, COMET is also the official evaluation metric used in the shared task competition, ensuring alignment between our development-time evaluation and the final scoring criteria.

2.3 Transcription

We use the Whisper large-v3 model (Radford et al., 2022) for speech transcription. Whisper provides state-of-the-art performance in multilingual speech recognition and serves as a reliable backbone for converting audio input into text.

2.4 Machine Translation

For translation, we employ three variants of the NLLB model (Team et al., 2022): the 600M distilled, 1.3B distilled, and 3.3B versions. The 600M model is fine-tuned directly, while the 1.3B and 3.3B models are fine-tuned using QLoRA (Dettmers et al., 2023) to facilitate efficient adaptation under limited computational resources.

Task	Type	Augmented Training sample
original training sample	source	roberto ma kienx jidher inkwitat daqs kuġinuh dwar dan
	target	Roberto didn't seem as worried as his cousin about this
swap	target	Roberto about seem his worried as as cousin didn't this
token	target	UNK UNK UNK as worried UNK his UNK about this .
source	target	roberto ma kienx jidher inkwitat daqs kuġinuh dwar dan
reverse	target	this about cousin his as worried as seem didn't Roberto
rephrase	target	but Joe Calleja did not let him continue
	rephrased	But Joe Calleja wouldn't let him go on

Table 1: A Maltese–English, word-aligned training sample (first row) and the result of applying the transformations described in Sec. 2.5 using hyperparameter = 0.4 for the swap task and = 0.5 for the token task. Words modified by each transformation are coloured; for swap, a different colour identifies each pair of words that are swapped together; for rephrased, a different colour identifies each pair of words rephrased.

2.5 Data Augmentation

We follow the multi-task data augmentation (MTL DA) framework proposed by Sánchez-Cartagena et al. (2021) (Sánchez-Cartagena et al., 2021), where several auxiliary tasks are defined to modify target sequences in ways that challenge the decoder and reinforce encoder reliance. Among the auxiliary tasks the *swap* and *token* are controlled by a hyperparameter α, which determines the proportion of tokens in the target sentence that are affected. For instance, in the *swap* task, α defines the fraction of target words whose positions are altered; similarly, in the *token* task, it defines the proportion of target words replaced by the [UNK] symbol.

Swap	Random swapping of target tokens to disrupt sequence order.
Token	Replacement of target tokens with the [UNK] symbol.
Source	Copying the source sentence to the target side.
Reverse	Reversal of the target token order.
Paraphrase	As an additional augmentation method, we employ a paraphrasing approach using NLLB for back-translation, which translates the target sentence to Italian and then back to English.

Although we did not conduct hyperparameter tuning in our setup, we adopted $\alpha = 0.4$ for the *swap* task and $\alpha = 0.5$ for the *token* task, which fall within the optimal range (typically $\alpha \in [0.1, 0.9]$) explored in the original study. These values were chosen based on their reported performance and balancing between task disruption and learnability as described in (Sánchez-Cartagena et al., 2021). The choice allows us to benefit from the task's intended regularization effect without introducing excessive noise.

Fine-tuning is conducted in two stages: an initial phase on a mixture of the main and auxiliary tasks, followed by a final phase focused solely on the primary translation task.

3 Results

Model Size and Fine-Tuning Strategy. Our results indicate that the larger 3.3B NLLB model, fine-tuned using QLoRA, outperforms the smaller 600M model that is fully fine-tuned. While the larger models achieve higher overall performance after fine-tuning, this may partly reflect its stronger baseline performance. The performance gain from fine-tuning is actually greater for the smaller 600M model, suggesting that smaller models benefit more directly from the fine-tuning process, while larger models rely more on their pretrained capacity.

Effect of Data Augmentation. For the 3.3B model, none of the tested data augmentation techniques such as paraphrasing, token swapping, UNK token insertion, or sentence reversal led to noticeable gains, with the highest improvement being

Model	Baseline	1st-Stage (DA)					2nd-Stage (DA)				
	(No DA)	Swap	Token	Source	Reverse	Paraphrase	Swap	Token	Source	Reverse	Paraphrase
NLLB 3.3B pretrained	0.8056	–	–	–	–	–	–	–	–	–	–
NLLB 1.3B distilled	0.8018	–	–	–	–	–	–	–	–	–	–
NLLB 600M distilled	0.7858	–	–	–	–	–	–	–	–	–	–
NLLB 3.3B fine-tuned	0.8323	0.8320	0.8310	0.8275	0.8316	0.8196	0.8322	0.8323	0.8320	0.8321	**0.8324**
NLLB 1.3B fine-tuned	0.8275	–	–	–	–	–	–	–	–	–	–
NLLB 600M fine-tuned	0.8223	0.8235	0.8221	0.8198	0.8229	0.8186	0.8240	**0.8250**	0.8229	0.8249	0.8241
Whisper to NLLB 3.3B fine-tuned	0.7602	**0.7608**	0.7595	0.7512	0.7601	0.7499	0.7604	0.7602	0.7607	0.7601	0.7601
Whisper to NLLB 600M fine-tuned	0.7472	0.7507	0.7477	0.7452	0.7495	0.7481	0.7501	0.7495	0.7493	**0.7529**	0.7503

Table 2: COMET scores for two-stage fine-tuning. The first three rows show pretrained NLLB models without fine-tuning. The next three rows show the NLLB models after fine-tuning. Baseline: no data augmentation; 1st-Stage: scores with data augmentation (DA); 2nd-Stage: another fine-tuning without DA.

just 0.001 COMET points from paraphrasing. The 600M model, on the other hand, showed slightly better results, with consistent but small improvements across all methods, reaching up to 0.0026 COMET points. While the gains for the smaller model are more apparent, they remain modest. These results suggest that data augmentation may be more useful for smaller models, which benefit more from the added variability due to their limited capacity. This aligns with prior findings (Sánchez-Cartagena et al., 2021), where augmentation strategies had a greater effect on less-pretrained models.

Impact of Multi-Stage Fine-Tuning. The two-stage fine-tuning approach, where models are first trained on a mix of auxiliary and primary translation tasks and then fine-tuned solely on the main task, resulted in performance improvements across all model sizes. This shows that a final alignment phase focused on the primary objective enhances model performance and task-specific adaptation.

End-to-End Performance. Table 2 shows that feeding Whisper transcriptions into the NLLB models lowers COMET by around 0.07–0.076 points across all settings. This degradation is most likely caused by transcription errors from the ASR stage, which the MT component cannot fully recover from. Notably, the highest end-to-end COMET score achieved was 0.7608, obtained using Whisper to NLLB 3.3B fine-tuned model with swap-based augmentation in the first stage. For the official test set submission in the unconstrained setting, this same system achieved 45.4 BLEU and 65.11 chrF.

4 Limitations

The limitation of our study is the lack of extensive qualitative analysis due to limited language proficiency. Since we do not fully understand the language in the dataset, our analysis primarily relies on quantitative methods.

5 Conclusion

In this paper, we explore the use of pre-trained models—Whisper for ASR and NLLB for MT—alongside data augmentation and parameter-efficient fine-tuning methods. Our experiments show that fine-tuning larger NLLB models using QLoRA outperforms full fine-tuning on smaller models. Two-stage fine-tuning also provides consistent performance improvements across model sizes. In contrast, data augmentation offers only marginal benefits, limited to the smaller 600M model, and the improvements appear inconsistent.

These findings highlight the promise of scalable fine-tuning techniques for translation in low-resource settings. However, our focus on MT fine-tuning overlooks the more significant impact of ASR errors, which remain a primary source of performance degradation in the end-to-end pipeline. This suggests that future research should prioritize improvements in the ASR component. Further work could also explore more targeted data augmentation strategies, end-to-end fine-tuning approaches, and incorporate qualitative evaluations with native speakers to better capture translation quality nuances.

References

Tim Dettmers, Artidoro Pagnoni, Ari Holtzman, and Luke Zettlemoyer. 2023. Qlora: Efficient finetuning of quantized llms. *Preprint*, arXiv:2305.14314.

Injy Hamed, Nizar Habash, and Thang Vu. 2023. Data augmentation techniques for machine translation of code-switched texts: A comparative study. In *Findings of the Association for Computational Linguistics: EMNLP 2023*, pages 140–154, Singapore. Association for Computational Linguistics.

Zeyu Han, Chao Gao, Jinyang Liu, Jeff Zhang, and Sai Qian Zhang. 2024. Parameter-efficient fine-tuning for large models: A comprehensive survey. *arXiv preprint arXiv:2403.14608*.

Alec Radford, Jong Wook Kim, Tao Xu, Greg Brockman, Christine McLeavey, and Ilya Sutskever. 2022. Robust speech recognition via large-scale weak supervision. *Preprint*, arXiv:2212.04356.

Ricardo Rei, Craig Stewart, Ana C Farinha, and Alon Lavie. 2020. Comet: A neural framework for mt evaluation. *Preprint*, arXiv:2009.09025.

Mike Rosner and Claudia Borg. 2022. Report on the maltese language. Language Technology Support of Europe's Languages in 2020/2021. Available online at `https://european-language-equality.eu/deliverables/`.

Víctor M. Sánchez-Cartagena, Miquel Esplà-Gomis, Juan Antonio Pérez-Ortiz, and Felipe Sánchez-Martínez. 2021. Rethinking data augmentation for low-resource neural machine translation: A multi-task learning approach. In *Proceedings of the 2021 Conference on Empirical Methods in Natural Language Processing*, pages 8502–8516, Online and Punta Cana, Dominican Republic. Association for Computational Linguistics.

Kyosuke Takahagi and Hiroyuki Shinnou. 2023. Data augmentation by shuffling phrases in recognizing textual entailment. In *Proceedings of the 37th Pacific Asia Conference on Language, Information and Computation*, pages 194–200, Hong Kong, China. Association for Computational Linguistics.

Wenyi Tang and Yves Lepage. 2023. A dual reinforcement method for data augmentation using middle sentences for machine translation. In *Proceedings of Machine Translation Summit XIX, Vol. 1: Research Track*, pages 48–58, Macau SAR, China. Asia-Pacific Association for Machine Translation.

NLLB Team, Marta R. Costa-jussà, James Cross, Onur Çelebi, Maha Elbayad, Kenneth Heafield, Kevin Heffernan, Elahe Kalbassi, Janice Lam, Daniel Licht, Jean Maillard, Anna Sun, Skyler Wang, Guillaume Wenzek, Al Youngblood, Bapi Akula, Loic Barrault, Gabriel Mejia Gonzalez, Prangthip Hansanti, John Hoffman, Semarley Jarrett, Kaushik Ram Sadagopan, Dirk Rowe, Shannon Spruit, Chau Tran, Pierre Andrews, Necip Fazil Ayan, Shruti Bhosale, Sergey Edunov, Angela Fan, Cynthia Gao, Vedanuj Goswami, Francisco Guzmán, Philipp Koehn, Alexandre Mourachko, Christophe Ropers, Safiyyah Saleem, Holger Schwenk, and Jeff Wang. 2022. No language left behind: Scaling human-centered machine translation. *Preprint*, arXiv:2207.04672.

Xinyi Wang, Hieu Pham, Zihang Dai, and Graham Neubig. 2018. SwitchOut: an efficient data augmentation algorithm for neural machine translation. In *Proceedings of the 2018 Conference on Empirical Methods in Natural Language Processing*, pages 856–861, Brussels, Belgium. Association for Computational Linguistics.

Xiangpeng Wei, Heng Yu, Yue Hu, Rongxiang Weng, Luxi Xing, and Weihua Luo. 2020. Uncertainty-aware semantic augmentation for neural machine translation. In *Proceedings of the 2020 Conference on Empirical Methods in Natural Language Processing (EMNLP)*, pages 2724–2735, Online. Association for Computational Linguistics.

LIA and ELYADATA systems for the IWSLT 2025 low-resource speech translation shared task

Chaimae Chellaf[*,1,4], **Haroun Elleuch**[*,1,2], **Othman Istaiteh**[*,1], **Fortuné Kponou**[*,1,3]
Fethi Bougares[1,2], **Yannick Estève**[1], **Salima Mdhaffar**[1]

[1]LIA (France), [2]Elyadata (Tunisia), [3]UAC/IMSP (Benin), [4]LundiMatin (France)
Correspondence: salima.mdhaffar@univ-avignon.fr

Abstract

In this paper, we present the approach and system setup of our participation in the IWSLT 2025 low-resource speech translation shared task. We submitted systems for three language pairs, namely Tunisian Arabic to English, North Levantine Arabic to English, and Fongbé to French. Both pipeline and end-to-end speech translation systems were explored for Tunisian Arabic to English and Fongbé to French pairs. However, only pipeline approaches were investigated for the North Levantine Arabic–English translation direction. All our submissions are based on the usage of pre-trained models that we further fine-tune with the shared task training data.

1 Introduction

The International Workshop on Spoken Language Translation (IWSLT) is an annual scientific conference dedicated to the study and advancement of spoken language translation technologies. It serves as a platform for researchers and practitioners to present their work on speech translation, encompassing areas such as automatic speech recognition (ASR) and machine translation (MT). IWSLT has played a pivotal role in the advancement of spoken language translation (ST) by providing a structured environment to evaluate and compare different approaches. Its emphasis on real-world challenges, such as low-resource languages and real-time translation, has contributed to the development of more robust and versatile translation systems. IWSLT 2025 (Abdulmumin et al., 2025) proposes two shared tasks: High-resource ST and Low-resource ST. Several language pairs were proposed this year for the low-resource task. In this paper, we focus on Tunisian Arabic-English, North Levantine-English and Fongbé-French language pairs. This paper describes the approach and system setup of the joint participation of LIA and Elyadata in the tasks as mentioned earlier.

For the Tunisian Arabic-English and Fongbé–French tracks, both end-to-end (E2E) and pipeline approaches were explored. In contrast, only pipeline approaches were investigated for the North Levantine Arabic–English track. For E2E approaches, we focus on fine-tuning self-supervised learning (SSL) models and Whisper models (Radford et al., 2023a). All systems are trained with an unconstrained setup, which means that any resource, including pre-trained language models, can be used, except for evaluation sets. We particularly investigate the SAMU-like approach (Khurana et al., 2022) to enrich the SSL speech encoder with semantic information. For pipeline approaches, we focus on fine-tuning large language models (LLMs).

The remaining of the paper is structured as follows: Section 2 presents the related work. Section 3 is dedicated to describe our systems for Tunisian Arabic to English. The experiments for Fongbé to French and for North Levantine to English are presented, respectively, in sections 4 and 5. Section 6 concludes the paper and discusses future work.

2 Related Work

The Speech Translation task has received considerable attention from the research community, and numerous approaches have been proposed. Traditional speech translation (ST) approaches follow a cascade architecture (Matusov et al., 2005; Kumar et al., 2015; Laurent et al., 2023), where an automatic speech recognition (ASR) system is followed by a machine translation (MT) module applied to the ASR output. Recent advances in deep neural networks for both ASR and MT have led to substantial improvements in the overall performance of ST systems.

More recently, end-to-end speech translation

*These authors contributed equally to this work

Proceedings of the 22nd International Conference on Spoken Language Translation (IWSLT 2025), pages 274–281
July 31 - August 1, 2025 ©2025 Association for Computational Linguistics

models (Bérard et al., 2018; Duong et al., 2016; Bérard et al., 2016) have gained attention as an alternative to the traditional cascade architecture. These models aim to directly translate speech in a source language into text or speech in the target language without requiring intermediate text transcriptions. End-to-end models reduce latency, avoid error propagation between ASR and MT components, and can be optimized globally for the final translation objective.

With the emergence of robust transformer-based architectures and multilingual pretraining methods, such as those used in SeamlessM4T (Seamless Communication et al., 2023), speech translation systems have gained momentum, leading to diversity in model architectures and training methods. Meta's SeamlessM4T stands out as a unified multimodal system capable of handling speech-to-text translation across 101 input and 96 output languages. OpenAI's Whisper (Radford et al., 2023a) is an automatic speech recognition (ASR) system that also offers speech-to-text translation capabilities. Trained on 680,000 hours of multilingual and multitask supervised data, Whisper demonstrates robustness to accents, background noise, and technical language. It supports transcription in multiple languages and translation from those languages into English. Of the 680,000 hours of labelled audio used by Whisper, 117,000 hours cover 96 other languages. The dataset also includes 125,000 hours of X→EN translation data. Beyond Whisper and SeamlessM4T, several other models have emerged that employ self-supervised learning (SSL) to enhance performance in speech translation. Wav2vec 2.0 (Baevski et al., 2020), introduced by Facebook AI, is one of the earliest SSL-based models that significantly improved ASR performance. Wav2vec 2.0 is typically coupled with a Transformer decoder for speech translation. Building on this foundation, w2v-BERT (Chung et al., 2021) and HuBERT (Hsu et al., 2021) models have been developed. In this paper, we investigate these recent advances in speech-to-text translation systems to participate in the IWSLT low-resource speech translation shared task.

3 Tunisian Arabic-English Experiments

3.1 Data

The Tunisian Arabic dataset (LDC2022E01) used in our experiments was developed and provided by LDC2 to the IWSLT 2025 participants. It comprises 383h of Tunisian conversational speech with manual transcripts, from which 160h are also translated into English. Thus, it is a three-way parallel corpus, comprising audio, transcript, and translation. This LDC data constitutes the basic condition of the dialect task. Arabic dialects are the informal form of communication in everyday life in the Arab world. Tunisian Arabic is one of several Arabic dialects. There is no standard written Arabic form that all Tunisian speakers share. However, the transcripts of Tunisian conversations of the LDC2022E01 Tunisian Arabic dataset follow the rules of the Tunisian Arabic CODA – Conventional Orthography for Dialectal Arabic (Habash et al., 2012).

3.2 Pipeline ST

3.2.1 ASR systems

Two ASR systems have been trained for the Tunisian dialect. The first ASR system **(Primary)** is based on the w2v_Bert 2.0 (Barrault et al., 2023) speech encoder. In addition to the speech encoder model, we incorporate an extra layer with 1024 neurons and LeakyReLU as the activation function, followed by a fully-connected layer and a final 37-dimensional softmax layer, each dimension corresponding to a character. The weights of these two additional layers were randomly initialized. In contrast, the weights of the speech encoder part for SSL models in the neural architecture were initialized using pre-trained weights. The fine-tuning is done with the LDC2022E01 training set using a character-level CTC loss function. We optimize the loss with an Adam optimizer of learning rate equal to 1×10^{-5} for both the speech encoder and Adadelta with learning rate equal to 1.0 for the linear layer.

The second ASR system **(contrastive 1)** is trained with the same dataset and is based on the Whisper-large-v3 model (Radford et al., 2023b).

We fine-tune this Whisper model for the ASR task with the LDC2022E01 dataset. we used AdamW optimizer (Loshchilov and Hutter, 2017) with a learning rate of $1e-5$ and weight decay of 0.01. The encoder was left unfrozen throughout the training, which consisted of 10 epochs with a warmup of 500 steps, a patience of two epochs for early stopping, and a maximum gradient norm of 2.0. Training was performed using FP16 precision with a sampling rate of 16 kHz, and the data was randomly sorted. We set the batch size per GPU to 8 and used 4 H100 80GB GPUs with a gradient accumulation factor of 4, resulting in an effective batch size of 128 (8 × 4 GPUs × 4 accumulation steps). We used a beam size of 8 for decoding, with decode ratios ranging from 0.0 to 1.0. The model was optimized using a negative log-likelihood loss.

We use the SpeechBrain toolkit to train ASR systems (Ravanelli et al., 2024).

3.2.2 MT model

We fine-tuned a machine translation model (**contrastive3**) based on the NLLB-200 1.3B architecture (Costa-Jussà et al., 2022), a multilingual transformer model designed to support high-quality translation across over 200 languages, including many low-resource ones. This model was specifically adapted for the task of translating Tunisian Arabic into English.

Fine-tuning was performed using the LDC2022E01 translation training set, with optimization carried out using the Cross-Entropy loss function. We used the AdamW optimizer with a learning rate of 1×10^{-5} and a batch size of 16, with a beam size of 8 for decoding. We use the HuggingFace framework to train the MT model.

3.3 End-to-end ST

The entire dataset used to train the E2E system includes 160 hours of data with gold translations provided for the task, and 223 hours without translations, which we automatically translated using the MT system described in Section 3.2.2. We filter a portion of the 223 hours of translated data using the BLASER score to improve translation quality.

SAMU-XLSR (Khurana et al., 2022) is a multilingual multimodal semantic speech representation learning framework where the speech transformer encoder XLS-R is fine-tuned using semantic supervision from the pre-trained multilingual semantic text encoder LaBSE (Feng et al., 2022a). The training and modeling details follow the original paper (Khurana et al., 2022). In this work, we use the same training framework except that we trained our model starting from another speech encoder: w2v_Bert 2.0 (Barrault et al., 2023) and another semantic text encoder BGE M3-Embedding (Chen et al., 2024). We use the CommonVoice-v19 (Ardila et al., 2020) to train this model. In this paper, we refer to this model as SAMU-BGE.

We use the standard encoder-decoder architecture for our translation model. The training of our E2E ST model is divided into three stages. First, we specialize the SAMU-BGE model with the Tunisian ST dataset. Second, we fine-tune the mBart model for text-to-text translation from Tunisian to English. Once our speech encoder (SAMU-BGE) and our decoder (mBart) are fine-tuned, we initialize the encoder and decoder using these models. A feed-forward network projection layer is used to connect the encoder and decoder, bridging the two modules. The described system presents our **Primary** ST system.

For the **contrastive 1** system, we use Whisper-large-v3 to train the ST model. The training of our model is separated into two stages. First, we train an end-to-end ASR model (the ASR model is described in Section 3.2.1). Then, once our ASR model is trained, we fine-tune this Whisper model for the translation task. We used AdamW optimizer (Loshchilov and Hutter, 2017) with a learning rate of 1e-5 and weight decay of 0.01. The encoder was left unfrozen throughout the training, which ran for 10 epochs with a warmup of 500 steps, a patience of two epochs for early stopping, and a max gradient norm of 2.0. Training used FP16 precision with a sampling rate of 16 kHz, and the data was randomly sorted. We set the batch size per GPU to 8 and used 4 H100 80GB GPUs with a gradient accumulation factor of 4, resulting in an effective batch size of 128 (8 × 4 GPUs × 4 accumulation steps). We used a beam size of 8 for decoding, with decode ratios ranging from 0.0 to 1.0. The model was optimized using a negative log-likelihood loss. We combined different augmentations to perform data augmentation: speed perturbation (resample the audio signal at a rate that is similar to the original rate, to achieve a slightly slower or slightly faster signal), frequency drop (randomly drops several frequency bands to zero) and chunk drop (an augmentation strategy that helps a model learn to rely on all parts of the signal, since it can't expect a given part to be present).

For the **contrastive 2** system, we use Whisper-large-v3 to train the ST model without the step of ASR fine-tuning and without data augmentation. We apply the same parameters described for the **contrastive 1** system.

3.4 Results

3.4.1 Results for ASR

The ASR results in terms of word error rate (WER) are reported in Table 1 on the development datasets and the internal test provided by the organisers.

Table 1: WER (%) results for Tunisian dialect ASR.

	Dev	Test Int	Test1	Test2
Primary	36.3	39.63	38.6	40
Contrastive 1	36.78	40.43	39.2	40.3

3.4.2 Results for ST

The ST results in terms of BLEU scores are reported in Table 2 on the development datasets and the internal test provided by the organisers.

Table 2: BLEU results for Tunisian dialect to English translation.

	Dev	Test Int	Test1	Test2
Primary	25.04	21.41	22.3	21
Contrastive 1	24.72	21.12	22	20.3
Contrastive 2	24.63	20.40	21.6	19.2
Contrastive 3	23.77	20.23	21.4	19.6

4 Fongbé-French Experiments

4.1 Data

The dataset used in our experiments comprises a total of 61 hours of speech. For the end-to-end speech translation (ST) task, we used the entire dataset. We also used internal data for the automatic speech recognition (ASR) task, by using Fongbé transcripts we collected for a 36 hour subset. To ensure a fair comparison between the end-to-end and cascade systems, we excluded the validation and test portions of the ST dataset from the ASR training set.

Table 3: ST and ASR dataset description

Experiments	Split	Hours	Sentences
ASR	Train	29	19.9k
ASR	Valid	3.54	2.4k
ASR	Test	3.93	2.5k
ST	Train	48	29.5k
ST	Valid	6.1	4.1k
ST	Test	5.9	3.9k

4.2 Pipeline ST

4.2.1 ASR system

We conducted three automatic speech recognition (ASR) experiments for ASR. In the first experiment, Fongbé transcripts containing diacritics were used to establish a baseline, referred to as ASR With Diacritics. The second experiment was performed using transcripts without diacritics (ASR Without Diacritics). In the third, we introduced a novel diacritic substitution strategy: monosyllabic words containing diacritics were systematically replaced by their base syllables appended with a unique numerical identifier (ASR with Sub). This method was designed to retain key linguistic distinctions while modifying the representation of diacritics, potentially improving the model's ability to generalize across phonetically similar patterns. For each setting, we trained a separate *SentencePiece* tokenizer (Kudo and Richardson, 2018) at the character level using the combined training and validation sets. The resulting vocabulary sizes were 62, 44, and 36 for the diacritics, no-diacritics, and substitution settings, respectively. All ASR models shared the same architecture, consisting of an AfriHuBERT speech encoder followed by three fully connected layers with 1024 dimensions. Training was performed using Connectionist Temporal Classification (CTC) loss over 50 epochs. The ASR model trained without diacritics achieved the lowest WER of 17.02%, outperforming both the model trained with diacritics (21.98%) and the substitution-based model (22.18%), as detailed in Table 4.

Table 4: WER (%) results for Fongbé ASR

	Dev	Test
ASR with Diacritics	17.25	21.89
ASR without Diacritics	12.71	17.02
ASR with Sub	24.63	22.18

4.2.2 MT model

We fine-tuned three versions of the NLLB-200 1.3B model on Fongbé manual transcriptions: one with diacritics, the second without diacritics, and a third using diacritic-substituted sentences, as described in the previous section. The model trained on diacritic transcriptions achieved the best performance, followed by the substitution-based model. The results show in Table 5 highlight the importance of diacritics in Fongbé for translation quality, while also demonstrating that the substitution approach offers a competitive alternative positioned between the performance of models trained with and without diacritics.

Table 5: BLEU (%) results for Fongbé MT

	Dev	Test
MT With Diacritics	58.9	55.41
MT Without Diacritics	47.39	44.95
MT with Sub	57.56	53.88

Table 6: BLEU results for Fongbé to French translation.

	Dev	Test
Primary	59.24	39.6
Contrastive 1	54.87	37.23
Contrastive 2	48.39	32.76
Contrastive 3	41.60	28.32

4.3 Fongbe Speech Translation system

We explored the use of various speech encoders—specifically HuBERT-147, AfriHuBERT, and XLS-R-1B in combination with different text decoders, including mBART and NLLB. All experimental results are presented in Table 6.

For the cascade experiments, we paired each ASR system with its corresponding machine translation (MT) system. The best-performing cascade system combines ASR with diacritics and MT with diacritics, and is designated as the **Primary** system. The second-best system, referred to as **Contrastive 1**, used both ASR and MT models trained on diacritic-substituted data. The third system, **Contrastive 2**, employed ASR and MT models trained on data without diacritics.

In the end-to-end setting, for experiments involving XLS-R-1B, we applied a semantic alignment strategy inspired by the method proposed in Khurana et al. (2022), using translated labels. SAMU, which builds on XLS-R-1B, integrates a frozen Language-Agnostic BERT Sentence Encoder (LaBSE) (Feng et al., 2022b) as the master model to align Fongbé speech embeddings and French text embeddings in a shared XLS-R representation space.

We also investigated the impact of several data augmentation techniques, including speed perturbation, frequency drop, and chunk drop. Our best end-to-end systems combined the AfriHuBERT encoder with the NLLB decoder, and the SAMU model with NLLB, both enhanced by these augmentations. Among them, the SAMU-NLLB system achieved the highest performance in the end-to-end speech translation task, ranking fourth overall among all submitted systems. Consequently, we selected the SAMU-NLLB end-to-end system as the **Contrastive 3** submission.

4.4 Results

Overall, for the Fongbé Speech Translation task, we proposed both cascade and end-to-end systems. All cascade systems outperformed the end-to-end approach, with a gap of approximately ~11 BLEU points between the best-performing cascade system and the submitted end-to-end system (SAMU-NLLB + Data Augmentation). This performance difference highlights the potential for improving end-to-end models through more effective encoder adaptation techniques for the decoder, aiming to narrow the gap between end-to-end and cascade performance. The superiority of cascade systems can be attributed, in part, to the use of in-domain ASR data for fine-tuning the decoder, which provides a more aligned and semantically rich input for the translation model.

5 North Levantine-English Experiments

5.1 Data

5.1.1 ASR dataset

The training data consisted of the Babylon Levantine corpus (LDC2005S08) and the Levantine Arabic QT (LDC2006T07), both provided by LDC, along with an additional 23 hours of Levantine speech automatically extracted from the QASR dataset using the best performing dialect identification model from Elleuch et al. (2025) [1]. QASR is the largest publicly available Arabic speech recognition dataset, consisting of 2,000 hours of transcribed speech collected from the broadcast domain. It includes both dialectal and Modern Standard Arabic (MSA) speech, as well as code-switching (Mubarak et al., 2021).

5.1.2 MT dataset

The training data for the North Levantine to English machine translation task consisted of two distinct corpora. The first is the **UFAL Parallel Corpus of North Levantine 1.0**, provided to participants in the IWSLT 2025 shared task. This corpus

[1]Whisper-large-v3 encoder trained on the ADI-20-53 dataset for Arabic dialect identification. This dataset comprises 53 hours of speech for 20 country-level dialects. The Levantine subset included speech segments identified as Jordanian, Palestinian, Syrian, and Lebanese.

comprises approximately 120,000 lines of parallel North Levantine, MSA, and English textual data.

The second corpus is **Levanti**[2], which includes 500,000 sentence pairs in Levantine colloquial Arabic (covering Palestinian, Syrian, Lebanese, Jordanian, and Egyptian dialects) and their English translations. Levanti comprises 42,000 real sentences that have been manually translated and validated. Additionally, it includes 466,000 high-quality synthetic sentence pairs, carefully generated using Claude Sonnet 3.5 (Anthropic, 2024). These synthetic examples were created based on diverse dictionary entries and carefully curated examples to enhance the semantic and lexical diversity of the corpus.

5.2 Pipeline ST

5.2.1 ASR systems

We submitted two ASR systems for the North Levantine Arabic to English track, employing the Whisper-large-v3 in an encoder-decoder configuration, trained on a dataset that combines dialectal and Modern Standard Arabic (MSA) transcribed speech. The first system, **contrastive 1**, augmented the Levantine dataset with an equal number of MSA utterances, while the second system, **primary**, further fine-tuned **contrastive 1** solely on the Levantine datasets (LDC2005S08 and LDC2006T07) to specialize the model for Levantine dialects.

5.2.2 MT model

We trained two machine translation (MT) models using the HuggingFace framework, both based on the NLLB-200 1.3B model. The first MT model was fine-tuned on the entire Levanti dataset using a learning rate of 1×10^{-5} and a batch size of 8. The second MT model was fine-tuned on the UFAL Parallel Corpus and the non-synthetic portion of the Levanti dataset, using the same learning rate 1×10^{-5} and a batch size of 6, with a beam size of 5 for decoding.

Following extensive experimentation on the development and test sets, we selected the second MT model (trained on the UFAL Corpus and non-synthetic Levantine data) for the final Levantine-to-English translation task, as it outperformed the first model in terms of translation quality.

We then constructed two cascaded systems (**contrastive 1** and **contrastive 2**) using the trained ASR systems.

[2]https://huggingface.co/datasets/guymorlan/levanti

5.3 ST candidates selection

To evaluate and rank outputs from different ASR-MT combinations, we used the BLASER-REF quality estimation model (Dale and Costa-jussà, 2024; Seamless Communication et al., 2023). BLASER-REF is a reference-based model that estimates translation quality using SONAR embeddings (Duquenne et al., 2023), which map both speech and text from different languages into a shared latent space, making the model inherently language and modality-agnostic.

The model takes three inputs: the original speech signal, a system-generated translation, and a reference translation. As human reference translations were unavailable, we used the transcription as the reference. The speech input was encoded using the SONAR Arabic speech encoder, which was trained on Modern Standard Arabic (MSA); we applied it to Levantine speech due to the lack of a Levantine-specific encoder. The transcription and translation were encoded using the SONAR text encoder, which supports the source (North Levantine Arabic) and target (English) languages.

For each utterance, we generated 10 candidate outputs from five ASR and two MT models—the same systems described in Sections 5.2.1 and 5.2.2 with additional variants—and selected the output with the highest BLASER-REF score on a scale from 1 to 5, where higher scores indicate better quality; this combination is considered our **primary** system for ST.

5.4 Results

5.4.1 Results for ASR

The ASR results in terms of word error rate (WER) are reported in Table 7 on the development set 2024 (Dev), test set 2024 (Test), and test set 2025 (Test 2025) provided by the organisers. The **Primary** system outperformed the **Contrastive 1** system on both Dev and Test sets.

Table 7: WER (%) results for North Levantine dialect ASR.

	Dev	**Test**
Primary	38.43	41.06
Contrastive 1	38.92	42.86

5.4.2 Results for ST

The ST results in terms of BLEU score (BLEU) are reported in Table 8 on the development set 2024

(Dev), test set 2024 (Test), and test set 2025 (Test 2025) provided by the organisers.

Table 8: BLEU results for North Levantine dialect to English translation.

	Dev	Test	Test 2025
Primary	29.64	28.02	22.56
Contrastive 1	28.74	26.87	21.02
Contrastive 2	28.88	26.61	21.45

6 Conclusion

This paper describes the translation systems developed by LIA and ELYADATA for three tracks of the IWSLT 2025 Evaluation Campaign, focusing on low-resource speech translation. The targeted language pairs are Tunisian Arabic–English, North Levantine Arabic–English, and Fongbé–French.

Acknowledgments

This work was funded by the French Research Agency (ANR) through the TRADEF project. It used HPC resources from GENCI-IDRIS: grants AD011012551R3, AD011015051R1, AD011012108R3, AD011014814R1, and AD011015509.

References

Idris Abdulmumin, Victor Agostinelli, Tanel AlumÃ€e, Antonios Anastasopoulos, Ashwin, Luisa Bentivogli, OndÅej Bojar, Claudia Borg, Fethi Bougares, Roldano Cattoni, Mauro Cettolo, Lizhong Chen, William Chen, Raj Dabre, Yannick EstÃšve, Marcello Federico, Marco Gaido, DÃ¡vid JavorskÃœ, Marek Kasztelnik, and 30 others. 2025. Findings of the iwslt 2025 evaluation campaign. In *Proceedings of the 22nd International Conference on Spoken Language Translation (IWSLT 2025)*, Vienna, Austia (in-person and online). Association for Computational Linguistics. To appear.

AI Anthropic. 2024. The claude 3 model family: Opus, sonnet, haiku. *Claude-3 Model Card*, 1:1.

Rosana Ardila, Megan Branson, Kelly Davis, Michael Kohler, Josh Meyer, Michael Henretty, Reuben Morais, Lindsay Saunders, Francis Tyers, and Gregor Weber. 2020. Common voice: A massively-multilingual speech corpus. In *Proceedings of the Twelfth Language Resources and Evaluation Conference*, pages 4218–4222.

Alexei Baevski, Yuhao Zhou, Abdelrahman Mohamed, and Michael Auli. 2020. wav2vec 2.0: A framework for self-supervised learning of speech representations. In *Advances in Neural Information Processing Systems (NeurIPS)*, volume 33, pages 12449–12460.

Loïc Barrault, Yu-An Chung, Mariano Coria Meglioli, David Dale, Ning Dong, Mark Duppenthaler, Paul-Ambroise Duquenne, Brian Ellis, Hady Elsahar, Justin Haaheim, and 1 others. 2023. Seamless: Multilingual expressive and streaming speech translation. *arXiv preprint arXiv:2312.05187*.

Alexandre Bérard, Laurent Besacier, Ali Can Kocabiyikoglu, and Olivier Pietquin. 2018. End-to-end automatic speech translation of audiobooks. In *2018 IEEE International Conference on Acoustics, Speech and Signal Processing (ICASSP)*, pages 6224–6228. IEEE.

Alexandre Bérard, Olivier Pietquin, Christophe Servan, and Laurent Besacier. 2016. Listen and translate: A proof of concept for end-to-end speech-to-text translation. *arXiv preprint arXiv:1612.01744*.

Jianlv Chen, Shitao Xiao, Peitian Zhang, Kun Luo, Defu Lian, and Zheng Liu. 2024. BGE M3-Embedding: Multi-lingual, multi-functionality, multi-granularity text embeddings through self-knowledge distillation. *arXiv preprint arXiv:2402.03216*.

Yu-An Chung, Wei-Ning Hsu, Hank Liao Tang, and James Glass. 2021. w2v-bert: Combining contrastive learning and masked language modeling for self-supervised speech pre-training. In *Proceedings of the Annual Conference of the International Speech Communication Association (INTERSPEECH)*, pages 2445–2449.

Marta R Costa-Jussà, James Cross, Onur Çelebi, Maha Elbayad, Kenneth Heafield, Kevin Heffernan, Elahe Kalbassi, Janice Lam, Daniel Licht, Jean Maillard, and 1 others. 2022. No language left behind: Scaling human-centered machine translation. *arXiv preprint arXiv:2207.04672*.

David Dale and Marta Costa-jussà. 2024. Blaser 2.0: a metric for evaluation and quality estimation of massively multilingual speech and text translation. In *Findings of the Association for Computational Linguistics: EMNLP 2024*, pages 16075–16085.

Long Duong, Antonios Anastasopoulos, David Chiang, Steven Bird, and Trevor Cohn. 2016. An attentional model for speech translation without transcription. In *Proceedings of the 2016 conference of the North American chapter of the association for computational linguistics: human language technologies*, pages 949–959.

Paul-Ambroise Duquenne, Holger Schwenk, and Benoît Sagot. 2023. Sonar: sentence-level multimodal and language-agnostic representations. *arXiv preprint arXiv:2308.11466*.

Haroun Elleuch, Salima Mdhaffar, Yannick Estève, and Fethi Bougares. 2025. ADI-20: Arabic Dialect Identification dataset and models. In *Proceedings of Interspeech 2025*, Rotterdam, The Netherlands. Submitted to Interspeech 2025.

Fangxiaoyu Feng, Yinfei Yang, Daniel Cer, Naveen Arivazhagan, and Wei Wang. 2022a. Language-agnostic bert sentence embedding. In *Proceedings of the 60th Annual Meeting of the Association for Computational Linguistics (Volume 1: Long Papers)*, pages 878–891.

Fangxiaoyu Feng, Yinfei Yang, Daniel Cer, Naveen Arivazhagan, and Wei Wang. 2022b. Language-agnostic BERT sentence embedding. In *Proceedings of the 60th Annual Meeting of the Association for Computational Linguistics (Volume 1: Long Papers)*, pages 878–891, Dublin, Ireland. Association for Computational Linguistics.

Nizar Habash, Mona Diab, and Owen Rambow. 2012. Conventional orthography for dialectal Arabic. In *Proceedings of the Eighth International Conference on Language Resources and Evaluation (LREC'12)*, pages 711–718, Istanbul, Turkey. European Language Resources Association (ELRA).

Wei-Ning Hsu, Benjamin Bolte, Yao-Hung Hubert Tsai, Kushal Lakhotia, Ruslan Salakhutdinov, and Abdelrahman Mohamed. 2021. Hubert: Self-supervised speech representation learning by masked prediction of hidden units. In *Proceedings of the Annual Conference of the International Speech Communication Association (INTERSPEECH)*, pages 1474–1478.

Sameer Khurana, Antoine Laurent, and James Glass. 2022. Samu-xlsr: Semantically-aligned multimodal utterance-level cross-lingual speech representation. *IEEE Journal of Selected Topics in Signal Processing*, 16(6):1493–1504.

Taku Kudo and John Richardson. 2018. SentencePiece: A simple and language independent subword tokenizer and detokenizer for neural text processing. In *Proceedings of the 2018 Conference on Empirical Methods in Natural Language Processing: System Demonstrations*, pages 66–71, Brussels, Belgium. Association for Computational Linguistics.

Gaurav Kumar, Graeme Blackwood, Jan Trmal, Daniel Povey, and Sanjeev Khudanpur. 2015. A coarse-grained model for optimal coupling of asr and smt systems for speech translation. In *Proceedings of the 2015 Conference on Empirical Methods in Natural Language Processing*, pages 1902–1907.

Antoine Laurent, Souhir Gahbiche, Ha Nguyen, Haroun Elleuch, Fethi Bougares, Antoine Thiol, Hugo Riguidel, Salima Mdhaffar, Gaëlle Laperrière, Lucas Maison, and 1 others. 2023. On-trac consortium systems for the iwslt 2023 dialectal and low-resource speech translation tasks. In *International Conference on Spoken Language Translation (IWSLT) 2023*.

Ilya Loshchilov and Frank Hutter. 2017. Decoupled weight decay regularization. *arXiv preprint arXiv:1711.05101*.

Evgeny Matusov, Stephan Kanthak, and Hermann Ney. 2005. On the integration of speech recognition and statistical machine translation. In *Interspeech*, pages 3177–3180.

Hamdy Mubarak, Amir Hussein, Shammur Absar Chowdhury, and Ahmed Ali. 2021. Qasr: Qcri aljazeera speech resource a large scale annotated arabic speech corpus. In *Proceedings of the 59th Annual Meeting of the Association for Computational Linguistics and the 11th International Joint Conference on Natural Language Processing (Volume 1: Long Papers)*, pages 2274–2285.

Alec Radford, Jong Wook Kim, Tao Xu, Greg Brockman, Christine Mcleavey, and Ilya Sutskever. 2023a. Robust speech recognition via large-scale weak supervision. In *Proceedings of the 40th International Conference on Machine Learning*, volume 202 of *Proceedings of Machine Learning Research*, pages 28492–28518. PMLR.

Alec Radford, Jong Wook Kim, Tao Xu, Greg Brockman, Christine McLeavey, and Ilya Sutskever. 2023b. Robust speech recognition via large-scale weak supervision. In *International conference on machine learning*, pages 28492–28518. PMLR.

Mirco Ravanelli, Titouan Parcollet, Adel Moumen, Sylvain de Langen, Cem Subakan, Peter Plantinga, Yingzhi Wang, Pooneh Mousavi, Luca Della Libera, Artem Ploujnikov, and 1 others. 2024. Open-source conversational ai with speechbrain 1.0. *Journal of Machine Learning Research*, 25(333):1–11.

Seamless Communication, Barrault, Loïc, Chung, Yu-An, Meglioli, Mariano Cora, Dale, David, Dong, Ning, Duquenne, Paul-Ambroise, Elsahar, Hady, Gong, Hongyu, Heffernan, Kevin, Hoffman, John, Klaiber, Christopher, Li, Pengwei, Licht, Daniel, Maillard, Jean, Rakotoarison, Alice, Sadagopan, Kaushik Ram, Wenzek, Guillaume, Ye, Ethan, and 49 others. 2023. Seamlessm4t—massively multilingual & multimodal machine translation. *ArXiv*.

CUNI-NL@IWSLT 2025: End-to-end Offline Speech Translation and Instruction Following with LLMs

Nam Luu and **Ondřej Bojar**
Institute of Formal and Applied Linguistics
Faculty of Mathematics and Physics
Charles University
namhoang.luu700@student.cuni.cz, bojar@ufal.mff.cuni.cz

Abstract

This paper describes the CUNI-NL team's submission to the IWSLT 2025 Offline Speech Translation and Instruction Following tasks, focusing on transcribing the English audio and translating the English audio to German text. Our systems follow the end-to-end approach, where each system consists of a pretrained, frozen speech encoder, along with a medium-sized large language model fine-tuned with LoRA on three tasks: 1) transcribing the English audio; 2) directly translating the English audio to German text; and 3) a combination of the above two tasks, i.e., simultaneously transcribing the English audio and translating the English audio to German text.

1 Introduction

End-to-end speech translation (ST) is a growing research direction that aims to ignore the intermediate speech recognition (ASR) step to directly translate the audio input into the corresponding text in another language. This approach simplifies the overall architecture and has been shown to match the performance of the cascaded counterpart (Bérard et al., 2018; Liu et al., 2019; Gaido et al., 2020).

Large language models (LLMs) have demonstrated their good performance in a large number of complex natural language tasks, including machine translation (Minaee et al., 2024; Zhang et al., 2024; Zhao et al., 2023; Naveed et al., 2024). With the ever-improving potential of LLMs, researchers have been trying to integrate different components used for other modalities, in order to extend their abilities to go beyond text-only tasks (Li et al., 2023a; Gao et al., 2023; Liu et al., 2023; Li et al., 2023c; Zhang et al., 2023).

Motivated by recent contributions in speech representation learning and LLMs, to participate in the IWSLT 2025 Offline Speech Translation and Instruction Following tasks, we aim to investigate an end-to-end architecture that can perform both ASR and ST. This architecture combines the high-quality audio representation from the pre-trained acoustic models with the excellent performance of LLMs to serve as an end-to-end speech translation system, while still having the ability to transcribe from the audio signal. Our systems, after being fine-tuned with the Low-Rank Adaptation (LoRA; Hu et al., 2021) technique, achieve a solid performance in both speech recognition and translation.

The paper is structured as follows:

- Section 2 describes the details of our chosen network architecture, along with the dataset used for its training and evaluation.
- Section 3 provides the ASR and ST evaluation results of the model in different public test sets.
- Section 4 proposes possible directions to improve the architecture.

2 Methods and Dataset

2.1 Architecture

The overall architecture is illustrated in Figure 1. For each training sample, given the speech signal, its corresponding transcript, and the translated text, the speech hidden features are obtained using a speech encoder. In this step, we experimented with SeamlessM4T (Barrault et al., 2025) and Whisper encoder (Radford et al., 2022).

Next, the speech features represented as a time sequence of vectors, at the "frame rate" of 20ms, are fed to a projection layer, in order to convert the feature dimension to match the LLM's embedding dimension. For a better match between the speech encoder and the LLM, we use a length adapter which effectively reduces the "frame rate" of the sequence. The resulting speech embeddings are subsequently given to the LLM as the prompt for it to generate the corresponding transcription and the translated text simultaneously. The LLM is fine-tuned in the next-token-prediction fashion to

Proceedings of the 22nd International Conference on Spoken Language Translation (IWSLT 2025), pages 282–288
July 31 - August 1, 2025 ©2025 Association for Computational Linguistics

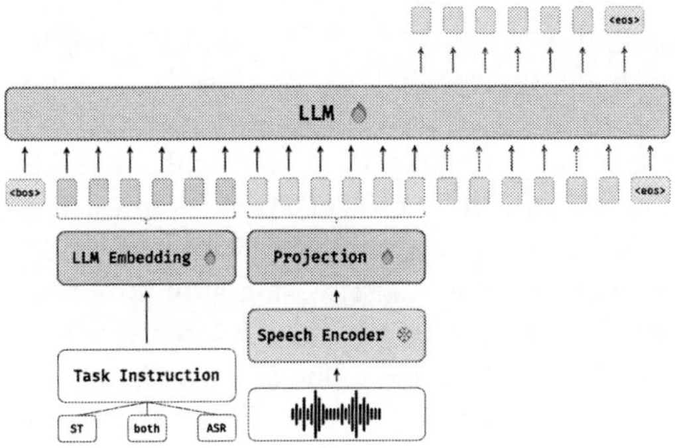

Figure 1: The overall architecture includes a frozen speech encoder component, a modal projection layer, and a fine-tuned LLM. **Red** arrows denote the usage of tokens during training, and **blue** arrows indicate tokens generated during inference; while **black** arrows represent the prompt fed to the LLM. The original modality of the model is indicated by the token color, from left to right: violet for text instruction, blue for source-language speech tokens, green for target-language text tokens. Length adapter is a part of the Projection step.

complete the sequence with the translation into the target language.

2.2 Speech Encoder

We adopted SeamlessM4T (Barrault et al., 2025) and Whisper (Radford et al., 2022) as the speech encoders, utilizing their capability of extracting high-quality representation from audio data. From both architectures, we only employed the encoder part of the pre-trained `seamless-m4t-v2-large`[1] and `whisper-large-v3`,[2] respectively, in order to extract the audio hidden features.

2.3 Length Adapter

The length of the speech feature sequence can be longer than the supported length of the LLM, as a result, it is more favorable to shorten it beforehand.

Because the speech encoder part of the SeamlessM4T architecture already contains a length adapter layer (Figure 2), we decided not to add any adapter layer, but used it as-is for SeamlessM4T-based models.

For Whisper-based models, a convolution-based downsampling layer with a kernel size of 25x5 and a stride of 25 is used to reduce the length of the speech feature sequence from 1500 tokens (each corresponds to 20ms) to 60 tokens (each encodes 500ms). The detail of the convolution adapter layer is illustrated in Figure 3.

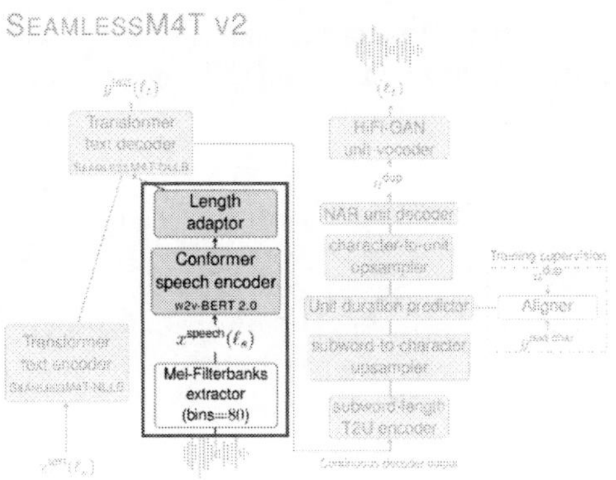

Figure 2: Details of the SeamlessM4T-v2 architecture,[3] where the red region is the speech encoder part

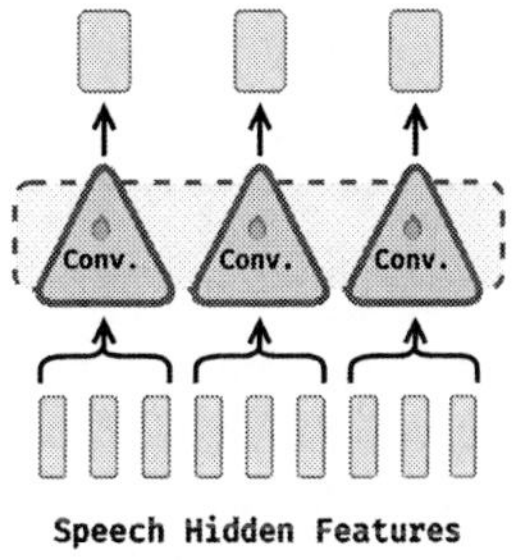

Figure 3: Details of the convolution adapter. Note that the convolution windows do not overlap.

2.4 Projection Layer

For the projection layer, we used only one simple three-layer ReLU-activated feed-forward network, with the hidden size of 4096, to map from the encoder's hidden size to the corresponding LLM's hidden size. This layer ensures the resulting speech representation is well integrated into the LLM's embedding space, giving it enough information for the downstream task.

2.5 LLMs

We experimented with three different pre-trained LLMs available on HuggingFace, namely `Llama-3.1-8B-Instruct`,[4]

[1] `https://huggingface.co/facebook/seamless-m4t-v2-large`

[2] `https://huggingface.co/openai/whisper-large-v3`

[3] `https://github.com/facebookresearch/seamless_communication/blob/main/docs/m4t/README.md`

[4] `https://huggingface.co/meta-llama/Llama-3.1-8B-Instruct`

EuroLLM-9B-Instruct,[5] and gemma-3-12b-it.[6] We summarize the examined combinations of components in Table 1.

Speech Enc.	LLM	Adapter
seamless-m4t -v2-large Ⓢ	Llama-3.1-8B-Instruct Ⓛ EuroLLM-9B-Instruct Ⓔ gemma-3-12b-it Ⓖ	N/A
whisper -large-v3 Ⓦ	Llama-3.1-8B-Instruct Ⓛ EuroLLM-9B-Instruct Ⓔ gemma-3-12b-it Ⓖ	25x5 Convolution

Table 1: Details of our six examined combinations of components, testing each of the speech encoders (Ⓢ, Ⓦ) with each of the LLMs (Ⓛ, Ⓔ, Ⓖ).

2.6 Dataset

All models were trained using the CoVoST2 dataset (Wang et al., 2020), a large multilingual corpus built from the Common Voice corpora (Ardila et al., 2020), which contains the audio data, the English transcription of such audio and the translation of the transcription into multiple languages. Specifically, we used the English-to-German subset of the dataset, with approximately 184 hours of audio data.

For evaluation, we used the test sets from the Offline Speech Translation track of IWSLT 2021[7] and 2022,[8] because they are the two latest development sets whose golden labels are available. These datasets are from the TED domain, in which the audios contain clean speech from the speaker mixed with some occasional noise from the audience; thus, we believe these are suitable for development. As all models can perform both ASR and ST, evaluation results for both tasks are described in Sections 3.2 and 3.3, respectively.

2.7 Multi-task Training

To obtain a system that can perform both ASR and ST tasks, we decided to train the model on the following three tasks:

① Transcribing the English audio to English text;

② Directly translating the English audio to German text; and

③ Simultaneously transcribing the English audio to English text, and translating such audio to German text.

[5]https://huggingface.co/utter-project/EuroLLM-9B-Instruct

[6]https://huggingface.co/google/gemma-3-12b-it

[7]https://iwslt.org/2021/offline

[8]https://iwslt.org/2022/offline

With tasks ① and ③, the LLM is given corresponding instructions depending on each task. For task ②, we used two different prompts in either English or German, to prepare the model for processing both English and German instructions. With this setup, we randomly divided the training dataset into four subsets using a uniform distribution, where each part was associated with an instruction according to the task and the relevant language. We decided to split the dataset and train the model on only one epoch, instead of duplicating the dataset four times and training for four epochs, due to limited time and resources. Details about each task and the corresponding instructions are described in Table 2.

Task	Instruction	# examples
transcribe ①	Transcribe the English audio	72,067
translate_en ②	Translate the English audio to German	72,600
translate_de ②	Übersetzen Sie den englischen Ton ins Deutsche	72,455
both ③	Transcribe then translate the following English audio to German	72,291

Table 2: Details of our four tasks, each demonstrated by roughly a quarter of the fine-tuning items

2.8 Training and Inference Details

All systems were fine-tuned using 16-bit LoRA (Hu et al., 2021) adapters in bfloat16 precision, with the following LoRA parameters: rank of $r = 256$, alpha of $\alpha = 256$. The effective batch size was set to 8. Other training hyperparameters included the learning rate of $1e - 5$ with 100 warmup steps, and an AdamW optimizer (Loshchilov and Hutter, 2019) with a cosine scheduler (Loshchilov and Hutter, 2017). All systems were trained for 1 epoch.

For each example, the training data is formatted as follows: "<bos> {user_header} {instruction} {audio_features} {assistant_header} {output} <eos>". The cross-entropy loss was computed only for the tokens following "{assistant_header}". Each system's training loss details are illustrated in Figure 4.

During inference, for each audio data, the LLMs were prompted using the following format: "<bos> {user_header} {instruction} {audio_features} {assistant_header}", then generated the output, subject to the task, in an autoregressive manner. We performed inference using the beam search algorithm, with a beam size of 2

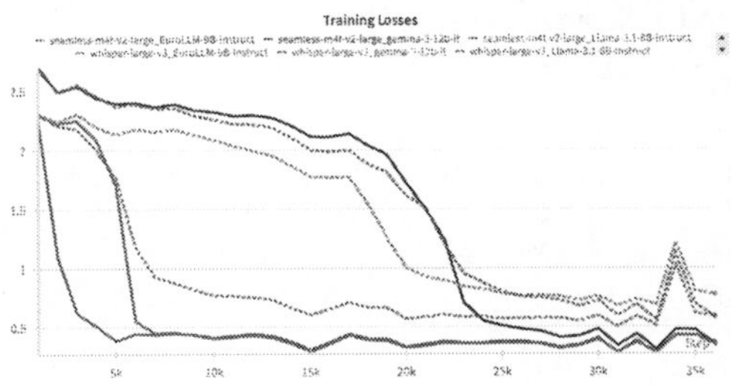

Figure 4: Training loss of systems

for all systems. All evaluation results are described in Sections 3.2 and 3.3.

3 Evaluation

3.1 Metrics and Tools

For the Offline Speech Translation task, we evaluated all models using standard metrics, namely BLEU (Papineni et al., 2002), $\text{COMET}_{22}^{\text{DA}}$ (Rei et al., 2022a),[9] and $\text{COMET}_{22}^{\text{KIWI-DA}}$ (Rei et al., 2022b).[10] For the Automatic Speech Recognition task, we used WER, the standard metric for speech recognition.

For the evaluation purpose, we used the SLTev (Ansari et al., 2021) library,[11] because it supports both MT and ASR evaluation in one package, using sacreBLEU (Post, 2018) to calculate BLEU score. However, since SLTev does not report any COMET-family metrics, we had to change the structure of the sentence with mwerSegmenter,[12] to automatically resegment the models' output according to the reference, before evaluating with the unbabel-comet[13] package. The evaluation was done using python-3.11.5, SLTev-1.2.3, and unbabel-comet-2.2.2.

3.2 ASR Results

Table 3 details the ASR evaluation results against the IWSLT 2022 test set (tst2022). We reported the WER score after applying the "LPW" preprocessing strategy available in SLTev, which first lowercased every character, removed all punctuation, then used the built-in mwerSegmenter tool to resegment the output transcripts. Due to some bugs when processing the IWSLT 2021 test set (tst2021), mwerSegmenter failed to run during evaluation, hence we could not obtain the results. It can be seen that the model with seamless-m4t-v2-large as the speech encoder and EuroLLM-9B-Instruct as the decoder has the best result among all systems.

3.3 Offline ST Results

Tables 4 and 5 report the BLEU and COMET-family scores, respectively, on the two test sets, with two corresponding instructions. For evaluating with BLEU, we included both docAsWhole score, which concatenated all reference segments and candidate complete segments as two documents, and mwerSegmenter score, which resegments complete candidate segments according to reference segments to minimize WER. Similar to Section 3.2, mwerSegmenter scores for IWSLT 2021 test set could not be obtained, hence we did not include them.

We observe that the system with seamless-m4t-v2-large as the encoder and EuroLLM-9B-Instruct as the language model achieves the best scores in all evaluation metrics, compared to the other systems. With the instruction associated with the task "both" (Table 2), the system excels in translation results, suggesting that the inclusion of English transcript provided useful assistance in translation.

Comparing between the two prompt variations "translate_en" and "translate_de" for this task, the latter one leads to more solid overall results. For example, consider the Ⓢ+Ⓔ system: for tst2022, while "translate_en" instruction might outperform that of "translate_de", but the difference is small; while results for tst2021 shows a contrastive situation, where "translate_de" surpasses "translate_en' by a considerable amount. This behavior also appears in other systems, leading us to believe that the system can perform better when the instruction provided is in the relevant target language. As a result, we chose "translate_de" prompt with Ⓢ and Ⓔ as our submission to the Offline Speech Translation and Instruction Following task, under the "*constrained+LLM*" evaluation condition.

4 Future Work

For the IWSLT 2025 Offline Speech Translation and Instruction Following tasks, we have only conducted experiments for the English-to-German di-

[9] https://huggingface.co/Unbabel/wmt22-comet-da

[10] https://huggingface.co/Unbabel/wmt22-cometkiwi-da

[11] https://github.com/ELITR/SLTev

[12] https://www-i6.informatik.rwth-aachen.de/web/Software/mwerSegmenter.tar.gz

[13] https://github.com/Unbabel/COMET

Model		transcribe	both
Enc.	LLM	tst2022	tst2022
	Ⓛ	14.1%	17.3%
Ⓢ	Ⓔ	**13.4%**	16.7%
	Ⓖ	20.0%	24.2%
	Ⓛ	24.3%	26.6%
Ⓦ	Ⓔ	47.9%	47.5%
	Ⓖ	38.6%	38.5%

Table 3: ASR evaluation results (WER↓)

Model		translate_en		translate_de		both	
Enc.	LLM	tst2021	tst2022	tst2021	tst2022	tst2021	tst2022
	Ⓛ	39.53 / -	37.55 / 26.58	39.50 / -	37.58 / 26.66	42.01 / -	38.15 / 29.78
Ⓢ	Ⓔ	41.50 / -	**38.47 / 30.65**	**41.94** / -	37.73 / 29.83	44.28 / -	40.82 / 32.33
	Ⓖ	37.37 / -	33.72 / 24.93	36.70 / -	33.66 / 25.25	42.17 / -	37.70 / 29.73
	Ⓛ	33.02 / -	31.54 / 19.47	33.64 / -	30.02 / 19.62	39.48 / -	37.76 / 26.64
Ⓦ	Ⓔ	22.43 / -	22.02 / 9.24	22.21 / -	23.32 / 9.83	32.91 / -	31.50 / 19.56
	Ⓖ	27.23 / -	27.34 / 14.67	27.34 / -	27.81 / 14.67	35.37 / -	34.72 / 22.95

Table 4: Offline ST en2de BLEU results, with both `docAsWhole`↑ and `mwerSegmenter`↑ scores, respectively

Model		translate_en		translate_de		both	
Enc.	LLM	tst2021	tst2022	tst2021	tst2022	tst2021	tst2022
	Ⓛ	61.11 / 53.85	68.05 / 62.38	68.69 / 62.63	67.88 / 62.02	69.49 / 64.66	69.48 / 64.80
Ⓢ	Ⓔ	62.57 / 56.13	**71.06 / 66.04**	**70.38 / 65.11**	70.62 / 65.46	71.59 / 66.93	71.05 / 66.53
	Ⓖ	59.09 / 51.87	66.01 / 60.33	66.33 / 60.48	66.08 / 60.10	67.90 / 62.75	68.20 / 63.28
	Ⓛ	52.80 / 43.13	61.99 / 53.47	62.73 / 54.55	62.02 / 53.73	66.66 / 60.71	66.38 / 60.00
Ⓦ	Ⓔ	42.73 / 30.45	48.33 / 35.93	48.22 / 35.80	49.48 / 36.95	58.35 / 47.78	56.85 / 46.70
	Ⓖ	48.10 / 36.40	55.36 / 44.11	55.75 / 44.10	54.10 / 42.70	61.49 / 52.65	61.54 / 52.86

Table 5: Offline ST en2de $\text{COMET}_{22}^{\text{DA}}$↑ and $\text{COMET}_{22}^{\text{KIWI-DA}}$↑ results, respectively

rection; hence, in the future, we will expand our experiments to more language pairs and directions. In addition, we have some ideas to improve the pipeline:

- Try other modal adapter methods, like Q-Former (Li et al., 2023b).
- Experiment with smaller variants of the LLMs for faster training and inference, while retaining the quality in translation, by distilling knowledge from fine-tuned systems.
- Build a Direct Preference Optimization (DPO; Rafailov et al., 2024) or Contrastive Preference Optimization (CPO; Xu et al., 2024) dataset to apply into the training pipeline. Xu et al. (2024) showed that their CPO approach improved the performance of medium-sized LLMs, so we will try following the same idea.

5 Conclusion

In this paper, we leveraged pre-trained speech encoders and LLMs and connected them into an end-to-end architecture to participate in the IWSLT 2025 Offline Speech Translation and Instruction Following tasks. Our primary goal was to develop a system that could perform both ASR for English audio, and ST from English audio to German text. In our experiments, the model with `seamless-m4t-v2-large` as the speech encoder and `EuroLLM-9B-Instruct` as the LLM yielded the best results in evaluation of both ASR and ST tasks, suggesting that this pair could be a promising combination for end-to-end models.

6 Acknowledgment

Computational resources were provided by the e-INFRA CZ project (ID:90254), supported by the Ministry of Education, Youth and Sports of the Czech Republic.

Nam Luu has been supported by the Erasmus Mundus program in Language and Communication Technologies (LCT).

Ondřej Bojar has received funding from the Project OP JAK Mezisektorová spolupráce Nr. CZ.02.01.01/00/23_020/0008518 named "Jazykověda, umělá inteligence a jazykové a řečové technologie: od výzkumu k aplikacím."

References

Ebrahim Ansari, Ondřej Bojar, Barry Haddow, and Mohammad Mahmoudi. 2021. SLTEV: Comprehensive Evaluation of Spoken Language Translation. In *Proceedings of the 16th Conference of the European Chapter of the Association for Computational Linguistics: System Demonstrations*, pages 71–79, Online. Association for Computational Linguistics.

Rosana Ardila, Megan Branson, Kelly Davis, Michael Henretty, Michael Kohler, Josh Meyer, Reuben Morais, Lindsay Saunders, Francis M. Tyers, and Gregor Weber. 2020. Common Voice: A Massively-Multilingual Speech Corpus.

Loïc Barrault, Yu-An Chung, Mariano Coria Meglioli, David Dale, Ning Dong, Paul-Ambroise Duquenne, Hady Elsahar, Hongyu Gong, Kevin Heffernan, John Hoffman, Christopher Klaiber, Pengwei Li, Daniel Licht, Jean Maillard, Alice Rakotoarison, Kaushik Ram Sadagopan, Guillaume Wenzek, Ethan Ye, Bapi Akula, Peng-Jen Chen, Naji El Hachem, Brian Ellis, Gabriel Mejia Gonzalez, Justin Haaheim, Prangthip Hansanti, Russ Howes, Bernie Huang, Min-Jae Hwang, Hirofumi Inaguma, Somya Jain, Elahe Kalbassi, Amanda Kallet, Ilia Kulikov, Janice Lam, Daniel Li, Xutai Ma, Ruslan Mavlyutov, Benjamin Peloquin, Mohamed Ramadan, Abinesh Ramakrishnan, Anna Sun, Kevin Tran, Tuan Tran, Igor Tufanov, Vish Vogeti, Carleigh Wood, Yilin Yang, Bokai Yu, Pierre Andrews, Can Balioglu, Marta R. Costa-jussà, Onur Çelebi, Maha Elbayad, Cynthia Gao, Francisco Guzmán, Justine Kao, Ann Lee, Alexandre Mourachko, Juan Pino, Sravya Popuri, Christophe Ropers, Safiyyah Saleem, Holger Schwenk, Paden Tomasello, Changhan Wang, Jeff Wang, Skyler Wang, and SEAMLESS Communication Team. 2025. Joint speech and text machine translation for up to 100 languages. *Nature*, 637(8046):587–593.

Alexandre Bérard, Laurent Besacier, Ali Can Kocabiyikoglu, and Olivier Pietquin. 2018. End-to-End Automatic Speech Translation of Audiobooks.

Marco Gaido, Mattia Antonino Di Gangi, Matteo Negri, and Marco Turchi. 2020. End-to-End Speech-Translation with Knowledge Distillation: FBK@IWSLT2020.

Peng Gao, Jiaming Han, Renrui Zhang, Ziyi Lin, Shijie Geng, Aojun Zhou, Wei Zhang, Pan Lu, Conghui He, Xiangyu Yue, Hongsheng Li, and Yu Qiao. 2023. LLaMA-Adapter V2: Parameter-Efficient Visual Instruction Model.

Edward J. Hu, Yelong Shen, Phillip Wallis, Zeyuan Allen-Zhu, Yuanzhi Li, Shean Wang, Lu Wang, and Weizhu Chen. 2021. LoRA: Low-Rank Adaptation of Large Language Models.

Junnan Li, Dongxu Li, Silvio Savarese, and Steven Hoi. 2023a. BLIP-2: Bootstrapping Language-Image Pre-training with Frozen Image Encoders and Large Language Models.

Junnan Li, Dongxu Li, Silvio Savarese, and Steven Hoi. 2023b. BLIP-2: bootstrapping language-image pre-training with frozen image encoders and large language models. In *Proceedings of the 40th International Conference on Machine Learning*, ICML'23. JMLR.org.

Yuang Li, Yu Wu, Jinyu Li, and Shujie Liu. 2023c. Prompting Large Language Models for Zero-Shot Domain Adaptation in Speech Recognition.

Haotian Liu, Chunyuan Li, Qingyang Wu, and Yong Jae Lee. 2023. Visual Instruction Tuning.

Yuchen Liu, Hao Xiong, Zhongjun He, Jiajun Zhang, Hua Wu, Haifeng Wang, and Chengqing Zong. 2019. End-to-End Speech Translation with Knowledge Distillation.

Ilya Loshchilov and Frank Hutter. 2017. SGDR: Stochastic Gradient Descent with Warm Restarts.

Ilya Loshchilov and Frank Hutter. 2019. Decoupled Weight Decay Regularization. ArXiv:1711.05101 [cs, math].

Shervin Minaee, Tomas Mikolov, Narjes Nikzad, Meysam Chenaghlu, Richard Socher, Xavier Amatriain, and Jianfeng Gao. 2024. Large Language Models: A Survey.

Humza Naveed, Asad Ullah Khan, Shi Qiu, Muhammad Saqib, Saeed Anwar, Muhammad Usman, Naveed Akhtar, Nick Barnes, and Ajmal Mian. 2024. A Comprehensive Overview of Large Language Models.

Kishore Papineni, Salim Roukos, Todd Ward, and Wei-Jing Zhu. 2002. BLEU: a method for automatic evaluation of machine translation. In *Proceedings of the 40th Annual Meeting on Association for Computational Linguistics*, ACL '02, page 311–318, USA. Association for Computational Linguistics.

Matt Post. 2018. A Call for Clarity in Reporting BLEU Scores.

Alec Radford, Jong Wook Kim, Tao Xu, Greg Brockman, Christine McLeavey, and Ilya Sutskever. 2022. Robust Speech Recognition via Large-Scale Weak Supervision.

Rafael Rafailov, Archit Sharma, Eric Mitchell, Stefano Ermon, Christopher D. Manning, and Chelsea Finn. 2024. Direct Preference Optimization: Your Language Model is Secretly a Reward Model.

Ricardo Rei, José G. C. de Souza, Duarte Alves, Chrysoula Zerva, Ana C Farinha, Taisiya Glushkova, Alon Lavie, Luisa Coheur, and André F. T. Martins. 2022a. COMET-22: Unbabel-IST 2022 Submission for the Metrics Shared Task. In *Proceedings of the*

Seventh Conference on Machine Translation (WMT), pages 578–585, Abu Dhabi, United Arab Emirates (Hybrid). Association for Computational Linguistics.

Ricardo Rei, Marcos Treviso, Nuno M. Guerreiro, Chrysoula Zerva, Ana C. Farinha, Christine Maroti, José G. C. de Souza, Taisiya Glushkova, Duarte M. Alves, Alon Lavie, Luisa Coheur, and André F. T. Martins. 2022b. CometKiwi: IST-Unbabel 2022 Submission for the Quality Estimation Shared Task.

Changhan Wang, Anne Wu, and Juan Pino. 2020. CoVoST 2 and Massively Multilingual Speech-to-Text Translation.

Haoran Xu, Amr Sharaf, Yunmo Chen, Weiting Tan, Lingfeng Shen, Benjamin Van Durme, Kenton Murray, and Young Jin Kim. 2024. Contrastive Preference Optimization: Pushing the Boundaries of LLM Performance in Machine Translation.

Dong Zhang, Shimin Li, Xin Zhang, Jun Zhan, Pengyu Wang, Yaqian Zhou, and Xipeng Qiu. 2023. SpeechGPT: Empowering Large Language Models with Intrinsic Cross-Modal Conversational Abilities.

Shengyu Zhang, Linfeng Dong, Xiaoya Li, Sen Zhang, Xiaofei Sun, Shuhe Wang, Jiwei Li, Runyi Hu, Tianwei Zhang, Fei Wu, and Guoyin Wang. 2024. Instruction Tuning for Large Language Models: A Survey.

Wayne Xin Zhao, Kun Zhou, Junyi Li, Tianyi Tang, Xiaolei Wang, Yupeng Hou, Yingqian Min, Beichen Zhang, Junjie Zhang, Zican Dong, Yifan Du, Chen Yang, Yushuo Chen, Zhipeng Chen, Jinhao Jiang, Ruiyang Ren, Yifan Li, Xinyu Tang, Zikang Liu, Peiyu Liu, Jian-Yun Nie, and Ji-Rong Wen. 2023. A Survey of Large Language Models.

GMU Systems for the IWSLT 2025 Low-Resource Speech Translation Shared Task

Chutong Meng and Antonios Anastasopoulos
George Mason University
{cmeng2,antonis}@gmu.edu

Abstract

This paper describes the GMU systems for the IWSLT 2025 low-resource speech translation shared task. We trained systems for all language pairs, except for Levantine Arabic. We fine-tuned SeamlessM4T-v2 (Seamless Communication et al., 2023b) for automatic speech recognition (ASR), machine translation (MT), and end-to-end speech translation (E2E ST). The ASR and MT models are also used to form cascaded ST systems. Additionally, we explored various training paradigms for E2E ST fine-tuning, including direct E2E fine-tuning, multi-task training, and parameter initialization using components from fine-tuned ASR and/or MT models. Our results show that (1) direct E2E fine-tuning yields strong results; (2) initializing with a fine-tuned ASR encoder improves ST performance on languages SeamlessM4T-v2 has not been trained on; (3) multi-task training can be slightly helpful.[1]

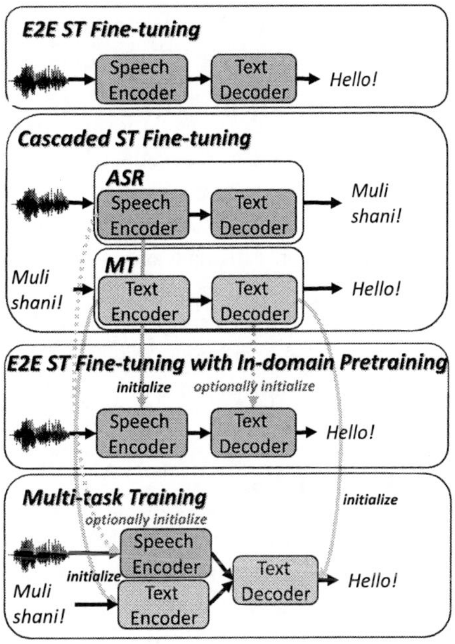

Figure 1: Illustration of our SeamlessM4T-v2 fine-tuning strategies. Speech Encoder, Text Encoder, and Text Decoder refer to the corresponding components of SeamlessM4T-v2.

1 Introduction

Speech translation (ST) is a task that aims to translate speech in one language into text in another language. It can be addressed by either an end-to-end (E2E) ST model or a cascaded system that combines an automatic speech recognition (ASR) model and a machine translation (MT) model. Recent advances in E2E ST have been driven by the development of large multilingual models trained on large amounts of multilingual datasets (Seamless Communication et al., 2023a,b; Radford et al., 2023). Similar trends can be observed in ASR (Radford et al., 2023) and MT (NLLB Team et al., 2022) as well. Despite these models have covered a wide range of languages, many low-resource languages remain underrepresented and are not yet well supported by existing models.

The IWSLT low-resource speech translation shared tasks (Abdulmumin et al., 2025; Ahmad et al., 2024; Agarwal et al., 2023; Anastasopoulos et al., 2022) are designed to advance ST technology for low-resource languages. To address the challenge of data scarcity, previous submissions have explored various pre-trained models, including multilingual self-supervised speech models such as XLSR (Conneau et al., 2021), multilingual ASR models such as Whisper (Radford et al., 2023), multilingual MT models such as NLLB (NLLB Team et al., 2022), and multilingual ST models such as SeamlessM4T (Seamless Communication et al., 2023a,b). These pre-trained models were then fine-tuned on ST datasets for low-resource languages. Among them, SeamlessM4T-v2 has demonstrated superior performance, according to last year's evaluations (Ahmad et al., 2024).

[1]We release our code for reproducibility: https://github.com/mct10/IWSLT2025_LowRes_ST.

Proceedings of the 22nd International Conference on Spoken Language Translation (IWSLT 2025), pages 289–300
July 31 - August 1, 2025 ©2025 Association for Computational Linguistics

This paper describes GMU submissions to the IWSLT 2025 low-resource speech translation task (Abdulmumin et al., 2025). Our work focuses on fine-tuning the SeamlessM4T-v2 model (Seamless Communication et al., 2023b) for all language pairs except Levantine Arabic-to-English. We fine-tuned the model for both E2E and cascaded systems. For E2E ST fine-tuning, we explored multiple strategies, including multi-task training with MT and knowledge distillation objectives, as well as initializing model components with those from fine-tuned ASR and/or MT models, trying to utilize all available datasets. Figure 1 illustrates our strategies. Our results show that direct E2E fine-tuning SeamlessM4T-v2 yields strong performance across all languages pairs, except Quechua, which has too little training data. For languages not seen during SeamlessM4T-v2 pre-training, we show that fine-tuning the model on ASR data and initializing the ST encoder with the ASR encoder improves performance significantly. We also show that multi-task training offers some performance gains when the MT model significantly outperforms the E2E ST model.

2 Task Descriptions

The IWSLT 2025 low-resource ST task (Abdulmumin et al., 2025) covers 10 language pairs: (North) Levantine Dialectal Arabic to English (apc-eng), Tunisian Arabic Dialect to English (aeb-eng), Bemba to English (bem-eng), Fongbe to French (fon-fra), Irish to English (gle-eng), Bhojpuri to Hindi (bho-hin), Estonian to English (est-eng), Maltese to English (mlt-eng), Marathi to Hindi (mar-hin), and Quechua to Spanish (que-spa). In each of these language pairs, the source language is low-resource while the target language is high-resource. We trained systems for all language pairs except for apc-eng.[2]

Formally, E2E ST is defined as translating a speech utterance x^{sp} in the source language into text y in the target language. For cascaded ST, a source speech utterance x^{sp} is first transcribed into text x^{text} in the source language using an ASR model, which is then translated into the target-language text y using an MT model.

The datasets we used are summarized in Table 1. Each of the official datasets provided by the organizers is either a 2-way ST or a 3-way ST dataset. A 2-way ST data sample is represented as a tuple (x^{sp}, y), while a 3-way ST data sample refers to a triple $(x^{\text{sp}}, x^{\text{text}}, y)$. 3-way ST datasets are available for aeb-eng, bem-eng, est-eng, mlt-eng, and que-spa. The other languages are provided with 2-way ST datasets. Among these, est-eng has the largest dataset with more than 1,000 hours of speech. Both aeb-eng and bem-eng have more than 100 hours of data, while datasets for other languages are limited and having only about 10 hours of speech. In addition, the organizers provide pointers to additional ASR and MT datasets. An ASR data sample is represented as $(x^{\text{sp}}, x^{\text{text}})$, while an MT data sample is represented as (x^{text}, y). It is evident that both ASR and MT datasets can be derived from 3-way ST datasets.

The task allows submissions under two conditions: constrained and unconstrained. Under the constrained condition, only the provided dataset can be used and no pre-trained models are allowed. The unconstrained condition allows the use of any models and any datasets. All of our submissions fall under the unconstrained condition.

3 Methods

Our methods focus on fine-tuning the SeamlessM4T-v2 model (Seamless Communication et al., 2023b). We explore 4 different fine-tuning strategies: (1) E2E ST fine-tuning; (2) ASR and MT fine-tuning for the cascaded system; (3) multi-task training similar to Seamless Communication et al. (2023b); (4) initializing ST model components with those from ASR and/or MT models. We fine-tune the model on a single language pair at a time. Due to the dataset availability and model performance for each language pair, not all strategies have been tried for every pair.

Although the MT components of SeamlessM4T-v2 are initialized by the NLLB model (NLLB Team et al., 2022), SeamlessM4T-v2 has been trained on less languages and supports MT for only 4 out of the 10 language pairs in this shared task. In contrast, the NLLB model supports MT for all 10 pairs. To evaluate whether the smaller language coverage of SeamlessM4T-v2 impacts performance, we additionally fine-tuned an NLLB model on the MT datasets, using it as the MT baseline. Section 3.1 introduces the NLLB and SeamlessM4T-v2 models. Section 3.2 through Section 3.5 elaborate our fine-tuning strategies.

[2]The LDC resources for apc cannot be obtained for free this year.

Language	Task	Amount	Sources
aeb-eng	ASR 3-way ST	156 hours 161 hours/202k lines	LDC2022E01
bem-eng	3-way ST	167 hours/82k lines	Sikasote et al. (2023)
fon-fra	2-way ST	47 hours	IWSLT2025 (Abdulmumin et al., 2025)
gle-eng	ASR 2-way ST 3-way ST	5 hours 7 hours 202 hours	CommonVoice 21.0 IWSLT2025 Moslem (2024)
bho-hin	2-way ST ASR	20 hours 60 hours	IWSLT2025 ULCA
est-eng	3-way ST	1213 hours/581k lines	IWSLT2025
mlt-eng	3-way ST	12 hours/9k lines	IWST2025
mar-hin	ASR 2-way ST	15 hours 16 hours	CommonVoice 21.0; He et al. (2020) IWSLT2025
que-spa	MT ASR 3-way ST	46k lines 48 hours 9 hours/2k lines	Ortega et al. (2020); NLLB Team et al. (2022) Cardenas et al. (2018) IWSLT2025; Zevallos et al. (2022)

Table 1: Summary of datasets used for training. 2-way ST refers to datasets with paired source speech and target text, while 3-way ST includes paired source speech, source text, and target text. The 3-way ST datasets can be used for ASR and MT training as well.

3.1 Base Models

NLLB (NLLB Team et al., 2022). NLLB is a multilingual MT model supporting over 200 languages, including all language pairs in this shared task. The model is available in two architecture variants: a sparsely gated mixture-of-experts (MoE) one and a set of dense transformer models. The dense transformer architecture comprises a text encoder and a text decoder. While the MoE variant (NLLB-200) achieves the strongest performance, it has 54.5B parameters and is not practical for fine-tuning. Therefore, in our experiments, we choose the 1.3B dense transformer model distilled from NLLB-200, referred to as `NLLB-200-Distilled-1.3B`.

SeamlessM4T-v2 (Seamless Communication et al., 2023b). SeamlessM4T-v2 is the state-of-the-art foundation model for ST. While it supports into-speech translation, we only focus on its into-text translation capabilities for the purpose of this shared task. SeamlessM4T-v2 is composed of a speech encoder, a text encoder, and a shared text decoder. Its `Large` variant has 2B parameters in total and we refer to it as `SeamlessM4T-v2-Large`. The speech encoder is pre-trained on 4.5M hours of unlabeled audio with the w2v-BERT 2.0 objective. The text encoder and decoder are initialized by the NLLB model. During fine-tuning, a multi-task training strategy is employed, incorporating ASR, MT, ST, and knowledge distillation (KD) objectives. We also explore this strategy in our experiments. The model supports 101 languages for speech input and 96 languages for text input and output. Among the low-resource languages in this shared task, SeamlessM4T-v2 supports `est`, `gle`, `mar`, and `mlt`, but does not support `aeb`, `bem`, `bho`, `fon`, and `que`.

3.2 E2E ST Fine-tuning

For E2E fine-tuning, we utilize 2-way ST data samples (x^{sp}, y). We use Equation 1 as the loss function to optimize the speech encoder and the text decoder.

$$L_{\text{E2E}} = -\frac{1}{|y|}\log p(y|x^{\text{sp}};\theta_{\text{se}},\theta_{\text{td}}) = -\frac{1}{|y|}\sum_{i=1}^{|y|}\log p(y_i|y_{<i},x^{\text{sp}};\theta_{\text{se}},\theta_{\text{td}}) \quad (1)$$

θ_{se} and θ_{td} denote the parameters of the speech encoder and the text decoder, respectively.

3.3 ASR and MT Fine-tuning for the Cascaded ST System

Since SeamlessM4T-v2 also supports multilingual ASR and MT, it is suitable for being fine-tuned on the low-resource languages for ASR and MT as well. Specifically, ASR data samples $(x^{\text{sp}}, x^{\text{text}})$ and MT data samples (x^{text}, y) are used. A cascaded system can then be built by a fine-tuned ASR and a fine-tuned MT model. The corresponding loss functions for ASR and MT fine-tuning are defined in Equation 2 and Equation 3, respectively. Equation 3 is also used for NLLB MT fine-tuning.

$$L_{\text{ASR}} = -\frac{1}{|x^{\text{text}}|}\log p(x^{\text{text}}|x^{\text{sp}};\theta_{\text{se}},\theta_{\text{td}}) \\ = -\frac{1}{|x^{\text{text}}|}\sum_{i=1}^{|x^{\text{text}}|}\log p(x_i^{\text{text}}|x_{<i}^{\text{text}},x^{\text{sp}};\theta_{\text{se}},\theta_{\text{td}}) \quad (2)$$

$$L_{\text{MT}} = -\frac{1}{|y|}\log p(y|x^{\text{text}};\theta_{\text{te}},\theta_{\text{td}}) \\ = -\frac{1}{y}\sum_{i=1}^{|y|}\log p(y_i|y_{<i},x^{\text{text}};\theta_{\text{te}},\theta_{\text{td}}) \quad (3)$$

θ_{te} refers to the parameters of the text encoder. We use $\theta_{\text{se}}^{\text{ASR}}$ and $\theta_{\text{td}}^{\text{ASR}}$ to denote the fine-tuned ASR components, $\theta_{\text{te}}^{\text{MT}}$ and $\theta_{\text{td}}^{\text{MT}}$ to denote the fine-tuned MT components.

3.4 Multi-task Fine-tuning

Inspired by the multi-task fine-tuning strategy in Seamless Communication et al. (2023b), we adopt a similar approach and explore its effect in the low-resource ST setting.

Our approach includes ST, MT, and KD objectives, using paired 3-way ST data samples $(x^{\text{sp}}, x^{\text{text}}, y)$. The ST objective follows Equation 1 and the MT objective follows Equation 3. The goal of applying the KD objective is to use the MT components to enhance the ST components. The motivation is that MT is generally an easier task than ST and often yields better performance, and we hope to mitigate this performance gap. In order to have a strong MT teacher, we initialize the text encoder and the text decoder in SeamlessM4T-v2 with $\theta_{\text{te}}^{\text{MT}}$ and $\theta_{\text{td}}^{\text{MT}}$ from Section 3.3, respectively. Optionally, to help with convergence, we can initialize the speech encoder with $\theta_{\text{se}}^{\text{ASR}}$. Equation 4 explains how we obtain the teacher probability distribution from the MT components.

$$p_{\text{teacher}}(\cdot|y_{<i},x^{\text{text}}) \\ = \text{stop-gradient}\left(p(\cdot|y_{<i},x^{\text{text}};\theta_{\text{te}},\theta_{\text{td}})\right) \quad (4)$$

stop-gradient$(\cdot)$ means that we detach the resultant tensor from the computation graph, thereby preventing the gradients from the teacher probability distribution being propagated to the MT teacher parameters θ_{te} and θ_{td}. We tried without stop-gradient$(\cdot)$ but observed a performance drop.

Then, we compute KL-Divergence between the student and the teacher probability distributions with Equation 5.

$$L_{\text{KD}} \\ = \frac{1}{|y|}\sum_{i=1}^{|y|} D_{\text{KL}}\left[p_{\text{teacher}}(\cdot|y_{<i},x^{\text{text}})||p(\cdot|y_{<i},x^{\text{sp}};\theta_{\text{se}},\theta_{\text{td}})\right] \\ = \frac{1}{|y|}\sum_{i=1}^{|y|}\left[p_{\text{teacher}}(\cdot|y_{<i},x^{\text{text}})\cdot\log\frac{p_{\text{teacher}}(\cdot|y_{<i},x^{\text{text}})}{p(\cdot|y_{<i},x^{\text{sp}};\theta_{\text{se}},\theta_{\text{td}})}\right] \quad (5)$$

The student probability distribution comes from the ST components θ_{se} and θ_{td}.

During fine-tuning, θ_{se} and θ_{td} are updated while θ_{te} is kept frozen. The final loss function is a linear combination of the three losses:

$$L = \alpha \cdot L_{\text{E2E}} + \beta \cdot L_{\text{MT}} + \gamma \cdot L_{\text{KD}} \quad (6)$$

where α, β, and γ are constants which can be tuned on the development set. Empirically, we found that $\alpha = 1$, $\beta = 1$, and $\gamma = 2$ worked best.

3.5 E2E ST Fine-tuning with In-domain Pre-trained Components

As mentioned in Section 3.1, the SeamlessM4T-v2 model has not been trained on 5 low-resource languages of interest. To better adapt the model to new languages for ST, we fine-tune it on in-domain ASR data with Equation 2, such that the fine-tuned speech encoder $\theta_{\text{sp}}^{\text{ASR}}$ can better capture semantics from the speech in the new language. Then, we can initialize the speech encoder of the ST model with $\theta_{\text{sp}}^{\text{ASR}}$ for E2E ST fine-tuning. Optionally, we can also initialize the text decoder by $\theta_{\text{td}}^{\text{MT}}$. However, we do not expect the fine-tuned decoder to be as helpful as the fine-tuned speech encoder, as the target language is always high-resource and the SeamlessM4T-v2 model has been trained on a lot of that. After the initializations, we perform E2E ST fine-tuning with Equation 1.

4 Experiments

We describe the additional datasets we used in Section 4.1. In Section 4.2, we describe the fine-tuning hyperparameters. The evaluation metrics are described in Section 4.3.

4.1 Dataset

All datasets are summarized in Table 1. Besides the official ST datasets provided by the organizers, we use the following additional datasets.

gle-eng. We use the synthetic 3-way ST dataset from Moslem (2024). The text is extracted from OPUS (Tiedemann, 2012), covering portions of the Wikimedia, Tatoeba, and EUbbookshop corpora. The speech is synthesized using the Azure Speech service. This synthetic dataset has about 202 hours of speech. We also use the `gle` ASR dataset from CommonVoice 21.0[3] (Ardila et al., 2020) to include real speech data.

bho-hin. We use the bho dataset from the ULCA corpus.[4] It has 60 hours of speech.

mar-hin. We collect Marathi ASR data from CommonVoice (Ardila et al., 2020) and OpenSLR64 (He et al., 2020), totaling 15 hours of speech.

que-spa. The official 3-way ST dataset has merely 1.6 hours of speech, so we try to find and use as much data as possible. We use the additional synthetic 3-way ST dataset (Zevallos et al., 2022), whose Spanish translations are generated by Google Translate. We also include the additional 48-hour ASR dataset (Cardenas et al., 2018). For MT, we use the additional MT dataset (Ortega et al., 2020) extracted from JW300 and Hinantin. The data is very noisy, so we apply extensive text cleaning strategies inspired by Koehn et al. (2018). Furthermore, we obtain the NLLB Quechua-English dataset from OPUS[5] (Tiedemann, 2012). This dataset is obtained by text mining (Fan et al., 2020; Schwenk et al., 2021). We translate the English text into Spanish by applying `NLLB-200-Distilled-1.3B`, creating a synthetic Quechua-Spanish MT dataset having approximately 34k lines.

In general, for ASR, MT, and E2E ST experiments, we use their designated datasets as well as subsets extracted from the 3-way ST datasets if available.

In our experiments, we keep the text in their original form. No text normalization is performed, except for apostrophe normalization in `fon`. All speech files are resampled to 16khz if they originally have a different sampling rate.

4.2 Experiment Setup

We fine-tune `SeamlessM4T-v2-Large` for all language pairs. Two codebases are used in our experiments. One is the official repository,[6] which is for E2E ST fine-tuning (Section 3.2) only. To support all fine-tuning strategies, we have implemented a second codebase based on the HuggingFace Transformers toolkit[7] (Wolf et al., 2020). The HuggingFace codebase is designed to be identical to the official fine-tuning script. However, in practice, we observed some performance gaps between the two codebases, which we discuss in detail in Appendix A.

Additionally, we fine-tune `NLLB-200-Distilled-1.3B` as the MT baseline (the reason is discussed in Section 3).

For all experiments, we use the AdamW optimizer (Loshchilov and Hutter, 2019) with betas $(0.9, 0.98)$, and no weight decay. Models are trained for a maximum of 10 epochs. We use a learning rate of 1e-4, with the first epoch being the warmup phase. For E2E ST fine-tuning with model components initialized by ASR and/or MT components, we use a smaller learning rate of 6e-5. We use the inverse square root learning rate scheduler. The batch size is 120 utterances for speech input tasks (ASR and ST) and 256 sentences for text input tasks (MT). The label smoothing weight is 0.2. These hyperparameters can be slightly adjusted for different language pairs depending on dataset characteristics. For instance, for `que-spa`, we use a learning rate of 1e-5 for ST fine-tuning and the maximum epoch number is 200. For ASR fine-tuning on `est-eng` and `que-spa`, the batch size is 72 utterances due to longer input durations. Lastly, for MT fine-tuning, the hyperparameters for NLLB are exactly the same as `SeamlessM4T-v2`. During inference, we use a beam size of 5 and length penalty of 1.0.

4.3 Evaluation Metrics

We evaluate ASR performance using word error rate (WER) and character error rate (CER) with the `jiwer`[8] package. For MT performance, we use SacreBLEU[9] (Post, 2018) to compute BLEU[10] scores. For both evaluations, text is lowercased and punctuations are removed before scoring.

[3] https://commonvoice.mozilla.org/en/datasets

[4] https://github.com/Open-Speech-EkStep/ULCA-asr-dataset-corpus

[5] https://opus.nlpl.eu/NLLB/qu&en/v1/NLLB

[6] https://github.com/facebookresearch/seamless_communication

[7] https://huggingface.co/docs/transformers/main/model_doc/seamless_m4t_v2

[8] https://github.com/jitsi/jiwer

[9] https://github.com/mjpost/sacrebleu

[10] Signature: nrefs:1 + case:lc + eff:no + tok:13a + smooth:exp + version:2.5.1

Lang	System	Dev		Public Test	
		CER	WER	CER	WER
aeb	Seamless-FT	20.7	41.2	24.6	49.0
bem	Seamless-FT	9.27	31.08	8.86	30.40
gle	Seamless-0s	14.27	23.90	14.79	24.61
	Seamless-FT	5.51	9.47	4.71	8.39
bho†	Seamless-FT	32.68	41.86	-	-
est	Seamless-0s	12.94	22.22	-	-
	Seamless-FT	3.06	8.59	-	-
mlt	Seamless-0s	8.57	20.68	-	-
	Seamless-FT	3.69	12.12	-	-
mar†	Seamless-0s	4.28	17.40	4.73	18.44
	Seamless-FT	1.90	8.42	8.15	2.08
que	Seamless-FT	15.54	37.80	-	-

Table 2: ASR results for languages with available ASR datasets. †: Models are **not** evaluated on official IWSLT2025 datasets but on additional ASR datasets. The bho model is evaluated on ULCA, and the mar model is evaluated on CommonVoice. **0s** denotes a zero-shot model, while **FT** denotes a fine-tuned model.

Lang	System	Eval 1		Eval 2	
		CER	WER	CER	WER
aeb	Seamless-FT	19.7	38	22.3	39.9
bem	Seamless-FT	8.96	30.62	-	-

Table 3: Official ASR Evaluation results for aeb and bem. We did not submit hypothesis for other language pairs unfortunately.

5 Results and Analysis

We first present the ASR and MT performance in Section 5.1 and 5.2, respectively. Then, we summarize the ST performance in Section 5.3. The ablation study of using additional datasets is presented in Appendix B.

5.1 Automatic Speech Recognition

Internal evaluation results are presented in Table 2, and the official evaluation results (Abdulmumin et al., 2025) are in Table 3. **Seamless-FT** refers to SeamlessM4T-v2-Large fine-tuned on all available ASR datasets, while **Seamless-0s** refers to SeamlessM4T-v2-Large evaluated in a zero-shot manner without fine-tuning. Languages without zero-shot results are not supported by SeamlessM4T-v2's ASR capability. For bho and mar, no official ASR datasets are provided by the organizers, so we evaluate them on held-out subsets from ULCA and CommonVoice, respectively.

The zero-shot performances on gle, est, mlt, and mar are relatively strong, all with WER around 20% and CER around 10%. Further fine-tuning on in-domain ASR datasets yields substantial improvements, reducing both CER and WER by about 50% in relative value. For languages that SeamlessM4T-v2 has not been trained on, ASR performance is poorer. aeb and bho are particularly challenging, with WERs greater than 40%. que also has a high WER of 37.8%. The model performs relatively well on bem, achieving a low CER of approximately 9%, although its WER remains high at around 30%. We can conclude from these results that the fine-tuned SeamlessM4T-v2-Large performs better on languages it has been trained on.

Lang	System	Dev BLEU	Public Test BLEU
aeb	NLLB-0s	11.05	8.98
	NLLB-FT	**30.48**	27.11
	Seamless-FT	30.39	**27.54**
bem	NLLB-0s	8.57	8.58
	NLLB-FT	**29.20**	**30.42**
	Seamless-FT	28.86	29.27
est	NLLB-0s	31.60	-
	Seamless-0s	30.33	-
	NLLB-FT	32.85	-
	Seamless-FT	**40.23**	-
mlt	NLLB-0s	50.39	-
	Seamless-0s	53.96	-
	NLLB-FT	**64.29**	-
	Seamless-FT	62.13	
que	NLLB-0s	5.05	-
	NLLB-FT	**15.98**	-
	Seamless-FT	15.29	-

Table 4: MT results for languages with available MT datasets. **0s** denotes a zero-shot model, while **FT** denotes a fine-tuned model. There are only small gaps between NLLB-FT and Seamless-FT.

5.2 Text Machine Translation

Table 4 presents MT performance for languages with available MT datasets. We report both 0-shot and fine-tuned results for SeamlessM4T-v2-Large and NLLB-200-Distilled-1.3B. **NLLB-0s** and **Seamless-0s** refer to the zero-shot performance, while **NLLB-FT** and **Seamless-FT** refer to the fine-tuned results. Note that NLLB results are used only for reference. The fine-tuned NLLB-200-Distilled-1.3B are neither used for submissions nor for model initialization.

Fine-tuning on the in-domain MT datasets leads to substantial improvements. NLLB-200-Distilled-1.3B achieves +10 BLEU for all languages, except for est, where the

Lang	Dev	Public Test
aeb	4.29	3.22
bem	0.93	0.93
fon	1.09	-
gle	28.98	47.66
bho	25.28	-
est	26.21	-
mlt	50.02	-
mar	24.07	31.77
que	1.47	-

Table 5: Zero-shot SeamlessM4T-v2-Large ST results for all languages. Results are obtained using the official codebase.

gain is +1.25 BLEU. For aeb and bem, the improvements even reach approximately +20 BLEU. Despite being trained on fewer languages, the fine-tuned SeamlessM4T-v2-Large achieves performance comparable to that of the fine-tuned NLLB-200-Distilled-1.3B. This justifies our choice of adopting SeamlessM4T-v2-Large as the MT model.

5.3 Speech Translation

Internal evaluation and official evaluation (Abdulmumin et al., 2025) results are presented in Table 6. The **HF** prefix indicates models fine-tuned using the HuggingFace toolkit, while the **OFF** prefix refers to models fine-tuned with the official codebase. For a fair comparison, we compare results obtained from the same codebase. **E2E** refers to E2E ST fine-tuning (Section 3.2), **Cascaded** refers to the cascaded ST system (Section 3.3), and **MLT** denotes multi-task fine-tuning (Section 3.4). $\mathbf{ASR_{init}}$ and $\mathbf{MT_{init}}$ indicate that the speech encoder and the text decoder are initialized with the fine-tuned ASR encoder and MT decoder, respectively (Section 3.5). For gle, results are reported without using the synthetic ST dataset (Moslem, 2024), as we observed a performance drop when including it. Additionally, we report the zero-shot performance of SeamlessM4T-v2-Large in Table 5.

The official codebase yields stronger performance. In Table 6, E2E ST fine-tuning using the official codebase performs strongest in 5 out of 9 languages. It is unexpected that the official codebase (OFF-E2E) outperforms the HuggingFace codebase (HF-E2E) in all languages except for bem and mar. We discuss the discrepancies in Appendix A.

E2E ST fine-tuning produces strong models in general. Compared to the zero-shot SeamlessM4T-v2-Large performance in Table 5, E2E ST fine-tuning leads to substantial improvements. For aeb, bem, fon, and que whose zero-shot BLEU scores are close to 0, E2E fine-tuning improves by about +20, +30, +40, and +10 BLEU, respectively. For languages where SeamlessM4T-v2-Large has good performance already, E2E fine-tuning yields improvements of at least +10 BLEU, except for gle, which has a modest gain of +1 BLEU. Overall, E2E ST fine-tuning (including both OFF-E2E and HF-E2E) achieves the best performance in 6 out of the 9 languages. Notably, for bem, the E2E ST result even surpasses the MT result by about 2 BLEU.

E2E ST fine-tuning performs best for languages with ASR support. Next, we compare different fine-tuning strategies. For a fair comparison, we compare results obtained by the HF codebase. HF-E2E performs best in gle, mlt and mar, exactly the languages that SeamlessM4T-v2-Large provides ASR support. Having been trained on large amounts of ASR data, SeamlessM4T-v2-Large already has a strong capability to extract semantics from speech in those languages. Further fine-tuning on our own small ASR datasets may just hurt the model's generalization capability. However, ASR encoder initialization has only a minor negative effect, with a performance drop less than 1 BLEU.

In-domain pre-training improves performance for languages without ASR support. For languages that SeamlessM4T-v2-Large does not support ASR for, fine-tuning on in-domain ASR datasets improve the ST performance. Specifically, for bho and aeb, ASR training improves performance by about +5 and +3 BLEU, respectively. Smaller gains of about +1 BLEU are observed for bem and que, while the remaining languages see improvements of less than 1 BLEU. In contrast, text decoder initialization is less effective. It provides a slight improvement for que but hurts aeb performance.

Multi-task training is beneficial when MT performance is strong. We explored multi-task training for aeb, mlt, and que, languages for which fine-tuned MT models outperform E2E ST models. The gaps are approximately 8, 5, and 2 BLEU, respectively. Multi-task improves aeb performance by 2 BLEU and improves que by about 0.7 BLEU. However, there is no improvement for mlt.

Cascaded systems are competitive but generally underperform E2E ST fine-tuning. We evaluate cascaded systems for aeb, bem, est, mlt, and que. Among these, the cascaded system only outperforms E2E ST fine-tuning in est, with a

Lang	System	Submission	Dev	Public Test	Eval 1	Eval 2
aeb	HF-E2E-ASR$_{init}$	Primary	**25.48**	**21.41**	**20.30**	**17.8**†
	HF-MLT-ASR$_{init}$	Contrastive 1	24.64	21.18	19.2	17.3
	HF-Cascaded	Contrastive 2	24.42	21.01	18.90	17.3
	HF-MLT	-	24.23	20.33	-	-
	HF-E2E-ASR$_{init}$-MT$_{init}$	-	24.08	20.41	-	-
	OFF-E2E	-	23.76	19.67	-	-
	HF-E2E	-	22.73	18.35	-	-
bem	HF-E2E-ASR$_{init}$	Primary	**31.96**	**32.12**	**31.7**	-
	HF-E2E	Contrastive 1	31.14	30.93	30.6	-
	HF-Cascaded	Contrastive 2	28.02	28.02	27.9	-
	OFF-E2E	-	30.69	31.23	-	-
fon	OFF-E2E	Primary	**40.86**	-	**31.96**	-
gle*	OFF-E2E	Primary	**29.63**	51.91	**13.4**	-
	HF-E2E	Contrastive 1	24.07	51.21	8.4	-
	HF-E2E-ASR$_{init}$	Contrastive 2	23.34	51.43	6.7	-
bho	OFF-E2E	Primary	**41.96**	-	**3.9**	-
	HF-E2E-ASR$_{init}$	Contrastive 1	39.04	-	3.4	-
	HF-E2E	Contrastive 2	33.92	-	2	-
est	OFF-E2E	Primary	**38.07**	-	29.8	-
	HF-Cascaded	Contrastive 1	38.00	-	**30.2**	-
	HF-E2E-ASR$_{init}$	Contrastive 2	36.97	-	29.6	-
	HF-E2E	-	36.89	-	-	-
mlt	OFF-E2E	Primary	**57.92**	-	**67.1**	**47.87**‡
	HF-E2E	Contrastive 1	57.65	-	64.21	48.53
	HF-E2E-ASR$_{init}$	Contrastive 2	57.57	-	63.23	48.65
	HF-MLT	-	57.46	-	-	-
	HF-Cascaded	-	57.04	-	-	-
mar	HF-E2E	Primary	**44.84**	**53.80**	43.4	-
	HF-E2E-ASR$_{init}$	Contrastive 1	44.72	53.77	**44.3**	-
	OFF-E2E	Contrastive 2	42.52	51.34	41.5	-
que	HF-E2E-ASR$_{init}$-MT$_{init}$	Primary	**13.37**	-	12.7	-
	HF-MLT-ASR$_{init}$	Contrastive 1	13.03	-	12.9	-
	HF-E2E-ASR$_{init}$	Contrastive 2	13.00	-	**13.0**	-
	HF-Cascaded	-	13.15	-	-	-
	HF-E2E	-	12.32	-	-	-

Table 6: ST results for all languages. **HF-*** means the model is trained with HuggingFace toolkit, while **OFF-*** refers to the official codebase. **Eval** refers to the official evaluation result. *For gle, the results are obtained without using the synthetic data (Moslem, 2024). †For aeb, Eval 1 refers to LDC20022E02 and Eval 2 refers to LDC2023E09. ‡For mlt, Eval 1 refers to CV and Eval 2 refers to Masri.

modest gain of +1 BLEU. For bem and mlt, cascaded systems even underperform direct E2E ST fine-tuning. For aeb and que, although cascaded systems are better than direct E2E ST fine-tuning, they fall short compared to ST models initialized with in-domain pre-trained components.

6 Conclusion and Future Work

In this paper, we describe GMU systems for the IWSLT 2025 Low-resource ST shared task. We focus on fine-tuning the SeamlessM4T-v2-Large model and explore four fine-tuning strategies. We find that E2E ST fine-tuning performs best on languages with ASR support. For languages without ASR support, we can fine-tune the model on in-domain ASR datasets first and then initialize the ST encoder with the ASR encoder, which significantly improves performance. Multi-task training and cascaded systems are not as good as E2E fine-tuning in general. We hypothesize that it is because SeamlessM4T-v2-Large is strong enough on ST, and the fine-tuned MT performance is not strong enough to provide useful additional performance gains.

For future work, we could explore better pre-training methods to mitigate the gap between the speech encoder and the text decoder (Le et al., 2023). We could also explore the use of speech large language models, as large language models have recently achieved success in MT tasks (Kocmi et al., 2024).

Acknowledgements

We are thankful to the Shared Task organizers and the anonymous reviewers for their valuable feedback. This work is supported by the National Science Foundation under awards IIS-2327143 and CIRC-2346334.

References

Idris Abdulmumin, Victor Agostinelli, Tanel Alumäe, Antonios Anastasopoulos, Ashwin, Luisa Bentivogli, Ondřej Bojar, Claudia Borg, Fethi Bougares, Roldano Cattoni, Mauro Cettolo, Lizhong Chen, William Chen, Raj Dabre, Yannick Estève, Marcello Federico, Marco Gaido, Dávid Javorský, Marek Kasztelnik, and 30 others. 2025. Findings of the iwslt 2025 evaluation campaign. In *Proceedings of the 22nd International Conference on Spoken Language Translation (IWSLT 2025)*, Vienna, Austria (in-person and online). Association for Computational Linguistics. To appear.

Milind Agarwal, Sweta Agrawal, Antonios Anastasopoulos, Luisa Bentivogli, Ondřej Bojar, Claudia Borg, Marine Carpuat, Roldano Cattoni, Mauro Cettolo, Mingda Chen, William Chen, Khalid Choukri, Alexandra Chronopoulou, Anna Currey, Thierry Declerck, Qianqian Dong, Kevin Duh, Yannick Estève, Marcello Federico, and 43 others. 2023. FINDINGS OF THE IWSLT 2023 EVALUATION CAMPAIGN. In *Proceedings of the 20th International Conference on Spoken Language Translation (IWSLT 2023)*, pages 1–61, Toronto, Canada (in-person and online). Association for Computational Linguistics.

Ibrahim Said Ahmad, Antonios Anastasopoulos, Ondřej Bojar, Claudia Borg, Marine Carpuat, Roldano Cattoni, Mauro Cettolo, William Chen, Qianqian Dong, Marcello Federico, Barry Haddow, Dávid Javorský, Mateusz Krubiński, Tsz Kin Lam, Xutai Ma, Prashant Mathur, Evgeny Matusov, Chandresh Maurya, John McCrae, and 25 others. 2024. FINDINGS OF THE IWSLT 2024 EVALUATION CAMPAIGN. In *Proceedings of the 21st International Conference on Spoken Language Translation (IWSLT 2024)*, pages 1–11, Bangkok, Thailand (in-person and online). Association for Computational Linguistics.

Antonios Anastasopoulos, Loïc Barrault, Luisa Bentivogli, Marcely Zanon Boito, Ondřej Bojar, Roldano Cattoni, Anna Currey, Georgiana Dinu, Kevin Duh, Maha Elbayad, Clara Emmanuel, Yannick Estève, Marcello Federico, Christian Federmann, Souhir Gahbiche, Hongyu Gong, Roman Grundkiewicz, Barry Haddow, Benjamin Hsu, and 24 others. 2022. Findings of the IWSLT 2022 evaluation campaign. In *Proceedings of the 19th International Conference on Spoken Language Translation (IWSLT 2022)*, pages 98–157, Dublin, Ireland (in-person and online). Association for Computational Linguistics.

Rosana Ardila, Megan Branson, Kelly Davis, Michael Kohler, Josh Meyer, Michael Henretty, Reuben Morais, Lindsay Saunders, Francis Tyers, and Gregor Weber. 2020. Common voice: A massively-multilingual speech corpus. In *Proceedings of the Twelfth Language Resources and Evaluation Conference*, pages 4218–4222, Marseille, France. European Language Resources Association.

Ronald Cardenas, Rodolfo Zevallos, Reynaldo Baquerizo, and Luis Camacho. 2018. Siminchik: A speech corpus for preservation of southern quechua. *ISI-NLP 2*, page 21.

Alexis Conneau, Alexei Baevski, Ronan Collobert, Abdelrahman Mohamed, and Michael Auli. 2021. Unsupervised Cross-Lingual Representation Learning for Speech Recognition. In *Interspeech 2021*, pages 2426–2430.

Angela Fan, Shruti Bhosale, Holger Schwenk, Zhiyi Ma, Ahmed El-Kishky, Siddharth Goyal, Mandeep Baines, Onur Celebi, Guillaume Wenzek, Vishrav Chaudhary, Naman Goyal, Tom Birch, Vitaliy Liptchinsky, Sergey Edunov, Edouard Grave, Michael Auli, and Armand Joulin. 2020. Beyond English-Centric Multilingual Machine Translation. *Preprint*, arXiv:2010.11125.

Fei He, Shan-Hui Cathy Chu, Oddur Kjartansson, Clara Rivera, Anna Katanova, Alexander Gutkin, Isin Demirsahin, Cibu Johny, Martin Jansche, Supheakmungkol Sarin, and Knot Pipatsrisawat. 2020. Open-source multi-speaker speech corpora for building Gujarati, Kannada, Malayalam, Marathi, Tamil and Telugu speech synthesis systems. In *Proceedings of the Twelfth Language Resources and Evaluation Conference*, pages 6494–6503, Marseille, France. European Language Resources Association.

Tom Kocmi, Eleftherios Avramidis, Rachel Bawden, Ondřej Bojar, Anton Dvorkovich, Christian Federmann, Mark Fishel, Markus Freitag, Thamme Gowda, Roman Grundkiewicz, Barry Haddow, Marzena Karpinska, Philipp Koehn, Benjamin Marie, Christof Monz, Kenton Murray, Masaaki Nagata, Martin Popel, Maja Popović, and 3 others. 2024. Findings of the WMT24 general machine translation shared task: The LLM era is here but MT is not solved yet. In *Proceedings of the Ninth Conference on Machine Translation*, pages 1–46, Miami, Florida, USA. Association for Computational Linguistics.

Philipp Koehn, Huda Khayrallah, Kenneth Heafield, and Mikel L. Forcada. 2018. Findings of the WMT 2018 shared task on parallel corpus filtering. In *Proceedings of the Third Conference on Machine Translation: Shared Task Papers*, pages 726–739, Belgium, Brussels. Association for Computational Linguistics.

Phuong-Hang Le, Hongyu Gong, Changhan Wang, Juan Pino, Benjamin Lecouteux, and Didier Schwab. 2023. Pre-training for speech translation: CTC meets optimal transport. In *International Conference on Machine Learning*, pages 18667–18685. PMLR.

Ilya Loshchilov and Frank Hutter. 2019. Decoupled Weight Decay Regularization. *Preprint*, arXiv:1711.05101.

Yasmin Moslem. 2024. Leveraging synthetic audio data for end-to-end low-resource speech translation. In *Proceedings of the 2024 International Conference on Spoken Language Translation (IWSLT 2024)*, Bangkok, Thailand.

NLLB Team, Marta R. Costa-jussà, James Cross, Onur Çelebi, Maha Elbayad, Kenneth Heafield, Kevin Heffernan, Elahe Kalbassi, Janice Lam, Daniel Licht, Jean Maillard, Anna Sun, Skyler Wang, Guillaume Wenzek, Al Youngblood, Bapi Akula, Loic Barrault, Gabriel Mejia-Gonzalez, Prangthip Hansanti, and 20 others. 2022. No language left behind: Scaling human-centered machine translation.

John E Ortega, Richard Castro Mamani, and Kyunghyun Cho. 2020. Neural machine translation with a polysynthetic low resource language. *Machine Translation*, 34(4):325–346.

Matt Post. 2018. A call for clarity in reporting BLEU scores. In *Proceedings of the Third Conference on Machine Translation: Research Papers*, pages 186–191, Brussels, Belgium. Association for Computational Linguistics.

Alec Radford, Jong Wook Kim, Tao Xu, Greg Brockman, Christine Mcleavey, and Ilya Sutskever. 2023. Robust Speech Recognition via Large-Scale Weak Supervision. In *Proceedings of the 40th International Conference on Machine Learning*, volume 202 of *Proceedings of Machine Learning Research*, pages 28492–28518. PMLR.

Holger Schwenk, Guillaume Wenzek, Sergey Edunov, Edouard Grave, Armand Joulin, and Angela Fan. 2021. CCMatrix: Mining billions of high-quality parallel sentences on the web. In *Proceedings of the 59th Annual Meeting of the Association for Computational Linguistics and the 11th International Joint Conference on Natural Language Processing (Volume 1: Long Papers)*, pages 6490–6500, Online. Association for Computational Linguistics.

Seamless Communication, Loïc Barrault, Yu-An Chung, Mariano Cora Meglioli, David Dale, Ning Dong, Paul-Ambroise Duquenne, Hady Elsahar, Hongyu Gong, Kevin Heffernan, John Hoffman, Christopher Klaiber, Pengwei Li, Daniel Licht, Jean Maillard, Alice Rakotoarison, Kaushik Ram Sadagopan, Guillaume Wenzek, Ethan Ye, and 49 others. 2023a. SeamlessM4T: Massively Multilingual & Multimodal Machine Translation. *Preprint*, arXiv:2308.11596.

Seamless Communication, Loïc Barrault, Yu-An Chung, Mariano Coria Meglioli, David Dale, Ning Dong, Mark Duppenthaler, Paul-Ambroise Duquenne, Brian Ellis, Hady Elsahar, Justin Haaheim, John Hoffman, Min-Jae Hwang, Hirofumi Inaguma, Christopher Klaiber, Ilia Kulikov, Pengwei Li, Daniel Licht, Jean Maillard, and 46 others. 2023b. Seamless: Multilingual Expressive and Streaming Speech Translation. *Preprint*, arXiv:2312.05187.

Claytone Sikasote, Eunice Mukonde, Md Mahfuz Ibn Alam, and Antonios Anastasopoulos. 2023. BIG-C: a multimodal multi-purpose dataset for Bemba. In *Proceedings of the 61st Annual Meeting of the Association for Computational Linguistics (Volume 1: Long Papers)*, pages 2062–2078, Toronto, Canada. Association for Computational Linguistics.

Jörg Tiedemann. 2012. Parallel data, tools and interfaces in OPUS. In *Proceedings of the Eighth International Conference on Language Resources and Evaluation (LREC'12)*, pages 2214–2218, Istanbul, Turkey. European Language Resources Association (ELRA).

Thomas Wolf, Lysandre Debut, Victor Sanh, Julien Chaumond, Clement Delangue, Anthony Moi, Pierric Cistac, Tim Rault, Remi Louf, Morgan Funtowicz, Joe Davison, Sam Shleifer, Patrick von Platen, Clara Ma, Yacine Jernite, Julien Plu, Canwen Xu, Teven Le Scao, Sylvain Gugger, and 3 others. 2020. Transformers: State-of-the-art natural language processing. In *Proceedings of the 2020 Conference on Empirical Methods in Natural Language Processing: System Demonstrations*, pages 38–45, Online. Association for Computational Linguistics.

Rodolfo Zevallos, Luis Camacho, and Nelsi Melgarejo. 2022. Huqariq: A multilingual speech corpus of native languages of peru forspeech recognition. In *Proceedings of the Thirteenth Language Resources and Evaluation Conference*, pages 5029–5034.

A Discrepancies between codebases

There are three discrepancies between our HuggingFace codebase and the official codebase.

Loss on the target language code. During training, the target sequence is formatted as $[< /\mathrm{s} >, < \mathrm{lang} >, \mathrm{token}_1, \ldots, \mathrm{token}_n, < /\mathrm{s} >]$, where $< /\mathrm{s} >$ is both the start-of-sentence and end-of-sentence token, and $< \mathrm{lang} >$ denotes the language code. The text decoder takes as input $[< /\mathrm{s} >, < \mathrm{lang} >, \mathrm{token}_1, \ldots, \mathrm{token}_n]$. The losses described in Section 3 are computed using $[< \mathrm{lang} >, \mathrm{token}_1, \ldots, \mathrm{token}_n, < /\mathrm{s} >]$ as the label. The official codebase ignores the loss on the first label, i.e., $< \mathrm{lang} >$. However, we still include this loss, because we use the same codebase for ASR and we want to train the language code embedding for newly added languages like <aeb>.

Parameter sharing of word embeddings. There are three word embeddings in a SeamlessM4T model: a text encoder embedding, a text decoder input embedding, and a text decoder output embedding (also termed `lm_head`). These three embeddings are intended to share the same weight matrix. However, in the official codebase, the `lm_head` is accidentally untied from the other two embeddings during model initialization, resulting in additional 262M trainable parameters. In contrast, the HuggingFace codebase still ties all three embeddings.

Dropout modules. There are a few dropout modules in the HuggingFace model that differ from the official model.

1. `ffn_dropout` in the decoder layers: The HuggingFace model uses $p = 0.0$, whereas the official model uses $p = 0.1$.

2. `dropout` in the `self_attn` module of the adapter layer: The HuggingFace model uses $p = 0.0$, while the official model uses $p = 0.1$.

3. `intermediate_dropout` in the `ffn` module of the adapter layer: The HuggingFace model uses $p = 0.1$, while the official model uses $p = 0.0$.

4. There is a dropout module with $p = 0.1$ applied to the text decoder input word embedding in the official model, but it is missing in the HuggingFace model.

We are able to fix the first 3 dropout modules easily. However, adding a missing dropout module for the last one would require some more efforts, so we leave it unresolved for now.

We also present experiment results on aeb after addressing these discrepancies. As Table 7 shows, the HuggingFace model achieves performance comparable as the official model for E2E ST after resolving all three discrepancies (+`lm_head`+dropout+lang). Addressing only a single or two of the discrepancies does not have a significant effect.

System	Dev BLEU	Public Test BLEU
OFF-E2E	23.76	19.67
HF-E2E	22.73	18.35
+`lm_head`	22.88	19.14
+dropout	22.88	19.22
+lang	22.36	18.86
+dropout	**23.50**	**20.12**
+dropout	22.58	19.52

Table 7: ST results for aeb. **+lm_head** means the lm_head is untied from word embeddings. **+dropout** means we use the same drop modules as in the official model. **+lang** means we do not compute loss on the target language code. Combining all three changes yields comparable performance as the official codebase.

B Ablation study of using additional datasets

In this section, we present results when using different amounts of ST training data for `gle` and que.

gle-eng. There are approximately 7 hours of official 2-way ST data and about 200 hours of synthetic 3-way ST data (Moslem, 2024) available for `gle`. We attempted to incorporate the synthetic 3-way ST data into E2E ST fine-tuning. However, it did not help as shown in Table 8. When training on the official ST dataset only, the dev set performance is 29.63 BLEU. In contrast, training on both the official and synthetic data results in a performance drop of 1 BLEU.

Datasets	Dev BLEU	Public Test BLEU
IWSLT2025	**29.63**	51.91
+Moslem (2024)	28.69	51.46

Table 8: gle-eng results on the IWSLT2025 dev set. All models are trained using the official codebase.

que-spa. There are only 1.67 hours of official 3-way ST data for que. Additional resources include approximately 8 hours of synthetic 3-way data (Zevallos et al., 2022), about 12k lines of MT data (Ortega et al., 2020), and about 48 hours of ASR data (Cardenas et al., 2018). We also created a synthetic que-spa MT dataset using the NLLB (NLLB Team et al., 2022) que-eng alignments, resulting in approximately 34k lines of bitext. Details have been described in Section 4.1.

The ASR, MT, and E2E ST results are presented in Table 9, Table 10, Table 11, respectively, which show that incorporating all available datasets improve the performance across all three tasks. For ASR, using additional data reduces CER by 3.65 and WER by 12.98 in absolute value. For MT, incorporating Zevallos et al. (2022) and Ortega et al. (2020) substantially improves the performance by 8.5 BLEU. Although the synthetic NLLB dataset is the largest, adding it only yields a marginal further improvement of 0.91 BLEU. For ST, adding the synthetic dataset significantly improves E2E ST by 8.59 BLEU. While the gains are smaller for E2E-ASR$_{\text{init}}$ and E2E-ASR$_{\text{init}}$-MT$_{\text{init}}$, the additional data still improves the performance by 3.16 and 2.95 BLEU, respectively. The ASR and MT models used for initialization are the best ones from Table 9 and Table 10, respectively.

Datasets	Dev	
	CER	WER
IWSLT2025	19.19	50.78
+Zevallos et al. (2022)	16.97	41.14
+Cardenas et al. (2018)	**15.54**	**37.80**

Table 9: ASR results on the ASR split of the official 3-way ST dev set.

Datasets	Dev BLEU
IWSLT2025	5.88
+Zevallos et al. (2022) +Ortega et al. (2020)	14.38
+NLLB Team et al. (2022)	**15.29**

Table 10: MT results on the MT split of the official 3-way ST dev set.

Datasets	System	Dev BLEU
IWSLT2025	E2E	3.73
	E2E-ASR$_{\text{init}}$	9.84
	E2E-ASR$_{\text{init}}$-MT$_{\text{init}}$	10.42
+Zevallos et al. (2022)	E2E	12.32
	E2E-ASR$_{\text{init}}$	13.00
	E2E-ASR$_{\text{init}}$-MT$_{\text{init}}$	**13.37**

Table 11: ST results on the ST split of the official 3-way ST dev set. Models are trained using the HuggingFace codebase. The ASR and MT models are the best ones trained on all available ASR and MT datasets, respectively.

BeaverTalk: Oregon State University's IWSLT 2025 Simultaneous Speech Translation System

Matthew Raffel, Victor Agostinelli, and Lizhong Chen
Oregon State University
{raffelm, agostinv, chenliz}@oregonstate.edu

Abstract

This paper discusses the construction, fine-tuning, and deployment of BeaverTalk[1], a cascaded system for speech-to-text translation as part of the IWSLT 2025 simultaneous translation task. The system architecture employs a VAD segmenter for breaking a speech stream into segments, Whisper Large V2 for automatic speech recognition (ASR), and Gemma 3 12B for simultaneous translation. Regarding the simultaneous translation LLM, it is fine-tuned via low-rank adaptors (LoRAs) for a conversational prompting strategy that leverages a single prior-sentence memory bank from the source language as context. The cascaded system participated in the English→German and English→Chinese language directions for both the low and high latency regimes. In particular, on the English→German task, the system achieves a BLEU of 24.64 and 27.83 at a StreamLAAL of 1837.86 and 3343.73, respectively. Then, on the English→Chinese task, the system achieves a BLEU of 34.07 and 37.23 at a StreamLAAL of 2216.99 and 3521.35, respectively.

1 Introduction

This paper covers Oregon State University's simultaneous translation system, BeaverTalk, for IWSLT 2025. The system constructed takes in a speech stream input and outputs text translation in a cascaded manner for two language pairs, those being English→German (en→de) and English→Chinese (en→zh). Unique to IWSLT 2025's simultaneous translation task (Abdulmumin et al., 2025), this system generates translation for unsegmented audio. Architecture-wise, the system includes a VAD speech segmenter (Team, 2024), breaking a speech stream into segments, Whisper Large V2 (Radford et al., 2022) performing automatic speech recognition (ASR), and a fine-tuned Gemma 3 12B model (Team et al., 2025) that performs context-aware conversational prompting to generate a simultaneous translation.

The simultaneous translation portion of this cascaded system is fine-tuned on OpenSubtitles v2018 (Lison et al., 2018) across both language pairs. Given the unsegmented source for this task, leveraging additional context is possible and likely to improve results, based on prior work (Papi et al., 2024). As such, our system utilizes a single-sentence memory bank for the source language as context. This memory bank required modifying the typical conversational prompting structure for simultaneous translation(Wang et al., 2024).

Although a fine-tuned Gemma 3 12B leveraging conversational prompting is a powerful model for simultaneous translation, its application in a cascaded architecture suffers from typical issues of error propagation (Tran et al., 2022; Zhou et al., 2024). As such, maximizing the capabilities of a powerful simultaneous translation LLM requires minimizing these errors in the preceding steps, consisting of the VAD segmenter and Whisper ASR model. As such, we conduct an extensive inference time hyperparameter search aimed at minimizing error propagation. From the joint contributions of our cascaded simultaneous translation system and minimization of error propagation, we achieve impressive results on the ACL 60/60 development set. For example, on the English→German language pair, our cascaded system achieves a BLEU of 24.64 and 27.83 at a streamLAAL of 1837.86 and 3343.73. Furthermore, on the English→Chinese task, our system achieves a BLEU of 34.07 and 37.23 at a streamLAAL of 2216.99 and 3521.35.

2 Task Description

Simultaneous translation, generally speaking, is the process of taking in some source context and making translation decisions to another language

[1]Our fine-tuning and evaluation code is available at `https://github.com/OSU-STARLAB/BeaverTalk`

Proceedings of the 22nd International Conference on Spoken Language Translation (IWSLT 2025), pages 301–308
July 31 - August 1, 2025 ©2025 Association for Computational Linguistics

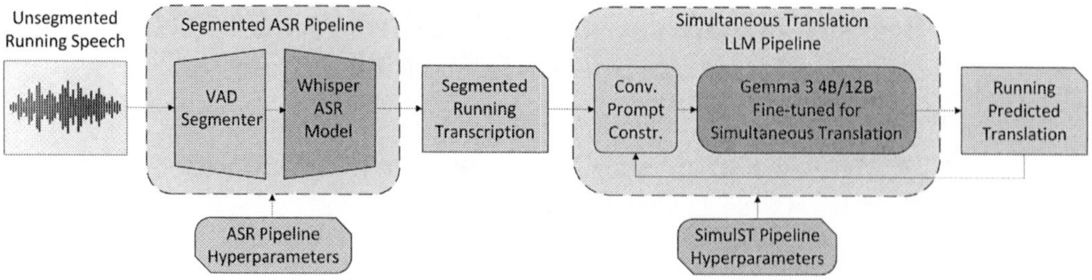

Figure 1: Depiction of the cascaded system described in this technical paper. Unsegmented source audio is taken in and fed into an ASR pipeline that segments the audio and then transcribes it into a hard text data modality. This segmented, running transcription is then fed into a simultaneous translation pipeline powered by Gemma 3. The transcription and current translation are fed into a conversational prompt constructor, adapted from prior work.

in a manner that does not rely on that source context being complete. For example, typical neural machine translation (NMT) might act on a sentence-to-sentence basis, taking in a source sentence and outputting a target sentence. In comparison, a simultaneous translation must balance the lagging factor of output translations (i.e., the time it takes from a piece of source context to a corresponding piece of the output translation) with translation quality, making translation decisions with only partial context.

As previously mentioned, the IWSLT 2025 simultaneous translation task (Abdulmumin et al., 2025) is fundamentally a speech-to-text task with two tracks governing what systems participants are expected to build: text-to-text where participants only construct a simultaneous agent for text data and prepend this system with an ASR model and speech-to-text where the simultaneous system takes in raw speech and outputs target translations in text without the need for a conversion to a text data modality. Our constructed system targets the text-to-text track, and since it is applied to the English→German (en→de) and English→Chinese (en→zh) language directions, it is restricted to predefined high and low latency regimes specified by the task. These two latency regimes, as specified below, are governed by non-computationally aware StreamLAAL in seconds (s):

- en→de: 0-2s (low), 2-4s (high);
- en→zh: 0-2.5s (low), 2.5-4s (high).

The required development set for en→de and en→zh is ACL 60/60. A blind test set is employed for final evaluations.

3 BeaverTalk: A System Description

Our simultaneous translation system consists of a cascaded architecture, which is divided into a VAD segmenter utilizing a Silero VAD model (Team, 2024), Whisper Large V2 (Radford et al., 2022), and a fine-tuned Gemma 3 (Team et al., 2025) for simultaneous translation. In the system, Gemma 3 was fine-tuned for a conversational prompting strategy (Wang et al., 2024), which is designed to mimic a streaming setting. Our complete system is provided in Figure 1.

Our choice of a cascaded architecture rather than an end-to-end system hinges on our desire to (1) leverage the language modeling capabilities of an LLM to overcome contextual obstacles faced during simultaneous translation, (2) take advantage of an LLMs context understanding capabilities to harness prior sentence context in a stream of data, and (3) benchmark the fine-tuning and multilingual capabilities of the recent Gemma 3 (Team et al., 2025). To provide a deeper understanding of our designed system, we will first explain the fine-tuning approach for our translation LLM to enable conversational prompting, followed by a deeper explanation of our cascaded translation system.

3.1 SFT Conversational Prompting

We conduct supervised fine-tuning (SFT) for our Gemma 3 LLM for translation using a conversational prompting strategy that leverages a prior sentence memory bank as context. The prompting strategy is designed whereby provided a source sequence $S = [s_1, s_2, ..., s_{|S|}]$ and a target sequence $T = [t_1, t_2, ..., t_{|T|}]$ the prompt will interleave subsequences from S and T leveraging delimiting tokens to separate the subsequences. Now suppose we had prior sentence context $C = [c_1, c_2, ..., c_{|C|}]$,

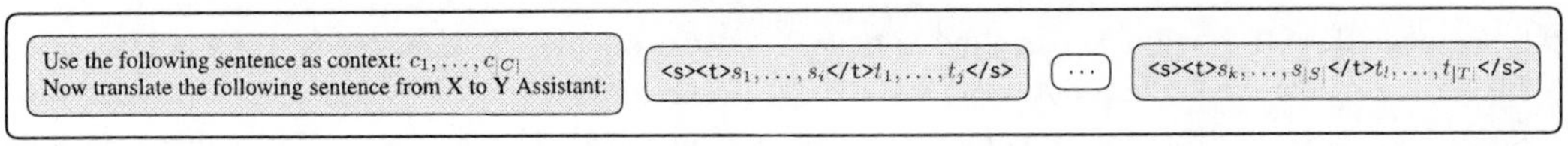

Figure 2: An example conversational prompt for translating for source language X to target language Y using source and target sequences $S = [s_1, s_2, ..., s_{|S|}]$ and $T = [t_1, t_2, ..., t_{|T|}]$ with context $C = [c_1, c_2, ..., c_{|C|}]$.

then an example of a conversational prompt constructed from these components is provided in Figure 2.

Aside from the prior sentence memory bank, which we inject into our prompt, our conversational prompting follows a similar implementation to Wang et al. (2024). The approach for generating this conversational prompting (the green region in Figure 2) can be broken into the following three steps:

1. Generate the alignments between words in the source and the target sequences. Unlike Wang et al. (2024), which uses fast-align (Dyer et al., 2013), we use the Itermax method from the SimAlign toolkit leveraging XLM-RoBERTa base to align words due to their work reporting better alignments (Jalili Sabet et al., 2020; Conneau et al., 2019).

2. Segment the graph into subsequences such that all the word dependencies for each target subsequence are available in or before the respective source subsequence. For example, assuming we did not perform step 3, in Figure 2 every word in the subsequence $t_1, ...t_j$ aligns with each word in $s_1, ..., s_i$.

3. Merge and shift subsequences to break the ideal alignments. Such a step is necessary to aid in making the LLM flexible for different variations of subsequences received during inference.

Once the prompt is constructed, we fine-tune our LLM using a causal language modeling objective using cross-entropy loss. We ensure that loss is only computed for tokens between the delimiting tokens </t>, not inclusive, and </s>, inclusive. Suppose our conversational prompt possesses K conversation intervals (ie. the number of times<s> appears in the prompt of Figure 2), where the beginning and end of each conversation interval are at index s_k and e_k. Then we can represent such a loss objective with Equation 1.

$$\mathcal{L} = \sum_{k=1}^{K} \sum_{i=s_k}^{e_k} \log p_\theta(t_i \mid s_{<i}) \quad (1)$$

The purpose of such a loss is to ensure that the model learns to predict </s> whenever it has insufficient context at inference. In doing so our LLM learns a portion of the decision policy in conjunction with the translation objective.

3.2 Streaming Cascaded SimulST System

As we leverage a cascaded architecture we will break our explanation into (1) the Segmented ASR Pipeline, the part responsible for segmenting and transcribing a speech stream (shown in the left half of Figure 1), and (2) the Simultaneous Translation LLM Pipeline, the part responsible for translating the transcribed speech (shown in the right half of Figure 1).

3.2.1 Segmented ASR Pipeline

The first part of our Segmented ASR Pipeline is the VAD segmenter. As previously mentioned, it segments a speech signal. This segmentation is based on (1) the maximum segment duration, (2) the maximum unvoiced duration, and (3) the voice probability threshold. As the name implies, the maximum segment duration determines the maximum length of a valid segment. If the segment duration exceeds the maximum segment duration, it is cut. The maximum unvoiced duration and the voice probability threshold alternatively rely on one another to determine when to segment the speech input prior to reaching the maximum segment duration. The first part of this second facet of segmentation begins with the Silero VAD model (Team, 2024). This VAD model outputs a probability score of a specific sample containing audio of a speaker's voice. If the score falls below the voice probability threshold, it is determined that there is currently no voice from the speaker. When the score has been below the probability threshold for longer than the maximum unvoiced duration, the speech is segmented. Such a condition would be ideally met between pauses in speech or at the end of a sentence.

The Whisper ASR model (Radford et al., 2022) interacts with the VAD segmenter by receiving the segmented audio inputs. The Whisper portion of the Segmented ASR Pipeline is designed to have Whisper transcribe the audio input using a stable transcription policy, leveraging a context mechanism. The stable transcription policy followed aims to create consistent, accurate transcriptions. It works by committing a transcription to a stable transcription buffer once it repeats a transcription for a given audio interval. For example, if on the first interval Whisper transcribes the sequence s_1, s_2, s_3, s_4 and then on the second interval it transcribes $s_1, s_2, s_3, s'_4, s_5, s_6$, only the s_1, s_2, s_3 will be committed to the stable transcription. Once committed as a stable transcription, it becomes available to the Simultaneous Translation LLM Pipeline for translation. To further improve transcription quality, Whisper is also provided with additional context from a context buffer. The context buffer is designed to provide Whisper with the transcript from the previous segment. However, if the previous segment exceeds the cutoff threshold, the number of context words is limited to be equal to the cutoff threshold.

3.2.2 Simultaneous Translation LLM Pipeline

As previously explained in Section 3.1, our Gemma 3 (Team et al., 2025) based simultaneous translation model follows a conversational prompting strategy utilizing a prior sentence memory bank as context. It is designed to firstly place the running stream of transcription chunks from the Segmented ASR Pipeline into a buffer upon receipt. Such a buffer will retain already translated portions of the transcript so long as the sentence these translated portions are associated with has yet to be completed.

Once the buffer has been extended, it is passed to a Spacy sentence tokenizer, which splits the buffer of words into sentences. Upon splitting the buffer into sentences, the pipeline will enter a translation generation loop, where a translation action will occur if one of two conditions is met. These conditions consist of (1) the length of untranslated words in the buffer has exceeded a prespecified minimum chunk size or (2) the sentence tokenizer has split the buffer into more than 1 sentence.

Once a translation action is triggered, the first step is to construct a conversational prompt. The conversational prompt is constructed identically to the one in Figure 2 by appending the new source subsequence from the oldest sentence in the buffer after a <t> delimiter following the previous translation action conversational prompt. In order to ensure the model understands it is a conversation phase after the source sequence, the </t> delimiter is appended. The new source subsequence length is equal to the untranslated word count present in the current sentence. We require such a condition as allowing for multiple sentences in the source subsequence would deviate from the fine-tuning setting, where only a single sentence was allowed at any time in the conversational prompt (a restriction by the dataset). Once constructed, the prompt is provided to the LLM to produce a translation until it outputs the delimiting token </s>. The output translation is added to a running translation to be reused in prompt construction for subsequent translation phases.

Upon completing the translation, if the sentence tokenizer determined there was more than a single sentence in the buffer, it would signify that the current sentence had completed translation. As such, the translated sentence transcript is cached to be used as context for the subsequent sentence. Additionally, its contents would be removed from the transcription buffer. Further translation phases would occur if conditions (1) and (2) were once again met.

4 Experimental Setup

The dataset of choice for fine-tuning is OpenSubtitles v2018. This corpus is particularly noisy (e.g. some Chinese translations are almost entirely English, mismatched translations to transcriptions, etc.), rendering it difficult to achieve reasonable initial results. Given that, some cleaning of the dataset is required. This occurs in four steps, the third of which only occurs for the en→zh dataset split:

1. Filtering all samples on length such that the source and memory bank sequence are greater than or equal to 25 characters.
2. Filtering all samples with '...', '[', ']', '(', ')', or consisting of only capital letters and replacing '- ' with empty space.
3. Filtering all samples in the en→zh language split that contain English words in the target column.
4. Filtering all remaining samples via CometKiwi (Rei et al., 2022) with a thresholding score of 0.6 to ensure semantic similarity between the transcription and

Table 1: Comparison table for simultaneous translation experiments, organized by language pair and model size.

Language Pair	Model Size	Latency Regime	BLEU ↑	StreamLAAL ↓
en–de	4B	low	23.64	1958.22
		high	25.22	3503.46
	12B	low	24.64	1837.86
		high	27.83	3343.73
en–zh	4B	low	32.81	2249.32
		high	34.62	3190.68
	12B	low	34.07	2216.99
		high	37.23	3521.35

the reference translation. This is meant to minimize the likelihood of a mismatched transcription and translation.

The fine-tuning pipeline that employs the aforementioned dataset is based on frameworks for simultaneous translation with LLMs provided in prior work (Agostinelli et al., 2024; Raffel et al., 2024), which were then adapted for unsegmented fine-tuning and evaluation.

Fine-tuning occurred on Gemma 3 4B/12B via LoRAs with quantization (Hu et al., 2021; Dettmers et al., 2023). The LoRA adapters were applied to all attention projections and all the feed-forward network linear projections. We chose a LoRA r of 64, a LoRA α of 16, and a LoRA dropout of 0.1. Our quantization quantized to 4-bit floating point via NormalFloat with a compute data type of bfloat16. We used the Paged 32-bit Adamw optimizer and an inverse sqrt learning rate scheduler with an effective batch size of 64, a learning rate of $2e^{-4}$, a weight decay of 0.1, a max gradient norm of 1, and a warm-up ratio of 0.03.

We evaluate the translation quality of our models using BLEU score with sacreBLEU (Post, 2018). The latency is reported using StreamLAAL (Papi et al., 2024). For the en→de language direction, the latency and BLEU scores are reported at the word level using the 13a tokenizer. Alternatively, for the en→zh language direction, the latency and BLEU scores are reported at the character level.

Our fine-tuning and evaluation for the Gemma 12B models was conducted on an NVIDIA H200. Alternatively, the Gemma 4B models were trained on a NVIDIA A40 and evaluated on a NVIDIA V100.

5 Results

5.1 Inference Hyperparameter Tuning

For our system, we tuned the maximum unvoiced duration (MUD), the voice probability threshold (VPT), the maximum segment duration (MSD), and the minimum chunk size (MCS). We immediately found that a maximum unvoiced duration greater than 0.1 s would deteriorate performance, so we kept that constant for our experimentation. Due to our 12B Gemma 3 model requiring an H200 to evaluate (a byproduct of memory requirements), we selected inference hyperparameters using a 4B Gemma 3 model, which could run on a V100. Such a choice is feasible due to the cascaded structure of our architecture. This is a byproduct of the maximum unvoiced duration, voice probability threshold, and maximum segment duration only influencing the quality of the transcriptions from the Segmented ASR Pipeline. If the transcription related hyperparameters are tuned properly, the Gemma 3 translation model will perform better irrespective of the model size.

We began our inference hyperparameter search by fixing our translation minimum chunk size to 3 words on the en→de language pair and 5 words on the en→zh language pair. These minimum chunk sizes were chosen to accommodate the en→de language pair, having a low latency cutoff of 2s, and the en→zh language pair, having a low latency cutoff of 2.5s. We then iteratively searched for the optimal maximum segment duration and voice probability threshold for both the low and high latency regimes. We report these results in Tables 2 and 3 for en→de and en→zh language pairs, respectively.

From observing, Table 2 we can see for the low latency regime of the en→de language pair the only selection of hyperparameters that fall below the 2s threshold is with a voice probability threshold of

Table 2: Simultaneous translation results for **en→de** organized by voice probability threshold (VPT) and maximum segment duration (MSD) with a minimum chunk size of 3.

VPT	MSD	BLEU ↑	StreamLAAL ↓
0.1	0.5	23.43	2079.14
0.1	1	24.86	2677.30
0.1	1.5	25.02	3114.15
0.3	0.5	23.36	2047.62
0.3	1	25.01	2477.67
0.3	1.5	25.05	2877.81
0.5	0.5	23.59	1940.58
0.5	1	24.96	2356.68
0.5	1.5	24.82	2804.01

Table 3: Simultaneous translation results for **en→zh** organized by voice probability threshold (VPT) and maximum segment duration (MSD) with a minimum chunk size of 5.

VPT	MSD	BLEU ↑	StreamLAAL ↓
0.1	0.5	33.16	2294.95
0.1	1	33.57	2979.20
0.1	1.5	34.11	3382.83
0.3	0.5	32.47	2307.56
0.3	1	33.36	2851.60
0.3	1.5	33.70	3206.28
0.5	0.5	32.81	2249.32
0.5	1	33.31	2728.01
0.5	1.5	34.62	3190.68

0.5 and a maximum segment duration of 0.5s. Alternatively, for the high latency regime, we select a voice probability threshold of 0.3 and a maximum segment duration of 1. We chose the maximum segment duration of 1s rather than 1.5s due to the increase in StreamLAAL. We report our final selected maximum unvoiced duration, voice probability threshold, and maximum segment duration in Table 4 for the en→de language pair.

Table 4: Inference hyperparameters for **en→de**.

Latency	MUD	VPT	MSD	MCS
low	0.1	0.5	0.5	3
high	0.1	0.3	1	7

On the high latency regime of the en→zh from observing Table 3 we chose a voice probability threshold of 0.5 with a maximum segment duration of 1.5s due to the high BLEU achieved. Then, for the low-latency regime, we chose a voice probability threshold of 0.5 and a maximum segment duration of 0.5 to align with our high-latency regime. We report our final selected maximum unvoiced duration, voice probability threshold, and maximum segment duration in Table 5 for the en→zh language pair.

Table 5: Inference hyperparameters for **en→zh**.

Latency	MUD	VPT	MSD	MCS
low	0.1	0.5	0.5	5
high	0.1	0.5	1.5	7

Using the optimal maximum unvoiced duration, voice probability threshold, and maximum segment duration from Tables 4 and 5 of our previous search, we iteratively step through a minimum chunk size of 1, 3, 5, and 7. We report the results for the BLEU and StreamLAAL for each given chunk size for both language pairs at the low and high latency regimes in Figure 3. Our final selected minimum chunk size for each latency regime is reported in Tables 2 and 3.

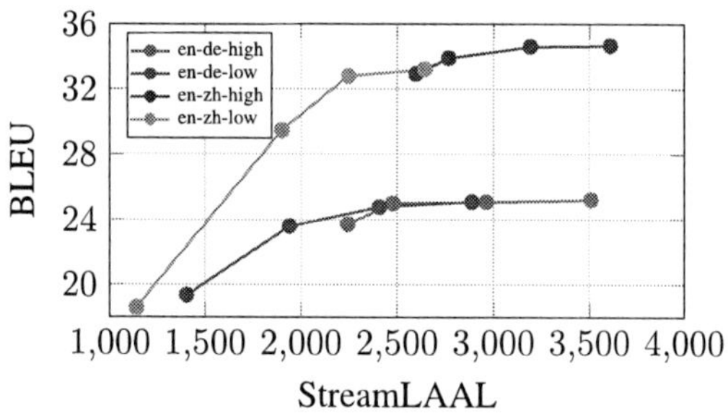

Figure 3: BLEU score plotted against StreamLAAL on the **en→de** and **en→zh** language pairs for minimum chunk sizes of 1, 3, 5, 7.

5.2 Quality and Latency Results on Dev set

We provide the quality and latency of our system in Table 1 on the ACL 60/60 dev set for the en→de and en→zh language pairs. For each language pair, we show the influence of model size on our system's BLEU score. From the results in Table 1, we can see that increasing the model size from 4B to 12B can offer approximately a 2 BLEU increase. We choose to submit the 12B Gemma 3 translation model version of our cascaded architecture to the IWSLT 2025 simultaneous track (Abdulmumin et al., 2025). On the en→de language pair, we achieve a BLEU of 24.64 and 27.83 on the low and high latency regimes. Then on the en→zh language pair, we achieve a BLEU of 34.07 and 37.23 on the low and high latency regimes.

6 Conclusion

In this paper, we provide Oregon State University's system, BeaverTalk, designed for the low and high latency regimes of the en→de and en→zh language pairs as a part of the IWSLT 2025 simultaneous track. Our system consists of a cascaded architecture composed of a VAD speech segmenter, a Whisper ASR model, and a Gemma 3 translation LLM using conversational prompting. We provide an extensive inference hyperparameter search for our system and demonstrate its performance utilizing a 4B and 12B translation LLM. Our final submitted model, composed of the 12B translation LLM, demonstrates strong results on the en→de and en→zh language pairs for both the low and high latency categories.

Acknowledgements

This research was supported, in part, by the National Science Foundation grants 2223483 and 2223484.

References

Idris Abdulmumin, Victor Agostinelli, Tanel Alumäe, Antonios Anastasopoulos, Ashwin, Luisa Bentivogli, Ondřej Bojar, Claudia Borg, Fethi Bougares, Roldano Cattoni, Mauro Cettolo, Lizhong Chen, William Chen, Raj Dabre, Yannick Estève, Marcello Federico, Marco Gaido, Dávid Javorský, Marek Kasztelnik, and 30 others. 2025. Findings of the iwslt 2025 evaluation campaign. In *Proceedings of the 22nd International Conference on Spoken Language Translation (IWSLT 2025)*, Vienna, Austia (in-person and online). Association for Computational Linguistics. To appear.

Victor Agostinelli, Max Wild, Matthew Raffel, Kazi Fuad, and Lizhong Chen. 2024. Simul-LLM: A framework for exploring high-quality simultaneous translation with large language models. In *Proceedings of the 62nd Annual Meeting of the Association for Computational Linguistics (Volume 1: Long Papers)*, pages 10530–10541, Bangkok, Thailand. Association for Computational Linguistics.

Alexis Conneau, Kartikay Khandelwal, Naman Goyal, Vishrav Chaudhary, Guillaume Wenzek, Francisco Guzmán, Edouard Grave, Myle Ott, Luke Zettlemoyer, and Veselin Stoyanov. 2019. Unsupervised cross-lingual representation learning at scale. *CoRR*, abs/1911.02116.

Tim Dettmers, Artidoro Pagnoni, Ari Holtzman, and Luke Zettlemoyer. 2023. Qlora: Efficient finetuning of quantized llms. *Advances in neural information processing systems*, 36:10088–10115.

Chris Dyer, Victor Chahuneau, and Noah A. Smith. 2013. A simple, fast, and effective reparameterization of IBM model 2. In *Proceedings of the 2013 Conference of the North American Chapter of the Association for Computational Linguistics: Human Language Technologies*, pages 644–648, Atlanta, Georgia. Association for Computational Linguistics.

Edward J. Hu, Yelong Shen, Phillip Wallis, Zeyuan Allen-Zhu, Yuanzhi Li, Shean Wang, Lu Wang, and Weizhu Chen. 2021. Lora: Low-rank adaptation of large language models. *Preprint*, arXiv:2106.09685.

Masoud Jalili Sabet, Philipp Dufter, François Yvon, and Hinrich Schütze. 2020. SimAlign: High quality word alignments without parallel training data using static and contextualized embeddings. In *Findings of the Association for Computational Linguistics: EMNLP 2020*, pages 1627–1643, Online. Association for Computational Linguistics.

Pierre Lison, Jörg Tiedemann, and Milen Kouylekov. 2018. OpenSubtitles2018: Statistical rescoring of sentence alignments in large, noisy parallel corpora. In *Proceedings of the Eleventh International Conference on Language Resources and Evaluation (LREC 2018)*, Miyazaki, Japan. European Language Resources Association (ELRA).

Sara Papi, Marco Gaido, Matteo Negri, and Luisa Bentivogli. 2024. Streamatt: Direct streaming speech-to-text translation with attention-based audio history selection. *Preprint*, arXiv:2406.06097.

Matt Post. 2018. A call for clarity in reporting bleu scores. *arXiv preprint arXiv:1804.08771*.

Alec Radford, Jong Wook Kim, Tao Xu, Greg Brockman, Christine McLeavey, and Ilya Sutskever. 2022. Robust speech recognition via large-scale weak supervision. *arXiv preprint*.

Matthew Raffel, Victor Agostinelli, and Lizhong Chen. 2024. Simultaneous masking, not prompting optimization: A paradigm shift in fine-tuning LLMs for simultaneous translation. In *Proceedings of the 2024 Conference on Empirical Methods in Natural Language Processing*, pages 18302–18314, Miami, Florida, USA. Association for Computational Linguistics.

Ricardo Rei, Marcos Treviso, Nuno M Guerreiro, Chrysoula Zerva, Ana C Farinha, Christine Maroti, José GC De Souza, Taisiya Glushkova, Duarte M Alves, Alon Lavie, and 1 others. 2022. Cometkiwi: Ist-unbabel 2022 submission for the quality estimation shared task. *arXiv preprint arXiv:2209.06243*.

Gemma Team, Aishwarya Kamath, Johan Ferret, Shreya Pathak, Nino Vieillard, Ramona Merhej, Sarah Perrin, Tatiana Matejovicova, Alexandre Ramé, Morgane Rivière, Louis Rouillard, Thomas Mesnard, Geoffrey Cideron, Jean bastien Grill, Sabela Ramos, Edouard

Yvinec, Michelle Casbon, Etienne Pot, Ivo Penchev, and 197 others. 2025. Gemma 3 technical report. *Preprint*, arXiv:2503.19786.

Silero Team. 2024. Silero vad: pre-trained enterprise-grade voice activity detector (vad), number detector and language classifier. https://github.com/snakers4/silero-vad.

Viet Anh Khoa Tran, David Thulke, Yingbo Gao, Christian Herold, and Hermann Ney. 2022. Does joint training really help cascaded speech translation? In *Proceedings of the 2022 Conference on Empirical Methods in Natural Language Processing*, pages 4480–4487, Abu Dhabi, United Arab Emirates. Association for Computational Linguistics.

Minghan Wang, Thuy-Trang Vu, Yuxia Wang, Ehsan Shareghi, and Gholamreza Haffari. 2024. Conversational simulmt: Efficient simultaneous translation with large language models. *Preprint*, arXiv:2402.10552.

Giulio Zhou, Tsz Kin Lam, Alexandra Birch, and Barry Haddow. 2024. Prosody in cascade and direct speech-to-text translation: a case study on korean wh-phrases. *arXiv preprint arXiv:2402.00632*.

CMU's IWSLT 2025 Simultaneous Speech Translation System

Siqi Ouyang Xi Xu Lei Li
Language Technologies Institute, Carnegie Mellon University, USA
{siqiouya,xixu}@andrew.cmu.edu

Abstract

This paper presents CMU's submission to the IWSLT 2025 Simultaneous Speech Translation (SST) task for translating unsegmented English speech into Chinese and German text in a streaming manner. Our end-to-end speech-to-text system integrates a chunkwise causal Wav2Vec 2.0 speech encoder, an adapter, and the Qwen2.5-7B-Instruct as the decoder. We use a two-stage simultaneous training procedure on robust speech segments curated from LibriSpeech, CommonVoice, and VoxPopuli datasets, utilizing standard cross-entropy loss. Our model supports adjustable latency through a configurable latency multiplier. Experimental results demonstrate that our system achieves 44.3 BLEU for English-to-Chinese and 25.1 BLEU for English-to-German translations on the ACL60/60 development set, with computation-aware latencies of 2.7 seconds and 2.3 seconds, and theoretical latencies of 2.2 and 1.7 seconds, respectively.

1 Introduction

CMU's submission to the IWSLT 2025 Simultaneous Speech-to-Text Translation track (Abdulmumin et al., 2025)[1] is an end-to-end model that effectively translates unbounded English speech input into German and Chinese text without speech segmentation.

Translating unbounded speech presents unique challenges. Unlike segmented speech translation, it requires the model to maintain and process the speech and translation history so that translation quality, theoretical latency, and computation cost can be balanced (Papi et al., 2024a,b). Large language models (LLMs) have recently shown strong performance in improving speech translation quality (Zhang et al., 2023; Chen et al., 2024; Huang et al., 2023; Xu et al., 2024; Ahmad et al., 2024), and modern LLMs now support long-context inference due to architectural and algorithmic advances (Han et al., 2024; Su et al., 2024). These two advantages were recently unified in InfiniSST (Ouyang et al., 2025), which frames simultaneous translation as a multiturn dialogue and enables inference on unbounded speech with minimal computational overhead.

Our system is built upon the InfiniSST framework and consists of:

1. A chunkwise causal Wav2Vec 2.0 Large encoder (Baevski et al., 2020b), which incrementally processes the unbounded speech input.

2. The Qwen2.5-7B-Instruct LLM (Qwen et al., 2025), which receives the encoded speech features and performs simultaneous translation using a specially designed key-value (KV) cache management strategy.

However, a major limitation in speech translation research is the scarcity of high-quality parallel speech-text data. Only several hundred hours are available on resources such as EuroParl-ST (Iranzo-Sánchez et al., 2020) and CoVoST2 (Wang et al., 2021b). To scale InfiniSST training beyond this constraint, we synthesize training data by translating transcripts from automatic speech recognition (ASR) datasets into target-language text using an LLM.

Our experiments on the ACL60/60 development set (Salesky et al., 2023) demonstrate that increasing the amount of synthesized speech translation data consistently improves translation quality, with gains observed even beyond 3,000 hours of training data. Additionally, we find that Qwen2.5-7B-Instruct significantly outperforms Llama3.1-8B-Instruct (Grattafiori et al., 2024) on English-to-Chinese translation and achieves comparable performance on English-to-German translation.

[1] https://iwslt.org/2025/simultaneous

Proceedings of the 22nd International Conference on Spoken Language Translation (IWSLT 2025), pages 309–314
July 31 - August 1, 2025 ©2025 Association for Computational Linguistics

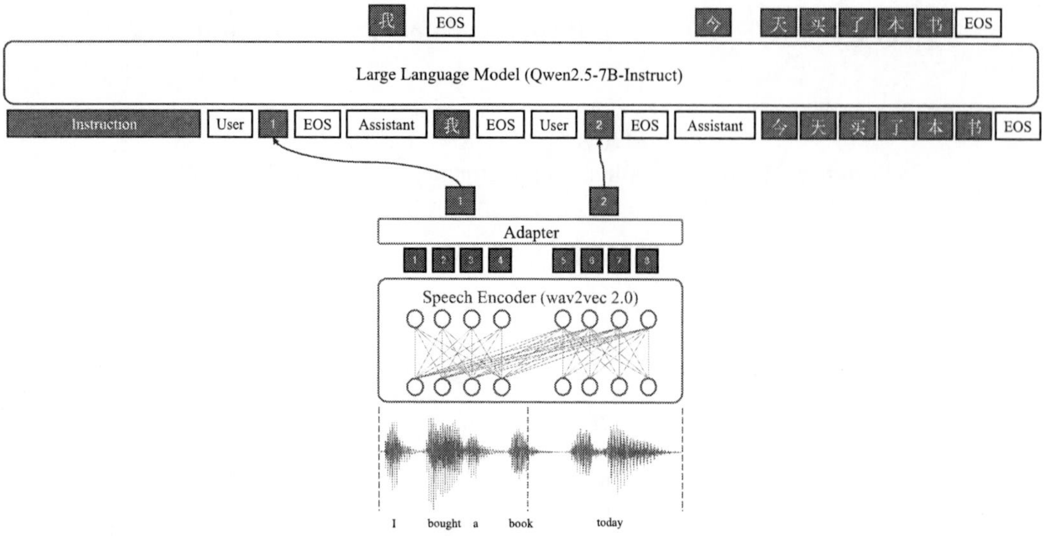

Figure 1: Model Architecture

2 Task Description

The IWSLT 2025 Simultaneous Speech-to-Text Translation track[2] focuses on translating unsegmented speech into target-language text using pre-trained large language models (LLMs) and speech encoders. The evaluation data consists of unsegmented ACL talks. For English-to-German, systems are additionally tested on accented speech, while a dedicated development set is provided for Czech-to-English.

Systems are evaluated on both translation quality and latency. Latency is measured using StreamLAAL (Papi et al., 2024a), while translation quality is assessed using BLEU (Papineni et al., 2002) and neural metrics such as COMET (Guerreiro et al., 2024), BLEURT (Sellam et al., 2020), etc.

We participate in two language directions: English-to-Chinese and English-to-German. For both directions, we submit models operating in the low-latency regime—achieving StreamLAAL ≤ 2 seconds for German and ≤ 2.5 seconds for Chinese on the development set.

3 System Description

3.1 Model Architecture

Our model architecture builds upon InfiniSST (Ouyang et al., 2025), a simultaneous speech translation system designed to efficiently handle unbounded streaming speech input and generate target text incrementally. The architecture comprises three primary components: 1) a streaming speech encoder that incrementally computes representations from partial speech without redundant computations; 2) a speech-to-token embedding adapter that aligns speech representations with the LLM's token embedding space; and 3) a multi-turn LLM decoder that dynamically processes speech inputs and produces translations interactively, as shown in Figure 1.

Streaming Speech Encoder We adapt the pretrained Wav2Vec 2.0 speech encoder (Baevski et al., 2020a)[3] with several modifications. First, we replace the convolutional positional embedding with rotary positional embeddings (RoPE), due to its better performance on long sequence tasks. Second, we replace the original bidirectional attention with chunk-wise causal attention, where each chunk consists of 48 frames from wav2vec (equivalent to 960 ms). In chunk-wise causal attention, each frame can attend to frames within the same chunk and all preceding chunks, but not future ones. Third, to limit the context length and computational load, we use a sliding window approach, allowing chunk i to attend only to the hidden states from chunks within the window $[i - w^s + 1, i]$, where $w^s = 10$ represents the window size.

Speech-to-Token Embedding Adapter Outputs from the speech encoder typically have longer se-

[2] https://iwslt.org/2025/simultaneous

[3] https://dl.fbaipublicfiles.com/fairseq/wav2vec/wav2vec_vox_960h_pl.pt

quence lengths compared to the corresponding transcripts, and their embedding dimensions differ from those expected by the LLM. To address this, we incorporate two 1D convolutional layers with kernel size 2 and stride 2, effectively reducing the length of the encoder output sequence. Subsequently, a linear projection layer maps these convolutional outputs to match the LLM embedding space. This adapter downsamples input sequences by a factor of 4, converting each speech chunk of 48 frames into 12 embedding vectors.

Multi-turn LLM Decoder The decoder generates the target text and emits a special EOS token when additional speech input is needed. We utilize the Qwen2.5-7B-Instruct (Qwen et al., 2025)[4] and structure the inputs using a multi-turn dialogue format. We also report results obtained with Llama-3.1-8B-Instruct (Grattafiori et al., 2024)[5] used as the decoder.

3.2 Data Synthesis

We utilize three ASR datasets for data synthesis: LibriSpeech-v12 (Panayotov et al., 2015), CommonVoice-v11.0 (Ardila et al., 2020), and VoxPopuli (Wang et al., 2021a). The English transcripts are translated into Chinese and German using the 4-bit quantized `Qwen2.5-32B-Instruct` model[6]. For LibriSpeech and VoxPopuli, whose utterances are segmented from longer speech recordings, we condition the translation on up to three preceding utterances to provide additional context. The prompt is shown below.

```
<|im_start|>system
You are a professional translator.
<|im_end|>
<|im_start|>user
Given an English sentence along with its
preceding sentences, translate the given
sentence into Chinese. Do not include any
other text.

|Preceding Sentences|
{}
|End of Preceding Sentences|

|Sentence to Translate|
{}
|End of Sentence to Translate|
<|im_end|>
<|im_start|>assistant
```

[4]https://huggingface.co/Qwen/Qwen2.5-7B-Instruct

[5]https://huggingface.co/meta-llama/Llama-3.1-8B-Instruct

[6]https://huggingface.co/Qwen/Qwen2.5-32B-Instruct-AWQ

Dataset	# Robust Segments	Hours
LibriSpeech	174112	1393
VoxPopuli	85874	687
CommonVoice	221717	1774
Total	481703	3854

Table 1: Statistics of synthesized data for model training.

Given (speech, transcript, translation) triplets, we first use Montreal Forced Aligner (McAuliffe et al., 2017) to align speech and transcript words, and then align transcript words with translation words using SimAlign (Jalili Sabet et al., 2020) with LaBSE model (Feng et al., 2022). In this way, we obtain a mapping between speech and each translation word.

Let m_i denote the right boundary timestamp of the speech segment aligned with the i-th translation word. To ensure monotonic alignment, we enforce $m_i = \max(m_i, m_{i-1})$. We then divide each utterance into fixed-duration chunks of 960 ms and construct a translation trajectory $(s_1, y_1), (s_2, y_2), \cdots$, where each s_j is a 960 ms speech chunk and $y_j = (y_{l_j}, \cdots, y_{r_j})$ is the translation span such that $m_i \leq 960 \cdot j$ for all $i \in [l_j, r_j]$.

While segmented utterances mostly consist of clean human speech, real-world scenarios often include non-speech segments. To improve model robustness, we create robust segments by slicing unsegmented speech from LibriSpeech and VoxPopuli into 30-chunk segments[7]. If a segment starts in the middle of an utterance, we shift the start to align with the utterance boundary. The trajectory for a robust segment is constructed by concatenating the trajectories of all included utterances.

Since CommonVoice consists of short, single-sentence utterances not derived from long speech, we simulate robust segments by concatenating randomly sampled utterances interleaved with randomly inserted silence intervals.

The data statistics are shown in Table 1.

[7]$30 \cdot 960$ ms = 28.8 seconds.

LLM	Data	English-Chinese	English-German
Llama-3.1-8B-Instruct	LS+CV	39.3 / 2092 / 2691	21.1 / 1430 / 2183
	LS+CV+VP	40.8 / 2159 / 2673	23.7 / 1503 / 2109
Qwen2.5-7B-Instruct	LS+CV+VP	44.3 / 2189 / 2739	25.1 / 1689 / 2306

Table 2: Translation quality and latency across different combinations of LLMs and training data evaluated on ACL60/60 development set. LS, CV, and VP refer to the LibriSpeech, CommonVoice, and VoxPopuli datasets, respectively. Metrics are reported as A / B / C, where A is BLEU, B is StreamLAAL, and C is StreamLAAL_CA. Incorporating synthetic speech translation data from VP leads to an improvement of at least 1 BLEU point. Additionally, Qwen2.5-7B-Instruct significantly outperforms Llama-3.1-8B-Instruct in Chinese translation, with a gain of approximately 4 BLEU points.

3.3 Training

We train our model using standard cross-entropy loss on the target translation tokens, including the special EOS token, derived from robust speech segments we constructed. Additionally, for each robust segment, we randomly sample a latency multiplier $m \leq 12$ and merge every m consecutive chunks as the data augmentation.

The training is conducted in two stages. Initially, we freeze the LLM and only train the speech encoder and adapter components. In the subsequent stage, we freeze the speech encoder, adapter and LLM, and conduct LORA finetuning (Hu et al., 2022).

3.4 Inference on Unbounded Speech

During inference, we segment the continuous input speech into fixed-length chunks of 960 ms. To manage latency, we vary the latency multiplier, ensuring translations are generated only after accumulating a predefined number of chunks. At each inference step, the newly received speech chunks are processed by both the speech encoder and the LLM, where KV caching is used to avoid redundant computations.

The speech encoder first processes new chunks along with relevant cached context. The resulting speech features are then downsampled by the adapter into a reduced set of embeddings, matching the LLM's input requirements. The LLM subsequently generates translations based on these embeddings.

The decoder uses a sliding window strategy to maintain context, combining the cached representations of initial system instructions with the most recent generated tokens similar to Han et al. (2024). We concatenate the KV cache of instruction with those of the most recent 1K tokens and apply RoPE on top of them. Then the LLM generates translations conditioned on this combined KV cache.

4 Experiments

4.1 Setup

We use the Adam optimizer (Kingma and Ba, 2015) with cosine learning rate decay and 1,000 warmup steps. Training is conducted in two stages. In Stage 1, we update only the speech encoder and adapter, using a maximum learning rate of 2e-4. In Stage 2, we freeze the speech encoder and train the LLM with LoRA (Hu et al., 2022)[8], using a maximum learning rate of 1e-4. Each stage is trained for one epoch with a maximum effective batch size of 57.6K tokens. We leverage PyTorch Lightning[9] and DeepSpeed ZeRO[10] to train the model on a node of 8 NVIDIA L40S GPUs.

During inference, we use beam search with beam size 4, repetition penalty 1.2, and ngram_no_repeat 5. We set test-time latency multiplier to 3 for English-to-Chinese and 2 for English-to-German. The results are evaluated with BLEU, StreamLAAL and StreamLAAL_CA.

4.2 Results

Results are presented in Table 2. While the synthetic speech translation data from LibriSpeech and CommonVoice already includes over 3K hours of speech, adding additional synthetic data from VoxPopuli consistently improves BLEU scores by at least 1 point. Moreover, replacing Llama-3.1-8B-Instruct with Qwen2.5-7B-Instruct leads to a notable gain in translation quality, particularly for

[8]rank = 32, alpha = 16, dropout = 0.1, applied to all linear layers.

[9]https://github.com/Lightning-AI/pytorch-lightning

[10]https://github.com/deepspeedai/DeepSpeed

English–Chinese, with an improvement of over 3 BLEU points.

5 Conclusion

In this paper, we presented CMU's simultaneous speech translation system built upon the InfiniSST framework for the IWSLT 2025 SST task. Our end-to-end model employs a chunkwise causal Wav2Vec 2.0 encoder, a adapter, and the Qwen2.5-7B-Instruct decoder. We demonstrated that synthesizing training data by translating large-scale ASR datasets significantly alleviates the limitations posed by limited parallel data, achieving substantial improvements in translation quality. Our experiments indicated that the addition of synthesized data from VoxPopuli provided consistent gains, and the Qwen2.5-7B-Instruct decoder notably outperformed alternatives, particularly in English-to-Chinese translation. The proposed model effectively balances translation quality and computational latency, showcasing strong performance in a realistic, unbounded speech scenario.

References

Idris Abdulmumin, Victor Agostinelli, Tanel Alumäe, Antonios Anastasopoulos, Ashwin, Luisa Bentivogli, Ondřej Bojar, Claudia Borg, Fethi Bougares, Roldano Cattoni, Mauro Cettolo, Lizhong Chen, William Chen, Raj Dabre, Yannick Estève, Marcello Federico, Marco Gaido, Dávid Javorský, Marek Kasztelnik, and 30 others. 2025. Findings of the iwslt 2025 evaluation campaign. In *Proceedings of the 22nd International Conference on Spoken Language Translation (IWSLT 2025)*, Vienna, Austia (in-person and online). Association for Computational Linguistics. To appear.

Ibrahim Said Ahmad, Antonios Anastasopoulos, Ondřej Bojar, Claudia Borg, Marine Carpuat, Roldano Cattoni, Mauro Cettolo, William Chen, Qianqian Dong, Marcello Federico, Barry Haddow, Dávid Javorský, Mateusz Krubiński, Tsz Kin Lam, Xutai Ma, Prashant Mathur, Evgeny Matusov, Chandresh Maurya, John McCrae, and 25 others. 2024. FINDINGS OF THE IWSLT 2024 EVALUATION CAMPAIGN. In *Proceedings of the 21st International Conference on Spoken Language Translation (IWSLT 2024)*, pages 1–11, Bangkok, Thailand (in-person and online). Association for Computational Linguistics.

Rosana Ardila, Megan Branson, Kelly Davis, Michael Kohler, Josh Meyer, Michael Henretty, Reuben Morais, Lindsay Saunders, Francis Tyers, and Gregor Weber. 2020. Common voice: A massively-multilingual speech corpus. In *Proceedings of the Twelfth Language Resources and Evaluation Conference*, pages 4218–4222, Marseille, France. European Language Resources Association.

Alexei Baevski, Henry Zhou, Abdelrahman Mohamed, and Michael Auli. 2020a. wav2vec 2.0: A framework for self-supervised learning of speech representations. *Preprint*, arXiv:2006.11477.

Alexei Baevski, Yuhao Zhou, Abdelrahman Mohamed, and Michael Auli. 2020b. wav2vec 2.0: A framework for self-supervised learning of speech representations. In *Advances in Neural Information Processing Systems*, volume 33, pages 12449–12460. Curran Associates, Inc.

Zhehuai Chen, He Huang, Andrei Andrusenko, Oleksii Hrinchuk, Krishna C. Puvvada, Jason Li, Subhankar Ghosh, Jagadeesh Balam, and Boris Ginsburg. 2024. Salm: Speech-augmented language model with in-context learning for speech recognition and translation. In *ICASSP 2024 - 2024 IEEE International Conference on Acoustics, Speech and Signal Processing (ICASSP)*, pages 13521–13525.

Fangxiaoyu Feng, Yinfei Yang, Daniel Cer, Naveen Arivazhagan, and Wei Wang. 2022. Language-agnostic BERT sentence embedding. In *Proceedings of the 60th Annual Meeting of the Association for Computational Linguistics (Volume 1: Long Papers)*, pages 878–891, Dublin, Ireland. Association for Computational Linguistics.

Aaron Grattafiori, Abhimanyu Dubey, Abhinav Jauhri, Abhinav Pandey, Abhishek Kadian, Ahmad Al-Dahle, Aiesha Letman, Akhil Mathur, Alan Schelten, Alex Vaughan, Amy Yang, Angela Fan, Anirudh Goyal, Anthony Hartshorn, Aobo Yang, Archi Mitra, Archie Sravankumar, Artem Korenev, Arthur Hinsvark, and 542 others. 2024. The llama 3 herd of models. *Preprint*, arXiv:2407.21783.

Nuno M. Guerreiro, Ricardo Rei, Daan van Stigt, Luisa Coheur, Pierre Colombo, and André F. T. Martins. 2024. xcomet: Transparent machine translation evaluation through fine-grained error detection. *Transactions of the Association for Computational Linguistics*, 12:979–995.

Chi Han, Qifan Wang, Hao Peng, Wenhan Xiong, Yu Chen, Heng Ji, and Sinong Wang. 2024. LM-infinite: Zero-shot extreme length generalization for large language models. In *Proceedings of the 2024 Conference of the North American Chapter of the Association for Computational Linguistics: Human Language Technologies (Volume 1: Long Papers)*, pages 3991–4008, Mexico City, Mexico. Association for Computational Linguistics.

Edward J Hu, yelong shen, Phillip Wallis, Zeyuan Allen-Zhu, Yuanzhi Li, Shean Wang, Lu Wang, and Weizhu Chen. 2022. LoRA: Low-rank adaptation of large language models. In *International Conference on Learning Representations*.

Zhichao Huang, Rong Ye, Tom Ko, Qianqian Dong, Shanbo Cheng, Mingxuan Wang, and Hang Li. 2023. Speech translation with large language models: An industrial practice. *Preprint*, arXiv:2312.13585.

Javier Iranzo-Sánchez, Joan Albert Silvestre-Cerdà, Javier Jorge, Nahuel Roselló, Adrià Giménez, Albert Sanchis, Jorge Civera, and Alfons Juan. 2020. Europarl-st: A multilingual corpus for speech translation of parliamentary debates. In *ICASSP 2020 - 2020 IEEE International Conference on Acoustics, Speech and Signal Processing (ICASSP)*, pages 8229–8233.

Masoud Jalili Sabet, Philipp Dufter, François Yvon, and Hinrich Schütze. 2020. SimAlign: High quality word alignments without parallel training data using static and contextualized embeddings. In *Findings of the Association for Computational Linguistics: EMNLP 2020*, pages 1627–1643, Online. Association for Computational Linguistics.

Diederik P. Kingma and Jimmy Ba. 2015. Adam: A method for stochastic optimization. In *3rd International Conference on Learning Representations, ICLR 2015, San Diego, CA, USA, May 7-9, 2015, Conference Track Proceedings*.

Michael McAuliffe, Michaela Socolof, Sarah Mihuc, Michael Wagner, and Morgan Sonderegger. 2017. Montreal forced aligner: Trainable text-speech alignment using kaldi. In *Interspeech 2017*, pages 498–502.

Siqi Ouyang, Xi Xu, and Lei Li. 2025. Infinisst: Simultaneous translation of unbounded speech with large language model. *Preprint*, arXiv:2503.02969.

Vassil Panayotov, Guoguo Chen, Daniel Povey, and Sanjeev Khudanpur. 2015. Librispeech: An asr corpus based on public domain audio books. In *2015 IEEE International Conference on Acoustics, Speech and Signal Processing (ICASSP)*, pages 5206–5210.

Sara Papi, Marco Gaido, Matteo Negri, and Luisa Bentivogli. 2024a. StreamAtt: Direct streaming speech-to-text translation with attention-based audio history selection. In *Proceedings of the 62nd Annual Meeting of the Association for Computational Linguistics (Volume 1: Long Papers)*, pages 3692–3707, Bangkok, Thailand. Association for Computational Linguistics.

Sara Papi, Peter Polák, Dominik Macháček, and Ondřej Bojar. 2024b. How "real" is your real-time simultaneous speech-to-text translation system? *Transactions of the Association for Computational Linguistics*, 13:281–313.

Kishore Papineni, Salim Roukos, Todd Ward, and Wei-Jing Zhu. 2002. Bleu: a method for automatic evaluation of machine translation. In *Proceedings of the 40th Annual Meeting of the Association for Computational Linguistics*, pages 311–318, Philadelphia, Pennsylvania, USA. Association for Computational Linguistics.

Qwen, :, An Yang, Baosong Yang, Beichen Zhang, Binyuan Hui, Bo Zheng, Bowen Yu, Chengyuan Li, Dayiheng Liu, Fei Huang, Haoran Wei, Huan Lin, Jian Yang, Jianhong Tu, Jianwei Zhang, Jianxin Yang, Jiaxi Yang, Jingren Zhou, and 25 others. 2025. Qwen2.5 technical report. *Preprint*, arXiv:2412.15115.

Elizabeth Salesky, Kareem Darwish, Mohamed Al-Badrashiny, Mona Diab, and Jan Niehues. 2023. Evaluating multilingual speech translation under realistic conditions with resegmentation and terminology. In *Proceedings of the 20th International Conference on Spoken Language Translation (IWSLT 2023)*, pages 62–78, Toronto, Canada (in-person and online). Association for Computational Linguistics.

Thibault Sellam, Dipanjan Das, and Ankur Parikh. 2020. BLEURT: Learning robust metrics for text generation. In *Proceedings of the 58th Annual Meeting of the Association for Computational Linguistics*, pages 7881–7892, Online. Association for Computational Linguistics.

Jianlin Su, Murtadha Ahmed, Yu Lu, Shengfeng Pan, Wen Bo, and Yunfeng Liu. 2024. Roformer: Enhanced transformer with rotary position embedding. *Neurocomput.*, 568(C).

Changhan Wang, Morgane Riviere, Ann Lee, Anne Wu, Chaitanya Talnikar, Daniel Haziza, Mary Williamson, Juan Pino, and Emmanuel Dupoux. 2021a. VoxPopuli: A large-scale multilingual speech corpus for representation learning, semi-supervised learning and interpretation. In *Proceedings of the 59th Annual Meeting of the Association for Computational Linguistics and the 11th International Joint Conference on Natural Language Processing (Volume 1: Long Papers)*, pages 993–1003, Online. Association for Computational Linguistics.

Changhan Wang, Anne Wu, Jiatao Gu, and Juan Pino. 2021b. Covost 2 and massively multilingual speech translation. In *Interspeech 2021*, pages 2247–2251.

Xi Xu, Siqi Ouyang, Brian Yan, Patrick Fernandes, William Chen, Lei Li, Graham Neubig, and Shinji Watanabe. 2024. CMU's IWSLT 2024 simultaneous speech translation system. In *Proceedings of the 21st International Conference on Spoken Language Translation (IWSLT 2024)*, pages 154–159, Bangkok, Thailand (in-person and online). Association for Computational Linguistics.

Hao Zhang, Nianwen Si, Yaqi Chen, Wenlin Zhang, Xukui Yang, Dan Qu, and Xiaolin Jiao. 2023. Tuning large language model for end-to-end speech translation. *Preprint*, arXiv:2310.02050.

JHU IWSLT 2025 Low-resource System Description

Nathaniel R. Robinson*[1] Niyati Bafna* Xiluo He* Tom Lupicki*
Lavanya Shankar* Cihan Xiao Qi Sun Kenton Murray David Yarowsky
Johns Hopkins University Center for Language and Speech Processing
*Equal contribution, [1]Contact author
{nrobin38,nbafna1,xhe69,tlupick1,ls1,cxiao7,qsun29,kenton,yarowsky}@jhu.edu

Abstract

We present the Johns Hopkins University's submission to the 2025 IWSLT Low-Resource Task. We competed on all 10 language pairs. Our approach centers around ensembling methods – specifically Minimum Bayes Risk Decoding. We find that such ensembling often improves performance only slightly over the best performing stand-alone model, and that in some cases it can even hurt performance slightly.

1 Introduction and Background

Despite many recent advances in deep learning and artificial intelligence, challenges in low-resource and dialectal speech translation still preclude high-quality automated translation systems for many language communities. Cross-lingual transfer and multilingual models have allowed for recent progress in scarce data settings, but performance still lags significantly behind that of higher resource languages (Ziems et al., 2023; Joshi et al., 2024).

Due to a lack of training resources, low-resource languages systems tend to generate hypotheses with higher variance than is seen in higher-resourced conditions. In other words, different models might generate diverse outputs; hence a single system might not be optimal in all scenarios. This motivates attempting to select the best option from multiple potential systems—i.e., ensembling.

For this year's IWSLT low-resource speech translation campaign (Abdulmumin et al., 2025), we, the Johns Hopkins University (JHU) team decided to focus on Minimum Bayes Risk Decoding (MBR) with the interest in exploring in-depth how combining methods across a range of language pairs can improve performance in a low-resource setting (Bickel and Doksum, 1977; Kumar and Byrne, 2004).

Following our approach from last year (Robinson et al., 2024), we submitted systems for all language pairs, with a focus on seeing how robust our

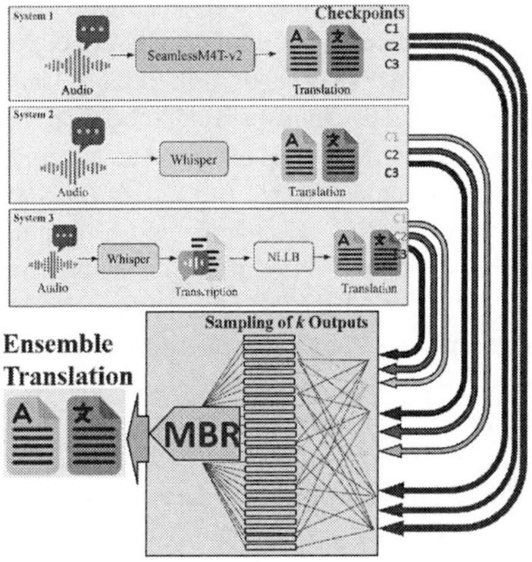

Figure 1: We apply Minimum Bayes Risk (MBR) ensembling to a variety of systems.

methods are across a wide range of data settings and typologically diverse languages. Rather than focusing on a specific language, our line of inquiry was geared towards broader exploration, with the interest of discovering language-agnostic trends in mind.

Our approach in 2024 focused on fine-tuning pre-trained models Whisper (Radford et al., 2023a), NLLB (NLLB Team et al., 2022), and SEAMLESSM4T v2 (Barrault et al., 2023) for both ASR+MT cascading and end-to-end speech translation. We also incorporated joint training for language pairs with common targets, as well as fine-tuning with a regularization technique known as intra-distillation (Xu et al., 2022, 2023; Robinson et al., 2024). In this year's submission, we similarly gather a variety of different systems for each translation language pair. We use these to obtain a diverse set of outputs for the language pairs sampled from various checkpoints of the different cascaded and end-to-end fine-tuned systems. To maximize variety of systems, and following our submission

Proceedings of the 22nd International Conference on Spoken Language Translation (IWSLT 2025), pages 315–323

from last year, we experimented with combining fine-tuning data for language pairs with a common target language, and with use of additional or supplementary training data. Rather than comparing these diverse systems directly, however, we ensembled them into a single inference method. We used MBR to select the best performing candidate translation from the resulting pool for each source audio.

Our decision to attempt an ensemble approach was inspired by other team submissions from last year. Our submissions performed best in last year's evaluation campaign (Ahmad et al., 2024) for Irish-to-English (gle-eng), Bemba-to-English (bem-eng), and Bhojpuri-to-Hindi (bho-hin) translation. However the teams that performed best for Levantine Arabic-to-English (apc-eng), Maltese-to-English (mlt-eng), and Quechua-to-Spanish (que-spa) all employed ensemble models. Ben Kheder et al. (2024) ensembled 26 model checkpoints for their apc-eng system, and E. Ortega et al. (2024) ensembled 10 checkpoints for their que-spa system. For their mlt-eng system, Li et al. (2024) ensembled cascade systems with end-to-end models (just as we attempt to do in this work).

2 Methodology and Experiments

Our methodology is illustrated in Figure 1. Given any language pair, we have a number of cascade and end-to-end systems (three in the figure). These systems employ either Whisper ST, Whisper ASR with NLLB MT, or SeamlessM4T v2 ST, and may have other more minor variations differentiating them. The number of systems varies between one and four, depending on the language pair. The systems we use for each language pair are listed in Table 2.

We keep three fine-tuning checkpoints from the final model of each of the systems (NLLB in the case of the bi-model cascade) and for each input audio, we sample five hypothesis translations from each system checkpoint, resulting in a total of 15 hypotheses per system for each input. In the case of language pairs like apc-eng, for which we ensembled four different systems, this amounted to $15 * 4 = 60$ hypotheses for each input audio, which are reduced to a single hypothesis via the MBR process.

2.1 Task description and data

This year's task focuses on speech translation for ten language pairs: Levantine Arabic to English (apc-eng), Tunisian Arabic to English (aeb-eng), Bemba to English (bem-eng), Fongbe to French (fon-fra), Irish to English (gle-eng), Bhojpuri to Hindi (bho-hin), Estonian to English (est-eng), Maltese to English (mlt-eng), Marathi to Hindi (mar-eng), and Quechua to Spanish (que-spa). Fongbe and Estonian are new as source languages in this year's task. Fongbe is a Gbe language of the Niger-Congo family spoken in Benin; while Estonian is a Uralic language spoken in Estonia.

In developing our systems, we utilize a combination of organizer-provided data as well as some external data. We summarize our data sources in Table 1.

Lang.	Type	Amount	Sources
apc-eng	ASR MT	28h 120k lines	Makhoul et al. (2005) Sellat et al. (2023)
aeb-eng	E2E ASR	167h 324h	Anastasopoulos et al. (2022) Anastasopoulos et al. (2022)
bem-eng	ST ASR	180h 24h	Sikasote et al. (2023) Sikasote and Anastasopoulos (2022)
fon-fra	E2E	57h	Kponou et al. (2024)
gle-eng	E2E	11h	Agarwal et al. (2023)
bho-hin	E2E	25h	Agarwal et al. (2023)
est-eng	E2E	1262h	Sildam et al. (2024)
mlt-eng	ST MT	14h 2.1M lines	CV; Hernandez Mena et al. (2020) Bañón et al. (2023, 2020)
mar-hin	E2E ASR	30h 1300h	Agarwal et al. (2023) CV; He et al. (2020); Bhogale et al. (2022)
que-spa	ST ASR MT	1.7h 48h 26k lines	Ortega et al. (2020) Cardenas et al. (2018) Tiedemann (2012); Ortega et al. (2020)

Table 1: Data information for each language pair. "CV" refers to Common Voice (https://commonvoice.mozilla.org/).

2.2 Seamless E2E systems

We detail the different systems listed in Table 2.

The SeamlessM4T v2 model (Barrault et al., 2023) is a state-of-the-art multilingual model developed specifically for speech translation (ST). It supports both speech-to-text and speech-to-speech translation, enabling direct translation of spoken language in 143 languages. The model is trained on a large and diverse corpus that combines supervised and semi-supervised data, allowing it to perform well even on low-resource language pairs. Its architecture is optimized for end-to-end processing of speech inputs, without relying on intermediate

Lang.	Systems	Lang.	Systems
aeb-eng	Seamless Whisper+NLLB (2023)	gle-eng	Seamless Seamless comb.
apc-eng	Seamless Seamless comb. Whisper+NLLB Whisper+NLLB+ID	mar-hin	Seamless Seamless comb. Seamless Shrutilipi Whisper MTL
bem-eng	Seamless Whisper+NLLB Whisper+NLLB+ID Whisper MTL	mlt-eng	Seamless Seamless comb. Whisper MTL
bho-hin	Seamless Seamless comb. Whisper E2E	que-spa	Seamless Whisper+NLLB Whisper+NLLB+ID
est-eng	Seamless	fon-fra	Seamless

Table 2: Systems used for ensembling. For each system we sample five outputs from three model checkpoints and perform MBR on the total sets of sampled outputs (which vary in number from 15 to 60, since the number of systems varies from one to four).

text transcriptions. This design makes it suitable for real-time applications and improves translation accuracy by minimizing error propagation across stages (Barrault et al., 2023).

Similar to Robinson et al. (2024), we employ SEAMLESSM4T v2 for our multilingual translation experiments. We re-fine-tuned SEAMLESSM4T v2 models, training most language pairs for 10 epochs (contrasting the 4 epochs of Robinson et al. (2024)). We found that dev BLEU scores continued to increase with longer train times and hence selected 10 epochs instead of 4. We generally used the same learning rates detailed by Robinson et al. (2024): 1×10^{-6} for almost all language pairs.The following language pairs used the standard learning rate and number of epochs: gle-eng, mlt-eng, bho-hin, mar-hin, apc-eng, fon-fra, and aeb-eng.

As Robinson et al. (2024), for the bem-eng pair, we used a reduced learning rate of 1×10^{-7} while keeping the number of epochs fixed at 10. We also trained the (que-spa) system for 100 epochs due to the small dataset size. Our Estonian ASR system was trained for only 0.5 epochs with a learning rate of 1×10^{-6}, due to the massive dataset size and computational constraints.

A more comprehensive list of all hyperparameters used for these experiments is provided in Appendix A.

Mixed data Training We also experimented with combining data for different language pairs for mixed data training. In this configuration, we explored the effect of combining similar languages for joint training. Specifically, we trained the following groups together:

- bem, mlt, gle, est, aeb, apc $\rightarrow$ eng
- bho, mar $\rightarrow$ hin

The rationale behind this setup is that grouping related languages can lead to more robust representations, particularly in low-resource settings, by effectively increasing the size of the training data and enhancing cross-lingual generalization.

For the into-Hindi combined system, we fine-tuned SEAMLESSM4T v2 for 10 epochs in the standard way. For the into-English combined system, trained on a mixture of data that included the full standard fine-tuning sets for mlt-eng, gle-eng, and apc-eng; and we added 5.2% of the Estonian ASR files[1], 36.1% of the bem-eng files, and 38.8% of the Tunisian Arabic-to-English (aeb-eng) files. This was done for the language pairs with the largest datasets to prevent data imbalance, and the percentages were selected to keep the dataset size withing roughly 250 hours total (about 25 times the size of the gle-eng dataset). We fine-tuned SEAMLESSM4T v2 for $\sim$ 1.3 epochs on this combined dataset. Both of these combined-data systems are denoted "Seamless comb." in Table 2.

We also experimented with fine-tuning SEAMLESSM4T v2 on additional data. We attempted to augment the gle-eng dataset (11 hours of audio, as in the 2024 shared task (Ahmad et al., 2024)) with the synthetic data provided by the task organizers for 2025. However, we met this attempt with little success. After more than a full epoch of training, the dev BLEU score had not increased above 1.0 BLEU, so we decided to terminate fine-tuning to preserve our computational resources for other experiments. We did, however, include among our Marathi-to-Hindi (mar-hin) systems a SEAMLESSM4T v2 model that was fine-tuned using the massive Shrutilipi dataset (Bhogale et al., 2022), which contains 1280 hours of Marathi ASR data. In this approach we were inspired by ?, who employed this dataset among others to develop a successful mod-hin submission in 2023. We used NLLB (NLLB Team et al., 2022) off-the-shelf for Marathi-to-Hindi translation to translate the transcription labels of the dataset to Hindi, and then we employed it as ST data for SEAMLESSM4T v2 fine-tuning (combined with the original mar-hin

[1]This was a mistake, as we mistakenly thought the Estonian ASR data was Estonian-to-English ST data, due to a miscommunication in our team.

data). We trained this model for approximately 2 epochs, and we denote it "Seamless Shrutilipi".

Our apc-eng SEAMLESSM4T v2 model was also trained on synthetic labels. Robinson et al. (2024) did not fine-tune a SEAMLESSM4T v2 model for apc-eng because of the nature of the apc-eng data (only ASR and MT datasets separately, with no ST labels). This year we bypassed this challenge by using Robinson et al.'s (2024) NLLB model fine-tuned for apc-eng MT to translate all the transcriptions in the provided apc ASR dataset into English. Then we fine-tuned SEAMLESSM4T v2 on the resulting dataset.

2.3 Whisper and NLLB

Whisper (Radford et al., 2023b) is a speech recognition model created by OpenAI. It is trained on a large amount of audio data—around 680,000 hours—from the internet. This includes many languages and different types of speech, such as conversations, lectures, and translations. Whisper works well in many languages without needing extra training for each new language. In our work, we use Whisper for both ASR and ST. Whisper's strength is its robustness—it can understand different accents, background noise, and even low-quality recordings. During pretraining, the model was already trained on data from over 90 languages such as English, Marathi, Hindi, Maltese, and Modern Standard Arabic. However, it lacks exposure to several low-resource languages like Bemba, Bhojpuri, and Quechua.

In this work we employed the same Whisper models used by Robinson et al. (2024). Whisper used in tandem with NLLB is used only as an ASR module to convert from the speech domain for text translation. "Whisper E2E" in Table 2 refers to using Whisper as an end-to-end translator via "psuedo-translation" (Robinson et al., 2024). This is the practice of fine-tuning Whisper on bho-hin data with a Hindi ASR objective. "Whisper MTL" also refers to using Whisper as an end-to-end ST system but with a mixed ASR and ST fine-tuning objective. This approach is typically most suitable for into-English ST, since English is the only ST target language officially supported by Whisper.

We also employ NLLB (NLLB Team et al., 2022), an extensive multilingual machine translation system, just as Robinson et al. (2024). NLLB covers more than 200 languages, including Arabic, Quechua, and Bemba. (We use the 600M-parameter release of the model, fine-tuned by Robinson et al. (2024).)

While "NLLB" refers to use of these fine-tuned NLLB model checkpoints in Table 2, "NLLB+ID" refers to the use of NLLB fine-tuned on the same data, but with intra-distillation (Xu et al., 2022; **?**), a regularlization technique designed to ensure that all network parameters contribute equally to successful inference. Intra-distillation was effective in enhancing MT performance in the 2024 shared task campaign.

2.4 System ensembling via MBR

Minimum Bayes Risk Decoding (MBR) (Bickel and Doksum, 1977) is a method of ensembling that aims to choose candidates that have the lowest risk – i.e., high probability but also consistent with other candidates. In other words, if multiple candidates are similar, they are more likely to be correct and it is not too risky to select one of them (Bertsch et al., 2023). It was originally used in machine translation in the early days of phrase-based, statistical methods (Kumar and Byrne, 2004), but has been shown to be very robust to common errors in neural methods (Müller and Sennrich, 2021), explored in-depth theoretically (Ohashi et al., 2024), as well as correlated well with human judgments (Freitag et al., 2022).

See a depiction of traditional MBR in Algorithm 1. $p(c_i)$ is usually set as the posterior probability of the translation candidate when ensembling candidates from a single system; in our case, since we are ensembling different systems, we simply set $p(c_i) = 1$; i.e. we apply a uniform weighting scheme to our candidates. We experiment with using both BLEU (Papineni et al., 2002) and chrF (Popović, 2015) as our similarity metric.

Algorithm 1 Minimum Bayes Risk (MBR) Decoding for Ensembling

Require: Candidate translations $C = \{c_1, c_2, \ldots, c_n\}$
Require: A similarity metric $\text{sim}(\cdot,\cdot)$ (e.g., BLEU, chrF)
Ensure: MBR-selected translation c^*
1: **for all** $c_i \in C$ **do**
2: Compute risk for c_i:
3: $R(c_i) = \sum_{c_j \in C} (1 - \text{sim}(c_i, c_j)) \cdot p(c_j)$
4: **end for**
5: $c^* \leftarrow \arg\min_{c_i \in C} R(c_i)$
6: **return** c^*

3 Results and Conclusions

The results of our different language systems are in Table 3. We used MBR ensembling with a BLEU objective as our primary system for each language pair, and MBR with chrF as our "contrastive 1" submission. In cases where the best performing of the newly fine-tuned SEAMLESSM4T v2 models outperformed all of the systems using Whisper and NLLB from Robinson et al. (2024) (using dev BLEU of the final checkpoint to compare), we selected that system's final checkpoint as our "contrastive 2" submission.

In Table 3, "Test 1" denotes our internal test set, while "Eval" denotes the official evaluation set for the shared task, given by Abdulmumin et al. (2025). We had no internal test set for `apc-eng` since our only ST data for this language pair was synthetically labeled. We also exclude the standard SEAMLESSM4T v2 system for `mar-hin` from our internal test set evaluation since this model was trained on the internal test set.[2]

We see that MBR generally improves performance by a small amount over the best stand-alone system (as can be seen for `bem-eng`, `bho-hin`, `fon-fra`, and `mar-hin`). However, we also see that MBR can also hurt performance (usually slightly), as seen in the remaining language pairs. Disappointingly, we do not see any dramatically higher results on our internal test sets due to MBR, indicating that its benefit in these settings may be smaller than we had originally hypothesized. We point out that ensembling still provides a clear advantage to practitioners, in that they do not need to know which individual system performs best, and can still reach performance on par with whichever the best-performing model is, via this method. However, it does not itself appear to increase scores dramatically.

We also note that while there are significant score differences between different systems (such as SEAMLESSM4T v2 vs. Whisper or cascaded vs. end-to-end), training with combined language data or supplementary data (i.e. Shrutilipi) also did not cause any drastic score increases. Given the scantness of these results, we conclude that methods such as ensembling and multilingual training either have limited use in some low-resource speech translation settings, or that they require more creative and effective applications than those we explored here in order to be optimally useful. We encourage researchers to explore such creative applications of these techniques, as well as other techniques to improve low-resource systems, in the future.

[2]This was another mistake due to a file path misunderstanding.

Acknowledgments

We thank Neha Verma, Henry Li, Philipp Koehn, Yaohan Guan, Sanjeev Khudanpur, and Amir Hussein for their contributions to this work.

References

Idris Abdulmumin, Victor Agostinelli, Tanel Alumäe, Antonios Anastasopoulos, Ashwin, Luisa Bentivogli, Ondřej Bojar, Claudia Borg, Fethi Bougares, Roldano Cattoni, Mauro Cettolo, Lizhong Chen, William Chen, Raj Dabre, Yannick Estève, Marcello Federico, Marco Gaido, Dávid Javorský, Marek Kasztelnik, and 30 others. 2025. Findings of the iwslt 2025 evaluation campaign. In *Proceedings of the 22nd International Conference on Spoken Language Translation (IWSLT 2025)*, Vienna, Austia (in-person and online). Association for Computational Linguistics. To appear.

Milind Agarwal, Sweta Agrawal, Antonios Anastasopoulos, Luisa Bentivogli, Ondřej Bojar, Claudia Borg, Marine Carpuat, Roldano Cattoni, Mauro Cettolo, Mingda Chen, William Chen, Khalid Choukri, Alexandra Chronopoulou, Anna Currey, Thierry Declerck, Qianqian Dong, Kevin Duh, Yannick Estève, Marcello Federico, and 43 others. 2023. FINDINGS OF THE IWSLT 2023 EVALUATION CAMPAIGN. In *Proceedings of the 20th International Conference on Spoken Language Translation (IWSLT 2023)*, pages 1–61, Toronto, Canada (in-person and online). Association for Computational Linguistics.

Ibrahim Said Ahmad, Antonios Anastasopoulos, Ondřej Bojar, Claudia Borg, Marine Carpuat, Roldano Cattoni, Mauro Cettolo, William Chen, Qianqian Dong, Marcello Federico, Barry Haddow, Dávid Javorský, Mateusz Krubiński, Tsz Kin Lam, Xutai Ma, Prashant Mathur, Evgeny Matusov, Chandresh Maurya, John McCrae, and 25 others. 2024. FINDINGS OF THE IWSLT 2024 EVALUATION CAMPAIGN. In *Proceedings of the 21st International Conference on Spoken Language Translation (IWSLT 2024)*, pages 1–11, Bangkok, Thailand (in-person and online). Association for Computational Linguistics.

Antonios Anastasopoulos, Loïc Barrault, Luisa Bentivogli, Marcely Zanon Boito, Ondřej Bojar, Roldano Cattoni, Anna Currey, Georgiana Dinu, Kevin Duh, Maha Elbayad, Clara Emmanuel, Yannick Estève, Marcello Federico, Christian Federmann, Souhir Gahbiche, Hongyu Gong, Roman Grundkiewicz, Barry Haddow, Benjamin Hsu, and 24 others. 2022. Findings of the IWSLT 2022 evaluation campaign. In *Proceedings of the 19th International Conference on*

Language Pair	System	Submission	Test1 BLEU	Eval BLEU
aeb-eng	JHU-cascade-2023		-	-
	Seamless	contr. 2	11.47	6.70
	MBR-BLEU	primary	10.73	8.20
	MBR-CHRF	contr. 1	10.76	8.90
apc-eng	Seamless		-	-
	Seamless comb.		-	-
	Whisper ASR + NLLB		-	-
	Whisper ASR + NLLB + ID		-	-
	MBR-BLEU	primary	-	14.64
	MBR-CHRF	contr. 1	-	15.39
bem-eng	Seamless		14.67	-
	Whisper MTL		17.76	-
	Whisper ASR + NLLB		27.58	-
	Whisper ASR + NLLB + ID		29.39	-
	MBR-BLEU	primary	28.80	26.8
	MBR-CHRF	contr. 1	27.84	28.1
bho-hin	Seamless	contr. 2	37.39	7.8
	Seamless comb.		39.08	-
	Whisper MTL		24.19	-
	MBR-BLEU	primary	39.38	10.5
	MBR-CHRF	contr. 1	39.39	10.7
fon-fra	Seamless	contr. 2	5.34	5.60
	MBR-BLEU	primary	4.76	5.96
	MBR-CHRF	contr. 1	5.57	6.26
gle-eng	Seamless	contr. 2	51.80	12.3
	Seamless comb.		47.65	-
	MBR-BLEU	primary	50.37	11.6
	MBR-CHRF	contr. 1	51.13	12.0
mar-hin	Seamless		-	-
	Seamless comb.		44.98	-
	Seamless Shrutilipi	contr. 2	43.17	40.0
	Whisper MTL		28.06	-
	MBR-BLEU	primary	45.64	41.4
	MBR-CHRF	contr. 1	45.27	40.7
mlt-eng	Seamless	contr. 2	40.62	56.10
	Seamless comb.		38.57	-
	Whisper MTL		21.37	-
	MBR-BLEU	primary	40.02	56.80
	MBR-CHRF	contr. 1	38.98	55.98
que-spa	Seamless		1.05	-
	Whisper ASR + NLLB		6.08	-
	Whisper ASR + NLLB + ID		10.69	-
	MBR-BLEU	primary	7.87	9.0
	MBR-CHRF	contr. 1	10.29	11.0

Table 3: BLEU score results. "Test BLEU" refers to our internal tests, while "Eval BLEU" refers to the evaluation run by Abdulmumin et al. (2025)

Spoken Language Translation (IWSLT 2022), pages 98–157, Dublin, Ireland (in-person and online). Association for Computational Linguistics.

Marta Bañón, Pinzhen Chen, Barry Haddow, Kenneth Heafield, Hieu Hoang, Miquel Esplà-Gomis, Mikel L. Forcada, Amir Kamran, Faheem Kirefu, Philipp Koehn, Sergio Ortiz Rojas, Leopoldo Pla Sempere, Gema Ramírez-Sánchez, Elsa Sarrías, Marek Strelec, Brian Thompson, William Waites, Dion Wiggins, and Jaume Zaragoza. 2020. ParaCrawl: Web-scale acquisition of parallel corpora. In *Proceedings of the 58th Annual Meeting of the Association for Computational Linguistics*, pages 4555–4567, Online. Association for Computational Linguistics.

Marta Bañón, Malina Chichirau, Miquel Esplà-Gomis, Mikel L. Forcada, Aarón Galiano-Jiménez, Cristian García-Romero, Taja Kuzman, Nikola Ljubešić, Rik van Noord, Leopoldo Pla Sempere, Gema Ramírez-Sánchez, Peter Rupnik, Vít Suchomel, Antonio Toral, and Jaume Zaragoza-Bernabeu. 2023. Maltese-english parallel corpus MaCoCu-mt-en 2.0. Slovenian language resource repository CLARIN.SI.

Loïc Barrault, Yu-An Chung, Mariano Cora Meglioli, David Dale, Ning Dong, Paul-Ambroise Duquenne, Hady Elsahar, Hongyu Gong, Kevin Heffernan, John Hoffman, and 1 others. 2023. Seamlessm4t: Massively multilingual & multimodal machine translation. *arXiv preprint arXiv:2308.11596*.

Waad Ben Kheder, Josef Jon, André Beyer, Abdel Messaoudi, Rabea Affan, Claude Barras, Maxim Tychonov, and Jean-Luc Gauvain. 2024. ALADAN at IWSLT24 low-resource Arabic dialectal speech translation task. In *Proceedings of the 21st International Conference on Spoken Language Translation (IWSLT 2024)*, pages 192–202, Bangkok, Thailand (in-person and online). Association for Computational Linguistics.

Amanda Bertsch, Alex Xie, Graham Neubig, and Matthew R Gormley. 2023. It's mbr all the way down: Modern generation techniques through the lens of minimum bayes risk. In *The Big Picture Workshop*, page 108.

Kaushal Santosh Bhogale, Abhigyan Raman, Tahir Javed, Sumanth Doddapaneni, Anoop Kunchukuttan, Pratyush Kumar, and Mitesh M. Khapra. 2022. Effectiveness of mining audio and text pairs from public data for improving asr systems for low-resource languages. *arXiv preprint*.

Peter J Bickel and Kjell A Doksum. 1977. *Mathematical statistics: basic ideas and selected topics*. Holden-Day Inc.

Ronald Cardenas, Rodolfo Zevallos, Reynaldo Baquerizo, and Luis Camacho. 2018. Siminchik: A speech corpus for preservation of southern quechua. *ISI-NLP 2*, page 21.

John E. Ortega, Rodolfo Joel Zevallos, Ibrahim Said Ahmad, and William Chen. 2024. QUESPA submission for the IWSLT 2024 dialectal and low-resource speech translation task. In *Proceedings of the 21st International Conference on Spoken Language Translation (IWSLT 2024)*, pages 125–133, Bangkok, Thailand (in-person and online). Association for Computational Linguistics.

Markus Freitag, David Grangier, Qijun Tan, and Bowen Liang. 2022. High quality rather than high model probability: Minimum Bayes risk decoding with neural metrics. *Transactions of the Association for Computational Linguistics*, 10:811–825.

Fei He, Shan-Hui Cathy Chu, Oddur Kjartansson, Clara Rivera, Anna Katanova, Alexander Gutkin, Isin Demirsahin, Cibu Johny, Martin Jansche, Supheakmungkol Sarin, and Knot Pipatsrisawat. 2020. Open-source multi-speaker speech corpora for building Gujarati, Kannada, Malayalam, Marathi, Tamil and Telugu speech synthesis systems. In *Proceedings of the Twelfth Language Resources and Evaluation Conference*, pages 6494–6503, Marseille, France. European Language Resources Association.

Carlos Daniel Hernandez Mena, Albert Gatt, Andrea DeMarco, Claudia Borg, Lonneke van der Plas, Amanda Muscat, and Ian Padovani. 2020. MASRI-HEADSET: A Maltese corpus for speech recognition. In *Proceedings of the Twelfth Language Resources and Evaluation Conference*, pages 6381–6388, Marseille, France. European Language Resources Association.

Aditya Joshi, Raj Dabre, Diptesh Kanojia, Zhuang Li, Haolan Zhan, Gholamreza Haffari, and Doris Dippold. 2024. Natural language processing for dialects of a language: A survey. *arXiv preprint arXiv:2401.05632*.

D. Fortuné Kponou, Fréjus A. A. Laleye, and Eugène Cokou Ezin. 2024. FFSTC: Fongbe to French speech translation corpus. In *Proceedings of the 2024 Joint International Conference on Computational Linguistics, Language Resources and Evaluation (LREC-COLING 2024)*, pages 7270–7276, Torino, Italia. ELRA and ICCL.

Shankar Kumar and Bill Byrne. 2004. Minimum bayes-risk decoding for statistical machine translation. In *Proceedings of the Human Language Technology Conference of the North American Chapter of the Association for Computational Linguistics: HLT-NAACL 2004*, pages 169–176.

Zhaolin Li, Enes Yavuz Ugan, Danni Liu, Carlos Mullov, Tu Anh Dinh, Sai Koneru, Alexander Waibel, and Jan Niehues. 2024. The KIT speech translation systems for IWSLT 2024 dialectal and low-resource track. In *Proceedings of the 21st International Conference on Spoken Language Translation (IWSLT 2024)*, pages 221–228, Bangkok, Thailand (in-person and online). Association for Computational Linguistics.

John Makhoul, Bushra Zawaydeh, Frederick Choi, and David Stallard. 2005. Bbn/aub darpa babylon levantine arabic speech and transcripts. *Linguistic Data Consortium (LDC), LDC Catalog No.: LDC2005S08.*

Mathias Müller and Rico Sennrich. 2021. Understanding the properties of minimum Bayes risk decoding in neural machine translation. In *Proceedings of the 59th Annual Meeting of the Association for Computational Linguistics and the 11th International Joint Conference on Natural Language Processing (Volume 1: Long Papers)*, pages 259–272, Online. Association for Computational Linguistics.

NLLB Team, Marta R. Costa-jussà, James Cross, Onur Çelebi, Maha Elbayad, Kenneth Heafield, Kevin Heffernan, Elahe Kalbassi, Janice Lam, Daniel Licht, Jean Maillard, Anna Sun, Skyler Wang, Guillaume Wenzek, Al Youngblood, Bapi Akula, Loic Barrault, Gabriel Mejia-Gonzalez, Prangthip Hansanti, and 20 others. 2022. No language left behind: Scaling human-centered machine translation.

Atsumoto Ohashi, Ukyo Honda, Tetsuro Morimura, and Yuu Jinnai. 2024. On the true distribution approximation of minimum bayes-risk decoding. In *Proceedings of the 2024 Conference of the North American Chapter of the Association for Computational Linguistics: Human Language Technologies (Volume 2: Short Papers)*, pages 459–468.

John E Ortega, Richard Castro Mamani, and Kyunghyun Cho. 2020. Neural machine translation with a polysynthetic low resource language. *Machine Translation*, 34(4):325–346.

Kishore Papineni, Salim Roukos, Todd Ward, and Wei-Jing Zhu. 2002. Bleu: a method for automatic evaluation of machine translation. In *Proceedings of the 40th Annual Meeting of the Association for Computational Linguistics*, pages 311–318, Philadelphia, Pennsylvania, USA. Association for Computational Linguistics.

Maja Popović. 2015. chrF: character n-gram F-score for automatic MT evaluation. In *Proceedings of the Tenth Workshop on Statistical Machine Translation*, pages 392–395, Lisbon, Portugal. Association for Computational Linguistics.

Alec Radford, Jong Wook Kim, Tao Xu, Greg Brockman, Christine Mcleavey, and Ilya Sutskever. 2023a. Robust speech recognition via large-scale weak supervision. In *Proceedings of the 40th International Conference on Machine Learning*, volume 202 of *Proceedings of Machine Learning Research*, pages 28492–28518. PMLR.

Alec Radford, Jong Wook Kim, Tao Xu, Greg Brockman, Christine McLeavey, and Ilya Sutskever. 2023b. Robust speech recognition via large-scale weak supervision. In *International conference on machine learning*, pages 28492–28518. PMLR.

Nathaniel Romney Robinson, Kaiser Sun, Cihan Xiao, Niyati Bafna, Weiting Tan, Haoran Xu, Henry Li Xinyuan, Ankur Kejriwal, Sanjeev Khudanpur, Kenton Murray, and 1 others. 2024. Jhu iwslt 2024 dialectal and low-resource system description. In *Proceedings of the 21st International Conference on Spoken Language Translation (IWSLT 2024)*, pages 140–153.

Hashem Sellat, Shadi Saleh, Mateusz Krubiński, Adam Pospíšil, Petr Zemánek, and Pavel Pecina. 2023. UFAL parallel corpus of north levantine 1.0. LINDAT/CLARIAH-CZ digital library at the Institute of Formal and Applied Linguistics (ÚFAL), Faculty of Mathematics and Physics, Charles University.

Claytone Sikasote and Antonios Anastasopoulos. 2022. BembaSpeech: A speech recognition corpus for the Bemba language. In *Proceedings of the Thirteenth Language Resources and Evaluation Conference*, pages 7277–7283, Marseille, France. European Language Resources Association.

Claytone Sikasote, Eunice Mukonde, Md Mahfuz Ibn Alam, and Antonios Anastasopoulos. 2023. BIG-C: a multimodal multi-purpose dataset for Bemba. In *Proceedings of the 61st Annual Meeting of the Association for Computational Linguistics (Volume 1: Long Papers)*, pages 2062–2078, Toronto, Canada. Association for Computational Linguistics.

Tiia Sildam, Andra Velve, and Tanel Alumäe. 2024. Finetuning end-to-end models for Estonian conversational spoken language translation. In *Proceedings of the Seventh Workshop on Technologies for Machine Translation of Low-Resource Languages (LoResMT 2024)*, pages 166–174, Bangkok, Thailand.

Jörg Tiedemann. 2012. Parallel data, tools and interfaces in OPUS. In *Proceedings of the Eighth International Conference on Language Resources and Evaluation (LREC'12)*, pages 2214–2218, Istanbul, Turkey. European Language Resources Association (ELRA).

Haoran Xu, Philipp Koehn, and Kenton Murray. 2022. The importance of being parameters: An intra-distillation method for serious gains. In *Proceedings of the 2022 Conference on Empirical Methods in Natural Language Processing*, pages 170–183, Abu Dhabi, United Arab Emirates. Association for Computational Linguistics.

Haoran Xu, Jean Maillard, and Vedanuj Goswami. 2023. Language-aware multilingual machine translation with self-supervised learning. *arXiv preprint arXiv:2302.05008.*

Caleb Ziems, William Held, Jingfeng Yang, Jwala Dhamala, Rahul Gupta, and Diyi Yang. 2023. Multi-VALUE: A framework for cross-dialectal English NLP. In *Proceedings of the 61st Annual Meeting of the Association for Computational Linguistics (Volume 1: Long Papers)*, pages 744–768, Toronto, Canada. Association for Computational Linguistics.

A SEAMLESSM4T v2 hyperparameters

In our experiments, we use the SEAMLESSM4T v2 model. To keep things consistent, we cut off audio that is longer than 30 seconds. We also use a fixed random seed of 42 so that the results can be repeated.

We try different learning rates from the set $\{10^{-6}, 10^{-7}\}$ to see which works best. For most language pairs, we fine-tune the `SEAMLESSM4T v2-large` model for 10 epochs using a learning rate of 1×10^{-6} and a batch size of 32.

During training, we use a constant learning rate schedule and set 50 warm-up steps. When generating translations, we use greedy decoding and limit the output to 256 tokens.

SYSTRAN @ IWSLT 2025 Low-resource track

Marko Avila and Josep Crego
SYSTRAN by ChapsVision
5 rue Feydeau, 75002 Paris (France)

Abstract

SYSTRAN submitted systems for one language pair in the 2025 Low-Resource Language Track. Our main contribution lies in the tight coupling and light fine-tuning of an ASR encoder (Whisper) with a neural machine translation decoder (NLLB), forming an efficient speech translation pipeline. We present the modeling strategies and optimizations implemented to build a system that, unlike large-scale end-to-end models, performs effectively under constraints of limited training data and computational resources. This approach enables the development of high-quality speech translation in low-resource settings, while ensuring both efficiency and scalability. We also conduct a comparative analysis of our proposed system against various paradigms, including a cascaded Whisper+NLLB setup and direct end-to-end fine-tuning of Whisper.

1 Introduction

The goal of the IWSLT'2025 low-resource shared task is to benchmark and promote speech translation technology for a diverse range of dialects and low-resource languages. While significant research progress has been demonstrated recently on popular datasets, many of the world's dialects and low-resource languages lack the parallel data at scale needed for standard supervised learning. Thus, this share task requires creative approaches in leveraging disparate resources. The low-resource shared task will involve two tracks:

- Track 1: A "traditional" speech-to-text translation track focusing on XX typologically diverse language-pairs.
- Track 2: A data track, inviting participants to provide open-sourced speech translation datasets for under-resourced languages.

SYSTRAN participates exclusively in the "traditional" Tunisian Arabic-to-English speech translation track. Our system employs a tightly coupled architecture wherein the automatic speech recognition (ASR) encoder directly interfaces with the neural machine translation (NMT) encoder-decoder module. This end-to-end pipeline has demonstrated robust performance in prior evaluations under low-resource conditions. The primary objective is to build a high-performance speech-to-text translation (S2TT) system optimized for constrained computational environments and limited annotated data, while effectively leveraging the representational power of large-scale pretrained models.

In Section 2, we describe the corpora used in this study, as well as the pre-processing steps applied to improve their relevance and quality for the target tasks (see Section 3). Section 4 introduces the proposed system, which combines a speech encoder with neural machine translation components. Section 5 presents the experimental setup and reports the results obtained. Finally, Section 6 summarizes the main findings and concludes the paper.

2 Dataset Description

This work is conducted as part of a shared task aimed at advancing the state of the art in ASR and speech S2TT for low-resource dialects, with a particular focus on Tunisian Arabic. To ensure comparability and fairness, all experiments are conducted under the *constrained condition*, using exclusively the Tunisian-English resources provided by the Linguistic Data Consortium (LDC) for this challenge.

2.1 Corpus Overview

The dataset comprises manually transcribed and translated audio resources in two language varieties: Tunisian Arabic (TA) and Modern Standard Arabic (MSA). Although MSA content originates from broadcast news (BN), TA is represented through conversational telephone speech (CTS), offering rich linguistic variability. English transla-

Proceedings of the 22nd International Conference on Spoken Language Translation (IWSLT 2025), pages 324–332
July 31 - August 1, 2025 ©2025 Association for Computational Linguistics

tions are available for all MSA transcripts and for a large portion of TA segments, enabling the training of end-to-end speech translation models.

2.2 Audio Data

MSA Broadcast News (BN): This portion includes two single-channel recordings totaling approximately 1 hour of audio. The recordings consist of multi-speaker news broadcasts and interviews, sampled at 16 kHz and stored as FLAC-compressed MS-WAV files with 16-bit PCM encoding.

TA Conversational Telephone Speech (CTS): The core of the dataset consists of 387 hours of two-channel telephone conversations, distributed across 2,198 dialogues (4,396 single-channel files). These were collected in Tunisia via an automated robot operator that interfaced directly with the regional public telephone network. Each call involves:

- Side A: A "claque" speaker, a recruited participant tasked with initiating conversations.
- Side B: A callee, selected naturally by the claque from their personal contacts.

Claques completed 8 to 15 distinct calls, each lasting 8–10 minutes, and were encouraged to dominate the discourse to ensure informative linguistic content. The TA audio files are encoded in A-law format at 8 kHz with NIST SPHERE headers.

2.3 Segmentation and Speaker Annotation

Broadcast News (BN). Manual segmentation and speaker turn identification were performed using the LDC-developed *XTrans* tool (Glenn et al., 2009). Speakers were identified by name when available; otherwise, anonymous labels indicating speaker and gender (e.g., *speaker1/male*) were used.

Conversational Telephone Speech (CTS). Segmentation followed a three-stage process: (i) automatic speech activity detection (SAD) with a minimum silence threshold of 0.5 seconds was applied to each single-channel audio file; (ii) segments longer than 15 seconds were re-segmented with a relaxed silence threshold of 0.3 seconds; (iii) final segment boundaries were manually verified and corrected in XTrans by expert annotators.

2.4 Transcription Protocol

BN transcripts were generated in Arabic script using XTrans. **CTS** segments, alternating between speakers A and B, were transcribed using a contextual navigation web interface. Transcripts were in Buckwalter transliteration, with some segments also featuring broad IPA transcriptions. A verification pass ensured alignment between orthographic and phonemic transcripts and enabled token-level annotation for MSA, foreign language, and uncertain items.

2.5 Transcription Statistics

Manual transcriptions were provided for both MSA and TA recordings. Table 4 summarizes the number of segments, duration of speech-only segments, and number of files per genre.

Table 1: Transcription statistics per genre.

Type	Segments	Hours	Files
MSA / BN	420	0.96	2
TA / CTS	398,064	323.73	4,396
Total	398,484	324.69	4,398

2.6 Translation Statistics

English translations are provided for the full set of MSA segments and a substantial subset of TA transcripts, supporting supervised ST model training. Table 2 reports the number of translated segments, duration of time-stamped speech, and corresponding files.

Table 2: Translation statistics per genre.

Type	Segments	Hours	Files
MSA / BN	420	0.96	2
TA / CTS	210,901	167.48	2,284
Total	211,321	168.44	2,286

In total, this release provides:

- **323.73 hours** of Tunisian Arabic CTS audio with manual transcriptions, suitable for ASR development.
- **167.48 hours** of translated Tunisian Arabic audio, enabling end-to-end ST modeling.
- **1 hour** of Modern Standard Arabic broadcast news audio, fully transcribed and translated.

This resource offers a rare and valuable foundation for research in dialectal ASR and ST, bridging the gap between underrepresented spoken varieties and high-resource translation targets.

3 Data Cleaning and Annotation

3.1 Token-Level Annotations and Markup

Arabic transcripts include token-level annotations to reflect linguistic variability:

- `M/` — Modern Standard Arabic
- `O/` — Foreign word
- `U/` — Uncertain token
- `UM/`, `UO/` — Combined uncertainty

BN transcripts use XML-style tags (`<non-MSA> ... </non-MSA>`) to flag non-MSA spans. These annotations were removed in our pre-processing pipeline to ensure clean input for downstream modeling.

3.2 Translation Annotations

English translations are aligned at the segment level. Annotation conventions include:

- `(())`: Uncertain words
- `%pw`: Partial word
- `#`: Untranslated foreign word
- `+`: Mispronunciation
- =: Typographic errors from the transcript
- *uh, um, eh, ah*: Filled pauses

All special symbols were removed in a pre-processing step.

3.3 Text Pre-processing and Token Filtering

To ensure consistency and reduce noise introduced by transcription and translation annotation artifacts, we applied language-specific filtering rules to clean both Arabic and English segments. These regular expressions were crafted based on the known annotation conventions of the dataset.

We defined the following regular expression used for Arabic transcripts:

$$re.compile(r'[OUM]+/*|\backslash u061F|\backslash ?|\backslash !|\backslash .')$$

This expression targets and removes annotation prefixes such as $O/$, $U/$, and $M/$, which denote foreign language tokens, uncertain words, and Modern Standard Arabic (MSA), respectively. It also eliminates punctuation marks including the Arabic question mark (Unicode $\backslash u061F$) as well as Western punctuation symbols (?, !, .), which are inconsistently used and not linguistically informative for model training.

For English translations, we defined the following filter:

$$re.compile(r'\backslash (|\backslash)|\backslash |\backslash +|\backslash =|\backslash ?|\backslash !|\backslash ;|\backslash .|\backslash ,|\backslash "|\backslash :')$$

This regular expression removes special characters and annotation markers such as # (foreign words), + (mispronunciations), = (typographical errors), and common punctuation symbols. These annotations were introduced during the manual translation process to capture spoken language phenomena but are not useful for token-level alignment or model training.

This pre-processing step allowed us to normalize the text, reduce vocabulary sparsity, and ensure cleaner input for downstream Automatic Speech Recognition (ASR) and Speech Translation (ST) tasks.

After filtering, preprocessing, and splitting the data according to the partitions provided by the organizers, we obtained the following subsets: training, development, and test.

Table 3: Transcription statistics per genre after filtering for train/dev/test.

Type	Segments	Hours
MSA / BN	410	0.94
TA / CTS	390,021/3833/4220	317.19/3.12/3.43
Total	390,431/3833/4220	318.13/3.12/3.43

Table 4: Translation statistics per genre after filtering for train/dev/test.

Type	Segments	Hours
MSA / BN	409	0.937
TA / CTS	202,504/3833/4204	160.81/3.12/3.42
Total	202,913/3833/4204	161.747/3.12/3.42

After filtering, the dataset comprises 318.13 hours of transcribed Tunisian Arabic audio for ASR training, with 3.12 and 3.42 hours for development and test, respectively. Additionally, it includes 161.75 hours of parallel audio-translation pairs for ST training, with the same dev/test splits.

3.4 Known Issues

- **Partial Call Coverage:** Some CTS calls are only partially annotated due to transcription kit omissions.

- **Stranded Diacritic Marks:** 158 instances of diacritic-prefixed tokens (e.g., a, i, o) persist in 134 files.
- **Empty Segments:** 714 CTS segments contain only a hyphen ("-"), signaling rejected or unusable segments.
- **Missing Translations:** 10 BN segments lack translations due to English speech in the source audio.

4 Coupling Whisper and NLLB

This work introduces a hybrid solution designed for parameter-efficient training in low-resource language scenarios inspired by the integration strategy presented in (Avila and Crego, 2025) , integrating speech representation features from a pre-trained speech model into a multilingual NMT system. Our approach integrates speech representation features from a pre-trained speech model encoder such as Whisper into a multilingual Neural Machine Translation system such as NLLB, enabling both ASR and S2TT capabilities.

4.1 Motivation and Context

The primary goal of this shared task is to benchmark and foster advancements in speech translation technologies for a wide spectrum of dialects and low-resource languages. In particular, this initiative focuses on improving automatic speech transcription and translation for the Tunisian dialect, a variety of Arabic that remains significantly underrepresented in existing resources.

Low-resource conditions such as those encountered with Tunisian Arabic pose substantial challenges for conventional speech translation pipelines, which typically rely on large-scale annotated corpora. In this context, pre-trained models like Whisper, despite their multilingual design, lack direct support for Tunisian. Conversely, the NLLB model provides explicit support for Tunisian text and English, enabling translation in both directions.

This complementary nature of Whisper and NLLB forms the foundation of our hybrid approach. By leveraging Whisper for robust audio feature extraction and NLLB for multilingual text translation, we bridge the gap between speech and text modalities. The integration of high-quality speech representations into a powerful text-based multilingual translation model allows us to address the limitations of current systems in low-resource environments.

4.2 Speech Representation via Whisper

In our hybrid approach, Whisper encoder is kept frozen and used to generate speech representations, which substitute the input word embedding of the NLLB network.

The speech representations X consist of the outputs after the K lower encoder layers:

$$\texttt{Whisper}_{ENC}^{K}(a) = X, \text{ with } X \in \mathcal{R}^{N \times M}$$

with a the audio signal, N the sequence length and M the embedding dimension.

`Whisper`[1] (Radford et al., 2023) is a speech recognition model tailored for multilingual recognition, translation, and language identification. Its Transformer-based architecture integrates multiple speech processing tasks into a single, unified model.

We use two variants of Whisper (**Medium** and **Large-v3**) to evaluate the impact of model scale on representation quality. Both models take 30-second segments of audio resampled at 16kHz and convert them into 80-channel log-magnitude Mel spectrograms. The Whisper encoder outputs are extracted from the final Transformer layer: the K=24th layer for **Medium** ($M = 1024$) and the K=32nd for **Large-v3** ($M = 1280$). The output is a fixed-length sequence of $N = 1500$ vectors.

To align Whisper outputs with the NLLB encoder input we employ a `Reshape` module consisting of:

- A **convolutional layer** with kernel size = 3 and stride = 1 is used to reduce the sequence length from 1500 to 100.
- A **linear projection layer** ($M \times 2048$) is applied to match the expected embedding dimension of the NLLB 3.3B encoder.

4.3 Neural Machine Translation with NLLB

We employ `NLLB`[2] (team et al., 2022), a multilingual NMT model developed by Meta AI, designed to support direct translation between more than 200 languages, including many low-resource and underrepresented languages. Based on a Transformer architecture, NLLB employs language-specific tokens and dense representations to handle diverse

[1]https://huggingface.co/openai/whisper-medium,https://huggingface.co/openai/whisper-large-v3

[2]https://huggingface.co/facebook/nllb-200-3.3B

linguistic structures. Its 3.3B parameter version, used in this work, provides strong performance across a wide range of language pairs, making it well-suited for multilingual and low-resource translation tasks.

In NLLB, we prepend a special token $\langle \text{lang}_{src} \rangle$ at the beginning of the source sentence to specify the source language and another special token $\langle \text{lang}_{tgt} \rangle$ to specify the target language. During inference, this last token guides the decoder to produce output in the desired language.

The NLLB encoder is partially fine-tuned during training, specifically the lower L layers, while the higher layers remain frozen to retain multilingual generalization. The Whisper encoder remains completely frozen and is used purely for speech feature extraction.

4.4 Language Conditioning and Token Embeddings

To handle multilingual input and output, we append the source language token $\langle \text{lang}_{src} \rangle$ to the reshaped speech representation and use $\langle \text{lang}_{tgt} \rangle$ in the decoder. Both tokens are embedded using NLLB's embedding layer. This token-based control mechanism enables seamless switching between languages during both training and inference.

Source and target training pairs are formatted as follows:

$$\begin{aligned} source &= \langle lang_{src} \rangle \; src\_sentence \; \langle eos \rangle \\ target &= \langle bos \rangle \; \langle lang_{tgt} \rangle \; tgt\_sentence \; \langle eos \rangle \end{aligned}$$

4.5 Hybrid Architecture

This hybrid configuration transforms the multilingual NLLB 3.3B model into a multi-functional system capable of both ASR and S2TT. The architecture leverages pre-trained speech representations from Whisper (specifically the Medium and Large-v3 variants) and integrates them into the NLLB framework. This design enables the system to operate in low-resource settings with minimal parameter updates. In this setup, high-level audio features are extracted from a frozen Whisper encoder, which serves solely as a feature extractor. These representations are then reshaped to align with the input format expected by the NLLB encoder. Crucially, this reshaped output replaces the traditional word embedding layer in the NLLB encoder, allowing the model to process audio input instead of text, and the efficiency of parameter training is achieved by only modifying the parameters of reshape module and the lower layers of the NLLB encoder. The architecture consists of three main components:

- A frozen Whisper encoder (either Medium or Large-v3),
- A reshape module that projects the audio embeddings into the required format,
- A multilingual NLLB 3.3B encoder-decoder model.

Figure 1 (right block) illustrates the complete hybrid S2TT architecture. Speech representations X, visualized as black squares, are generated by the Whisper encoder. These are subsequently reshaped X' and passed to the NLLB encoder, which processes them and generates translations from the outputs Z by applying a linear projection followed by a softmax function. By limiting fine-tuning to only the lower layers of the NLLB encoder and the reshape module, the model achieves parameter-efficient training while retaining multilingual capabilities.

The Whisper encoder outputs high-dimensional speech representations that are reshaped to match the input format expected by the NLLB encoder. This replaces the word embedding layer in NLLB with audio-derived embeddings. Mor formally:

$$X = \texttt{Whisper}^{K}_{ENC}(a) \quad (1)$$

$$X' = \texttt{EMB}(\langle lang_{src} \rangle) \cdot \texttt{Reshape}(X) \quad (2)$$

$$Y = \texttt{NLLB}_{ENC}(X') \quad (3)$$

$$Z = \texttt{NLLB}_{DEC}(Y) \quad (4)$$

Here, a is the input audio signal, X is the speech representation, and X' is the concatenated input embedding. Y and Z represent the encoded and decoded outputs, respectively.

4.6 Parameter-Efficient Training Scenarios

We consider two training scenarios for low-resource adaptation:

- **Zero-shot:** Whisper and NLLB are used as is, without fine-tuning. Figure 1 illustrates this scenario.
- **Domain adaptation:** Parameter-efficient fine-tuning is performed:
  - Whisper is fine-tuned over Tunisian audio/transcription examples obtained from LDC in-domain data (LDC ASR).

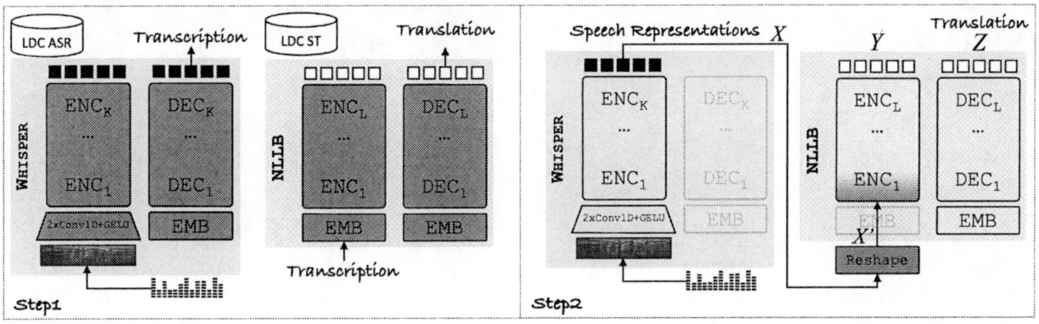

Figure 1: Overview of the Hybrid Whisper+NLLB Approach in a parameter-efficient domain adaptation scenario. The Whisper encoder/decoder is fine-tuned using LDC ASR data, while NLLB is fine-tuned on both transcription and translation text from LDC ASR and S2TT datasets (step1). Both models are then coupled to enable hybrid processing (step2). Red color indicates model weights being updated (the rest are kept freezed).

- NLLB is fine-tuned using in-domain transcription/translation examples.

Figure 1 illustrates the adaptation in domain for Whisper ASR tunisian and NLLB adaption to translate english or tunisian in LDC domain. In both cases, a last adaptation for coupling these two models is achieved by updating only a small subset of model parameters (e.g., the reshape module and lower layers of the NLLB encoder), enabling effective learning from limited resources.

5 Experimental work

5.1 Networks

Our **Coupling Hybrid** models are trained using a single NVIDIA H100 GPU (80GB) during up to 20 epochs, with a maximum batch size of 64 utterances and updates of the model after accumulating 64 batches. We validate every $1,000$ updates and perform early stopping on a separate validation set excluded from the training set. We use the lazy Adam algorithm (Kingma and Ba, 2014) for optimization. In inference, we use a beam size of 5.

5.2 Results

Table 5 summarizes the results obtained across various model configurations and architectures. We report BLEU scores (Post, 2018) and word error rates (WER)[3] as evaluation metrics for S2TT and ASR, respectively. WER is computed on normalized transcriptions[4].

BLEU and WER results are indicated over internal development and test sets, as provided by the task organizers. These splits are considered in our analysis. Best scores for each development/test set are highlighted in bold.

Columns *Whisper Inf Enc* and *Dec* indicate the number of encoder/decoder layers used during inference by Whisper. Similarly, *NMT Opt Enc* and *Dec* specify the number of encoder and decoder layers fine-tuned in the NLLB model. Note that we always use the 3.3B parameter version of NLLB.

During inference, NLLB consistently employs all its encoder/decoder layers. The *Size* column reports the total number of parameters used by each system during inference.

System **`Whisper M`** indicates the original Whisper Medium model, used for both ASR and S2TT tasks. Without fine-tuning the model obtains very poor transcription and translation scores. This is mainly because Whisper was pre-trained in modern standard Arabic (MSA) and lacks exposure to the Tunisian dialect, which severely limits its ability to handle dialectal input.

Systems **`Whisper M`**^{FT} and **`Whisper L`**^{FT} involve full fine-tuning of `Whisper Medium` and `Whisper Large v3` for ASR using the complete cleaned speech-transcription training data introduced in Section 2. These are the only two configurations in which Whisper is fine-tuned, resulting in considerably longer training times (nearly 2 days). Although their BLEU scores remain very low, similar to those of the baseline Whisper model, their ASR performance improves significantly after fine-tuning. Compared to the baseline **`Whisper M`**, which was not fine-tuned, both fine-tuned systems show significant improvements in ASR per-

[3]`https://huggingface.co/spaces/evaluate-metric/wer`

[4]Normalization is performed by `BasicTextNormalizer` from the `transformers.models.whisper` module.

Model	Data	Whisper Inf		NLLB Opt		Size	BLEU↑		WER↓	
		Enc	*Dec*	*Enc*	*Dec*		*dev*	*tst*	*dev*	*tst*
`Whisper M`	-	24	24	-	-	769M	1.18	1.14	157.28	168.23
`Whisper` *fine-tunned*										
`Whisper` $\texttt{M}^{FT}$	ASR	24	24	-	-	769M	1.17	1.15	44.31	53.41
`Whisper` $\texttt{L}^{FT}$	ASR	32	32	-	-	1550M	2.13	1.86	**43.70**	**50.23**
Cascade										
`Whisper` $\texttt{M}^{FT}$ `+ NLLB`	ASR	24	24	0	0	4.07B	5.45	4.64	44.31	53.41
`Whisper` $\texttt{L}^{FT}$ `+ NLLB`	ASR	32	32	0	0	4.85B	5.68	5.07	43.70	50.23
`Whisper` $\texttt{M}^{FT}$ `+` $\texttt{NLLB}^{FT}$	ASR+MT	24	24	24	24	4.07B	19.25	16.44	44.31	53.41
`Whisper` $\texttt{L}^{FT}$ `+` $\texttt{NLLB}^{FT}$	ASR+MT	32	32	24	24	4.85B	**19.77**	17.39	43.70	50.23
Hybrid										
`Whisper M + NLLB`	ST	24	-	2	0	4.07B	12.39	9.92	-	-
`Whisper M + NLLB`	ASR+ST	24	-	2	0	4.07B	9.10	7.44	77.71	85.07
`Whisper` $\texttt{M}^{FT}$ `+` $\texttt{NLLB}^{FT}$	ST	24	-	2	0	4.07B	19.22	16.62	126.57	121.41
`Whisper` $\texttt{L}^{FT}$ `+` $\texttt{NLLB}^{FT}$	ST	32	-	2	0	4.35B	19.37	**17.52**	149.31	139.48

Table 5: Translation (BLEU) and recognition (WER) results across various model configurations. The column *Data* shows data used for each configuration, the column *Whisper Inf* specifies the number of Whisper encoder/decoder layers used during inference, while *NMT Opt* shows the number of NLLB encoder/decoder layers optimized during training. The *Size* column denotes the total number of parameters used during inference.

formance. Specifically, **`Whisper`** $\texttt{M}^{FT}$ achieves WERs of 44.31 and 53.41 on the dev and test sets, while **`Whisper`** $\texttt{L}^{FT}$ further improves to 43.70 and 50.23. These results demonstrate the effectiveness of fine-tuning even without changes to the model architecture. However, BLEU scores remain low for in both cases as these models are not explicitly optimized for translation. The slight increase in BLEU for the larger model is likely due to more accurate transcriptions feeding into the implicit translation process, but overall, these scores confirm that fine-tuning Whisper solely for ASR is insufficient for reliable S2TT performance.

In the *Cascade* setup, systems **`Whisper`** $\texttt{M}^{FT}$**`+NLLB`** and **`Whisper`** $\texttt{L}^{FT}$**`+NLLB`** combine fine-tuned Whisper models (for ASR) with the base NLLB model (for MT). In this approach, Whisper is first fine-tuned on the LDC ASR dataset to generate transcriptions, which are then passed to the unadapted NLLB model for translation. These configurations do not yield strong translation performance, primarily due to the mismatch between the transcription domain and the NLLB training data. However, performance could be improved through domain adaptation of the NLLB component. When adapting the NLLB model with the available in-domain datasets, systems **`Whisper`** $\texttt{M}^{FT}$**`+`**$\texttt{NLLB}^{FT}$ and **`Whisper`** $\texttt{L}^{FT}$**`+`**$\texttt{NLLB}^{FT}$ clearly improve their translation performance. The NLLB model is fine-tuned on transcription-translation pairs from the LDC ASR and ST datasets. Thus, transcriptions produced by Whisper are then translated using the adapted NLLB network. These latter systems demonstrate the effectiveness of adapting NLLB to the ASR/ST domain using LDC transcriptions and translations. However, despite the improved accuracy, the inherent latency introduced by cascading models makes them less suitable for real-time or industrial applications, where efficiency is critical. WER scores remain constant across all cascade systems because the Whisper component, responsible for transcription, is identical within each Whisper variant. This consistency further confirms that BLEU gains are due solely to the adaptation of the translation model.

The next set of results pertains to our hybrid systems. We utilize fine-tuned versions of Whisper (Medium and Large v3) tightly coupled with NLLB as detailed in section 4. Similarly to the cascade setup, the first two systems use the original, pretrained Whisper and NLLB models, while the latter two are hybrid systems that combine Whisper and NLLB models which have been previously fine-tuned.

One key advantage of the hybrid models lies in their compactness: they require significantly fewer parameters than the cascade counterparts. Furthermore, coupling optimization is computationally efficient. The Whisper speech encoder is kept frozen, while only 2 out of 24 layers in the NLLB encoder are fine-tuned. This strategy drastically reduces training time and computational cost. Fine-tuning with the LDC ST dataset required only 1 to 3 days, depending on the configuration and number of trainable parameters.

The first two hybrid systems, where Whisper and NLLB models are used without any fine-tuning, output moderate improvements over the raw Whisper model but significantly lower performance than domain-adapted cascade approaches. The system trained on both ASR and ST objectives (ASR+ST) exhibits a significant drop in both translation and transcription quality compared to the version trained solely on the ST objective (ST). This suggests that, in the absence of domain adaptation, multitask training may lead to interference between the tasks.

When hybridizing the adapted networks (last two rows), where both Whisper and NLLB are fine-tuned using in-domain LDC data, systems attain BLEU scores nearly equivalent to the best-performing cascade systems. These results validate the effectiveness of our lightweight hybrid fine-tuning strategy, which freezes most Whisper and NLLB layers, optimizing only a minimal subset. Notably, these hybrid models operate with lower parameter counts and exhibit superior latency characteristics compared to their cascade counterparts. WER scores, however, are higher in the hybrid domain-adapted models (ranging from 121 to 149), reflecting a trade-off in ASR accuracy potentially introduced by tighter integration and shared optimization. This is also partly due to the fact that the hybrid models were exclusively fine-tuned using speech translation (ST) data, without direct supervision on ASR objectives. As a result, while the models are optimized for generating accurate translations, their raw transcription outputs may be less precise, contributing to higher WER.

As expected, the hybrid models achieve S2TT performance comparable to the cascade systems. For example, the best hybrid domain adaptation configuration attains BLEU scores of 19.37 and 17.52 on the development and test sets, respectively. Importantly, these hybrid models offer superior latency characteristics, making them more suitable for deployment in real-time or resource-constrained environments compared to their cascade counterparts.

Finally, it is important to note that the results submitted for the evaluation of this task were obtained several epochs prior to the final version of the model. At that stage, the model achieved a BLEU score of 18.96 on the development set and 16.94 on the test set. The current version of our model outperforms the submitted one by approximately 0.5 BLEU points.

6 Conclusions and further work

We presented SYSTRAN's submitted systems for the 2025 Low-Resource Language Track, targeting the task of Tunisian Arabic to English speech translation. Our approach combines an ASR encoder (Whisper) with a neural machine translation decoder (NLLB), using light fine-tuning to create an efficient and compact speech translation pipeline. The resulting Speech-to-Text Translation system is designed to operate with minimal computational resources and limited training data. We evaluated our system against several alternative configurations, including a cascaded Whisper+NLLB setup and direct end-to-end fine-tuning of Whisper. Our results demonstrate that it is possible to achieve high translation quality under low-resource constraints, enabling broader accessibility without the need for large-scale infrastructure.

Acknowledgments

This work has been funded by the French Ministry of Defense through the DGA-RAPID 2022190955, COMMUTE project.

References

Marko Avila and Josep Crego. 2025. Leveraging large pre-trained multilingual models for high-quality speech-to-text translation on industry scenarios. In *Proceedings of the 31st International Conference on Computational Linguistics*, pages 7624–7633, Abu Dhabi, UAE. Association for Computational Linguistics.

Meghan Lammie Glenn, Stephanie Strassel, and Haejoong Lee. 2009. Xtrans: a speech annotation and transcription tool. In *Interspeech*.

Diederik P Kingma and Jimmy Ba. 2014. Adam: A method for stochastic optimization. *arXiv preprint arXiv:1412.6980*.

Matt Post. 2018. A call for clarity in reporting BLEU scores. In *Proceedings of the Third Conference on Machine Translation: Research Papers*, pages 186–191, Brussels, Belgium. Association for Computational Linguistics.

Alec Radford, Jong Wook Kim, Tao Xu, Greg Brockman, Christine McLeavey, and Ilya Sutskever. 2023. Robust speech recognition via large-scale weak supervision. In *Proceedings of the 40th International Conference on Machine Learning*, ICML'23. JMLR.org.

Nllb team, Marta Ruiz Costa-jussà, James Cross, Onur cCelebi, Maha Elbayad, Kenneth Heafield, Kevin Heffernan, Elahe Kalbassi, Janice Lam, Daniel Licht, Jean Maillard, Anna Sun, Skyler Wang, Guillaume Wenzek, Alison Youngblood, Bapi Akula, Loïc Barrault, Gabriel Mejia Gonzalez, Prangthip Hansanti, and 20 others. 2022. No language left behind: Scaling human-centered machine translation. *ArXiv*, abs/2207.04672.

IIITH-BUT system for IWSLT 2025 low-resource Bhojpuri to Hindi speech translation

Bhavana Akkiraju[1], Aishwarya Pothula[1], Santosh Kesiraju[2], Anil Kumar Vuppala[1]
[1]International Institute of Information Technology, Hyderabad, India
[2]Speech@FIT, Brno University of Technology, Czechia
{bhavana.akkiraju,aishwarya.pothula}@research.iiit.ac.in
kesiraju@fit.vut.cz,anil.vuppala@iiit.ac.in

Abstract

This paper presents the submission of IIITH-BUT to the IWSLT 2025 shared task on speech translation for the low-resource Bhojpuri-Hindi language pair. We explored the impact of hyperparameter optimisation and data augmentation techniques on the performance of the SeamlessM4T model fine-tuned for this specific task. We systematically investigated a range of hyperparameters including learning rate schedules, number of update steps, warm-up steps, label smoothing, and batch sizes; and report their effect on translation quality. To address data scarcity, we applied speed perturbation and SpecAugment and studied their effect on translation quality. We also examined the use of cross-lingual signal through joint training with Marathi and Bhojpuri speech data. Our experiments reveal that careful selection of hyperparameters and the application of simple yet effective augmentation techniques significantly improve performance in low-resource settings. We also analysed the translation hypotheses to understand various kinds of errors that impacted the translation quality in terms of BLEU.

1 Introduction

Speech translation (ST) transforms spoken language into written text in a different language, serving as a critical component in breaking down communication barriers. While significant advancements have been made for high-resource language pairs (Jia et al., 2019; Bentivogli et al., 2021), developing effective ST systems for low-resource and dialectal languages remains challenging due to scarce parallel data, inconsistent orthography, and substantial linguistic variation.

We address the low-resource scenario of Bhojpuri speech to Hindi text translation within the Indian linguistic context. Despite being spoken by over 50 million people, Bhojpuri suffers from limited quality and diversity in available speech-text corpora (Wikipedia contributors, 2025). In contrast, Hindi possesses relatively abundant resources, making it an ideal target language for translation. Our system, developed for the IWSLT 2025 shared task, addresses these resource disparities through a combination of transfer learning from linguistically similar languages, data augmentation techniques, and hyperparameter optimization.

Recent end-to-end ST models, such as the Speech-to-Text Transformer (Wang et al., 2020b) and SeamlessM4T (Communication et al., 2023) effectively replace traditional cascade pipelines by jointly modelling ASR and MT, reducing error propagation and latency. However, these approaches typically require substantial labelled data unavailable for most low-resource languages, often leading to overfitting and poor generalisation.

Our contributions include:

- A systematic investigation of hyperparameter optimization for low-resource ST, identifying that configuration choices such as batch sizes, moderate label smoothing values, and extended warmup periods significantly impact performance on the Bhojpuri-Hindi language pair.

- An analysis of data augmentation techniques - SpecAugment (Park et al., 2019) and speed perturbation (Ko et al., 2015) for low-resource speech translation, demonstrating their effectiveness in expanding our training data by 3x and improving BLEU scores by an average of 2.1 points.

- An evaluation of cross-lingual transfer learning through joint fine-tuning with Marathi-Hindi data, empirically showing how linguistic similarities between related Indo-Aryan languages can be leveraged to improve low-resource speech translation performance.

Proceedings of the 22nd International Conference on Spoken Language Translation (IWSLT 2025), pages 333–339
July 31 - August 1, 2025

The remaining of this paper is organized as follows: Section 2 provides a comprehensive review of related work, Section 3 describes our system including hyperparameter optimization, data augmentation techniques, and joint fine-tuning approach, Section 4 details our experimental setup, Section 5 presents results and analysis, and Section 6 concludes with future directions.

2 Related work

Low-resource speech translation (ST) has garnered significant attention through IWSLT shared tasks (Agarwal et al., 2023; Ahmad et al., 2024; Gow-Smith et al., 2023). The field has evolved from traditional pipeline approaches (Post et al., 2013) to end-to-end architectures such as Listen Attend and Spell (LAS) (Bérard et al., 2016), fairseq S2T (Wang et al., 2020a; E. Ortega et al., 2023),(Radhakrishnan et al., 2023), and transfer learning based methods (Kesiraju et al., 2023b,a). In (Mbuya and Anastasopoulos, 2023), explored fine-tuning self-supervised models by incorporating a linear layer for the ST task, which streamlined workflows while maintaining specialized strategies for low-resource scenarios. (Shanbhogue et al., 2023), implemented various data augmentation techniques including audio stretching, back-translation, and paraphrasing.

Contemporary approaches to low-resource ST can be categorized into several methodological frameworks. The SETU-DCU submission (Zafar et al., 2024) enhanced ST robustness through CTC loss integration and rigorous data cleaning protocols. (Post et al., 2013) incorporated pseudo-labelling techniques to expand their training corpus. The JHU IWSLT 2024 system (Robinson et al., 2024) demonstrated the efficacy of Whisper-style large models with domain-adaptive pretraining methodologies. Meanwhile, the QUESPA team (Ortega et al., 2024) implemented ensemble decoding with cross-lingual knowledge transfer mechanisms. SeamlessM4T (Communication et al., 2023) presents a comprehensive approach handling ASR, MT, and ST across more than 100 languages, though its performance on genuinely low-resource languages necessitates substantial adaptation strategies.

Our approach focuses on systematically exploring hyperparameter optimization and data augmentation techniques for low-resource speech translation. Unlike previous work that often applies general strategies such as default hyperparameter values, generic data augmentation, standard transfer learning without language-specific considerations and using default model architectures and training strategies without adaptation to low-resource constraints, we conduct a comprehensive investigation specifically tailored to the challenges of the Bhojpuri-Hindi language pair. Our experimentation includes a detailed analysis of learning rates, batch sizes, label smoothing values, and warmup periods, and used two data augmentation techniques (Speed Perturb, SpecAug). Additionally, we examine how cross-lingual transfer from Marathi can supplement these optimizations, leveraging the linguistic proximity between these Indo-Aryan languages.

3 Methodology

3.1 Model architecture

Our experiments used SeamlessM4T as the backbone. We experimented with medium (1.2B parameters) and large (2.3 B parameters) variants. The medium consists of a 24-layer conformer speech encoder, 12-layer Transformer text decoder, with 1024-dimensional hidden states, and 16 attention heads.

3.2 Fine-tuning

For most of the experiments, we fine-tuned all the parameters on the target language pair, i.e. Bhojpuri–Hindi. We also conducted experiments where fine-tuned on both language pairs Marathi–Hindi and Bhojpuri–Hindi. This model was further fine-tuned for few epochs for the target pair Bhojpuri–Hindi.

3.3 Evaluation

We used the standard objective metrics BLEU (Papineni et al., 2002) and chrF++ (Popović, 2017) implemented in sacrebleu (Post, 2018) to objectively evaluate the translation quality against the reference.

4 Experiments

4.1 Datasets

We used only the official IWSLT 2025 shared task dataset for Bhojpuri $\rightarrow$ Hindi speech translation: For our multilingual experiments, we incorporated an additional Marathi $\rightarrow$ Hindi[1] parallel corpus

[1] IWSLT Marathi-Hindi Dataset

Dataset	Duration (hrs)	No. of utterances
Training	20.00	10,171
Dev	2.07	1,056
Test	0.87	750

Table 1: Data split statistics for Bhojpuri-Hindi ST task.

from IWSLT, consisting of 16 hours (7,990 utterances) of training data, 3.6 hours (2,103 utterances) of development data, and 0.45 hours (286 utterances) of test data.

4.2 Implementation

Our code was based on the original seamless library written in PyTorch. Our experiments used two NVIDIA A100 GPUs (40GB each), employing data parallel training, synchronised batch normalisation, and FP16 mixed precision for optimal computational efficiency.

4.3 Pre-trained model selection

Here we report the fine-tuning results for Seamless medium and large v2 variants. We observed that the medium model consistently yielded better translation results than the large one. Hence, we used the medium variant for all subsequent experiments and analysis.

Model	lr	BLEU	chrF++
Medium	1e-5	**30.5**	**54.6**
Large	1e-5	25.5	50.5

Table 2: Translation scores on dev set after fine-tuning seamless medium and large variants on Bhojpuri–Hindi.

4.4 Hyperparameter optimisation

Our hyperparameter optimisation investigation focused on several critical training parameters. The **learning rate** (LR) was evaluated across three settings (1e-6, 1e-5, and 2e-5), with the moderate rate of **1e-5** consistently yielding the best performance as shown in Table 3, achieving a balance between training stability and domain adaptation. For **label smoothing** (LS), we tested values of 0, 0.1, and 0.2, with **0.1** offering the best generalisation and robustness (Table 4). We explored **warmup steps** (100, 250, 350, and 400) to stabilise the learning rate schedule, finding **250 steps** produced optimal convergence without extending training time. To mitigate overfitting, we experimented with **early stopping patience** values (5, 10, and 20 epochs), where **10 epochs** struck the best trade-off between overtraining and early termination. Finally, we examined **training batch size** (5, 10, 32, and 64), with a batch size of **32** demonstrating the most favourable performance (Table 3), balancing gradient update stability with computational efficiency.

LR	batch size	BLEU	chrF++
1e-5	5	30.5	54.5
1e-5	10	33.8	56.9
1e-5	32	**35.1**	58.2
1e-6	5	18.2	48.4
1e-6	10	20.1	49.1
1e-6	32	26.7	51.2

Table 3: Effect of learning rate (LR) and training batch size (batch size) on Bhojpuri-Hindi fine-tuning performance

LS	BLEU	chrF++
0.0	30.9	55.3
0.1	**33.8**	**56.9**
0.2	31.8	56.6

Table 4: Effect of label smoothing (LS) on Bhojpuri–Hindi fine-tuning performance with LR = 1e-5 and batch size = 10.

4.5 Data augmentation

To address the limited training data for the Bhojpuri-Hindi language pair, we implemented two established speech augmentation techniques.

4.5.1 SpecAugment

We applied spectrogram masking with time masks (max 30 frames) and frequency masks (max 30 mel-frequency bins), creating diverse variations that forced the model to rely on broader contextual information rather than specific acoustic features.

4.5.2 Speed perturbation

We implemented speed factors of 0.9x, 1.0x, and 1.1x to simulate different speaking rates without changing pitch, effectively tripling our training data with realistic variations and improving the robustness of the model to natural speaking rate differences among Bhojpuri speakers.

By combining these complementary methods, we expanded the diversity of training data without requiring additional recordings. The impact on translation quality is shown in Table 5.

SP	SA	BLEU
False	False	31.8
False	**True**	**33.7**
True	False	32.7
True	True	32.4

Table 5: Effect of Speed perturb (SP) and SpecAugment (SA) on Bhojpuri–Hindi fine-tuning performance with LR = 1e-5, batch size = 10, and LS = 0.1

4.6 Joint-finetuning approach

We implemented cross-lingual transfer learning by integrating Marathi-Hindi and Bhojpuri-Hindi language pairs into a unified training framework. This approach leverages the linguistic similarities between these Indo-Aryan languages, which share phonological characteristics, lexical resources, and syntactic structures.

Our methodology combined the Marathi-Hindi parallel corpus with the limited Bhojpuri-Hindi dataset during SeamlessM4T model adaptation, thereby expanding the training data while introducing linguistically relevant patterns from Marathi. To mitigate catastrophic forgetting, we implemented sequential fine-tuning with an initial joint training phase followed by Bhojpuri-only finetuning. We tested this approach under three conditions: one epoch, two epochs, and training until convergence, as shown in Table 7.

5 Results and analysis

This section presents an analysis of the experimental results obtained from our primary and contrastive models. The **primary model** encompasses an optimized combination of hyperparameter configuration and data augmentation techniques that yielded the highest BLEU score in our evaluations.

As demonstrated in Table 5, the application of SpecAugment during fine-tuning produced superior performance compared to other augmentation strategies. During inference, we systematically evaluated translation quality across multiple beam search configurations (sizes 1, 5, and 10) to determine the optimal decoding approach.

Table 6 represents a comprehensive comparison of various experimental configurations and their corresponding performance metrics. Increasing the beam size from 5 to 10 while maintaining all other parameters constant yielded a modest improvement in translation quality. Subsequently, with beam size fixed at 10, enlarging the training batch size from 10 to 32 further enhanced performance by 0.21 BLEU points. The combination of beam size 10, batch size 32, increased warmup steps from 100 to 250, and the introduction of SpecAugment collectively improved the BLEU score from 34.01 to 35.38. Our optimal configuration, which additionally increased early stopping patience from 5 to 10, achieved the highest performance with 36.41 BLEU. Notably, further extending patience to 20 epochs resulted in performance degradation, suggesting potential overfitting.

For our **contrastive model**, we implemented a multilingual fine-tuning strategy that jointly trained on Marathi and Bhojpuri data using the hyperparameter configuration that previously achieved the highest performance (36.4 BLEU). This multilingual model initially underperformed compared to our monolingual system, potentially due to catastrophic forgetting. To mitigate this issue, we conducted additional fine-tuning on Bhojpuri data exclusively for various epoch counts.

As shown in Table 7, performance peaked after a single epoch of Bhojpuri-specific fine-tuning and subsequently declined with additional epochs, suggesting that extended training on previously observed data may lead to overfitting. Consequently, our contrastive submission consisted of the joint Marathi-Bhojpuri model with one additional epoch of Bhojpuri–Hindi exclusive finetuning, which produced results comparable to our optimised monolingual configuration.

Table 8 presents the BLEU scores obtained on both test and development datasets. In the IWSLT 2025 shared task (Abdulmumin et al., 2025), the highest reported BLEU score was 10.7, representing a significant decrease compared to IWSLT 2024 (Ahmad et al., 2024), where scores reached approximately 24.4. Our primary and contrastive models achieved BLEU scores of 9.9 and 10.2 respectively on the test set, while demonstrating substantially higher performance on the development set with scores of 36.4 and 36.0. The considerable performance gap between development and test sets suggests potential domain mismatch between the datasets or possible data quality issues in the test set, warranting further investigation.

LR	LS	Batch size	SP	SA	Warm up steps	Patience	Beam size	BLEU
1e_5	0.1	10	False	False	100	5	5	33.1
1e_5	0.1	10	False	False	100	5	10	33.8
1e_5	0.1	32	False	False	100	5	10	34.0
1e_5	0.1	32	False	True	250	5	10	35.3
1e_5	**0.1**	**32**	**False**	**True**	**250**	**10**	**10**	**36.4**
1e_5	0.1	32	False	True	250	20	10	35.6

Table 6: BLEU scores for various hyperparameter configurations during fine-tuning of SeamlessM4T. We varied the learning rate (LR), label smoothing (LS), batch size, speed perturbation (SP), SpecAugment (SA), warm-up steps, early stopping patience, and beam size. The highest BLEU score (36.41) was obtained with SA enabled, patience set to 10, and a beam size of 10.

Strategy	Epochs	BLEU
Joint finetuning (JF)	Convergence	34.6
JF + monolingual bhoj	**1**	**36.0**
JF + monolingual bhoj	2	35.6
JF + monolingual bhoj	Convergence	35.4

Table 7: BLEU scores for contrastive model with the same configuration as highest BLEU in Table 6

Model	Dev BLEU	Test BLEU
Primary	36.4	9.9
Contrastive	36.0	10.2

Table 8: BLEU scores for primary and contrastive models using the same configuration as highest BLEU scores in Table 6 and Table 7 for both dev and test dataset

5.1 Error analysis

Our systematic examination of translation outputs revealed several factors in the development dataset that affected ST performance. Analysis of audio-transcript relationships identified multiple inconsistencies impacting model performance. We observed three key patterns when comparing reference and target word counts: (1) When reference counts exceeded target counts, low BLEU scores often resulted from incomplete audio recordings paired with complete reference transcripts, audio-transcript misalignment, or redundant reference content; (2) Equal word counts with low BLEU scores frequently corresponded with noisy recordings; (3) Cases where target counts exceeded reference counts typically involved recordings with significant acoustic interference.

Numerical content presented particular challenges. We identified inconsistent representation formats (e.g., "8 crores 74 lakhs" in audio versus "87.4 lakhs" in text), incomplete numerical transcription (e.g., in audio, numbers are spoken in English as "Fifteen" whereas in reference text they appear in Hindi as "Pandrah(hindi)"), and instances where equal numerical representation corresponded with degraded audio quality. These findings highlight the importance of audio-transcript alignment and standardized numerical representation in speech translation datasets, particularly for low-resource language evaluation.

6 Conclusion

Our submission to the IWSLT 2025 evaluation campaign for low-resource and dialectal speech translation advances Bhojpuri–Hindi ST through a combination of hyperparameter optimisation, data augmentation, and cross-lingual joint fine-tuning. By leveraging the SeamlessM4T medium model (1.2B parameters) and systematically exploring optimal training configurations, we demonstrate significant performance gains despite the challenges posed by limited parallel data. Our results show that even established techniques like SpecAugment and speed perturbation, when carefully implemented, can lead to substantial improvements in low-resource speech translation tasks, expanding our effective training data threefold. Additionally, we found that joint training with Marathi—a linguistically related Indo-Aryan language—followed by sequential Bhojpuri-specific adaptation provides an effective strategy to mitigate data sparsity and improve generalisation across diverse speech patterns.

For future work, we plan to explore more sophisticated augmentation techniques such as noise injection, pitch shifting, and cross-speaker synthesis. We also intend to investigate self-supervised pretraining on monolingual Bhojpuri speech data and further extend our cross-lingual approach to additional Indo-Aryan languages. As low-resource ST continues to evolve, we believe that modular, linguistically informed adaptation pipelines will play a key role in advancing the real-world applicability of such systems for under represented language communities.

7 Acknowledgements

Santosh Kesiraju was supported by Ministry of Education, Youth and Sports of the Czech Republic (MoE) through the OP JAK project "Linguistics, Artificial Intelligence and Language and Speech Technologies: from Research to Applications" (ID:CZ.02.01.01/00/23_020/0008518).

References

Idris Abdulmumin, Victor Agostinelli, Tanel Alumäe, Antonios Anastasopoulos, Ashwin, Luisa Bentivogli, Ondřej Bojar, Claudia Borg, Fethi Bougares, Roldano Cattoni, Mauro Cettolo, Lizhong Chen, William Chen, Raj Dabre, Yannick Estève, Marcello Federico, Marco Gaido, Dávid Javorský, Marek Kasztelnik, and 30 others. 2025. Findings of the iwslt 2025 evaluation campaign. In *Proceedings of the 22nd International Conference on Spoken Language Translation (IWSLT 2025)*, Vienna, Austia (in-person and online). Association for Computational Linguistics. To appear.

Milind Agarwal, Sweta Agrawal, Antonios Anastasopoulos, Luisa Bentivogli, Ondřej Bojar, Claudia Borg, Marine Carpuat, Roldano Cattoni, Mauro Cettolo, Mingda Chen, William Chen, Khalid Choukri, Alexandra Chronopoulou, Anna Currey, Thierry Declerck, Qianqian Dong, Kevin Duh, Yannick Estève, Marcello Federico, and 43 others. 2023. FINDINGS OF THE IWSLT 2023 EVALUATION CAMPAIGN. In *Proceedings of the 20th International Conference on Spoken Language Translation (IWSLT 2023)*, pages 1–61, Toronto, Canada (in-person and online). Association for Computational Linguistics.

Ibrahim Said Ahmad, Antonios Anastasopoulos, Ondřej Bojar, Claudia Borg, Marine Carpuat, Roldano Cattoni, Mauro Cettolo, William Chen, Qianqian Dong, Marcello Federico, Barry Haddow, Dávid Javorský, Mateusz Krubiński, Tsz Kin Lam, Xutai Ma, Prashant Mathur, Evgeny Matusov, Chandresh Maurya, John McCrae, and 25 others. 2024. FINDINGS OF THE IWSLT 2024 EVALUATION CAMPAIGN. In *Proceedings of the 21st International Conference on Spoken Language Translation (IWSLT 2024)*, pages 1–11, Bangkok, Thailand (in-person and online). Association for Computational Linguistics.

Luisa Bentivogli, Mauro Cettolo, Marco Gaido, Alina Karakanta, Alberto Martinelli, Matteo Negri, and Marco Turchi. 2021. Cascade versus direct speech translation: Do the differences still make a difference? *arXiv preprint arXiv:2106.01045*.

Alexandre Bérard, Olivier Pietquin, Christophe Servan, and Laurent Besacier. 2016. Listen and translate: A proof of concept for end-to-end speech-to-text translation. *arXiv preprint arXiv:1612.01744*.

Seamless Communication, Loïc Barrault, Yu-An Chung, Mariano Cora Meglioli, David Dale, Ning Dong, Paul-Ambroise Duquenne, Hady Elsahar, Hongyu Gong, Kevin Heffernan, John Hoffman, Christopher Klaiber, Pengwei Li, Daniel Licht, Jean Maillard, Alice Rakotoarison, Kaushik Ram Sadagopan, Guillaume Wenzek, Ethan Ye, and 49 others. 2023. Seamlessm4t: Massively multilingual & multimodal machine translation. *arXiv preprint arXiv:2308.11596*.

John E. Ortega, Rodolfo Zevallos, and William Chen. 2023. QUESPA submission for the IWSLT 2023 dialect and low-resource speech translation tasks. In *Proceedings of the 20th International Conference on Spoken Language Translation (IWSLT 2023)*, pages 261–268, Toronto, Canada (in-person and online). Association for Computational Linguistics.

Edward Gow-Smith, Alexandre Berard, Marcely Zanon Boito, and Ioan Calapodescu. 2023. NAVER LABS Europe's multilingual speech translation systems for the IWSLT 2023 low-resource track. In *Proceedings of the 20th International Conference on Spoken Language Translation (IWSLT 2023)*, pages 144–158, Toronto, Canada (in-person and online). Association for Computational Linguistics.

Ye Jia, Ron J Weiss, Fadi Biadsy, Wolfgang Macherey, Melvin Johnson, Zhifeng Chen, and Yonghui Wu. 2019. Direct speech-to-speech translation with a sequence-to-sequence model. *arXiv preprint arXiv:1904.06037*.

Santosh Kesiraju, Karel Beneš, Maksim Tikhonov, and Jan Černocký. 2023a. BUT systems for IWSLT 2023 Marathi - Hindi low resource speech translation task. In *Proceedings of the 20th International Conference on Spoken Language Translation (IWSLT 2023)*, pages 227–234, Toronto, Canada (in-person and online). Association for Computational Linguistics.

Santosh Kesiraju, Marek Sarvaš, Tomáš Pavlíček, Cécile Macaire, and Alejandro Ciuba. 2023b. Strategies for improving low resource speech to text translation relying on pre-trained asr models. In *Interspeech 2023*, pages 2148–2152.

Tom Ko, Vijayaditya Peddinti, Daniel Povey, and Sanjeev Khudanpur. 2015. Audio augmentation for speech recognition. In *Interspeech*, volume 2015, page 3586.

Jonathan Mbuya and Antonios Anastasopoulos. 2023. GMU systems for the IWSLT 2023 dialect and low-resource speech translation tasks. In *Proceedings of the 20th International Conference on Spoken Language Translation (IWSLT 2023)*, pages 269–276, Toronto, Canada (in-person and online). Association for Computational Linguistics.

John E Ortega, Rodolfo Joel Zevallos, Ibrahim Sa'id Ahmad, and William Chen. 2024. QUESPA Submission for the IWSLT 2024 Dialectal and Low-resource Speech Translation Task. In *Proceedings of the 21st International Conference on Spoken Language Translation (IWSLT 2024)*, pages 125–133.

Kishore Papineni, Salim Roukos, Todd Ward, and Wei-Jing Zhu. 2002. Bleu: a method for automatic evaluation of machine translation. In *Proceedings of the 40th Annual Meeting of the Association for Computational Linguistics*, pages 311–318, Philadelphia, Pennsylvania, USA. Association for Computational Linguistics.

Daniel S Park, William Chan, Yu Zhang, Chung-Cheng Chiu, Barret Zoph, Ekin D Cubuk, and Quoc V Le. 2019. Specaugment: A simple data augmentation method for automatic speech recognition. *arXiv preprint arXiv:1904.08779*.

Maja Popović. 2017. chrF++: words helping character n-grams. In *Proceedings of the Second Conference on Machine Translation*, pages 612–618, Copenhagen, Denmark. Association for Computational Linguistics.

Matt Post. 2018. A call for clarity in reporting BLEU scores. In *Proceedings of the Third Conference on Machine Translation: Research Papers*, pages 186–191, Brussels, Belgium. Association for Computational Linguistics.

Matt Post, Gaurav Kumar, Adam Lopez, Damianos Karakos, Chris Callison-Burch, and Sanjeev Khudanpur. 2013. Improved speech-to-text translation with the fisher and callhome spanish-english speech translation corpus. In *Proceedings of the 10th international workshop on spoken language translation: papers*.

Balaji Radhakrishnan, Saurabh Agrawal, Raj Prakash Gohil, Kiran Praveen, Advait Vinay Dhopeshwarkar, and Abhishek Pandey. 2023. SRI-B's systems for IWSLT 2023 dialectal and low-resource track: Marathi-Hindi speech translation. In *Proceedings of the 20th International Conference on Spoken Language Translation (IWSLT 2023)*, pages 449–454, Toronto, Canada (in-person and online). Association for Computational Linguistics.

Nathaniel Romney Robinson, Kaiser Sun, Cihan Xiao, Niyati Bafna, Weiting Tan, Haoran Xu, Henry Li Xinyuan, Ankur Kejriwal, Sanjeev Khudanpur, Kenton Murray, and 1 others. 2024. JHU IWSLT 2024 Dialectal and Low-resource System Description. In *Proceedings of the 21st International Conference on Spoken Language Translation (IWSLT 2024)*, pages 140–153.

Akshaya Vishnu Kudlu Shanbhogue, Ran Xue, Soumya Saha, Daniel Zhang, and Ashwinkumar Ganesan. 2023. Improving low resource speech translation with data augmentation and ensemble strategies. In *Proceedings of the 20th International Conference on Spoken Language Translation (IWSLT 2023)*, pages 241–250, Toronto, Canada (in-person and online). Association for Computational Linguistics.

Changhan Wang, Yun Tang, Xutai Ma, Anne Wu, Dmytro Okhonko, and Juan Pino. 2020a. Fairseq S2T: Fast speech-to-text modeling with fairseq. In *Proceedings of the 1st Conference of the Asia-Pacific Chapter of the Association for Computational Linguistics and the 10th International Joint Conference on Natural Language Processing: System Demonstrations*, pages 33–39, Suzhou, China. Association for Computational Linguistics.

Changhan Wang, Yun Tang, Xutai Ma, Anne Wu, Sravya Popuri, Dmytro Okhonko, and Juan Pino. 2020b. Fairseq s2t: Fast speech-to-text modeling with fairseq. *arXiv preprint arXiv:2010.05171*.

Wikipedia contributors. 2025. 2011 census of india — Wikipedia, the free encyclopedia. `https://en.wikipedia.org/w/index.php?title=2011_census_of_India&oldid=1289695299`. [Online; accessed 1-June-2025].

Maria Zafar, Antonio Castaldo, Prashanth Nayak, Rejwanul Haque, Neha Gajakos, and Andy Way. 2024. The SETU-DCU submissions to IWSLT 2024 low-resource speech-to-text translation tasks. In *Proceedings of the 21st International Conference on Spoken Language Translation (IWSLT 2024)*, pages 80–85.

MLLP-VRAIN UPV system for the IWSLT 2025 Simultaneous Speech Translation Translation task

Jorge Iranzo-Sánchez*◇ and **Javier Iranzo-Sánchez**◇
and **Adrià Giménez**† and **Jorge Civera**◇ and **Alfons Juan**◇
◇Machine Learning and Language Processing, VRAIN, Universitat Politècnica de València
†Departament d'Informàtica, Escola Tècnica Superior d'Enginyeria, Universitat de València
{jorirsan,jairsan,jorcisai,ajuanci}@upv.es, adria.gimenez@uv.es

Abstract

This work describes the participation of the MLLP-VRAIN research group in the shared task of the IWSLT 2025 Simultaneous Speech Translation track. Our submission addresses the unique challenges of real-time translation of long-form speech by developing a modular cascade system that adapts strong pre-trained models to streaming scenarios. We combine Whisper Large-V3-Turbo for ASR with the multilingual NLLB-3.3B model for MT, implementing lightweight adaptation techniques rather than training new end-to-end models from scratch. Our approach employs document-level adaptation with prefix training to enhance the MT model's ability to handle incomplete inputs, while incorporating adaptive emission policies including a wait-k strategy and RALCP for managing the translation stream. Specialized buffer management techniques and segmentation strategies ensure coherent translations across long audio sequences. Experimental results on the ACL60/60 dataset demonstrate that our system achieves a favorable balance between translation quality and latency, with a BLEU score of 31.96 and non-computational-aware StreamLAAL latency of 2.94 seconds. Our final model achieves a preliminary score on the official test set (IWSLT25Instruct) of 29.8 BLEU. Our work demonstrates that carefully adapted pre-trained components can create effective simultaneous translation systems for long-form content without requiring extensive in-domain parallel data or specialized end-to-end training.

1 Introduction

In this paper we describe the participation of the MLLP-VRAIN research group in the shared tasks of the 22th International Conference on Spoken Language Translation (IWSLT) (Abdulmumin et al., 2025). We participated on the Simultaneous Speech Translation (SimulST) task in the English to German direction. Compared to other years, two aspects were changed in the shared task which guided the construction of our system: The usage of pretrained open weight models and the evaluation of long-form audio. Our participation this year was an attempt of creating a production ready model based on the minimal adaptation of offline ASR and MT (Papi et al., 2022). Recent years have seen a rise in the usage of end-to-end approaches[1] which, in theory, can offer a better integration and can avoid error compounding between ASR and MT components. However, they typically require large quantities of parallel speech-to-text translation data, which is often scarce and costly to obtain. Cascade systems, on the other hand, while they are more data-efficient due to the abundance of separate ASR and MT training resources, may suffer from error propagation and lack of joint optimization. Nevertheless, recent shared tasks and evaluation campaigns continue to show that cascade systems generally achieve superior performance over current end-to-end alternatives (Salesky et al., 2023b, 2024). As such, we model our system based on the cascaded approach, in which we take a special keen interest due to its inherent modularity and easier reuse of strong pre-trained components. Figure 1 shows the overall architecture of our system.

2 System Architecture

2.1 ASR system

For the choice of the ASR components, we select our model based on the results of public ASR systems on common benchmarks available at the Hugging Face Open ASR Leaderboard (Srivastav et al., 2023). After some initial tests and taking into account our computing limitations, we selected Whisper-Large-V3-Turbo (Radford et al., 2023) [2]

[1]As defined by IWSLT `https://iwslt.org/2025/offline#evaluation-conditions`.

[2]`https://huggingface.co/openai/whisper-large-v3-turbo`

Proceedings of the 22nd International Conference on Spoken Language Translation (IWSLT 2025), pages 340–346

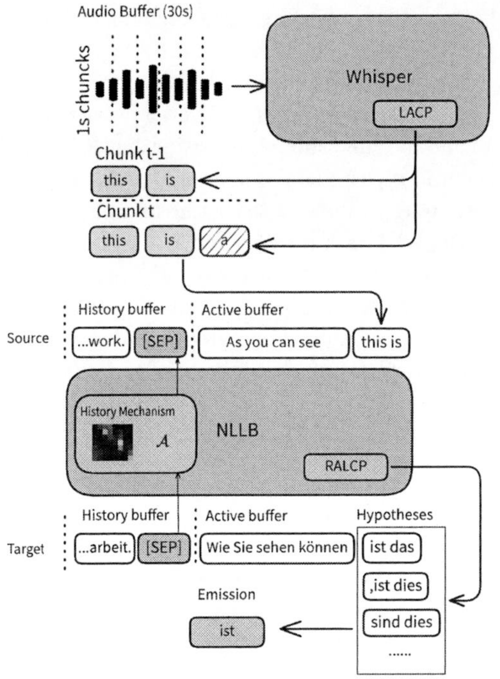

Figure 1: System diagram of our cascaded system for the SimulST track.

as our final ASR model. We use the model as it is, and we do not make usage of any of the English audio data provided by the organizers for finetunning of the model. There are two reasons for this decision. First, when looking at the provided datasets, we conjecture that the Whisper model has probably have already seen this data; and second, that we fear that we may end up lowering the performance of the system as there is a domain mismatch between the provided datasets and evaluation set, with the latter being scientific talks of the ACL.

The adaptation for streaming is done in a similar way to the one described in Macháček et al. (2023), where a Longest Common Prefix policy along some heuristics are combined for the usage in a streaming fashion. Inference is done via the Faster-Whisper library [3]. We select a maximum audio buffer of 30 seconds and a minimum chunk size of one second and deactivate the usage of VAD filtering. The audio buffer is cleaned when a end of sentence is detected by external sentence splitter or the 30 seconds window is full. The audio stream is then updated accordingly to the timestamps obtained by the typical DTW procedure used in Whisper.

During development we detected that this base system had sometimes very unreliable behaviour due to latency spikes derived from indecisions of the LCP policy on the punctuation, casing and styling of some words. To alleviate this, we relaxed the LCP policy so that it is done on lower cased input, with no punctuation signs, and with the additional constraint of a threshold by Levenshtein Distance to consider if a word in the prefix is sufficiently different. We select a Levenshtein Distance threshold of two so that if the distance of the words to be checked is less or equals to it, then they are to be considered the same by the policy.

The ASR system obtains a WER of 8.54% on the ACL60/60 (Salesky et al., 2023a) development set.

2.2 MT system

During recent years a series of works have appeared exploring realistic scenarios for SimulST where models are evaluated on long-form speech scenarios. (Schneider and Waibel, 2020; Sen et al., 2022; Papi et al., 2024; Polák and Bojar, 2023; Iranzo-Sánchez et al., 2024; Ouyang et al., 2025). Taking this into consideration, for our MT model, we adapt an offline MT model to streaming through a lightweight procedure inspired to that of Iranzo-Sánchez et al. (2024), which presents an easy to adapt pipeline for the creation of an MT component in SimulST system which we further adapt and simplify it to our given conditions. Overall, through training with prefix-training (Niehues et al., 2018) and document level metadata, the model is able to learn to work with an incomplete stream and control a history stream (Iranzo-Sánchez et al., 2022) by emitting a sentinel token [SEP] which then serves to call a lightweight log-linear model to take into account which part of the stream has already been translated. When a certain threshold of size in the buffer reached, the oldest pairs of identified segments can easily be discarded without any fear of possible mismatches in the stream.

Model: Instead of training from scratch, we make use of the multilingual system NLLB-3.3B (Team, 2024). We also explored the usage of MADLAD-400 (Kudugunta et al., 2023), but discarded it after founding BLEU scores of over 95 points when evaluation of the system in an offline scenario for the ACL60/60 dataset, which indicated a possible data contamination of the test set. We also tested some LLMs, but found early results too unsatisfactory for our computing budget.

[3]https://github.com/SYSTRAN/faster-whisper

History Mechanism: Inspired by the usage of attention maps of Papi et al. (2023), for the log-feature model, instead of the described reverse translation model of the original paper, we found that a single feature which looks at the most attended position of the previous token before the sentinel [SEP] token to be more simpler and effective to determine the segmentation position of the source stream. To be more precise, the position of the last source word $\hat{a}$ to be moved to the streaming history buffer for the current active source and target chunks x and $\hat{y}$ is

$$\hat{a} = \underset{i}{\operatorname{argmax}} \mathcal{A}(x_i, y_{[SEP]-1}) \quad (1)$$

with $\mathcal{A}$ being the attention score function and i indicates the position of source word x in the active chunk.

Data and Training: For the document level data, we take the available News Comentary[4] and Europarl[5] datasets with their reconstructed document level information extracted from Paradocs (Wicks et al., 2024) for a total of 36225 documents. While not in the target domain of ACL talks, we hope that our adaptation is able to move the model from offline inference domain to simultaneous with the usage of history context. Additionally, we want to adapt the multilingual model so that it can better focus on the English to German direction. Prefix augmented data with document level information is created as in the original work, but is dynamically generated at training time. For each document, which represents a data sample, we select a sentence and randomly prepend from 1 up to 10 of the previous phrases of the document with the corresponding sentinel token [SEP]. Then, for the corresponding phrase we create the prefix by taking into account the ratio of the length of the active source and target phrase. During training, the usage of prefix training is triggered at a rate of 50%. As for the training procedure, we make use DoRA (Mao et al., 2024) to fine-tune our MT model. Training hyperparameters are shown in Appendix A.

Policy: For our policy in the MT component, we make use of RALCP (Wang et al., 2024) using the hypotheses of the system beam search in combination with a *wait-k* policy (Ma et al., 2019), the latter being active only during the beginning of a new phrase (that is after emitting a [SEP] token) to prevent system hallucination. We also clean "invalid" empty beam hypotheses, which were very frequent on the baseline model, adjusting the RALCP λ accordingly so that the ratio of hypotheses and λ stays roughly the same as before filtering.

The final peak memory usage during inference of both ASR and MT models combined is of 20GB of VRAM [6], with values fluctuating between 1-3GiB depending on the current audio and translation history buffers. We leave further optimization for future work.

3 Evaluation

For our baselines, we searched for any other public simultaneous speech translation systems capable of long form translation. However, we only found the system described in Papi et al. (2024) available, and in this case, we observed that the system had strong hallucinations that ended up in an unrecoverable state for long enough audios. Due to this, we instead build a "naive" baseline for our system which make use of the plain translation system without any additional training. For controlling the history buffers, we simply remove from the source and target text history buffers after a maximum number of words is reached in each buffer. In practice, we surpassingly found that while the system will end up with slight mismatches between the source and target stream at the head position, systems are still able to work in a streaming scenario. We additionally add the offline inference of the model before and after fine-tuning and the best baseline from the IWSLT organizers that achieved a similar latency-quality tradeoff matching our own.[7]. Best hyperparameters with the optimal quality/latency are shown in Appendix A.

Table 1 shows the results of the baseline and our adapted model, the stream LAAL, both computationally an computationally aware, BLEU (Papineni et al., 2002) as calculated with SacreBLEU (Post, 2018)[8] and the COMET-22 (Rei et al., 2022)[9]. We follow the recomendations of Zouhar

[4]https://data.statmt.org/news-commentary/v18/training/

[5]https://www.statmt.org/europarl/v10/training/europarl-v10.de-en.tsv.gz

[6]On a Nvidia GTX 4090 with a Intel(R) Core(TM) i9-10920X CPU @3.50GHz

[7]Organizer baseline results extracted from https://github.com/pe-trik/iwslt25-baselines/tree/master/experiments/acl6060_dev/de/cascade

[8]Python3.12.9|BLEU|nrefs:1|case:mixed|eff:no|tok:13a|smooth:exp|version:2.5.1

[9]Python3.12.9|Comet2.2.6|fp16|Unbabel/wmt22-comet-da|r1

			StreamLAAL	
	BLEU	COMET	NCA	CA
Offline	43.12	0.833	—	—
Offline$^{(A)}$	41.48	0.836	—	—
Baseline^{iwslt}	25.47	—	3.67	—
Baseline^{upv}	26.10	0.642	3.61	4.35
Adapted	31.96	0.732	2.94	4.20

Table 1: Quality (BLEU, COMET↑) and non-computational and computational aware (NCA/CA) latency (StreamLAAL (secs)↓) results on the ACL60/60 development set. Offline models take the golden reference source text. The Offline$^{(A)}$ model refers to the results of our adapted model when doing offline inference. Offline models results are obtained given the golden source reference transcription.

model	M	mdn	p90	p95	p99	max
			NCA			
Baseline	3.61	2.96	6.57	9.14	13.51	16.59
Adapted	2.94	2.65	4.30	5.38	7.59	9.25
			CA			
Baseline	4.35	3.62	7.65	10.51	14.58	18.52
Adapted	4.20	3.55	5.98	7.64	10.73	15.00

Table 2: StreamLAAL mean (M), median (mdn), percentiles 90%, 95% and 99%, and maximum value (in seconds) for the Baseline^{upv} and Adapted system.

et al. (2024) and set the COMET score to 0 for samples where the target translation is empty after re-segmentation with mWERSegmenter (Matusov et al., 2005).

First of all, impact of the translation quality degradation in the offline mode seems to minimal, with deltas of 1.64 BLEU and 0.03 of COMET respectively. As for our baseline and adapted models, we can see that there is a significant quality degradation. We can attribute this to multiple factors, but we would like to highlight two aspects. First, is that we are comparing ourselves to offline systems that take the golden reference transcription, and thus, transcriptions errors from the ASR and possible resegmentation errors introduced by StreamLAAL are not taken into account in the evaluation of our offline baseline. The second factor which may explain this gap is the mere nature of the ACL60/60 dataset. We would like to highlight this one in particular since the translations where originally based on post-edits from offline translation models and thus more suited for the evaluation of offline speech translation compared to that of SimulST. Thus, we think that the resulting translations from our SimulST system, which should be more monotonic in nature compared to the offline baselines and ACL60/60 references, maybe be more penalized in a similar way to the observations of Doi et al. (2024).

In terms of baselines, we can see that our naive baseline slight beats the organizers baseline in the selected quality-latency range. When comparing our baseline and adapted model, we can see a considerable increase in both quality and reduction of latency. Our adapted model ends up scoring 31.96 BLEU and 0.732 COMET and StreamLAAL scores of 2.94 and 4.20 seconds depending on the computational awareness of the metric calculation. This places our model on the high latency regime as defined by the shared task description.

To better study the latency of our system, Table 2 shows the top percentiles of StreamLAAL as well as their medians and maximum recorded values. We can see how for all of these metrics our adapted system consistently beats our baseline and ensures a better performance on the worst case scenarios, with these delays being the more impactful for the end user of SimulST systems.

An observation that can be made in this table is that of the considerable increase of latency for the worst cases between the NCA and CA metrics. After investigating, we discovered the temperature fallback mechanism of Whisper to seem to cause this phenomena, resulting in some rare cases where latency spikes occur and can only be observed when taking computational costs into account. Despite this, we found that in practice the performance is really poor with this feature disabled. In general, we observed that the ASR emission policy highly influenced the system performance, with hyperparameter changes on the MT system having less of an overall impact.

Regarding the official test set (IWSLT25Instruct), preliminary results by the organizers indicate that our model achieved a final score of 29.8 BLEU.

4 Conclusions

In this paper we described our SimulST system for the IWSLT 2025 Simultaneous Speech Translation task. Preliminary results show that our cascaded based system using Whisper and NLLB showed a good performance and achieved a good balance between translation quality and latency. We see how through adaptive policies and very computationally cheap adaptation a long-form speech SimulST system can be created from offline models. Future work could be expand to see the robustness of this methodology, such as the usage of synthetic document level bitext data (Post and Junczys-Dowmunt, 2024) or speech data. Investigating more robust adaptive latency policies or techniques which better optimize ASR and MT components (Tran et al., 2022) while preserving the benefits of the cascaded approach could further greatly enhance the system performance. Also, a gap still exists compared to offline translation, which should be further explore d more detail.

Additionally, the usage of LLMs to serve as all in one transcriber, translator and re-scorer in a cascaded pipeline along their robustness and usage of long context shows promising results for their usage in long-form speech translation if computational costs can be taken into account.

5 Limitations

Due to time constraints, hyperparameters search for trade-offs between translation and latency of models was limited, as well as the tuning of the ASR system. In our participation, we restricted ourself to the English to German direction, but we think that our approach could be generalized to the other language pairs in the competition. We hope to participate in future editions covering all language pairs available and expanding the breadth and scale of the studied models.

Acknowledgments

The research leading to these results has received funding from EU4Health Programme 2021–2027 as part of Europe's Beating Cancer Plan under Grant Agreements nos. 101056995 and 101129375; and from the Government of Spain's grant PID2021-122443OB-I00 funded by MICIU/AEI/10.13039/501100011033 and by "ERDF/EU", and grant PDC2022-133049-I00 funded by MICIU/AEI/10.13039/501100011033 and by the "European Union NextGenerationEU/PRTR". The authors gratefully acknowledge the financial support of Generalitat Valenciana under project IDIFEDER/2021/059.

References

Idris Abdulmumin, Victor Agostinelli, Tanel Alumäe, Antonios Anastasopoulos, Ashwin, Luisa Bentivogli, Ondřej Bojar, Claudia Borg, Fethi Bougares, Roldano Cattoni, Mauro Cettolo, Lizhong Chen, William Chen, Raj Dabre, Yannick Estève, Marcello Federico, Marco Gaido, Dávid Javorský, Marek Kasztelnik, Tsz Kin Lam, Danni Liu, Evgeny Matusov, Chandresh Kumar Maurya, John P. McCrae, Salima Mdhaffar, Yasmin Moslem, Kenton Murray, Satoshi Nakamura, Matteo Negri, Jan Niehues, Atul Kr. Ojha, John E. Ortega, Sara Papi, Pavel Pecina, Peter Polák, Piotr Połeć, Beatrice Savoldi, Nivedita Sethiya, Claytone Sikasote, Matthias Sperber, Sebastian Stüker, Katsuhito Sudoh, Brian Thompson, Marco Turchi, Alex Waibel, Patrick Wilken, Rodolfo Zevallos, Vilém Zouhar, and Maike Züfle. 2025. Findings of the iwslt 2025 evaluation campaign. In *Proceedings of the 22nd International Conference on Spoken Language Translation (IWSLT 2025)*, Vienna, Austia (in-person and online). Association for Computational Linguistics. To appear.

Tim Dettmers, Mike Lewis, Sam Shleifer, and Luke Zettlemoyer. 2022. 8-bit optimizers via block-wise quantization. In *The Tenth International Conference on Learning Representations, ICLR 2022, Virtual Event, April 25-29, 2022*. OpenReview.net.

Kosuke Doi, Yuka Ko, Mana Makinae, Katsuhito Sudoh, and Satoshi Nakamura. 2024. Word order in English-Japanese simultaneous interpretation: Analyses and evaluation using chunk-wise monotonic translation. In *Proceedings of the 21st International Conference on Spoken Language Translation (IWSLT 2024)*, pages 254–264, Bangkok, Thailand (in-person and online). Association for Computational Linguistics.

Javier Iranzo-Sánchez, Jorge Civera, and Alfons Juan. 2022. From simultaneous to streaming machine translation by leveraging streaming history. In *Proceedings of the 60th Annual Meeting of the Association for Computational Linguistics (Volume 1: Long Papers)*, pages 6972–6985, Dublin, Ireland. Association for Computational Linguistics.

Javier Iranzo-Sánchez, Jorge Iranzo-Sánchez, Adrià Giménez, Jorge Civera, and Alfons Juan. 2024. Segmentation-free streaming machine translation. *Transactions of the Association for Computational Linguistics*, 12:1104–1121.

Sneha Kudugunta, Isaac Caswell, Biao Zhang, Xavier Garcia, Derrick Xin, Aditya Kusupati, Romi Stella, Ankur Bapna, and Orhan Firat. 2023. MADLAD-400: A multilingual and document-level large audited dataset. In *Advances in Neural Information Processing Systems 36: Annual Conference on Neural Information Processing Systems 2023, NeurIPS 2023, New Orleans, LA, USA, December 10 - 16, 2023*.

Mingbo Ma, Liang Huang, Hao Xiong, Renjie Zheng, Kaibo Liu, Baigong Zheng, Chuanqiang Zhang,

Zhongjun He, Hairong Liu, Xing Li, Hua Wu, and Haifeng Wang. 2019. STACL: Simultaneous translation with implicit anticipation and controllable latency using prefix-to-prefix framework. In *Proceedings of the 57th Annual Meeting of the Association for Computational Linguistics*, pages 3025–3036, Florence, Italy. Association for Computational Linguistics.

Dominik Macháček, Raj Dabre, and Ondřej Bojar. 2023. Turning whisper into real-time transcription system. In *Proceedings of the 13th International Joint Conference on Natural Language Processing and the 3rd Conference of the Asia-Pacific Chapter of the Association for Computational Linguistics: System Demonstrations*, pages 17–24, Bali, Indonesia. Association for Computational Linguistics.

Yulong Mao, Kaiyu Huang, Changhao Guan, Ganglin Bao, Fengran Mo, and Jinan Xu. 2024. Dora: Enhancing parameter-efficient fine-tuning with dynamic rank distribution. In *Proceedings of the 62nd Annual Meeting of the Association for Computational Linguistics (Volume 1: Long Papers), ACL 2024, Bangkok, Thailand, August 11-16, 2024*, pages 11662–11675.

Evgeny Matusov, Gregor Leusch, Oliver Bender, and Hermann Ney. 2005. Evaluating machine translation output with automatic sentence segmentation. In *Proceedings of the Second International Workshop on Spoken Language Translation*, Pittsburgh, Pennsylvania, USA.

Jan Niehues, Ngoc-Quan Pham, Thanh-Le Ha, Matthias Sperber, and Alex Waibel. 2018. Low-latency neural speech translation. In *19th Annual Conference of the International Speech Communication Association, Interspeech 2018, Hyderabad, India, September 2-6, 2018*, pages 1293–1297.

Siqi Ouyang, Xi Xu, and Lei Li. 2025. Infinisst: Simultaneous translation of unbounded speech with large language model. *Preprint*, arXiv:2503.02969.

Sara Papi, Marco Gaido, Matteo Negri, and Luisa Bentivogli. 2024. StreamAtt: Direct streaming speech-to-text translation with attention-based audio history selection. In *Proceedings of the 62nd Annual Meeting of the Association for Computational Linguistics (Volume 1: Long Papers)*, pages 3692–3707, Bangkok, Thailand. Association for Computational Linguistics.

Sara Papi, Marco Gaido, Matteo Negri, and Marco Turchi. 2022. Does Simultaneous Speech Translation need Simultaneous Models? In *Findings of the Association for Computational Linguistics: EMNLP 2022*, pages 141–153.

Sara Papi, Marco Turchi, and Matteo Negri. 2023. AlignAtt: Using Attention-based Audio-Translation Alignments as a Guide for Simultaneous Speech Translation. In *INTERSPEECH 2023*, pages 3974–3978.

Kishore Papineni, Salim Roukos, Todd Ward, and Wei-Jing Zhu. 2002. Bleu: a method for automatic evaluation of machine translation. In *Proceedings of the 40th Annual Meeting of the Association for Computational Linguistics*, pages 311–318, Philadelphia, Pennsylvania, USA. Association for Computational Linguistics.

Peter Polák and Ondřej Bojar. 2023. Long-Form End-to-End Speech Translation via Latent Alignment Segmentation. *Preprint*, arXiv:2309.11384.

Matt Post. 2018. A call for clarity in reporting BLEU scores. In *Proceedings of the Third Conference on Machine Translation: Research Papers*, pages 186–191, Brussels, Belgium. Association for Computational Linguistics.

Matt Post and Marcin Junczys-Dowmunt. 2024. Escaping the sentence-level paradigm in machine translation. *Preprint*, arXiv:2304.12959.

Alec Radford, Jong Wook Kim, Tao Xu, Greg Brockman, Christine McLeavey, and Ilya Sutskever. 2023. Robust speech recognition via large-scale weak supervision. In *International Conference on Machine Learning, ICML 2023, 23-29 July 2023, Honolulu, Hawaii, USA*, pages 28492–28518.

Ricardo Rei, José G. C. de Souza, Duarte Alves, Chrysoula Zerva, Ana C Farinha, Taisiya Glushkova, Alon Lavie, Luisa Coheur, and André F. T. Martins. 2022. COMET-22: Unbabel-IST 2022 submission for the metrics shared task. In *Proceedings of the Seventh Conference on Machine Translation (WMT)*, pages 578–585, Abu Dhabi, United Arab Emirates (Hybrid). Association for Computational Linguistics.

Elizabeth Salesky, Kareem Darwish, Mohamed Al-Badrashiny, Mona Diab, and Jan Niehues. 2023a. Evaluating multilingual speech translation under realistic conditions with resegmentation and terminology. In *Proceedings of the 20th International Conference on Spoken Language Translation (IWSLT 2023)*, pages 62–78, Toronto, Canada (in-person and online). Association for Computational Linguistics.

Elizabeth Salesky, Marcello Federico, and Marine Carpuat, editors. 2023b. *Proceedings of the 20th International Conference on Spoken Language Translation (IWSLT 2023)*. Association for Computational Linguistics, Toronto, Canada (in-person and online).

Elizabeth Salesky, Marcello Federico, and Marine Carpuat, editors. 2024. *Proceedings of the 21st International Conference on Spoken Language Translation (IWSLT 2024)*. Association for Computational Linguistics, Bangkok, Thailand (in-person and online).

Felix Schneider and Alexander Waibel. 2020. Towards stream translation: Adaptive computation time for simultaneous machine translation. In *Proceedings of the 17th International Conference on Spoken Language Translation*, pages 228–236, Online. Association for Computational Linguistics.

Sukanta Sen, Ondřej Bojar, and Barry Haddow. 2022. Simultaneous translation for unsegmented input: A sliding window approach. *Preprint*, arXiv:2210.09754.

Vaibhav Srivastav, Somshubra Majumdar, Nithin Koluguri, Adel Moumen, Sanchit Gandhi, et al. 2023. Open automatic speech recognition leaderboard. `https://huggingface.co/spaces/hf-audio/open_asr_leaderboard`.

NLLB Team. 2024. Scaling neural machine translation to 200 languages. *Nat.*, 630(8018):841–846.

Viet Anh Khoa Tran, David Thulke, Yingbo Gao, Christian Herold, and Hermann Ney. 2022. Does joint training really help cascaded speech translation? In *Proceedings of the 2022 Conference on Empirical Methods in Natural Language Processing*, pages 4480–4487, Abu Dhabi, United Arab Emirates. Association for Computational Linguistics.

Minghan Wang, Thuy-Trang Vu, Jinming Zhao, Fatemeh Shiri, Ehsan Shareghi, and Gholamreza Haffari. 2024. Simultaneous machine translation with large language models. In *Proceedings of the 22nd Annual Workshop of the Australasian Language Technology Association*, pages 89–103, Canberra, Australia. Association for Computational Linguistics.

Rachel Wicks, Matt Post, and Philipp Koehn. 2024. Recovering document annotations for sentence-level bitext. In *Findings of the Association for Computational Linguistics: ACL 2024*, pages 9876–9890, Bangkok, Thailand. Association for Computational Linguistics.

Vilém Zouhar, Pinzhen Chen, Tsz Kin Lam, Nikita Moghe, and Barry Haddow. 2024. Pitfalls and outlooks in using COMET. In *Proceedings of the Ninth Conference on Machine Translation*, pages 1272–1288, Miami, Florida, USA. Association for Computational Linguistics.

A Hyperparameters

Hyperparameter	Baseline	Adapted
ASR VAD	✗	
ASR Initial Wait	1s	
ASR LCP Chunk	1s	
ASR Beam Size	5	
MT Wait-k	3	
MT RALCP λ	0.5	
MT Beam Size	10	
MT Attention Head Layer	6	
MT Max Buffer	80 words	
MT History Remove	20 words	1 sentence

Table 3: Inference hyperparameters for the baseline and adapted models

Hyperparameter	Value
Optimizer	8bit-AdamW (Dettmers et al., 2022)
Warm up Ratio	0.06
LR Schedule	Linear
Effective Batch Size	64
Epochs	3 or until convergence
Initial Learning Rate	2e-4
DoRA Dropout	0
Target Modules	$\boldsymbol{Q}, \boldsymbol{V}$ and Vocabulary Embeddings $\boldsymbol{E}$
DoRA rank config.	$r_Q = r_K = r_E = 16$
DoRA α	32
Bias	✗

Table 4: DoRA hyperparameters for the trained adapted model.

Instituto de Telecomunicações at IWSLT 2025: Aligning Small-Scale Speech and Language Models for Speech-to-Text Learning

Giuseppe Attanasio[♣], Sonal Sannigrahi[♣♠], Ben Peters[♣], André F.T. Martins[♣♠◇]
[♣]Instituto de Telecomunicações, Lisbon, Portugal
[♠]Instituto Superior Técnico, Universidade de Lisboa, Portugal
[◇]Unbabel, Lisbon, Portugal
giuseppe.attanasio@lx.it.pt

Abstract

This paper presents Instituto de Telecomunicações's submission to the IWSLT 2025 Shared Task on Instruction Following Speech Processing. We submit results for the Short Track, i.e., speech recognition, translation, and spoken question answering. Our model is a unified speech-to-text model that integrates a pretrained continuous speech encoder and text decoder through a first phase of modality alignment and a second phase of instruction fine-tuning. Crucially, we focus on using small-scale language model backbones (< 2B) and restrict to high-quality, CC-BY data along with synthetic data generation to supplement existing resources.[1]

1 Introduction

This paper presents our submission to the IWSLT 2025 Instruction Following track for the tasks of Automatic Speech Recognition (ASR), Speech Translation (ST), and Spoken Question Answering (SQA) for English, Chinese, and German. Our work builds upon a long line of previous research equipping LMs with additional multimodal capabilities, aligning an LM's semantic spaces with that of a pretrained speech encoder (Tang et al., 2023; Huang et al., 2023; Hu et al., 2024; Chu et al., 2024; Grattafiori et al., 2024, *inter alia)*. Our contribution is particularly motivated by *efficiency*, i.e., the goal of achieving strong performance using small-scale (< 2B) models. Recent work has explored audio quantization techniques (Zhang et al., 2024; Défossez et al., 2023, *inter alia)*, quantized input mel spectrograms (Shen et al., 2024), or extreme compression of input data over the time dimension through convolutional kernels paired with strong small-scale LM backbones (Abouelenin et al., 2025).

[1]Code and data at `https://github.com/deep-spin/it-iwslt-2025`.

We take stock of such advancements and propose a model for even smaller scales. We use established methods for speech integration in LMs (Gaido et al., 2024; Grattafiori et al., 2024) using pretrained base models of up to 1.5B learnable parameters, finding empirically that with highly filtered and synthetic data, we can enable similar results at a fraction of the cost of larger LMs. The main contributions of our system are as follows:

- **Adapting pretrained, small-scale LMs:** We experiment with Qwen 2.5 1.5B and 0.5B (Yang et al., 2024a) as our LM of choice and use w2v-BERT 2.0 (Barrault et al., 2023) as our speech encoder.
- **Two-stage Training Curriculum:** We use a *modality alignment* and *instruction fine tuning* (IFT) phase for training our models, where the first equips the model with general speech capabilities and the second enables multi-task capabilities.
- **Training on open-licensed data:** To guarantee reproducibility and facilitate future research, we train on established CC-BY data collections and synthetic data filtered for quality. We release training and modeling artefacts under a permissive license.

2 Related Work

Efficient LMs. Recent works on efficient, small-scale language models (SLMs) have shown impressive knowledge compression capabilities by maintaining similar performance to larger, more computationally-intensive models. Models such as Phi-4 Mini (Abouelenin et al., 2025) and Gemma 2 (Gemma Team et al., 2024) have reported strong performance relative to size with a focus on computational efficiency. Lu et al. (2024) have shown how scaling laws operate differently for SLMs and

Proceedings of the 22nd International Conference on Spoken Language Translation (IWSLT 2025), pages 347–353
July 31 - August 1, 2025

have further demonstrated the efficiency of such models in subsequent reasoning tasks.

Multimodal LM Extension. Equipping a text-based model with multimodal capabilities is often done using an auxiliary modality encoder that is then used to jointly learn a semantic mapping between speech and text. Early works in joint text-speech modeling include AudioPaLM (Rubenstein et al., 2023), VioLA (Wang et al., 2023), and VoxtLM (Maiti et al., 2024). Other approaches combine a pretrained continuous speech encoder with an LM by concatenating speech embeddings to the text context (Tang et al., 2023; Huang et al., 2023; Hu et al., 2024; Chu et al., 2024; Grattafiori et al., 2024, *inter alia)*. Such works rely on strong multilingual capabilities of the speech encoder and those of large-scale LMs (i.e., 7B or more) to learn how to use speech-related parts of the context (Grattafiori et al., 2024). Our system echoes this compositional approach to speech and language modeling but leverages recent language models in the scale 0.5-1.5B.

3 System Overview

3.1 Model Architecture

Our model follows a standard speech encoder, text decoder architecture (e.g., Tang et al., 2023; Grattafiori et al., 2024; Chu et al., 2024).

Speech stack. We extract 80-dimensional Mel-filterbank audio representations with a stride of 2 using w2v-BERT 2.0's standard processor. Then we compress the audio over the time dimension using three 1D convolutional layers with a kernel width of 3 and a stride of 2. This input is then processed by the pretrained w2v-BERT 2.0 model. The output representations are processed by a modality and length adapter composed of two Conformer-like (Gulati et al., 2020) layers that further compress the audio representations on the time dimension and project them into the embedding space of the language model.

Text stack. We prepend the audio representations computed from the audio stack to the text input embeddings extracted from the input embedding matrix of the language model. We use a bidirectional self-attention for the audio positions and a causal (autoregressive) one for the text part of the context. Following prior work (Chu et al., 2023; Radford et al., 2022), we constrain text generation using a target language and task token. Figure 1 illustrates the model architecture.

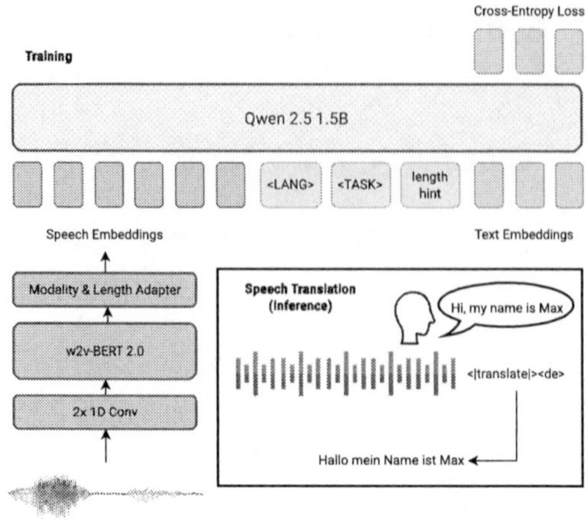

Figure 1: Illustration of our model. During training, the speech stack (red) generates speech representations which are prepended to task and language tags and an (optional) length hint (yellow), and text tokens (green). At inference time, we only provide the language and task tokens.

3.2 Training Curriculum

We train our model in two stages: a modality alignment stage followed by an instruction fine-tuning (IFT) stage.

Modality Alignment. This first stage aligns the speech stack output representations to the language model's embedding space. We use the pretrained w2v-BERT 2.0 (v2)[2] as our speech encoder and randomly initialize the pre-encoder convolutional layers and the modality adapter. We choose Qwen 2.5 1.5B,[3] a multilingual LM, as our text decoder. Choosing a small ($<$ 2B) model allows for the exploration of more efficient alternatives and is often overlooked in the literature.

In this phase, we train only the pre-encoder convolutional layers and the modality adapter with a learning rate of 3×10^{-3} for a single epoch. We train the model only on ASR data. The model is trained using standard cross-entropy loss on the reference transcript tokens. With a 95% chance, we prepend to the language and task tags a *length hint*, as suggested by Deitke et al. (2024), to let the model learn a length distribution. This stage leads to a model that can perform ASR but does not yet have other capabilities.

[2]https://huggingface.co/facebook/w2v-bert-2.0
[3]https://huggingface.co/Qwen/Qwen2.5-1.5B

Task	Data	License	Hours
	Modality Alignment (MA)		
ASR	LibriSpeech (LS)	CC-BY 4.0	1K
	Multilingual LS	CC-BY 4.0	2K
	FLEURS	CC-BY 4.0	24
	CommonVoice 16.1	CC-BY 4.0	4K
	Instruction Fine-Tuning (IFT)		
ASR	*All MA data*		
	VoxPopuli	CC-BY 4.0	1.8K
	Peoples Speech	CC-BY 4.0	12K
	CV 16.1 PL	-	30K
ST	CoVoST-2	CC-BY NC 4.0	3K
	CoVoST-2 PL	CC-BY NC 4.0	3K
SQA	SpokenSQuAD	-	-
	Generated Data	-	-

Table 1: Data statistics with licence, hours of speech data across all languages, and task splits.

Instruction Fine-Tuning. Following the modality alignment phase, we perform IFT using speech-to-text tasks included in the IWSLT campaign (AST, SQA) in English, German, and Chinese. During this stage, we train every component jointly end-to-end.[4]

Generation Parameters. For all tasks, we let the model generate up to 1024 tokens with beam search decoding (beam size of 3), a repetition penalty of 1.6, and nucleus sampling with temperature of 1.2.

3.3 Data

Where possible, we use CC-BY licensed data across all tasks. When sufficient data is not available, we generate synthetic corpora using the procedures described below. Table 1 provides an overview of the data sources used for each task and training phase.

Speech Recognition. We use CommonVoice 16.1 (Ardila et al., 2020), FLEURS (Conneau et al., 2023), MLS (Pratap et al., 2020), and LibriSpeech (Panayotov et al., 2015) for the modality alignment (MA) data mixture. For IFT, we reuse all MA data plus VoxPopuli (Wang et al., 2021) and The People's Speech (clean) (Galvez et al., 2021).

Speech Translation. We use CoVoST2 (Wang et al., 2020) as gold-standard AST data across English, Chinese, and German. We supplement this gold standard parallel data by **pseudolabeling** ASR transcriptions. This technique has proven effective for previous systems (Barrault et al., 2023; Ambilduke et al., 2025) and is simple to implement. Concretely, we translate all transcriptions from the English portion of CommonVoice 16.1 using four strong MT models: the 13B and Mistral-7B versions of TowerInstruct (Alves et al., 2024), EuroLLM-9B-Instruct (Martins et al., 2024), and NLLB-3.3B (NLLB Team et al., 2022). For each transcription, we use a COMETKiwi (Rei et al., 2022) oracle to select the best translation among the four systems. We then filter out examples for which the best translation records a score under 0.85. This process allows for fewer examples to be filtered than in conventional single-model pseudolabeling, as is shown in Table 2, and also increases diversity because the translations come from a mixture of several models.

Model	% Kept en→de	% Kept en→zh
NLLB-3B	58.1	34.3
TowerInstruct-Mistral-7B	60.0	51.5
TowerInstruct-13B	59.4	49.9
EuroLLM-9B-Instruct	62.5	52.3
Oracle	71.0	64.3

Table 2: Percentage of English transcriptions in CommonVoice 16.1 for which various models produce a translation with a COMETKiwi score of at least 0.85. The oracle keeps a much larger share of hypotheses than any individual model.

Spoken Question Answering. We use the Spoken SQuAD (Lee et al., 2018) dataset for English SQA. This dataset consists of several texts which are synthesized into speech and has a total of 37K questions and answers. Due to the limited availability of multilingual SQA datasets, we follow the same pseudolabeling process as for ST to create synthetic German and Chinese questions and answers for each example. The question and answer were translated separately using the same mixture of models as for ST. Question-answer pairs were kept if the best translated question had a COMETKiwi score of at least 0.80. The same system was used to translate the answer regardless of how it compared to the translated answers from other systems.[5] As the SQA task also includes questions where the answer cannot be inferred from the context, we additionally generate synthetic *unanswerable* questions for each context in English, German, and Chinese using Qwen2.5-

[4]MA and IFT runs required a total of three days using four H100 GPUs in an in-house infrastructure.

[5]As the answers were generally very short, we found that COMETKiwi performed unreliably for them.

Given a text passage and some questions about it, write 2 questions in [LANG_ID] as close to the style of the original questions as possible but that are not answerable. The questions must be of similar difficulty as the example questions, i.e., they have to mention aspects and topics of the passage, but the answer cannot be inferred from the text. Be creative. Provide one question per line.

Text passage: [CONTEXT]

Example questions: [QUESTION]
Unanswerable questions:

Figure 2: Prompt used to generate unanswerable questions from Qwen2.5-70B where **context** is the transcript used to synthesize speech in Spoken SQuAD, **question** is an answerable question from Spoken SQuAD, and **lang id** is the language in which we want to generate questions.

70B (Yang et al., 2024a). Following insights from (Sannigrahi et al., 2024), we provide the LM with context along with example questions to guide the style and quality of the generated answers. We find that without example questions based on the original dataset, the LM often produces i) questions not adhering to the topic of the context and ii) verbose questions. We also experiment with prompts that do not explicitly request the model to mention aspects/topics of the context provided and find this to be suboptimal. As the number of positive instances in the Spoken QA dataset is small, in order to maintain a balanced dataset, we limit unanswerable questions to two per context. We further experimented with using the audio directly as opposed to the text transcript for context, but found this approach to be more prone to errors, as the Spoken SQuAD dataset is *not* a native spoken dataset but rather a synthesized QA dataset, often leading to minor pronunciation errors. The final prompt used to obtain additional questions is shown in Figure 2.

Preprocessing. We restrict our model to process audio of up to 120 seconds, discarding all training input longer than that. We preprocess all the instances appending to the speech embeddings (and prepending to the text embeddings) the task and language tags following the input template in Figure 1. The task task tag can be either <|transcribe|>, <|translate|>, or <|reply|> for ASR, AST, and SQA, respectively, and the language tag is <|en|>, <|de|>, or <|zh|>.

en		en-de		en-zh	
ASR	SQA	ST	SQA	ST	SQA
0.15	0.14	0.34	0.22	0.34	0.21

Table 3: Official normalized ASR (WER (↓)), ST (COMET (↑)), and SQA (BertScore (↑)) scores.

4 Results

Our results for all three short-track tasks are in Table 3. For further details about the evaluation campaign as well as the metrics, we refer readers to Abdulmumin et al. (2025).

Our model obtains **reasonably good ASR scores for English**. This result is particularly relevant, considering that the test data originate from the technical domain, exhibit high speaker variability, and consist primarily of spontaneous speech. However, while the model successfully performs ASR, **SQA and ST prove to be more complex**. Through manual inspection, we observed poor quality outputs for ST. At times, the model repeats the same word or ignores the task tag and transcribes the audio segment rather than translating it. This finding aligns with prior work that has found ASR data dominates the multitask capabilities of models (Tang et al., 2023). Moreover, it emphasizes the importance of a more carefully designed training curriculum, where SQA, ST, and ASR data are more evenly distributed. Lastly, due to the audio length cutoff—set to 120 seconds due to technical limitations—we were unable to use all of the available SQA data. At test time, when prompted to perform the SQA task, the model sometimes generates the question itself, rather than the answer. We believe that by utilizing a combination of more data, enhanced base models with stronger multilingual capabilities, and extended context support, we will be able to improve upon these results substantially.

5 Conclusions

We have presented our submission for the IWSLT 2025 Instruction Following Short Track. We explored the usage of a small-scale LM in modality adaptation through a continuous speech encoder. In particular, we equip an existing text model, Qwen 2.5 1.5B, with the speech modality for a joint multilingual and multitask model.

We used standard modality alignment approaches, including building on pretrained speech encoders and autoregressive text decoder models, and a two-stage curriculum learning. In future work, we plan to support longer contexts, better filtered data, and further push small-scale LMs to be fully multimodal. We will incorporate more high-quality multilingual data to enhance the model's language identification capabilities. Additionally, we will extend the evaluation beyond standard performance-oriented benchmarks, e.g., by accounting for safety (Yang et al., 2024b) and fairness (Koudounas et al., 2024; Attanasio et al., 2024).

Acknowledgements

We thank Duarte Alves and Patrick Fernandes for their feedback and insightful discussions in the earlier versions of the paper. This work was supported by the Portuguese Recovery and Resilience Plan through project C645008882-00000055 (Center for Responsible AI), by EU's Horizon Europe Research and Innovation Actions (UTTER, contract 101070631), by the project DECOLLAGE (ERC-2022-CoG 101088763), and by FCT/MECI through national funds and when applicable cofunded EU funds under UID/50008: Instituto de Telecomunicações.

Limitations

Currently, our model supports audio up to 2 minutes in length. Ideally, we would also like to support longer audio contexts while maintaining computationally inexpensive training. With the current length filters, we do not see much of the SQA data, which hinders the model's multi-task capabilities. Additionally, we have worked with a small LM (1.5B) in our model, which did not have the best language modeling capabilities. We plan to run additional experiments within the 3B scale. Lastly, there is limited research on the filtering of synthetically generated data for the QA domain. For future work, we plan to further refine the pipeline to generate synthetic QA data from spoken contexts.

References

Idris Abdulmumin, Victor Agostinelli, Tanel Alumäe, Antonios Anastasopoulos, Ashwin, Luisa Bentivogli, Ondřej Bojar, Claudia Borg, Fethi Bougares, Roldano Cattoni, Mauro Cettolo, Lizhong Chen, William Chen, Raj Dabre, Yannick Estève, Marcello Federico, Marco Gaido, Dávid Javorský, Marek Kasztelnik, and 30 others. 2025. Findings of the iwslt 2025 evaluation campaign. In *Proceedings of the 22nd International Conference on Spoken Language Translation (IWSLT 2025)*, Vienna, Austria (in-person and online). Association for Computational Linguistics. To appear.

Abdelrahman Abouelenin, Atabak Ashfaq, Adam Atkinson, Hany Awadalla, Nguyen Bach, Jianmin Bao, Alon Benhaim, Martin Cai, Vishrav Chaudhary, Congcong Chen, and 1 others. 2025. Phi-4-mini technical report: Compact yet powerful multimodal language models via mixture-of-loras. *arXiv preprint arXiv:2503.01743*.

Duarte Miguel Alves, José Pombal, Nuno M Guerreiro, Pedro Henrique Martins, João Alves, Amin Farajian, Ben Peters, Ricardo Rei, Patrick Fernandes, Sweta Agrawal, Pierre Colombo, José G. C. de Souza, and Andre Martins. 2024. Tower: An open multilingual large language model for translation-related tasks. In *First Conference on Language Modeling*.

Kshitij Ambilduke, Ben Peters, Sonal Sannigrahi, Anil Keshwani, Tsz Kin Lam, Bruno Martins, Marcely Zanon Boito, and André FT Martins. 2025. From tower to spire: Adding the speech modality to a text-only llm. *arXiv preprint arXiv:2503.10620*.

Rosana Ardila, Megan Branson, Kelly Davis, Michael Kohler, Josh Meyer, Michael Henretty, Reuben Morais, Lindsay Saunders, Francis Tyers, and Gregor Weber. 2020. Common voice: A massively-multilingual speech corpus. In *Proceedings of the Twelfth Language Resources and Evaluation Conference*, pages 4218–4222, Marseille, France. European Language Resources Association.

Giuseppe Attanasio, Beatrice Savoldi, Dennis Fucci, and Dirk Hovy. 2024. Twists, humps, and pebbles: Multilingual speech recognition models exhibit gender performance gaps. In *Proceedings of the 2024 Conference on Empirical Methods in Natural Language Processing*, pages 21318–21340, Miami, Florida, USA. Association for Computational Linguistics.

Loïc Barrault, Yu-An Chung, Mariano Coria Meglioli, David Dale, Ning Dong, Mark Duppenthaler, Paul-Ambroise Duquenne, Brian Ellis, Hady Elsahar, Justin Haaheim, and 1 others. 2023. Seamless: Multilingual expressive and streaming speech translation. *arXiv preprint arXiv:2312.05187*.

Yunfei Chu, Jin Xu, Qian Yang, Haojie Wei, Xipin Wei, Zhifang Guo, Yichong Leng, Yuanjun Lv, Jinzheng He, Junyang Lin, and 1 others. 2024. Qwen2-audio technical report. *arXiv preprint arXiv:2407.10759*.

Yunfei Chu, Jin Xu, Xiaohuan Zhou, Qian Yang, Shiliang Zhang, Zhijie Yan, Chang Zhou, and Jingren Zhou. 2023. Qwen-audio: Advancing universal audio understanding via unified large-scale audio-language models. *arXiv preprint arXiv:2311.07919*.

Alexis Conneau, Min Ma, Simran Khanuja, Yu Zhang, Vera Axelrod, Siddharth Dalmia, Jason Riesa, Clara Rivera, and Ankur Bapna. 2023. Fleurs: Few-shot learning evaluation of universal representations of speech. In *2022 IEEE Spoken Language Technology Workshop (SLT)*, pages 798–805. IEEE.

Alexandre Défossez, Jade Copet, Gabriel Synnaeve, and Yossi Adi. 2023. High fidelity neural audio compression. *Transactions on Machine Learning Research*. Featured Certification, Reproducibility Certification.

Matt Deitke, Christopher Clark, Sangho Lee, Rohun Tripathi, Yue Yang, Jae Sung Park, Mohammadreza Salehi, Niklas Muennighoff, Kyle Lo, Luca Soldaini, and 1 others. 2024. Molmo and pixmo: Open weights and open data for state-of-the-art multimodal models. *arXiv preprint arXiv:2409.17146*.

Marco Gaido, Sara Papi, Matteo Negri, and Luisa Bentivogli. 2024. Speech translation with speech foundation models and large language models: What is there and what is missing? In *Proceedings of the 62nd Annual Meeting of the Association for Computational Linguistics (Volume 1: Long Papers)*, pages 14760–14778, Bangkok, Thailand. Association for Computational Linguistics.

Daniel Galvez, Greg Diamos, Juan Ciro, Juan Felipe Cerón, Keith Achorn, Anjali Gopi, David Kanter, Maximilian Lam, Mark Mazumder, and Vijay Janapa Reddi. 2021. The people's speech: A large-scale diverse english speech recognition dataset for commercial usage. *Preprint*, arXiv:2111.09344.

Gemma Team, Morgane Riviere, Shreya Pathak, Pier Giuseppe Sessa, Cassidy Hardin, Surya Bhupatiraju, Léonard Hussenot, Thomas Mesnard, Bobak Shahriari, Alexandre Ramé, and 1 others. 2024. Gemma 2: Improving open language models at a practical size. *arXiv preprint arXiv:2408.00118*.

Aaron Grattafiori, Abhimanyu Dubey, Abhinav Jauhri, Abhinav Pandey, Abhishek Kadian, Ahmad Al-Dahle, Aiesha Letman, Akhil Mathur, Alan Schelten, Alex Vaughan, and 1 others. 2024. The llama 3 herd of models. *arXiv preprint arXiv:2407.21783*.

Anmol Gulati, James Qin, Chung-Cheng Chiu, Niki Parmar, Yu Zhang, Jiahui Yu, Wei Han, Shibo Wang, Zhengdong Zhang, Yonghui Wu, and Ruoming Pang. 2020. Conformer: Convolution-augmented transformer for speech recognition. *Preprint*, arXiv:2005.08100.

Shujie Hu, Long Zhou, Shujie Liu, Sanyuan Chen, Lingwei Meng, Hongkun Hao, Jing Pan, Xunying Liu, Jinyu Li, Sunit Sivasankaran, Linquan Liu, and Furu Wei. 2024. WavLLM: Towards robust and adaptive speech large language model. In *Findings of the Association for Computational Linguistics: EMNLP 2024*, pages 4552–4572, Miami, Florida, USA. Association for Computational Linguistics.

Zhichao Huang, Rong Ye, Tom Ko, Qianqian Dong, Shanbo Cheng, Mingxuan Wang, and Hang Li. 2023. Speech translation with large language models: An industrial practice. *arXiv preprint arXiv:2312.13585*.

Alkis Koudounas, Eliana Pastor, Giuseppe Attanasio, Vittorio Mazzia, Manuel Giollo, Thomas Gueudre, Elisa Reale, Luca Cagliero, Sandro Cumani, Luca de Alfaro, and 1 others. 2024. Towards comprehensive subgroup performance analysis in speech models. *IEEE/ACM Transactions on Audio, Speech, and Language Processing*, 32:1468–1480.

Chia-Hsuan Lee, Szu-Lin Wu, Chi-Liang Liu, and Hung-yi Lee. 2018. Spoken squad: A study of mitigating the impact of speech recognition errors on listening comprehension. *Proc. Interspeech 2018*, pages 3459–3463.

Zhenyan Lu, Xiang Li, Dongqi Cai, Rongjie Yi, Fangming Liu, Xiwen Zhang, Nicholas D Lane, and Mengwei Xu. 2024. Small language models: Survey, measurements, and insights. *CoRR*.

Soumi Maiti, Yifan Peng, Shukjae Choi, Jee-weon Jung, Xuankai Chang, and Shinji Watanabe. 2024. Voxtlm: Unified decoder-only models for consolidating speech recognition, synthesis and speech, text continuation tasks. In *ICASSP 2024-2024 IEEE International Conference on Acoustics, Speech and Signal Processing (ICASSP)*, pages 13326–13330. IEEE.

Pedro Henrique Martins, Patrick Fernandes, João Alves, Nuno M. Guerreiro, Ricardo Rei, Duarte M. Alves, José Pombal, Amin Farajian, Manuel Faysse, Mateusz Klimaszewski, Pierre Colombo, Barry Haddow, José G. C. de Souza, Alexandra Birch, and André F. T. Martins. 2024. Eurollm: Multilingual language models for europe. *Preprint*, arXiv:2409.16235.

NLLB Team, Marta R Costa-jussà, James Cross, Onur Çelebi, Maha Elbayad, Kenneth Heafield, Kevin Heffernan, Elahe Kalbassi, Janice Lam, Daniel Licht, Jean Maillard, Anna Sun, Skyler Wang, Guillaume Wenzek, Al Youngblood, Bapi Akula, Loic Barrault, Gabriel Mejia-Gonzalez, Prangthip Hansanti, and 20 others. 2022. No language left behind: Scaling human-centered machine translation. *arXiv preprint arXiv:2207.04672*.

Vassil Panayotov, Guoguo Chen, Daniel Povey, and Sanjeev Khudanpur. 2015. Librispeech: an asr corpus based on public domain audio books. In *2015 IEEE international conference on acoustics, speech and signal processing (ICASSP)*, pages 5206–5210. IEEE.

Vineel Pratap, Qiantong Xu, Anuroop Sriram, Gabriel Synnaeve, and Ronan Collobert. 2020. MLS: A Large-Scale Multilingual Dataset for Speech Research. In *Proc. Interspeech 2020*, pages 2757–2761.

Alec Radford, Jong Wook Kim, Tao Xu, Greg Brockman, Christine McLeavey, and Ilya Sutskever. 2022. Robust speech recognition via large-scale weak supervision. In *International Conference on Machine Learning*.

Ricardo Rei, Marcos Treviso, Nuno M. Guerreiro, Chrysoula Zerva, Ana C Farinha, Christine Maroti, José G. C. de Souza, Taisiya Glushkova, Duarte

Alves, Luisa Coheur, Alon Lavie, and André F. T. Martins. 2022. CometKiwi: IST-unbabel 2022 submission for the quality estimation shared task. In *Proceedings of the Seventh Conference on Machine Translation (WMT)*, pages 634–645, Abu Dhabi, United Arab Emirates (Hybrid). Association for Computational Linguistics.

Paul K Rubenstein, Chulayuth Asawaroengchai, Duc Dung Nguyen, Ankur Bapna, Zalán Borsos, Félix de Chaumont Quitry, Peter Chen, Dalia El Badawy, Wei Han, Eugene Kharitonov, and 1 others. 2023. Audiopalm: A large language model that can speak and listen. *arXiv preprint arXiv:2306.12925*.

Sonal Sannigrahi, Thiago Fraga-Silva, Youssef Oualil, and Christophe Van Gysel. 2024. Synthetic query generation using large language models for virtual assistants. In *Proceedings of the 47th International ACM SIGIR Conference on Research and Development in Information Retrieval*, pages 2837–2841.

Kai Shen, Zeqian Ju, Xu Tan, Eric Liu, Yichong Leng, Lei He, Tao Qin, Sheng Zhao, and Jiang Bian. 2024. Naturalspeech 2: Latent diffusion models are natural and zero-shot speech and singing synthesizers. In *The Twelfth International Conference on Learning Representations*.

Changli Tang, Wenyi Yu, Guangzhi Sun, Xianzhao Chen, Tian Tan, Wei Li, Lu Lu, Zejun Ma, and Chao Zhang. 2023. Salmonn: Towards generic hearing abilities for large language models. *arXiv preprint arXiv:2310.13289*.

Changhan Wang, Morgane Rivière, Ann Lee, Anne Wu, Chaitanya Talnikar, Daniel Haziza, Mary Williamson, Juan Pino, and Emmanuel Dupoux. 2021. Voxpopuli: A large-scale multilingual speech corpus for representation learning, semi-supervised learning and interpretation. *Preprint*, arXiv:2101.00390.

Changhan Wang, Anne Wu, and Juan Pino. 2020. Covost 2 and massively multilingual speech-to-text translation. *arXiv preprint arXiv:2007.10310*.

Tianrui Wang, Long Zhou, Ziqiang Zhang, Yu Wu, Shujie Liu, Yashesh Gaur, Zhuo Chen, Jinyu Li, and Furu Wei. 2023. Viola: Unified codec language models for speech recognition, synthesis, and translation. *arXiv e-prints*, pages arXiv–2305.

An Yang, Baosong Yang, Beichen Zhang, Binyuan Hui, Bo Zheng, Bowen Yu, Chengyuan Li, Dayiheng Liu, Fei Huang, Haoran Wei, Huan Lin, Jian Yang, Jianhong Tu, Jianwei Zhang, Jianxin Yang, Jiaxi Yang, Jingren Zhou, Junyang Lin, Kai Dang, and 22 others. 2024a. Qwen2.5 technical report. *arXiv preprint arXiv:2412.15115*.

Hao Yang, Lizhen Qu, Ehsan Shareghi, and Reza Haf. 2024b. Towards probing speech-specific risks in large multimodal models: A taxonomy, benchmark, and insights. In *Proceedings of the 2024 Conference on Empirical Methods in Natural Language Processing*, pages 10957–10973, Miami, Florida, USA. Association for Computational Linguistics.

Xin Zhang, Dong Zhang, Shimin Li, Yaqian Zhou, and Xipeng Qiu. 2024. Speechtokenizer: Unified speech tokenizer for speech language models. In *ICLR*.

Bemba Speech Translation: Exploring a Low-Resource African Language

Muhammad Hazim Al Farouq
Kreasof AI
Research Labs
Jakarta, Indonesia

Aman Kassahun Wassie
African Institute for
Mathematical Sciences (AIMS)
Addis Ababa, Ethiopia

Yasmin Moslem[✩]
ADAPT Centre
Trinity College Dublin
Dublin, Ireland

Abstract

This paper describes our system submission to the International Conference on Spoken Language Translation (IWSLT 2025), low-resource languages track, namely for Bemba-to-English speech translation. We built cascaded speech translation systems based on Whisper and NLLB-200, and employed data augmentation techniques, such as back-translation. We investigate the effect of using synthetic data and discuss our experimental setup.

1 Introduction

Low-resource languages face critical limitations due to the scarcity and scattered nature of the available data (Haddow et al., 2022). Speech translation for low-resource languages involves similar challenges (Ahmad et al., 2024; Moslem, 2024; Lovenia et al., 2024; Abdulmumin et al., 2025), Similarly, speech applications for African languages are very limited due to the lack of linguistic resources. For example, Bemba is an under-resourced language spoken by over 30% of the population in Zambia (Sikasote and Anastasopoulos, 2022). Hence, the IWSLT shared task on speech translation for low-resource languages aims to benchmark and promote speech translation technology for a diverse range of dialects and low-resource languages.

We participated in the Bemba-to-English language pair through building cascaded speech translation systems. In other words, we employed Whisper (Radford et al., 2022) for automatic speech recognition (ASR), and NLLB-200 (Costa-jussà et al., 2022) for text-to-text machine translation (MT). For ASR, we fine-tuned Whisper models using two datasets, BembaSpeech and BIG-C. For MT, we fine-tuned the NLLB-200 models using the bilingual segments of the BIG-C dataset, and the "dev" split of the FLORES-200 dataset. In addition, we augmented the Bemba-to-English training data with back-translation of a portion of the Tatoeba dataset from English into Bemba. The back-translated data was filtered based on cross-entropy scores. As Table 4 shows, the systems we submitted to the shared tasks are as follows:

- Primary: It uses Whisper-Medium for ASR and NLLB-200 3.3B for MT.
- Contrastive 1: It uses Whisper-Small for ASR and NLLB-200 3.3B for MT.
- Contrastive 2: It uses Whisper-Small for ASR and NLLB-200 600M for MT.

2 Data

The data we used to train our Bemba-to-English speech translation models can be categorized into: (1) authentic data, and (2) synthetic data. The following sections provide more details (cf. Table 1).

Dataset	Language	Train	Dev	Test	Audio
Big-C	Bem-Eng	82,371	2,782	2,763	✓
BembaSpeech	Bem	12,421	1,700	1,359	✓
FLORES-200	Bem-Eng	997	0	1,012	✗
Tatoeba	Eng	20,121	0	0	✗

Table 1: Data Statistics: The "Language" column specifies which languages are originally available in each dataset. "Train", "Dev", and "Test" represent the dataset sizes. The "Audio" column indicates whether each dataset includes audio signals.

2.1 Authentic Data

We filtered the authentic data by removing any overlaps between the training data and test data based on the text transcript. For building our models, we used the following data sources.

- **Big-C** is a parallel corpus of speech and transcriptions of image-grounded dialogues between Bemba speakers and their corresponding English translations. It contains 92,117

✩Correspondence: yasmin[at]machinetranslation.io

Proceedings of the 22nd International Conference on Spoken Language Translation (IWSLT 2025), pages 354–359
July 31 - August 1, 2025 ©2025 Association for Computational Linguistics

Training Dataset(s)	FLORES-200			BIG-C		
	BLEU	**chrF++**	**COMET**	**BLEU**	**chrF++**	**COMET**
Big-C	18.13	42.11	53.25	27.83	51.08	53.28
Big-C + Tatoeba	21.67	45.25	55.64	27.82	50.98	**53.39**
Big-C + FLORES-200	25.21	47.31	57.23	27.96	51.03	53.29
Big-C + FLORES-200 + Tatoeba	**25.70**	**47.75**	**58.29**	**28.60**	**51.38**	53.08

Table 2: MT Evaluation: In general, the models trained with both authentic data (Big-C & FLORES-200) and back-translated data (Tatoeba) outperform the models trained with the authentic data only. All the models in this table uses NLLB-200 600M.

spoken utterances of both complete and incomplete dialogues, amounting to 187 hours of speech data grounded on 16,229 unique images. The dataset aims to enable the development of speech recognition, speech, and text translation systems for Bemba, as well as facilitate research in language grounding and multimodal model development (Sikasote and Anastasopoulos, 2022).[1] Since this dataset includes audio and transcription in Bemba as well as translation into English, we could use it to build both modules of our cascaded systems, i.e. ASR and MT. Table 7 shows examples of sentence pairs from the Big-C datasets.

- **BembaSpeech** is an ASR corpus for the Bemba language of Zambia. It contains read speech from diverse publicly available Bemba sources; literature books, radio/TV shows transcripts, YouTube video transcripts as well as various open online sources. Its purpose is to enable the training and testing of automatic speech recognition (ASR) systems in Bemba language. The corpus has 14,438 utterances, culminating into 24.5 hours of speech data (Sikasote et al., 2023).[2] We used the BembaSpeech dataset in addition to the Big-C dataset to build our ASR models.

- **FLORES-200** (Goyal et al., 2022) is a bilingual text-only dataset for machine translation. We used the Bemba-to-English "dev" split for training, and the "devtest" split for testing.

- **Tatoeba** (Tiedemann, 2020) is a monolingual dataset in English. We used a portion of it for back-translation (cf. Section 2.2).

[1]https://github.com/csikasote/bigc

[2]https://github.com/csikasote/BembaSpeech

2.2 Synthetic Data

We augmented our authentic data (cf. Section 2.1) with synthetic data created with back-translation. To this end, we fine-tuned the NLLB-200 600M model in the other direction, i.e. for the English-to-Bemba language pair. Thereafter, we translated the English sentences from Tatoeba into Bemba using the fine-tuned English-to-Bemba NLLB-200 model. For translation, we used CTranslate2 (Klein et al., 2020), generating the prediction cross-entropy scores for each sentence, and calculating the exponential of the scores for better readability. We filtered data based on the cross-entropy scores, removing low-quality segments. We removed segments with scores less than 0.77 based on manual exploration of samples of the generated back-translations. While the unfiltered back-translated data consists of 85,000 segments, the filtered back-translated data consists of 20,000 segments. Finally, we prepended the source side (Bemba) with the <*bt*> tag to indicate that the data is synthetic. Moreover, we experimented with removing the <*bt*> tag and found that this achieves slightly better results when testing with the FLORES-200's "devtest" split, as the data was already filtered (cf. Table 3).

3 Experiments and Results

As illustrated by Figure 1, our cascaded systems involve two components, an ASR model based on Whisper to generate transcriptions and an MT model based on NLLB-200 to generate text translation. We experimented with different versions of these models, namely Whisper Small and Medium, and NLLB-200 with 600M and 3.3B parameters. Our code for data preparation, training, and evaluation is publicly available.[3]

[3]https://github.com/cobrayyxx/Bemba-IWSLT2025

Datasets	BT Size	Filtered	<bt> tag	FLORES-200 BLEU	FLORES-200 chrF++	FLORES-200 COMET	BIG-C BLEU	BIG-C chrF++	BIG-C COMET
BIG-C + Tatoeba	85,155	⊗	✓	20.96	45.06	**55.92**	**28.17**	**51.26**	53.45
	20,121	✓	✓	19.82	44.09	54.79	28.04	51.20	**53.51**
	20,121	✓	⊗	**21.67**	**45.25**	55.64	27.82	50.98	53.39

Table 3: Performance of MT models that are based on NLLB-200 600M and trained using both authentic data and augmented back-translated data. There are two pre-processing aspects applied to the augmented data, filtering the data based on cross-entropy scores, and prepending the source sentence with the *<bt>* tag. Evaluating the models with the devtest split of the FLORES-200 dataset, the highest evaluation scores, in terms BLEU and chrF++, are achieved when the back-translated data is filtered and the *<bt>* tag is removed. Meanwhile, the AfriCOMET score (COMET) of this model is comparable to the model where the back-translated data is not filtered and the source is prepended with the *<bt>* tag. Evaluating the models with the hold-out test split of Big-C reveals a different outcome where using the *<bt>* tag results in relatively higher scores, although the scores of the three experiments are relatively comparable. It is worth noting that the filtered back-translated data consists of only 20k segments, while the unfiltered back-translated data consists of 85k segments.

Training: We trained our models for 3 epochs, saving the best checkpoint based on the chrF++ score during training on the validation dataset. Our training arguments were chosen based on both manual exploration and automatic hyperparameter optimization using the Optuna framework (Akiba et al., 2019). The most important arguments are a learning rate of 1e-4 and a warm-up ratio of 0.03.

Inference: For inference, we used Faster-Whisper [4] with the default VAD[5] arguments, and 5 for the "beam size". The model was quantized with the float16 precision for more efficient inference.

Evaluation: To evaluate our systems, we calculated BLEU (Papineni et al., 2002), and chrF++ (Popović, 2017), as implemented in the sacreBLEU library[6] (Post, 2018). For semantic evaluation, we used AfriCOMET (Wang et al., 2024). We conducted ASR evaluation (cf. Table 5) and MT evaluations (cf. Table 2 and Table 3). Finally, we evaluated the whole cascaded systems (cf. Table 4).

3.1 Data Augmentation

As explained in Section 2.2, we created synthetic data using back-translation to augment our training data (Sennrich et al., 2016; Edunov et al., 2018; Poncelas et al., 2019; Haque et al., 2020). Then, we filtered this back-translated data based on generation cross-entropy scores. In our experiments, data augmentation improved the translation quality.

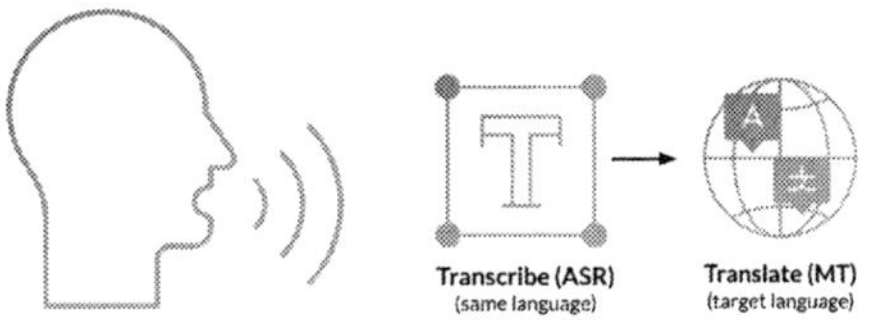

Figure 1: Cascaded speech translation systems use two models, an ASR model to generate audio transcriptions in the same language, and then an MT model to translate the generated transcriptions into the target language.

As shown in Table 2, when fine-tuning NLLB-200 600M, the models trained with back-translated data outperformed the models trained with only the authentic data.

We tried prepending the back-translated source with the *<bt>* tag, but found removing it achieves better results (cf. Table 3). This might be because we filtered the back-translated data, so its quality is good enough that it does not require distinguishing from the authentic data with the *<bt>* tag.

3.2 Whisper and NLLB-200 Models

We experimented with both Whisper Small and Whisper Medium to train ASR models. Similarly, we experimented with both NLLB-200 600M and 3.3B to train MT models. For our datasets, the results are comparable (cf. Table 4).

3.3 End-to-End vs. Cascaded System

Unlike a cascaded system, an end-to-end speech translation system requires only one model to perform audio-to-text translation (Agarwal et al., 2023;

[4] https://github.com/SYSTRAN/faster-whisper

[5] Voice Audio Detection (VAD) removes low-amplitude samples from an audio signal, which might represent silence or noise.

[6] https://github.com/mjpost/sacrebleu

System	ASR	MT	Type	BLEU	chrF++	COMET
Primary	Whisper-Medium	NLLB 200 3.3B	Baseline	0.72	14.28	16.23
			Finetuned	**27.45**	**49.64**	**51.74**
Contrastive 1	Whisper-Small	NLLB 200 3.3B	Baseline	0.51	13.41	11.9
			Finetuned	**27.39**	**49.65**	**52.01**
Contrastive 2	Whisper-Small	NLLB 200 600M	Baseline	0.41	13.21	10.69
			Finetuned	**27.30**	**50.17**	**51.91**

Table 4: Performance of the baseline and finetuned cascaded systems based on BLEU, chrF++, and AfriCOMET (COMET) scores. The approaches we followed, including fine-tuning and data augmentation, have considerably improved the quality of Bemba-to-English speech translation. The models were evaluated using the test split of the Big-C dataset.

Model	Type	WER
Whisper-Small	Baseline	157.5
	Finetuned	35.64
Whisper-Medium	Baseline	150.92
	Finetuned	**36.19**

Table 5: ASR Evaluation: The models were trained with Big-C and BembaSpeech. The performance of the finetuned models outperform the baseline models, indicated by the lower Word Error Rate (WER) scores of the finetuned models compared to the baseline models. The models were evaluated using the test split of the Big-C dataset.

Ahmad et al., 2024; Moslem et al., 2025). We fine-tuned Whisper directly on the Bemba-to-English Big-C dataset. Table 6 compares the results of the two systems. Where there is a slight increase in the scores of BLEU And chrF++ of the end-to-end model, the cascaded system outperforms the end-to-end system in terms of the COMET score, while the BLEU score of the end-to-end model is slightly higher.

Model	Type	BLEU	chrF++	COMET
End-to-End	Baseline	0.09	11.85	6.9
	Finetuned	**28.08**	**49.68**	48.36
Cascaded	Baseline	0.51	13.41	11.9
	Finetuned	27.39	49.65	**52.01**

Table 6: Comparison of the end-to-end speech translation using Whisper-Small, and the cascaded system that uses Whisper-Small for transcription and then NLLB-200 3.3B for translation. The evaluation uses the test split of the Big-C dataset.

Bemba	nafwala na amakalashi ku menso
Big-C	he is wearing glasses as well
Generated	He is wearing glasses.
Bemba	Imbwa iyafonka pamoona, ilebutuka palunkoto lwamucibansa
Big-C	A dog with a wide nose is running on the lawns of the football ground
Generated	A dog with a pointed nose is running on the lawn
Bemba	Akamwanakashi nakemya ukuulu mumuulu ukulwisha ukutoba aka lipulanga.
Big-C	She has her leg in the air attempting to break a board.
Generated	A child has lifted one leg in an attempt to hit a wood.
Bemba	Kunuma yabo kuli notu ma motoka tulya ba bonfya mu ncende iya talala nge iyi baliko.
Big-C	There are also small vehicles that they use in cold places behind them.
Generated	Behind them are vehicles that they use in cold places like this one.
Bemba	abaume Bali pa mutenge yanganda umo afwele ishati lya mitomito ilyamaboko ayatali elyo me tolishi lya makumbimakumbi
Big-C	Of the men on the roof of the house, ine is wearing a long sleeved grey shirt and a blue trousers.
Generated	Men are on the roof of the house, one is wearing a grey long sleeved shirt and a blue trousers.
Bemba	Ifi bafwele kunsapato fyakutelelela nga baya mukwangala umu mwine muli ice.
Big-C	These on their shoes are for sliding when the to play on the ice.
Generated	These shoes they are wearing are for sliding when they are going to play in ice.
Bemba	Namayo ale enda mumusebo nabika nomwana pamabeya.
Big-C	A woman is walking in the road with a child on her showders.
Generated	A woman is walking in the road with a child on her shoulder.
Bemba	Namayo naikata ifyakulya pa mbale mukati ke tuuka.
Big-C	A woman is holding food on a plate inside a shop.
Generated	A woman is holding food on a plate inside a shop.
Bemba	Nangu limbi kuli bamo abamufulwishe.
Big-C	Or maybe someone has made him upset.
Generated	Or maybe someone has upset her.
Bemba	Abantu bane bali umuli ifimabwe ifikulu nga nshi kabili nafwala ne fimpopo ku mitwe yabo
Big-C	four people are inside an area with large rocks and they are wearing helmets
Generated	Four people are in a place full of rocks and they are wearing helmets.
Bemba	Akamwana kambi balekafuula amasapato kuli kafundisha wakako.
Big-C	Another child's shoes being taken off by the instructor.
Generated	One of the pupils is being removed the shoes by the teacher.
Bemba	Afwile alefwaya afike pampela ya lumpili. Pantu icishimbi ekete.Eco babomfya abatemwa ukuniine mpili
Big-C	Maybe he wants to reach the top of the mountain. The rode metal he is carrying, it is mostly used when one is climbing the mountains.
Generated	Obviously he wants to reach the top of the mountain because this metal he is holding is used by mountain climbers.

Table 7: Examples of sentences in Bemba, their English translations from the Big-C dataset, and generated translations using Whisper-Medium and NLLB-200 3.3B.

Acknowledgements

We would like to thank Kreasof AI for supporting this work through providing the first author with computational resources.

References

Idris Abdulmumin, Victor Agostinelli, Tanel Alumäe, Antonios Anastasopoulos, Ashwin, Luisa Bentivogli, Ondřej Bojar, Claudia Borg, Fethi Bougares, Roldano Cattoni, Mauro Cettolo, Lizhong Chen, William Chen, Raj Dabre, Yannick Estève, Marcello Federico, Marco Gaido, Dávid Javorský, Marek Kasztelnik, Tsz Kin Lam, Danni Liu, Evgeny Matusov, Chandresh Kumar Maurya, John P. McCrae, Salima Mdhaffar, Yasmin Moslem, Kenton Murray, Satoshi Nakamura, Matteo Negri, and 20 others. 2025. Findings of the iwslt 2025 evaluation campaign. In *Proceedings of the 22nd International Conference on Spoken Language Translation (IWSLT 2025)*, Vienna, Austia (in-person and online). Association for Computational Linguistics.

Milind Agarwal, Sweta Agrawal, Antonios Anastasopoulos, Luisa Bentivogli, Ondřej Bojar, Claudia Borg, Marine Carpuat, Roldano Cattoni, Mauro Cettolo, Mingda Chen, William Chen, Khalid Choukri, Alexandra Chronopoulou, Anna Currey, Thierry Declerck, Qianqian Dong, Kevin Duh, Yannick Estève, Marcello Federico, Souhir Gahbiche, Barry Haddow, Benjamin Hsu, Phu Mon Htut, Hirofumi Inaguma, Dávid Javorský, John Judge, Yasumasa Kano, Tom Ko, Rishu Kumar, and 33 others. 2023. FINDINGS OF THE IWSLT 2023 EVALUATION CAMPAIGN. In *Proceedings of the 20th International Conference on Spoken Language Translation (IWSLT 2023)*, pages 1–61, Toronto, Canada (in-person and online). Association for Computational Linguistics.

Ibrahim Said Ahmad, Antonios Anastasopoulos, Ondřej Bojar, Claudia Borg, Marine Carpuat, Roldano Cattoni, Mauro Cettolo, William Chen, Qianqian Dong, Marcello Federico, Barry Haddow, Dávid Javorský, Mateusz Krubiński, Tsz Kim Lam, Xutai Ma, Prashant Mathur, Evgeny Matusov, Chandresh Maurya, John McCrae, Kenton Murray, Satoshi Nakamura, Matteo Negri, Jan Niehues, Xing Niu, Atul Kr Ojha, John Ortega, Sara Papi, Peter Polák, Adam Pospíšil, and 15 others. 2024. FINDINGS OF THE IWSLT 2024 EVALUATION CAMPAIGN. In *Proceedings of the 21st International Conference on Spoken Language Translation (IWSLT 2024)*, pages 1–11, Stroudsburg, PA, USA. Association for Computational Linguistics.

Takuya Akiba, Shotaro Sano, Toshihiko Yanase, Takeru Ohta, and Masanori Koyama. 2019. Optuna: A next-generation hyperparameter optimization framework. In *The 25th ACM SIGKDD International Conference on Knowledge Discovery & Data Mining*, pages 2623–2631.

Marta R Costa-jussà, James Cross, Onur Çelebi, Maha Elbayad, Kenneth Heafield, Kevin Heffernan, Elahe Kalbassi, Janice Lam, Daniel Licht, Jean Maillard, Anna Sun, Skyler Wang, Guillaume Wenzek, Al Youngblood, Bapi Akula, Loic Barrault, Gabriel Mejia Gonzalez, Prangthip Hansanti, John Hoffman, Semarley Jarrett, Kaushik Ram Sadagopan, Dirk Rowe, Shannon Spruit, Chau Tran, Pierre Andrews, Necip Fazil Ayan, Shruti Bhosale, Sergey Edunov, Angela Fan, and 9 others. 2022. No Language Left Behind: Scaling human-centered machine translation. *arXiv [cs.CL]*.

Sergey Edunov, Myle Ott, Michael Auli, and David Grangier. 2018. Understanding Back-Translation at Scale. In *Proceedings of the 2018 Conference on Empirical Methods in Natural Language Processing*, pages 489–500, Brussels, Belgium. Association for Computational Linguistics.

Naman Goyal, Cynthia Gao, Vishrav Chaudhary, Peng-Jen Chen, Guillaume Wenzek, Da Ju, Sanjana Krishnan, Marc'aurelio Ranzato, Francisco Guzmán, and Angela Fan. 2022. The Flores-101 evaluation benchmark for low-resource and multilingual machine translation. *Trans. Assoc. Comput. Linguist.*, 10:522–538.

Barry Haddow, Rachel Bawden, Antonio Valerio Miceli Barone, Jindřich Helcl, and Alexandra Birch. 2022. Survey of Low-Resource Machine Translation. *Computational Linguistics*, 06:1–67.

Rejwanul Haque, Yasmin Moslem, and Andy Way. 2020. Terminology-Aware Sentence Mining for NMT Domain Adaptation: ADAPT's Submission to the Adap-MT 2020 English-to-Hindi AI Translation Shared Task. In *Proceedings of the 17th International Conference on Natural Language Processing (ICON): Adap-MT 2020 Shared Task*, pages 17–23, Patna, India. NLP Association of India (NLPAI).

Guillaume Klein, Dakun Zhang, Clément Chouteau, Josep Crego, and Jean Senellart. 2020. Efficient and high-quality neural machine translation with OpenNMT. In *Proceedings of the Fourth Workshop on Neural Generation and Translation*, pages 211–217, Stroudsburg, PA, USA. Association for Computational Linguistics.

Holy Lovenia, Rahmad Mahendra, Salsabil Maulana Akbar, Lester James V Miranda, Jennifer Santoso, Elyanah Aco, Akhdan Fadhilah, Jonibek Mansurov, Joseph Marvin Imperial, Onno P Kampman, Joel Ruben Antony Moniz, Muhammad Ravi Shulthan Habibi, Frederikus Hudi, Railey Montalan, Ryan Ignatius, Joanito Agili Lopo, William Nixon, Börje F Karlsson, James Jaya, Ryandito Diandaru, Yuze Gao, Patrick Amadeus, Bin Wang, Jan Christian Blaise Cruz, Chenxi Whitehouse, Ivan Halim Parmonangan, Maria Khelli, Wenyu Zhang, Lucky Susanto, and 32 others. 2024. SEACrowd: A Multilingual Multimodal Data Hub and Benchmark Suite for Southeast Asian Languages. *arXiv [cs.CL]*.

In *Proceedings of the 61st Annual Meeting of the Association for Computational Linguistics (Volume 1: Long Papers)*, pages 2062–2078, Toronto, Canada. Association for Computational Linguistics.

Yasmin Moslem. 2024. Leveraging Synthetic Audio Data for End-to-End Low-Resource Speech Translation. In *Proceedings of the 21st International Conference on Spoken Language Translation (IWSLT 2024)*, pages 265–273.

Yasmin Moslem, Juan Julián Cea Morán, Mariano Gonzalez-Gomez, Muhammad Hazim Al Farouq, Farah Abdou, and Satarupa Deb. 2025. SpeechT: Findings of the first mentorship in speech translation. In *Proceedings of Machine Translation Summit XX, Implementations and Case Studies Track*.

Kishore Papineni, Salim Roukos, Todd Ward, and Wei-Jing Zhu. 2002. Bleu: a Method for Automatic Evaluation of Machine Translation. In *Proceedings of the 40th Annual Meeting of the Association for Computational Linguistics*, pages 311–318, Philadelphia, Pennsylvania, USA. Association for Computational Linguistics.

Alberto Poncelas, Gideon Maillette de Buy Wenniger, and Andy Way. 2019. Adaptation of Machine Translation Models with Back-Translated Data Using Transductive Data Selection Methods. In *Proceedings of the 20th International Conference on Computational Linguistics and Intelligent Text Processing CICLing 2019: Computational Linguistics and Intelligent Text Processing*, pages 567–579, La Rochelle, France. Springer Nature Switzerland.

Maja Popović. 2017. chrF++: words helping character n-grams. In *Proceedings of the Second Conference on Machine Translation*, pages 612–618, Copenhagen, Denmark. Association for Computational Linguistics.

Matt Post. 2018. A Call for Clarity in Reporting BLEU Scores. In *Proceedings of the Third Conference on Machine Translation: Research Papers*, pages 186–191, Brussels, Belgium. Association for Computational Linguistics.

Alec Radford, Jong Wook Kim, Tao Xu, Greg Brockman, Christine McLeavey, and Ilya Sutskever. 2022. Robust Speech Recognition via Large-Scale Weak Supervision. *arXiv [eess.AS]*.

Rico Sennrich, Barry Haddow, and Alexandra Birch. 2016. Improving Neural Machine Translation Models with Monolingual Data. In *Proceedings of the 54th Annual Meeting of the Association for Computational Linguistics (Volume 1: Long Papers)*, pages 86–96, Berlin, Germany. Association for Computational Linguistics.

Claytone Sikasote and Antonios Anastasopoulos. 2022. Bembaspeech: A speech recognition corpus for the bemba language. In *Proceedings of the Language Resources and Evaluation Conference*, pages 7277–7283, Marseille, France. European Language Resources Association.

Claytone Sikasote, Eunice Mukonde, Md Mahfuz Ibn Alam, and Antonios Anastasopoulos. 2023. BIG-C: a multimodal multi-purpose dataset for Bemba.

Jörg Tiedemann. 2020. The Tatoeba Translation Challenge – Realistic Data Sets for Low Resource and Multilingual MT. In *Proceedings of the Fifth Conference on Machine Translation*, pages 1174–1182, Online. Association for Computational Linguistics.

Jiayi Wang, David Adelani, Sweta Agrawal, Marek Masiak, Ricardo Rei, Eleftheria Briakou, Marine Carpuat, Xuanli He, Sofia Bourhim, Andiswa Bukula, Muhidin Mohamed, Temitayo Olatoye, Tosin Adewumi, Hamam Mokayed, Christine Mwase, Wangui Kimotho, Foutse Yuehgoh, Anuoluwapo Aremu, Jessica Ojo, Shamsuddeen Muhammad, Salomey Osei, Abdul-Hakeem Omotayo, Chiamaka Chukwuneke, Perez Ogayo, Oumaima Hourrane, Salma El Anigri, Lolwethu Ndolela, Thabiso Mangwana, Shafie Mohamed, and 29 others. 2024. AfriMTE and AfriCOMET: Enhancing COMET to embrace under-resourced African languages. In *Proceedings of the 2024 Conference of the North American Chapter of the Association for Computational Linguistics: Human Language Technologies (Volume 1: Long Papers)*, pages 5997–6023, Stroudsburg, PA, USA. Association for Computational Linguistics.

NAIST Offline Speech Translation System for IWSLT 2025

Ruhiyah Faradishi Widiaputri[1], Haotian Tan[1], Jan Meyer Saragih[1], Yuka Ko[1], Katsuhito Sudoh[1,2], Satoshi Nakamura[1,3], Sakriani Sakti[1],
[1]Nara Institute of Science and Technology, Japan,
[2]Nara Women's University, Japan,
[3]Chinese University of Hong Kong, Shenzhen, China,
Correspondence: ruhiyah.faradishi.rc2@naist.ac.jp, ssakti@is.naist.jp

Abstract

This paper presents NAIST's submission to the offline speech translation task of the IWSLT 2025 evaluation campaign, focusing on English-to-German and English-to-Chinese translation. We implemented both cascade and end-to-end frameworks using various components. For the cascade approach, we used Whisper and SALMONN as automatic speech recognition systems, each paired with Qwen2.5 large language model (LLM) for translation. In the end-to-end setting, we used SALMONN as speech translation and also built a custom model combining the Whisper encoder, DeCo projector, and Qwen2.5 LLM. To further leverage the large language model capabilities, we experimented with different prompting strategies. Additionally, since long speech inputs are segmented for processing, we applied hypothesis combination techniques to generate the final translation output. Our results show that combining Whisper and LLMs can yield strong translation performance, even without further fine-tuning in the cascade setup. Moreover, our proposed end-to-end architecture achieved competitive results, despite being trained on significantly less data compared to SALMONN. Finally, we decided to use both SALMONN as an end-to-end speech translation model and our proposed end-to-end model for our IWSLT 2025 submission for both language pairs.

1 Introduction

Spoken Language Translation (SLT) refers to the process of automatically converting spoken audio into written text in another language. Within the IWSLT Shared Task, the Offline Speech Translation Task stands out as one of the longest-running tracks. Its goal is to offer a consistent evaluation setting for speech translation, without the timing and structural limitations typically associated with other tasks—such as real-time constraints in simultaneous interpretation, space restrictions in subtitling, duration matching in dubbing, or the challenges posed by limited data in low-resource language scenarios.

In the 2025 edition of the Offline Speech Translation Task (Abdulmumin et al., 2025), three translation directions are included: English to German, Chinese, and Arabic. This year's challenge places particular emphasis on tackling more practical translation scenarios, such as content from TV shows, academic talks, business news, and speech with diverse accents. Our team at NAIST is participating in the English-German and English-Chinese tracks. Unfortunately, due to limited preparation time, we were not able to take part in the English-Arabic track.

To address these translation tasks, we explore two widely used SLT frameworks: the cascade and end-to-end approaches. The cascade method separates the process into two stages—first transcribing speech using automatic speech recognition (ASR), followed by translating the transcription with a machine translation (MT) system. In contrast, the end-to-end approach generates translations directly from the speech input, integrating both steps into a single model. While the cascade framework benefits from modularity and reuse of existing ASR and MT models, it is susceptible to error propagation. End-to-end systems can mitigate such issues, but they often struggle with data scarcity, as large-scale parallel speech-to-text corpora remain limited.

In particular, we implemented both frameworks using a range of components. For the cascade approach, we explored two ASR systems — Whisper[1] (Radford et al., 2023) and SALMONN[2] (Tang et al., 2024) — each paired with the Qwen2.5[3] (Yang et al., 2024) LLM for machine translation. In the end-to-end setting, we treated SALMONN as a unified speech translation system. Addition-

[1]https://github.com/openai/whisper
[2]https://github.com/bytedance/SALMONN
[3]https://github.com/QwenLM/Qwen2.5

Proceedings of the 22nd International Conference on Spoken Language Translation (IWSLT 2025), pages 360–368
July 31 - August 1, 2025 ©2025 Association for Computational Linguistics

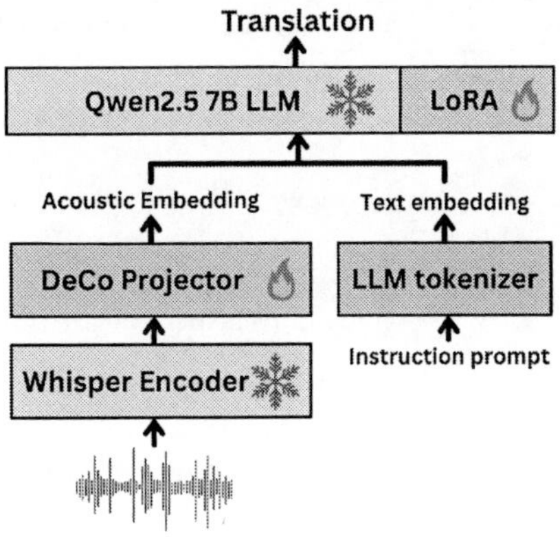

Figure 1: Our proposed end-to-end ST.

ally, we developed a custom end-to-end model that integrates the Whisper encoder, a DeCo (Yao et al., 2024) projection module, and Qwen2.5 as the decoder. To further investigate the capabilities of large language models, we conducted experiments with different prompting strategies and analyzed their impact on translation performance. Since long speech inputs are segmented and processed separately, we also explore hypothesis combination strategies to produce the final translation output.

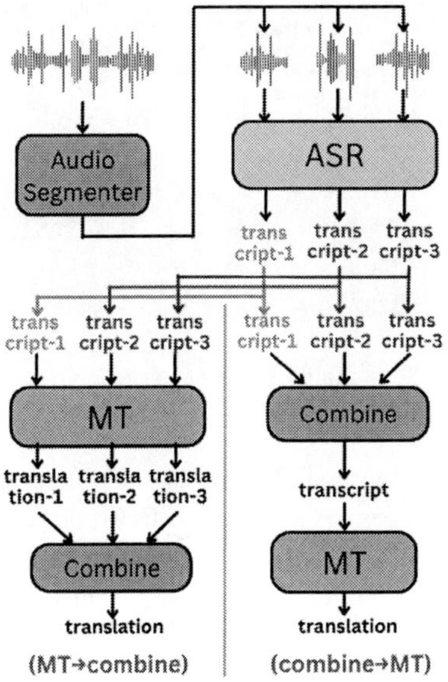

Figure 2: Two strategies for combining outputs of short segments in cascaded speech translation: (left) each short ASR outputs is translated individually, and the translations are merged afterward; (right) ASR outputs are first merged into a single text before translation.

2 System Description

As outlined earlier, this work explores both cascade and end-to-end approaches to speech translation, utilizing a range of components including Whisper, SALMONN, Qwen2.5, and others. In the following sections, we first describe the model architectures of these components in Section 2.1. We then explain our methods for applying zero-shot, few-shot learning, or fine-tuning to both the cascaded and end-to-end speech translation settings in Sections 2.2 and 2.3, respectively.

2.1 Model Architecture

Whisper is an encoder-decoder Transformer model (Vaswani et al., 2017), trained on a wide range of speech processing tasks, including multilingual speech recognition, speech translation, spoken language identification, and voice activity detection, using up to 680,000 hours of weakly-supervised labeled audio data. Whisper is highly robust across diverse environments and performs well in zero-shot settings without the need for fine-tuning. The model is available in various sizes, from `tiny` to `large`. Additionally, improved versions of the `large` model have been released, known as `large-v2` and `large-v3`. In this work, we experimented with both Whisper `large-v2` and `large-v3` as ASR.

SALMONN is a multimodal LLM that can perceive and understand general audio inputs including speech, audio events, and music. The model integrates two auditory encoders: a Whisper `large-v2` speech encoder and a fine-tuned BEATs (Chen et al., 2022) encoder for non-speech audio. These are connected to a Vicuna 13B LLM (Chiang et al., 2023) via a window-level Q-Former module (Li et al., 2023). SALMONN is pre-trained through a three-stage cross-modal learning process on diverse datasets. In this work, we use SALMONN for both ASR and end-to-end ST.

Qwen2.5 is the latest series of large language models from the Qwen LLM family, which has demonstrated top-tier performance across various benchmarks. The open-sourced Qwen2.5 models are dense, Transformer-based decoder architectures. Two types of Qwen2.5 models have been released: base models and instruction-tuned models, available in sizes ranging from 0.5B to 72B parameters. For the cascade system, we used the instruction-tuned version of Qwen2.5 with 7B parameters as MT.

In addition to existing models, we propose a

Split	en-de		en-zh	
	Dataset	Size	Dataset	Size
Train	CoVoST + Europarl	261526	CoVoST	229347
Dev	CoVoST + Europarl	16530	CoVoST	15233
	tst2022	2045		
Test	tst2021	2025	tst2022	2130

Table 1: Data statistics.

ASR	en-de tst2021	en-zh tst2022
SALMONN	16.33	15.9
Whisper large-v2	9.79	**10.33**
Whisper large-v3	**8.89**	10.77

Table 2: WER scores of Whisper and SALMONN ASRs.

novel end-to-end ST model that integrates the Whisper `large-v3` encoder, a DeCo projector, and the Qwen2.5 LLM. As illustrated in Figure 1, the Whisper encoder first extracts acoustic features from the input speech. The DeCo projector, consisting of a 2D adaptive average pooling layer for downsampling followed by two linear projection layers, bridges the speech-text modality gap by mapping the acoustic features from the Whisper encoder into the LLM embedding space as acoustic embeddings. Qwen2.5 then performs the translation based on prompt instructions. In this system, we use the base Qwen2.5 7B model.

2.2 Zero-shot and Few-shot Learning for Cascaded ST

For ASR, we used Whisper `large-v2`, Whisper `large-v3`, and SALMONN in a zero-shot setting (without fine-tuning). After we segmented long audio into shorter clips (see Subsection 3.2) and generated the transcription for each segment individually, we experimented with two hypothesis combination methods, as illustrated in Figure 2: (1: MT$\rightarrow$combine) translating each transcription segment individually and then combining the translations, or (2: combine$\rightarrow$MT) combining the transcriptions and translating the merged text using MT. The combination was performed by simply concatenating the transcriptions or translations of each speech segment in their original order.

For LLM-based MT, we initially experimented with the instruction-tuned version of Qwen2.5 7B using seven zero-shot prompts, ranging from simple to detailed instructions, as listed in Appendix A. For English-to-German, we selected the two best-performing prompts based on average BLEU and COMET scores, and then applied few-shot learning with $k = 1, 3, 5, 7$, and 10, using examples derived from transcriptions generated by the best ASR on the development set (en-de `tst2022`).

2.3 Zero-shot and Fine-tuning for End-to-end ST

For end-to-end ST, we used SALMONN and our proposed end-to-end ST model. SALMONN was evaluated under two settings: zero-shot and fine-tuning, using the datasets described in Section 3.1. Inference and fine-tuning of SALMONN followed the default settings and hyperparameters provided in the official SALMONN source code, except that we used a maximum of 22 and 30 epochs for fine-tuning with CoVoST + Europarl en-de as the validation set, and 22 epochs for fine-tuning with en-zh data (see Table 4).

Our proposed ST model was also fine-tuned. During the fine-tuning phase, we fully trained the projector while fine-tuning the LLM using LoRA (Hu et al., 2022), with the parameters of both the Whisper encoder and the LLM kept frozen. To improve translation performance and simplify training, we incorporated ASR as an auxiliary task. Specifically, we used a single prompt that instructed the LLM to output both the transcription and its corresponding translation, separated by the <end> symbol. This symbol then served as the stopping criterion during inference.

3 Experiment Setup

3.1 Dataset

The training and development datasets used in this work consist of speech-to-text parallel data listed under the IWSLT 2025 constrained setup, namely CoVoST v2 (Wang et al., 2020) and Europarl v1.1 (Iranzo-Sánchez et al., 2020). For development and test sets, we used the most recent past development sets provided by IWSLT 2025, tst2022 and tst2021. Specifically, for end-to-end English-to-German speech translation, we used the en-de CoVoST v2 and en-de Europarl v1.1 train sets for training, either the en-de CoVoST v2 dev set or the en-de tst2022 set for validation, and en-de tst2021 for testing. For end-to-end English-to-Chinese speech

en-de tst2021				
Prompt	MT→combine		combine→MT	
	BLEU	COMET	BLEU	COMET
1	24.90	78.12	27.72	**85.56**
2	25.59	77.15	**29.18**	84.22
3	26.04	79.43	28.54	83.58
4	21.53	73.71	27.84	82.90
5	**28.36**	**81.11**	26.80	83.46
6	26.91	78.92	27.86	83.62
7	26.13	77.79	28.87	82.59
en-zh tst2022				
Prompt	MT→combine		combine→MT	
	BLEU	COMET	BLEU	COMET
1	41.41	86.17	44.66	86.10
2	43.48	85.44	46.37	**86.81**
3	45.86	84.36	46.83	86.75
4	41.20	82.99	45.60	86.24
5	44.45	**86.24**	46.01	86.66
6	**46.10**	83.55	**47.15**	86.71
7	44.92	83.87	45.71	86.39

Table 3: BLEU and COMET scores of Qwen2.5 7B Instruct as zero-shot MT with seven prompts. Inputs are Whisper large-v3 ASR outputs.

translation, we used the en-zh CoVoST v2 train and dev sets for training and validation, and en-zh tst2022 as the test set. For the cascade speech translation system, since both the ASR and MT components were evaluated in zero-shot or few-shot settings, no training data was used. Instead, we evaluated directly on the test set. Few-shot examples were selected from the development set randomly.

For CoVoST v2 and Europarl v1.1, we preprocessed the datasets by removing samples with missing audio or target text, samples with audio that was too short or too long, and samples with noisy audio. We also performed basic text cleaning. Table 1 presents the details of the data used in this work.

3.2 Model Setup

Since Whisper was trained on 30-second audio chunks and cannot process longer input directly, we segmented long audio into shorter clips of less than 30 seconds before feeding them into the ASR or the end-to-end ST system. Segmentation for en-de tst2021, en-de tst2022, and en-zh tst2022 was performed using the Gentle forced aligner based

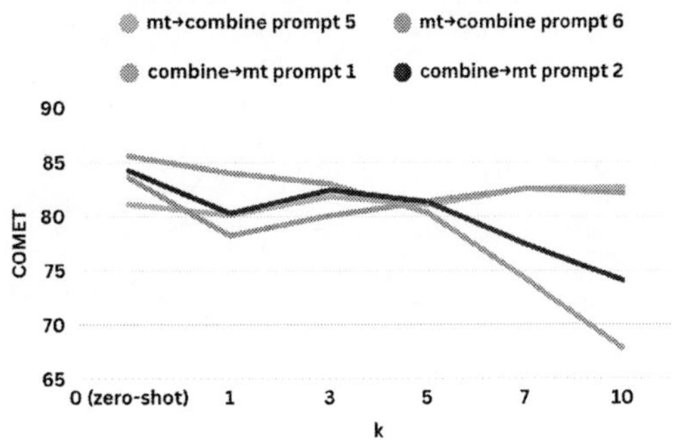

Figure 3: COMET Scores for English-to-German few-shot translation.

on the provided reference transcripts[4]. For audio without reference transcriptions, segmentation was carried out using the Silero Voice Activity Detector[5] (Silero Team, 2024).

For cascaded ST, we first performed zero-shot inference using the ASR models Whisper `large-v2`, Whisper `large-v3`, and SALMONN on the test set of each language pair. We then calculated the WER based on the transcriptions of the long audio inputs, where individual segment transcriptions were first merged using simple string concatenation before computing WER. Next, we selected the better-performing transcriptions between Whisper `large-v3` and SALMONN (Whisper `large-v2` was used solely for comparison with SALMONN, as SALMONN's speech encoder is based on Whisper `large-v2`) and used them as input for the Qwen2.5 7B Instruct MT.

We evaluated seven zero-shot prompts for both hypothesis combination methods (Figure 2). Subsequently, we calculated BLEU and COMET scores (Rei et al., 2020) for the long audio translations. BLEU scores were computed using SacreBLEU (Post, 2018), and COMET scores were obtained using the default COMET model `Unbabel/wmt22-comet-da`. For the English-to-German pair, we further explored few-shot learning with $k = 1, 3, 5, 7$, and 10 using the two prompts that achieved the highest average BLEU and COMET scores.

For the end-to-end model, we first evaluated the SALMONN checkpoint in a zero-shot setting. We then fine-tuned both SALMONN and our proposed end-to-end ST model for each language pair and calculated BLEU and COMET scores on the long

[4] `https://github.com/strob/gentle`
[5] `https://github.com/snakers4/silero-vad`

Languages and Data	Model	Detail	BLEU	COMET
en-de train: -CoVoST en-de -Europarl en-de test: tst-2021	SALMONN	Zeroshot	22.33	71.86
		Dev: CoVoST + Europarl en-de (Max epoch: 22)	31.20	86.19
		Dev: CoVoST + Europarl en-de (Max epoch: 30)	**31.76**	86.21
		Dev: tst-2022 en-de	30.81	**86.25**
	OUR-ST	Dev: CoVoST + Europarl en-de	28.84	84.73
		Dev: tst-2022 en-de	29.03	85.05
en-zh train: CoVoST en-zh test: tst-2022	SALMONN	Zeroshot	46.97	76.77
		Dev: CoVoST en-zh (Max epoch: 22)	**48.63**	80.47
	OUR-ST	Dev: CoVoST en-zh	44.78	**83.47**

Table 4: BLEU and COMET scores of SALMONN and ours in end-to-end ST.

audio translations.

We then compared the best-performing cascade combination, the best SALMONN results, and the best fine-tuned version of our end-to-end model for each language pair with two strong baselines—Whisper `large-v3` ASR + NLLB 3.3B (Costa-Jussà et al., 2022) and SeamlessM4T v2 Large (Barrault et al., 2023). Both baselines were evaluated in zero-shot settings, and the cascaded system used the MT→combine scenario due to the NLLB models' limited maximum input lengths. We also compared them with the top three models from previous IWSLT submissions that used the same test sets: IWSLT 2021 (Anastasopoulos et al., 2021) for English-to-German and IWSLT 2022 (Anastasopoulos et al., 2022) for English-to-Chinese.

It is important to note that, since we assumed the use of pre-trained acoustic models (i.e., Whisper in this case) is allowed under the "constrained with large language models" setting, we submitted the fine-tuned SALMONN results under the "unconstrained" track, and our proposed end-to-end ST model under the "constrained with large language models" track for IWSLT 2025.

4 Experiment Results

4.1 Cascaded ST

Table 2 presents the WER scores of Whisper and SALMONN as ASR systems, evaluated on the en-de tst2021 and en-zh tst2022 sets in a zero-shot setting. As shown in the table, Whisper `large-v2` and Whisper `large-v3` performed comparably, and both models outperformed SALMONN, despite SALMONN incorporating a Whisper `large-v2` encoder and an LLM.

Table 3 presents the BLEU and COMET scores of Qwen2.5 7B Instruct as MT across seven zero-shot prompt variations, using the output of Whisper `large-v3` as input. Interestingly, although the WER for en-de tst2021 is lower than that for en-zh tst2022, Qwen's translation performance for the latter is significantly better. In other words, Qwen translates English to Chinese more effectively than English to German. It can also be observed that combining the ASR transcriptions for a single input audio before translation yields better translation results than combining the translations afterward. Furthermore, the the fourth prompt is shown to give slightly lower performance compared to other prompts. In the MT→combine scenario, prompts that perform well for English-to-German also work well for English-to-Chinese, and vice versa. However, this relationship does not hold in the combine-before-translate scenario (combine→MT).

Figure 3 shows COMET scores for MT with few-shot learning for English to German, using the two best prompts for each hypothesis recombination strategy: prompts 5 and 6 for `MT→combine`, and prompts 1 and 2 for `combine→MT`. As shown in the figure, adding examples in the `MT→combine` strategy improves translation quality. However, the opposite trend is observed for `combine→MT`. This is possibly due to the fact that, in `combine→MT`, the MT input becomes significantly longer, which can affect the model's ability to effectively utilize few-shot examples.

4.2 End-to-end ST

Table 4 shows the BLEU and COMET scores for two end-to-end ST models—SALMONN and our

en-de (test: tst2021)			BLEU	COMET
Baseline	Baseline cascade	Whisper large-v3 ASR + NLLB 3.3B MT	**34.04**	84.62
	Baseline end-to-end	SeamlessM4T v2 Large	31.37	74.45
Existing IWSLT submissions	HW-TSC	Constrained - cascade	20.30	-
	KIT (Nguyen et al., 2021)	Constrained - cascade	19.00	-
	AppTek (Bahar et al., 2021)	Constrained - end-to-end	18.30	-
Our best systems	Our best cascade	Whisper large-v3 ASR + Qwen2.5 7B Inst MT (prompt: 2 - scenario: combine→MT - k: 0)	29.18	84.22
	Our best SALMONN	Dev: CoVoST + Europarl en-de - max epoch=30	31.76	**86.21**
	Our best end-to-end ST	Dev: tst-2022 en-de - max step: 100,000	29.03	85.05
en-zh (test: tst2022)			**BLEU**	**COMET**
Baseline	Baseline cascade	Whisper large-v3 ASR + NLLB 3.3B MT	30.31	76.48
	Baseline end-to-end	SeamlessM4T v2 Large	32.81	68.12
Existing IWSLT submissions	USTC-NELSLIP cascade (Zhang et al., 2022a)	Cascade	35.70	-
	YI cascade (Zhang et al., 2022b)	Cascade	35.00	-
	HW-TSC (Li et al., 2022)	Cascade	33.40	-
Our best systems	Our best cascade	Whisper large-v3 ASR + Qwen2.5 7B Inst MT (prompt 6 - scenario: combine→MT - k: 0)	47.15	**86.81**
	Our best SALMONN	Dev: CoVoST en-zh - max epoch: 22	**48.63**	80.47
	Our best our end-to-end ST	Dev: tst-2022 en-zh - max step: 100,000	44.78	83.47
	Our submitted end-to-end ST	Dev: tst-2022 en-zh - max step: 51,000	40.69	83.03

Table 5: Performance comparison between our best ST systems, baselines, and previous IWSLT submissions. Our submitted systems are shaded in gray.

proposed model. As shown in the table, fine-tuning the publicly released SALMONN checkpoint with additional ST data improves translation performance. Similar to the results observed when using Qwen as the MT component in the cascaded approach, the end-to-end models also achieve significantly higher BLEU scores for English-to-Chinese translation than for English-to-German. However, the COMET scores show the opposite trend. Additionally, for English-to-German translation, the choice of development set had minimal impact on performance. Lastly, despite being fine-tuned on substantially less data than SALMONN, our proposed end-to-end models achieve competitive results, especially compared to the zero-shot SALMONN.

4.3 Comparison with Baselines and Previous Submissions

Table 5 shows the comparison between our best cascaded ST, our best SALMONN end-to-end ST, our best proposed end-to-end ST, with two strong baselines: Whisper ASR + NLLB 3.3B cascade baseline and SeamlessM4T v2 Large end-to-end baseline, as well as the top three previous IWSLT submissions (from IWSLT 2021 for en-de and IWSLT 2022 for en-zh)[6]. As shown in the table, for both en-de and en-zh pairs, our cascaded and end-to-end ST systems performed significantly better than the IWSLT submissions.

For the en-de pair, despite using the same ASR, the cascaded Whisper ASR + NLLB 3.3B system achieved a higher BLEU score than our best cascaded model. This suggests that for English-to-German MT, NLLB 3.3B still outperforms Qwen2.5 7B Instruct. Our end-to-end models, on the other hand, achieved comparable BLEU scores to SeamlessM4T v2 Large and outperformed it in terms of COMET scores. In contrast, for the en-zh pair, both our cascaded and end-to-end ST systems performed significantly better than the baselines, indicating that Qwen2.5 7B Instruct outperforms NLLB 3.3B for English-to-Chinese translation.

We decided to use end-to-end models (SALMONN and our proposed end-to-end ST) for our IWSLT 2025 submission, which are shaded in

[6]The IWSLT submissions were selected based on their BLEU NewRef scores as reported in the official findings; however, the scores shown in the table are BLEU TEDRef to allow fair comparison with our systems.

gray in the table. However, due to time constraints, the submission for English-to-Chinese using our proposed model did not use the best-performing checkpoint, but rather the best checkpoint at step 51,000.

5 Conclusion

This paper describes NAIST's submission to the IWSLT 2025 offline speech translation task, focusing on English-to-German and English-to-Chinese translation. We found that using Whisper as the ASR combined with Qwen2.5 LLM as the MT in a zero-shot setting was already capable of producing good translations. Furthermore, in the zero-shot setting, translation quality for long audio was better when the transcriptions of individual segments were combined first and then translated together, compared to translating each segment individually and combining the translations afterward. However, few-shot learning yielded better results in the latter case. Fine-tuning the SALMONN model further improved its translation quality. Additionally, our custom end-to-end model demonstrated competitive performance with SALMONN, despite being trained on significantly less data. Finally, we observed that both Qwen2.5 and SALMONN performed better on English-to-Chinese translation than on English-to-German.

Acknowledgments

Part of this work is supported by JSPS KAKENHI Grant Numbers JP21H05054 and JP23K21681.

References

Idris Abdulmumin, Victor Agostinelli, Tanel Alumäe, Antonios Anastasopoulos, Ashwin, Luisa Bentivogli, Ondřej Bojar, Claudia Borg, Fethi Bougares, Roldano Cattoni, Mauro Cettolo, Lizhong Chen, William Chen, Raj Dabre, Yannick Estève, Marcello Federico, Marco Gaido, Dávid Javorský, Marek Kasztelnik, and 30 others. 2025. Findings of the iwslt 2025 evaluation campaign. In *Proceedings of the 22nd International Conference on Spoken Language Translation (IWSLT 2025)*, Vienna, Austria (in-person and online). Association for Computational Linguistics.

Antonios Anastasopoulos, Loc Barrault, Luisa Bentivogli, Ondřej Bojar, Roldano Cattoni, Anna Currey, Georgiana Dinu, Kevin Duh, Maha Elbayad, Clara Emmanuel, and 1 others. 2022. Findings of the iwslt 2022 evaluation campaign. In *Proceedings of the 19th international conference on spoken language translation (IWSLT 2022)*, pages 98–157. Association for Computational Linguistics.

Antonios Anastasopoulos, Ondřej Bojar, Jacob Bremerman, Roldano Cattoni, Maha Elbayad, Marcello Federico, Xutai Ma, Satoshi Nakamura, Matteo Negri, Jan Niehues, Juan Pino, Elizabeth Salesky, Sebastian Stüker, Katsuhito Sudoh, Marco Turchi, Alexander Waibel, Changhan Wang, and Matthew Wiesner. 2021. FINDINGS OF THE IWSLT 2021 EVALUATION CAMPAIGN. In *Proceedings of the 18th International Conference on Spoken Language Translation (IWSLT 2021)*, pages 1–29, Bangkok, Thailand (online). Association for Computational Linguistics.

Parnia Bahar, Patrick Wilken, Mattia A Di Gangi, and Evgeny Matusov. 2021. Without further ado: Direct and simultaneous speech translation by apptek in 2021. In *Proceedings of the 18th International Conference on Spoken Language Translation (IWSLT 2021)*, pages 52–63.

Loïc Barrault, Yu-An Chung, Mariano Coria Meglioli, David Dale, Ning Dong, Mark Duppenthaler, Paul-Ambroise Duquenne, Brian Ellis, Hady Elsahar, Justin Haaheim, and 1 others. 2023. Seamless: Multilingual expressive and streaming speech translation. *arXiv preprint arXiv:2312.05187*.

Sanyuan Chen, Yu Wu, Chengyi Wang, Shujie Liu, Daniel Tompkins, Zhuo Chen, and Furu Wei. 2022. Beats: Audio pre-training with acoustic tokenizers. *arXiv preprint arXiv:2212.09058*.

Wei-Lin Chiang, Zhuohan Li, Zi Lin, Ying Sheng, Zhanghao Wu, Hao Zhang, Lianmin Zheng, Siyuan Zhuang, Yonghao Zhuang, Joseph E. Gonzalez, Ion Stoica, and Eric P. Xing. 2023. Vicuna: An open-source chatbot impressing gpt-4 with 90%* chatgpt quality.

Marta R Costa-Jussà, James Cross, Onur Çelebi, Maha Elbayad, Kenneth Heafield, Kevin Heffernan, Elahe Kalbassi, Janice Lam, Daniel Licht, Jean Maillard, and 1 others. 2022. No language left behind: Scaling human-centered machine translation. *arXiv preprint arXiv:2207.04672*.

Edward J Hu, Yelong Shen, Phillip Wallis, Zeyuan Allen-Zhu, Yuanzhi Li, Shean Wang, Lu Wang, Weizhu Chen, and 1 others. 2022. Lora: Low-rank adaptation of large language models. *ICLR*, 1(2):3.

J. Iranzo-Sánchez, J. A. Silvestre-Cerdà, J. Jorge, N. Roselló, A. Giménez, A. Sanchis, J. Civera, and A. Juan. 2020. Europarl-st: A multilingual corpus for speech translation of parliamentary debates. In *ICASSP 2020 - 2020 IEEE International Conference on Acoustics, Speech and Signal Processing (ICASSP)*, pages 8229–8233.

Junnan Li, Dongxu Li, Silvio Savarese, and Steven Hoi. 2023. Blip-2: Bootstrapping language-image pre-training with frozen image encoders and large language models. In *International conference on machine learning*, pages 19730–19742. PMLR.

Yinglu Li, Minghan Wang, Jiaxin Guo, Xiaosong Qiao, Yuxia Wang, Daimeng Wei, Chang Su, Yimeng Chen,

Min Zhang, Shimin Tao, and 1 others. 2022. The hw-tsc's offline speech translation system for iwslt 2022 evaluation. In *Proceedings of the 19th International Conference on Spoken Language Translation (IWSLT 2022)*, pages 239–246.

Tuan-Nam Nguyen, Thai-Son Nguyen, Christian Huber, Ngoc-Quan Pham, Thanh-Le Ha, Felix Schneider, and Sebastian Stüker. 2021. Kit's iwslt 2021 offline speech translation system. In *Proceedings Of The 18th International Conference On Spoken Language Translation (IWSLT 2021)*, pages 125–130.

Matt Post. 2018. A call for clarity in reporting BLEU scores. In *Proceedings of the Third Conference on Machine Translation: Research Papers*, pages 186–191, Belgium, Brussels. Association for Computational Linguistics.

Alec Radford, Jong Wook Kim, Tao Xu, Greg Brockman, Christine McLeavey, and Ilya Sutskever. 2023. Robust speech recognition via large-scale weak supervision. In *International conference on machine learning*, pages 28492–28518. PMLR.

Ricardo Rei, Craig Stewart, Ana C Farinha, and Alon Lavie. 2020. Comet: A neural framework for mt evaluation. *arXiv preprint arXiv:2009.09025*.

Silero Team. 2024. Silero vad: pre-trained enterprise-grade voice activity detector (vad), number detector and language classifier. `https://github.com/snakers4/silero-vad`.

Changli Tang, Wenyi Yu, Guangzhi Sun, Xianzhao Chen, Tian Tan, Wei Li, Lu Lu, Zejun MA, and Chao Zhang. 2024. SALMONN: Towards generic hearing abilities for large language models. In *The Twelfth International Conference on Learning Representations*.

Ashish Vaswani, Noam Shazeer, Niki Parmar, Jakob Uszkoreit, Llion Jones, Aidan N Gomez, Łukasz Kaiser, and Illia Polosukhin. 2017. Attention is all you need. *Advances in neural information processing systems*, 30.

Changhan Wang, Anne Wu, and Juan Pino. 2020. Covost 2 and massively multilingual speech-to-text translation. *arXiv preprint arXiv:2007.10310*.

An Yang, Baosong Yang, Beichen Zhang, Binyuan Hui, Bo Zheng, Bowen Yu, Chengyuan Li, Dayiheng Liu, Fei Huang, Haoran Wei, Huan Lin, Jian Yang, Jianhong Tu, Jianwei Zhang, Jianxin Yang, Jiaxi Yang, Jingren Zhou, Junyang Lin, Kai Dang, and 22 others. 2024. Qwen2.5 technical report. *arXiv preprint arXiv:2412.15115*.

Linli Yao, Lei Li, Shuhuai Ren, Lean Wang, Yuanxin Liu, Xu Sun, and Lu Hou. 2024. Deco: Decoupling token compression from semantic abstraction in multimodal large language models. *arXiv preprint arXiv:2405.20985*.

Weitai Zhang, Zhongyi Ye, Haitao Tang, Xiaoxi Li, Xinyuan Zhou, Jing Yang, Jianwei Cui, Pan Deng, Mohan Shi, Yifan Song, and 1 others. 2022a. The ustc-nelslip offline speech translation systems for iwslt 2022. In *Proceedings of the 19th International Conference on Spoken Language Translation (IWSLT 2022)*, pages 198–207.

Ziqiang Zhang, Junyi Ao, Long Zhou, Shujie Liu, Furu Wei, and Jinyu Li. 2022b. The yitrans end-to-end speech translation system for iwslt 2022 offline shared task. *arXiv preprint arXiv:2206.05777*.

A Prompts for LLM MT

Table 6 shows seven zero-shot prompts for LLM MT. `<tgt-lang>` denotes the target language for the translation, which may be either "German" or "Chinese". For few-shot prompting, we add some examples in the format of Prompt 1 right before the input.

For example, using Prompt 3 with few-shot prompting, the full prompt will be:

> You are given a source English sentence. It is a transcription of spontaneous speech, which may include repetitions, fillers, or disfluencies. Translate it into `<tgt-lang>` as it is. Do not change the structure or nuance.
>
> English: `<example-src-text-1>`
> `<tgt-lang>`: `<example-tgt-text-1>`
> ...
> English: `<example-src-text-k>`
> `<tgt-lang>`: `<example-tgt-text-k>`
> English: `<input>`
> `<tgt-lang>`:

Prompt 1	English: { } <tgt-lang>:
Prompt 2	"Translate the sentence from English to <tgt-lang>. English: { } <tgt-lang>: "
Prompt 3	"You are given a source English sentence. It is a transcription of spontaneous speech, which may include repetitions, fillers, or disfluencies. Translate it into <tgt-lang> as it is. Do not change the structure or nuance. English: { } <tgt-lang>: "
Prompt 4	"You are given a source English sentence. It is a transcription of spontaneous speech, which may include repetitions, fillers, or disfluencies. Your task is to: 1. Translate it into <tgt-lang> as it is. Do not change the structure or nuance. 2. Convert any written-out numbers (e.g., one, twenty) into numerical digits (e.g., 1, 20). 3. If you detect any indirect words, enclose them in „“. 4. Add punctuations '.', ',' if necessary. English: { } <tgt-lang>: "
Prompt 5	"Translate from English to <tgt-lang>, using the appropriate tone for the topic. Do not mention the topic. Output only the <tgt-lang> translation. English: { } <tgt-lang>: "
Prompt 6	"You are given a source English sentence. It is a transcription of spontaneous speech, which may include repetitions, fillers, or disfluencies. Translate it into <tgt-lang> as it is. Do not change the structure or nuance. Do not mention the topic. Output only the <tgt-lang> translation. English: { } <tgt-lang>: "
Prompt 7	"You are given a source English sentence. It is a transcription of spontaneous speech, which may include repetitions, fillers, or disfluencies. Your task is to: 1. Translate it into <tgt-lang> as it is. Do not change the structure or nuance. Do not mention the topic. Output only the <tgt-lang> translation. 2. Convert any written-out numbers (e.g., one, twenty) into numerical digits (e.g., 1, 20). 3. If you detect any indirect words, enclose them in „“. 4. Add punctuations '.', ',' if necessary. English: { } <tgt-lang>: "

Table 6: Zero-shot prompts for Qwen2.5 LLM as MT.

NAIST Simultaneous Speech Translation System for IWSLT 2025

Haotian Tan[1], Ruhiyah Faradishi Widiaputri[1], Jan Meyer Saragih[1], Yuka Ko[1], Katsuhito Sudoh[1,2], Satoshi Nakamura[1,3], Sakriani Sakti[1],
[1]Nara Institute of Science and Technology, Japan,
[2]Nara Women's University, Japan,
[3]Chinese University of Hong Kong, Shenzhen, China,
Correspondence: tan.haotian.tf5@naist.ac.jp, ssakti@is.naist.jp

Abstract

This paper describes the NAIST submission to the English-to-{German, Japanese, Chinese} Simultaneous Speech-to-Text track at IWSLT 2025. Last year, our system was based on an end-to-end speech-to-text translation model that combined HuBERT and mBART. This year, the system consists of a Whisper encoder, the DeCo compressive projector, and the Qwen large language model. The simultaneous translation (SimulST) system is implemented by applying a local agreement policy to an offline-trained translation model. For the streaming translation (StreamST) system, we integrate an online version of the SHAS segmenter into our SimulST architecture. Our results demonstrate that adopting LLMs as the backbone architecture for speech translation tasks yields strong translation performance. Additionally, leveraging robust segmentation capability of SHAS for StreamST achieves good quality-latency trade-off when processing unbounded audio streams.

1 Introduction

Simultaneous speech-to-text translation (SimulST) aims to mimic human interpreters by providing real-time translation with low latency while maintaining high translation quality. In SimulST, the system generates translation before receiving the full source utterance. A decision policy is required to determine whether to generate partial output or wait for additional source context to improve reliability.

Some prior studies train dedicated models for SimulST using specialized training strategies and architecture designs to learn a data-driven decision policy (Ma et al., 2020b; Ren et al., 2020; Zeng et al., 2021; Liu et al., 2021; Zhang et al., 2024). However, their performance heavily depends on the design of training strategies, which is a complex and challenging task. Furthermore, achieving different latency regimes typically requires training multiple separate models, substantially increasing computational requirements and complicating practical deployment.

Due to the aforementioned reasons, approaches using a single model for different simultaneous scenarios have become popular (Papi et al., 2022a). These methods train the speech translation (ST) model using offline translation data and then apply a manually designed decision policy to this offline ST model for SimulST inference. In this way, a single ST model can adapt to different latency requirements in practical use. Designing an optimal decision policy is significant to their performance. Among several existing decision policies (Ma et al., 2019; Liu et al., 2020; Nguyen et al., 2021), Local Agreement (LA) (Liu et al., 2020; Polák et al., 2022) is one of the most popular method and won the SimulST track of IWSLT 2022 (Polák et al., 2022). It makes decisions by establishing an agreement between two consecutive chunks and only emitting their longest common prefixes. Additionally, the attention-based decision policies, EDAtt (Papi et al., 2023a) and AlignAtt (Papi et al., 2023b), have been proposed for encoder-decoder ST models. They leverage the cross-attention mechanism to make decisions based on the idea that if the model attends to the tail end of the incomplete input speech, the generated hypothesis is unreliable and more context is needed. These attention-based decision policies have shown good performance and have been widely adopted for SimulST tasks (Ko et al., 2024; Tan and Sakti, 2024).

Most recently, several studies have explored the use of pre-trained large language models (LLMs) for SimulST, capitalizing on their powerful generative and zero-shot transfer capabilities. Koshkin et al. (2024) proposes a cascaded architecture combining an ASR model with a decoder-only LLM to perform SimulST. However, this cascaded approach is hindered by error propagation and additional latency. A few works have instead focused

Proceedings of the 22nd International Conference on Spoken Language Translation (IWSLT 2025), pages 369–378
July 31 - August 1, 2025 ©2025 Association for Computational Linguistics

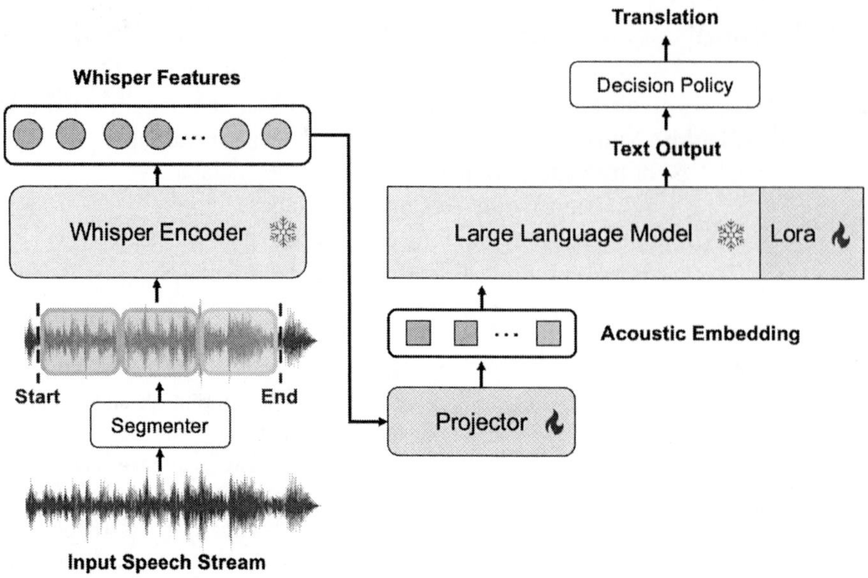

Figure 1: Architecture of our LLM-based StreamST system. The model integrates a Whisper encoder with the LLM via the projector module. The decision policy enables simultaneous translation capabilities, while an online segmenter processes unbounded audio streams for real-time streaming translation.

on end-to-end LLM-based SimulST systems. Xu et al. (2024) trains an offline LLM-based ST model and extends it to SimulST using the Hold-n (Liu et al., 2020) decision policy. Fu et al. (2025) develops a fully end-to-end system through a specialized multi-step training strategy. Another line of work by Ouyang et al. (2025) reformulates SimulST as a multi-turn dialogue task, enabling the LLM to make translation decisions by predicting an end-of-turn token.

Nevertheless, most of the aforementioned SimulST systems are designed to work on pre-segmented speech. Streaming speech-to-text translation (StreamST), the task of automatically translating speech while incrementally receiving an audio stream, remains a challenging problem due to the need for effectively processing the history audio and text contexts. Papi et al. (2024) introduces the first StreamST policy to deal with the unbounded audio stream via audio and textual history selection. Ouyang et al. (2025) utilizes a LLM cache management module to handle the unbounded audio stream during inference.

This paper describes the NAIST submission for the English-to-{German, Japanese, Chinese} Simultaneous Speech-to-Text Track at IWSLT 2025. In our last year's system (Ko et al., 2024), we applied the LA policy to an encoder-decoder model to do SimulST. For the IWSLT 2025 Evaluation Campaign, we explore employing LLM in our system to conduct translation in real time. We construct an end-to-end LLM-based ST model, trained on offline data, and—similar to our previous system—enable it to perform simultaneous translation using the LA policy. To handle the unbounded audio stream in real-world settings, we adopt an online version of the SHAS segmentation method (Tsiamas et al., 2022) to identify the speech segments in the audio stream and present the SHAS-based StreamST.

2 System Description

In this section, we first describe the model architecture of our system and its training methodology. Then we present the detailed implementation of our simultaneous speech-to-text translation and streaming speech-to-text translation approaches.

2.1 Model Architecture

As illustrated in Figure 1, the translation model of our system comprises three principal components: a Whisper encoder, a projector, and a large language model. The Whisper output features of the input speech are transformed into acoustic embeddings, which are subsequently integrated with the prompt textual embeddings and fed into the LLM to generate the target translation.

Whisper Encoder: The Whisper model (Radford et al., 2023) is an open-source speech model trained on a large amount of speech recognition and translation data. The output features of the Whisper encoder have demonstrated superior performance in modeling speech information and have been widely adopted for downstream speech processing tasks. In our submission system, we utilize the Whisper-large-v3[1] architecture to extract high-fidelity acoustic features from the source speech signal.

Projector: The projector serves as a critical bridging mechanism to address the speech-text modality gap between the source speech and the text-driven LLM by mapping the acoustic features into the LLM embedding space. In our system, we implement DeCo (Yao et al., 2024) as the projector between the Whisper encoder and the LLM. DeCo is a compressive projector originally proposed for visual-language models that exhibits a remarkably efficient structure: a 2D adaptive averaging pooling (AdaptiveAvgPool) layer functioning as a down-sampler, followed by two linear projection layers. These linear projection layers constitute the only trainable parameters in this module, making it computationally efficient while effectively aligning the speech representations with the LLM embedding space.

Large Language Model: The Qwen-2.5-7B LLM[2] (Yang et al., 2024) is employed in our system to function as an expert translator. The model processes the acoustic embeddings alongside textual prompts to generate high-quality translations based on the prompt instruction. The generative capabilities of the LLM enable flexible adaptation to various translation scenarios while maintaining semantic accuracy and linguistic fluency in the target language.

2.2 Model Training

2.2.1 Training Objective

We train our system in an offline manner using supervised learning with parallel speech-text data. Specifically, given the training dataset $D = \{(\mathbf{S}, \mathbf{Y}_{src}, \mathbf{Y}_{tgt})\}$, the Whisper encoder $\mathcal{F}_e(\cdot)$ consumes the complete source speech signal $\mathbf{S} = \{s_1, s_2, ..., s_T\}$ to extract acoustic features:

$$\mathbf{X_s} = \mathcal{F}_e(\mathbf{S}) = \{x_1, x_2, ...x_L\}. \tag{1}$$

[1]https://huggingface.co/openai/whisper-large-v3
[2]https://github.com/QwenLM/Qwen2.5

The projector $\mathcal{F}_p(\cdot)$ subsequently maps these acoustic features into the LLM embedding space with length compression to generate the acoustic embedding of the source speech:

$$\mathbf{E}(\mathbf{X_s}) = \mathcal{F}_p(\mathbf{X_s}) = \{e_1, e_2, ..., e_M\}, M < L. \tag{2}$$

We integrate the acoustic embedding $\mathbf{E}(\mathbf{X_s})$ with the textual embedding of the LLM prompt and the prefix tokens to form the composite input for the LLM:

$$\mathbf{I}_{llm} = \{\mathbf{E}(\mathbf{X_s}), \mathbf{E}(Prompt), \mathbf{E}(Prefix)\}. \tag{3}$$

The LLM then processes this multimodal input to autoregressively get the model output:

$$P(\mathbf{Y}|\mathbf{I}_{llm}) = \mathcal{F}_{llm}(\mathbf{I}_{llm}), \tag{4}$$

where $\mathbf{Y} = \{y_1, y_2, ..., y_N\}$ denotes the target textual sequence during training. Given the composite LLM input $\mathbf{I}_{llm}$, we optimize the system by minimizing the token-level negative log-likelihood loss over the target output sequence:

$$\mathcal{L} = -\frac{1}{|\mathbf{Y}|}\sum_{i=1}^{|\mathbf{Y}|} \log P(y_i|\mathbf{I}_{llm}, y_{<i}). \tag{5}$$

2.2.2 ASR Joint Training

To enhance the performance of the translation system and facilitate training, we implement a multi-task learning approach utilizing automatic speech recognition (ASR) as an auxiliary task. Unlike approaches proposed by Chen et al. (2024) and Huang et al. (2024), which employ a dedicated prompt for the transcription task to augment the training data, we utilizes a single unified prompt that instructs the LLM to generate the transcription immediately following its translation output. The target sequence for training is specifically formatted as:

$\mathbf{Y}$ = Translation:$\mathbf{Y}_{tgt}$ <end> Transcription:$\mathbf{Y}_{src}$,

where the <end> token denotes the end of the translation, which is a signal to terminate the decoding process during inference when only the translation component is required for deployment scenarios.

2.2.3 Fine-tuning

During the training phase, the pretrained weights of both the whisper encoder and the core LLM architecture are frozen to maintain their representational capabilities. We fine-tune the LLM using Low-Rank Adaptation (LoRA) (Hu et al., 2022) and optimize the complete parameter set of the projector module.

2.3 Simultaneous Speech-to-text Translation

We enable our offline-trained ST system to do simultaneous speech-to-text translation via Local Agreement (LA) (Liu et al., 2020; Polák et al., 2022), which is one of the most commonly used decision policy in recent years. It compares the generated hypotheses of two consecutive chunks and only emit their longest common prefixes (i.e., agreement). A fixed length chunk size (speech segment size) is tuned to control the quality-latency trade-off for SimulST.

2.4 Streaming Speech-to-text Translation

The SimulST system is assumed to work on pre-segmented speech and it is not practical to directly process a long audio stream in real-world scenarios due to latency and computational resources. We develop the StreamST system by integrating an automatic segmenter module into our SimulST system to detect the speech segments $\mathbf{S} = \{s^1, s^2, ...s^N\}$ in real-time. As illustrated in Figure 1, once the segmenter module detect the start point s_1^i of a speech segment s^i, the subsequent modules process the speech chunk-by-chunk in a SimulST manner to emit translations. When the speech segment endpoint is detected, both of the speech and text history buffers are reset, and the translation stops until the start point of the next speech segment is detected.

We use Supervised Hybrid Audio Segmentation (SHAS) (Tsiamas et al., 2022) as the segmentation method for our StreamST system. SHAS is a neural-based method that can effectively learn the optimal segmentation from manually segmented speech corpus to achieve the state-of-the-art segmentation performance. It uses a pre-trained wav2vec 2.0 (Baevski et al., 2020) to extract acoustic features and a SHAS classifier to obtain the probabilities for each audio frame. SHAS determines the speech offset τ and duration Δt of an input audio with a probability threshold θ. However, the SHAS is designed to segment a long audio into multiple speech segments that are shorter than a predefined maximum length L_{max} using the probabilistic Divide-and-Conquer (pDAC) algorithm, while in StreamST, the length of the audio stream increases incrementally.

We enable the SHAS to perform real-time segmentation for StreamST. Specifically, we apply SHAS on the incrementally increasing audio stream until it detects a speech segment offset. The first detected offset is treated as the segment start point, $\mathbf{Seg}_{start}$. Then the subsequent modules of the StreamST system process the speech chunk-by-chunk to generate translations until the segment endpoint $\mathbf{Seg}_{end} = (\tau + \Delta t)$ is detected. However, we observed that SHAS consistently returns an offset-duration pair even when processing incomplete audio streams where speech has not yet finished. In these cases, the SHAS-detected speech segments become too short, negatively impacting the overall performance of the StreamST system. To address this issue, we leverage our empirical observation that when speech is ongoing, the SHAS-detected segment endpoint $\mathbf{Seg}_{end}$ typically falls very close to the length of the currently available audio stream L_{stream}. We therefore introduce a

Algorithm 1 SHAS-based StreamST

Require: Audio stream $\mathbf{X}$, pause length L_{pause}, minimum segment length L_{min}, maximum segment length L_{max}, chunk size C
Ensure: Translation output $\mathbf{Y}$

while processing audio stream **do**
  $\tau, \Delta t \leftarrow$ SHAS($\mathbf{X}$) ▷ Get offset and duration
  if no speech detected **then**
    Continue reading stream
    continue
  end if
  $\mathbf{Seg}_{start} \leftarrow \tau$
  $\mathbf{Seg}_{end} \leftarrow \tau + \Delta t$
  $L_{stream} \leftarrow$ length($\mathbf{X}$)
  segmentComplete $\leftarrow$ False
  if $\mathbf{Seg}_{end} - \mathbf{Seg}_{start} \geq L_{max}$ **then**
    segmentComplete $\leftarrow$ True ▷ Maximum length reached
  else if $\mathbf{Seg}_{end} + L_{pause} < L_{stream}$ **and** $\mathbf{Seg}_{end} - \mathbf{Seg}_{start} > L_{min}$ **then**
    segmentComplete $\leftarrow$ True ▷ Valid pause detected
  end if
  Segment $\leftarrow \mathbf{X}[\mathbf{Seg}_{start} : L_{stream}]$
  if length(Segment) $\geq$ *PrevLength*+C **then**
    Process segment chunk-by-chunk
    $\mathbf{Y} \leftarrow$ SimulST(Segment)
    PrevLength $\leftarrow$ length(Segment)
  end if
  if segmentComplete **then**
    Reset buffers and prepare for next segment
  end if
end while

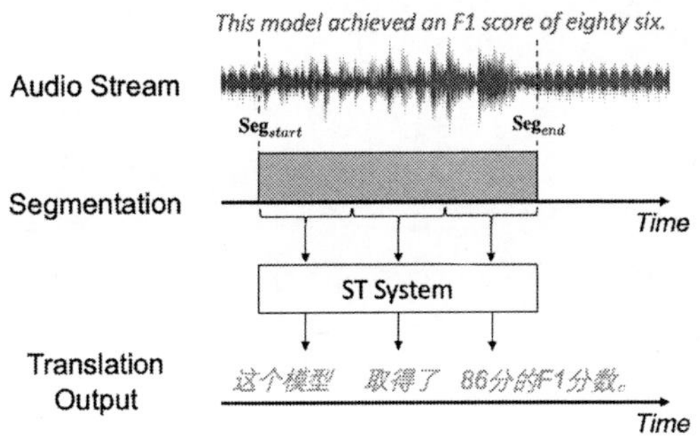

Figure 2: An English-Chinese translation example demonstrating our StreamST system workflow. Upon detecting the speech start point $\mathbf{Seg}_{start}$, the SHAS segmenter triggers the translation system to process incoming speech incrementally, chunk-by-chunk, generating translations continuously until a valid endpoint $\mathbf{Seg}_{end}$ is detected.

pause length parameter L_{pause} and consider a detected segment endpoint $\mathbf{Seg}_{end}$ to be valid only when:

$$\mathbf{Seg}_{end} + L_{pause} < L_{stream}. \quad (6)$$

We demonstrate the significance of the parameter L_{pause} in Section 4.3.3. For practical implementation, we set maximum and minimum segment length constraints to prevent excessively long or short segmentation. Algorithm 1 provides the complete inference procedure for our StreamST system, while Figure 2 illustrates a representative English-Chinese translation example.

3 Experiments Setup

3.1 Data

We used CoVoST-2 (Wang et al., 2020) for all language pairs: English-to-German (En→De), English-to-Japanese (En→Ja), and English-to-Chinese (En→Zh) and also included Europarl-ST (Iranzo-Sánchez et al., 2020) for En→De. We followed our previous submission (Ko et al., 2024) to conduct data filtering based on Bilingual Prefix Alignment (Kano et al., 2022). We used ACL 60/60 (Salesky et al., 2023) data for both validation and evaluation. All of the text data was tokenized using LLM's default tokenizer.

3.2 Evaluation Setup

We assessed the system performance using metrics for both translation quality and latency. For translation quality, we employed BLEU (↑) calculated with SacreBLEU (Post, 2018). For latency evaluation, we used the Length Adaptive Average Lagging (LAAL) (↓) (Papi et al., 2022b) for the SimulST and StreamLAAL (↓) (Papi et al., 2024) for our StreamST system. Additionally, we report the computation-aware versions of both LAAL and StreamLAAL to account for processing overhead. All experiments were conducted using the SimulEval (Ma et al., 2020a) toolkit, providing a standardized evaluation framework.

<System>: You are a professional interpreter who is good at simultaneous interpretation and translation. The user will provide you with a speech in English, which is enlosed within <Speech> and </Speech> tags. And you need to provide both the translation and transcription.

<User>: Based on this original English speech <Speech><SpeechHere></Speech>, complete its translation into <tgt_lang>.

Figure 3: LLM prompt used for both training and evaluation.

3.3 Offline Model

We trained the model of our system in an offline manner. The speech input was provided as waveforms with 16kHz sampling rate. The Whisper encoder processed this input using a causal attention mask to prevent the model from utilizing future information. The LLM then processed the acoustic embeddings produced by the DeCo projector to generate translations based on a prompt instruction as shown in Figure 3. During training, we used the Adam optimizer with $\beta_1 = 0.9$, $\beta_2 = 0.98$. The learning rate was controlled by a cosine scheduler with a base learning rate of 2.0×10^{-4} and 3,000 warming-up steps within the total 100,000 updates. Validation was performed every 1,500 updates, and model checkpoints were saved based on the best BLEU scores. We averaged the parameters of the ten best-performing checkpoints to create the best model.

3.4 Simultaneous Speech-to-Text Translation

We adapted our offline-trained model for SimulST by applying the local agreement policy to the LLM-based translation system. To control the quality-latency trade-off, we used variable chunk sizes of $\{0.5s, 0.75s, 1.0s, 1.5s, 2.0s, 2.5s, 3.0s\}$. During inference, we employed beam search with a beam size of 4 to generate translation hypotheses for each input chunk.

We compare our SimulST system with our submission from the previous year. The primary dis-

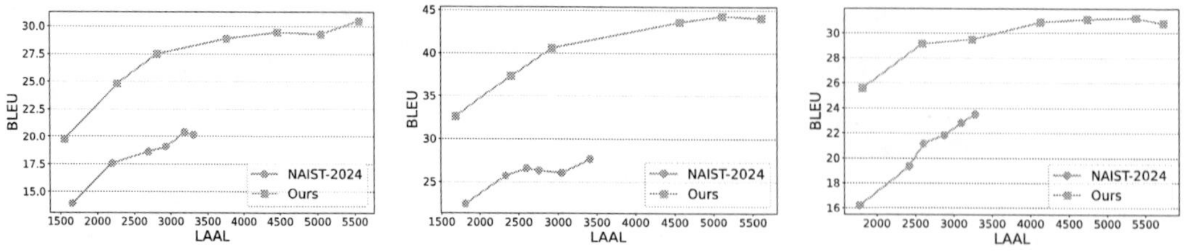

(a) BLEU and LAAL in En-De (b) BLEU and LAAL in En-Zh (c) BLEU and LAAL in En-Ja

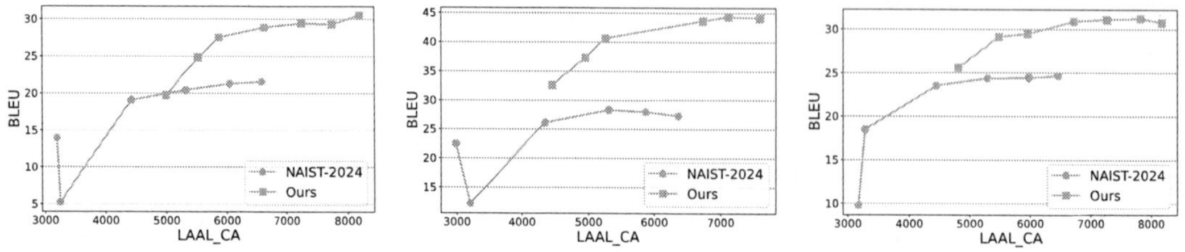

(d) BLEU and LAAL_CA in En-De (e) BLEU and LAAL_CA in En-Zh (f) BLEU and LAAL_CA in En-Ja

Figure 4: Quality-latency trade-off of our **SimulST** system compared to our last year's system on ACL 60/60 dev set.

tinction between the two systems lies in the adoption of an LLM-based model architecture.

3.5 Streaming Speech-to-Text System

We developed our submitted StreamST system by integrating an online version SHAS segmenter with our SimulST model. The pause length L_{pause} and the segmentation threshold θ parameters of SHAS were set differently for each language pair: $\{0.025s, 0.2\}$ for En→De and $\{0.025s, 0.4\}$ for both En→Zh and En→Ja. The impact of these hyperparameters (L_{pause} and θ) is analyzed in Section 4.3.3.

We compare our submitted system with the IWSLT 2025 baseline systems[3]. The baselines implement StreamST using either a naive fixed-length segmenter or a Voice Activity Detection (VAD) segmenter applied to the SeamlessM4T model (Barrault et al., 2023) for all language pairs. An additional cascaded model, which comprises a Whisper ASR model and a M2M100 (Fan et al., 2021) machine translation model, is included for the En→De language pair.

4 Experimental Results

4.1 Offline Results of Topline

The offline performance of our model establishes an upper bound for both the SimulST and StreamST systems by utilizing manual segmentation and processing the complete context to generate translations. Table 1 presents the results of the offline model on the ACL 60/60 dataset.

Table 1: Offline results of our model in the submitted system on ACL 60/60 dev set.

Language Pair	BLEU Score
En–De	28.2
En–Zh	43.9
En–Ja	30.3

4.2 Simultaneous Speech-to-text Translation

4.2.1 NAIST 2024 Model vs. 2025 Model

Non-computation-aware latency: We managed to improve our system compared to our system of last year on non-computation-aware latency setting. As can be seen in Figure 4a through Figure 4c, our system outperforms our previous year system by a margin of 6.4 BLEU score on En-De language pair, 12.3 BLEU score on En-Zh language pair, and 5.2 BLEU score on En-Ja language pair when compared at equivalent latency levels. **Computation-aware latency:** We managed to improve our system compared to our system of last year on computation-aware latency setting. As can be seen in Figure 4d through Figure 4f, our current year system managed to improve the overall BLEU score in all pairs of languages with a greater difference in En-Zh translation, as shown by 4e. In computationa-aware setting, our system managed to improve the 6.6 BLEU score on latency

[3]https://github.com/pe-trik/iwslt25-baselines

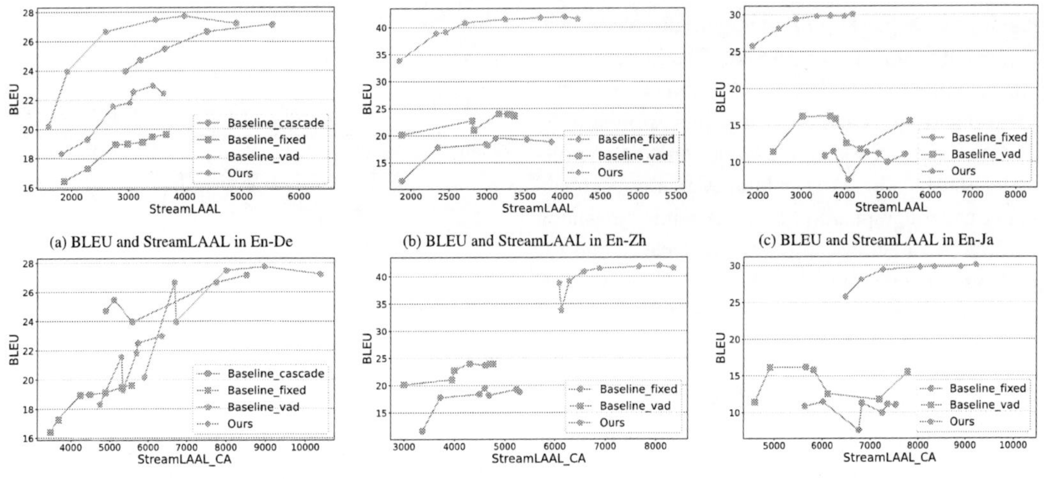

(a) BLEU and StreamLAAL in En-De
(b) BLEU and StreamLAAL in En-Zh
(c) BLEU and StreamLAAL in En-Ja
(d) BLEU and StreamLAAL_CA in En-De
(e) BLEU and StreamLAAL_CA in En-Zh
(f) BLEU and StreamLAAL_CA in En-Ja

Figure 5: Quality-latency trade-off of our submitted streaming speech-to-text translation (**StreamST**) system compared to IWSLT2025 baseline systems on ACL 60/60 dev set.

Table 2: Results of the submitted streaming speech-to-text translation (**StreamST**) system on ACL 60/60 dev set.

Language Pair	Latency Regime	Chunk Size (s)	BLEU	StreamLAAL (ms)
En–De	Low (0–2s)	0.62	23.92	1921
	High (2–4s)	2.0	27.74	3988
En–Zh	Low (0–2.5s)	0.85	39.17	2455
	High (2.5–4s)	2.0	41.80	3699
En–Ja	Low (0–3.5s)	1.5	29.78	3348
	High (3.5–4s)	2.5	29.81	3982

around 4.35 s and the 12.3 BLEU score on latency around 5.3 s on that particular language pair. Despite not showing as much of a difference, on En-De and En-Ja language pair similar pattern could be observed where our current year system gives better BLEU score overall on similar latency. However, our LLM-based model architecture is more computationally expensive than last year's encoder-decoder model, resulting in higher latency under computation-aware evaluation conditions.

4.3 Submitted StreamST System

In this section, we report the results of our submitted system for IWSLT 2025 simultaneous track. We followed the data condition for both training and evaluation as well as the allowed pre-trained models and therefore our submission is constrained.

4.3.1 Main Results

Figure 5a through Figure 5c illustrate the non-computation-aware quality-latency tradeoff between our StreamST system and the baselines. For the En→De language pair, our system outperforms all three baseline systems in both translation quality and latency metrics, while achieving slightly better peak translation quality compared to the cascaded baseline model. For the En→Zh and En→Ja language pairs, our system also demonstrates substantially superior performance compared to both of the baseline systems.

For each language pair, we select two submission with configurations satisfying the low latency and high latency regimes. Table 2 presents the scores of our submitted StreamST system.

4.3.2 Computation-aware Latency

We also evaluate the computation-aware[4] quality-latency trade-off of our StreamST system, as illustrated in Figures 5d through 5f. While our system demonstrates strong performance under non-computation-aware conditions, it exhibits higher

[4]The computation-aware evaluation was conducted using an NVIDIA RTX A5000 GPU.

latency across all three language pairs when real computation time is considered. This increased latency stems from the LA policy's substantial computational requirements in practical applications. Unfortunately, cross-attention-based decision policies (EDAtt, AlignAtt), which typically perform better under computation-aware conditions, cannot be directly integrated into our LLM-based end-to-end system. This limitation highlights the need to develop more efficient decision policies specifically designed for LLM-based systems in future work.

4.3.3 Ablation Study for SHAS

As mentioned in Section 2.4, we implemented a short pause length to prevent premature segment termination in our SHAS-based StreamST system. To understand the influence of the critical SHAS parameters, we conducted a comprehensive ablation study examining both pause length (L_{pause}) and SHAS threshold (θ). We evaluated offline translation quality across various segmentation configurations with different (L_{pause}, θ) combinations. As shown in Table 3 through Table 5, we identified optimal configurations for each language pairs, $\{0.025s, 0.2\}$ for En→De and $\{0.025s, 0.4\}$ for both En→Zh and En→Ja. Notably, when the pause length parameter L_{pause} was disabled ($L_{pause} = 0.0s$), translation quality decreased significantly across all three language pairs due to premature segment termination. This finding underscores the importance of properly configuring the pause length parameter in SHAS-based segmentation for StreamST systems.

Table 3: Impact of SHAS hyperparameters on En→De.

L_{pause}	Threshold (θ)					
	0.6	**0.5**	**0.4**	**0.3**	**0.2**	**0.1**
0.0s	14.58	14.85	15.06	15.09	14.53	14.48
0.025s	27.14	28.40	29.82	30.04	**30.85**	30.16
0.05s	27.74	28.80	30.03	30.07	30.78	30.55
0.1s	28.41	28.96	29.06	30.20	30.39	29.38

Table 4: Impact of SHAS hyperParameters on En→Zh.

L_{pause}	Threshold (θ)					
	0.6	**0.5**	**0.4**	**0.3**	**0.2**	**0.1**
0.0s	33.20	33.85	33.65	33.73	32.84	32.67
0.025s	41.84	42.43	**43.60**	42.03	37.18	34.45
0.05s	41.32	43.09	42.71	41.38	37.40	33.94
0.1s	41.73	42.04	41.40	41.02	36.42	28.98

Table 5: Impact of SHAS hyperParameters on En→Ja.

L_{pause}	Threshold (θ)					
	0.6	**0.5**	**0.4**	**0.3**	**0.2**	**0.1**
0.0s	25.62	25.74	25.83	25.39	25.27	24.78
0.025s	37.09	37.57	**38.61**	38.27	37.02	36.25
0.05s	37.25	37.45	38.17	38.31	36.74	35.97
0.1s	37.15	37.77	38.19	38.44	36.24	34.95

5 Conclusion

This paper presents our StreamST system developed for the IWSLT 2025 Simultaneous Speech Translation Track. Experimental results demonstrated the effectiveness of employing an large language model (LLM) as the backbone for the speech translation tasks. Our system also showed the effectiveness of applying SHAS segmentation method in real time to handle unbounded audio stream during streaming speech translation. This time, we used the Local Agreement (LA) for our LLM-based system, which results in a higher computational latency in real condition. In the future, we will investigate better decision policy methods for the LLM-based StreamST system.

Acknowledgments

Part of this work is supported by JSPS KAKENHI Grant Numbers JP21H05054 and JP23K21681.

References

Alexei Baevski, Yuhao Zhou, Abdelrahman Mohamed, and Michael Auli. 2020. wav2vec 2.0: A framework for self-supervised learning of speech representations. *Advances in neural information processing systems*, 33:12449–12460.

Loïc Barrault, Yu-An Chung, Mariano Cora Meglioli, David Dale, Ning Dong, Paul-Ambroise Duquenne, Hady Elsahar, Hongyu Gong, Kevin Heffernan, John Hoffman, and 1 others. 2023. Seamlessm4t: Massively multilingual & multimodal machine translation. *arXiv preprint arXiv:2308.11596*.

Xi Chen, Songyang Zhang, Qibing Bai, Kai Chen, and Satoshi Nakamura. 2024. LLaST: Improved end-to-end speech translation system leveraged by large language models. In *Findings of the Association for Computational Linguistics: ACL 2024*, pages 6976–6987, Bangkok, Thailand. Association for Computational Linguistics.

Angela Fan, Shruti Bhosale, Holger Schwenk, Zhiyi Ma, Ahmed El-Kishky, Siddharth Goyal, Mandeep Baines, Onur Celebi, Guillaume Wenzek, Vishrav

Chaudhary, and 1 others. 2021. Beyond english-centric multilingual machine translation. *Journal of Machine Learning Research*, 22(107):1–48.

Biao Fu, Donglei Yu, Minpeng Liao, Chengxi Li, Yidong Chen, Kai Fan, and Xiaodong Shi. 2025. Efficient and adaptive simultaneous speech translation with fully unidirectional architecture. *arXiv preprint arXiv:2504.11809*.

Edward J Hu, Yelong Shen, Phillip Wallis, Zeyuan Allen-Zhu, Yuanzhi Li, Shean Wang, Lu Wang, Weizhu Chen, and 1 others. 2022. Lora: Low-rank adaptation of large language models. *ICLR*, 1(2):3.

Chao-Wei Huang, Hui Lu, Hongyu Gong, Hirofumi Inaguma, Ilia Kulikov, Ruslan Mavlyutov, and Sravya Popuri. 2024. Investigating decoder-only large language models for speech-to-text translation. *arXiv preprint arXiv:2407.03169*.

Javier Iranzo-Sánchez, Joan Albert Silvestre-Cerdà, Javier Jorge, Nahuel Roselló, Adrià Giménez, Albert Sanchis, Jorge Civera, and Alfons Juan. 2020. Europarl-st: A multilingual corpus for speech translation of parliamentary debates. In *ICASSP 2020 - 2020 IEEE International Conference on Acoustics, Speech and Signal Processing (ICASSP)*, pages 8229–8233.

Yasumasa Kano, Katsuhito Sudoh, and Satoshi Nakamura. 2022. Simultaneous neural machine translation with prefix alignment. In *Proceedings of the 19th International Conference on Spoken Language Translation (IWSLT 2022)*, pages 22–31, Dublin, Ireland (in-person and online). Association for Computational Linguistics.

Yuka Ko, Ryo Fukuda, Yuta Nishikawa, Yasumasa Kano, Tomoya Yanagita, Kosuke Doi, Mana Makinae, Haotian Tan, Makoto Sakai, Sakriani Sakti, Katsuhito Sudoh, and Satoshi Nakamura. 2024. NAIST simultaneous speech translation system for IWSLT 2024. In *Proceedings of the 21st International Conference on Spoken Language Translation (IWSLT 2024)*, pages 170–182, Bangkok, Thailand (in-person and online). Association for Computational Linguistics.

Roman Koshkin, Katsuhito Sudoh, and Satoshi Nakamura. 2024. TransLLaMa: LLM-based simultaneous translation system. In *Findings of the Association for Computational Linguistics: EMNLP 2024*, pages 461–476, Miami, Florida, USA. Association for Computational Linguistics.

Dan Liu, Mengge Du, Xiaoxi Li, Yuchen Hu, and Lirong Dai. 2021. The USTC-NELSLIP systems for simultaneous speech translation task at IWSLT 2021. In *Proceedings of the 18th International Conference on Spoken Language Translation (IWSLT 2021)*, pages 30–38.

Danni Liu, Gerasimos Spanakis, and Jan Niehues. 2020. Low-Latency Sequence-to-Sequence Speech Recognition and Translation by Partial Hypothesis Selection. In *Proc. Interspeech*, pages 3620–3624.

Mingbo Ma, Liang Huang, Hao Xiong, Renjie Zheng, Kaibo Liu, Baigong Zheng, Chuanqiang Zhang, Zhongjun He, Hairong Liu, Xing Li, Hua Wu, and Haifeng Wang. 2019. STACL: Simultaneous translation with implicit anticipation and controllable latency using prefix-to-prefix framework. In *Proceedings of the 57th Annual Meeting of the Association for Computational Linguistics*, pages 3025–3036.

Xutai Ma, Mohammad Javad Dousti, Changhan Wang, Jiatao Gu, and Juan Pino. 2020a. SIMULEVAL: An evaluation toolkit for simultaneous translation. In *Proceedings of the 2020 Conference on Empirical Methods in Natural Language Processing: System Demonstrations*, pages 144–150, Online. Association for Computational Linguistics.

Xutai Ma, Juan Pino, and Philipp Koehn. 2020b. SimulMT to SimulST: Adapting simultaneous text translation to end-to-end simultaneous speech translation. In *Proceedings of the 1st Conference of the Asia-Pacific Chapter of the Association for Computational Linguistics and the 10th International Joint Conference on Natural Language Processing*, pages 582–587.

Thai-Son Nguyen, Sebastian Stüker, and Alex Waibel. 2021. Super-Human Performance in Online Low-Latency Recognition of Conversational Speech. In *Proc. Interspeech*, pages 1762–1766.

Siqi Ouyang, Xi Xu, and Lei Li. 2025. Infinisst: Simultaneous translation of unbounded speech with large language model. *arXiv preprint arXiv:2503.02969*.

Sara Papi, Marco Gaido, Matteo Negri, and Luisa Bentivogli. 2024. StreamAtt: Direct streaming speech-to-text translation with attention-based audio history selection. In *Proceedings of the 62nd Annual Meeting of the Association for Computational Linguistics (Volume 1: Long Papers)*, pages 3692–3707, Bangkok, Thailand. Association for Computational Linguistics.

Sara Papi, Marco Gaido, Matteo Negri, and Marco Turchi. 2022a. Does simultaneous speech translation need simultaneous models? In *Findings of the Association for Computational Linguistics: EMNLP*, pages 141–153.

Sara Papi, Marco Gaido, Matteo Negri, and Marco Turchi. 2022b. Over-generation cannot be rewarded: Length-adaptive average lagging for simultaneous speech translation. In *Proceedings of the Third Workshop on Automatic Simultaneous Translation*, pages 12–17, Online. Association for Computational Linguistics.

Sara Papi, Matteo Negri, and Marco Turchi. 2023a. Attention as a guide for simultaneous speech translation. In *Proceedings of the 61st Annual Meeting of the Association for Computational Linguistics (Volume 1: Long Papers)*, pages 13340–13356, Toronto, Canada. Association for Computational Linguistics.

Sara Papi, Marco Turchi, and Matteo Negri. 2023b. AlignAtt: Using Attention-based Audio-Translation

Alignments as a Guide for Simultaneous Speech Translation. In *Proc. INTERSPEECH*, pages 3974–3978.

Peter Polák, Ngoc-Quan Pham, Tuan Nam Nguyen, Danni Liu, Carlos Mullov, Jan Niehues, Ondřej Bojar, and Alexander Waibel. 2022. CUNI-KIT system for simultaneous speech translation task at IWSLT 2022. In *Proceedings of the 19th International Conference on Spoken Language Translation (IWSLT 2022)*, pages 277–285, Dublin, Ireland (in-person and online). Association for Computational Linguistics.

Matt Post. 2018. A call for clarity in reporting BLEU scores. In *Proceedings of the Third Conference on Machine Translation: Research Papers*, pages 186–191, Brussels, Belgium. Association for Computational Linguistics.

Alec Radford, Jong Wook Kim, Tao Xu, Greg Brockman, Christine Mcleavey, and Ilya Sutskever. 2023. Robust speech recognition via large-scale weak supervision. In *Proceedings of the 40th International Conference on Machine Learning*, volume 202 of *Proceedings of Machine Learning Research*, pages 28492–28518. PMLR.

Yi Ren, Jinglin Liu, Xu Tan, Chen Zhang, Tao Qin, Zhou Zhao, and Tie-Yan Liu. 2020. Simulspeech: End-to-end simultaneous speech to text translation. In *Proceedings of the 58th Annual Meeting of the Association for Computational Linguistics*, pages 3787–3796.

Elizabeth Salesky, Kareem Darwish, Mohamed Al-Badrashiny, Mona Diab, and Jan Niehues. 2023. Evaluating multilingual speech translation under realistic conditions with resegmentation and terminology. In *Proceedings of the 20th International Conference on Spoken Language Translation (IWSLT 2023)*, pages 62–78, Toronto, Canada (in-person and online). Association for Computational Linguistics.

Haotian Tan and Sakriani Sakti. 2024. Contrastive feedback mechanism for simultaneous speech translation. In *Interspeech 2024*, pages 852–856.

Ioannis Tsiamas, Gerard I. Gállego, José A. R. Fonollosa, and Marta R. Costa-jussà. 2022. SHAS: Approaching optimal Segmentation for End-to-End Speech Translation. In *Proc. Interspeech 2022*, pages 106–110.

Changhan Wang, Juan Pino, Anne Wu, and Jiatao Gu. 2020. CoVoST: A diverse multilingual speech-to-text translation corpus. In *Proceedings of the Twelfth Language Resources and Evaluation Conference*, pages 4197–4203, Marseille, France. European Language Resources Association.

Xi Xu, Siqi Ouyang, Brian Yan, Patrick Fernandes, William Chen, Lei Li, Graham Neubig, and Shinji Watanabe. 2024. CMU's IWSLT 2024 simultaneous speech translation system. In *Proceedings of the 21st International Conference on Spoken Language Translation (IWSLT 2024)*, pages 154–159, Bangkok, Thailand (in-person and online). Association for Computational Linguistics.

An Yang, Baosong Yang, Beichen Zhang, Binyuan Hui, Bo Zheng, Bowen Yu, Chengyuan Li, Dayiheng Liu, Fei Huang, Haoran Wei, and 1 others. 2024. Qwen2. 5 technical report. *arXiv preprint arXiv:2412.15115*.

Linli Yao, Lei Li, Shuhuai Ren, Lean Wang, Yuanxin Liu, Xu Sun, and Lu Hou. 2024. Deco: Decoupling token compression from semantic abstraction in multimodal large language models. *arXiv preprint arXiv:2405.20985*.

Xingshan Zeng, Liangyou Li, and Qun Liu. 2021. RealTranS: End-to-end simultaneous speech translation with convolutional weighted-shrinking transformer. In *Findings of the Association for Computational Linguistics: ACL-IJCNLP*, pages 2461–2474.

Shaolei Zhang, Qingkai Fang, Shoutao Guo, Zhengrui Ma, Min Zhang, and Yang Feng. 2024. StreamSpeech: Simultaneous speech-to-speech translation with multi-task learning. In *Proceedings of the 62nd Annual Meeting of the Association for Computational Linguistics (Volume 1: Long Papers)*, pages 8964–8986, Bangkok, Thailand. Association for Computational Linguistics.

Efficient Speech Translation through Model Compression and Knowledge Distillation

Yasmin Moslem
ADAPT Centre
School of Computer Science and Statistics
Trinity College Dublin
Dublin, Ireland

Abstract

Efficient deployment of large audio-language models for speech translation remains challenging due to their significant computational requirements. In this paper, we address this challenge through our system submissions to the "Model Compression" track at the International Conference on Spoken Language Translation (IWSLT 2025). We experiment with a combination of approaches including iterative layer pruning based on layer importance evaluation, low-rank adaptation with 4-bit quantization (QLoRA), and knowledge distillation. In our experiments, we use Qwen2-Audio-7B-Instruct for speech translation into German and Chinese. Our pruned (student) models achieve up to a 50% reduction in both model parameters and storage footprint, while retaining 97-100% of the translation quality of the in-domain (teacher) models.

1 Introduction

Multimodal foundation models have shown powerful capabilities in different tasks, including speech translation. However, these models are often large and computationally intensive, making them impractical to use in real-world settings with limited resources. To enhance the efficiency of these models, researchers have been investigating diverse approaches to model compression that aim to reduce the computational requirements while retaining performance (Gandhi et al., 2023; Peng et al., 2023b,a; Treviso et al., 2023; Wang et al., 2023).

Qwen2-Audio (Chu et al., 2023, 2024) is a state-of-the-art foundation model that accepts various audio signal inputs and performs audio analysis or direct textual responses to speech instructions. In the IWSLT 2025's Model Compression track (Abdulmumin et al., 2025), the organizers required that all submissions must be derived from the Qwen2-Audio model. The official languages of the task are English-to-German (EN-DE) and English-to-Chinese (EN-ZH).

We experimented with various approaches including efficient fine-tuning using quantized low-rank adapters with 4-bit quantization (QLoRA) (Hu et al., 2021; Dettmers et al., 2023), iterative layer pruning based on layer importance evaluation (Peer et al., 2022; Gandhi et al., 2023; Sajjad et al., 2023), and sequence-level knowledge distillation (Kim and Rush, 2016; Crego and Senellart, 2016; Jooste et al., 2022; Gandhi et al., 2023). Our experiments are mainly based on *Qwen2-Audio-7B-Instruct*.[1] While Section 3 elaborates on our experiments, we can summarize our two submissions for German and Chinese as follows:

- **Setup 1:** This model is the outcome of fine-tuning *Qwen2-Audio-7B-Instruct* in two stages: (a) full fine-tuning with the ACL 60/60 dataset, and (b) QLoRA fine-tuning with 4-bit quantization using the ACL 60/60 dataset augmented with data knowledge distillation from the fully fine-tuned model. This process has achieved 40% compression in terms of both model parameters and storage size. We discuss the details of this model in Section 3.2.
- **Setup 2:** This model is a pruned version of *Qwen2-Audio-7B-Instruct*, and was created in multiple stages: (a) full fine-tuning of the baseline model with the ACL 60/60 dataset, (b) layer pruning of the decoder into 24 layers, while all 32 encoder layers were kept intact, (c) full fine-tuning of the pruned model, and (d) QLoRA fine-tuning with the ACL 60/60 dataset augmented with data knowledge distillation from the fully fine-tuned model and a portion of the CoVoST2 dataset to restore the quality of the teacher model. This process has achieved 50% compression in terms of both model parameters and storage size. We discuss the details of this model in Section 3.3.

[1] `https://hf.co/Qwen/Qwen2-Audio-7B-Instruct`

Proceedings of the 22nd International Conference on Spoken Language Translation (IWSLT 2025), pages 379–388
July 31 - August 1, 2025

Model	EN-DE BLEU	EN-DE chrF++	EN-DE COMET	EN-ZH BLEU	EN-ZH chrF	EN-ZH COMET	Params (B)	Storage (GB)
Baseline	22.96	49.88	8.61	38.73	32.53	17.38	8.40	16.79
+ Full Fine-tuning	39.28	65.27	56.32	58.54	52.54	65.97		
+ QLoRA Fine-tuning	41.52	66.25	53.47	57.65	51.08	65.77	**4.95**	**9.64**
+ Knowledge Distillation	**43.25**	**68.02**	**59.36**	**59.60**	**53.94**	**68.42**		

Table 1: Evaluation of the experiment that employs QLoRA with 4-bit quantization and augments the authentic data with knowledge distillation. This approach reduces the model size by more than 40% in terms of both the number of parameters (params) and storage footprint, while achieving the best translation performance for both English-to-German (EN-DE) and English-to-Chinese (EN-ZH) language pairs.

2 Data

2.1 In-Domain Data

The ACL 60/60 dataset[2] (Salesky et al., 2023) is used in all of our experiments as the in-domain data. ACL 60/60 contains multilingual translation of ACL 2022 technical presentations into 10 target languages. The dataset consists of two splits, "dev" and "eval", which together comprise 884 utterances. We merged the two splits, and randomly sampled 100 utterances for testing, which left us with 784 utterances for training. For test data sampling, we used the *train_test_split* method from the *datasets*[3] library (Lhoest et al., 2021), setting the random seed option to zero. The ACL 60/60 dataset was required for "constrained" submissions to the IWSLT's "Model Compression" track.

2.2 Out-of-Domain Data

After layer pruning of the *Qwen2-Audio-7B-Instruct* model (cf. Section 3), we needed to use more training data to restore the translation quality of the unpruned model. In addition to knowledge distillation data from the teacher model, we used a portion of the CoVoST2 dataset (Wang et al., 2021) (cf. Section 3.3). CoVoST2 is a large-scale multilingual speech-to-text translation corpus, covering translations from English into 15 languages, including German and Chinese.

3 Methodologies

We experiment with diverse methods to compress *Qwen2-Audio-7B-Instruct* while maintaining the translation quality. This section covers our two main experimental setups, while Section 4 discusses several ablation studies and elaborates on intermediate experiments.

Our first experimental setup (cf. Section 3.2) employs QLoRA fine-tuning with 4-bit quantization, while the other experimental setup (cf. Section 3.3) conducts layer importance evaluation and applies iterative layer pruning of the model, followed by QLoRA fine-tuning. Both setups use knowledge distillation to recover the translation quality of the in-domain teacher model.

3.1 Full-Parameter Fine-tuning

In all of our experiments, we start by full-parameter fine-tuning of the *Qwen2-Audio-7B-Instruct* model on the ACL 60/60 dataset. This step is essential to ensure the foundation model is familiar with the downstream task and in-domain data. In particular, we train the baseline model on the in-domain data for 3 epochs, using a batch size of 4, learning rate of 1e-5, weight decay of 0.001, and no warm-up steps. The model is initially loaded in *bfloat16* data type. As shown in Table 1 and Table 2, the fully fine-tuned model clearly outperforms the baseline by an average of 48 COMET points for translation into German and Chinese. Hence, this fully fine-tuned model is used as a foundation for both our experiments in Section 3.2 and Section 3.3. It is also used as a "teacher" for knowledge distillation into the compressed "student" models. We conduct the training on one H200 SXM GPU, using the Transformers framework[4] (Wolf et al., 2020).

3.2 QLoRA with 4-bit Quantization

This experimental setup employs quantization, accompanied by efficient fine-tuning, and knowledge distillation techniques. We start with full-parameter

[2] https://hf.co/datasets/ymoslem/acl-6060
[3] https://github.com/huggingface/datasets
[4] https://github.com/huggingface/transformers

Model	Data	EN-DE BLEU	EN-DE chrF++	EN-DE COMET	EN-ZH BLEU	EN-ZH chrF	EN-ZH COMET	Params (B)	Storage (GB)
Baseline	-	22.96	49.88	8.61	38.73	32.53	17.38	8.40	16.79
+ Full FT	ACL	39.28	65.27	56.32	58.54	52.54	65.97		
+ Pruning	ACL	10.78	39.58	-44.4	42.52	36.92	39.42	6.78	13.55
+ FT	ACL	32.16	60.39	39.08	53.05	47.23	56.72		
	+ KD	33.44	60.91	39.23	53.41	48.20	54.94		
+ QLoRA	+ CV	39.59	65.14	59.21	56.52	50.74	64.34	**4.12**	**8.65**

Table 2: Evaluation of the iterative layer pruning experiment. We started by full-parameter fine-tuning (Full FT) of the baseline model *Qwen2-Audio-7B-Instruct* on the in-domain dataset ACL 60/60. Pruning 8 layers of the decoder of the model achieved approx. 20% reduction in the model size; however, it affected the quality of the model. Hence, we fine-tuned the pruned model again on the in-domain dataset to restore as much as possible of the quality of the fully fine-tuned model. Finally, we fine-tuned the resulting model with low-rank adaptation after quantizing it into the 4-bit precision (QLoRA) on a mix of the in-domain data, knowledge distillation data (KD) and out-of-domain data, namely the CoVoST2 (CV) dataset. The whole process of pruning followed by QLoRA fine-tuning with 4-bit quantization has resulted in approx. 50% reduction in the model size, while retaining 97% and 100% of the translation quality for Chinese and German, respectively, compared to the teacher model.

fine-tuning of *Qwen2-Audio-7B-Instruct* (cf. Section 3.1). Afterwards, the fine-tuned model is quantized into the 4-bit precision and then fine-tuned with low-rank adapters (QLoRA) (Hu et al., 2021; Dettmers et al., 2023). Moreover, we use the fully fine-tuned model as a "teacher" in the knowledge distillation process.

Knowledge distillation: To restore the quality of the in-domain fully fine-tuned teacher models (cf. Section 3.1), sequence-level knowledge distillation is applied (Kim and Rush, 2016; Gandhi et al., 2023). In other words, we translate the ACL 60/60 training data with the "teacher" model. The training data is then augmented with the knowledge distillation data, and duplicates are filtered out. As a result, the augmented data after knowledge distillation comprises 1,568 segments for German and 1,069 segments for Chinese. Finally, "student" models are fine-tuned with QLoRA on the augmented data.

QLoRA fine-tuning: First, we enable 4-bit quantization through *BitsAndBytes* (Dettmers et al., 2023) while loading the in-domain fully fine-tuned model. In the configuration of *BitsAndBytes*, we set the quantization type to "nf4", and use the "double_quant" option, where the quantization constants from the first quantization are quantized again. For LoRA configuration, we set the rank to 64, alpha to 128, and dropout to 0. We target all linear modules. Overall, this configuration results in 2.41% trainable parameters of the model. Moreover, we enable Rank-Stabilized LoRA (rsLoRA) (Kalajdzievski, 2023). We train the model for 4 epochs, using a batch size of 4, and a learning rate of 1e-5.

As Table 1 illustrates, the combination of QLoRA with 4-bit quantization and knowledge distillation has achieved the highest translation performance into both German and Chinese across all evaluation metrics while reducing the model size in terms of both the number of parameters and storage requirements by more than 40% compared to the baseline model.[5]

3.3 Iterative Layer Pruning

In this experimental setup, we apply iterative layer pruning to the fully fine-tuned "teacher" model (cf. Section 3.1). This approach incrementally identifies and removes layers with minimal contribution to translation quality, one layer at a time. The pruned model resulting from this process is then fine-tuned on both the ACL 60/60 training dataset and knowledge distillation data from the teacher model. Finally, the model is further fine-tuned with QLoRA, leveraging 4-bit quantization for efficient

[5]For consistency, our storage footprint calculations are based only on the size of model files (**.safetensors*), including the adapter of QLoRA models. We exclude the tokenizer and configuration files, as their contribution to the overall size is relatively small ($\sim$ 13 MB) and they are unaffected by our optimization methods. All sizes are computed using the decimal definition of gigabytes, where 1 GB $= 1000^3$ bytes.

low-rank adaptation. Pruning 8 layers achieves a 20% reduction in model size, which increases to 50% when combined with 4-bit quantization. Fine-tuning the pruned model restores between 97% and 100% of the teacher model's translation quality for Chinese and German, respectively. The following points elaborate on the process.

Layer importance evaluation: We conduct layer importance evaluation by measuring translation performance without each layer. In this greedy layer pruning approach (Peer et al., 2022; Rostami and Dousti, 2024), to prune $n + 1$ layers, only a single optimal layer to prune must be added to the already known solution for pruning n layers. After identifying and removing the least critical layer, we repeat the layer importance evaluation on the remaining layers until reaching our n pruning target. We observe that while removing certain layers of the model (e.g. the first or last layer) substantially degrades translation performance, others result in minimal performance drops. When experimenting with using either the chrF/chrF++ or COMET metric for layer importance evaluation, the models pruned based on chrF/chrF++ outperform those pruned based on COMET.

Layer pruning: We iteratively prune one decoder layer at a time, selecting the layer whose removal has the least negative impact on translation quality, measured by chrF/chrF++ scores. At each iteration, we evaluate the translation performance of the pruned model on the test split of the ACL 60/60 dataset, after removing each candidate layer. The layer whose removal yields the best performance is eventually pruned. This process continues until a predefined number of layers (8 in the main experiments) have been removed. By iteratively removing the least important layers, this performance-guided method produces a more compact model that can be fine-tuned further to recover the translation quality of the teacher model. We observe that the performance of the English-to-German model is more impacted by pruning than the English-to-Chinese model, which might be attributed to the pre-training process (cf. Table 2).

Knowledge distillation: Knowledge distillation is the process of transferring knowledge from a large model (teacher) to a smaller one (student). In our case, the teacher is the fully fine-tuned model, and the student is the model resulting from iterative pruning. We translate the in-domain data with the teacher model to augment the authentic data. As the process can result in duplicate translations, we remove duplicate segments from the training data. This step is similar to what we did in the first experimental setup (cf. Section 3.2).

Fine-tuning: The pruning step is followed by fine-tuning the pruned model for 4 epochs using the in-domain ACL 60/60 dataset augmented with the knowledge distillation data (Kim et al., 2023; Gandhi et al., 2023). This step recovers most of the translation quality of the teacher model.

QLoRA fine-tuning: This step serves two purposes, improving both the compression level and translation performance of the pruned model. After quantizing the model resulting from the previous step, low rank adaptation is used for fine-tuning it further. The training data consists of the ACL 60/60 dataset augmented with the knowledge distillation data from the fully fine-tuned "teacher" model (oversampled by a factor of 10), as well as a portion of the CoVoST2 dataset (100k utterances). We fine-tune the model for 1 epoch, using a batch size of 8 (to make use of the computing resources, since the model is much smaller now), and a learning rate of 1e-5.

This whole process of iterative layer pruning followed by fine-tuning has achieved up to 50% compression in terms of both model parameters and storage size.[6] Moreover, the quality degradation caused by pruning has been mitigated through multi-stage fine-tuning on diverse data. As demonstrated by Table 2, by the end of the process, the pruned model could recover most of the translation quality of the fully fine-tuned teacher model (97% for Chinese and 100% for German).

Our ablation study (cf. Section 4) demonstrates that iterative layer pruning considerably outperforms fixed middle-layer pruning (cf. Section 4.3). Moreover, it clarifies that pruning exclusively decoder layers yields better performance than pruning both encoder and decoder layers (cf. Section 4.2). While our main experiments in this section prune only 8 layers, resulting in a model with 24 decoder layers and 32 encoder layers, the ablation study investigates pruning up to 16 layers (cf. Section 4.5).

[6]To achieve these compression gains from layer pruning, the Qwen2-Audio model must initially be loaded in *bfloat16* data type. For other tasks like fine-tuning and inference, *bfloat16* precision is not required, although it may be necessary when computing resources are limited, potentially at the cost of reduced quality.

Encoder	Decoder	BLEU	chrF++	COMET	Params	Storage
24 ↓	24 ↓	26.44	54.67	13.90	6.62 B	13.24 GB
32 =	24 ↓	**30.81**	**58.45**	**31.95**	6.78 B	13.55 GB

Table 3: Comparison of layer pruning of both the encoder and decoder with layer pruning of the decoder only. Both models are fine-tuned before and after layer pruning on the EN-DE ACL 60/60 dataset. This experiment uses middle layer pruning. The model that prunes the layers of only the decoder outperforms the model that prunes both the encoder and decoder, although the former has a slightly higher number of parameters and storage size.

4 Ablation Study

This section elaborates on some intermediate experiments that led us to the final models in Section 3.2 and Section 3.3. These experiments include comparing the performance of the Qwen2-Audio base model with Qwen2-Audio-Instruct (cf. Section 4.1), comparing encoder-decoder pruning with decoder-only pruning (cf. Section 4.2), comparing "iterative" layer pruning with fixed middle-layer pruning (cf. Section 4.3), iterative pruning of up to 16 layers (cf. Section 4.5), fine-tuning before and after pruning (cf. Section 4.6), and using different sizes of out-of-domain data to fine-tune the pruned models (cf. Section 4.7).

4.1 Qwen2-Audio Base vs Instruct

We experimented with both *Qwen2-Audio-7B* and *Qwen2-Audio-7B-Instruct* for English-to-German speech translation. As Table 4 the "Instruct" model outperforms its base version. Hence, we use *Qwen2-Audio-7B-Instruct* in all of our experiments throughout the paper.

We follow the prompt requirements of the *Qwen2-Audio* models. For the base model, Qwen2-Audio-7B, the prompt is as follows:

```
"<|audio_bos|><|AUDIO|><|audio_eos|>Translate the English speech into {language}:"
```

For the instruction-following model, *Qwen2-Audio-7B-Insruct*, the prompt is as follows:

```
[
  {"role": "system", "content": "You are a professional translator."},
  {"role": "user", "content": [
    {"type": "audio", "audio_url": audio_path},
    {"type": "text", "text": "Translate the English speech into {language}:"},
  ]},
]
```

Language	Model	BLEU	chrF/++	COMET
EN-DE	base	6.15	32.10	-58.34
	instruct	**22.96**	**49.88**	**8.61**
EN-ZH	base	7.23	10.62	-52.06
	instruct	**38.73**	**32.53**	**17.38**

Table 4: Evaluation of the Qwen2-Audio-7B (base) and Qwen2-Audio-7B-Instruct (instruct) models before fine-tuning. The "instruct" model outperforms the "base" model for both English-to-German (EN-DE) and English-to-Chinese (EN-ZH) speech translation.

4.2 Encoder-Decoder Layer Pruning

The Qwen2-Audio is based on the encoder-decoder Transformer architecture (Vaswani et al., 2017). It consists of an encoder for audio (*audio_tower*) and a decoder for text generation (*language_model*), each of which comprises 32 layers. We first experimented with layer pruning of both the encoder and decoder. However, inspired by the Distil-Whisper work (Gandhi et al., 2023), we experimented with pruning decoder layers only, which achieved better results. In other words, pruning only the decoder from 32 layers to 24 layers outperformed pruning both the encoder and decoder into 24 layers.

In this experiment, we pruned 8 fixed middle layers, from the 12th to the 19th layer, inclusively. After fine-tuning both models with the English-to-German ACL 60/60 dataset, the model where only the decoder layers were pruned achieved 4+ additional points in terms of BLEU and chrF++ and 18+ points of COMET. It is worth noting that both the number of parameters and the storage footprint of this model is only 1% larger than the model with both the encoder and decoder were pruned. Table 3 shows the performance evaluation results of fine-tuning the English-to-German model after middle-layer pruning.

Language	Pruning	Metric	Pruned Layers	Model	BLEU	chrF/++	COMET
EN-DE	Middle	n/a	[12, 13, 14, 15, 16, 17, 18, 19]	Pruned	0.13	6.13	-162.44
				+ FT	30.81	58.45	31.95
	Iterative	COMET	[12, 1, 9, 15, 20, 27, 29, 5]	Pruned	6.53	31.15	-41.96
				+ FT	30.97	59.67	34.39
		chrF++	[13, 3, 20, 9, 29, 1, 19, 27]	Pruned	10.78	39.58	-44.40
				+ FT	**32.16**	**60.39**	**39.08**
EN-ZH	Middle	n/a	[12, 13, 14, 15, 16, 17, 18, 19]	Pruned	1.3	3.8	-94.05
				+ FT	45.84	40.48	40.37
	Iterative	COMET	[7, 9, 24, 3, 28, 6, 15, 18]	Pruned	21.1	27.25	28.26
				+ FT	51.85	46.36	**58.64**
		chrF	[7, 25, 3, 4, 29, 15, 26, 20]	Pruned	42.52	36.92	39.42
				+ FT	**53.05**	**47.23**	56.72

Table 5: Comparison between **middle-layer pruning** and **iterative layer pruning**, with either COMET or chrF/chrF++ as the metric for measuring layer importance. Iterative layer pruning, i.e. removing layers one by one, and then evaluating the resulting model, outperforms middle-layer pruning. In particular, when chrF/chrF++ is used for layer importance evaluation, the resulting pruned model achieves better speech translation quality after fine-tuning on the ACL 60/60 dataset.

4.3 Iterative vs Middle Layer Pruning

In this section, we compare two common approaches to layer-wise pruning, namely iterative layer pruning and middle-layer pruning. Moreover, we compare using chrF/chrF++ and COMET for layer importance evaluation during iterative layer pruning. In all cases, we only work on decoder layers (cf. Section 4.2).

As discussed in Section 3.3, we experimented with iterative pruning based on layer importance evaluation to identify and remove the layers that contribute least to translation quality. In contrast, in middle-layer pruning, we simply remove the 8 middle layers of the model, namely layers 12 through 19 out of the 32 decoder layers of the model.

Since the bottom layers of a model are closer to the input and the top layers are closer to the output, it is possible that both the top layers and the bottom layers are more important than the middle layers. In practice, the impact on model performance after pruning the middle layers varies across different models (Sajjad et al., 2023).

In iterative layer pruning based on performance evaluation (using chrF++ for German and chrF for Chinese), the pruned layers are [1, 3, 9, 13, 19, 20, 27, 29] for German, and [3, 4, 7, 15, 20, 25, 26, 29] for Chinese. This shows a diverse layer selection that is not concentrated solely in the middle. As Table 5 illustrates, iterative layer pruning yields much better results than middle-layer pruning. For example, when pruning 8 middle layers of the English-to-Chinese model, the final evaluation scores of the resulting model are so low across all metrics (BLEU: 1.3, chrF: 3.8, COMET -94.05), compared to the scores achieved when the same number of layers is iteratively removed based on layer importance (BLEU: 42.52, chrF: 36.92, COMET 39.42).

Moreover, we experimented with both using chrF/chrF++ and COMET for evaluating pruned models during the iterative process. Interestingly, the final model obtained by using chrF/chrF++ for layer importance evaluation achieves better results (cf. Table 5). This might be due to the scientific nature of the ACL 60/60 dataset, and it requires future exploration with other datasets.

4.4 Immediate Recovery

In our main experiments, we fine-tuned the pruned models only after completing the entire pruning process (cf. Section 3.3). In order to understand the effect of accompanying iterative pruning with iterative recovery (Wibowo et al., 2025), we conducted an extra experiment where we immediately fine-tuned the model after each layer pruning iteration. In other words, when pruning 8 layers, the

Model	Layers	EN-DE BLEU	EN-DE chrF++	EN-DE COMET	EN-ZH BLEU	EN-ZH chrF	EN-ZH COMET	Params (B)	Storage (GB)
Pruned [8]	24/32	10.78	39.58	-44.4	42.52	36.92	39.42	6.78	13.55
+ Fine-tuned		32.16	60.39	39.08	53.05	47.23	56.72		
Pruned [10]	22/32	4.54	26.33	-114.73	16.51	23.02	5.89	6.37	12.74
+ Fine-tuned		30.90	59.80	33.74	51.97	47.19	59.57		
Pruned [12]	20/32	3.08	19.45	-154.69	5.97	10.14	-62.50	5.97	11.93
+ Fine-tuned		31.05	58.68	30.03	52.43	47.03	56.15		
Pruned [16]	16/32	0.06	10.44	-182.25	1.99	4.26	-124.75	5.16	10.32
+ Fine-tuned		22.15	50.90	-6.92	47.33	42.13	42.51		

Table 6: Comparison of iterative **pruning of 8 decoder layers** (which is the foundation of our pruning experiments) against **pruning 10, 12, and 16 decoder layers**. We observe that the quality of German degrades much more rapidly than that of Chinese, after pruning more than 8 layers. Moreover, pruning 16 layers from the Chinese model results in notably worse performance compared to pruning only 8, 10, or 12 layers, even after fine-tuning. When iteratively removing 16 layers from the German model, the removed layers are: [13, 3, 20, 9, 29, 1, 19, 27, 7, 26, 15, 18, 10, 17, 14, 30]. For the Chinese model, the removed layers are [7, 25, 3, 4, 29, 15, 26, 20, 24, 5, 10, 9, 27, 28, 18, 13]. The layers are listed from most to least important (left to right), according to the layer importance evaluation used in our iterative pruning method. In this experiment, all 32 encoder layers are kept intact; therefore, the table reports the remaining decoder layers as 24/32, 22/32, 20/32, and 16/32 encoder/decoder layers.

fine-tuning is performed 8 times, once after each pruning step.

By the end of the process, the pruned layers for German are [13, 1, 3, 17, 12, 4, 14, 21], based on layer importance evaluation. These layers differ from those selected when pruning without immediate recovery (cf. Section 4.3), since fine-tuning after each iteration changes the relative importance of the remaining layers.

Model	BLEU	chrF++	COMET
pruned	10.78	39.58	-44.40
+ FT [after]	**32.16**	**60.39**	**39.08**
pruned	30.96	59.02	30.07
↻ FT [immediate]	31.67	59.76	36.13

Table 7: Comparison of fine-tuning after the end of the pruning process (+ FT [after]) against immediate fine-tuning after each pruning iteration (↻ FT [immediate]). Fine-tuning only after completing the pruning process achieves better final performance. The results are for iterative pruning of 8 decoder layers from the English-to-German model.

While this immediate recovery approach improved evaluation scores of the pruned model, it did not achieve performance gains over our standard method of fine-tuning only once after complete pruning. This might be due to overfitting caused by fine-tuning several times on the small in-domain dataset. Moreover, immediate recovery through fine-tuning after each pruning iteration is much more computationally intensive.

4.5 Pruning more layers

In our main pruning experiments (cf. Section 3.3), we pruned only 8 layers based on layer importance evaluation. We decided to experiment with pruning more layers to explore the level to which a model can be pruned while keeping a similar level of translation performance. As Table 6 illustrates, we compare pruning 8, 10, 12, and 16 layers. We observe that the quality after pruning up to 12 layers and fine-tuning the pruned model on the ACL 60/60 dataset is close to pruning 8 layers. However, when pruning 16 layers, the quality starts to degrade considerably. It is worth noting that the results reported in Table 6 are only for the pruning and initial fine-tuning steps, while Section 3.3 describes the whole process that involves knowledge distillation, extra compression with quantization, and further fine-tuning with QLoRA.

Pruning reduces storage footprint while accelerating inference speed by approximately 20% and 40% when 8 and 16 layers are pruned, respectively, compared to the unpruned baseline, after full-parameter fine-tuning of both models on the

English-to-German in-domain data. In contrast, 4-bit quantization as implemented in QLoRA reduces storage at the cost of inference speed. Given that the shared task prioritized minimizing storage requirements, we applied QLoRA to the pruned model in the final fine-tuning stage. For deployment scenarios where inference speed is critical, however, the pruned model can be fine-tuned with standard LoRA instead of QLoRA to avoid quantization overhead.

4.6 Fine-tuning before/after pruning

It is common to fine-tune pruned models *after* pruning (Kim et al., 2023). As we pruned 1/4 of the decoder layers, obtaining valid translations for German was not possible without further training (cf. Table 2). Similarly, fine-tuning the teacher model on in-domain data *before* pruning is especially recommended for downstream tasks (Li et al., 2020).

4.7 Out-of-Domain Data Size

After layer pruning, we added more data for fine-tuning the pruned model to recover the translation quality of the teacher model. We mixed the in-domain data (ACL 60/60), knowledge distillation data, and out-of-domain data from the CoVoST2 dataset. We experimented with different sizes of out-of-domain data, namely 10k, 50k, 80k and 100k randomly sampled segments.

Data Size	BLEU	chrF++	COMET
10k	37.83	63.84	48.90
50k	38.47	64.09	54.56
80k	**40.24**	65.04	54.75
100k	39.59	**65.14**	**59.21**

Table 8: Investigating the effect of the data sizes used from the out-of-domain CoVoST2 dataset. Increasing out-of-domain data from 10k to 50k or 80k improves the translation quality on the English-to-German test split of the ACL 60/60 dataset. When increasing the out-of-domain data from 80k to 100k, this only improves the COMET score, but not the BLEU and chrF++ scores.

As Table 8 shows, for English-to-German translation, increasing the data size from 10k to 50k and 80k segments improves the overall performance. However, increasing the data size to 100k has diminishing returns, especially in terms of BLEU and chrF++ scores, while it improves the COMET score.

5 Inference and Evaluation

For inference, we use greedy generation by disabling the sampling options. We apply the prompt illustrated in Section 4.1. We use a batch size of 1, and set the generation max length to 1024 tokens.

To evaluate our systems, we calculated BLEU (Papineni et al., 2002), chrF++ (Popović, 2017), as implemented in the sacreBLEU library[7] (Post, 2018). While we use chrF++ for German, we use raw chrF for Chinese, following the author of the metric who noted that "the concept of *Chinese words* is generally not clear" (Popović, 2017). For semantic evaluation, we use COMET (Rei et al., 2020).[8] Table 1 and Table 2 report the results of the main experiments. Moreover, we conduct an ablation study (cf. Section 4) to investigate the effect of modifying some aspects of our experiments, such as the baseline model, the pruning approach, the number of pruned layers, and the data size.

6 Conclusions and Future Work

In this work, we showed that combining multiple compression techniques enables substantial model size reduction with minimal impact on speech translation performance. To conclude, QLoRA fine-tuning with knowledge distillation achieved superior translation quality compared to layer pruning alone, though with reduced model compression. To achieve higher compression ratios while preserving translation quality, we employed a combined approach using iterative layer pruning, quantization, knowledge distillation, and multi-stage fine-tuning. The code of our experiments is publicly available.[9]

In future work, we plan to explore adaptive compression strategies that dynamically adjust pruning levels and quantization precision based on real-time deployment constraints such as memory limits and latency requirements. Additionally, we aim to evaluate our compression techniques across more diverse datasets, including both authentic and synthetic training data, to better understand the generalization capabilities of our approach. Given that Qwen2-Audio-Instruct relies on text prompts for generation, it would be interesting to investigate retrieval-augmented generation with few-shot prompting to improve the translation quality of compressed models.

[7]https://github.com/mjpost/sacrebleu

[8]In particular, we used the *"wmt20-comet-da"* model.

[9]https://github.com/ymoslem/Model-Compression

References

Idris Abdulmumin, Victor Agostinelli, Tanel Alumäe, Antonios Anastasopoulos, Ashwin, Luisa Bentivogli, Ondřej Bojar, Claudia Borg, Fethi Bougares, Roldano Cattoni, Mauro Cettolo, Lizhong Chen, William Chen, Raj Dabre, Yannick Estève, Marcello Federico, Marco Gaido, Dávid Javorský, Marek Kasztelnik, Tsz Kin Lam, Danni Liu, Evgeny Matusov, Chandresh Kumar Maurya, John P McCrae, Salima Mdhaffar, Yasmin Moslem, Kenton Murray, Satoshi Nakamura, Matteo Negri, Jan Niehues, Atul Kr Ojha, John E Ortega, Sara Papi, Pavel Pecina, Peter Polák, Piotr Połeć, Beatrice Savoldi, Nivedita Sethiya, Claytone Sikasote, Matthias Sperber, Sebastian Stüker, Katsuhito Sudoh, Brian Thompson, Marco Turchi, Alex Waibel, Patrick Wilken, Rodolfo Zevallos, Vilém Zouhar, and Maike Züfle. 2025. Findings of the IWSLT 2025 Evaluation Campaign. In *Proceedings of the 22nd International Conference on Spoken Language Translation (IWSLT 2025)*, Vienna, Austria (in-person and online). Association for Computational Linguistics.

Yunfei Chu, Jin Xu, Qian Yang, Haojie Wei, Xipin Wei, Zhifang Guo, Yichong Leng, Yuanjun Lv, Jinzheng He, Junyang Lin, Chang Zhou, and Jingren Zhou. 2024. Qwen2-Audio Technical Report. *arXiv [eess.AS]*.

Yunfei Chu, Jin Xu, Xiaohuan Zhou, Qian Yang, Shiliang Zhang, Zhijie Yan, Chang Zhou, and Jingren Zhou. 2023. Qwen-audio: Advancing universal audio understanding via unified large-scale audio-language models. *arXiv [eess.AS]*.

Josep Crego and Jean Senellart. 2016. Neural Machine Translation from Simplified Translations. *arXiv [cs.CL]*.

Tim Dettmers, Artidoro Pagnoni, Ari Holtzman, and Luke Zettlemoyer. 2023. QLoRA: Efficient Finetuning of Quantized LLMs. *arXiv [cs.LG]*.

Sanchit Gandhi, Patrick von Platen, and Alexander M Rush. 2023. Distil-Whisper: Robust knowledge distillation via large-scale pseudo labelling. *arXiv [cs.CL]*.

Edward J Hu, Yelong Shen, Phillip Wallis, Zeyuan Allen-Zhu, Yuanzhi Li, Shean Wang, Lu Wang, and Weizhu Chen. 2021. LoRA: Low-Rank Adaptation of Large Language Models. *arXiv [cs.CL]*.

Wandri Jooste, Andy Way, Rejwanul Haque, and Riccardo Superbo. 2022. Knowledge Distillation for Sustainable Neural Machine Translation. In *Proceedings of the 15th Biennial Conference of the Association for Machine Translation in the Americas (Volume 2: Users and Providers Track and Government Track)*, pages 221–230, Orlando, USA. Association for Machine Translation in the Americas.

Damjan Kalajdzievski. 2023. A rank stabilization scaling factor for fine-tuning with LoRA. *arXiv [cs.CL]*.

Dahyun Kim, Chanjun Park, Sanghoon Kim, Wonsung Lee, Wonho Song, Yunsu Kim, Hyeonwoo Kim, Yungi Kim, Hyeonju Lee, Jihoo Kim, Changbae Ahn, Seonghoon Yang, Sukyung Lee, Hyunbyung Park, Gyoungjin Gim, Mikyoung Cha, Hwalsuk Lee, and Sunghun Kim. 2023. SOLAR 10.7B: Scaling large language models with simple yet effective depth upscaling. *arXiv [cs.CL]*.

Yoon Kim and Alexander M Rush. 2016. Sequence-Level Knowledge Distillation. In *Proceedings of the 2016 Conference on Empirical Methods in Natural Language Processing*, pages 1317–1327, Austin, Texas. Association for Computational Linguistics.

Quentin Lhoest, Albert Villanova del Moral, Yacine Jernite, Abhishek Thakur, Patrick von Platen, Suraj Patil, Julien Chaumond, Mariama Drame, Julien Plu, Lewis Tunstall, Joe Davison, Mario Šaško, Gunjan Chhablani, Bhavitvya Malik, Simon Brandeis, Teven Le Scao, Victor Sanh, Canwen Xu, Nicolas Patry, Angelina McMillan-Major, Philipp Schmid, Sylvain Gugger, Clément Delangue, Théo Matussière, Lysandre Debut, Stas Bekman, Pierric Cistac, Thibault Goehringer, Victor Mustar, François Lagunas, Alexander Rush, and Thomas Wolf. 2021. Datasets: A community library for natural language processing. In *Proceedings of the 2021 Conference on Empirical Methods in Natural Language Processing: System Demonstrations*, pages 175–184, Stroudsburg, PA, USA. Association for Computational Linguistics.

Zhuohan Li, Eric Wallace, Sheng Shen, Kevin Lin, K Keutzer, D Klein, and Joseph E Gonzalez. 2020. Train large, then compress: Rethinking model size for efficient training and inference of transformers. In *Proceedings of the 37th International Conference on Machine Learning (ICML 2020)*, pages 5958–5968, Virtual.

Kishore Papineni, Salim Roukos, Todd Ward, and Wei-Jing Zhu. 2002. Bleu: a Method for Automatic Evaluation of Machine Translation. In *Proceedings of the 40th Annual Meeting of the Association for Computational Linguistics*, pages 311–318, Philadelphia, Pennsylvania, USA. Association for Computational Linguistics.

David Peer, Sebastian Stabinger, Stefan Engl, and Antonio Rodríguez-Sánchez. 2022. Greedy-layer pruning: Speeding up transformer models for natural language processing. *Pattern Recognit. Lett.*, 157:76–82.

Yifan Peng, Jaesong Lee, and Shinji Watanabe. 2023a. I3D: Transformer architectures with input-dependent dynamic depth for speech recognition. In *ICASSP 2023 - 2023 IEEE International Conference on Acoustics, Speech and Signal Processing (ICASSP)*, pages 1–5. IEEE.

Yifan Peng, Yui Sudo, Shakeel Muhammad, and Shinji Watanabe. 2023b. DPHuBERT: Joint Distillation and Pruning of Self-Supervised Speech Models. In *Proceedings of the 24th Annual Conference of the*

International Speech Communication Association, InterSpeech 2023, pages 62–66.

Maja Popović. 2017. chrF++: words helping character n-grams. In *Proceedings of the Second Conference on Machine Translation*, pages 612–618, Copenhagen, Denmark. Association for Computational Linguistics.

Matt Post. 2018. A Call for Clarity in Reporting BLEU Scores. In *Proceedings of the Third Conference on Machine Translation: Research Papers*, pages 186–191, Brussels, Belgium. Association for Computational Linguistics.

Ricardo Rei, Craig Stewart, Ana C Farinha, and Alon Lavie. 2020. COMET: A Neural Framework for MT Evaluation. In *Proceedings of the 2020 Conference on Empirical Methods in Natural Language Processing (EMNLP)*, pages 2685–2702, Online. Association for Computational Linguistics.

Pedram Rostami and Mohammad Javad Dousti. 2024. CULL-MT: Compression using language and layer pruning for machine translation. *arXiv [cs.CL]*.

Hassan Sajjad, Fahim Dalvi, Nadir Durrani, and Preslav Nakov. 2023. On the effect of dropping layers of pre-trained transformer models. *Comput. Speech Lang.*, 77(101429):101429.

Elizabeth Salesky, Kareem Darwish, Mohamed Al-Badrashiny, Mona Diab, and Jan Niehues. 2023. Evaluating multilingual speech translation under realistic conditions with resegmentation and terminology. In *Proceedings of the 20th International Conference on Spoken Language Translation (IWSLT 2023)*, pages 62–78, Stroudsburg, PA, USA. Association for Computational Linguistics.

Marcos Treviso, Ji-Ung Lee, Tianchu Ji, Betty van Aken, Qingqing Cao, Manuel R Ciosici, Michael Hassid, Kenneth Heafield, Sara Hooker, Colin Raffel, Pedro H Martins, André F T Martins, Jessica Zosa Forde, Peter Milder, Edwin Simpson, Noam Slonim, Jesse Dodge, Emma Strubell, Niranjan Balasubramanian, Leon Derczynski, Iryna Gurevych, and Roy Schwartz. 2023. Efficient methods for natural language processing: A survey. *Transactions of the Association for Computational Linguistics*, 11:826–860.

Ashish Vaswani, Noam Shazeer, Niki Parmar, Jakob Uszkoreit, Llion Jones, Aidan N Gomez, Lukasz Kaiser, and Illia Polosukhin. 2017. Attention Is All You Need. In *Advances in Neural Information Processing Systems (NIPS 2017)*, volume 30. Curran Associates, Inc.

Changhan Wang, Anne Wu, and Juan Pino. 2021. CoVoST 2 and Massively Multilingual Speech-to-Text Translation. In *Proceedings of the 22nd Annual Conference of the International Speech Communication Association, InterSpeech 2021*, pages 2247–2251.

Haoyu Wang, Siyuan Wang, Wei-Qiang Zhang, Suo Hongbin, and Yulong Wan. 2023. Task-Agnostic Structured Pruning of Speech Representation Models. In *Proceedings of the 24th Annual Conference of the International Speech Communication Association, InterSpeech 2023*, pages 231–235.

Haryo Akbarianto Wibowo, Haiyue Song, Hideki Tanaka, Masao Utiyama, Alham Fikri Aji, and Raj Dabre. 2025. IteRABRe: Iterative recovery-aided block reduction. *arXiv [cs.CL]*.

Thomas Wolf, Lysandre Debut, Victor Sanh, Julien Chaumond, Clement Delangue, Anthony Moi, Pierric Cistac, Tim Rault, Remi Louf, Morgan Funtowicz, Joe Davison, Sam Shleifer, Patrick von Platen, Clara Ma, Yacine Jernite, Julien Plu, Canwen Xu, Teven Le Scao, Sylvain Gugger, Mariama Drame, Quentin Lhoest, and Alexander Rush. 2020. Transformers: State-of-the-art natural language processing. In *Proceedings of the 2020 Conference on Empirical Methods in Natural Language Processing: System Demonstrations*, pages 38–45, Stroudsburg, PA, USA. Association for Computational Linguistics.

Simultaneous Translation with Offline Speech and LLM Models in CUNI Submission to IWSLT 2025

Dominik Macháček and Peter Polák

Charles University, Faculty of Mathematics and Physics,
Institute of Formal and Applied Linguistics, Czech Republic
{machacek,polak}@ufal.mff.cuni.cz

Abstract

This paper describes Charles University submission to the Simultaneous Speech Translation Task of the IWSLT 2025. We cover all four language pairs with a direct or cascade approach. The backbone of our systems is the offline Whisper speech model, which we use for both translation and transcription in simultaneous mode with the state-of-the-art simultaneous policy AlignAtt. We further improve the performance by prompting to inject in-domain terminology, and we accommodate context. Our cascaded systems further use EuroLLM for unbounded simultaneous translation. Compared to the Organizers' baseline, our systems improve by 2 BLEU points on Czech to English and 13-22 BLEU points on English to German, Chinese and Japanese on the development sets. Additionally, we also propose a new enhanced measure of speech recognition latency.

1 Introduction

In this paper, we describe the submission of the Charles University (CUNI) system to IWSLT 2025 Simultaneous Speech Translation Task (Abdulmumin et al., 2025). Our system is built on top of Whisper (Radford et al., 2022) with AlignAtt (Papi et al., 2023) simultaneous policy. To achieve higher translation quality, we apply beam search and prompting for in-domain terminology. In our end-to-end system for the Czech-to-English translation, we also exploit previous translations as a context. For the translation into German, Chinese, and Japanese, we adopted a cascaded approach consisting of Whisper for English ASR and EuroLLM (Martins et al., 2025) for translation. We validate our systems' latency in computationally unaware simulation. Our Czech-to-English systems work both in 2-second and 4-second latency regimes required by IWSLT 2025 ("low" and "high"). The English-to-German, Chinese and Japanese systems are available only in the high-latency regime of 4-5 seconds. For an overview of our systems, see Table 1.

Our main goal in this submission is to create a robust and straightforward implementation that can be used in further research as well as in many realistic use cases. We name the implementation **SimulStreaming** and publish it at `https://github.com/ufal/SimulStreaming`.

Among the strengths of our submitted system is very high quality, because of using high-performing foundation models, and very high multilinguality. Whisper allows direct translation from 99 speech source languages to English, and EuroLLM allows English translation into 35 languages. Our systems are also adaptable; the prompts and in-context learning allow injecting specific in-domain terminology.

Moreover, although we primarily focus on computationally unaware latency, our system is practically usable in real time only with feasible hardware resources. It requires hosting Whisper large 1.6B parameters model and and the EuroLLM 9B parameters model.

Our second goal is to evaluate the state-of-the-art methods in combination. Our results show improvements by 2 BLEU points on Czech to English over the organizers baseline, and 13-22 BLEU points on English to German, Chinese, and Japanese, which highlights the effectiveness of our systems.

We conclude we have reached both goals. The original contributions of this work is the SimulStreaming implementation and evaluation, and also a new enhanced method for measuring ASR latency using Continuous Levenshtein Alignment (see Section 5.1).

2 Background

Whisper is among the top-performing ASR and speech translation models for 99 languages. It has the ability to use initial and context prompts,

Proceedings of the 22nd International Conference on Spoken Language Translation (IWSLT 2025), pages 389–398
July 31 - August 1, 2025

		Cs-En	En-{De,Zh,Ja}
Speech-to-text	model	Whisper large-v3	Whisper large-v3
	task	translate to En	transcribe En
	beam	yes	no
	prompt	yes	no
	context	yes	no
	simult. policy	AlignAtt	AlignAtt
+ Text-to-text	model	-	EuroLLM-9B-Instruct
	prompt	-	yes
	context	-	yes
	simult. policy	-	LocalAgreement
Latency regime	2 seconds ("low")	yes	no
	4-5 seconds ("high")	yes	yes

Table 1: Overview of CUNI systems submissions to IWSLT 2025 Simultaneous Speech Translation Task.

which makes it adaptable for in-domain terminology. Works such as Macháček et al. (2023b) and Wang et al. (2024) show that Whisper is adaptable to simultaneous mode, although it is primarily designed for offline mode. Whisper is available in multiple model versions that differ in size and quality. We use the large-v3 model, which achieves the highest quality.

AlignAtt (Papi et al., 2023) is a simultaneous policy. Given an offline translation model, partial source and previous target, it detects where to stop generating the partial target, which is when the most attended source frame by the decoder is behind a threshold. Papi et al. (2023) shows that this policy outperforms all previously proposed policies. Wang et al. (2024) later showed that AlignAtt also works with Whisper.

LocalAgreement (Polák et al., 2022, 2023) is a simultaneous policy that considers the target prefixes of two subsequent updates, each processing a newly incoming source chunk. It emits their longest common prefix as confirmed and uses it in forced decoding of the latter chunks.

Simul-Whisper (Wang et al., 2024) is an implementation of the simultaneous mode with Whisper using AlignAtt. It is an extension of the original OpenAI Whisper inference using the Torch deep learning framework. Simul-Whisper supports only ASR of speech that is segmented into individual sentences, and computationally unaware simulation, while the IWSLT 2025 Simultaneous Task focuses on a more realistic case of unbounded speech (Papi et al., 2025) without any explicit sentence boundaries. On the other hand, **Whisper-Streaming** (Macháček et al., 2023b) is our implementation of Whisper with the LocalAgreement simultaneous policy and reprocessing the audio buffer from the beginning with every incoming source chunk, which is less computationally effective than AlignAtt. On the other hand, Whisper-Streaming supports both computationally aware and unaware simulations, as well as unbounded speech. It integrates Silero VAD (Team, 2024) that incrementally detects silence and non-voice sounds vs. voice.

EuroLLM (Martins et al., 2025) is a recent large language model for text-to-text translation between 35 EU and non-EU languages, including English, German, Japanese, and Chinese. It is a decoder-only model of the LLaMA family. We use its 9B parameter version with instruction tuning. It supports a system prompt, which can be used to suggest the domain, and a maximum context of 4096 tokens, which spans over 10 minutes of English source and German target of ACL 6060 (Salesky et al., 2023) dev set reference (see estimation in Appendix A). We use EuroLLM with the fast inference framework CTranslate2. It enables fast computation and efficient memory usage; however, it currently does not provide access to attention weights. Therefore, we can not apply the AlignAtt policy to EuroLLM, so we use it with the LocalAgreement simultaneous policy, which is the best-performing policy that does not require attention weights.

3 Direct Simultaneous Speech-to-Text with Whisper and AlignAtt

Let us describe the process of simultaneous speech-to-text processing, which we apply to direct Czech-to-English translation and to English ASR in the cascaded system for English to German, Chinese, and Japanese.

Our system uses our implementation called SimulStreaming which merges the Simul-Whisper AlignAtt policy with the Whisper-Streaming interface to support unbounded speech processing. Moreover, we extend the original Simul-Whisper with the following enhancements. First, we added support for the Whisper large-v3 model. Second, in addition to transcription, we enabled translation. Then, to improve quality, we implement beam search decoding. Finally, we incorporate support for initial prompts and contextual information from the preceding audio buffers.

Our simultaneous speech-to-text pipeline consists of the prototypical processing steps that are described in Papi et al. (2025), Section 3.1.

1. Audio acquisition.

2. Audio segmentation. Silero Voice Activity Detection (VAD) iterator with the same default parameters as in Whisper-Streaming is applied (minimum chunk size 0.04 seconds, minimum non-voice duration 500 ms, voice is padded with 100 ms). When VAD detects non-voice in the 0.04-second chunk, the chunk is discarded. When VAD detects voice, it holds it until *MinChunkSize*[1] seconds of voiced audio accumulate, or until the end of voice is detected. The accumulated voiced audio is passed to the next step.

3. Speech buffer update. The incoming chunk, which has *MinChunkSize* seconds if the end of voice is not detected, or less otherwise, is concatenated with the speech buffer.

4. Hypothesis generation. Whisper large-v3 model encodes the speech buffer and populates the decoder's Key-Value cache with the representation of the optional initial prompt, previous context, and forced-decoded target prefix. Then the model decodes the target as long as the AlignAtt policy allows. If the current chunk is not final, the decoding continues until the most attended source frame is close to the end of the audio, which is indicated by the *Frames* parameter. In our proposed beam search implementation, we decode until the top beam hypothesis is attended behind the threshold. In case the current chunk is final, we decode until the last 4 frames, as the Simul-Whisper authors propose.

5. Buffers selection. There are the following four buffers in our implementation: (1) source audio buffer, (2) forced decoding target buffer that contains the stable part of the hypothesis that was decoded from current audio buffer, (3) context buffer, which is the transcript or translation from the audio segments that were pushed away from the audio buffer, and (4) initial prompt, for example a text that can contain terminology or initiate the style of decoding.

   If the audio buffer has the length of *BufferLength* seconds or more, we remove the first speech chunk from the source audio buffer. At the same time, we move the text that was decoded with the first chunk from the forced decoding to the context buffer. If the initial prompt and context are longer than *MaxContextLength*, we trim the complete words from the beginning. A parameter *StaticPrompt* specifies whether the initial prompt is pushed away with the context or not.

   If finalization is triggered, that is, when the source recording is finished, or when the end of voice was detected, the buffers are cleared.

4 Simultaneous Translation with EuroLLM

We implement EuroLLM simultaneous translation using a chat template. We design a system prompt asking the model to perform simultaneous interpreting at a conference and specifying the translation direction. The chat is followed by the user's message containing the source prefix, and by the assistant's reply that contains the previous target prefix to continue. The chat is initiated with one sentence pair as an in-context example because we observed that without that, the model tends to produce text that is not a translation, especially for a short source.

Our simultaneous translation consists of steps that are analogous to the prototypical ones in Papi et al. (2025):

1. Source acquisition: The punctuated text produced by the simultaneous Whisper English ASR.

2. Segmentation: Because we assume computational unaware mode and English as the

[1]We mark the system parameters that we tune with italics.

source language, we segment the source into individual words by spaces. A parameter *MinChunkSize* specifies the number of new words in each update.

3. Buffer update: The newly incoming source words are appended to the previous source.

4. Buffer trimming: In our initial experiments, we observed that the model tends to hallucinate with larger context. Therefore, we trim the source-target buffer if it has more tokens than *MaxContextLength*. We apply one of the two buffer trimming strategies:

   (a) *Sentences*: Detect sentences by punctuation in the source and target, trim the first sentence in the source and target, while the context length is too large and there is at least one sentence left in each buffer. This strategy assumes that there is a one-to-one correspondence between the source and target sentences. This strategy seems to be sufficient for English-to-German translation, but not for English to Chinese and Japanese.

   (b) *Segments*: The source-target buffer contains the source-target pairs as they were received and generated, including empty targets. If the buffer is too long, one pair is trimmed. Although the buffer is not completely parallel and the source is typically more ahead, this strategy appears to be more optimal for English-to-Chinese and Japanese translations than *Sentences*. Additionally, this strategy does not require processing a slow parallel word-alignment model.

5. Hypothesis generation: The source and target buffers are transformed into the chat tokens as described above. EuroLLM's reply is generated. The new target prefix is compared to the one from the previous update, and their longest common prefix (LocalAgreement policy) is considered as a newly confirmed hypothesis. The unconfirmed hypothesis suffix is held for confirmation with the following update.

5 Development

Dev sets For English-to-German, Chinese, and Japanese translations, we use the ACL6060 development set as provided by the IWSLT organizers. For Czech-to-English translation, we use the IWSLT 2025 dev set. However, we found that the ParCzech subset is segmented in this dev set, while the 2025 test set will be unsegmented. Therefore, we merged the subsequent segments from the same speech. Since there were two very diverse subsets, ParCzech and Robothon, we selected the final candidate based on the average of quality scores on the merged ParCzech and Robothon. Finally, to meet the shared task conditions, we filtered out the candidates that did not meet the latency criteria on the unsegmented dev set.

MT metric We selected the primary candidates using ChrF because ChrF tends to be more reliable than BLEU in simultaneous translation (Macháček et al., 2023a).

Translation Latency For translation latency, we use the StreamLAAL metric (SLAAL, Papi et al., 2024) as proposed by IWSLT organizers. For English ASR latency, we use the following algorithm.

5.1 ASR Latency with Continuous Levenshtein Alignment

We propose an improvement of the algorithm for the average word latency of the ASR. We call it "ASR Latency with Continuous Levenshtein Alignment." The improvement over existing methods stems from (1) the more accurate character-level alignment and (2) minimum edit distance alignment that prefers continuous sequences of edit operations to prevent coincident alignment to deleted or inserted segments that would contribute to unrealistic latency. The algorithm is as follows.

Assume a gold transcript with word-level timestamps and an ASR transcript where each word is assigned its emission time.

First, create a dynamic programming matrix for the Levenshtein minimum edit distance alignment of the gold and ASR transcript at the character level. Character-level alignment is more accurate than word-level because it is more robust to minor deviations from the gold transcripts, such as suffixes, when the other part of the word is correct. The disadvantage is computation and memory complexity, which is quadratic, and therefore much higher on characters than on words. However, we were able to compute roughly 12 minutes of transcripts in a feasible time. Longer transcripts can be segmented.

gold	t h e ␣ t a b l e
interrupted alignment	t a b l e
edit operations	C D D D D C C C C
continuous alignment	t a b l e
edit operations	D D D D C C C C C

Figure 1: Illustration of interrupted vs. continuous alignment of the ASR candidate "table" to the gold "the table". Both alignments have identical edit distance (4 Deletions, 5 Copies), but the bottom one includes a longer continuous sequence of Copies. The interrupted alignment is incorrect.

Second, when generating the minimum distance alignment, prioritize continuous sequences of Copy or Substitute operations over interruptions with Deletes or Inserts. The illustration is in Figure 1. The reason is to prevent alignment to deleted segments too far ahead or behind, which would lead to incorrect latency.

Third, convert aligned characters to the sequence of aligned words. Fourth, for each word in the transcript that is aligned to any gold word, estimate its latency as the word's emission time minus the timestamp of its gold-aligned word. Fifth, report the average word latency.

We publish an implementation of the ASR Latency with Continuous Levenshtein Alignment at `https://github.com/ufal/asr_latency`.

6 Results

6.1 Czech-to-English Translation

For the Czech-to-English translation, we use the direct speech translation with Whisper and AlignAtt policy. First, we investigate the impact of *Beams* and *BufferLength*. For that, we use a 30-minute subset of the merged ParCzech dev set.

Beam search We set the *MaxContextLength* to 0, *BufferLength* to 25 seconds, *Frames* threshold to 4, and *MinChunkSize* to 3 seconds. Table 2 contains MT quality scores with different *Beams*. We observe a ChrF score improvement by 1.04 with 5 beams compared to 1. With *Beams* 4 and 8, we observe analogous gains, with maximum at 5 beams. The latency (SLAAL) decreases negligibly with higher beams.

Buffer Length Then, we investigated the *BufferLength* parameter. The setup is the same as with beam search, except that we set *MinChunkSize* to 1.75 seconds and *Frames* to 4. Table 3 shows the results. Maximum quality is with *BufferLength* 30 seconds. We observe analogous results with *Frames* set to 80.

Beams	1	2	6	5
ChrF	48.03	48.77	48.89	**49.07**
SLAAL	2373	2393	2308	2285

Table 2: Impact of beam search on MT quality (ChrF) and latency (SLAAL) in milliseconds.

BufferLength	15	20	25	28	30
ChrF	47.65	48.09	48.24	48.67	**48.78**
SLAAL	2698	2627	2830	2920	2928

Table 3: Impact of *BufferLength* on MT quality (ChrF) and latency (SLAAL) in milliseconds.

Therefore, we further set *BufferLength* to 30 seconds.

Grid search Then, we perform grid search to find the optimal *MinChunkSize*, *Frames*, and *Beams* parameters to meet the low-latency threshold of the IWSLT 2025 Simultaneous task, which is below SLAAL 2000ms, and the high-latency threshold below 4000ms SLAAL. For that, we used the merged ParCzech and Robothon portions of the dev set, and we averaged their ChrF score. We found 4 candidates for the low-latency regime that were near 2000 SLAAL. Their scores are in Table 4. For high latency, we selected one candidate.

Prompt and Context We experimented with *MaxContextLength*, which can be between 0 and 255 tokens, as Whisper's documentation suggests, and *Prompt*, which can be any text that initiates decoding. Moreover, the prompt can be *StaticPrompt*, which stays at the beginning of decoding for all buffers, or *NonStaticPrompt*, which means it is pushed away by context that reaches maximum

MinChunkSize	*Frames*	ChrF	SLAAL
1.2	25	49.72	1715
1.4	35	49.75	2091
1.6	25	49.83	2166
1.4	30	49.83	2067
1.8	25	49.93	2636

Table 4: Pre-selected top candidates for low latency (upper part of table, with SLAAL near 2000) and high latency (lower part) by average ChrF on the merged ParCzech and Robothon portions of the dev set. All of them are with 2 *Beams*.

length.

We optimize for two subsets of the Czech-to-English test set in IWSLT 2025: the native ParCzech subset, and the non-native subset for which we have no other information. We assume that the ParCzech are speeches from the plenary sessions of the Chamber of Deputies, Parliament of the Czech Republic, similarly to the dev set. We noticed a specific terminology that the Whisper model is not aware of. For example, the terms "Chamber of Deputies," "deputy," and "chairman" are often missing. They are alternated with terms such as "Senate", "MP", "Ambassador", and "President", which are wrong in the ParCzech domain. Therefore, we attempted to inject these terms via prompting.

We proposed 13 prompts, 9 of which were specific to the ParCzech, and 4 of them were general, applicable to any domain. We evaluated these prompts on the ParCzech portion of the dev set with all static or non-static prompts and varying context lengths. We discovered that half of the prompts increased the performance over the baseline, while the other half decreased it.

In the end, the prompt "This is Chamber of Deputies." reached the highest quality score. We use this as the static prompt for the ParCzech domain with *MaxContextLength* 20 for high latency, where it increased ChrF by 0.45, and with *MaxContextLength* 250 for low latency, where it increased ChrF by 0.61. For the general domain, we use no context and no prompt for the high latency, and the non-static prompt "He starts." with *MaxContextLength* 250 for the low latency, as it gained 0.24 ChrF improvement. Table 5 summarizes our observations.

Comparison to the IWSLT 2025 Baseline Although we do not consider validation on the segmented dev set as the most relevant for evaluation on unbounded speech, which is the primary objective in the IWSLT 2025 Simultaneous task, we validate our primary candidate on the segmented dev set and compare it to the IWSLT 2025 organizers' baseline. Their system that reached the highest BLEU score while having SLAAL below 4000 (high latency) was a cascade system with Whisper ASR and M2M100 MT (Fan et al., 2021). Similarly, their top-scoring system for the low-latency regime was the SeamlessM4T (Seamless Communication et al., 2023) direct speech translation model with VAD Segmenter. The scores are compared in Table 6.

	low	**high**
baseline ChrF	49.67	49.78
context	0	0
prompt	-	-
ChrF	**50.28**	**50.23**
context	250	20
prompt	ParCzech, static	ParCzech, st.
ChrF	49.91	49.78
context	250	0
prompt	general, non-st.	-

Table 5: ChrF on the merged ParCzech portion of the dev set with the top performing prompt and context setup with the prompt adapted to the ParCzech domain (middle section of the table), or a general prompt (lower section).

	BLEU	ChrF	SLAAL
baseline low	15.16	-	1777
our low	**18.49**	48.51	1763
baseline high	16.63	-	3996
our high	**18.83**	48.86	2630

Table 6: Comparison of IWLST 2025 organizers' baseline on the segmented Czech-to-English dev set.

We conclude that in the Czech-to-English simultaneous translation, we outperformed the organizers' baseline by 3.3 BLEU in the low latency and by 2.2 BLEU in the high latency regime.

6.2 English ASR

We use Whisper with AlignAtt for simultaneous English ASR. We set *BufferLength* to 30 seconds (maximum). Since Whisper with AlignAtt reached very high quality on the English ASR of the ACL6060 domain with no prompt and no context, we did not attempt to improve it with prompt or context. We perform a grid search for the parameters *MinChunkSize*, *Frames*, and *Beams*. Unlike for Czech to English, *Beams* set to 1 performed the best in this case of English ASR. We validate with ACL6060 English dev set in computational unaware mode, measuring latency with the algorithm in Section 5.1.

Meanwhile, we validated the simultaneous translation of English to German with the gold transcripts. Given the minimum translation latency, we determined the span of latency for ASR in the cascade to fit the high latency regime of IWSLT 2025 Simultaneous task. We selected the top-performing

ref.	Chunk	Frame	WER	CER	latency
#00	0.05	4	14.22	5.10	494
#10	0.15	4	13.33	4.75	596
#11	0.25	15	13.10	4.66	754
#12	0.25	20	13.09	4.63	845
#20	0.5	10	13.40	4.81	1037
#21	0.5	15	13.35	4.71	1149
#22	0.5	20	13.06	4.64	1262
#23	1.4	15	12.98	4.76	1389
#24	1.5	10	12.92	4.85	1461
#25	1.4	25	12.77	4.76	1522
#30	2.0	20	12.69	4.77	2143

Table 7: Selected top performing English ASR candidates with various latency levels. We report % WER (range 0%-100%, the lower, the better), % CER, and latency in milliseconds on ACL6060 English dev set. The first column "ref." is a reference under which we will refer this ASR candidate.

ASR systems from the grid search with various latency levels, each roughly 100 milliseconds from the others. The scores are in Table 7. We observe very high ASR quality, around 5% CER (character error rate.

When we looked at the differences in the ASR and gold transcripts, we noticed that the differences are often not errors but a consequence of unspecified orthographical conventions, for example, swapping numerals and digits, capitalization of titles, use of quotation marks, etc. We also noticed that named entities and acronyms tend to be more often incorrect with small *MinChunkSize* than with large. This is an expected consequence of shorter context.

6.3 English to German, Chinese, and Japanese

The text-to-text simultaneous translation component of our cascade has the parameters *MinChunkSize*, *MaxContextLength*, and *BufferTrimmingStrategy*. We do not tune the system prompt nor the in-context example because we do not presume to have any further background information about the content to be translated.

Latency regime First, we processed English-to-German translation with gold ASR. We realized that the lowest possible latency, with *MinChunkSize* 1 and *MaxContextLength* 300, is 2471 SLAAL, which means that we can not fit under the low-latency threshold of 2000 SLAAL. We can target only the high-latency regime that requires SLAAL under 4000. Furthermore, we observed a lower

context	BLEU	ChrF	SLAAL
300	39.84	**67.88**	2472
500	39.71	67.44	2461
700	16.24	48.54	< 0
1000	34.51	61.35	< 0

Table 8: English to German scores with gold ASR input, *MinChunkSize* 1, and various *MaxContextLength*. The scores are on ACL6060 dev set with 5 documents. SLAAL scores less than zero (< 0) indicate hallucinations in at least one document.

quality score with *MaxContextLength* 500 than with 300, and even lower performance with longer context due to hallucinations, mostly repetitions of long sentences. The results are summarized in Table 8.

Buffer Trimming Strategy We observed many hallucinations with English-to-Chinese and Japanese with the buffer trimming strategy *Sentences*, because the assumption of matching number of source and target sentences was wrong. The buffer often contained only one source sentence and many short sentences in Chinese or Japanese. However, there were no hallucinations when we applied the *Segments* strategy instead.

Primary Candidates Finally, we performed a grid search with *MinChunkSize*, *MaxContextLength*, and the ASR candidates, and found the best ChrF scoring setup on the dev set that met the high-latency criterion. See results in Table 9, where we also compare to contrastive systems and the organizers' baseline.

We observe high improvement on each language pair, nearly 13 BLEU points on English to German, 22 BLEU on Chinese, and 18 BLEU point on Japanese. We presume that the baseline was not very strong, likely due to hallucinations of the SeamlessM4T model.

7 Conclusion

In this paper, we presented our submission to the Simultaneous Speech Translation Task of the IWSLT 2025. Using the combination of the direct approach for Czech-to-English translation and the cascaded approach for English to German, Chinese, and Japanese, we cover all language pairs of the task. To leverage the strong offline Whisper speech model and the large language model EuroLLM, we applied state-of-the-art onlinization techniques and

		BLEU	ChrF	SLAAL	ASR latency
EnDe	baseline	25.64	-	3464	-
	ASR #25, chunk 1, context 300	**38.46**	66.59	3934	1522
	ASR gold, chunk 1, context 300	39.84	67.88	2472	0
EnZh	baseline	23.96	-	3275	-
	ASR #22, chunk 1, context 100	**46.44**	40.05	3698	1262
	ASR #11, chunk 3, context 100	49.91	43.08	5449	754
EnJa	baseline	16.19	-	3662	-
	ASR #22, chunk 2, context 200	**34.69**	42.89	4654	1262

Table 9: High-latency simultaneous translation results for English to German, Chinese, and Japanese on ACL6060 dev set compared to the IWSLT 2025 organizer's baseline and the contrastive systems (grey background). The English-to-German contrastive system uses gold ASR. The English-to-Chinese one does not meet the SLAAL high latency limit of 4000 ms.

further advancements such as prompting for context and domain adaptation. Our systems achieve a substantial improvement of 2 to 22 BLEU points over the IWSLT Organizers' baseline. Moreover, we propose a new robust approach to measure speech recognition latency.

Acknowledgements

This paper has received funding from the Project OP JAK Mezisektorová spolupráce Nr. CZ.02.01.01/00/23_020/0008518 named "Jazykověda, umělá inteligence a jazykové a řečové technologie: od výzkumu k aplikacím." The authors also acknowledge the support of National Recovery Plan funded project MPO 60273/24/21300/21000 CEDMO 2.0 NPO.

References

Idris Abdulmumin, Victor Agostinelli, Tanel AlumÃ¤e, Antonios Anastasopoulos, Ashwin, Luisa Bentivogli, OndĹ™ej Bojar, Claudia Borg, Fethi Bougares, Roldano Cattoni, Mauro Cettolo, Lizhong Chen, William Chen, Raj Dabre, Yannick EstÃ¨ve, Marcello Federico, Marco Gaido, DÃ¡vid JavorskÃ½, Marek Kasztelnik, and 30 others. 2025. Findings of the iwslt 2025 evaluation campaign. In *Proceedings of the 22nd International Conference on Spoken Language Translation (IWSLT 2025)*, Vienna, Austia (in-person and online). Association for Computational Linguistics. To appear.

Angela Fan, Shruti Bhosale, Holger Schwenk, Zhiyi Ma, Ahmed El-Kishky, Siddharth Goyal, Mandeep Baines, Onur Celebi, Guillaume Wenzek, Vishrav Chaudhary, Naman Goyal, Tom Birch, Vitaliy Liptchinsky, Sergey Edunov, Edouard Grave, Michael Auli, and Armand Joulin. 2021. Beyond english-centric multilingual machine translation. *J. Mach. Learn. Res.*, 22(1).

Dominik Macháček, Ondřej Bojar, and Raj Dabre. 2023a. MT metrics correlate with human ratings of simultaneous speech translation. In *Proceedings of the 20th International Conference on Spoken Language Translation (IWSLT 2023)*, pages 169–179, Toronto, Canada (in-person and online). Association for Computational Linguistics.

Dominik Macháček, Raj Dabre, and Ondřej Bojar. 2023b. Turning whisper into real-time transcription system. In *Proceedings of the 13th International Joint Conference on Natural Language Processing and the 3rd Conference of the Asia-Pacific Chapter of the Association for Computational Linguistics: System Demonstrations*, pages 17–24, Bali, Indonesia. Association for Computational Linguistics.

Pedro Henrique Martins, Patrick Fernandes, João Alves, Nuno M. Guerreiro, Ricardo Rei, Duarte M. Alves, José Pombal, Amin Farajian, Manuel Faysse, Mateusz Klimaszewski, Pierre Colombo, Barry Haddow, José G.C. de Souza, Alexandra Birch, and André F.T. Martins. 2025. Eurollm: Multilingual language models for europe. *Procedia Computer Science*, 255:53–62. Proceedings of the Second EuroHPC user day.

Sara Papi, Marco Gaido, Matteo Negri, and Luisa Bentivogli. 2024. StreamAtt: Direct Streaming Speech-to-Text Translation with Attention-based Audio History Selection. In *Proceedings of the 62nd Annual Meeting of the Association for Computational Linguistics (Volume 1: Long Papers)*, Bangkok, Thailand.

Sara Papi, Peter Polák, Dominik Macháček, and Ondřej Bojar. 2025. How "real" is your real-time simultaneous speech-to-text translation system? *Transactions of the Association for Computational Linguistics*, 13:281–313.

Sara Papi, Marco Turchi, and Matteo Negri. 2023. AlignAtt: Using Attention-based Audio-Translation Alignments as a Guide for Simultaneous Speech Translation. In *Proc. INTERSPEECH 2023*.

Peter Polák, Ngoc-Quan Pham, Tuan Nam Nguyen, Danni Liu, Carlos Mullov, Jan Niehues, Ondřej Bojar, and Alexander Waibel. 2022. CUNI-KIT system for simultaneous speech translation task at IWSLT 2022. In *Proceedings of the 19th International Conference on Spoken Language Translation (IWSLT 2022)*, pages 277–285, Dublin, Ireland (in-person and online). Association for Computational Linguistics.

Peter Polák, Brian Yan, Shinji Watanabe, Alex Waibel, and Ondřej Bojar. 2023. Incremental Blockwise Beam Search for Simultaneous Speech Translation with Controllable Quality-Latency Tradeoff. In *Proc. INTERSPEECH 2023*, pages 3979–3983.

Alec Radford and 1 others. 2022. Robust speech recognition via large-scale weak supervision. *Preprint*, arXiv:2212.04356.

Elizabeth Salesky, Kareem Darwish, Mohamed Al-Badrashiny, Mona Diab, and Jan Niehues. 2023. Evaluating multilingual speech translation under realistic conditions with resegmentation and terminology. In *Proceedings of the 20th International Conference on Spoken Language Translation (IWSLT 2023)*, pages 62–78, Toronto, Canada (in-person and online). Association for Computational Linguistics.

Loïc Barrault Seamless Communication and 1 others. 2023. Seamless: Multilingual expressive and streaming speech translation.

Silero Team. 2024. Silero vad: pre-trained enterprise-grade voice activity detector (vad), number detector and language classifier. `https://github.com/snakers4/silero-vad`.

Haoyu Wang, Guoqiang Hu, Guodong Lin, Wei-Qiang Zhang, and Jian Li. 2024. Simul-whisper: Attention-guided streaming whisper with truncation detection. In *Interspeech 2024*, pages 4483–4487.

A Maximum Context Duration of EuroLLM

How long is the maximum context of EuroLLM in simultaneous mode, expressed in duration of long-form speech?

Consider the ACL6060 dev set reference in English, German, Japanese, and Chinese. It consists of five recordings with an average duration of 11.5 minutes. The average number of tokens per recording with the EuroLLM tokenizer for English, German, Japanese, and Chinese is in Table 10.

EuroLLM has a maximum context length of 4096 tokens. If the context contains parallel text in the source and target language, which is x-times English tokens plus x-times target tokens, and they sum up to 4096, x is the maximum proportion of recording that fits into the context. Considering average recording, EuroLLM is able to fit a maximum of 10.5 minutes of English to German translation, 10.7 minutes of English to Chinese, or 10.0 minutes of English to Japanese.

language	En	De	Zh	Ja
tokens per avg. recording (11.5 minutes)	1 963	2 550	2 423	2 637
proportion of avg. recording in context	1.04	0.91	0.93	0.87
max duration in context [minutes]	11.96	10.5	10.7	10.0

Table 10: Estimation of maximum context duration of EuroLLM translation from English to German (De), Chinese (Zh), and Japanese (Ja), considering 11.5 minutes of average ACL6060 recording, and 4096 maximum context tokens containing the same content of the source and target.

Effectively combining Phi-4 and NLLB for Spoken Language Translation: SPRING Lab IITMs submission to Low Resource Multilingual Indic Track

Sankalpa Sarkar, Samriddhi Kashyap, Advait Joglekar, S. Umesh

SPRING Lab, Indian Institute of Technology Madras

Abstract

This paper presents the methodologies implemented for Spoken Language Translation for the language pairs Hindi-English, Bengali-English and Tamil-English for the Low Resource Multilingual Indic Track of The International Conference on Spoken Language Translation (IWSLT) for 2025. We adopt a cascaded approach and use a fine-tuned Phi-4 multimodal instruct model for Automatic Speech Recognition(ASR) and a fine-tuned NLLB model for Machine Translation(MT). Finally, we discuss targeted solutions (e.g. data augmentation, multilingual training, targeted fine-tuning) to boost low-resource translation, noting that significant retraining on additional Tamil data is likely needed.

1 Introduction

India is home to an incredibly diverse linguistic landscape, with over 100 officially recognized languages and thousands of dialects spoken across its vast geographic and cultural expanse. This linguistic richness reflects the countrys deep-rooted cultural heritage and regional diversity, but it also presents considerable challenges for Natural Language Processing (NLP) applications, particularly for tasks like Automatic Speech Recognition (ASR) and Machine Translation (MT).

Unlike monolingual or relatively linguistically homogeneous countries, India's multilingualism requires NLP systems to handle a wide variety of linguistic variations from phonetic and grammatical differences to script variations and region-specific vocabulary. ASR systems must account for varied accents, pronunciation patterns, and speech styles, while MT systems are required to preserve contextual accuracy and fluency across structurally and syntactically diverse language pairs.

This diversity becomes even more complex due to situations like speakers alternate between languages mid-sentence, highly inflected words and complex verb conjugations, and lexical words from one language are integrated into another. Such features are common in Indian speech and text, making the development of robust, generalizable ASR and MT models particularly challenging.

Despite these obstacles, these technologies are crucial for millions of Indians who do not speak English or other dominant languages. ASR and MT systems can help bridge the communication barrier, enabling equal access to information, digital services, and opportunities across Indias diverse population.

The "Low Resource Multilingual Indic" track proposed by IWSLT 2025 tasked participants with developing innovative methods to work with the sparse and varied resources available for three Indian languages: Hindi, Bengali, and Tamil. The participants were required to submit under various different conditions constrained or unconstrained, end-to-end or cascaded, and monolingual or multilingual. Our team participated under the unconstrained, cascaded, and monolingual category for the language pairs Hindi to English, Bengali to English, and Tamil to English. This paper outlines the implementation of our ASR and MT systems designed for these language pairs.

2 ASR

2.1 Datasets

2.1.1 SpringLab/Hindi-1482hrs

The dataset contains 1,482 hours of quality Hindi audio, and is specifically built for performing ASR tasks.

- Curated by: SPRING Lab
- Language: Hindi

Proceedings of the 22nd International Conference on Spoken Language Translation (IWSLT 2025), pages 399–404
July 31 - August 1, 2025 ©2025 Association for Computational Linguistics

2.1.2 AI4Bharat/SeamlessAlign [1]

BhasaAnuvaad (Jain et al., 2024), is the largest Indic-language AST dataset spanning over 44,400 hours of speech and 17M text segments for 13 of 22 scheduled Indian languages and English. This repository consists of parallel data for Speech Translation from SeamlessAlign, a subset of BhasaAnuvaad. The dataset contains 5 separate splits for different languages namely: Hindi, Tamil, Telugu, Kannada and Urdu, out of which only the Hindi split is used for training the model. Although it is an AST dataset , to perform finetuning for ASR task, we utilized the audio and the transcription column.

- Curated by: AI4Bharat
- Language: Hindi

2.1.3 SKNahin/open-large-bengali-asr-data [2]

This is a collection of publicly available ASR data for Bengali. It contains 5000 hours of audio. The dataset is divided into 9 different splits namely: commonvoice (Ardila et al., 2020), openslr (Panayotov et al., 2015), madasr, shrutilipi (Bhogale et al., 2023), kathbath (Javed et al., 2022), fleurs (Conneau et al., 2022), indictts (Conneau et al., 2022), ucla and gali, out of which only the commonvoice and ucla split were used for training. We have a filtering column called is-better to filter good-quality audio from the corpus. It is set based on the wer between original transcription and prediction taken from a Bengali-Wav2Vec2 model and word-per-second (wps).

- Curated by: SKNahin
- Language: Bengali

2.1.4 Prajwal-143/ASR-Tamil-cleaned [3]

This dataset is a combination of the Common Voice 16.0 and Open SLR datasets which is of 534 hours. It has been meticulously curated, normalized to a 16kHz sampling rate, and cleaned for better usability. This dataset aims to provide a comprehensive collection of speech data for various applications, including speech recognition, natural language processing, and machine learning research.

- Curated by: Prajwal N. Pharande
- Language: Tamil

2.2 Training

In our submission, we have fine-tuned the Phi-4 Multimodal Instruct(5.57B) (Marah Abdin, 2024) to obtain three fine-tuned models for ASR Hindi, Bengali and Tamil.

The following hyper-parameters were used during training of all the models:

- Train Epochs: 1
- Learning Rate: 4.0e-5
- Batch Size: 8
- Gradient Accumulation Steps: 4
- Optimizer: Paged Adamw 32-bit with betas=(0.9,0.999)
- LR scheduler type: cosine
- LR scheduler warmup steps: 1000
- Weight Decay: 0.01
- Max Grad Norm: 1.0

We trained the Hindi model for a total of 28263 steps on the SpringLab/Hindi-1482 hrs dataset and 31911 on the AI4Bharat/SeamlessAlign (Jain et al., 2024) dataset, the Bengali model for a total of 30113 steps on the commonvoice (Ardila et al., 2020) split and 60035 steps on the ucla split for SKNahin/open-large-bengali-asr-data dataset, finally the Tamil model for a total of 7018 steps on the Prajwal-143/ASR-Tamil-cleaned dataset. We trained the model only for 1 epoch to avoid overfitting

2.3 Evaluation

The Evaluation results for all the three models were performed on the mozilla-foundation/common-voice-17-0 (Ardila et al., 2020) [4] dataset (test split). The scores for the ASR are recorded in terms of WER and CER, listed in Table 1

[1] https://huggingface.co/datasets/ai4bharat/SeamlessAlign

[2] https://huggingface.co/datasets/SKNahin/open-large-bengali-asr-data

[3] https://huggingface.co/datasets/Prajwal-143/ASR-Tamil-cleaned

[4] https://huggingface.co/datasets/mozilla-foundation/common-voice-17-0

Language	WER	CER
Hindi	0.15156	0.06526
Bengali	0.21968	0.06288
Tamil	0.41953	0.07078

Table 1: Scores for the ASR in terms of WER and CER.

2.3.1 ASR Performance

The ASR outputs were passed to the MT stage. Errors in ASR propagate to MT, so ASR accuracy is critical. ASR errors included substitutions (e.g., similar-sounding words), deletions (inflectional suffixes), and insertions (extra syllables). Tamil had the highest WER, indicating more ASR errors.

The relatively high WER for Tamil ASR (over 0.4) can be attributed to the limited training dataonly about 200 hours were available for Tamil, in contrast to over 1,000 hours used for Hindi and Bengali. Furthermore, the Phi-4 base model used does not offer native support for Indic languages, which meant the performance for Tamil relied solely on the quality of fine-tuning.

To assess the generalization ability of our ASR models and avoid overfitting, we chose to train all language models for only one epoch. For Hindi and Bengali, which had large training sets, this approach provided sufficient exposure while maintaining regularization. Although this uniform strategy may have under exploited the Tamil dataset, it allowed us to clearly isolate data volume as a primary variable in performance.

3 MT

3.1 Datasets

3.1.1 SPRINGLab/shiksha [5]

This is a Technical Domain focused Translation Dataset for 8 Indian Languages. It consists of more than 2.5 million rows of translation pairs between all 8 languages and English.

This data has been derived from raw NPTEL documents. More information on this can be found in our paper: (Joglekar and Umesh, 2024)

[5] https://huggingface.co/datasets/SPRINGLab/shiksha

3.1.2 SPRINGLab/BPCC-cleaned [6]

A curated subset of Bharat Parallel Corpus Collection (BPCC) for 8 Indian languages. Translation pairs are filtered with LABSE score(>0.9) and further preprocessed. Useful for training high-quality translation models.

3.2 Training

For the Machine Translation of the transcriptions generated by the ASR model, we are using a fine-tuned NLLB model (3.3B) (NLLB Team, 2022) trained on the Shiksha (Joglekar and Umesh, 2024) and BPPC cleaned (English→Indic, Indic→Indic) dataset in both directions. The fine-tuned model is then used to translate transcriptions obtained through Whisper (Radford et al., 2022), Phi-4 multimodal instruct (Marah Abdin, 2024), and Data2Vec (Alexei Baevski, 2022).

Following were the training arguments that were used to fine-tune both the NLLB models:

- Learning Rate: 5e-5
- Batch Size: 8
- Weight Decay: 0.01
- Train Epochs: 5

4 Evaluation

The Evaluation results for the models were performed on the facebook/flores dataset (NLLB Team, 2022) (Goyal et al., 2021) (Guzmán et al., 2019). The scores for the MT are recorded in terms of Chrf++ and BLEU, listed in Table 2

4.0.1 Qualitative Error Analysis

Unlike purely numerical metrics like BLEU or WER, qualitative error analysis explores what kinds of errors the models make and helps identify patterns that can guide targeted improvements. We also analyzed how metric-based evaluation can sometimes fail to reflect semantic adequacy due to stylistic or lexical variation.

The figure 1 below shows a few examples of English-Hindi translation tasks where the BLEU scores are low despite reasonably acceptable translations:

These examples show that even when translations preserve meaning, surface-level metrics may penalize valid variations. Incorporating semantic

[6] https://huggingface.co/datasets/SPRINGLab/BPCC_cleaned

Source	Reference	Prediction	BLEU	chrF	Comment
Let me talk to Dad.	पहले पिताजी से बात कर लूं।	मुझे पापा से बात करने दो।	16.23	28.77	Lexical variation (formal/informal)
Yeah, I am in my second year.	हाँ, ये मेरा दूसरा साल है।	हां, मैं अपने दूसरे वर्ष में हूं।	5.52	16.96	Stylistic differences and structure shift
Am I too late?	क्या मुझे बहुत देर हो गई?	क्या मैं बहुत देर से आया हूं?	13.13	39.64	Perspective/gender difference
————	————	————	——	——	————
Come and have a seat.	এসো, এসে বোসো।	আসুন বসুন।	0	5.85	Register mismatch (formal vs. informal) --> semantically correct but stylistically different
Where are they heading to?	তারা কোথায় যাচ্ছে?	তারা কোথায় যাচ্ছে?	35.36	70.97	Metrics pick up tiny encoding differences; meaning is identical
Let us wait and watch.	চলো অপেক্ষা করি , দেখি।	আসুন অপেক্ষা করি এবং দেখি।	23.64	57.05	Both sentences are valid but differ in tone and conjunction style. informal vs. formal invitation and , vs. এবং — stylistic variation ("and")
————	————	————	——	——	————
It is a holiday.	ஸ்கூல் லீவு.	இது ஒரு விடுமுறை.	15.97	4.24	Reference has loan phrase, lexical mismatch and contextual variation
Why is it a holiday though?	ஆனால், நாளைக்கு ஏன் லீவு?	இது ஏன் ஒரு விடுமுறை?	10.4	11.42	Rephrased but semantically equivalent
Yes mom, I can't wait for it.	ஆமாம் அம்மா, நானும் அதற்காகவே காத்திருக்கிறேன்.	ஆம் அம்மா, என்னால் காத்திருக்க முடியாது.	14.54	41.95	Different idiomatic phrasing, meaning preserved, The prediction is idiomatic (lit. "I can't wait") whereas reference is literal ("I am waiting for it").

Figure 1: Sentence-level MT evaluation for Hindi, Tamil, and Bengali examples showing BLEU and chrF scores.

Language	Chrf++	BLEU
Hindi-English	0.83	0.62
Bengali-English	0.55	0.41
Tamil-English	0.79	0.85

Table 2: Datasets used for Evaluating the MT Models.

similarity metrics or human judgment could provide a more robust evaluation framework.

5 Final Evaluation

After Fine-tuning and evaluating the ASR and MT model separately, we conducted a final evaluation to test how the models were performing collectively with models namely: whisper-large-v2, data2vec-aqc[7] and NLLB. We cascaded the fine-tuned Phi-4 multimodal instruct (Marah Abdin, 2024) with NLLB and our fine-tuned NLLB model (3.3B), whisper-large-v2 (Radford et al., 2022) with NLLB (NLLB Team, 2022) and our fine-tuned NLLB model (3.3B) and data2vec-aqc with NLLB and our fine-tuned NLLB model (3.3B),

The metrics used for the evaluation were BLEU and chrf++, the results for the Bengali to English translation are listed in Table 3

6 Results

On final evaluation on the IWSLT 2025 leaderboard, with chrf as the ranking metric, we find that we perform the best on Indic to English translations, achieving first place for both Hindi to English and Bengali to English, and achieving second place for Tamil to English. However, we rank last on English to Indic evaluation. Our Evaluation results are listed in Table 4 .

[7] https://huggingface.co/SPRINGLab/data2vec_aqc

ASR	MT	chrf++	BLEU
whisper	FT NLLB	52.5917	18.3550
whisper	NLLB	44.7125	16.7514
Data2vec-aqc	FT NLLB	53.3732	21.0471
Data2vec-aqc	NLLB	44.1628	16.3213
FT Phi-4	FT NLLB	55.2648	22.9005
FT Phi-4	NLLB	47.3048	18.3701

Table 3: Final Evaluation results for the cascaded models on Bengali to English translation task, whisper denotes the base model whisper-large-v2 (1.54B) , F denotes fine-tuned model,

6.0.1 Several factors likely contributed to the low English-Indic performance:

- Data Imbalance: While the IndicEnglish direction had sufficient high-quality training data, the EnglishIndic direction, particularly EnglishTamil, suffered from limited parallel corpora. For our MT model, we had increased the number of Indic-Indic corpora by leveraging parallel translations of the same sentence across various Indian languages. Therefore, our MT model had a much better understanding with regard to Indic languages. Same is reflected in the result, where Indic-English is performing well during evaluation. This constrained the model's ability to generalize.

- Limited Training Epochs: The ASR model was trained for only one epoch to avoid overfitting, which may have led to undertrainingespecially problematic in already low-resource settings (e.g Tamil).

Task	chrf++	BLEU
Bn-En	55.2648	22.9005
Hi-En	68.144	41.5874
Ta-En	42.0195	13.4667
En-Bn	60.8094	26.6685
En-Hi	62.3016	41.0865
En-Ta	62.3335	21.3543

Table 4: IWSLT 2025 leaderboard results for our cascaded models,

- Lack of Multilingual Transfer: Fine-tuning was done monolingually. Multilingual fine-tuning across related Indic languages could have allowed knowledge transfer and improved low-resource directions.
- Linguistic Complexity: Tamil's rich morphology and syntactic structure (e.g., SOV order) increased the difficulty of accurate translation from English without dedicated architectural or preprocessing adaptations.

Together, these limitations explain the performance gap between the two translation directions and emphasize the need for multilingual strategies and additional data in future work.

Conclusion

In this paper, we have presented our Speech Translation Systems for the low-resource Indic Languages track of IWSLT 2025 employing a cascaded ap- proach using fine-tuned models for both ASR and MT. Moving Forward we will try to employ a SLAM-ASR (Ziyang Ma, 2024) based approach to our ASR model, to get better ASR results and try to train the models more on indic languages data to generalize better.

References

Idris Abdulmumin, Victor Agostinelli, Tanel Alumäe, Antonios Anastasopoulos, Ashwin, Luisa Bentivogli, Ondej Bojar, Claudia Borg, Fethi Bougares, Roldano Cattoni, Mauro Cettolo, Lizhong Chen, William Chen, Raj Dabre, Yannick Estève, Marcello Federico, Marco Gaido, Dávid Javorský, Marek Kasztelnik, and 30 others. 2025. Findings of the iwslt 2025 evaluation campaign. In *Proceedings of the 22nd International Conference on Spoken Language Translation (IWSLT 2025)*, Vienna, Austia (in-person and online). Association for Computational Linguistics. To appear.

Qiantong Xu Arun Babu Jiatao Gu Michael Auli Alexei Baevski, Wei-Ning Hsu. 2022. data2vec: A general framework for self-supervised learning in speech, vision and language. *Machine Learning (cs.LG)*.

R. Ardila, M. Branson, K. Davis, M. Henretty, M. Kohler, J. Meyer, R. Morais, L. Saunders, F. M. Tyers, and G. Weber. 2020. Common voice: A massively-multilingual speech corpus. In *Proceedings of the 12th Conference on Language Resources and Evaluation (LREC 2020)*, pages 4211–4215.

Kaushal Santosh Bhogale, Abhigyan Raman, Tahir Javed, Sumanth Doddapaneni, Anoop Kunchukuttan, Pratyush Kumar, and Mitesh M. Khapra. 2023. Effectiveness of mining audio and text pairs from public data for improving ASR systems for low-resource languages. In *ICASSP*, pages 1–5. IEEE.

Alexis Conneau, Min Ma, Simran Khanuja, Yu Zhang, Vera Axelrod, Siddharth Dalmia, Jason Riesa, Clara Rivera, and Ankur Bapna. 2022. Fleurs: Few-shot learning evaluation of universal representations of speech. *arXiv preprint arXiv:2205.12446*.

Naman Goyal, Cynthia Gao, Vishrav Chaudhary, Peng-Jen Chen, Guillaume Wenzek, Da Ju, Sanjana Krishnan, Marc'Aurelio Ranzato, Francisco Guzmán, and Angela Fan. 2021. The flores-101 evaluation benchmark for low-resource and multilingual machine translation.

Francisco Guzmán, Peng-Jen Chen, Myle Ott, Juan Pino, Guillaume Lample, Philipp Koehn, Vishrav Chaudhary, and Marc'Aurelio Ranzato. 2019. Two new evaluation datasets for low-resource machine translation: Nepali-english and sinhala-english. *arXiv preprint arXiv:1902.01382*.

Sparsh Jain, Ashwin Sankar, Devilal Choudhary, Dhairya Suman, Nikhil Narasimhan, Mohammed Safi Ur Rahman Khan, Anoop Kunchukuttan, Mitesh M Khapra, and Raj Dabre. 2024. Bhasaanuvaad: A speech translation dataset for 14 indian languages. *arXiv preprint arXiv: 2411.04699*.

Tahir Javed, Kaushal Santosh Bhogale, Abhigyan Raman, Anoop Kunchukuttan, Pratyush Kumar, and Mitesh M. Khapra. 2022. Indicsuperb: A speech processing universal performance benchmark for indian languages. *arXiv preprint*.

Advait Joglekar and Srinivasan Umesh. 2024. Shiksha: A technical domain focused translation dataset and model for indian languages. *Preprint*, arXiv:2412.09025.

Harkirat Behl Sébastien Bubeck Ronen Eldan Suriya Gunasekar Michael Harrison Russell J. Hewett Mojan Javaheripi Piero Kauffmann James R. Lee Yin Tat Lee Yuanzhi Li Weishung Liu Caio C. T. Mendes Anh Nguyen Eric Price Gustavo de Rosa Olli Saarikivi Adil Salim Shital Shah Xin Wang Rachel Ward Yue Wu Dingli Yu Cyril Zhang Yi Zhang

Marah Abdin, Jyoti Aneja. 2024. Phi-4 technical report. *Computation and Language (cs.CL); Artificial Intelligence (cs.AI)*, arXiv:2412.08905. Version 1.

James Cross Onur Çelebi Maha Elbayad Kenneth Heafield Kevin Heffernan Elahe Kalbassi Janice Lam Daniel Licht Jean Maillard Anna Sun Skyler Wang Guillaume Wenzek Al Youngblood Bapi Akula Loic Barrault Gabriel Mejia Gonzalez Prangthip Hansanti John Hoffman Semarley Jarrett Kaushik Ram Sadagopan Dirk Rowe Shannon Spruit Chau Tran Pierre Andrews Necip Fazil Ayan Shruti Bhosale Sergey Edunov Angela Fan Cynthia Gao Vedanuj Goswami Francisco Guzmán Philipp Koehn Alexandre Mourachko Christophe Ropers Safiyyah Saleem Holger Schwenk Jeff Wang (NLLB Team) NLLB Team, Marta R. Costa-jussà. 2022. No language left behind: Scaling human-centered machine translation. *Computation and Language (cs.CL); Artificial Intelligence (cs.AI)*, arXiv:2207.04672. Version 2.

Vassil Panayotov, Guoguo Chen, Daniel Povey, and Sanjeev Khudanpur. 2015. Librispeech: an asr corpus based on public domain audio books. In *Acoustics, Speech and Signal Processing (ICASSP), 2015 IEEE International Conference on*, pages 5206–5210. IEEE.

Alec Radford, Jong Wook Kim, Tao Xu, Greg Brockman, Christine McLeavey, and Ilya Sutskever. 2022. Robust speech recognition via large-scale weak supervision. *arXiv preprint*.

Yifan Yang Zhifu Gao Jiaming Wang Zhihao Du Fan Yu Qian Chen Siqi Zheng Shiliang Zhang Xie Chen Ziyang Ma, Guanrou Yang. 2024. An embarrassingly simple approach for llm with strong asr capacity. *arXiv preprint arXiv:2402.08846*.

HITSZ's End-To-End Speech Translation Systems Combining Sequence-to-Sequence Auto Speech Recognition Model and Indic Large Language Model for IWSLT 2025 in Indic Track

Xuchen Wei, Yangxin Wu, Yaoyin Zhang, Henglyu Liu,
Kehai Chen*, Xuefeng Bai, Min Zhang,
School of Computer Science and Technology, Harbin Institute of Technology, Shenzhen, China
{2023311524,2023311526,2023313720,23s151043}@stu.hit.edu.cn,
{chenkehai,baixuefeng,zhangmin2021}@hit.edu.cn

Abstract

This paper presents HITSZ's submission for the IWSLT 2025 Indic track, focusing on speech-to-text translation (ST) for English-to-Indic and Indic-to-English language pairs. To enhance translation quality in this low-resource scenario, we propose an end-to-end system integrating the pre-trained Whisper automated speech recognition (ASR) model with Krutrim, an Indic-specialized large language model (LLM). Experimental results demonstrate that our end-to-end system achieved average BLEU scores of 28.88 for English-to-Indic directions and 27.86 for Indic-to-English directions. Furthermore, we investigated the Chain-of-Thought (CoT) method. While this method showed potential for significant translation quality improvements on successfully parsed outputs (e.g. a 13.84 BLEU increase for Tamil-to-English), we observed challenges in ensuring the model consistently adheres to the required CoT output format.

1 Introduction

Speech-to-text translation plays a vital role in overcoming language barriers in multilingual and international contexts, such as real-time translation during online meetings. Although translation systems for high-resource language pairs have achieved impressive performance, low-resource language pairs, particularly those involving Indic languages, continue to face significant challenges (Radford et al., 2023; Joshi et al., 2020).

This paper presents HITSZ's submission to the Indic Track of IWSLT 2025, covering bidirectional speech translation between English and three major Indic languages: Hindi, Bengali, and Tamil. An overview of the end-to-end system is illustrated in Figure 1.

Data scarcity poses a significant challenge for speech translation (ST) between English and Indic languages, primarily due to the low-resource nature of these language pairs and the reliance on data-driven neural models (Ahmad et al., 2024). Acknowledging this, we collected available parallel corpus from the official IWSLT data releases for effective end-to-end ST model training.

Cascade and end-to-end (E2E) systems represent two prominent paradigms in ST, each offering distinct advantages (Ney, 1999; Mathias and Byrne, 2006; Bérard et al., 2016). While cascaded systems typically achieve higher translation quality (Agarwal et al., 2023), E2E systems are favored for their lower latency and reduced modeling complexity (Ahmad et al., 2024; Xu et al., 2023). This work focuses exclusively on the end-to-end paradigm for the bidirectional speech translation task. We adopt an *unconstrained* setting and utilize state-of-the-art pre-trained models, including Whisper (Radford et al., 2023) and Krutrim (Kallappa et al., 2025), to develop E2E systems for both English-to-Indic and Indic-to-English directions. Although additional resources such as the IndicVoices (Javed et al., 2024) dataset are available, we deliberately exclude them due to concerns about potential overlap with the test set.

The remainder of this paper is structured as follows: Section 2 reviews related work on speech translation, particularly in low-resource and Indic language settings. Section 3 describes the datasets and data pre-processing. Section 4 introduces our end-to-end system. Section 5 presents the experimental settings, results, and analysis. Lastly, Section 6 concludes the paper.

2 Related Work

Recent advances in end-to-end speech translation (ST) have demonstrated the effectiveness of combining large pre-trained models with task-

*Corresponding author

Proceedings of the 22nd International Conference on Spoken Language Translation (IWSLT 2025), pages 405–411
July 31 - August 1, 2025

specific adaptation (Wang et al., 2017; Bérard et al., 2018; Bansal et al., 2019; Wang et al., 2020; Alinejad and Sarkar, 2020), especially in low-resource and multilingual settings (Marie et al., 2019; Sun et al., 2020; Tsiamas et al., 2024; Li et al., 2025). Among them, several works stand out for their innovative training paradigms and architectural choices that have directly influenced our approach. These include NICT's submission to IWSLT 2024 (Dabre and Song, 2024), which leverages decoder-side fine-tuning of Whisper with pseudo-labels from IndicTrans2 (Gala et al., 2023); ZeroSwot, which introduces an encoder-centric alignment method for zero-shot ST (Tsiamas et al., 2024); and SALMONN, a multimodal framework that uses a lightweight training pipeline to adapt frozen encoders and LLMs through cross-modal instruction tuning (Tang et al., 2024). In what follows, we briefly review each of these works and highlight their relevance to our system design.

2.1 NICT's E2E ST System in IWSLT 2024

One of the most relevant works to our approach is the IWSLT 2024 submission by NICT, which developed end-to-end speech translation systems for English to Hindi, Bengali, and Tamil. A key contribution was their fine-tuning strategy for Whisper: instead of using human-annotated translations, they first fine-tuned IndicTrans2 to generate pseudo-translations from English transcripts. These synthetic targets were then used to train Whisper in a speech-to-text translation setting, effectively distilling knowledge and improving decoder performance beyond what reference translations alone could achieve.

2.2 ZeroSwot

Another influential work is ZeroSwot, which proposes a novel zero-shot end-to-end ST framework by aligning speech representations with the embedding space of a multilingual MT model. In their setup, the speech encoder is initialized from a CTC-finetuned wav2vec 2.0 model (Baevski et al., 2020) and trained using a combination of CTC loss and Optimal Transport loss (Graves et al., 2006; Peyré et al., 2019). The goal is to produce subword-level acoustic representations that match those expected by a frozen multilingual MT encoder (NLLB) (Team et al., 2022). In addition, a compression adapter (Liu et al., 2020) is introduced to map variable-length audio sequences into subword-aligned embeddings, bridging both length and representation mismatches between modalities. In contrast to NICT's decoder-focused fine-tuning, ZeroSwot emphasizes encoder-side alignment, enabling zero-shot translation without requiring any parallel ST data.

2.3 SALMONN

We also take inspiration from SALMONN, a multimodal framework that integrates Whisper and BEATs (Chen et al., 2023) encoders with a large language model (Vicuna) (Chiang et al., 2023) to enable general auditory understanding across speech, audio events, and music. Although SALMONN targets a broader set of audio-language tasks beyond ST, its modular design and training strategy are particularly relevant. SALMONN adopts a three-stage training pipeline—pre-training (Zhu et al., 2024), instruction tuning, and activation tuning—where only lightweight modules (Q-Former and LoRA adaptors (Li et al., 2023; Hu et al., 2022)) are updated while the encoders and LLM remain frozen. This design enables efficient adaptation with minimal parameter updates. Our work builds on this principle by leveraging pre-trained components and applying modular fine-tuning in a similarly efficient manner, tailored to low-resource, bidirectional speech translation between English and Indic languages.

3 Data

In this section, we present the statistics of the initial corpora and describe our methods for pre-processing the raw data.

3.1 Dataset

Direction	Train	Dev	Test	Total Speech Hours
en → bn	680.9	40.8	93.2	814.9
en → hi	680.9	40.8	93.2	814.9
en → ta	680.9	40.8	93.2	814.9
bn → en	158.0	1.0	1.3	160.3
hi → en	653.9	1.0	1.3	656.2
ta → en	478.2	1.0	2.2	481.4

Table 1: Statistics of dataset for training, development, and test sets. The abbreviations *en*, *bn*, *hi*, and *ta* stand for English, Bengali, Hindi, and Tamil, respectively.

We rely solely on the corpus provided by the organizers, with its statistics detailed above. Although we did not incorporate any supplementary data, our model remains *unconstrained* by leveraging the pre-trained Whisper ASR model, the Krutrim large language model, and adapters trained specifically for the spoken language translation task based on these two models. The audio segments corresponding to textual sentences are extracted from the original files based on the given offset and duration details. Post-segmentation, each dataset entry includes an audio clip in the source language, its transcription, and a translation in the target languages.

3.2 Pre-processing

We find that some audio clips in the English-to-Indic corpus are very long, indicating a very large consumption of GPU memory. To accelerate the fine-tuning process, we separate the data with English transcription length less than and above 400 characters, which allows us to increase the batch size during the training process.

4 Method

Our model builds upon the *Dhwani* model (Shah et al., 2025), which is trained for speech translation tasks in Indic languages and is itself derived from the SALMONN architecture. To effectively process and align multimodal audio data with textual outputs, the architecture integrates several specialized components. For speech signals, it leverages the Whisper speech encoder (WhisperSE) to extract robust linguistic representations. In parallel, non-speech audio inputs, such as environmental sounds and music, are processed using the BEATs encoder, which is optimized for general audio understanding.

These two audio streams are subsequently bridged to the language model via a Window-Level Query Transformer (Q-Former), which acts as a connection module to transform modality-specific features into a unified representation space. The transformed tokens are then passed to the Krutrim LLM, a 7-billion-parameter dense transformer model built on a multilingual foundation and optimized for Indic language tasks. Trained on a corpus of 2 trillion tokens with extensive coverage of native Indian languages, Krutrim demonstrates strong performance across multilingual benchmarks in both Indic and English, despite being relatively lightweight in terms of training compute.

To enable efficient domain-specific adaptation without retraining the entire model, Low-Rank Adaptation (LoRA) is employed during fine-tuning. This technique aligns the LLM's outputs with the semantics of the input audio, facilitating robust and adaptable performance.

5 Experiments and Results

This section details the experimental setup and presents the results for our monolingual speech translation models, trained individually for each translation direction. We follow the settings of the *Dhwani* model, employing the *Whisper-large-v2* model as the speech encoder and the *Krutrim-1-instruct* model as the text decoder branch.

5.1 English-Indic Translation

For the English-to-Indic translation task, we adopted a fine-tuning strategy where both the WhisperSE and the BEATs audio encoders were kept frozen. Training focused exclusively on the Q-Former module, which connects the speech encoder to the language model, and a LoRA adapter integrated into the LLM branch. We configured the LoRA adapter with a rank (r) of 8 and an alpha (α) of 32.

The learning rate schedule commenced with a linear warmup phase over the initial 3,000 training steps, increasing from a base rate of $1e^{-6}$ to the peak learning rate of $3e^{-5}$. Subsequently, the learning rate followed a cosine decay schedule, oscillating between the maximum rate ($3e^{-5}$) and a minimum rate ($1e^{-5}$), before finally decaying to the minimum rate of $1e^{-5}$.

Direction	Dev	Test
en → bn	30.61	27.00
en → hi	37.83	33.84
en → ta	25.97	22.81

Table 2: BLEU scores on the development and test set in English-to-Indic directions.

We initiated training using only the *short* audio segments from our dataset. This allowed for a larger batch size of 4, thereby accelerating the training process. Models were trained independently for three language pairs: English-to-Bengali, English-to-Hindi, and English-to-Tamil. For each pair, the checkpoint yielding the highest BLEU score on the development set was selected for subsequent incremental fine-tuning on the dataset containing *long* audio segments. Detailed results are presented in Table 2.

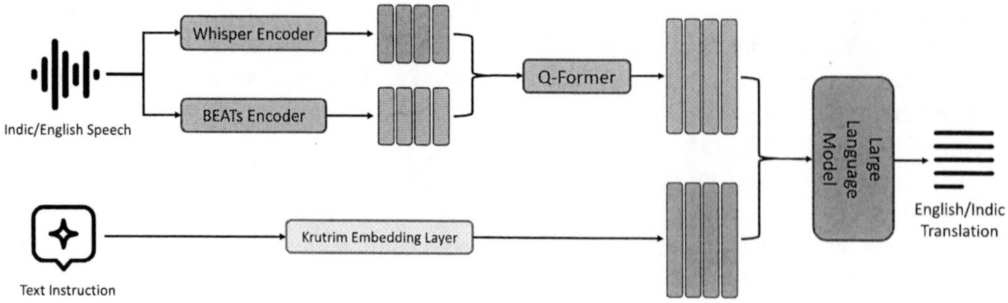

Figure 1: Overview of the our end-to-end spoken language translation system.

5.2 Indic-to-English Translation

The experimental setup for Indic-to-English translation largely mirrored the English-to-Indic configuration. However, a key difference was the absence of exceptionally *long* audio clips in the Indic-to-English corpus. Consequently, we did not employ the two-stage (*short/long*) training strategy used for the English-to-Indic directions.

Recognizing that the Whisper model exhibits comparatively lower performance on Indic languages than high-resource languages, we set the WhisperSE module to be trainable for the first epoch. Using a batch size of 1 with gradient accumulation over 4 steps helped conserve GPU memory while enabling updates to the WhisperSE, aiming for improved feature extraction from Indic audio inputs. The evaluation results are presented in Table 3.

To mitigate the challenge of limited training data and to better exploit the inherent bilingual capabilities of the LLM, we explored the Chain-of-Thought (CoT) prompting and fine-tuning technique. Specifically, this approach involved fine-tuning the model to first produce a transcription of the speech in the source language, followed by the English translation. Our findings indicate that the automatic parsing of the generated responses for the reliable extraction of the final translation output was not consistently successful.

Our experiments on the development set demonstrate that, on average, 66.54% of the responses generated by our E2E system adhere to the Chain-of-Thought (CoT) format constraints and can be successfully parsed. For the subset of responses that are parsable, results indicate notable improvements in BLEU scores. Specifically, in the Tamil-to-English translation direction, we observe a significant BLEU score improvement of 13.84 points.

Direction	Dev	Test
bn → en	25.38	25.02
hi → en	31.71	39.29
ta → en	20.93	19.27

Table 3: BLEU scores on the development and test set in Indic-to-English directions.

Direction	CoT Parsing Success Rate	BLEU Score	Δ
bn → en	68.18%	28.13	2.592
hi → en	71.00%	38.49	6.780
ta → en	60.43%	34.77	13.84

Table 4: Parsing success rate of Chain of Thought responses in Indic-to-English directions; BLEU scores of successfully parsed CoT responses on the development set; and the corresponding BLEU score improvements of the CoT method.

6 Conclusion

This paper presented HITSZ's submission to the IWSLT 2025 speech-to-text translation task in the Indic track. We leveraged recent advancements in Indic LLM by integrating the Whisper model and the Krutrim model into our end-to-end system. Future work will primarily focus on two key directions: first, enhancing the instruction-following capability of the specialized LLM for Indic languages to facilitate the development of a Spoken Language Translation system utilizing the Chain-of-Thought (CoT) method; and second, improving its generation capabilities in Indic languages to boost performance in English-to-Indic translation tasks.

Acknowledgement

We sincerely thank the shared task organizers for their efforts in designing and coordinating the task, as well as the reviewers for their valuable work that made this technical report possible. This work is supported in part by the National Natural Science Foundation of China (62276077, 62406091, and U23B2055), the Guangdong Basic and Applied Basic Research Foundation (2024A1515011205), the Shenzhen Science and Technology Program (KQTD20240729102154066 and ZDSYS20230626091203008), and Shenzhen College Stability Support Plan (GXWD20220817123150002 and GXWD20220811170358002).

References

Milind Agarwal, Sweta Agarwal, Antonios Anastasopoulos, Luisa Bentivogli, Ondřej Bojar, Claudia Borg, Marine Carpuat, Roldano Cattoni, Mauro Cettolo, Mingda Chen, and 1 others. 2023. Findings of the iwslt 2023 evaluation campaign. Association for Computational Linguistics.

Ibrahim Said Ahmad, Antonios Anastasopoulos, Ondřej Bojar, Claudia Borg, Marine Carpuat, Roldano Cattoni, Mauro Cettolo, William Chen, Qianqian Dong, Marcello Federico, Barry Haddow, Dávid Javorský, Mateusz Krubiński, Tsz Kin Lam, Xutai Ma, Prashant Mathur, Evgeny Matusov, Chandresh Maurya, John McCrae, and 25 others. 2024. FINDINGS OF THE IWSLT 2024 EVALUATION CAMPAIGN. In *Proceedings of the 21st International Conference on Spoken Language Translation (IWSLT 2024)*, pages 1–11, Bangkok, Thailand (in-person and online). Association for Computational Linguistics.

Ashkan Alinejad and Anoop Sarkar. 2020. Effectively pretraining a speech translation decoder with machine translation data. In *Proceedings of the 2020 Conference on Empirical Methods in Natural Language Processing (EMNLP)*, pages 8014–8020.

Alexei Baevski, Henry Zhou, Abdelrahman Mohamed, and Michael Auli. 2020. wav2vec 2.0: a framework for self-supervised learning of speech representations. *arXiv preprint*. ArXiv:2006.11477 [cs].

Sameer Bansal, Herman Kamper, Karen Livescu, Adam Lopez, and Sharon Goldwater. 2019. Pre-training on high-resource speech recognition improves low-resource speech-to-text translation. In *2019 Annual Conference of the North American Chapter of the Association for Computational Linguistics*, pages 58–68. Association for Computational Linguistics.

Alexandre Bérard, Laurent Besacier, Ali Can Kocabiyikoglu, and Olivier Pietquin. 2018. End-to-end automatic speech translation of audiobooks. In *2018 IEEE International Conference on Acoustics, Speech and Signal Processing (ICASSP)*, pages 6224–6228. IEEE.

Alexandre Bérard, Olivier Pietquin, Laurent Besacier, and Christophe Servan. 2016. Listen and translate: A proof of concept for end-to-end speech-to-text translation. In *NIPS Workshop on end-to-end learning for speech and audio processing*.

Sanyuan Chen, Yu Wu, Chengyi Wang, Shujie Liu, Daniel Tompkins, Zhuo Chen, Wanxiang Che, Xiangzhan Yu, and Furu Wei. 2023. BEATs: audio pre-training with acoustic tokenizers. In *Proceedings of the 40th International Conference on Machine Learning*, pages 5178–5193. PMLR. ISSN: 2640-3498 shortConferenceName: ICML.

Wei-Lin Chiang, Zhuohan Li, Zi Lin, Ying Sheng, Zhanghao Wu, Hao Zhang, Lianmin Zheng, Siyuan Zhuang, Yonghao Zhuang, Joseph E. Gonzalez, Ion Stoica, and Eric P. Xing. 2023. Vicuna: An open-source chatbot impressing gpt-4 with 90%* chatgpt quality.

Raj Dabre and Haiyue Song. 2024. NICT's cascaded and end-to-end speech translation systems using whisper and IndicTrans2 for the Indic task. In *Proceedings of the 21st International Conference on Spoken Language Translation (IWSLT 2024)*, pages 17–22, Bangkok, Thailand (in-person and online). Association for Computational Linguistics.

Jay Gala, Pranjal A. Chitale, Raghavan Ak, Varun Gumma, Sumanth Doddapaneni, Aswanth Kumar, Janki Nawale, Anupama Sujatha, Ratish Puduppully, Vivek Raghavan, Pratyush Kumar, Mitesh M. Khapra, Raj Dabre, and Anoop Kunchukuttan. 2023. IndicTrans2: towards high-quality and accessible machine translation models for all 22 scheduled indian languages. *arXiv preprint*. ArXiv:2305.16307 [cs].

Alex Graves, Santiago Fernández, Faustino Gomez, and Jürgen Schmidhuber. 2006. Connectionist temporal classification: labelling unsegmented sequence data with recurrent neural networks. In *Proceedings of the 23rd international conference on Machine learning*, pages 369–376.

Edward J Hu, Yelong Shen, Phillip Wallis, Zeyuan Allen-Zhu, Yuanzhi Li, Shean Wang, Lu Wang, and Weizhu Chen. 2022. LoRA: Low-rank adaptation of large language models. In *International Conference on Learning Representations*.

Tahir Javed, Janki Atul Nawale, Eldho Ittan George, Sakshi Joshi, Kaushal Santosh Bhogale, Deovrat Mehendale, Ishvinder Virender Sethi, Aparna Ananthanarayanan, Hafsah Faquih, Pratiti Palit, Sneha Ravishankar, Saranya Sukumaran, Tripura Panchagnula, Sunjay Murali, Kunal Sharad Gandhi, Ambujavalli R, Manickam K M, C Venkata Vaijayanthi, Krishnan Srinivasa Raghavan Karunganni, and 2 others. 2024. Indicvoices: Towards building an inclusive multilingual speech dataset for indian languages. *Preprint*, arXiv:2403.01926.

Pratik Joshi, Sebastin Santy, Amar Budhiraja, Kalika Bali, and Monojit Choudhury. 2020. The state and fate of linguistic diversity and inclusion in the nlp world. In *Proceedings of the 58th Annual Meeting of the Association for Computational Linguistics*, page 6282. Association for Computational Linguistics.

Aditya Kallappa, Palash Kamble, Abhinav Ravi, Akshat Patidar, Vinayak Dhruv, Deepak Kumar, Raghav Awasthi, Arveti Manjunath, Himanshu Gupta, Shubham Agarwal, Kumar Ashish, Gautam Bhargava, and Chandra Khatri. 2025. Krutrim LLM: multilingual foundational model for over a billion people. *arXiv preprint*. ArXiv:2502.09642 [cs].

Bo Li, Shaolin Zhu, and Lijie Wen. 2025. MIT-10M: A large scale parallel corpus of multilingual image translation. In *Proceedings of the 31st International Conference on Computational Linguistics*, pages 5154–5167, Abu Dhabi, UAE. Association for Computational Linguistics.

Junnan Li, Dongxu Li, Silvio Savarese, and Steven Hoi. 2023. BLIP-2: bootstrapping language-image pre-training with frozen image encoders and large language models. In *Proceedings of the 40th International Conference on Machine Learning*, pages 19730–19742. PMLR. ISSN: 2640-3498 shortConferenceName: ICML.

Yuchen Liu, Junnan Zhu, Jiajun Zhang, and Chengqing Zong. 2020. Bridging the modality gap for speech-to-text translation. *arXiv preprint arXiv:2010.14920*.

Benjamin Marie, Haipeng Sun, Rui Wang, Kehai Chen, Atsushi Fujita, Masao Utiyama, and Eiichiro Sumita. 2019. NICT's unsupervised neural and statistical machine translation systems for the WMT19 news translation task. In *Proceedings of the Fourth Conference on Machine Translation (Volume 2: Shared Task Papers, Day 1)*, pages 294–301, Florence, Italy. Association for Computational Linguistics.

Lambert Mathias and William Byrne. 2006. Statistical phrase-based speech translation. In *2006 IEEE International Conference on Acoustics Speech and Signal Processing Proceedings*, volume 1, pages I–I. IEEE.

Hermann Ney. 1999. Speech translation: Coupling of recognition and translation. In *1999 IEEE International Conference on Acoustics, Speech, and Signal Processing. Proceedings. ICASSP99 (Cat. No. 99CH36258)*, volume 1, pages 517–520. IEEE.

Gabriel Peyré, Marco Cuturi, and 1 others. 2019. Computational optimal transport: With applications to data science. *Foundations and Trends® in Machine Learning*, 11(5-6):355–607.

Alec Radford, Jong Wook Kim, Tao Xu, Greg Brockman, Christine Mcleavey, and Ilya Sutskever. 2023. Robust speech recognition via large-scale weak supervision. In *Proceedings of the 40th International Conference on Machine Learning*, pages 28492–28518. PMLR. ISSN: 2640-3498 shortConferenceName: ICML.

Sanket Shah, Kavya Ranjan Saxena, Kancharana Manideep Bharadwaj, Sharath Adavanne, and Nagaraj Adiga. 2025. IndicST: Indian multilingual translation corpus for evaluating speech large language models. In *Proc. ICASSP*.

Haipeng Sun, Rui Wang, Kehai Chen, Masao Utiyama, Eiichiro Sumita, and Tiejun Zhao. 2020. Knowledge distillation for multilingual unsupervised neural machine translation. In *Proceedings of the 58th Annual Meeting of the Association for Computational Linguistics*, pages 3525–3535, Online. Association for Computational Linguistics.

Changli Tang, Wenyi Yu, Guangzhi Sun, Xianzhao Chen, Tian Tan, Wei Li, Lu Lu, Zejun MA, and Chao Zhang. 2024. SALMONN: Towards generic hearing abilities for large language models. In *The Twelfth International Conference on Learning Representations*.

NLLB Team, Marta R. Costa-jussà, James Cross, Onur Çelebi, Maha Elbayad, Kenneth Heafield, Kevin Heffernan, Elahe Kalbassi, Janice Lam, Daniel Licht, Jean Maillard, Anna Sun, Skyler Wang, Guillaume Wenzek, Al Youngblood, Bapi Akula, Loic Barrault, Gabriel Mejia Gonzalez, Prangthip Hansanti, and 20 others. 2022. No language left behind: Scaling human-centered machine translation. *Preprint*, arXiv:2207.04672.

Ioannis Tsiamas, Gerard I. Gállego, José A. R. Fonollosa, and Marta R. Costa-jussà. 2024. Pushing the limits of zero-shot end-to-end speech translation. In *Findings of the Association for Computational Linguistics: ACL 2024*, pages 14245–14267, Bangkok, Thailand. Association for Computational Linguistics.

Changhan Wang, Yun Tang, Xutai Ma, Anne Wu, Dmytro Okhonko, and Juan Pino. 2020. Fairseq s2t: Fast speech-to-text modeling with fairseq. In *Proceedings of the 1st Conference of the Asia-Pacific Chapter of the Association for Computational Linguistics and the 10th International Joint Conference on Natural Language Processing: System Demonstrations*, pages 33–39.

Rui Wang, Masao Utiyama, Lemao Liu, Kehai Chen, and Eiichiro Sumita. 2017. Instance weighting for neural machine translation domain adaptation. In *Proceedings of the 2017 Conference on Empirical Methods in Natural Language Processing*, pages 1482–1488, Copenhagen, Denmark. Association for Computational Linguistics.

Chen Xu, Rong Ye, Qianqian Dong, Chengqi Zhao, Tom Ko, Mingxuan Wang, Tong Xiao, and Jingbo

Zhu. 2023. Recent advances in direct speech-to-text translation. In *Proceedings of the Thirty-Second International Joint Conference on Artificial Intelligence*, pages 6796–6804.

Shaolin Zhu, Menglong Cui, and Deyi Xiong. 2024. Towards robust in-context learning for machine translation with large language models. In *Proceedings of the 2024 Joint International Conference on Computational Linguistics, Language Resources and Evaluation (LREC-COLING 2024)*, pages 16619–16629, Torino, Italia. ELRA and ICCL.

Findings of the IWSLT 2025 Evaluation Campaign

Idris Abdulmumin[37] Victor Agostinelli[35] Tanel Alumäe[5] Antonios Anastasopoulos[1] Luisa Bentivogli[3] Ondřej Bojar[4] Claudia Borg[7] Fethi Bougares[6] Roldano Cattoni[3] Mauro Cettolo[3] Lizhong Chen[35] William Chen[9] Raj Dabre[33] Yannick Estève[16] Marcello Federico[12] Mark Fishel[39] Marco Gaido[3] Dávid Javorský[4] Marek Kasztelnik[36] Fortuné Kponou[16] Mateusz Krubiński[38] Tsz Kin Lam[18] Danni Liu[23] Evgeny Matusov[21] Chandresh Kumar Maurya[32] John P. McCrae[22] Salima Mdhaffar[16] Yasmin Moslem[31] Kenton Murray[15] Satoshi Nakamura[20] Matteo Negri[3] Jan Niehues[23] Atul Kr. Ojha[22] John E. Ortega[24] Sara Papi[3] Pavel Pecina[4] Peter Polák[4] Piotr Połeć[36] Ashwin Sankar[33] Beatrice Savoldi[3] Nivedita Sethiya[32] Claytone Sikasote[26] Matthias Sperber[27] Sebastian Stüker[28] Katsuhito Sudoh[34] Brian Thompson Marco Turchi[28] Alex Waibel[9] Patrick Wilken[21] Rodolfo Zevallos[29] Vilém Zouhar[30] Maike Züfle[23]

[1]GMU [3]FBK [4]Charles U. [5]TalTech [6]Elyadata [7]U. Malta [9]CMU [12]Amazon [15]JHU [16]Avignon U. [18]U. Edinburgh [20]CUHK Shenzhen [21]AppTek [22]U. Galway [23]KIT [24]Northeastern U. [26]U. Cape Town [27]Apple [28]Zoom [29]U. Pompeu Fabra [30]ETH Zurich [31]ADAPT Centre [32]IIT Indore [33]IIT Madras [34]Nara Women's U. [35]Oregon State U. [36]ACC Cyfronet AGH [37]U. Pretoria [38]Snowflake [39]U. Tartu

Abstract

This paper presents the outcomes of the shared tasks conducted at the 22nd International Workshop on Spoken Language Translation (IWSLT). The workshop addressed seven critical challenges in spoken language translation: simultaneous and offline translation, automatic subtitling and dubbing, model compression, speech-to-speech translation, dialect and low-resource speech translation, and Indic languages. The shared tasks garnered significant participation, with 32 teams submitting their runs. The field's growing importance is reflected in the increasing diversity of shared task organizers and contributors to this overview paper, representing a balanced mix of industrial and academic institutions. This broad participation demonstrates the rising prominence of spoken language translation in both research and practical applications.

1 Introduction

The International Conference on Spoken Language Translation (IWSLT) stands as the leading annual scientific conference dedicated to advancing all aspects of spoken language translation (SLT). Operating under the auspices of the Special Interest Group on Spoken Language Translation (SIGSLT), the conference receives support from three prestigious organizations: the Association for Computational Linguistics (ACL), the International Speech Communication Association (ISCA), and the European Language Resources Association (ELRA). Maintaining its 22-year tradition, the 2025 conference was preceded by a comprehensive evaluation campaign designed to address critical scientific challenges in SLT. This paper presents the outcomes of the 2025 IWSLT Evaluation Campaign, which comprised seven distinct shared tasks organized into three primary research areas:

- **High-resource ST**
  - **Offline track**, with focus on speech-to-text translation of recorded scientific presentations, TV series, and business news from English to German, Arabic and Chinese.
  - **Simultaneous track**, focusing on speech-to-text translation of streamed audio of conferences and interviews from English to German, Japanese and Chinese, and from Czech to English.
  - **Subtitling track**, with focus on speech-to-subtitle translation of audio-visual documents from English to German and Spanish and on compression of pre-generated German and Spanish subtitles.
  - **Model compression**, with focus on speech-to-text translation of recorded scientific presentations, TV series, and business news from English to German and Chinese, achieved by reducing the size of a large mul-

Proceedings of the 22nd International Conference on Spoken Language Translation (IWSLT 2025), pages 412–481
July 31 - August 1, 2025

tilingual speech-to-text foundation model.

- **Low resource ST**
  - **Low-resource SLT**, focusing on the translation of recorded speech from North Levantine Arabic to English, Tunisian Arabic to English, Bemba to English, Fongbe to French, Irish to English, Bhojpuri to Hindi, Estonian to English, Maltese to English, Marathi to Hindi, and Quechua to Spanish. It also included a data track, inviting participants to submit newly collected speech translation datasets of under-resourced language pairs.

  - **Indic Languages Track** focuses on English and multiple Indic languages. The speech translations are from English speech to Indic language text and from Indic speech to English language text. Indic languages include Bengali, Hindi, and Tamil.
- **Instruction-following Speech Processing**
  - **Speech Recognition, Translation, Question Answering, and Summarization**, with focus on Scientific talk audios from English to German, Italian, and Chinese languages.

The shared tasks drew participation from 32 diverse teams (detailed in Table 1), encompassing both academic institutions and industry leaders. In the following sections, we provide comprehensive coverage of each shared task, including detailed descriptions of the research challenges, specifications of training and testing datasets, evaluation methodologies, and submission analyses. Each task discussion concludes with a thorough results summary, with additional detailed performance metrics available in the corresponding appendices. This structure ensures a systematic presentation of the tasks while maintaining accessibility to both high-level findings and granular technical details.

2 Evaluation

The evaluation campaign features both automatic and human evaluation. To support automatic evaluation, we developed a dedicated evaluation server this year, as detailed in Section 2.1. The server was piloted in the *Offline*, *Model Compression*, and *Instruction Following* tracks. For the other tracks, submission and evaluation processes were managed by the respective organizers, following the procedure used in previous campaigns. In addition, we performed a human evaluation across several tracks as described in 2.2

2.1 SPEECHM-IWSLT2025 Evaluation Server

The Evaluation Server is a suite of datasets and metrics designed to measure and monitor the performance of task-specific systems. It is part of the "SPEECHM" platform, developed under the Meetween European Project.[1] For the IWSLT-2025 Evaluation Campaign, a dedicated instance—SPEECHM-IWSLT2025[2]—was created. This instance features a web-based user interface that allows participants to submit system outputs and track their performance via a leaderboard. The implemented evaluation metrics depend on the task: COMET, BLEURT, BLEU and CharacTER are used in the Offline and the Model Compression tasks, while WER, COMET and BERT scores are used Instruction Following task.

The Evaluation Server is described in detail in Appendix B.1.

2.2 Human Evaluation

Similar to last year's round, a human evaluation through direct assessment is performed on the primary submissions of each participant in order to verify the soundness and completeness of the results. We include most tasks and test sets for human evaluation. We follow Sperber et al. (2024)'s approach to handle the automatically segmented long-form speech in a robust manner. Details are provided in Section A.

3 Offline track

The Offline Speech Translation task at IWSLT, a cornerstone of the conference's tradition, aims to establish a robust evaluation framework for monitoring advancements in spoken language translation. Its core focus lies in unconstrained speech translation, distinguishing it from tasks with inherent temporal and structural limitations such as simultaneous translation or subtitling. While maintaining a consistent task formulation, the emphasis over time has incrementally shifted towards increasing task difficulty to better align with real-world demands, encompassing the translation of

[1] www.meetween.eu
[2] iwslt2025.speechm.cloud.cyfronet.pl

Team	Organization	Tracks	Reference
AIB-MARCO		🔋	
ALADAN	ALADAN	🔋	Kheder et al. (2025)
APPTEK	AppTek	🅲🅲	Petrick et al. (2025)
BUINUS	University of Indonesia and Bina Nusantara University	🔋	Tjiaranata et al. (2025)
CDAC-SVNIT	Center for Development of Advance Computing & Sardar Vallabhbhai National Institute of Technology	🌏	Roy et al. (2025)
CMU	Carnegie Mellon University	⏱	Ouyang et al. (2025)
CUNI	Charles University	⏱	Macháček and Polák (2025)
CUNI-NL	Charles University	🔌 ☰	Luu and Bojar (2025)
FFSTC-2		🔋	Kponou et al. (2025b)
GMU	George Mason University	🔋	Meng and Anastasopoulos (2025)
HITSZ	Harbin Institute of Technology, Shenzhen	🌏	Wei et al. (2025)
IIITH-BUT	International Institute of Information Technology Hyderabad (IIITH) and Brno University of Technology (BUT)	🔋	Akkiraju et al. (2025)
IITM	SPRING Lab, IIT Madras	🌏	Sarkar et al. (2025)
IST	Instituto Superior Tecnico	☰	Attanasio et al. (2025)
JHU	Johns Hopkins University	🔋	Robinson et al. (2025)
JU	Jadavpur University	🌏	Das et al. (2025)
JU-CSE-NLP	Jadavpur University	🌏	Dhar et al. (2025)
KIT	Karlsruhe Institute of Technology	🔌 🔋 ☰	Koneru et al. (2025); Li et al. (2025)
KREASOF-TCD	Kreasof AI, Trinity College Dublin, and African Institute for Mathematical Sciences	🔋	Farouq et al. (2025)
KUVOST		🔋	Mohammadamini et al. (2025)
LIA	University of Avignon	🔋	Chellaf et al. (2025)
MBZAI	Mohamed bin Zayed University of Artificial Intelligence	🔋	
MEETWEEN	MeetWeen	☰	
NAIST	Nara Institute of Science and Technology	🔌 ⏱	Widiaputri et al. (2025); Tan et al. (2025)
NLE	NAVER LABS Europe	☰	Lee et al. (2025)
NYA	Netease YiDun AI Lab	🔌	Wang et al. (2025)
OSU	Oregon State University	⏱	Raffel et al. (2025)
QUESPA	QUESPA	🔋	Ortega et al. (2025)
SYSTRAN	company for translation technology	🔋	Avila and Crego (2025)
TCD	Trinity College Dublin	🏋	Moslem (2025)
UPV	Universitat Politècnica de València	⏱	Sanchez et al. (2025)
URDU		🔋	Mehmood and Rauf (2025)

Table 1: List of participants to the IWSLT 2025 shared tasks (🔌 Offline track; ⏱ Simulultaneous track; 🅲🅲 Subtitle track; 🏋 Compression track; 🔋 Low-resource track; 🌏Indic track; ☰ Instruction-following track

new and diverse languages, domains, and speaking styles.

This section provides an overview of this year's task characteristics, along with a summary of the participating systems and their respective results.

3.1 Challenge

In line with the track's emphasis on the challenges posed by diverse and increasingly complex evaluation scenarios, this year's round focused on incorporating a new language, Arabic, into an evaluation setting designed to capture the complexity of real-world speech. This scenario encompassed diverse language settings (English → Arabic/Chinese/German) and domains (scientific presentations, TV series, and business news), alongside varied speaking styles and challenging recording conditions (e.g., single speakers, multiple overlapping speakers, background noise, and accent data).

Within this framework, participants were tasked with developing their system(s) for any of the three language combinations, selecting one from three distinct training data conditions (i.e., constrained, constrained with large language models, unconstrained), which differed in terms of allowed training resources. Consistent with previous rounds, the task welcomed participation with both cascade and end-to-end models, the latter being defined as solutions that eschew intermediate discrete representations (e.g., source language transcripts), instead employing joint training of all parameters and components used during decoding. Multiple submissions to the "SPEECHM" centralized evaluation server[3] were permitted, with the requirement of designating one as the *primary* submission and any others as *contrastive*.

[3]iwslt2025.speechm.cloud.cyfronet.pl

3.2 Data and Metrics

Test Data Also this year, participants were provided with test data representative of diverse domains and conditions, namely:

- **Scientific Presentations** – This dataset, derived from the Instruction Following task (Section 9), comprises 21 recordings, each lasting approximately 5.5 minutes, featuring transcripts of scientific oral presentations and their corresponding translations into several languages. The talks encompass a variety of technical content delivered by speakers from around the world.
- **TV Series** from ITV Studios[4] – This dataset includes 3 recordings, each approximately 40 minutes in length, featuring multiple individuals interacting in various scenarios. The speech translation system needs to handle challenges such as overlapping speakers, different accents, and background noise.
- **Business News** from Asharq Business with Bloomberg[5] – This dataset comprises two recordings, each approximately 2.5 hours in duration, and specifically focuses on the economy domain. The content is derived from a TV channel and distributed through various digital and social media platforms.
- **Accented English Conversations** sampled from the Edinburgh International Accents of English Corpus (EdAcc, Sanabria et al., 2023) – This dataset provides approximately 3.5 hours of conversations, each featuring two friends interacting on daily topics such like hobbies and vacation. The speakers were selected to cover a wide range of English accents from around the globe. In addition to the variety of accents (33 in total), another major challenge presented is the presence of spontaneous speech.

Contingent on data availability, each language direction was evaluated across distinct scenarios, specifically:

- English → German: TV series, scientific presentations, business news, and accent challenge.
- English → Arabic: business news.
- English → Chinese: scientific presentations.

Continuing the practice of previous years, the test sets were either entirely or partially shared with other tasks. This included the subtitling track (for TV series and business news data), the simultaneous, instruction-following, and model compression tracks (for scientific presentations). This collaborative approach significantly fosters broader integration and comparability across the various components of the evaluation campaign.

Training and Development Data As in the last two rounds of the challenge, participants were offered the possibility to submit systems built under three training data conditions:

1. **Constrained**: In this condition, permitted training data is limited to a medium-sized framework to ensure manageable training time and resource requirements. The comprehensive list[6] of allowed training resources (speech, speech-to-text-parallel, text-parallel, text-monolingual) explicitly excludes any pre-trained language models.
2. **Constrained with large language models** (constrained^{+LLM}): This condition allows all training data permitted in the constrained setup, with the addition of any other LLMs, provided they are freely accessible and released under a permissive license. This setup aims to enable participants to leverage accessible LLMs in a standardized evaluation scenario.
3. **Unconstrained**: Under this condition, any resource, including pre-trained language models, may be utilized, with the sole exception of the evaluation sets. This setup is designed to allow the participation of teams equipped with high computational power and capable of developing effective solutions leveraging additional in-house resources.

Development data were supplied only for English-German and English-Chinese. For English-German, they comprise the development set from IWSLT 2010, along with the test sets released for the 2010, 2013-2015, and 2018-2022 IWSLT campaigns. For English-Chinese, they consist of the test set used for the 2022 round.

Evaluation Metrics Systems were evaluated based on their ability to produce translations similar to the target-language references. This similarity was quantified using multiple automatic metrics: COMET[7] (Rei et al., 2020), BLEU[8](Papineni et al., 2002), BLEURT (Sellam et al., 2020), Char-

[4]www.itvstudios.com

[5]asharqbusiness.com

[6]See the IWSLT 2025 offline track: iwslt.org/2025/offline

[7]huggingface.co/Unbabel/wmt22-comet-da

[8]BLEU+case.mixed+numrefs.1+smooth.exp+tok.13a +version.1.4.14

acTER (Wang et al., 2016), chrF[9](Popović, 2015), and TER[10](Snover et al., 2006). COMET was again chosen as the primary evaluation metric this year. It was calculated on the test set using automatic resegmentation of the hypothesis based on the reference translation by mwerSegmenter,[11] employing a detailed script made accessible to participants.[12] To enhance the soundness and completeness of the evaluation, human assessment was also conducted on the best-performing submission from each participant.

3.3 Submissions

This year, 7 teams participated in the offline task, submitting a total of 30 runs through the "SPEECHM" evaluation server. Table 2 provides a breakdown of the participation in each subtask showing, for each training data condition, the number of participants, the number of submitted runs and, for each training data condition (constrained, constrained^{+LLM}, unconstrained), the number of submitted runs. Below, we provide a short description of the systems, whose creators submitted a system description paper.

CUNI-NL (Luu and Bojar, 2025) participated with an end-to-end en-de system trained under the "constrained with Large Language Models" condition. The model consists of an audio encoder that transforms the input audio into embeddings that are then passed to the LLM, which generates the output texts (transcript or translation). Both a length adapter and a modality adapter are added to facilitate the integration of the audio embeddings into the LLM. Two speech encoders (Seamless-v2-large and Whisper-v3-large) and three LLMs (Llama3 8B Instruct, EuroLLM 9B Instruct, and gemma3 12B Instruct) have been tested. To enhance the performance, multitask training was performed, teaching the model to transcribe, translate, and simultaneously transcribe and translate. The training data are limited to the CoVoST2 dataset and a large multilingual corpus built from the Common Voice corpora.

[9]nrefs:1+case:mixed+eff:yes+nc:6+nw:0+space:no +version:2.4.2

[10]nrefs:1+case:lc+tok:tercom+norm:no+punct:yes+asian:no +version:2.4.2

[11]www-i6.informatik.rwth-aachen.de/web/Software/mwerSegmenter.tar.gz

[12]github.com/isl-mt/SLT.KIT/blob/master/scripts/evaluate/Eval.sh

KIT (Koneru et al., 2025) participated with a cascade en-de system trained under the "unconstrained" condition. The cascade model comprises several components. The segmenter aims to identify the optimal point at which to segment an audio file. Various techniques were tested, demonstrating that fixed-window chunking with a chunk size of 25 consistently yields the best performance. The second component is an ensemble of ASR systems trained under different conditions, which is used to transcribe the audio. The produced transcripts are then recombined by a task-adapted LLM based on Llama3 8 B. The final transcripts are translated using a version of Tower 7B enhanced for the en-de translation direction. A final component was introduced to post-edit the translations with an APE model based on Tower 13 B. All the data used to train each component has been previously cleaned and selected to obtain high-quality samples.

NAIST (Widiaputri et al., 2025) participated with end-to-end en-de, en-zh systems, where the version based on SALMONN technology was trained under the "unconstrained" condition, while the in-house version was trained under the "constrained with Large Language Models" condition. SALMONN is an end-to-end speech-to-text model that integrates Whisper large-v2 as the speech encoder, a fine-tuned BEATs encoder for non-speech audio and the Vicuna 13B LLM as the decoder. The two audio encoders and the LLM are connected via a window-level Q-Former module. The customised end-to-end version is based on the Whisper large-v3 encoder, a DeCo projector, and the Qwen2.5 LLM. The en-de models are fine-tuned using a combination of CoVoST and Europarl, while the en-zh models are fine-tuned only on CoVoST. Different prompts have been tested to maximise translation performance.

NYA (Wang et al., 2025) participated with cascade en-ar, en-de, en-zh systems trained under the "unconstrained" condition. The ASR is based on Whisper medium, while the MT system combines an NMT model based on the Transformer technology and an LLM model based on X-ALMA. The NMT model is enhanced by leveraging data augmentation with backwards and forward translations and domain adaptation via data filtering. The LLM model is obtained by fine-tuning X-ALMA on in-domain data and leveraging Low-

English-German				
Participants	Runs	Constrained	Constrained^{+LLM}	Unconstrained
6	16	0	4	12
English-Chinese				
Participants	Runs	Constrained	Constrained^{+LLM}	Unconstrained
4	10	0	2	8
English-Arabic				
Participants	Runs	Constrained	Constrained^{+LLM}	Unconstrained
2	4	0	0	4

Table 2: Breakdown of the participation in each sub-task (English→German, English→Chinese, English→Arabic) of the IWSLT offline ST track. For each language direction, we report the number of participants, the number of submitted runs and, for each training data condition (constrained, constrained^{+LLM}, unconstrained), the number of submitted runs.

Rank Adaptation fine-tuning. The NMT n-best and the LLM list of candidates are merged and reranked using COMET-based MBR decoding. The MT training data are filtered using a semantic metric based on sBERT. The in-domain specific data are generated by crawling domain-specific videos and leveraging the existing bilingual subtitles. The audio is segmented using SHAS.

3.4 Results

3.4.1 English to German

Overall result Table 21 shows the aggregated result of the systems participated in the four test sets. In terms of ranking based on automatic evaluation metrics, KIT is ranked 1st, followed by NYA and NeMo. These top-3 systems perform better than the others by a large margin, e.g., a 0.1 COMET score, and most of them are based on the cascaded architecture rather than end-to-end. Unlike last year, where the winning system is metric dependent, the ranking between the top-3 systems remains consistent across all six metrics.

Unlike the top-3 systems, NAIST (U) and CUNI-NL presents a scenario where the ranking is metric dependent. In particular, NAIST (U) performs better in both COMET and BLEURT (neural metrics) but worse in both BLEU and chrF (string-based metrics).

Domains This year, a new set of domains has been introduced for evaluation. The long-standing TED domain has been removed, whereas the accent (data) and the ITV (only the domain) remain. Similar to last year's edition, we evaluated each submitted system on different domains.

In spite of having diverse set of domains, the top-3 systems (KIT, NYA and NeMo) perform consistently well. The much better numbers on the evaluation metrics indicate that both Scientific Presentations and Business News domains are less challenging to translate than the accent and ITV domains. Although the top-3 systems perform similarly in both the accent and ITV domains, the remaining systems achieve far worse scores on the ITV domain, making ITV possibly the most challenging domain.

Furthermore, the ranking across domains is quite consistent meaning that a system performing good in one domain as performs good in the other domain. The only exception is AIB, which performs good on three domains, but has challenges in the ITV domain.

Data conditions On top of the above, we can also observe the improvement of translation quality by increase the training data size. In all the test domains, the top three systems are from the "unconstrained" conditions, whereas the "constrained LLMs" submissions are ranked the bottom, except in the ITV domain. Among all the participants, NAIST is the only team which submitted both "unconstrained" and "constrained with LLMs" conditions. Their "unconstrained" system outperforms the constrained condition substantially in all metrics, showing the importance of training data size despite using LLMs for the tasks. However, it is worth noting that the pretrained models and the architectures between the two conditions are quite dissimilar. Another noteworthy comparison is between the CUNI-NL and the NAIST (U). Despite being a "constrained with LLMs" submission, the CUNI-NL performs better in Business News, ITV and Scientific Presentations domains in almost all metrics. This smaller performance gap could be attributed to the choice of the pretrained models, which the CUNI-NL has substantially tested on.

3.4.2 English to Arabic

For the en-ar direction, we evaluate the submitted systems on the Business News domain. This is a newly added language pair this year, and there are 3 submissions that are all based on "unconstrained" conditions.

Table 22 summarizes the results. The NYA is ranked 1st, followed by the NeMo and the AIB. The ranking is consistent across all the evaluation metrics. Furthermore, the ranking is also consistent with the ranking in English to German.

3.4.3 English to Chinese

For the en-zh direction, we evaluate the submitted systems on the Scientific Presentations domain. Unlike last year, there are both cascaded and end-to-end submissions this year.

Table 23 summarizes the results. The NYA is ranked 1st in the COMET metric among the six submitted systems. In addition to COMET, it is also ranked 1st in both BLEU and character-TER. While it does not score the highest on chrF and BLEURT, it ranks second overall. The AIB takes the second place with performance similar to the NYA in most evaluation metrics, and it is even ranked 1st according to BLEURT.

Regarding the data condition, NAIST submitted both "unconstrained" and "constrained with LLMs" conditions. Similar to en-de language direction, their "unconstrained" system outperforms the "constrained with LLMs" system substantially in all metrics. Despite the stronger performance, possibly caused by the larger training data size, NAIST (U) and NAIST (C^+) use different pre-trained components.

3.5 Human Evaluation

Similar to previous editions, each participant's primary submission has been further assessed by professional translators. The details of the human evaluation and its results are described in A.

Examining the results, it is interesting to note that, in most cases, human evaluation confirms the ranking provided by automatic metrics, with only minor discrepancies. This is true for the English to Arabic direction, where NYA outperforms other models, and for the English to Chinese direction, where only the top position shifted in favour of NYA, leading to a better average DA score than AIB (despite automatic metrics showing minimal difference between the two submissions). The human evaluation also corroborates the findings from the automatic metrics regarding the impact of data conditions: the models trained in the unconstrained data condition generally outperform those trained in the constrained condition.

For English to German, the results confirm the trends observed in other language directions for the TV series test set, with human evaluation validating the rankings generated by the automatic metrics. More variations are shown for the accent and scientific presentation test sets.[13] For the accent test set, KIT outperforms all other systems, achieving the best score. The most surprising results concern the AIB submission, which, despite a significant difference from the best model in terms of COMET score (5.4 points), is indistinguishable from KIT from the human evaluation standpoint. It is difficult to hypothesise a possible reason for this discrepancy due to the lack of a system description paper, but this confirms the need to test a model under different conditions and validate its results with human evaluation. The AIB submission also shows similar behaviour for the scientific presentation test set, where it is penalised by the automatic evaluation (fourth with a gap of 3.8 COMET scores from the top-ranked system), but rewarded by human evaluation.

The fact that some of the test sets are shared across different tasks gives us the possibility to present a single ranking including systems developed under different conditions and tasks. Examining Tables 14, 15 and 17 shows that the systems built for the offline task without any latency (simultaneous task), task-sharing (instruction task), and length (subtitling task) constraints attain the best performance, with a margin of more than 1 average DA score over the other submissions.

4 Simultaneous track

Simultaneous speech translation focuses on translating speech in real-time, in a manner similar to simultaneous interpreting. The system is designed to begin translating before the end of an utterance. This technology is particularly useful in scenarios such as international conferences, personal travel, or public emergency events.

The task included two tracks: cascaded and direct. Submissions to the cascaded track contain systems that produce intermediate text, i.e. the transcription of the source audio, that is imme-

[13]The Asharq News test set has not been human-evaluated due to budget constraints.

diately consumed by a simultaneous text-to-text agent. In contrast, direct, or end-to-end, systems avoid any intermediate text and directly generate target-language (text) translations from the source audio. Both tracks covered four language directions as in the previous year: English to German, English to Chinese, English to Japanese, and Czech to English.

4.1 Challenge

4.1.1 Changes from the last year

This year's simultaneous translation task had two major changes compared to the last year:

Long-form speech We introduced a more realistic condition for simultaneous speech translation on unsegmented speech (Papi et al., 2025a). Participants had to develop streaming translation systems processing long-form speech.

Large language models Participants were allowed to use LLMs under the same conditions as *Constrained with large language models* in the Offline task described in Section 3.2.

4.1.2 Latency regimes

Two latency regimes, *low* and *high*, were introduced for each of the tracks to evaluate translation quality in different latency conditions.

English-to-German and Czech-to-English 0 to 2 seconds (low), 2 to 4 seconds (high)

English-to-Chinese 0 to 2.5 seconds (low), 2.5 to 4 seconds (high)

English-to-Japanese 0 to 3.5 seconds (low), 3.5 to 5 seconds (high)

4.1.3 Submission

Participants were allowed to submit no more than one system per track, language direction, and latency regime. The latency regime of a submission was determined by its results on the development set. This year, we allowed two submission options: *Docker image* and *System log* submissions. The latter option was easier for the participants because they did not need to wrap their systems into a deployable form. Systems of the Docker image submissions were executed by the organizers on the blind-test set in a controlled environment using a NVIDIA H200 GPU. An example implementation was provided using the SimulEval toolkit (Ma et al., 2020).

4.2 Data

To simplify the setting and allow participants to focus on the new modeling aspects of simultaneous translation, we adhere to the constraints with large language models as defined for the offline SLT task, see Section 3.2 above. This is the only data condition for the task. The test and dev sets differ across language pairs:

English to German, Chinese, and Japanese The test data are the speech translation section of the IWSLT25Instruct benchmark created for the Instruction Following task (Section 9) and derived from scientific talks (ACL Anthology presentations). The dev data are the ACL 60/60 benchmark (Salesky et al., 2023). In addition, we use *Accented English Conversations* test set for English to German.

split	domain	#utter.	#words/ utter.	duration (min)
dev	ParCzech	276	24	56
	ELITR	314	13	28.6
test	ParCzech	636	20.53	108.58
	Non-Native	1298	6.33	86.85

Table 3: Statistics of the dev and test sets for the Czech-English simultaneous task.

Czech to English The dev set was created from two sources:

- From ParCzech 3.0 (Kopp et al., 2021), we took a subset of the test recordings in the variant called "context", which consists of parliamentary speeches in their original partitioning, preserving the natural flow of the speech.
- From the ELITR test set (Ansari et al., 2021),[14] we took an entire recording of a debate about AI.

The reference translations of the devset were done by students of translation studies from the Faculty of Arts at Charles University.

The test set was also collected from two sources:

- Selected recordings (complete speeches) of the Parliament of the Czech Republic, ensuring that there is no speaker overlap with the recordings allowed for training.
- Recordings of Czech language proficiency exams at the A2 level (Novák et al., 2024).

[14]github.com/ELITR/elitr-testset/tree/master/documents/2021-theaitre-related/robothon-debate

The reference translations of the testset were provided by a professional translation agency. The statistics of both sets are provided in Table 3.

4.3 Evaluation

4.3.1 Automatic Evaluation

We automatically evaluate two aspects of models: quality and latency.

Quality We conducted both automatic and human evaluation. BLEU (Papineni et al., 2002) and COMET (Rei et al., 2022a) are used for automatic quality evaluation. The ranking of the submission is based on the BLEU score on the blind test set.

Latency We only conducted automatic evaluation using StreamLAAL (Papi et al., 2024).

4.3.2 Human evaluation

For English-to-German and Czech-to-English, human evaluation was conducted using the Continuous Rating method proposed by Javorský et al. (2022). Further details on the method and score calculation are provided in Appendix A.2. This evaluation covered systems operating in the high-latency regime (with the exception of the CMU submission, which participated only in the low-latency regime).

For Czech-to-English, we additionally collected two independent human interpretations—one by a professional and one by a student interpreter—and evaluated them in the exact same manual evaluation style as system outputs, i.e. presenting them as gradually growing text in their authentic timing. The professional interpreter has been working full-time in the field since 2013, has been accredited by EU institutions since 2018, and regularly interprets for clients such as Czech Television, Czech Radio, CNN, and the World Bank. The student interpreter was a second-year master's student at the Institute of Translation Studies, with three completed semesters of simultaneous interpreting training. The interpreting was carried out remotely, transcribed by WhisperX (Bain et al., 2023) and post-edited by an annotator fluent in English. For preparation of the sessions, both interpreters got a brief summary of each speech in three sentences using Llama 3.3 language model (Grattafiori et al., 2024). According to the professional interpreter, the interpretation differed from real-world conditions for three main reasons: (1) the absence of visual input, as the recordings were provided in audio-only format; (2) the absence of a second interpreter, who would normally assist by noting down numbers and looking up specific terminology; and (3) limited preparation time, as the speeches covered a wide range of topics — unlike in real interpreting settings, where the subject matter is typically more stable.

For English-to-Japanese, another human evaluation was conducted by a professional interpreter using MQM-based metric (JTF, 2018) as in the last years.

Human evaluation using Direct Assessment was also conducted for comparison with other tasks, as described in A.1.

4.4 Submissions

Five teams in total participated this year, with three of those participating submissions containing testable systems for computationally-aware latency measurements. All teams entered the English-to-German track; four teams entered the English-to-Chinese, two teams entered the English-to-Japanese tracks; and one team entered the Czech-to-English track.

BASELINES were built for all directions. We use two approaches, a cascaded and a direct one. Both approaches used simultaneous segmenters to accommodate the long-form regime. We used fixed-length and VAD segmenters as described in Polák and Bojar (2024). For the cascaded system, we use Whisper-Large-V3-Turbo (Radford et al., 2023) for ASR and M2M100 (Fan et al., 2021) for MT. Both the Whisper and M2M100 models were onlinized using the Local Agreement policy (Polák et al., 2022, 2023). To make the ASR more robust to segmentation, we used the transcript of the previous segment as a context. For the direct approach, we selected SeamlessM4T (Seamless Communication et al., 2023) as the backbone of our system. We also used the Local Agreement policy for onlinizing the offline SeamlessM4T model.

CUNI **(Macháček and Polák, 2025)** participated in the direct track for English to German, Chinese, and Japanese, as well as Czech to English directions. They proposed two system architectures based on the language direction. For the from-English direction, their system is based on Whisper-Large-V3 (Radford et al., 2022) in the role of ASR and EuroLLM (Martins et al., 2024) as MT. The Whisper model was onlinized using the AlignAtt (Papi et al., 2023) policy, while the EuroLLM model was onlinized using the Local Agreement policy (Polák et al., 2022, 2023). For the Czech-to-English direction, they used a direct approach, leveraging Whisper-Large-V3. They also explored improving translation quality by including previous translation as context and prompting for in-domain terminology.

CMU **(Ouyang et al., 2025)** participated in the direct track for the English to Chinese and German directions. Their system integrates a chunk-wise causal Wav2Vec2.0 speech encoder (Baevski et al., 2020), an adapter, and the Qwen2.5-7B-Instruct (Qwen et al., 2025) as the decoder. The training is conducted in two stages on speech segments curated from LibriSpeech (Panayotov et al., 2015), CommonVoice (Ardila et al., 2020b), and VoxPopuli (Wang et al., 2021) datasets, which are translated into Chinese and German with the 4-bit quantized Qwen2.5-32B-Instruct. The latency is controlled through a configurable latency multiplier, ensuring translations are generated after accumulating a predefined number of chunks, and the decoder uses a sliding window strategy to maintain the context through KV cache concatenation.

OSU **(Raffel et al., 2025)** participated in the cascaded track for the English-to-German and Chinese directions. Their system employs Whisper-Large-V2 (Radford et al., 2022) with a voice-activity-detection (VAD) segmenter (Silero Team, 2021) for ASR with a 4-bit quantized Gemma3-12B-Instruct (Team et al., 2025) and context-aware conversational prompting (Wang et al., 2024a) for translation. For fine-tuning, they re-purpose a prior framework (Agostinelli et al., 2024; Raffel et al., 2024) and its conversational prompting implementation alongside semantic similarity-based filtering to curate noisy subtitling data (Lison et al., 2018) before fine-tuning with LoRAs (Hu et al., 2021). In addition, this system augments basic conversational prompting for ST by leveraging a single-sentence sliding window memory bank for prior context.

UPV **(Sanchez et al., 2025)** participated in the cascaded track for the English-to-German direction. Their system employs Whisper-Large-V3-Turbo (Radford et al., 2022) with a modified longest-common-prefix (LCP) decoding policy for ASR alongside NLLB-3.3B (NLLB Team et al., 2022) with relaxed-agreement LCP (RALCP) (Wang et al., 2024b) with a *wait-k* policy (Ma et al., 2019) for simultaneous translation. Additionally, this system features a similar, but simplified and more efficient, segmentation process to AlignAtt (Papi et al., 2023), leveraging attention maps to judge necessary model context. For training, they randomly prepended up to 10 sentences of prior context to a given sample so as to better leverage the unsegmented audio of this year's task.

NAIST **(Tan et al., 2025)** participated in English-to-German, Chinese, and Japanese language directions of the direct track. Their system employs SHAS (Tsiamas et al., 2022) for speech segmentation, Whisper-large-v3 (Radford et al., 2022) for encoding input speech, DeCo (Yao et al., 2024) for projecting Whisper features into acoustic embeddings for the LLM, and Qwen-2.5-7B-Instruct (Qwen et al., 2025) LLM. It was fine-tuned with LoRA by joint training of ST and ASR, and the offline-trained ST system was used for simultaneous translation using Local Agreement (Liu et al., 2020; Polák et al., 2022).

4.5 Results

4.5.1 Automatic Evaluation

We rank the system performance based on BLEU scores. Cascaded systems are marked with an asterisk ($*$). The detailed results can be found in the respective tables in Appendix B.3.

Low-Latency The ranking of systems for the the low-latency condition is as follows:

- English to German (Table 24):
  CMU, NAIST, OSU *, BASELINES-Direct
- English to Chinese (Table 25):
  CMU, NAIST, OSU *, BASELINES-Direct
- English to Japanese (Table 26):
  NAIST, BASELINES-Direct
- Native Czech to English (Table 27):
  CUNI, BASELINES-Direct
- Non-native Czech to English (Table 28):
  CUNI, BASELINES-Direct
- Accented English to German (Table 29):
  OSU *, NAIST, CMU, BASELINES-Direct

High-Latency The ranking of systems for the high-latency condition is as follows:

- English to German (Table 24):
  CUNI *, UPV *, OSU *, BASELINES-Casc.*, NAIST, BASELINES-Direct
- English to Chinese (Table 25):
  CUNI *, NAIST, OSU *, BASELINES-Direct

- English to Japanese (Table 26):
  CUNI, NAIST, BASELINES-Direct
- Native Czech to English (Table 27):
  BASELINES-Direct, CUNI, BASELINES-Casc.*
- Non-native Czech to English (Table 28):
  CUNI, BASELINES-Casc.*, BASELINES-Direct
- Accented English to German (Table 29):
  OSU *, UPV *, BASELINES-Casc. *, NAIST, CUNI *, BASELINES-Direct

4.5.2 Human Evaluation

Details of the human evaluation are provided in Section A.2 of the Appendix and results are shown in Table 18 for Czech-to-English, in Table 19 for English-to-German, and in Table 20 for English-to-Japanese. For Czech-to-English and English-to-German, we selected only one baseline that has a higher BLEU score.

4.6 Conclusions

This year's simultaneous translation shared task marks a significant shift in the focus of simultaneous translation system evaluations. With the introduction of unsegmented source audio in the test-set, participants are incentivized to address critical opportunities and challenges in real applications that have largely been avoided in prior years at the IWSLT. Unlike last year, submissions for this year's shared task all feature large language models (LLMs), with the exception of the CUNI Czech-to-English submission, which were tailored for simultaneous translation in a variety of ways. Interestingly, a range of LLMs were represented in this year's submissions. CUNI's submission leveraged EuroLLM, a model built for translation across numerous languages, whereas other teams employed more general-purpose models.

On the IWSLT25Instruct test set, the CUNI submission outperformed almost all other systems at high-latency regimes, aside from on English-to-Chinese, where the NAIST submission produced a slightly higher BLEU score. At low-latency regimes, CMU produced the highest quality translations at comparatively low latency for English-to-German and English-to-Chinese. While the OSU and UPV submissions performed worse on the IWSLT25Instruct test set, they both performed significantly better on the challenging accented English-to-German test set, with the OSU system performing best at the cost of comparably high latency.

Human evaluation of the Czech-to-English language pair shows that the quality of CUNI is comparable to that of the student interpreter but worse than that of the professional interpreter. However, the latency of CUNI is 1.51, approximately three times lower, i.e. faster than human interpreting.[15] BLEU scores for human interpretations are very low, which is expected, as interpreting often involves paraphrasing, summarization, and explanation. While both latency and BLEU favor CUNI, the professional interpreting still delivers the highest overall quality and in the shortest time, by going beyond the literal translation and conveying information in a more comprehensive way.

Human evaluation for English-to-German and English-to-Japanese aligns well with the results of automatic evaluation. Neural network-based evaluations are similarly aligned with automatic evaluations, yielding no major surprises.

Regarding promising directions for investigations and improvements to the shared task, the accented and non-native test sets emerged as the most difficult for current systems, and more studies on these scenarios could drive simultaneous translation models to be more robust. Moreover, enhancing the task accessibility–such as allowing log-based submissions as this year–can encourage broader participation. However, this comes at the cost of losing compatibility in computationally-aware latency metrics, which are crucial for simultaneous translation systems. Striking a balance between accessibility and fair evaluation will be key to enabling more meaningful progress in future editions.

5 Subtitling track

In recent years, the task of automatically creating subtitles for audiovisual content in another language has gained a lot of attention due to the rapid increase in the global distribution and streaming of movies, series, and user-generated videos. Reflecting these trends, the **automatic subtitling track** was introduced for the first time in 2023 (Agarwal et al., 2023) and proposed again in 2024 (Ahmad et al., 2024) as part of the IWSLT Evaluation Campaigns.

The automatic subtitling task has been continued this year.[16] Participants were asked to gen-

[15]The latency is even lower than 2 seconds. The reason is that the systems were bucketed according to the latency on the devset, which for CUNI is 2.63.

[16]The **subtitle compression** sub-track, introduced in 2024, was proposed this year as well but we received no submis-

erate subtitles in German and/or Arabic from English speech in audiovisual documents.

5.1 Challenge

The task of automatic subtitling is multifaceted: starting from speech, not only must the translation be generated, but it must also be segmented into subtitles that comply with constraints ensuring a high-quality user experience. These constraints include proper reading speed, synchrony with the voices, the maximum number of subtitle lines, and characters per line. Most audio-visual companies define their own subtitling guidelines, which can slightly differ from each other. In the case of IWSLT participants, we asked to generate subtitles according to specific guidelines provided by TED, including:

- The maximum subtitle reading speed is 21 characters per second;
- Lines cannot exceed 42 characters, including white spaces;
- Subtitles cannot exceed 2 lines.

Participants were expected to use only the audio track from the provided videos (dev and test sets), as the video track could be of low quality and primarily intended to check the temporal synchronicity and other aspects of displaying subtitles on screen.

The subtitling track required participants to automatically subtitle audio-visual documents in German and/or Arabic, where the spoken language is always English. The documents were collected from the following sources:

- TV series from **ITV** Studios;[17]
- Financial news content recordings from the **Asharq Business with Bloomberg** media group.[18]

5.2 Data and Metrics

Data. This track proposed two training data conditions:

- **Constrained**: the official training data condition, in which the allowed training data is limited to a medium-sized framework[19] to keep the training time and resource requirements manageable;
- **Unconstrained**: a setup without data restrictions (any resource, pre-trained language models included, can be used) to allow also the participation of teams equipped with high computational power and effective in-house solutions built on additional resources.

For each language and domain, a development set and three test sets were released, those of previous evaluations (**tst2023** and **tst2024**), used for measuring progress over years, and a new one (**tst2025**). Table 4 provides some statistics on these sets.

domain	set	AV docs	hh:mm	#ref subtitles de	#ref subtitles ar
ITV	dev	7	06:01	4489	-
	tst23	7	05:08	4807	-
	tst24	7	05:54	4564	-
	tst25	3	02:07	1845	-
Asharq--Bloomberg	dev	2	03:01	3662	2974
	tst25	2	03:03	3543	2759

Table 4: Statistics of the dev and evaluation sets for the subtitling task.

Metrics. The evaluation was carried out from three perspectives, subtitle quality, translation quality, and subtitle compliance, through the following automatic measures:

- Subtitle quality vs. reference subtitles:
  - **SubER**, primary metric, used also for ranking (Wilken et al., 2022);[20]
- Translation quality vs. reference translations:
  - **BLEU**[21] and **CHRF**[22] via sacreBLEU (Post, 2018);
  - **BLEURT** (Sellam et al., 2020).

  Automatic subtitles are realigned to the reference subtitles using mwerSegmenter (Matusov et al., 2005)[23] before running sacreBLEU and BLEURT.
- Subtitle compliance:[24]
  - rate of subtitles with more than 21 characters per second (**CPS**);
  - rate of lines longer than 42 characters, whitespace included (**CPL**);
  - rate of subtitles with more than 2 lines (**LPB**).

sion for it.

[17] www.itvstudios.com

[18] asharqbusiness.com

[19] iwslt.org/2025/subtitling#training-and-data-conditions

[20] github.com/apptek/SubER

[21] sacreBLEU signature: `nrefs:1|case:mixed|eff:no|tok:13a|smooth:exp|version:2.0.0`

[22] sacreBLEU signature: `nrefs:1|case:mixed|eff:yes|nc:6|nw:0|space:no|version:2.0.0`

[23] www-i6.informatik.rwth-aachen.de/web/Software/mwerSegmenter.tar.gz

[24] github.com/hlt-mt/FBK-fairseq/blob/master/examples/speech_to_text/scripts/subtitle_compliance.py

5.3 Submissions

The subtitling track saw the participation of only one team: APPTEK (Petrick et al., 2025). Details about their systems follow.

AppTek: The APPTEK cascaded system includes the AppTek[25] production ASR and MT systems, adapted to the domains of this evaluation (ITV and Asharq-Bloomberg).

- **ITV**: In addition to other speech data from various domains, APPTEK's hybrid ASR system was trained on entertainment data (audio and corresponding subtitles) provided by AppTek's major media and entertainment localization customer. Similar data, in the form of professionally created English and German subtitle files, was used to adapt the English-to-German Transformer-based neural MT system.
- **Asharq-Bloomberg en-de**: The cascade of the AppTek's general domain ASR system and an adapted English-German MT system was used. The MT model was adapted on a subset of parallel data selected from available public sources (like CCMatrix), based on semantic similarity with the Asharq-Bloomberg en-de parallel development data (clustering based on sentence embedding similarity).
- **Asharq-Bloomberg en-ar**: In this case too, the cascade consisted of the AppTek's general domain ASR system and an adapted English-Arabic MT system. Here, the MT model was adapted on parallel data of human-curated (post-edited) Asharq-Bloomberg financial news programs. This data was available to AppTek as part of their cooperation with Asharq business with Bloomberg.

AppTek's Intelligent Line Segmentation (ILS, proprietary technology) neural model was used in the source language after ASR to create subtitle blocks, timed mostly according to word boundaries but extended where possible for a comfortable (lower) reading speed. ILS was also used to segment the translated sentences into these blocks, optimizing line breaks for human acceptance and readability while, at the same time, respecting the subtitling constraints.

AppTek's NMT systems support length control. For all primary submissions, whenever the default translation violated either the lines-per-block (LPB) limit or the characters-per-second (CPS) limit, the source transcript was re-translated with a stricter length control parameter (e.g., "short", "shorter", "shortest").

For the primary ITV submission, an increased reading speed limit of 23 CPS was chosen for a better translation quality/subtitle compliance trade-off. The `Contrastive 1` submission is without MT length control, while the `Contrastive 2` submission uses the default CPS value of 21. For Asharq-Bloomberg, the `Contrastive 1` is without domain adaptation, en-ar `Contrastive 2` is without length control, en-de `Contrastive 2` differs in setting MT meta-data controls to genre "news" and style "formal".

5.4 Results

5.4.1 Automatic Evaluation

Scores on tst2025 of all APPTEK runs calculated using automatic metrics are shown in Tables 30 and 31. Tables 32 and 33 refer to progressive tst2024 and tst2023 sets, respectively, where the primary runs of 2024 and 2023 participants are reported as well to allow comparisons and quantification of progresses.

tst2025 ITV en-de (Table 30, ITV rows): Scores confirm the expectations based on the setups of the various runs. The primary run actually provides the best trade-off between translation quality and subtitle compliance using a smoothed setup of the length control mechanism: indeed, its BLEURT score lies between those of `Contrastive 1` (for which translation quality was the priority, obtained by disabling the length control mechanisms) and `Contrastive 2` (for which subtitle compliance was prioritized using the default setup of the length control mechanism). On the other side, the CPS of the primary run is better than that of `Contrastive 1` but worse than `Contrastive 2`. The SubER value, being the best among all, confirms that the working point of the primary run optimizes the compromise between the two contrasting features.

tst2025 Asharq-Bloomberg en-de (Table 30, Asharq-Bloomberg rows): In the financial news domain, the length control configuration is common to all runs and so it is not surprising to observe CPS values that are close to each other. The MT model used to produce the `Contrastive 1` submission was not domain-adapted, which caused the lowest BLEURT value. It is evident

[25] www.apptek.com

that the generation of translations according to the "news" genre and "formal" style (`Contrastive 2`) does not have effects that automatic metrics can capture.

tst2025 Asharq-Bloomberg en-ar (Table 31): In this case, the domain adaptation does not help too much for the primary run as compared to the use of the original generic MT model (`Contrastive 1`). The deactivation of the length control mechanism (`Contrastive 2`) allows to obtain the best translation quality at the expense of the lowest CPS.

tst2024 ITV en-de (Table 32): The results of APPTEK's runs on the tst2024 essentially confirm the main outcome from the 2025 testset, i.e. that the length control mechanism allows to adjust the subtitle compliance at the expense of translation quality. The main difference observed between tst2025 and tst2024 results is that, for the latter, the best SubER—corresponding to the optimal trade-off between the two contrastive features—is obtained with the `Contrastive 2` setup, not the primary one.

Concerning the comparison with the primary submission of the past edition, the improvement observed for the 2025 APPTEK system is impressive from all point of views, including translation quality, subtitle compliance, and trade-off between them. The only 2024 system that beats the primary AppTek 2025 submission is HW-TSC in terms of (only) BLEURT, but at the cost of significantly worse subtitle compliance values.

tst2023 ITV en-de (Table 33): The same considerations made on APPTEK's runs for tst2024, in particular on the impact of the length control mechanism, also apply to tst2023.

The results on tst2023 also assess the progress among all participants of the current and past two editions of the subtitling track. As noted last year, the two best primary 2024 systems (APPTEK and HW-TSC) achieved SubER values similar to those of the two best 2023 systems (APPTEK and TLT), having generally better translation quality but worse subtitle compliance. This seemed to indicate that in 2024 more attention was paid to the quality of translation than to subtitle compliance. On the contrary, this year both aspects were taken into consideration, allowing to establish working points that are better than in the past from all perspectives.

Overall, the results discussed here demonstrate a clear evolution in subtitling technology over the years. Despite limited participation, the task appears to have successfully met its objectives of fostering research in this area by providing a shared evaluation framework for sound comparisons across diverse and challenging settings, as well as enabling comparative analyses of progress on blind test sets from previous years.

5.4.2 Human Evaluation

Human evaluation was also conducted for the subtitling task, with the aim of gaining a general and purely indicative understanding of the quality of the systems' output in this challenging condition, as compared to systems developed under different conditions, including the much less restrictive ones of the offline task. A crucial premise in interpreting the results reported in Section A.1 is that these results stem from an evaluation setup that is inherently penalizing for subtitling systems. The scores shown in Tables 13 and 16 were obtained by asking human assessors to compare the systems' outputs against verbatim translations, without access to the reference transcripts in the source language - a process that inevitably disadvantages the often shortened or condensed outputs produced by subtitling systems. That said, the results are not surprising. On the en-ar task (Table 13), the gap with the three competitive, unconstrained offline systems is substantial. On the en-de task (Table 16), the APPTEK system obtains rank 4 out of the 8 evaluated systems.

6 Model compression track

The Model Compression Track, introduced for the first time at IWSLT 2025, addresses a growing concern in the NLP community: how to reconcile the impressive capabilities of foundation models with the practical constraints of real-world deployment. As a matter of fact, while large-scale text and speech models have revolutionized tasks such as end-to-end speech-to-text translation, their substantial size and computational demands introduce significant challenges in resource-constrained settings—including mobile devices, embedded systems, and edge computing environments. This is particularly problematic when low-latency, on-device inference is required. Model compression offers a promising path forward, enabling reductions in model size and complexity while striving to minimize performance degradation as much as possible. By foregrounding this challenge, the track aims to establish a shared evaluation framework for monitoring future advancements in the development of more efficient, accessible, and deployable SLT systems.

6.1 Challenge

This year's objective was to assess participants' ability to reduce the size of a large multilingual speech-to-text foundation model while minimizing performance degradation in English→German and English→Chinese speech translation settings. The chosen model, Qwen2-Audio (Chu et al., 2024), was selected due to its substantial yet manageable size (8.2 billion parameters, requiring approximately 16 GB of memory storage), its support for various speech processing task across multiple language directions, and its permissive Apache 2.0 license. Altogether, its computational cost, memory-intensive nature, and versatility make it an ideal candidate for task-oriented model compression.

Regarding compression techniques, admissible approaches were required to exclusively focus on modifying or optimizing the model's internal parameters, ensuring that the final compressed model remained strictly derived from the original Qwen2-Audio. Therefore, eligible techniques included pruning (i.e. the removal of less important neurons and/or entire layers within the model, by identifying and eliminating parameters that contribute minimally to its output), quantization (i.e. the reduction of the numerical precision of the model's weights–e.g., from 32-bit to 16-bit, 8-bit, or less–to lower its memory footprint), distillation (i.e. the creation of a smaller "student" model derived from Qwen2-Audio, for instance through pruning, trained to replicate the behavior of the original "teacher" model), as well as any other method that produces a compressed counterpart of the original model. Compression techniques could be applied either individually or in combination.

6.2 Data and Metrics

Test Data Participants were provided with test data representative of a specific domain, **scientific presentations**, which is shared across other tracks–specifically, the offline, simultaneous, and instruction-following tracks. This dataset (IWSLT25Instruct, fully described in Section 9) comprises 21 recordings, each approximately 5.5 minutes in length, featuring transcripts of scientific oral presentations along with their corresponding translations from English into several languages (including German and Chinese).

Training and Development Data Participants were offered the possibility to submit systems developed under two distinct training data conditions, which differed in the datasets allowed to support the model compression process. Specifically, while the **unconstrained** condition imposed no restrictions on data usage, the **constrained** condition limited the permitted training data to the ACL60/60 dataset.[26] This dataset is identical in both size and source audio content for the two language directions involved in the task and, although small, is domain-consistent with the evaluation sets.

Evaluation As an initial step toward a comprehensive evaluation framework for benchmarking compression techniques that strike a balance between compactness and performance, this first round of the task focused on a subset of the relevant dimensions of the problem,[27] specifically addressing two interconnected challenges, each with its own evaluation criteria:

- **Model Reduction**: Reduce the size of the foundation model, defined by its number of parameters and memory usage, to improve suitability for deployment in resource-limited settings.
- **Translation Performance**: Preserve translation quality despite model size reduction, ensuring that the compressed models remain both practically valuable and reliable.

Focusing on these two dimensions, the evaluation protocol was designed to follow a two-step approach.

STEP 1: Categorization of the submitted models into five size bins based on their storage requirements (S),[28] representing increasingly aggressive levels of compression. The bins were defined as follows:

- Bin1: 2 GB $\leq$ S $<$ 4 GB
- Bin2: 1 GB $\leq$ S $<$ 2 GB
- Bin3: 500 MB $\leq$ S $<$ 1 GB

[26] https://aclanthology.org/attachments/2023.iwslt-1.2.dataset.zip

[27] While computational efficiency (i.e., speed) is recognized as a critical factor for deploying models in resource-constrained environments, it was excluded from the evaluation framework in this initial round. However, we plan to adopt a phased evaluation strategy in future editions, with subsequent rounds incorporating computational efficiency and thereby broadening the overall evaluation scope.

[28] Self-reported by participants at the submission stage.

Model	Num. Params (↓)	Storage (↓)	en-de (↑)	en-zh (↑)
Qwen2-Audio-7B-Instruct	8.4B	16.8GB	0.672	0.743
TCD_constrained_primary	5.0B	9.7GB	0.764	0.806
TCD_unconstrained_contrastive	4.1B	8.8GB	0.693	-

Table 5: Results on the IWSLT25-Instruct ST test set in terms of translation quality (COMET-22 scores) and model size (expressed in terms of number of parameters and storage size).

- Bin4: 200 MB ≤ S < 500 MB
- Bin5: S < 200 MB

STEP 2: Translation quality assessment using COMET, following the same procedure adopted in the offline track (i.e., computing COMET scores on the test sets after automatically resegmenting the system hypotheses and aligning them with the reference translations using mwerSegmenter[29]).

The rationale behind this evaluation protocol was to enable an independent assessment of models within the same size bin, thereby ensuring fairness and meaningfulness in the comparisons.

6.3 Submissions and Results

The task had only one participant, **TCD** (Moslem, 2025), that submitted a constrained primary system and an unconstrained contrastive one. The constrained system reduced the number of parameters by 40% by means of 4-bit quantization and QLoRa finetuning, after a full-finetuning of the base model (Qwen2-Audio-7B-Instruct) on the in-domain data. During the QLoRa finetuning, sequence-level knowledge distillation from the full-finetuned model is employed. For the unconstrained system, the method is similar, but after the first finetuning of the whole model a layer pruning strategy on the decoder (from 32 to 24 layers) is applied to further streamline the model, followed by another full-finetuning of the resulting model.

As seen from Table 5, the submitted runs exhibit mixed results with respect to our two evaluation dimensions. On the one hand, looking at **model reduction**, the number of parameters (5.0B for the constrained submission, 4.1B for the unconstrained one) and storage usage (9.7 GB and 8.8 GB, respectively) of the compressed models are notable but insufficient to meet the most relaxed size requirements defined by Bin1 (i.e., a maximum of 4 GB of storage). This highlights the difficulty of the task and the need to further explore more aggressive techniques, as there remains significant room for improvement.

On the other hand, considering **translation performance**, it is encouraging to observe that, although the reductions were insufficient to fall into any of the target compression bins, the output quality across both target languages is even higher than the original model, thanks to dedicated finetuning on in-domain data, despite the applied compression techniques. The COMET scores show relative increases up to 13.43% on English→German and 9.46% on English→Chinese compared to the original, uncompressed Qwen2-Audio model. This is a non-trivial outcome, especially given the typical trade-offs involved when attempting to reduce the computational requirements of a large model.

In light of these findings, we believe that the challenges introduced in this first round of the model compression track remain open. The substantial margin for improvement observed should encourage broader participation in future rounds, driven by the growing need for efficient, accessible, and deployable SLT systems.

7 Low-resource SLT

The 5th edition of the Low-resource Spoken Language Translation track focused on the translation of speech from a variety of data-scarce languages. The target language is typically a higher-resource one, generally of similar geographical or historical linkages. The goal of this shared task is to benchmark and promote speech translation technology for a diverse range of dialects and low-resource languages. While significant research progress has been demonstrated recently, many of the world's languages and dialects lack the parallel data at scale needed for standard supervised learning.

Recognizing that the biggest bottleneck towards truly language-inclusive speech translation systems is data availability, this year's edition included a data track, inviting participants to contribute newly collected speech translation datasets

[29]www-i6.informatik.rwth-aachen.de/web/Software/mwerSegmenter.tar.gz

for under-resourced language pairs.

7.1 Challenge

Systems Track This year's task significantly expanded the typological and geogrpahical diversity of the languages, language families, and scripts represented. The ten subtasks were:

- North Levantine Arabic → English (apc-eng)
- Tunisian Arabic → English (aeb-eng)
- Bemba → English (bem-eng)
- Fongbe → French (fon-fra)
- Irish → English (gle-eng)
- Bhojpuri → Hindi (bho-hin)
- Estonian → English (est-eng)
- Maltese → English (mlt-eng)
- Marathi → Hindi (mar-hin)
- Quechua → Spanish (que-spa)

Teams were allowed to submit to as few as one language pair, up to all ten. Both constrained and unconstrained submissions were allowed, to be separately ranked. For the constrained scenario, teams were only allowed to submit systems using the data provided by the shared task. For the unconstrained systems, teams were allowed to use any data as well as any pre-trained models.

Data Track This track aimed to empower language communities to contribute datasets. Such datasets are essential for expanding the reach of spoken language technology to more languages and varieties.

Participants of this track were encouraged to get creative with data creation strategies, while also ensuring data quality. As such, data track instructions included the following:

- Translations should be performed, wherever possible, by qualified, native speakers of the target language. We strongly encouraged verification of the data by at least one additional native speaker.
- Submitted datasets should be accompanied by dataset cards.[30] These should detail precise language information and the translation workflow that was employed. In particular, we asked participants to identify the language with both an ISO 639-3 individual language tag and a Glottocode. The script should be identified with an ISO 15924 script code.
- We highly encouraged new contributions to be released under CC BY-SA 4.0 or other similarly permissive licenses. By contributing data to this shared task, participants agreed to have this data released under these terms. At a minimum, data should be made available for research use.
- While post-editing of automatic output was allowed, we required that any data submitted for the shared task are 100% verified by humans, if not directly created by humans. Raw, unverified machine translated outputs were not allowed. If using MT, we tasked participants with ensuring that the terms of service of the model they used allow re-using its outputs to train other machine translation models (for example, popular commercial systems such as DeepL, Google Translate and ChatGPT explicitly disallow this).

7.2 Data and Metrics

Table 6 provides a summary of the training data that were part of the shared task. We describe in more detail the data for each language pair below.

***North* Levantine Arabic–English (apc-eng)** Levantine Arabic (ISO code: `apc`) is a well-established unit within the Arabic dialectal continuum, spoken mainly in Syria, Jordan, Lebanon, and Palestine. Although historically often split into *North* and *South* sub-dialects, recent ISO categorizations unite them under a common variant. Nonetheless, we maintain this finer split to emphasize the distinct phonological features and linguistic variations that characterize regional accents.

As in the first run of the *apc–eng* language pair, participants were provided with the UFAL Parallel Corpus of North Levantine 1.0 (Sellat et al., 2023), which includes about 120k lines of multi-parallel North Levantine-Modern Standard Arabic-English textual data, that can be downloaded from the LINDAT/CLARIAH-CZ Repository.[31] For additional speech data in Levantine Arabic, participants were pointed to two LDC resources: the BBN/AUB DARPA Babylon Levantine corpus (Makhoul et al., 2005) and the Levantine Arabic QT Training Data Set 5 corpus (Maamouri et al., 2006). Participants were also encouraged to make use of the Tunisian Arabic and Modern Standard Arabic resources made available in previous IWSLT editions.

Given the limited amount of publicly available corpora, we adopted the design of the initial *apc–eng* language pair run and focused exclusively on the unconstrained scenario.

[30] github.com/openlanguagedata/oldi.org/blob/main/resources/dataset-card-template.md

[31] hdl.handle.net/11234/1-5033

The development[32] and test[33] data consist of recordings of native speakers of the dialect and are a mix of spontaneous monologues and dialogues on topics of everyday life (health, family life, sports) as well as characteristics of the country of origin (Syrian traditions, education system, culture, etc.). The transcription and translation team consisted of students of Arabic at Charles University, with an additional quality check provided by the native speakers of the dialect.

Tunisian Arabic–English (aeb-eng) Tunisian Arabic (ISO code: aeb) is the main spoken language in Tunisia. It is heavily influenced by the Arabic language. Due to its geographic position, the spoken language of Tunisia was also influenced by other languages including Tamazight, French and Turkish. As was the case of IWSLT22 and 23, the provided Tunisian Arabic–English corpus consists of around 323 hours of Tunisian Conversational Telephone Speech (CTS) along with manual transcripts made available by LDC. A subset of the above transcript (200k lines that represent 167 hours of speech) was manually translated into English and provided as training data for the speech translation task. In this 2025 evaluation campaign, participants also had access to an additional Tunisian dialect corpus of manually transcribed 08 hours of conversational speech (Mdhaffar et al., 2024).

All train and test sets are time-segmented at the utterance level. The development and test sets are the same official sets used during IWLST 2022 and 2023.

Bemba–English (bem-eng) Bemba (also known as IciBemba) is a Bantu language (ISO code: `bem`), spoken predominantly in Zambia and other parts of Africa by over 10 million people. It is the most populous indigenous language spoken by over 30% of the population in Zambia where English is the lingua franca and official high-resourced language of communication. Bemba is native to the people of Northen, Luapula and Muchinga provinces of Zambia but also spoken in other parts of the country including urban areas such as Copperbelt, Central and Lusaka provinces by over 50% of the population (ZamStats, 2012).

The provided Bemba-English corpus (Sikasote et al., 2023a) consists of over 180 hours of Bemba audio data, along with transcriptions and translations in English. The dataset is comprised of recorded multi-turn dialogues between native Bemba speakers grounded on images.

In addition, we provided transcribed (28 hours) and untranscribed (60 hours) monolingual Bemba speech from Zambezi Voice (Sikasote et al., 2023b) and BembaSpeech (Sikasote and Anastasopoulos, 2022) datasets.

Fongbe–French (fon-fra) Fongbé (also spelled Fongbè or Fon) is a Gbe language (ISO 639-3: fon). Fongbe, a tonal African language, is the most spoken dialect of Benin, by more than 50% of Benin's population, including 8 million speakers. Fongbe is also spoken in Nigeria and Togo. The provided dataset contains over 48 hours of Fongbe audio recordings aligned with French translations. Additionally, a validation set of over 6 hours is included. The data used for this shared task is the extended version of the FFSTC corpus recently released (Kponou et al., 2025a). All recordings are derived from reading sessions by native Fongbe speakers, making this dataset a valuable resource for speech translation and low-resource language processing research.

Irish–English (gle-eng) Irish (also known as Gaeilge; ISO code: `gle`) has around 170,000 L1 speakers and 1.85 million people (37% of the population) across the island (of Ireland) claim to be at least somewhat proficient with the language. In the Republic of Ireland, it is the national and first official language. It is also one of the official languages of the European Union (EU) and a recognized minority language in Northern Ireland with the ISO `ga` code.

The provided Irish audio data were compiled from the news domain, Common Voice (Ardila et al., 2020a),[34] and Living-Audio-Dataset.[35] The Irish-to-English corpus comprises approximately 12 hours of Irish speech data (see Table 6), translated into English texts.[36] This year, we also provided the participants of three synthetic audio Irish-to-English datasets comprising 196 hours (Moslem, 2024). The synthetic data was created by synthesizing audio from parallel textual datasets obtained from OPUS (Tiedemann, 2012), namely EUbookshop, Tatoeba, and Wikimedia.[37]

[32]IWSLT 2024 devset and testset (with references): hdl.handle.net/11234/1-5518, hdl.handle.net/11234/1-5519
[33]hdl.handle.net/11234/1-5924

[34]commonvoice.mozilla.org/en/datasets
[35]github.com/Idlak/Living-Audio-Dataset
[36]github.com/shashwatup9k/iwslt2025_ga-eng
[37]hf.co/collections/ymoslem/irish-english-speech-

Bhojpuri–Hindi (bho-hin) Bhojpuri (ISO code: `bho`) belongs to the Indo-Aryan language group. It is dominantly spoken in India's western part of Bihar, the north-western part of Jharkhand, and the Purvanchal region of Uttar Pradesh. As per the 2011 Census of India, it has around 50.58 million speakers (Ojha and Zeman, 2020). Bhojpuri is spoken not just in India but also in other countries such as Nepal, Trinidad, Mauritius, Guyana, Suriname, and Fiji. Since Bhojpuri was considered a dialect of Hindi for a long time, it did not attract much attention from linguists and hence remains among the many lesser-known and less-resourced languages of India.

The provided Bhojpuri–Hindi corpus consists of 23.31 hours of Bhojpuri speech data (see Table 6) from the news domain, extracted from News On Air[38] and translated into Hindi texts.[39] Additionally, the participants were directed that they may use monolingual Bhojpuri audio data (with transcription) from ULCA-asr-dataset-corpus[40] as well as Bhojpuri Language Technological Resources (BHLTR) (Ojha et al., 2020; Ojha, 2019)[41] and Bhojpuri-wav2vec2 based model.[42]

Estonian–English (est-eng) Estonian (ISO code: `est`) belongs to Finnic branch of the Uralic language family. It is the official language of Estonia and is spoken natively by about one million people.

The provided training set consists of 581,647 utterances (1,258 hours), while the development set includes 1,601 utterances (3.6 hours). The training data is sourced from the TalTech Estonian Speech Dataset 1.0 (Alumäe et al., 2023), a manually transcribed corpus primarily comprising broadcast material, created for training speech recognition models. All recordings are long-form speech, transcribed and time-aligned at the utterance level. In this dataset, long recordings have been segmented into individual utterances. The transcripts have been automatically translated into English using Google Translate in 2024 (Sildam et al., 2024).

The development and test sets include speech from government and municipal press conferences, TV news, radio shows and talk shows, covering a variety of topics (sports, AI, international relations). The English translations have been manually created by professional translation agencies, instructed to translate without using any MT systems for post-editing. Both the original Estonian transcriptions and their English translations are provided for all utterances.

Maltese–English (mlt-eng) Maltese (ISO code: `mlt`) is a Semitic language with a heavy influence from Italian and English. It is spoken primarily in Malta, as well as in migrant communities abroad, notably in Australia, parts of the United States, and Canada.

The data release for this shared task comprises over 14 hours (split into development and training sets) of audio data, along with their transcription in Maltese and translation into English. Participants were allowed to use additional Maltese data, including the text corpus used to train BERTu (Micallef et al., 2022), a Maltese monolingual BERT model, the MASRI Data speech recognition data (Hernandez Mena et al., 2020), and any data available at the Maltese Language Resource Server.[43]

Marathi–Hindi (mar-hin) Marathi (ISO code: `mar`) is an Indo-Aryan language and is dominantly spoken in the state of Maharashtra in India. It is one of the 22 scheduled languages of India and the official language of Maharashtra and Goa. As per the 2011 Census of India, it has around 83 million speakers which covers 6.86% of the country's total population.[44] Marathi is the third most spoken language in India.

The provided Marathi–Hindi corpus consists of 25.12 hours of Marathi speech data (see Table 6) from the news domain, extracted from News On Air[45] and translated into Hindi texts.[46] The dataset was manually segmented and translated by Panlingua.[47] Additionally, the participants were directed that they may use monolingual Marathi audio data (with transcription) from Common Voice (Ardila et al., 2020a),[48] as well as the corpus provided by He et al. (2020)[49] and the Indian Language Cor-

translation-datasets-665dd9e8fbaa279db3474ca0

[38] newsonair.gov.in

[39] github.com/panlingua/iwslt2025_bho-hi

[40] github.com/Open-Speech-EkStep/ULCA-asr-dataset-corpus

[41] github.com/shashwatup9k/bho-resources

[42] www.openslr.org/64/

[43] mlrs.research.um.edu.mt/

[44] censusindia.gov.in/nada/index.php/catalog/42561

[45] newsonair.gov.in

[46] github.com/panlingua/iwslt2025_mr-hi

[47] panlingua.co.in/

[48] commonvoice.mozilla.org/en/datasets

[49] www.openslr.org/64/

Language Pairs		Train Set	Dev Set	Test Set	Additional Data
North Levantine–English	apc–eng	-	2.5	1.39	IWSLT 2024 test set (with references)
Tunisian Arabic–English	aeb–eng	323.0	-	-	A 160 hours out of this 323 hours are manually translated into English. 8h of transcribed speech from TARIC data set are also provided. Evaluation sets are same as IWSLT23.
Bemba–English	bem–eng	167.17	5.89	5.83	28.12 hours of monolingual audio with transcriptions (ASR) and 60 hours of untranscribed audio data.
Fongbe–French	fon–fra	48	6.1	5.9	A 57 hours of spoken Fongbe with corresponding French translations
Irish–English	ga–eng	9.46	1.03	0.66	A 196 hours of Synthetic Data, IWSLT 2023 and 2024 test set (with references) and MT data (monolingual and parallel corpora)
Bhojpuri–Hindi	bho–hi	19.88	2.07	0.54	IWSLT 2024 test set (with references) and Monolingual audio with transcription (ASR) and monolingual text
Estonian–English	est-eng	1258.0	3.6	4.22	Remark: training data is synthetic (ASR data, machine-translated to English)
Maltese–English	mlt–eng	11.83	2.52	2.0	Monolingual audio with transcriptions (ASR), monolingual text
Marathi–Hindi	mr–hi	15.88	3.66	0.46	Monolingual audio with transcriptions (ASR), IWSLT 2023 and 2024 test set (with references) and monolingual text
Quechua–Spanish	que–spa	1.60	1.03	1.03	48.0 hours of monolingual audio with transcriptions (ASR) and post-edited translations (new) along with extra MT data

Table 6: Training, development and test data details (hours) for the language pairs of the low-resource shared task.

pora (Abraham et al., 2020).[50]

Quechua–Spanish (que-spa) Quechua (macrolaguage ISO code: `que`) is an indigenous language spoken by more than 8 million people in South America. It is mainly spoken in Peru, Ecuador, and Bolivia where the official high-resource language is Spanish. It is a highly inflective language based on its suffixes which agglutinate and are found to be similar to other languages like Finnish. The average number of morphemes per word (synthesis) is about two times larger than in English. English typically has around 1.5 morphemes per word and Quechua has about 3 morphemes per word.

There are two main regional divisions of Quechua known as Quechua I and Quechua II. This data set consists of two main types of Quechua spoken in Ayacucho, Peru (Quechua Chanka ISO: `quy`) and Cusco, Peru (Quechua Collao ISO: `quz`) which are both part of Quechua II and, thus, considered a "southern" language. We label the data set with `que` - the ISO norm for Quechua II mixtures.

Due to the lack of data and low performance in previous work ((Salesky et al., 2024; E. Ortega et al., 2024)), the organizers decided to allow only *unconstrained* submissions this year. The unconstrained setting consists of 1 hour and 40 minutes of training data and divided into 573 training files, 125 validation files, and 125 test files which are excerpts from the Siminchik corpus translated by native Quechua speakers. (Cardenas et al., 2018) Additionally, participants were directed to another larger data set from the Siminchik corpus which consisted of 48 hours of fully transcribed Quechua audio (monolingual). In this year's task (2025), the organizers also included post-edited translation from Google of the 48 Siminchik hours which did not have translations last year (2024). Another MT dataset is offered in a parallel format, similar to last year. (Ortega et al., 2020) It consists of 100 daily magazine article sentences and 51140 sentences which are of religious context in nature.

[50]www.cse.iitb.ac.in/~pjyothi/indiccorpora/

7.2.1 Metrics

We use standard lowercase BLEU with no punctuation to automatically score all submissions. Additional analyses for some language pairs are provided below. Were applicable, we also report chrF++ (Popović, 2015).

7.3 Submissions

The Shared Task received a record 109 submissions (for speech translation) from 12 teams for all 10 language pairs. The submissions that provided an accompanying system paper are described in detail below and outlined in Table 7.

AIB-MARCO This team employed a cascade speech translation system consisting of Whisper/SeamlessM4T and Qwen2.5-7B-instruct. They performed sliding window ASR on the input audio then segment-level translation based on the transcription from the ASR model.

For primary systems of apc-eng and est-eng they used Whisper-large as the ASR model, whereas for gle-eng they used SeamlessM4T as the ASR model. For the contrastive systems, they employed different ASR models. The LLM used in translation is an optimized Qwen2.5-7B-instruct model.[51]

ALADAN (Kheder et al., 2025) provided a submission for the North Levantine Arabic to English direction, building on the same team's efforts from last year (Kheder et al., 2024). It is a cascade of ASR and MT systems. For the MT part data sparsity is alleviated via a crowd-sourced parallel corpus that covers five major Arabic dialects (Tunisian, Levantine, Moroccan, Algerian, Egyptian), curated via rigorous qualification and filtering. They also include an additional experiment with a large, high-quality Levantine Arabic corpus from LDC, which does not benefit from adding the crowdsourced data. ASR is done with a TDNN-F model and a Zipformer, whereas compared to the previous year's submission, a 4-times bigger model is taken for Zipformer (253M parameters). The methodology also includes dialect-specific normalization of Arabic text.

BUINUS (Tjiaranata et al., 2025) focused on the mlt-eng direction. Their system employs a cascade architecture, combining ASR and translation to handle the low-resource setting better. For ASR, they use Whisper (Radford et al., 2022), which was further fine-tuned with the data provided in the shared task. For the translation step, they use NLLB model (NLLB Team et al., 2022), employing both direct fine-tuning and data augmentation techniques designed to modify the target sequences and thereby reinforce encoder reliance and decoder robustness. Fine-tuning of NLLB was carried out in two stages: an initial stage used a combination of real and augmented data, followed by a second stage fine-tuning exclusively on the main task to refine the model further. To efficiently fine-tune larger models under computational constraints, they used QLoRA (Dettmers et al., 2023), achieving better performance with the 3.3B parameter model compared to smaller versions. Notably, their analysis revealed that data augmentation yielded comparatively greater performance gains for smaller models, underscoring the value of data-driven strategies in resource-constrained scenarios. They note, however, that the performance difference between the larger and smaller NLLB models was modest, and the errors at the ASR stage hurt the translation component.

GMU (Meng and Anastasopoulos, 2025) submitted systems for all language pairs except apc-eng. Their approach focuses on fine-tuning SeamlessM4T-v2 for ASR, MT, and ST tasks. The fine-tuned ASR and MT models are used to construct cascaded ST systems. They also explored various training paradigms for ST fine-tuning, including direct end-to-end (E2E) fine-tuning, parameter initialization using fine-tuned ASR and/or MT model components, and multi-task training. The multi-task training setup includes ST, MT and knowledge distillation (KD) objectives, where KD leverages the MT components to enhance the ST components. They found that direct E2E fine-tuning yielded strong overall results, and initializing the ST encoder with an in-domain fine-tuned ASR encoder further improved performance on languages SeamlessM4T-v2 had not been previously trained on. Multi-task training, on the other hand, provided marginal improvements.

JHU Johns Hopkins University's team, (Robinson et al., 2025), participated in all language pairs continuing their tradition from last year (Romney Robinson et al., 2024). As with the previous year, the motivation was to assess the robustness of the methods they were employing across a variety of domains and typologically diverse languages. However, the main focus this year was on ensembling methods, and in particular, Minimum Bayes Risk (MBR) decoding (Bickel and Doksum, 1977; Kumar and Byrne, 2004). In order to do so, they aimed to gather a variety of different submissions

[51]This description was provided by the participants. No associated paper was submitted.

Team Name	Language Pairs									
	apc-eng	aeb-eng	bem-eng	fon-fra	bho-hin	gle-eng	est-eng	mlt-eng	mar-hin	que-spa
Systems Track										
AIB-MARCO	✓					✓	✓			
ALADAN (Kheder et al., 2025)	✓	✓								
BUINUS (Tjiaranata et al., 2025)								✓		
GMU (Meng and Anastasopoulos, 2025)		✓	✓	✓	✓	✓	✓	✓	✓	✓
IIITH-BUT (Akkiraju et al., 2025)					✓					
JHU (Robinson et al., 2025)	✓	✓	✓	✓	✓	✓	✓	✓	✓	✓
KIT (Li et al., 2025)	✓	✓	✓							
KREASOF-TCD (Farouq et al., 2025)			✓							
LIA (Chellaf et al., 2025)	✓	✓		✓						
QUESPA (Ortega et al., 2025)										✓
SYSTRAN (Avila and Crego, 2025)		✓								
Teams per Pair:	5	6	4	3	3	3	3	3	2	3
Data Track										
KUVOST (Mohammadamini et al., 2025)	English - Central Kurdish									
URDU (Mehmood and Rauf, 2025)	Urdu - English									
FFSTC-2 (Kponou et al., 2025b)	Fongbe - French									

Table 7: Breakdown of the teams and the language pairs subtasks that they participated in for the Low-Resource Shared Task.

for each language pair. They relied on both end-to-end translation systems, as well as cascaded systems. In addition, they looked at combining similar languages for mixed data training. Overall, the results were mixed with ensembling helping in some language pairs and hurting in others. However, a key takeaway is that for practioners, MBR is still helpful because you do not need to know which system is the best in advance.

LIA (Chellaf et al., 2025) participated in three language pairs - both of the arabic dialects, as well as Fongbe to French. All of their submissions were in the unconstrained setting relying on pretrained models. They explored both pipelined systems and end-to-end systems. They investigated various ways of augmenting systems with varying data, such as combining Modern Standard Arabic (MSA) data with dialectal arabic, or looking at including Fongbe transcriptions both with and without diacritics. For the Tunisian-to-English translation task, their primary system was an end-to-end system based on a language-agnostic semantically aligned speech encoder. They trained it following the SAMU-XSLR framework (Khurana et al., 2022) from the w2v-bert 2.0 (Seamless Communication et al., 2023) model as a student and BGE-M3 text model (Chen et al., 2024) as a teacher. For the North Levantine-to-English task, their primary system was based on a combination of cascaded systems. The two ASR modules were based on Whisper-large-v3: these models have been fine-tuned on the Levantine data released by the organizers but also on Modern Standard Arabic data. The two MT models applied to the ASR outputs were based on NLLB-200 1.3B fine-tuned on the official data augmented with the Levanti corpus, available on Hugging Face [52]. Each MT model fed by different ASR output generated 10 translation hypotheses. The final selection was made by using BLASER (Chen et al., 2023). Last, for the Fongbe to French translation task, their primary system was also a cascaded system using an ASR module built on the AfriHuBERT SSL speech encoder (Alabi et al., 2024) and an MT module based on the NLLB model.

KIT (Li et al., 2025) participated in the Bemba-to-English, North Levantine Arabic-to-English, and Tunisian Arabic-to-English tasks under the unconstrained condition. They explored both cascaded and end-to-end ST systems. All approaches were based on pretrained models: SeamlessM4T (Seamless Communication et al., 2023) for end-to-end ST, NLLB (NLLB Team et al., 2022) for MT, and MMS (Pratap et al., 2024) and XEUS[53] for ASR. The main focus was on using synthetic data for data augmentation and applying model regularization techniques. Two types of synthetic data generation were studied: (1) translating source language ASR data using MT systems to create ST training data, and (2) generating source lan-

[52] huggingface.co/datasets/guymorlan/levanti

[53] huggingface.co/espnet/xeus

guage speech via text-to-speech from MT training data. Results showed that ST models trained only on synthetic data can outperform cascaded systems, provided that a strong MT system is used. The impact of TTS-based augmentation varied: it was effective only when the TTS quality was high. Regularization experiments used intradistillation (Romney Robinson et al., 2024), which proved to be a reliable and broadly applicable method across all tasks in low-resource settings.

IIITH-BUT (Akkiraju et al., 2025) fine-tuned SeamlessM4T models for Bhojpuri-Hindi speech translation. To address data scarcity, they applied speed perturbation and SpecAugment data augmentation techniques. Moreover, they examined cross-lingual transfer learning through joint training with Marathi and Bhojpuri speech data.

The team experimented with two variants of SeamlessM4T, medium (1.2B parameters) and large v2 (2.3B parameters). For hyperparameter optimisation, they explored a range of values for batch size, learning rate, label smoothing, and warmup steps. For data augmentation, they used SpecAugment to apply spectrogram masking with time masks and frequency masks, and implemented speed perturbation with speed factors of 0.9x, 1.0x, and 1.1x. This data augmentation process resulted in expanding the training data by three times. Finally, they combined the Marathi-Hindi parallel data with the limited Bhojpuri-Hindi dataset to fine-tune the SeamlessM4T models.

KREASOF-TCD (Farouq et al., 2025) This team participated in the Bemba-to-English shared task under unconstrained conditions. The team submitted three speech translation systems based on the cascading method. The *Primary* submission system is based on medium-sized Whisper for the ASR and NLLB-200 3.3B for the MT. The *Contrastive 1* and *Contrastive 2* systems use the small-sized Whisper model for the ASR, while the MT systems are based on the NLLB-200 3.3B and NLLB-200 600M models, respectively. The team explored fine-tuning pre-trained models and data augmentation for their strategy to develop the systems. The ASR systems were obtained by fine-tuning the Whisper models on the data from the BembaSpeech (Sikasote and Anastasopoulos, 2022) and BIG-C (Sikasote et al., 2023a) datasets. The MT systems are based on the NLLB-200 (NLLB Team et al., 2022) model, which is fine-tuned on bilingual segments of the BIGC and "dev" split of the FLORES-200 (Goyal et al., 2022) datasets. To improve the quality of speech translations, the team explored augmenting the Bemba-to-English training data with the portion of the Tatoeba (Tiedemann, 2020) dataset that was back-translated from English into Bemba using the NLLB-200 600M model. The back-translations were filtered using cross-entropy scores.

SYSTRAN (Avila and Crego, 2025) participated in one language pair, Tunisian Arabic to English, under the *constrained* condition using the resources provided by LDC for this task that included MSA data from broadcast news and Tunisian Arabic conversational telephone speech. The focus of their contribution was on tightly coupling an ASR encoder (Whisper, the Medium and Large-v3 versions tested) with an NMT decoder (NLLB, the 3.3B parameter version). Embeddings from the Whisper encoder are fed into the NLLB decoder via a Reshape module consisting of a convolutional layer and liner projection layer instead of using the standard word embeddings. The motivation is for parameter-efficient training in low-resource settings, ensuring quality translations while being scalable. They fine-tuned their model using the available LDC parallel corpora, with additional filtering and cleaning strategies to optimize domain robustness and translation consistency.

QUESPA (Ortega et al., 2025) submitted three *unconstrained* systems this year as the Quechua–Spanish shared task organizers only allowed unconstrained setting submissions. Team QUESPA were able to improve the previous year's results despite the baseline task data remaining mostly the same with exception of newly machine-translated text from the original Siminchik corpus. The three unconstrained systems ranged from 14.8 BLEU to 26.7 BLEU where QUESPA's best performing systems from last year (2024) ranged from 11.1 to 19.7 BLEU. The 7 BLEU points of improvement of their best system is attributed to a new ASR dataset released from the "quy" ISO code called Collao, a dialect of Quechua spoken mostly in southern Peru. (Paccotacya-Yanque et al., 2022)

QUESPA's *unconstrained* systems were once again a novel introduction for the QUE–SPA

Language Pair	Winning Team	System	Constrained	BLEU
apc-eng	KIT	primary	no	23.3
aeb-eng	KIT	primary	no	21.4
bem-eng	GMU	primary	no	31.7
fon-fra	LIA	primary	no	39.6
bho-hin	JHU	primary	no	10.7
gle-eng	GMU	primary	no	13.4
est-eng	AIB-MARCO	primary	no	30.9
mlt-eng	GMU	primary	no	57.5
mar-hin	GMU	contrastive1	no	44.3
que-spa	QUESPA	contrastive2	no	26.7

Table 8: Winning submissions for each language pair of the Low-Resource Shared Task.

task and outperformed last year's best systems. The Primary System was not previously used by QUESPA in IWSLT. It is comprised of a cascaded ASR + MT system where ConMamba (Jiang et al., 2024), based on a Conformer architecture (Gulati et al., 2020) is used for ASR using publicly available recipes[54], experimenting with small (S) and large (L) configurations (144/512 dimensions, 12+4/12+6 layers). The resulting transcribed text is then passed into a newly created (fine-tuned) NLLB (NLLB Team et al., 2022) machine translation system that was tested in development with several combinations that finally resulted in 18 BLEU on the test set. The *Contrastive 1* system is similar to QUESPA's submission from 2024, however, Whisper **Version 3** is used this year along with ESPnet (Watanabe et al., 2018). Results from the Whisper V3 model were then passed into the NLLB-based MT model used in the Primary system. The *Contrastive 2* system is QUESPA's biggest achievement yet and can be considered the most novel system to data for speech translation on the Quechua–Spanish language pair. It is a pre-trained SpeechT5 (Ao et al., 2022) model fine-tuned for Speech Translation using the unconstrained training data along with the 48 hours of newly created post-edited MT data. Furthermore, they applied a data augmentation technique called *nlpaug* (noise, distortion, duplication)(Ma, 2019) which resulted in a total of 96h: 48h original + 48h of new synthetic data. Lastly, their best addition to the Contrastive 2 system was the inclusion of a Collao speech translation corpus that contains 15 hours of Quechua Collao translated speech (quz). The resultant training data set for the Contrastive 2 system thus was: 96 + 15 (111) total hours of Quechua speech translations. (Paccotacya-Yanque et al., 2022)

[54]github.com/xi-j/Mamba-ASR

7.4 Results

General Notes Table 8 summarizes the winning submissions for each language pair. Detailed results for all teams' systems and settings are available in Appendix B.5.

Of the 10 language pairs, 6 different teams had the top performing system on at least one language pair. This shows how competitive the shared task was, and that a multitude of approaches are helpful for low-resource speech translation.

Compared to previous iterations of the shared task, some of the language pairs had marked improvements with large gains in the official automatic metrics. For example, BLEU scores for Quechua-Spanish, the least resourced language pair, improved from 19.7 to 26.7 BLEU points (this was largely the result of the use of additional data by the winning team). However, for other continuing language pairs, performance is rather stagnated, remaining in exactly the same levels (if not worse) for Bemba-English, Bhojpuri-Hindi, Irish-English, and the two Arabic dialects language pairs. This might suggest that we have perhaps reached a performance ceiling of sorts in the current datasets under the current data-scarce conditions, especially for the language pairs that lie in the low-end of data availability. It should be noted, though, that this "ceiling" performance nevertheless still lags substantially behind the translation quality we observe for high-resource pairs, still reinforcing the need for further data collection and research in the area.

For the language pairs included for the first time in the shared task, we find that Estonian-English, our highest resourced language pair with more than 1,200 hours of translated audio, ends up with speech translation systems of decent quality with BLUE scores in the 29–31 range by multiple participants. On the other hand lies Fongbe-Frnech, which even though does end up with decent systems yielding BLEU scores over 30 by two participants. Similar to last year's findings, we see our current technologies can produce good ST systems for language pairs with more than 50 hours of high-quality translated speech.

We note that almost all submissions followed the unconstrained setting – a clear indication that pre-trained multilingual systems seem to be the best option for building ST for low-resource languages, at least under the current data, architectural, and compute constraints.

Notes on apc-eng Compared to the initial run of the *apc-eng* language pair in the previous year, the performance gap between the top-ranked system (KIT) and the remaining participants has narrowed. The second-place team (LIA) achieved results within 1 BLEU point of the winner, while the third-place team (ALADAN, last year's champion) trailed by only 3.5 BLEU points. Although the absolute BLEU score achieved by the top-performing system is notably lower than that of the previous year (23.34 vs. 28.71), we attribute this discrepancy not to a decline in overall system quality (quite the contrary!) but rather to differences in the test set composition (2024: 974 lines, 12,263 words; 2025: 1,026 lines, 8,833 words). Although the ranking based on chrF corresponds with the BLEU evaluation, COMET indicates that the LIA system surpasses KIT, emphasizing the minimal performance differences among the leading submissions. The integration of end-to-end and cascaded systems, particularly through MBR decoding to combine translation hypotheses, proved to be a successful strategy for enhancing overall system performance. Due to their strong multilingual capabilities, the Whisper and NLLB models continue to be among the most widely adopted solutions for ASR and MT, respectively. Top-performing systems demonstrated substantial quality improvements through the use of additional speech and text resources, often curated internally. Notably, LIA showcased the benefits of carefully filtering a general Arabic corpus using a dialect identification system. The generation of synthetic textual data via back-translation, forward-translation, and paraphrasing remains an effective method. The winning team, KIT, also experimented with synthetic speech data generation using a TTS model; however, this approach was found to be ineffective, primarily due to the lack of high-quality speech data, leading to an under-trained TTS system. Several teams also reported findings regarding the impact of domain alignment in training and evaluation datasets, emphasizing the critical importance of developing resources for low-resource languages that are tailored to the practical needs of end users.

7.5 Data Track Results and Discussion

The data track received 3 submissions, each producing usable datasets for 3 low-resource language pairs: English-Central Kurdish, Urdu-English, and Fongbe-French. This successful first iteration reinforces the desire by researchers and communities to contribute open-source datasets. The organizers will plan to use these datasets in future iterations of the low-resource shared task as appropriate. We discuss the submissions below.

KUVOST (Mohammadamini et al., 2025) produced a large-scale English speech to Central Kurdish dataset by relying on the publicly available Common Voice dataset. This effort produced more than 1,000 hours of parallel speech translation data, by leveraging community volunteer work: more than 230 volunteers manually translated and revised more than 240k English sentences, which were then paired with their utterances in Common Voice. The effort included an extensive data validation process. The participants also ensure the quality of the data by producing pre-determined train-dev-test splits, and building baseline systems on top of fine-tuned Whisper v3 and Seamless M4T, leading to BLEU scores over 32 on the test set.

Note that this effort, in contrast to the norm for the systems track, produced data where the low-resource language (Central Kurdish) is on the target side and the high-resource one (English) is on the source speech side.

URDU (Mehmood and Rauf, 2025) produced an Urdu-English speech translation dataset. They relied on Common Voice 13.0 and its Urdu speech portion. The Urdu transcripts were first automatically translated into English, but then checked and corrected by 19 bilingual volunteers, as well as validated by a professional translator. This multi-stage quality assurance approach disentangles the correction of potential syntactic or grammatical errors from a secondary stage that ensures high-quality, fluent translations for idiomatic or poetic texts, highlighting the potential need for more careful handling of some data subdomains.

FFSTC-2 (Kponou et al., 2025b) presented an extension of the previous FFSTC dataset, adding another 36 hours to bring the available total to 61 hours of Fongbe-French data. Unlike the other two submissions, this team started with target-side text (French), which was first automatically translated to Fongbe. Then the text translations were reviewed by bilingual experts, and only at the end was read speech of these Fongbe translations collected. The effort included a validation process, e.g. to remove utterances with excessive background noise, where the validators re-recorded the utterances, yielding an additional 42k recordings.

The participants also confirmed the utility of these additional data, developing ST systems (both cascade and end-to-end) as well as ASR systems that improve over systems trained on the previous iteration of the corpus.

8 Indic Languages Track

The growing demand for inclusive digital access has highlighted the need for seamless cross-lingual communication, especially in linguistically rich regions like India. While English dominates global technology and information spheres, millions of speakers of Indic languages such as Bengali, Hindi, and Tamil still lack adequate speech and language technologies. Despite their large combined speaker base of over 700 million and significant cultural and economic importance, these languages remain underrepresented in NLP and speech research due to limited high-quality parallel text and audio data.

Compounding this challenge are the inherent complexities of Indic languages including rich morphology, high inflection, and frequent code-mixing in real-world discourse, which make Spoken Language Translation (SLT) development especially difficult (Sethiya and Maurya, 2024). Addressing this gap, the Indic Shared Task track at IWSLT 2025 focuses on SLT for Bengali, Hindi, and Tamil in both English→Indic and Indic→English directions. The latter is emphasized due to its higher complexity and the inclusion of STEM and broadcast media domains, demanding systems capable of handling technical vocabulary and varied speech styles.

By releasing the first benchmark dataset tailored to these low-resource languages across critical domains, this task aims to drive research that tackles real-world multilingual challenges. It seeks to advance digital inclusion, foster equitable access to global knowledge, and support the preservation and technological integration of Indic languages.

8.1 Challenge

The IWSLT 2025 Indic Shared Task track focuses on speech-to-text translation (ST) across six language directions: English-to-Bengali (en→bn), English-to-Hindi (en→hi), English-to-Tamil (en→ta), Bengali-to-English (bn→en), Hindi-to-English (hi→en), and Tamil-to-English (ta→en). This year's challenge expands beyond previous iterations by including both Indic-to-English and English-to-Indic directions, though the data sources for each direction are distinct.

The track allows participants to submit in both the constrained and unconstrained conditions. The constrained condition permits only the use of the provided dataset, while the unconstrained condition allows the incorporation of additional external resources and pre-trained models. Systems can be either end-to-end (E2E) or cascaded, and participants may submit both monolingual and multilingual systems across any or all of the six language directions.

8.2 Data and Metrics

The Indic track at IWSLT 2025 provides a comprehensive speech-to-text translation (ST) corpus spanning three Indic languages: Bengali, Hindi, and Tamil. The dataset is constructed from two distinct sources, reflecting the two translation directions.

For the English-to-Indic (en→xx) direction, the data is derived from the Indic-ST corpus (Sethiya et al., 2024), which consists English speech paired with English transcripts and Indic translations. These data is from domains like Mann ki Baat, and NPTEL, unlike IWSLT 2024, which had data from TED talks (Sethiya et al., 2024). The dataset is segmented using provided YAML files, ensuring consistent alignment across audio, English transcripts, and Indic translations. Table 9 reports the number of lines and audio hours, partitioned into training, validation, and test splits. Note that due to linguistic differences, the token counts between English and the target Indic languages naturally vary.

For the Indic-to-English (xx→en) direction, the data is sourced from a curated subset of the BhasaAnuvaad dataset (Sankar et al., 2025), which draws from rich educational and broadcast domains. Specifically, it includes material from the National Programme on Technology Enhanced Learning (NPTEL), the Spoken-Tutorial project, and Mann-ki-Baat addresses, covering specialized STEM content as well as public broadcast speech. This direction provides a new challenge for participants, requiring systems to handle domain-specific terminology, varied accents, and spontaneous speech phenomena.

English-Bengali (en↔bn): Bengali, the seventh most spoken language globally, has around 228 million speakers and belongs to the Indo-Aryan family. It is the official language of Bangladesh and is widely spoken in the Bengal region of India, written in the Bengali-Assamese script. The en→bn dataset comprises 815 hours of English speech aligned to Bengali translations, while the bn→en set contains 157.95 hours of Bengali speech aligned to English text.

English-Hindi (en↔hi): Hindi is the third most spoken language in the world, with approximately 615 million speakers. It belongs to the Indo-Aryan family and is primarily spoken in India, where it serves as one of the official languages, written in Devanagari script. The en→hi dataset contains 815 hours of English speech and Hindi translations, while the hi→en dataset provides 653.88 hours of Hindi speech with aligned English translations.

English-Tamil (en↔ta): Tamil, a classical Dravidian language with approximately 91 million speakers, is spoken predominantly in the Tamil Nadu state of India and parts of Sri Lanka. It is written in the Tamil script derived from Brahmi. The en→ta dataset offers 815 hours of English speech with aligned Tamil translations, whereas the ta→en data includes 378.16 hours of Tamil speech with English translations.

Evaluation Metrics: For system evaluation, we primarily employ the chrF++ metric (Popović, 2017), chosen for its high correlation with human judgments—especially in the context of Indian languages (Sai B et al., 2023)—making it particularly well-suited to our task. All chrF++ scores are computed using the standardized `sacreBLEU` toolkit (Post, 2018) to ensure consistency and reproducibility. In addition, we report BLEU scores for completeness, although they are not used in ranking the systems.

Lang.	Train		Valid		Test	
	Hours	Samples	Hours	Samples	Hours	Samples
en→hi	680.54	205.2k	40.48	11.67k	93.13	36.25k
en→bn	680.54	205.2k	40.48	11.67k	93.13	36.25k
en→ta	680.54	205.2k	40.48	11.67k	93.13	36.25k
bn→en	157.95	64.8k	1.00	395	1.25	858
hi→en	653.88	248.8k	1.00	397	1.34	579
ta→en	478.16	211.3k	1.00	457	2.18	956

Table 9: Summary of provided data for each language direction, including hours and number of samples.

8.3 Submissions

The 2nd edition of the Indic shared task track of IWSLT received 32 submissions for all six language pairs from five teams: the CDAC-SVNIT team from SNLP Lab, the CDAC Noida and SVNIT, Surat; the JU-CS-NLP team from Jadavpur University; another team, JU from Jadavpur University; team IITM from Speech Lab, IIT Madras; and team HITSZ from Harbin Institute of Technology, Shenzhen. The participants submitted their results under various constraints, including end-to-end constrained and unconstrained, cascaded constrained, and unconstrained approaches. Below, we provide an overview of each team's approach and their results.

CDAC-SVNIT (Roy et al., 2025): This team submitted 12 systems, two for each of the six language pairs. Their submissions featured both cascaded and end-to-end approaches. The cascaded systems operated under an unconstrained setting, while the end-to-end systems adhered to a constrained setup. For the cascaded approach, they fine-tuned a pre-trained CLSRIL-23 model for ASR and a pre-trained IndicTrans2 model for MT. The end-to-end systems utilized a transformer-based encoder-decoder architecture from the Fairseq toolkit, pretrained on the provided data.

JU-CS-NLP (Dhar et al., 2025): This team submitted six systems, one for each language pair, under the unconstrained cascaded setting. For En → xx translation, the system employed OpenAI's pre-trained Whisper Base model for ASR and a fine-tuned version of Meta's NLLB-200-distilled-600M model for MT. For xx → En, it used the pre-trained IndicConformer model for ASR and the fine-tuned IndicTrans2 model for MT, both developed by AI4Bharat. The MT models are fine-tuned on the provided dataset.

JU (Das et al., 2025): The submission includes

Direction	Team ID	chrF++ / BLEU
en→bn	CDAC-SVNIT	62.21 / 36.96
	JU-CSE-NLP	**74.58 / 51.70**
	IITM	60.81 / 26.67
en→hi	CDAC-SVNIT	64.17 / 44.09
	JU-CSE-NLP	**72.98 / 57.61**
	IITM	62.30 / 41.09
en→ta	CDAC-SVNIT	66.15 / 29.34
	JU-CSE-NLP	**73.81 / 36.17**
	IITM	62.33 / 21.35
bn→en	CDAC-SVNIT	44.89 / 14.77
	JU-CSE-NLP	53.99 / 23.69
	JU	35.56 / 8.69
	IITM	**55.27 / 22.90**
hi→en	CDAC-SVNIT	67.06 / 41.04
	JU-CSE-NLP	67.91 / 44.13
	IITM	**68.14 / 41.59**
ta→en	CDAC-SVNIT	41.16 / 15.70
	JU-CSE-NLP	**49.34 / 17.66**
	JU*	39.02 / 13.39
	IITM	47.44 / 18.41

Table 10: Performance of unconstrained cascaded systems on different language pairs in terms of chrF++ and BLEU scores. The * symbol denotes a system that used a multilingual base model without any finetuning.

an unconstrained cascade setting for 2 language pairs from Bengali and Tamil to English. A pretrained Whisper Small model is used for ASR, which is pretrained for Bengali on the Bangla Mozilla Common Voice dataset and for Tamil on multiple publicly available datasets. For MT, the system utilized the fine-tuned MarianMT model for Bengali to English translation and the fine-tuned facebooknllb-200-distilled-600M model for Tamil to English translation.

IITM (Sarkar et al., 2025): The team submitted six systems under the unconstrained cascaded setting. For ASR, they used the Phi-4 model, fine-tuned separately for each language: Bengali using SKNahin/open-large-bengali-asr-data, Hindi using SpringLab/Hindi-1482hrs and AI4Bharat/SeamlessAlign, and Tamil using Prajwal-143/ASR-Tamil-cleaned. For MT, they employed the NLLB model, fine-tuned on the SPRINGLab/shiksha and SPRINGLab/BPCC-cleaned datasets for xx → English translation.

HITSZ (Wei et al., 2025): The team made 6 submissions for the unconstrained end-to-end setting for each of the 6 language pairs. The end-to-end system utilizes the encoder-decoder based Dhwani model, where the speech signals are encoded using the whisper speech encoder and the non-speech audio signals are encoded using the BEAT's encoder, which are bridged to the language model with the help of Q-former. The transformed tokens are decoded using the Krutrim large language instruct model.

Direction	chrF++ / BLEU
en→bn	52.69 / 27.00
en→hi	52.50 / 33.84
en→ta	54.67 / 22.81
bn→en	53.07 / 25.02
hi→en	62.94 / 39.29
ta→en	43.91 / 19.27

Table 11: Performance of unconstrained end-to-end systems by HITSZ on different language pairs in terms of chrF++ and BLEU scores.

8.4 Results

Tables 10, 11 & 12 present the performance of the submitted systems across six translation directions, evaluated primarily using the chrF++ (Popović, 2017) metric. Each direction was evaluated under both unconstrained and constrained settings, and systems were categorized as either cascaded or end-to-end (E2E) in design. The unconstrained setting permitted the use of any external data, while the constrained setting required systems to be trained using only the provided shared data. Below, we summarize the key findings per translation direction.

en→bn In the English-to-Bengali direction, the highest chrF++ score was achieved by the JU-CSE-NLP team using a cascaded system in the unconstrained setting, with a score of 74.58. CDAC-SVNIT and IITM also submitted strong cascaded systems, achieving 62.21 and 60.81 chrF++, respectively. Among end-to-end (E2E) systems, HITSZ obtained a chrF++ of 52.69, while in the constrained setting, CDAC-SVNIT's E2E model led with 58.22 chrF++, indicating the effectiveness of their model despite the data restrictions.

en→hi For English-to-Hindi, the best chrF++ score again came from JU-CSE-NLP's cascaded system under the unconstrained condition, reaching 72.98. CDAC-SVNIT and IITM followed closely with scores of 64.17 and 62.30, respectively. The E2E system from HITSZ achieved 52.50 chrF++, and CDAC-SVNIT's constrained E2E model attained a respectable 54.48, outperforming several unconstrained E2E systems.

Direction	chrF++ / BLEU
en→bn	58.22 / 31.57
en→hi	54.48 / 34.61
en→ta	56.08 / 21.35
bn→en	14.30 / 00.46
hi→en	42.97 / 15.42
ta→en	26.25 / 05.05

Table 12: Performance of constrained systems submitted by CDAC-SVNIT using an end-to-end (E2E) approach. Only the provided shared data was used for training.

en→ta In the English-to-Tamil direction, JU-CSE-NLP led with a chrF++ of 73.81 using a cascaded approach under the unconstrained setting. This was followed by IITM (62.33) and HITSZ's E2E model (54.67). Under the constrained condition, CDAC-SVNIT's E2E model achieved 56.08 chrF++, showing competitive performance despite being limited to shared training data.

bn→en For Bengali-to-English, the highest chrF++ score was reported by HITSZ's E2E system with 53.07, outperforming all cascaded systems including CDAC-SVNIT (44.89), IITM (55.27), and JU (35.56). Under the constrained condition, the best result was 14.3 chrF++ from CDAC-SVNIT's E2E model, underscoring the difficulty of this direction when relying solely on shared data.

hi→en In the Hindi-to-English direction, the top-performing system was submitted by IITM with a chrF++ of 68.14 using a cascaded architecture under the unconstrained setting. This was closely followed by JU-CSE-NLP (67.91) and CDAC-SVNIT (67.06). HITSZ's E2E model achieved 62.94 chrF++, while CDAC-SVNIT's constrained E2E system reached 42.97, indicating a substantial drop in performance under constrained data.

ta→en For Tamil-to-English, JU-CSE-NLP's cascaded system achieved the highest chrF++ score under the unconstrained setting with 49.34. Other strong systems included IITM (41.16) and JU* (47.44), the latter of which utilized a multilingual model without fine-tuning. Among E2E approaches, HITSZ led with 43.91. CDAC-SVNIT's constrained E2E system attained 26.25 chrF++, again reflecting the challenges imposed by data limitations in this direction.

8.5 Conclusion

This edition of the Low-Resource Indic Multilingual Speech Translation track marked the first time that translation from Indic languages to English was included alongside the English-to-Indic directions. This expansion provided a more comprehensive evaluation of multilingual translation capabilities and highlighted the unique challenges of translating into English from morphologically rich and syntactically diverse Indic languages.

Across the six language directions, systems demonstrated strong performance in both unconstrained and constrained settings, with cascaded architectures generally outperforming end-to-end approaches in the unconstrained track. However, several constrained end-to-end systems showed promising results, indicating progress toward robust low-resource translation without reliance on external data.

The wide range of approaches submitted—spanning cascaded pipelines, multilingual pretraining, and direct speech-to-text modeling—reflects growing diversity in system design for low-resource speech translation. These results offer valuable insights into the current state of the field and set a strong baseline for future editions of the task, especially in further improving Indic-to-English performance and in exploring more unified multilingual modeling techniques.

9 Instruction-Following Track

In recent years, large language models (LLMs) have redefined the landscape of natural language processing by demonstrating the ability to perform a wide range of tasks without requiring task-specific architectures or fine-tuning. These models offer a single, unified interface for diverse applications such as translation, summarization, and question answering, simply by conditioning on textual instructions (Hendy et al., 2023). Initially restricted to textual input, LLMs are now evolving into multimodal systems, incorporating modalities such as vision and speech to expand their applicability beyond the text domain (Li et al., 2024). In parallel, speech foundation models (SFMs) have emerged as powerful architectures capable of processing spoken language at scale (Latif et al., 2023). When combined with the instruction-following capabilities of LLMs (Ouyang et al., 2022), they open new opportunities for building general-purpose speech models that are not limited to handling a pre-defined set of tasks (Rubenstein et al., 2023). This integration, often referred to as SpeechLLM or SFM+LLM (Gaido et al., 2024), promises to deliver very versatile systems, making it possible to interact with spoken language in flexible and controllable ways.

To explore this promising direction, this year we introduce, for the first time at IWSLT, a new shared task focused on evaluating instruction-following models for the speech modality. The goal is to assess models that can perform multiple speech-to-text tasks–such as automatic speech recognition, speech translation, spoken question answering, and summarization–by following natural language prompts, using either short audio segments or long-form spoken content as input.

9.1 Task Description

In the Instruction-Following (IF) task, participants had to develop a single instruction-following model that can perform multiple speech-to-text tasks based on a natural language prompt. The model receives both an audio input and a task instruction in textual form and is expected to follow the instruction to produce the appropriate output.

Sub-Tracks. The task is divided into two sub-tracks based on the nature of the input audio: `SHORT`, where the input is represented by automatically segmented audio (usually of a few seconds), and `LONG`, where the input is a long-form audio. Depending on the sub-track, the following tasks have to be supported by the model:

- `SHORT` Sub-Track
  - **Automatic Speech Recognition (ASR)**: the speech is transcribed into the same language;
  - **Speech-to-text Translation (S2TT)**: the speech is translated into the target language;
  - **Spoken Question Answering (SQA)**: textual questions have to be answered based on the spoken content in the same language and in a language different from the speech (questions and answers are always in the same language);
- `LONG` Sub-Track
  - **Automatic Speech Recognition (ASR)**: the speech is transcribed into the same language;
  - **Speech-to-text Translation (S2TT)**: the speech is translated into the target language;
  - **Spoken Question Answering (SQA)**: textual questions have to be answered based on the spoken content in the same language and in a language different from the speech (questions and answers are always in the same language);
  - **Speech-to-text Summarization (S2TSUM)**: a summary has to be provided from the spoken content in the same language and in a language different from the speech.

All tasks listed for each sub-track were mandatory; that is the model must be capable of handling each task type when prompted appropriately.

Languages. The tasks involve both monolingual and cross-lingual processing. The supported languages are English (en) for ASR, monolingual SQA, and S2TSUM, and English to German (de), Italian (it), and Chinese (zh) for S2TT, multilingual SQA, and multilingual S2TSUM. Participants were allowed to submit results for a subset of language directions.

Prompts. For each sample in the test set, there is no information about the specific task to be performed (e.g., ASR) or the language pair to support (e.g., en); rather, the model has to correctly interpret and fulfill diverse instructions across the supported language pairs (e.g., "Traduci questo audio in inglese"[it], "Translate this audio into English"[en]).

9.2 Data and Metrics

Training and Development Data. We adopt two evaluation conditions: constrained and unconstrained. In the *constrained* condition, participants are allowed to use the specified Speech Foundation Model[55] and Large Language Model[56], training their systems on designated datasets:

- EuroParl-ST (Iranzo-Sánchez et al., 2020) and CoVoST2 (Wang et al., 2020) for ASR/S2TT[57] tasks,
- Spoken-SQuAD (Li et al., 2018) for SQA,
- NUTSHELL (Züfle et al., 2025) for S2TSUM.

Development data is provided through the ACL 60/60 dataset (Salesky et al., 2023), which contains transcripts, translations, and summaries that can be retrieved using video IDs. Importantly, the use of the pre-trained SFM and LLM is not mandatory, and submissions with models trained from scratch on the allowed data are accepted, as are systems using only one of the two pre-trained

[55]hf.co/facebook/seamless-m4t-v2-large

[56]hf.co/meta-llama/Llama-3.1-8B-Instruct

[57]EuroParl-ST: en→{it, de}, CoVoST2: en→{zh, de}

models. No training data is provided for cross-lingual SQA or S2TSUM tasks where the output languages differ from the source speech language, which is designed to test the models' zero-shot cross-lingual abilities. The *unconstrained* condition places no limitations on model architectures, pre-trained models, or training data.

The constrained evaluation condition is meant for providing a controlled environment for comparing different approaches without the confounding effects of varying data sources or model scales. On the other hand, the unconstrained condition reflects real-world deployment scenarios where practitioners may leverage cutting-edge models, proprietary datasets, and computational scaling to achieve optimal performance.

Evaluation Data. We evaluate the submitted models with IWSLT25Instruct, a novel resource, representing the first cross-lingual multimodal benchmark for instruction-following tasks across speech, text, and vision modalities in four languages: English, German, Italian, and Chinese. IWSLT25Instruct is extracted from the ASR, S2TT, SQA, and S2TSUM sections of the MMIF benchmark (Papi et al., 2025b), built upon scientific domain data retrieved from the ACL Anthology.[58] The dataset contains 21 videos, corresponding to 2 hours. Source audio and video content in English (talks of about 5-6 minutes each) are enriched with multilingual annotations and translations to support: *i)* ASR (en→en); *ii)* S2TT (en→de, it, zh), *iii)* S2TSUM (en→es, de, it, zh); *iv)* SQA (en→es, de, it, zh). In SQA, questions (about 10 for each video) are provided both in the speech language (English) and in other target languages (German, Italian, Chinese), and answers must be given in the same language as the one of the question (e.g., Italian questions require answers in Italian). The SQA task includes unanswerable questions, to which the only correct response is "*Not answerable* or its corresponding translations in the other languages.[59] For S2TSUM, the dataset contains 100 abstracts (including those of the 21 videos), for a total of 17k words. The audio data are provided as complete audio files (5-6 minutes, WAV format) for the `LONG` sub-track, and as automatically segmented audio (of 15-20 seconds) using SHAS (Tsiamas et al., 2023) for the `SHORT` sub-track.

We release the videos, source audio, and task instructions to participate in the shared task. Also, we provide an example submission for the `LONG` sub-track, which could be used as a 1-shot task demonstration. Participants submit their system outputs and may adjust instructions to suit their models' prompts. The evaluation is conducted via the SPEECHM platform, presented in Section 2.

Metrics. The evaluation was carried out by computing separate scores for each of the tasks involved. Namely, for ASR, we computed WER using the jiWER library[60] after normalizing the test using the Whisper normalizer[61] (Radford et al., 2022). For S2TT, we used COMET[62] (Rei et al., 2020) after concatenating all segments belonging to the same talk in the case of the `SHORT` sub-track and resegmenting the text with `mwerSegmenter` to pair them with the reference sentences. Lastly, for SQA and S2TSUM, we computed BERTScore (Zhang* et al., 2020) rescaling the scores with baselines to obtain more interpretable scores in a wider range (typically, in the [0, 1] range).[63] The code used for the evaluation is available at: github.com/hlt-mt/if-iwslt2025.

9.3 Submissions

In total, we received 16 submissions from 5 different teams. Two teams submitted under the constrained setting. Only one submission was contrastive. Two teams (NLE and KIT) participated in all language directions, while others (CUNI-NL and IST) submitted for a subset. One team (MEETWEEN) submitted for English only. The participants' systems in the `SHORT` (CUNI-NL, IST, MEETWEEN, NLE) and `LONG` (KIT) sub-tracks are detailed below.

CUNI-NL (Luu and Bojar, 2025) participated in the unconstrained `LONG` sub-track, submitting to ASR (en→en) and S2TT (en→de). Their submission explores the combination of speech encoders and instruction-tuned LLMs. Specifically, they compare Whisper and Seamless as encoders, alongside LLaMA, EuroLLM-9B-Instruct (Martins et al., 2024), and Gemma-3-12B-IT (Team

[58] aclanthology.org

[59] Namely, in Italian "*Non è possibile rispondere*", German "Nicht zu beantworten.", and Chinese 无法回答。.

[60] github.com/jitsi/jiwer

[61] Specifically, we used version `0.0.10`.

[62] With model `Unbabel/wmt22-comet-da`.

[63] See github.com/Tiiiger/bert_score/blob/master/journal/rescale_baseline.md

et al., 2025) as LLMs. For Seamless, the original length adapter is used, while for Whisper, a convolution-based length adapter is applied. A trainable feed-forward projection connects the frozen encoder with the frozen LLM, and LoRA adapters (Hu et al., 2021) are applied on top of the LLM. Training is conducted exclusively on the CoVoST dataset. Their results show that combining Seamless as the encoder with EuroLLM as the LLM yields the strongest performance.

IST (Attanasio et al., 2025) participated in the SHORT unconstrained sub-track, submitting to the en→en, de, and zh language pairs. Their system adapts small language models: audio is encoded with wav2vec 2.0 (Baevski et al., 2020), and a two-layer MLP projects features into the input space of a frozen Qwen2.5–1.5B (Qwen et al., 2025). Seven ASR datasets are used, along with CoVoST2 for S2TT, and Spoken-SQuAD for SQA. To increase coverage, ASR transcripts and Spoken-SQuAD are translated into German and Chinese using multiple LLMs and unanswerable questions are synthesized to improve SQA robustness. Task and language tags are prepended to prompts to enable multilingual, multitask instruction following. Training then proceeds in two stages: first, the speech encoder and MLP are jointly trained on ASR data for modality alignment; then, the encoder is frozen and only the MLP is fine-tuned on ASR, AST, and SQA.

MEETWEEN participated in the SHORT unconstrained sub-track, submitting to the ASR and SQA tasks. The system[64] combines the Seamless speech encoder with a Q-Former (Li et al., 2023; Tang et al., 2024) modality adapter and a LLaMA decoder. Training is performed in three stages. In the first stage, an ASR warmup is conducted with the encoder and LLM frozen and only the modality adapter is trained. The second stage, all-task warmup, retains the frozen encoder and LLM while training the adapter across ASR, S2TT, SQA, S2TSUM, MT, SLU, and lip reading tasks. Finally, in end-to-end training, the encoder remains frozen while both the adapter and LLM are fine-tuned on the same set of tasks.

NLE (Lee et al., 2025) participated in the SHORT constrained sub-track, submitting to all language pairs: en→en, de, it, zh. They augmented training data by translating SpokenSQuAD and generating more fluent, abstractive answers. Their model employs a Seamless encoder with additional downsampling, a Transformer-based projection module, and LLaMA with LoRA (Hu et al., 2021) applied. Training occurs in three stages using two-level sampling process (Zanon Boito et al., 2024): first, the projector is trained with frozen encoder and LLM on ASR+ST or ASR+ST+SQA data; second, LoRA adapters are trained on the LLM using text-only MT and QA data; finally, both are jointly fine-tuned on all tasks for 1000 steps, with strong performance evident after 100 steps. Models trained with SQA in stage two initially underperform on SQA. However, after final tuning, all models perform similarly, with those trained only on ASR and S2TT slightly better on S2TT.

[64]huggingface.co/meetween/Llama-speechlmm-1.0-l

KIT Koneru et al. (2025) participated in the LONG constrained sub-track, submitting to all language pairs: en→en, de, it, zh. They augmented data by synthesizing NUTSHELL speech with TTS for ASR adaptation, and using LLaMA to generate multilingual QA pairs and translated summaries from NUTSHELL for SQA and S2TSUM. Their architecture connects Seamless and LLaMA via a trainable Q-Former (Li et al., 2023; Tang et al., 2024). Training involved contrastive pretraining (Züfle and Niehues, 2025) on ASR data followed by task-specific fine-tuning. Chain-of-thought reasoning was applied to improve SQA robustness by detecting unanswerable questions. For long audio, VAD-based segmentation (Sohn et al., 1999) was used in ASR and S2TT. For SQA and S2TSUM, audio segments were encoded separately, with embeddings concatenated before projection and LLM input to maintain end-to-end trainability. A context-aware post-editing model trained on NUTSHELL TTS data improved domain-specific terminology and restored context lost to segmentation.

9.4 Results

9.4.1 Automatic Evaluation

The complete results for both SHORT and LONG sub-tracks are presented in Table 47. For comparison, we include the results of the Phi4-Multimodal model (Abouelenin et al., 2025), a state-of-the-art baseline model trained on a broader range of tasks (including the IF task) and datasets (both in-house and public).

Monolingual English. In the monolingual scenario–comprising ASR and SQA in the SHORT sub-track, and ASR, SQA, and S2TSUM in the LONG sub-track–all participating teams submitted systems, including a contrastive submission (CUNI-NL). In the SHORT sub-track, the best ASR performance is achieved by the baseline (7 WER). Among participants, NLE obtains the best result (13 WER), followed by CUNI-NL and IST, both with 15 WER. For SQA, NLE outperforms all other systems with a BERTScore of 0.50–exceeding the baseline by 0.04 points. Notably, the NLE's system, even if trained in the constrained settings, still emerged as the top-performing participant, though it lagged behind the baseline in ASR by nearly double the WER. In the LONG sub-track, KIT, which is the only team that submitted a system, is able to outperform the baseline in two out of three tasks (ASR and S2TSUM), and its SQA performance (0.41 BERTScore) is nearly on par with the baseline (0.42). Nonetheless, there remains a performance gap compared to short-form processing: for example, the constrained systems NLE (SHORT) and KIT (LONG) differ by 0.02 WER in ASR and 0.08 BERTScore in SQA.

Crosslingual German. In the English-to-German (en-de) direction, the best S2TT result in the SHORT sub-track is achieved by the baseline (0.77 COMET). Among participants, CUNI-NL's primary submission (0.72 COMET), NLE (0.71), and CUNI-NL's contrastive (0.69) perform similarly. For SQA, NLE achieves the best score, surpassing the baseline by 0.02 BERTScore. In the LONG sub-track, KIT outperforms the baseline in all three tasks (ST, SQA, and S2TSUM), with substantial margins in some cases (e.g., 0.74 vs. 0.55 COMET in S2TT). While short-form processing remains easier for current systems, the gap is smaller in this case, with the constrained NLE system achieving only 0.03 COMET improvement on S2TT and 0.03 BERTScore in SQA compared to the constrained KIT.

Crosslingual Italian. In the English-to-Italian (en-it) direction, the baseline again achieves the best S2TT result in the SHORT sub-track, outperforming the only participant (NLE) by 0.06 COMET. However, NLE surpasses the baseline in SQA with a 0.02 BERTScore improvement. In the LONG sub-track, KIT outperforms the baseline across all three tasks, including a large gain of 0.21 COMET in S2TT. As with other language directions, performance on long-form input remains consistently lower than short-form.

Crosslingual Chinese. In the English-to-Chinese (en-zh) direction, the baseline also leads in S2TT for the SHORT sub-track, outperforming NLE–the best-performing participant–by 0.05 COMET. For SQA, however, NLE achieves a 0.02 BERTScore improvement over the baseline. In the LONG sub-track, KIT once again outperforms the baseline and, interestingly, achieves better performance in long-form SQA (0.41) than those obtained by NLE in the short-form SQA (0.35), suggesting that the system was able to effectively exploit the long context.

9.4.2 Human Evaluation

Similar to the other tracks of this year's IWSLT Evaluation Campaign, each participant's primary submission[65] has been manually evaluated. The human evaluation involves the speech translation outputs in German and Chinese, and the manual process that has been conducted is explained in Appendix A. The results are also compared with those of the other tracks in Table 15 and Table 17.

The human evaluation results largely confirm the trends observed in automatic evaluation. For en-de, the top-ranked KIT system (with a COMET score of 0.74) achieved the best human-evaluated performance, followed by CUNI primary and NLE (with a COMET of 0.72 and 0.71, respectively). However, human evaluators found the second and third-ranked systems indistinguishable, suggesting that COMET score differences of 0.01 fall below the threshold of human perceptual sensitivity. Similarly, for en-zh, the KIT and NLE systems were perceived as equivalent by humans, confirming their close automatic scores (of 0.77 and 0.76, respectively). Compared to the other tracks, the IF track results align with expectations, performing worse than the systems of the offline track but better than those of the simultaneous track, especially under low-latency constraints. This performance reflects two key factors: offline and simultaneous tracks' systems benefit from larger training datasets and task-specific optimization for speech

[65]We have excluded from the human evaluations the submissions with COMET scores below 0.4, as they were significantly worse than other participants, making the comparison meaningless.

translation, while IF models are more general-purpose architectures, supporting multiple tasks. These findings highlight that while automatic metrics provide valuable performance insights, human perception may be less sensitive to small metric differences, particularly when systems achieve relatively high performance levels.

9.5 Discussion and Conclusions

As this was the first edition of the Instruction-Following (IF) shared task at IWSLT, our primary goal was to understand the interest of our community in evaluating general-purpose speech models across a variety of tasks and languages, and explore the feasibility of leveraging these models for long-form speech processing. The task was met with strong interest, with 16 submissions from 5 teams, and provided valuable insights into the current capabilities and limitations of IF systems for speech-based tasks.

Among the four tasks, ASR emerged as the most accessible, with most participants achieving a WER below 18. Monolingual SQA was also relatively approachable, with BERTScores up to 0.50. In contrast, crosslingual SQA proved more challenging, with best-case BERTScores between 0.38 and 0.41. The S2TT task showed consistent translation quality across language pairs, with best COMET scores ranging from 0.74 to 0.77. S2TSUM, however, stood out as the most difficult task, with no system exceeding a score of 0.37–even in the best case (en-zh).

Comparing performance across tracks, short-form processing (`SHORT`) consistently outperformed long-form (`LONG`) processing in all languages. Surprisingly, the difference appears to be more pronounced in the monolingual tasks instead of the crosslingual tasks, which are inherently more difficult, suggesting that ASR and monolingual SQA are better mastered by current short-form models. It is also noteworthy that the best results in both tracks were achieved by systems trained under constrained settings, demonstrating that these settings represent a promising *starter pack* for IF model development, allowing for building competitive systems even with limited resources.

In terms of top-performing systems, NLE's submissions led the `SHORT` track across all language directions. In the `LONG` track, the KIT system–despite being the only submission–outperformed the state-of-the-art Phi4-Multimodal baseline in nearly every task.

Given the success of this first edition and the encouraging level of participation, we plan to continue the IF shared task in future editions of IWSLT, expanding its scope and challenges to further advance research in speech processing.

Acknowledgements

We gratefully acknowledge the Polish high-performance computing infrastructure PLGrid (HPC Center: ACK Cyfronet AGH) for providing computer facilities and support within computational grant no. PLG/2025/018002. The work by FBK has received funding from the PNRR project FAIR - Future AI Research (PE00000013), under the NRRP MUR program funded by the NextGenerationEU, and from the European Union's Horizon research and innovation programme under grant agreement No 101135798, project Meetween (My Personal AI Mediator for Virtual MEETings BetWEEN People). The work by Charles University received funding from the Project OP JAK Mezisektorová spolupráce Nr. CZ.02.01.01/00/23_020/0008518 named "Jazykověda, umělá inteligence a jazykové a řečové technologie: od výzkumu k aplikacím" (Ondřej Bojar), from the grant 272323 of the Grant Agency of Charles University (Dávid Javorský), and the National Recovery Plan funded project MPO 60273/24/21300/21000 CEDMO 2.0 NPO (Peter Polák). The work was also supported by the internal university grant number 260 821 (SVV). The work by Mateusz Krubiński and Pavel Pecina was funded by the European Commission via its H2020 Program (contract no. 870930: WELCOME).

Atul Kr. Ojha and John P. McCrae would like to thank Research Ireland under Grant Number SFI/12/RC/2289_P2 Insight_2 and thank RTÉ/TG4 for sharing the Irish speech data. We would also like to thank Panlingua for providing the Marathi-Hindi and Bhojpuri-Hindi speech translation data.

The work by Tsz Kin Lam was funded by UK Research and Innovation (UKRI) under the UK government's Horizon Europe funding guarantee (grant number 10039436: UTTER)

References

Abdelrahman Abouelenin, Atabak Ashfaq, Adam Atkinson, Hany Awadalla, Nguyen Bach, Jianmin Bao, Alon Benhaim, Martin Cai, Vishrav Chaudhary, Congcong Chen, et al. 2025. Phi-4-mini technical report: Compact yet powerful multimodal language models via mixture-of-loras. *arXiv preprint arXiv:2503.01743*.

Basil Abraham, Danish Goel, Divya Siddarth, Kalika Bali, Manu Chopra, Monojit Choudhury, Pratik Joshi, Preethi Jyoti, Sunayana Sitaram, and Vivek Seshadri. 2020. Crowdsourcing speech data for low-resource languages from low-income workers. In *Proceedings of the Twelfth Language Resources and Evaluation Conference*, pages 2819–2826, Marseille, France. European Language Resources Association.

Milind Agarwal, Sweta Agrawal, Antonios Anastasopoulos, Luisa Bentivogli, Ondřej Bojar, Claudia Borg, Marine Carpuat, Roldano Cattoni, Mauro Cettolo, Mingda Chen, William Chen, Khalid Choukri, Alexandra Chronopoulou, Anna Currey, Thierry Declerck, Qianqian Dong, Kevin Duh, Yannick Estève, Marcello Federico, Souhir Gahbiche, Barry Haddow, Benjamin Hsu, Phu Mon Htut, Hirofumi Inaguma, Dávid Javorský, John Judge, Yasumasa Kano, Tom Ko, Rishu Kumar, Pengwei Li, Xutai Ma, Prashant Mathur, Evgeny Matusov, Paul McNamee, John P. McCrae, Kenton Murray, Maria Nadejde, Satoshi Nakamura, Matteo Negri, Ha Nguyen, Jan Niehues, Xing Niu, Atul Kr. Ojha, John E. Ortega, Proyag Pal, Juan Pino, Lonneke van der Plas, Peter Polák, Elijah Rippeth, Elizabeth Salesky, Jiatong Shi, Matthias Sperber, Sebastian Stüker, Katsuhito Sudoh, Yun Tang, Brian Thompson, Kevin Tran, Marco Turchi, Alex Waibel, Mingxuan Wang, Shinji Watanabe, and Rodolfo Zevallos. 2023. FINDINGS OF THE IWSLT 2023 EVALUATION CAMPAIGN. In *Proceedings of the 20th International Conference on Spoken Language Translation (IWSLT 2023)*, pages 1–61, Toronto, Canada (in-person and online). Association for Computational Linguistics.

Victor Agostinelli, Max Wild, Matthew Raffel, Kazi Fuad, and Lizhong Chen. 2024. Simul-LLM: A framework for exploring high-quality simultaneous translation with large language models. In *Proceedings of the 62nd Annual Meeting of the Association for Computational Linguistics (Volume 1: Long Papers)*, pages 10530–10541, Bangkok, Thailand. Association for Computational Linguistics.

Ibrahim Said Ahmad, Antonios Anastasopoulos, Ondřej Bojar, Claudia Borg, Marine Carpuat, Roldano Cattoni, Mauro Cettolo, William Chen, Qianqian Dong, Marcello Federico, Barry Haddow, Dávid Javorský, Mateusz Krubiński, Tsz Kin Lam, Xutai Ma, Prashant Mathur, Evgeny Matusov, Chandresh Maurya, John McCrae, Kenton Murray, Satoshi Nakamura, Matteo Negri, Jan Niehues, Xing Niu, Atul Kr. Ojha, John Ortega, Sara Papi, Peter Polák, Adam Pospíšil, Pavel Pecina, Elizabeth Salesky, Nivedita Sethiya, Balaram Sarkar, Jiatong Shi, Claytone Sikasote, Matthias Sperber, Sebastian Stüker, Katsuhito Sudoh, Brian Thompson, Alex Waibel, Shinji Watanabe, Patrick Wilken, Petr Zemánek, and Rodolfo Zevallos. 2024. FINDINGS OF THE IWSLT 2024 EVALUATION CAMPAIGN. In *Proceedings of the 21st International Conference on Spoken Language Translation (IWSLT 2024)*, pages 1–11, Bangkok, Thailand (in-person and online). Association for Computational Linguistics.

Farhad Akhbardeh, Arkady Arkhangorodsky, Magdalena Biesialska, Ondřej Bojar, Rajen Chatterjee, Vishrav Chaudhary, Marta R. Costa-jussa, Cristina España-Bonet, Angela Fan, Christian Federmann, Markus Freitag, Yvette Graham, Roman Grundkiewicz, Barry Haddow, Leonie Harter, Kenneth Heafield, Christopher Homan, Matthias Huck, Kwabena Amponsah-Kaakyire, Jungo Kasai, Daniel Khashabi, Kevin Knight, Tom Kocmi, Philipp Koehn, Nicholas Lourie, Christof Monz, Makoto Morishita, Masaaki Nagata, Ajay Nagesh, Toshiaki Nakazawa, Matteo Negri, Santanu Pal, Allahsera Auguste Tapo, Marco Turchi, Valentin Vydrin, and Marcos Zampieri. 2021. Findings of the 2021 conference on machine translation (WMT21). In *Proceedings of the Sixth Conference on Machine Translation*, pages 1–88, Online. Association for Computational Linguistics.

Bhavana Akkiraju, Aishwarya Pothula, Santosh Kesiraju, and Anil Vuppala. 2025. IIITH-BUT system for IWSLT 2025 low-resource Bhojpuri to Hindi speech translation. In *Proceedings of the 22th International Conference on Spoken Language Translation (IWSLT)*.

Jesujoba O Alabi, Xuechen Liu, Dietrich Klakow, and Junichi Yamagishi. 2024. Afrihubert: A self-supervised speech representation model for african languages. *arXiv preprint arXiv:2409.20201*.

Tanel Alumäe, Joonas Kalda, Külliki Bode, and Martin Kaitsa. 2023. Automatic closed captioning for Estonian live broadcasts. In *Proceedings of the 24th Nordic Conference on Computational Linguistics (NoDaLiDa)*, pages 492–499, Tórshavn, Faroe Islands. University of Tartu Library.

Ebrahim Ansari, Ondřej Bojar, Barry Haddow, and Mohammad Mahmoudi. 2021. SLTev: Comprehensive Evaluation of Spoken Language Translation. In *Proceedings of the 16th Conference of the European Chapter of the Association for Computational Linguistics: Demo Papers*, Kyiv, Ukraine. Association for Computational Linguistics.

Junyi Ao, Rui Wang, Long Zhou, Chengyi Wang, Shuo Ren, Yu Wu, Shujie Liu, Tom Ko, Qing Li, Yu Zhang, Zhihua Wei, Yao Qian, Jinyu Li, and Furu Wei. 2022. SpeechT5: Unified-modal encoder-decoder pre-training for spoken language processing. In *Proceedings of the 60th Annual Meeting of the Association for Computational Linguistics (Volume 1: Long Papers)*, pages 5723–5738, Dublin, Ireland. Association for Computational Linguistics.

Rosana Ardila, Megan Branson, Kelly Davis, Michael Henretty, Michael Kohler, Josh Meyer, Reuben Morais, Lindsay Saunders, Francis M Tyers, and Gregor Weber. 2020a. Common voice: A massively-multilingual speech corpus. In *Lrec*.

Rosana Ardila, Megan Branson, Kelly Davis, Michael Kohler, Josh Meyer, Michael Henretty, Reuben Morais, Lindsay Saunders, Francis Tyers, and Gregor Weber. 2020b. Common voice: A massively-multilingual speech corpus. In *Proceedings of The 12th Language Resources and Evaluation Conference*, pages 4218–4222.

Giuseppe Attanasio, Sonal Sannigrahi, Ben Peters, and André F.T. Martins. 2025. IST at IWSLT 2025: Multilingual Efficient Learning for Speech-Text Models. In *Proceedings of the 22th International Conference on Spoken Language Translation (IWSLT)*.

Marko Avila and Josep Crego. 2025. SYSTRAN @ IWSLT 2025 Low-resource track. In *Proceedings of the 22nd International Conference on Spoken Language Translation (IWSLT)*.

Alexei Baevski, Yuhao Zhou, Abdelrahman Mohamed, and Michael Auli. 2020. wav2vec 2.0: A framework for self-supervised learning of speech representations. In *Advances in Neural Information Processing Systems*, volume 33, pages 12449–12460. Curran Associates, Inc.

Max Bain, Jaesung Huh, Tengda Han, and Andrew Zisserman. 2023. Whisperx: Time-accurate speech transcription of long-form audio. *arXiv preprint arXiv:2303.00747*.

Bbc. 2019. BBC Subtitle Guidelines. BBC © 2018 Version 1.1.8.

Peter J Bickel and Kjell A Doksum. 1977. *Mathematical statistics: basic ideas and selected topics*. Holden-Day Inc.

Ronald Cardenas, Rodolfo Zevallos, Reynaldo Baquerizo, and Luis Camacho. 2018. Siminchik: A speech corpus for preservation of southern quechua. *Isi-nlp 2*, page 21.

Mauro Cettolo, Marcello Federico, Luisa Bentivogli, Jan Niehues, Sebastian Stüker, K. Sudoh, K. Yoshino, and Christian Federmann. 2017. Overview of the IWSLT 2017 Evaluation Campaign. In *Proceedings of the 14th International Workshop on Spoken Language Translation (IWSLT 2017)*, pages 2–14, Tokyo, Japan.

Chaimae Chellaf, Haroun Elleuch, Othman Istaiteh, D. Fortuné Kponou, Fethi Bougares, Yannick Estève, and salima Mdhaffar. 2025. LIA and ELYADATA systems for the IWSLT 2025 low-resource speech translation shared task. In *Proceedings of the 22th International Conference on Spoken Language Translation (IWSLT)*.

Jianlv Chen, Shitao Xiao, Peitian Zhang, Kun Luo, Defu Lian, and Zheng Liu. 2024. Bge m3-embedding: Multi-lingual, multi-functionality, multi-granularity text embeddings through self-knowledge distillation. *arXiv preprint arXiv:2402.03216*.

Mingda Chen, Paul-Ambroise Duquenne, Pierre Andrews, Justine Kao, Alexandre Mourachko, Holger Schwenk, and Marta R. Costa-jussà. 2023. BLASER: A text-free speech-to-speech translation evaluation metric. In *Proceedings of the 61st Annual Meeting of the Association for Computational Linguistics (Volume 1: Long Papers)*, pages 9064–9079, Toronto, Canada. Association for Computational Linguistics.

Yunfei Chu, Jin Xu, Qian Yang, Haojie Wei, Xipin Wei, Zhifang Guo, Yichong Leng, Yuanjun Lv, Jinzheng He, Junyang Lin, Chang Zhou, and Jingren Zhou. 2024. Qwen2-audio technical report.

Sayan Das, Soham Chaudhuri, Dipanjan Saha, Dipankar Das, and Sivaji Bandyopadhyay. 2025. IWSLT 2025 Indic Track System Description Paper: Speech-to-Text Translation from Low-Resource Indian Languages (Bengali and Tamil) to English. In *Proceedings of the 22th International Conference on Spoken Language Translation (IWSLT)*.

Tim Dettmers, Artidoro Pagnoni, Ari Holtzman, and Luke Zettlemoyer. 2023. Qlora: efficient finetuning of quantized llms. In *Proceedings of the 37th International Conference on Neural Information Processing Systems*, Nips '23, Red Hook, NY, USA. Curran Associates Inc.

Daniel Deutsch, Rotem Dror, and Dan Roth. 2021. A statistical analysis of summarization evaluation metrics using resampling methods. *Transactions of the Association for Computational Linguistics*, 9:1132–1146.

Debjit Dhar, Soham Lahiri, Tapabrata Mondal, and Sivaji Bandyopadhyay. 2025. JU-CSE-NLP's Cascaded Speech to Text Translation Systems for IWSLT 2025 in Indic Track. In *Proceedings of the 22th International Conference on Spoken Language Translation (IWSLT)*.

David Draper, James S Hodges, Colin L Mallows, and Daryl Pregibon. 1993. Exchangeability and data analysis. *Journal of the Royal Statistical Society Series A: Statistics in Society*, 156(1):9–28.

John E. Ortega, Rodolfo Joel Zevallos, Ibrahim Said Ahmad, and William Chen. 2024. QUESPA submission for the IWSLT 2024 dialectal and low-resource speech translation task. In *Proceedings of the 21st International Conference on Spoken Language Translation (IWSLT 2024)*, pages 125–133,

Bangkok, Thailand (in-person and online). Association for Computational Linguistics.

Angela Fan, Shruti Bhosale, Holger Schwenk, Zhiyi Ma, Ahmed El-Kishky, Siddharth Goyal, Mandeep Baines, Onur Celebi, Guillaume Wenzek, Vishrav Chaudhary, et al. 2021. Beyond english-centric multilingual machine translation. *Journal of Machine Learning Research*, 22(107):1–48.

Muhammad Hazim Al Farouq, Aman Kassahun Wassie, and Yasmin Moslem. 2025. Bemba Speech Translation: Exploring a Low-Resource African Language. In *Proceedings of the 22th International Conference on Spoken Language Translation (IWSLT)*.

RA Fisher. 1935. *The design of experiments*. Oliver & Boyd.

Markus Freitag, George Foster, David Grangier, Viresh Ratnakar, Qijun Tan, and Wolfgang Macherey. 2021a. Experts, errors, and context: A large-scale study of human evaluation for machine translation. *Transactions of the Association for Computational Linguistics*, 9:1460–1474.

Markus Freitag, Nitika Mathur, Daniel Deutsch, Chi-Kiu Lo, Eleftherios Avramidis, Ricardo Rei, Brian Thompson, Frederic Blain, Tom Kocmi, Jiayi Wang, David Ifeoluwa Adelani, Marianna Buchicchio, Chrysoula Zerva, and Alon Lavie. 2024. Are LLMs breaking MT metrics? results of the WMT24 metrics shared task. In *Proceedings of the Ninth Conference on Machine Translation*, pages 47–81, Miami, Florida, USA. Association for Computational Linguistics.

Markus Freitag, Nitika Mathur, Chi-kiu Lo, Eleftherios Avramidis, Ricardo Rei, Brian Thompson, Tom Kocmi, Frederic Blain, Daniel Deutsch, Craig Stewart, Chrysoula Zerva, Sheila Castilho, Alon Lavie, and George Foster. 2023. Results of WMT23 metrics shared task: Metrics might be guilty but references are not innocent. In *Proceedings of the Eighth Conference on Machine Translation*, pages 578–628, Singapore. Association for Computational Linguistics.

Markus Freitag, Ricardo Rei, Nitika Mathur, Chi-kiu Lo, Craig Stewart, George Foster, Alon Lavie, and Ondřej Bojar. 2021b. Results of the WMT21 metrics shared task: Evaluating metrics with expert-based human evaluations on TED and news domain. In *Proceedings of the Sixth Conference on Machine Translation*, pages 733–774, Online. Association for Computational Linguistics.

Marco Gaido, Sara Papi, Matteo Negri, and Luisa Bentivogli. 2024. Speech translation with speech foundation models and large language models: What is there and what is missing? In *Proceedings of the 62nd Annual Meeting of the Association for Computational Linguistics (Volume 1: Long Papers)*, pages 14760–14778, Bangkok, Thailand. Association for Computational Linguistics.

Phillip Good. 2002. Extensions of the concept of exchangeability and their applications. *Journal of Modern Applied Statistical Methods*, 1:243–247.

Phillip Good. 2013. *Permutation tests: a practical guide to resampling methods for testing hypotheses*. Springer Science & Business Media.

Naman Goyal, Cynthia Gao, Vishrav Chaudhary, Peng-Jen Chen, Guillaume Wenzek, Da Ju, Sanjana Krishnan, Marc'Aurelio Ranzato, Francisco Guzmán, and Angela Fan. 2022. The Flores-101 evaluation benchmark for low-resource and multilingual machine translation. *Transactions of the Association for Computational Linguistics*, 10:522–538.

Yvette Graham, Timothy Baldwin, Alistair Moffat, and Justin Zobel. 2013. Continuous measurement scales in human evaluation of machine translation. In *Proceedings of the 7th Linguistic Annotation Workshop and Interoperability with Discourse*, pages 33–41, Sofia, Bulgaria. Association for Computational Linguistics.

Aaron Grattafiori, Abhimanyu Dubey, Abhinav Jauhri, Abhinav Pandey, Abhishek Kadian, Ahmad Al-Dahle, Aiesha Letman, Akhil Mathur, Alan Schelten, Alex Vaughan, et al. 2024. The llama 3 herd of models. *arXiv preprint arXiv:2407.21783*.

Anmol Gulati, James Qin, Chung-Cheng Chiu, Niki Parmar, Yu Zhang, Jiahui Yu, Wei Han, Shibo Wang, Zhengdong Zhang, Yonghui Wu, and Ruoming Pang. 2020. Conformer: Convolution-augmented transformer for speech recognition. *arXiv preprint arXiv:2005.08100*.

Fei He, Shan-Hui Cathy Chu, Oddur Kjartansson, Clara Rivera, Anna Katanova, Alexander Gutkin, Isin Demirsahin, Cibu Johny, Martin Jansche, Supheakmungkol Sarin, and Knot Pipatsrisawat. 2020. Open-source multi-speaker speech corpora for building Gujarati, Kannada, Malayalam, Marathi, Tamil and Telugu speech synthesis systems. In *Proceedings of the Twelfth Language Resources and Evaluation Conference*, pages 6494–6503, Marseille, France. European Language Resources Association.

Amr Hendy, Mohamed Abdelrehim, Amr Sharaf, Vikas Raunak, Mohamed Gabr, Hitokazu Matsushita, Young Jin Kim, Mohamed Afify, and Hany Hassan Awadalla. 2023. How good are gpt models at machine translation? a comprehensive evaluation. *arXiv preprint arXiv:2302.09210*.

Carlos Daniel Hernandez Mena, Albert Gatt, Andrea DeMarco, Claudia Borg, Lonneke van der Plas, Amanda Muscat, and Ian Padovani. 2020. Masri-headset: A maltese corpus for speech recognition. In *Proceedings of The 12th Language Resources and Evaluation Conference*, pages 6381–6388, Marseille, France. European Language Resources Association.

Edward J Hu, Yelong Shen, Phillip Wallis, Zeyuan Allen-Zhu, Yuanzhi Li, Shean Wang, Lu Wang, and Weizhu Chen. 2021. Lora: Low-rank adaptation of large language models. *arXiv preprint arXiv:2106.09685*.

Javier Iranzo-Sánchez, Joan Albert Silvestre-Cerdà, Javier Jorge, Nahuel Roselló, Adrià Giménez, Albert Sanchis, Jorge Civera, and Alfons Juan. 2020. Europarl-st: A multilingual corpus for speech translation of parliamentary debates. In *ICASSP 2020 - 2020 IEEE International Conference on Acoustics, Speech and Signal Processing (ICASSP)*, pages 8229–8233.

Dávid Javorský, Dominik Macháček, and Ondřej Bojar. 2022. Continuous rating as reliable human evaluation of simultaneous speech translation. In *Proceedings of the Seventh Conference on Machine Translation (WMT)*, pages 154–164, Abu Dhabi, United Arab Emirates (Hybrid). Association for Computational Linguistics.

Xilin Jiang, Yinghao Aaron Li, Adrian Nicolas Florea, Cong Han, and Nima Mesgarani. 2024. Speech slytherin: Examining the performance and efficiency of mamba for speech separation, recognition, and synthesis. *arXiv preprint arXiv:2407.09732*.

Japan Translation Federation JTF. 2018. JTF Translation Quality Evaluation Guidelines, 1st Edition (in Japanese).

Waad Ben Kheder, Josef Jon, André Beyer, Abdel Messaoudi, Rabea Affan, Claude Barras, Maxim Tychonov, and Jean-Luc Gauvain. 2024. ALADAN at IWSLT24 Low-resource Arabic Dialectal Speech Translation Task. In *Proceedings of the 21th International Conference on Spoken Language Translation (IWSLT)*.

Waad Ben Kheder, Josef Jon, André Beyer, Abdel Messaoudi, Rabea Affan, Claude Barras, Maxim Tychonov, and Jean-Luc Gauvain. 2025. ALADAN at IWSLT25 Low-resource Arabic Dialectal Speech Translation Task. In *Proceedings of the 22nd International Conference on Spoken Language Translation (IWSLT)*.

Sameer Khurana, Antoine Laurent, and James Glass. 2022. Samu-xlsr: Semantically-aligned multimodal utterance-level cross-lingual speech representation. *IEEE Journal of Selected Topics in Signal Processing*, 16(6):1493–1504.

Tom Kocmi, Eleftherios Avramidis, Rachel Bawden, Ondřej Bojar, Anton Dvorkovich, Christian Federmann, Mark Fishel, Markus Freitag, Thamme Gowda, Roman Grundkiewicz, Barry Haddow, Philipp Koehn, Benjamin Marie, Christof Monz, Makoto Morishita, Kenton Murray, Masaaki Nagata, Toshiaki Nakazawa, Martin Popel, Maja Popović, Mariya Shmatova, and Jun Suzuki. 2023. Findings of the 2023 conference on machine translation (WMT23): LLMs are here but not quite there yet. In *Proceedings of the Eighth Conference on Machine Translation*, pages 1–42, Singapore. Association for Computational Linguistics.

Sai Koneru, Maike Züfle, Thai-Binh Nguyen, Seymanur Akti, Jan Niehues, and Alexander Waibel. 2025. KIT's Offline Speech Translation and Instruction Following Submission for IWSLT 2025. In *Proceedings of the 22th International Conference on Spoken Language Translation (IWSLT)*.

Matyáš Kopp, Vladislav Stankov, Ondřej Bojar, Barbora Hladká, and Pavel Straňák. 2021. ParCzech 3.0. LINDAT/CLARIAH-CZ digital library at the Institute of Formal and Applied Linguistics (ÚFAL), Faculty of Mathematics and Physics, Charles University.

D. Fortune Kponou, Salima Mdhaffar, Fréjus A. A. Laleye, Eugène C. Ezin, and Yannick Estève. 2025a. Extending the fongbe to french speech translation corpus: Resources, models and benchmark. In *Proceedings of Interspeech 2025*.

D. Fortuné Kponou, Salima Mdhaffar, Fréjus A. A. Laleye, Eugène Cokou Ezin, and Yannick Estève. 2025b. FFSTC 2: Extending the Fongbe to French Speech Translation Corpus. In *Proceedings of the 22th International Conference on Spoken Language Translation (IWSLT)*.

Shankar Kumar and Bill Byrne. 2004. Minimum bayes-risk decoding for statistical machine translation. In *Proceedings of the Human Language Technology Conference of the North American Chapter of the Association for Computational Linguistics: HLT-NAACL 2004*, pages 169–176.

Siddique Latif, Moazzam Shoukat, Fahad Shamshad, Muhammad Usama, Heriberto Cuayáhuitl, and Björn W Schuller. 2023. Sparks of Large Audio Models: A Survey and Outlook. *arXiv preprint arXiv:2308.12792*.

Beomseok Lee, Marcely Zanon Boito, Laurent Besacier, and Ioan Calapodescu. 2025. NAVER LABS Europe Submission to the Instruction Following Track. In *Proceedings of the 22th International Conference on Spoken Language Translation (IWSLT)*.

Chia-Hsuan Li, Szu-Lin Wu, Chi-Liang Liu, and Hung-yi Lee. 2018. Spoken squad: A study of mitigating the impact of speech recognition errors on listening comprehension. In *19th Annual Conference of the International Speech Communication Association, Interspeech 2018, Hyderabad, India, September 2-6, 2018*, pages 3459–3463. Isca.

Chunyuan Li, Zhe Gan, Zhengyuan Yang, Jianwei Yang, Linjie Li, Lijuan Wang, and Jianfeng Gao. 2024. Multimodal foundation models: From specialists to general-purpose assistants. *Found. Trends. Comput. Graph. Vis.*, 16(1–2):1–214.

Junnan Li, Dongxu Li, Silvio Savarese, and Steven C. H. Hoi. 2023. Blip-2: Bootstrapping language-image pre-training with frozen image encoders and large language models. In *International Conference on Machine Learning*.

Zhaolin Li, Yining Liu, Danni Liu, Tuan Nam Nguyen, Enes Yavuz Ugan, Tu Anh Dinh, Carlos Mullov, Alexander Waibel, and Jan Niehues. 2025. KIT's Low-resource Speech Translation Systems for IWSLT2025: System Enhancement with Synthetic Data and Model Regularization. In *Proceedings of the 22th International Conference on Spoken Language Translation (IWSLT)*.

Pierre Lison, Jörg Tiedemann, and Milen Kouylekov. 2018. OpenSubtitles2018: Statistical rescoring of sentence alignments in large, noisy parallel corpora. In *Proceedings of the Eleventh International Conference on Language Resources and Evaluation (LREC 2018)*, Miyazaki, Japan. European Language Resources Association (ELRA).

Danni Liu, Gerasimos Spanakis, and Jan Niehues. 2020. Low-latency sequence-to-sequence speech recognition and translation by partial hypothesis selection. In *Proceedings of Interspeech 2020*, pages 3620–3624.

Arle Lommel, Hans Uszkoreit, and Aljoscha Burchardt. 2014. Multidimensional Quality Metrics (MQM): A Framework for Declaring and DescribingTranslation Quality Metrics. *Revista Tradumàtica: tecnologies de la traducció*, 12:455–463.

Nam Luu and Ond˘rej Bojar. 2025. CUNI-NL@IWSLT 2025: End-to-end Offline Speech Translation and Instruction Following with LLMs. In *Proceedings of the 22th International Conference on Spoken Language Translation (IWSLT)*.

Edward Ma. 2019. Nlp augmentation. https://github.com/makcedward/nlpaug.

Mingbo Ma, Liang Huang, Hao Xiong, Renjie Zheng, Kaibo Liu, Baigong Zheng, Chuanqiang Zhang, Zhongjun He, Hairong Liu, Xing Li, Hua Wu, and Haifeng Wang. 2019. STACL: Simultaneous translation with implicit anticipation and controllable latency using prefix-to-prefix framework. In *Proceedings of the 57th Annual Meeting of the Association for Computational Linguistics*, pages 3025–3036, Florence, Italy. Association for Computational Linguistics.

Xutai Ma, Mohammad Javad Dousti, Changhan Wang, Jiatao Gu, and Juan Pino. 2020. SIMULEVAL: An evaluation toolkit for simultaneous translation. In *Proceedings of the 2020 Conference on Empirical Methods in Natural Language Processing: System Demonstrations*, pages 144–150, Online. Association for Computational Linguistics.

Mohamed Maamouri, Tim Buckwalter, David Graff, and Hubert Jin. 2006. Levantine arabic qt training data set 5. *Speech Linguistic Data Consortium, Philadelphia*.

Dominik Macháček and Peter Polák. 2025. Simultaneous Translation with Offline Speech and LLM Models in CUNI Submission to IWSLT 2025. In *Proceedings of the 22nd International Conference on Spoken Language Translation (IWSLT)*.

John Makhoul, Bushra Zawaydeh, Frederick Choi, and David Stallard. 2005. Bbn/aub darpa babylon levantine arabic speech and transcripts. *Linguistic Data Consortium (LDC), LDC Catalog No.: LDC2005S08*.

Pedro Henrique Martins, Patrick Fernandes, João Alves, Nuno M. Guerreiro, Ricardo Rei, Duarte M. Alves, José Pombal, Amin Farajian, Manuel Faysse, Mateusz Klimaszewski, Pierre Colombo, Barry Haddow, José G. C. de Souza, Alexandra Birch, and André F. T. Martins. 2024. Eurollm: Multilingual language models for europe.

Evgeny Matusov, Gregor Leusch, Oliver Bender, and Hermann Ney. 2005. Evaluating machine translation output with automatic sentence segmentation. In *Proc. of the International Workshop on Spoken Language Translation (IWSLT)*, pages 138–144.

Salima Mdhaffar, Fethi Bougares, Renato De Mori, Salah Zaiem, Mirco Ravanelli, and Yannick Estève. 2024. Taric-slu: A tunisian benchmark dataset for spoken language understanding. In *Proceedings of the 2024 Joint International Conference on Computational Linguistics, Language Resources and Evaluation (LREC-COLING 2024)*, pages 15606–15616.

Humaira Mehmood and Sadaf Abdul Rauf. 2025. Human-Evaluated Urdu-English Speech Corpus: Advancing Speech-to-Text for Low-Resource Languages. In *Proceedings of the 22th International Conference on Spoken Language Translation (IWSLT)*.

Chutong Meng and Antonios Anastasopoulos. 2025. GMU Systems for the IWSLT 2025 Low-Resource Speech Translation Shared Task. In *Proceedings of the 22th International Conference on Spoken Language Translation (IWSLT)*.

Kurt Micallef, Albert Gatt, Marc Tanti, Lonneke van der Plas, and Claudia Borg. 2022. Pre-training data quality and quantity for a low-resource language: New corpus and BERT models for Maltese. In *Proceedings of the Third Workshop on Deep Learning for Low-Resource Natural Language Processing*, pages 90–101, Hybrid. Association for Computational Linguistics.

Mohammad Mohammadamini, Daban Jaff, Sara Jamal, Ibrahim Ahmed, Hawkar Omar, Darya Sabr, Marie Tahon, and Antoine Laurent. 2025. Kuvost: A Large-Scale Human-Annotated English to Central Kurdish Speech Translation Dataset Driven from

English Common Voice. In *Proceedings of the 22th International Conference on Spoken Language Translation (IWSLT)*.

Yasmin Moslem. 2024. Leveraging synthetic audio data for end-to-end low-resource speech translation. In *Proceedings of the 21st International Conference on Spoken Language Translation (IWSLT 2024)*, pages 265–273, Bangkok, Thailand (in-person and online). Association for Computational Linguistics.

Yasmin Moslem. 2025. Efficient Speech Translation through Model Compression and Knowledge Distillation. In *Proceedings of the 22th International Conference on Spoken Language Translation (IWSLT)*.

NLLB Team, Marta R. Costa-jussà, James Cross, Onur Çelebi, Maha Elbayad, Kenneth Heafield, Kevin Heffernan, Elahe Kalbassi, Janice Lam, Daniel Licht, Jean Maillard, Anna Sun, Skyler Wang, Guillaume Wenzek, Al Youngblood, Bapi Akula, Loic Barrault, Gabriel Mejia-Gonzalez, Prangthip Hansanti, John Hoffman, Semarley Jarrett, Kaushik Ram Sadagopan, Dirk Rowe, Shannon Spruit, Chau Tran, Pierre Andrews, Necip Fazil Ayan, Shruti Bhosale, Sergey Edunov, Angela Fan, Cynthia Gao, Vedanuj Goswami, Francisco Guzmán, Philipp Koehn, Alexandre Mourachko, Christophe Ropers, Safiyyah Saleem, Holger Schwenk, and Jeff Wang. 2022. No language left behind: Scaling human-centered machine translation. *arXiv preprint*.

Michal Novák, Peter Polák, Kateřina Rysová, Magdaléna Rysová, and Ondřej Bojar. 2024. Towards automated spoken language assessment: A study of asr transcription of examinations for non-native speakers of czech.

Atul Kr. Ojha. 2019. English-Bhojpuri SMT System: Insights from the Kāraka Model. *arXiv preprint arXiv:1905.02239*.

Atul Kr. Ojha, Valentin Malykh, Alina Karakanta, and Chao-Hong Liu. 2020. Findings of the LoResMT 2020 shared task on zero-shot for low-resource languages. In *Proceedings of the 3rd Workshop on Technologies for MT of Low Resource Languages*, pages 33–37, Suzhou, China. Association for Computational Linguistics.

Atul Kr. Ojha and Daniel Zeman. 2020. Universal Dependency treebanks for low-resource Indian languages: The case of Bhojpuri. In *Proceedings of the WILDRE5– 5th Workshop on Indian Language Data: Resources and Evaluation*, pages 33–38, Marseille, France. European Language Resources Association (ELRA).

John E Ortega, Richard Castro Mamani, and Kyunghyun Cho. 2020. Neural machine translation with a polysynthetic low resource language. *Machine Translation*, 34(4):325–346.

John E. Ortega, Rodolfo Joel Zevallos, William Chen, and Idris Abdulmumin. 2025. QUESPA Submission for the IWSLT 2025 Dialectal and Low-resource Speech Translation Task. In *Proceedings of the 22th International Conference on Spoken Language Translation (IWSLT)*.

Long Ouyang, Jeffrey Wu, Xu Jiang, Diogo Almeida, Carroll Wainwright, Pamela Mishkin, Chong Zhang, Sandhini Agarwal, Katarina Slama, Alex Ray, et al. 2022. Training language models to follow instructions with human feedback. *Advances in neural information processing systems*, 35:27730–27744.

Siqi Ouyang, Xi Xu, and Lei Li. 2025. CMU's IWSLT 2024 Simultaneous Speech Translation System. In *Proceedings of the 22nd International Conference on Spoken Language Translation (IWSLT)*.

Rosa YG Paccotacya-Yanque, Candy A Huanca-Anquise, Judith Escalante-Calcina, Wilber R Ramos-Lovón, and Álvaro E Cuno-Parari. 2022. A speech corpus of quechua collao for automatic dimensional emotion recognition. *Scientific Data*, 9(1):778.

Vassil Panayotov, Guoguo Chen, Daniel Povey, and Sanjeev Khudanpur. 2015. Librispeech: An asr corpus based on public domain audio books. *2015 IEEE International Conference on Acoustics, Speech and Signal Processing (ICASSP)*, pages 5206–5210.

Sara Papi, Marco Gaido, Matteo Negri, and Luisa Bentivogli. 2024. StreamAtt: Direct streaming speech-to-text translation with attention-based audio history selection. In *Proceedings of the 62nd Annual Meeting of the Association for Computational Linguistics (Volume 1: Long Papers)*, pages 3692–3707, Bangkok, Thailand. Association for Computational Linguistics.

Sara Papi, Peter Polák, Dominik Macháček, and Ondřej Bojar. 2025a. How "real" is your real-time simultaneous speech-to-text translation system? *Transactions of the Association for Computational Linguistics*, 13:281–313.

Sara Papi, Marco Turchi, Matteo Negri, et al. 2023. AlignAtt: Using attention-based audio-translation alignments as a guide for simultaneous speech translation. In *Proceedings of Interspeech 2023*. Isca.

Sara Papi, Maike Züfle, Marco Gaido, Beatrice Savoldi, Danni Liu, Ioannis Douros, Luisa Bentivogli, and Jan Niehues. 2025b. MCIF: Multimodal Crosslingual Instruction-Following Benchmark from Scientific Talks.

Kishore Papineni, Salim Roukos, Todd Ward, and Wei-Jing Zhu. 2002. Bleu: a method for automatic evaluation of machine translation. In *Proceedings of the 40th Annual Meeting of the Association for Computational Linguistics*, pages 311–318, Philadelphia, Pennsylvania, USA. Association for Computational Linguistics.

Frithjof Petrick, Patrick Wilken, Evgeny Matusov, Nahuel Roselló, and Sarah Beranek. 2025. AppTek's Automatic Speech Translation: Generating Accurate and Well-Readable Subtitles. In *Proceedings of the 22nd International Conference on Spoken Language Translation (IWSLT)*.

Edwin James George Pitman. 1937. Significance tests which may be applied to samples from any populations. ii. the correlation coefficient test. *Supplement to the Journal of the Royal Statistical Society*, 4(2):225–232.

Peter Polák, Ngoc-Quan Pham, Tuan Nam Nguyen, Danni Liu, Carlos Mullov, Jan Niehues, Ondřej Bojar, and Alexander Waibel. 2022. CUNI-KIT system for simultaneous speech translation task at IWSLT 2022. In *Proceedings of the 19th International Conference on Spoken Language Translation (IWSLT 2022)*, pages 277–285, Dublin, Ireland (in-person and online). Association for Computational Linguistics.

Peter Polák, Brian Yan, Shinji Watanabe, Alex Waibel, and Ondřej Bojar. 2023. Incremental blockwise beam search for simultaneous speech translation with controllable quality-latency tradeoff. In *Proc. INTERSPEECH 2023*, pages 3979–3983.

Peter Polák and Ondřej Bojar. 2024. Long-form end-to-end speech translation via latent alignment segmentation. In *2024 IEEE Spoken Language Technology Workshop (SLT)*, pages 1076–1082.

Maja Popović. 2015. chrf: character n-gram f-score for automatic mt evaluation. In *Proceedings of the tenth workshop on statistical machine translation*, pages 392–395.

Maja Popović. 2017. chrF++: words helping character n-grams. In *Proceedings of the Second Conference on Machine Translation*, pages 612–618, Copenhagen, Denmark. Association for Computational Linguistics.

Matt Post. 2018. A call for clarity in reporting BLEU scores. In *Proceedings of the Third Conference on Machine Translation: Research Papers*, pages 186–191, Brussels, Belgium. Association for Computational Linguistics.

Vineel Pratap, Andros Tjandra, Bowen Shi, Paden Tomasello, Arun Babu, Sayani Kundu, Ali Elkahky, Zhaoheng Ni, Apoorv Vyas, Maryam Fazel-Zarandi, et al. 2024. Scaling speech technology to 1,000+ languages. *Journal of Machine Learning Research*, 25(97):1–52.

Qwen, An Yang, Baosong Yang, Beichen Zhang, Binyuan Hui, Bo Zheng, Bowen Yu, Chengyuan Li, Dayiheng Liu, Fei Huang, Haoran Wei, Huan Lin, Jian Yang, Jianhong Tu, Jianwei Zhang, Jianxin Yang, Jiaxi Yang, Jingren Zhou, Junyang Lin, Kai Dang, Keming Lu, Keqin Bao, Kexin Yang, Le Yu, Mei Li, Mingfeng Xue, Pei Zhang, Qin Zhu, Rui Men, Runji Lin, Tianhao Li, Tianyi Tang, Tingyu Xia, Xingzhang Ren, Xuancheng Ren, Yang Fan, Yang Su, Yichang Zhang, Yu Wan, Yuqiong Liu, Zeyu Cui, Zhenru Zhang, and Zihan Qiu. 2025. Qwen2.5 technical report.

Alec Radford, Jong Wook Kim, Tao Xu, Greg Brockman, Christine McLeavey, and Ilya Sutskever. 2022. Robust Speech Recognition via Large-Scale Weak Supervision.

Alec Radford, Jong Wook Kim, Tao Xu, Greg Brockman, Christine McLeavey, and Ilya Sutskever. 2023. Robust speech recognition via large-scale weak supervision. In *International Conference on Machine Learning*, pages 28492–28518. Pmlr.

Matthew Raffel, Victor Agostinelli, and Lizhong Chen. 2024. Simultaneous masking, not prompting optimization: A paradigm shift in fine-tuning LLMs for simultaneous translation. In *Proceedings of the 2024 Conference on Empirical Methods in Natural Language Processing*, pages 18302–18314, Miami, Florida, USA. Association for Computational Linguistics.

Matthew Raffel, Victor Agostinelli, and Lizhong Chen. 2025. BeaverTalk: Oregon State University's IWSLT 2025 Simultaneous Speech Translation System. In *Proceedings of the 22nd International Conference on Spoken Language Translation (IWSLT)*.

Ricardo Rei, José G. C. de Souza, Duarte Alves, Chrysoula Zerva, Ana C Farinha, Taisiya Glushkova, Alon Lavie, Luisa Coheur, and André F. T. Martins. 2022a. COMET-22: Unbabel-IST 2022 submission for the metrics shared task. In *Proceedings of the Seventh Conference on Machine Translation (WMT)*, pages 578–585, Abu Dhabi, United Arab Emirates (Hybrid). Association for Computational Linguistics.

Ricardo Rei, Craig Stewart, Ana C Farinha, and Alon Lavie. 2020. COMET: A neural framework for MT evaluation. In *Proceedings of the 2020 Conference on Empirical Methods in Natural Language Processing (EMNLP)*, pages 2685–2702, Online. Association for Computational Linguistics.

Ricardo Rei, Marcos Treviso, Nuno M. Guerreiro, Chrysoula Zerva, Ana C Farinha, Christine Maroti, José G. C. de Souza, Taisiya Glushkova, Duarte Alves, Luisa Coheur, Alon Lavie, and André F. T. Martins. 2022b. CometKiwi: IST-unbabel 2022 submission for the quality estimation shared task. In *Proceedings of the Seventh Conference on Machine Translation (WMT)*, pages 634–645, Abu Dhabi, United Arab Emirates (Hybrid). Association for Computational Linguistics.

Nathaniel Romney Robinson, Niyati Bafna, Xiluo He, Tom Lupicki, Lavanya Shankar, Cihan Xiao, Qi Sun, Kenton Murray, and David Yarowsky. 2025. JHU IWSLT 2025 Low-resource System Description. In *Proceedings of the 22th International Conference on Spoken Language Translation (IWSLT)*.

Nathaniel Romney Robinson, Kaiser Sun, Cihan Xiao, Niyati Bafna, Weiting Tan, Haoran Xu, Henry Li Xinyuan, Ankur Kejriwal, Sanjeev Khudanpur, Kenton Murray, and Paul McNamee. 2024. JHU IWSLT 2024 dialectal and low-resource system description. In *Proceedings of the 21st International Conference on Spoken Language Translation (IWSLT 2024)*, pages 140–153, Bangkok, Thailand (in-person and online). Association for Computational Linguistics.

Mukund K Roy, Karunesh K Arora, Praveen Kumar Chandaliya, Rohit Kumar, and Pruthwik Mishra. 2025. CDAC-SVNIT submission for IWSLT 2025 Indic track shared task. In *Proceedings of the 22th International Conference on Spoken Language Translation (IWSLT)*.

Paul K. Rubenstein, Chulayuth Asawaroengchai, Duc Dung Nguyen, Ankur Bapna, Zalán Borsos, Félix de Chaumont Quitry, Peter Chen, Dalia El Badawy, Wei Han, Eugene Kharitonov, Hannah Muckenhirn, Dirk Padfield, James Qin, Danny Rozenberg, Tara Sainath, Johan Schalkwyk, Matt Sharifi, Michelle Tadmor Ramanovich, Marco Tagliasacchi, Alexandru Tudor, Mihajlo Velimirović, Damien Vincent, Jiahui Yu, Yongqiang Wang, Vicky Zayats, Neil Zeghidour, Yu Zhang, Zhishuai Zhang, Lukas Zilka, and Christian Frank. 2023. Audiopalm: A large language model that can speak and listen.

Ananya Sai B, Tanay Dixit, Vignesh Nagarajan, Anoop Kunchukuttan, Pratyush Kumar, Mitesh M. Khapra, and Raj Dabre. 2023. IndicMT eval: A dataset to meta-evaluate machine translation metrics for Indian languages. In *Proceedings of the 61st Annual Meeting of the Association for Computational Linguistics (Volume 1: Long Papers)*, pages 14210–14228, Toronto, Canada. Association for Computational Linguistics.

Elizabeth Salesky, Kareem Darwish, Mohamed Al-Badrashiny, Mona Diab, and Jan Niehues. 2023. Evaluating multilingual speech translation under realistic conditions with resegmentation and terminology. In *Proceedings of the 20th International Conference on Spoken Language Translation (IWSLT 2023)*, pages 62–78, Toronto, Canada (in-person and online). Association for Computational Linguistics.

Elizabeth Salesky, Marcello Federico, and Marine Carpuat, editors. 2024. *Proceedings of the 21st International Conference on Spoken Language Translation (IWSLT 2024)*. Association for Computational Linguistics, Bangkok, Thailand (in-person and online).

Ramon Sanabria, Nikolay Bogoychev, Nina Markl, Andrea Carmantini, Ondrej Klejch, and Peter Bell. 2023. The edinburgh international accents of english corpus: Towards the democratization of english asr. In *ICASSP 2023-2023 IEEE International Conference on Acoustics, Speech and Signal Processing (ICASSP)*, pages 1–5. Ieee.

Jorge Iranzo Sanchez, Jorge Civera Saiz, and Adrià Giménez Pastor. 2025. MLLP-VRAIN UPV System for the IWSLT 2025 Simultaneous Speech Translation Task. In *Proceedings of the 22nd International Conference on Spoken Language Translation (IWSLT)*.

Ashwin Sankar, Sparsh Jain, Nikhil Narasimhan, Devilal Choudhary, Dhairya Suman, Mohammed Safi Ur Rahman Khan, Anoop Kunchukuttan, Mitesh M Khapra, and Raj Dabre. 2025. Towards building large scale datasets and state-of-the-art automatic speech translation systems for 13 Indian languages. In *The 63rd Annual Meeting of the Association for Computational Linguistics*.

Sankalpa Sarkar, Samriddhi Kashyap, Advait Joglekar, and Srinivasan Umesh. 2025. Effectively combining Phi-4 and NLLB for Spoken Language Translation: SPRING Lab IITM's submission to Low Resource Multilingual Indic Track. In *Proceedings of the 22th International Conference on Spoken Language Translation (IWSLT)*.

Seamless Communication, Loïc Barrault, Yu-An Chung, Mariano Cora Meglioli, David Dale, Ning Dong, Paul-Ambroise Duquenne, Hady Elsahar, Hongyu Gong, Kevin Heffernan, John Hoffman, Christopher Klaiber, Pengwei Li, Daniel Licht, Jean Maillard, Alice Rakotoarison, Kaushik Ram Sadagopan, Guillaume Wenzek, Ethan Ye, Bapi Akula, Peng-Jen Chen, Naji El Hachem, Brian Ellis, Gabriel Mejia Gonzalez, Justin Haaheim, Prangthip Hansanti, Russ Howes, Bernie Huang, Min-Jae Hwang, Hirofumi Inaguma, Somya Jain, Elahe Kalbassi, Amanda Kallet, Ilia Kulikov, Janice Lam, Daniel Li, Xutai Ma, Ruslan Mavlyutov, Benjamin Peloquin, Mohamed Ramadan, Abinesh Ramakrishnan, Anna Sun, Kevin Tran, Tuan Tran, Igor Tufanov, Vish Vogeti, Carleigh Wood, Yilin Yang, Bokai Yu, Pierre Andrews, Can Balioglu, Marta R. Costa-jussà, Onur Celebi, Maha Elbayad, Cynthia Gao, Francisco Guzmán, Justine Kao, Ann Lee, Alexandre Mourachko, Juan Pino, Sravya Popuri, Christophe Ropers, Safiyyah Saleem, Holger Schwenk, Paden Tomasello, Changhan Wang, Jeff Wang, and Skyler Wang. 2023. Seamlessm4t: Massively multilingual & multimodal machine translation.

Thibault Sellam, Dipanjan Das, and Ankur Parikh. 2020. BLEURT: Learning robust metrics for text generation. In *Proceedings of the 58th Annual Meeting of the Association for Computational Linguistics*, pages 7881–7892, Online. Association for Computational Linguistics.

Hashem Sellat, Shadi Saleh, Mateusz Krubiński, Adam Pospíšil, Petr Zemánek, and Pavel Pecina. 2023. UFAL parallel corpus of north levantine 1.0. LINDAT/CLARIAH-CZ digital library at the Institute of Formal and Applied Linguistics (ÚFAL), Faculty of Mathematics and Physics, Charles University.

Nivedita Sethiya and Chandresh Kumar Maurya. 2024. End-to-end speech-to-text translation: A survey. *Computer Speech & Language*, page 101751.

Nivedita Sethiya, Saanvi Nair, and Chandresh Maurya. 2024. Indic-TEDST: Datasets and baselines for low-resource speech to text translation. In *Proceedings of the 2024 Joint International Conference on Computational Linguistics, Language Resources and Evaluation (LREC-COLING 2024)*, pages 9019–9024, Torino, Italia. ELRA and ICCL.

Claytone Sikasote and Antonios Anastasopoulos. 2022. BembaSpeech: A speech recognition corpus for the Bemba language. In *Proceedings of the Thirteenth Language Resources and Evaluation Conference*, pages 7277–7283, Marseille, France. European Language Resources Association.

Claytone Sikasote, Eunice Mukonde, Md Mahfuz Ibn Alam, and Antonios Anastasopoulos. 2023a. BIG-C: a multimodal multi-purpose dataset for Bemba. In *Proceedings of the 61st Annual Meeting of the Association for Computational Linguistics (Volume 1: Long Papers)*, pages 2062–2078, Toronto, Canada. Association for Computational Linguistics.

Claytone Sikasote, Kalinda Siaminwe, Stanly Mwape, Bangiwe Zulu, Mofya Phiri, Martin Phiri, David Zulu, Mayumbo Nyirenda, and Antonios Anastasopoulos. 2023b. Zambezi Voice: A Multilingual Speech Corpus for Zambian Languages. In *Proc. INTERSPEECH 2023*, pages 3984–3988.

Tiia Sildam, Andra Velve, and Tanel Alumäe. 2024. Finetuning end-to-end models for Estonian conversational spoken language translation. In *Proceedings of the Seventh Workshop on Technologies for Machine Translation of Low-Resource Languages (LoResMT 2024)*, pages 166–174, Bangkok, Thailand. Association for Computational Linguistics.

Silero Team. 2021. Silero vad: pre-trained enterprise-grade voice activity detector (vad), number detector and language classifier.

Matthew Snover, Bonnie Dorr, Rich Schwartz, Linnea Micciulla, and John Makhoul. 2006. A study of translation edit rate with targeted human annotation. In *Proceedings of the 7th Conference of the Association for Machine Translation in the Americas: Technical Papers*, pages 223–231, Cambridge, Massachusetts, USA. Association for Machine Translation in the Americas.

Jongseo Sohn, Nam Soo Kim, and Wonyong Sung. 1999. A statistical model-based voice activity detection. *IEEE Signal Processing Letters*, 6(1):1–3.

Matthias Sperber, Ondřej Bojar, Barry Haddow, Dávid Javorský, Xutai Ma, Matteo Negri, Jan Niehues, Peter Polák, Elizabeth Salesky, Katsuhito Sudoh, and Marco Turchi. 2024. Evaluating the IWSLT2023 speech translation tasks: Human annotations, automatic metrics, and segmentation. In *Proceedings of the 2024 Joint International Conference on Computational Linguistics, Language Resources and Evaluation (LREC-COLING 2024)*, pages 6484–6495, Torino, Italia. ELRA and ICCL.

Haotian Tan, Ruhiyah Faradishi Widiaputri, Jan Meyer Saragih, Yuka Ko, Katsuhito Sudoh, Satoshi Nakamura, and Sakriani Sakti. 2025. NAIST Simultaneous Speech Translation System for IWSLT 2025. In *Proceedings of the 22nd International Conference on Spoken Language Translation (IWSLT)*.

Changli Tang, Wenyi Yu, Guangzhi Sun, Xianzhao Chen, Tian Tan, Wei Li, Lu Lu, Zejun MA, and Chao Zhang. 2024. SALMONN: Towards generic hearing abilities for large language models. In *The Twelfth International Conference on Learning Representations*.

Gemma Team, Aishwarya Kamath, Johan Ferret, Shreya Pathak, Nino Vieillard, Ramona Merhej, Sarah Perrin, Tatiana Matejovicova, Alexandre Ramé, Morgane Rivière, Louis Rouillard, Thomas Mesnard, Geoffrey Cideron, Jean bastien Grill, Sabela Ramos, Edouard Yvinec, Michelle Casbon, Etienne Pot, Ivo Penchev, Gaël Liu, Francesco Visin, Kathleen Kenealy, Lucas Beyer, Xiaohai Zhai, Anton Tsitsulin, Robert Busa-Fekete, Alex Feng, Noveen Sachdeva, Benjamin Coleman, Yi Gao, Basil Mustafa, Iain Barr, Emilio Parisotto, David Tian, Matan Eyal, Colin Cherry, Jan-Thorsten Peter, Danila Sinopalnikov, Surya Bhupatiraju, Rishabh Agarwal, Mehran Kazemi, Dan Malkin, Ravin Kumar, David Vilar, Idan Brusilovsky, Jiaming Luo, Andreas Steiner, Abe Friesen, Abhanshu Sharma, Abheesht Sharma, Adi Mayrav Gilady, Adrian Goedeckemeyer, Alaa Saade, Alex Feng, Alexander Kolesnikov, Alexei Bendebury, Alvin Abdagic, Amit Vadi, András György, André Susano Pinto, Anil Das, Ankur Bapna, Antoine Miech, Antoine Yang, Antonia Paterson, Ashish Shenoy, Ayan Chakrabarti, Bilal Piot, Bo Wu, Bobak Shahriari, Bryce Petrini, Charlie Chen, Charline Le Lan, Christopher A. Choquette-Choo, CJ Carey, Cormac Brick, Daniel Deutsch, Danielle Eisenbud, Dee Cattle, Derek Cheng, Dimitris Paparas, Divyashree Shivakumar Sreepathihalli, Doug Reid, Dustin Tran, Dustin Zelle, Eric Noland, Erwin Huizenga, Eugene Kharitonov, Frederick Liu, Gagik Amirkhanyan, Glenn Cameron, Hadi Hashemi, Hanna Klimczak-Plucińska, Harman Singh, Harsh Mehta, Harshal Tushar Lehri, Hussein Hazimeh, Ian Ballantyne, Idan Szpektor, Ivan Nardini, Jean Pouget-Abadie, Jetha Chan, Joe Stanton, John Wieting, Jonathan Lai, Jordi Orbay, Joseph Fernandez, Josh Newlan, Ju yeong Ji, Jyotinder Singh, Kat Black, Kathy Yu, Kevin Hui, Kiran Vodrahalli, Klaus Greff, Linhai Qiu, Marcella Valentine, Marina Coelho, Marvin Ritter, Matt Hoffman, Matthew Watson, Mayank Chaturvedi, Michael Moynihan, Min Ma, Nabila Babar, Natasha Noy, Nathan Byrd, Nick Roy, Nikola Momchev, Nilay Chauhan, Noveen Sachdeva, Oskar Bunyan, Pankil Botarda, Paul Caron, Paul Kishan Rubenstein, Phil Culliton, Philipp Schmid, Pier Giuseppe Sessa, Pingmei Xu, Piotr Stanczyk, Pouya Tafti, Rakesh Shivanna, Renjie Wu, Renke Pan, Reza Rokni, Rob Willoughby, Rohith Vallu, Ryan Mullins, Sammy Jerome, Sara Smoot, Sertan Girgin, Shariq Iqbal, Shashir Reddy, Shruti Sheth, Siim Põder, Sijal Bhatnagar, Sindhu Raghuram Panyam, Sivan Eiger, Susan Zhang, Tianqi Liu, Trevor Yacovone, Tyler Liechty, Uday Kalra, Utku Evci, Vedant Misra, Vincent Roseberry, Vlad Feinberg, Vlad Kolesnikov, Woohyun Han, Woosuk Kwon, Xi Chen, Yinlam Chow, Yuvein Zhu, Zichuan Wei, Zoltan Egyed, Victor Cotruta, Minh Giang, Phoebe Kirk, Anand Rao, Kat Black, Nabila Babar, Jessica Lo, Erica Moreira, Luiz Gustavo Martins, Omar Sanseviero, Lucas Gonzalez, Zach Gleicher, Tris Warkentin, Vahab Mirrokni, Evan Senter, Eli Collins, Joelle Barral, Zoubin Ghahramani, Raia Hadsell, Yossi Matias, D. Sculley, Slav Petrov, Noah Fiedel, Noam Shazeer, Oriol Vinyals, Jeff Dean, Demis Hassabis, Koray Kavukcuoglu, Clement Farabet, Elena Buchatskaya, Jean-Baptiste Alayrac, Rohan Anil, Dmitry, Lepikhin, Sebastian Borgeaud, Olivier Bachem, Armand Joulin, Alek Andreev, Cassidy Hardin, Robert Dadashi, and Léonard Hussenot. 2025. Gemma 3 technical report.

Brian Thompson, Nitika Mathur, Daniel Deutsch, and Huda Khayrallah. 2024. Improving statistical significance in human evaluation of automatic metrics via soft pairwise accuracy. In *Proceedings of the Ninth Conference on Machine Translation*, pages 1222–1234, Miami, Florida, USA. Association for Computational Linguistics.

Jörg Tiedemann. 2012. Parallel data, tools and interfaces in OPUS. In *Proceedings of the Eighth International Conference on Language Resources and Evaluation (LREC'12)*, pages 2214–2218, Istanbul, Turkey. European Language Resources Association (ELRA).

Jörg Tiedemann. 2020. The tatoeba translation challenge – realistic data sets for low resource and multilingual MT. In *Proceedings of the Fifth Conference on Machine Translation*, pages 1174–1182, Online. Association for Computational Linguistics.

Filbert Aurelian Tjiaranata, Vallerie Alexandra Putra, Eryawan Presma Yulianrifat, and Ikhlasul Akmal Hanif. 2025. BUINUS System Description for IWSLT 2025 Maltese to English Low-Resource Speech Translation Track. In *Proceedings of the 22th International Conference on Spoken Language Translation (IWSLT)*.

Ioannis Tsiamas, José Fonollosa, and Marta Costa-jussà. 2023. SegAugment: Maximizing the utility of speech translation data with segmentation-based augmentations. In *Findings of the Association for Computational Linguistics: EMNLP 2023*, pages 8569–8588, Singapore. Association for Computational Linguistics.

Ioannis Tsiamas, Gerard I. Gállego, José A. R. Fonollosa, and Marta R. Costa-jussà. 2022. SHAS: Approaching optimal Segmentation for End-to-End Speech Translation. In *Proc. Interspeech 2022*, pages 106–110.

Changhan Wang, Morgane Riviere, Ann Lee, Anne Wu, Chaitanya Talnikar, Daniel Haziza, Mary Williamson, Juan Pino, and Emmanuel Dupoux. 2021. VoxPopuli: A large-scale multilingual speech corpus for representation learning, semi-supervised learning and interpretation. In *Proceedings of the 59th Annual Meeting of the Association for Computational Linguistics and the 11th International Joint Conference on Natural Language Processing (Volume 1: Long Papers)*, pages 993–1003, Online. Association for Computational Linguistics.

Changhan Wang, Anne Wu, and Juan Miguel Pino. 2020. Covost 2: A massively multilingual speech-to-text translation corpus. *CoRR*, abs/2007.10310.

Minghan Wang, Thuy-Trang Vu, Yuxia Wang, Ehsan Shareghi, and Gholamreza Haffari. 2024a. Conversational simulmt: Efficient simultaneous translation with large language models.

Minghan Wang, Thuy-Trang Vu, Jinming Zhao, Fatemeh Shiri, Ehsan Shareghi, and Gholamreza Haffari. 2024b. Simultaneous machine translation with large language models. In *Proceedings of the 22nd Annual Workshop of the Australasian Language Technology Association*, pages 89–103, Canberra, Australia. Association for Computational Linguistics.

Weiyue Wang, Jan-Thorsten Peter, Hendrik Rosendahl, and Hermann Ney. 2016. CharacTer: Translation edit rate on character level. In *Proceedings of the First Conference on Machine Translation: Volume 2, Shared Task Papers*. Association for Computational Linguistics.

Wenxuan Wang, Yingxin Zhang, Yifan Jin, Binbin Du, and Yuke Li. 2025. NYA's Offline Speech Translation System for IWSLT 2025. In *Proceedings of the 22th International Conference on Spoken Language Translation (IWSLT)*.

Shinji Watanabe, Takaaki Hori, Shigeki Karita, Tomoki Hayashi, Jiro Nishitoba, Yuya Unno, Nelson Enrique Yalta Soplin, Jahn Heymann, Matthew Wiesner, Nanxin Chen, Adithya Renduchintala, and Tsubasa Ochiai. 2018. ESPnet: End-to-end speech processing toolkit. In *Proceedings of Interspeech*, pages 2207–2211.

Xuchen Wei, Yangxin Wu, Yaoyin Zhang, Henglyu Liu, Kehai Chen, Xuefeng Bai, and Min Zhang. 2025. HITSZ's End-To-End Speech Translation Systems Combining Sequence-to-Sequence Auto Speech Recognition Model and Indic Large Language Model for IWSLT 2025 in Indic Track. In *Proceedings of the 22th International Conference on Spoken Language Translation (IWSLT)*.

Ruhiyah Faradishi Widiaputri, Haotian Tan, Jan Meyer Saragih, Yuka Ko, Katsuhito Sudoh, Satoshi Nakamura, and Sakriani Sakti. 2025. NAIST Offline Speech Translation System for IWSLT 2025. In *Proceedings of the 22nd International Conference on Spoken Language Translation (IWSLT)*.

Patrick Wilken, Panayota Georgakopoulou, and Evgeny Matusov. 2022. SubER - a metric for automatic evaluation of subtitle quality. In *Proceedings of the 19th International Conference on Spoken Language Translation (IWSLT 2022)*, pages 1–10, Dublin, Ireland (in-person and online). Association for Computational Linguistics.

Linli Yao, Lei Li, Shuhuai Ren, Lean Wang, Yuanxin Liu, Xu Sun, and Lu Hou. 2024. Deco: Decoupling token compression from semantic abstraction in multimodal large language models.

ZamStats. 2012. 2010 census of population and housing - national analytical report.

Marcely Zanon Boito, Vivek Iyer, Nikolaos Lagos, Laurent Besacier, and Ioan Calapodescu. 2024. mhubert-147: A compact multilingual hubert model. In *Interspeech 2024*, pages 3939–3943.

Tianyi Zhang*, Varsha Kishore*, Felix Wu*, Kilian Q. Weinberger, and Yoav Artzi. 2020. Bertscore: Evaluating text generation with bert. In *International Conference on Learning Representations*.

Vilém Zouhar, Peng Cui, and Mrinmaya Sachan. 2025a. How to select datapoints for efficient human evaluation of nlg models?

Vilém Zouhar, Maike Züfle, Beni Egressy, Julius Cheng, and Jan Niehues. 2025b. Early-exit and instant confidence translation quality estimation.

Maike Züfle, Sara Papi, Beatrice Savoldi, Marco Gaido, Luisa Bentivogli, and Jan Niehues. 2025. NUTSHELL: A dataset for abstract generation from scientific talks. *CoRR*, abs/2502.16942.

Maike Züfle and Jan Niehues. 2025. Contrastive learning for task-independent speechllm-pretraining.

Appendix A. Human Evaluation

A Human Evaluation

Human evaluation includes direct assessment for offline, simultaneous, subtitling, and instruction following tasks (A.1), in addition to continuous rating and MQM for the simultaneous task (A.2, A.3).

A.1 Direct Assessment

For the offline translation track (Section 3), simultaneous translation track (Section 4), subtitling track (Section 5), and instruction following track (Section 9), we conduct a human evaluation of primary submissions. Human graders are asked for direct assessment (DA) (Graham et al., 2013; Cettolo et al., 2017; Akhbardeh et al., 2021), expressed as scores ranging from 0 to 100. The *business news* test set does not include reference transcripts, so the human assessment is performed monolingually, comparing the system outputs against reference translations. We exclude the English to German direction from this test set for budget reasons. All other sets are graded in full, with no subsampling performed. No annotator normalization was performed this year.

Since many tasks have standardized their test sets, we evaluate all outputs for a given testset, across any task that used said testset. This gives us the opportunity to compare across tasks and get a general sense of the relative progress across tasks. Caution should be exercised when comparing systems across tasks, as the tasks have different objectives – for example, length in the case of subtitling and latency in the case of online systems. Additionally, in the case of the *business news* testset, we use the verbatim version of the reference; the subtitle systems would likely have been judged more favorably if we had instead used the more terse subtitle reference.

A.1.1 Automatic Segmentation

We collect segment-level annotations based on the re-segmentated test data, generating automatic resegmentations of the hypothesis based on the reference translation by mwerSegmenter.[66] Because we do not want issues from the segmentation to influence scores negatively, we follow Sperber et al. (2024) and provide translators not only with the source sentence and system translation but also with the system translation of the previous and following segments. Annotators are then instructed as follows: *"Sentence boundary errors are expected and should not be taken into account when judging translation quality. This is when the target appears to be adding or missing words (including being completely empty) while the source was segmented in a different place. To this end, we have included the previous and next sentence targets for context. If the content of the source and target are only different because of sentence boundary issues, do not let this affect your scoring judgement.*
Example of a good translation (shown English-only for illustration purposes) suffering only from sentence boundary issues that should not be penalized:
Source: you'll see that there's actually a sign near the road.
Target: is a sign near the
Previous target: [...] and you will see that there actually Next target: road. [...]
No video or audio context is provided. Segments are shuffled and randomly assigned to annotators to avoid bias related to the presentation order. Annotation is conducted by professional translators fluent in the source language and native in the target language.

For monolingual grading (*business news* test set, English to Arabic), we add the following instruction: *"You'll be shown a candidate translation from English into Arabic, while the "source" is the Arabic reference translation. Please rate the correctness of the candidate, given the reference.."*

A.1.2 Computing Pairwise Statistical Significance and System Rankings

Last year, we used the Wilcoxon rank-sum test (also called the Mann-Whitney U) to determine statistical significance of the human evaluation scores. The Wilcoxon rank-sum test is non-parametric, which is advantageous because DA scores do not follow a normal or other known distribution (see Figure 1).

[66] www-i6.informatik.rwth-aachen.de/web/Software/mwerSegmenter.tar.gz

However, the Wilcoxon rank-sum test also assumes independent samples, whereas our data samples are not in fact independent. This is because a given source sentence is translated by two or more MT systems and then those outputs are scored by a human annotator. We generally expect correlation between scores for the same source sentence (e.g. a source sentence which is very difficult to translate will likely result in lower than average scores for all MT systems).

An alternative to the Wilcoxon rank-sum test is the Wilcoxon signed-rank test, which assumes dependent (i.e. paired) data, but it adds an assumption that the distribution of scores is symmetric around a mean, which Figure 1 illustrates is not true in our case.

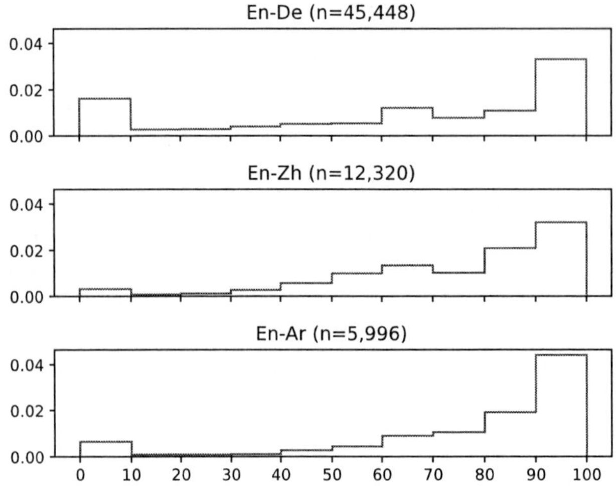

Figure 1: Direct assessment score histograms, normalized, per language pair.

This year, we chose to use a permutation test (Fisher, 1935) to estimate the statistical significance of the difference in the means of the segment-level DA scores for each pair of MT systems. Permutation tests are appealing because they don't require any assumptions about the underlying distribution of the data. Instead, they have the assumption of exchangeability (Pitman, 1937; Draper et al., 1993; Good, 2002)—that is, under the null hypothesis (in our case, that the two MT systems are of equal quality) the joint distribution of the observations is invariant under permutations of the data labels. We first randomly split the segment-level scores (ignoring the labels, i.e. which MT system produced each segment) into two parts and compute the difference in DA score mean. Repeating this process many times provides a set of mean differences we can reasonably expect under the null hypothesis that the two systems are of the same quality. We compute a one-tailed p-value by calculating the fraction of the time that the random splits produce differences greater than or equal to the mean difference we observe for the two systems. To help ensure exchangeability, we perform permutations such that each split has exactly one translation of each test set sentence, commonly referred to as a paired permutation test (Good, 2013). In the context of machine translation, paired permutation tests are widely used in automatic metric evaluation (Deutsch et al., 2021; Freitag et al., 2023, 2024; Thompson et al., 2024). We use the paired permutation implementation from Thompson et al. (2024).[67]

Given the p-values from all pairwise system comparisons, system rankings are trivially computed by ordering the systems by mean DA score and then finding the rank of the highest and lowest ranked system(s) that are not statistically significantly different from each system. We use a 95% confidence (i.e. p-value < 0.05).

English → Arabic, *business news* testset rankings are given in Table 13, with p-values in Figure 2. English → German, *accented English conversations* testset rankings are given in Table 14, with p-values in Figure 3. English → German, *scientific presentations* testset rankings are given in Table 15, with p-

[67] github.com/thompsonb/mt-metrics-eval/blob/main/mt_metrics_eval/pairwise_paired_permutation_test.py

values in Figure 4. English → German, *TV series* testset rankings are given in Table 16, with p-values in Figure 5. English → Chinese, *scientific presentations* testset rankings are given in Table 17, with p-values in Figure 6.

As one would expect, we find that across all language pairs / test sets, offline systems tend to be the highest ranked, and high-latency online systems tend to rank higher than low-latency online systems.

Table 13: English → Arabic, *business news* testset. Human direct assessment scores and corresponding rankings. Rank range based on 95% confidence interval, from pairwise p-values in Figure 2.

Task	System	Data/Condition	Human Score	Human Rank
Offline	NYA	unconstrained	84.451	1
Offline	NEMO	unconstrained	82.017	2
Offline	AIB-MARCO	unconstrained	80.228	3
Subtitling	APPTEK		60.524	4

Table 14: English → German, *accent English conversations* testset. Human direct assessment scores and corresponding rankings. Rank range based on 95% confidence interval, from pairwise p-values in Figure 3.

Task	System	Data/Condition	Human Score	Human Rank
Offline	KIT	unconstrained	74.865	1-2
Offline	AIB-MARCO	unconstrained	74.705	1-2
Offline	NYA	unconstrained	72.576	3-4
Offline	NEMO	unconstrained	72.298	3-4
Simultaneous	UPV	high	70.679	5-6
Simultaneous	OSU	high	70.372	5-6
Simultaneous	OSU	low	67.550	7
Offline	NAIST	unconstrained	63.622	8
Offline	NAIST	constrained	58.610	9
Offline	CUNI	constrained	51.407	10
Simultaneous	CMU	low	44.099	11

Table 15: English → German, *scientific presentations* testset. Human direct assessment scores and corresponding rankings. Rank range based on 95% confidence interval, from pairwise p-values in Figure 4.

Task	System	Data/Condition	Human Score	Human Rank
Offline	KIT	unconstrained	90.626	1
Offline	NEMO	unconstrained	86.583	2-4
Offline	NYA	unconstrained	86.536	2-4
Offline	AIB-MARCO	unconstrained	85.372	2-5
Simultaneous	CUNI	high	84.309	4-5
Simultaneous	UPV	high	78.662	6
Simultaneous	OSU	high	76.923	7-10
Instruction.long	KIT	primary	76.382	7-10
Offline	NAIST	unconstrained	75.432	7-11
Offline	CUNI	constrained	75.367	7-11
Simultaneous	OSU	low	74.397	9-11
Simultaneous	NAIST	high	71.166	12-15
Instruction.short	CUNI-NL	primary	70.702	12-15
Simultaneous	CMU	low	70.372	12-15
Instruction.short	NLE	primary	69.607	12-16
Offline	NAIST	constrained	67.801	15-18
Simultaneous	NAIST	low	67.197	16-18
Instruction.short	CUNI-NL	contrastive	66.280	16-18

Table 16: English → German, *TV series* testset. Human direct assessment scores and corresponding rankings. Rank range based on 95% confidence interval, from pairwise p-values in Figure 5.

Task	System	Data/Condition	Human Score	Human Rank
Offline	KIT	unconstrained	61.379	1
Offline	NYA	unconstrained	56.801	2-3
Offline	NEMO	unconstrained	56.395	2-3
Subtitling	APPTEK		53.992	4
Offline	CUNI	constrained	32.278	5
Offline	NAIST	unconstrained	27.174	6
Offline	NAIST	constrained	21.674	7
Offline	AIB-MARCO	unconstrained	12.122	8

Table 17: English → Chinese, *scientific presentations* testset. Human direct assessment scores and corresponding rankings. Rank range based on 95% confidence interval, from pairwise p-values in Figure 6.

Task	System	Data/Condition	Human Score	Human Rank
Offline	AIB-MARCO	unconstrained	85.918	1
Offline	NYA	unconstrained	84.044	2-4
Offline	BIGWATERMELON	unconstrained	83.338	2-4
Offline	NEMO	unconstrained	83.009	2-4
Simultaneous	CUNI	high	77.805	5
Offline	NAIST	unconstrained	71.593	6-9
Instruction.short	NLE	primary	70.465	6-10
Instruction.long	KIT	primary	69.995	6-10
Simultaneous	CMU	low	69.812	6-10
Simultaneous	OSU	high	69.415	7-11
Simultaneous	NAIST	high	67.761	10-12
Simultaneous	OSU	low	67.519	11-12
Simultaneous	NAIST	low	65.487	13
Offline	NAIST	constrained	58.831	14

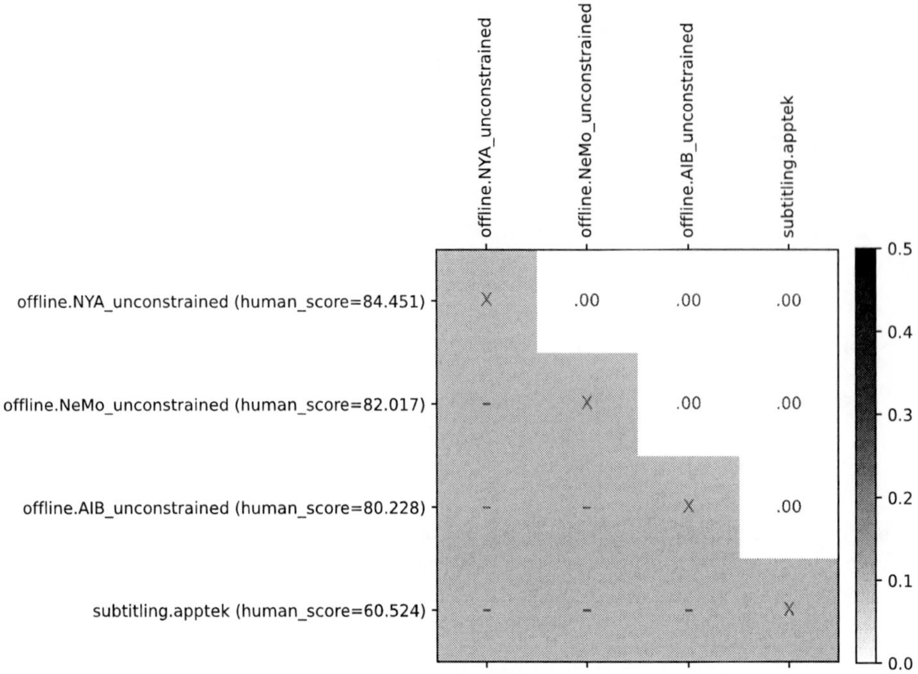

Figure 2: English → Arabic, *business news* testset, pairwise p-values from paired permutation tests. p-values < 0.05 are shown in green, while p-values $>= 0.05$ are shown in red. For system rankings computed from these p-values, see Table 13.

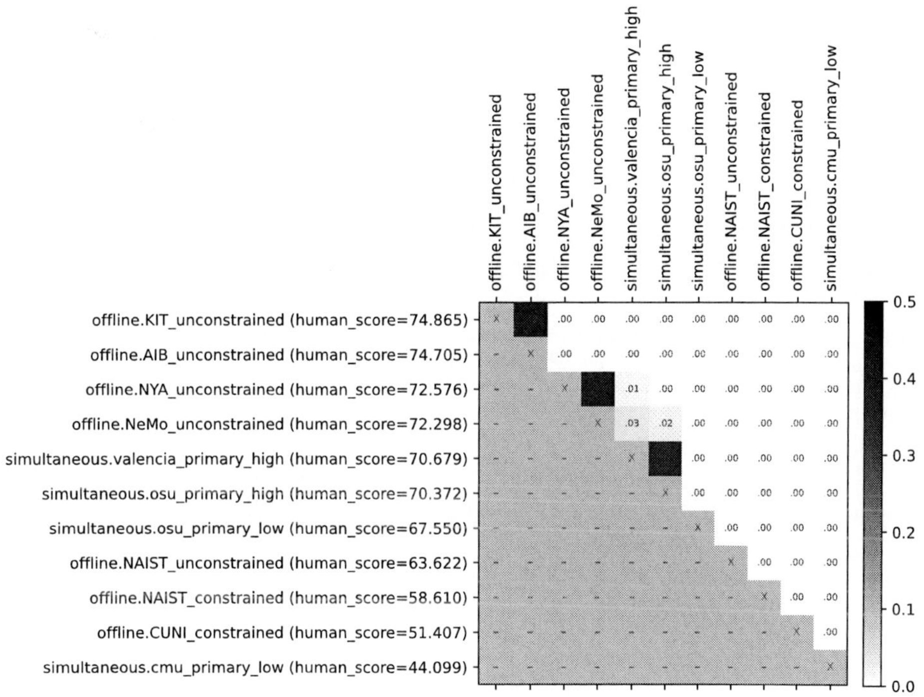

Figure 3: English → German, *accented English conversations* testest, pairwise p-values from paired permutation tests (n=10,000). p-values < 0.05 are shown in green, while p-values >= 0.05 are shown in red. For system rankings computed from these p-values, see Table 14.

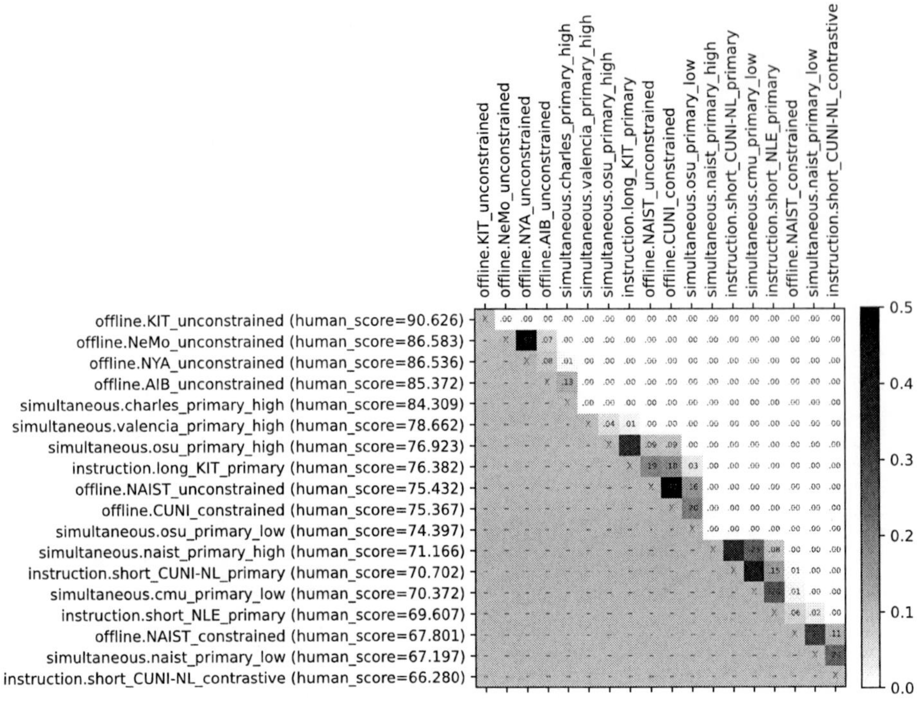

Figure 4: English → German, *scientific presentations* testset, pairwise p-values from paired permutation tests (n=10,000). p-values < 0.05 are shown in green, while p-values >= 0.05 are shown in red. For system rankings computed from these p-values, see Table 15.

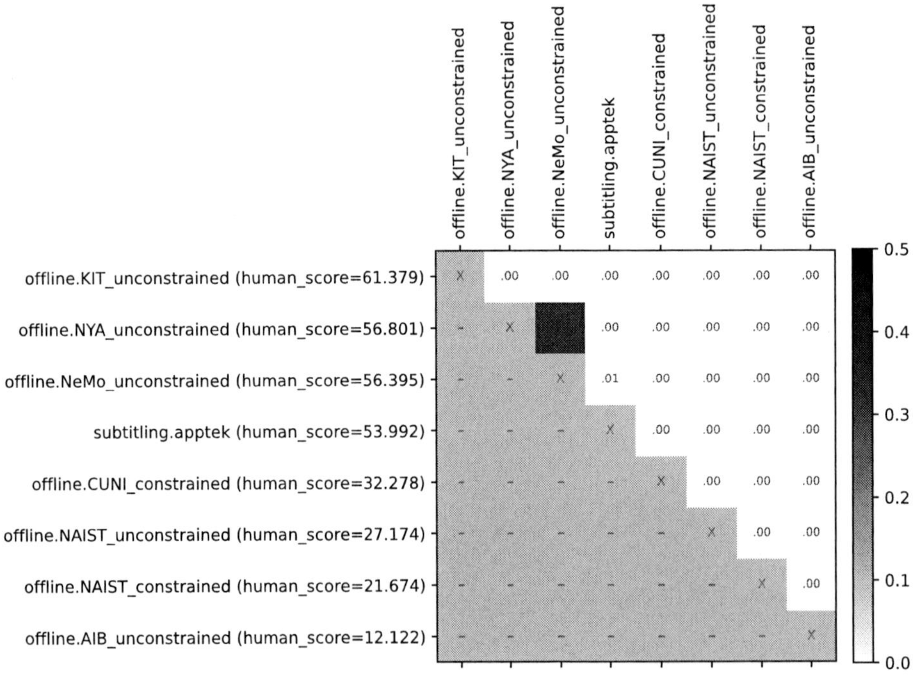

Figure 5: English → German, *TV series* testset, pairwise p-values from paired permutation tests (n=10,000). p-values < 0.05 are shown in green, while p-values >= 0.05 are shown in red. For system rankings computed from these p-values, see Table 16.

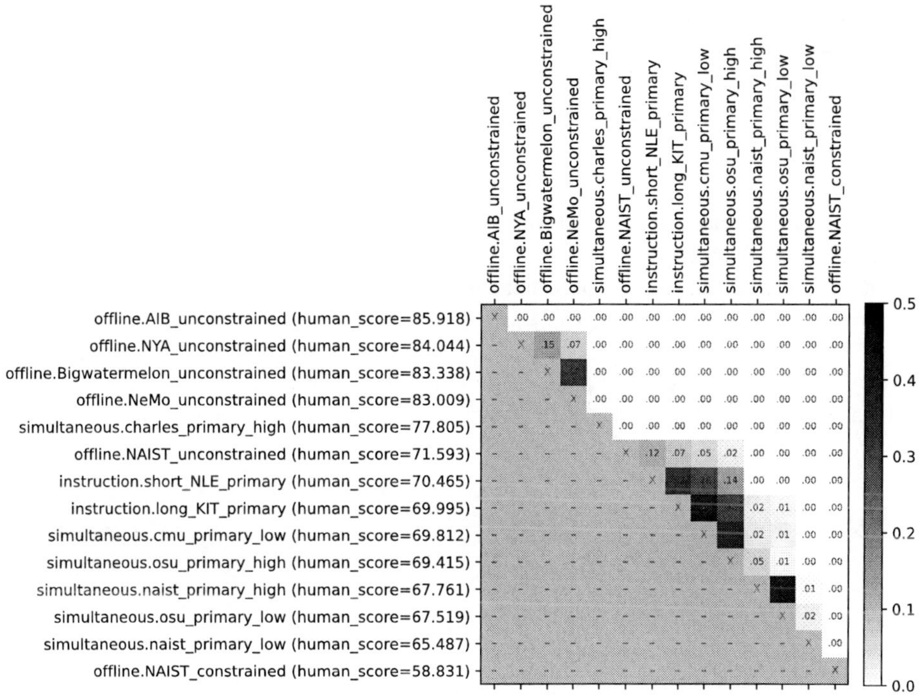

Figure 6: English → Chinese, *scientific presentations* testset, pairwise p-values from paired permutation tests (n=10,000). p-values < 0.05 are shown in green, while p-values $>= 0.05$ are shown in red. For system rankings computed from these p-values, see Table 17.

A.1.3 Deciding Which Segments to Human-Evaluate

Each year, the shared task size is limited by the amount that can be human-evaluated. Oftentimes, a random subset of segments is chosen for human evaluation to fit a specific budget. However, this uninformed selection might be suboptimal and previous works showed promise for efficient subset selection for machine translation and summarization. While the IWSLT 2025 evaluation has not used informed subset selection, this section investigates its potential for future IWSLT human evaluation campaigns.

Setup. Given a large set of evaluatable items $\mathcal{X}$, the task is to select $\mathcal{Y} \subseteq \mathcal{X}$ such that $|\mathcal{Y}|$ fits a specific budget. Then, all systems participating in the shared task are evaluated on $\mathcal{Y}$. We consider the following methods for subset selection (Zouhar et al., 2025a):

- **Metric average**: Selecting examples with lowest average quality estimation scores across systems (highest difficulty). Based on wmt22-cometkiwi-da (Rei et al., 2022b).
- **Metric variance**: Selecting examples with largest variance among the quality estimation scores across systems. Same metric.
- **Metric consistency**: Selecting examples where the item-level metric ranking is predictive of the final aggregated system ranking. Same metric.
- **Diversity**: Selecting examples with which lead to most different system outputs (measured with pairwise ChrF).
- **K-means**: Selecting examples that are most dissimilar to each other (using k-means clustering).

We simulate the selection at a particular budget (subset size). We measure the success of subset selection in three ways. In all cases, the higher the better.

- **Cluster count:** Number of statistically significant clusters, as computed by Kocmi et al. (2023).
- **Kendall's τ_b rank correlation:** Similarity of final system ranking based on the subset and based on the full set.
- **Soft Pairwise Accuracy** (Thompson et al., 2024): Similarity of final system ranking based on the subset and based on the full set but with statistical significance taken into account.

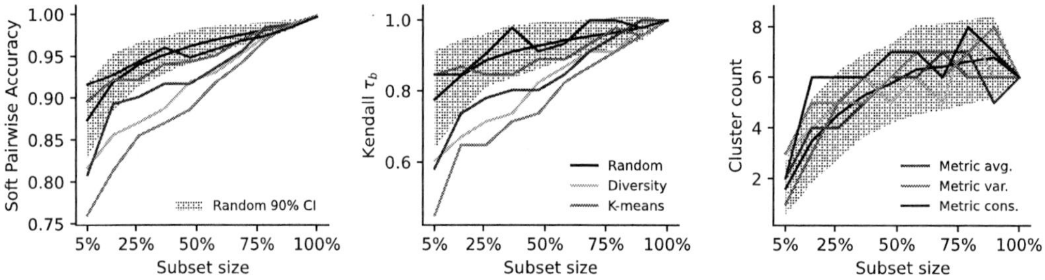

Figure 7: Results of informed subset selection for English→Arabic human-evaluated testset.

Results. The results in Figure 7 show that, by far, random selection remains the most robust selection, with metric consistency being on par to random when measured by soft pairwise accuracy or Kendall's τ_b and slightly better when measured by cluster count.

This can be partly explained by the evaluation segments not being aligned. For other tasks, such as text-to-text machine translation, given a single input, the systems produce outputs that can be compared to each other. In the current speech translation setup, the segmentation makes it so that segments with the same force-aligned source have very different outputs across systems. For example, the following are the 8 system translations aligned to the same source segment "*There were tough fights, even blood flowed.*", which sometimes include non-relevant content, likely from previous or subsequent segments:

viel Geld verschwendet. Scham!
zu Besuch Sie kommen heute Nacht zu uns
Harte Kämpfe. Es wurde Blut vergossen.
Schwer erkämpfte Kämpfe. Es wurde Blut vergossen.
hart umkämpfte Schlachten, Blut wurde vergossen. Ich schäme
Hart gekämpfte Schlachten. Das Blut wurde vergossen,
Hart gekämpfte Schlachten. Das Blut wurde vergossen,
war glücklich. Vier Schlachten. Es wurde geschrieben. Schande!

Comparing the segment-level quality estimation using automatic metrics (necessary for metric average, metric variance, and metric consistency) then becomes difficult. The primary noise for the metrics comes from noisy prefixes and suffixes. Some metrics, such as COMET-partial (Zouhar et al., 2025b, Appendix G) show promise to this kind of noise, though do not improve meaningfully the subset selection. The biggest hurdle to informed subset selection is thus a better alignment of system output, or the selection at higher-level units where the alignment is implicitly correct, such as the level of documents or whole audio files.

A.2 Continuous Rating for Czech-to-English and English-to-German

Manual evaluation of English-to-German Simultaneous Task uses Continuous Rating as described by Javorský et al. (2022).

For both translation directions (Czech-to-English and English-to-German), we solicited students of translation studies from the Faculty of Arts, Charles University, as evaluators. All were native speakers of Czech, studying for English and (those evaluating German) also German translation.

During the evaluation, annotators were presented with the source audio and subtitles. The subtitles were displayed in two lines below the audio following the guidelines for video subtitling (Bbc, 2019). The annotators were asked to score the quality of the live-presented text output while listening to the input sound. Specifically, the instructions explicitly asked to focus on *content preservation*, or roughly the *adequacy*:

- We ask you to provide your assessment using so-called "continuous rating", which *continuously indicates the quality of the text output given the input utterance you hear* in the range from 1 (the worst) to 4 (the best) by clicking the corresponding buttons or pressing the corresponding keys.
- The rate of clicking/pressing depends on you. However, we suggest clicking *each 5-10 seconds* or when your assessment has changed. We encourage you to provide feedback *as often as possible* even if your assessment has *not changed.*
- The quality scale should reflect primarily the meaning preservation (i.e. evaluating primarily the "content" or very approximately the "adequacy") and the grammaticality and other qualitative aspects like punctuation (i.e. the "form" or extremely roughly the "fluency") should be the secondary criterion.

Processing of Collected Rankings Once the results are collected, they are processed as follows. We first inspect the timestamps on the ratings, and remove any that appeared more than 20 seconds than the end of the audio. Because of the natural delay and because the collection process is subject to network and computational constraints, there can be ratings that are timestamped greater than the audio length. If the difference is however too high, we judge it to be an annotation error. We also remove any annotated audio where there is fewer than one rating per 20 seconds because the annotators were instructed to annotate every 5-10 seconds.

Obtaining Final Scores To calculate the final score for each system, we average the ratings across each annotated audio, then average across all the annotated audios pertaining to each system-latency combination. This type of averaging renders all input speeches equally important and it is not affected by the speech length or the eagerness of the annotator.

The final scores for Czech-to-English and English-to-German are provided further below in Tables 18 and 19, respectively.

A.3 MQM-based Human Evaluation for English-to-Japanese

For the English-to-Japanese Simultaneous Translation Task, we conducted a human evaluation using a variant of Multidimensional Quality Metrics (MQM; Lommel et al., 2014). MQM has been used in recent MT evaluation studies (Freitag et al., 2021a) and WMT Metrics shared task (Freitag et al., 2021b). For the evaluation of Japanese translations, we used *JTF Translation Quality Evaluation Guidelines* (JTF, 2018), distributed by Japan Translation Federation (JTF). The guidelines are based on MQM but include some modifications in consideration of the property of the Japanese language.

We hired a Japanese-native professional interpreter as the evaluator. The evaluator checked translation hypotheses along with their source speech transcripts and chose the corresponding error category and severity for each translation hypothesis on a spreadsheet. Here, we asked the evaluator to focus only on *Accuracy* and *Fluency* errors, because other types of errors in Terminology, Style, and Locale convention would not be so serious in the evaluation of simultaneous translation. Finally, we calculated the cumulative error score for each system based on the error weighting presented by Freitag et al. (2021a), where *Critical* and *Major* errors have the same level of error scores. The results are shown in Table 20.

Test Set Part	Team	CR (↑)	BLEU (↑)	StreamLAAL (↓)
Non-Native	Baseline-VAD	2.34	16.46	1.85
	CUNI	3.02	24.53	1.79
ParCzech	Baseline-VAD	3.04	23.55	3.68
	Interpreting-Student	3.35	11.31	4.34
	CUNI	3.36	21.94	1.51
	Interpreting-Professional	3.51	10.09	4.16

Table 18: Human evaluation using Continuous Rating (CR) for systems from the high-latency regime of simultaneous speech-to-text translation contrasted with two variants of human interpreting, Czech-to-English. The Continuous Rating values range from 1 (worst) to 4 (best).

Team	CR (↑)	BLEU (↑)	COMET (↑)	StreamLAAL (↓)
Baseline-Fixed	3.02	19.15	0.593	3.54
NAIST	3.25	24.58	0.717	3.71
CMU	3.39	22.63	0.697	1.47
OSU	3.56	25.80	0.729	3.21
UPV	3.63	29.81	0.739	2.90
CUNI	3.72	35.25	0.790	3.32

Table 19: Human evaluation using Continuous Rating (CR) for systems from the high-latency regime (except CMU which was only in low-latency regime) of simultaneous speech-to-text translation, English-to-German. The Continuous Rating values range from 1 (worst) to 4 (best).

System	BLEU (on two ACL talks)	Error score	# Errors		
			Critical	Major	Minor
CUNI	39.4	32	0	3	17
NAIST (high)	32.8	123	8	12	23
NAIST (low)	33.1	129	12	9	24

Table 20: Human evaluation results on two ACL talks (91 lines) in the English-to-Japanese Simultaneous speech-to-text translation task. Error weights are 5 for Critical and Major errors and 1 for Minor errors.

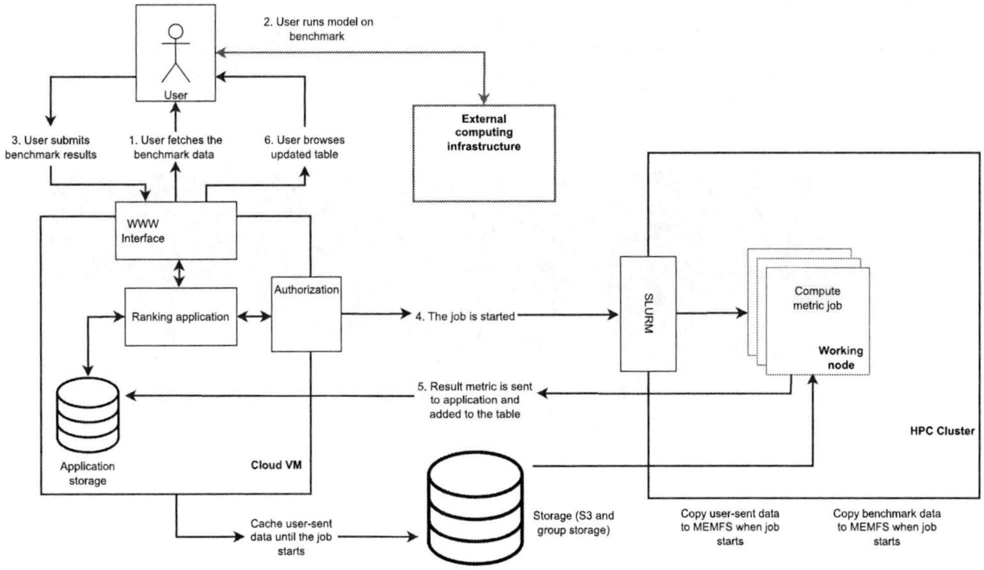

Figure 8: SPEECHM architecture. The platform is composed of the WebUI for managing user submissions and showing evaluation results, produced by the evaluation scripts executed in the scope of Slurm jobs on the HPC Ares (for CPU-based calculations) and Athena (for GPU-based calculations) HPC clusters.

Appendix B. Automatic Evaluation Results and Details

B.1 Evaluation Server

B.1.1 Introduction

The Evaluation Server is a collection of benchmarking resources and tools to evaluate the capability of user systems with respect to a set of tasks. It is part of the SPEECHM platform, released by the Meetween European Project[68], which consists of (a) ten downstream tasks, (b) a set of task-dependent evaluation metrics and (c) a WebUI for submissions and performance tracking by means of a leaderboard.

For the IWSLT-2025 Evaluation Campaign a dedicate instance of the SPEECHM has been developed, named SPEECHM-IWSLT2025[69]. It supports three of the IWSLT-2025 shared tasks, namely the *Offline*, the *Model Compression* and the *Instruction Following* tasks.

B.1.2 User operations

Given a task testset (e.g. the TvSeries English-German testset for the Offline SLT task), users typically perform the following operations:

1. download the source data (i.e. the English audios archive);
2. run their system and produce the hypothesis output (i.e. the German translations)
3. submitt their system output (i.e. the German translations);
4. wait for the evaluation process and read the evaluation scores (e.g. the COMET, and BLEU scores).

The SPEECH-IWSLT2025 allows the users to perform the above operations except the 2. one (users are expected to run their systems outside the Evaluation Server). In addition users can also delete and replace a submission with another one.

Submissions are managed trough the concept of user *models*, a user-defined entity that describes the main features of a given user system. By means of models, users can submitt multiples hypothesis

[68]www.meetween.eu
[69]iwslt2025.speechm.cloud.cyfronet.pl

Figure 9: SPEECHM leaderboard.

outputs for the same task testset, one for each different developed system.

B.1.3 The Web UI

The Web UI facilitates the submission process, manages evaluation submissions, and monitors interactions with the external HPC cluster. This workflow is illustrated in Figure 8. Initially, users must create an account in the SPEECHM system, a straightforward process due to its integration with PLGrid, GitHub, and Google identity providers. Once registered, users can download the challenge input files (Step 1). These files serve as input for the participant's model inference (Step 2), which must currently be performed outside the SPEECHM system. In future iterations, SPEECHM aims to integrate this step as well.

After generating the outputs, users can conveniently upload them to the SPEECHM portal (Step 3). At this stage, challenge owners initiate the hypothesis evaluation process (Step 4). This step is restricted to challenge owners since they alone have access to the HPC computational resources required for evaluation. SPEECHM employs *slurmrestd*[70] to submit SLURM jobs to HPC clusters and to monitor job execution status.

Upon completion of the evaluations, the scores are stored in the SPEECHM database (Step 5). These scores contribute to generating various leaderboards, such as those specific to a task, testset, or model. An example leaderboard is shown in Figure 9.

B.1.4 The evaluation scripts

The evaluation metrics are computed through a set of scripts that run on the PLGRID clusters[71]. Scripts to compute the metrics that benefit from usage of GPU cards (such as COMET, BLEURT and BERT scores) run on the *Athena*[72] cluster while the other scripts (computing ASR, BLEU and CharacTER scores) are executed on the *Ares* cluster[73].

It is worth noticing here that while the references of the Offline and Model Compression task testsets are typically unstructured plain files, those of the Instruction Following task are structured as XML files. Therefore, the evaluation script for the Instruction Following task testsets has been developed specifically in order to manage the XML input structure.

B.2 Offline SLT

- Systems are ordered according to the COMET score (denoted by <u>COMET</u>, the first column).
- The "Joint" table is computed by averaging the scores of the 4 test sets, aka macro-averaging.

[70] slurm.schedmd.com/slurmrestd.html

[71] portal.plgrid.pl

[72] www.cyfronet.pl/en/19073,artykul,athena.html

[73] www.cyfronet.pl/en/computers/18827,artykul,ares_supercomputer.html

- The "D" column indicates the data condition in which each submitted run was trained, namely: Constrained (C), Constrained^{+LLM} (C^+), Unconstrained (U).
- This year, we have submissions of both cascade and end-to-end architectures.

System	D	Joint					
		COMET (↑)	BLEU (↑)	BLEURT (↑)	chrF (↑)	CharacTER (↓)	TER (↓)
KIT	U	0.783	30.2	0.660	57.4	0.451	63.1
NYA	U	0.780	28.9	0.646	56.5	0.463	64.6
NeMo	U	0.765	28.7	0.638	56.1	0.465	67.1
AIB	U	0.676	22.0	0.520	47.8	0.548	77.4
NAIST	U	0.644	17.9	0.469	43.0	0.628	77.1
CUNI-NL	C^+	0.632	19.4	0.465	44.3	0.634	73.2
NAIST	C^+	0.594	13.4	0.400	37.9	0.693	83.3

System	D	Accent					
		COMET	BLEU	BLEURT	chrF	CharacTER	TER
NYA	U	0.742	20.7	0.595	52.0	0.543	78.3
KIT	U	0.733	21.8	0.603	52.3	0.54	76.2
NeMo	U	0.712	18.4	0.579	51.0	0.549	92.5
NAIST	U	0.695	16.7	0.551	46.8	0.598	81.2
AIB	U	0.688	19.4	0.533	50.2	0.569	79.7
NAIST	C^+	0.672	13.7	0.518	43.8	0.628	86.8
CUNI-NL	C^+	0.628	15.3	0.473	40.6	0.676	80.5

System	D	Asharq News					
		COMET	BLEU	BLEURT	chrF	CharacTER	TER
KIT	U	0.833	36.2	0.722	65.0	0.382	54.5
NYA	U	0.832	37.5	0.708	64.7	0.396	52.8
NeMo	U	0.826	38.1	0.708	64.7	0.384	51.1
AIB	U	0.811	35.8	0.686	62.1	0.416	53.3
NAIST	U	0.601	18.3	0.408	40.9	0.677	74.6
CUNI-NL	C^+	0.583	21.8	0.432	47.5	0.629	71.8
NAIST	C^+	0.503	10.3	0.282	30.3	0.804	81.8

System	D	ITV					
		COMET	BLEU	BLEURT	chrF	CharacTER	TER
KIT	U	0.722	21.8	0.579	44.3	0.546	74.7
NYA	U	0.704	19.1	0.551	42.9	0.564	78.4
NeMo	U	0.695	19.8	0.546	42.2	0.571	75.8
CUNI-NL	C^+	0.544	10.6	0.318	29.7	0.778	83.3
NAIST	U	0.513	8.20	0.287	25.7	0.787	93.8
NAIST	C^+	0.491	6.90	0.249	25.4	0.786	97.5
AIB	U	0.401	2.60	0.172	17.9	0.788	121

System	D	Scientific Presentations					
		COMET	BLEU	BLEURT	chrF	CharacTER	TER
KIT	U	0.842	40.9	0.735	68.0	0.337	47.0
NYA	U	0.840	38.4	0.730	66.4	0.348	48.9
NeMo	U	0.828	38.4	0.718	66.3	0.355	49.0
AIB	U	0.804	30.0	0.688	61.0	0.418	56.1
CUNI-NL	C^+	0.772	29.9	0.638	59.4	0.453	57.1
NAIST	U	0.766	28.6	0.630	58.5	0.448	59.0
NAIST	C^+	0.710	22.8	0.550	52.2	0.554	67.1

Table 21: Official results of the automatic evaluation for the Offline Speech Translation Task on official test sets, **English to German**.

System	D	Asharq News					
		COMET (↑)	BLEU (↑)	BLEURT (↑)	chrF (↑)	CharacTER (↓)	TER (↓)
NYA	U	0.839	22.1	0.665	55.4	0.440	64.4
NeMo	U	0.820	19.7	0.644	52.7	0.461	66.2
AIB	U	0.812	17.2	0.627	50.3	0.496	67.0

Table 22: Official results of the automatic evaluation for the Offline Speech Translation Task on official test set, **English to Arabic**.

System	D	Scientific Presentations					
		COMET (↑)	BLEU (↑)	BLEURT (↑)	chrF (↑)	CharacTER (↓)	TER (↓)
NYA	U	0.860	56.7	0.713	49.1	0.418	32.9
AIB	U	0.856	55.7	0.719	49.1	0.427	33.0
BigWaterMelon	U	0.845	56.2	0.703	49.5	0.436	34.1
NeMo	U	0.844	46.3	0.699	40.6	0.481	39.0
NAIST	U	0.771	40.2	0.590	33.4	0.600	48.4
NAIST	C^{+}	0.711	31.0	0.487	26.6	0.724	56.7

Table 23: Official results of the automatic evaluation for the Offline Speech Translation Task on official test set, **English to Chinese**. When computing the TER scores via sacreBLEU, we provide these two additional arguments: "–ter-normalized" and "–ter-asian-support"

B.3 Simultaneous SLT

Latency Regime	Team	Quality Metrics BLEU (↑)	COMET (↑)	StreamLAAL dev (↓)	test (↓)
Low-Latency	Baseline-Fixed	15.74	0.551	1.87	1.70 (2.61)
	Baseline-VAD	17.81	0.595	1.82	1.99 (3.10)
	NAIST	20.85	0.680	1.92	1.82 (N/A)
	OSU *	22.04	0.708	1.84	1.73 (2.47)
	CMU	22.63	0.697	1.69	1.47 (1.81)
High-Latency	Baseline-Casc.*	24.89	0.699	3.23	3.20 (4.59)
	Baseline-Fixed	19.15	0.593	2.35	3.54 (4.57)
	Baseline-VAD	22.07	0.644	3.43	2.95 (3.82)
	NAIST	24.58	0.717	3.99	3.71 (N/A)
	OSU *	25.80	0.729	3.34	3.21 (4.41)
	UPV *	29.81	0.739	2.94	2.90 (3.37)
	CUNI *	35.25	0.790	3.77	3.32 (N/A)

Table 24: English-to-German simultaneous speech-to-text translation divided by latency regimes. Latency is measured in seconds. Values in parentheses are computationally aware latency and are provided for system submissions only on the test set. Cascaded systems are marked with an asterisk (∗).

Latency Regime	Team	Quality Metrics BLEU (↑)	COMET (↑)	StreamLAAL dev (↓)	test (↓)
Low-Latency	Baseline-Fixed	20.42	0.568	2.35	3.76 (4.64)
	Baseline-VAD	22.63	0.588	1.88	1.96 (2.74)
	OSU *	34.06	0.705	2.22	2.20 (3.34)
	NAIST	37.82	0.747	2.46	2.28 (N/A)
	CMU	43.26	0.773	2.19	2.15 (2.66)
High-Latency	Baseline-Fixed	21.84	0.595	3.12	3.11 (3.98)
	Baseline-VAD	26.19	0.638	3.28	3.15 (3.91)
	OSU *	37.07	0.733	3.52	3.49 (4.82)
	CUNI *	39.07	0.808	3.54	2.94 (N/A)
	NAIST	39.41	0.761	3.70	3.20 (N/A)

Table 25: English-to-Chinese simultaneous speech-to-text translation divided by latency regimes. Latency is measured in seconds. Values in parentheses are computationally aware latency and are provided for system submissions only on the test set. Cascaded systems are marked with an asterisk (∗).

Latency Regime	Team	Quality Metrics BLEU (↑)	COMET (↑)	StreamLAAL dev (↓)	test (↓)
Low-Latency	Baseline-VAD	11.32	0.591	2.35	2.21 (3.25)
	NAIST	23.84	0.786	3.34	2.83 (N/A)
High-Latency	Baseline-Fixed	10.05	0.610	3.74	4.62 (5.89)
	Baseline-VAD	13.76	0.667	3.66	3.54 (4.62)
	NAIST	23.99	0.787	3.98	3.25 (N/A)
	CUNI *	33.44	0.841	4.48	4.23 (N/A)

Table 26: English-to-Japanese simultaneous speech-to-text translation divided by latency regimes. Values in parentheses are computationally aware latency and are provided for system submissions only on the test set. Cascaded systems are marked with an asterisk (*).

Latency Regime	Team	Quality Metrics BLEU (↑)	COMET (↑)	StreamLAAL dev (↓)	test (↓)
Low-Latency	Baseline-Fixed	19.96	0.647	1.87	2.31 (3.26)
	Baseline-VAD	19.94	0.642	1.78	2.46 (3.70)
	CUNI	20.78	0.715	1.76	1.41 (N/A)
High-Latency	Baselines-Casc.*	19.92	0.675	3.64	4.29 (8.11)
	Baseline-Fixed	21.44	0.662	3.41	3.34 (4.22)
	Baseline-VAD	23.55	0.677	3.34	3.68 (4.67)
	CUNI	21.94	0.729	2.63	1.51 (N/A)

Table 27: Czech-to-English simultaneous speech-to-text translation for the native speakers test set divided by latency regimes. Latency is measured in seconds. Values in parentheses are computationally aware latency and are provided for system submissions only on the test set.

Latency Regime	Team	Quality Metrics BLEU (↑)	COMET (↑)	StreamLAAL dev (↓)	test (↓)
Low-Latency	Baseline-Fixed	8.84	0.568	1.87	3.33 (4.53)
	Baseline-VAD	12.84	0.589	1.78	1.00 (1.88)
	CUNI	21.59	0.704	1.76	3.30 (N/A)
High-Latency	Baselines-Casc.*	24.00	0.698	3.64	5.30 (9.43)
	Baseline-Fixed	18.02	0.612	3.41	5.19 (6.22)
	Baseline-VAD	16.46	0.626	3.34	1.85 (2.62)
	CUNI	24.53	0.749	2.63	1.79 (N/A)

Table 28: Czech-to-English simultaneous speech-to-text translation for the non-native speakers test set divided by latency regimes. Latency is measured in seconds. Values in parentheses are computationally aware latency and are provided for system submissions only on the test set.

Latency Regime	Team	Quality Metrics BLEU (↑)	COMET (↑)	StreamLAAL dev (↓)	test (↓)
Low-Latency	Baseline-Fixed	10.89	0.490	1.87	2.48 (3.57)
	Baseline-VAD	10.22	0.487	1.82	3.43 (4.41)
	CMU	11.18	0.525	1.87	1.74 (2.26)
	NAIST	12.15	0.570	1.92	1.89 (N/A)
	OSU *	16.11	0.618	1.84	2.06 (2.90)
High-Latency	Baselines-Casc.*	13.99	0.583	3.23	3.09 (4.37)
	Baseline-Fixed	13.03	0.520	2.35	4.06 (4.92)
	Baseline-VAD	11.07	0.500	3.43	3.33 (4.33)
	CUNI *	12.51	0.626	3.77	2.99 (N/A)
	NAIST	12.92	0.585	3.99	3.70 (N/A)
	UPV *	16.26	0.599	2.94	3.58 (N/A)
	OSU *	18.73	0.643	3.34	3.81 (4.83)

Table 29: English-to-German simultaneous speech-to-text translation for the challenging accented test set divided by latency regimes. Latency is measured in seconds. Values in parentheses are computationally aware latency and are provided for system submissions only on the test set. Cascaded systems are marked with an asterisk ($*$).

B.4 Automatic Subtitling

Team	Cndt	System	Domain	Sub. qual. SubER	Translation quality Bleu	ChrF	Bleurt	Subtitle compliance CPS	CPL	LPB
AppTek	U	prmry	ITV	62.86	19.11	40.62	.4899	93.78	100.00	100.00
			Asharq-Bloomberg	50.87	35.21	59.03	.6057	92.44	100.00	99.19
AppTek	U	cntrstv1	ITV	63.57	20.65	42.94	.5043	82.36	100.00	97.55
			Asharq-Bloomberg	51.93	34.28	57.83	.5869	95.69	100.00	99.85
AppTek	U	cntrstv2	ITV	63.31	18.06	39.16	.4767	97.40	100.00	100.00
			Asharq-Bloomberg	50.94	35.02	58.99	.6052	92.13	100.00	99.07

Table 30: Subtitling Task: automatic evaluation scores on tst2025 en→de. *U* stands for *unconstrained* training condition; *prmry* and *cntrstv* for *primary* and *contrastive* systems.

Team	Cndt	System	Domain	Sub. qual. SubER	Translation quality Bleu	ChrF	Bleurt	Subtitle compliance CPS	CPL	LPB
AppTek	U	prmry	Asharq-Bloomberg	62.13	21.56	52.74	.5995	99.81	100.00	99.97
AppTek	U	cntrstv1	Asharq-Bloomberg	62.62	21.22	52.25	.5982	99.81	100.00	99.97
AppTek	U	cntrstv2	Asharq-Bloomberg	62.57	21.87	53.27	.6044	96.28	100.00	99.38

Table 31: Subtitling Task: automatic evaluation scores on tst2025 en→ar. *U* stands for *unconstrained* training condition; *prmry* and *cntrstv* for *primary* and *contrastive* systems.

Team	Cndt	System	Domain	Sub. qual. SubER	Translation quality Bleu	ChrF	Bleurt	Subtitle compliance CPS	CPL	LPB
AppTek	U	prmry	ITV	66.55	18.86	41.71	.5053	93.50	100.00	100.00
AppTek	U	cntrstv1	ITV	69.32	19.07	43.08	.5164	83.53	100.00	97.87
AppTek	U	cntrstv2	ITV	65.97	18.33	40.96	.5008	97.07	100.00	100.00
Submissions 2024										
AppTek	U	prmry	ITV	72.38	16.98	40.42	.4683	69.23	100.00	99.92
FBK-AI4C$_{DIR}$	C	prmry	ITV	78.90	9.67	28.43	.2911	70.45	90.04	99.97
FBK-AI4C$_{CSC}$	U	prmry	ITV	79.92	14.86	35.16	.4048	54.20	91.12	100.00
HW-TSC	U	prmry	ITV	76.04	16.09	41.34	.5098	61.72	61.80	100.00

Table 32: Subtitling Task: automatic evaluation scores on tst2024 en→de. *C* and *U* stand for *constrained* and *unconstrained* training condition, respectively; *prmry* and *cntrstv* for *primary* and *contrastive* systems.

Team	Cndt	System	Domain	Sub. qual. SubER	Translation quality Bleu	ChrF	Bleurt	Subtitle compliance CPS	CPL	LPB
AppTek	U	prmry	ITV	65.26	18.79	41.62	.5064	93.32	100.00	100.00
AppTek	U	cntrstv1	ITV	66.97	20.27	43.73	.5219	82.02	100.00	97.69
AppTek	U	cntrstv2	ITV	65.01	18.26	40.77	.5003	97.12	100.00	100.00
Submissions 2024										
AppTek	U	prmry	ITV	69.21	17.97	41.27	.4790	67.64	100.00	99.96
HW-TSC	U	prmry	ITV	72.16	18.35	42.95	.5244	60.15	62.37	100.00
FBK-AI4C$_{CSC}$	U	prmry	ITV	74.91	16.19	35.91	.3996	54.70	92.97	100.00
FBK-AI4C$_{DIR}$	C	prmry	ITV	77.15	10.40	29.13	.2939	68.73	91.00	99.97
Submissions 2023										
AppTek	U	prmry	ITV	69.83	14.43	35.27	0.4028	86.01	100.00	100.00
TLT	U	prmry	ITV	73.11	14.92	37.13	0.4501	80.21	99.47	100.00
AppTek	C	prmry	ITV	80.87	9.08	27.74	0.2612	91.14	100.00	100.00
FBK $_{DIR}$	C	prmry	ITV	82.67	8.05	26.10	0.2255	67.75	85.12	100.00

Table 33: Subtitling Task: automatic evaluation scores on tst2023 en→de. *C* and *U* stand for *constrained* and *unconstrained* training condition, respectively; *prmry* and *cntrstv* for *primary* and *contrastive* systems.

B.5 Low-Resource SLT

North Levantine Arabic→English (Unconstrained Condition)

Team	System	BLEU↓	COMET	chrF2
KIT	primary	23.34	0.704	45.09
LIA	primary	22.56	0.719	44.72
KIT	contrastive2	21.93	0.697	44.67
LIA	contrastive2	21.45	0.694	43.13
LIA	contrastive1	21.02	0.698	42.92
ALADAN	primary	20.02	0.661	39.91
KIT	contrastive1	19.11	0.683	40.95
AIB_Marco	contrastive4	16.47	0.683	37.96
AIB_Marco	contrastive3	16.22	0.667	37.48
AIB_Marco	contrastive1	15.82	0.646	36.23
JHU	contrastive1	15.39	0.657	35.91
JHU	primary	14.64	0.649	36.23
AIB_Marco	primary	12.01	0.655	34.19
AIB_Marco	contrastive2	10.53	0.573	27.69

Table 34: Automatic evaluation results for the North Levantine Arabic to English task, unconstrained Condition. A lowercase, no-punctuation variant of chrF2 is reported. The `Unbabel/wmt22-comet-da` model was used for COMET computation, with the source side (Arabic transcript) unmodified and the target side lowercased and with removed punctuation. The *AIB_Marco* team did not submit a system description paper.

Bemba→English (Unconstrained Condition)

Team	System	BLEU
JHU	primary	32.6
KIT	primary	28.8
KIT	contrastive2	28.1
JHU	contrastive1	27.0
KIT	contrastive1	27.0
JHU	contrastive2	26.7

Team	System	WER
KIT ASR	primary	33.2
JHU ASR	primary	35.7

Table 35: Automatic evaluation results for the Bemba to English task, unconstrained Condition.

Bhojpuri→Hindi (Unconstrained Condition)

Team	System	BLEU	chrF2
GMU	contrastive1	3.4	23.0
GMU	contrastive2	2.0	16
GMU	primary	3.9	24.0
JHU	contrastive1	10.7	34.0
JHU	contrastive2	7.8	32.0
JHU	primary	10.5	34.0
IIITH_BUT	contrastive1	10.2	32.0
IIITH_BUT	primary	9.9	33.0

Table 36: Automatic evaluation results for the Bhojpuri to Hindi task, unconstrained Condition.

Estonian→English (Unconstrained Condition)

Team	System	BLEU	chrF2	COMET
AIB_Marco	contrastive1	29.3	55.8	0.7944
AIB_Marco	contrastive2	23.3	48.3	0.7601
AIB_Marco	primary	30.9	57.4	0.7958
GMU	contrastive1	30.2	53.4	0.7746
GMU	contrastive2	29.6	52.9	0.7760
GMU	primary	29.8	53.1	0.7767

Table 37: Automatic evaluation results for the Estonian to English task, unconstrained condition.

Irish→English (Unconstrained Condition)

Team	System	BLEU	chrF2
AIB_Marco	contrastive1	7.8	32.0
AIB_Marco	contrastive2	12.5	34.0
AIB_Marco	primary	12.5	34.0
GMU	contrastive1	8.4	32.0
GMU	contrastive2	6.7	30.0
GMU	primary	13.4	34.0
JHU	contrastive1	12.0	33.0
JHU	contrastive2	12.3	33.0
JHU	primary	11.6	33.0

Table 38: Automatic evaluation results for the Irish to English task, unconstrained Condition.

Maltese→English (Unconstrained Condition)

Team	System	BLEU	chrF2
KIT	primary	58.9	76.5
SETU-DCU	primary	56.7	81.9
KIT	contrastive2	56.2	75.0
KIT	contrastive1	55.2	74.4
SETU-DCU	contrastive1	52.6	72.1
UoM	primary	52.4	72.3
UoM	contrastive1	52.4	72.3
UoM	contrastive2	52.3	72.1
SETU-DCU	contrastive2	44.7	65.5
JHU	primary	41.4	68.6
JHU	contrastive1	36.5	64.2
UoM-DFKI	primary (e2e)	35.1	59.0
JHU	contrastive2	24.8	55.8
UoM-DFKI	contrastive1 (e2e)	18.5	42.0

Table 39: Automatic evaluation results for the Maltese to English task, Unconstrained Condition. e2e denotes end-to-end system.

Maltese→English (Constrained Condition)

Team	System	BLEU	chrF2
UoM	primary	0.5	15.6

Table 40: Automatic evaluation results for the Maltese to English task, Constrained Condition.

Marathi→Hindi (Constrained Condition)

Team	System	BLEU	chrF2
SRI-B	contrastive1	22.6	50.0
SRI-B	contrastive2	24.0	52.0
SRI-B	primary	23.7	52.0

Table 41: Automatic evaluation results for the Marathi to Hindi task, Constrained Condition.

Marathi→Hindi (Unconstrained Condition)

Team	**System**	**BLEU**	**chrF2**
GMU	contrastive1	44.3	68.0
GMU	contrastive2	41.5	66.0
GMU	primary	43.4	67.0
JHU	contrastive1	40.7	65.0
JHU	contrastive2	40.0	65.0
JHU	primary	41.4	65.0

Table 42: Automatic evaluation results for the Marathi to Hindi task, Unconstrained Condition.

Quechua→Spanish (Unconstrained Condition)

Team	**System**	**BLEU**	**chrF2**
GMU	contrastive1	12.9	46.4
GMU	contrastive2	13.0	46.4
GMU	primary	12.7	46.2
JHU	contrastive1	11.0	46.7
JHU	primary	9.0	43.5
QUESPA	contrastive1	15.0	52.4
QUESPA	contrastive2	26.7	48.6
QUESPA	primary	14.8	51.8

Table 43: Automatic evaluation results for the Quechua to Spanish task, Unconstrained Condition.

Fongbe→French (Unconstrained Condition)

Team	**System**	**BLEU**	**chrF2**
LIA	primary	**39.6**	**56.7**
LIA	contrastive1	37.23	54.96
LIA	contrastive2	32.76	50.09
LIA	contrastive3	28.32	46.08
GMU	primary	31.96	48.01
JHU	primary	5.96	23.21
JHU	contrastive1	6.26	23.27
JHU	contrastive2	5.6	23.27

Table 44: Automatic evaluation results for the Fongbe to French task, Unconstrained Condition.

B.6 Dialectal SLT

Tunisian Arabic→English (Unconstrained Condition)

		test22		test23	
Team	System	BLEU	chrF	BLEU	chrF
KIT	primary	**22.7**	**44.4**	**21.4**	42.3
KIT	contrastive1	21.2	43	19.3	40.9
KIT	contrastive2	21.4	43.7	19.2	41.1
LIA	primary	22.3	44.3	21.0	**42.5**
LIA	contrastive1	22.0	43.9	20.3	41.6
LIA	contrastive2	21.6	43.4	19.2	40.3
LIA	contrastive3	21.4	43.2	19.6	41.2
GMU	primary	20.3	43.2	17.8	40.6
GMU	contrastive1	19.2	42.8	17.3	40.0
GMU	contrastive2	18.9	42.4	17.3	40.1
SYSTRAN	primary	19.2	36.0	17.5	33.9
MBZAI	primary	11.7	34.0	10.4	32.2
JHU	primary	8.2	30.4	6.8	27.6
JHU	contrastive1	30.7	42.8	7.3	27.9
JHU	contrastive2	28.6	42.4	5.5	26.1

Table 45: Automatic evaluation results for the Tunisian to English Speech Translation task, Unconstrained Condition. Primary systems are ordered in terms of the official metric BLEU on test23. We also report chrF score.

Tunisian Arabic ASR (Unconstrained Condition)

		test22		test23	
Team	System	WER	CER	WER	CER
GMU	primary	**38.0**	19.7	**39.9**	22.3
LIA	primary	38.6	**19.2**	40.0	**21.4**
LIA	contrastive1	39.2	44.4	40.3	22.5
AMIRBEK	primary	39.9	20.0	41.0	22.3
SYSTRAN	primary	40.6	21.0	41.8	23.3

Table 46: Word Error Rate (WER) and Character Error Rate (CER) of the ASR component of submitted cascaded systems on test22 and test23 after Arabic-specific normalization for e.g. Alif, Ya, Ta-Marbuta on the hypotheses and transcripts before computing WER/CER. Systems are ordered in terms of the official metric WER on test23.

B.7 Instruction Following

en-en					
Model			**Metric**		
Organization	*Condition*	*Role*	*ASR-WER* ↓	*SQA-BERTScore* ↑	*S2TSUM-BERTScore* ↑
SHORT					
MICROSOFT-PHI	UNCONSTRAINED	BASELINE	**0.07**	0.46	-
MEETWEEN	UNCONSTRAINED	PRIMARY	0.18	0.17	-
NLE	CONSTRAINED	PRIMARY	0.13	**0.50**	-
CUNI-NL	UNCONSTRAINED	PRIMARY	0.15	0.21	-
		CONTRASTIVE	0.25	0.15	-
IST	UNCONSTRAINED	PRIMARY	0.15	0.14	-
LONG					
MICROSOFT-PHI	UNCONSTRAINED	BASELINE	0.17	**0.42**	0.17
KIT	CONSTRAINED	PRIMARY	**0.15**	0.41	**0.23**

en-de					
Model			**Metric**		
Organization	*Condition*	*Role*	*S2TT-COMET* ↑	*SQA-BERTScore* ↑	*S2TSUM-BERTScore* ↑
SHORT					
MICROSOFT-PHI	UNCONSTRAINED	BASELINE	**0.77**	0.36	-
NLE	CONSTRAINED	PRIMARY	0.71	**0.38**	-
CUNI-NL	UNCONSTRAINED	PRIMARY	0.72	0.21	-
		CONTRASTIVE	0.69	0.21	-
IST	UNCONSTRAINED	PRIMARY	0.34	0.22	-
LONG					
MICROSOFT-PHI	UNCONSTRAINED	BASELINE	0.55	**0.35**	0.16
KIT	CONSTRAINED	PRIMARY	**0.74**	**0.35**	**0.21**

en-it					
Model			**Metric**		
Organization	*Condition*	*Role*	*S2TT-COMET* ↑	*SQA-BERTScore* ↑	*S2TSUM-BERTScore* ↑
SHORT					
MICROSOFT-PHI	UNCONSTRAINED	BASELINE	**0.81**	0.40	-
NLE	CONSTRAINED	PRIMARY	0.75	**0.42**	-
LONG					
MICROSOFT-PHI	UNCONSTRAINED	BASELINE	0.56	0.36	0.19
KIT	CONSTRAINED	PRIMARY	**0.77**	**0.39**	**0.25**

en-zh					
Model			**Metric**		
Organization	*Condition*	*Role*	*S2TT-COMET* ↑	*SQA-BERTScore* ↑	*S2TSUM-BERTScore* ↑
SHORT					
MICROSOFT-PHI	UNCONSTRAINED	BASELINE	**0.81**	0.33	-
NLE	CONSTRAINED	PRIMARY	0.76	**0.35**	-
IST	UNCONSTRAINED	PRIMARY	0.34	0.21	-
LONG					
MICROSOFT-PHI	UNCONSTRAINED	BASELINE	0.51	0.39	0.04
KIT	CONSTRAINED	PRIMARY	**0.77**	**0.41**	**0.37**

Table 47: Complete results for the IF Task, including the BASELINE (Phi4-Multimodal). For each team, it is indicated whether the submission was under CONSTRAINED or unconstrained settings, and if it was PRIMARY or CONTRASTIVE. **Bold** indicates the best track-wise (SHORT and LONG) result per language direction, and underline indicates the overall best result among tracks.

Author Index